A COMPANION TO THE HISTORY
OF ECONOMIC THOUGHT

Blackwell Companions to Contemporary Economics

The *Blackwell Companions to Contemporary Economics* are reference volumes accessible to serious students and yet also containing up-to-date material from recognized experts in their particular fields. These volumes focus on basic bread-and-butter issues in economics as well as popular contemporary topics often not covered in textbooks. Coverage avoids the overly technical, is concise, clear, and comprehensive. Each *Companion* features an introductory essay by the editor, extensive bibliographical reference sections, and an index.

A Companion to
the History of
Economic Thought

Edited by

WARREN J. SAMUELS,
JEFF E. BIDDLE
Michigan State University

JOHN B. DAVIS
Marquette University, Wisconsin

Blackwell
Publishing

350 Main Street, Malden, MA 02148-5018, USA
108 Cowley Road, Oxford OX4 1JF, UK
550 Swanston Street, Carlton South, Melbourne, Victoria 3053, Australia
Kurfürstendamm 57, 10707 Berlin, Germany

First published 2003 by Blackwell Publishing Ltd
First published in paperback 2007 by Blackwell Publishing Ltd

3 2008

Library of Congress Cataloging-in-Publication Data

Samuels, Warren J., 1933–
A companion to the history of economic thought / edited by Warren J.
Samuels, Jeff E. Biddle and John B. Davis.
p. cm.
Includes bibliographical references and index.
ISBN 978-1-4051-3459-0
1. Economics–History. 2. Economics–Historiography. I. Biddle,
Jeff. II. Davis, John Bryan. III. Title.

HB75 .S29 2003
330.1–dc21

2002151895

A catalogue record for this title is available from the British Library.

Set in 10/12pt Book Antique
by Graphicraft Limited, Hong Kong

For further information on
Blackwell Publishing, visit our website:
http://www.blackwellpublishing.com

FSC
Mixed Sources
Product group from well-managed
forests and other controlled sources
Cert no. SGS-COC-2953
www.fsc.org
© 1996 Forest Stewardship Council

Contents

List of Figures

List of Tables

List of Contributors

Roger E. Backhouse is Professor of the History and Philosophy of Economics at the University of Birmingham, England. He specializes in the history of economics and economic methodology.

William J. Barber is Andrews Professor of Economics, Emeritus, at the Wesleyan University, Connecticut. He specializes in the history of American economics.

Jeff E. Biddle is Professor of Economics at Michigan State University. He specializes in the history of economic thought, labor economics, and econometrics.

Mark Blaug is Visiting Professor of Economics at the University of Amsterdam and Erasmus University, Rotterdam, The Netherlands. He specializes in methodology and the history of economic thought.

Peter J. Boettke is Deputy Director, The James M. Buchanan Center for Political Economy, and Associate Professor of Economics at George Mason University, Virginia. He specializes in comparative political economy, market process theory, the history of economic thought, and methodology.

Anthony Brewer is Professor of the History of Economics at the University of Bristol, England. He specializes in the history of economics.

Vivienne Brown is Senior Lecturer in the Faculty of Social Sciences at The Open University, England. She specializes in intellectual history, including the history of economics.

José Luís Cardoso is Professor of Economics at the Technical University of Lisbon, Portugal. He specializes in the history of economic thought, economic history, and economic methodology.

A. W. Bob Coats is Emeritus Professor of Economic and Social History at the University of Nottingham, England. He specializes in the methodology and history of economic thought.

John B. Davis is Professor of Economics at Marquette University, Wisconsin. He specializes in the history of economic thought and methodology.

Robert W. Dimand is Professor of Economics at Brock University, St. Catharines, Ontario, Canada. He specializes in macroeconomics and the history of economic thought.

Sheila C. Dow is Professor of Economics at the University of Stirling, Scotland. She specializes in the methodology and history of economic thought, monetary theory, and regional finance.

Ross B. Emmett is John P. Tandberg Chair and Associate Professor of Economics at Augustana University College, Camrose, Alberta, Canada. He specializes in twentieth-century history of economic thought, Chicago economics, and Frank H. Knight.

Craufurd D. W. Goodwin is James B. Duke Professor of Economics, Duke University, North Carolina. He specializes in the history of economic thought and international education.

Peter Groenewegen is Professor of Economics, University of Sydney. He specializes in the history of economic thought.

G. C. Harcourt is Emeritus Reader in the History of Economic Theory, University of Cambridge (1998); Emeritus Fellow, Jesus College, Cambridge (1998); and Professor Emeritus, University of Adelaide (1988). He specializes in post-Keynesian theory applications and policy, intellectual biography, and the history of economic theory.

Geoffrey M. Hodgson is Research Professor, The Business School, University of Hertfordshire, England. He specializes in institutional economics, evolutionary economics, methodology of economics, history of economic thought, and business economics.

Kevin D. Hoover is Professor of Economics at the University of California at Davis. He specializes in monetary and macroeconomics, economic methodology, and the history of economic thought.

Steven Horwitz is Professor of Economics at St. Lawrence University, Canton, New York. He specializes in monetary theory and macroeconomics.

Hamid S. Hosseini is John Davis Distinguished Professor of Economics, King's College, Pennsylvania. He specializes in economic development, international economics, the history of economic analysis, and Islamic economics.

Prue Kerr is Fellow, Centro Richerche Studi e Documentazione Piero Sraffa, Rome. She specializes in the history of economic thought, classical political economy, and post-Keynesian economics.

J. E. King is Professor of Economics at La Trobe University, Victoria, Australia. He specializes in the history of economic thought, with special reference to heterodox schools of thought, Marxian political economy, and post-Keynesian economics.

Matthias Klaes is Lecturer at the University of Stirling, Scotland. He specializes in economic methodology, historiography, economy of knowledge and social epistemology, and transaction cost theory.

Heinz D. Kurz is Full Professor of Economics at the University of Graz, Austria. He specializes in economic theory (production, income distribution, technical change, growth) and the history of economic thought (classical political economy, marginalist economics, German–Austrian school).

Peter T. Leeson is a graduate student in the Department of Economics at George Mason University, Virginia. He is specializing in Austrian economics and methodology.

David M. Levy is Professor of Economics at George Mason University, Virginia. He specializes in metaeconomics, the history of economics, statistical ethics, robust regression, and economics and language.

John Lodewijks is Associate Professor of Economics at the University of New South Wales, Australia. He specializes in the history and methodology of modern economics.

S. Todd Lowry is Professor of Economics Emeritus at Washington and Lee University, Virginia. He specializes in the history of economic thought, law and economics, and environmental studies.

Lars G. Magnusson is Professor of Economic History at Uppsala University, Sweden. He specializes in the history of economic thought and general economic history.

Maria Cristina Marcuzzo is Professor of the History of Economic Thought at the Università degli Studi di Roma "La Sapienza," Rome, Italy. She specializes in classical monetary theory and the Cambridge school of economics.

Steven G. Medema is Professor of Economics at the University of Colorado at Denver. He specializes in the history of economic thought, law and economics, and public economics.

D. E. Moggridge is Professor of Economics at the University of Toronto, Canada. He specializes in twentieth-century economic thought and international economic history.

Denis P. O'Brien is Professor of Economics, Emeritus, at the University of Durham, England. He specializes in the history of economic thought, industrial economics, and international economics.

Sandra J. Peart is Professor of Economics at Baldwin-Wallace College, Ohio. She specializes in nineteenth-century history of economic thought.

Mark Perlman is University Professor of Economics (Emeritus) at the University of Pittsburgh, Pennsylvania. He specializes in the history of economic thought and demographic economics.

Bruce Pietrykowski is Associate Professor of Economics at the University of Michigan–Dearborn. His research specializes in labor economics, the methodology and history of economic thought, and economic geography.

Geert Reuten is Associate Professor in the history and methodology of economics at the University of Amsterdam, The Netherlands. He specializes in the history and methodology of Marx's and Marxian theory, and dialectical research methods.

S. Abu Turab Rizvi is Associate Professor of Economics at the University of Vermont. He specializes in microeconomic theory and the history of economic thought.

Malcolm Rutherford is Professor of Economics at the University of Victoria, Canada. He specializes in the history of economics, institutional economics, and the history of American economics.

Warren J. Samuels is Professor Emeritus of Economics at Michigan State University. He specializes in the history of economic thought, methodology, and the economic role of government.

Janet A. Seiz is Associate Professor of Economics at Grinnell College, Iowa. She specializes in the history of economic thought, methodology, and feminist economics.

Andrew S. Skinner is Adam Smith Professor of Economics Emeritus at the University of Glasgow, Scotland. He specializes in eighteenth-century economic thought.

Philippe Steiner is Professor of Sociology at the Université de Lille 3, France. He specializes in the history of economic thought and economic sociology.

Keith Tribe is presently an unaffiliated scholar. He specializes in the history of European economics, 1600–1950; Max Weber and German economics; and the formation of economics as a university discipline.

Donald A. Walker is University Professor and Professor of Economics, Emeritus, at the Indiana University of Pennsylvania. He specializes in microeconomic theory and history.

A. M. C. Waterman is Professor of Economics at the University of Manitoba, Canada. He specializes in the history of economic thought, eighteenth- and early nineteenth-century economic thought, Malthus, political economy, and Christian theology.

Preface

The purpose of this *Companion* is threefold: to introduce the history of economic thought, the interpretive problems facing historians of economic thought, and the work of historians of economic thought to interested and competent nonspecialists, including other economists, graduate students, advanced undergraduate students, and lay people (including noneconomists), as well as specialists seeking a review of a topic.

The design strategy for this *Companion* is simple and straightforward. The chapters comprising part I are historical surveys of major topics in the history of economic thought. Their purpose is to report on the present state of understanding and interpretation of those topics. That there is a history of understanding and interpretation for each topic is an important point, one that leads to several of the topics of part II. These topics reflect a situation – much more evident in the work of historians of economics since, roughly, the early 1960s – in which it is recognized that the history of economic thought is laden with interpretation and is not, in important matters, self-evident. That history is socially constructed, embodying interpretive strategies that are either explicit or implicit in how historians of economic thought pursue their work. The result is that we have the history of economic thought (the history of ideas), the history of economics as a discipline (the sociology of economics and economists), and the history of the history of economic thought. Something of the latter two is presented in the chapters comprising the second part. All of the foregoing is preceded by an introduction to the variety of research styles of historians of economic thought (originally prepared as a regular essay). Wm. Roger Louis writes that "historiography is, in a sense, the art of explaining why historians wrote as they did," that "[i]n still another sense, historiography is the art of depicting historical controversy," and that [h]istoriography may also be regarded as the way certain historians have left a mark on the subject" (Louis, 1999, pp. vii–ix). These considerations surely apply to the present *Companion*. [Different research styles of historians of economic thought are presented and interpreted in Samuels (1983) and in Medema and Samuels (2001).]

All individual essays are, not surprisingly, in light of the themes of the chapters of part II, a product of the negotiations among the co-editors and between them and prospective contributors. The contributors were chosen because of their mastery of the materials on which they were invited to write, and their relative willingness to transcend their own perspectives in order to prepare texts that the editors felt would provide meaningful starting points for scholars. So long as their individual chapters served such purpose, the individual authors were given complete discretion, subject to the suggestions of the co-editors and to the mandatory limits of 8,000 words for all essays other than the group comprising Postwar Heterodox Economics, each of which has a limit of 4,000 words (reference lists included in both groups). No single model was imposed on the authors, although the genre itself conveys some elements of design, and no attempt was made to enforce the editors' own views – although such inevitably entered the design of the volume. Accordingly, some degree of idiosyncrasy will be found, as well as differences of interpretation.

One feature of the collection is the attempt to include aspects of the period following World War II. Indeed, a substantial interpretive literature already exists. We envision, in the not too distant future, a *Companion* dealing more or less exclusively with that period. Yet, as several chapters in this collection reveal, we are only now achieving meaningful insight into the interwar period. And surely, by the time a sequel is contemplated, new interpretations of the entire history of economic thought and new research strategies will have arisen.

One consideration should be understood, that of multiplicity. Clearly, not all historians of economic thought agree with and practice their discipline in the light of all the positions surveyed in the historiographic chapters of part II. Similarly, not all historians of economic thought agree with the particular interpretations necessarily expressed in the chapters of part I. Historians of economic thought and of economics are much more diverse in their modes of work at the start of the twenty-first century than their counterparts were at either the beginning of the twentieth century or during the early postwar period.

The reader should treat these chapters as suggestive, not complete; general, not fully nuanced; and so on. Every topic is much more complex once you get into it. One chapter can do only so much. Each is best treated by the reader as a series of pointers and not a treatise. As definitive as one would prefer the chapters to be, they are best seen as sophisticated introductions – as companions to, not substitutes for, serious further intellectual effort.

We are appreciative of the hard work and cooperative spirit of the contributors to this *Companion* and of the staff of Blackwell Publishing.

WARREN J. SAMUELS, JEFF E. BIDDLE
Michigan State University

JOHN B. DAVIS
Marquette University, Wisconsin

References

Louis, W. R. 1999: Foreword. In R. Winks (ed.), *Historiography*, vol. V, *The Oxford History of the British Empire*. New York: Oxford University Press, vii–vi.

Medema, S. G. and Samuels, W. J. (eds.) 2001: *Historians of Economics and Economic Thought: The Construction of Disciplinary Memory*. New York: Routledge.

Samuels, W. J. (ed.) 1983: *Research in the History of Economic Thought and Methodology*, vol. 1, *The Craft of the Historian of Economic Thought*. Greenwich, CN: JAI Press.

CHAPTER ONE

Research Styles in the History of Economic Thought

Jeff E. Biddle

What is the history of economic thought? One could answer, paraphrasing Jacob Viner's answer to the question "What is economics?," that the history of thought is "what historians of economic thought do." One purpose of this *Companion* is to acquaint those unfamiliar with the field with what historians of economic thought do. The first part of the *Companion* does this by surveying the body of knowledge that has been built up by historians of economic thought. It consists of a series of individual essays that partition that body of knowledge along several lines, such as time period, school of thought, and nation of origin. Other ways of dividing the field could have been chosen, but the one employed here is broadly consistent with the way in which the field is currently comprehended by practitioners.

In most of the chapters of this first part, readers will find evidence that the history of economic thought as a body of knowledge is not settled; that although there are many areas of consensus, the field is also home to numerous controversies and open questions. This is perhaps even more apparent when one compares essays that overlap in terms of coverage. Different authors may have surprisingly different ideas about the central themes or the most significant ideas of a particular school, national tradition, or time period. A comparison of the several contributions dealing with aspects of or contributors to classical economics will amply illustrate this point.

The second part of the *Companion*, with which this introduction is mainly concerned, explores more explicitly the question of "what historians of thought do" with a group of essays designed to offer readers an introduction to the varieties of research styles employed by historians of economic thought. These essays make it clear that there is, in fact, a fair amount of methodological diversity to be found in the field of the history of economic thought, a diversity that is in no small part responsible for the unsettled nature of the field referred to above. [Samuels (1983) and Medema and Samuels (2001) reveal in more detail the variety of approaches employed by historians of economic thought, through examinations of the work of notable practitioners.]

Those who have contributed to writing the history of economic thought over the decades have been motivated by a variety of questions and purposes, and have used a variety of research strategies and source materials. This variety stems in part from the fact that historians of economic thought have had different interests and thus different ideas about what types of historical phenomena are most intriguing. But it also results from the fact that they have explicitly or implicitly adopted different answers to fundamental historiographic questions, questions about the purposes for which history is written and about the best methods for accomplishing those purposes. A number of the chapters of part II, in particular those of Matthias Klaes and Anthony Waterman, deal with the basic historiographic issues that have generated and are revealed by the many research styles found in the literature of the history of economic thought.

Research in the history of economics has for the most part been research in intellectual history; that is, an attempt to understand the ideas of past thinkers and how and why those ideas have developed and changed through time. In particular, research in the history of economics has been concerned with discovering what people in the past have believed about phenomena that either they or the researcher regard as economic activity, and why they have believed it. Notwithstanding the above-mentioned diversity of research approaches that can be observed among the scholars engaged in this task of discovery, however, there has traditionally been one task that has dominated the work in the field: that of developing a more complete and more correct understanding of the theoretical creations of those whom history has identified as great and/or influential economists.

So, a central question that has motivated most research efforts in the history of economic thought has been of the form "What was Adam Smith's (or Karl Marx's, or John Maynard Keynes's) theory of X?" And by far the most commonly adopted approach to answering questions of this type has been to examine the published works of the economist in question. This means that most research in the history of economic thought has involved textual exegesis or interpretation; that in a sense the work of most historians of economic thought has been similar to the work of theologians seeking the true interpretations of scriptural writings, or legal scholars and judges seeking the true intent of legislators. And while it may be argued that the material with which the historians of economics work is of less significance, the intellectual problems that they face in the task of interpretation are much the same. As is clear from a number of the contributions to the first part of this *Companion*, many of the debates in the field arise from differences over the correct interpretation of a particular text or texts and, by implication, the exegetical or interpretive guidelines that one should follow in interpreting texts. The essays of Ross Emmett and Vivienne Brown deal with some of the basic (and rather perplexing) issues that face the historian of economic thought in the process of textual exegesis. Waterman's essay also discusses the uses of and problems associated with a form of interpretation that emerged as important in the second half of the last century, that of translating theories presented in literary form into mathematical models.

The search for clues and insights into what an economist really believed, or for the correct interpretation of his or her theories, will sometimes take the historian of economic thought beyond the published works of his or her subjects. Archival material, such as letters or unpublished manuscripts and lectures, has been used to clarify vague statements or sketchy concepts found in the published works of economists, or to offer evidence that resolves apparent contradictions in those works. Recent decades have seen a significant increase the use of archival material by historians of economics, as well as greater efforts by the research community to assemble and to make such material more accessible to scholars. With the increasing use of archival material has come controversy over the weights to be assigned in the interpretive task to evidence from unpublished versus published writings. A related argument concerns the relative value of more broadly biographical evidence, material that may not explicate or even mention economic theories and ideas, but sheds light on other aspects of the economist's life, such as upbringing, social interactions, hobbies, or political views. Does such material also help to contribute to understanding the ideas of a past economist, or to explaining the theoretical choices made by that economist? The various views on this matter and the roles played by biography in understanding the history of economic thought are explored in Don Moggridge's essay.

Historians often seek a deeper understanding of an economist's ideas by searching for possible intellectual influences on the thought of the subject, perhaps by reading books that the subject read or might have read, or familiarizing him- or herself with the philosophical systems and political ideologies that dominated intellectual discourse during the subject's life. Such research may, for example, reveal parallels between the subject's conceptual framework or theoretical assumptions and some contemporary philosophical system. The argument that a particular interpretation of an ambiguous passage would represent a similar parallel can then be offered as evidence for that interpretation. Or, if interpretive differences arise because a key assumption was left unstated or unclear in the published work, an understanding of the preconceptions or ideological beliefs that prevailed in the subject's social or intellectual circles might provide the foundation for reasonable conjectures about what the subject was assuming.

Although explications and interpretations of the work of those that current opinion regards as great economists dominate the literature of the history of economic thought, the ideas of others have also received attention. One finds studies of "neglected" economists, for example, those whose ideas the researcher does not feel have achieved the attention they deserved. Sometimes the ideas of people whom history has not identified as economists, but remembers for some other reason – political figures, philosophers, scientists, novelists, and so on – have been the object of research. Instead of the conventional question "What did

Y really think about *X*?" a scholar may ask "What did the general public (or the typical businessman, or influential policy-makers) think that *Y* was saying about *X*?" Such information is of interest for its own sake, and because it may provide an understanding of the impact of the economic thought of a particular author on the public discourse and perhaps on public policy.

Of course, whether the object of research is the *Wealth of Nations* or a little known work by an American legal scholar, the difficulties of determining the author's intended meaning, and the many alternative approaches to overcoming these difficulties, remain. It is also worth noting that the concept of "the author's intended meaning" is not an unproblematic one – some historians of thought have argued that the true meaning intended by a writer either does not exist or cannot be definitively established; others that the author's intended meaning, even if it could be established, is of no greater significance than what the researcher or anyone else thinks the author meant. Such assertions do not go uncontested, of course, and the arguments to which they give rise make for thought-provoking reading. Brown's essay provides an introduction to this area of controversy.

It is not uncommon that an article in a journal devoted to the history of economic thought will have as its sole purpose a careful and well documented explication of some aspect of a past economist's ideas, but often such exegetical work is a means to a larger purpose. It may be a prelude to the identification of the economist or one of his or her theories with some larger movement in economics – a certain school of economic thought, for example, or a particular approach to economic theorizing that has persisted through time. Historians of economic thought also attempt to reveal the links between economic theories and aspects of the world of ideas beyond economic thought, including philosophical movements, theological traditions, political ideologies, and developments in the natural sciences. Such links have been found to run both ways, as economists' ideas and theories have both reflected and influenced the ideas of those writing in other fields.

Historians of economic thought frequently give accounts of the theories of past economists or the general approaches of schools of economic thought in order to evaluate them. The goal may be to critique the work of past economists (and perhaps, by implication, the work of later economists who have built upon it) or to show the superiority of past theories or approaches to some modern alternative, be it heterodox or orthodox. Related to this type of work is that which seeks to provide an historical pedigree for a novel theory of, or approach to explaining, some phenomenon. In the process of recounting the ideas of the past the author may attempt, as it were, to portray him- or herself, or some admired colleague, as one who is working within an established and respected intellectual tradition. The general value of history written for such purposes is a matter of disagreement among historians of economic thought, but be that as it may, a great deal of it has been written. John Lodewijks's contribution discusses the general approach and some of the literature that has resulted from applying it.

The history of economic thought is concerned not only with what people believed in the past, but why they believed it; not just how beliefs changed over time, but also why the changes occurred. These "why" questions are both fascinating and difficult, and proposed answers have been yet another source of controversy in the field. For example, a researcher's attempt to place economic theories and ideas in the context of the philosophical, theological, or ideological systems of their day may be, as mentioned above, an exegetical strategy, but it may also be part of an effort to explain why an economist made particular theoretical or methodological choices in attempting to explain economic phenomena, and why the intended audiences either believed or did not believe the explanations that the economist offered. The justification for this is that what people (i.e., both economists and their audiences) consider plausible is a function of their economic or class interests, the ethical or philosophical systems they learned in their youths, and so on. Marx's notion of the intellectual superstructure of a society being derivative of its economic base and system of class relations is one influential version of this argument; another version of this argument underlies Mark Perlman's essay and its attention to the role of a few key *authority-systems* in shaping the development of economic thought. A third rationale for studying the times in which an economist lived is associated most notably with Wesley Mitchell, who argued that the economic theories proposed and accepted at a particular time are best understood as responses to what are seen at the time as the most pressing political and economic problems (Mitchell, 1967, ch. 1). Such arguments about what causes people to propose or believe a particular explanation of economic activity at a moment in time can also be applied to explaining changes over time in economic theories, in the fortunes of particular schools of or approaches to economic thought, and so on; that is, they are held to be due to changes over time in philosophical fashion, ideology, religious beliefs, or events in political and economic history.

These sorts of arguments do not go unchallenged. An alternative view is that economists' choices of theoretical problems to solve and methods of solving them have, at least for the past 200 years, been driven mainly by a desire to improve or expand the theoretical corpus created by their predecessors and contemporaries with respect to such things as descriptive accuracy, logical coherence, or range of applicability. As it has sometimes been expressed, theoretical choices of economists are best explained by factors internal to the activity of economic thought. Similarly, the main factors that govern whether a theory comes to be widely believed (at least within the community of economists and among the more thoughtful members of their audiences) are things such as the logical coherence and generality of a theory, and the extent to which, in one sense or another, it fits the facts (which are held to be perceived in an objective fashion). Theories that perform better in these respects eventually drive out inferior theories. Factors "external" to the realm of economic thought – such as current events, political ideologies, or class interests – play only a minor role in determining changes over time in orthodox economic thought. A careful analysis of the debate concerning the relative importance of internal versus external factors in governing what economic theories people believe can be found in Klaes's essay, but it is clear that a historian's own opinion as to which factors are more important will influence the historical questions that he or she chooses to explore, and the sources and methods that he or she uses in exploring them.

During the 1960s and 1970s, historians of economic thought become more aware of the work of historians and philosophers of science in trying to explain why scientific theories changed over time and how the scientific community chose between competing theories of the same phenomena, along with the associated normative questions of how scientists should seek to improve their theories and what criteria should be used to choose between competing theories. This work teemed with ideas, arguments, and conceptual frameworks that could arguably be applied in attempts to explain and evaluate the historical development of economic theory, and such attempts were made in a number of influential studies. References to Thomas Kuhn, Karl Popper, and Imre Lakatos, and attention to developments in the literature of the history and philosophy of science, have since become standard features of the literature on the history of economic thought. A number of the part II essays, in particular that of John Davis, discuss details of this phenomenon.

As noted earlier in this introduction, the majority of published research in the history of economic thought is devoted to explicating the theories and ideas of famous economists, mainly through careful readings of their published works. Furthermore, discussions of the impact or influence of the theories and ideas of famous economists have largely been limited to their impact on other famous economists. It has been suggested from time to time, and with more or less forcefulness, that such activity might have reached the point of diminishing returns, or at the very least that the understanding of the history of economics provided by this traditional research approach could be enriched considerably through the application of alternative research strategies. These sorts of suggestion have not gone unheeded, and several of the part II essays describe and survey the results of alternative approaches. Whereas the modal research approach in the history of economics has implicitly begun with the concept of economic theories being produced by individual economists armed only with books and intellect, these alternative approaches begin with other pictures of the process through which knowledge is produced, and/or attempt to follow more carefully the processes through which this knowledge is transferred within and beyond the community of economists.

Just as the basic concepts of and ongoing developments in the history and philosophy of science have become part of the working knowledge of many historians of economic thought, so too have many of the fundamental ideas and methods employed by sociologists of scientific knowledge. Those attracted to the research approaches of the sociology of knowledge have argued that it is fruitful to conceptualize economic knowledge as something that is produced in a group setting, through cooperative activity structured by social institutions. So, for example, in trying to understand the choices made by economists at a certain moment in time about what questions to pursue and how best to pursue them, and the choices made by members of their audiences about what to believe, the historian might study the reward structures inherent in the academic setting in which the economists worked, the editorial processes through which books and journal articles containing research findings were published, or the structure and functioning of professional societies in which the economists interacted. Some, following the work of Robert Merton in the sociology of science, have argued that economic thought since the start of the twentieth century has been embodied or reflected in the output of large numbers of workers whose research is standardized in many ways by a shared institutional framework. As such, it becomes possible and worthwhile to portray certain aspects of economic thought with statistical measures, and to test hypotheses about changes in economic thought with statistical methods. A. W. Bob Coats's contribution to this *Companion* provides more detail on how concepts from sociology have been applied to the study of the history of economics. A sociological view of the activities of the economic profession and the processes that govern the transmission and acceptance of ideas has also motivated much of the work on the transmission of ideas across international boundaries, work that is surveyed by José Luís Cardoso.

Economists write to influence other economists, and historians of thought have rightly given a great deal of attention to the success, or lack of success, that they have experienced in that effort, looking into matters such as how Adam Smith was influenced by William Petty, or how the models and methods of Alfred Marshall reflected the influence of Augustin Cournot. But the economists themselves from before the time of Adam Smith have been very much concerned with another audience as well: those who make economic policy. In light of that, it seems obvious that the study of the history of economic thought should include attention to the ideas of all those who, directly or indirectly, play a role in making economic policy, and research on the processes through which their actions and decisions have been influenced by, and perhaps have influenced, economists. Craufurd Goodwin's essay shows that this has indeed become a rich research vein for historians of economics. Scholars have gone into the archives of governmental agencies and the personal papers of governmental officials, from which they have emerged with stories of economists acting directly as policy-makers or as advisors to policy-makers, participating with more or less effectiveness in an environment governed by very different rules than those that prevail in the world of scientific discourse. Historians have followed the ideas of economists as they passed into and through the hands of – and were often transformed by – popularizers, intellectuals-at-large, literary figures, and others who influence the course of policy, from presidents and cabinet members to the people in the street who make up the electorate.

The first paragraphs of this introduction made reference to the diversity of research styles in the history of thought. Klaes offers some evidence that this diversity is increasing. I am not at this point going to join the argument over which of these research methods are more fruitful or productive. I am, however, willing to argue that within the history of economic thought the increase in methodological pluralism has been a good thing. In particular, the impression that a wider array of research topics and methods are coming to be accepted within the field has attracted people with a wider array of intellectual interests and aptitudes to the study of the general questions with which the field has traditionally been concerned. At the same time, the literature of the field is becoming more interesting, as previously unappreciated or under-researched aspects of those questions are being explored in new ways.

Bibliography

Medema, S. G. and Samuels, W. G. (eds.) 2001: *Historians of Economics and Economic Thought: The Construction of Disciplinary Memory.* London and New York: Routledge.

Mitchell, W. C. 1967: *Types of Economic Theory from Mercantilism to Institutionalism*, ed. J. Dorfman, 2 vols. New York: Augustus M. Kelley.

Samuels, W. J. (ed.) 1983: *The Craft of the Historian of Economic Thought.* Vol. 1 of *Research in the History of Economic Thought and Methodology.* Greenwich, CN: JAI Press.

PART I

Historical Surveys

CHAPTER TWO

Ancient and Medieval Economics

S. Todd Lowry

2.1 INTRODUCTION

When dealing with the economic thought of antiquity, we must give primary attention to the ancient Greeks, whose writings have been preserved and form an integral part of our European intellectual heritage. Unfortunately, the two most prominent contemporary classical scholars who deal with the issue, M. I. Finley and Scott Meikle, emphatically deny that the Greeks had any relevant economic thought (Finley, 1970; Meikle, 1995). The problem is, however, definitional. These writers insist on defining economics in terms of Marx's "bourgeois exchange," characterized by late-eighteenth-century international markets. They ignore the broader conceptual perspective of most modern economists and of the earlier political economists such as Marx with his interaction between the "relations" and the "factors" of production; paralleled by Veblen, the interaction between "institutions" and "technology," and Lionel Robbins, the interaction between "unlimited wants" and "limited resources."

This survey focuses on the concepts reflected in policies and institutions applied to economic processes. Outright analyses framed in jurisprudential and political terms have also contributed to modern formulations of economic problems. We can best organize the discussion in terms of three categories – the administrative, the moral, and the analytic – that are frequently intertwined.

2.2 THE ADMINISTRATIVE TRADITION

Ancient administration emphasized personal leadership and decision-making involving labor, materials, and efficient organization.

In retrospect, the best evidence shows that primitive human beings and their hominid ancestors evolved in East Africa as hunter–gatherers in simple extended family groups. In such a system, anthropological studies indicate that social bonding and informal leadership roles provided the organizational cohesion necessary for survival (Reader, 1998 [1997]).

The first records of formal economic organization and accompanying intellectual frameworks come from the ancient river basin economies where grain was produced in coordination with the annual flooding that left raw mudflats as a seedbed. In the Nile and Euphrates Valleys, high yields and dry conditions for storage resulted in stable populations that required land measurement (geometry) and public regulation. The population concentrations and cultural accumulation made possible by this form of agriculture are reflected in the *Old Testament* account of Joseph, in the role of an economic advisor, administering the storage of surplus grain to withstand future famines (Paris, 1998).

Egyptian literature documents the annual accounting of keepers of the royal granaries, whose inventory was measured with giant scales that acquired the status of symbols of justice. Note that the "scales of justice" were an administrative tool for annual accounting, achieving a role as a religious symbol, not as a symbol of exchange (Brandon, 1969).

In the Euphrates Valley, some recently studied clay tablets dating from about 2,200–2,100 B.C. give a clear picture of the administrative thought and practices of a Sumerian city–state. The Erlenmeyer Tablets, which became available for study in 1988, constitute a collection of 88 tablets found in a large jar. These tablets provide a set of written records of production for a three-year period (Nissen et al., 1994). The records show yields from about 75,000 acres, with target amounts and shortfalls in yield from year to year. Average yields were about 12.5 bushels per acre, with three-quarters of a bushel retained for seed (6 percent!).

In addition, records for a milling operation show grain and labor inputs, with product valued in "female labor days." The shortfall from the target efficiency for one year was carried over as a deficit to the next year and was measured at 7,420 female labor days (Nissen et al., 1994, p. 54).

These records show the precision of administrative organization and the origins of both writing and arithmetic for identifying stored produce and its quantity. Marx called this administrative tradition that dominated Near Eastern economic organization "the Asiatic mode of production"(Krader, 1975). Silver, who searches for expressions of natural market forces, finds that political and economic instabilities resulted in nonmarket institutions dominating the economies of antiquity (Silver, 1995).

Most important are these mathematical, graphic, and administrative skills that passed from the Sumerians to the Babylonian culture, whose sexigesimal system has influenced modern measurement of degrees, minutes, and seconds (Nugebauer, 1969). This administrative and mathematically sophisticated tradition continued in the Near East into the Islamic culture. Note that since administration and mathematical procedures are products of human understanding and policy, they are clear repositories of the level of economic thought. Note as well that the development of the zero, or cipher, was irrelevant to arithmetic as long as a placement system with columns was used, crystallized in the abacus or counting board. The zero only became important in Europe when northern African Arabic arithmetic and bookkeeping were brought into northern Italy from Algiers by Leonardo of Pisa (Fibonacci) in the early thirteenth century. When cumulative written records were kept, Roman numerals proved too cumbersome for running accounts in neat columns. It has also been argued that increasingly varied Arabic commerce led to the development of algebra and gave rise to the mechanistic generalization of economic processes in the late Middle Ages (Hadden, 1994). In addition, the thirteenth century saw the shift from tally sticks to account books, and from the itinerant trader to the sedentary merchant who used credit instruments such as bills of exchange.

The best record of the tradition of training in administrative economics is found in Xenophon's treatise, the *Oeconomicus*, written in the mid-fourth century B.C. (Pomeroy, 1994). He also draws on the Babylonian and Persian tradition in his biography of Cyrus the Great, the *Cyropaedia*, that emphasizes the training of Cyrus for administration and military leadership. Xenophon's *Hiero* contains discussions of the administrative stimulus of private production and technology through public recognition and prizes. His *Ways and Means* was a treatise on economic development, emphasizing economies of scale, programming, and promotion. The *Oeconomicus* is a systematic treatment of the organization and administration of the agricultural estate, emphasizing human capital and organizational efficiency (Lowry, 1965; 1987, ch. 3). The family farm was the backbone of the economy and booty from military operations was the prime source of surplus for farm and city (Hanson, 1995). The details of many of Xenophon's ideas must be treated under the heading of analysis.

The tradition of an efficiently managed agrarian estate surfaced in the twelfth century in the Cistercian monasteries that spread across Europe. This order, initiated in 1084 and dedicated to prayer and work, specialized in developing new land with a rational integration of crafts and agriculture (Baeck, 1994, ch. V). Baeck documents some indications of Muslim correlations with the Cistercian movement through Spanish Islam. The managerial uniqueness of the Cistercians might well be studied along with E. E. Cohen's work on Athenian banking to question Polanyi's thesis that early economic activities were "embedded" in broader social structures, and not in dominant forces (Cohen, 1992).

Plato's contribution to administration acquires significance because he incorporated the Pythagorean mathematical tradition into a near-mystical formulation of ideal models. This view of a rational perfectible administration is elaborated below in the discussion of analysis. The Platonic theory of the "Ideas," clearly expounded in Adam Smith's inaugural lecture for his professorship in logic at Glasgow (*The History of the Ancient Logics and Metaphysics*) has its parallels in modern economic theory. Plato's theoretical perspective produced the concept of a perfectible efficient state directed toward optimality through specialization and training. His concept of "justice" was colored by his premise of order and efficiency supervised by the prime intellect with a single value criterion. His famous image of the "ship of state" directed by the technically skilled pilot or captain (the philosopher king) was properly questioned by one authority, who pointed out that some of the passengers might want to have some influence on where they were going (Lowry, 1987, pp. 111–14).

The concept of plural values introduced a dynamic into political economy. When irrational numbers were demonstrated in the Pythagorean societies in the late fifth or early fourth century B.C., Platonic absolutism was shaken to the core. It was partially salvaged by Eudoxus' importation from Chaldea of a dialectical approach to irrationals that became a mathematical image for judicial, legislative, and bargaining processes, to be discussed under analyses.

The pseudo-Platonic dialogue *Alcibiades Major* (ca. 340 B.C.) discusses the need for formal training of those who presume to be "politicos" or "oikonomicos"; that is, politicians or economists in the city–state. This document influenced the Greco-Roman educational tradition for 900 years. The dialogue emphasizes Plato's concept of individualistic authoritarian virtue, but it also discusses an apparently broader tradition that prescribed "looking into the eyes of others" to get a reflection or social criterion for managing one's conduct as administrator. The concept became known as "the mirror for princes," naming a rich body of literature on political and economic administration (Lowry, 2001). A famous example was the Arabic pseudo-Aristotelian advice to Alexander the Great, the *Secretum Secretorum*, dating from the eighth century A.D. It reached England in Latin translation after the Crusades. Erasmus's *The Education of a Christian Prince*, dedicated to the young Emperor Charles V in 1518, was also an influential example of the genre (Born, 1936). These tracts emphasized leadership, human capital, personnel policy, taxation, trade, and control of the military.

2.3 THE MORAL TRADITION

The Eden story in *Genesis* provides basic imagery in the Judeo-Christian tradition. As with most cultural myths, it is a collage of concepts, including a parallel with the female blame tradition of the Greek Pandora myth (Norris, 1999). The dominant thesis is, however, the challenge to divine authority by the beneficiaries of the abundance of the Garden of Eden. When Adam and Eve ate the forbidden fruit of the tree of knowledge and asserted the right to choose for themselves, they were cast out of the world of abundance into scarcity; to "eat bread in the sweat of their faces." The moral theme is that knowledge and the exercise of choice are burdens in a world of divinely imposed or natural scarcity. This picture of economics is usually found in the introductory chapter of sophisticated introductory economics textbooks, although contradicted by subjective relativism in later chapters. An unfortunate spinoff of the Eden story is the "curse of work" with its simplistic tension between work and leisure, in a world in which most people find fulfillment and self-definition in their work.

In contrast to the bounty of the Nile and Euphrates, the near-subsistence level in the small agrarian communities in Greece gave rise to a moral emphasis on allocation that is the real issue behind the more superficial concept of objective scarcity. Aristotle framed this issue very carefully in book I of his *Politics*. Consumption was the objective of production and the surplus should be allocated to rearing children (Lowry, 1995). Aristotle found this natural moral commitment illustrated by the yolk in eggs that sustained the embryo. This was a real issue in eastern Mediterranean societies, where newborns were not named until the eighth day, when the family patriarch evaluated sex, health, and food supply before ceremonially accepting them into the family circle. Unwanted children were set adrift in baskets or left on the mountainside.

Exchange within the village and the use of money facilitated distribution, but satiation provided a natural limit on consumption that left surpluses for the "offspring." By contrast, foreign merchants who accumulated money were not subject to this natural limit of physical satiation. Therefore, this kind of trade fell outside the natural regulatory process.

In book VII of the *Politics*, Aristotle clearly formulated the concept of diminishing marginal utility and an ordinal hierarchy of values, an influential conceptual framework that has been attributed to Maslow in contemporary motivation theory (Maslow, 1943; Lowry, 1998, p. 32).

The importance of Aristotle's distinction is its basis for the moral repudiation of usury, in which money loans are condemned as immoral and extortionate. As in Judaic doctrine, money cannot breed, and should not be expected to grow when a consumption loan is made to a needy person within the community.

The moral validity of a claim for subsistence grew into a natural right of appropriation in the writings of Thomas Aquinas and John Locke (Lowry, 1995). In addition, the usury issue is largely a retrospective emphasis. Medieval Muslims developed the justification for charging borrowers for the sacrifice suffered by the lender, adopted by Scholastics as "lucrum cessans." The moral issue persisted when considering the extortion implicit in subsistence loans to the starving. In commerce, however, the institution of the commendam partnership demonstrates the irrelevance of the usury issue and the sharing of surpluses generated by capital advances for trade. The "commendam" was a commercial partnership in which one party advanced the capital for a trading venture and the other provided the personal service. As in modern partnership law, profits were divided equally between the partners after the voyage. The commendam contract, of Arabian origin, neutralized the usury issue in commerce through the Middle Ages. It also provided a mechanism for limiting liability to achieve economies of scale – a device that fueled the development of the modern corporation. Several persons could invest money in a commendam partnership with a broker, who would then advance the sum to a trader in another commendam partnership. The initial investors were insulated from personal liability for losses beyond their specific investment (Udovitch, 1970).

The moral reinforcement of this system was provided by the "unwritten law," an ancient Near Eastern custom that guaranteed hospitality to strangers, the honoring of parents, and respect for gods (Lowry, 1987, pp. 142–3). In his *Memorabilia* (IV, 4, 19–20), Xenophon argues that the unwritten law must have come from the gods, since it was universal among all peoples, who could not have met together and agreed on it. The point emphasizes that the rule of hospitality made merchant travelers safe and gave people a source of news, trade goods, and entertainment provided by itinerant bards. It supported the institution of "guest friendship" that served to initiate exchange through reciprocal gift-giving (Lowry, 1987, pp. 147–9). Through the Middle Ages, much trade was supported by special relationships between commercial families, with long traditions reminiscent of the ancient "guest friendship" relationship.

It is important to emphasize that the Near Eastern tradition of personal honor, associated with the early Persians, provided a basis for commercial exchange using tokens or tallies as credit instruments. Deposits could be left with an individual and the depositing party could take a split piece of the tally stick, the dividend. The split could be transferred to an agent or third party who could claim the deposit with the unforgeable match of the dividend with the stock. This system was also used as a record of payments or simple accounting by notching the matched pieces. The personal pledge behind letters of credit and bills of exchange became the foundation of commercial relations in a world in which transfers of bullion were risky. By the thirteenth century, annual fairs for clearing bills of exchange were held in Champagne (Postan, 1928). The growth in importance of bills of exchange under the "Law Merchant" is documented in Gerard Malynes's *Lex Mercatoria* of 1620. The moral force behind the personal pledge to honor the claim represented by the paper document permitted transferable paper to circulate internationally in the late Middle Ages under the rules of the Law Merchant. Every endorser added his personal pledge to the paper and the accepter took his rights "from the face of the document." By the sixteenth century, the Common Law of England was enforcing "actions on account," providing a remedy beyond the merchant courts (Rogers, 1995).

A further insight into the practical conflict between economic reality and the usury issue is to be found in the institution of the *Mons Pietas*. In the mid-fifteenth century in central Italy, San Bernardino of Siena launched a campaign to drive out Jewish pawnshops. The success of this project resulted in such popular protest that local municipalities developed public pawnshops, *Monti di Piete*, which provided 5 percent annual loans. The institution spread to Spain and elsewhere in the sixteenth century. Historically, many fifteenth-century commercial cities arranged for Jews to enter and set up sources of credit. Credit was needed by rich and poor alike.

2.4 The Analysis of Economic Interactions

The earliest economic relationships were distributive or allocative within the family. Without food collection and distribution to dependent children as unearned increments, there would be no surviving progeny. Beyond the family there evolved a formal system of distributive economics, geared to interactions between unrelated individuals or groups. The basic arrangement, divide and choose, was well developed in antiquity and presaged the analysis of exchange.

In Hesiod's *Theognis* (335–60), the myth of Prometheus dividing an ox with Zeus is presented (Lowry, 1987, ch. 5; 1991). As with myths generally, this account is multi-layered and sometimes contradictory, but it is one of the earliest presentations of the formal system used to divide game, booty, and inheritances.

Prometheus skins the ox and divides the meat into two piles. He then invites Zeus to choose the pile he prefers. The beauty of the system is that both parties receive shares based on voluntary choice, which limits the likelihood of disputes. As indicated in the myth, however, the system contains elements of exchange. Prometheus aggregates the bones under a layer of fat in one pile, and the lean meat covered by the stomach and tripe in the other. As anthropologists remind us, Zeus, as with other Near Eastern gods, could only receive his share of sacrificed animals via "burnt offerings," which was best achieved by burning the bones and some fat. On the other hand, humans of that era highly valued a dish similar to the Scottish "haggis" and also used the lean meat grilled on spits. The result was a voluntary exchange of subjective preferences. The system established the principle of volition as the measure of fairness that was transferred to exchange, despite the many subtleties in the inequality of informed choice in most exchanges for necessaries.

Some of Aesop's *Fables* elucidate the way in which this system, as with exchange, could be corrupted by the exercise of raw power. One fable presents the case of a lion and three other animals participating in a joint hunt. One of the animals divides the meat into four piles. The lion chooses the first share as "the King of Beasts," the second as leader of the hunt, the third as a participant, and, finally, he places a paw on the fourth pile and, after hesitating, he dares anyone to try and take it away from him. This and a similar fable are the source of the adage "taking the lion's share."

The principle of voluntary choice was used in more complex systems such as the Athenian "antidosis," where the ostensibly wealthiest citizen was called on to finance public festivals. He could try to opt out by offering to trade his total wealth with that of another citizen whom he considered wealthier. The latter could accept the trade or assume responsibility for the event (Lowry, 1987, p. 129).

This principle was used as a basis for a national political system by James Harrington in his *Oceana* of 1656. Harrington referred to the process as "cake cutting," as when two little girls divided a single small cake – one divided and the other chose. This has been the point of departure for extensive modern mathematical examination of the process in multiple distributions and arbitration. Brams and Taylor developed the modern implications of this distributive process in political theory (Brams and Taylor, 1996). It can also be surmised that the system of public auctions evolved from dividing booty among a group of raiders, where goods were offered and added to until one party accepted them as his share.

In Xenophon's *Oeconomicus*, subjective value or individual use value is specifically analyzed and compared with exchange value. If a man owns a horse and does not know how to handle it, and is even likely to be injured by it, is it useful to him? But if he knows how to sell it, it has exchange value (*Oeconomicus*, I.5–6, 8; Lowry, 1987, pp. 76–9). This idea broadens the concept of individual use value to a general social use value that the individual can reach through exchange. It is not, however, a market theory of value.

The foundation for a theory of fair exchange in the market is laid out in the widely cited incident from the *Cyropaedia* where Cyrus, as a boy, is assigned the responsibility of judging the fairness of a forced exchange. A tall boy with a short tunic forcibly exchanges tunics with a short boy who has a long one. Cyrus rules that the exchange is fair because it results in both boys having better fitting tunics. His mentors flog him for his decision, pointing out that he was asked to judge the justice of the case, not the enhanced use values involved. To be just, an exchange must be voluntary (*Cyropaedia*, I.3.15–17)!

The most important legacy of Xenophon's thought in the history of economic ideas is his formulation of the division of labor. In the *Cyropaedia*, Xenophon comments on the quality of the different dishes prepared by the specialized cooks in Cyrus' kitchen. He then describes a shoemaking workshop in which standard parts are cut out and assembled in stages by different workmen. The discussion is extended to remark on the fact that carpenters are "jacks of all trades" in small communities, but specialists in larger cities (*Cyropaedia*, VIII.2.5–6). Adam Smith's discussion of the pin factory is frequently credited with characterizing modern economic theory, since it was in this context that he elaborated the point that specialization is limited by the extent of the market. Meek and Skinner's publication of a new set of dated notes of Smith's lectures identifies his development of this point in 1763, and his lecture reads like a paraphrase of Xenophon's discussion of the role of the carpenter in small and large cities (Lowry, 1979, p. 77; 1987, pp. 68–73). Marx quoted the passage from Xenophon in full and attributed to it the formulation of division of labor as correlated with the extent of the market while emphasizing quality, not quantity, in production (Marx, 1930, v. 1, p. 388, n. 1). Marx distinguished the workshop from the mechanized factory when characterizing modern economics. "Bourgeois exchange," as opposed to simple specialization, was what made the social division of labor possible (Marx, 1847, pp. 128–39). Classical scholars such as Finley have ignored this distinction when rejecting the importance of Xenophon's exposition, which Marx accepted as important to political economy. The undue emphasis on quality by analysts of Xenophon's discussion is put in serious question by his shoemaking illustration. A shop using an assembly line production process with interchangeable parts is very close to Eli Whitney's breakthrough of "replaceable parts." Modern industrialization is built on mass production with standardized parts and assembly lines.

While it is clear that Xenophon and his contemporaries limited their analyses of transactions to "isolated exchange" – that is, to individualized transactions – their grasp of the nuances of social efficiency is convincing. In Xenophon's *Banquet* (VII, 1–5) a Syracusan impresario challenges Socrates to validate his reputation as a theorist. Socrates obliges by pointing out that since the impresario seeks to entertain, having his slave boy do acrobatics over swords is inefficient. The increment in entertainment value is trivial, while the increased risk of injury to the boy is great. This comparison of marginal revenue with marginal cost as a formal analytic contribution has been ignored by modern classicists and economists alike. However, the principle was repeated as an abstraction in a sixteenth-century English agricultural manual, where it is pointed out that when one has a great number of things to do on the farm, priority should be given to those that would result in the greatest loss in the shortest time if not done. In the context of choice, the marginal nature of costs and benefits is formulated clearly (Fitzherbert, 1534, p. 146, L. 63–75: p. 97 of reprint).

Another analytic contribution in Xenophon's writings that has been strangely ignored is a remarkable presentation of mutual advantage from exchange. The *Cyropaedia* (III. 2. 17–33) contains an account of Cyrus administratively structuring an exchange of lands, surplus farmland from a herding people and surplus pasture from a farming people. The Armenians and the Chaldeans both benefit, demonstrating a productive surplus from exchange that can also support the necessary administrative superstructure (Lowry, 1987, pp. 64–5).

Plato's most important and enduring contribution to formal thought was his elevation of mathematics to a primary position in scientific inquiry. All sciences, including economics, which use mathematical analyses must comprehend the essence of Platonic idealism in order to properly evaluate the significance and limits of mathematics in their disciplines. Plato was basically elaborating the ideas of the secret Pythagorean societies. They held that the world was a rational entity built by the "great Geometer" from the basic unit; that is, the point or the "one." A series of points made a line, a series of adjacent lines made a plane, and a series of superimposed planes made a solid. All shapes or "forms" were divisible by the unit, the "one" or the "point," and definable in terms of each other by "whole number ratios," and therefore "rational" and commensurable! By the same token, the integer "1" was the building block of all numbers, paralleling the materialist's atom. All physical entities and social structures, therefore, existed as ideas or forms – in essence, blueprints – developed by a divine power. As a result, inquiry into physical and social relationships was more effective through mathematical formulations and analyses. The theory was that worldly expressions of things were somewhat imperfect and observation was unreliable, so it was preferable to go straight to the essence toward which dynamic processes gravitated dialectically.

By medieval times, this perspective had become known as Platonic "realism" and it lies behind the somewhat erroneous tradition that the Greeks in general did not believe in experimentation. The Pythagoreans experimented extensively with musical intervals, seeking to "discover" natural proportions. Of course, this attitude flies in the face of those who consider mathematics a synthetic science, artificially elaborating rational consistency. Plato's and the Pythagoreans' influence was very persistent, but it primarily appealed to an elitist perspective. Since there was only one true reality, the most discerning and intelligent person was the best source of supervision. Efficiency was an absolute with only one true measure of rational utility and departures from it occurred only through ignorance. Of course, the ignorant who could not accept revealed truth should be dismissed. Jeremy Bentham absorbed this perspective as the basis for neoclassical utility theory (Lowry, 1987, p. 266, n. 22).

As discussed above, the discovery of irrational numbers upset Pythagorean absolutism, but the problem was resolved by embracing the Eudoxan dialectic that approached the "truth." The most famous of these number ladders, the Fibonacci Series, approaches the "Golden Section" (0.618 . . . /1). The dialectic is formed by the series 1/2, 2/3, 3/5, 5/8; each fraction being alternately a "little more" and a "little less," but closing on the irrational, 0.618. . . . This ratio occurs in nature, was accepted aesthetically in art and architecture, and was revived in the Renaissance (Taylor, 1949).

The democratic school of thought in antiquity, articulated by Protagoras, held that human understanding was best achieved by a dialectic between two perspectives as in the opposing sides in a law suit, an assembly, or a bargaining process (Lowry, 1987, chs. 6 and 7). In this view, good laws and justice were a popular consensus, not an abstract absolute.

The most economically provocative analytic writing in ancient Greece was book V.v of Aristotle's *Nicomachean Ethics*, which discusses justice in exchange. Aristotle surveyed justice in distribution, correction, and exchange. He contended that the mathematics of proportion illustrated these relationships. Commentaries on the sketchy survivals of this exposition dominated Scholastic treatments of exchange when Aristotelianism was revived in European academic centers. Odd Langholm's systematic analysis of the many Scholastic commentaries on book V demonstrated that the vagueness of the manuscript promoted a variety of criteria for just price, including labor value, subjective value, and scarcity theory (Langholm, 1979). Many economists, most conspicuously, J. A. Schumpeter, have labeled Aristotle's book V as hopelessly obscure and have put Aristotle down as a purveyor of "pompous common sense." It is anachronistic, however, to evaluate this suggestive material in terms of modern market theory. The analysis deals with justice in an isolated exchange in the context of legal arbitration, not fair market price. Having been exposed to the breakdown of simplistic rationality in Plato's Academy, the problem was how to define a fair exchange price between two parties with different subjective perspectives toward goods or money.

There are two relevant mathematical insights into Aristotle's analysis of exchange. Both are ignored by most modern classical scholars (Meikle, 1995). The first is the dilemma of irrational numbers and commensurability that was ameliorated by Eudoxus. Secondly, Aristotle's statement that he was using three different proportions to analyze distributive, corrective, and reciprocal or exchange transactions has strangely befuddled most classical scholars. Only a few have recognized the harmonic proportion as the one that Aristotle intended to use to illustrate exchange. What is mystifying is that Boethius wrote a summary of ancient arithmetic in the sixth century A.D. that was well known in medieval intellectual circles. He specifically stated that all the ancients knew three major proportions – the arithmetic, the geometric, and the harmonic – and used them to elucidate social and political relations (Masi, 1983). The harmonic is frustrating because it implicitly assimilates the concept of subjectivity. The illustration used by Boethius is 16, as the harmonic mean between 10 and 40. The mean term (16) is a particular proportion (60 percent [6]) larger than the smaller term (10) and that same proportion (60 percent [24]) smaller than the larger term (40). Thus the harmonic proportion can suggest that a price exists that is proportional to the subjective perspectives of the two bargainers. Surprisingly, this nuance does not show up in the medieval commentaries as rendered by modern scholars, although Olivi's work suggests a grasp of it. Furthermore, Buridan's anecdotal formulation of the dilemma of an ass that got caught equidistant between two equally attractive piles of hay – and starved to death, suspended in indecision – suggests a sophisticated understanding of the pitfalls that are inherent in mathematizing subjective demand.

Another nuance in Aristotle's analysis of exchange is the concept of consumer's surplus. This is not strange, since he was not burdened with the presumption of a single market exchange price. His point was that parties were drawn together because they both saw a potential advantage in exchanging. There was, therefore, a zone of surplus that had to be divided by a judge (Lowry, 1969; 1987, ch. 7). Aristotle indicated that this mutual advantage should be "halved" when settling an exchange in arbitration. The idea was clearly articulated by Xenophon in his discussion of the arrangement that Cyrus negotiated between the Armenians and the Chaldeans, described above.

2.5 ROMAN LAW AND MARKET THEORY

It must be observed that modern neoclassical economic theory frames transactions as simple sales. Early Greek and Judaic law, following the voluntaristic principle of just exchange, held that a party could back out of an arrangement before its execution; that is, the point of sale. Roman law developed contract. Contract recognizes that the economy requires planning and that without commitments over time, complex chains of production and trade cannot take place at an individual level. Contract discounts the presumption of a stable market and builds commitments as isolated exchanges, similar to modern international trade agreements.

The massive body of Roman law was brought together in the 530s A.D. by Justinian, Emperor of the Eastern Roman Empire in Byzantium from 527–65 A.D. Along with the *Digest*, he also produced a one-volume text, *The Institutes*, which served as the basic legal text in the universities in the Middle Ages. The Roman law nominally identified a "natural law" or "jus gentium," but this was a concept in the Protagorean and Aristotelian tradition, where "natural" meant what people tended to develop for themselves or that which was inherently rational (Kelley, 1990). This is echoed in Judaic literature, where Jewish elders, debating a point of theological doctrine, rejected the arguments by an individual who demonstrated divine authority by calling down a heavenly sign. A sage, supporting rational discourse, quoted the Torah, "After the Majority one must incline.(Ex.23:2)" (Ohrenstein, 1998, p. 215). Stein has succinctly analyzed the Sabinian school of Roman law with its institutionalist orientation, and after his definitive compendium of Scholastic thought, Odd Langholm has abstracted the institutional aspects of Scholastic thought that carried on into modern economics (Langholm, 1992, 1998a; Stein, 1995).

Further comment should be made on the spirit of trade and the alleged suppressive influence of the prohibition of usury. The respectability of the merchant was well established in the medieval Islamic world. The commonality of commercial culture in the Mediterranean was demonstrated by the development of trade languages, *lingua franca* in the eastern and *sabir* in the western Mediterranean. As cited above, most trade was organized under the façade of the commendam partnership system (Udovitch, 1970). We should also consider the possible influence of the decentralized individualistic Islamic religious tradition on European Protestantism and the spirit of capitalism.

Joel Kaye has demonstrated the emerging concept of the market process reflected in literature and scholastic writings in late medieval times (Kaye, 1998a,b). It is also important to recognize the municipal organization from the Greco-Roman world that was indigenous in Muslim North Africa, Italy, and Spain. This tradition provided a prototype for the small medieval commercial towns that flourished in eleventh- and twelfth-century Europe. The municipal commitment to regulating prices of subsistence goods for the poor was part of the tradition. Also, the English rules that specify market locations and days, with provisions against "forestalling, cornering, and regrating," dating from the thirteenth and fourteenth centuries, are replicas of North African market regulations (Essid, 1995, pp. 156–8).

In his compact but detailed summary of the debates over Scholastic economic influences, Julius Kirshner reminds us that medieval doctors followed the Roman law on just price (Kirshner, 1974, p. 24). The rule is stated in Justinian's *Institutes* (3.305); "*tantum bona valent, quantum vendi possunt*" ("goods are worth as much as they can be sold for"). The theory, however, assumes a rational market atmosphere and, as Kirshner reminds us, there was no hesitation in assuming that any body of rational individuals, whether buyers, judges, or legislators, could arrive at a rational price. The contributions of Raymond de Roover focus on the influence of Scholastic thought on modern economics. He emphasizes that San Bernardino's development of utility theory brings out the role of bills of exchange in circumventing the usury problem (Kirshner, 1974, p. 32).

2.6   MONEY AND THE ECONOMY

Money is reputed to have emerged shortly before 600 B.C. in Lydia, possibly to pay soldiers in pre-measured amounts of precious metals. Minted money, however, spread over the Mediterranean basin during the following century as a convenience in local trade. Ed Will has contended that the concept of credit preceded minted money (Will, 1955). This is supported by the early references to tally sticks and tokens that suggest fiat money.

Aristotle's discussion of money has been widely recognized. He identified the uses of money as a medium of exchange, a unit of measure, and a store of value for future purchases. In listing these concepts, Schumpeter contended that Aristotle failed to identify money as a means of deferred payment, and labeled him a metalist (Lowry, 1987, pp. 223, 226–30). These two contentions can be put into question by Aristotle's treatment of usury and his treatment of money as a product of law (Gordon, 1961). In addition, the many discussions of fiat money in Aristotle's time suggest that the pervasiveness of eighteenth-century naturalism and bullionism has influenced moderns to refuse to give credence to earlier monetary sophistication. We recognize Gresham's Law in Aristophanes' *Frogs*, and fiat money in Plato's recommendation of a cartel money system for domestic trade in his *Laws* (742a–b) and in the pseudo-Platonic dialogue, *Eryxias*.

An additional example of monetary theory that shows an amazing macroeconomic grasp is Plutarch's biography of Lycurgus, the legendary Spartan lawgiver

(Plutarch's *Lives*, I; *Lycurgus*, VIII–X). Lycurgus introduced the iron obol as part of an economic reform. The iron money had its commodity value destroyed with vinegar and its exchange value was less than the commodity value of iron, so that counterfeiting was thwarted. Foreign trade was limited to barter, stimulating domestic production since outsiders would not take the money. This analysis was available in English as early as 1579 in Sir Thomas North's translation, but the only economist who noted it was Cantillion (*Essai*, I, XVII; see Lowry, 1987, pp. 226–7). The act of ignoring such a comprehensive macroeconomic analysis by classical economists, who undoubtedly read Plutarch as students, can only be explained by bullionist presumptions and by naturalistic rejection of an administered monetary policy.

In his *Politics*, Aristotle built an economic system based on aggregations of human units into families, villages, and cities. Associated with these levels were "goods of the body," (consumption) "amenities" (traded for in the village), and "psychic goods" (products of city culture). The first two of these are limited by natural satiation or diminishing utility and the third, although unlimited, requires no money since it involves improving the mind. This ordinal hierarchy of values is concisely developed in book VII of the *Politics* and closely follows Maslow's groundbreaking ordinal analysis of human motivation (Maslow, 1943).

Marx understood Aristotle's distinctions clearly. Foreign merchants bought commodities and sold them for more money. They were not subject to any natural limit, because there is no limit on the desire for money. Therefore, $M - C - M'$, as Marx put it in *Capital*, crossed a threshold into another type of economic process (Marx, 1930, vol. I, pp. 83ff. and 131–41; Lowry, 1974a; 1987, pp. 123ff.). Aristotle's emphasis on satiety or diminishing utility is echoed in Adam Smith's contention that landlords consume a limited amount and therefore, as if guided by an invisible hand, they contribute the balance for productive investment (Smith, 1976, pp. 219–21).

After the deaths of Alexander the Great in 323 and of Aristotle in 322 B.C., the Hellenistic period was characterized by economic thought oriented toward kingship and administration. War was the primary source of imperial wealth, supported by agriculture and people. Ultimately, in Imperial Rome, a breakthrough occurred in fiscal policy as productive land was taxed as the source of wealth instead of relying on booty and levies on the assets of wealthy citizens (Vivenza, 1998). The assumption that agriculture was the source of surpluses for investment dominated economic writings through Smithian times and was theoretically structured by Quesnay and the physiocrats (McNally, 1988).

The medieval literature on money is characterized by nascent nationalism, with the imagery of the body applied to the kingdom, and of money as the blood moving through its parts. Nicole Oresme's *De Moneta* pointed out that if money is accumulated in the king's treasury and withdrawn from circulation, it constitutes an abscess in the body. Copernicus also wrote a sophisticated tract on money (Lowry, 1974b). These ideas culminated in Thomas Hobbes's *Leviathan* and were ultimately worked out by Quesnay (Lowry, 1974b).

The sophistication of late medieval thought regarding money deserves special attention. Sovereigns who controlled mints were aware of the short-term advantages of 10 percent and 20 percent debasements. Reminted issues could be spent before prices adjusted upward.

   Three significant phenomena further indicate the economic understanding of the time. First, discussions of "vellon" or "billon" that initially referred to debased copper money (black money) began to note the importance of small coins to foster beneficial exchange among the common people. Secondly, imaginary monies of account began to be used as common denominators for the dozens of coinages in circulation (Einaudi, 1953). Thirdly, bills of exchange were developed that replaced tally sticks as merchants ceased to travel with money and goods. Annual fairs were held in Champagne as early as the thirteenth century for clearing or settling accounts based on bills of exchange, thus minimizing the hazardous physical transfer of minted money (Postan, 1928). These financial instruments were pledges of credit from responsible merchants and circulated widely with endorsements before being presented for payment. This created a paper currency that strengthened with each additional endorsement. *Cambio secco* and *cambio fictitio* were names given to bills that did not grow out of a substantive exchange of goods. These synthetic bills circulated with their pledge of credit, anticipating nineteenth-century bank notes. Bills were enforced by the Law Merchant, an international fraternal system, but Rogers finds that English courts were enforcing negotiable instruments by the fifteenth century (Boyer-Xambeu et al., 1994; Rogers, 1995).

2.7   CONCLUSION

After a surge of interest in experimentation in the late Renaissance and Enlightenment, an emphasis on romantic naturalistic theory dominated eighteenth-century thought. Particularly in the English tradition, this theme was influenced by Deists, who conceived of a world operating like a giant clock that had been wound up by God and left to run on its own rational basis. Such a perspective served as a basis for rejecting the "Divine Right of Kings" and government intervention. Predictably, the Platonic philosophical view tended to creep into this materialist perspective. It was characterized by the notion of an ideal blueprint of perfect processes toward which the real world should be allowed to gravitate. Aspects of this ideal naturalism persist to this day. Their shadow is understandable when we remember that both Adam Smith and Karl Marx, the two most influential classical economists, were primarily trained in the Greek classics. The ubiquity of classical literature in the educational foundation of nineteenth-century Europeans, including Englishmen, explains the surfacing of Thucidides' theory of challenge from the introductory lines of his history in the work of Arnold Toynbee, and the specific embracing of Xenophon's work by John Ruskin. Meanwhile, the more realistic tradition of administrative efficiency and leadership has probably dominated pragmatic decision-making in business and government without the credentials of an institutionalized philosophy, except for grudging concessions to organization theory and human capital.

Bibliography

Baeck, L. 1994: *The Mediterranean Tradition in Economic Thought*. London and New York: Routledge.

Born, L. K. 1936: *The Education of a Christian Prince by Deciderius Erasmus*, translated and introduced. New York: Columbia University Press.

Boyer-Xambeu, M. T., Deleplace, G., and Gillard, L., 1994: *Money and Public Currencies: The 16th Century Challenge*, trans. A. Azodi. Armonk, New York: M. E. Sharpe (review by S. T. Lowry in *History of Political Economy*, 28(2), 1996, 310–13).

Brams, S. J. and Taylor, A. D. 1996: *Fair Division: From Cake-Cutting to Dispute Resolution*. Cambridge, UK: Cambridge University Press.

Brandon, S. G. F. 1969: The weighing of the soul. In J. M. Kitagawa and C. H. Long (eds.), *Myths and Symbols*. Chicago: The University of Chicago Press.

Cohen, E. E., 1992: *Athenian Economy and Society: A Banking Perspective*. Princeton, NJ: Princeton University Press.

Einaudi, L. 1953: The theory of imaginary money. In F. C. Lane and J. C. Riemersma (eds.), *Enterprise and Secular Change*. Homewood, IL: Richard D. Irwin, 229–61.

Essid, M. Y. 1995: *A Critique of the Origins of Islamic Economic Thought*. New York and Köln: E. J. Brill.

Finley, M. I. 1970: Aristotle and economic analysis. *Past & Present*, no. 70, 3–25.

Fitzherbert, M. 1534: *The Book of Husbandry*, ed. W. W. Skeat. Vaduz: Kraus Reprint Ltd, 1965 reprint.

Gordon, B. 1961: Aristotle, Schumpeter, and the metallist tradition. *Quarterly Journal of Economics*, 75, 608–14.

Hadden, R. W. 1994: *On the Shoulders of Merchants*. Albany, NY: State University of New York Press.

Hanson, V. D. 1995: *The Other Greeks*. New York: The Free Press.

Kaye, J. 1998a: Monetary and market consciousness in thirteenth and fourteenth century Europe. In Lowry and Gordon, op. cit., pp. 371–404.

—— 1998b: *Economy and Nature in the Fourteenth Century*. Cambridge, UK: Cambridge University Press.

Kelley, D. R. 1990: *The Human Measure: Social Thought in the Western Legal Tradition*. Cambridge, MA: Harvard University Press.

Kirshner, J. 1974: Raymond de Roover on Scholastic economic thought. In J. Kirshner (ed.), *Business, Banking, and Economic Thought in Late Medieval and Early Modern Europe*. Chicago: The University of Chicago Press, 15–36.

Krader, L., 1975: *The Asiatic Mode of Production: Sources, Development, and Critique in the Writings of Karl Marx*. Assen: Van Gorcum.

Langholm, O., 1979: *Price and Value in the Aristotelian Tradition: A Study in Scholastic Sources*. Bergen, Oslo, Tromso: Universitetsforlaget.

—— 1992: *Economics in the Medieval Schools*. New York: E. J. Brill.

—— 1998a: *The Legacy of Scholasticism in Economic Thought*. Cambridge, UK: Cambridge University Press.

—— 1998b: The medieval schoolmen (1200–1400). In Lowry and Gordon, op. cit., pp. 439–502.

Lowry, S. T. 1965: The classical Greek theory of natural resources. *Land Economics*, 41, 204–8.

—— 1969: Aristotle's mathematical analysis of exchange. *History of Political Economy*, 1, 44–66.

—— 1974a: Aristotle's "natural limit" and the economics of price regulation. *Greek, Roman and Byzantine Studies*, 15, 57–63.

—— 1974b: The archaeology of the circulation concept in economic theory. *Journal of the History of Ideas*, 35, 422–44.

—— 1979: Recent literature on ancient Greek economic thought. *Journal of Economic Literature*, 17, 65–86.

—— 1981: The roots of hedonism. *History of Political Economy*, 13, 812–23.

—— 1987: *The Archaeology of Economic Ideas: The Classical Greek Tradition*. Durham, NC: Duke University Press.

—— 1991: Distributive economics and the Promethean meat division. In M. Silver (ed.), *Ancient Economy in Mythology: East and West*. Savage, MD: Rowman and Littlefield, 45–58.

—— 1995: Social justice and the subsistence economy. In K. D. Irani and M. Silver (eds.), *Social Justice in the Ancient World*. Westport, CT: Greenwood Press, 9–24.

—— 1998: The economic and jurisprudential ideas of the ancient Greeks: our heritage from Hellenic thought. In Lowry and Gordon, op. cit., pp. 11–37.

—— 2001: The training of the economist in antiquity: "The Mirror for Princes" tradition in *Alcibiades Major* and Aquinas' *On Kingship*. In J. E. Biddle, J. B. Davis, and S. G. Medema (eds.), *Economics Broadly Considered: Essays in Honor of Warren J. Samuels*. London and New York: Routledge, 33–48.

—— and B. Gordon (eds.) 1998: *Ancient and Medieval Economic Ideas and Concepts of Social Justice*. New York: E. J. Brill.

Marx, K. 1847: *The Poverty of Philosophy*, translated from the corrected French and German editions, 1885 and 1892. Moscow: Foreign Languages Publishing House, no date.

—— 1930: *Capital: A Critique of Political Economy*, Everyman's Library edn., 2 vols. London and Toronto: J. M. Dent.

Masi, M. 1983: *Boethian Number Theory: A Translation of the* De Institutione Arithmetica. Amsterdam: Editions Rodopi.

Maslow, A. H. 1943: A theory of human motivation. *Psychological Review*, 50(4), 370–96.

McNally, D. 1988: *Political Economy: A Reinterpretation*. Berkeley, CA: University of California Press.

Meikle, S. 1995: *Aristotle's Economics*. Oxford: Oxford University Press.

Neugebauer, O. 1969: *The Exact Sciences in Antiquity*, 2nd edn. New York: Dover.

Nissen, H. J., Damerow, P., and Englund, R. K., 1993: *Ancient Bookkeeping: Early Writing and Techniques of Economic Administration in the Ancient Near East*. Chicago: The University of Chicago Press.

Norris, P. 1999: *Eve: A Biography*. New York: New York University Press.

Ohrenstein, R. A. 1998: "Talmud and Talmudic tradition: a socio-economic perspective. In Lowry and Gordon, op. cit., pp. 209–67.

Paris, D. 1998: An economic look at the Old Testament. In Lowry and Gordon, op. cit., pp. 39–104.

Pomeroy, S. B. 1994: *Xenophon Oeconomicus: A Social and Historical Commentary with a New English Translation*. Oxford: The Clarendon Press.

Postan, M. 1928: Credit in medieval trade. *Economic History Review*, 1(2), 234–61 (on money).

Reader, J. 1998 [1997]: *Africa: The Biography of a Continent*. New York: Alfred A. Knopf, 29–105. First published London: Hamish Hamilton.

Rogers, J. S. 1995: *The Early History of the Law of Bills and Notes: A Study of the Origins of Anglo-American Commercial Law*. Cambridge, UK: Cambridge University Press.

Silver, M. 1995: *Economic Structures of Antiquity*. Westport, CT, and London: Greenwood Press.

Smith, A., 1976: *The Theory of Moral Sentiments*, ed. R. H. Campbell, A. S. Skinner, and W. B. Todd. Glasgow edition. Oxford: The Clarendon Press.

Stein, P. 1995: Interpretation and legal reasoning in Roman law. *Chicago/Kent Law Review: Symposium on Ancient Law, Economics & Society*, 70(4), 1539–56.

Taylor, A. E. 1949: *Plato: The Man and his Work*. London: Methuen.

Udovitch, A. L. 1970: *Partnership and Profit in Medieval Islam*. Princeton, NJ: Princeton University Press.

Vivenza, G. 1998: Roman thought on economics and justice. In Lowry and Gordon, op. cit., pp. 269–332.

Will, E. 1955: Reflexions et hypotheses sur les origines du monnayage. *Revue Numismatique*, 17, 5–23.

CHAPTER THREE

Contributions of Medieval Muslim Scholars to the History of Economics and their Impact: A Refutation of the Schumpeterian Great Gap[1]

Hamid S. Hosseini

No historical student of the culture of Western Europe can ever reconstruct for himself the intellectual values of the later Middle Ages unless he possesses a vivid awareness of Islam in the background.

Pierce Butler (1933), quoted by Mirakhor

3.1 THE GREAT GAP THESIS AS THE PROBLEM

In his seminal 1954 work *History of Economic Analysis*, Joseph Schumpeter proposes a historical gap of some five hundred years in the history of economics after its beginnings in ancient Greece. "Nothing was said, written, or practiced which had any relevance to economics" (Mirakhor, 1988 [1983], p. 301) within this "historical gap," which stretched from the demise of Greek civilization to the writings of Thomas Aquinas (1225–74). For, according to Schumpeter (1954, p. 74), many centuries within that span are blanks. Emphasizing the contributions of Thomas Aquinas, which, to Schumpeter, were instrumental in ending that five hundred years of "historical discontinuity," the author of *History of Economic Analysis* writes: "so far as our subject is concerned we may leap over 500 years to the epoch of St. Thomas Aquinas (1225–74) whose *Summa Theologica* is in the history of thought what the South-Western spire of the Cathedral of Chartres is in the history of architecture" (Schumpeter, p. 74).

According to Schumpeter, what distinguished the thirteenth century from the twelfth, eleventh, and earlier centuries was the revolution that took place due to Aquinas and the Scholastics in theological and philosophical thought. This revolution, Schumpeter maintains, had two causes: the rediscovery of Aristotle's writings, and what he calls the towering achievements of St. Thomas Aquinas (Schumpeter, p. 87). De-emphasizing the first cause, Schumpeter writes that: "The reader will observe that I do not assign to the recovery of Aristotle's writings the role of chief cause of the 13th century developments" (Schumpeter, p. 88).

Adherence to the Schumpeterian Great Gap thesis has by no means been restricted to Schumpeter's 1954 book. As several writers – Mirakhor, Essid, Ghazanfaar, Islahi, and Hosseini – have demonstrated, the thesis, which ignores the contributions of medieval Muslim scholars, has been "deeply entrenched" (at least until recently) as part of the accepted tradition among historians of economic thought. Although it became more explicit and was perhaps strengthened by Schumpeter's *History of Economic Analysis*, the thesis was well established in the nineteenth century, as is evident in William Ashley's 1988 book on the history of economics. According to Ghazafar, "Even Jacob Viner, proclaimed by Blaug as the greatest historian of economic thought that ever lived, unhesitatingly accepts the gap thesis" (Ghazanfar, 1995, p. 241). In fact, in a review essay on Schumpeter's *History of Economic Analysis*, Viner simply accepts the "gap" and acknowledges Schumpeter's claim of having accounted for "every writer who made a significant contribution to the development of economic theory" (quoted by Ghazanfar, 1995, p. 241). Whatever his reason, Viner, like Schumpeter, also ignores Islamic contributions to economics during the blank centuries (ibid.). Of course, the same can also be said of the texts in the history of economic thought, at least until recently.

The Schumpeterian Great Gap thesis is problematic, for there was no historical discontinuity in those "blank" centuries; it is certainly not true that "many centuries within that span are blanks" (Schumpeter, p. 74). Furthermore, the Thomasian revolution suggested by Schumpeter was a reaction to the Greco-Islamic influence in the Latin West and was impacted by it.

Notwithstanding Karl Polanyi's substantive and formalistic distinctions in economics, it is a fact that many non-Western civilizations made contributions to the development of economics within those "blank" centuries (Hosseini, 1995, p. 539). This is particularly true of medieval Muslim scholars – theologians, jurists, Greek-inspired philosophers, and authors of the (Persian) mirrors for princes. Those writers – who reflected Greek rationality, a sense of realism and practicality characteristic of the Persian-originated mirrors, the worldly teachings of Islam, and the "modernistic" economic institution present in medieval Islamic society – produced theories closer to the economic concepts of the more recent centuries than those of the Greeks or pre-modern Latin Christianity. That, of course, occurred before economics had become an independent discipline.

Medieval Muslims also influenced Christian scholasticism and Thomas Aquinas in their economic views, another point also neglected by Schumpeter and other historians of economics. For scholasticism was a form of ecclesiasticism that contained various elements, including Islamic thought (Mirakhor, 1988 [1983], p. 304). Furthermore, medieval Islamic influence in economics may even have extended to centuries beyond the age of Thomas Aquinas, as Hosseini has demonstrated in his paper on the division of labor (Hosseini, 1998, pp. 653–81).

Interestingly enough, Latin Scholastics had initially found Islam and the philosophic works of Muslims to be threats to Christian dogma (Ghazanfar, 1991, p. 130), evidenced by over two hundred condemnations, called Averroestic heresies, published by the then Bishop of Paris. The numerous translations in the eleventh, twelfth, and thirteenth centuries into Latin of the works of Muslim and Greek philosophers were so different from Christianity that, in the words of Will Durant, "they threatened to sweep away the whole theology of Christiandom unless Christianity could construct a counterphilosophy" (quoted by Ghazanfar, 1991, p. 130). To overcome that fear, Aquinas used the views developed by the prominent (Persian-speaking) medieval Muslim theologian Ghazali. For in writing his book *The Incoherence of Philosophers* (1927), Ghazali had placed science, philosophy, and reason in a position inferior to religion and theology. According to Meyers, the Scholastics accepted this view of Ghazali and made it a characteristic of much of their philosophy (Ghazanfar, 1991, p. 130). The works of Ghazali and other prominent Muslim scholars had been translated into Latin before 1150.

Muslim scholars were also instrumental in the transmission of Aristotelian ideas to the Latin West, a point also ignored by Schumpeter. Jourdain's study of the scholars of the eleventh and twelfth centuries found not even "a single passage to suggest any of these authors suspected that the pursuit of riches, which they despised, occupied a sufficiently large place in national as well as individual life to offer to the philosopher a subject fruitful in reflection and result" (Mirakhor, 1988 [1983], p. 308). It is well documented that all of the European scholars mentioned in chapter 2 of Schumpeter were in fact influenced by Muslim thinkers (Hosseini, 1998, p. 675).

The following sections will discuss the contributions of medieval Muslim scholars, the causes and roots of those contributions, and their impact on European scholasticism. We will also explore the reasons why these contributions have not been acknowledged during the past few centuries. We will, however, discuss first the significance of Joseph Spengler's 1964 path-breaking article on Ibn Khaldun (1332–1406). But, because Spengler's 1964 article failed to prove the historical continuity of economic thought and thereby refute the Schumpeterian thesis in its totality, we will also discuss the impact of the more serious challenges to the gap thesis that emerged later on.

3.2 JOSEPH SPENGLER'S 1964 ARTICLE: OVEREMPHASIZING THE GREEK ELEMENT IN ISLAMIC ECONOMIC THOUGHT AND MORE

Joseph Spengler's 1964 article dealt the first blow to the Schumperian Great Gap thesis, without even mentioning it. By writing this article, Spengler became the first Western historian of economics to acknowledge the contribution of a "medieval" Muslim thinker and to view it as significant. For Spengler believed that, among other things, Ibn Khaldun "had a deep insight into the essentials of the accumulated knowledge of his time, could evaluate the manifestations of the culture of his day, could reflect faithfully the understanding which contemporary lawyers and jurists had of practical economic and financial matters that normally were not treated in books" (Spengler, 1964, p. 269).

Spengler's article, while important in acknowledging the neglected contributions of various Muslim scholars, was not without its share of problems. According to Mirakhhor, "Perhaps due to his zeal to show the influence of Greek writings on Muslims, which he does on every page of the first section of his paper, Spengler only considered some of the available evidence from the ninth century onwards" (p. 309).

While we cannot deny the impact of Greek thought on Islamic civilization – for the latter is a confluence of Arab, Greek, and Persian (i.e., Iranian) elements – we should at the same time not overemphasize the share of individual components in that synthesis. However, by exaggerating the Greek share in that totality, Spengler diminishes the extent of the contributions of the pre-Ibn Khaldun Muslim scholars that he surveys: "Such attention as was given to theoretical economics seems to have been prompted less by an early and persisting interest in taxation than by contact with Greek philosophical and scientific writings, especially those of later Platonic and neo-Platonic orientation" (Spengler, 1964, p. 270).

Spengler, being aware that Ibn Khaldun's knowledge of economic behavior was superior to that of Bryson of Heraclea and other Greek thinkers, fails to understand that Ibn Khaldun's substantial knowledge of economic matters reflected the realities of medieval Islamic society and the knowledge of many Muslim scholars of the "Gap" centuries.

Furthermore, by concentrating on the contributions of Ibn Khaldun – who lived after the Schumpeterian blank centuries – Spengler, in effect, did not provide sufficient ammunition to negate the Schumpeterian Great Gap thesis; Spengler's article was not in total support of the historical continuity of economic thought, although it was a step in the right direction. In addition, by overemphasizing the impact of Greek thought, Spengler downplayed the contributions of Muslims who were not affected (at all or very much) by Greek thought. He also ignored the contributions of those scholars who wrote during the first two and a half centuries of Islamic history, since it was some two and a half centuries after the rise of Islam that the works of Greek thinkers were translated into the Arabic language.

In spite of the significance of the 1964 path-breaking article by Spengler, the real challenge to the Schumpeterian Great Gap thesis came about as a result of the work done by a few economists with roots in Muslim lands (although the work of the Belgian economist Leuis Baeck and the personal encouragement of Todd Lowry should not go unnoticed). These historians of economics, in addition to demonstrating the contributions of medieval Muslim scholars, also challenged the accuracy of the Schumpeterian thesis, and tried to show the impact of medieval Islamic scholarship on Aquinas and Christian scholasticism.

3.3 Economic Activity in Medieval Islam

Jourdain's observation (above) was indicative of the medieval Christian scholars' disapproval of the pursuit of riches. The Greeks too were less approving of the pursuit of riches than medieval Muslims. In Plato, we see a derogation of economic activity, reinforced by his description of the property arrangements for each class. For him, only the lowest classes – farmers and artisans – were allowed to work for profit and accumulate property; the pursuit of money by the base would not arouse the envy of wise rulers more than the prudent exercise of power by the latter would antagonize artisans and farmers (Hosseini, 1998, p. 66). And, as stated by McNulty (1975), for Plato, the desire to engage in exchange is not a universal human characteristic; rather, it is a specialized activity. This view is obvious in the *Republic*, in the discussion between Socrates and Adiemantus. Plato rejected private property, at least for the upper class, because it causes selfishness. Although Aristotle defended private property, he rejected exchange and had no Platonic appreciation of the division of labor (Hosseini, 1998, p. 66).

Medieval Muslim scholars viewed wealth and gainful activity more positively. This was partly because Islam had mercantile roots. It is worth mentioning that the Quran (believed by Muslims to be the direct words of God) and the Hadith (reported words and acts of the Prophet) have a negative view of what the Quran calls Riba (interest, or as some argue, only excessive usury). However, these two highest sources of Islamic law regard wealth and profit, on both exchange and productive activity, very positively (Hosseini, 1988, p. 58).

In the Quran and the Hadith, production and trade are viewed as noble practices (Essid, 1987, p. 78). (In contrast, the medieval Christian Church was insisting that no Christian ought to be a merchant.) According to Sami Zubaida, "The Meccan milieu of Mohammad and his followers was a business milieu. Before the call to Islam, Mohammad and his companion engaged in trade extensively. Mohammad was a relatively small merchant, but also worked as agent for other merchants in trade with Syria. The early Muslims of Mecca and Medina continued in trade" (Zubaida, 1972, p. 321).

According to Maxime Rodinson, in medieval Islamic society, "the capitalist sector was undoubtedly well-developed in a number of aspects, the most obvious being the commercial one" (Rodinson, 1978, p. 28). According to Nasser Khusraw (1003–60) – a Persian poet, essayist, and traveler – in the year 1052 there existed in the central Persian city of Isfahan some two hundred money changers, although usury is forbidden in Islam (see Hosseini, 1995, p. 543). Many economic historians – such as Udovitch (1970), Labib (1969), Tuma, and S. G. Goitein – have elaborated on these aspects of medieval Islamic society. These writers have demonstrated attempts by early Muslim leaders at enforcing fiscal and monetary policies, deficit financing, the use of taxation to encourage production, and the existence of credit and credit instruments for the rudiments of checking and saving accounts, banking institutions, and procedures for the formation of partnerships, commendam contracts, and monopolies, all of which developed before the ninth century. By the ninth century, these developments had been enshrined in Islamic law (i.e., fiqh manuals).

According to S. G. Goitein: "A subject worthy of such special study is the merchant class and bourgeoisie of early Islam. This class developed slowly during the first hundred and fifty years of the Muslim era, emerged into the full light of history at the end of the second, became socially admitted during the third and asserted itself as a most powerful socioeconomic factor during the fourth" (Goitein, 1957, p. 584).

Of course, the early Islamic bourgeoisie was not able to obtain political power, nor was it able to enjoy other powers necessary to become as effective as the type that eventually emerged in Western Europe centuries later. This is because this early bourgeoisie "never became an organized body and, as a class, never obtained political power, although many of its members occupied positions as the highest executives of the state" (Goitein, 1957, p. 584).

As stated by Goitein, "Before all this happened, however, Islam as a religion and civilization, had fully taken shape, and it was largely members of the bourgeoisie, who had developed Muslim religious law, which is the backbone and very essence of Islam" (Goitein, 1957, p. 584).

3.4 ISLAMIC VIEWS OF THE ECONOMY AND ECONOMIC POLICY PRIOR TO THE NINTH CENTURY

Medieval Muslims had already held and expressed a positive view of economic activity before the ninth century, when the Abbasid Caliph Maamoun ordered the translation of the works of the Greeks into Arabic. In fact, numerous scholars and jurists had written on economic issues, almost from the inception of Islam (Mirakhor, 1988 [1983]; Ghazanfar, 1991; Hosseini, 1995).

Prophet Mohammad is reputed to have said that the state should have only a limited role in the productive process, in market structure, and in the movement of prices. According to Elias Tuma, the role of the state "was restricted to factors which distorted normal conditions, these being competition and price determination through invisible forces such as God's will and the interaction of supply and demand. However, when intervention by the state was deemed necessary it was usually kept at a minimum and exercised through the market" (Tuma, 1965, pp. 10–18).

Mohammad, as the prophet and political leader of the Islamic community, refused to combat price rises by direct action, stating that only God alone sets prices (i.e., invisible hand? – see Tuma, 1965, p. 14). Mohammad is believed to have declared that one who supplies the market with a commodity receives his income as a blessing, but the monopolist who withholds his supplies receives his income as a curse (Tuma, 1965, p. 15).

Among the pre-ninth-century Muslim scholars endowed with a deep understanding of economic issues and matters, the Iraqi jurist Abu Yusuf (731–98) stands out. Having studied Islamic jurisprudence under Abu Hanifah (founder of the Hanafi Sunni School of thought), Abu Yusuf, a judge for several Abbasid Caliphs, was eventually chosen by Abbasid Caliph Harun al-Rashid as his chief jurist (Qadi al Qudat) in Baghdad, the capital. It was in his capacity as chief jurist that Abu Yusuf composed *The Book of Taxation* (*Kitab al-Kharaj*), addressing Caliph Harun al-Rashid. In this volume, the eighth-century jurist exhibits his understanding of taxation, public finance, agricultural production, and other related economic issues (Ghazanfaar, 1991, p. 125; also see M. N. Siddiqui, 1964; S. A. Siddiqui, 1968). In *Kitab al-Kharaj*, Abu Yusuf shows his preference for a proportional tax on agricultural produce, instead of a fixed rent on land. He finds a proportional tax on agricultural produce more just and, at the same time, as providing a greater incentive for bringing more land into cultivation, thus creating more revenues for the government. Abu Yusuf strongly opposes tax farming – a practice by which the tax collector could confiscate land in case of delinquency (Ghazanfar, 1991, p. 5). Interestingly enough, this eighth-century Muslim jurist suggested certain principles that anticipated those proposed 1,000 years later by Adam Smith (1985 [1776]) as the four canons of taxation; namely, equity, certainty, convenience, and economy. As a result of these principles and to ease the burden of taxes on taxpayers, Abu Yusuf proposed the ability-to-pay principle of taxation and convenience regarding time, space, and the manner of payment of these taxes. Furthermore, to reduce the likelihood of corruption in the collection of taxes, Abu Yusuf proposed a centralized tax administration and the use of strictly supervised salaried workers as tax collectors.

Abu Yusuf also provided a deep insight into issues such as the distribution of tax revenues, government responsibilities concerning societal welfare, the promotion of economic development, and the building of socioeconomic infrastructure and public works such as roads, bridges, and canals for irrigation or transportation purposes. He also discussed various types of taxes, including specific taxes on commodities, death taxes, and import duties, and problems related to water supply, fisheries, and forest and pasture lands.

Concerning private projects and state responsibilities, he writes: "As for smaller canals from which people obtain water for their own farms, fruit orchards, vineyards, vegetable gardens, etc., the expense of cleaning and restoring them should be borne by the residents themselves. There should be no burden on the state treasury" (*Kitab al-Kharaj*; quoted by Ghazanfar, 1998, p. 22).

To Abu Yusuf, no part of the expense should be borne by the taxpayers if the project benefits the entire Muslim community.

3.5   MEDIEVAL MUSLIM CONTRIBUTIONS TO THE HISTORY OF ECONOMICS BEYOND THE EIGHTH CENTURY

Although scholars in the first two and a half centuries of Islamic history demonstrated a thorough understanding of the economy of their age, their understanding of the economy was enhanced when they witnessed the rise of non-Islamic thought in their midst. Islamic understanding of economic matters benefited from the works of Greek masters, and the mirrors of Persian origin which were translated into Arabic.[2]

Philosophy entered Islam when, during the ninth century, the Abbasid Caliph Maamoun ordered Syrian Christians at Baghdad to translate the works of the Greeks into Arabic. These translations gave rise to a great deal of philosophic activity and some of the greatest philosophers in history, who debated, reproduced, added to, and wrote commentaries on the philosophic works of the ancient Greeks. The first Greek-inspired Muslim philosopher was (Arab) Al-Kindi (d. 870), who was soon joined by many others, mostly of Persian origin. However, even before Al-Kindi, a rationalist Islamic "philosophic school" – the Mutazeleh school – had emerged, peaking when scholar Abd al-Jabbar composed a volume in dialectical form.

The Islamic mirrors for princes literature was "an important and characteristic branch of Persian belles letters" (Lambton, 1980, p. 449). It entered Islamic thought when the Iranian Ibn Muqaffa (724–57), a Zoroastrian convert, translated four Persian (of pre-Islamic Sassanid-age) books of moral counsel into Arabic, and wrote two more mirrors in Arabic himself. Soon Ibn Muqaffa was joined by numerous other writers who – writing in Persian, Arabic, and other Islamic languages – produced a branch of thought that was rich in an understanding of economic activity (Hosseini, 2001).

The availability of Persian and Greek sources in Arabic, the language of intellectual discourse among all scholars of medieval Islamic society, introduced these scholars to the issues (economic or otherwise) debated by ancient Greek thinkers or raised in the pre-Islamic Persian books of counsel. Such availability enriched the economic discussions of Muslim scholars and elevated their discussions to a higher plane.

From the ninth century onward, early writers were joined by many more scholars, such as theologians and Muslim jurists, as well as philosophers and authors of the mirrors. Of course, they were also occasionally joined by writers who did not fit any of those categories, such as the Persian scientist and essayist Biruni (b. 973), the twelfth-century Syrian merchant Dimishqhi, or the North African historian and social theorist Ibn Khaldun.

Among the theologian/jurists who contributed to the development of economic thought, we can include Ghazali (1058–1111), al-Mawardi (1075–1158), Ibn Taimiyah (1263–1328), and al-Maqrizi. Among many philosophers who made contributions we can include Farabi (873–950), Ibn Sina or Avicenna (980–1037), Ibn Miskaway (b. 1030), Nasir Tusi (1201–74), Asaad Davani (b. 1444), and many more. After Ibn Muqaffa translated a few pre-Islamic books of counsel and wrote the first two Islamic mirrors, various Muslim scholars, of different languages, composed numerous mirrors for princes. These works of an expedient edifying and moralizing nature Islamized pre-Islamic (and thus Zoroastrian) Persian maxims and made impartial use of examples of Sassani Persian kings, as well as those of Arabic (i.e., Islamic) Caliphs, Sufi saints, and Persian sages. These included a great many economic concepts. Interestingly, the pre-Islamic Persian materials that found their way in the mirrors also influenced Iranian and non-Iranian theologians. One example is the theologian Ghazali, who wrote *Nasihat al Muluk*. Yassine Essid's 1995 book discusses the Arab theologian al-Mawardi, whose works were influenced by pre-Islamic Iranian sources (Essid, 1995, p. 37).

Muslim scholars after the first two and a half centuries of Islamic history provide a surprisingly detailed discussion of various economic issues. The following are examples of these discussions.

3.5.1   Wealth, poverty, and acquisitiveness

In contrast to their European counterparts, medieval Muslim writers praised economic activity and the accumulation of wealth, viewed individuals as acquisitive, and scorned poverty. Kai Kavus, in *Qabus Nameh*, gives his son the following advice: "My son, do not be indifferent to the acquisition of wealth. Assure yourself that everything you acquire shall be the best quality and is likely to give you pleasure" (Kai Kavus, 1951, p. 91). To Khajeh Nasir Tusi (1985, p. 159), "The intelligent man should not neglect to store up provisions and property." According to the theologian Ghazali, "man loves to accumulate wealth and possessions of all kinds of property. If he has two valleys of gold, he wants to have a third" (translation, from the *Ihya*, by Ghazanfar and Islahi, 1990, pp. 384–5). According to Kai Kavus, "you must realize that the common run of men have an affection for the rich, without regard to their personal concern, and that they dislike poor men, even when their own interests are at stake. The reason is that poverty is man's worst evil and any quality which is to the credit of the wealthy is itself a derogation of the poor" (Kai Kavus, p. 92). Like a post-Smithian proponent of self-interest, Kai Kavus writes: "And never, in anything you do, lose sight of your own interest – to do so is superfluous folly" (Kai Kavus, p. 109). Or, according to the philosopher Ibn Miskaway, "The creditor desires the well-being of the debtor in order to get his money back rather than because of his love for him. The debtor, on the other hand, does not take great interest in the creditor" (Ibn Miskaway, undated, p. 137).

3.5.2   The division of labor

Various medieval Muslims discussed the division of labor and its benefits in the economic process. Among them are Kai Kavus, Ghazali, and the philosophers–ethicists Farabi, Ibn Sina (Avicenna), Ibn Miskaway, Nasir Tusi, and Davani. The discussions provided by these authors of the division of labor were much more sophisticated than those of the Greeks, and included division of labor within the household, within society (i.e., social), within the factory (manufacturing or technical), and among nations (Hosseini, 1998, section 4, p. 670). While it is believed that it was Thomas Hodgskin (1787–1869) who, in 1829, applied the division of labor to the household for the first time (see Hodgskin, 1966 [1829]), Hosseini has argued that this was discussed by the Persian Muslims Avicenna and Nasir Tusi several centuries earlier (Hosseini, 1998, p. 668). All of these writers have discussed the social division of labor; and Farabi, Ghazali, and Kai Kavus have applied it to the international arena. According to Farabi, each society is imperfect because they all lack all of the necessary resources. A perfect society can only be achieved when domestic, regional, and international trade all take place (Farabi, 1982, p. 25). The same view is expressed in Kai Kavus' *Qabus Nameh*: "To benefit the inhabitants of the west they import the wealth of the east and for those of the east the wealth of the west, and by doing so become the instruments of the world's civilization" (Kai Kavus, p. 156). Thus, like Adam Smith, these two medieval authors view international trade as a nonzero-sum game.

Although writing before the age of industry, medieval Muslim writers understood the application of the division of labor to a productive unit (such as a factory), and its usefulness, rather well. Recognizing that "there are a thousand things to be done before anyone can put a morsel of bread in his mouth," they recognized that it is useful to assign different tasks to different workers (Hosseini, 1998, p. 671). Reminiscent of Adam Smith's statement in *The Wealth of Nations* about the woolen coat being the joint product of a multitude of workers, Ghazali argues that "you should know that plants and animals cannot be eaten and digested as they are. Each needs some transformation, cleaning, mixing, and cooking, before consumption. For a bread, for example, first . . . Just imagine how many tasks are involved; and we mentioned only some. And, imagine the number of people performing these various tasks" (Ghazanfar and Islahi, 1990; quoted by Hosseini, 1998, p. 672).

For Ghazali and Tusi, as for Smith, exchange and division of labor are related (Hosseini, 1998, p. 672). Interestingly enough, Tusi, like Smith, argues that exchange and division of labor are the necessary consequences of the faculties of reason and speech. And both indicate that animals, such as dogs, do not exchange one bone for another (ibid., p. 672).

Smith's substantive economic analysis of the division of labor appears with the celebrated illustration of the productivity of the pin factory (Lowry, 1979, p. 73). This example is very similar to Ghazali's discussion in his *Ihya al-Ulum al-Din* that: "Even the small needle becomes useful only after passing through the hand of needle makers about twenty-five times, each time going through a different process" (Hosseini, 1998, p. 673, quoting Ghazanfar and Islahi's translation).

3.5.3   Barter and money

Ibn Khaldun, and various medieval Muslims before him, had understood the problems of barter and the importance and functions of money in a more complex economy. For example, Ghazali (1058–1111), in his *Ihya*, identified three problems associated with barter – the lack of double coincidence of wants, the indivisibility of goods due to the lack of a common denominator, and limited specialization (Ghazanfar and Islahi, 1990, p. 391). Ghazali was able to trace the evolution of a money-exchange system and the functions of money in modern terms; in particular, its being a means of exchange. Ghazali also discussed the use of gold and silver as money and the harmful effects of counterfeiting and currency debasement (Ghazanfar and Islahi, 1990, p. 392). Ghazali was able to develop an early version of Gresham's Law (Ghazanfar and Islahi, 1990, p. 394).

3.5.4 Demand, supply, and the market mechanism

Medieval Muslim scholars demonstrated an understanding of the forces of supply and demand, and their role in price determination. For many of these thinkers, there are only free markets and voluntary exchange. Providing advice to his son, Kai Kavus states: "Further you must buy when the market is slack and sell when the market is brisk" (in Hosseini, 1995, p. 553). According to Ibn Taimiyah, "If desire for goods increases while its availability decreases, its price rises. On the other hand, if availability of the good increases and the desire for it decreases, the price comes down." Ibn Taimiyah and other writers also understood shifts in supply and demand (Hosseini, 1995, p. 553).

Ghazali also understood the same forces and causes. In the *Ihya* we read: "If the farmer does not get a buyer for produce, then he sells at a very low price" (Hosseini, 1995, p. 557). In the *Ihya*, Ghazali seems to have understood what we now call price elasticity of demand, when he suggested that a cut in profit margin by price reduction will cause an increase in sales and thus in profits (ibid.). Ibn Miskaway even discusses equilibrium price, a price that Ghazali calls the "prevailing" price (Hosseini, 1996b, p. 74).

Medieval Muslim thinkers discuss various other issues, including production and its efficiency, the economic function of the state and regulation, diversification of assets as a hedge against loss, and many more. They also anticipated many modern economic concepts, including the Malthusian theory of population. Several writers – Ibn Miskaway, Nasir Tusi, Asaad Davani, and Biruni – presented arguments resembling that introduced by Thomas Malthus centuries later, even utilizing mathematical calculations to prove their arguments. In fact, Spengler, in his article about the Iranian thinker Biruni, brought to our attention that this eleventh-century thinker can be regarded as the precursor to Darwin and Malthus. In his book on India, Biruni warned of the problem of overpopulation, argued that the growth of anything is limited by the environment accessible to it, and recognized that since the capacity for growth of a species in number is unlimited, its actual growth is restrained by limiting and (apparently) almost exclusively external agents. Biruni observed, as did Charles Darwin upon reading Malthus, that the pressure of increasing numbers will give rise to natural selection (Hosseini, 1996b, pp. 78–9).

Although political economy as an independent branch of thought goes back to Adam Smith, and the first use of the term (in 1615) can be attributed to the French writer Antoyne de Montchrétien, some medieval Muslims were at least implicitly aware of the need for such as a discipline. In fact, Nasir Tusi discusses the need for a science that he calls *hekmat-e-madani* (the science of city life), whose definition very much resembles Marshall's definition of economics. In discourse three of his book *Ethics* (in Persian), Tusi defines this science as: "the study of universal laws governing the public interest (welfare?) in so far as they are directed, through cooperation, toward the optimal (perfection)" (in Hosseini, unpublished paper).

3.6 TRANSMISSION OF KNOWLEDGE AND INFLUENCE ON THE SCHOLASTICS

The revolution brought about by Aquinas and the Scholastics was influenced by medieval Muslim scholars; it was also a reaction to the Greco-Islamic rationalism that was initially introduced to medieval Latin Christianity by the likes of Ibn Sina, Farabi, and Ibn Rushd. But how did that influence come about?

First, as we are reminded by historians such as Butler, Harkins, Leff, Ronan, Hitti, and others, scholars in medieval Islam were "bearers of the torch of culture and civilization throughout the world" (Hitti, 1943, p. 143). Secondly, for various reasons, medieval Western Europe could not escape that influence. Muslim and Christian lands were adjacent; Spain was under Islamic rule for well over seven centuries, as were parts of southern Italy for about a century; the Crusades, which lasted for a long time, introduced Christians to various Islamic concepts and institutions; the works of major scholars of the Muslim world were translated into Latin; and there were various other types of contacts between the two civilizations.

It was during the late eleventh and the twelfth centuries that Western Europe became interested in science, mathematics, and philosophy – when these branches of thought were at their height in the Muslim world. The Europeans had to learn all they could from the Muslims before they themselves could make further advances. The transmission of knowledge from Muslims to Western Europeans took several forms:

1 During the late eleventh and early twelfth centuries, various Christian scholars traveled to Muslim lands to study Arabic and "Islamic sciences," in order to write and teach upon their return. One example is Leonardo Fibonacci (of Pisa, d. after 1240), who traveled to study mathematics in Algeria and upon his return wrote a book (*Liber Abaci*) in 1202 (Watt, 1972, p. 43). Interestingly, Harro Bernardelli traces the beginning of economic analysis in Europe to Leonardo's *Liber Abaci* (Bernadelli, 1961, p. 320).
2 Many students from Italy, Spain, and southern France attended Muslim seminaries in order to study mathematics, philosophy, medicine, and the sciences. In due course, many of these students "became candidates for professorships in the first Western Universities to be established after the pattern of the Muslim seminaries" (Mirakhor, 1988 [1983], p. 325).

3 Upon receiving a petition from Raymond Lully (1232–1315), who had traveled widely in Muslim lands, the Council of Vienne (1311) set up five schools of oriental languages in Rome, Bologna, Paris, Oxford, and Salamanca, in which Arabic was taught to the students (Durant, 1950, p. 979).
4 Many manuscripts by Muslims were brought to Northern Europe beginning from the twelfth century onward. During that time, "Europe discovered the wealth of Spain in books. Scholars descended upon Toledo, Cordova, and Seville; and a flood of new learning poured up over the Pyrenees to revolutionize the intellectual life of the adolescent North" (Durant, 1950, p. 979).
5 Europe during "the late twelfth and all through the thirteenth and fourteenth centuries saw a great translation movement by which much of the works of Muslim scholars were translated to Latin" (Mirakhor, 1988 [1983], p. 326). These translations were made in various places in Europe – in particular, Toledo and Burgos in Spain and Sicily and Naples in Italy – during the first two of those three centuries. Later, the Arabic manuscripts that had previously been translated into Hebrew were translated into Latin (Mirakhor, 1988 [1983], p. 326). This suggests an end to intellectual isolation from the Muslim world (Leff, 1958, p. 141).

Muslim thinkers influenced Christian scholars in many fields. Crombie (1963), Sarton (1931), and Winter (1950), for example, have shown the influence of Muslim scholars on the development of physics, chemistry, astronomy, and cosmology in Europe during medieval times (Crombie, 1963, p. 61). Sharif has shown influences in many more areas, including the historical sciences, scientific method, and the harmonization of faith and philosophy (as in the case of Ghazali's influence on Aquinas) (Sharif, 1966, p. 1349).

If, as is generally believed, Muslims influenced the Scholastics in philosophy, ethics, and the sciences, could there be any reason why Muslim scholars would not have influenced Christian scholars in their economic thought? We can make the case that more reasons existed for Muslims to influence Christian scholars in economic matters than in philosophy, ethics, and the sciences. Two additional avenues existed for this economic influence: trade and the cultural diffusion of Muslim economic institutions and processes into medieval European societies (Mirakhor, 1988 [1983], p. 327).

Concerning these influences, Spuler (1970) maintains that everywhere medieval Islam entered, "it activated business life, fostered an increasing exchange of goods, and played an important part in the development of credit" (in Mirakhor, 1988 [1983], p. 329). To Spuler, through Spain, the Mediterranean, and the Baltic, the merchants of the Islamic world became indispensable middlemen to the trade of the West.

A consequence of that trade was the diffusion of economic institutions and processes. The more advanced and flexible commercial techniques of the Muslim East and Muslim Spain soon spread to Latin Europe. The commendam contracts that became prevalent in medieval Latin Europe are believed to have Roman origins. However, as demonstrated by Udovitch, the commendam and other partnership contracts were Muslim inventions that moved through medieval

Europe because of contacts between Muslims and Latin Europe, including the writings of medieval Muslim scholars (in Richards, 1970, pp. 37–62). The same was also true of other types of institutions – commercial and consumer credits as well as such credit instruments as *suftaja* and *hawala* (bills of exchange and letters of credit) – means of commerce developed by Muslims and borrowed by Europeans (Mirakhor, 1988 [1983], p. 330). Udovitch and other economic historians have also demonstrated the diffusion of other Muslim institutions to Latin Europe.

The foregoing lends support to our argument that Christian Scholastics were influenced by medieval Muslims in their views of economic matters. Citations of the works of these Muslim scholars cannot be found in the writings of the Scholastics for several reasons:

1 As epitomized by the Crusades, Christians – Scholastics included – denigrated Islam and the Muslim peoples. Perhaps as a result of this negative view of Muslims, Europe "exaggerated its dependence on its Greek and Roman heritage," thereby belittling its Islamic influence.

2 The Scholastics perceived that Islam and the ideas of Muslim scholars threatened Christian dogma. The list of condemnations of ideas published by Stephen Tampier, Bishop of Paris, in 1277 (and other similar condemnations at Oxford and elsewhere) was a manifestation of these fears. Thus, Aquinas wrote his Summas to halt the threatened liquidation of Christian theology by Muslim interpretation of Aristotle; the industry of Aquinas was due not to love of the Greek Aristotle, but to fear of the Muslim Averroes. If a Christian scholar referred to a Muslim scholar (usually when writing about theology), it was to show how he had erred, as in Aquinas' *Summa Contra Gentiles* (Durant, p. 954). Otherwise, Christian scholars borrowed Muslim ideas without citing any references.

3 Borrowing without acknowledging the source was a general practice on the part of the Scholastics. Richard Dales (1971) provides examples of thirteenth-century Scholastic authors who were greatly "pillaged" by their contemporary scholars (Mirakhor, 1988 [1983], p. 324). Many historians have demonstrated that, with amazing openness, the medieval European mind borrowed, explored, assimilated, and elaborated the writings and teachings of Muslim scholars (Mirakhor, p. 334). For example, Bar Hebraeus, a minister at a Syriac Jacobite Church and famous during the thirteenth century, copied chapters of Abu Hamed Ghazali's *Ihya al-Ulum-al-Din* – including a chapter containing Ghazali's economic ideas – without referring to him. Bar Hebraeus' book was considered fundamental in monastery teachings (Mirakhor, p. 334). Another example is the Spanish Dominican Monk Raymond Martini, who borrowed from Ghazali's *Tahasof al-Filasofia* and three other books, including the *Ihya*, without providing any reference. In fact, Robert Hammond (1947) has demonstrated the extent of the borrowing and assimilation of ideas of Muslim thinkers by placing some of the arguments of St. Thomas Aquinas opposite those of Farabi and showing that they are virtually the same (see Mirakhor, p. 334). Authors such as Brifault, Crombie, Harris (1959), Sarton (1931), Sharif and others have done the same, tracing the ideas of Grosseterste, Albertus Magnus, Roger Bacon, and Wittelo to the writings of Muslim scholars.

3.7   CONCLUDING REMARKS

The Great Gap thesis, which has been implicit in the history of economic thought since at least the nineteenth century, was made explicit by Joseph Schumpeter in 1954. But demonstrations of the historical continuity of economic thought have led to rejection of the thesis. These demonstrations have included the contributions of medieval Muslim scholars to the history of economics during the five centuries of the alleged Great Gap, the transmission of medieval Muslim knowledge to Western Europe during the eleventh, twelfth, and thirteenth centuries, and the impact of this body of thought on Christian scholasticism and Thomas Aquinas.

Historians of economics are intellectually curious, inclined in part to seek the precursors of various theories. Until recently, this curiosity was not observed in dealing with the contributions of medieval Muslim scholars. Historians of economics, "usually so quick to find a deceased precursor for every theorist," had remained silent about medieval Islamic contributions (Essid, 1992, p. 39). How do we explain this silence on the part of historians of economics?

It is likely true that believers in the Gap were generally not aware of the evidence against the Gap thesis, which proves the historical continuity of economic thought. However, the same perhaps cannot be said of Schumpeter, for several reasons. First, Schumpeter was not totally unaware of the contributions of medieval Muslims. Otherwise, he would not have mentioned Ibn Khaldun in two footnotes in his 1954 seminal work (pp. 136 and 788) in reference to historical sociology. Secondly, during his formative period Schumpeter spent some time in Egypt (1907–8, working for an Italian law firm). Since Arab Egypt is an extremely important country in terms of both Arab and Islamic studies and culture, it is hard to believe that Schumpeter who, according to Viner, was to account for every writer who made a significant contribution to the development of economic analysis, would not have heard, in Egypt, of the contributions of Ibn Khaldun or other significant medieval Muslim scholars. Thirdly, Schumpeter was a professor, from 1932 to 1950, at Harvard University. Since Harvard has attracted, and produced, some of the best historians of medieval Europe and medieval Islam, and its libraries are among the best in the world for medieval Islamic studies, could Schumpeter not have become aware of the medieval Muslim contributions to the history of economics while at Harvard, even if he had not been introduced to them in Egypt? If these arguments are correct, the unanswered question is: Why did Schumpeter not include non-Europeans, particularly medieval Muslims, among the writers who made contributions to the development of economics?

Notes

1   Some authors have preferred to use Arab or Arab-Islamic rather than Islamic. Since Islamic civilization has always been diverse and Arabs only constitute a minority of Muslims (somewhere around 20 percent) and the scholars often were not native Arab

speakers, I find the use of Arab or Arab-Islamic inappropriate. Writing in Arabic, the language of theology, the Prophet and the Caliphs until the Ottoman days, and the medieval international language of Muslims from Spain to the Far East, should not make one Arab.

2   Although the overwhelming majority of the medieval scholars of the Muslim world were Muslims, some non-Muslim scholars, such as the Jewish Maimonides in Muslim Spain, also existed in that society.

Bibliography

Ashley, W. J. 1988, 1993: *An Introduction to English Economic History*, 2 vols. New York: G. P. Putnam.

Bernardelli, H. 1961: The origins of modern economic theory. *Economic Record*, 37, 320–38.

Butler, P. 1933: *Fifteenth Century Editions of Arabic Authors in Latin Translation*, McDonald Presentation Volume. Freeport, NY: Books For Libraries Press.

Crombie, A.-C. 1963: *Medieval and Early Modern Science*, 2 vols. Cambridge, MA: Harvard University Press.

Dales, R. 1971: The influence of Grossetesste's *Hexaemeron* on the Sentences, Commentaries of Richard Fishaire, O.P., and Richard Rufus of Crownwall, O.F.M. *Viator*, 21, 271–300.

Durant, W. 1950: *The Age of Faith*. New York: Simon and Schuster.

Essid, Y. 1987: Islamic economic thought. In S. T. Lowry (ed.), *Pre-Classical Economic Thought*. Boston, MA: Kluwer, 77–113.

—— 1992: Greek economic thought in Islamic milieu: Bryson and Dimishqi. In S. T. Lowry (ed.), *Perspectives on the History of Economic Thought*, vol. 7. Northampton, MA: Edward Elgar, 39–45.

—— 1995: *A Critique of the Origins of Islamic Economics*. New York: E. J. Brill.

Farabi, Abu Nassr 1982: *Madineh Fazeleh (Good City)*, Persian translation by Sajadi. Teheran, Iran: Zuhuri.

Ghazali, Abu Hamed undated: *Ihya-al-Ulum al-Din (Revival of the Religious Sciences)*, 4 vols. Beirut, Lebanon: Dar al Nadwaa.

—— 1927: *Kitab Tahafut al, Falasafah (The Incoherence of Philosophers)*. Beirut, Lebanon.

Ghazanfar, S. M. 1991: Scholastic economics and Arab scholars: the Great Gap thesis reconsidered. *Diogenes: International Review of Human Sciences*, no. 154, 117–40.

—— 1995: History of economic thought: the Schumpeterian Great Gap, the lost Arab–Islamic legacy, and the literature gap. *Journal of Islamic Studies*, 6(2), 234–53.

—— 1998: Early medieval Arab–Islamic economic thought: Abu Yusuf's (731–798 AD) economics of public finance. University of Idaho Discussion Paper #98/5.

—— and Islahi, A. 1990: Economic thought of an Arab Scholastic: Abu Hamed Ghazali. *History of Political Economy*, 22(2), 381–403.

—— and Islahi, A. 1992: Explorations in medieval Arab–Islamic economic thought: some aspects of Ibn Taimmiyah's economics. In S. T. Lowry (ed.), *Perspectives on the History of Economic Thought*, vol. 7. Northampton, MA: Edward Elgar, 45–63.

Goitein, S. G. 1957: The rise and fall of Middle Eastern bourgeoisie in early Islamic times. *Journal of World History*, 3 (Spring), 583–604.

Hammond, R. 1947: *The Philosophy of Alfarabi and its Influence on Medieval Thought*. New York: Hobson Press.

Harris, C. R. S. 1959: *Duns Scotus*, 2 vols. New York: Humanities Press.

Haskins, C. H. 1927: *The Renaissance of the Twelfth Century*. Cambridge, UK: Cambridge University Press.

Hitti, P. 1943: *The Arabs: A Short History*. Princeton, NJ: Princeton University Press.

Hodgskin, T. 1966 [1829]: *Popular Political Economy*. London: Charles Tait. Reprinted New York: Augustus M. Kelley.

Hosseini, H. 1988: Notions of private property in Islamic economics. *International Journal of Social Economics*, 115(9), 51–61.

—— 1995: Understanding the market mechanism before Adam Smith: economic thought in medieval Islam. *History of Political Economy*, 27(3), 539–61.

—— 1996a: Economics and household management in the works of philosophers Ibn Sina and Nasir Tusi: a further reason for rejecting the Schumpeterian Great Gap thesis. Unpublished paper, presented at the History of Economics Society Conference, Vancouver, 1996.

—— 1996b: The inaccuracy of the Schumpeterian Great Gap thesis: economic thought in medieval Iran (Persia), In L. Moss (ed.), *Schumpeter: Historian of Economics*. New York: Routledge, 63–82.

—— 1998: Seeking the roots of Adam Smith's division of labor in medieval Persia. *History of Political Economy*, 30(4), 653–81.

—— 2001: Medieval Islamic (Persian) mirrors for princes and the history of economics. *Journal of South Asian and Middle Eastern Studies*, XXIV(4), summer.

Ibn Sina, Abu Ali Hossein (Avicenna) 1940: *Tadbir-e-Manzel (Household Management)* (in Persian). Tehran, Iran: Sina.

Ibn Miskaway, Abu Ali Mohammad undated: *Tahdib al-Akhlar (Ethics)* (Persian translation). Tehran, Iran: Zurooyk.

Kai Kavus Ibn Eskandar (Prince of Gurgan) 1951: *A Mirror for Princes*, translated from the Persian *Qabus Nameh* by R. Levy. New York: Dutton.

Labib, S. 1969: Capitalism in medieval Islam. *Journal of Economic History*, 29, 77–98.

Lambton, A. K. S. 1980: *Theory and Practice in Medieval Persian Government*. London: Variorum Reprints.

Leff, G. 1958: *Medieval Thought*. Chicago, IL: Quadrangle Books.

Lewis, T. 1978: Acquisition and anxiety: Aristotle's case against the market. *Canadian Journal of Economics*, 11(1), 69–90.

Lowry, S. T. 1979: Recent literature on ancient Greek economic thought. *Journal of Economic Literature*, 27, 65–86.

McNulty, P. 1975: A note on the division of labor in Plato and Adam Smith. *History of Political Economy*, 7(3), 372–8.

Mirakhor, A. 1988 [1983]: Muslim scholars and the history of economics: a need for reconsideration. Published in English in *Papers on Islamic Banking*, Tehran, Iran: Central Bank of Iran, 299–354. Original paper presented in 1983 at the Annual Meetings of Southwestern and Midwestern Economic Associations (US).

Richards, D. S. (ed.) 1970: *Islam and Trade of Asia*. Philadelphia, PA: University of Pennsylvania Press.

Rodinson, M. 1978: *Islam and Capitalism*. Austin, TX: University of Texas Press.

Sarton, G. 1931: *Introduction to the History of Science*, 3 vols. Baltimore, MD: Williams and Wilkins.

Schumpeter, J. 1954: *History of Economic Analysis*. New York: Oxford University Press.

Sharif, M. M. (ed.) 1966: *A History of Muslim Philosophy*, vol. 2. Wiesbaden, Germany: Otto Harrassowitz.

Siddiqi, N. M. 1964: Economic thought of Abu-Yusuf. *Fikl-O-Nazal* (Aligorh, India), January.

Siddiqi, S. A. 1968: *Public Finance in Islam*. Lahore, Pakistan: S. M. Ashraf.

Smith, A. 1985 [1776]: *An Inquiry into the Nature and Causes of the Wealth of Nations*. New York: Modern Library.

Spengler, J. J. 1964: Economic thought of Islam: Ibn Khaldun. *Comparative Studies in Society and History*, VI(3), 264–306.

—— 1971: Alberuni: eleventh century Iranian Malthusian? *History of Political Economy*, 3(1) (Spring), 92–104.

Spuler, B. 1970: Trade in the eastern Islamic countries. In D. S. Richards (ed.), *Islam and Trade of Asia*. Philadelphia, PA: University of Pennsylvania Press, 11–20.

Tuma, E. 1965: Early Arab economic policies. *Islamic Studies*, 6(1), 1–23.

Tusi, Khajeh Nasir 1985: *Ahlagh-e-Nasseri (Nassireean Ethics)* (in Persian), Tehran, Iran: Minavi; English translation, 1964.

Udovitch, A. 1970: Commercial techniques in the early Islamic centuries. In D. S. Richards (ed.), *Islam and Trade of Asia*. Philadelphia, PA: University of Pennsylvania Press.

Watt, W. W. 1972: *The Influence of Islam on Medieval Europe*. Edinburgh, UK: Edinburgh University Press.

White, L., Jr. 1969: Medieval borrowings from further Asia. *Medieval and Renaissance Studies*, 5: Proceedings of the Southern Institute for Medieval and Renaissance Studies, Summer (Chapel Hill), 3–26.

Winter, H. J. 1950: the Arabic achievement in physics. *Endeavor*, 9.

Zubaidah, S. 1972: Economic and political activism in Islam. *Economy and Society*, I(3), 308–37.

Mercantilism

Lars G. Magnusson

4.1   THE HISTORY OF THE CONCEPT

In common scholarly and popular vocabulary, the concept of "mercantilism" designates either a system of economic policy or an epoch in the development of economic doctrine during the seventeenth and eighteenth centuries, or both of them, before the publication of Adam Smith's path-breaking *Wealth of Nations* (1776). The bulk of what is commonly known as "mercantilist literature" appeared in Britain from the 1620s up until the middle of the eighteenth century. However, the concept also appeared as a label for trade protection and *dirigiste* views during later periods, most often as "neo-mercantilism." Among the first mercantilist writers, who are explicitly named as such, we find two Englishmen, Thomas Mun and Edward Misselden in the 1620s, while James Steuart's *Principles of Political Oeconomy* (1767) is conventionally perceived as perhaps the last major "mercantilist" work. Most of the mercantilist writers during the seventeenth and eighteenth centuries were businessmen, merchants and government officials. They wrote mainly about practical matters concerning trade, shipping, the economic effects of tariffs and protection of industries, monetary issues (the devaluation of coins), interest rates, and so on (Magnusson, 1994).

The concept of "mercantilism" first appeared in print in Marquis de Mirabeau's *Philosophie Rurale* in 1763 as *systeme mercantile*, although it was used by other physiocrats during the same period as well. In France during this period, the concept was utilized in order to describe an economic policy regime characterized by direct state intervention, intended to protect domestic merchants and manufacturers. This system, which was designed primarily to finance state manufactories, was more commonly known as "Colbertism," after the famous seventeenth-century French finance minister. However, the main creator of "the mercantile system" was Adam Smith. According to Smith, the core of the mercantile system – "the commercial system" as he called it – consisted of the popular folly of confusing wealth with money. He argued that even though mercantilist writers mainly were practically oriented, they nevertheless proposed an analytic principle; namely, that a country must export more than it imported, which would lead to net inflow of bullion. This goal would be achieved through an active policy and thus make the state – or commonwealth – richer. This was the core argument of the much debated so-called "positive balance of trade theory."

According to Adam Smith, the main architect of the mercantile system of economic thinking was the English writer and tradesman Thomas Mun (1571–1641). His main published writings appear in two short treatises, *A Discourse of Trade from England unto the East Indies* (1621) and perhaps the more important *England's Treasure by Forraign Trade* (1664). Adam Smith picked out this last tract – published posthumously after Mun's death, but probably written during the late 1620s – as the archetype of mercantilist texts; its manifesto. Underlying this erroneous theory of the favorable gains from a positive trade balance lurked – further according to Smith – a mercantile special interest, which used the idea of a positive balance of trade in order to propagate a protective trade policy in general, including duties on imports, tariffs, bounties, and so on. According to Smith, the mercantile system implied a gigantic conspiracy on behalf of master manufacturers and merchants in order to cheat the public and consumers. This view of mercantilism as a policy of rent-seeking developed by special interests has in recent times been further elaborated by economists inspired by positive and public-choice theory; especially by Robert E. Eklund and Robert D. Tollison, who have defined mercantilism as "a rent-seeking society." Hence, according to their view, rent-seeking was the real, but most often hidden, agenda behind the mercantilist doctrines and, especially, the view that trade among nations, by and large, was a zero-sum game; what one gained in trade someone else lost, as stated by many pamphleteers during this period (Ekelund and Tollison, 1997).

From Smith and onwards the view of the mercantile system, or simply mercantilism, as state *dirigisme*, and sometimes also protectionism, in order to support a special interest with the aid of the positive balance of trade, was carried further by classical political economy. In France, Auguste Blanqui and, in Britain, J. R. McCulloch were those who were most influential in creating this image of mercantilism. In the 1830s, Richard Jones argued that the seventeenth century had seen the emergence of a protective trade system that built on "the almost romantic value which our ancestors set upon the possessions of the precious metals" (Jones, 1964 [1859], p. 312). Hence, mercantilism was based on the King Midas folly and could be described as a mere fallacy. Certainly, already Hume and others before him had used a simple specie-flow argument to correct this mistake: a net inflow of bullion must certainly mean a relative increase in prices, which through the export and import mechanism will tend to correct itself. Smith and his followers were thus quite content to draw the conclusion that the argument for protection and against free trade was based on a mere intellectual and analytic mistake.

During the nineteenth century, this viewpoint was contested by the German historical school, which preferred to define mercantilism as state-making in a general sense. Hence, the doctrines of mercantilism were no mere folly. Instead, they were the rational expression of nation-building during the early modern period (i.e., 1500–1750). The definition of mercantilism as a process of state-making during a specific historical epoch first appeared in a series of articles published from 1884 to 1887 by the German historical economist Gustav Schmoller. These were translated into English as *The Mercantile System and its Historical Significance* (1896). "Mercantilism" was the term that Schmoller used to designate the policy of unity and centralization pursued by the Prussian government in particular during the seventeenth and eighteenth centuries. Hence, mercantilism expressed the economic interest of the state and regarded economic wealth as a rational means to achieve political power. According to Schmoller, mercantilism expressed the "... economic interests of the whole states" (Schmoller, 1896, p. 59). With his roots in the older German historical school – which included such outstanding figures as Wilhelm Roscher and Friedrich List – Schmoller argued that the core of mercantilism consisted of *dirigiste* ideas propounding the active role of the state in economic modernization and growth. Although the balance of trade theory was perhaps an analytic blind shot, it was rational in a more general and historical sense, as it emphasized the pivotal role of protectionism and tariffs to protect new, emerging infant industries in order to create a modern industrial nation.

These two widely different definitions of mercantilism are certainly not easy to combine. However, an attempt was made by the Swedish economic historian Eli Heckscher, who in his massive *Mercantilism* (1955, first published in 1931) aimed to present mercantilism both as a system of economic thought and of economic policy. As a broader school of economic doctrine, he principally accepted Adam Smith's description. He was in agreement with the balance of trade theory being at the core of the mercantilist doctrine. Moreover, he agreed that it was a folly that later on was upset by modern thinking, such as Hume's specie-flow mechanism. His explained the core of the positive balance of trade theory by pointing at what he believed was a distinct "fear of goods" that dominated the popular mind of the seventeenth century. According to him, the fear of goods and love of money was an expression of the transition from a barter economy to a money (gold and silver) economy, which took place during this period.

However, Heckscher also regarded mercantilism as a system of economic policy. And as such its core logic was – as the historical economists emphasized – state-building. Hence, with the aim of pursuing the goal of state power, the mercantilists developed a number of nationalist economic policy tools, including tariffs. Therefore, the British Navigation Act of 1651, as well as the establishment of national standards of weights and measurements, a national monetary system, and so on, could be viewed as the outcome of the same mercantilist policies.

It is not easy to grasp, in Heckscher's synthesis, how mercantilism as a system of economic theory, a system of economic policy, and a world-view (moral philosophy) relate to each other. Unfortunately, and for this reason, his grand construction has caused grave misunderstandings. For example, Jacob Viner has therefore unfairly interpreted Heckscher as a follower of Schmoller and the historical school (Viner, 1991). Following Smith, Viner was eager to point out that a main characteristic of the mercantilist writers was their confusion of wealth and money. Unlike Heckscher's more complicated picture, he thus portrayed the mercantilist writers as bullionists pure and simple (Viner, 1937).

Another response to Heckscher became common in the heated discussion over mercantilism in the 1950s and 1960s. As early as 1939, A. V. Judges had vigorously rejected the notion of a particular mercantilist doctrine or system. He stated that mercantilism had neither a common theoretical core nor any priests to defend it (Judges, 1969 [1939]). His rejection of mercantilism as a coherent system was later taken up by a number of British economic historians. For example, D. C. Coleman denounced the usefulness of mercantilism outright, both as a description of economic policy and of economic theory; it was "a red-herring of historiography," he stated. The main problem with using this concept was that it gave a false unity to disparate events and ideas. Coleman argued that mercantilism was not a school of economic thinking and doctrine as was, for example, the physiocratic school of the eighteenth century. It was a concept invented by Adam Smith, and its core was a literature of seventeenth-century pamphlets that dealt mainly with practical matters. This literature was neither analytic nor can we here find any definite theoretical propositions (Coleman, 1969).

The majority of modern interpreters seem to agree with Coleman that mercantilism was no finished system or coherent doctrine in the nineteenth- and twentieth-century sense. Although "mercantilist" views mainly appeared in pamphlets that dealt with contemporary economic and political issues, this does not – as several authors have pointed out – necessarily imply that economic writers during the seventeenth and eighteenth centuries composed economic texts without some common objectives, views, and shared concepts in order to make intelligible the complex world of economic phenomena. Hence, it is perhaps more fruitful to perceive the situation as if mercantilist writers shared a common vocabulary in order to argue for specific political and economic viewpoints. On the other hand, Coleman and others were certainly right when they stressed that commentators such as Schmoller and Heckscher overemphasized the systematic character of mercantilism as a coherent system both of economic ideas and of economic policy that stemmed more or less directly from these doctrines.

Moreover, it seems evident that Smith and his followers helped to cement a view of the mercantilist writers that made them more "old-fashioned" than they actually were. As we shall see, rather than being in complete opposition to Smith, they can – to some extent – be regarded as forerunners of both Smith and the liberal school. Any first-hand knowledge of their texts will suggest that they were not totally devoted to *dirigisme*. Moreover, their methodology and supply-and-demand analysis has formed the nucleus of modern theorizing ever since.

4.2 THE ENGLISH CONTEXT

Mercantilism is thus perhaps best understood as a literature of pamphlets and books, mainly of English origin, which primarily dealt with practical political and economic policy issues, roughly between 1620 and 1750. However, an overall objective in much of this literature was the question how England should be able to achieve national wealth and power. In the bulk of this literature, these two goals of achieving wealth and power were looked upon as identical. To some extent, this was perhaps not anything that distinguishes the generation after Mun from its predecessors or, indeed, from much later "schools" of economic writers. Such an identity can be traced in English, Italian, French, and other European economics texts from the sixteenth century and onward. Interpreted in this sense, Italian writers such as Giovanni Botero (1544–1617) and Antonio Serra (1580–?), as well as Spanish writers such as de Vitoria, de Soto, de Azpilcueta, and Luis de Ortiz during the sixteenth century, were perhaps the first "mercantilists." Nor were such ideas absent in later economic writing and thinking, including that of members of the German historical school from List and onwards, and followers of the "American system" as well as the British "free-trade imperialists" during the nineteenth century. Hence, the recommendation that a state should try to keep as much gold and silver as possible within the country, or to organize its foreign trade in such a manner that the net export of manufactured goods is maximized, seems to have been common parlance all over Europe since at least the early sixteenth century.

However, in the English discussion from the 1620s and onwards we can identify a number of other topics as well. Hence, the Dutch example provided an argument for how economic wealth could be achieved through increased international trade and a great population, as well as more manufactories utilizing increased division of labor. Moreover, an increase in trade and manufacture could only be accomplished by propounding sound laws and establishing effective institutions. Thus, most writers were unwilling to put their sole faith in the self-equilibrating forces of the marketplace in order to achieve wealth and growth. On the other hand, as many argued, too much interference in the laws of supply and demand could be just as harmful as none at all. Hence, it is a mistake to interpret all "mercantilists" as protectionists. After all, during the seventeenth century "protectionism" was still not a clear-cut concept, and few argued that duties should be introduced in order to protect domestic industries from foreign competition. It was only gradually that this viewpoint won ground during that century and the next. On the contrary, according to most writers on the subject the main objective of duties was to increase the income of the state.

Hence, English "mercantilism" can to some extent be seen as a special national case of a broader *dirigiste* literature, which appeared in a number of European countries during the sixteenth, seventeenth, and eighteenth centuries, with the overall aim of making the state powerful and rich, and to this effect proposing a number of policy recommendations. Among these were included different proposals for what we perhaps today would call "administered" foreign trade, as well as the notion of keeping money within the country as much as possible. Such writers, who appeared all over Europe, were called "consultant administrators" by Joseph Schumpeter. They were especially common in Spain, Austria, France, and the German states, including Austria (Schumpeter, 1954, pp. 143–207).

However, it is clear that English mercantilist literature also included some additional features. As proposed by for instance Joyce Appleby, this was perhaps due to the fact that many of the English writers were not consultants in any true sense; that is, they were not civil servants, working in the interests of the state or prince. Rather, many of the English writers during the seventeenth century – including Mun and Misselden – were tradesmen and merchants (although this certainly does not exclude them from having political views and objectives as well as a stake in a certain kind of policy). Their different social and occupational makeup might very well have made a difference, and it may have implied that many of them were more clear about how the marketplace actually worked and were less enthusiastic about state intervention as a general principle (Appleby, 1978).

Be that as it may, it is clear that the mercantilist literature from the 1620s gradually introduced analytic ideas and concepts which, 150 years later, became part of the classical synthesis. Hence, as early as during the 1620s in the writings of Mun and Misselden, we can detect a number of new viewpoints that would be developed later on by many writers. To a large extent, the economic depression of the early 1620s was pivotal in inaugurating the famous debate between Gerrard de Malynes (1583–1641), in one corner, and Thomas Mun and Edward Misselden, in the other, which most often has been regarded as the starting point of mercantilism proper as an economic doctrine. Being asked by the Crown to provide explanations for the ongoing depression at the beginning of the 1620s, Malynes and Mun (and Misselden) came up with totally divergent viewpoints. In the heated discussion, Malynes repeated an argument for which he was well known; namely, that the main cause of the depression was the deteriorating terms of trade for English wares caused by foreign money speculators (especially Dutch merchants and Jews). He argued that abroad there was a conspiracy to lower the value of English money. Furthermore, according to Malynes, money speculation was a form of usury and, as such – to use the title of one of his earliest treatises from 1601 – "the Canker of England's Commonwealth." Mun, together with Misselden, had come up with another explanation as early as 1622, when he chaired a Privy Council committee aimed at finding remedies for the crisis. Both Mun and Misselden agreed with Malynes that the terms of trade had worked against England during recent years. However, the main reason for this was not evil speculation by foreign usurers, but that the "real" trade balance between England and other European countries had developed in a negative way since the beginning of the Thirty Years' War. Thus, an earlier English trade surplus had been transformed into a negative balance of trade. They argued that it was this negative balance that had made English exchange rates less favorable and caused a general crisis.

In this context, we are not concerned with whether or not this interpretation was correct. Obviously, one reason why Mun and Misselden differed so much in their interpretation from that of Malynes was that they placed much more emphasis on the problem of why foreign buyers showed so little interest in buying English wares, such as wool and cloth, than on the issue of why these wares were exchanged for a lower price than before. It was this loss of demand from abroad that caused a negative trade balance, an outflow of bullion, deflation, and a general economic crisis. However, as Raymond de Roover among others emphasized, the worsening terms of trade for England certainly had a great deal to do with monetary chaos triggered by the Thirty Years' War (de Roover, 1974).

It is more important here, perhaps, that by introducing the "real" economy into the picture, Mun and Misselden introduced ideas that would be further elaborated during the seventeenth century and, certainly, serve as a main stimulus to what, for England, Terence Hutchison has called "the economic boom of economic thinking" from the 1690s onwards, including such authors as Josiah Child, Charles Davenant, Nicholas Barbon, Sir Dudley North, John Martyn, and William Petty, whose work became known to a larger circle especially during that decade (Hutchison, 1988). First, as we have seen, mercantilists such as Mun and Misselden believed that the "real" balance of payments was the main cause for the over- or under-valuation of the English currency. Secondly, and in line with this, they recognized the overall importance of the supply-and-demand principle and applied this to price formation in general (at least concerning commodities and money). Thirdly, unlike Malynes and many before him, they did not perceive the "economy" as primarily a moral order. Men were certainly self-interested – and some were evil – but the economic system was a self-regulating order in which supply and demand ruled. Hence, to some extent they perceived the economy as an independent system with its own laws and orders, its "springs and balances." This view was certainly developed much further by later writers during the seventeenth (Barbon, North) and eighteenth centuries (Martyn, Gervaise, Decker, Tucker Hume, Smith), but we can already detect these ideas at a much earlier date. Fourthly, and last, Mun and Misselden proposed a methodology for studying economic phenomena which was clearly inspired by a Baconian program, and which also included a critique of Aristotlean formalism, and they hailed empiricism as a general methodological principle. Certainly, as Finkelstein has propounded most recently, much of the vocabulary used by seventeenth-century writers on economic phenomena was still borrowed from Aristotle, including concepts such as "balance," the use of bodily metaphors in order to describe economic relations (blood or dung as money, and so on; Finkelstein, 2000). However, the understanding of what "economy" was in relation to state, morals, politics, and so on had slowly begun to change.

4.3   INTERPRETATION OF THE MERCANTILIST DOCTRINE

The mercantilist writers – in Britain and elsewhere – were preoccupied with the question of how the nation should become prosperous, wealthy, and powerful. To this effect, they proposed, among other things, the doctrine of a favorable balance of trade mentioned above. As this theory seems to be in total contrast to later theories, such as Hume's specie-flow mechanism, numerous interpreters have tried hard to make sense of why the mercantilist would hold such (errant) beliefs as the positive advantage of having a long-run trade surplus.

First, from Adam Smith to Jacob Viner in the 1930s, the orthodox view that the mercantilist writers confused money with wealth has been repeated over and over again. However, more recent research has been in agreement about how this explication fails for empirical reasons. Although Viner brings forward a number of citations to support his view, they are taken out of context and do not really provide a fair illustration of the contemporary opinions. In fact, the Midas interpretation has no real support at all in actual texts from this period. For example, in 1699 Charles Davenant – one of the most famous "reform" or "tory mercantilists" – wrote: "Gold and Silver are indeed the Measure of Trade, but that the Spring and Original of it, in all nations is the Natural or Artificial Product of the Country; that is to say, what this Land or what this Labour and Industry Produces" (Davenant, 1771 [1699], p. 171). It is quite clear that a majority of writers from Thomas Mun and Edward Misselden in the 1620s largely agreed with this statement. Some of them might have added that having an abundance of money in the country was of great importance for economic progress and for the wealth of the nation. However, this did not imply that money was identical with wealth. Rather, writers such as Davenant and Child argued that a net inflow of money was a barometer that signaled whether a nation won or lost in its trade with other countries. Others would say that an abundance of money would help to speed up interaction in the marketplace, and stimulate growth and development. Thus, a net inflow of money could be a means of *procuring* wealth; but wealth itself was always the result of production and consumption. Bruno Suviranta's interpretation from 1923 – which probably inspired Heckscher to follow the same line of thinking – of the balance theory being a natural folly, considering the preoccupation with money during this period (money fetishism), is also problematic for the same reason; after all, very few of the mercantilist writers seem to have confused money with riches (Suviranta, 1923).

Secondly, as we have seen, during the nineteenth century historical economists such as Roscher and Schmoller interpreted mercantilism as the theory and practice of state-making. Rather than being a shallow camouflage of private rent-seeking – as envisaged by Smith – mercantilism was a reflection of the modern state bureaucracy and its interests. To some extent, this interpretation was also incorporated into Heckscher's synthesizing work on mercantilism: "mercantilism as a system of power." However, this was only one of several aspects mentioned by Heckscher in order to understand what mercantilism really was. Hence, it is wrong to see Heckscher as a mere fellow-traveling historical economist. On the contrary, he objected loudly to being placed within this tradition, as Viner and other writers have tended to do.

It is not easy to say to what extent this interpretation of mercantilism as state-making is accurate. However, if we undertake a careful reading of the British mercantilist literature in particular, it is notable how seldom these authors refer to a particular state interest when they put forward their policy recommendations. Certainly, it is the aim of these writers to find means and ways to enrich the nation. Moreover, they often emphasize how increased wealth is a precondition for a strong and militarily powerful state. However, in the bulk of this literature, to enrich the state or prince is by no means an end in itself. Hence, there seems to be quite a big difference between this literature and, for example, the German cameralist literature of the eighteenth century or, for that matter, the French *economique politique* as it was developed by Laffemas and Montchrétien in the early seventeenth century.

From another point of view, it is of course also debatable whether it is possible to see a clear and direct line between mercantilism perceived as a set of economic ideas and the policies of the seventeenth- and eighteenth-century states. Especially for the historical school – as well as for Heckscher – it seemed natural to draw a clear line of correspondence from economic *ideas* to economic *policies*. Hence, mercantilism has often been regarded as an excuse for protective policies by the state during the *l'ancien régime*. On the contrary, most of the leading English mercantilist writers seem to have been quite critical of the protective policies of the early modern state. Although they can by no means be characterized as free traders in the modern sense, the most significant feature was their attempt to locate the limits of *dirigisme* rather than to praise it in all circumstances. In this respect, there is no significant difference between the early- and late-seventeenth-century English writers. Hence, it is misleading for several interpreters to have drawn a clear line of demarcation between a more "liberal" and a more "protectionist" phase during the seventeenth century, and to have said that it was not until the late seventeenth century that "mercantilism proper" emerged. Certainly, from the 1690s and onwards, many writers drew the conclusion that the British textile industry must be protected from the inflow of cheap calicoes from India. Furthermore, during the same period many writers argued that England had lost out in its trade with France and for that reason must protect itself. Nevertheless, a majority of the discussants seem to have been hesitant to allow state policies to interfere too much in the workings of the economy. A minority was even against protection as a general principle. Among them, we especially find the so-called "Tory free traders," to use W. J. Ashley's famous phrase (Ashley, 1900), a group that included Davenant, Child, North, Barbon, and so on. To cite Davenant once more: "Trade is in its nature free, finds its own channels, and best directeth its own course: and all laws to give it rules and directive . . . may serve the particular ends of private men, but are seldom advantageous to the public" (Davenant, 1699, p. 98).

Thirdly, it is sometimes proposed that the English mercantilist writers supported a favorable balance of trade because they saw an advantage in higher prices. According to such an interpretation, the mercantilists were thus nothing more than supporters of price inflation. However, it is difficult to find any hard evidence for such a view. For example, Mun fully understood that part of the specie-flow argument which stated that an inflow of money would necessarily imply rising prices. For the bulk of the seventeenth-century writers on economic and trade issues, the quantity theory of money was a standard point of departure. As Viner correctly stated, there were in fact very few price inflationists among the English mercantilists (Viner, 1937). Instead, the majority were in agreement about how high prices would cause lower exports – that is, they argued that elasticity of demand was considerable in most export markets.

Hence, neither the Midas folly nor the idea that the mercantilists sought to fill the princely coffers with bullion or believed in price inflation seems to have any real support in the texts themselves. In his *Early British Economics* (1938), Max Beer suggested that in order to find a more realistic understanding of the doctrine of the favorable balance of trade, the crux of this "doctrine" was the idea of the need to have more money in circulation: "a struggle for liquid assets."

Hence, a main concern for writers on economics in seventeenth- and eighteenth-century England was that the shortage of money would curtail economic development. This was a major problem for England in particular, as it had no silver or gold mines of its own. The only solution to this dilemma was to import money from abroad. As bullion only could be obtained in exchange for goods, *one* possible interpretation of the favorable balance idea might be the existence of an export surplus of *goods*, which would mean that gold and silver could be obtained without having to sell more wares than were being brought into the country. The kingdom's stock would therefore be enlarged both in wares *and* in money.

Another interpretation – first suggested by J. D. Gould – takes Thomas Mun's complex discussion in his *England's Treasure by Forraign Trade* (1664) as a point of departure. As pointed out by Viner, Mun was certainly aware of both the quantity theory of money and the existence of demand elasticity. So the puzzle is why he did not follow this line of thought and state that an inflow of money could not be obtained over a longer period, as an increase in prices would only lead to less foreign demand, in accordance with the specie-flow mechanism developed later on by Hume and others. According to Gould, the reason for this was simply that Mun believed that an increased stock of bullion could be used as liquid capital to finance a greater volume of trade. This would then imply that Mun – perhaps reflecting the contemporary factual circumstances that the bulk of the capital stock consisted of liquid capital assets – identified money with capital (Gould, 1955).

However, it is possible to interpret Mun in another way as well. Along with many others during this period, Mun seems to have feared that without a steady inflow of money originating from a favorable balance of trade, trade and industry would stagnate, land prices would fall, and so on. Thus, the predicament might arise that the circulation of goods would expand so fast that it would lead to a shortage of money. For practical reasons, this could not easily be remedied by an increase in the velocity of money – the importance of which in the quantity theory of money equation was acknowledged as early as in the sixteenth century. Another alternative was to counter this shortage of bullion in circulation by allowing a steady inflow of money through a net trade surplus. Hence no inflation would occur as a consequence of the positive net inflow of bullion, since the new money was necessary in order to cope with increased levels of trade activity.

Fourthly, it is questionable whether we really can talk of a full-fledged, favorable balance theory dominating economic thinking during the period, say, from 1620 to 1750 (or 1776!). The idea of a specific mercantilist "central theory" in the modern sense has already been rejected by Suviranta, but has been hard to root out. It is true that Mun and Misselden evidently seemed to believe in a positive trade balance – whatever they meant by that concept – but it is also clear that this "theory" was abandoned in its most simple form by most writers as early as the late seventeenth century. Some argued that this principle was impractical as a policy goal since it was impossible to account for a trade surplus in quantitative terms. Others found problems on more theoretical grounds – that is, directly or indirectly agreed with the specie-flow argument. Instead, from the 1690s, writers such as Josiah Child (1630–99), Charles Davenant (1656–1714), and Nicholas Barbon (1640–98) developed a new idea that has alternatively been called "the theory of foreign-paid incomes," the "labor balance of trade theory," or "the export of work theory." Instead of holding on to the dogma that a country should strive to receive an inflow of bullion through the balance of trade, these authors stressed that a country should export products with as much value-added content as possible and import as little of such products as they could. They thought that the export of more manufactured goods would lead to an increase in England's income. The profit would stem from the importers – Spain, Portugal, or other countries – not only paying England for its raw materials, but also for its labor costs. Certainly, such a "labor balance theory" – which found its most mature version with James Steuart in the 1760s – is distinctively different in kin from the "bullionist" idea of an inflow of money making the country rich. Most certainly, it served as an excuse both for high duties on the import of manufactured wares and for subsidies for infant manufactures.

4.4 POWER AND PROTECTION

A picture emerges that emphasizes how mercantilism – both as a doctrine and as a system of economic policy – was not at all particularly cohesive. It is true that, to some extent, many writers on economic topics in England as well as other countries shared a common vocabulary and some common ideas. As we have seen, many of them were preoccupied with the importance of trade and payment balances, defined either as a positive balance of trade theory or as a positive balance of labor theory. However, what they mainly shared was a preoccupation with the question of how a nation could become rich and thus also achieve greater national power and glory.

Thomas Mun was especially interested in how the Dutch republic had become such an island of plenty. In fact, his famous *England's Treasure by Forraign Trade* (1664) was – as we saw – posthumously published by his son at a time when England was more or less constantly at war with Holland over trade issues. His explanation was, of course, that the secret of the Dutch success was that it had driven the English out of competition and forced them out of many profitable trades, including the North Sea herring fishery. Moreover, less export trade meant that more had to be bought from the outside, with expensive money. During the same period, William Temple's *Observations upon the United Provinces of the Netherlands* (1673) was highly influential in cementing the view that the prosperity of the Dutch republic lay in its trading and industrial competitiveness. Later on, during the seventeenth and eighteenth centuries, the assumed unbalanced trade with France became the most important policy concern. It was Samuel Fortrey's pamphlet from 1673, *England's Interest and Improvement*, in particular that signaled the shift from Holland to France as the evil "other." Written by Theodore Jansen as a commentary on the Peace of Utrecht between England and France in 1713, the influential *General Maxims of Trade* published some years later discussed how different nationalist economic strategies could be used in order to drive the French out of competition. Among those strategies, tariffs, support for domestic manufacturers, and so on were mentioned in particular (Janssen, 1721 [1713]).

4.5   THE LATER HISTORY OF MERCANTILISM

As we have seen, mercantilism has often been regarded as an ideology for economic protection in order to achieve domestic growth. In this sense, "mercantilist ideas" are not at all only applicable to the period prior to Adam Smith. As mentioned above, the nineteenth century saw the rise of a strong reaction toward the gospels of free trade propounded by British classical economy. Hence, both in Germany and America, a protectionist school emerged that had much in common with eighteenth-century mercantilists such as James Steuart at the very least.

However, the rise of a special school of "national economics" was mainly something that occurred outside England. Hence, a string of foreign writers, among whom the most prominent were the Americans Alexander Hamilton (1757–1804), Matthew Carey, and Henry Carey (1793–1879), as well as the adventurer and economist Friedrich List (1789–1846), who was born in Württemberg in Germany, developed ideas that were based on the quest for national industrial protection. Although quite distinct in temper, style, and ideas, they shared the view that an agricultural economy was always inferior to an industrial economy. Moreover, List and the Careys (father and son) in particular stressed that the "cosmopolitanism" developed in much English economics during the time was false and in reality concealed the fact that free trade was a tool for preserving England's superiority as an industrial nation. It is usually emphasized that the first "national economist" was the American Alexander Hamilton, the first finance minister of the USA. At the American Congress in 1790, he presented a "Report on Manufactures." Hamilton was familiar with Smith's *Wealth of Nations*; ". . . so well in fact as to be able to mold it to his own visions of practical possibilities or necessities and to perceive its limitations" (Schumpeter, 1954, p. 199). In this report, Hamilton presents a number of arguments for the protection of infant industries, which have been commonplace ever since.

In the middle of the nineteenth century, Hamilton's followers argued that British free trade was injurious to less-developed countries and, secondly, that economic theory and practice should be relative to the particular stage of economic development that a certain nation had reached. Such ideas of "national economics" were even more pronounced in the work of Friedrich List, who in fact was highly influenced by the American discussion about free trade and protection. In his still highly controversial contribution to the history of economic doctrines, *Das Nationale System der Politischen Ökonomie* (1846), List constructed a stage theory of economic development in which a nation started out from free trade in its agricultural stage, turned protectionist during its early days of industrialization, and then in its mature stage returned to free trade. He fiercely attacked the false or "chimerical cosmopolitanism" of the British, which he regarded as a cloak for self-interest – that nation's peculiar version of "individualism." Instead, each state must concentrate on the building-up of its own "productive forces" and not neglect the future by focusing on the immediate present. Furthermore, he argued that it was only through such a national build-up of productive forces that true cosmopolitanism could be achieved in the future.

Certainly, mercantilist ideas can also be traced in modern forms of protectionism, which appeared during the nineteenth century. For example, Heckscher's synthesis was aimed at propagating liberal and free trade ideas against protectionism, and against the economic nationalism that was so characteristic of the interwar period. Although Hecksher's insistence upon that mercantilism was a false ideology – free trade was better for economic growth, at least in the long run – he regarded it as an almost ageless form of commonsensical popular economics. According to Heckscher, it presents itself especially during periods of economic problems and crises – such as during the 1920s and 1930s.

Such ideas have also become common since World War II, and are now called "neo-mercantilism" or "strategic-trade theory." From the late 1970s onward, economists such as Lester Thurow, James Brander, Barbara Spencer, and Paul Krugman have sought to replace Torrens's and Ricardo's theory of comparative advantages with something that Michael E. Porter has called "competitive advantage" (Porter, 1985). They argue that the pattern of international trade cannot be explained on the basis of comparative advantage, or with the help of the simple Heckscher–Ohlin theorem. Instead, the flow of international trade is a consequence of scale and scope, economic strength, and increasing returns to scale. Thus, the basis of the Brander–Spencer model and "the new trade theory's" plea for "strategic trade policy" was that countries which, through early investments, had reached a strong position in a certain export market for a particular good would tend to keep such a leading position. In such contexts, in which competition is not perfect (and who cannot find such instances?), sunk investments will lead to barriers to entry – at least in industries with a high value-added or knowledge content – which in its turn will serve as a competitive advantage.

The political implications of the "new trade theory" have been pretty straightforward, although some of its originators (Krugman, for example) have been reluctant to go so far as to state that governmental support could bring forward a competitive advantage for a certain industry, which could be beneficial for a specific nation in the long term (Krugman, 1986). However, against this background, the radical American economist Robert Kuttner has argued for (state) "administrated" foreign trade, especially in his *The End of Laissez-faire. National Purpose and the Global Economy after the Cold War* (1991). Certainly, this is another way to defend the infant-industry argument, with clear implications for trade policy. An often-used example propounded by the strategic trade policy theorists is the current fierce competition between the airplane builders Boeing in America and Airbus in Europe. As these theorists would argue, the active support of the government is doubtless of great importance for a certain nation's position in the international division of labor.

4.6 PROTECTION AND UNDERDEVELOPMENT

As we have seen, free-trade liberalism and the theory of comparative advantages has often been challenged during the nineteenth and twentieth centuries with arguments of mercantilist stance. Such a "Third World" critique with a mercantilist flavor has been developed in order to explain development and underdevelopment as a consequence of economic globalization. Hence, scholars have insisted that old mercantilist ideas were inspired by the same arguments that were propounded during the nineteenth-century discussion on the role of import substitution as a means for underdeveloped countries to become more developed, and ultimately rich. Thus, for example, the Italian economist Cosimo Perrotta insists that the core of the favorable balance theory "really" was what E. A. Johnson conceptualized as a "labor balance theory" (Johnson, 1937). Thus, the main concern of mercantilism was industrial development. Its core was the development of national industries through international trade. Perrotta defines the mercantilist doctrine as a theory of development, stressing that a ". . . country gains in exchange if the value of the matter imported is greater than that of the matter exported, whereas it loses if the labor put into the product imported is greater than put into the product exported" (Perrotta, 1991, p. 321; 1993). So depicted, mercantilism becomes nothing other than a proxy for import substitution policies. According to such lines of thought – which, says Perrotta, connect the seventeenth-century mercantilists with nineteenth- and twentieth-century protectionism – the establishment of industry will give rise to value-adding production and more employment.

Hence, according to such a view, as early as the seventeenth century the mercantilists had a clear picture of the importance of those factors that development economists critical of free trade, such as Paul Prebisch and Gunnar Myrdal, stressed 300 years later, namely that in international trade there is an unequal advantage for those parties involved that depend on the commodities exchanged or, to put it differently, on the different productive potentials and linkage effects. Perrotta and others are doubtlessly correct in emphasizing that many mercantilists were aware of how a higher productive potential in the form of "modern" industry, apart from causing more employment, provided the more developed country with a technological monopoly, which could be used for exploitation or improvements in terms of trade.

Interpreted in this way, mercantilism once again becomes state-building by economic means: a promotion of growth and economic modernization in an internationally competitive *milieu*. To some extent, it also becomes identical to protectionism. However, the danger of this approach is that mercantilism becomes too broad and encompassing a concept. Once again, it turns into a wide description of an economic policy that has been pursued by nation–states throughout history. Instead, I would argue that it is more fruitful and revealing to undertake a more historical reading of what mercantilism really was. Hence, in a historical sense, it was a discussion that emphasized the role of trade and manufacture in economic growth and modernization. However – in the sense in which Adam Smith and others have tended to interpret it over the past two centuries – it was never a coherent theory, with a "favorable balance of trade" theory at its core.

Bibliography

Appleby, J. O. 1978: *Economic Thought and Ideology in Seventeenth Century England*. Princeton, NJ: Princeton University Press.

Ashley, W. J. 1900: The Tory origin of free trade policy. In *Surveys. Historical and Economic*. London: Longman.

Beer, M. 1938: *Early British Economics*. London: George Allen & Unwin.

Coleman, D. C. (ed.) 1969: *Revisions in Mercantilism*. London: Methuen.

Davenant, C. 1771 [1699]: An essay upon the probable methods of making a people gainers in the ballance of trade. In *The Political and Commercial Works of that Celebrated Writer Charles D'Avenant*, vol. 1. London.

de Roover, R. 1974: Gerrard Malynes as an economic writer. In J. Kirschner (ed.), *Business, Banking and Economic Thought in Late Medieval and Early Modern Europe*. Chicago: The University of Chicago Press.

Ekelund, R. E. and Tollison, R. K. 1997: *Politicized Economics. Monarchy, Monopoly and Mercantilism*. College Station, TX: Texas A&M University Press.

Finkelstein, A. 2000: *Harmony and the Balance. An Intellectual History of Seventeenth-Century English Economic Thought*. Ann Arbor, MI: The University of Michigan Press.

Gould, J. D. 1955: The trade crisis of the early 1620's and the English economic thought. *Journal of Economic History*, XV, 121–33.

Heckscher, E. F. 1955: *Mercantilism*, 2 vols. London: George Allen & Unwin.

Hutchison, T. 1988: *Before Adam Smith. The Emergence of Political Economy 1662–1776*. Oxford: Blackwell.

Janssen, T. 1721 [1713]: Maxims of trade. In C. King (ed.), *The British Merchant*, vol. IV. London.

Johnson, E. A. 1937: *Predecessors of Adam Smith. The Growth of British Economic Thought*. New York: Prentice-Hall.

Jones, R. 1964 [1859]: Primitive political economy of England. In *Literary Remains Consisting of Lectures and Tracts on Political Economy*. New York: Augustus M. Kelley.

Judges, A. V. 1969 [1939]: The idea of a mercantile state. In Coleman, op. cit.

Krugman, P. (ed.) 1986: *Strategic Trade Policy and the New International Economics*. Cambridge, MA: The MIT Press.

Kuttner, R. 1991: *The End of Laissez-faire. National Purpose and the Global Economy after the Cold War*. New York: Knopf.

Magnusson, L. 1994: *Mercantilism: The Shaping of Economic Language*. London: Routledge.

Perrotta, C. 1991: Is the mercantilist theory of the favourable balance of trade really erroneous? *History of Political Economy*, 23(2), 301–36.

—— 1993: Early Spanish mercantilism: the first analysis of underdevelopment. In L. Magnusson (ed.), *Mercantilist Economics*. Boston: Kluwer.

Porter, M. E. 1985: *Competitive Advantage*. New York: The Free Press.

Schmoller, G. 1896: *The Mercantile System and its Historical Significance*. London: Macmillan.

Schumpeter, J. A. 1954: *History of Economic Analysis*. New York: Oxford University Press.

Suviranta, B. 1923: *The Theory of the Balance of Trade in England*. Dissertation, Helsinki.

Viner, J. 1937: Early English theories of trade. In *Studies in the Theory of International Trade*. New York: Harper and Brothers.

—— 1991: Power versus plenty as objectives of foreign policy in the seventeenth and eighteenth centuries. In *Essays on the Intellectual History of Economics*. Princeton, NJ; Princeton University Press.

CHAPTER FIVE

Physiocracy and French Pre-Classical Political Economy

Philippe Steiner

5.1 INTRODUCTION

The final part of Louis XIV's reign saw the development of major economic works with the contributions of Pierre de Boisguilbert (1646–1714) and Sébastien le Prestre, Marshall Vauban (1633–1707). A member of the local administration, the former wrote several pamphlets and booklets on economic administration (taxation, grain trade, and money) in which several market mechanisms were studied with great insight (Boisguilbert, 1966). Following the Jansenist approach – according to which a good society may work well without virtuous behavior, since self-love is enough – Boisguilbert explained that wealth did not result from benevolence and charity, but from self-interest (Faccarello, 1986). Since corn does not grow like mushrooms, the price paid to the farmer should be high enough to cover the cost of production. With the concept of proportionate prices (*prix de proportion*), Boisguilbert pointed out that markets were connected by money flows: an expense for the buyer of grain is a revenue for the farmer. Thus, lowering the price of corn – a usual claim in periods of grain shortage – was a dangerous economic policy, since farmers would stop producing corn. More generally, Boisguilbert warned the government that any active policy on the grain market (for example, buying corn abroad) would give birth to anticipations (a likely shortage) and would prevent the policy from being effective (buyers eager to obtain a stock of grain would increase their demands, prices would rise, and a shortage would be created). Free trade thus appeared to be a sound policy. In line with English political arithmetic, Marshall Vauban, a great military engineer, grounded his proposal for a new fiscal system, known as *La dîme royale* (Vauban, 1992 [1707]), on calculations. He suggested that an increase in the military and economic power of the king could be achieved together with an increase in the well-being of the population through an appropriate taxation system: the state would collect a moderate percentage (from 5 to 10 percent) of the agricultural produce, whereas commerce and industry would contribute a very small amount to the royal revenues.

These reflections on economic affairs likely were related, on the one hand, to the poor situation of the realm (with a series of bad weather conditions in 1693–4, 1698–9, and 1709–10, accompanied by famines and a huge mortality – up to one-tenth of the population) and, on the other, to continuous warfare with the continental power (the Austrian Empire) or with the maritime power (The Netherlands). The situation in the 1750s was again marked by military conflict – the Seven Years' War (1756–63) between France and England – but, as recent French historiography has demonstrated (Perrot, 1992; Théré, 1998), economic affairs were then a public concern.

First, several journals appeared, such as the *Journal Œconomique* (1751–72), the *Journal du commerce* (1759–62), the *Journal de l'agriculture, du commerce et des finances* (1765–74), and the *Ephémérides du citoyen* (1767–72; second series 1774–6). The first promoted agronomy and pushed for more rational husbandry; and the second, in which one may find influences from Cantillon's work, was devoted to the science of commerce; whereas the last two were partially or completely dominated by the physiocrats. Secondly, the Intendant du commerce, Jacques Vincent de Gournay (1712–59), gathered a group of young men, including François Véron de Forbonnais (1722–1800) and Anne-Robert-Jacques Turgot (1727–81), in order to promote the study of commerce. Finally, the number of economic publications exploded after the middle of the century (table 5.1), the authors coming from all of the enlightened strata of French society: out of 1587 authors during the period 1750–89, about 10 percent were landowners, farmers, or manufacturers, 10 percent were ecclesiastics, and 6.5 percent were military officers, but the vast majority came from intellectual strata, with educators and men of letters (14.5 percent), lawyers, judicial officers, or financial magistrates (21 percent), or doctors and surgeons (6.5 percent).

This very active period in French political economy was dominated by François Quesnay and Turgot, whose work we will now consider in greater detail.

Table 5.1 Ten-yearly movements in economic publications, 1700–1789

	1700–10	1710–20	1720–30	1730–40	1740–50	1750–60	1760–70	1770–80	1780–89
	60	54	77	72	85	349	560	627	1284
(%)	2	1.5	2.5	2	2.5	10.5	17	19	39

Source: Based on Théré (1998), table 1.2.

5.2 QUESNAY AND THE ECONOMIC THEORY OF AN AGRICULTURAL KINGDOM

François Quesnay (1694–1774) began his career as a surgeon, and then became a physician, working for the nobility and finally at the court in Versailles, where he was the protégé of Mme de Pompadour, the favorite of the king, Louis XV (Weulersse, 1910). He was well established in his profession, a member of the Académie des sciences (Paris) and of the Royal Academy of Sciences (London), and author of several books on medical subjects. Why he left this domain to become an economic thinker remains unclear.

The first step came with a new, enlarged, edition of his *Traité de l'œconomie animale* (Quesnay, 1747), in which he introduced considerations related to the theory of knowledge and rational behavior. He critically examined major philosophers of the day (Nicolas Malebranche and John Locke) in order to deliver his own interpretation of Condillac's sensualism, to which he added the concept of order borrowed from Malebranche's Cartesianism. This approach was reassessed in his first contribution to the *Encyclopédie* ("Evidence," 1756), in which Quesnay stressed the difference between self-interest and enlightened self-interest or rational behavior, the one needed amongst landlords and the administration in order to reach the state of bliss.

The second and decisive step came when Quesnay wrote five papers ("Fermier," "Grains," "Hommes," "Impôts," and "Intérêt de l'argent") to be published in the *Encyclopédie*: due to difficulties with the royal censorship, only the first two papers were published; nevertheless, all of them circulated and the last one appeared in the *Ephémérides du citoyen* in 1765. Quesnay then met the Marquis de Mirabeau (1715–89), whose fame was high after the publication of *L'ami des hommes* (1756–60), and turned the populationist into a fierce advocate of the new science. They jointly wrote two major books (*Théorie de l'impôt* in 1760 and *Philosophie rurale* in 1763) and a school grew up, with Pierre-Samuel Dupont de Nemours (1739–1817), l'Abbé Baudeau (1730–92), whose journal (*Ephémérides du citoyen*) became the journal of the school, and Pierre-Paul le Mercier de la Rivière (1727–1801), whose book (*L'ordre naturel et essentiel des sociétés politiques*, 2001 [1767]) gave a general and methodical exposition of the whole doctrine. At their height, the physiocrats were sufficiently influential to promote a free trade policy, with an Act passed in 1764 concerning the freedom of the grain and flour trade.

5.2.1 Economic policy, the price of grain, and taxation

In the papers written in the years 1756–7, Quesnay was busy with economic government, defined thus:

> The state of the population and of the employment of men is therefore the principal matter of concern in the economic government of states, for the fertility of the soil, the market value of the products, and the proper employment of monetary wealth

are the results of the labour and industry of men. These are the four sources of abundance, which co-operate in bringing about their own mutual expansion. But they can be maintained only through the proper management of the general administration of *men and products; a situation in which monetary wealth is valueless* is a clear evidence of some unsoundness in government policy, or oppression, and of a nation's decline. (Quesnay, 1958, p. 512; Meek, 1964, p. 88; emphasis in the original)

He strongly rejected the economic policy of the French kingdom, a policy too close to the commercial interest, what Quesnay labeled the merchant's system (*le système des commerçants*, Quesnay, 1958, p. 555), with monopolies, chartered companies, and the like (ibid., p. 523). Mesmerized by Amsterdam, with its commercial and monetary wealth, French governments since the time of Colbert, the great minister of Louis XIV, had been misled. Dutch economic government did not fit the French situation, claimed Quesnay, since The Netherlands was a commercial republic with few lands, whereas France was an agricultural kingdom, a large country with a rich soil, in need of an economic policy that favored a large volume of agricultural production that could be sold at a good price (*bon prix*).

In order to ground his view on economic policy, Quesnay reconsidered some basic theoretical issues. In "Hommes" and in chapter VII of the *Philosophie rurale*, he made a distinction between use value and monetary value, the latter being the true subject matter of political economy. Wealth is then defined as the goods exchanged on the market against money, in conformity to their value (ibid., p. 526); however, he had no explicit theory of value and price formation. He noted that use value cannot explain market value, since the latter is continuously changing whereas the former does not, but he contented himself with stating that prices were evolving according to a large number of unspecified circumstances (ibid., p. 526). He later urged his adversaries to write an "Essay on prices" that would offer "a fundamental contribution in order to close the discussions in this domain" (ibid., p. 750). Quesnay overcame the lack of a theory of price by presenting a large number of specific prices combined in an insightful comparison between two economic governments, autarky and free trade (Vaggi, 1987; Steiner, 1994, 1998b), the core of which is given in two tables, here presented in a slightly modified form (table 5.2).

In a manner reminiscent of Cantillon's definition of the entrepreneur (Cantillon, 1997, pp. 28–33), Quesnay's farmer has to assume certain costs (the fundamental price or the production cost plus rent – accordingly, the fundamental price is a production price, since it contains a part of the net surplus) with uncertain revenues, depending on the climate and the actual economic policy. Given a stable distribution of the climate over a period of five years, the model focuses on prices and revenues, the economic policy being considered as the independent variable.

In the absence of free trade, current market prices within the nation differ from international prices and, except in the case of a bad harvest, the former is below the latter since the nation is rich and fertile; this situation is detrimental to both the seller (the farmer, since the merchant is left out) and the buyer (the final consumer). The consumer is supposed to buy the same quantity of corn (three units) each year in order to fulfill his basic needs. Accordingly, the current sum

Table 5.2 Economic government: autarky and free trade compared

Fundamental price (in livres)	Autarky				Free trade	
	Quality of the climate	Quantity produced by unit of land, q_t	Market prices, p_t (in livres)	Net surplus (in livres) by unit of land	Market prices, p'_t (in livres)	Net surplus (in livres) by unit of land
	Plentiful	7	10	−4	16	28
	Good	6	12	−2	17	28
74	Average	5	15	1	18	6
	Poor	4	20	6	19	2
	Bad	3	30	16	20	−14

Source: Based on Quesnay (1958), pp. 532–3.

spent, or the *consumer price*, is equal to the quantity times the market price (p_t) and the average cost of one unit of corn for the consumer, or the *average consumer price*, is $1/5 \ \Sigma p_t = 17.4$ livres, according to Quesnay's data. The situation is substantially different for the producer, since his annual revenue depends on prices and on the quantity produced (q_t); accordingly, the average revenue that he gets for one unit of corn, or the *average producer price*, is $\Sigma p_t q_t / \Sigma q_t = 15.48$ livres. The same unit of corn costs more to the consumer than it yields to the producer; this is due to the price–quantity relationship, which is the core element of the model. Quesnay's price–quantity relationship is a King–Davenant relation, with a weaker price elasticity (Steiner, 1994), which means that prices overreact to a fall in production. Finally, in the situation of autarky, net product (annual gross revenue minus fundamental price) is positive but, on the one hand, there is an inverse relation between net product and quantity produced and, on the other hand, producers and consumers have a direct opposition of interest: when the crop is plentiful, the consumer enjoys abundance and low prices, which means a loss for the producer, whereas the producer gets a large surplus when the crop is bad – that is, when there is a shortage and a high price.

Under free trade policy, with the broadening of the market, a different price–quantity relationship is at work together with a higher current price (p'_t), except in the case of a bad harvest. Nevertheless, the average consumer price is not substantially modified (from 17.4 livres to 18 livres) due to the disappearance of the very high price that was formerly associated with bad harvest. Meanwhile, the average producer price jumps from 15.48 livres to 17.6 livres, and the net product is greater, with 50 livres for 5 years instead of 17 livres formerly. Finally, consumers and producers have the same interest in a plentiful harvest, since the inverse net product–quantity produced relation has disappeared with the King–Davenant price–quantity relation.

Without the help of a theory of price, Quesnay produced a fine piece of economic analysis showing the benefits associated with free trade. The improvement in the situation of the farmer comes from a small increase in the average price of corn, which means that wages have no reason to rise substantially, permitting the export sector to remain competitive abroad. Furthermore, if one takes the size of the net product as the yardstick for evaluating policy, the system of merchants appears to be disastrous: in order to get a small net product from commerce, based on a low cost in manufacturing and in maritime commerce (Steiner, 1997) – that is, with a low price for corn and low wages – the French kingdom deprives itself of the large agricultural net product associated with a free trade policy.

According to Quesnay, farmers constitute the core of the productive class, since the level of production depends on the size of their capital once the correct economic policy is implemented. In "Fermier," Quesnay explained that when farmers are poor (do not have capital of their own), they cannot produce with a good technique (*grande culture*), which is characterized by a net product to circulating capital ratio equal to 100 percent, and they must content themselves with a less productive technique (*petite culture*), with a lower ratio equal to 35 percent. The productive sector (agriculture) must be given the priority over the sterile one (manufacture), and thus Quesnay asked for institutional reforms in favor of this class, because their wealth was the basic fuel for the recovery of the French nation. In a period during which France was involved in a costly war against England, this policy would appeal to a kingdom in need of the financial resources necessary to cope with the high costs of maritime and continental wars (Steiner, 2002). Nonetheless, it raised some important problems related to the distribution of wealth.

Rent is determined though a bargaining process between the landlord and the farmer, but Quesnay did not introduce any specific revenue for the farmer. In his papers, farmers are supposed to pay both the taxes (whether to the state or to the Church) and the rent out of the net product; a profit could be conceived as the remaining part of the net product accruing to the farmer. In the following period, Quesnay went in a different direction with the single-tax doctrine.

This fiscal doctrine was aimed at diminishing the economic and social costs of fiscal administration, notably for the people living in the countryside, through a tax directly paid by those who were the effective taxpayers, the landlords. Quesnay's single tax doctrine was a bold policy according to which farmers would pay the whole net product to the landlords, so that the latter could pay all of the taxes to the king and the Church. Then farmers would no longer fear the tax administrators and their capital would be free of any threat, as would be the agricultural net product that was so important for restoring the nation. The theoretical cost of this solution was important: from an analytic point of view; this meant that there was no room for a genuine concept of profit, since all of the surplus was paid as rent to the landlords. In this respect, the only possible remaining profit was the temporary profit that the farmer would retain as long as the productivity of his farm was enhanced, but he had yet to bargain anew his lease with the landlord (Meek, 1964; Eltis, 1975). In *Philosophie rurale*, Quesnay, followed by Dupont's *De l'importation et de l'exportation des grains* (1910 [1764]), used this temporary profit argument to explain how farmers would find the necessary capital for progressively restoring the agricultural sector: as soon as a free trade policy was implemented, farmers would receive a larger revenue while paying rent on the former and less profitable basis; this extra revenue could be invested, permitting them to use more efficient techniques (Eltis, 1996).

The political cost of this solution was high, since it demanded that landlords, many of whom were members of the nobility, pay the taxes. Indeed, Quesnay carefully explained that his tax system was the best solution for them, since, directly or indirectly, taxes were being paid by them. It is difficult to believe, however, that they would have welcomed such a proposal, at least without any political compensation in terms of the rights of citizenship and political representation. It is true that the physiocrats were looking for such political representation (Charles and Steiner, 1999), but they were not very successful in this respect.

5.2.2 The *Tableau économique*: capital and the circulation process

Quesnay devoted much effort to understanding the functioning of a large agricultural kingdom in which the government has implemented free trade: the *Tableau économique* was the result of this effort.

In line with his theory of knowledge, Quesnay considered that genuine economic science should be grounded on sensations; or, more precisely, on facts grasped through a quantitative dimension. In this respect, Quesnay was close to Petty's political arithmetic, in which the latter characterized his approach by the use of weights and numbers instead of superlatives.

Empirical relevance was a methodological prerequisite for accurate economic calculations, out of which evidence could make its way through the misleading arguments that vested interests often spread about during economic debates. As Quesnay put it in the preface of the *Philosophie rurale*, "Calculations are to the science of political economy, what bones are to the human body." Conscious of the specificity of the social sciences, he added a rhetorical dimension: "It takes calculations to critique calculations" (Quesnay, in Mirabeau, 1763, pp. xix–xx). Nevertheless, calculation was limited to arithmetic and geometry; in his book on mathematics Quesnay (1773, vol. 5, pp. 26–7) explained that calculus was a metaphysical tool, free of any sensationalistic basis, and useless in political economy.

Empirical accuracy and rhetorical advantage were important aims, but Quesnay added a theoretical one to his approach as far as his economic table was concerned. In the final remark in his first edition, he told the reader that, by hypothesis, agricultural techniques permitted the net product to circulating capital ratio to reach 100 percent but, whatever the actual ratio, wrote Quesnay, the principles at work in the table were correct (Quesnay, 1958, p. 673). As in Ricardian "strong cases," the economic table was constructed to explain the functioning of basic principles. Which ones? Two kinds of economic table can be distinguished (Cartelier, 1984; Herlitz, 1996), even if, as indicated above, one can make room for a third kind using the disequilibrium approach in *Philosophie rurale*, "Premier problème économique" (1766) and "Second problème économique" (1767) (Eltis, 1996). The first kind is given in the three successive editions of the zig-zag

Table 5.3   Two economic tables: the zig-zag (1758–9) and the formula (1765)

The zig-zag			The arithmetic formula		
Productive expenses	Landlords' expenses	Sterile expenses	Productive class	Landlords	Sterile class

The zig-zag:

Revenue

Annual advances		Annual advances
600 reproduce 600		300
300 reproduce 300		300
150 reproduce 150		150
75 reproduce 75		75

The arithmetic formula:

2 a 2 b 1
1   c   d   1
1   1
1
2
Total: 5

Total: 2

e

formulated in the years 1758–9; the second is limited to the "Analyse de la formule arithmétique du tableau économique."

In the zig-zag (table 5.3), the major concern was spending. The formalization shows how the rent paid by farmers to landlords (600 livres) is successively received and spent by two other classes (the agricultural or productive class and the artisan or sterile class), giving rise to the same amount of net product (600 livres). The initial expenditure of the landlords is divided into two equal sums (300 livres), one for the luxury consumption of food and the other for the luxury consumption of furniture, clothes, and the like. Then, the sterile class spends half of the money received (150 livres) to buy food and raw materials from the productive class; the other 150 livres is used to reconstitute the capital of the sterile class, eventually with some goods being bought abroad (Meek, 1964). The productive class spends 150 livres to get manufactured goods from the sterile class, whereas the 150 livres that are left are spent within the sector. The two classes go on spending half of the money received until all of the money is finally spent. When this spending process is complete, the gross total revenue received by the productive class (300 livres from the landlords and 300 livres from the sterile class) is equal to the circulating capital (or "annual advances" in Quesnay's language) of this class; consequently, the reproduction of the capital generates a net product of an equal amount, as shown in the central column of the table. In line with Keynesian insights (a multiplier equal to two), Quesnay showed that the sums spent by the landlords are crucial: the various classes are related by flows of money and, to use Michal Kalecki's language, those in possession of money (landlords) earn what they spend, whereas others spend what they earn. Nevertheless, as recognized by François Véron de Forbonnais (1767), who carefully studied this version of the economic table, the table is not correct as far as the reproduction of capital is concerned. In the table, the gross revenue (600 livres) and the net revenue (300 livres) of both the sterile class and the productive class are equal, a result clearly at variance with the principle of exclusive productivity of the productive class. Aware of this fact, in his commentary on the table, Quesnay introduced an extra flow (300 livres) from the sterile class to the productive class in such a way that the latter obtain a net revenue equal to the initial amount of the net product (600 livres). This is a clear sign that the economic table cannot prove the exclusive productivity of one sector alone, but that this exclusive productivity was only an hypothesis – a weak one, according to many contemporaries (Galiani, 1984 [1770]).

Hence, the formula can be considered as an attempt to overcome the remaining difficulty in the zig-zag: how the reproduction of capital (circulating and fixed capital, money capital) results from the monetary flows between the three classes. At the outset, the productive class has two units of money, and has advanced ten units of fixed capital and two units of circulating capital; the sterile class has only one unit of circulating capital; this capital generates a gross production of five units of agricultural goods and two units of manufactured goods. Then the productive class pays the rent or net produce to the landlords, with the two units of money. The circulation process begins with (a) landlords spending half of their rent to get luxury food from the farmers (one unit) and (b) luxury goods from the artisans (one unit); thereafter, artisans buy one unit of agricultural produce for their food (c), while farmers reconstitute their fixed capital with one unit of manufactured goods (d), since this capital suffers from an annual depreciation of one-tenth of its value. Finally, (e) artisans spend this unit of money buying one unit of agricultural produce in order to reconstitute their circulating capital.

Summing up, the landlords have spent all the money received as rent in order to consume; the artisans have sold two units of manufactured goods, and have spent a corresponding amount of money in order to buy food and to reconstitute their capital; the circulation process has thus allowed these two classes in the end to get what they had in the beginning. What about the productive class? They have sold three of the five units of the agricultural goods produced, they have bought the necessary manufactured goods in order to reconstitute their fixed capital, while the two remaining units of agricultural goods reconstitute their circulating capital. Finally, the money capital is reconstituted as well, since they have two units of money equal to their gross revenue (three units) minus their expenses (one unit). Every form of capital is thus reproduced, in value and in use value, by the class that formerly possessed it: the process of circulation has reproduced the initial conditions of production.

The effective spending of *all* of the money received by the various classes is a crucial hypothesis; however, Quesnay adds a further hypothesis, since landlords have to spend half of their rent in each sector. If they do not, if they spend more in manufactured goods than in food, then, according to Quesnay, the reproduction of agricultural advances cannot be achieved and a process of decline necessarily ensues. Modern analysis does not confirm this point, since if artisans were to go on spending all their money buying agricultural produce, agricultural revenue would be left unchanged and the only effect would be a modification of the proportion of both sectors in the economy (Cartelier, 1984, 1991).

It was a substantial *tour de force* to set out the circulation process of a whole nation within three nodes and five lines. It is no surprise that the formula has since attracted the attention of major theoreticians: Karl Marx, when he built his reproduction model (Gehrke and Kurz, 1995); Joseph Schumpeter, when he praised Quesnay for this first attempt to set forth the general equilibrium approach, which he considered as the economists' *Magna carta*; and Wassily Leontief, when he modeled the American economy with his input–output table.

5.3 TURGOT: TOWARD A THEORY OF A CAPITALIST ECONOMY

After brilliant academic studies, Anne-Robert-Jacques Turgot gave up his anticipated ecclesiastical career and became a member of the high governmental administration. He was personally acquainted with Gournay, traveling with him during the years 1756–7; his first notes on trade, wealth, and money, and several entries ("Etymologie," "Existence," "Expansibilité," "Foires," and "Fondation") for the *Encyclopédie* date from that period. Appointed intendant in Limousin, one of the poorest parts of France, a position in which he remained from 1761 to 1774, he became an emblematic figure of the reformer. Nevertheless, he often stayed in Paris and was well acquainted with the physiocrats, Dupont in particular, and other Parisian salons (he met Adam Smith during the latter's stay in Paris in 1765) through which he met Condorcet, one of his major intellectual heirs. During this period, he wrote his major essays in political economy: on taxes (*Observations sur les mémoires de Graslin et de Saint-Péravy*, 1767), on the grain trade (*Lettres au Contrôleur général sur le commerce des grains*, 1770), on money and interest (*Valeur et monnaie*, 1769; *Mémoire sur les prêts d'argent*, 1770), and his most comprehensive book, *Réflexions sur la formation et la distribution des richesses* (1766). Louis XVI appointed him Contrôleur général and he served from August 1774 to May 1776: he reestablished the freedom of the internal grain trade, which had been suppressed by the former Contrôleur général (Abbé Terray), and he worked for the freedom of the labor market.

A correct assessment of Turgot's political economy must cope with his relation to physiocracy. Recent research emphasizes his differences with Quesnay's political economy (Faccarello, 1992; Ravix and Romani, 1997), suggesting that Turgot was directly in line with classical political economy (Groenewegen, 1969, 1983b;

Brewer, 1987), notably for his theory of capital. Turgot's *Lettres au Contrôleur général sur le commerce des grains* offers a good opportunity to see his intellectual relations to Quesnay, while his theories of value and capital highlight Turgot's originality. Hastily written in three weeks at the request of the Abbé Terray, Turgot endorsed Quesnay's view of free trade.

5.3.1   Markets and competition

Turgot made intensive use of Quesnay's concepts of producer and consumer prices, fundamental prices, and net product; and, according to Dupont's summary of one lost letter, Turgot used a table similar to Quesnay's in "Grains" and "Hommes," and endorsed those fundamental ideas according to which free trade offered what could be now labeled a Pareto-improving policy. However, he added new insights on the functioning of free trade.

Quesnay had explained why price volatility will diminish, but Turgot raised a new problem: How could one explain that free trade did not raise the average price of corn in France? Turgot argued that price would rise only due to a change between supply and demand. Internal demand had no reason to change, he said, since the consumer would not change the quantity consumed, and since, in the short run, there was no reason to believe that producers would change the quantity produced. What about foreign consumers? Are they not ready to buy a large quantity of French corn at a low price, leaving French consumers short of their basic foodstuff? Turgot discarded the common argument with which traditional thinkers opposed free trade: foreign consumers would not buy French corn unless its price fell below the international price to such an extent that the French price plus the profit of the capital of the merchant would be inferior to foreign prices. As simple as it may appear, this reasoning is quite original: it contains the basic principles of the theory of price and profits that were lacking in Quesnay's approach. It also reveals that Turgot was in full command of the principle of spatial arbitrage between two marketplaces. Furthermore, his letters show that Turgot had benefited from Boisguilbert's works, notably the concept of proportionate prices, as is clear from his analysis of the relations between the labor market and the grain market.

Turgot did not content himself with a static approach; he introduced the necessary outcome related to a higher average producer price. With the rise of the producer price, profits accruing to farmers give them the possibility of increasing production when it is in their interest. As a consequence, the demand for labor will rise, while the supply of grain will do the same: What will be the result of such a situation? With the rise in farmers' demand for labor, a rise in either the number of wage earners or a rise in wages, or both, will ensue; in any case, there will be a rise in the demand for corn, facing the rise in the quantity produced. Turgot was not able to provide a solution to this dynamic system, but he argued that the two market prices (the wage rate and the price for corn) would be proportionate to each other, and would exist in an "advantageous equilibrium" in which wages would allow laborers to buy corn, and the price of corn would be high enough for farmers to make a profit on the cultivation of land:

> Since society subsists, then as a rule the necessary proportion between the price
> of foodstuff and the price of labour must subsist. However, this proportion is not
> so strictly determined that it cannot vary and become around the most just and
> advantageous equilibrium. (Turgot, 1770; in 1913–23, vol. III, p. 315)

Indeed, though the proportionate-prices theory is not fully worked out, and
there is no demonstration of the existence and stability of equilibrium, Turgot's
analysis of competition in terms of the relations between two markets was path-
breaking. Competition, wrote Turgot to Dupont (ibid., vol. II, p. 507), was a less
abstract but simpler and more powerful principle than the economic table.

In the longer run, Turgot considers the case in which population growth
becomes a condition of economic growth through a growing supply of labor in
the nation, even though the lag between birth and capacity to work introduces
some stickiness in the labor market. This growth, together with an increasing
quantity of capital, ensures the possibility of economic growth, and is in line
with the philosophy of progress that he had developed as early as his discourse
in the Sorbonne in 1750 (Meek, 1973), and which he fully worked out in his
four-stage theory in *Reflections*. Nevertheless, this growth is limited by natural
constraints. In comments in two essays on indirect taxes, Turgot made a
fundamental remark concerning the net product–capital ratio. Contrary to what
Quesnay and the physiocrats had said, it is not possible to say that this ratio is
constant:

> If the soil were tilled once, the produce would be greater; tilling it a second and
> third time would not just double or triple, but quadruple or decuple the produce,
> which will thus increase in a much larger proportion than the expenditure, and this
> would be the case up to a certain point, at which the produce would be as large as
> possible relative to the advances. Past this point, if the advances are still further
> increased, the product will still increase, but less so, and continuously less and less
> until an addition to the advances would add nothing further to the produce. (Turgot,
> 1767; in 1913–23, vol. II, p. 645; Groenewegen, 1977, p. 112)

To this very clear statement regarding nonproportional returns, Turgot adds a
further remark, according to which the best economic situation is not the one
determined by the best production ratio (net product on capital), since it is likely
that a further quantity of capital would provide enough net product to be
a valuable investment. However, since Turgot did not introduce the price of
the product, there was, once again, no precise determination of the equilibrium
point.

5.3.2   Value, capital, profit, and interest

In *Valeur et monnaie*, Turgot coped with an intricate problem in the theory of
value: How can a social evaluation – the current price – be the result of individual evaluation? Like several other economists of the period (Graslin, 1911
[1767]; Condillac, 1980 [1776]), Turgot developed a theory of value grounded on
utility. First, with the sensualistic conception of man as a bundle of desires,

man's relation to wealth is conceived in terms of needs and utility. Secondly, Turgot considers a pure exchange model in which two agents have a fixed initial stocks of two goods, corn and wood: the process begins with the ordering of the goods by each agent according his perception of scarcity (*rareté*); that is, the utility of the goods balanced by the difficulty of obtaining them. Out of this preference ordering, there appears an estimated value (*valeur estimative*) with which each agent relates the utility of the good to him and the disutility of obtaining one unit of the good; indeed, the estimated value of one unit of corn (wood) is smaller than the estimated value of wood (corn) for the agent whose initial endowment is in corn (wood). Exchange appears as a social relation, as a result of which agents are better off for two reasons: because they can exchange, which means that they can benefit from the higher productivity related to the division of labor (Turgot, 1913–23, vol. III, p. 93; Groenewegen, 1977, p. 144), and because they exchange less for more, in terms of estimated value. Thirdly, the bargaining process proper takes place: this process, considered as the working of competition, is capable of revealing the true price of the good; that is, the exchange ratio between corn and wood. This ratio, or appreciative value (*valeur appréciative*), is the social result of two subjective evaluations of the scarcity of goods. Since Francis Y. Edgeworth's formalization of this process, we know that no single solution exists in this pure exchange model; Turgot's own solution introduced something like an equity principle, according to which the difference between each agent's estimated value of the good bought and the good sold is equal. Unfortunately, Turgot's manuscript stops after a programmatic sentence according to which he would have considered the general case involving more than two agents and more than two goods.

Capital theory was Turgot's second major achievement. Turgot considered his *Reflections* to be a general overview of the subject, while also claiming to have examined in detail the formation and the working of capital and the interest rate. As a matter of fact, while the physiocrats focused on Quesnay's economic table – a tool that Turgot never made use of – he left out algebra, only considering the "metaphysics of the economic table" (Turgot to Dupont; in Turgot, 1913–23, vol. II, p. 519). Quesnay had done much on capital theory, but Turgot's contribution was much more encompassing and accurate, since he considered all the forms of capital involved in the functioning of a commercial society, and because he had a clear concept of profit.

After the various agricultural stages, Turgot examines the commercial stage characterized by market relations; that is, by the value relations between goods and money (ibid., §XXXI–LXVIII). When members of commercial society receive more money than they spend for the satisfaction of their needs, and can spare this extra money, they transform a part of their revenue into capital. With this clear definition Turgot offers a simple explanation of the formation of capital, instead of the physiocratic one which is grounded on imperfections in the competition between farmers and landlords; furthermore, saving is no longer associated with hoarding; that is, a diminution in the circulation. According to his stage theory of progress (Fontaine, 1992), Turgot explains how wealthy people can earn a living out of land or out of money; this means that any amount of accumulated wealth is equivalent to land whenever the revenue that the owner obtains at the end of the period is equal (ibid., §LVIII). How is profit explained? Like any entrepreneur investing capital, the farmer waits for three different elements, apart from the return of the value of the initial capital:

> firstly, a profit equal to the revenue they would be able to acquire with their capital without any labour; secondly, the wages and the price of their labour, of their risk and their industry; thirdly, the wherewithal to replace annually the wear and tear of their property. (ibid., §LXII)

Thus profit is different from wages, since it is a revenue associated with the possession and the investment of capital, and has nothing to do with the revenue of labor. As far as rent and profit are concerned, Turgot explains that profit is a necessary part of the fundamental price, which means that profit does not belong to the net product; as in the Ricardian approach, rent becomes a residual category:

> the surplus serves the farmer to pay the proprietor for the permission he has given to use his field for establishing his enterprise. This is the price of the lease, the revenue of the proprietor, the *net product* . . . and the profits of every kind due to him who made the advances cannot be regarded as a *revenue*, but only as the *return of the expenses of cultivation*, considering that if the cultivator did not get them back, he would be loath to risk his wealth and trouble in cultivating the field of another. (ibid., §LXII)

Turgot generalizes his approach to any form of investment, from land to money-lending, and explains that there exists a stable hierarchy of rates of return associated with the risk and the trouble assumed. These rates are in mutual relation, through a process of allocation of resources among the different investment opportunities and the basic mechanism of competition and economic equilibrium:

> The different uses of the capitals produce, therefore, very unequal products; but this inequality does not prevent them from having a reciprocal influence on each other, nor for establishing a kind of equilibrium amongst themselves. (ibid., §LXXXVII)

In his paper on the interest rate, Quesnay had made a distinction between merchants and the rest of the population: while the former could lend at a rate that was freely determined by market forces, the rate of interest for the latter should be legally maintained below the rate of rent, in such a way as to make investment in land more attractive than financial activities. Turgot did not endorse such an approach: freely determined by the market forces, the rate of interest is inferior to the rate of profit in manufacture or agriculture because the risk and trouble assumed are less important; and there is no need for state intervention. A low interest rate is a clear indication that capital is abundant in a nation, and that entrepreneurs can expand their businesses since they can easily borrow the capital they need.

5.4 CONCLUSION

French political economy was particularly brilliant in the last period of *l'ancien régime*; this is especially true if one also considers the works written by the adversaries of the physiocrats, Ferdinando Galiani (1984 [1770]) and Jacques Necker (1986 [1775]), who objected to their abstract approach of political economy and to their way of implementing reform, discarding both political elements such as power relationships and disturbing anticipations on the market (Faccarello, 1998; Steiner, 1998a, ch. 2). However, the writings of Quesnay and Turgot were the most important and influential, whether for their contemporaries or for the generations that followed.

It is not an overstatement to say that Quesnay and Turgot offered the most innovative pieces of political economy prior to the work of Adam Smith. Many commentators on the great Scottish political economist have mentioned his debts to them (Gronewegen, 1969; Skinner, 1995), while others have stressed how much the two French economists contributed to the formation of classical political economy (Groenewegen, 1983b; Brewer, 1987; Cartelier, 1991; Faccarello, 1992). Their impact was obviously strong in France, whether on economic theory or on political debate. In the former domain, the works of Condorcet are important, at least for the movement toward social mathematics, in which Arrow's impossibility theorem is found in a reasonably well developed form. In a different direction, one can find many links between Jean-Baptiste Say's *Traité d'économie politique* (1803) and Turgot, through the influence of Pierre Louis Roederer, notably for his theory of value grounded on utility.

Among the major points debated in the following decades was the physiocratic theory of taxation: this is not by chance, since taxation links pure analysis and political reform. Furthermore, in that period of political turmoil, taxation was a strong political concern, since citizens were supposed to pay taxes. As a consequence, the "new science" of political economy, to use Dupont's words, was directly involved in the transformation of political discourse. Physiocracy, Turgot included, had created a new political vision, grounded on self-interest, and opposed to Montesquieu's and Rousseau's visions grounded on honor or virtue (Charles and Steiner, 1999). In order to promote this vision of society, they were so eager to turn all the traditional elements of the social hierarchy upside down that Alexis de Tocqueville wittily considered them to have been major promoters of the revolutionary spirit in France.

Bibliography

Primary literature

Boisguilbert, P. de 1966: *Pierre de Boisguilbert ou la naissance de l'économie politique*. Paris: INED.
Cantillon, R. 1997: *Essai sur la nature du commerce en général*. Paris: INED.
Condillac, Etienne Bonnot, abbé de 1980 [1776]: *Le commerce et le gouvernement*. Genève: Slatkine. English translation, Cheltenham: Edward Elgar.

Dupont de Nemours, P. S. 1910 [1764]: *De l'exportation et de l'importation des grains*. Paris: Geuthner.

Galiani, F. 1984 [1770]: *Dialogues sur le commerce*. Paris: Fayard.

Graslin, J.-J. 1911 [1767]: *Essai analytique sur la richesse et sur l'impôt*. Paris: Geuthner.

Le Mercier de la Rivière, P.-P. 2001 [1767]: *L'ordre naturel et essentiel des sociétés politique*. Paris: Fayard.

Mirabeau, Victor Riquetti, marquis de 1760: *Théorie de l'impôt*. Paris.

—— 1763: *Philosophie rurale*. Amsterdam: Libraires associés.

—— 1999 [1758–60]: *Traité de la monarchie*. Paris: L'Harmattan.

Necker, J. 1986 [1775]: *Sur la législation et le commerce des grains*. Roubais: Edires.

Quesnay, F. 1747: *Essai physique sur l'œconomie animale*. Paris, Cavelier.

—— 1773: *Recherches philosophiques sur l'évidence des vérités géométriques*. Amsterdam and Paris: Knapper et Delagnette.

—— 1958: *François Quesnay et la Physiocratie*, vol. 2. Paris: INED.

Turgot, A.-R.-J. 1913–1923: *Œuvres de Turgot et documents le concernant*. Paris: Alcan.

Vauban, Sébastien le Prestre 1992 [1707]: *La dîme royale*. Paris: Imprimerie Nationale.

Véron de Forbonnais, F. 1767: *Principes et observations économiques*. Amsterdam: Chez Marc Michel Rey.

English translations

Groenewegen, P. 1977: The *Economics of A. R. J. Turgot*. The Hague: Martinus Nijhoff.

—— 1983a: *Quesnay "Farmers" and Turgot "Sur la grande et la petite culture."* Sydney: University of Sydney.

Kuczynski, M. and Meek, R. L. 1972: *Quesnay's tableau économique*. London: Macmillan, for the Royal Economic Society and the American Economic Association.

Meek, R. 1964: *The Economics of Physiocracy. Essays and Translation*. London: George Allen & Unwin.

—— 1973: *Turgot on Progress, Sociology and Economics*. Cambridge, UK: Cambridge University Press.

Secondary literature

Barna, T. 1975: Quesnay's Tableau in modern guise. *Economic Journal*, 85, 485–96.

Brewer, A. 1987: Turgot: founder of classical economics. *Economica*, 54(4), 417–28.

Cartelier, J. 1984: Les ambiguités du Tableau économique. *Cahier d'économie politique*, 9, 39–63.

—— 1991: L'économie politique de Quesnay ou l'Utopie du Royaume agricole. In *François Quesnay, Physiocratie*. Paris: Flammarion, 9–64.

Charles, L. and Steiner, P. 1999: Entre Montesquieu et Rousseau. La Physiocratie parmi les origines de la révolution française. *Etudes Jean-Jacques Rousseau*, 11, 83–159.

Eltis, W. 1975: Quesnay: a reinterpretation. *Oxford Economic Papers*, 27(2), 167–200; 27(3), 327–51.

—— 1996: The *Grand Tableau* of François Quesnay's economics. *European Journal of the History of Economic Thought*, 3(1), 21–43.

Faccarello, G. 1986: *Aux origines de la pensée économique libérale: Pierre de Boisguilbert*. Paris: Anthropos.

—— 1992: Turgot et l'économie politique sensualiste. In A. Béraud and G. Faccarello (eds.), *Nouvelle histoire de la pensée économique*, vol. 1. Paris: La découverte, 254–88.

—— 1998: Turgot, Galiani and Necker. In G. Faccarello (ed.), *Studies in the History of French Political Economy. From Bodin to Walras*. London: Routledge, 120–95.

Fontaine, P. 1992: Social progress and economic behaviour in Turgot. In S. T. Lowry (ed.), *Perspectives on the History of Economic Thought*, vol. 7: *Perspectives on the Administrative Tradition: From Antiquity to the Twentieth Century: Selected Papers from the History of Economics Conference 1990*. Aldershot, UK: Edward Elgar, for the History of Economics Society, 76–93.

Fox-Genovese, E. 1976: *The Origins of Physiocracy. Economic Revolution and Social Order in Eighteenth Century France*. Ithaca, NY: Cornell University Press.

Gehrke, C. and Kurz, H. D. 1995: Karl Marx on physiocracy. *European Journal of the History of Economic Thought*, 2(1), 53–90.

Groenewegen, P. 1969: Turgot and Adam Smith. *Scottish Journal of Political Economy*, 16(3), 271–87.

—— 1983b: Turgot's place in the history of economics: A bi-centenary estimate. *History of Political Economy*, 15(4), 585–616.

Herlitz, L. 1996: From spending to reproduction. *European Journal of the History of Economic Thought*, 3(1), 1–20.

Larrère, C. 1992: *L'invention de l'économie au 18e siècle*. Paris: Presses universitaires de France.

Perrot, J.-C. 1992: *Une histoire intellectuelle de l'économie politque*. Paris: Editions de l'Ecole des Hautes Etudes en Sciences Sociales.

Ravix, J.-T. and Romani, P.-M. 1997: Le "système économique" de Turgot. In Turgot, *Formation et distribution des richesses*. Paris: Flammarion, 1–63.

Skinner, A. 1995: Adam Smith and François Quesnay. In B. Delmas, T. Demals, and P. Steiner (eds.), *La diffusion internationale de la Physiocratie: 18e–19e siècles*. Grenoble: Presses universitaires de Grenoble, 33–57.

Steiner, P. 1994: Demand, price and net product in the early writings of Quesnay. *European Journal of the History of Economic Thought*, 1(2), 231–51.

—— 1997: Quesnay et le commerce. *Revue d'économie politique*, 107(5), 695–713.

—— 1998a: *Sociologie de la connaissance économique. Essai sur les rationalisations de la pensée économique (1750–1850)*. Paris: Presse universitaires de France.

—— 1998b: *La "Science nouvelle" de l'économie politique*. Paris: Presses universitaires de France.

—— 2002: Wealth and power: Quesnay's Political Economy of the agricultural kingdom. *Journal of the History of Economic Thought*, 24(1), 91–110.

Théré, C. 1998: Economic publishing and authors, 1566–1789. In G. Faccarello (ed.), *Studies in the History of French Political Economy. From Bodin to Walras*. London: Routledge, 1–56.

Vaggi, G. 1987: *The Economics of François Quesnay*. London: Macmillan.

Weulersse, G. 1910: *Le mouvement physiocratique en France*. Paris: Alcan.

CHAPTER SIX

Pre-Classical Economics in Britain

Anthony Brewer

The early development of economics in Britain falls into two distinct phases, before and after 1700. The seventeenth-century literature is almost wholly English and London-centered – mainly pamphlets or short books arguing a particular viewpoint or tackling a particular policy issue. There was a first flush of activity in the 1620s, a lull during the civil war and the Cromwellian republic, and sustained debate after 1660, reaching a climax in the 1690s, "the first *major* concentrated burst of development in the history of the subject" (Hutchison, 1988, p. 56). The London-centered debates of the 1690s came to an abrupt end at the turn of the century. The early eighteenth century saw little of note apart from two rather eccentric works by Law and Mandeville, and when the subject came to life again in the middle of the century the most important contributions came from Scotland. The economic thinking of the Scottish Enlightenment was less oriented to immediate policy issues and more concerned to locate economic issues in a wider ethical and historical framework.

It makes no sense to look at the economic writings of this time in isolation from their context. Britain's situation was changing rapidly. At the start of the seventeenth century, England and Scotland were separate countries, and were in almost all respects marginal to the European system – prosperous but intellectually rather backward, and politically and militarily negligible on the European stage. Trade was dominated by Dutch ships and merchants, and Britain exported little but wool and woolen textiles. By the later seventeenth century things were changing on almost every front. England became the center of the new science, with the foundation of the Royal Society (1662) and the publication of Newton's *Principia* (1687). New institutions were emerging, such as the Bank of England (1694). London overtook Amsterdam as a trading center, three naval wars with the Dutch opened the way to British control of the seas, and the Navigation Act of 1660 ensured that British ships and merchants were the beneficiaries. The intense debates of the 1690s reflected the uncertainties of a period of change. By the early eighteenth century the pattern was set, as Marlborough's victories on land made Britain, now united by the Act of Union of 1707, a major European power. The main aims of British policy – to maintain control of the seas and to prevent France dominating continental Europe – were set for a century or more (Wilson, 1984; J. Brewer, 1989). As Daniel Defoe observed in 1724, England was "the most flourishing and opulent country in the world." The relative stability and continuing growth of the eighteenth century allowed a more reflective (and perhaps a more complacent) approach to economic issues.

6.1 Seventeenth-Century England: The Making of a Great Power

6.1.1 Trade and the trade balance

To understand the voluminous literature on trade in seventeenth-century England, one must first understand the way contemporary Englishmen saw their situation relative to the Dutch. The United Provinces (the modern Netherlands) had finally established their independence in 1648 after a ferocious 80-year war against Spain. They were the trading and financial center of Northern Europe and, in per capita terms, the richest place in Europe. English merchants obsessively scrutinized the Dutch to discover the secret of their success. Thus, Child's *Brief Observations* (1668) starts: "The prodigious increase of the Netherlanders in their domestick and forreign Trade, Riches, and multitude of Shipping, is the envy of the present and may be the wonder of all future Generations" but, he continued, the Dutch could be imitated "by us of this Kingdom of *England*" (1668, p. 3). If seventeenth-century writers thought that trade was the route to wealth, it was because of the Dutch example. By the eighteenth century, England had less cause to be envious and the debate subsided.

The seventeenth-century literature (or part of it) has often been labeled "mercantilist" (see Magnusson, ch. 4, this volume), but the writers of the time were too varied to be treated as a unified school of thought. There was indeed widespread support for active policies of one sort or another to promote English trade, usually at the expense of the Dutch and the French, but that is as far as it goes.

Applying modern methods of analysis to seventeenth-century conditions, it is not hard to make a case for "mercantilist" policies to promote Britain's trade and market share. The big profits were in trading with the Far East and the Americas, using armed convoys and fortified settlements. Free trade in the modern sense was not an option. More generally, there were economies of scale and scope in entrepôt trade, and real opportunities to diversify England's exports, with associated infant-industry arguments for protection. Seventeenth-century writers were dimly aware of these issues, but lacked the analytic apparatus to discuss them in terms acceptable to modern critics. Active policies were nonetheless adopted and did in fact have the desired results.

Many seventeenth-century debates focused on the balance of trade; that is, the excess (or shortfall) of export revenue over import spending. The basic idea can be traced back to the Middle Ages (Viner, 1937, p. 6). The metaphor of a "balance" seems to have been introduced by Malynes in 1601, in the phrase "overballancing" of trade. Much the most influential work on the subject was Thomas Mun's *England's Treasure by Forraign Trade*, written in the 1620s but published (in a quite different context) in 1664. The notion of an overall balance of trade was undoubtedly an analytic advance. Mun contrasted the overall balance tellingly with the balance on specific trades or the bilateral balance with any particular country, and used it to distinguish between gains to merchants, gains to the king, and gains to the nation as a whole. For a country that used metallic money and had no domestic sources of precious metals, the balance of trade really did determine the net inflow of specie and hence the change in the money stock (neglecting nonmonetary uses of gold and silver, which could be accounted for separately, and capital account transactions).

Unfortunately, it was fatally easy to confuse the balance of trade with the gains from trade, and to treat it as an aim in itself. The simplest way to fall into this trap would be to confuse wealth with money, or with precious metals. This is the charge that Adam Smith brought against Mun and other writers of the seventeenth century, and it is hard to acquit them completely (Viner, 1937, pp. 15–22). They did not think of precious metals as desirable in themselves, but they did, it seems, find it difficult to distinguish between the stock of money and a stock of wealth or capital. Thus, Mun argued that the "stock of a Kingdom" was like that of a private man who becomes richer by spending less than he earns and adding the difference to the "ready money in his chest" (1664, p. 5). In mitigation, one might point out that it was important to have reserves of internationally accepted metallic money in case of war, and that an inflow of money would stimulate the domestic economy, but one would then have to meet the objection that an inflow of money would raise the price level and make exports less competitive. Mun was aware of this possibility, but seems to have seen it as no more than a minor qualification, perhaps limiting the inflow of money rather than eliminating or reversing it. Not everyone accepted the balance of trade as a relevant policy aim and those who did could not agree on the policy conclusions. The issues involved were not sorted out satisfactorily until Hume (1752; see below).

The "mercantilist" writers of the seventeenth century are often described as opponents of free trade, but this is a misleading way to categorize them. Trade had always been taxed and regulated, and there was no established notion of free trade to act as a benchmark. What was new in the seventeenth century was not the regulation of trade but the development of a vocabulary and a framework for discussing the economic effects of regulation. In general, debates did not turn on freedom of trade as a general alternative to regulation or protection, but on the best policies to follow in particular cases. Thus Child (1693) recognized that where trade was free the cheapest suppliers would prevail, but since the Dutch were likely to be cheapest he saw that as an argument against free trade, while Barbon (1690) was against the prohibition of imports to protect domestic suppliers but in favor of using high duties to have the same effect. Early in the century,

Misselden (1622) did indeed argue for free trade, but what he meant by it was the opening of monopolistic companies such as the East India Company to other (English) merchants. Where trade was "disordered" and "ungoverned," however, it should be brought to order.

It was from precisely these "mercantilist" debates that the concept of free trade, in something like its modern sense, emerged at the end of the century; in, for example, North (1691) and Martyn (1701). North led up to the conclusion that "we may labour to hedge in the Cuckow, but in vain; for no People ever yet grew rich by Policies; but it is Peace, Industry, and Freedom that brings Trade and Wealth, and nothing else" (North, 1691, p. 28). North and Martyn, however, had little impact at the time. Ironically, the main protective legislation, the Navigation Act, was progressively amended to make it more effective and was enforced more rigorously thereafter, while tariffs were raised significantly to raise revenue for military purposes. The case for free trade emerged just as trade was becoming less free.

6.1.2   Money and the interest rate

Money was a perennial topic of discussion for a number of reasons. Money consisted of coins at that time, and the English coinage was in a very poor state because of wear and clipping. By the time of the eventual recoinage in 1696, coins had on average fallen to half their supposed weight. Gresham's Law (named after Sir Thomas Gresham, advisor to Queen Elizabeth), that "bad money drives out good" because it pays to pass on coins with a low metal content and melt down better coins for the metal, was at work – the mint issued full weight coins, but 99 percent vanished from circulation. Consideration of the amount of money needed for circulation naturally led toward seeing the economy as a single whole, while consideration of changes in the money stock connected it to the trade balance and the relation between price levels in different countries. Fluctuations in the relative value of gold and silver also posed problems.

The interest rate was also an issue. In medieval Europe, "usury," or lending at interest, had often been forbidden, at least in theory. By the seventeenth century, financial markets were becoming quite well organized but the law still set a maximum to interest rates. Repeated proposals to lower the maximum legal rate to what would certainly have been an unsustainably low level came very close to being passed in the 1690s. There were at least three views about interest rates: (a) that they reflected the "plenty or scarcity" of money, providing a possible motive for aiming at a positive trade balance to increase the money stock and allow lower interest rates; (b) that they depended on supply and demand of loans, and hence on net saving and on profit opportunities open to borrowers; and (c) the naive view that they could be set by legal fiat.

From the 1660s on, Josiah Child (1630–99) argued for reducing the interest rate by law, claiming that the rate had fallen as wealth increased, that it was lower in rich than poor countries, and that the time was now ripe for it to fall again. Low interest was the "*causa causans*" of prosperity because it would encourage merchants and farmers to expand their businesses, and it would also encourage those with money to use it productively rather than simply letting it out at interest. There are clearly the makings of the notion of a demand and a supply function for investible funds here, but what is lacking is a clear notion of equilibrium between the two. Critics agreed that Holland had a low interest rate but pointed out that this was achieved without legal compulsion. Child replied that legislation might not be needed in Holland but it was in England, to allow England to match Holland as a center of trade.

The opposing case, and much more, is to be found in some of the most important economic writings of the seventeenth century, by John Locke (1632–1704). As early as 1668, he had prepared an unpublished draft on an earlier proposal to reduce interest rates, but he was forced into exile until after the revolution of 1688, when his main philosophic works appeared in quick succession, followed by a return to monetary issues in his *Considerations* (1691).

The basic idea of the quantity theory of money, that an increased quantity of money will lead to a fall in its value and a rise in the prices of goods, had been understood in general terms from early on. Locke argued it very clearly for an isolated economy. Whatever the quantity of gold and silver, it "will be a steady standing measure of the value of all other things" and can "drive any proportion of trade" (Locke, 1691, pp. 75–6), since a smaller quantity will be valued more highly. In modern terms, the nominal quantity of money is unimportant since prices adjust to it. In an open economy, however, he argued that the value of money was set at a world level. He thought that a country with a relatively small money stock would be at a disadvantage, but hovered between arguing that its prices would be low and its terms of trade unfavorable or that its trade would be limited and resources unemployed. Either way, he supported the common complaint that a shortage of money was a problem. Both Locke and his contemporary William Petty discussed the institutional determinants of the velocity of circulation and hence the amount of money needed to drive a given amount of trade. Both failed to grasp the specie-flow mechanism that Hume was later to state so clearly.

Locke thought that setting a low legal maximum to the interest rate would be ineffective in practice, and harmful if it were effective. In the absence of regulation, interest rates are determined by demand and supply, explained in what, to a modern reader, seem to be two different and conflicting ways. First, he claimed that when money is scarce, its price (the interest rate) must rise, like any scarce commodity. Interest is high when "Money is little in proportion to the Trade of a Country" (Locke, 1691, pp. 10–11). Secondly, he explained interest rates in terms of demand from borrowers who see profitable uses for capital and supply from those who have more wealth than they can (or want to) employ themselves, comparing it to rent, determined by the balance between potential tenants and landowners with land to rent out (pp. 55–7). The explanation of this apparent inconsistency between monetary and real theories of interest is that he seems to have confused wealth or loanable funds with the stock of circulating money. "My having more Money in my hand than I can . . . use in buying and selling, makes me able to lend" (p. 55). If there were a "million of money" in England, but debts of two millions were needed "to carry on the trade" – that is, if one million were available for lending, but borrowers needed to borrow two millions – the interest rate must rise (p. 11). A low legal maximum would only make matters worse, because it would reduce the amount people were willing to lend, leaving the increased demand unsatisfied.

Dudley North (1641–91) presented an analysis (North, 1691) that has striking similarities to Locke's on some points, but which is diametrically opposed to him on others. Interest rates, he argued, are determined by supply and demand for loans. As in Locke, the supply comes from those who have more resources than they want to employ themselves, and demand from those who see opportunities but need to borrow to take advantage of them. Unlike Locke, however, North saw that it was "stock" (capital or wealth) – not the quantity of money – that determined the supply. Low interest rates, as in Holland, are the result, not the cause, of wealth. Success in trade is the result of thrift and hard work, and leads to the accumulation of wealth and hence to a large supply of loans.

North argued that shortage of money is never a problem, focusing not on international movements of gold and silver but on movements of metal between coins in circulation and hoards of bullion or plate. A shortage of coin will bring out bullion and plate to be coined, while a surplus will be absorbed into hoards. He was able to support the argument by pointing out that large amounts of silver had been coined but that the new coins had disappeared to be melted down. The flow of money accommodates itself, he claimed, without any help from politicians.

6.1.3 Political arithmetic and the state

Sir William Petty (1623–87) was trained as a doctor, became Professor of Anatomy at Oxford and Professor of Music at Gresham College, and was one of the founder members of the Royal Society. His key idea was to apply Baconian scientific method, the use of "number, weight and measure," to social and political issues. This was "political arithmetic," which aimed to provide impersonal, numerical facts as a basis for policy.

His great early achievement, the mapping of Ireland, illustrates his attitude. He had gone to Ireland as physician to Cromwell's army, but he bid for and won the contract to survey the country. His map was an outstanding scientific and organizational achievement – perhaps the best map of any country at the time, finished on time and within budget – but its purpose was to help with the distribution of land to members of the victorious army. Petty himself emerged with extensive lands in Ireland. He was fiercely ambitious, and attached himself to whoever was in power, switching allegiance from Cromwell to Charles II at the Restoration (as, of course, many others did). His policy proposals were designed to strengthen the state, almost regardless of individual rights or interests. To make Ireland more secure and profitable for the British state, for example, he advocated transferring most of the Irish to England, to be absorbed into the much larger English population and eliminated as a separate people with a different language and culture.

The most important of the state's resources is its population, so population estimates were the backbone of political arithmetic. The key work was the

Observations on the Bills of Mortality (1662), by John Graunt (1620–74). Petty certainly collaborated with Graunt and made similar calculations of his own, but their exact roles are unclear. Records of deaths and christenings showed that England as a whole produced a healthy surplus of births over deaths, but that London could only maintain and increase its population by migration from the rest of the country. Petty went on to use estimates of population and assumed per capita income levels to make pioneering estimates of total national income.

What use Petty made of these estimates, and the way they fit into the context of his time, can best be seen in his *Political Arithmetick* of 1676 (published post-humously in 1690; see Petty, 1899, pp. 233–313). He stated and supported ten conclusions, including:

> That a small Country, and few People, may . . . be equivalent in Wealth and Strength to a far greater People and Territory. . . . That France cannot . . . be more powerful at Sea than the English or Hollanders. . . . That the People and Territories of the King of England are naturally near as considerable, for Wealth and Strength, as those of France. . . . That one tenth part, of the whole Expence of the King of England's subjects; is sufficient to maintain one hundred thousand Foot, thirty thousand Horse, and forty thousand Men at Sea, and to defray all other Charges, of the Government. . . . That the King of England's Subjects have Stock, competent, and convenient to drive the Trade of the Whole Commercial World. (Petty, 1899, pp. 247–8)

To see this in context, note that Parliament held the purse strings and would not allow Charles II the funds to pursue an active policy. He accepted a subsidy from Louis XIV, effectively making Britain a passive junior partner in French expansionary plans. Petty's calculations showed that England need not be anyone's junior partner. A small country it might be, but it could (and, under a new king, did) aim to control the seas and to dominate the trade of the "commercial world" (essentially the sea-borne trade of Europe). Petty estimated the requirements and the costs with striking accuracy. In the wars around the turn of the eighteenth century, Britain's navy employed just about the 40,000 he proposed. The land army was smaller than his 130,000, but Britain was effectively paying for its allies' troops as well. To do it, taxes had to rise from 3–4 percent of GNP to just about the 10 percent that Petty proposed (Holmes, 1993, p. 439). Petty saw no objection to allowing France to expand on the continent since England's interests lay at sea (Petty, 1927, vol. 1, p. 262), but later generations disagreed.

Petty's writings contain a few digressions that have attracted (perhaps disproportionate) attention. There is a suggestion of a labor theory of value (Petty, 1899, vol. 1, pp. 43, 50–1, 90) and a (conflicting) suggestion that the value of a good might be determined by the labor and land required to produce it, leading Petty to speculate about a "par" or value-conversion factor between labor and land (vol. 1, p. 181). This was later followed up by Cantillon, who referred to Petty's par as "fanciful" (Cantillon, 1755, p. 43). There are also passages that describe some notion of a surplus of output over necessary subsistence (e.g., Petty, 1899, vol. 1, pp. 30, 118). Petty did not follow up any of these in a systematic way and nor did anyone else, at least in Britain (there may be a line of descent via Cantillon and Quesnay in France). To some who think that the labor theory of value and the notion of surplus are particularly important, these digressions seem significant. Seen in the context of the time, however, what is important in Petty is, rather, his emphasis on quantification and on the role of different sectors (agriculture, trade) in the economy as measured by their contribution to income and to tax revenue.

Petty and Graunt had a number of successors. Edmund Halley (the astronomer, 1656–1742) improved on Graunt's population modeling using better data (from Silesia). Gregory King (1648–1712) produced updated estimates of population and national income, which were not published until later but were drawn on by Charles Davenant (1656–1714) in the 1690s. "Political Arithmetic," as defined by Petty, did not survive long beyond the end of the seventeenth century and was harshly criticized in the eighteenth century for excessive reliance on unreliable data.

6.1.4   The seventeenth-century achievement

The seventeenth century inherited a medieval ideal of a static, hierarchical society with well-defined functions, rights, and duties. Economic considerations came second to the maintenance of a social order consecrated by custom and religion. This was never more than an abstract ideal, but it shaped people's thinking and underlay legislation such as the Statute of Artificers of 1563, which regulated entry and wages in different trades, backed up by the Poor Laws and by regulation of foreign trade. Finkelstein (2000) has argued that much seventeenth-century economic thought can be seen as an attempt to maintain the old order in changing times.

At the same time, the debates of the seventeenth century produced, bit by bit, a radically new idea, of "a natural order of economic relations impervious to social engineering and political interference" (Appleby, 1978, p. 242). Interest rates, for example, are governed by supply and demand, so attempts to fix them by law are bound to fail or to damage the economy. Similarly, net flows of monetary metals depend on the trade balance, and hence on a whole complex of trading relations. Crude attempts to interfere may be counterproductive. The idea of a national economy was emerging as a subject of discussion and as a legitimate concern of government. Petty tried to estimate population and income on a national level. The balance of trade is a genuinely national aggregate, and Mun identified a national interest, distinct from the interest of individual merchants or the king. Discussion of monetary issues led to a conception of a national money stock, a nationwide circulation of money, and a national price level distinct from the price level in other countries.

If the seventeenth century saw the emergence of the idea of an autonomous sphere of economic relations, and hence, in a sense, the birth of economics as a subject (not yet named or even recognized as such), this achievement was not matched by any real attempt to trace the causal processes involved beyond a rather superficial level. Thus, for example, Locke stated the basic idea of the quantity theory of money very clearly, but it was not until Hume, half a century on, that the links between the quantity of money, the price level, and the balance of payments were clarified. Many elements of later theories of capital accumulation surfaced in the debates over interest rates without being brought together. It was just at this point, when the makings of a real advance seem, in retrospect, so obvious, that the advance of the 1690s fizzled out. Policy debates continued, of course, but nothing really new or substantial emerged from them for many years.

What went wrong? Several key figures died before they could take the debate further – Petty in 1687, North in 1691, Barbon in 1698, Child in 1699, and Locke in 1704 – but that does not explain why they left no successors. The key point may be that the debates were driven by immediate policy problems. Once the main issues of the 1690s were settled – the legal interest rate was not lowered after all, the recoinage was carried out, and so on – there was no immediate stimulus to take the argument further. Other, noneconomic, issues took center stage. There were advances in the following period, but in France (Cantillon and others) or Scotland (Hume and others).

6.2   TRANSITION: LAW AND MANDEVILLE

6.2.1   John Law

John Law (1671–1729) was an extraordinary character. A Scot by origin, he killed a man in a duel in London in 1694 and had to flee for his life. For a while he was safe in Scotland, then a separate country, but had to flee again on the Act of Union in 1707. He wandered around Europe peddling proposals for monetary reform and supporting himself as a professional gambler, before gaining the confidence of the French regent. The results were dramatic. He founded a state-backed bank in 1716 and then a joint-stock company, the Mississippi Company, to take over French state debt in return for concessions in the overseas empire. By manipulating monetary conditions, he engineered a spectacular speculative boom in the shares of his company and was briefly able to replace the whole French currency with notes issued by his bank. The bubble burst in 1720. Law was ruined and the scandal rocked the French state. The collapse of Law's "system" left France, in particular, with a deep suspicion of monetary experiments.

His *Money and Trade Considered* (1705) was aimed at a Scottish audience, but Law saw it as more widely applicable. He argued that Scotland was potentially rich but its resources were underemployed. His answer was to expand the money supply by issuing paper money. He is sometimes described as a proto-Keynesian, but he seems to have seen a lack of supply, not demand, as the problem. Thus, discussing price cuts to expand exports, he argued:

> It may be alleg'd, we have more Product and Manufacture, than is consum'd or exported; and selling cheaper, would occasion a greater demand for our Goods Abroad. . . . Product and Manufacture might be much encreas'd, if we had Money to imploy the People: But I'm of Opinion we have not any great Quantity of Goods, more than what is consum'd or exported. (Law, 1705, p. 62)

If output (the "yearly value" of the nation) were increased by £500,000, and if a quarter of the increased income were spent on a greater consumption of home-produced goods, a quarter on consumption of imports, and a quarter on building up stocks of imported goods ("Magazines of Forreign Goods"), there would still be an improvement in the balance of trade of a quarter of the increase in output (Law, 1705, p. 146; see also pp. 16–18; Locke had a similar argument). The numbers were only illustrative, but the theoretical point is clear: increased demand is the consequence, not the cause, of increased output. Increasing the money supply would increase the supply of goods. Like others at the time, Law seems to have thought of money and capital as interchangeable, so extra money would employ more people and allow increased output.

For all its faults, Law's theory raised real macroeconomic questions and suggested ways of thinking about them, but after the collapse of his system his ideas were discredited and had little impact.

6.2.2 Bernard Mandeville

Bernard Mandeville (1671–1733) was a doctor of Dutch origin, who had settled in England. His verse satire, *The Grumbling Hive*, of 1705 was reissued repeatedly as *The Fable of the Bees: Or Private Vices, Public Benefits* after 1714 with added material by way of elaboration and defense of the original. The basic fable has a thriving, growing, hive of bees, clearly representing England, which is permeated with "vice" at every level. A puritanical reformation brings luxury, crime, and war to an end, but the result is mass unemployment (of bees!), falling population, and decline.

Mandeville defined vice very broadly to make his satirical point, including almost anything that the most extreme puritan could possibly object to – luxury and extravagance as well as war and crime. His main line of argument is clearly demand-orientated: ostentation creates a demand for fine clothes and other accoutrements, burglars create a demand for locks and hence work for locksmiths, and so on. Little needs to be said about this, beyond noting that he missed the obvious point that if people did not need locks they might buy something else instead. A second, implicit, argument is that the desire for luxury gives naturally lazy men an incentive to work. These two lines of argument are logically distinct, though they are often hard to separate in Mandeville's text. Neither was wholly new, but Mandeville stated them more forcefully than before.

Mandeville's provocative style aroused general hostility but his arguments bore fruit in the work of later writers, however unwilling they might be to admit it. At the center is the idea of unintended consequences, which became a theme of Scottish Enlightenment thought and of all subsequent economics – individual motives and intentions may have no relation to the overall outcome. Specifically, the actions of selfish individuals, driven by pride and avarice, may have socially desirable results. Adam Smith's invisible hand is clearly a less paradoxical development of the same idea.

Mandeville typified the eighteenth-century approach in another way. The seventeenth-century literature was driven by a conviction that England was not doing well enough and had to improve. Mandeville, like his successors, assumed that England was doing well and getting even better. He sought to explain that success and to argue against any basic change. Law, although he was an exact contemporary, clearly belongs to the earlier tradition, perhaps because the one place he could not settle was England.

6.3 THE EIGHTEENTH CENTURY AND THE SCOTTISH ENLIGHTENMENT

6.3.1 Population and economic growth

There was no population census in England before 1801, and few anywhere else. Eighteenth- (and seventeenth-) century writers did not know what the population was or whether it was increasing. Graunt and Petty had made a start, but their estimates were open to criticism. Steuart, for example, rejected Petty's results because they clashed with his theory. There was even debate about whether population had grown by comparison with classical antiquity. One of Hume's essays dealt with this question.

Population size and growth was widely used as an index of economic success, since reliable estimates of income and output were even scarcer than estimates of population, but there was no agreement on the direction of causality. The Graunt–Petty estimates of population growth used estimates of births and deaths, which Petty treated as essentially independent of economic success. Population growth, he thought, would certainly increase total income, and perhaps income per head. His notorious proposal to ship most of the Irish to England was based on the assumption that an increase in the population of England would be a good thing. Many seventeenth-century writers shared this opinion.

The alternative view, which was to dominate classical economics, saw population as endogenous. Steuart, like Smith and Malthus a few years later, thought that population presses against the limits set by subsistence, so that economic success would automatically lead to population growth. On the other hand, Josiah Tucker (1713–99), one of the few significant English economic writers of the mid-eighteenth century, wanted to encourage immigration because he saw an enlarged population as an asset. Whether population is seen as exogenous or endogenous matters to the emergence of a concept of economic growth in the late eighteenth century. Sustained economic growth was not taken for granted then, as it has been in later centuries, and there was no agreement on whether population and output had grown or would grow in the future (A. Brewer, 1995).

6.3.2 David Hume

David Hume (1711–76) was a central figure in the "Scottish Enlightenment." With Francis Hutcheson (Adam Smith's teacher and predecessor at Glasgow), Adam Ferguson, and others, he pioneered an approach that was historical, in that it saw human societies as the result of a long process of development, and rational, in that it refused to accept tradition or authority as a guide. His main contributions to economics are to be found in a number of short but pointed essays (1752).

His most influential contribution to economics was his magisterial treatment of the interaction between money, prices, and the balance of trade. The basic argument was simple. In a closed economy, the quantity of money is of no importance, since prices adjust proportionately (as Locke had argued). In an open economy, a change in the money supply causes a corresponding price change, which in turn affects competitiveness:

> Suppose four-fifths of all the money in Great Britain to be annihilated in one night ... Must not the price of all labour and commodities sink in proportion? ... What nation could then dispute with us in any foreign market? ... In how little time, therefore, must this bring back the money which we had lost, and raise us to the level of all the neighbouring nations? Where, after we have arrived, we immediately lose the advantage of the cheapness of labour and commodities; and the farther flowing in of money is stopped. (Hume, 1752, p. 311)

Similarly, any excess of money flows out. The conclusion is simple. There is no need to worry about the balance of trade or about a scarcity of money. The system is self-adjusting. The elements of the argument were not new, but they had never been stated so clearly, nor had their full consequences been worked out and presented in the way that Hume did. He effectively settled the issue for a century or more.

Europe was a single system, with a system-wide general price level. India and China were only loosely connected to the European price level, because transport costs were high and trade was restricted by monopolistic companies. Within the European system, money was more or less abundant in different areas according to demand. Austria, for example, had a small money stock because it was relatively underdeveloped. Within a country, the capital and the major ports had a larger share of the money stock because more business was done there. The introduction of paper money would not increase the money stock within a single country, but would simply displace metallic money within a total determined by real factors. Hume's arguments provided an important, if implicit, methodological lesson in the use of the conditions of equilibrium to derive a series of conclusions.

Hume conceded that there would be some stimulus to economic activity during the process of monetary expansion, because prices and wages are slow to adjust. Extra spending is initially perceived as an increase in real demand. Output and employment rise, but when the price increases have fully worked their way through the system, everything returns to normal. Similarly, monetary contraction causes a temporary depression.

A second major theme in Hume's economic essays was the case for a "commercial" society, and for what he called "refinement," or sometimes "luxury." He started from the simple observation that people working in agriculture could feed themselves and have plenty left over which could feed others. This prompts the question: Why should they produce such a surplus and whom should it be used to support? Without coercion, if there is nothing that cultivators want to buy, they will have no incentive to produce a surplus at all:

> Where manufactures and mechanic arts are not cultivated, the bulk of the people must apply themselves to agriculture; and if their skill and industry encrease, there must arise a great superfluity from their labour beyond what suffices to maintain them. They have no temptation, therefore, to encrease their skill and industry; since they cannot exchange that superfluity for any commodities. . . . A habit of indolence naturally prevails. (Hume, 1752, pp. 260–1)

This is the case of a "simple" (underdeveloped) society. (It is also rather like Mandeville's imaginary puritanical revolution.) Hume did not see it as a purely theoretical case, but as a description of England (and other places) in earlier centuries. Force could be used to elicit a surplus, as in feudal society, but Hume thought the results would be meager. Self-interest is a better motivator.

Once attractive manufactures become available, everything changes. Farmers work hard and find better methods of cultivation. Spending by farmers and landlords supports a growing body of urban merchants and manufacturers. The effects go further:

> The spirit of the age affects all the arts; and the minds of men, being once roused from their lethargy . . . turn themselves on all sides, and carry improvements into every art and science. Profound ignorance is totally banished, and men enjoy the privilege of rational creatures, to think as well as to act, to cultivate the pleasures of the mind as well as those of the body. (p. 271)

How does the process start? A backward economy will not advance spontaneously, because manufactures will not develop without a market and farmers will not demand what they have never seen. The impetus, Hume thought, usually comes from outside. Luxury imports provide the incentive to produce a surplus, and then local producers step in. International trade continues to promote development, introducing novelties and offering foreign markets to domestic producers. Competition induces improvement and innovation all round.

Hume linked the decline of feudalism to this process. In a world in which manufactures were few and crude, feudal lords maintained gangs of retainers and soldiers. Once offered more "refined" manufactures, they switched to buying from independent merchants and manufacturers, living a better life but sacrificing their personal power.

Military power was still an issue. Hume worked through a neat example. War threatens a developed commercial society, so taxes are increased and taxpayers have to spend less. Producers of luxuries lose their jobs and must either join the army or move to agriculture, displacing others who enlist. In effect, the luxury sector provides a reservoir of people available for military service, supported by the large surplus generated in a commercial society. There is no conflict between power and wealth.

The contrast between Hume and the seventeenth-century literature is complete. The balance of trade is not a problem. Trade is not a zero-sum game but a mutually beneficial stimulus to economic, cultural, and political advance.

6.3.3   James Steuart

Sir James Steuart (1713–80) was Scottish but spent most of his adult life on the continent and little in Britain, still less in England. While traveling as a young man he met the Stuart claimant to the British throne and committed himself to the Jacobite cause. After the defeat of the 1745 rebellion he was in exile, starting work on his *Inquiry into the Principles of Political Oeconomy* (1767) well before he returned to Scotland in 1762. He did not take British (really, English) success as the norm, which may explain his pessimism about the commercial economies of his day. He constantly emphasized the complexity of economic affairs, and refused to support or advance simple theories. His main theme was the need for a "statesman" to keep watch over the system and ward off the many problems that were sure to arise. He was, one might say, a throwback to seventeenth-century attitudes, which were still prevalent on the continent.

Steuart's *Principles* starts with a discussion of population that is very reminiscent of Cantillon. Humans, like animals, multiply within the limits set by food supply, so "the numbers of mankind must depend on the quantity of food produced by the earth for their nourishment" (p. 36). This was combined with an account of the development of food production, and hence population, closely based on Hume. Where people "live in such simplicity of manners, as to have few wants" (p. 41) production stagnates. Once a taste for luxuries emerges, farmers produce more and support a growing nonagricultural population in "the regular progress of mankind, from great simplicity to complicated refinement" (p. 28). Much of Europe, however, was still well below its potential due to "moral incapacity."

Steuart rejected Hume's account of the specie-flow mechanism and the quantity theory, arguing that prices depend on supply and demand, which depend in turn on various nonmonetary factors. Rich people, for example, may hoard their wealth, reducing demand. The quantity of money could multiply ten-fold without this having any necessary effect on prices. Overall supply and demand matter, because a deficiency of demand (caused by any of the varied factors that he thought relevant) could lead to unemployment. It was the duty of the statesman to ensure that the people were employed.

Steuart had a very ambivalent attitude to luxury and to international trade. A taste for (modest) luxuries is needed to stimulate development, examples from outside are needed to arouse demand in the first place, and demand from foreign markets increases employment. However, success in trade leads to wealth, which induces a demand for foreign luxuries, laziness, and high prices. The balance of trade will turn against a rich country in the end. "No trading state has ever been of long duration, after arriving at a certain height of prosperity" (p. 195). At this stage, the statesman must turn away from foreign trade and guide the county toward "inland commerce."

Steuart's *Principles* was the first full-length treatise on political economy in Britain. It attracted a fair amount of attention when it was first published, but was superseded by Adam Smith's *Wealth of Nations* within a decade. It is a fascinating work, but it lacks the analytic substance of the *Wealth of Nations* and it lost out because it seemed old-fashioned and stylistically clumsy.

6.3.4   Eighteenth-century British economics

This essay ends on the eve of the real breakthrough, Adam Smith's *Wealth of Nations*. The story told here, of the development of economic thought in Britain before Smith, is one of rather erratic and uncertain advance. After the intense debates of the seventeenth century, England, the most successful economy of the time, contributed surprisingly little to the development of economic thinking in the eighteenth century. The important advances came from Scotland and France. The French contribution (Cantillon, Quesnay, and Turgot) is well known (see Steiner, ch. 5, this volume). In Scotland, Hume's treatment of money and the trade balance largely resolved the issues that had worried seventeenth-century writers and left the field clear for Smith to shift the emphasis to capital accumulation and the case for "natural liberty." Smith undoubtedly drew on his predecessors in Britain and France, but the *Wealth of Nations* had a breadth and coherence that easily surpassed anything that had gone before and started a new epoch in the history of economics.

Note

Roger Backhouse, Mark Blaug, and the editors of this volume made helpful suggestions. The remaining errors, however, are mine.

Bibliography

Primary sources are cited by date of first publication, and collections by publication date. There is a flourishing secondary literature on early economics. Hutchison (1988) gives the best overview. Here are a few other starting points: on the seventeenth century, Finkelstein (2000) and Appleby (1978); on mercantilism, Magnusson (ch. 4, this volume); on the Scottish Enlightenment, Campbell and Skinner (1982); on Petty, Aspromourgos (1996); on Locke, Vaughn (1980); and on Law, Murphy (1997).

Appleby, J. 1978: *Economic Thought and Ideology in Seventeenth-Century England*. Princeton, NJ: Princeton University Press.

Aspromourgos, T. 1996: *On the Origins of Classical Economics: Distribution and Value from William Petty to Adam Smith*. London: Routledge.

Barbon, N. 1690: *A Discourse of Trade*. London: Tho. Milbourne.

Brewer, A. 1995: The concept of growth in eighteenth century economics. *History of Political Economy*, 27, 609–38.

Brewer, J. 1989: *The Sinews of Power: War, Money and the English State 1688–1783*. London: Unwin Hyman.

Campbell, R. H. and Skinner, A. (eds.) 1982: *The Origins and Nature of the Scottish Enlightenment*. Edinburgh: J. Donald.

Cantillon, R. 1755: *Essai sur la nature du commerce en général*. English translation by H. Higgs. New York: Augustus M. Kelley, 1964.

Child, J. 1668: *Brief Observations Concerning Trade and Interest of Money*. London. Reprinted in *Selected Works 1668–1697*. Farnborough, UK: Gregg Press, 1968.

—— 1693: *A New Discourse of Trade*. London. Reprinted in *Selected Works 1668–1697*. Farnborough, UK: Gregg Press, 1968.

Finkelstein, A. 2000: *Harmony and the Balance: an Intellectual History of Seventeenth-Century English Economic Thought*. Ann Arbor: University of Michigan Press.

Graunt, J. 1662: *Natural and Political Observations upon the Bills of Mortality*. In Petty (1899), op. cit., vol. 2, 314–435.

Holmes, G. 1993: *The Making of a Great Power: Late Stuart and Early Georgian Britain, 1660–1722*. Harlow: Longman.

Hume, D. 1752: *Essays: Moral, Political and Literary*. Indianapolis, IN: Liberty Classics, 1987.

Hutchison, T. 1988: *Before Adam Smith: the Emergence of Political Economy, 1662–1776*. Oxford: Blackwell.

Law, J. 1705: *Money and Trade Considered with a Proposal for Supplying the Nation with Money*. In J. Law, *Oeuvres Complètes*, 3 vols, ed. P. Harsin. Paris: Librarie du Recueil Sirey, 1934.

Locke, J. 1691: *Some Considerations of the Consequences of the Lowering of Interest and Raising the Value of Money*. In *Several Papers Relating to Money, Interest and Trade, &c*. London, 1696. Reprinted New York: Augustus M. Kelley, 1968.

Mandeville, B. 1714: *The Fable of the Bees: Or Private Vices, Public Benefits*, 2 vols, ed. F. B. Kaye. Oxford: Oxford University Press, 1924.

Martyn, H. 1701: *Considerations on the East India Trade*. Reprinted in J. McCulloch 1861: *A Select Collection of Early English Tracts on Commerce*. London: Political Economy Club; reprinted Cambridge University Press, 1970, 541–630.

Misselden, E. 1622: *Free Trade or the Meanes to Make trade Florish*. London. Reprinted New York: Augustus M. Kelley, 1971.

Mun, T. 1664: *England's Treasure by Forraign Trade*. London. Reprinted Fairfield, NJ: Augustus M. Kelley, 1986.

Murphy, A. 1997: *John Law: Economic Theorist and Policy-Maker*. Oxford: The Clarendon Press.

North, D. 1691: *Discourses upon Trade*. London. Reprinted Wakefield: S. R. Publishers, n.d.

Petty, W. 1899: *The Economic Writings of Sir William Petty*, 2 vols, ed. C. Hull. Cambridge, UK: Cambridge University Press.

—— 1927: *The Petty Papers: Some Unpublished Writings of Sir William Petty*, 2 vols, ed. the Marquis of Lansdowne. London: Constable.

Steuart, J. 1767: *An Inquiry into the Principles of Political Oeconomy*, 2 vols, ed. A. Skinner. Edinburgh: Oliver and Boyd, 1966.

Vaughn, K. 1980: *John Locke: Economist and Social Scientist*. London: Athlone Press.

Viner, J. 1937: *Studies in the Theory of International Trade*. London: George Allen & Unwin.

Wilson, C. 1984: *England's Apprenticeship 1603–1763*. Harlow: Longman.

CHAPTER SEVEN

Adam Smith (1723–1790): Theories of Political Economy

Andrew S. Skinner

7.1 SYSTEM

This chapter is primarily concerned with Smith's approach to political economy seen as theory. It is also designed to draw attention to Smith's wider purposes and to confirm the significance of Edwin Cannan's discoveries of 1895.

Adam Smith was elected to the Chair of Logic and Rhetoric in the University of Glasgow on January 9, 1751. In the following year he was translated to the Chair of Moral Philosophy. His pupil John Millar recalled:

> His course of lectures on this subject was divided into four parts. The first contained Natural Theology; in which he considered the proofs of the being and attributes of God, and those principles of the human mind upon which religion is founded. The second comprehended Ethics strictly so called, and consisted chiefly of the doctrines which he afterwards published in his Theory of Moral Sentiments. In the third part, he treated at more length of that branch of morality which relatives to *justice*, and which, being susceptible of precise and accurate rules, is for that reason capable of a full and particular explanation. (Stewart, I.18)

> In the last part of his lectures, he examined those political regulations which are founded, not upon the principle of *justice*, but that of *expediency*, and which are calculated to increase the riches, the power, and the prosperity of a State ... What

he delivered on these subjects contained the substance of the work he afterwards published under the title of An Inquiry into the Nature and Causes of the Wealth of Nations. (Stewart, I.20)

It only became possible to evaluate the third part of the major program when Edwin Cannan discovered the *Lectures on Jurisprudence*. Cannan recalled that:

On April 21, 1895, Mr Charles C. Maconochie, whom I then met for the first time, happened to be present when in course of conversation with the literary editor of the Oxford Magazine, I had occasion to make some comment about Adam Smith. Mr Maconochie immediately said that he possessed a manuscript report of Adam Smith's lectures on jurisprudence, which he regarded as of considerable interest. (Cannan, 1896, p. xv)

Cannan's reaction can be imagined.

7.2 ETHICS AND JURISPRUDENCE

One of the most interesting sections of the course is that which deals with public jurisprudence. Smith began by discussing the pattern of development known to have taken place in the classical world, before going on to consider those forces which caused the decline and fall of the Roman Empire in the West. This argument, with its emphasis on the "four stages," made it possible to appreciate the significance of, and the interrelations between, books V and III of the *Wealth of Nations* (WN). The first two socioeconomic stages, hunting and pasture, are most fully developed in the treatment of justice and defense. Book III and parts of book V, on the other hand, contain one of the most sophisticated analyses of the origin and breakdown of the agrarian (allodial and feudal) stage before going on to consider the emergence of the exchange economy – the "final" stage of commerce.

The links between the first two parts of the great plan are many and various. *The Theory of Moral Sentiments* (TMS), for example, may be regarded as an exercise in social philosophy, designed in part to show the ways in which so self-regarding a creature as man erects barriers against his own passions, thus explaining the fact that he is typically found in "troops and companies." The argument places great emphasis on the importance of general rules of behavior that are related to experience, and may thus vary in content, together with the need for some system of government as a precondition of social order.

The historical analysis, with its four socioeconomic stages, complements this argument by formally considering the origin of government and by explaining to some extent the forces that cause variations in accepted standards of behavior over time. Both are related in turn to Smith's treatment of political economy. There are a number of links.

First, Smith suggests that the economic structure consistent with the stage of commerce is not to be regarded as a model but, rather, as a structure with a history. The historical process outlined in WN book III culminates in a system wherein all goods and services command a price.

Secondly, he argued that this new structure would feature new forms of activity and sources of wealth; developments that would feature a shift in the balance of economic and therefore of political power. The point owed much to David Hume, as Smith acknowledged. Hume wrote that in England, "the lower house is the support of our popular governments, and all the world acknowledges, that it owned its chief influence and consideration to the increase of commerce, which threw such a balance into the hands of the commons" (Hume, 1987 [1741], 277–8).

Thirdly, Smith confirmed that in the case described there must be a major change in the pattern of dependence and subordination as compared to the feudal period. Since all goods and services command a price, it follows that while the farmer, tradesman, or artificer must depend upon his customers, "though in some measure obliged to them all, ... he is not absolutely dependent upon any one of them" (WN, III.iv.12).

Finally, it is suggested that the type of institutional structure described will be associated with what Hume described as a particular set of "customs and manners." The link here is once again with the analysis of the TMS and man's desire for social approbation.

For Smith, "Power and riches appear ... then to be, what they are, enormous and operose machines contrived to produce a few trifling conveniences to the body, consisting of springs the most nice and delicate" (TMS, IV.i.8). But Smith continued to emphasize that the pursuit of wealth is related not only to the desire to acquire the means of purchasing "utilities" but also to the need for status:

> From whence, then arises that emulation which runs through all the different ranks of men, and what are the advantages which we propose by that great purpose of human life which we call bettering our condition? To be observed, to be attended to, to be taken notice of ... are all the advantages which we can propose to derive from it. (TMS, I.iii.2.1)

Smith also suggested that in the modern economy, men tend to admire not only those who have the capacity to enjoy the trappings of wealth, but also the qualities that contribute to that end.

Smith recognized that pursuit of wealth and "place" was a basic human drive that would involve sacrifices likely to be supported by the approval of the spectator. The "habits of oeconomy, industry, discretion, attention and application of thought, are generally supposed to be cultivated from self-interested motives, and at the same time are apprehended to be very praiseworthy qualities, which deserve the esteem and approbation of everybody" (TMS, IV.2.8). Smith developed this theme in a passage added to the TMS in 1790:

> In the steadiness of his industry and frugality, in his steadily sacrificing the ease and enjoyment of the present moment for the probable expectation of the still greater ease and enjoyment of a more distant but more lasting period of time, the prudent man is always both supported and rewarded by the entire approbation of the impartial spectator. (TMS, VI.1.11)

The most polished accounts of the emergence of the exchange economy and of the psychology of the "economic man" are to be found, respectively, in the third book of WN and in part VI of TMS that was added in 1790. Yet both areas of analysis are old, and their substance would have been communicated to Smith's students and understood by them to be a preface to the treatment of political economy.

Taken as a whole, it is a subtle argument. Nicholas Phillipson has argued that Smith's ethical theory "is redundant outside the context of a commercial society with a complex division of labour" (1983, pp. 179, 182). John Pocock concluded that:

> A crucial step in the emergence of Scottish social theory, is, of course, that elusive phenomenon, the advent of the four stages scheme of history. The progression from hunter to farmer, to merchant offered not only an account of increasing plenty, but a series of stages of increasing division of labour, bringing about in their turn an increasingly complex organisation of both society and personality. (Pocock, 1983, p. 242)

Others have associated these trends with the emergence of what has been described as a particular pattern of "manners" – a bourgeois ideology.

It is against this background that Smith presented his economic analysis.

7.3   ECONOMICS: HUTCHESON

The early analyses of questions relating to political economy are to be found in three documents: The *Early Draft* (Scott, 1937), the lectures delivered in 1762–3 (Lothian, LJ(A)), and the text discovered by Cannan (1896, LJ(B)). Cannan's discovery is the most significant in respect of both date and content. The version contained in LJ(B) is the most complete and polished and provides an invaluable record of Smith's teaching in this branch of his project in the last year of his Professorship (1763–4).

The Cannan version yielded two important results.

First, Cannan confirmed Smith's debts to Francis Hutcheson. Hutcheson's economic analysis was not presented by him as a separate discourse but, rather, woven into the broader fabric of his lectures on jurisprudence. Perhaps it was for this reason that historians of economic thought had rather neglected him. But the situation was transformed as a result of the work of Cannan, who first noted that the *order* of Smith's lectures on "expediency" followed that suggested by Hutcheson; albeit, significantly, in the form of a single discourse. The importance of the connection was noted by Cannan (1896, xxv–xxvi; 1904, xxxvi–xli). Cannan was soon followed by the entry in the *Palgrave* (1899). Hutcheson's economic analysis received its most elaborate treatment in W. R. Scott's *Francis Hutcheson* (1900) in this period.

Renewed interest in Hutcheson's *economic* analysis revealed its history. Hutcheson admired the work of his immediate predecessor in the Chair of Moral Philosophy, Gerschom Carmichael (1672–1729), and especially his translation of, and commentary on, the works of Pufendorf. In Hutcheson's address to the "students in Universities," the *Introduction to Moral Philosophy* (1742) is described thus:

> The learned will at once discern how much of this compend is taken from the writings of others, from Cicero and Aristotle, and to name no other moderns, from Pufendorf's small work, *De Officio Hominis et Civis Juxta Legem Naturalem* which that worthy and ingenious man the late Professor Gerschom Carmichael of Glasgow, by far the best commentator on that book, has so supplied and corrected that the notes are of much more value than the text. (Taylor, 1965, p. 25)

It is to W. L. Taylor that we are indebted for the reminder that Carmichael and Pufendorf may have shaped Hutcheson's economic *ideas*, thus indirectly influencing Smith (op. cit., pp. 28–9).

Both men followed a particular *order* of argument. Starting with the division of labor, they explained the manner in which disposable surpluses could be maximized, thereafter emphasizing the importance of security of property and freedom of choice. This analysis led naturally to the problem of value and hence to the analysis of the role of money. The analysis is distinctive in the attention given to value *in exchange*; both writers emphasized the role of utility and disutility: perceived utility attaching to the commodities to be acquired, and perceived disutility embodied in the labor necessary to create the goods to be exchanged. The distinction between utility anticipated and realized is profoundly striking (Skinner, 1996, ch. 5). This tradition was continued by Smith in both LJ and WN, but with a change of emphasis toward the *measurement* of value – thus explaining Terence Hutchison's point that Smith retained *some* of his heritage (1988, p. 199; see ch. 11). Hutchison has noted that the Pufendorf/Hutcheson line was continued most notably by Beccaria and Condillac (and much later by Walras; see ch. 17).

Secondly, it is apparent that the account that Smith provides in LJ(B) is concerned with the *economic* system that features the activities of agriculture, manufacture, and commerce (LJ(B), p. 210) where these activities are characterized by a division of labor (LJ(B), pp. 211–23), with the patterns of exchange facilitated by the use of money (LJ(B), pp. 235–43). Three main features of the central analysis are the treatment of the division of labor, the analysis of price and allocation, and the exposure of the mercantile fallacy.

The institution of the division of labor is central to Smith's explanation of the growth in opulence associated with the development of the arts under the stimulus of the "natural wants" of man (LJ(B), pp. 209–11).

As in the *Wealth of Nations*, Smith's handling of price theory is amongst the most successful aspects of the study, featuring a clear distinction between natural and market price and an examination of their interdependence. *Natural* price is defined in effect as the supply price of a commodity, where the latter refers to labor cost (LJ(B), p. 227).

Market price is the price that may prevail at any given moment in time and will be determined by the "demand or need for the commodity," its abundance or scarcity in relation to the demand (a point that is used to explain the "paradox" of value), and, finally, the "riches or poverty of those who demand" (LJ(B), pp. 227–8). Smith then suggested that although the two prices were logically distinct, they were also "necessarily connected." In the event of market price rising above the natural level, the reward of labor in this employment will rise above its natural (long-run equilibrium) rate, leading to an inflow of labor and an expansion in supply (and vice versa). In equilibrium, therefore, the market and natural prices will be the same; a point that allowed Smith to go on to argue that "whatever police" tends to prevent this coincidence will "diminish public opulence" (LJ(B), p. 230). The familiar examples that contributed to keep the market above the natural price include taxes on industry, monopolies, and the exclusive privileges of corporations, all of which affect price through their direct impact on selling price.

These examples refer to particular cases. Smith added a further dimension to the argument by showing that the economic system can be seen under a more general aspect. This much is evident in his objection to particular regulations of "police" on the ground that they distorted the use of resources by breaking what he called the "natural balance of industry," while interfering with the "natural connexion of all trades in the stock" (LJ(B), pp. 233–4). He concluded: "Upon the whole, therefore, it is by far the best police to leave things to their natural course" (LJ(B), p. 235).

Smith's understanding of the interdependence of economic phenomena was quite as sophisticated as that of his master. Yet his lecture notes confirm neither a clear distinction between factors of production (land, labor, and capital) nor between the categories of return corresponding to them (rent, wages, and profit). Nor is there any evidence of a macroeconomic model of the system as a whole: a model that Smith first met during his visit to France.

7.4 ECONOMICS: THE PHYSIOCRATS AND QUESNAY

Adam Smith's visit to France was his only journey outside Great Britain. The fact that the visit took place at all was due to the success of the *Theory of Moral Sentiments*. Hume reported that "Charles Townshend, who passes for the cleverest Fellow in England, is so taken with the Performance, that he said to Oswald he wou'd put the Duke of Buccleugh under the Author's care." Hume bestirred himself on Smith's behalf, but assumed that he would wish to welcome the Duke as a student in Glasgow, as distinct from giving up his chair. This was a reasonable assumption, bearing in mind Smith's enjoyment of his post and the program of publication announced in the closing pages of the first edition of *The Theory of Moral Sentiments*.

Smith's resignation from the Chair at the early age of 41 no doubt surprised Hume, but it may well be that the proposed visit to France was attractive precisely because it afforded an opportunity to meet a group of thinkers whom Smith so much admired.

Smith left Glasgow in January 1764 and arrived in Paris on February 13. He resigned from his academic post the following day (Corr., letter 81). On March 4 he was in Toulouse, his base for many months. Hume arranged a number of introductions but few of his contacts were available, causing Smith to write to Hume that the "life which I led at Glasgow was a pleasurable dissipated life, in comparison of that which I lead here at present." He added that "I have begun to write a book in order to pass away the time. You may believe I have very little to do" (Corr., letter 82). But the situation soon improved, partly due to a series of expeditions to Bordeaux, the Pyrenees, and Montpelier.

Smith arrived back in Paris in February 1766, to begin a stay of some ten months. The visit was clouded by the developing quarrel between Rousseau and Hume. In August, Smith was caused real anxiety by the illness of the Duke. The Duke recovered, but sadly his brother was taken ill in October and died on the 19th of the month. At this point, the party left for home, reaching London on November 1. Smith never left Britain again.

From an intellectual point of view, the visit was a resounding success. Hume's contacts and the reputation of TMS ensured entry to both English and French circles. The latter were especially important in that Smith was afforded an opportunity to meet Diderot, Helvetius, and Holbach. Other important contacts were made, of particular interest to the economist and to commentators on WN. These included Quesnay, Mirabeau, Dupont de Nemours, and, amongst others, Mercier de la Rivière, whose book *L'ordre naturel et essentiel des sociétés politiques* (1767) was considered by Smith to be "the most distinct and best connected account" of physiocratic doctrine.

When Smith arrived in Paris, the physiocratic school was at the zenith of its influence. Two journals, the *Journal d'Agriculture* and the *Ephemerides du Citoyen* carried articles of a professional nature, while the central texts were already published, most notably Quesnay's *Tableau* (1758), Mirabeau's *Friend of Man* (1756, 1760), and the *Philosophie rurale* (1763).

The content of Smith's library confirms his interest in the school. Smith especially enjoyed the friendship of Quesnay, whom he described as "one of the worthiest men in France and one of the best physicians that is to be met with in any country. He was not only physician but the friend and confident of Madam Pompadour, a woman who was no contemptible judge of merit" (Corr., letter 97). In addition, we have Dugald Stewart's authority that "Mr Smith had once an intention (as he told me himself) to have inscribed to him his *Wealth of Nations*" (Stewart, III.12).

Much physiocratic writing was to prove unattractive to some; most obviously, perhaps, the doctrine of legal despotism and a political philosophy that envisaged a constitutional monarch modeled upon the Emperor of China. The uncritical attitudes of the disciples to the teaching of the master, Quesnay, were also a source of aggravation.

But Smith did recognize that the system:

> with all its imperfections, is, perhaps, the nearest approximation to the truth that has yet been published upon the subject of political economy, and is upon that account well worth the consideration of every man who wishes to examine with attention the principles of that very important science. (WN, IV.ix.38)

The reason for this assessment may be found in the physiocratic definition of wealth, in their liberal attitude to trade policy, but above all in the quality of the basic model (in sharp contrast to Linguet, who wrote off the *Tableau* as "an insult to common sense, to reason, and philosophy"; Rothbard, 1995, p. 377). Quesnay's purpose was both practical and theoretical. As Meek has indicated, Quesnay announced his purpose in a letter to Mirabeau that accompanies the first edition of the *Tableau*:

> I have tried to construct a fundamental *Tableau* of the economic order for the purpose of displaying expenditure and products in a way which is easy to grasp. And for the purpose of forming a clear opinion about the organisation and disorganisation which the government can bring about. (Meek, 1962, p. 108)

7.5 Economics: Turgot

The model in question sought to explore the interrelationships between output, the generation of income, expenditure, and consumption – or, in Quesnay's words, a "general system of expenditure, work, gain and consumption" (Meek, 1962, p. 374) which would expose the point that "the whole magic of a well ordered society is that each man works for others, while believing that he is working for himself" (Meek, 1962, p. 70).

Peter Groenewegen has confirmed that *Turgot* was in Paris between July and September 1766 (Groenewegen, 1969, p. 272). The belief that the two men met and discussed economic questions is supported by the Abbé Morellet who, in a passage that refers to Smith, confirmed that:

> M. Turgot, who like me loved things metaphysical, estimated his talents greatly. We saw him several times; he was presented at the house of M. Helvetius; we talked of commercial theory, banking, public credit and several points in the great work he was meditating. (Morellet, 1823, vol. I, p. 244)

But it is not known how often the two men met, and it appears that they did not correspond. In a letter to the Duc de la Rochefoucauld, dated November 1, 1785, Smith referred to the "ever-to-be-regretted Mr Turgot" and added that "tho" I had the happiness of his acquaintance, and I flattered myself, even of his friendship and esteem, I never had that of his correspondence" (Corr., letter 248). But if the two men *were* friends it is perhaps hardly surprising in view of the fact that their scientific temperaments were so similar.

The purely economic analysis must also have made an immediate impact on Smith not least because Turgot opened his argument, as he had originally done, with the division of labor. Here, Turgot drew attention to the causes of increased productivity and to the associated point that "the reciprocal exchange of needs, renders men necessary to one another and constitutes the bond of society" (Meek, 1973, p. 122).

Turgot offered a more familiar account of that "bond" in a model linking the different sectors of activity, and the various socioeconomic groups, in a cycle of activities that involve the generation of income, expenditure, and productive activity.

The first class is that of the cultivators. Turgot effectively restated the by-now time-honored dictum that "it is always the land which is the primary and unique source of all wealth" (Meek, p. 147). Strictly speaking, the *Husbandman*:

> is therefore the unique source of all wealth, which, through its circulation, animates all the industry of society; because he is the only one whose labour produces any-thing over and above the wages of labour. (Meek, p. 123)

As before, the *Cultivators* are designated as the "productive class."

The second social group is the *Proprietors* of land (the disposable class), who receive an income in the form of *rent*. This class:

> may be employed to meet the general needs of the Society, for example, in war and the administration of justice, whether through personal service, or through the pay-ment of a part of its revenue. (Meek, p. 127)

Turgot added, in a passage whose implications would be uncomfortable for some, that:

> The Proprietor enjoys nothing except through the labour of the Cultivator . . . but the cultivator has need of the Proprietor only by virtue of human conventions and the civil laws. (Meek, p. 128)

Finally there are the *artisans*, who do not generate any net revenue; and also the *stipendiary* class, who are "supported by the product of the land" (Meek, p. 127).

These would have been regarded as fairly conventional points; so too would Turgot's emphasis on the role of capital (fixed and circulating). But it is at this stage that Turgot advanced beyond Quesnay, by introducing a distinction between entrepreneurs and wage labor, and, therefore, a further distinction between profits and wages as categories of return.

It is worthy of note that Turgot defined *profit* as the reward accruing to Entrepreneurs for the risks incurred in combining the factors of production (i.e., fixed and circulating capitals), while the "simple workman, who possesses only his hands and his industry, has nothing except in so far as he succeeds in selling his toil to others" (Meek, p. 122).

The relevant passages deserve some elaboration. The industrial *stipendiary* class:

> finds itself, so to speak, subdivided into two orders: that of the Entrepreneurs, Manufacturers and Masters who are all possessors of large capitals which they turn to account by setting to work, through the medium of their advances the second order, which consists of ordinary Artisans who possess no property but their own hands, who advance nothing but their daily labour, and who receive no profit but their wages. (Meek, p. 153)

Turgot also remarked that the position of the Entrepreneurs engaged in agriculture "must be the same as that of the Entrepreneurs in Factories" (Meek, p. 153), adding that:

> We also see that it is capitals alone which establish and maintain great Agricultural enterprises, which give the land, so to speak, an invariable rental value, and which ensure to the Proprietors a revenue which is always regular and as high as it is possible for it to be. (Meek, p. 155)

Turgot isolated four distinct factors of production (land, labor, capital, and entrepreneurship), and three categories of return (rent, wages, and profit). He also supplied a distinctive version of the circular flow.

If we map these points against Quesnay's basic model, it emerges that the entrepreneurs engaged in agriculture advance rent to the proprietors, thus providing this group with an income available for use in a given time period. The Entrepreneurs advance wages to labor as a group and also affect purchase both *between* the sectors and *within* the sectors to which they belong.

Looked at from another point of view, Turgot's model indicates that output is made up of consumer and investment goods; that the income thus generated may be divided into two streams (consumption and saving) and used to make purchases of consumer and investment goods. The goods withdrawn from the market in a given period are then replaced by virtue of current productive activity. While aware of the possibility of contraction, it is interesting that Turgot believed that savings will normally be converted into capital expenditure "sur le champ" (Schumpeter, 1954, p. 324; Groenewegen, 1969, p. 279).

Smith's commentary on physiocratic teaching is readily accessible and provided his readers with a broadly accurate account of the *Analyse*. The detailed account that Smith offered (WN, IV.ix) is made even more intriguing by the fact that while remaining faithful to the original, he went to great pains to associate the "super model" with a clear division between factors of production and categories of return – the Turgot version, although he did not directly cite his authority.

7.6 ECONOMICS: THE *WEALTH OF NATIONS*

That Smith benefited from his examination of the French system was quickly noted by Cannan. In referring to the theories of distribution and to the macroeconomic dimension, Cannan noted that:

> When we find that there is no trace of these theories in the **Lectures**, and that in the meantime Adam Smith had been to France . . . it is difficult to understand, why we should be asked, without any evidence, to refrain from believing that he came under physiocratic influence after and not before or during his Glasgow period.

He added:

Adam Smith, as his chapter on agricultural systems shows, did not appreciate the minutiae of the table very highly, but he certainly took these main ideas and adapted them as well as he could to his Glasgow theories. (Cannan, 1904, p. xxxi)

Smith's debts to the physiocratic *model* may be seen in the content of the analytic apparatus developed in the first two books of WN. In these books, Smith in effect transformed his earlier, sophisticated, analysis of the interdependence of economic phenomena in such a way as to permit him to create a system that was at once descriptive and analytic. Building upon an analysis that owed much to the *Lectures* and to the physiocrats, Smith developed a synthetic system that offered an opportunity to understand the full range of problems that should be encountered by "economists" if the economy as a system is to be fully understood.

7.6.1   A model of conceptualized reality

The concept of an economy involving a flow of goods and services, and the appreciation of the importance of intersectoral dependencies, were familiar in the eighteenth century. Such themes are dominant features of the work done, for example, by Sir James Steuart and David Hume. Smith's work was distinctive, at least as compared to his *Scottish* contemporaries, in the emphasis given to the importance of *three distinct factors* of production (land, labor, and capital) and to the three categories of return (rent, wages, and profit) corresponding to them. Distinctive to the modern eye is how Smith deployed these concepts in providing an account of the flow of goods and services between the sectors involved and between the different socioeconomic groups (proprietors of land, capitalists, and wage labor). The approach is also of interest in that Smith, following the lead of the French economists, worked in terms of period analysis – the year was typically chosen, so that the working of the economy is examined within a significant time dimension as well as over a series of time periods. Both versions of the argument emphasize the importance of capital, fixed and circulating.

Taking the economic system as a whole, Smith suggested that the *total stock of society* could be divided into three parts. There is, first, that part of the total stock which is reserved for immediate *consumption*, and which is held by all consumers (capitalists, labor, and proprietors), reflecting purchases made in previous time periods. The characteristic feature of this part of the total stock is that it affords no revenue to its possessors, since it consists in the stock of "food, cloaths, household furniture, etc, which have been purchased by their proper consumers, but which are not yet entirely consumed" (WN, II.i.12).

Secondly, there is that part of the total stock which may be described as *fixed capital* and which is distributed between the various groups in society. This part of the stock, Smith suggested, is composed of the "useful machines" purchased in preceding periods but currently held by the undertakers engaged in manufacture, the quantity of useful buildings, and of "improved land" in the possession of the "capitalist" farmers and the proprietors, together with the "acquired and useful abilities" of all the inhabitants (WN, II.i.13–17); that is, human capital.

Thirdly, there is that part of the *total* stock which may be described as *circulating capital*, and which again has several components, these being:

1. The quantity of money necessary to carry on the process of circulation.
2. The stock of provisions and other agricultural products available for sale during the current period, but are still in the hands of either the farmers or merchants.
3. The stock of raw materials and work in process, held by merchants, undertakers, or those capitalists engaged in the agricultural sector (including mining).
4. The stock of manufactured goods (consumption and investment goods) created during the previous period, but which remain in the hands of undertakers and merchants at the beginning of the period examined. (WN, II.i.19–22)

The logic of the process can be best represented by separating the activities along the lines of the physiocratic model with which Smith was familiar. Suppose that, at the beginning of the time period in question, the major capitalist groups possess the net receipts earned from the sale of products in the previous period, and that the undertakers engaged in agriculture initiate activity by transmitting the total rent due to the proprietors of land for the current use of that factor. The income thus provided will enable the proprietors to make the necessary purchases of consumption (and investment) goods in the current period, thus contributing to reduce the stocks of such goods with which the undertakers and merchants began the period.

Secondly, assume that the undertakers engaged in both sectors, together with the merchant groups, transmit to wage labor the content of the wages fund, thus providing this socioeconomic class with an income that can be used in the current period. Notable in this connection is that the capitalist groups transmit a fund to wage labor that forms a part of their *savings*, providing by this means an income that is available for current *consumption*.

Thirdly, the undertakers engaged in agriculture and manufactures will purchase consumption and investment goods from each other, through the medium of retail and wholesale merchants, thus generating a series of expenditures linking the two major sectors. Finally, the process of circulation is completed by the purchases made by individual undertakers within their own sectors. These purchases will again include consumption and investment goods, contributing still further to reduce the stocks of commodities available for sale when the period under examination began, and which forms part of the circulating capital of the society. Looked at in this way, the "circular flow" could be seen to involve purchases that take goods from the circulating capital of society, which are in turn matched by a continuous process of *replacement* through current production of materials and finished goods – where both types of production require the use of the fixed and circulating capitals of *individual entrepreneurs*, while generating the income flows needed to purchase commodities (and services). Smith elaborated on the argument.

In effect, the expenditure of the consumers of particular commodities replaces the outlays of those who retail them, just as the capital of the retailer replaces, together with its profits, that of the wholesale merchant from whom he purchases goods, thereby enabling him to continue in business (WN, II.v.9). In turn, the capital of the wholesale merchant replaces, together with their profits, the capitals of the farmers and manufacturers of whom he purchases the rude and manufactured products that he deals in, and thereby enables them to continue their respective trades (WN, ii.v.10). At the same time, part of the capital of the master manufacturer is "employed as a fixed capital in the instruments of his trade, and replaces, together with its profits, that of some other artificer from whom he purchases them. Part of this circulating capital is employed in purchasing materials, and replaces, with profits, the capitals of the farmers and miners from whom he purchases them. But a great part of it is always, either annually, or in a much shorter period, distributed among the different workmen whom he employs" (WN, II.iv.11). The farmers perform a similar function with regard to the manufacturing sector.

Smith can be seen to have addressed a series of problems that begin with an analysis of the division of labor, before proceeding to the discussion of value, price, and allocation, and thence to the issue of distribution in any single time period and over time.

The analysis offered in the first book enabled Smith to proceed to the discussion of both macrostatics and macrodynamics, in the context of a model in which all magnitudes are dated. Smith produced a model of conceptualized reality that was essentially descriptive, and which was further illustrated by reference to an *analytic* system that, if on occasion subject to ambiguity, was nonetheless so organized as to meet the requirements of the Newtonian ideal. The system was intended to be *comprehensive*.

7.7   THE IMPLICATIONS OF THE ANALYSIS

John Stuart Mill, the archetypal classical economist of a later period, is known to have remarked that "The *Wealth of Nations* is in many parts obsolete and in all, imperfect." Writing in 1926, Edwin Cannan observed:

> Very little of Adam Smith's scheme of economics has been left standing by subsequent enquirers. No one now holds his theory of value, his account of capital is seen to be hopelessly confused, and his theory of distribution is explained as an ill-assorted union between his own theory of prices and the Physiocratic fanciful Economic Table. (p. 123)

In view of authoritative judgments such as these, it is perhaps appropriate to ask what elements in this story should command the attention of the historian and economist. A number of points might be suggested.

First, there is the issue of *scope*. Smith's approach to the study of political economy was through the examination of history and ethics. The historical analysis is important in that he set out to explain the origins of the commercial stage. The ethical analysis is important to the economist because it is here that Smith identifies the values that are appropriate to the modern situation. It is here that we confront the emphasis on the desire for status (which is essentially Veblenesque) and the qualities of mind that are necessary to attain this end: industry, frugality, and prudence.

The TMS also reminds us that the pursuit of economic ends takes place within a *social* context, and that men maximize their chances of success by respecting the rights of others. In Smith's sense of the term, "prudence" is essentially rational self-love. In a famous passage from the TMS (II.ii.2.1), Smith noted, with regard to the competitive individual, that:

> In the race for wealth, and honours, and preferments, he may run as hard as he can, and strain every nerve and every muscle, in order to outstrip all his competitors. But if he should justle, or throw down any of them, the indulgence of the spectators is entirely at an end. It is a violation of fair play, which they cannot admit of.

Smith's emphasis upon the fact that self-interested actions take place within a social setting, and that men are motivated (generally) by a desire for approval by their fellows, raises some interesting questions of continuing relevance. For example, in an argument that bears upon the analysis of the TMS, Smith noted in effect that the rational individual may be constrained by the reaction of the spectator of his conduct – a much more complex case than that which more modern approaches may suggest. Smith made much of the point in his discussion of Mandeville's "licentious system," that supported the view that private vices were public benefits, in suggesting that the gratification of desire should be consistent with observance of the rules of propriety – as defined by the spectator; that is, by an external agency. In an interesting variant on this theme, Etzioni has recently noted that we need to recognize "at least two irreducible sources of valuation or utility: pleasure and morality" (Etzioni, 1988, pp. 21–4).

Secondly, there is a series of issues that arise from Smith's interest in political economy as a system. The idea of a single all-embracing conceptual system, whose parts should be mutually consistent, is not easily attainable in an age in which the division of labor has increased the quantity of science through specialization. Smith was aware of the division of labor in different areas of science, and of the fact that specialization often led to systems of thought which were inconsistent with each other (*Astronomy*, IV.35, 52, 67; see also Skinner, 1996, p. 43). But the division of labor within a *branch* of science – for example, economics – has led to a situation in which sub-branches of a single subject may be inconsistent with one another.

As a third point, one of the most significant features of Smith's vision of the economic process lies in the fact that it has a significant time dimension. For example, in dealing with the problem of value in exchange, Smith made due allowance for the fact that the process involves judgments with regard to the utility of the commodities to be acquired, and the disutility involved in creating the goods to be exchanged. In the manner of his predecessors (Hutcheson, Carmichael, and Pufendorf), Smith was aware of the distinction between utility (and disutility) anticipated and realized, and, therefore, of the process of adjustment that would inevitably take place through time.

Smith's theory of price, which allows for a wide range of changes in taste, is also distinctive in that it allows for competition *among* and *between* buyers and sellers, while presenting the allocative mechanism as one that involves simultaneous and interrelated adjustments in *both* factor and commodity markets (Skinner, 1996).

As befits a writer concerned to address the problems of change, including adjustment to change, Smith's position was also distinctive in that he was not directly concerned with phenomenon even of *partial* equilibrium. For Smith, the "natural" (supply) price was, as it were:

> the central price, to which the prices of all commodities are continually gravitating ... whatever may be the obstacles which hinder them from settling in this centre of response and continuance, they are constantly tending towards it. (WN, I.vii.15)

But perhaps the most intriguing feature of the *macro*model is found in the manner of its linkage to the analytics of book I and in the way in which it was specified. Smith argued that incomes are generated as a result of productive activity, thus making it possible for commodities to be withdrawn from the "circulating" capital of society. The consumption goods withdrawn from the existing stock may be used up in the present period, or added to the stock reserved for immediate consumption; or used to replace more durable goods that have reached the end of their lives in the current period. In a similar manner, undertakers and merchants may also add to their stocks of materials, or to their holdings of fixed capital, while replacing the plant that has reached the end of its operational life. It is equally obvious that undertakers and merchants may add to, or reduce their *inventories* in ways that will reflect the changing patterns of demand for consumption and investment goods, and their past and current levels of production.

Smith's emphasis that different "goods" have different life-cycles (which may derive from Steuart) also means that the pattern of purchase and replacement may vary continuously as the economy moves through different time periods, and in ways that reflect the various age profiles of particular products as well as the pattern of demand for them. If Smith's model of the circular flow is to be seen as a spiral, rather than a circle, it soon becomes evident that this spiral is likely to expand (and contract) through time at variable rates.

It is perhaps this total vision of the complex working of the economy that led Mark Blaug to comment on Smith's distinctive and sophisticated grasp of the economic *process* and to distinguish this from his contribution to particular *areas* of economic analysis.

Blaug noted that:

> In appraising Adam Smith, or any other economist, we ought always to remember that brilliance in handling purely economic concepts is a very different thing from a firm grasp of the essential logic of economic relationships. Superior technique does not imply superior insight and vice-versa. Judged by standard of analytical competence, Smith is not the greatest of eighteenth century economists. But for an acute

insight into the nature of the economic process, it would be difficult to find Smith's equal. (Blaug, 1985, p. 57)

Joseph Schumpeter was not always a warm critic of "A. Smith," and yet regarded the WN as "the peak success of [the] period":

> [T]hough the *Wealth of Nations* contained no really novel ideas, and though it cannot rank with Newton's *Principia* or Darwin's *Origin* as an intellectual achievement, it is a great performance all the same and fully deserved its success. (Schumpeter, 1954, p. 185)

Bibliography

This list contains authorities cited in the text and also additional references that the reader may find helpful.

References to Smith's *Works and Correspondence* conform to the usages of the Glasgow edition (Oxford: The Clarendon Press, 1976–83). These include:

1976: *The Theory of Moral Sentiments*, ed. D. D. Raphael and A. L. Macfie, cited as "TMS."

1976: *The Wealth of Nations*, ed. R. H. Campbell, A. S. Skinner, and W. B. Todd, cited as "WN."

1977: *The Correspondence of Adam Smith*, ed. E. C. Mossner and I. S. Ross, cited as "Corr."

1978: *Lectures on Jurisprudence*, ed. R. L. Meek, D. D. Raphael, and P. G. Stein, cited as "LJ(A)" and "LJ(B)."

1980: *Essays on Philosophical Subjects*, general editors D. D. Raphael and A. S. Skinner. This volume contains Smith's essay on the *History of Astronomy*, cited as "Astronomy."

References to Corr. give the number of the letter. References to LJ(A), the report dated 1762–3, give the volume and page number of the manuscript. References to LJ(B) add the page number in the Cannan edition.

References to the other works cited above provide the relevant section and paragraph. Thus:

Astronomy, II.4 = *History of Astronomy*, section II, paragraph 4

Stewart, I.12 = *Account of the Life and Writings of Adam Smith*, section I, paragraph 12 (in *Essays on Philosophical Subjects*)

TMS, I.i.5.5 = part I, section i, chapter 5, paragraph 5

WN, V.i.f.26 = book V, chapter i, sixth division, paragraph 26

Black, R. D. C. 1976: Smith's contribution in historical perspective. In A. S. Skinner and T. Wilson (eds.), *The Market and the State: Essays in Honour of Adam Smith*. Oxford: Oxford University Press.

Blaug, M. 1985: *Economic Theory in Retrospect*, 4th edn. Cambridge, UK: Cambridge University Press.

—— 1999: The formalist revolution. In R. E. Backhouse and J. Creedy (eds.), *From Classical Economics to the Theory of the Firm*. Cheltenham, UK: Edward Elgar.

Cannan, E. (ed.) 1896: Adam Smith's *Lectures on Justice, Police, Revenue and Arms*. Oxford: The Clarendon Press.

—— (ed.) 1904: Adam Smith's *The Wealth of Nations*. London: Methuen.

—— 1926: Adam Smith as an economist. *Economica*, 6, 123–34. Reprinted in Wood, op. cit., vol. 2, pp. 20–8.

Etzioni, A. 1988: *The Moral Dimension: Towards a New Economics*. London: Collier Macmillan.

Fleischacker, S. 2001: Adam Smith's influence on the American Founders. Paper delivered at the ECSSS meeting, Arlington, 2001.

Groenewegen, P. 1969: Turgot and Adam Smith. *Scottish Journal of Political Economy*, 16, 271–87. Reprinted in Wood, op. cit., vol. 4, pp. 106–19.

Hume, D. 1987 [1741]: *Essays: Moral, Political and Literary*, ed. E. Miller. London: Oxford University Press (1963)/Indianapolis, IN: Liberty Classics.

Hutchison, T. 1988: *Before Adam Smith*. Oxford: Blackwell.

Jeck, A. 1994: The macrostructure of Adam Smith's theoretical system: a reconstruction. *European Journal of the History of Economic Thought*, 1, 551–76.

Jensen, H. E. 1976: Sources and contours in Adam Smith's conceptualised reality in the *Wealth of Nations*. *Review of Social Economy*, 34, 259–74. Reprinted in Wood, op. cit., vol. 2, pp. 193–204.

McLaurin, C. 1775 [1748]: *An Account of Sir Isaac Newton's Philosophical Discoveries*, 3rd edn. Edinburgh.

Meek, R. L. 1962: *The Economics of Physiocracy*. London: Harvard University Press.

—— 1973: *Turgot on Progress, Sociology and Economics*. Cambridge, UK: Cambridge University Press.

Morellet, Abbé de 1823: *Memoires*. Paris: Baudouin frères.

Phillipson, N. 1983: Adam Smith as a civic moralist. In I. Hont and M. Ignatieff (eds.), *Wealth and Virtue*. Cambridge, UK: Cambridge University Press.

Piel, J. 1999: *Adam Smith and Economic Science: A Methodological Interpretation*. Cheltenham, UK: Edward Elgar.

Pocock, J. 1983: Cambridge paradigms and Scotch philosophers. In I. Hont and M. Ignatieff (eds.), *Wealth and Virtue*. Cambridge: Cambridge University Press.

Randive, K. R. 1977: The *Wealth of Nations*: the vision and the conceptualisation. *Indian Economic Journal*, 24, 295–332. Reprinted in Wood, op. cit., vol. 2, pp. 244–79.

Robbins, L. 1953: *The Theory of Economic Policy in English Classical Political Economy*. London: Macmillan.

Rothbard, M. 1995: *Economic Thought before Adam Smith*. Cheltenham, UK: Edward Elgar.

Schumpeter, J. A. 1954: *A History of Economic Analysis*. London: Oxford University Press.

Scott, W. R. 1900: *Francis Hutcheson*. Cambridge, UK: Cambridge University Press.

—— 1937: *Adam Smith as Student and Professor*. Glasgow: Jackson, Son & Co.

Shackle, G. L. S. 1967: *The Years of High Theory*. Cambridge, UK: Cambridge University Press.

Skinner, A. S. 1987: Adam Smith. In J. Eatwell, M. Milgate, and P. Newman (eds.), *The New Palgrave: A Dictionary of Economics*. London: Macmillan.

—— 1996: *A System of Social Science: Papers Relating to Adam Smith*, 2nd edn. Oxford: Oxford University Press.

Stephens, W. W. 1895: *The Life and Writings of Turgot*. London: Longmans, Green.

Steuart, Sir James 1966 [1767]: *An Inquiry into the Principles of Political Oeconomy*, ed. A. S. Skinner. Edinburgh: The University of Chicago Press.

Stevens, D. 1975: Adam Smith and the colonial disturbances. In A. S. Skinner and T. Wilson (eds.), *Essays on Adam Smith*. Oxford: The Clarendon Press.

Taylor, W. L. 1965: *Francis Hutcheson and David Hume as Predecessors of Adam Smith*. Durham, NC: Duke University Press.

Teichgraeber, R. F., III 1987: "Less abused than I had reason to expect": the reception of the *Wealth of Nations*. *Historical Journal*, 30, 337–66.

Tribe, K. 1988: *Governing Economy: The Reformation of German Economic Discourse, 1750–1840*. Cambridge, UK: Cambridge University Press.

Turgot, A. R. J. 1973 [1766]: *Reflections on the Formation and Distribution of Riches*. In Meek (1973), op. cit.

Viner, J. 1927: Adam Smith and laisser-faire. In J. M. Clark, P. H. Douglas, J. H. Hollander, G. R. Morrow, M. Palyi, and J. Viner, *Adam Smith, 1776–1926: Lectures to Commemorate the Sesquicentennial of the Publication of* "The Wealth of Nations." Chicago: The University of Chicago Press.

Winch, D. 1994: Nationalism and cosmopolitanism in the early histories of political economy. In M. Albertone and A. Masoero (eds.), *Political Economy and National Realities*. Turin: Fondazione Luigi Einaudi.

Wood, J. C. (ed.) 1984: *Adam Smith: Critical Assessments*, 4 vols. London: Croom Helm.

Young, J. 1997: *Economics as a Moral Science: The Political Economy of Adam Smith*. Cheltenham, UK: Edward Elgar.

CHAPTER EIGHT

Classical Economics

Denis P. O'Brien

8.1 Introduction

Classical economics ruled economic thought for about 100 years. It focused on macroeconomic issues and economic growth. Because the growth was taking place in an open economy, with a currency that (except during 1797–1819) was convertible into gold, the classical writers were necessarily concerned with the balance of payments, the money supply, and the price level. Monetary theory occupied a central place, and their achievements in this area were substantial and – with their trade theory – are still with us today. Those ideas developed amid an international economy free from major wars. However, the French wars of 1793–1815 had a powerful influence on classical economics, leading to major problems with public finance, and to a significant national debt. Because convertibility of the note issue into gold was suspended, it was necessary to develop a theory of the operation of an inconvertible paper currency.

8.2 Foundations

The intellectual basis for virtually all classical economics is found in Adam Smith's *Wealth of Nations* of 1776 (O'Brien, 1975). Earlier work, including that by Smith himself (his *Theory of Moral Sentiments*, 1759, and *Lectures*, 1763) and of David Hume (1711–76) can be seen in the context of the research program that Smith established.

Apart from Adam Smith (1723–90), the most famous and influential figure was David Ricardo (1772–1823). There are several views of Ricardo. Schumpeter (1954) regarded Ricardo's work as essentially a detour. The Sraffians regard it as the start of the only valid tradition in economics, running from Ricardo to Marx and thence to Sraffa. Alfred Marshall and Samuel Hollander (1979) have interpreted Ricardo as a neoclassical economist.

Ricardo excelled in model building, but his restrictive type of model grafted uneasily on to the main part of classical economics, and the work of later writers such as J. R. McCulloch (1789–1864) and J. S. Mill (1806–73) owed much more to Smith than to Ricardo.

To interpret classical economics in terms of Smith and Ricardo alone is a mistake (O'Brien, 1988). Contemporary with Ricardo were T. R. Malthus (1766–1834), James Mill (1773–1836), Nassau Senior (1770–1864), Robert Torrens (1780–1864), and numerous writers on special topics, especially monetary theory.

Most classical economists had intellectual interests besides economics. Few had academic employment. Journalism, the law, and business – especially banking – were mostly their occupations. Yet these writers formed a "scientific community." With the exception of the French economist J.-B. Say (1776–1832), they lived in the British Isles. They read the literary reviews of the day, and there was an active circulation of pamphlets. They met at the Political Economy Club and in other societies such as the [Royal] Statistical Society.

Economics grew out of philosophy. Smith and Hume were the products of a distinctive Scottish philosophical school. The influence of Smith's teacher, Francis Hutcheson, is discussed in Skinner's contribution to this *Companion*. In addition, the utilitarian strain in the classical literature, usually associated with Jeremy Bentham (1748–1832), has its origins in this Scottish philosophical tradition, leading to Smith's stress on the welfare of the laboring classes.

Absorbed into this philosophical background were ideas from more narrowly economic literature that developed during the century before Smith's great work. The most important example is the work of the physiocrats and A. R. J. Turgot (1727–1781) in France (Turgot, 1769), whose ideas and influence on Smith are described elsewhere in this volume. In some respects, what was borrowed from France merely reinforced ideas that Smith had developed earlier, as is clear from notes on lectures that Smith delivered in 1763.

Smith's debt to some of his English predecessors is not always so clear, although it is hard to ignore the likely influence of Bernard Mandeville's (1660–1733) *Fable of the Bees* (1714). Smith's emphasis on individual self-interest as productive of social benefit reflects that of Mandeville. Smith avoids mentioning Mandeville and Sir William Petty (1623–87), who undoubtedly influenced Smith's views on public finance, if only on the treatment of equality in taxation.

The wide-ranging basic concepts of the *Wealth of Nations* set the agenda for the whole classical era. The individual pursues self-interest that, constrained by a framework of law, religion, and custom, and an inherent moral sense (sympathy), brings about a coincidence of private and public satisfaction. Competition in response to price signals allocates resources as capital pursues profit opportunities, and the search for greater output from the resources commanded by capital leads to specialization and division of labor, the mainspring of technical progress. Freedom of trade stimulates technical progress and widens the market, allowing disposal of the increased output – division of labor depends on the extent of the market.

Ricardo, reading Smith with the mind of a model builder (Ricardo, 1815, 1817–21), was to have a huge, if ultimately transient, influence on the way in which that agenda was developed. For Ricardo was concerned with two immediate practical problems, inflation and agricultural protection; and he found that the material in the *Wealth of Nations* failed to provide clear-cut answers.

In the Bullion Controversy, the price level in relation to the balance of payments was critical. Smith had argued that a rise in wages would ultimately raise the price level. But Ricardo concluded that, in an open economy on the gold standard, the price level could not rise permanently; after an initial increase, a balance-of-payments deficit would ensue, gold would flow out, the money supply would be reduced, and prices would return to the initial level. This insight, it has been plausibly argued (Hollander, 1979; cf., Peach, 1988), led Ricardo to argue that profits would be compressed by a rise in wages.

Applying the argument to agricultural protection, one could predict dire consequences for growth. Protection increased agricultural costs as inferior land was brought into use to feed a growing population; this meant a rising price of corn. For the laborer to purchase the same amount of corn, money wages would have to rise. Profits would fall and accumulation of capital would slow and ultimately stop. The economy would reach a stationary state.

The landlords' share of total output, rent, would increase as diminishing returns ensured a growing gap between total product and the net product shared between profit and wages. With wages at subsistence, profits would fall to a minimum. The landlords' interests conflicted with the rest of society – to the extent, as Ricardo argued (wrongly, because he neglected the economic interests of *individual* landlords) that improvements in agricultural technology were against their interests.

Ricardo's model had a considerable impact on economic thought over perhaps two decades. But there was misunderstanding. Ricardo was believed to have developed theorems consistent with Smith's basic program, in some instances correcting Smith's conclusions. But it eventually became apparent that Ricardo had constructed an analytic framework that was qualitatively different from Smith's, and classical economics developed along a path increasingly divergent from that laid down by Ricardo.

Malthus's work also enjoyed this ambiguous position in relation to the body of classical literature. Malthus's core ideas go back at least to Cantillon, writing in about 1730. But Malthus provided the version of the population theory underlying classical economics, articulating a conflict between a geometric rate of increase of population and an arithmetic increase in food supply. This had the analytic advantage, especially for Ricardo, of leading to the conclusion that population would increase to the point at which wages were at subsistence, allowing the wage level to be treated as a constant.

The second edition of his *Essay on Population* (1803) removed this certainty. Malthus introduced the idea that population might, or might not (if moral restraint, as distinct from vice, limited procreation), press up against the limits of the food supply. In this form the population theory was incorporated into nineteenth-century economics. According to Senior, population might be limited not by actual shortage, but by anticipation of it. J. S. Mill allowed Malthus an honored place in his *Principles* (1848) while denying that Malthus had attached any importance to his arithmetical and geometric ratios, restating the tautological "tendency" as an economic law that could be modified only by the spread of methods of family limitation.

To understand how all these threads fit together, it is best to look at the classical treatment of particular aspects of economic analysis.

8.3   VALUE AND DISTRIBUTION

8.3.1   Value

Smith designed his value theory to produce a theory of relative price, on the basis of adding up the per-unit costs of the labor, capital, and land inputs into production, the valuation of the inputs being determined separately. He explained the value of commodities in long-run equilibrium, in terms of wages, profit, and rent. Market price fluctuated around long-run equilibrium price, with departures from long-run equilibrium eliminated by the mobility of capital in response to profit opportunities or losses.

Ricardo attempted to replace Smith's adding-up approach with a labor theory of value, creating problems for his contemporaries and successors. Even if capital amortization were treated as payments to stored-up labor, relative values could change without any change in labor input, if the capital–labor ratios were not uniform across all commodities. This would happen when wages rose and profits fell. Ricardo claimed that this would only produce variations of 6 or 7 percent in value. But the problems were tied up with the basic Ricardian model: for money wages were *supposed* to rise with the growth of population and the rising cost of obtaining food, thus altering values. Ricardo further posited an average capital–labor ratio, and the existence of a commodity produced under such conditions – the "Invariable Measure." He then decided that gold would fit that specification, and treated agriculture as operating with the same capital–labor ratio. Thus a rise in wages would not, of its own, alter the money price of corn. If the money price of food did rise, this must signal the existence of diminishing returns in agriculture.

In analyzing rent, Ricardo introduced one of the longest-lasting fallacies in the history of economics. Rent, he argued, was an intramarginal surplus, due to the existence of diminishing returns in agriculture. Economists now conventionally envisage this as a rising agricultural supply schedule, with an area of producer surplus lying between the supply schedule and the market price. Because rent was a surplus, Ricardo argued that it did not determine price but was *determined by* price. The argument neglected transfer earnings: to grow one crop, land had to be paid sufficient to prevent it being used for another crop. The cost of the land did enter into the cost of production when where there were many agricultural products, rather than the single product "corn" of Ricardo's model.

All this has to be seen in the context of Ricardo's overriding aim – to produce a model of growth and stagnation. This was not understood by his contemporaries, who were concerned with *relative* price and saw no role for "Absolute Value" in terms of the "Invariable Measure." McCulloch clearly envisioned an improved cost of production theory: accepting the elimination of rent from cost, he wrestled vainly with the problem of capital and the nature of profit. Torrens adopted a different approach and argued that relative amounts of *capital*, rather than *labor*, determined relative price. However, since the valuation of the capital turned out to depend upon the number of days of labor "stored up," this was no advance.

J. S. Mill's treatment of the cost of production approach to value provides insight into Ricardo's influence. First, Mill rejected Ricardo's "Invariable Measure" and insisted that value was only a relative term. Secondly, Mill emphasized the fluctuation of market price around the long-run natural (cost of production) price; but cost could vary with output, and some products could command a scarcity value. Cost of production comprised wages and profits (depreciation was seen as wages and profits incurred in the past); rent was *not* an element of cost of production. Things could only differ in relative value if they required more labor, or labor paid at higher wages, differed with respect to the capital–labor ratio, or were the products of industries that required a higher rate of profit. Ricardo's influence is apparent both in the "getting rid of rent" and the recognition that varying capital–labor ratios would produce changes in relative values if average wages rose and profits fell: but his contributions only modified a basically Smithian cost of production approach.

The French tradition of J.-B. Say had a wholly different approach, one consistent with the post-1870 approach to value theory: of the interaction of subjective valuation (underlying demand) and limitations in supply. Say argued that both goods and productive services derived their value from the utility of the final product. Price was determined by the intersection of a negatively sloped demand curve (described verbally) and a rising supply schedule.

Say (1817) explained the declining demand schedule in terms of income distribution, not utility. Two later writers developed the argument further. Nassau Senior explained the idea of diminishing marginal utility, although he did not relate it to a demand curve (Senior, 1836), while the Irish economist Mountifort Longfield put forward a strikingly modern subjective value theory (Longfield, 1834). Value depends upon demand and supply: cost of production limits supply, and demand depends upon diminishing marginal utility. Marginal utility varies between units of a commodity and between persons. Rather than relying upon income distribution to derive a negatively sloped demand schedule, Longfield derived it explicitly from diminishing marginal utility. Longfield was followed by others in this tradition (Black, 1945).

8.3.2 Distribution

To avoid explaining prices by prices, the cost-of-production theorists had to provide a theory of the valuation of factor services.

WAGES

The main development followed two lines. One involved the concept of subsistence wages. Commentators disagree about the extent to which the subsistence was physical, although if it were merely conventional (psychological) subsistence, including some luxuries, it is difficult to see why a fall in wages below *that* level should reduce population, unless perhaps through postponement of marriage.

The concept of subsistence provided a theory of the long-run equilibrium wage. But the classical literature focused mainly on the market period, and the so-called wage fund. In the market period, the supply of labor could be taken as fixed; the wage rate was then determined by the intersection of a vertical market supply of labor and a demand curve for labor of unit elasticity, its position being dependent on the size of funds pre-accumulated to employ labor. Thus capital, not demand for commodities, constituted demand for labor.

This approach left open many questions, including the determination of the size of the labor force given the population, the determination of the size of the wage fund itself (particularly as, in the classical analysis, a tax on wage goods was generally to be passed on, implying that it increased the size of the wage fund), and the division of a given stock of capital between fixed and variable capital.

PROFIT

Profit, as distinct from wages of management, was the return on capital, identified as interest plus a risk premium. The source of the interest element in profit still needed analysis. Some writers recognized that capital increased total output, thus sensing that its reward must be linked in some way to productivity. But Samuel Bailey (1791–1870) and, more importantly, Nassau Senior developed the idea of time-preference, which limited the supply of this productivity-enhancing (and thus demanded) factor (Bailey, 1825; Senior, 1836). The combination of limited supply and positive demand gave rise to a positive price for the services of capital.

J. S. Mill's more elaborate treatment analyzed the motives for saving, considered the power to save out of income, and equated the rate of interest with the marginal supply price of saving. Longfield had argued that demand for capital at the margin could be identified with the marginal product of capital; Mill independently advanced the same argument.

The level of profit was thus dependent on both the demand for investment (in relation to the available supply of investment funds) and the demand for consumption goods (which influenced the productivity of that investment), as the classicists from Smith onward recognized. Ricardo argued differently, that the rate of profit for the economy as a whole was determined by the marginal rate of profit in the agricultural sector. This was consistent with showing how diminishing returns in agriculture would bring the economy to a stationary state. His contemporaries felt that increasing manufacturing productivity would offset diminishing returns in agriculture. Ricardo's view was arrived at by dividing the whole economy into one giant farm and a series of manufacturing tributaries. Then the profit-raising effect of innovation in any tributary would be swamped by both capital inflow and the effect of rising wages (due to agricultural diminishing returns), both of which raised costs and lowered the relative value of (capital-intensive) manufactures.

Rent

The Ricardian theory of rent as intramarginal surplus was due at least equally to Sir Edward West, Malthus, and Torrens; all four men published in 1815.

Given the classical treatment of rent, wages, and profits, the treatment of relative shares was easily discernable. Wages would eventually reach subsistence (although perhaps not *physical* subsistence); but wage-earners would enjoy spells during which wages were greater than subsistence as capital accumulation ran ahead of population increase. Profits would fall to a minimum, as a result of both capital accumulation in relation to investment opportunities (Smith, Malthus, and J. S. Mill) and diminishing returns in agriculture (Ricardo). Rent would rise both as a share of national income and in absolute amount.

8.4 Money

8.4.1 Background

Classical monetary theory focused on gold and silver money and bank notes, treating bank deposits as devices for increasing the velocity of circulation, even though the concept of the deposit multiplier was put forward in the 1820s by James Pennington (1777–1862) (Pennington, 1826–40) and Robert Torrens (1837).

The theory, stemming from Hume (1752), became known as the price specie-flow mechanism: A country's price level is a function of its money supply; the equilibrium price level depends upon its balance-of-payments equilibrium. If the price level is too high, an outflow of metal will reduce the money supply (and the price level) to equilibrium, and vice versa. Worldwide, the value of gold and silver depend on their cost of production. But the relative value of gold and silver on the one hand, and of commodities on the other, within a country, is defined by balance-of-payments equilibrium. This mechanism proved to be the pivotal idea in the two great monetary controversies of classical economics.

8.4.2 The Bullion Controversy

In 1797 the Bank of England suspended convertibility of its notes into gold, leading to the first major controversy between those who believed that causality ran from the money supply to the price level and those who believed the money supply responded passively to the price level. Those in the first camp, the Bullionists, blamed the Bank of England for generating inflation by over-issuing notes. Following Hume, for the Bullionists causality ran from the money supply to the price level. But their policy prescriptions differed. Some held to this position rigidly, and their position has come to be called the Ricardian Definition of Excess: *whenever* there are two symptoms of excess (paper) money supply – a high value of gold bullion (a low value of bank notes) and a depreciated exchange rate – then, *by definition*, the currency supply (Bank of England notes) is excessive, and the Bank should contract its issues.

The other group of Bullionists, led by Henry Thornton (1760–1815), argued that while these tests were valid if the symptoms were sustained, they could, in the short run, arise from other causes (Thornton, 1939 [1802]), such as harvest failure or financial panic. Severe damage to the economy could be caused by contracting the note issue in response to transient causes of pressure.

Nevertheless, both groups agreed that in the long run the Bank must restrict its note issue sufficiently to permit a return to convertibility of its notes into gold.

The Anti-Bullionists, by contrast, argued that the Bank's note issue was simply responding to "the needs of trade" as indicated by the "real bills" presented to it for discount. The "real bills" were bills of exchange resulting from real transactions in goods and services.

Their position was not sustainable. First, many of the notes issued had nothing whatever to do with "real" transactions, but were ultimately a consequence of the Bank's position both as the government's bank and as lender of last resort to the financial sector, a position recognized since statements of it by Francis Baring (1797) and Thornton. Secondly, as Thornton pointed out, even had the Bank confined itself to "real bills," the transactions to which they related had to take place at some absolute price level – and in the Bullionist analysis the price level depended on the money supply. Thirdly, Anti-Bullionists argued that the Bank could not over-issue its notes because it charged interest (discount) when issuing notes, so no one would demand notes for which they had no need. But, as Thornton indicated, there was an indefinitely large demand for loans and discounts if the rate that the Bank charged was less than the marginal rate of profit.

Ultimately the Bullionist case triumphed. Convertiblity was progressively restored from 1819. However, the 1820s and 1830s witnessed a series of financial crises and brought convertibility into question, as the Bank of England became hard pressed for gold. The debate on the terms on which the Bank's charter would be renewed in 1844 formed the basis of the next controversy.

8.4.3   The Currency and Banking Debate

Issues from the Bullion Controversy reappeared in the Currency and Banking Debate. The Currency school, positing an endogenous cycle of real income (O'Brien, 1995), argued that if the money supply (Bank of England notes) were regulated in accordance with the Ricardian definition of excess – contracted whenever there was a balance-of-payments deficit – this could act countercyclically. A balance-of-payments deficit was due to a rising price (and income) level, indicating the need for monetary contraction. The Banking school's prescription of allowing the money supply to respond to the "needs of trade" would magnify the cycle and, by intensifying the price-level rise that had produced the balance-of-payments deficit, result in a gold outflow endangering the convertibility of the note issue into gold.

The Banking school maintained that the money supply depended on the price level, that the balance of payments did not depend upon the price level, and that deficits were self-reversing. Over-issue of notes was impossible if the Bank adhered to discounting only "real bills" – any over-issue would automatically return to the Bank under the so-called Doctrine of Reflux.

Both disputants shared certain assumptions, including acceptance of the need for convertibility and of the key role of the Bank of England note issue in the money supply. Neither assumption went completely unquestioned. Thomas Joplin (ca. 1790–1847) argued that the country bank notes were not, as both the Bullionists and the Currency school believed, controlled by the high-powered money base of the Bank of England notes; even more damagingly, he argued that the predominant influence on the price level was these country bank notes rather than those issued by the Bank (O'Brien, 1993).

Joplin accepted that the link with gold should be maintained under normal circumstances. Members of the Birmingham school, notably Thomas Attwood (1783–1856), did not even go this far (Attwood, 1816–43). They urged an inconvertible paper currency to inflate aggregate demand, with the aim of reducing unemployment. This idea had respectable antecedents: Hume and Malthus had argued that increases in the money supply would increase output and employment. But inflation as a policy had few supporters – the experience of the Assignats in Revolutionary France had demonstrated the danger of hyperinflation.

Aggregate demand was not ignored by the classical writers. Say's Law provided an explanation of the underlying circularity of the economic system. But the classical writers, especially J. S. Mill in his *Unsettled Questions* (1844), recognized that outside a barter system there could be excess demand for money, and that market clearing in a monetary, as distinct from a hypothetical barter, economy was an equilibrium proposition. Monetary changes were not neutral – if the classical economists had believed they were, the Bullion and Currency and Banking Controversies would have been pointless.

8.5   TRADE

8.5.1   Smith and the gains from trade

Perhaps the most prominent feature of classical economics is the central importance attached to trade, and the corollary that trade should be free of restrictions. The intellectual underpinnings of this position are complex.

Adam Smith set the tone by offering a critique of existing restrictionist trade policy, sustained and defended as it was by interest groups. The basic grounds for Smith's position, however, involved a blurring of the distinction between home and foreign trade. Specialization and division of labor increased output per head, but were limited by the extent of the market. Freedom of trade increased the extent of that market, allowing greater division of labor. International trade, like interregional trade, was thus based upon the source of supply being the producer with absolute advantage. An international outlet for the increased output was offered by trade – this was later called the Vent-for-Surplus doctrine – in exchange for goods (and raw materials) produced more efficiently abroad. But for sources of supply to be absolutely the most efficient, it was necessary for factors to migrate to where they could work most efficiently, which labor could not. J. S. Mill explained that for trade to be based upon absolute advantage, labor would have to migrate in search of its highest productivity, as its output would have to be sold in the same market wherever it worked, but the return to capital would be higher, the lower the resource input.

8.5.2 Comparative advantage

If resources were not fully mobile internationally, it was still possible for trade to yield advantages for all parties, even though some of them were not the most efficient in terms of resource use. This idea, developed as the principle of comparative advantage, is usually associated with Ricardo's *Principles* of 1817. However, Robert Torrens published the idea two years before Ricardo (Torrens, 1815; Robbins, 1958). The argument was basically that if one country were generally more efficient than another, it would initially run a balance-of-payments surplus and gold would flow to it. This would inflate its money supply and raise its price level, with this process continuing until both countries were in balance-of-payments equilibrium. The more efficient country would import those commodities in which its productivity advantage was least, and export those in which its superiority was greatest.

8.5.3 The terms of trade

Division of the gains from trade between countries depended on the terms of trade, but Ricardo left unexplained the forces determining them. J. S. Mill explored the limiting case where a small country traded at a larger one's internal price ratio, in which all gains went to the smaller country.

Senior attempted to explain the terms of trade via relative labor productivity in export industries – which left unresolved the question of which *were* the export industries, since this depended on the terms of trade. Torrens (1827) and Joplin (1828) perceived that the key resided in the reciprocal demand of each country for the products of its trading partners, and James Pennington identified the outer limits of the terms of trade as being the different comparative cost ratios of the trading countries. J. S. Mill explained the analysis of reciprocal demand completely, his analysis being permeated by a complete understanding of the importance of the elasticity of offer curves (as they are now called) for the terms of trade.

TRADE POLICY

These developments had important implications for the analysis of trade policy, and somewhat undermined the Smithian case for free trade. Torrens showed that *unilateral* free trade would lead to a balance-of-payments deficit, which would cause an outflow of metal, reducing the money supply, lowering the price level, and turning the terms of trade against the free-trade country (O'Brien, 1977). Moreover, the fall in the price level would increase the weight of fixed charges, such as taxes, and produce economic depression. Conversely, a country would benefit from protection.

Torrens's work was comprehensively criticized. Senior (1843) argued that a country imposing protectionist duties would lose the advantage of specialization; the reduction in output per head could lead to a balance-of-payments deficit with third countries, to offset the gain of metal from the country whose products were now duntied. George Warde Norman (1860) showed that the effects assumed by Torrens would be much reduced if the assumption of constant outlay (a reciprocal demand curve of unit elasticity) were abandoned, and argued that Torrens's case led to retaliation on the part of a country faced with new import duties on its exports, with the prospect of a tariff war, the original terms of trade restored, but international trade at much reduced levels – a welfare loss for all participants.

8.6   Economic Growth

8.6.1   Adam Smith

The *Wealth of Nations* established that economics is about economic growth. Smith pays attention to both the required institutional framework and the mechanics that operate within that framework. The framework included well-defined and secure property rights, diffusion of agricultural property through control over the concentration of inheritance, and the provision of an infrastructure. (Here government had a key role to play.) Within this framework, individuals pursued their self-interest, as limited by law, religion, and custom (Robbins, 1952), allocating capital to where the return was greatest. Capital employed labor, and the output per head from a given population determined national income. The determinants of output per head were the proportion of the labor force employed productively, and its productivity when employed.

For Smith, the distinction between productively and unproductively employed labor is basically that between labor that adds value (and/or produces a vendible or storable product) and labor employed in areas such as government. There are obvious objections to this generalization, but Smith saw the big picture well enough: the state accumulated no capital, and its appropriation of labor, which might otherwise be employed productively, was not conducive to economic growth.

At the core of the argument, specialization and division of labor – the source of labor productivity and the mainspring of technology – depended on the supporting capital and the extent of the market. Smith's immortal example of the specialization of tasks in pin manufacturing has tended to obscure the bigger point that division of labor was even more important *between* occupations, thus requiring a developed market system.

As output per head rose, wages were slow to adjust, capital was accumulated, extra labor was demanded, wages rose, and population increased in response. The larger population, receiving increased wages, increased the extent of the market. Economic growth involved simultaneous supply-side and demand-side mechanisms.

Welfare improved with rising wages and the psychological subsistence level increased; subsistence in England would, Smith observed, seem the lap of luxury to an African chief. The welfare effects of rising national income were not completely unambiguous; division of labor confined people to monotonous and dulling work. Nonetheless, economic growth had a tendency to raise wages and to accustom people to small luxuries. Growth would not continue indefinitely – the stationary state would come about through the exhaustion of investment opportunities, but this was a fairly distant prospect.

8.6.2   Smith's successors

Smith's book set the agenda for subsequent discussions of economic growth, with the exception of Ricardo, who focused instead on the mechanics of his model, in which economic growth came to an early halt because of agricultural protection. The rest manifest a continuation of Smith's research program, though now bearing Ricardian marks.

Malthus also stressed security of property, capital accumulation, natural resources, and trade; and, given the technical explosion of the Industrial Revolution, he added invention. His treatment of population went beyond Smith. The most novel element in his approach (also stressed by Lauderdale) was the need to ensure sufficient aggregate demand, an important element of which was the existence of what Smith had classified as unproductive labor.

McCulloch added religious tolerance, an expanded role for government, and a banking system. He stressed the importance of invention, and introduced the concept of human capital (which assisted invention), and thus emphasized the importance of education. Like some other writers (notably Say), he rejected Smith's distinction between productive and unproductive labor – his grounds being that the desire for the products of unproductive labor could stimulate activity.

J. S. Mill's treatment of economic growth, like that of Ricardo, stressed the inevitability of diminishing returns in agriculture, despite asserting that technical progress held them in abeyance for the 20 years before the appearance of his *Principles*. The stationary state might not be as miserable as Ricardo had envisaged – family limitation would ensure that wages were not unduly depressed, and legacy duties could redistribute wealth. Despite Ricardian elements, the majority of Mill's treatment could be described as Smith brought up to the 1840s. Mill borrowed material relating to technology, scale, organization, and joint stock companies from Babbage (1832). From John Rae (1796–1872) he borrowed material on invention and a remarkable treatment of capital (Rae, 1834), to produce a theory of investment that involved the interaction of time-preference and the marginal productivity of investment.

Ricardo, drawing on John Barton (1789–1852), had advanced, in the third edition (1821) of his *Principles*, a numerical example in which the introduction of machinery resulted in unemployment that was not temporary (Barton, 1817; Ricardo, 1817– 21). Most other classical writers were not convinced: it was obvious from recent economic history that employment had increased hugely in parallel with the employment of machinery. Several writers also noted the special nature of Ricardo's assumptions.

The possibility of demand-deficient unemployment elicited more concern. Malthus worried that capital accumulation would proceed so fast that there could be no market for the output of the expanding industries, and prices would be depressed to the point at which the marginal return on capital was negative. He looked to "unproductive consumption" to maintain a sufficient level of aggregate demand *and* to keep some resources away from production. Malthus also envisaged a role for public works.

8.7   Public Finance

Smith devoted the final book of the *Wealth of Nations* to public finance, and after him an extensive literature on taxation developed (O'Brien, 1999). The starting point for classical tax analysis was Smith's four maxims of taxation – equality, certainty, convenience, and economy. Equality could mean taxation according to either equal benefit received or equal ability to pay. Smith did not make the distinction; later classical economists adopted one standpoint or the other. The benefit theorists included Hume, Bentham, and Say. McCulloch and J. S. Mill both favored an ability-to-pay approach, although they meant different things by it. For McCulloch, it meant equality of burdens on different sectors of the economy, so as not to distort the process of economic growth. For Mill, it meant that taxpayers should suffer equal sacrifices of utility, leaving unclear whether these sacrifices should be equal absolute ones or equal proportional ones.

The majority opinion favored indirect taxes over direct taxes, despite the recognition that the former distorted relative prices, gave rise to smuggling, and could be levied in oppressive ways. McCulloch thought moderate indirect taxes avoided investigation, were convenient, could be used for sumptuary purposes, and that they stimulated effort and ingenuity. He also believed that indirect taxes, which discouraged consumption, could stimulate saving.

The main exception to the general approval of such taxes was Ricardo, who believed that a tax on wages (which in his model would be passed on and paid out of profit, a conclusion telescoping the long run and short run), together with a tax on rent, and one on interest on government securities, was the ideal tax system. J. S. Mill favored only a limited use of direct taxes on houses, land, and increments of rental value.

The classical economists approached the analysis of taxation in two different ways. The first was taxation of factor rewards – wages, profits, and rent. The second was particular modes of taxation, such as the income tax. While the majority covered taxation in both ways, the more empirically oriented economists, especially McCulloch (1845–63), paid particular attention to forms of revenue raising.

8.7.1   Functional rewards

Smith and Ricardo believed that a tax on *wages* would be passed on, because in the long run wages could not be pressed below subsistence. Hume, and later, McCulloch, disagreed. With the exception of Ricardo, there was general opposition to such taxes. Nor was there any enthusiasm for taxing *profits*. To Smith, profits were undiscoverable and contained a necessary reward to risk-bearing that was part of the supply price of capital to different occupations. Taxes on profits might also affect resource allocation; Ricardo argued that a tax on profits in particular trades would alter relative prices through capital mobility, reducing the supply of commodities that generated taxed profits to the point at which price had risen far enough to restore profit to the same level as in other employments of capital. Both McCulloch and J. S. Mill were critical of this conclusion, noting barriers to capital mobility and the possibility that technical progress might offset the tax. It was generally accepted that a tax on agricultural profits not offset by technical progress would increase rent by raising marginal cost in agriculture.

A tax on *rent* was theoretically ideal; it would not affect factor allocation, being an intramarginal surplus. But in practice economic rent often could not be distinguished from returns on capital invested in improvements; a tax on rent would act as a disincentive to improvements in agricultural technology.

8.7.2   Revenue raising

The *income tax* was a matter of serious controversy during the classical era. Introduced in 1799, abandoned in 1816, and then reintroduced in 1842, it eventually became a mainstay of public revenue. Characterized by widespread fraud and evasion, it found little support amongst the classical economists. There was little enthusiasm for progression in such a tax, apart from that implied by the exemption of a subsistence minimum.

Commodity taxes were seen as the major source of revenue. It was generally argued that these taxes should be at low levels (to avoid the obvious disadvantages of regressivity and the danger of smuggling). Some writers, particularly McCulloch, argued that such taxes should be on both home and imported sources of commodities, to avoid a protective effect.

Taxes on home-produced commodities were generally held to raise price by the full amount of the tax. McCulloch, consistently with his retention of Smith's absolute advantage trade model, held that import duties were also paid entirely by the home consumer; and argued for balancing duties on home-produced and imported commodities. The reciprocal demand analysis of J. S. Mill and Torrens, however, showed that this symmetry did not necessarily exist. It was generally agreed that such taxes should be on "luxuries" – tobacco, tea, beer, and sugar – rather than on "necessaries" (basic foodstuffs), taxes on which might raise wages even if not fully passed on.

8.8   POLICY PRESCRIPTIONS

The classical economists were the first group of writers to appreciate fully the allocative role of the market. But the market operated within a framework of law, which was properly subject to development, pragmatically, as needs were discovered. Thus from Smith onward, a legitimate role for the state was recognized.

Bentham and J. S. Mill distinguished between what the state should do and what it should leave alone, the contents of each list depending upon the stage of economic and political development.

Classical economists did not assume an omniscient, benevolent, state; government intervention had to be justified. Moreover, there was the ever-present danger of abuse of public authority for rent-seeking – the mercantilism that Smith had attacked so vigorously.

Smith stressed the role of the state in the provision of defense, justice, a legal system, infrastructure, and coinage, and even advocated the regulation of inheritance and of leases. He defended shipping restrictions (the Navigation Laws), and legal limitations on the rate of interest. Here, he was not followed by later classical writers. His advocacy of public health regulation and banking regulation was supported, and a number of writers went further – McCulloch advocating employer accident liability and laws to prevent the overloading of ships. Even the regulation of public utility charges was approved by McCulloch and J. S. Mill. In part, they were simply following the trend of public opinion, but they were not hampered by any *laissez-faire* dogmatism: they examined the economic implications of possible legislative remedies to amend and regulate a functioning price system. Socialism held no attraction for them, although J. S. Mill flirted with cooperation. Centralized and totalitarian socialism was completely foreign to their outlook.

8.8.1 Factories

The classical economists were reluctant to endorse intervention in industrial organization. Although they supported the regulation of child labor, they were ambiguous about regulation of women's work, and opposed the limitation of factory hours – Torrens and Senior opposed the Ten Hour Bill on grounds that the resultant increase in costs would reduce exports, causing a balance-of-payments deficit, an outflow of metal, a fall in the price level, and a reduction in profitability.

However, they had no objection to measures to cushion unemployment resulting from mechanization, through the provision of alternative employment (Bentham), unemployment relief (Torrens), or even slowing the pace of mechanization if necessary (J. S. Mill). When intervention was not recommended (as in the report on the plight of the handloom weavers, written by Senior) there was no belittling of the hardships involved; what was presented was an economic analysis of the likely effects of intervention. There was no objection in principle to intervention; merely pessimism about the likely outcome.

Some, however, objected in principle to the provision of poor relief – notably Ricardo and Malthus, based on the idea that poor relief subsidized population growth out of net rent. Other writers, led by Senior, favored making poor relief available, but only in the workhouse, a view that triumphed in the New Poor Law of 1834. The disincentive to seeking relief that this "indoor relief" provided was held to neutralize the adverse effects on labor supply and population control of providing poor relief.

8.8.2   Education

Education could raise the psychological subsistence level, thus providing a major check to population; and all the classical economists favored public provision of education – though not a state monopoly. There were differences over whether fees should be paid. Smith and McCulloch argued that reliance upon income from fees was a necessary incentive for the teachers. But Senior and J. S. Mill believed that education was an instance of market failure – those paying fees could not tell the difference between good and bad suppliers – and argued for state-funded education.

In addition to its beneficial effect on population, education would provide investment in human capital. This was a theme of Smith, McCulloch, and also J. S. Mill, who saw education as supplying potential managers as well as increasing equality of income through erosion of the rents enjoyed by those with favored access to education. Education also enabled people to understand the need for security of property, thus favoring economic growth.

8.9   CONCLUSION

Classical economics covered virtually all areas of concern to later economists, laying the foundations for the development of economics since. Some parts of it – essentially the microeconomics – were submerged in the course of that development; but the work on trade, growth, and money has proved to be extremely durable.

Bibliography

See O'Brien (1975) for further references.

Attwood, T. 1816–43: *Selected Economic Writings*, ed. F. W. Fetter. London: London School of Economics.

Babbage, C. 1832: *On the Economy of Machinery and Manufactures*. London: Knight.

Bailey, S. 1825: *A Critical Dissertation on the Nature, Measure and Causes of Value*. Reprinted London: London School of Economics, 1931.

Baring, F. 1797: *Observations on the Establishment of the Bank of England & the Paper Circulation of the Country*. Reprinted New York: Augustus M. Kelley, 1967.

Barton, J. 1817: *Observations on the Circumstances which Influence the Condition of the Labouring Classes*. London: J. and A. Arch.

Black, R. D. C. 1945: Trinity College, Dublin, and the theory of value, 1832–1863. *Economica*, NS, 12, 140–8.

Cantillon, R. ca. 1730: *Essai sur la Nature du Commerce en Général*, trans. H. Higgs. Reprinted New York: Augustus M. Kelley, 1964.

Hollander, S. 1979: *The Economics of David Ricardo*. Toronto: University of Toronto Press.

Hume, D. 1752: *Writings on Economics*, ed. E. Rotwein. Edinburgh: Nelson, 1955.

Joplin, T. 1828: *Views on the Corn Bill of 1827, and Other Measures of Government*. London: Ridgway.

Longfield, M. 1834: *Lectures on Political Economy*. In R. D. C. Black (ed.), *The Economic Writings of Mountifort Longfield*. New York: Augustus M. Kelley, 1971.

McCulloch, J. R. 1845–63: *A Treatise on the Principles and Practical Influence of Taxation and the Funding System*, ed. D. P. O'Brien. Edinburgh: Scottish Academic Press, for the Scottish Economic Society, 1975.

Malthus, T. R. 1803: *An Essay on the Principle of Population*, 2nd edn. London: Johnson.

—— 1815: *An Inquiry into the Nature and Progress of Rent, and the Principles by which it is Regulated*. London: Murray.

Mandeville, B. 1714–29: *The Fable of the Bees*, ed. F. B. Kaye. Reprinted Indianapolis: Liberty Press, 1988.

Mill, J. S. 1844: *Unsettled Questions of Political Economy*, ed. J. M. Robson. In *Collected Works*, vol. IV. Toronto: University of Toronto Press, 229–339.

—— 1848: *The Principles of Political Economy*, ed. W. J. Ashley. London: Longman, 1923.

Norman, G. W. 1860: *Remarks on the Incidence of Import Duties*. Privately printed.

O'Brien, D. P. 1975: *The Classical Economists*. Oxford: The Clarendon Press; in particular, see additional references therein.

—— 1977: Torrens, McCulloch and Disraeli. *Scottish Journal of Political Economy*, 24, 1–8.

—— 1988: Classical reassessments. In W. O. Thweatt (ed.), *Classical Political Economy*. Boston: Kluwer, 179–220.

—— 1993: *Thomas Joplin and Classical Macroeconomics*. Aldershot: Edward Elgar.

—— 1995: Long-run equilibrium and cyclical disturbances: the currency and banking controversy over monetary control. In M. Blaug, W. Eltis, D. O'Brien, D. Patinkin, R. Skidelsky, and G. Wood (eds.), *The Quantity Theory of Money*. Aldershot, UK: Edward Elgar.

—— (ed.) 1999: *The History of Taxation*. London: Pickering & Chatto.

Peach, T. 1988: David Ricardo: a review of some interpretative issues. In W. O. Thweatt (ed.), *Classical Political Economy*. Boston: Kluwer, 103–31.

Pennington, J. 1826–40: *Economic Writings*, ed. R. S. Sayers. London: London School of Economics, 1963.

Rae, J. 1834: *Statement of Some New Principles of Political Economy*. Reprinted New York: Augustus M. Kelley, 1964.

Ricardo, D. 1815: *An Essay on the Influence of a Low Price of Corn on the Profits of Stock*. In P. Sraffa (ed.), *Works and Correspondence of David Ricardo*, vol. IV. Cambridge, UK: Cambridge University Press, 1951, 1–41.

—— 1817–21: *On the Principles of Political Economy and Taxation*. In P. Sraffa (ed.), *Works and Correspondence of David Ricardo*, vol. I. Cambridge, UK: Cambridge University Press, 1951.

Robbins, L. C. 1952: *The Theory of Economic Policy in English Classical Political Economy*. London: Macmillan.

—— 1958: *Robert Torrens and the Evolution of Classical Economics*. London: Macmillan.

Say, J.-B. 1817: *A Treatise on Political Economy*, 4th edn., trans. C. R. Prinsep, 1821. Reprinted New York: Augustus M. Kelley, 1971.

Schumpeter, J. A. 1954: *A History of Economic Analysis*. London: George Allen & Unwin.

Senior, N. W. 1836: *An Outline of the Science of Political Economy*. London: William Clowes.

—— 1843: Free trade and retaliation. *Edinburgh Review*, 88, 1–47.

Smith, A. 1759: *The Theory of Moral Sentiments*, ed. D. D. Raphael and A. L. Macfie. Oxford: Oxford University Press, 1976.

—— 1763: *Lectures on Justice, Police, Revenue and Arms*, ed. E. Cannan. Oxford: The Clarendon Press, 1896.

—— 1776. *An Inquiry into the Nature and Causes of the Wealth of Nations*, ed. R. H. Campbell, A .S. Skinner, and W. B. Todd. Indianapolis: Liberty Press, 1981.

Thornton, H. 1939 [1802]: *An Enquiry into the Nature and Effects of the Paper Credit of Great Britain*, ed. F. A. Hayek. London: George Allen & Unwin.

Torrens, R. 1815: *An Essay on the External Corn Trade*. London: J. Hatchard.

—— 1827: *An Essay on the External Corn Trade*, 4th edn. London: Longman.

—— 1837: *A Letter to the Right Honourable Lord Viscount Melbourne on the Causes of the Recent Derangements in the Money Market and on Bank Reform*. London: Longman.

Turgot, A. R. J. 1769: *Reflections on the Formation and the Distribution of Wealth*, trans. R. L. Meek. In Meek, R. 1973: *Turgot on Progress, Sociology and Economics*. Cambridge, UK: Cambridge University Press.

West, E. 1815: *An Essay on the Application of Capital to Land*. London: Underwood.

CHAPTER NINE

Post-Ricardian British Economics, 1830–1870

Sandra J. Peart and David M. Levy

9.1 INTRODUCTION

Ours is a story that begins with hegemony, and continues with attack, defense, and defeat. The intellectual composition of classical economics by 1830 is complex, and it is not our intention to minimize substantive differences amongst Adam Smith, Thomas Robert Malthus, David Ricardo, Nassau William Senior, John Stuart Mill, or less well-known but nonetheless important contributors. Some of these will become apparent in what follows. Yet, differences notwithstanding, by 1830 the analytics of classical growth, distribution, and value theories were well-developed, reflecting a preoccupation with land scarcity and diminishing returns, and formulated with the problem of population growth in mind. We choose to focus on what united the economists of the time to help clarify what separated them from their critics. Between 1830 and 1870, classical analytic machinery, its methodological underpinning (abstraction), and the policy recommendations that flowed from the analytics, came under fire from many directions: the literary community; the anthropological and biological sciences that produced eugenics; and within the economics community itself.

To a large extent, the controversy surrounding post-Ricardian economics occurred over the presumption of equal competence, or homogeneity. On the side of homogeneity, we locate the great classical economists, who presumed that economic agents are all equipped with a capacity for language and trade, and observed outcomes are explained by incentives, luck, and history. In opposition, we find many "progressives" (Thomas Carlyle, John Ruskin, Charles Dickens, and Charles Kingsley), whose explanation for the observed heterogeneity of custom and behavior was race. In our period, the notion of "race" is rather ill defined, but the argument played out both in terms of the Irish and the former slaves in Jamaica (Curtis, 1997). In addition, the "laboring classes" were sometimes included in discussions of incompetence.

The economists' explanation for observed heterogeneity was to appeal to the incentives associated with different institutions. Classical economists such as John Stuart Mill struggled with the problem of transition from one set of institutions to another: How are new habits formed as institutions change? Economists who have become accustomed to institution-free analysis may fail to appreciate how much of classical economics is designed to deal precisely with this problem of self-motivated human development in the context of institutional change. Examples in what follows include the Irish land question, slavery, Mill's higher and lower pleasures, his analysis of economic growth, and Thornton's famous challenge to classical economics at the end of our period.

In the period that we study, economic analysis also supposed – as Mill put it in his *Essay on the Definitions of Political Economy; and on the Method of Investigation Proper to It* (1836; hereafter, *Essay*) – that it treats "man's nature as modified by the social state" (Mill, 1967a, p. 321). This supposition enabled classical economists such as Richard Whately and his student, Senior, to develop and improve the science of exchange, "catallactics." The catallactic tradition retained a key role for nonmaterial concerns, what Smith had called "sympathy" as well as the desire for approbation. As the period comes to a close, social sentiments disappear from economics and material concerns become singularly important.

It is widely accepted that the boundary of economic science was narrowed throughout the nineteenth century (Winch, 1972). This narrowing occurred with the removal of sympathy and the rise in materialism from 1830 to 1870, as well as the removal of institutional concerns from economic analysis, and the presumption of reversibility that underscores early neoclassical analysis by Fleeming Jenkin. Jenkin's argument was a critical blow against the classical supposition of the importance of the status quo.

Homogeneity was not simply an analytic tool. The methodological position in Mill's *Essay* was that the economist must abstract from differences to focus on the common. The method of abstraction was denounced throughout the period, and early critiques of abstract economic man were made in the context of the Irish question. The political economist and co-founder (with Francis Galton) of the eugenics movement, W. R. Greg, attacked classical political economy for its assumption that the Irishman is an "average human being," rather than one prone to "idleness," "ignorance," "jollity," and "drink."

9.2　HEGEMONY: GROWTH, DISTRIBUTION, AND VALUE

By 1830, classical analytic machinery consisted of well developed theories of growth, distribution, and value – all formulated with the population mechanism and land scarcity yielding diminishing returns in mind. Importantly for our argument that follows, these theories abstract from race or any other features such as religion or gender.

Classical growth theory presupposes a functional relationship between the average real wage and population growth. Land scarcity (and the absence of prudential population control) are said to create secular downward pressure on the wage (and profit, or interest) rates. Presuming single-use land, rent is a differential surplus. Increasing land scarcity reduces the growth rate of capital accumulation and, consequently, the growth of labor demand. As what would later be known as the marginal product of the composite labor and capital input falls, this drives the returns to the variable factors, labor and capital, down. The secular fall in the real wage is smaller than the fall in the marginal product, so the wage share rises and profits fall, a result widely known today as the fundamental theorem on distribution. The incidence of diminishing returns is thus shared by capital (as lower profit rates) and labor (as lower wage rates or increased prudential control). In a stationary state setting with zero net accumulation and zero population growth, the subsistence wage pertains, along with a corresponding subsistence rate of profit. In this – and other – details, our summary of classical analytics follows the "New View" developed by Hollander, Levy (Levy, 1976; Hollander, 2001), and others. For a restatement by Hollander, and for extensions and criticisms, see Forget and Peart (2001).

In the simplest case when money and corn are produced with equal capital–labor ratios, a labor theory of exchange value holds and any change in wages leaves relative prices unaffected. If the labor embodied in gold remains constant while diminishing returns pertains in corn production, then the (gold) value of corn rises as a result of the reduction in labor's productivity in the corn sector. The (gold) value of the output of a unit of labor is invariable.

Using the gold measure of value, classical growth analysis also yields the inverse wage–profit relationship: the profit rate is inversely related to the proportion of output devoted to laborers as a whole. Thus, the inverse wage–profit relationship holds both in value and physical terms. In these terms, growth again implies the profit rate tends downward. Laborers receive a higher money wage rate. But since the money value of the marginal output is constant, profits must also fall.

In classical analysis, "natural" – or cost – prices include both "ordinary" or average wages and profits; natural price is achieved through an allocative process by which capital flows from low to high return industries until a uniform rate of profit is achieved. In the event that factor proportions are fixed and uniform, long-run equilibrium prices are proportionate to relative labor inputs. When factor proportions differ, prices are no longer proportionate to relative labor inputs but, instead, reflect all costs. But the mechanism that ensures that cost prices will emerge remains the same: profit rate differentials cause flows from low- to high-profit sectors until equality is restored and a new set of relative prices emerges.

In large measure, the hegemony of classical analytics was due to the influence of John Stuart Mill, whose refinements and restatements proved definitive throughout the period. At the end of our period, William Stanley Jevons railed at the "noxious influence" of Ricardo's "equally able but wrong-headed admirer" (1871, pp. 275, li). But Mill's influence, as will become clear below, extended beyond pure analytics to the defense of the classical presumption of homogeneity against its racist critics, and to methodology and the hard problem of the "improvement of mankind" (Robson, 1968).

Much of the coherence in the period was also the result of Nassau Senior's wide-ranging contributions, a fact that is appreciated by considering which "Ricardians" Frank Knight selects as targets (Knight, 1935). Famously, Senior's abstinence theory of interest brought the real cost doctrine to savings, but his contributions also tied together many loose threads of classical analysis. His controversy with T. R. Malthus over the "tendency" for population to outrun subsistence made it clear that a "tendency" became "forecast" only when the cost of a family vanished, as it would under what Malthus referred to as "systems of equality" – without government or property (Senior, 1998b [1829], pp. 87–9).

Senior's contribution to the analysis of aggregate economic activity was equally important to the classical system. Smith and Ricardo supposed a metallic money provided by a competitive market (Smith, 1976, p. 435). But they failed to explain how this works in a Britain without mines. Senior answered:

> The mine worked by England is the general market of the world: the miners are those who produce those commodities by the exportation of which the precious metals are obtained. (Senior, 1998c [1830], p. 15)

Smith had supposed that the market for money cleared quickly (Smith, 1976, pp. 435–6).

If we start with the supposition that the excess demand for money equals the aggregate excess supply of goods (known today as Walras's Law), then Smith's adjustment principle suffices to obtain Say's Law – the aggregate excess supply of goods is zero. Senior worked an example of how equilibrium in the classical system is affected when a sudden contraction of the money supply resulted from a bank panic:

> A great portion . . . of what acted as the circulating medium of exchange throughout the country becomes valueless; and the effects are precisely the same as if an equal portion of the metallic currency of the country had been suddenly annihilated or exported.

Then the classical price adjustment mechanism is called into play:

> Prices fall, the importation of commodities is checked, and their exportation is encouraged. The foreign exchanges become universally favourable, and the precious metals flow in until the void, occasioned by the destruction of the paper currency, has been filled. (Senior, 1998a [1828], p. 27)

9.3   HOW ECONOMICS BECAME THE "DISMAL SCIENCE"

Perhaps the hegemony of classical thought on population growth and the stationary state is in part responsible for today's misconceptions on the origins of the "dismal science" phrase. Certainly, critics of the classical system would have us believe so. And almost everyone believes that Carlyle called classical political economy the "dismal science" as a response to T. R. Malthus's prediction that population would always grow faster than food, dooming mankind to unending poverty.

In fact, Carlyle's target was not Malthus, but economists such as John Stuart Mill, who argued that it was institutions, not race, that explained why some nations were rich and others poor. It was the fact that economics assumed that people were all the same, and were all entitled to liberty, that led Carlyle to label economics the "dismal science." It is too rarely appreciated (Persky, 1990; Levy, 2001; Levy and Peart, 2001–2) that economics became the "dismal science" in this period because of a view of human nature that abstracted away from the possibility of racial difference. Classical economists were committed to the hardest possible doctrine of analytic homogeneity. As a consequence, they opposed racial slavery and paternalism, and they favored markets instead.

Here is the paragraph in which Carlyle first uses the "dismal science" phrase as part of his attack on the anti-slavery stance of political economy:

> Truly, my philanthropic friends, Exeter Hall Philanthropy is wonderful; and the Social Science – not a "gay science," but a rueful – which finds the secret of this universe in "supply-and-demand," and reduces the duty of human governors to that of letting men alone, is also wonderful. Not a "gay science," I should say, like some we have heard of; no, a dreary, desolate, and indeed quite abject and distressing one; what we might call, by way of eminence, the *dismal science*. These two, Exeter Hall Philanthropy and the Dismal Science, led by any sacred cause of Black Emancipation, or the like, to fall in love and make a wedding of it, – will give birth to progenies and prodigies; dark extensive moon-calves, unnameable abortions, wide-coiled monstrosities, such as the world has not seen hitherto! (Carlyle, 1849, pp. 672–3)

Carlyle was the greatest enemy of the anti-slave coalition of political economists and Christian evangelicals centered at Exeter Hall. His "Negro Question" revived the pro-slavery movement in mid-century Britain (Denman, 1853, p. 12).

Mill's response comes into print a month after Carlyle's "Negro Question." In it, he condemned what he called "the vulgar error of imputing every difference which he finds among human beings to an original difference of nature" (Mill, 1850, p. 29). He supposes that black people in Jamaica, being competent to make economic decisions, respond to incentives just as any other people would.

The real meaning of the Carlyle–Mill debate became clear during the "Governor Eyre Controversy" of 1865. The controversy was triggered by a seemingly trivial event in the British colony of Jamaica. After minor skirmishes, the island's Governor, Edward James Eyre, took command, imposing martial law and calling in the army. Over 400 Jamaicans were massacred, wire whips were used as instruments of terror, and thousands were left homeless. In England, the Jamaica Committee was formed to demand an investigation. Its members included every classical political economist of note living at the time – J. S. Mill (its head), John Bright, Henry Fawcett, J. E. Cairnes, Thorold Rodgers, and Herbert Spencer – as well as Charles Darwin and T. H. Huxley. On the other side, the Eyre Defence

Fund was led by Carlyle, assisted by Ruskin. Additional literary figures on the Eyre Defence included Dickens, Kingsley, and Alfred Lord Tennyson (Semmel, 1962). As the Jamaica Committee failed to obtain an indictment of Eyre and Mill lost his seat in Parliament, the controversy was a great defeat for classical political economy.

9.4 CATALLACTIC THEORY AND POLICY: STARTING WITH TWO EXCHANGING

When Whately opened his Oxford lectures on political economy, he began with Adam Smith's teaching that exchange is a uniquely human activity. He also explained in this context that political economy "takes no cognizance" of isolated individuals, such as "Robinson Crusoe" (Whately, 1831, p. 7). Catallactics carries with it the connotation of reciprocity. For Whately, as for Smith, dogs do not exchange because they lack language and the concept of "fair." Catallactics comes with desires, including the desire for reciprocity.

Whately took the next step in the argument when he generalized from purely voluntary exchanges to such involuntary exchanges as the provision of tax-financed government services:

> And it is worth remarking, that it is just so far forth as it is an exchange, – so far forth as protection, whether adequate or not, is afforded in exchange for this payment, – that the payment itself comes under the cognizance of this science. There is nothing else that distinguishes taxation from avowed robbery. (Whately, 1832, pp. 10–11)

The government service that he considered in detail was protection (Whately, 1833). For catallactic theorists, the question is not whether exchange is voluntary, but whether it is mutually beneficial. Viewing government as an exchange has a dramatic consequence: hierarchy vanishes and the consumer becomes sovereign. Carlyle appreciated this consequence (Carlyle, 1987, p. 31), and he objected to the analytic egalitarianism in catallactics; he realized that classical political economy – the economics of exchange with reciprocity – provided a key weapon in the war against slavery. If exchange with reciprocity is the mark of the human, then slavery is a perversion of the social order.

9.4.1 Catallactic policy

Two acts of political exchange are central to the period: the 1833 Act of Emancipation and the 1834 New Poor Law. As these are not customarily seen as exchanges, we shall expand upon this view.

The abolition of slavery – a seven-year "apprenticeship" – was accompanied by a £20 million "indemnity" to the slave-owners and a protective tariff on West Indian sugar (Denman, 1853). The compensation principle of catallactics is exchange. Here is Mill's analysis in his 1848 *Principles*, in which he maintains that emancipation, like all reforms, requires compensation: "Whether the object be education; a more efficient and accessible administration of justice; reforms of any kind which, like the Slave Emancipation, require compensation to individual interests" (Mill, 1965, pp. 865–6).

Government as exchange requires the recognition of constraints. The problem that Senior found with the "old" poor law was that it imposed only benefits on recipients and, as a consequence, it created the incentive for indigence. As Senior saw it, poor relief is desirable for those "poor" who are unable to earn their own subsistence:

> In one sense of that word, ["poor"] means merely the aggregate of the individuals who, from infirmity, or accident, or misconduct, have lost their station as independent members of society, and are really unable to earn their own subsistence. These persons form, in every well-ordered community, a small minority – a minority which it is in the power, and therefore within the duty of society, to relieve; but, if possible, to reduce, and certainly not to encourage. (Senior, 1998e [1841], p. 14)

But how can society separate the indigent, whom society stands willing to assist, from those larger numbers who would simply like to be assisted? Senior proposed a test, in the form of a trade:

> ... to connect the relief of the able-bodied with a condition which no man not in real want would accept, or would submit to when that want had ceased. . . . the able-bodied application, with his family, should enter a workhouse – should be supported there by a diet ample indeed in quantity, but from which the stimulations which habit had endeared to him were excluded – should be subjected to habits of cleanliness and order, be separated from his former associates, and debarred from his former amusements. (Senior, 1998e [1841], p. 30)

One proves one is destitute by trading, by accepting a wholesome life. In Senior's view, the New Poor Law provided the safety net of social insurance with the quid pro quo of "indoor relief" in exchange for strict sumptuary controls. In his review of Mill on intervention, Senior provided an additional example of exchange-oriented government policy:

> another exception is . . . [t]he observance of Sunday as a day of rest. . . . There is probably no institution so beneficial to the labouring classes; and they are aware of it. But without the assistance of law they would probably be unable to enforce it. In the few businesses in which Sunday trading is allowed, every shop is open. Though it would be beneficial to the whole body of druggists that every druggist's shop should be shut on Sunday, it is the immediate interest of every individual that his own shop should be open. And the result is that none are closed. (Senior, 1998f [1848], p. 338)

9.5   Abstract Economic Man

Classical economists put forward a doctrine of abstract economic man, an analytic egalitarianism that explains behavior in terms of incentives, luck, and history

(Smith, 1976, p. 28). Mill's famous *Essay* provides a defense of the method of abstraction (Blaug, 1980; Hausman, 1981). He maintains that the "assumed" hypotheses of political economy include a set of behavioral assumptions:

> Political economy does not treat of the whole of man's nature as modified by the social state, nor of the whole conduct of man in society. It is concerned with him solely as a being who desires to possess wealth, and who is capable of judging of the comparative efficacy of means for obtaining that end. . . . It makes entire abstraction of every human passion or motive; except those which may be regarded as perpetually antagonizing principles to the desire of wealth, namely, aversion to labour, and desire of the present enjoyment of costly indulgences. (Mill, 1967a, p. 321)

The wealth-maximization axiom is selected because it is "the main and acknowledged end" in "certain departments of human affairs" (p. 323). Perhaps more than any economist of his time or since, Mill was a synthesizer. But, for reasons of practicality in the face of multiple causation, he called for specialization in the social sciences (Hollander and Peart, 1999).

In his 1848 *Principles,* Mill outlined the implication of such a method: it implies a rejection of racial "explanations" of outcomes, which he condemned:

> Is it not, then, a bitter satire on the mode in which opinions are formed on the most important problems of human nature and life, to find public instructors of the greatest pretensions, imputing the backwardness of Irish industry, and the want of energy of the Irish people in improving their condition, to a peculiar indolence and *insouciance* in the Celtic race? Of all vulgar modes of escaping from the consideration of the effect of social and moral influences on the human mind, the most vulgar is that of attributing the diversities of conduct and character to inherent natural differences. (Mill, 1965, p. 319)

Mill's abstraction from race and his focus instead on property rights were sharply disputed in the decades that followed the publication of his *Essay*. W. R. Greg objected specifically to the abstract accounts of human beings put forward by classical economists on the grounds that they abstract from *race*:

> "Make them peasant-proprietors," says Mr. Mill. But Mr. Mill forgets that, till you change the character of the Irish cottier, peasant-proprietorship would work no miracles. He would fall behind the instalments of his purchase-money, and would be called upon to surrender his farm. He would often neglect it in idleness, ignorance, jollity and drink, get into debt, and have to sell his property to the newest owner of a great estate. . . . Mr. Mill never deigns to consider that an Irishman is an Irishman, and not an average human being – an idiomatic and idiosyncratic, not an abstract, man. (Greg, 1869, p. 78)

James Hunt, the influential owner of the *Anthropological Review,* also repeatedly attacked race-neutral accounts of human nature: "Mr. Mill, who will not admit that the Australian, the Andaman islander, and the Hottentot labour under any *inherent* incapacity for attaining the highest culture of ancient Greece or modern Europe!" (Hunt, 1866, p. 122; see Levy, 2001).

The Irish question raised the issue of whether the conclusions of political economy might be considered universally relevant or of limited applicability (Bagehot, 1876). In the latter half of the century, attacks on the nature and scope of economics focused on the relative roles of induction and deduction in economics, and on the legitimacy of studying economic phenomena separately from social phenomena (Peart, 2001, pp. 362–5). Mill's proposal for widespread land reform in Ireland as well as his 1870 review essay, *Leslie on the Land Question*, argued, in line with the historicists such as T. E. C. Leslie (1873) and J. K. Ingram (1878), that institutional differences in Ireland rendered the conclusions of political economy invalid there.

In response to such concerns, Jevons's recommendation went farther than Mill, calling for even more specialization, now *within* the discipline (1871, xvi–xvii). Jevons also insisted that mathematical methods be used in economic theory (Schabas, 1990), commencing his 1866 *Brief Account of a General Mathematical Theory of Political Economy* with a call to reduce the "main problem" of economics to "mathematical form" (1866, p. 282). Perhaps most significantly, Ireland provides a rare instance in which Jevons objected to Mill's policy recommendation (land tenure reform) (see Peart, 1990).

Thus, notwithstanding his own significant contributions to applied analysis (Black, 1981; Peart, 2002), Jevons succeeded in taking a methodological step toward narrowing economics, insulating economic analysis from institutional concerns (Peart, 2001). For an additional example, consider his comparison of Cairnes's opposition to slavery with his own neutrality: "Though I greatly admire 'Slave Power' as a piece of reasoning, I hardly go with you in your Northern Sympathies. I am strictly neutral" (correspondence, April 23, 1864; Jevons, 1972–81, vol. 3, p. 53).

9.6 Materialism and Sympathy: The Occupational Structure of Wages

This narrowing of the discipline also entailed the removal from economics of non-material concerns. It is a commonplace to read the utilitarian economists of our period as simple materialists, concerned only with the aggregate wealth produced by society. But recent scholars have distinguished utilitarians from Adam Smith, for whom the desire for approbation is foundational and for whom approbation is incommensurate with income. Smith's treatment of the desire for approbation carried by cultural norms extends to occupational choice. This begins one of the great set topics in our period: the explanation of occupational wage differences.

As noted above, Smith holds that people are physically the same. If all people are the same and labor markets are competitive, then wouldn't wages equalize across occupations? Indeed, Smith claims this is so when we take "wages" to reflect the net advantages to employments, including nonpecuniary considerations such as "the ease or hardship, the cleanliness or dirtiness, the honourableness or dishonourableness of the employment" (Smith, 1976, p. 117). Smith does *not* make the leap from the assertion that an occupation is useful to the assertion that the occupation is approved, and this is where the materialism reading fails.

In our period, Smith's results are accepted by a host of writers. Mountiford Longfield argued that Smith's conclusions follow from the assumption of *local* mobility:

> Increased profits of bricklayers, or the diminished gains of barristers, will not induce any person to become a bricklayer who would otherwise become a barrister. Neither will the diminished profits of bricklayers, to pursue the profession of the bar, and by his competition reduce the gains of the profession to their proper level. This may be the case, and yet the due proportion between the gains of those two professions, so remote from each other, may be preserved by means of the intermediate professions. These act as media of communication. (Longfield, 1834, pp. 84–5)

E. G. Wakefield called Smith's analysis "one of the most admired and admirable chapters," "free from error," and "complete" (Wakefield, in Smith, 1835, vol. 1, p. 328). As the consulting economist behind the New Poor Law, Senior had reflected carefully upon the impact of disapprobation on our choices. His 1836 *Outline* added texture to Smith's account (Senior, 1998d [1836], p. 201).

In 1852, in the first edition of the work following his exchange with Carlyle on slavery, Mill added to his analysis of this issue in the *Principles*. He remained committed to the doctrine as "tolerably successful" (Mill, 1965, p. 380). But he now alluded to the difference between theory and fact, and he sharpened his statement of noncompeting groups:

> But it is altogether a false view of the state of facts, to present this [inequality of remuneration] as the relation which generally exists between agreeable and dis- agreeable employments. The really exhausting and the really repulsive labours, instead of being better paid than others, are almost invariably paid the worst of all, because performed by those who have no choice. (Mill, 1965, p. 383)

The debate with Carlyle over the "Gospel of Labour" raised this point with a vengeance.

Since the analytic device of sympathy falls out of economic analysis as the transition to neoclassicism occurs, the question that arises is where does sympathy go? It enters into debates in evolutionary biology. In 1864, A. R. Wallace claimed that natural selection did not apply to humans because of sympathy, morality, and the division of labor (1864, p. clxii). Wallace's demonstration that natural selection stops at the edge of sympathy is the beginning of the eugenics movement. As Greg (1874) put it, sympathy blocked the "survival of the fittest," and therefore these sentiments ought to be suppressed.

9.7   Institutional Reform and Higher and Lower Pleasures

When we neglect the problem of institutional reform, we lose the context in which the analytic machinery of classical economics was developed. Mill's notorious statement of the difference between higher and lower pleasures in his 1861 *Utilitarianism* provides a case in point (Mill, 1969, p. 211). But the same idea first appears in the 1848 *Principles*. The context is not of Mill's making. Here is Senior's statement of the consequences of slavery on people's habits:

> [slavery] destroys all the nobler virtues, both moral and intellectual; that it leaves the slave without energy, without truth, without honesty, without industry, without providence; in short, without any of the qualities which fit men to be respected or even esteemed. But mischievous as slavery is, it has many plausible advantages, and freedom many apparent dangers. The subsistence of a slave is safe; he cannot suffer from insufficient wages, or from want of employment; he has not to save for sickness or old age; he has not to provide for his family; he cannot waste in drunkenness the wages by which they were to be supported; his idleness or dishonesty cannot reduce them to misery; they suffer neither from his faults nor his follies. (Senior, 1998e [1841], p. 2)

How do people make themselves into competent optimizers? Senior provides no answer.

Mill tackles the problem in the same context. Emancipation is justified by the increase in human happiness – the statement in response to Carlyle's 1849 proposal for reenslavement (Mill, 1850) is considerably sharper on this regard – not by any increase in material output. To civilize a man, one immerses him in material desires:

> To civilize a savage, he must be inspired with new wants and desires, even if not of a very elevated kind, provided that their gratification can be a motive to steady and regular bodily and mental exertion. If the negroes of Jamaica and Demerara, after their emancipation, had contented themselves, as it was predicted they would do, with the necessaries of life, and abandoned all labour beyond the little which in a tropical climate, with a thin population and abundance of the richest land, is sufficient to support existence, they would have sunk into a condition more barbarous, though less unhappy, than their previous state of slavery. (Mill, 1965, p. 104)

While these material desires might not be approved in Mill's society, they are critical steps in the development of the capacity for self-reliance:

> The motive which was most relied on for inducing them to work was their love of fine clothes and personal ornaments. No one will stand up for this taste as worthy of being cultivated, and in most societies its indulgence tends to impoverish rather than to enrich; but in the state of mind of the negroes it might have been the only incentive that could make them voluntarily undergo systematic labour, and so acquire or maintain habits of voluntary industry which may be converted to more valuable ends. (Mill, 1965, pp. 104–5)

If one can move to self-government entailing far-sighted concern for one's own interest, can one not take the additional step toward concern for others? Materialism is a only a step toward this end (Mill, 1965, p. 105).

Whether Mill succeeds or fails – authorities are divided (Jevons, 1879; Schumpeter, 1954; McPherson, 1982) – he points to a real difficulty in the transition between social states: habits that evolve for sensible reasons in one state might be counterproductive in another.

9.8   Classical Growth Theory

Mill integrates the problem of transformation from one set of institutions to another into the classical theory of growth and distribution. As a Ricardian, he holds that a tax on profits will slow growth and therefore be shared by the workers in terms of wage reduction (Mill, 1965, p. 827). His distinction between higher and lower wants enters into the analysis of growth in the first edition of *Principles*, when he looks forward to a stationary state entailing the cultivation of the Art of Living, and easing the labor burden upon the poor (Mill, 1965, p, 756). But just as "lower" wants help educate freed slaves to discipline themselves, so too the "trampling, crushing, elbowing, and treading on each other's heels, which form the existing type of social life" may play a vital role in the development of a society's norms. This is the lesson that Mill draws from the American Civil War (Mill, 1965, p. 754). For Mill, higher aspirations encompass a willingness to sacrifice for the happiness of others. This would hardly surprise the moralist, Adam Smith, who begins the classical period of British economics (Smith, 1976, p. 9).

9.9   The Popularizers: Martineau on Slavery

While this was a period of sustained challenge to classical economics, it was also a period of great popularizers of political economy. It is, however, a disservice to view Harriet Martineau as merely a re-teller of the stories of economics. We consider her work for the same reason that Stigler (1949) chose to illustrate the best of classical economics with Senior on the handloom weavers: practical problems tended to bring out their best work. For Martineau and her peers, the question of great import was how the institution of slavery mattered. We point to two nice pieces of analysis.

9.9.1   Harem economics

In her 1830s visit to America, Martineau found compelling evidence against paternalistic accounts of slavery: fathers do not use their daughters sexually. As a Malthusian, Martineau attended to the tradeoff between sex and material income. She found in America an instance in which a man can have more of both sex and material income by acquiring additional families, only one of which will be white:

> Every man who resides on his plantation may have his harem, and has every inducement of custom, and of pecuniary gain,* to tempt him to the common practice.

*[The law declares that the children of slaves are to follow the fortunes of the mother. Hence the practice of planters selling and bequeathing their own children. – Martineau] (Martineau, 1837, vol. 2, p. 223)

Martineau is responding here to the slavery apologists' claim that the morality of slavery can be judged by the relative infrequency of prostitution in Southern cities (Martineau, 1837, vol. 2, p. 325). So it can, she argues, but not in the way the slavery apologists thought. The relative infrequency of prostitution in slave cities provides evidence that slaves were used sexually in sufficient numbers to affect the market demand for prostitution.

9.9.2   Market slavery

In her novel *Demerara* (1832), Martineau introduces a character, Alfred, who seems to have studied political economy in Britain and who persuades his father to try something Smithian:

> "Task-work with wages," said Alfred, pointing to his own gang; "eternal labor, without wages," pointing to the other. "It is not often that we have an example of the two systems before our eyes at the same moment. I need not put it to you which plan works the best." (Martineau, 1832–4, vol. 2, pp. 70–1)

In America, the task work that she saw worried her. Is an efficient slavery good (1837, vol. 2, pp. 157–8)?

9.10   To What are Multiple Equilibria a Challenge?

It is commonly held that the most famous single challenge to classical economics in this period came in the form of an attack on classical wage theory launched by William Thomas Thornton in 1869. Thornton begins with the now-famous denunciation of the notion of supply and demand. He considers two methods of auction: one that starts high and moves down; another that starts low and moves up. Why, he asks, do we believe that the results from the two methods of auction will always be the same (1869, pp. 47–8)? The question was particularly important in the light of the classical doctrine of the importance of the status quo: if the only difference is where we begin the auction, and Thornton is correct that this affects the resulting price, then the status quo matters.

Was Thornton's challenge really a difficulty for classical economics? Two important classical economists responded to his argument. John Stuart Mill's judgment was that Thornton had identified the possibility of multiple equilibria, a nice addition to the standard doctrine:

> [Mr. Thornton] has proved that the law of equalisation of supply and demand is not the whole theory of the particular case. He has not proved that the law is not strictly conformed to in that case. In order to show that the equalisation is not the law of price, what he has really shown is that the law is, in this particular case, consistent

with two different prices, and is equally and completely fulfilled by either of them. The demand and supply are equal at twenty shillings, and equal also at eighteen shillings. The conclusion ought to be, not that the law is false, for Mr. Thornton does not deny that in the case in question it is fulfilled; but only, that it is not the entire law of the phenomenon. (Mill, 1967b, p. 637)

John Elliott Cairnes was more emphatic in endorsing Thornton's "solution" to the problem of the determination of price (1874, p. 110). Thus, two classical economists of high regard considered the possibility of multiple equilibria with considerable composure.

But it would not be long before Thornton's case would be challenged, and the importance of the status quo would be dismissed. Fleeming Jenkin begins his 1870 article with a methodological attack. Like Jevons, he traced the difficulties of the recent debates to insufficient mathematical machinery (1887 [1870], vol. 2, p. 76). After explaining how demand and supply curves can be used to describe choice, Jenkin considers Thornton's example:

In a Dutch auction buyers are as likely at first tentatively to let the seller offer below the market price as to close with him above that price.

In an English auction, buyers are as likely to first to run up above the market price as to stop bidding below it. . . .

The device by which Mr. Thornton has made it appear that in a Dutch and English auction there might be two market prices, is to assume that the demand at prices in the neighbourhood of the market price is constant at all prices; that the same number, and no more, fish would be bought at 18s. as at 20s. In this case the demand curve becomes horizontal near the market price; and as the supply curve is also horizontal, the market price is indeterminate. This case is not peculiar to any form of bargain, but represents an unusual state of mind. (Jenkin, 1887 [1870], vol. 2, pp. 84–5)

Jenkin's conclusion – that Thornton assumes "an unusual state of mind" – is the basis of Stigler's (1954) judgment that Thornton depends upon a "bizarre" demand curve.

Jenkin has transformed a difficult probabilistic problem – What are the other bidders going to do? – into a demand curve in which probabilistic elements have vanished. He does not allow for the possibility that bidders form different beliefs in the different institutional setting, since, if this happens, there is no reason to predict that bidders will behave the same way in the two types of auction. For Jenkin's argument, and the neoclassical arguments to come, Thornton's counter-example had to be dispatched.

Neoclassical economics thus begins with the claim, *contra* Thornton and the classical consensus, that the status quo does not matter. The question of the English and Dutch auction has since become a staple of the experimental economics literature, and the answer is in. The classics were right: the method of auction matters. This difference can be routinely replicated (V. Smith, 1982, pp. 943–4). Thus, in the context of the attack on classical theory, we find an additional, and misguided, case of denial of the significance of institutions.

9.11 Conclusion: Trapped in the Status Quo

We have applied the classical insight that the status quo is important to our reading of the classics. From *our* status quo, in which racial explanations are anathema, we see nothing unusual in the classical doctrine that racial explanations are the height of "vulgarity," as John Stuart Mill put it. Philosophers who radically move the status quo tend to seem commonplace when viewed from the status quo of their creation. But this supposition of unoriginality cannot survive immersion in the context of mid-nineteenth-century controversy: what one does not read can matter for what one does read. Thus, we hold that all texts are connected, and the history of economics ought to be a general equilibrium procedure.

Opponents of classical economics held that some races (blacks and the Irish) were child-like and thus ill equipped to make decisions on their own behalf. Such races required the benevolent master to guide their actions. The linchpin of the classical economists' opposition to both slavery and paternalism was their presumption of human competence which disallows masters, whether they own, rule, or look after their inferiors in a kindly fashion. For, supposing that the social world is composed of equally competent optimizers, there is no group that needs looking after and no group that can do the looking after. In post-Ricardian economics, there are no victims with whom to empathize: trades are voluntary and mutually beneficial.

This world without victims is surely what gives classical economics its reputation for hard-heartedness. By contrast, the great charm of paternalistic accounts is the compassion that they allow for the victims of voluntary transactions. And the temptation is to construct a class of victimizers ("parasites" is the term of choice in the literature of the time) who optimize all too well for their own interest (Levy and Peart, 2001–2). In the period that follows, social scientists succumbed to this temptation: eugenicists argued that society had the right to curtail breeding by such parasites, the "unfit" (Peart and Levy, 2003).

Note

We thank the editors of the volume for comments that led to significant improvements.

Bibliography

Bagehot, W. 1876: The postulates of political economy. *Fortnightly Review*, 21 o.s. (15 n.s.) (1), 215–42.

Black, R. D. C. 1981: William Stanley Jevons 1835–82. In D. P. O'Brien and J. R. Presley (eds.), *Pioneers of Modern Economics*. London: Macmillan, 1–35.

Blaug, M. 1980: *The Methodology of Economics, or How Economists Explain*. Cambridge, UK: Cambridge University Press.

Cairnes, J. E. 1874: *Some Leading Principles of Political Economy Newly Expounded*. London: Macmillan.

[Carlyle, T.] 1849: Occasional discourse on the Negro Question. *Fraser's Magazine for Town and Country*, 40, 670–9.

Carlyle, T. 1987: *Sartor Resartus*, ed. K. McSweeney and P. Sabor. Oxford: Oxford University Press.

Curtis, L. P. Jr. 1997: *Apes and Angels: The Irishman in Victorian Caricature*, rev. edn. Washington, DC: Smithsonian Institution Press.

Denman, Lord 1853: *Uncle Tom's Cabin, Bleak House, Slavery and Slave Trade*, 2nd edn. London: Longman, Brown, Green and Longmans.

Forget, E. L. and Peart, S. J. 2001: *Reflections on the Classical Canon in Economics: Essays in Honor of Samuel Hollander*. London: Routledge.

[Greg, W. R.] 1869: Realities of Irish life. *Quarterly Review*, 126, 61–80.

Greg, W. R. 1874: *Enigmas of Life*. Boston: J. R. Osgood.

Hausman, D. M. 1981: J. S. Mill's philosophy of economics. *Philosophy of Science*, 48(3), 363–85.

Hollander, S. 2001: Classical economics: a reification wrapped in an anachronism? In Forget and Peart, op. cit., 7–26.

—— and Peart, S. J. 1999: John Stuart Mill's method in principle and in practice. *Journal of the History of Economic Thought*, 21(4), 369–97.

Hunt, J. 1866: Race in legislation and political economy. *The Anthropological Review*, 4, 113–35.

Ingram, J. K. 1878: Address of the President of Section F of the British Association. *Journal of the Royal Statistical Society*, 41, 602–29.

Jenkin, F. 1887 [1870]: *Papers, Literary, Scientific, &c.* London: Longmans, Green and Co.

Jevons, W. S. 1866: Brief account of a general mathematical theory of political economy. *Journal of the Royal Statistical Society*, xxix, 282–7.

—— 1879: John Stuart Mill's philosophy tested. iv. Utilitarianism. *Contemporary Review*, 36, 521–38.

—— 1909 [1871]: *Theory of Political Economy*, 4th edn., ed. H. S. Jevons. London: Macmillan.

—— 1972–81. *Papers and Correspondence of William Stanley Jevons*, ed. R. D. C. Black. London: Macmillan.

Knight, F. H. 1935: The Ricardian theory of production and distribution. *Canadian Journal of Economics and Political Science*, 1, 3–25.

Leslie, T. E. C. 1873: Economic science and statistics. *Athenaeum*, September 27. Reprinted in *Essays in Political and Moral Philosophy*. Dublin: Hodges, Foster, and Figgis, 1879.

Levy, D. M. 1976: Ricardo and the Iron Law: a correction of the record. *History of Political Economy*, 8(2), 235–51.

—— 2001: *How the Dismal Science Got Its Name: Classical Economics and the Ur-Text of Racial Politics*. Ann Arbor, MI: University of Michigan Press.

—— and Peart, S. J. 2001–2: Secret history of the dismal science. Accessed at http://www.econlib.org

Longfield, M. 1834: *Lectures on Political Economy*. In R. D. C. Black (ed.), *The Economic Writings of Mountifort Longfield*. New York: Augustus M. Kelley, 1971.

Martineau, H. 1832–4: *Illustrations of Political Economy*. London: Charles Fox.

—— 1837: *Society in America*. London: Saunders and Otley.

McPherson, M. S. 1982: Mill's moral theory and the problem of preference change. *Ethics*, 92, 252–73.

[Mill, J. S.] 1850: The Negro Question. *Fraser's Magazine for Town and Country*, 41, 25–31.

Mill, J. S. 1965 [1848]: *The Principles of Political Economy with Some of Their Applications to Social Philosophy*. Robson, *Collected Works*, op. cit., vol. 2.

—— 1967a [1836]: On the definition of political economy; and on the method of investigation proper to it. In Robson, *Collected Works*, op. cit., vol. 4, *Essays on Economics and Society*, 1: *1824–1845*.

—— 1967b [1869]: Thornton on labour and its claims. In Robson, *Collected Works*, op. cit., vol. 5, *Essays on Economics and Society, 2: 1850–1879*, pp. 633–68.

—— 1967c [1870]: Leslie on the land question. In Robson, *Collected Works*, op. cit., vol. 5, *Essays on Economics and Society, 2: 1850–1879*, pp. 671–85.

—— 1969 [1861]: Utilitarianism. In Robson, *Collected Works*, op. cit., vol. 10, *Essays on Ethics, Religion and Society*, pp. 203–59.

Peart, S. J. 1990: Jevons's applications of utilitarian theory to economic policy. *Utilitas*, 2(2), 281–306.

—— 2001: Theory, application and the canon: the case of Mill and Jevons. In Forget and Peart, op. cit., 356–77.

—— 2002: "Facts carefully marshalled" in the empirical studies of William Stanley Jevons. In J. L. Klein and M. S. Morgan (eds.), *The Age of Economic Measurement*. Annual Supplement to *History of Political Economy*, 33. Durham, NC: Duke University Press, 252–76.

—— and Levy, D. M. 2003: "Not an average human being": how economics succumbed to racial accounts of economic man. In D. Colander, R. Prasch, and F. Sheth (eds.), *Race, Liberalism and Economics*. Ann Arbor, MI: University of Michigan Press, forthcoming.

Persky, J. 1990: Retrospectives: a dismal romantic. *The Journal of Economic Perspectives*, 4, 165–72.

Robson, J. M. (ed.) 1963– : *Collected Works of John Stuart Mill*. Toronto: University of Toronto Press.

—— 1968: *The Improvement of Mankind: The Social and Political Thought of John Stuart Mill*. Toronto: University of Toronto Press.

Rutherford, D. (ed.) 1998: *Collected Works of Nassau William Senior*, 3 vols. Bristol, UK: Theommes Press.

Schabas, M. 1990: *A World Ruled by Number: William Stanley Jevons and the Rise of Mathematical Economics*. Princeton, NJ: Princeton University Press.

Schumpeter, J. A. 1954: *History of Economic Analysis*. New York: Oxford University Press.

Semmel, B. 1962: *The Governor Eyre Controversy*. London: MacGibbon & Kee.

Senior, N. W. 1998a [1828]: Three lectures on the transmission of precious metals. In Rutherford, op. cit., vol. 2, *Money*.

Senior, N. W. 1998b [1829]: Two lectures on population. In Rutherford, op. cit., vol. 3, *Population and the Poor Laws*.

Senior, N. W. 1998c [1830]: Three lectures on the cost of obtaining money. In Rutherford, op. cit., vol. 2, *Money*.

Senior, N. W. 1998d [1836]: An outline of the science of political economy. In Rutherford, op. cit., vol. 1, *Political Economy*.

Senior, N. W. 1998e [1841]: Poor Law reform. In Rutherford, op. cit., vol. 3, *Population and the Poor Laws*.

Senior, N. W. 1998f [1848]: J. S. Mill on political economy. In Rutherford, op. cit., vol. 1, *Political Economy*.

Smith, A. 1835 [1776]: *An Inquiry into the Nature and Cause of the Wealth of Nations*, ed. E. G. Wakefield. London: Charles Knight and Co.

—— 1976 [1776]: *An Inquiry into the Nature and Causes of the Wealth of Nations*, ed. W. B. Todd. Oxford: The Clarendon Press.

Smith, V. 1982: Microeconomic systems as an experimental science. *The American Economic Review*, 75, 923–95.

Stigler, G. J. 1949: *Five Lectures on Economic Problems*. London: Longmans, Green.

—— 1954: The early history of empirical studies of consumer behavior. *The Journal of Political Economy*, 62, 95–113.

Thornton, W. T. 1869: *On Labour, Its Wrongful Claims and Rightful Dues, Its Actual Present and Possible Future*. London: Macmillan.

Wallace, A. R. 1864: The origin of human races and the antiquity of man deduced from the theory of "natural selection." *Journal of the Anthropology Society*, 2, clviii–clxx.

Whately, R. 1831: *Introductory Lectures on Political Economy*. London: B. Fellowes.

—— 1832: *Introductory Lectures on Political Economy*, 2nd edn. London: B. Fellowes.

—— 1833: *Easy Lessons on Money Matters; For the Use of Young People*. London: John W. Parker.

Winch, D. 1972: Marginalism and the boundaries of economic science. *History of Political Economy*, 4(2), 325–43.

CHAPTER TEN

Karl Marx: His Work and the Major Changes in its Interpretation

Geert Reuten

10.1 INTRODUCTION

Karl Marx is known for a 30-page political pamphlet, *The Communist Manifesto*, written in 1848 together with Friedrich Engels, and for a 2,200-page socio-economic work, *Capital*, published in three volumes in 1867, 1885, and 1894, the last two edited by Engels. The collected works of Marx and Engels extend to over 50 thick volumes.

Marx's *magnum opus*, *Capital*, is an analysis of the capitalist system (the term "communism" is mentioned some five times in notes; perhaps five out of 2,200 pages refer in passing to some future society). Marx wrote the work between 1857 and 1878 while living in London. British capitalism provided his main empirical material.

The changing appreciation of *Capital* throughout the twentieth century was influenced by both the degree to which other works of Marx were, or could be, taken into account (section 10.3) and, relatedly, developing methodological views (section 10.4). A reading of the work (section 10.5) is bound to take methodological sides.

10.2 ON MARX AND HIS *CAPITAL*

Marx was born in 1818 in Trier and died in 1883 in London. He studied law and philosophy and received a Ph.D. in 1841. Trained to pursue the positions of either a state official or university professor, both his studies and the repressive political climate in Prussia induced a different course. During his student years he helped fight for democratic rights, opposing the vested political regime. His subsequent writings and editorship of a liberal journal brought him into conflict with Prussian censorship. He sought refuge in Paris (1843–5), Brussels (1845–7), and Cologne (1848–9) and finally, in 1849, settled in London.

In the hectic 1842–9 period, Marx studied and wrote on philosophical, political, and economic issues, and developed his materialist conception of history (section 10.4.1). He also made contact with radical socialist groups, and met Friedrich Engels, his lifelong personal, political, and intellectual friend. In 1848, aged 30, he and Engels wrote the *Manifest der Kommunistischen Partei*.

From 1849 to about 1865, Marx reduced his political activities and concentrated on serious analysis of the capitalist system, combining research with journalistic work to earn his living. Many thousands of pages were drafted for his *magnum opus* in a creative and highly productive period. At the same time, he and his family lived in poverty. Income from Marx's journalistic work was scarce; to survive they relied on gifts from relatives and friends, especially Engels.

Marx's research plans were extremely ambitious. He aimed to write a complete systematic analysis of society: economic, social, political, and historical. By 1858 he planned to write six books. The first of these came to completely occupy his mind and energies. It grew to the three volumes of *Capital* that we now have, together with a sequel account of political economic theories (another three volumes). Marx brought to press himself only the first volume of *Capital* (1867).

After its 1867 publication, Marx continually revised volume I, especially its key value-theoretical Part 1 (the volumes are organized into parts). A second German edition dates from 1873 and a French, in installments, from 1872–5. This process of revision should be kept in mind for those who seek consistency between volume I and the manuscripts for volume III, composed in 1864–5.

In the years 1865–70 and 1877–8, Marx wrote much of volume II of *Capital*, without completing it. He had gotten re-involved in political activities, but his health also seriously deteriorated. As we will see below, Marx's *Capital* project employs a demanding systematic methodology. Toward the end of his life, the requirements for the organization of the work grew beyond his fading energy.

After Marx's death, the two remaining volumes of *Capital* were edited from Marx's drafts and notebooks by Engels (1885, 1894) and the sequel by Kautsky (1905–10). The drafts are in varied states of completion – the second half of both volumes II and III consists of reorganized notebooks – and the editors inevitably had their impact on the result. In fact, Marx had considered them unfit for publication.

Table 10.1 "Many Marxes": dates of publication of some major works

	1 First publication in German	2 Years 1–3	3 First English translation	4 Date of manuscript	5 Years 1–4 Ms–Ger.	6 Years 3–4 Ms–Engl.
1867	Das Kapital I	19	Capital I	1861, 1863, 1865–7[a]	0	19
1885	Das Kapital II	22	Capital II	1865–70, 1877–8	7	29
1894	Das Kapital III	15	Capital III	1864–5	29	44
1905–10	Theorien über den Mehrwert (3 vols.)	48–61	Theories of Surplus Value[b]	1862–3	47	108
1932	Pariser Manuskripte	31	Economic–Philosophical Manuscripts	1844	88	119
1932	Die deutsche Ideologie[c]	6	The German Ideology (Parts I and III)	1845–6	86	92
1953	Grundrisse[d]	20	Grundrisse[e]	1857–8	95	115
1992	Ökonomische Manuskripte 1863–7 (including the Capital III manuscripts)	–	–	1863–7	125–9	–

[a]Work on second German edition, 1867–72; and on French edition, 1872–5.
[b]First volume 1952, A History of Economic Theories; extracts 1951.
[c]Extracts 1902–3, 1921, and 1927.
[d]Earlier scarcely available edition, 1939–41; its Introduction was published in 1903.
[e]Extracts 1964 and 1971.

10.3 THE MANY MARXES, THE MANY *CAPITALS*

Developing historiographic views, as well as developing Marx scholarship, have affected the interpretation of Marx's *Capital* (section 10.4). This is no different from other authors. However, in the case of Marx especially, an additional factor is important: the time lags between the posthumous publications of his writings – as well as their translations into (for example) English. Table 10.1 provides examples.

A 27-year lag between the publication of volumes I and III meant that *Capital I* had a life of its own. In 1932 (1938 and 1963 in English), two works of Marx were published that shed new light on his views on money and the capitalist labor process. In 1953 (1973 in English) the *Grundrisse*, an early 800-page draft of *Capital* in dialectical style, was published, shedding new light on both the method and content of *Capital*. Even in the 1990s important new manuscripts were published, and others are still forthcoming. The result is that throughout the twentieth century, and continuing to the present day, there have been many Marxes and many *Capital*s.

It is illusory to think that new textual "evidence" changes views overnight, especially for path-breaking publications. The 1953/1973 publication of the *Grundrisse* has only had a major impact since the mid-1980s. Keynes, himself author of the path-breaking publication *The General Theory*, explained the reason in its Preface: "The difficulty lies, not in the new ideas, but in escaping from the old ones. . . ."

The early appreciation of the 1894 (English, 1909) *Capital* volume III, or even the 1867 (English, 1886) volume I of *Capital*, has shaped the interpretation of Marx in all standard histories of thought, in both the first half of the twentieth century and since. As difficult as it is to write a history, it is much harder to revise a history that has become part of the received view. Whatever textual "evidence" arises, a range of interpretations – perhaps a moving range – will likely ensue.

Table 10.1 requires a general historiographic note. Columns 1–3, ordered according to dates of publication, are its core. The order of publications – impact – is relevant for a general history of thought. A history of the intellectual development of Karl Marx, or of the "making" of *Capital*, requires an historical ordering by manuscripts dates (column 4). These are very different historiographic perspectives. (For the latter perspective, the making of *Capital*, Oakley's succinct 1983 book is very informative, even if at the time he lacked full information about Engels's editorial work.)

10.4 INTERPRETATIONS OF MARX'S METHOD IN *CAPITAL*

Interpretations of Marx's *Capital* are intimately related to interpretations of his method, of which five major aspects are examined below. Some version of the first, historical materialism (section 10.4.1), was shared by most commentators until around 1970. The interpretation of Marx's method in the following period is more complex. Subsequent subsections – roughly in historical order – add in these further complications, in each case building on the methodological aspect of the previous subsection.

10.4.1   Historical materialism

Marx embraced, and was the originator of, a materialist conception of history (often called "historical materialism" – the label is not Marx's). Analytically and institutionally, any society can be seen as a number of domains: political and legal, cultural including education, and economic. For Marx, the development of the economic domain (the "relations of production") is key to the development of a society at large (a "social formation," such as a feudal or a bourgeois/capitalist society). What happens in the "superstructure" – the juridico-political and cultural domains – is understood in terms of the "base structure" – the economic relations and their requirements. Two aspects are fundamental to the economic relations themselves: first, the relationship between (a) the social layer or class that does the actual work and (b) the layer or class that has the power to live off the surplus produced by the former, and that usually also possesses the means of production that the former works upon; and, secondly, the "forces of production," the amalgamation of the labor process in relation to technology (the latter understood in grand, epochal terms).

This schema is especially significant in analyzing *changes* in structures and their aspects, particularly their dynamic interaction during uneven development. "Grand" history can be seen in terms of revolutionary transitions – "restructuring" into more fitting aspects. (Note that especially in the first half of the twentieth century this schema was often interpreted monocausally, running from the forces of production, instead of as a dialectic between all structures and aspects.)

Marx developed these ideas when he was aged 25–30. They can be seen clearly in the *Manifesto*. One plausible reading of *Capital*, or one dimension of it, is as an analysis of the economic base structure of capitalism. Note, though, that the work does not contain an explicit analysis of social class (except for an unfinished "chapter" – just over one page long – on classes at the end of volume III of *Capital*, the term "class" is hardly ever used in *Capital*). Furthermore, even if there are a few – very few – mostly speculative references to transitional elements within capitalism, transition is not what the work is about.

10.4.2   Critique

Especially important in reading *Capital* is the methodology that Marx developed alongside his materialist conception of history, namely his method of "critique" – largely acquired from Hegel (post Kant – cf., Benhabib, 1986). Almost all of Marx's works carry the term "*Critique*" [*Kritik*], which is distinguishable from "criticism." The latter adopts a normative *external* criterion (ethical, aesthetic, or methodological) to evaluate society or such social products as artistic and scientific endeavors. The method of *critique* evaluates society and social products on the basis of the norms and standards of the object of inquiry itself. An object of inquiry is analyzed *from within itself*. Its norms and standards are taken to their logical conclusions, detecting possible inconsistencies and contradictions – as when capitalist business both lauds "market competition" and seeks to eliminate competitors and achieve monopolistic positions.

In *Capital* Marx addresses both a material ontological constellation and ideas about it. When the original title, *Das Kapital; Kritik der politischen Ökonomie*, is translated as *Capital; A Critique of Political Economy* (Penguin editions), the double meaning of the German is lost. The English translation correctly indicates that the work is a critique of a science, but omits that the work is as much – in my view, in the first place – an internal critique of "the political economy," an ontological constellation.

Marx scholars today accept "internal critique" as a major aspect of Marx's method in *Capital*. However, controversies remain over the method and content of *Capital*, since other aspects are not necessarily ruled out. For example, is "Marx's" "labor theory of value" (he never used the expression) still an external norm, or is the concept of value adopted from the object of inquiry? (See further section 10.4.4.)

10.4.3 Naturalistic versus socio-historical concepts

Marx simultaneously historicizes social and economic concepts – the critique is an historicized critique. Social self-understanding usually takes the current social constellation and its concepts for granted, as "natural," or as the norm ("ethnocentrism"). They are then used to evaluate history or other contemporary societies. (For example, some Americans deploy *their* notions of "market," "competition," "economic freedom," and "political democracy" to evaluate other societies.) Marx identified the "mainstream" political economy of his time as that body of self-understanding in Great Britain and France of 1850 set in ahistorical or *naturalistic* terms (cf., Mattick, 1986).

From this perspective, Marx sometimes distinguished a trans-historical, or general-material, denotation of concepts – "goods" and "work" – from their historical, in this case capitalist, counterpart – "commodities" and "labor" (Arthur, 1986; Murray, 1988). His aim was not to construct a second language, but to show that in the social domain naturalistic entities do not exist. No trans-historical "human needs," "utility," "wealth," "goods," "work," or "technology" exist; they are always "defined" and "subsumed" within a socio-historical constellation (on human needs, see Campbell, 1993; and on wealth and on subsumption generally, Murray, 2000, 2002). Whereas J. S. Mill historicizes "the laws of distribution" – still eternalizing/naturalizing "the laws of production" – Marx is a complete de-naturalizer. Anything human is set in an historically specific *social form*.

10.4.4 Value-form theory

The view that Marx's *critique* is an historicized critique, and that everything human takes on an historically specific *social form* (section 10.4.3), is highlighted in the recent "form theoretic" interpretation, for which *Capital* is an exposition of the capitalist social form "value" [early proponents are Eldred and Hanlon (1981) and Eldred et al. (1982–5), who build on work by Backhaus (1969); Rubin (1972 [1923]) is an important rediscovered precursor].

The general methodological idea of "form theory" (springing from Aristotle and Hegel – cf., Murray, 1997) is that "content" and "form" necessarily go together (for both natural–physical objects and anything created by human beings). "Form" is of the essence of content, just as much as form cannot exist without content. Any actual social formation requires an historically specific form of production and distribution (e.g., tradition, power, democratic decision-making), the capitalist form being *value as expressed in monetary dimension*. But isn't it the case that things – sugar, cigar, or car – already have a content and form? True. In fact, it is "truer" than the question purports. They surely have a physical form, but from Marx's viewpoint they necessarily also have a social form that can be *distinguished* but not *separated* from their physical being. In capitalist economies things are not merely exchanged in markets in terms of value, but are *produced as* values, which affects how things are qualitatively.

In a traditional interpretation of *Capital*, Marx introduces in its first chapters a "labor theory of value" – building on the classical political economy of Smith and especially Ricardo – "value" being a naturalistic concept, reckoned in a labor-time dimension. In this interpretation, Marx presents a "*positive*" theory of value. Hence the *materialist internal critique* aspect of Marx method must, for this part of *Capital* at least, be de-emphasized (note that the "labor-time theory" interpretation antedates the *critique* interpretation). For this traditional interpretation, later parts of *Capital* set out how concrete market phenomena can be "reconciled" with this "positive" theory.

For *value-form theory*, this first part of *Capital* is a key *materialist critique* text. When commodities are *produced* for sale – a specific characteristic of capitalism – the concrete, utility-producing character of labor is completely secondary to the producer; labor matters to the extent that it is value-producing "abstract labor," a mere expenditure of time. This same text also shows how value (the abstract time facet of labor) is necessarily expressed in abstract monetary terms – and in monetary terms *only*. Later parts of *Capital* set out even more complex forms, culminating in the *profit form* of value, in which things are not merely produced as values, but specifically according to the measure and success-norm of capital: profit and the rate of profit.

How can we appraise these two opposing interpretations? To any reader of *Capital* it will be obvious that for Marx value is not simply determined by labor time. The discussions of changing productivity and intensity of labor throughout volume I problematize such a notion. Nevertheless, Marx often uses the simplified notion as an analytic reference point. Thus whereas Marx's value-form theory is a fundamental break from classical political economy, he maintains remnants of a Ricardian labor-time theory of value (Backhaus, 1969).

I think that the "labor-time theory of value" interpretation cannot be maintained because too many texts are inconsistent with it. The same applies, however, to a comprehensive monetary value-form interpretation. There are two lines of reasoning within *Capital*. Marx shares the fate of those who made a fundamental break (a *césure*), or a paradigm shift, from past conceptions. New conceptions must be formulated in the inherited language. Initial breaks must be partial, inconsistent, or flawed, and need to be completed by researchers following up the break. This however, does not make the partial break less of an accomplishment (Reuten, 1993; for a different view, see Murray, 2000).

10.4.5   Systematic Dialectics

Also controversial is a final methodological interpretation, that arose in the mid-1980s, which views *Capital* as Systematic Dialectics. Historical Dialectics describes the evolution and succession of distinct social formations; Systematic Dialectics theorizes about one particular social formation, such as the capitalist system, setting out the whole of its object of inquiry as a completely *endogenous* system, or at least its necessary components and processes.

A major impetus for this interpretation was the 1953/1973 publication of Marx's *Grundrisse*, a rough draft of *Capital* that was, as mentioned in section 10.3, more so than *Capital* written in a dialectical style. As indicated, a publication, such as the *Grundrisse* in this case, will not change inherited interpretations overnight. A second impetus was the dedication by a number of scholars (some stimulated by the *Grundrisse* reading) to the study of the Hegel–Marx connection (cf., Burns and Fraser, 2000). As the studies of Marx's *Grundrisse* and Hegel's Systematic Dialectical works converged, the new interpretation of *Capital* gradually emerged. [For beginnings, see Banaji (1979), Arthur (1986), and Murray (1988). A comprehensive Systematic Dialectical interpretation is Smith (1990; cf., his 1993a,b). See Mattick (1993) for critique of the interpretation. For general accounts of the methodology of Systematic Dialectics, not necessarily related to *Capital*, see Reuten and Williams (1989, pp. 3–36), Arthur (1998), and Reuten (2000).]

A Systematic Dialectic operates on several conceptual levels, from abstract and simple to concrete and complex. Its starting point is also an entry into its whole object of inquiry, formulating that whole both abstractly and simply. Gradual concretion and increasing complexity are achieved at subsequent levels of abstraction; at a final level of "abstraction," the complexity of concrete empirical reality should be attained.

An un-theorized, or naive, empirical reality is the beginning of research. From that, after a complex and creative investigation, the initial highest level of abstraction is reached – the starting point of the systematic presentation (indicated in the previous paragraph). Thus empirical reality (at first naive, in the end systematically theorized) is both the beginning and the end of the research. A rough outline of this process from the empirical to the abstract to the concrete is found in one of Marx's few methodological texts (Marx, 1903).

Marx identifies neither these levels of abstraction in *Capital* nor how to get from one level to the next. So this must all be inferred in this interpretation of *Capital*.

The grand systematic of *Capital* is in terms of its three volumes: (I) "The production of capital" (from the commodity to money to capital, and from the production of capital through surplus value to the accumulation of capital); (II) "The circulation, or, the organic interconnections of capital"; and (III) "The destination and concrete shapes of capital" (profit and the rate of profit, and competition and the distribution of the fruits of capital into profits of enterprise, interest and rent). The three volumes are each made up of parts, which provide more detailed levels of abstraction.

Levels of abstraction are conceptual terrains. In dialectics, concepts are not fixed – as in conventional "linear logic" (cf., Arthur, 1997) – but manifest ongoing *conceptual progress* from one level of abstraction to another. An axiomatic translation of one level into another is inconsistent with the methodology. In general, when a level of abstraction insufficiently captures the whole, the process is driven forward. Capturing the whole means formulating "a system" that can, in principle, reproduce itself endogenously. At each operating level of abstraction, the "discovery" of its endogeneity limits pushes the process to a new, richer, more complex level. Such a level is institutionally more complex and requires new categories and concepts. With it come both a reconceptualization and the concretion of the conclusions of earlier levels of abstraction.

To *some* extent, the method may be envisioned as one of successive approximation (Sweezy, 1968 [1942]) – but only with the *major* proviso precluding fixed definitions (they only apply at their own level of abstraction). Indeed, a *recurrent reconceptualization* occurs. A succinct example comes from Marx's *Results* (1933, p. 969), when he contemplates volume I of *Capital*:

> Originally, we considered the *individual commodity in isolation*, as the direct product of a specific quantity of labour. Now, as the *result*, the *product of capital*, the commodity changes in form (and later on, in the price of production, it will be changed in *substance* too).

Earlier he had written (p. 954):

> The commodity may *now* be *further* defined as follows: . . . The labour expended on each commodity can no longer be calculated except as an average, i.e. an ideal estimate. . . . When determining the price of an individual article it appears as a merely ideal fraction of the total product in which the capital reproduces itself.

The manuscripts for the final versions of the three volumes of *Capital* that we have are dated in "odd" order (table 10.1). Inasmuch as Marx reworked and reconceptualized his manuscripts for volume I, this would have affected the re-study of the levels of abstraction in volumes II and III. The three volumes of *Capital* are not only in different states of draft (ranging from mere notes to final versions) but, more important for a Systematic Dialectic, in different states of conception. It is thus especially important to remember, for a Systematic Dialectical interpretation of *Capital*, that its last two volumes cannot be seen as conceptually final.

10.4.6   Conclusions

By the year 2000, Marx scholars had largely agreed that *Capital* analyzes its object of enquiry from within, aiming to drive *the object's* (capital's) own standards and processes to their logical conclusions. Marx's method of critique is largely an historicized critique. Whether it is a totally historicized critique – as highlighted in the value-form interpretation – is disputed. While most Marx scholars also agree that some type of conceptual development, or at least "successive approximation," exists in *Capital*, whether it is as rigorous as the Systematic Dialectical interpretation claims is disputed.

All of these different overall interpretations of *Capital* can find confirmations in Marx's texts. However, there is increasing evidence, from section 10.4.1 to section 10.4.5, falsifying each successive position. We might thus say that *Capital* is a rich heuristic source of a variety of different reconstructive theoretical approaches.

10.5   A SYNOPSIS OF THE SYSTEMATIC STRUCTURE OF CAPITAL

A synopsis of the general structure of Marx's *Capital* must be informed by some methodological interpretation. The present synopsis relies on the most recent Systematic Dialectical interpretation, not pushed too far, and with dialectical jargon avoided. Most Marx scholars will recognize the general outline of this structure – if perhaps not all of the details. The general scheme of the structure (see table 10.2) has some affinity with a sophisticated schema of Arthur (2002a).

The scheme shown in table 10.2 implies that, for example, the answer to the question "What is it?" at the first level (I-A) is insufficient. Subsequent levels (II-A, III-A) provide reconceptualization and concretion. The same applies to the question of "How it works" (I-B to III-B) and "The resulting process" (I-C to III-C). This involves a "vertical" conceptual progress; we also have a "horizontal" conceptual progress (from I-A to I-B, and so on). Below, each entry is considered in turn, with extra space devoted to the first (I-A).

References to *Capital* are by volume number and page number. References to the secondary literature are provided for the most controversial issues only. For various methodological aspects of *Capital* see Moseley (1993b) and Moseley and Campbell (1997); recent papers with further references on the three volumes can be found in Bellofiore and Taylor (2003), Arthur and Reuten (1998), Campbell and Reuten (2002), and Bellofiore (1998).

I-A: What is capital? – How it arises

"Capital" might be a sum of money, a quantity of means of production, or an investment in commodities. All such "shapes" of capital have in common that they are value-forms. For Marx "the commodity" is the elementary shape of the value-form. Therefore he starts with its analysis (*Capital I*, Part 1), turning in succession to money and capital.

There are two aspects to Part 1. First, Marx seeks in "value" a reference point for all of his volume I analysis. The problem of a suitable reference point has troubled all great economists, from Petty through Smith, Ricardo, and onward to Keynes and later. A main problem in understanding Marx's text is that he seeks (cf., section 10.4.2) an endogenous reference point, one *internal to his object of*

Table 10.2   The systematic of *Capital*

Capital	*A* *What it is*	*B* *How it works*	*C* *The resulting process*
Volume I Its production *How it arises*	Parts 1 and 2 From commodity to money; from money to capital	Parts 3–6 Production process of capital	Part 7 Accumulation of capital (Annex, Part 8)
Volume II Its circulation *How it operates*	Part 1 Capital as circuit	Part 2 Turnover of capital	Part 3 Extended social reproduction of capital
Volume III Its destination *How it culminates*	Part 1 Measure of capital – profit-form and rate of profit	Part 2 Competition and movement of capital; formation of general rate of profit	Part 3 Cyclical evolution of the rate of profit Parts 4–6 Industry, commerce, finance, landed property (Reflection, Part 7)

enquiry (in contradistinction to external constructs, such as – later on in history – index numbers, or Sraffa's standard commodity).

Secondly, Marx seeks *not* a naturalistic, but an historically specific social reference point (cf., section 10.4.3); one that applies to a society in which commodities are systematically *produced* with a view to sale (I, pp. 138–9, 153–4, 174). The two aspects appear to combine into one problematic, posing an even greater difficulty for the text.

The reference point for value is "abstract labor" measured by labor time (I, p. 129). (Therefore Marx's theory has often been interpreted as a "labor theory of value.") Simultaneously, Marx posits, first, that value exists only in a "value-relation or an exchange relation" and, secondly, that it is manifested in the value-form *par excellence*, the money form (I, pp. 138–9, 152, cf., 255). Indeed, throughout *Capital*, Marx always expresses value and value entities in monetary terms (£'s). (Thus it seems that Marx adopts a monetary measure of value.) I think, then, that we must accept that there is an ambiguity here, which can only be resolved in a reconstructive way (see, e.g., Backhaus, 1969; Bellofiore, 1989; Reuten, 1993; Smith, 1998; Bellofiore and Finelli, 1998; Arthur 2002b).

Note that, like the concept of capital, the concept of money – as introduced in Part 1, is developed throughout volumes II and III. Marx starts from a notion of commodity money; this is procedural within a "successive approximation" approach (cf., Campbell, 1997, 1998, 2002; Williams, 2000).

Marx develops the (level I) concept of capital in sequence from an analysis of the commodity and money. Part 2 of *Capital I* introduces capital proper. Marx's answer to the question "What is capital?" toward the end of this Part, is abstract and formal: it is inherent to capital that it expands "in movement": "The movement of capital is . . . the unceasing movement of profit-making" (I, pp. 253–4). It is a movement from money (M) into more money: $M \ldots M + \Delta M$. However, "unless it takes the form of some commodity, it does not become capital" (I, p. 256). Marx uses the formula $M - C - M'$ (where C is the value of a commodity, or of commodities, and $M' = M + \Delta M$). This is a formula of exchange, derived from the simpler $M - C - M$. The latter is a strange buying ($M - C$) in order to sell ($C - M$). It is an "inversion" of $C_i - M - C_j$; that is, selling C_i in order to buy a qualitatively different C_j (I, p. 258). Here, money is merely a facilitator – it does not really matter. In the strange, inverted form $M - C - M$, however, money is all that matters; by making sense only as $M - C - M'$, when the end result is an increment (ΔM), a "surplus-value" as Marx calls it. In $M - C - M'$ value is:

> the subject of a process in which, while constantly assuming the form in turn of money and commodities, it changes its own magnitude, throws off surplus-value from itself considered as original value, and thus valorizes itself independently. For the movement in the course of which it adds surplus-value is its own movement, its valorization is therefore self-valorization. (I, p. 255)

So capital is a movement of self-valorization, of throwing off surplus value. (Note that Marx has "bracketed" the notion of "profit" and replaced it by the more abstract notion of "surplus-value." Later on (III-A), we will see "surplus-value" transformed into "profit" and the latter again in the sum of "profit of enterprise," interest and rent. Before examining the processes of that distribution – in volume III – Marx's concern is to explain the abstract total. In volume I (and in volume II) he proceeds from the temporary assumption that each capitalist owns means of production and requires no hiring or borrowing of land, dwellings, or external finance (I, p. 710).)

Part 2 closes by formally introducing a particular commodity and commodity market, that of labor power, the existence of which is predicated on workers' lack of means of production. It includes a brief introduction to the value of labor power; that is, the wage that in principle should be sufficient to reproduce the labor power – "sufficient" depending on physical, historical, and moral elements (I, pp. 272–5).

I-B: How capital works – how it arises

Capital, we saw, is a movement of self-valorization, of throwing off surplus value. The middle part of volume I considers "not only how capital produces, but how capital is itself produced" (I, p. 280). How can surplus value be explained? Recall $M - C - M'$. "The change in value of the money . . . cannot take place in the money itself . . . The change must therefore take place in the commodity . . ." (I, p. 270). Hence the key to $M - C - M'$ lies in C. Marx next shows that the production process is the site at which the value of C is turned into C'.

In the exchange $M - C$, capital in money form is turned into capital in commodity form: means of production and labor power. Labor power is exchanged against the wage, and laborers sell their labor potential. During production, labor is "subordinated" to capital: "the worker works under the control of the capitalist . . . the product is the property of the capitalist and not that of the worker" (I, pp. 291–2). Because the means of production are static elements, a change in C can only be engendered by the *active* living element: labor. Labor alone can generate a surplus value beyond the wage. In labor resides the potential to produce a surplus product, or, in value terms, surplus value. Marx calls the ratio between the amount of surplus value and the capital laid out in wages the "rate of surplus-value" or the "degree of exploitation of labour-power by capital" (I, pp. 320–7).

The body of the middle part of *Capital I*, which is more than 400 pages long, consists of a detailed analysis of methods and (organizational) techniques for increasing the rate of exploitation. Throughout, Marx uses the labor-time reference point. Nevertheless, as previously indicated, all of his value entities are expressed in monetary terms (£'s); the same applies to all of his numerical examples (cf., Elson, 1979a).

I-C: Capital's resulting process – how it arises

"Earlier we considered how surplus-value arises from capital; now we have to see how capital arises from surplus-value. The employment of surplus-value as capital, or its reconversion into capital, is called accumulation of capital" (I, p. 725). In Part 7, Marx shows how capital's growth results in three simultaneous dynamic processes: (1) the propagation of a reserve army of unemployed labor, especially by way of the introduction of labor-expelling techniques of production pressing down the wage rate; (2) cyclical growth of capital; and (3) centralization of capital.

The final Part 8 provides an historical account of the conditions of the buying and sale of labor power: ownership of the means of production by capitalists. This is the precondition for the I-A starting point, and so rounds off this level of analysis as a circle.

II-A: What is capital? – How it operates

In I-A, Marx treats capital as "movement." Indeed, all of volume I describes movement, resulting in expanded movement (valorization and accumulation). In Part 1 of volume II this is made explicit. Capital is shown to be a continuous movement through four manifestations/shapes, together constituting the circuit of capital:

$$\text{—} M \text{—E—} C[\text{MP};\text{LP}] \cdots P \cdots C' \text{—E—} M' \text{—}$$

Capital in the shape of "money capital" (M) is transformed in the exchange process (–E–) into the shape of "production capital" (C); specifically, means of production (MP) and labor power (LP). The latter work up the former in the process of production (. . .) where we have the shape of "capital in process" (*P*); this constitutes a metamorphosis into valorized "commodity capital" (*C'*), with *C'* different qualitatively from *C*, as well as quantitatively in value terms (*C' > C*). Finally, another exchange transforms the expanded commodity value *C'* into a monetary value equivalent *M'*, the shape of expanded "money capital." The process can now resume on an expanded scale – wherein capital is accumulated.

II-B: How capital works – how it operates

Until Part 2, capital has been implicitly treated as an expanding flow (fixed capital as introduced in volume I was set to zero). Now Marx explicitly distinguishes circulating from fixed capital. It is shown how capital as movement works in production in terms of length of production periods and turnover times of capital. "Time" is key to capital. Speeding up any of the phases of the circuit means that a given quantity of capital can turn around more production.

II-C: Capital's resulting process – how it operates

Part 3 presents the circulation of capital in the context of the economy as a whole. Using a two-sector "model," Marx specifies dynamic interconnections pertinent to economic growth and conditions for balanced growth. These conditions are very severe and the implication is that balanced growth is possible, though unlikely.

III-A: What is capital? – How it culminates

Part 1 of volume III considers surplus value (flow) in relation to total capital invested (stock) and introduces the key capitalist *profit form*: "A sum of value is . . . capital if it is invested in order to produce a profit . . ." (III, p. 126). This involves a conceptual transformation of both "surplus-value" and "capital" such that the rate of profit measures the valorization of capital. Profit and the rate of profit are capital's continuity measures.

III-B: How capital works – how it culminates

The profit form brings a new dynamic (III, pp. 263, 267, 275); Part 2 shows how the profit rate measure works. Since for capital its particular physical content does not matter (bread, spirits, or bibles), another aspect of capital's movement is its flow to branches where it attains the highest profit rate. Thus competition between capitals produces an averaging of the profit rate. Concomitantly, we have a further commodification of workers who must move "from one sphere to another and from one local point of production to another" (III, p. 298).

  With the profit form, the concept of price developed in volume I is modified. After this, however, Marx surprisingly tries to make quantitative translations between the conceptual levels, comparing the transformed profit-form entities with a calculation prior to the profit form. In this Marx underscores the dynamic introduced at this level. [The literature on the interpretation and reconstruction of this "transformation" is enormous; for references, see Moseley (1993), Mohun (1994), Foley (2000), Bellofiore (2002), Laibman (2002), and various papers in Bellofiore (1998, vol. 1).]

III-C: Capital's resulting process – how it culminates

Part 3 presents the resulting dynamic of diachronic change in the average rate of profit through the profit-enforced introduction of cost-reducing techniques of production. These generate cyclical rate-of-profit increases to the *initiating* capital and a simultaneous cyclical *average* rate-of-profit decrease, as reversed in cyclical restructuring of capital (for this interpretation, see Reuten, 2002a, 2004 – cf., Lebowitz, 1976; Fine and Harris, 1979; Groll and Orzech, 1987).

No longer restricted to undifferentiated "industrial capital," Parts 4–6 show capital separated into functionally different and *conflicting* factions: industrial, commercial, financial, and real estate. Profit now separates and is distributed as profit of enterprise, interest and rent (Moseley, 2002). The final Part 7 is a draft for further concrete manifestations of the whole. It also emphasizes Marx's fundamental point that capitalism is an historically specific and mutable mode of production that conceals its class structure (Mattick, 2002; Murray, 2002).

Summary

In *Capital* the one-dimensionality of the capitalist social form – the value-form as expressed monetary terms – is the basis for capital as a "movement of self-valorization." Volume I treats the aspect of self-valorization as movement, volume II movement in a macrosocial context. In volume III these aspects are articulated in the working of the profit form and the "concrete abstraction" of a dimensionless rate of profit – money over money. That nondimensionality, indifferent to content, drives the base structure of a capitalist society.

10.6 MARX'S THEORY AND MARXIAN THEORY AS A STRAND

The main interpretations of Marx's work should be distinguished from the twentieth-century growth of "Marxian theory" as one strand alongside, in economics, the institutionalist, neoclassical, post-Keynesian, and others (for a historiography, see Howard and King, 1989–92). Marxian theory and institutionalism share an interdisciplinary emphasis, although Marxian theory is also a multidisciplinary project conducted by philosophers, economists, political scientists, sociologists, social geographers, and historians.

Current Marxian theory includes three types of research. A *first* type, nearest to Marx's work, is empirical research based on Marx's theory (such as the long-run development of the macroeconomic profit rate – e.g., Moseley, 1991; Duménil and Lévy, 1993; Wolff, 2001). Even more complicated than in mainstream economics, the concepts behind the statistical data differ from the theoretical concepts. Of course, such empirical studies involve interpretation of Marx's theory.

If one finds Marx's work to be inconsistent or unsatisfactory, a *second* type is theory reconstruction. Reconstructive work ranges across all fields of Marx's writings (particularly all components of table 10.2). Methodological work is a facet of this type (see, e.g., the contributions in Albritton and Simoulidis, 2002).

A *third* type is nonreconstructive theory development. For example, elements of business cycle theory – corresponding to their level of analysis (column 3 of table 10.2) – are found in all three volumes of *Capital*. Building on those elements, contemporary Marxian business cycle researchers may seek for an empirically testable theory of the cycle; this has requirements other than those intended, or at least reached, by Marx (for references, see Reuten, 2002b). Other examples are economic policy research (not reached in *Capital*) or, more generally, the study of the institutional conditions surrounding the accumulation of capital in different historical periods of capitalism ("phases," or "social structures," or "regimes" of accumulation; see the contributions in Albritton et al., 2001).

Although much of this work has drifted away from *Capital*, or at least beyond it, we nevertheless see in the former considerable reference to the latter (critically or complimentarily). This is an interesting aspect of Marx's status within the history of thought. It is also a fascinating aspect of the study of the history of thought generally, namely that it can serve as a rich heuristic source of inspiration for current ideas.

Note

I am grateful for comments by Chris Arthur, Mark Blaug, Gerald Levy, Paul Mattick, Patrick Murray, Tony Smith, Nicola Taylor, and the editors of this book, especially Warren Samuels and John Davis.

Bibliography

Albritton, R. and Simoulidis, J. (eds.) 2002: *New Dialectics and Political Economy*. Basingstoke and New York: Palgrave.

Albritton, R., Itoh, M., Westra, R., and Zuege, A. (eds.) 2001: *Phases of Capitalist Development; Booms, Crises and Globalizations*. Basingstoke and New York: Palgrave.

Arthur, C. J. 1986: *Dialectics of Labour; Marx and his Relation to Hegel*. Oxford and New York: Blackwell.

—— 1997: Against the logical–historical method: dialectical derivation versus linear logic. In Moseley and Campbell, op. cit., pp. 9–37.

—— 1998: Systematic Dialectic. *Science & Society*, 62(3), 447–59.

—— 2002a: Capital in general and Marx's *Capital*. In Campbell and Reuten, op. cit., pp. 42–64.

—— 2002b: The spectral ontology of value. In A. Brown, S. Fleetwood, and J. M. Roberts (eds.), *Critical Realism and Marxism*. London: Routledge, 215–33.

—— and Reuten, G. (eds.) 1998: *The Circulation of Capital: Essays on Volume II of Marx's "Capital."* London: Macmillan/New York: St. Martin's Press.

Backhaus, H.-G. 1969: Zur Dialektik der Wertform. In A. Schmidt (ed.), *Beiträge zur Marxistischen Erkenntnistheorie*. Frankfurt am Main: Suhrkamp Verlag. English translation: Eldred, M. and Roth, M. 1980: On the dialectics of the value-form. *Thesis Eleven*, 1, 99–120.

Banaji, J. 1979: From the commodity to capital: Hegel's dialectic in Marx's *Capital*. In Elson (1979b), op. cit., pp. 14–45.

Bellofiore, R. 1989: A monetary labor theory of value. *Review of Radical Political Economics*, 21(1–2), 1–25.

—— (ed.) 1998: *Marxian Economics: A Reappraisal*, 2 vols. London: Macmillan/New York: St. Martin's Press.

—— 2002: "Transformation" and the monetary circuit; Marx as a monetary theorist of production. In Campbell and Reuten, op. cit., pp. 102–27.

—— and Finelli, R. 1998: Capital, labour and time: the Marxian monetary labour theory of value as a theory of exploitation. In Bellofiore (1998), op. cit., vol. I, pp. 48–74.

—— and Taylor, N. (eds.) 2003: *The Constitution of Capital; Essays on Volume I of Marx's "Capital."* Basingstoke and New York: Palgrave.

Benhabib, S. 1986: *Critique, Norm, and Utopia*. New York: Columbia University Press.

Burns, T. and Fraser, I. (eds.) 2000: *The Hegel–Marx Connection*. London and New York: Macmillan.

Campbell, M. 1993: The commodity as necessary form of product. In R. Blackwell, J. Chatha, and E. J. Nell (eds.), *Economics as Worldly Philosophy; Essays in Political and Historical Economics in Honour of Robert L. Heilbroner*. New York: St. Martin's Press, 269–302.

—— 1997: Marx's theory of money: a defense. In Moseley and Campbell, op. cit., pp. 89–120.

—— 1998: Money in the circulation of capital. In Arthur and Reuten, op. cit., pp. 129–58.

—— 2002: The credit system. In Campbell and Reuten, op. cit., pp. 212–27.

—— and Reuten, G. (eds.) 2002: *The Culmination of Capital; Essays on Volume III of Marx's "Capital."* London and New York: Palgrave–Macmillan.

Duménil, G. and Lévy, D. 1993: *The Economics of the Profit Rate: Competition, Crises and Historical Tendencies in Capitalism*. Aldershot, UK: Edward Elgar.

Eldred, M. and Hanlon, M. 1981: Reconstructing value-form analysis. *Capital & Class*, 13, 24–60.

——, Hanlon, M., Kleiber, L., and Roth, M. 1982–5: Reconstructing value-form analysis 1–4. *Thesis Eleven*, 1982, 4; 1983, 7; 1984, 9; 1985, 11. Modified as "A value-form analytic reconstruction of *Capital*," in the appendix to M. Eldred, *Critique of Competitive Freedom and the Bourgeois-Democratic State*. København: Kurasje, pp. 350–487.

Elson, D. 1979a: The value theory of labour. In Elson (1979b), op. cit., pp. 115–80.

—— (ed.) 1979b: *Value, The Representation of Labour in Capitalism*. London: CSE Books.

Fine, B. and Harris, L. 1979: *Rereading Capital*. London: Macmillan.

Foley, D. 2000: Recent developments in the labor theory of value. *Review of Radical Political Economics*, 32(1), 1–39.

Groll, S. and Orzech, Z. B. 1987: Technical progress and values in Marx's theory of the decline in the rate of profit: an exegetical approach. *History of Political Economy*, 19(4), 591–613.

Howard, M. C. and King, J. E. 1989–92: *A History of Marxian Economics; Volume I, 1883–1929; Volume II 1929–1990*. London: Macmillan.

Laibman, D. 2002: Value and the quest for the core of capitalism. *Review of Radical Political Economics*, 34(2), 159–78.

Lebowitz, M. A. 1976: Marx's falling rate of profit: a dialectical view. *Canadian Journal of Economics*, 9(2), 232–54.

Marx, K. 1890 [1867]: *Das Kapital, Kritik der Politischen Ökonomie, Band I, Der Produktionsprozeß des Kapitals*, 4th edn., MEW 23 (first English translation: S. Moore and E. Aveling, 1886). Cited English edition 1976: *Capital, A Critique of Political Economy*, vol. I, trans. B. Fowkes. Harmondsworth: Penguin.

—— 1893 [1885]: *Das Kapital, Kritik der Politischen Ökonomie, Band II, Der Zirkulationsprozeß des Kapitals*, ed. F. Engels, 2nd edn., MEW 24 (first English translation: Ernest Untermann, 1907). Cited English edition 1978: *Capital, A Critique of Political Economy*, vol. II, trans. D. Fernbach. Harmondsworth: Penguin.

—— 1894: *Das Kapital, Kritik der Politischen Ökonomie, Band III, Der Gesamtprozeß der kapitalistischen Produktion*, ed. F. Engels, MEW 25 (first English translation: Ernest Untermann, 1909). Cited English edition 1981: *Capital, A Critique of Political Economy*, vol. III, trans. D. Fernbach. Harmondsworth: Penguin.

—— 1903: Einleitung (zu Grundrisse der Kritik der Politischen Ökonomie), ed. K. Kautsky, *Die Neue Zeit* (first English translation, 1904). Cited English translation: M. Nicolaus, 1973; see Marx (1953), op. cit., pp. 81–111.

—— 1933: *Resultate des Unmittelbaren Produktionsprozeßes*. Frankfurt: Verlag Neue Kritik. First English translation by R. Livingstone 1976: Results of the immediate process of production. In *Capital, A Critique of Political Economy*, vol. I, trans. B. Fowkes. Harmondsworth: Penguin, 948–1084.

—— 1953 [1939–41]: *Grundrisse der Kritik der Politischen Ökonomie (Rohentwurf)*. First English edition 1973: *Grundrisse*, trans. M. Nicolaus. Harmondsworth: Penguin.

—— and Engels, F. 1960– : *Werke* (MEW). Berlin: Dietz Verlag.

—— and —— 1975– : *Collected Works* (CW). London: Lawrence and Wishart/New York: International Publishers/Moscow: Progress Publishers.

—— and —— 1975– : *Gesamtausgabe (MEGA)*. Berlin: Dietz Verlag/Amsterdam: Internationales Institut für Sozialgeschichte Amsterdam.

—— and —— 1998: *Capital*, vols I–III. Essential Classics in Politics: Marx and Engels. London: The Electronic Book Company (ElecBook) [a CD-ROM version of the Lawrence and Wishart/International Publishers edition].

Mattick, P., Jr. 1986: *Social Knowledge; An Essay on the Nature and Limits of Social Science*. London: Hutchinson/Armonk, NY: M. E. Sharpe.

—— 1993: Marx's dialectic. In Moseley (1993b), op. cit., pp. 115–34.

—— 2002: Class, capital, and crisis. In Campbell and Reuten, op. cit., pp. 16–41.

Mohun, S. 1994: A re(in)statement of the labour theory of value. *Cambridge Journal of Economics*, 18, 391–412.

Moseley, F. 1991: *The Falling Rate of Profit in the Postwar United States Economy*. London: Macmillan.

—— 1993a: Marx's logical method and the "transformation problem." In Moseley (1993b), op. cit., pp. 157–84.

—— (ed.) 1993b: *Marx's Method in "Capital"; A reexamination*. Atlantic Highlands, NJ: Humanities Press.

—— 2002: Hostile brothers; Marx's theory of the distribution of surplus-value in volume III of *Capital*. In Campbell and Reuten, op. cit., pp. 65–101.

—— and Campbell, M. (eds.) 1997: *New Investigations of Marx's Method*. Atlantic Highlands, NJ: Humanities Press.

Murray, P. 1988: *Marx's Theory of Scientific Knowledge*. Atlantic Highlands, NJ: Humanities Press.

—— 1997: Redoubled empiricism: the place of social form and formal causality in Marxian theory. In Moseley and Campbell, op. cit., pp. 38–65.

—— 2000: Marx's "truly social" labor theory of value: abstract labor in Marxian value theory. *Historical Materialism*, 6, 27–66 (part 1); 7, 99–136 (part 2).

—— 2002: The illusion of the economic; the Trinity Formula and "the religion of everyday life." In Campbell and Reuten, op. cit., pp. 246–73.

Oakley, A. 1983: *The Making of Marx's Critical Theory; A Bibliographical Analysis*. London: Routledge and Kegan Paul.

Reuten, G. 1993: The difficult labour of a theory of social value; metaphors and Systematic Dialectics at the beginning of Marx's *Capital*. In Moseley (1993b), op. cit., pp. 89–113.

—— 2000: The interconnection of Systematic Dialectics and Historical Materialism. *Historical Materialism*, 7, 137–66.

—— 2002a: The rate of profit cycle and the opposition between managerial and finance capital; a discussion of *Capital III* Parts 3–5. In Campbell and Reuten, op. cit., pp. 174–211.

—— 2002b: Business cycles: Marxian approach. In B. Snowdon and H. Vane (eds.), *Encyclopedia of Macroeconomics*. Aldershot, UK: Edward Elgar, 73–80.

—— 2004: "Zirkel vicieux" or trend fall? – the course of the profit rate in Marx's *Capital III*. *History of Political Economy*, 36(1), forthcoming.

—— and Williams, M. 1989: *Value-Form and the State; the Tendencies of Accumulation and the Determination of Economic Policy in Capitalist Society*. London: Routledge.

Rubin, I. I. 1972 [1923]: *Essays on Marx's Theory of Value (Ocherki po teorii stoimosti Marksa)*, translation of 3rd edn. (Moscow, 1928) by M. Samardzija and F. Perlman. Detroit, MI: Black & Red.

Smith, T. 1990: *The Logic of Marx's Capital: Replies to Hegelian Criticisms*. Albany, NY: State University of New York Press.

—— 1993a: Marx's *Capital* and Hegelian Dialectical Logic. In Moseley (1993b), op. cit., pp. 15–36.

—— 1993b: *Dialectical Social Theory and its Critics*. Albany, NY: State University of New York Press.

—— 1998: Value theory and dialectics. *Science & Society*, 62(3), 460–70.

Sweezy, P. A. 1968 [1942]: *The Theory of Capitalist Development*. New York and London: Modern Reader Paperbacks.

Williams, M. 2000: Why Marx neither has nor needs a commodity theory of money. *Review of Political Economy*, 12(4), 435–51.

Wolff, E. 2001: The recent rise of profits in the United States. *Review of Radical Political Economics*, 33, 315–24.

CHAPTER ELEVEN

The Surplus Interpretation of the Classical Economists

Heinz D. Kurz

11.1 INTRODUCTION

The economy that the classical economists from William Petty to David Ricardo experienced typically generated an annual *social surplus*, which was distributed amongst the propertied classes in the form of rents or profits, and was used for the purposes of consumption and capital accumulation. The surplus refers to those quantities of the different commodities that were left over after the necessary means of production used up and the means of subsistence in the support of workers had been deducted from the gross outputs produced during a year. In this conceptualization, the necessary real wages of labor were considered no less indispensable as inputs and thus agents of production than raw materials, tools, or machines. What became known as the "surplus interpretation" of the classical economists focuses attention on the mature classical economists' approach to how the surplus is distributed and which system of exchange values of the different commodities can be expected to emerge as the result of the gravitation of "market" or "actual" prices to their "natural" or "ordinary" levels, or "prices of production." In conditions of free competition – that is, in the absence of significant barriers to entry and exit from markets – prices can be taken to oscillate around levels characterized by a *uniform rate of profits* on the value of the capital advanced at the beginning of the uniform production period and a uniform rate of rent for each of the different qualities of land.

The determination of the general rate of profits, the rents of land, and the corresponding system of relative prices constitutes the analytic centerpiece of classical political economy. It was designed to lay the foundation of all other economic analysis, including the investigation of capital accumulation and technical progress; of development and growth; of social transformation and structural change; and of taxation and public debt. The pivotal role of the theory of value and distribution can be inferred from the fact that the latter is typically developed right at the beginning of major classical works: think of Adam Smith's *Wealth of Nations* (WN, I.vi–xi), or of David Ricardo's *Principles* (*Works*, vol. I, chs. I–VI).

The importance of this part of classical analysis is also reflected in the following. When in 1951, in his introduction to Ricardo's *Principles* in volume I of *The Works and Correspondence of David Ricardo* (Sraffa, 1951), and then in 1960, in his book *Production of Commodities by Means of Commodities* (Sraffa, 1960), Piero Sraffa reestablished the surplus interpretation of the classical economists, which had been "submerged and forgotten since the advent of the 'marginal' method" (Sraffa, 1960, p. v), after some notable delay this caused a major controversy, the end of which is not yet in sight. (According to Sraffa, the classical approach to the theory of value and distribution was first submerged and forgotten shortly after Ricardo's death. He credited Marx (1954a) with having rediscovered and then further elaborated it.) Had Sraffa's historical and analytic reconstruction only been concerned with a peripheral aspect of classical economics, then it could have hardly attracted the attention and triggered the debate that it did. It was precisely because his interpretation concerned the very foundations of classical economics – its theory of value and distribution – that his alternative point of view caused a major stir amongst historians of economic thought and met with stiff opposition from those who advocated one form or other of the received Marshallian interpretation. The latter perceived the classical economists as essentially early and somewhat crude demand and supply theorists, with the demand side in its infancy. It was this interpretation and the underlying continuity thesis that Sraffa challenged.

If Sraffa was right, this would have important implications ranging far beyond the field of the history of economic thought. These implications began to emerge when, equipped with Sraffa's reformulation and generalization of the classical approach to the theory of value and distribution, a number of authors in the 1960s and 1970s successfully questioned the validity of the dominant long-period demand and supply theory in the so-called "Cambridge controversies in the theory of capital" (see, e.g., Kurz and Salvadori, 1995, ch. 14). This clearly demonstrated that a concern with the classical approach did not involve morbid antiquarianism.

In this essay, attention will focus exclusively on Sraffa's interpretation of the classical authors (see also Garegnani, 1984, 1987; Kurz and Salvadori, 1995, 1998a,b, 2002). As is well known, Sraffa published very little during his lifetime. What is less well known is that he left a huge amount of notes and manuscripts. Many of those that relate directly to our theme were written as early as the late 1920s. (A selection from his papers and correspondence is currently being prepared for publication.) Sraffa was then in the midst of recovering the classical approach to the theory of value and distribution from underneath thick layers of interpretation, a task the accomplishment of which was only aided when, in 1930, he was entrusted with the Ricardo edition on behalf of the Royal Economic Society. In private conversation, Sraffa is reported to have called his notes and papers the "iceberg," the tip of which is his published work.

The composition of this essay is as follows. Section 11.2 deals with important characteristic features of the classical method in the theory of value and distribution. Section 11.3 turns to the central classical concept of "physical real cost" and exemplifies its presence in the works of a number of major authors. Section 11.4 deals with some of the reasons why that concept was gradually abandoned and replaced by that of "labor." Section 11.5 shows that the classical approach to value and distribution can be adequately formulated in terms of simultaneous equations. Sraffa began to elaborate such equations from 1927 onward. Section 11.6 summarizes the analytic structure of the classical approach to the theory of value and distribution. Section 11.7 concludes with a few illustrations of how the classical authors employed this theory in an attempt to come to grips with the dynamism of the capitalist economy and the factors shaping its long-term trend.

11.2   THE SCOPE AND METHOD OF THE CLASSICAL APPROACH

The classical economists were concerned with the laws governing the emerging capitalist economy, characterized by: the stratification of society into three classes, workers, landowners, and the rising class of capitalists; wage labor as the dominant form of the appropriation of other people's capacity to work; an increasingly sophisticated division of labor within and between firms; the coordination of economic activity via a system of interdependent markets in which transactions were mediated through money; and significant technical, organizational, and institutional change. In short, they were concerned with an economic system that was incessantly in motion. How should one analyze such a system? The ingenious device of the classical authors for seeing through the complexities of the modern economy consisted in distinguishing between the "actual" values of the relevant variables – the distributive rates and prices – and their "normal" values. The former were taken to reflect all kinds of influences, many of an accidental or temporary nature, about which no general propositions were possible, whereas the latter were seen to express the persistent, nonaccidental, and nontemporary factors governing the economic system, which could be systematically studied.

The method of analysis adopted by the classical economists is known as the method of *long-period positions* of the economy. Any such position is one toward which the system is taken to gravitate as the result of the self-seeking actions of agents, thereby putting into sharp relief the fundamental forces at work. In conditions of free competition the resulting long-period position is characterized by a uniform rate of profits (subject, perhaps, to persistent inter-industry differentials reflecting different levels of risk) and uniform rates of remuneration for each particular kind of primary input. Competitive conditions were taken to engender *cost-minimizing behavior* from profit-seeking producers.

The classical economists proceeded essentially in two steps. In a first step, on which attention focuses in this essay, they isolated the kinds of factors that were seen to determine income distribution and the prices supporting that distribution in specified conditions; that is, *in a given place and time*. The theory of value and distribution was designed to identify *in abstracto* the dominant factors at work and to analyze their interaction. In a second step, the classical authors then turned to an investigation of the causes that, *over time*, systematically affected the factors at work from within the economic system. This involved the classical analysis of capital accumulation, technical change, economic growth, and socioeconomic development.

It is another characteristic feature of the classical approach to profits, rents, and relative prices that these are explained essentially in terms of magnitudes that can, in principle, be observed, measured, or calculated. The *objectivist* orientation of classical economics has received perhaps its strongest expression in a famous proclamation by William Petty, who was arguably its founding father. Keen to assume what he called the "physician's" outlook, Petty in his *Political Arithmetick*, published in 1690, stressed:

> The Method I take to do this, is not yet very usual; for instead of using only comparative and superlative Words, and intellectual Arguments, I have taken the course (as a Specimen of the Political Arithmetick I have long aimed at) to express my self in Terms of *Number, Weight* or *Measure*; to use only Arguments of Sense, and to consider only such Causes, as have visible foundations in Nature; leaving those that depend upon the mutable Minds, Opinions, Appetites and Passions of particular Men, to the Consideration of others . . . (Petty, 1986 [1899], p. 244; emphasis in original)

Notwithstanding their many differences, the classical economists generally shared in one form or another an essentially objectivist outlook on the problem of value and distribution. This will become clear when, in section 11.3, we turn to the concept of "cost" entertained by them.

Finally, the following aspect of the classical method deserves mention. In his 1960 book, which was explicitly designed to revive the "standpoint" of the old classical economists, Sraffa stressed: "the investigation is concerned exclusively with such properties of an economic system as do not depend on changes in the scale of production or in the proportion of 'factors'" (1960, p. v). To focus attention on these properties of an economic system does not mean, of course, that there are no such changes. It only means that these changes are set aside in the respective investigation. What is at stake is a method designed to analyze an aspect of the economic system under consideration. In contrast, the method adopted by the marginalist authors focuses attention on (marginal) changes in the scale of production and in the proportions of factors. It attempts to determine relative prices and the distributive variables in terms of incremental quantitative changes. This is in stark contrast to the classical method, which takes the levels of gross outputs as known magnitudes, reflecting, *inter alia*, the degree of the division of labor reached by a particular economy at a given stage of its development.

11.3   CIRCULAR FLOW AND PHYSICAL REAL COST

According to Sraffa, there are two especially important interrelated features characterizing the classical theory of production and cost. First, the classical concept of production is essentially that of a *circular flow*. This idea can be traced back to William Petty and Richard Cantillon and was most effectively expressed by François Quesnay (1972 [1759]) in the *Tableau économique* (see Aspromourgos, 1996). The classical view that commodities are produced by means of commodities is in stark contrast to the view of production as a one-way avenue leading from the services of original factors of production to consumption goods, as was entertained by the "Austrian" economists.

Secondly, the classical economists had a concept of *physical real cost*. Their starting point can be summarized in the following way. Man cannot create matter; man can only change its form and move it. Production involves destruction, and the real cost of a commodity consists in the commodities destroyed in the course of its production. This concept differs markedly from the later marginalist concepts, with their emphasis on "psychic cost," reflected in such notions as "utility" and "disutility," "abstinence," "waiting," or "opportunity cost."

We encounter the classical view in Petty, who reckoned the costs of a commodity as the means of production and the means of subsistence in support of the workers necessary in order to carry out production. Yet, as Sraffa noted, Petty was probably not the first author to have advocated such a point of view. Traces of it can also be found in the concept of "just price" in the canonists. After Petty, the new science of political economy was taken up and further developed by the physiocrats, who essentially adopted the received view.

The concept of physical real cost recurs in the writings of Adam Smith, James Mill, David Ricardo, Robert Torrens, and Karl Marx. Despite some ambiguities in Smith's argument, Sraffa insisted that the Scotsman's use of the term "natural" referred to that physical, purely natural relation between commodities. (The natural relation referred to is implicit in what Sraffa called the "first equations" of production; that is, production without a surplus – see section 11.5.1 below.) The same relation was intended when Ricardo spoke of "absolute value." The physical real cost approach is clearly discernible in the concept of "capital," which Ricardo defined as "the food and clothing consumed by the labourer, the buildings in which he works, the implements with which his labour is assisted" (*Works*, vol. I, p. 52). Particularly clear expressions of the physical real cost approach are encountered in James Mill's *Elements of Political Economy*, first published in 1821. Mill insisted that, in the last instance, "the agents of production are the commodities themselves" (Mill, 1844 [1826], p. 165): (i) the food of the laborer; (ii) the tools and the machinery with which he works; and (iii) the raw materials that he works upon.

Mill also drew the attention to a problem that was to become a major stumbling block for classical analysis: the tension between physical real costs, on the one hand, and labor, on the other. In the third edition, published in 1826, he wrote:

[T]he terms, Labour and Wages, are sometimes, incautiously used; and confusion of ideas, and some fundamental errors, are the consequence. It is clear that, when we speak of the labour of a man, for a day, or a month, or a year, the idea of his subsistence is as necessarily included, as that of the action of his muscles, or his life. . . . If wages be taken as synonymous with the consumption of the labourer, the labour cannot be taken, as one item of an aggregate, and its wages as another. As often as this is done, an error is the necessary consequence." (Mill, ibid., pp. 9–10)

While there is no reason to suppose that James Mill was fully aware of the deficiencies of the labor theory of value, he seems to have sensed that replacing physical real costs by, or confounding it with, quantities of labor might be the source of potential "error." We may now ask: What were the reasons for the shift from the concept of physical real costs to that of labor? A few observations must suffice.

11.4   FROM PHYSICAL REAL COSTS TO QUANTITIES OF LABOR

The move away from physical real costs and toward labor was first due to the fact that the relatively backward analytic tools at the disposal of the classical economists did not allow them to translate the former concept into an adequate analytic framework. In order to coherently determine the general rate of profits and the exchange ratios of different commodities in terms of given physical real costs of production, the problem would have to be stated in terms of a set of *simultaneous equations*. Lacking the proper tools, the classical authors attempted to cope with the problem of the heterogeneity of commodities by trying to reduce them to a common measure. Since labor was considered an indispensable input in the production of all commodities, labor was gradually identified as the common measure, or, in the case of Marx (1954b), as the "substance," of value.

Ricardo appears to have developed his theory of profits from one stage in which corn was considered the only means of production (wage good) in the system (see Sraffa, 1951, pp. xxxi–xxxii). Accordingly, the rate of profit in agriculture could be determined directly between quantities of corn (corn surplus relative to corn capital) without any question of valuation. Via an adjustment of the prices of their products to the price of corn, the other industries would receive the same rate of profit. Ricardo in the *Principles* then extended this theory and regarded labor as constituting the universal agent of production, with the consequence that the rate of profits was now seen to depend on the on the *proportion* of a day's or year's labor needed to produce the subsistence for a day or a year. The extension under consideration could only have been reaffirmed by the fact that Ricardo saw that workers could participate in the surplus product. In this case, wages could no longer be identified with mere subsistence. Ricardo therefore replaced the concept of a given real wage rate with that of a given share of wages in the social product. He identified this share with "the proportion of the result of labour that is given to the labourer" (*Works*, vol. VIII, p. 194).

The move away from the "loaf of bread" and toward "labor" may finally be illustrated in terms of Robert Torrens. [On Torrens, see de Vivo's commentaries in Torrens (2000).] In the 1820 edition of his *Essay on the External Corn Trade*, Torrens put forward the simplest possible conceptualization of the surplus approach to the theory of value and distribution: the *corn-ratio theory of profits*. He laid down, as a "general principle,"

> that in whatever proportion the quantity of produce obtained from the soil exceeds the quantity employed in raising it, in that proportion the value of the manufactured goods will exceed the values of the food and material expended in preparing them. (Torrens, 2000, vol. II, p. 362)

Here, the rate of profit in agriculture is determined as a ratio between two given quantities of corn: the surplus corn produced and the corn capital advanced in corn production (seed and corn wages). This rate of profit is then used in order to determine the price of manufactures, which – in competitive conditions – yields the manufacturer the same rate of return on his capital advances as the rate obtained by the farmer.

Torrens expressed his indebtedness to David Ricardo's "original and profound inquiry into the laws by which the rate of profit is determined" (ibid., p. xix). This provides indirect evidence in support of Sraffa's corn-profit interpretation of Ricardo (Sraffa, 1951, pp. xxxi–xxxiii). According to Sraffa, "The advantage of Ricardo's method of approach is that, at the cost of considerable simplification, it makes possible an understanding of how the rate of profit is determined without the need of a method for reducing to a common standard a heterogeneous collection of commodities" (ibid., p. xxxii). It also provides a first confirmation of Ricardo's conviction that the laws of distribution "are not essentially connected with the doctrine of value" (*Works*, vol. VII, p. 194).

It was, of course, clear to Ricardo and Torrens that, as Malthus had objected, the capital advanced in a single industry is never homogeneous with the industry's product. However, there may be homogeneity between product and capital in terms of a composite commodity with regard to the economy as a whole. In this case, the general rate of profits may again be conceived of in purely physical terms. In all three editions of Ricardo's *Principles* we encounter a numerical example that satisfies this requirement. In the example of every 100 units produced of three commodities – hats, coats, and quarters of corn – workers are paid 25 (or 22) units of each of them and landlords are also assumed to receive 25 (or 22) units; accordingly, profits consist of 50 (56) units of each commodity (see *Works*, vol. I, p. 50). On the assumption that capital consists only of the real wages bill, the rate of profits can be determined independently of the problem of the valuation of the different commodities and amounts to $50/25 = 2$ (or $56/22 = 28/11$). Similarly, in his *Essay on the Production of Wealth*, published in 1821, Torrens put forward an example with two industries, one producing corn and the other suits of clothing, where both industries use both products in the same proportions (and actually in the same absolute amounts) as inputs (see Torrens, 2000, vol. III, pp. 372–3). With the social surplus and the social capital consisting of the same commodities in the same proportions, the general rate of profits can be determined without having recourse to the system of relative prices. Moreover, given the exceedingly simple conditions underlying the example, the exchange ratio of the two commodities corresponding to a uniform rate of profits is obvious: since both commodities exhibit the same physical real costs per unit of output, a quarter of corn is necessarily exchanged for one suit of clothing.

[In the debate about whether Ricardo or Torrens or any other classical author had put forward a "corn model," this possibility is frequently, and surprisingly, overlooked by critics of Sraffa's interpretation. In order for a concept of the general rate of profits in purely physical terms to hold, there is no need to discern in the classical authors the fiction of a single industry whose product is physically homogeneous with its capital. (Corn models are, however, to be found in the works of these authors.) Therefore, concern with the corn model in the writings of some critics appears to be out of proportion in regard to the importance of that model in the works of the classical authors: helpful as it may have been at an early stage in the conceptual development of the classical approach to the theory of profits, that approach does very well without the corn model.]

Nor had it escaped Torrens's attention that physical homogeneity of product (and surplus) and capital cannot be expected to hold in any real economy. In his attempt to deal with more general cases, however, he was confronted with the complexity of the relationship between income distribution and relative prices. In yet another attempt to contain this complexity and arrive at a clear-cut deter-mination of the general rate of profits, Torrens resorted to the special assumption that we just encountered; namely, that in all lines of production the same commodity input proportions apply. This assumption implies, of course, that relative prices are correctly explained by the labor theory of value (see section 11.5 below). More specifically, echoing the physical real costs approach in labor terms, commodities exchange for one another according to the quantities of labor contained in the *capitals* (means of production and means of subsistence) used up in the course of their production. In the preface to the *Essay*, Torrens stressed:

> The principle that the *accumulated labour*, or, in other words, *the capital expended on production*, determines the exchangeable value of commodities, while it is derived from an extensive induction from particular cases, affords a *satisfactory solution* of some of the most important phenomena connected with the distribution of wealth. Without this correction or limitation of Mr. Ricardo's theory of value it is impossible to give a clear and unexceptionable demonstration of that gentleman's very original and valuable doctrine respecting the profits of stock." (Torrens, 2000, vol. III, p. vii; emphases added)

That this did not afford a generally "satisfactory solution," as Torrens was inclined to believe, was clear at the latest, if not earlier, in the context of the criticism of Marx's so-called "transformation" of labor values in "prices of production" (see below).

Not seeing their way through the complexities of the relation between relative prices and income distribution, given the system of production in use, without recourse to a "common measure" of value applies *cum grano salis* to all the clas-sical economists and Marx. [There is a notable exception: the critic of physiocratic doctrine, the French engineer Achille-Nicolas Isnard; see, e.g., Kurz and Salvadori (2000, pp. 159–61).] And all thought they had found such a measure in one way or another in terms of human labor. Some can even be said to have considered the problem of the "measure" of value as but another expression of the problem of the "cause" of value. Ricardo, as is well known, struggled with the problem of value and distribution until his death: the manuscript fragments on "Absolute value and exchangeable value" (see *Works*, vol. IV) document in detail his attempts to come to grips with this problem and his failure to elaborate a fully correct theory. They also contribute to a better understanding of why Ricardo (and other classical economists) were so "obsessed" with one version or another of the labor theory of value, as one commentator has remarked. This theory had allowed them, however imperfectly, to see through the complexities of the problem under consideration and determine the general rate of profits. As long as no better theory was available, there was no compelling reason to abandon the admittedly defective approach based on labor value.

However, granting for the moment – and for the sake of the argument – the alleged prior necessity of expressing the different commodity inputs in terms of labor quantities which could then be aggregated: How were those amounts of labor, or "labor values," to be ascertained when production is a circular flow? How can commodities that are produced by means of commodities be reduced to labor alone? Obviously, beside the labor term there will always be a "commodity residue" consisting of minute fractions of means of production and means of subsistence needed in the production of that residue. Is there reason to suppose that the sum total of the dated quantities of labor representing the production conditions of a given commodity converges to a finite limit, as Smith (WN, I.vi) and Ricardo (*Works*, vol. I, ch. I, section III) appear to have implicitly assumed? And does the determination of labor values not also presuppose the solution of a system of simultaneous equations, so that the route via "labor" that the classical economists had taken was not a way out of the impasse in which they found themselves?

The question, then, is how can the whole process of production be adequately analyzed and a coherent theory of value and distribution be elaborated that is faithful to what the classical economists appear to have been after, but were unable to express in a satisfactory way?

11.5   EQUATIONS OF PRODUCTION

What made it so difficult, if not impossible, for the classical authors to see how the theory of value and distribution could be firmly grounded in the concept of physical real cost? Given their primitive tools of analysis, they did not see that information about the system of production in use and the quantities of the means of subsistence in support of workers was all that was needed in order to *directly* determine the rate of profits and relative prices. Solving a set of simultaneous equations of production accomplishes this task in a straightforward manner. In the following, we deal only with single production and thus only circulating capital, and set aside joint production, fixed capital, and natural resources (see therefore Sraffa, 1960; Kurz and Salvadori, 1995).

11.5.1 Production without surplus

We may start from James Mill's case above with three kinds of commodities, tools (t), raw materials (m), and the food of the laborer (f). Production in the three industries may then be depicted by the following system of quantities:

$$T_t \oplus M_t \oplus F_t \to T,$$
$$T_m \oplus M_m \oplus F_m \to M, \qquad \text{(Q)}$$
$$T_f \oplus M_f \oplus F_f \to F,$$

where T_i, M_i, and F_i designate the inputs of the three commodities (employed as means of production and means of subsistence) in industry i ($i = t, m, f$), and T, M, and F are total outputs in the three industries; the symbol "$\oplus$" indicates that all inputs on the left-hand side of "$\to$," representing production, are required to generate the output on its right-hand side. Adopting the terminology of the classical authors, Sraffa called these relations "the methods of production and productive consumption" (Sraffa, 1960, p. 3). In the hypothetical case in which the economy is merely viable – that is, able to reproduce itself without any surplus (or deficiency) – we have $T = \Sigma_i T_i$, $M = \Sigma_i M_i$, and $F = \Sigma_i F_i$.

From this schema of reproduction and reproductive consumption we may *directly* derive the corresponding system of "absolute" or "natural" values, which expresses the idea of physical, real cost-based values in an unadulterated way. Denoting the value of one unit of commodity i by p_i ($i = t, m, f$), we have

$$T_t p_t + M_t p_m + F_t p_f = T p_t,$$
$$T_m p_t + M_m p_m + F_m p_f = M p_m,$$
$$T_f p_t + M_f p_m + F_f p_f = F p_f.$$

Only two of the three equations are independent of one another. Fixing a standard of value, whose price is *ex definitione* equal to unity, provides an additional equation without adding a further unknown and allows one to solve for the remaining dependent variables.

A numerical example taken from Sraffa's papers illustrates the important finding that the given socio-technical relations rigidly fix relative values:

	Values
$2p_t + 15p_m + 20p_f = 17p_t,$	$p_t = 3p_m,$
$5p_t + 7p_m + 4p_f = 28p_m,$	$p_m = {}^2\!/_3 p_f,$
$10p_t + 6p_m + 11p_f = 35p_f,$	$p_f = {}^1\!/_2 p_t.$

Hence values emerge as the solution to a system of simultaneous equations. These values depend exclusively on necessities of production. They are the only values that restore the initial distribution of resources.

Here the question of a "common measure" of commodities is of no real import, once the problem is approached from a rigorous physical real cost point of view. Or, rather, any valuable thing could serve as a "common measure" or standard of value. One may also "reduce" the value of one commodity to a certain amount of another commodity needed directly or indirectly in the production of the former. For example, one might reduce one unit of commodity t to an amount needed of commodity m. Hence one might say that each of the three commodities could serve as a "common measure," and that, for example, commodities t and f exchanged for one another in the proportion 1:2 because commodity t "contained" or "embodied" twice as much of commodity m as commodity f.

But what about the labor theory of value? Were the classical authors mistaken in thinking that in conditions without a surplus (profits) relative prices were proportional to the relative quantities of labor bestowed on, or "embodied" in, the different commodities? Obviously not. In the above equations, labor may be rendered visible by replacing the sustenance of producers in the different industries with the amount of labor employed in them and by adding a new equation that shows the "production" of the sum total of labor employed by means of the sum total of the means of subsistence in its support. In this way one would see how labor produces commodities (one equation for each commodity), so the commodities produce labor (one equation for labor). Hence in a system without a surplus (or a system in which the entire surplus is distributed to workers) a "Value Theory of Labour," as Sraffa dubbed it, holds. Labor values can rigorously be determined, but this involves solving a system of simultaneous equations.

11.5.2   Production with a surplus

We now turn to systems with a surplus and assume that there is free competition. The surplus is distributed in terms of a uniform rate of profits on the "capitals" advanced in the different industries.

We start again from system (Q), but now assume that $T \geq \Sigma_i T_i$, $M \geq \Sigma_i M_i$, and $F \geq \Sigma_i F_i$, where at least with regard to one commodity the strict inequality sign holds. The case of a uniform rate of physical surplus across all commodities contemplated by Ricardo and Torrens,

$$\frac{T - S_i T_i}{S_i T_i} = \frac{M - S_i M_i}{S_i M_i} = \frac{F - S_i F_i}{S_i F_i} = r, \tag{S}$$

denotes a very special constellation: in it the general rate of profits, r, equals the uniform material rate of produce. *Here we see the rate of profits in the commodities themselves, as having nothing to do with their values.* In general, however, the rates of physical surplus will be different for different commodities. It cannot even be excluded that some of these rates will be negative.

"Profits," Ricardo stressed, "come out of the surplus produce" (*Works*, vol. II, pp. 130–1; similarly vol. I, p. 95). Unequal rates of commodity surplus do not, however, by themselves imply unequal rates of profit across industries. In conditions of free competition the concept of "normal" prices, or "prices of production," implies that the social surplus is divided in such a way between the different employments of capital that a uniform rate of profits obtains. This is reflected by the following system of price equations:

$$(T_t p_t + M_t p_m + F_t p_f)(1 + r) = T p_t,$$
$$(T_m p_t + M_m p_m + F_m p_f)(1 + r) = M p_m, \qquad \text{(P)}$$
$$(T_f p_t + M_f p_m + F_f p_f)(1 + r) = F p_f.$$

Flukes apart, these three equations are independent of one another. Fixing a standard of value provides a fourth equation and no additional unknown, so that the system of equations can be solved for the dependent variables: the general rate of profits and prices.

The important point to note here is the following. With the real wage rate given and paid at the beginning of the periodical production cycle, the problem of the determination of the rate of profits consists in distributing the surplus product in proportion to the capital advanced in each industry. Obviously,

> such a proportion between two aggregates of heterogeneous goods (in other words, the rate of profits) cannot be determined before we know the prices of the goods. On the other hand, we cannot defer the allotment of the surplus till after the prices are known, for . . . the prices cannot be determined before knowing the rate of profits. *The result is that the distribution of the surplus must be determined through the same mechanism and at the same time as are the prices of commodities.* (Sraffa, 1960, p. 6; emphasis added)

This passage shows that the idea underlying Marx's so-called "transformation" of labor values into prices of production (see Marx, 1959, part II) cannot generally be sustained. Marx had proceeded in two steps; Ladislaus von Bortkiewicz (1906–7, essay II, p. 38) aptly dubbed his approach "successivist" (as opposed to "simultaneous"). In a first step Marx assumed that the general rate of profits is determined independently of, and prior to, the determination of prices as the ratio between the labor value of the social surplus and that of social capital, consisting of "constant capital" (means of production) and "variable capital" (wages or means of subsistence). In a second step, he then used this rate to calculate prices. Underlying his approach is the hypothesis that while the "transformation" of values into prices is relevant in regard to each single commodity, it is irrelevant in regard to commodity aggregates, such as the surplus product or the social capital, and the ratio of such aggregates. Yet this is not generally the case. It should be added, however, that with his formulation Marx came within one step of a correct solution of the problem (see Garegnani, 1987, pp. 567–8).

The passage quoted from Sraffa (1960) also contains the key to his critique of the long-period marginalist concept of capital. This concept crucially hinged on the possibility of defining the "quantity of capital," whose relative scarcity and thus marginal productivity was taken to determine the rate of profits, independently of the rate of profits. However, according to the logic of Sraffa's argument above, the rate of profits and the quantity (i.e., value) of capital can only be determined simultaneously.

11.5.3 Workers participating in the surplus

So far, we have assumed that wages are given at some level of subsistence. The classical economists, however, saw clearly that the share of wages in the product may rise above, or temporarily even fall below, mere sustenance of laborers (see, for example, Ricardo, *Works*, vol. I, p. 95). The question close at hand was (see, e.g., Mill, 1844 [1826], p. 105): How does the rate of profits and relative prices depend on wages?

The answer is close at hand: one simply plugs in the different level of wages in an appropriately reformulated system (P) and solves it for the rate of profits and prices. This can be done for any technically feasible wages. As a result of this analytic exercise we get the constraint binding changes in the distributive variables, wages, and the rate of profits. This constraint was discovered, though not consistently demonstrated, by Ricardo in terms of his labor-value-based approach: "The greater the portion of the result of labour that is given to the labourer, the smaller must be the *rate* of profits, and vice versa" (*Works*, vol. VIII, p. 194; emphasis added). He was thus able to dispel the idea, generated by Adam Smith's view of price as a sum of wages and profits (and rents) (WN, I.vi), that the wage and the rate of profits are determined independently of each other.

Ricardo also realized that the labor value principle cannot be sustained as a "general rule": it is considerably modified by different proportions of (direct) labor to means of production (and different degrees of durability of fixed capital items). The "variety of circumstances under which commodities are actually produced" (*Works*, vol. IV, p. 368) in conjunction with the fact that "profits [are] increasing at a compound rate[,] ... makes a great part of the difficulty" (*Works*, vol. IX, p. 387), and is responsible for the dependence of relative prices on distribution, given the system of production. This is so because, with different input proportions and compound interest, relative prices would not only depend on the quantities of labor "embodied" in the various commodities, but also on the level of the rate of profits, and would change with that level. Ricardo's search for a measure of value that is "invariable" with respect to changes in distribution may be considered a further attempt to simplify the theory of distribution (see Sraffa, 1951, pp. xxxi–xxxiii; also Kurz and Salvadori, 1993). The measure of value that he was in search of was meant to confirm his conviction, noted above, that the laws of distribution "are not essentially connected with the doctrine of value."

Here it suffices to note that Ricardo's problem of defining a measure of value that was invariable with respect to changes in distribution, given the system of production, was finally solved by Sraffa in terms of the "Standard commodity" (Sraffa, 1960, ch. IV). The corresponding Standard system is derived from the actual system by virtually re-proportioning the industries in such a way that uniform rates of surplus obtain with regard to all commodities which enter directly or indirectly in the production of all commodities (similar to (S) above).

11.6 THE ANALYTIC STRUCTURE OF THE CLASSICAL APPROACH TO VALUE AND DISTRIBUTION

According to Ricardo, an investigation of the laws governing the distribution of income was the "principal problem in Political Economy" (*Works*, vol. I, p. 6). This involved (1) isolating the factors determining that distribution *in a given place and time* and (2) studying the causes of changes in these factors *over time*. The analytic structure of the classical approach to the theory of value and distribution may now be summarized. In determining the distribution of income and relative prices in a given time and place, the classical authors isolated the following factors, or independent variables, or "data":

(a) The set of technical alternatives from which cost-minimizing producers can choose, reflecting the attained level of technical knowledge.

(b) The size and composition of the social product, reflecting, *inter alia* (together with (a)), the attained social division of labor, the needs and wants of the members of the different classes of society, and the requirements of reproduction and capital accumulation.

(c) The ruling real wage rate of common labor or the share of wages (and the scale of wage differentials), reflecting the balance of power between workers and the propertied classes in the conflict over the distribution of income.

(d) The quantities of different qualities of land available (and the known stocks of depletable resources, such as mineral deposits).

We may exemplify these givens in regard to Ricardo's writings. To him, the actual state of technical knowledge in a given situation was of great importance in ascertaining the levels of the rate of profits and the rents of different qualities of land. For instance, when discussing the tendency of the rate of profits to fall, Ricardo started from the assumption of a given technical knowledge and then added that this tendency "is happily checked at repeated intervals by the improvements in machinery . . . as well as by discoveries in the science of agriculture" (*Works*, vol. I, p. 120). The levels of total output were of great importance for the same purpose, because with diminishing returns in agriculture (and mining) it matters whether little or much corn is to be produced and little or much ore to be extracted, given the information summarized in (d). As Ricardo stressed: "The exchangeable value of all commodities, whether they be manufactured, or the produce of the mines, or the produce of land, is always regulated . . . by the most unfavorable circumstances, the most unfavorable under which *the quantity of produce required*, renders it necessary to carry on the production" (*Works*, vol. I, p. 73; emphasis added). Finally, Ricardo insisted that the rate of profits and relative prices depend on the level of wages (see Kurz and Salvadori, 1995, 472–3). Ricardo singled out these factors as the dominant ones determining the rate of profits, the rates of rent and prices in a given place and time.

It deserves to be stressed that Ricardo's intuition was correct: on the basis of the above data we can in fact determine in a coherent way the unknowns or dependent variables. No other information or data are needed. This is an important fact in itself. In addition, it should be emphasized that *any* coherent long-period theory of value and distribution must start from a set of data that implies the set (a)–(d) of variables that the classical authors took as given.

11.7   PUTTING THE THEORY OF VALUE AND DISTRIBUTION TO WORK

The overwhelming importance of the theory of value and distribution for the classical economists derives from the fact that all other economic analysis was developed in terms of it: the theory was indeed designed to provide a solid base from which such intricate problems as capital accumulation or different forms of technical change or various economic policy issues could be studied. A few illustrations must suffice.

The data (a)–(d) singled out in order to determine the rate of profits, rents, and relative prices in a given time and place at the same time contain the key to the problem of the long-run development of income distribution and relative prices. Any tendency of the rate of profits to fall or rise in Ricardo, for example, is traced back to the interaction of changes over time in techniques, output levels, and wages. Ricardo stressed: "If the necessaries of the workman could be constantly increased with the same facility, there could be no permanent alteration in the rate of profits or wages, to whatever amount capital might be accumulated" (*Works*, vol. I, p. 289). Yet, due to diminishing returns in agriculture (and mining), and setting aside technical progress, physical real costs of producing necessaries are bound to rise with rising output levels. With a given real wage rate, as less and less fertile lands (mines) are cultivated (worked), or given qualities of lands (mines) have to be cultivated (worked) more intensively, the rate of profits is bound to fall and rents must be paid to the owners of intramarginal lands (mines) as well as of lands (mines) cultivated (worked) intensively. This describes what Ricardo called the "natural course of events"; that is, the path the economy would take in the hypothetical case in which capital accumulates but there are no further technical improvements. In terms of the above schema, independent variable (b) changes (and, *a fortiori*, mines are depleted), but all other data are frozen.

Over time, the set of technical alternatives of production can be expected to change due to technical and organizational innovations of various kinds: see especially Ricardo's discussion of different forms of agricultural improvements and of machinery (*Works*, vol. I, chs. II and XXXI). Over time, the size and composition of output can be expected to change, reflecting a multitude of influences interacting in a complex way. The availability of entirely new commodities or of better qualities of known commodities would interact with the needs and wants of the different classes of society, and thus give rise to new patterns of consumption and a changing composition of output. (An approach that starts from given consumer preferences obviously cannot capture the changes under consideration.) Hence, what was taken as given in the determination of the rate of profits and the rates of rent in a given place and time under (b) is bound to change over time, involving changes in income distribution and relative prices. Obviously, the real wage rate of common labor is also not given and constant forever. As Ricardo kept stressing: "It is not to be understood that the natural price of labour, estimated even in food and necessaries, is absolutely fixed and constant. It varies at different times in the same country, and very materially differs in different countries. It essentially depends on the habits and customs of the people. . . . Many of the conveniences now enjoyed in an English cottage, would have been thought luxuries at an earlier period of our history" (*Works*, vol. I, pp. 96–7).

The classical economists studied the dynamics of the economic system essentially in terms of comparisons between different long-period positions characterized by different specifications of the "data" (a)–(c) (considering land as a nondepletable resource and setting aside exhaustible resources). The long-period method was seen as the best available for coming to grips with an ever-changing world characterized by ongoing technical progress, capital accumulation, and far-reaching structural change.

Bibliography

Aspromourgos, T. 1996: *On the Origins of Classical Economics. Distribution and Value from William Petty to Adam Smith*. London and New York: Routledge.

Bortkiewicz, L. von 1906–7: Wertrechnung und Preisrechnung im Marxschen System. *Archiv für Sozialwissenschaft und Sozialpolitik*, 23 (1906), 1–50 (essay I); 25 (1907), 10–51 (essay II) and 445–88 (essay III).

Garegnani, P. 1984: Value and distribution in the classical economists and Marx. *Oxford Economic Papers*, 36, 291–325.

—— 1987: Surplus approach to value and distribution. In J. Eatwell, M. Milgate, and P. Newman (eds.), *The New Palgrave. A Dictionary of Economics*, vol. 4. London: Macmillan, 560–74.

Kurz, H. D. and Salvadori, N. 1993: The "Standard commodity" and Ricardo's search for an "invariable measure of value." In M. Baranzini and G. C. Harcourt (eds.), *The Dynamics of the Wealth of Nations. Growth, Distribution and Structural Change. Essays in Honour of Luigi Pasinetti*. New York: St. Martin's Press, 95–123.

—— and —— 1995: *Theory of Production. A Long-Period Analysis*. Cambridge, UK: Cambridge University Press.

—— and —— 1998a: *Understanding "Classical" Economics: Studies in Long-Period Theory*. London: Routledge.

—— and —— (eds.) 1998b: *The Elgar Companion to Classical Economics*, 2 vols. Cheltenham and Northampton, MA: Edward Elgar.

—— and —— 2000: "Classical" roots of input–output analysis: a short account of its long prehistory. *Economic Systems Research*, 12, 153–79.

—— and —— 2002: The surplus interpretation of the classical economists: a reply to Mark Blaug. *History of Political Economy*, 34(1), 227–38.

Marx, K. 1954a: *Theories of Surplus Value*. Moscow: Progress Publishers. English translation of *Theorien über den Mehrwert*.

—— 1954b: *Capital*, vol. I. Moscow: Progress Publishers. English translation of *Das Kapital*, vol. I (1867). Hamburg: Meissner.

—— 1959: *Capital*, vol. III. Moscow: Progress Publishers. English translation of *Das Kapital*, vol. III, ed. F. Engels (1894). Hamburg: Meissner.

Mill, J. 1844: *Elements of Political Economy*, 1st edn. 1821; 3rd edn. 1826, reprinted 1844. London: Henry G. Bohn.

Petty, W. 1986: *The Economic Writings of Sir William Petty*, 2 vols, ed. C. H. Hull. Originally published in 1899, Cambridge, UK: Cambridge University Press. Reprinted in one volume, New York: Augustus M. Kelley, 1986.

Quesnay, F. 1972 [1759]: *Quesnay's Tableau économique*, ed. M. Kuczynski and R. L. Meek. London: Macmillan.

Ricardo, D. 1951–73: *The Works and Correspondence of David Ricardo*, 11 vols, edited by P. Sraffa with the collaboration of M. H. Dobb. Cambridge, UK: Cambridge University Press. This is referred to in the text as "*Works*," followed by the volume number.

Smith, A. 1976 [1776]: *An Inquiry into the Nature and Causes of the Wealth of Nations. The Glasgow Edition of the Works and Correspondence of Adam Smith*, 2 vols. Oxford: Oxford University Press. This is referred to in the text as "WN, book number, chapter number, section number, paragraph number."

Sraffa, P. 1951: Introduction. In Ricardo (1951), *Works*, vol. I, pp. xiii–lxii.

—— 1960: *Production of Commodities by Means of Commodities. Prelude to a Critique of Economic Theory*. Cambridge, UK: Cambridge University Press.

Torrens, R. 2000: *Collected Works of Robert Torrens*, 8 vols, edited and introduced by G. de Vivo. Bristol: Thoemmes Press.

CHAPTER TWELVE

Non-Marxian Socialism

J. E. King

12.1 INTRODUCTION

A socialist can be defined as anyone who asserts that capitalism has very serious problems, and who also believes that a substantial degree of common ownership is necessary if those problems are to be solved. Thus socialism covers a very wide range of opinions, from revolutionary anarcho-syndicalists to moderate social democrats and even (at the margin) some conservatives (Lichtheim, 1983 [1970]). It does exclude, however, the essentially neoliberal advocates of a (post-1989) "Third Way." Economics can also be defined very broadly, to include any discussion of production, consumption, distribution, or exchange, whether it is conducted by specialist economists, by political activists, or by social philosophers. Even "non-Marxist" is an elastic term, as the instances of Rudolf Hilferding, Oskar Lange, and John Roemer illustrate (see sections 12.3, 12.5, and 12.9). There is, inevitably, some overlap with Geert Reuten's chapter on Marxism and with Warren Samuels's chapter on utopian economics.

12.2 SOCIALISM BEFORE MARX, 1800–50

Arguments for some form of socialism date back to classical antiquity. The case for beginning this survey around 1800 is a simple one: all the writers considered here preached a socialism of affluence, denying the Malthusian claim that nature placed severe limits on material progress. For them, capitalism stood condemned for perpetuating poverty in the midst of potential plenty. The rise of modern industry, they asserted, demonstrated that human ingenuity was boundless; social, political, and (above all) economic institutions were to blame for the continuing misery of the mass of the population, not divine displeasure or the niggardliness of nature.

Among the most important of the early British socialists were John Francis Bray, John Gray, Thomas Hodgkin, Robert Owen, and William Thompson

(Thompson, 1998). They all attacked Malthus and his followers, sometimes drawing on Ricardo and other classical economists to substantiate their critique, and for this reason are frequently referred to as the "Ricardian socialists." The first and most serious defect of the existing order, they maintained, was an indefensible degree of inequality. At this point they often invoked the labor theory of value, interpreted (as it had been by John Locke) as a theory of natural right. Since each productive individual was entitled to the full fruits of his own labor, the working man was clearly receiving much less than his due. Most early socialists attributed the gross injustice of the contemporary income distribution to inequality in economic relations, in particular the prevalence of unequal exchange. Bray set out a very clear theory of exploitation, derived from a theory of surplus labor (Bray, 1931 [1839]; King, 1983).

The capitalist system was also criticized on efficiency grounds, since periodic industrial crises threw millions of working people into utter destitution and forced the economy to operate well below its potential capacity. Socialists frequently linked this phenomenon with the inequality of income, which they believed to be responsible for a chronic tendency to underconsumption. A similar point had been made in 1819 by J. C. L. Simonde de Sismondi and also by Robert Owen, who was equally convinced that unrestrained economic individualism was innately self-destructive. Owen added a further reason for supposing capitalism to be wasteful and inefficient, in that it failed miserably to develop the skills and make use of the intelligence of the workforce. Human potential was being squandered through constant overwork, malnutrition, and cultural and educational deprivation.

Claude-Henri de Saint-Simon came to the same conclusion by a different route. The principal defect of contemporary French society, he maintained, was the excessive influence of the aristocracy and the military. This came at the expense of the *industriels* or productive classes, which included not just the workers but also their capitalist employers, intellectuals, scientists, and artists. For Saint-Simon, economic efficiency required the concentration of decision-making in the hands of an enlightened (and well-paid) elite. His compatriot Charles Fourier proposed a much less authoritarian system in which work would be performed for its own sake and production organized by voluntary associations of free producers. Fourier was also no radical egalitarian: he believed in rewarding skill, responsibility, and managerial expertise, and even in the payment of interest on the capital invested in the Phalanstery, or productive community (Tugan-Baranovsky, 1966 [1910]).

While the early socialists disagreed on the defects of the status quo, there were even sharper differences of opinion on how things might be put right. Sismondi, famously described by Marx and Engels in *The Communist Manifesto* as a "petit-bourgeois socialist," advocated a return to a pre-capitalist and largely pre-industrial economy. Some British socialists favored an egalitarian society of independent artisans who could exchange their products among themselves in proportion to the labor time expended in producing them, with a monetary system (of "labor notes") designed to facilitate the process of equal exchange. Many, however, were convinced, like Saint-Simon, of the need for a collective solution that preserved the advantages of large-scale production and the social division of labor while eliminating the worst of the costs.

Some of the fault-lines that would later divide the socialist movement were already apparent. Was the new society to be egalitarian or stratified? Should it be democratic or authoritarian? Would it be based on market relations, or would nonmarket processes prevail? Could it be self-managed, or did it have to be run by the state? Would it be achieved by reform or revolution? These questions were to pose themselves over and over again, to every subsequent generation, right up to the present day.

Respectable economists reacted to "the people's political economy" with a mixture of fascination and horror. The socialist implications of the labor theory of value were vigorously denied, along with the theory itself, as was the viability of any alternative economic system. Socialism, the classical economists claimed, would destroy the incentive to produce, to save, and to exercise moral restraint in the matter of procreation. It would therefore have a disastrous effect on the level and rate of growth of output. Only John Stuart Mill responded at all sympathetically to socialist arguments, most strongly in the third edition of his *Principles*, where he rejected the Malthusian critique of socialism and accepted the possibility that public-spiritedness might well replace traditional economic incentives. Mill favored self-managed workers' cooperatives rather than state ownership of enterprises, and on this count can perhaps be seen as a forerunner of the syndicalists. Late in life, however, his doubts about the desirability of any form of socialism returned (Robbins, 1978 [1952]).

12.3 STATE SOCIALISM, 1850–1945

The case of Sismondi illustrates the potential for conservative critics of liberal individualism to take up socialist, or quasi-socialist, positions. By the 1870s there was in Germany a vigorous school of *Kathedersozialisten* (professorial socialists), led by Gustav von Schmoller and Adolph Wagner, who combined loyalty to the emperor with a deep suspicion of unbridled competition. These conservative state socialists advocated a substantial degree of state ownership and the encouragement of peasant proprietorship through state acquisition of large estates, supported tariff protection and government promotion of German trade and overseas colonies, and demanded strict regulation of hours and working conditions in factories and workshops. Wagner went much further, proposing the nationalization of all large-scale enterprises, including the banks (Dawson, 1972 [1890]).

In analytic terms the pioneers of the "marginalist revolution" in economics were a very long way from the German professorial socialists. The relationship between socialism and neoclassical economic theory was, however, ambivalent. On the one hand, the neoclassicals repudiated the labor theory of value and in most cases rejected the very concept of exploitation. Marginal productivity theory was sometimes consciously used to defend the justice of the existing distribution of income. On the other hand, some important elements of neoclassical theory pointed in a socialist direction. First, and most obviously, the diminishing marginal utility of money had inescapable egalitarian implications. Secondly, the Walrasian auctioneer who was supposed to establish the vector of competitive prices, although a phantom, could potentially be conjured into life in the service of a government planning bureau. General equilibrium theory could then be reinterpreted as a theory of socialism rather than as an account of the capitalist market process. Thirdly, the neoclassical concepts of marginal utility and marginal cost offered a rigorous foundation for collectivist economic planning (see section 12.5). This, perhaps, was what Léon Walras had in mind when he described himself as "a scientific socialist." Finally, since, in actually existing capitalism, monopoly power was widespread and growing rapidly, the conditions for efficient resource allocation were routinely violated. This pointed to the benefits of a very considerable degree of state intervention and also reinstated the fundamental socialist notion of exploitation, albeit in a very different form. Between 1870 and 1945 many socialists were attracted to marginalist economics (Steedman, 1995), while some of the best neoclassical theorists were committed socialists.

Fabians such as Sidney and Beatrice Webb and George Bernard Shaw were among the first to use neoclassical economics as an intellectual weapon against capitalism, which they believed to be both wasteful and unjust. In production, they argued, monopoly led to the curtailment of supply. In distribution, Ricardian rent theory could be extended from land to capital, providing a theory of exploitation independent of the labor theory of value, since the great bulk of property income was unrelated to any productive contribution or sacrifice. The anarchic nature of the capitalist economy generated enormous waste, because the coordination of individual decisions was necessarily highly imperfect. Thus the Fabians called for high rates of progressive taxation on unearned income and for the socialization of the means of production, which would be better employed under the direction of expert economic planners in the service of the state (Shaw, 1949). They regarded themselves as the true scientific socialists, since their analysis was based on modern economic theory and backed up by painstaking empirical research, in contrast with the speculative, Utopian, and Hegelian foundations of Marxian socialism.

Before long, neoclassical ideas began to infiltrate German social democracy. The key figure in this process was the former Marxist Eduard Bernstein, who was heavily influenced by the Fabian case for gradual, peaceful, piecemeal change. Bernstein abandoned the labor theory of value and the notions of surplus value and exploitation. He became skeptical of the Marxian doctrines of growing social polarization, the increasing severity of economic crises and the necessity – indeed, the inevitability – of violent revolution (Bernstein, 1909 [1899]). In the 1920s the formerly orthodox Marxian theorist Rudolf Hilferding pointed to the successful extension of state control over the economy during World War I and set out a new theory of "organised capitalism." The tyranny of the market, Hilferding proclaimed, had been overcome with the growth of private monopolies and public regulation and control of economic life. This process would culminate in a fully socialist economy, owned and managed by the state in the interests of the working class, without a revolutionary upheaval (Howard and King, 1992, ch. 1).

The socialist convictions of many neoclassical economists were reinforced by the emergence of Pigovian welfare economics, which highlighted the need for detailed and comprehensive state interference with the operation of many, if not all, markets. More important, perhaps, was the development of rigorous models of imperfect competition, revealing that prices were seldom equal to marginal costs and wage rates were almost invariably lower than the value of the marginal product of labor. Finally, Keynes's *The General Theory* demonstrated that involuntary unemployment was a recurrent fact of life in any capitalist economy in which the level of aggregate demand was not subject to conscious social control. In Britain, liberal socialists denounced unemployment, inequality, and monopoly as the three fundamental flaws of capitalist economies, and proposed a combination of public ownership, microeconomic planning, and Keynesian demand management to put them right (Meade, 1936; Robinson, 1943). In the United States, neoclassical theorists used the new analytic tools to outline an "economics of control" (Lerner, 1944) and to assert the feasibility of an efficient socialist economy (Bergson, 1948). Most neoclassical economists, however, remained opposed to socialism (Pigou, 1937). Equally, in the socialist camp it was not just the Marxists who dismissed contemporary economics as at best irrelevant and, at worst, little more than capitalist ideology (Cole, 1935).

12.4   LIBERTARIAN SOCIALISM, 1850–1945

There had always been an anti-statist element in socialist thought, reflected in the communitarianism of the Owenites and the supporters of Fourier and strengthened by anarchist suspicions of Marxism. Anarcho-communist ideas were propagated, from the early 1880s, by William Morris and Peter Kropotkin, who argued that human beings have a natural propensity for spontaneous cooperation to provide each other with "mutual aid" through voluntary and federative association (Kropotkin, 1902). In the early years of the twentieth century libertarian socialist arguments were advanced even more vigorously, by the syndicalists, Guild Socialists, and finally, after 1917, by Council Communists.

The syndicalists agreed with all the traditional socialist objections to capitalism: inequality, exploitation, unemployment, and poverty in the midst of potential plenty. But they had an additional complaint, against capitalism now and against state socialism as a vision of the future. In neither case were the interests of working people as *producers* taken at all seriously. Fabian (and all neoclassical) variants of socialism were based on the assumption that consumer interests were paramount, and implicitly placed a very low (or zero) value on the human need for self-realization though work. This need could be satisfied only through workers' control of the labor process, and it could not be traded away in exchange for higher levels of material consumption. An engaging account of the syndicalist vision was provided by Emile Pataud and Emile Pouget (1990 [1909]), who described the debates between those who argued for immediate free access to all consumer goods and more cautious syndicalists who believed this to be premature. A compromise would result, in which basic commodities such as food and clothing became available to all holders of a union card, free upon demand, while luxuries were rationed by price. Wage equality would ensure rough equality of consumption, according to individual taste, and the "free access" sector would continually expand as the productive potential of the new society increased. Working time would be greatly reduced, with the introduction of an eight-hour day and a much shorter working life.

A frequently voiced contemporary objection to syndicalism was that it privileged producer interests at the expense of consumers. Guild Socialism represented a compromise between the libertarians and the state socialists, on this and other issues. The Guild Socialists intended that consumer and producer interests be given equal weight in the making of economic decisions. The most eloquent defense of Guild Socialism came from the philosopher Bertrand Russell, who agreed with the anarchists that work should be undertaken voluntarily, as an end in itself, and should not be treated only as a means to the acquisition of consumer goods: "no community where most work is disagreeable can be said to have found a solution of economic problems" (Russell, 1920 [1918], p. 193). In a transitional phase it would be necessary to offer material incentives to compensate those workers in unpleasant or monotonous jobs, and also to encourage innovation. Everyone would receive a basic income and free access to some essential commodities (including education and child care), while those who chose to work would also be paid a wage and enjoy the right to a higher level of individual consumption. Receipt of the basic income, Russell noted, would give scientists and artists the freedom to pursue their interests unhindered by the need for state approval (or state finance). Payment for housework would "secure the complete economic independence of wives" (ibid., p. 196). He expected drudgery to decline very rapidly as leisure was given a higher priority than material consumption and less time was wasted on unproductive activities. People's characters would also improve, and the joy of life would be greater than it could ever be in a competitive world.

Like Russell, G. D. H. Cole proposed a form of market socialism based on workers' control of production but with the planning of investment, and the supply of credit, in the hands of the political authorities. Both the market and the inequalities that it engendered would eventually wither away, as more and more essential goods and services were supplied free, according to need (Cole, 1920, pp. 141–8). Reacting to the Russian Revolution, the Council Communists Anton Pannekoek and Herman Gorter rejected the authoritarianism and statism of mainstream communism, arguing instead for a form of nonmarket socialism based on self-management by mass assemblies of workers, represented where necessary by recallable delegates. A more detailed elaboration of an essentially similar vision guided the much more recent work of Albert and Hahnel (1991), which is discussed in section 12.9.

Fabians, Leninists, and conservatives were in broad agreement in criticizing libertarian socialism. Their principal objections concerned the lack of any provision for overall planning, the refusal to recognize the need for expert management, and – above all – the narrow sectionalism that syndicalist and kindred ideas would inevitably breed. In a generally rather sympathetic discussion of "collectivism," the liberal Treasury economist Ralph Hawtrey concluded that producer cooperatives would behave like a trade union engaged in collective bargaining with the state, which would bring all the dangers of injury to the community that were already posed by strikes under capitalism. Strike-breaking might have to be seen as a social virtue if the collectivist state were to survive (Hawtrey, 1926, p. 351).

12.5 THE LANGE CONTROVERSY, 1908–89

While the Fabians claimed that marginalism was entirely consistent with socialism, they made little progress in adapting neoclassical principles to serve as a guide to economic planning. In 1920 Ludwig von Mises attacked the very possibility of rational calculation in a socialist commonwealth. Without a market for producer goods, and a system of market prices, there was no rational method of pricing inputs, and thus no way in which costs of production could be calculated – or minimized. Socialists had simply evaded this problem, but no one any longer pretended that labor values offered a sensible measure of economic magnitudes. War communism in Russia was had involved the destruction of the existing division of labor and its replacement by "a closed peasant household economy" (von Mises, 1935 [1920], p. 125). Some socialists, such as von Mises's compatriot Otto Neurath, actually seemed to welcome this, making a virtue out of harsh necessity.

Unknown (apparently) to von Mises, this question had already been addressed by an Italian disciple of Pareto, Enrico Barone. If a socialist Ministry of Production wished to maximize social welfare, Barone argued, it would have to use the capitalist categories of prices, wages, interest, rent, and profit, and enforce the capitalist criteria of minimizing production costs and equating prices to costs. Thus socialism would look very much like capitalism. Even the much-vaunted gains from abolishing the "anarchy of the market" were illusory. The Ministry of Production would not be able to calculate economic magnitudes *a priori*; it would have to engage in precisely the same process of experimentation as occurred in capitalism, with identical consequences (Barone, 1935 [1908], pp. 287–9).

In 1935 Friedrich von Hayek published the first English translation of von Mises and Barone, together with similar criticisms by other writers (Hayek, 1935a). Hayek was prepared to concede the possibility of rational central planning, using a Barone-type system of simultaneous equations, but vehemently denied that it was practicable. A socialist planning authority would need "details of the most minute description"; it would have to undertake calculations that were "beyond human capacity" and "could not be carried out in a lifetime" (Hayek, 1935b, pp. 209, 211, 212). Some younger socialists had recognized this, and had repudiated planning in favor of market socialism. This, Hayek argued, was already a significant retreat. Neither was it any more practicable: without private property in the means of production, there could be nothing more than "pseudo-competition" (ibid., p. 217). The advocates of market socialism misunderstood the role of profits as "an inducement to change" (ibid., p. 230). There would be no incentive for socialist managers to take risks if successful innovation brought no reward; conversely, errors must not go unpunished. Hayek concluded by denying the existence of any middle way: "nobody has yet demonstrated how planning and competition can be rationally combined" (ibid., p. 241).

Oskar Lange (1938 [1936–7]) soon took up this challenge. He had no qualms about the restoration of markets and money under socialism; this, after all, is precisely what happened in the Soviet Union after 1921 once output had recovered from the disastrous consequences of the civil war. Lange set out a comprehensive model of market – or quasi-market – socialism with freedom of choice for consumers and workers, so that consumer goods and labor were allocated through markets, but all means of production and natural resources were owned by the state. Economic welfare would be maximized, Lange demonstrated, if socialist managers were required to follow Barone's two simple rules. First, minimize the average cost of production, thereby also minimizing the alternative opportunities forgone. Secondly, produce up to the point at which price equals marginal cost, thereby maximizing consumer welfare. Prices of producer goods and resources would be set by a Central Planning Board and therefore parametric to the managers, as would be the case in an ideal, perfectly competitive, capitalist economy. A process of trial and error could then be used to establish equilibrium. The Central Planning Board would play the role of the Walrasian auctioneer, carrying out a sort of socialist *tâtonnement*. It would not have to solve millions of equations, as had been alleged by Hayek; in fact, it would not have to solve any equations at all. The accumulation of capital could be determined by the Central Planning Board or simply left to the market, in which case the rate of interest would be established – as with all other prices – at the level necessary to equate the demand for capital with the supply.

The initial reaction of socialist economists was that Hayek had been routed. His reply can be interpreted either as reflecting a major shift in emphasis or simply as a clarification of the Austrian position. Either way, it required him to break explicitly with neoclassical economics. A successful attack on Lange, he came to realize, entailed a fundamental critique of equilibrium analysis and of the neoclassical conception of competition as a force which gives rise to equilibrium solutions. Competition, Hayek now argued, entails rivalry: it is a process of struggle, involving a clash of human purposes, and not a neutral progression of trial and error. Barone's equations were therefore irrelevant to the real world of continuous, rivalrous change – and so, too, were Lange's solutions to them (Hayek, 1940; Lavoie, 1985).

12.6 European Social Democracy After 1945

The postwar compromise between capital and labor led many Marxists to ask whether capitalism had changed, fundamentally and irreversibly (Howard and King, 1992, ch. 4), and social democrats also began to wonder whether it was still capitalism. The British politician (and former academic economist) Anthony Crosland (1956) argued that it was not. He claimed that economic power had been transferred from capitalists to the state, through nationalization and direct intervention in the private sector; to organized labor; and to a newly influential class of technicians and professional managers. This loss of power had produced an important change in the psychology and motivation of "the contemporary business leader," who was much less aggressive in the pursuit of profit and much more inclined to accept his social responsibilities. Poverty had declined greatly, Crosland noted, and the share of the very rich in income and wealth had been substantially reduced. Full employment had brought with it a shift from a buyers' to a sellers' market for labor, which had improved social welfare and further altered the balance of class power. Finally, almost everyone now accepted the need for some measure of economic planning by the state. If "capitalism" referred to decentralized economic decision-making by a tiny minority of private owners driven by individual greed in a climate of intense class antagonism, then capitalism was dead. Crosland concluded that ownership of the means of production was increasingly irrelevant, since *control* of large companies now rested with management. The traditional socialist concern with public ownership of the means of production, distribution, and exchange was misguided. Socialists should aim for greater equality, not for further nationalization.

Crosland had greatly exaggerated the extent to which the capitalist tiger's teeth had been drawn, as he himself was forced to acknowledge when international finance took its revenge on the British Labour government in the 1975 sterling crisis (Thompson, 1996, pp. 236–9). He had been remarkably complacent about the dangers of wage inflation, rejecting the necessity for an incomes policy on the grounds that demand management was sufficient to keep prices under control (Crosland, 1956, p. 461). He was at best lukewarm about industrial democracy, following the age-old Fabian line that self-management was simply not feasible in any large organization (ibid., pp. 333–50). Finally, his commitment to increased equality sat uneasily with his repudiation of further nationalization. If the distribution of wealth was to become much more equal, but industry was not (for the most part) to be owned by the state, what pattern of ownership *did* Crosland have in mind? Did he envisage a "share-owning democracy" or "people's capitalism," of the type supposedly favored by his Liberal and Conservative opponents?

More radical social democrats looked to Scandinavia for answers to these and other questions. Between 1945 and the late 1980s, when the Swedish model of socialism was at its strongest, unemployment was extremely low and incomes more equally distributed than anywhere else in the world, the self-proclaimed Communist bloc included. The most interesting part of the Swedish model, however, was the one that was never implemented: the proposal for wage-earners' funds. Under a "solidaristic" wages policy that benefited the low-paid, highly profitable firms were not subject to claims for higher pay from their workers. In the absence of a high excess profits tax, there was a real danger that the profit share in national income would rise continuously. To avoid this, the Swedish unions advocated a form of collective profit-sharing in which a proportion of a firm's profits would be allocated in the form of new shares to union-controlled trust funds. These wage-earners' funds, it was intended, would eventually own a significant percentage of equity in Swedish industry, offsetting the tendency to increasing concentration of wealth and strengthening the voice of employees in managerial decision-making (Meidner, 1993).

In the late 1970s and 1980s there was a deep crisis in European social democracy as a consequence of growing dissatisfaction with the welfare state, and especially with the high tax rates needed to finance it. The outcome was the adoption of neoliberal economic policies by ostensibly socialist governments and, on the left of social democracy, the articulation of an Alternative Economic Strategy (Aaronovitch, 1981) which combined an extension of public ownership with increased union rights at the workplace and proposals for detailed state intervention in the private sector to promote higher investment and more rapid technical change. Coupled with this "industry policy" was an essentially Keynesian macroeconomic strategy that relied upon fiscal and/or monetary policy to restore full employment and (for some) a consensual incomes policy – including control over prices and profits – to restrain inflation. Economic planning was to apply also to international trade and capital movements. To a very large extent, the Alternative Economic Strategy represented a restatement and modernization of the "liberal socialist" ideas of the 1930s (Thompson, 1996).

12.7   SELF-MANAGED SOCIALISM AFTER 1945

Largely in response to developments in Yugoslavia, a very substantial literature on the economics of self-management grew up in the 1970s (see Jaroslav Vanek, 1975). Branko Horvat argued that socialism required the replacement of *both* private *and* state ownership by "social ownership" of the means of production. This entailed that enterprises be self-managed, with their decisions coordinated by the market – but a market corrected and regulated by the state. Economic democracy, Horvat claimed, would lead to both increased efficiency and greater equity; it would also tend to reinforce political democracy (Horvat, 1982). A search for forerunners would have led him to Oskar Lange, whose first model of market socialism, written jointly (in Polish) with Marek Breit in 1934, had drawn on ideas dating back to Friedrich Engels's old enemy, Eugen Dühring, and further developed by Theodor Hertzka (1987 [1891]). In the Breit–Lange model, production was controlled by self-managed firms but membership of these enterprises was open to all-comers; any worker had the unconditional right to join (or leave) any firm. This right of free entry would automatically break down monopoly power. It would also provide the socialist National Bank with a ready-made investment criterion – direct resources to those enterprises with an inflow of members – since this would be an excellent indicator of the intensity of demand for the goods and services that they produced (Chilosi, 1986; Breit and Lange, 2003 [1934]).

The first formal analyses of the self-managed enterprise, using a neoclassical framework, came from Benjamin Ward (1958) and Evsey Domar (1966). A systematic and comprehensive neoclassical model of Yugoslav self-management was later published by Jaroslav Vanek, a trade theorist. Vanek's discussion was based on a comparative static analysis of a labor-managed firm that maximized net income per member, contrasting it with the behavior of the profit-maximizing capitalist firm of traditional theory. One potential problem was the supply response of the cooperative to an increase in product demand, which might be zero or even negative. On balance, though, a labor-managed economy would be "not only highly efficient in absolute terms but also more efficient than other existing economic systems," including Stalinist central planning (Vanek, 1970, p. 403).

Responding to Vanek, James Meade stressed the overriding importance of free entry in a labor-managed economy. He also discussed the possible incompatibility of self-management with labor discipline and the inescapable conflict between efficiency and equity, which implied a need for rules to govern the distribution of the surplus between established cooperative members and newcomers. There should also be some social provision for risk-sharing to prevent workers having all their eggs in one basket, which would be the case if all their assets, and their only source of income, came from their membership of a single cooperative enterprise (Meade, 1972). In later work Meade continued to advocate a decentralized, competitive society based on workers' cooperatives, in which economic incentives would restrain the cost-inflationary pressures that had ultimately destroyed the postwar social democratic consensus (Meade, 1989).

A much more conservative variant of Meade's analysis was supplied by Martin Weitzman (1984), who looked for inspiration to Japan, where workers received a significant proportion of their income in the form of annual bonuses related to their employer's profits. The marginal cost of labor, equal to the wage, was therefore substantially below the average cost, which included the bonus. Profit-maximizing Japanese firms had an incentive to employ more workers (*ceteris paribus*) than their Western counterparts. This pointed the way to a "share economy" in which full employment could be maintained without generating inflation.

Some theorists of self-management approached the question from a much more radical perspective. Jaroslav Vanek's brother Jan, for example, refused to be confined to a neoclassical straitjacket in his appraisal of the benefits from self-management, rejecting the single-maximand approach in favor of a "vectoral model" in which the self-managed enterprise pursued multiple goals. These included – in addition to current net income per worker – growth in income, long-term security of income, reduction in effort and work intensity, improvements in the work environment, acquisition of skills and career advancement for members, and welfare and social benefits provided by the cooperative. Self-managed enterprises would also strive for "the suppression of non-work," by which Vanek meant the elimination of the restrictive practices, featherbedding, and opportunistic withholding of effort that were characteristic of capitalist firms (Jan Vanek, 1972, ch. 9).

This last point was taken up, in a neoclassical framework, by Samuel Bowles and Herbert Gintis, who focused on the determination of effort levels in capitalist and "democratic" firms, the latter being owned and managed by the workforce. Bowles and Gintis identified several reasons why democratic enterprises might operate more efficiently, and induce higher inputs of effort, than their capitalist counterparts. These included the motivational impact of participation in decision-making, more effective mutual monitoring and the greater use of financial incentives by the democratic firm, relative to monitoring and disciplinary sanctions (Bowles and Gintis, 1993).

12.8   PLAN AND MARKET, 1953–89

Defenders of Soviet planning noted that while, under capitalism, the intertemporal allocation problem was solved by the uncoordinated individual decisions of capitalists and landlords, in communism the solution was imposed by the central planners in the interests of society as a whole. The relevant criteria had been specified by neoclassical theorists, but they could be implemented only under socialism (Dobb, 1960). In the Cambridge growth equation, $g = s_c r$, where g is the steady-state growth rate, r is the rate of profit, and s_c is the propensity to save out of profits. Eliminating capitalist consumption, so that $s_c = 1$, means that $g = r$ and a socialist "golden age" can be achieved (Nuti, 1970). After 1945 these arguments resonated powerfully in what soon came to be known as the Third World, since they appeared to offer a theoretical justification for applying the Soviet model to the ex-colonial countries, where rapid growth was the overriding political priority. Mao's China now provided a second major example of successful centrally planned industrialization (Baran, 1957).

The first doubts were expressed in Eastern Europe, not long after the death of Stalin in 1953. Here the static inefficiencies of the command economy were not only obvious but also large enough to reduce the growth rate (Nove and Nuti, 1972). Dissenting voices were heard first in Poland, where Michal Kalecki objected strongly to the "heroic" nature of Polish plan construction in the 1960s, which imposed enormous sacrifices on the working class and neglected both the productivity of new investment and its effect on the productivity of labor. Kalecki modified the Harrod–Domar growth equation to highlight the contribution of technical progress, and devised a planning algorithm allowing the authorities to economize on investment resources (Kalecki, 1992, 1993). Although he supported workers' management of production, Kalecki was not a market socialist. Neither was Oskar Lange (1967), who now believed that computers had made it possible to solve the classic socialist calculation problem directly. Some of Kalecki's younger colleagues, however, argued that markets should be given a much *greater* role in the increasingly complex and sophisticated economies of Central Europe (Brus, 1972).

This view proved more influential in those parts of Eastern Europe where far-reaching economic reforms were introduced. The economics minister in the ill-fated Dubček government in Czechoslovakia, Ota Šik (1976), advocated democratic market socialism as a "Third Way" between capitalism and Stalinism, in which production decisions would be made by independent enterprises. He proposed a combination of competitive markets and macroeconomic planning of incomes, credit, and foreign trade, all in the context of a democratic political system. According to Janos Kornai (1986), though, the record of economic reform in Hungary was not encouraging. Command planning had indeed been abolished, but state-owned enterprises had not achieved genuine independence. They operated under a system of "dual dependence," reliant vertically on the bureaucracy and horizontally on their suppliers and customers. Relative prices remained arbitrary and irrational, forcing firms to seek assistance from the state.

This reinforced the universal and pernicious phenomenon of the "soft budget constraint," which allowed enterprise managers to escape the consequences of their errors by obtaining subsidies from local and national government, renegotiating their tax liabilities, receiving credit on excessively generous terms from the state banking system, and benefiting from unduly favorable administered prices. The soft budget constraint, itself a major source of allocative inefficiency, further increased the influence of the political authorities. Pervasive excess demand created an insatiable appetite from enterprises for investment resources, and imposed frustrating and wasteful queuing upon consumers. Prices failed to converge to Walrasian prices; firms did not behave like profit-maximizers; and the planners were neither omniscient nor unselfish. For all these reasons it had proved impossible to simulate the market. The Austrian theorists had been right after all, in stressing that competitive rivalry required a hard budget constraint and a buyer's market.

In the Soviet Union the reforms had not gone even this far. Attempts had been made from the mid-1950s to apply optimizing techniques in the planning process, and Leonid Kantorovitch's work on programming theory won him a Nobel Prize in 1975. But no fundamental alterations to the command planning system were introduced until Mikhail Gorbachev came to power in 1985. Some of his advisers advocated decentralization and democratization of decision-making that went at least as far as anything that had been achieved in Hungary (Aganbegyan, 1988). The Soviet Union disintegrated before the economic theory of *perestroika* (reconstruction) was really put to the test, but early indications had been distinctly unfavorable.

What did all this imply for the feasibility of socialism in the West? Alec Nove offered a left social democratic perspective on the lessons of "actually existing socialism." Centralized planning had proved to be inconsistent with socialist democracy; rule by a self-perpetuating oligarchy had given rise to growing shortages, disequilibria, and imbalances. But the Hungarian reforms had proved relatively successful, and there was much to be learned also from the experience of Yugoslavia, Poland, and China. All relied, to a considerable extent, on the market, and all allowed for a range of different forms of productive unit. Nove's model of "feasible socialism" allowed for five species: state enterprises, centrally controlled and administered; state-owned enterprises with full autonomy and a management responsible to the workforce; cooperatives; small-scale private enterprise; and self-employed individuals. Each species would operate in the habitat most suited to it. Central planning of major investment projects was consistent with a general preference for small-scale production, and continued reliance on material incentives did not rule out the encouragement of moral incentives and conscious limitation of income inequalities (Nove, 1983).

12.9   After the Fall: Socialist Economics Since 1989

The sudden and unexpected collapse of the Communist system in 1989–91 was interpreted in various ways. Many economists concluded that the infeasibility of any form of socialism had been demonstrated for all eternity. Some were more thoughtful, and less triumphalist. Joseph Stiglitz (1994) argued that information problems constituted the most important reason for the failure of the socialist experiment; even Hayek had not recognized the full extent of the problem. The market socialists and the proponents of the standard neoclassical model of capitalism had made the same analytic mistakes. Stiglitz's conclusions were therefore not those of a neoliberal. He recognized that markets could not work without government intervention: the real question was, what sort of intervention, and how much.

Kornai was more pessimistic than Stiglitz about the prospects for any sort of socialism. The classical Soviet system, he suggested, had at least formed a coherent whole. The economic reforms had destroyed this coherence, but had proved incapable of establishing any new order in its place. There was no sign that the various contradictions of the reform process were being resolved; on the contrary, each inconsistency had bred new conflicts. Neither was there a "third road," as Gorbachev had proclaimed. The only outcome of the post-socialist transition was capitalism, even if some of the moral values associated with socialism would continue to exercise a considerable attraction to many in the transition economies (Kornai, 1992).

Attempts to rescue the socialist project were soon forthcoming. A nonmarket vision of a future socialist society came from Michael Albert and Robin Hahnel (1991), who drew on the vision of the Council Communists, reinforced by analytic tools taken from neoclassical economics. Their model of a participatory economy aimed to achieve equity, self-management, solidarity, efficiency, and a diversity of economic lifestyles. This was to be brought about through democratic planning, conducted by federations of workers' and consumers' councils using an iterative process in which production and consumption plans were repeatedly revised in the light of estimates of opportunity costs until excess demands and supplies were eliminated. Albert and Hahnel thus made use of Lange's neo-Walrasian trial-and-error methodology, but without recourse to markets, profits, or anything more than shadow prices. Equity at work would be established in the form of "balanced job complexes" – working lives in which the desirability of individual career paths was roughly equalized. Remuneration would be according to effort, as judged by one's workmates. Some of the objections to this model were considered, and rejected, by Hahnel (2000).

The alternative, market socialist, position was very clearly stated by Pranab Bardhan and John Roemer (1992, p. 101): "Our claim is that competitive markets are necessary to achieve an efficient and vigorous economy, but that full-scale private ownership is not necessary for the successful operation of competitive markets." The fundamental objective was to overcome the soft budget constraint, which (like Stiglitz) they interpreted as a principal–agent problem: How, short of bureaucratic controls, can socialist managers be kept on their toes? They set out two models, both incorporating some essential features of a capitalist economy, but without private ownership. One was bank-centered, while the other mimicked the operation of the capital market. In both variants, national and international competition would be encouraged to prevent the reemergence of soft budget constraints through the exercise of political influence.

A historical materialist could only agree – holding her nose, perhaps – with the market socialists. The Fabians had been quite wrong, along with the Marxists and many others, in believing that the development of the forces of production inside capitalism was leading inexorably to the suppression of competition and the elimination of market relations. In fact, the twentieth century had proved the opposite to be the case (Howard and King, 2003). This prompts a question raised by Weitzman against Bardhan and Roemer: Why go to all the trouble of simulating capitalism, when you can have the real thing? This is especially so when it can be reformed, along the lines proposed by Philippe Van Parijs (1995), to provide everyone with a "basic income" independent of their work or ownership of property, and thereby create "real freedom for all." This is, perhaps, the most fundamental challenge facing the advocates of non-Marxian socialism.

Bibliography

Aaronovitch, S. 1981: *The Road From Thatcherism*. London: Lawrence and Wishart.

Aganbegyan, A. G. 1988: *The Challenge: Economics of Perestroika*. London: Hutchinson.

Albert, M. and Hahnel, R. 1991: *The Political Economy of Participatory Economics*. Princeton, NJ: Princeton University Press.

Baran, P.A. 1957: *The Political Economy of Growth*. New York: Monthly Review Press.

Bardhan, P. and Roemer, J. E. 1992: Market socialism: a case for rejuvenation. *Journal of Economic Perspectives*, 6(3), 101–16.

Barone, E. 1935 [1908]: The Ministry of Production in the collectivist state. In Hayek (1935a), op. cit., pp. 245–90.

Bergson, A. 1948: Socialist economics. In H. S. Ellis (ed.), *A Survey of Contemporary Economics*, vol. 1. Homewood, IL: Richard D. Irwin/American Economic Association, 412–18.

Bernstein, E. 1909 [1899]: *Evolutionary Socialism*. New York: Huebsch.

Bowles, S. and Gintis, H. 1993: The democratic firm: an agency-theoretic evaluation. In S. Bowles, H. Gintis, and B. Gustafsson (eds.), *Markets and Democracy: Participation, Accountability and Efficiency*. Cambridge, UK: Cambridge University Press, 13–39.

Bray, J. F. 1931 [1839]: *Labour's Wrongs and Labour's Remedy*. London: London School of Economics, Reprints of Scarce Tracts in Economics and Political Science No. 6.

Breit, M. and Lange, O. 2003 [1934]: The way to the socialist planned economy (tr. J. Toporowski). *History of Economics Review*, 37, forthcoming.

Brus, W. 1972: *The Market in a Socialist Economy*. London: Routledge and Kegan Paul.

Chilosi, A. 1986: Self-managed market socialism with "free mobility of labour." *Journal of Comparative Economics*, 10(3), 237–54.

Cole, G. D. H. 1920: *Guild Socialism Re-Stated*. London: Leonard Parsons.

—— 1935: *Principles of Economic Planning*. London: Macmillan.

Crosland, C. A. R. 1956: *The Future of Socialism*. London: Cape.

Dawson, W. H. 1972 [1890]: *Bismarck and State Socialism*. New York: Howard Fertig.

Dobb, M. H. 1960: *An Essay on Economic Growth and Planning*. London: Routledge and Kegan Paul.

Domar, E. S. 1966: The Soviet collective farm as a producer cooperative. *American Economic Review*, 56(4, part 1), 734–57.

Hahnel, R. 2000: In defense of democratic planning. In R. Pollin (ed.), *Capitalism, Socialism, and Radical Political Economy*. Aldershot: Elgar, 318–39.

Hawtrey, R. G. 1926: *The Economic Problem*. London: Longmans, Green.

Hayek, F. A. (ed.) 1935a: *Collectivist Economic Planning*. London: Routledge and Kegan Paul.

—— 1935b: The present state of the debate. In Hayek (1935a), op. cit., pp. 201–43.

—— 1940: Socialist calculation: the competitive solution. *Economica*, n.s., 7(26), 125–49.

Hertzka, T. 1987 [1891]: *A Trip to Freeland*. Alexandria, VA: Chadwyck-Healey.

Horvat, B. 1982: *The Political Economy of Socialism*. Armonk, NY: M. E. Sharpe.

Howard, M. C. and King, J. E. 1992: *A History of Marxian Economics, Volume II, 1929–1990*. London: Macmillan/Princeton, NJ: Princeton University Press.

—— and —— 2003: The rise of neoliberalism: towards a materialist explanation. *International Papers in Political Economy*, forthcoming.

Kalecki, M. 1992: *Collected Works of Michal Kalecki*, vol. III. Oxford: The Clarendon Press.

—— 1993: *Collected Works of Michal Kalecki*, vol. IV. Oxford: The Clarendon Press.

King, J. E. 1983: A reconsideration of the Ricardian Socialists. *History of Political Economy*, 15(3), 345–73.

Kornai, J. 1986: The Hungarian reform process: visions, hopes, and reality. *Journal of Economic Literature*, 24(4), 1687–737.

—— 1992: *The Socialist System*. Princeton, NJ: Princeton University Press.

Kropotkin, P. 1902: *Mutual Aid*. London: Heinemann.

Lange, O. 1938 [1936–7]: On the economic theory of socialism. In B. E. Lippincott (ed.), *On The Economic Theory of Socialism*. New York: McGraw-Hill, 57–143.

—— 1967: The computer and the market. In C. H. Feinstein (ed.), *Socialism, Capitalism and Economic Growth; Essays Presented to Maurice Dobb*. Cambridge, UK: Cambridge University Press, 158–61.

Lavoie, D. 1985: *Rivalry and Central Planning: the Socialist Calculation Debate Reconsidered*. Cambridge, UK: Cambridge University Press.

Lerner, A. P. 1944: *The Economics of Control: Principles of Welfare Economics*. New York: Macmillan.

Lichtheim, G. 1983 [1970]: *A Short History of Socialism*. London: Fontana.

Meade, J. E. 1936: *An Introduction to Economic Analysis and Policy*. Oxford: Oxford University Press.

—— 1972: The theory of labour-managed firms and of profit-sharing. *Economic Journal*, 82 (325s), March (supplement), 402–28.

—— 1989: *Agathotopia: The Economics of Partnership*. Aberdeen: Aberdeen University Press.

Meidner, R. 1993: Why did the Swedish model fail? *Socialist Register*, 211–28.

Mises, L. von 1935 [1920]: Economic calculation in the socialist commonwealth. In Hayek (1935a), op. cit., pp. 87–130.

Nove, A. 1983: *The Economics of Feasible Socialism*. London: George Allen & Unwin.

—— and Nuti, D. M. (eds.) 1972: *Socialist Economics*. Harmondsworth: Penguin.

Nuti, D. M. 1970: Capitalism, socialism and steady growth. *Economic Journal*, 80(317), 32–57.

Pataud, E. and Pouget, E. 1990 [1909]: *How We Shall Bring About the Revolution?* London: Pluto.

Pigou, A. C. 1937: *Socialism Versus Capitalism*. London: Macmillan.

Robbins, L. 1978 [1952]: *The Theory of Economic Policy in English Classical Political Economy*. London: Macmillan.

Robinson, J. 1943: *Private Enterprise or Public Control*. London: English Universities Press, for the Association for Education in Citizenship.

Russell, B. 1920 [1918]: *Roads to Freedom*. London: George Allen & Unwin.

Shaw, G. B. 1949: *Essays In Fabian Socialism*. London: Constable.

Šik, O. 1976: *The Third Way*. London: Wildwood House.

Steedman, I. (ed.) 1995: *Socialism and Marginalism in Economics 1870–1930*. London: Routledge.

Stiglitz, J. 1994: *Whither Socialism?* Cambridge, MA: The MIT Press.

Thompson, N. 1996: *Political Economy and the Labour Party*. London: UCL Press.

—— 1998: *The Real Rights of Man*. London: Pluto.

Tugan-Baranovsky, M. I. 1966 [1910]: *Modern Socialism In Its Historical Development*. New York: Russell & Russell.

Van Parijs, P. 1995: *Real Freedom For All: What (if Anything) can Justify Capitalism?* Oxford: The Clarendon Press.

Vanek, Jan 1972: *The Economics of Workers' Management*. London: George Allen & Unwin.

Vanek, Jaroslav 1970: *The General Theory of Labor-Managed Market Economies*. Ithaca, NY: Cornell University Press.

—— (ed.) 1975: *Self-Management: Economic Liberation of Man*. Harmondsworth: Penguin.

Ward, B. 1958: The firm in Illyria: market syndicalism. *American Economic Review*, 48(4), 566–89.

Weitzman, M. L. 1984: *The Share Economy*. Cambridge, MA: Harvard University Press.

CHAPTER THIRTEEN

Utopian Economics

Warren J. Samuels

13.1 THE GENRE

Utopian economics is a distinctive genre of writings, a group of fictional accounts that can take two forms. A *utopia* is a good place that is, as yet, no place. A *dystopia* can be a bad place that is, as yet, no place; or it can be a pejorative interpretation of the author's status quo and its perceived trends. These writings, typically novels or novelettes, are fictional accounts that purport to describe and explain a particular community or state. The author usually stresses some principle of organization and control that serves as the basis of social, political, and/or economic structure or culture. The principle may express a particular authorial concern or theme and is often embodied in a distinctive set of arrangements, such as the equality of the sexes, reform of marriage, the brotherhood of mankind, toleration, reform of the institution of property, emphasis on education, advocacy and practice of eugenics, the hatred of tyranny, and so on.

In general, each utopian or dystopian community tends to be derivative of the author's status quo. It is an extension of the author's own country, on which it thereby serves as a commentary. The utopian community reflects that society or, more precisely, the problems, conflicts, and trends of the times, as perceived, evaluated, and projected by the author. The community is an extrapolation either to idealize and eulogize or to satirize and criticize certain aspects of the author's experience. The work is an exploration into the human condition and both the follies and prospects of mankind.

Utopias tend to be systems of consent, either volitional or induced; they also have solved, escaped, or transcended contemporary problems. Dystopias tend to be systems of regimented, authoritarian and totalitarian control; they also exhibit instability and other problems, often of an inhumane character.

A substantial historical, interpretive, and critical literature has developed with the utopian/dystopian literature as its subject of study (e.g., Hertzler, 1923; Russell, 1932; Buber, 1949; Popper, 1949; Berneri, 1950; Mumford, 1962; Negley and Patrick, 1962; Manuel, 1966, 1971; Eurich, 1967; Hillegas, 1967; Kateb, 1971, 1972; Negley,

1977; I. F. Clark, 1978; Manuel and Manuel, 1979; Aldridge, 1984; Kumar, 1987; Sargent, 1988; Booker, 1994a,b; Haschak, 1994; Hetherington, 1997; Mannheim, n.d.; see also an issue of *Daedalus*, 1965). Needless to say, interpretations vary, not least of Sir Thomas More's seminal work (e.g., Sullivan, 1983). Other literature is devoted to communities inspired by the utopian literature and impulse (e.g., McKinney, 1972; Moe, 1980; Guarneri, 1991). Centers and/or specialized collections for the study of utopian literature are found at Green Mountain College and Duke, Ohio, and Pennsylvania State Universities. Specialists may join the Society for Utopian Studies and the Associazione Internazionale per gli Studi sulle Utopie. Numerous sites (of various usefulness) are to be found on the web.

13.2 A LARGER CONCEPTION

A Platonic idealist element seems to pervade the exercise of the human intellect. One source is positivist and another is normative. The positivist source consists of efforts to distill the transcendent fundamental elements underlying the diverse and kaleidoscopic phenomena of experience in order to best describe what social "reality" is really all about. One version of this is Max Weber's notion of an "ideal type." The normative source is grounded in efforts to transform the imperfections of actual life into a perfect, ideal system. The latter is clearly a form of social constructivism; it embodies a philosophy of reform or of potential reform. The former may not be constructivist in motivation; but, in providing a particular definition of reality, it willy-nilly becomes the basis of policy and is, at least to that extent, constructivist with regard to the future. Social constructivism commences with the provision of a particular definition of reality and extends to the provision of a basis of policy.

Utopianism may be one form of Platonism in practice. Each utopist writing is a product, in part, of a belief, conscious or not, in the use of reason to critique and to re-create.

A feature, perhaps a problem, of idealist thought is that a given experience – that is, a given social situation, such as England in the sixteenth century or the United States in the nineteenth century or the 1930s – may give rise to a variety of idealizations. This is because not only does an actual situation not define itself but its fundamental elements may be perceived and identified differently by different people with different standpoints, who then proceed to construct both different definitions of reality and different pictures of its idealized form. The constructions are a function of both the particular multifaceted situation and the diverse imaginations, including values, of those who construct them.

One can interpret the Book of Isaiah and the Book of Ecclesiastes as, respectively, a utopian and a dystopian account of the human condition; the Book of Revelation projects a New Jerusalem. One can envision the writings that express Henry David Thoreau's return to nature as a utopian enterprise. One can perceive the agenda of the Enlightenment as utopian in the nonpejorative sense used here.

Science fiction, which is normally considered a literary genre unto itself, can also embody the utopian/dystopian dichotomy. While much science fiction portrays conflicts and other aspects of life hitherto explored in terrestrial terms – for example, cowboys versus Indians or ranchers versus farmers, but now in galactic or intergalactic terms – some portrays utopian and other dystopian arrangements. Isaac Asimov's *Foundation* (1951), for example, explores a utopia engendered by advanced mathematical social science – and profoundly influenced at least one economist, Roger B. Myerson (1998, p. 228).

Satire is another literary genre that can overlap (especially) the dystopian domain. Swift's *Gulliver's Travels* readily comes to mind. So, too, can irony, which can incorporate and project a utopian basis of judgment.

The motion picture industry has often been portrayed as presenting idealized, utopian characterizations of life; for example, "veritable machines of escapism and emotion that promotes images of a utopia in which everyone wants to live, if only for an instant, by proxy" (Attali, 2000, p. 84). Escapism, however, is not necessarily utopianism.

Utopianism is also known to the worlds of art and culture studies. In 2000 the Museum of Modern Art in New York City had an exhibition entitled "The Dream of Utopia/Utopia of the Dream." In the words of its promotional literature, the exhibition considered "the sharp opposition between the radical visions set for by Surrealism, on the one hand, and by the utopian abstraction of artists such as Piet Mondrian and Kazimir Malevich, on the other." And during the period October 14, 2000 to January 27, 2001, the New York Public Library had an exhibition entitled "Utopia: The Search for the Ideal Society in the Western World." Associated with it was a book of the same title (Schaer, Claeys, and Sargent, 2000; both the exhibit and the book are reviewed in Grafton, 2000).

Of a different nature are *The Good Society* by Walter Lippman (n.d.) and *The Economics of the Good Society* by Joseph Berliner (1999), each of which explores the nature of a better economic system. Geoffrey M. Hodgson's *Economics and Utopia* (1999) offers not a conventional utopian blueprint but a mode of utopian thinking. Hodgson critiques socialism and market individualism as two utopian visions and illusions. His approach stresses the incompleteness of the concepts of socialism and individualism, of private and public, and of the notion of a pure market. He stresses the importance of debate about the values to be institutionalized in actual markets and the role of social reform of market structures.

It is quite possible to think of the major schools of economic thought as Platonic idealizations, even though the disciples of several think of them as scientific. Thus, mercantilism, physiocracy, classical economics, Marxian and non-Marxian socialism, neoclassical economics, institutional economics, Keynesian economics, general equilibrium theory, Austrian economics, and such forms of economic theory as rational expectations economics, game theory, public choice theory, monetarism, and so on – indeed, all economic theory – can be comprehended as so many idealized representations of a much more complex, and messy, reality. Each of them is a particular specification of a utopia, with both affirmative and negative features. The same could be said of Henry George's *Progress and Poverty* (1880), the backward-looking utopias of early-nineteenth-century economic German and English Romanticism in economics, and the doctrines of libertarian economics (Tilman, 2001).

Neoclassical theories of price and market can be Weberian ideal types, methodo-logically limited formulations, and/or utopian idealist, ideological constructions. Neoclassical welfare maximization can be seen as an example of utopianism, however marked by its conventional omission of detailed institutions and however much neoclassical economists denigrate utopianism (Davis, 1988, p. 13). Through its emphasis on incremental change, benefit–cost calculations as a mode of decision-making, and on seeing the best as the enemy of the better, neoclassicism can be seen as affirming rationalistic, deliberative control of utopian exuberance.

Characterization may be subjective. The general social theory of Friedrich von Hayek – for example, his theory of spontaneous order – can be seen as (1) anti-utopian, (2) utopian in its anti-utopianism, and (c) the expression of a particular utopia.

(The foregoing may seem to equate economics, science, fiction, and utopia/ dystopia, but is intended to do so only in part. All have at least one foot in the "real world," but, given multiplicity of interpretation of the "real world," the identity of that foot seems always to be an issue.)

Apropos of conservatism in general, three views are possible. First, conserva-tism is a temperament that values stability and continuity, with no unique con-servative utopia, preferring to "use and enjoy what is available rather than to wish for or to look for something else; to delight in what is the present rather than what was or what may be" (Michael Oakeshott, quoted in Zakaria, 2000, p. 94). This would relegate utopianism to the "subjective imagination" of those who dream of "a radically different world" and "fantasise about a radically differ-ent future," writers "with vivid imaginations of the best of all possible worlds (or in a few cases, their dystopian opposite)" (Jay, 2000, p. 23). Secondly, insofar as a utopia reflects and/or is derived from a particular status quo whose idealization it represents, at least in part, in that respect, if in no other, it is conservative. Thirdly, particular conservative ideologies project their own specific idealized – that is, utopian – version of its status quo.

On the other side of the ideological spectrum, the liberal-left publisher, Verso, has a series entitled "The Real Utopias Project," edited by Erik Olin Wright. One blurb for the series that says it embraces the tension between dreams and practice, radical solutions to problems, and the pragmatically possible. Among the book topics are democracy, equal shares/egalitarianism, and universal basic income.

To the objection that the foregoing (the materials identified in the preceding five paragraphs) are not fictional accounts, one can respond that, while they certainly are not novels, each is fictional in the sense that it tells a particular story not about actual economies but of an abstracted rational reconstruction. Indeed, all science is fictional in pursuing abstraction and idealization – general models bearing no necessary relation to actual phenomena and experience. Much mod-ern economic theory is justified in precisely these terms (for further criticism, see Negley and Patrick, 1962, p. 3).

Friedrich Engels pejoratively called all versions of socialism other than his and Marx's "utopian socialism." He was referring to such authors as Abbé Morelly, Saint Simon, Charles Fourier, Etienne Cabet, and Louis Blanc, rather than to all utopists. But in the present context, Marxism is a dystopian representation of capitalism combined with a utopian portrayal of an economic system in which workers are no longer subjected to traditional property rights and a successor system in which they have rights over their own labor power. The writings of Josiah Warren portray the utopia in which each person is a property owner. The economics of Henry George includes a dystopia in which low wages and unemployment derive from the acquisition by private individuals of the unearned increment in the value of land, combined with the vision and promise of a utopia in which that problem is obviated by his "single tax" on land. Neoclassical economics is an idealization and thereby rationalization of the workings of a competitive, profit-oriented, materialist, private-property directed market economy. Given the statement that "Utopia is fiction in the classic sense of 'as if'; utopia is a world of *as if*" (Negley and Patrick, 1962, p. 4), then those who contemplate a market economy led *as if* by an invisible hand (not Adam Smith) are utopists. C. Wright Mills has been called "An American Utopian" (Horowitz, 1983); in his utopia forms of authoritarianism would be absent – as would be the case with a Hayekian system. An interesting and suggestive deconstruction of Marx and Hayek's respective critiques of utopianism is Sciabarra (1995).

In sum, religious and secular utopias (and fear of dystopia) pervade idealizations found in public discourse in many fields. Some are reactionary (ideological in Karl Mannheim's system); others are radical visions of the future (utopia in Mannheim's system). The emphasis is always on some definition of reality and some possibility for change – definitions and possibilities that are not always, indeed rarely, unequivocal and/or realistic.

13.3 THE LITERATURE AND ITS CHARACTER

Several thousand writings of the conventional genre exist, quite apart from science fiction. The best known – indeed, classic – literature includes Plato's *Republic* (360 B.C.), Sir Thomas More's *Utopia* (1516) (from which the genre acquires its name), Tomasso Campanella's *City of the Sun* (1637), Francis Bacon's *New Atlantis* (1626), Gerrard Winstanley's *The Law of Freedom in a Platform* (1652), James Harrington's *The Commonwealth of Oceana* (1656), Henry Neville's *The Isle of Pines* (1668), Jonathan Swift's *Gulliver's Travels* (1726), Robert Owen's *A New View of Society* (1813–14) and *Report to the County of Lanark* (1821), Etienne Cabet's *Voyage to Icaria* (1840), Samuel Butler's *Erewhon* (1872), Edward Bellamy's *Looking Backward* (1888), Theodor Hertzka's *Freeland* (1891), and H. G. Wells's *A Modern Utopia* (1905) and *New Worlds for Old* (1908). Less well known are Denis Diderot's *Supplement to Bougainville's Voyage* (1796), and William Morris's *News from Nowhere* (1891).

This literature – both the conventional genre and the extended group – can be understood as a part of the social valuational process, often but neither necessarily nor only, with regard to justice. Each piece provides a selective critique (in the sense of literary criticism) of a particular status quo either as received or as developing. This literature is an important vehicle for the expression of and quest for values. Each piece contributes in its own way to the exploration, identification, application, and critique of values. This literature is an important means by which authors can produce and express views for or against socio-politico-economic change.

This literature also can be understood not only as a quest for values but as a parallel and not unrelated quest for meaning. Each utopia or dystopia is an allegorical expression of a culture or civilization as individuals seek to divine its meaning; seeking, in part, a comprehension of its powers and its possibilities.

Latent within the members of every society are visions of the ideal and the just (and other values) and accounts of meaning. Some visions rise to the level of consciousness and become ensconced in the conscious, or self-conscious, utopias (dystopias) of a Godwin, a Saint-Simon or a Fourier; these visions are dreams, dreams of different futures, whose significance does not depend on their being directly acted upon (T. J. Clark, 2000, p. 9). They form a not inconsequential part of human intellectual baggage.

Accordingly, one can say, speaking quite broadly, that the main concern of this literature is the pursuit and achievement of human dignity (including "justice") in a well-ordered society. However, the meanings of both "human dignity" and "well-ordered society" are ambiguous and permit a great variety of specification. The problem is always one of stipulating the structure and system of freedom and control, with freedom both correlative to and derivative of control. This is no less true of the utopian/dystopian literature than of the literature of philosophy and social science.

While each piece of utopian/dystopian literature is a product of its times, a particular status quo can engender quite different utopias/dystopias. This is the case for at least two reasons: (1) each society or social status quo is heterogeneous and thus permits divergent perceptions and emphases; and (2) individual authors approach, interpret, and evaluate their society from different standpoints or perspectives. Thus, while conservative authors use the device to support established ideas, institutions, and ways of life, and radical authors employ the device to advocate change, each author is selective as to particular details and thereby contributes to both continuity and change.

Each author constructs their utopia or dystopia on the basis of some particular principle of organization, albeit typically supplemented by other ideas or themes. Among the principal historic types of principle are: religion, natural science, military organization, asceticism, political principle, and economic organization. The twentieth century – not without precursors, such as *Looking Backward* – saw a new type of principle, psychological or behavioral conditioning, found in Aldous Huxley's *Brave New World* (1932), B. F. Skinner's *Walden Two* (1948), George Orwell's *1984* (1949), and Ray Bradbury's *Fahrenheit 451* (1953). These tend to be dystopias, as are Matt Cohen's *The Colors of War* (1977), Hugh MacLennan's *Voices in Time* (1980), and William Gibson's *Count Zero* (1986). Ayn Rand's *Atlas Shrugged* (1957), which combined utopian and dystopian features, has influenced some, perhaps many, young economic thinkers.

Some writings are speculative and constructive (Plato, Bellamy); others are satirical and critical (Huxley, Orwell). Some are futuristic and progressive; others are retrogressive or reactionary, looking to reinstate a former condition of society, usually a nostalgic, idealized version (Negley and Patrick, 1962, pp. 5–6).

13.4   THE LITERATURE AND ITS EVOLUTION

Negley and Patrick (1962, pp. 6–8; cf., Hertzler, 1923; Kumar, 1987) distinguish between those utopias in which power is centralized and those in which power is decentralized. Progressive utopias tend to emphasize centralization and retrogressive, decentralization. The matter is subtle. Power is conspicuous when used to produce change and in articulating a new system. A revered old power structure is easily obfuscated by taking it for granted as part of the natural order of things. In either case, power may involve either an idealized new and different power structure or an idealized version of an old power structure.

It is difficult to generate a conclusive classification: each utopia is a product of a creative imagination applied in reaction to a complex set of experiences and phenomena. Nonetheless, Negley and Patrick distinguish between utopias written before and after roughly 1850 (their analysis is more elaborate than is presented here).

Utopias written during the period 1500–1850 tend to be characterized by decentralization of power, opposition to industrialization, and emphasis on the individual and ideal interpersonal relationships. Institutions are often denigrated and proper or ideal interpersonal relationships are put forth as the *sine qua non* of the good society. Although it is possible to argue that their "main theme . . . was advocacy, explicit or implicit, of the fullest possible, efficient utilization of the available resources of men and materials in a given society" (Negley and Patrick, 1962, pp. 290–1), economic considerations – scarcity, economic organization, and control – while not absent, are largely neglected, certainly in comparison with later utopias. Generally, the earlier utopias posited the "idea of a self-sufficient community of simple and uncomplicated economic structure, happy in the enjoyment of simple values of artisanship, family, and natural piety" – a vision that later became "the vehicle of satire or nostalgia" (Negley and Patrick, 1962, p. 13).

After roughly 1850, utopias are characterized by centralization of power, primacy of attention given to economic organization and control, the acceptance of industrialization and urbanization, emphasis on proper institutions as the basis of the good society and the full development of the individual, and anticipation of the welfare state.

As already noted, differentiation by period cannot be absolute; every characterization has its exceptions. Utopias always have been diverse in content, as well as sometimes dystopias. The increased importance of the economy in generating an organizing principle reflects the increased importance and differentiation of the economy and economic institutions – which means that both utopists and economists learned from and gave effect to modern economies. Increased centralization of power may actually reflect the arguable increased centralization in modern economic life. Since about 1850 the general problem has been that of promoting individualist values in a society with the institutional arrangements suitable to the conditions of mass production and mass consumption; that is, the problem of working out the meaning of individualism in modern bourgeois or nonbourgeois terms.

It seems that no utopias were written during the medieval period. If true, this may be due to the theological or mythopoetic mode of expression. Theology or supernaturalism is not only an alternative outlet for utopist strivings, but is the ultimate utopian literature. Another cause may be the medieval ideal of a static divinely sanctioned order, an ideal elevating continuity over change – notwithstanding the widespread actual changes then taking place, such that reification and idealization was of a changing reality. With the coming of the Renaissance and the Enlightenment – the actual history is more complicated than this – rationalism, humanism, naturalism, secularism, and individualism nurtured a revival of utilitarianism–pragmatism–instrumentalism and deliberative constructivism, aiming at progress, elevating change over continuity. Ruling classes had always been pragmatic and constructivist; with a growing consciousness that institutional arrangements were artifacts and were subject to change, the utopian urge was given freer, or at least wider, rein [although the emphasis on human social construction, over against divine origin, is found in More's *Utopia* – a point stressed by Grafton (2000, p. 4) – if not also in Plato's *Republic*].

Steven Weinberg (2000) has suggested that five nonsocialist types or styles of utopia seem to be emerging in public debate: the free-market utopia, the best-and-brightest utopia, the religious utopia, the Green utopia, and the technological utopia – and he offers his own "civilized egalitarian capitalist utopia."

13.5   Economics in the Utopian Literature

Utopist authors are more like social than economic theorists, and what economists of all schools would recognize as coming within their purview will vary, in part because of their diverse interests and perceptions, in part because of the heterogeneity of the ideas presented in the literature of utopia and dystopia, and in part because the central orientation and arguments, as it were, differ between utopias and dystopias. It is really impossible to generalize without exceptions. In general, however, economic ideas *per se* are much less important and salient than broadly political, social, and psychological ideas; ideas of political economy (as distinct from economics) are present, though typically largely implicit.

One pervasive theme is the importance of organization and structure. These authors do not project a pure conceptual a-institutional picture. Their overwhelming emphasis, often down to, if not centering upon, particular organizational details, is on structure.

Readers will find individualist and collectivist, or liberalist and socialist, features and themes. Among the individualist themes are enthusiasms for individual initiative, self-reliance, and self-development; economic (as well as political) criticisms of the state; and notions of spontaneous social order and harmony, once the proper set of institutions has been put in place. Among the collectivist themes are a hatred of the institution of private property and notions of class exploitation and domination. Still, whereas many criticize private property, others, such as Josiah Warren, propose a widespread distribution of property. Problems of class and inequality are frequent foundations for authorial motivation and design.

Nonetheless, for all the individualism and humanism to be found in this literature, appropriate social control is the core of the messages propounded by the utopist authors. The frequent anarchistic strains relate in part to psychological antipathy toward authority, especially its abuses, and in part to political antagonism toward concentrated political and economic power. Yet each utopian design has its own system of social control.

Frequently found ideas include various versions of the labor theory of value, but also – albeit to a lesser extent – an implicit reliance on properly structured markets. Also found are exploitation theories of property, state, religion, wealth and income distribution; beliefs in the destructive character of competition, unless properly institutionalized, and materialism. Some form of an ethical maldistribution theory is frequently encountered. Given the emphasis on the proper organization and control system, absent such system income and wealth may be distributed in such a manner and with such a result as to be unethical and unjust. Institutionally produced inequality is unjust, and poverty is inherently wrong and morally offensive in the face of great wealth. Often this inequality is attributed to ruling-elite control of the organs of social control.

Another idea, found, for example, in the work of Charles Fourier, is that the proper organization of life would promote abundance.

In various ways, therefore, utopist writers parallel political, economic, and social theorists (each a very diverse group) in the topics of their concern.

13.6   INTERPRETATION AND CRITIQUE

Utopist authors seem, individually and collectively, to have understood and posed certain basic questions: the status of the status quo, the distribution of power as a central problem, the quality of life, the quality of human beings as a product of the system, the process of leadership selection (including education for leadership), the dangers of extreme division of labor, the artifact nature of social institutions and their susceptibility to deliberative human modification, and the social valuation process. These authors, each in their own way, helped provide checks on their respective status-quo societies and articulations of values and of the possibilities of social change.

The conventional criticism of utopianism, and thereby the source of the pejorative use of the term, is that the utopist author is unrealistic as to how much social change is possible. This may well be true, though it may also be said that the authors so much appreciated the difficulties that they felt that their writing would help foment change. Bellamy's *Looking Backward*, in particular, sold millions of copies and apparently had enormous influence in providing the mental or ideological foundations for social reform.

The more interesting and more important criticism is that the typical utopia makes no provision for serious conflict and/or change once its system is put in place. It is a static once-and-for-all-time reconstruction. In this respect, it is equivalent to a libertarian *laissez-faire* in which the only function of officials is to see that the laws are kept, not to introduce social change. If change signifies change through law, as it often does in actuality and in instituting the projected utopia, then afterward there is nothing left for change through law to accomplish. It has been said that life in a utopia would be dull, for there would be no problems to solve (Harris, 1977, p. 74), and that "All the utopias are tame, just because vitality has been sacrificed to reduce risk" (Hartshorne, 1949, p. 448). It is not too much to think that some of the impetus behind the construction of a utopia is its author's effort at escapism from conflict and the ongoing necessity of choice in working things out.

The fundamental "utopian" character of this literature, in the pejorative sense, lies in its general neglect of the problem of change within the respective systems. The critical problem with this literature is not how difficult it is to generate change but that, typically, no further change is contemplated once the proposed system is put in place. This is often manifest in the human desire to establish *the* proper system or framework and then let it operate on its own accord, allowing individuals to act within it, with the confidence that the system will generate harmony, correct behavior, and the right goals.

This is too simplistic and disengaging a view of the complexity of real-world problems, the dynamics of change, and the need for collective decisions. Or, as Hertzler argued, social perfection is an illusion; there can only be social progress; "Utopia is not a social state, it is a state of mind" (Hertzler, 1923, p. 314).

Still, some utopists have considered the problem of change within their utopia. H. G. Wells is one author who did. Another (emphasized by J. C. Davis in Schaer, Chaeys, and Sargent, 2000), was More, who adopted a model of cumulative causation in which institutions helped to transform human nature and this in turn led to changes in institutions. And, inasmuch as many utopias have actual and/or potential contradictory elements, change within utopia is a logical possibility.

Per contra, one could argue that one function of utopist writing is to point out contradictions and faults in the author's society. Identifying a possible solution and contemplating it without change, under what amounts to a rule of "as is" or *ceteris paribus*, is a deft and heuristically useful mode of analysis – in literature and in science.

A correlative problem is that the posited utopia may not work out as intended, and for this if for no other reason may require institutional adjustments.

Perhaps second only to the problem of the neglect of change within the utopian system, and not unrelated thereto, is the temptation to hold that only one answer or solution is either possible or warranted for all problems, that only one utopia is possible. This begs the question of the possibility of diversity both within and between utopian societies. However, the neglect of both change and diversity can be attributed to the nature of the genre. Fiction can go only so far, presumably, in articulating alternatives; and literary license in such matters is neither unexpected nor to be condemned. Still, the utopian mentality may derive not only from a belief that one has found *the* solution to social problems but also from a desire to escape the burden of choice.

Another aspect of the complex dynamics of social change relevant to utopias is that social change toward an idealized image is often not perceived as change. The more successful a utopist, therefore, in altering a people's idealized image, the less the utopist's role will be recognized.

Although post-1850 utopias seem to have focused more on economic organization, overall one can say that the utopian literature has generally neglected problems of economic organization and control. Yet, most writers seem to have appreciated the need to organize production (though for some production is unimportant). As for the importance of distribution and incentives, two views are possible, often varying between writings: such considerations can appear to have been neglected; they may also be held to be a function of both institutions and the goals of the particular utopist author.

Correlative to the conventional criticism, one can say that the utopist authors failed to anticipate the opposition by the vested interests that their schemes threatened. Here, too, two views are possible: that they did fail to anticipate opposition, and that they considered their writings a device with which to challenge and weaken opposition (in some cases, with hoped-for immunity from persecution).

Another criticism is that the authors oversimplified the nature of human nature and exaggerated the possible impacts of changes in social institutions. Again, two views are possible: that the writers were naively over-optimistic, and that they were underscoring and enhancing the possibilities, however limited they might be – and/or that they sought to provide a check on the institutions that affected how human nature works out.

It should also be pointed out that utopist authors typically have complex notions of the nature of human nature – certainly in comparison with the conventional model deployed by most economists.

A powerful criticism, itself the basis for many dystopias, is that serious change may require concentrated power, a corollary of which is that any concentrated power (public ownership and mandatory central planning) is likely to engender abuse. This criticism is not unique to utopias, of course; it is a general social pathology. The totalitarian or authoritarian temptation, however, is not limited to utopian movements. The history of the genre is laden with ironies. For example, although Thomas Robert Malthus wrote his *Essay on Population* (1798) in criticism of William Godwin's emphasis in his *Enquiry Concerning Political Justice* (1793) on the moral improvement of man, in subsequent editions Malthus emphasized the preventive checks, including moral restraint. An irony of a different type is that for all their attention to specific arrangements, their overall import is not their blueprints but their "hazy recognition of the concrete potentialities and capacities immanent in what we already have" (Merrifield, 2000, p. 45). Thus, Hannah Arendt argued, in the words of one commentator, that "utopianism is grounded in the kind of political thinking that relies on the model of man in the singular as *homo faber*, who can fabricate his world, rather than men in the plural as political actors who can only contest it from a partial point of view" (Jay, 2000, p. 24). The opposite position, of course, is that the utopists are merely contributing their input to the process of working things out, in part by bringing out into the open and treating deliberatively what would otherwise be only latent and monopolized by established interests.

The significance, therefore, of the utopian literature resides in the following. It articulated values and possibilities; it has been idealism in literary practice. It has given vent for the imagination to develop possibilities for change. The utopian literature has emphasized the proposition that institutions matter. It has increasingly focused on the importance of psychology and the problems of identification and alienation in regard to the particulars of any status quo. It has focused on the problem of individualism within any given institutional structure. It has thereby raised the problems of power structure and the division of power. It has raised the question of the concentration of power both within a given utopia and in the process of creating an actual utopist society – including issues of utopian ends and of conflict resolution.

The utopian literature has, in effect, sought to provide answers to the problem posed by Jeremy Bentham's greatest happiness principle; namely, whether happiness is to be maximized by increasing the happiness of those made most happy or of the number of people made happy – that is, along the intensive or the extensive margins. In this respect, for all the greater centralization of power in modern utopias, many if not most authors have nonetheless sought to maximize the number of people made happy; that is, political and economic pluralism. But, again, the literature is so diverse that one must be wary of overemphasizing any single generalization.

A final principal problem is that the utopias promulgated by the various utopists are many and varied, indeed highly heterogeneous. This is, again, because of the heterogeneity of every status quo, the variety of authorial interpretive perspectives, and the fecundity of the human mind. Utopianism is idealism in practice and the enormous burden of idealism is the choice among apparent possible proposals for change. Utopist authors have helped promote the possibility of change, but have thereby compelled us to choose among quite different possibilities.

Bibliography

Aldridge, A. 1984: *The Scientific World View in Dystopia*. Ann Arbor, MI: UMI Research Press.

Attali, J. 2000: How Hollywood rules. *Civilization*, February–March, 644–65.

Berliner, J. S. 1999: *The Economics of the Good Society*. Malden, MA: Blackwell.

Berneri, M. L. 1950: *Journey Through Utopia*. London: Routledge and Paul.

Booker, M. K. 1994a: *The Dystopian Impulse in Modern Literature: Fiction as Social Criticism*. Westport, CT: Greenwood Press.

—— 1994b: *Dystopian Literature: A Theory and Research Guide*. Westport, CT: Greenwood Press.

Buber, M. 1949: *Paths in Utopia*. London: Routledge and Kegan Paul.

Clark, I. F. 1978: *Tales of the Future, from the Beginning to the Present Day*. London: The Library Association.

Clark, T. J. 2000: Reservations of the marvellous. *London Review of Books*, June 22, 3–9.

Daedalus 1965: Utopia. *Daedulus*, 94(2) (Spring).

Davis, J. B. 1988: *Looking Backward*: looking forward. *Forum for Social Economics*, 17(2), 13–22.

Eurich, N. 1967: *Science in Utopia: A Mighty Design*. Cambridge, MA: Harvard University Press.

George, H. 1880: *Progess and Poverty*. New York: D. Appleton.

Grafton, A. 2000: Over the rainbow. *The New York Review of Books*, November 30, 4–6.

Guarneri, C. 1991: *The Utopian Alternative: Fourierism in Nineteenth-Century America*. Ithaca, NY: Cornell University Press.

Haschak, P. G. 1994: *Utopian/Dystopian Literature: A Bibliography of Literary Criticism*. Metuchen, NJ: Scarecrow Press.

Harris, J. 1977: *William Beveridge: A Biography*. New York: Oxford University Press.

Hartshorne, C. 1949: Chance, love, and incompatibility. *The Philosophical Review*, 58 (no. 55), 429–50.

Hertzler, J. O. 1923: *The History of Utopian Thought*. New York: Macmillan.

Hetherington, K. 1997: *The Badlands of Modernity: Heterotopia and Social Ordering*. New York: Routledge.

Hillegas, M. R. 1967: *The Future as Nightmare: H. G. Wells and the Anti-Utopians*. New York: Oxford University Press.

Hodgson, G. M. 1999: *Economics and Utopia: Why the Learning Economy is Not the End of History*. London: Routledge.

Horowitz, I. L. 1983: *C. Wright Mills: An American Utopian*. New York: The Free Press.

Jay, M. 2000: The trouble with nowhere. *London Review of Books*, June 1, 23–4.

Kateb, G. (ed.) 1971: *Utopia*. New York: Atherton Press.

—— 1972: *Utopia and Its Enemies*. New York: Schocken Books.

Kumar, K. 1987: *Utopia and Anti-Utopia in Modern Times*. Cambridge, MA: Blackwell.

Lippmann, W. 1956: *The Good Society*. New York: Grosset's Universal Library.

Mannheim, K. n.d.: *Ideology and Utopia*. New York: Harvest Books.

Manuel, F. (ed.) 1966: *Utopias and Utopian Thought*. Boston: Houghton Mifflin.

—— (ed.) 1971: *Design for Utopia: Selected Writings of Charles Fourier*. New York: Schocken Books.

—— and Manuel, F. P. 1979: *Utopian Thought in the Western World*. Cambridge, MA: The Belknap Press.

McKinney, M. 1972: *Modern Communes, Utopian Societies, Utopian Thought: A Selected Bibliography of Green Mountain College Holdings*. Poultney, VT: Green Mountain College Library.

Merrifield, A. 2000: No exit? Dream on. *The Nation*, June 5, 44–9.

Moe, C. 1980: *New Towns and Utopias*. Monticello, IL: Vance Bibliographies.

Mumford, L. 1962: *The Story of Utopias*. New York: Viking.

Myerson, R. B. 1998: Working on game theory: a personal perspective. In M. Szenberg (ed.), *Passion and Craft: Economists at Work*. Ann Arbor, MI: University of Michigan Press, 227–33.

Negley, G. 1977: *Utopian Literature: A Bibliography with a Supplementary Listing of Works Influential in Utopian Thought*. Lawrence, KA: Regents Press of Kansas.

—— and Patrick, J. M. (eds.) 1962: *The Quest for Utopia*. Garden City, NY: Doubleday Anchor.

Popper, K. 1949: *The Open Society and Its Enemies*. London: Routledge and Kegan Paul.

Russell, F. T. P. 1932: *Touring Utopia, The Realm of Constructive Humanism*. New York: L. MacVeagh, Dial Press.

Sargent, L. T. 1988: *British and American Utopian Literature, 1516–1985: An Annotated Chronological Bibliography*. New York: Garland.

Schaer, R., Claeys, G., and Sargent, L. T. (eds.) 2000: *Utopia: The Search for the Ideal Society in the Western World*. New York: Oxford University Press.

Sciabarra, C. M. 1995: *Marx, Hayek, and Utopia*. Albany, NY: SUNY Press.

Sullivan, E. D. S. (ed.) 1983: *The Utopian Vision: Seven Essays on the Quincentennial of Sir Thomas More*. San Diego, CA: San Diego State University Press.

Tilman, R. 2001: *Ideology and Utopia in the Social Philosophy of the Libertarian Economists*. Westport, CT: Greenwood Press.

Weinberg, S. 2000: Five and a half utopias. *The Atlantic Monthly*, January, 107–14.

Zakaria, F. 2000: Whimper on the Right. *The New Yorker*, June 5, 85–90.

CHAPTER FOURTEEN

Historical Schools of Economics: German and English

Keith Tribe

14.1 INTRODUCTION

Identification with "historical economics" implies a critique of prevailing ortho-doxy. This reflex is as old as "modern economics"; arguments both for and against the progressive formalization of economics have gone hand in hand with either negative or positive reevaluations of the recent history of economic argument. Historical economics has developed in parallel with "abstract" economics, can be dated from the early nineteenth century, associated with the writings of Adam Müller and Friedrich List in Germany, and with William Whewell and Richard Jones in Britain. In their different ways, these and other writers argued that the work of Adam Smith, or of David Ricardo, sought a political economy founded upon economic laws that were valid for all times and all places. Political economy had become in this view "in a great measure a *deductive* science: that is, certain definitions were adopted, as of universal application to all countries upon the face of the globe and all classes of society; and from these definitions, and a few corresponding axioms, was deduced a whole system of propositions, which were regarded as of demonstrated validity" (Whewell, 1859, p. x). German historical economists took a similar position, but were more inclined to argue that classical economists assumed that their axioms represented the natural laws of economic life. To this was opposed the project of constructing an inductive, historical science, in which the diversity of economic circumstances was properly recog-nized. What therefore unites all those concerned with the project of a historical economics, then and now, is allegiance to an inductive, empiricist approach to economic theory, and hostility to a deductive, axiomatic economics. "Historical economists" are not, however, all of a piece; quite apart from variations in their degree of understanding of and sympathy with modern economics, the nature of "history" and "historical method" has altered substantially in the course of two centuries. Some caution is therefore in order when addressing the nature of "schools" of historical economics.

The most well known such school flourished in nineteenth-century Germany, from the 1840s to the early 1900s, and represented a national mainstream that was skeptical of classical economics as understood in Britain and France. Strictly speaking, there were two such schools: an "Older School," conventionally associated with the writings of Wilhelm Roscher, Carl Knies, and Bruno Hildebrand; and a "Younger School," whose foremost member was Gustav Schmoller, but which embraced most academic economists of the newly united Germany after 1871. Importantly, all these economists explicitly identified themselves as members of a "historical school" – Max Weber, in his inaugural lecture as Professor of Economics and Financial Science at the University of Freiburg, referred in passing to himself as one of "the younger representatives of the German historical school" (Weber, 1989, p. 200). That this school included primarily German nationals rather than German speakers was pointed up by the notorious "debate on method" between the Viennese economist Carl Menger and Gustav Schmoller, in which the former argued that historical and theoretical economics were complements, rather than substitutes, as Schmoller had suggested. Menger's argument that economic theory was not therefore susceptible to inductive development was abusively denounced by Schmoller, although the German project of historically founded economic theory, chartered by Wilhelm Roscher in 1843, remained an unfulfilled project to the very end. Nonetheless, although this project to refound economics upon an inductive basis failed, the project itself did have important consequences, not least that its proponents taught several generations of students.

The place of economics teaching in the late-nineteenth-century German university was secured by its place in the legal curriculum; not until the 1920s was a separate, nondoctoral qualification in economics introduced. Since a qualification in law was routinely required for posts in public administration, as well as the legal system itself, this ensured that large numbers of public servants and private employees were exposed to general economic principles. Furthermore, the German university was the international model, enjoying qualitative and quantitative supremacy over universities in Britain, France, and the United States. German universities were state universities, open to all with an appropriate educational background. Students in post-bellum America seeking advanced teaching in economics naturally gravitated to Germany, since in England there was very little systematic teaching of economics, and no graduate qualification as in Germany; while the French university system was then (and still is) firmly linked to a closed educational and cultural system. Many American students returned to teach in the rapidly expanding American university system, later contributing to the development of an American institutionalist economics that drew heavily on German historicism.

English historical economics was by contrast marginal to a mainstream represented by the work of John Stuart Mill, William Stanley Jevons, and Alfred Marshall. For the most part its roots lay in the work of Henry Maine and John Stubbs, and there was little direct connection with German historicism. Two leading proponents, William Cunningham and William Ashley, authored the first textbooks of economic history in the later nineteenth century, and the latter played an important role in the formation of the Economic History Society in 1926. The resulting institutional separation of economists and economic historians is thought to have facilitated in turn the accelerated development between the wars of an academic economics purged of historical content (Koot, 1987). The story is, however, more complex that that. William Ashley never did assign great importance to economic analysis, even when designing a business curriculum: at the Faculty of Commerce in Birmingham, which he founded in 1902, formal tuition in economic principles was confined to the first year (Ashley, 1902). William Cunningham repeatedly denounced the influence of Alfred Marshall's new economics, arguing that the new style of economic reasoning had prevented economists from "... attempting to imitate the careful observation of facts both in the past and the present, and limited generalisation from them, which has brought about progress in other sciences, and which has been the accepted method of study by the realistic or historical school of German economists for a generation or more" (Cunningham, 1894, p. 326). That Marshall was an inveterate collector of "facts" was ignored by Cunningham, as were the early chapters of Marshall's *Principles*, devoted as they were to a historical account of economic development. Above all, English economists whose work shared historicist features did not consider themselves to be members of any particular school, as did their German contemporaries. The "historicist critique" went through its most vociferous phase in Britain during the 1870s and 1880s, a time when there was little systematic teaching of economics in English universities and colleges, and hence little consequence in arguing one way or the other as far as employment and teaching went. During the 1890s regular teaching became more common, but the impulse to shape the new curricula in historicist terms was lacking. English historical economics, in short, failed to make the transition from a literature of controversy to one of pedagogy, a transition effected by "mainstream economics" at the turn of the century. As a tendency, English "historical economists" became quite marginal to the increasingly academic teaching of economics, which is not something one could say of their German counterparts; and, apart from the lack of academic posts in Britain, English historicists also lacked the organizational coherence that German economists gained with the foundation of the *Verein für Socialpolitik*. Strictly speaking, there never was an "English historical school of economics," but simply a series of authors with criticisms of the economics of their time and with a historical cast of mind.

This absence of an English "school" had therefore institutional as much as intellectual foundations. In Germany those who might be considered "economists" would by the later nineteenth century have been principally defined by their employment as a teacher of economics in one of the several state universities. Chairs of economics had existed in Germany since the eighteenth century, and although the teaching delivered from these posts was transformed over time along with the subject, the posts themselves were a constant feature of the university landscape. This teaching was for the benefit of students of law, attendance at a course of lectures in economics being a compulsory part of legal education. Those who studied economics for its own sake were by definition doctoral students, there being no other qualification; this was a formal requirement for university teaching, and it was also important for entry into some parts of state administration. When linked to the system of formal and informal contacts through which students entered employment, this added to the power and influence of professors such as Schmoller, who were able to assign doctoral topics to a growing band of students and draw upon public funds for the prosecution of research.

Nothing like this existed in Britain until later in the twentieth century. In the mid-1890s there were only two full-time Professors of Political Economy – Marshall in Cambridge and Gonner in Liverpool – although some teachers, such as Flux in Manchester, were fully occupied with a wide range of teaching (Tribe, 1993, pp. 200–2). When the British Economic Association was formed in 1890, its chief purpose was to secure the new *Economic Journal* from domination by any one particular tendency or group, not to promote public discussion of economics. Public discussion did take place at the annual meetings of the British Association for the Advancement of Science, but the *ad hoc* manner in which contributions were made and the diffuse background of the audience imposed inevitable limitations. Academic economists in Britain did not have their own organization until the formation of the Association of University Teachers of Economics in the 1920s; while the Political Economy Club had always been a private dining club dominated by nonacademic economists (Tribe, 2001, pp. 32–4). The major protagonists of historical economics in Britain – Ingram, Cliffe Leslie, Ashley, and Cunningham – made their presence felt through their writing, and the occasional speech. They had no national or institutional platform onto which they could draw younger adherents; nor, in truth, did the new academic economics until Alfred Marshall set about laying some foundations. The principal reason for the demise of English historical economics as a viable intellectual program in the early twentieth century was that the new economics succeeded in establishing itself academically, and historical economics did not. Instead, the heirs of Thorold Rogers and Cunningham went on to found the Economic History Society in 1926, a movement whose principal dynamic came from historians, rather than from disgruntled economists.

14.2 THE GERMAN HISTORICAL SCHOOL

By the 1830s, the economics taught and published in Germany was pragmatically eclectic, drawing widely on contemporary English and French political economy, but simply integrating this work with existing German work on the subject. As elsewhere in continental Europe, the writings of Jean-Baptiste Say had a greater substantive impact than that of the English writers, and Say's manner of combining the concept of value with utility and need, rather than labor, meant that patterns of consumption played a more prominent part in the development of continental political economy than was the case in Britain, where the emphasis was more on production and distribution, linking value to labor. In this light, Marx's political economy is a distant echo of earlier, English, preoccupations, detached from contemporary continental literature. This characteristic focus upon utility and need was to influence decisively the formation of a new subjective economics in the later nineteenth century, but in the early part of the century the controversy that had characterized English debates was absent. The leading German textbook was Rau's *Lehrbuch der politischen Oekonomie*, the first volume being published in 1826, reaching its ninth edition in 1876. Rau's text was "modern," and distinct from an eighteenth-century cameralistic tradition where the discussion of economic activity was linked to the work of economic administration; but although Rau incorporated elements of Smithian political economy, his book enumerates economic objects rather than presenting instruments of economic analysis (Tribe, 1988, ch. 9). More contentious in tone was Friedrich List's critique of Smithian "cosmopolitan political economy" presented in *Das nationale System der politischen Oekonomie* (1841), where he argued that the universal economic laws expounded in the *Wealth of Nations* failed properly to take account of national and historical differences. However, List was not strictly an exponent of a historical, let alone an inductive, approach to economics systems, and in any case the main lines of his critique of Adam Smith were borrowed from American, not German, writers.

It is generally agreed that the programmatic foundation of German historical economics can be found in a lecture outline published by Wilhelm Roscher in 1843. His prime objective in these lectures, he argued, was not a better understanding of national wealth and its increase, but instead

> ... a representation of the economic aspect of what peoples have thought, wanted and felt, what they have striven for and attained, why they have striven for it and why they have attained it. (Roscher, 1843, p. IV)

This involved more than mere chrematistics; it was a political science that would necessarily involve consideration of earlier cultural stages, for "a people is not simply the mass of individuals presently living." He also called for a comparative study of all peoples so that their "important, law-like features" might be discerned. These lectures were presented "according to historical method," and Roscher invoked the work of the Historical School of Law associated with Savigny and Eichhorn in his support. This method would illuminate

> ... the political impulses of men, impulses that can only be investigated on the basis of a comparison of all known peoples. The common features in the varied development of peoples summarised as a developmental law. (Roscher, 1843, p. 2)

State economy, argued Roscher, was concerned with "the developmental laws of the economy," while politics was the study of the developmental laws of the state, such that "state economy" was an especially important part of politics (Roscher, 1843, p. 2).

Even while arguing for a comparative, inductive approach to the "laws of development," Roscher recommended the writings of Smith, Say, and Ricardo; and in adopting this new position he avoided the blanket criticism of political economy typical of List. The program of comparative study that he sketched remained largely unfulfilled; instead, between 1854 and 1874 he devoted himself chiefly to study of the history of economic thought. During the same period he also wrote a textbook whose strictly historical foundation is the history of thought, not of peoples (Roscher, 1854). Later volumes were devoted to agriculture and to commerce, presented as a description of economic systems, not as a historicist foundation for the revision of all hitherto existing economic theory. This was also true of Bruno Hildebrand, whose name is usually linked with that of Roscher as a member of the "Older" historical school. His *Nationalökonomie der Gegenwart und Zukunft*, a projected reformulation of economics on historical lines as a "doctrine regarding the economic laws of developments of peoples," got no further than a first volume which presented a critical assessment of economic theories from Adam Smith to the present day (Hildebrand, 1848, p. V). His criticism of Smith was closely aligned with that of Roscher:

> The Smithian system represented itself as a general theory of human economy, but was only an expression of a money economy just become pre-eminent. . . . Economics was treated by the entire Smithian school as a natural science of commerce, in which the individual was assumed to be a purely selfish force, active like any natural force in a constant direction and which, given similar conditions, will produce the same results. For this reason its laws and regularities were called both in Germany and in England natural economic laws, and attributed eternal duration to them, like other natural laws. (Hildebrand, 1848, pp. 29, 33–4)

While this might recall List's own critique of Smith, Hildebrand devoted a critical chapter to List, noting that List's stages of economic development were simply borrowed from British history and lacked general validity, for "every people experiences a unique course of economic development" (p. 76). As elsewhere, therefore, we encounter a critique of prevailing classical orthodoxy, without any clear alternative being offered. Hildebrand did sketch later an evolutionary model of economic forms, but these – natural economy, money economy, and credit economy – were ultimately similar in kind and level of generality to the stages of economic development outlined by Adam Smith in book III of the *Wealth of Nations*. Nowhere did Hildebrand engage in the kind of detailed historical studies that were later typical of Schmoller and his students.

The third member of the "Older School" was Carl Knies, who likewise proposed that the task of political economy was not only to account for the historical development of economic theory, but also the economic conditions and development of different nations and periods (Knies, 1853, pp. 3–4). Whereas Roscher's influence was exercised largely through his writing, and Hildebrand's by founding the journal *Jahrbücher für Nationalökonomie und Statistik* in 1862, it was perhaps through his teaching in Heidelberg for over 30 years that Knies exercised his greatest influence – John Bates Clark, Eugen von Böhm-Bawerk, Friedrich Wieser, and Max Weber were among his students. Fortunately, student lecture notes from his course of 1886 have survived, and demonstrate that in his teaching Knies followed a predictable path, beginning with definitions of "wants" and "goods," just like any other German teacher of economics. Exposition of the leading concepts – of production, distribution, value, and price – are geared primarily to a critique of socialist theory, especially the doctrines of Marx, associated by Knies with the English classical economists. Rejecting the idea that price is determined by cost of production, Knies argues that if this were true, then prices would not fluctuate in the manner that they do while costs of production remain stable. Instead, he identifies the interaction of supply and demand as the dominant factor:

> The significance of production costs in price formation is determined by the extension or contraction of supply. . . . Where production cannot be expanded or reduced prices will rise with higher demand, or fall with less demand. If production can be varied, then prices do not vary so greatly, despite altered demand. (Knies, 2000, p. 48)

Knies' version of the relation of price to demand and supply is broadly continuous with those of other, pre-marginalist writers, and it might be noted that his discussion of these basic concepts remains unencumbered by assertions that such principles should be founded inductively. As with Roscher and Hildebrand, the principal historical component of his lecture course involves constant reference to the classics of economics such as the physiocrats, Adam Smith, and David Ricardo, and he generally eschews lengthy comparative analysis of, for example, patterns of trading, or property forms.

It can be argued that what divided the Older and the Younger Schools was precisely this: that the Older School was programmatic but failed to realize its vision; while the Younger School executed the program but lost the vision. The chief criticism made of the Older School was that they did not produce the systematic comparative histories of economic systems for which they called; while the chief criticism of the Younger School was to be that, while they certainly generated large quantities of economic–historical studies, it was never clear how these related to the historicist program as originally proclaimed by Roscher in 1843. When Carl Menger pointed this out (and offered a solution), he provoked what became known as the *Methodenstreit*, a dispute over the susceptibility of economic science to inductive development.

To understand the character of the Younger School one has to begin with Gustav Schmoller, founder of the Younger School by virtue of the role that he played in the formation of the *Verein für Socialpolitik* in 1872–3, and who subsequently became an academic impresario mediating between academic and official institutions, acquiring great influence over appointments and promotions in Prussian universities (Peukert, 2001). Schmoller studied history and state sciences in Tübingen, after which he entered the state administration of Württemberg, occupied chiefly with commercial statistics, moving in 1864 to a chair at Halle. In 1872 he made a politically significant move to the University of Straßburg, a cultural outpost in the newly occupied territories of Alsace-Lorraine; Schmoller identified himself in this way not only with a reunited Germany, but with Prussian domination, and ten years later, in 1882, he moved to a chair in the Prussian and German capital, Berlin, which he retained until his retirement in 1913. One year before the move to Berlin, he assumed the editorship of *Jahrbuch für Gesetzgebung, Verwaltung und Volkswirthschaft im Deutschen Reich*, renamed in 1913 *Schmollers Jahrbuch*, in the later nineteenth century the leading German journal for politics and economics.

The inaugural meeting of the *Verein für Socialpolitik* was held in Eisenach during October 1872; three years previously the German Social Democratic Party had been founded in the same town, dedicated to much the same purpose as the *Verein*, but differing in ideology, membership, and strategy. The *Verein* addressed itself to the "social question" – the social problems of industrialization and urbanization. In his opening speech, Schmoller identified the chief objective: to find a common basis among academics for the reform of social relations, a position from which one might then in turn influence public opinion (Schmoller, 2000, p. 595). He warned of the threat from social revolution engendered by the division between employer and worker, propertied and propertyless classes, and suggested that popular economic beliefs concerning commercial freedom and economic individualism could well create even greater disorder, rather than the rosy future they imagined. Germany unity had been realized the previous year; but social divisions already posed a threat to the young nation, and only the German state was in a position to reduce social tension and foster national unity, for it stood above selfish class interests, "legislating, guiding administration with a just hand, protecting the weak, raising the lower classes," the culmination of two centuries of Prussian endeavor (Schmoller, 2000, pp. 599–600). Economic doctrines hostile to state intervention might well have had their place when Germany was a nation of many small states; but with the new identity of nation and state "the conciliation of people and government, parliament and state power shed new light even on economic questions" (p. 596). Many in the *Kongreß der deutschen Volkswirte*, a relatively broadly based organization promoting free trade, understood the implications of these changes; but its leadership had become even more vociferous in defense of the dogma of economic individualism:

> There was no such thing as a labour problem – so they said – to talk in these terms was merely confused thinking or demagogic agitation, the working class now had all that they needed; those who did not get on in life only had themselves to blame; some suggested that workers' co-operatives were an affront to entrepreneurial profits because workers shared in the return, workers' unions were attacked because they were thought to revive guild organisation, any and every corporative body was reviled; likewise with factory legislation, it was denied that the factory inspectorate had any relevance to German conditions. The Berlin Economic Society denounced conciliation and arbitration tribunals as heresy. It almost seemed as if the party which had in the name of human rights once fostered the salvation of underprivileged classes were now only interested in the one-sided class standpoint of the

entrepreneur, as if economic freedom now meant only the freedom of big business, of large employers and owners of capital, to exploit the public. (Schmoller, 2000, p. 597)

Sharing socialist criticisms of the "Manchester school," but seeking the initiative for social reform from a strong state, the *Verein* was positioned from the beginning between liberals on the one side and socialists on the other (Hagemann, 2001). As noted above, as far as the Older School was concerned, these two polar extremes – economic liberals and Marxist socialists – in fact had a common source for their economic ideas: the classical economics of early-nineteenth-century Britain. German historical economics was therefore a path between these two extremes; and the economics of the *Verein*, characterized by the rejection both of *laissez-faire* liberalism and Marxist socialism, became by default one version or another of a German historicist tradition. That the *Verein* met annually during the summer vacation in the major cities of Germany to debate specific topics of social reform is indicative of the predominance of its academic members, lending economists an important forum both to discuss their common interests and hence establish a degree of identity. Although there was some initial success in exerting a direct influence upon legislation, from the early 1880s the *Verein* developed its work by commissioning studies of social problems that would form a basis for discussion at future meetings, in many cases receiving financial support from government departments for the collection of data. The empirical study of economic relationships and phenomena associated with the "social question" which the *Verein* fostered was well suited to the general understanding of economic development associated with German historicism.

Quite apart from the prominence that his role in the *Verein* gave him, Schmoller's own extensive writings were distinguished from those of his predecessors by their focus on the social and economic forces underlying the development of the German state, rather than on contemporary economic discussion of trade or wages. His early study of small enterprise (Schmoller, 1870) examined the pressures on small and craft businesses in increasingly international markets, arguing for a measure of protective legislation that would enable such enterprises to adapt to new conditions. Historical and comparative investigation of financial, agrarian, or industrial conditions was linked in this manner to the forces of industrialization and the role of the state in moderating the negative effects of economic progress. This approach was shared with others, such as Lujo Brentano, whose early studies of British trades unions prompted a comparative analysis of labor organization, establishing that British wages were higher and working hours shorter than those in Germany. His conclusion from this research, that economic progress would only result from a reduction of working hours in Germany, exemplifies the manner in which the comparative study originally envisaged by Roscher could be linked to social reform (Brentano, 1877). Academic economists of Schmoller's generation concerned themselves chiefly with empirical studies of this kind, and paid scant attention to the finer points of economic theory.

In time, a division emerged within the *Verein* between founding members who had experienced unification and who shared Schmoller's ethical evaluation of the state – Adolf Wagner, Wilhelm Lexis, and Johannes Conrad – and a younger generation, primarily of economists, more concerned with the social and political disintegration of the 1880s and 1890s – Eugen von Bortkiewicz, Carl Grünberg, Max Sering, Ferdinand Tönnies, and of course Max and Alfred Weber. Although these academics did conduct detailed empirical investigation, they were also more open to theoretical argument. Carl Menger's methodological critique of German historicism consequently prompted a violent response from Gustav Schmoller that was not echoed by the younger generation of economists.

The "dispute over method" is a landmark in the development of the social sciences, but when examined in detail it shrinks in significance. Menger made a methodological point that is today quite uncontroversial, making a clear distinction between the historical and statistical study of economic forms, theoretical economics, and practical fields such as economic policy and finance. Historical study of economic structures had its place, but was complementary to, not a substitute for, the development of theoretical principles (Menger, 1883, pp. 12–13). The prime task of economic analysis was therefore the elaboration of theory and policy, not the simple accumulation of economic facts. Empirical knowledge could not be acquired through reflection, and theoretical knowledge did not result from empirical work. This was the core of Menger's argument: not a rejection of historical economics *per se*, but a denial that "more" historical economics could lead to "better" theory (Tribe, 1995, pp. 77–8).

As noted above, Schmoller had largely abandoned the programmatic statements that were more typical of his predecessors and instead directed his efforts to detailed historical studies; nonetheless, his response to Menger's criticism was abrupt and dismissive. Schmoller simply reversed the point that Menger had made, and argued that economic analysis could not be derived from general principles of psychology, but must arise from the study of individual economic action. Historical study, he suggested, had no need of "theoretical" economics (Schmoller, 1883, pp. 976–7). His grasp of contemporary economic theory was in any case distinctly rudimentary, as evidenced by his 1897 inaugural lecture as *Rektor* of the University of Berlin. Couched in terms of a struggle between socialism and a classical economics associated with Smith and Ricardo, Schmoller looked back on the nineteenth century in terms that would not have been out of place 50 years earlier, or more:

> Contemporary economics has come to accept an historical and ethical view of state and society, in contrast to rationalism and materialism. From a mere doctrine of markets and exchange, a kind of business economics which threatened to become a class tool of the propertied, it has once more become a great moral and political science, a science which as well as investigating the production and distribution of goods, as well as the phenomena of value forms, investigates economic institutions, and which instead of the world of goods and capital places people at the centre of the science. (Schmoller, 1897, p. 26)

Of course, Schmoller never did study individual action (historical or otherwise) in the manner that he implied; to do so would have required a prior understanding of "economising activity," as Max Weber later pointed out in the second chapter of *Economy and Society*. There was no more to the *Methodenstreit* than this. Menger argued on the one hand that theory was not susceptible to inductive elaboration – something that Schmoller in truth never even attempted – while Schmoller's asserted that it was, but never sought to demonstrate how. Despite its insubstantial nature, this "dispute on method" came to symbolize the gulf that separated historical from theoretical economics in the later nineteenth century.

14.3   THE ENGLISH HISTORICAL SCHOOL

In the early 1890s John Neville Keynes published a survey of economic method that would remain a standard work until Lionel Robbins's *Nature and Significance of Economic Science* (1932). Keynes consistently contrasted deductive and inductive approaches to the subject, suggesting however that no reasonable practitioners adhered exclusively to the one or the other. Moreover, he noted a feature that was already evident in the German case: the greater the clarity and vehemence with which the one or the other was advocated, the less likely was it that anyone could be found who adhered to such prescriptions and injunctions. Keynes considered Schmoller to be an "extremist" who sought to collapse economic theory into economic history; he recommended instead the writings of Roscher and Wagner (Keynes, 1891, pp. 26, 298). This dismissal of Schmoller was linked with a similar judgment upon John Kells Ingram, suggesting that they were both in their different ways "arrogant and exclusive in their pretensions":

> The former would practically identify political economy and economic history, or at any rate resolve political economy into the philosophy of economic history. The latter, whose aim is somewhat different, though he is equally revolutionary in his tendency, would absorb political economy into sociology. (p. 27)

Ingram – a follower of Comte, hence the remark concerning sociology – had achieved a degree of notoriety with his robust, if wildly inaccurate, account of the parlous state of orthodox economics delivered as part of his Presidential Address to Section F of the British Association in 1878. In the previous year, Francis Galton had moved that this section, "Economic Science and Statistics," be wound up, his chief complaint being that the papers presented were quite heterogeneous and not suited to an organization dedicated to the advancement of scientific knowledge. In fact, Galton had passed no comment directly upon political economy, and his remarks were directed primarily at "statistical" contributions; but in his address Ingram represented Galton's intervention as one directed at political economy, employing this misrepresentation as the point of departure for his own critique of contemporary economics. He was undeniably successful in this rhetorical strategem: to this day the spin that he put upon Galton's intervention is dutifully repeated in the literature (Koot, 1987, p. 55). While such repetition does not alter the unreliability of Ingram's account of contemporary economics, the timing of his comments does suggest that there was a growing audience for some form of "alternative" political economy in the later 1870s and early 1880s. Furthermore, Ingram's address also made use of a standard refrain in such critiques: that while things might be in a sorry state "here," elsewhere affairs are better managed. Rather like Perry Anderson some 90 years later (1968), he suggested that there had occurred in continental Europe a revolt that had largely passed the English by:

> It is a characteristic result of the narrowness and spirit of routine which have too much prevailed in the dominant English school of economists, that they are either unacquainted with, or have chosen to ignore, this remarkable movement.
> The largest and most combined manifestation of the revolt has been in Germany, all whose ablest economic writers are in opposition to the methods and doctrines of the school of Ricardo. Roscher, Knies, Hildebrand, Nasse, Brentano, Held, Schmoller, Schäffle, Schönberg, Samter, and others, have taken up this attitude. (Ingram, 1962, p. 47)

The German historical school could therefore be introduced as an exemplary alternative, although as it happened none of those writers who became associated with "English historical economics" drew directly upon German writings (Tribe, 2000). Ingram went on to draw a line between Smith and Ricardo, suggesting that the former was broadly inductive and the latter relentlessly deductive; a line of argument that accounts for his statement that the German historical economists were hostile to the writings of Ricardo. This is very much an English preoccupation; the work of Ricardo was not especially influential in continental Europe, Adam Smith being consistently identified as the chief protagonist of classical economics. But it suited Ingram's purpose to argue in this way, for by associating Smith with inductivism he could appropriate Smith to the "alternative" canon.

Ingram warmly recommended the work of Cliffe Leslie, who had likewise drawn a line between deductive and inductive methods, between Ricardo on the one hand and Smith on the other. Leslie argued that Smith's work placed inductive investigation within a natural law framework, from which was drawn the conception of a natural harmony in economic life. This conception was later read in more providential terms, so that Smith's original ideas were reworked into a rigid doctrine of *laissez-faire*:

> The mischief done in political economy by this assumption respecting the benificent constitution of nature, and therefore of all human inclinations and desires, has been incalculable. It became an axiom of science with many economists, and with all English statesmen, that by a natural law the interests of individuals harmonise with the interests of the public; and one pernicious consequence is that the important department of the consumption of wealth has . . . been in reality either altogether set aside, as lying beyond the pale of scientific investigation, or passed over with a general assumption, after the manner of Mandeville, that private vices are public benefits. (Cliffe Leslie, 1879, p. 154)

Leslie elsewhere made clear that inductivism was equivalent to historicism, his understanding of historical study being stamped by his teacher Sir Henry Maine, and also the writings of Stubbs. When he identified sections of the *Wealth of Nations* with inductivism, this amounted to the claim that Smith could be regarded in a historicist light; and this itself indicates that the kind of historicism that he had in mind was quite distant from the social and economic history that Schmoller and his associates had already begun to publish.

The writings of both Ingram and Leslie had more in common with those of Roscher and Hildebrand than Schmoller and Wagner, since the organizing focus of Roscher and Hildebrand was primarily upon the history of economic doctrines, rather than historical study of manufacturing or trade. This was also true of Arnold Toynbee, whose 1881–2 course of Oxford lectures linked the study of economic history to the liberal concept of progress, in which he followed Macaulay, who in describing the English "Glorious Revolution" of 1688 argued that the history of England was a history of progress, "the history of a constant movement of the public mind" (Kadish, 1986, p. 105). His account of the Industrial Revolution linked the development of industrial history to the economic thinking that had accompanied it – Smith's *Wealth of Nations* was therefore linked to the impact of the steam engine, rejecting Carlyle's call for a halt to the onward march of industrialization and suggesting that the social division and fragmentation associated with it were transitional, that new economic freedoms were being generated. The literature of political economy provided an organizing framework to this history of industrial and social progress, with the work of Malthus presiding over the account of the main period of industrial change, and Ricardo taking care of the post-Napoleonic period. Toynbee also took a more conciliatory line on the question of deductivism and political economy, suggesting that the function of economic history was to test its principles, not provide a source for the inductivist reinvention of economics (Toynbee, 1884, p. 111). The historicization of political economy did not therefore necessarily imply a radical critique of the classical tradition, and Edwin Cannan – who at the time that Toynbee delivered his lectures was a student in Oxford – was later to take a very similar line on the relation of economic history and economic theory (Cannan, 1894).

Cannan's contemporary William Ashley took the notes from which Toynbee's lectures were posthumously reconstructed. Ashley took the historical route, contributing to the development of economic history in Britain, after inaugurating the chair of economic history at Harvard in 1893. Five years before this, at his Toronto inaugural, Ashley had expressed Ingram's sentiments in more measured tones:

> Ten or fifteen years ago Political Economy occupied, in English-speaking countries, no very dignified or useful position. In England it was represented by two very able men, Cairnes and Jevons. Neither of these, however, had any considerable influence upon the educated public; and the professorial teaching at Oxford and Cambridge was of but small scientific importance. In University and College instruction, Political Economy was the convenient stopgap. (Ashley, 1888, p. 10)

But at Harvard Ashley now spoke of the work of Ingram and Leslie as belonging to the past, that they shared a great deal with a classical orthodoxy that thought in terms of general propositions (Ashley, 1893, p. 3). Looking back on this evolution from the even later standpoint of 1907, Ashley noted the rise of marginalist economics, but emphasized a different set of questions:

> But *why* do people demand just those things? On what does the rapidity of satiation depend? Have their desires always been the same; or the possibilities of production in order to meet them? How are desires related to one another? What are they likely to become? What are the limits to demand set by the economic situation of the demanders? These are the things we really want to know. The problem is, in a wide sense of the term, an *historical* one; or, if you prefer the phrase, a *sociological* one, both "static" and "dynamic." Behind the workman's wife making up her mind on Saturday night whether to buy another loaf or a scrap more meat stand the whole of human nature and the whole of social history. (Ashley, 1907, p. 476)

The way in which Ashley casually links history here to sociology implies a different kind of history to the one with which he had started in the early 1880s. Only with the publication of Cunningham's *Growth of English Industry and Commerce* in 1882 was there a textbook available that outlined the "new" economic history; hitherto, history had been treated principally as the history of past politics.

While a specifically English reaction against the rigidities of classical economics occurred in the last third of the nineteenth century, the various writers and scholars who associated themselves with this response were intellectually diverse; they were united in this reaction, but little else. Some were historians first and foremost – Rogers, Ashley, and Cunningham – although these did not share a common view of the nature of historical method. Others were not historians – Ingram and Leslie. Ashley played an important part in the creation of the study of economic history in Britain; but then so did Clapham and Unwin, who are not usually included in accounts of the "English historical school"; while there is in any case a stronger argument that the study of economic history in Britain drew for the most part on changes in the study of history, not of economics. Some, like Hewins and Cunningham, were "neo-mercantilists," protectionists, and "fair-traders," as Koot suggests; but not Rogers or Ingram. Some, like Toynbee, were strong proponents of social reform, but then so were most economists in Britain. "History" as a critique of theory does not therefore serve us well in seeking to characterize the development of English economics in the later nineteenth century.

But this does not mean that history and economics did not enjoy a mutually reinforcing relationship. Edwin Cannan, perhaps the most influential teacher of economics in Britain up to his retirement as Professor of Political Economy at the LSE in 1926, edited what was until the 1970s the standard edition of Smith's *Wealth of Nations*, and he taught in London for many years a course on "Principles of Economics, including the History of Economic Theory." His *Theories of Production and Distribution in English Political Economy* was the first historical account of political economy to take its sources seriously, using the best texts available and in its exact reading of its sources demonstrating analytic errors that had not only eluded his predecessors, but which would also pass by his successors. To take another example, E. C. K. Gonner, Brunner Professor of Political Economy in Liverpool from 1891 to 1922, published an important study of the development of the English farming landscape, *Common Land and Inclosure* (Gonner, 1912). At first sight, the book appears to be related to a number of near-contemporary works of agrarian history; Gonner traces the gradual appropriation of common land for individual use, but in charting the impact of this transition upon cultivation and employment, he sets to work an explicitly analytic framework that owes much to his previous work in geography and economics. Gonner also edited Ricardo's *Principles of Political Economy*, and later published a collection of Ricardo's other writings, not the sort of thing that one would normally expect of a historically minded economist. Neither of these writers would conventionally be counted among "historical economists," nor do they self-consciously employ historical sources in developing a critique of contemporary economics. What does unite them, of course, is that they were both students of history and political economy in Oxford during the 1880s, as were Ashley, Price, Llewellyn Smith, and Hewins (Kadish, 1982, ch. 3). Political economy was in Oxford taught as part of history and of "Greats" until the foundation of "Modern Greats," the PPE course in 1920. In Cambridge it was part of history and the moral sciences until the inauguration of Marshall's Economics Tripos in 1903. In the London University BA degree before the turn of the century, the teaching of political economy was linked to history and moral philosophy.

In this perspective, the study of history and economics becomes part of the wider history of the social sciences, rather than a clash between inductive and deductive methods, or of historicism and rationalism. Whatever the relationship between economics and history might have been by the later twentieth century, economists of the earlier twentieth century continued as a reflex to draw upon historical materials and arguments in their work on practical economic problems – on unemployment, economic development, industrial decline, or poverty. The "historicist critique of economics" turns out on closer examination to be based largely on bad history: a faulty historical understanding of economics and history. And if this is true of the later nineteenth century, then it is even more so of the early twenty-first century.

Bibliography

Anderson, P. 1968: Components of the national culture. *New Left Review*, 50 (July–August), 3–57.

Ashley, W. J. 1888: *What is Political Science?* Toronto: Rowsell and Hutchison.

—— 1893: On the study of economic history. *Quarterly Journal of Economics*, 7, 115–36.

—— 1902: *The Faculty of Commerce in the University of Birmingham*. Birmingham.

—— 1907: The present position of political economy. *Economic Journal*, 17, 467–89.

Brentano, L. 1877: *Das Arbeitsverhältniss gemäss dem heutigen Recht*. Leipzig: Duncker und Humblot.

Cannan, E. 1894: *A History of the Theories of Production and Distribution in English Political Economy from 1776 to 1848*. London: Rivington, Percival & Co.

Cliffe Leslie, T. E. 1879: The political economy of Adam Smith. In *Essays in Political and Moral Philosophy*. Dublin: Hodges, Foster and Figgis, 148–66.

Cunningham, W. 1894: Why had Roscher so little influence in England? *Annals of the American Academy of Political and Social Science*, 5, 317–34.

Gonner, E. C. K. 1912: *Common Land and Inclosure*. London: Macmillan.

Hagemann, H. 2001: The Verein für Sozialpolitik from its foundation (1872) until World War I. In M. M. Augello and M. Guidi (eds.), *The Spread of Political Economy and the Professionalisation of Economists*. London: Routledge, 152–75.

Hildebrand, B. 1848: *Die Nationalökonomie der Gegenwart und Zukunft*. Frankfurt am Main: Literarische Anstalt.

Ingram, J. K. 1962: The present position and prospects of political economy. Reprinted in R. L. Smyth (ed.), *Essays in Economic Method*, London: Duckworth, 41–72.

Kadish, A. 1982: *The Oxford Economists in the Late Nineteenth Century*. Oxford: Oxford University Press.

—— 1986: *Apostle Arnold*. Durham, NC: Duke University Press.

Keynes, J. N. 1891: *The Scope and Method of Political Economy*. London: Macmillan.

Knies, K. 1853: *Die politische Oekonomie vom Standpunkte der geschichtlichen Methode*. Brunswick: C. A. Schwetschke und Sohn.

—— 2000: Allgemeine (theoretische) Volkswirtschaftslehre (1886). *Kyoto University Economic Review*, LXIX(1 & 2), 16–78.

Koot, G. M. 1987: *English Historical Economics, 1870–1926*. Cambridge, UK: Cambridge University Press.

Menger, C. 1883: *Untersuchungen über die Methode der Socialwissenschaften, und der Politischen Oekonomie insbesondere*. Leipzig: Duncker und Humblot.

Peukert, H. 2001: The Schmoller renaissance. *History of Political Economy*, 33, 71–116.

Robbins, L. 1932: *An Essay on the Nature and Significance of Economic Science*. London: Macmillan.

Roscher, W. 1843: *Grundriß zu Vorlesungen über die Staatswirthschaft. Nach geschichtlicher Methode*. Göttingen: Dieterische Buchhandlung.

—— 1854: *System der Volkswirthschaft Bd. I: Die Grundlagen der Nationalökonomie*. Stuttgart: J. G. Cotta.

Schmoller, G. 1870: *Zur Geschichte der deutschen Kleingewerbe im 19.Jahrhundert*. Halle: Verlag der Buchhandlung des Waisenhauses.

—— 1883: Zur Methodologie der Staats- und Sozialwissenschaften. *Jahrbuch für Gesetzgebung, Verwaltung und Volkswirtschaft*, N. F. Jg. 7, 975–94.

—— 1897: *Wechselnde Theorien und feststehende Wahrheiten im Gebiete der Staats- und Socialwissenschaften und die heutige deutsche Volkswirtschaftlehre*. Berlin: W. Büxenstein.

—— 2000: Eröffnungsrede auf der Eisenacher Versammlung zur Besprechung der sozialen Frage. In J. Burkhardt and B. P. Priddat (eds.), *Geschichte der Ökonomie*. Frankfurt am Main: Deutscher Klassiker Verlag, 595–603.

Toynbee, A. 1884: *Lectures on the Industrial Revolution in England*. London: Rivingtons.

Tribe, K. 1988: *Governing Economy*. Cambridge, UK: Cambridge University Press.

—— 1993: Political economy in the northern civic universities. In K. Tribe and A. Kadish (eds.), *The Market for Political Economy*. London: Routledge, 184–226.

—— 1995: *Strategies of Economic Order*. Cambridge, UK: Cambridge University Press.

—— 2000: The historicization of political economy? In B. Stuchtey and P. Wende (eds.), *British and German Historiography 1750–1950*. Oxford: Oxford University Press, 211–28.

—— 2001: Economic societies in Great Britain and Ireland. In M. M. Augello and M. Guidi (eds.), *The Spread of Political Economy and the Professionalisation of Economists*. London: Routledge, 32–52.

Weber, M. 1989: The national state and economic policy. In K. Tribe (ed.), *Reading Weber*. London: Routledge, 188–209.

Whewell, W. (ed.) 1859: *Literary Remains, Consisting of Lectures and Tracts on Political Economy, of the Late Rev. Richard Jones*. London: John Murray.

American Economics to 1900

William J. Barber

15.1 Introduction

To judge by the distribution of Nobel Prizes in economics over the past three decades or so, it would appear that American economics – for good or ill – has come to occupy a position of world preeminence. This has not always been so. To the contrary, if we roll the clock back to consider the "state of the art" during the first century of the nation's existence, the United States was largely on the periphery of major intellectual developments in the discipline. Indeed, when the country's centennial was celebrated in 1876, American economists had an inferiority complex. Writing on this occasion, Harvard's Charles F. Dunbar – the first American to be accorded the title of "Professor of Political Economy" – observed that American scholarship as yet had contributed nothing to fundamental economic knowledge. In his reading, American economics to date had been derivative, stagnant, and sterile. He further held that most of the domestic restatements of doctrines formulated abroad were flawed (Dunbar, 1876, pp. 124–54). Foreign observers tended to echo this appraisal.

The question thus needed to be asked: What could account for the backwardness of American intellectual achievement in this discipline? Numerous answers to this question were offered and each identified a pertinent aspect of the national reality. Creative intellectual production, it was suggested, should not be expected in an environment in which the challenge of taming a vast continent was the primary claimant on energies. "Do-ers," in other words, should not be expected to be "thinkers." The abundant resource endowment, so welcome in other respects, might also account for an apparent lack of original thinking in political economy. In the absence of perceived scarcity, stimuli to provoke hard-nosed analyses were blunted. Properties of America's federal system of government might also account for the country's seeming backwardness in economic analysis. Issues that deserved to be analyzed at the national level had been dispersed to the jealously guarded jurisdictions of individual states. This feature of the polity obstructed analytic progress on such matters as banking and currency. It could plausibly be argued as well that the politics of states' rights stunted detached reflection in debates over free trade versus protection, even though tariffs were within the constitutional mandate of the federal government.

International realities – not just national ones – framed the context for American political economy up to 1900. After all, those wishing to acquire insight into the discipline did not need to rely on home production. They could look overseas and import ideas ready made. Given the absence of copyright protection for foreigners, it may even have been more cost-effective for American publishers to pirate ideas in book form from abroad than to sponsor local authorship.

At the same time, there was always vigorous discourse on economic topics. Certainly colonial America did not lack for it. There were lively exchanges in public debates over such matters as the uses and abuses of paper money and over the "Mother Country's" practices in shaping colonial trade patterns. In the run-up to the American Declaration of Independence, protests over Britain's use of its taxing powers gathered considerable momentum. Moreover, the "Founding Fathers" in the first decades of the Republic had displayed a plenitude of ingenuity in crafting the instruments of a Federal political order and in establishing the credibility and creditworthiness of a novel form of government. Arguably, nothing in all this activity would qualify as a contribution to systematic economic analysis. Though a number of contemporary commentators took note of this shortcoming, the age of the economic treatise was not born until 1820.

As befitted the sectional diversity of the country, the first generation of Americans to produce systematic treatises on political economy did not speak with one voice. All of them, however, were obliged to come to grips with a common set of questions. Were economic concepts designed in the "Old World" transferable to the "New?" Should European formulations be rejected out of hand, or could they be made serviceable with modifications? Or was an altogether different approach to political economy called for in a young nation that had already severed its political links with the Mother Country? A review of the ways in which a representative sample of contributors responded will illustrate the variations played on these themes.

15.2   THE PIONEERING NATIVE VOICE: DANIEL RAYMOND (1786–1849)

The author of the first full-scale treatise produced on American soil, Daniel Raymond, chose to issue a full-throated plea for a declaration of American intellectual independence. His objective, as he put it in *Thoughts on Political Economy* (published in 1820), was "to break loose from the fetters of foreign authority – from foreign theories and systems of political economy, which from the dissimilarity in the nature of governments, renders them altogether unsuited to our country" (Raymond, 1820, pp. v–vi).

These were high aspirations indeed. They were expressed by a man who had decided to study the subject in order to relieve boredom as an under-employed lawyer in Baltimore. Persuaded that the absence of an American treatise on political economy was a "reproach to the nation," he persisted in his endeavor. Raymond mounted a frontal attack on core propositions that Adam Smith had advanced in the *Wealth of Nations*. The nation, in Raymond's view, should be understood as an organic "unity" which transcended the aggregate of its individual members. This conception suggested that the public interest and private interests might diverge. Optimal growth in national wealth – which he defined as the "capacity for acquiring the necessaries and comforts of life" – required guidance from above. He further charged Smith with error in the importance assigned to "parsimony" to fuel "accumulation." To the contrary, Raymond held that consumption was the force driving expansion in productive capacity. From that point of view, emphasis on saving invited disaster. The "present distress of our country," Raymond wrote, arose entirely from "the circumstance that consumption does not equal production." This led to "surplus" in the form of unsold output, which depressed economic activity. It was the duty of the legislator "to make provision . . . for its immediate consumption" (Raymond, 1820, p. 55). The measures that Raymond had in mind were shelters for home enterprise from foreign competition and spending on public works. For Raymond, "full employment" – and he used that expression – deserved top priority. That goal could be achieved if the informed legislator intervened to push production to the limits of its potential. The workings of an invisible hand could not be trusted to produce that result.

15.3   MUTATED CLASSICISM IN TEXTBOOK LITERATURE: THE CASE OF THE REVEREND FRANCIS WAYLAND (1796–1865)

Imported ideas got a more appreciative hearing from the first cohort of Americans authoring textbooks in political economy than they did from Raymond. The conditions of their production were such that more respectful references to learned authorities seemed appropriate. In the early American colleges, it was standard practice for the president – who, in the denominationally linked institutions, was invariably a clergyman – to lecture to seniors on "moral philosophy." The Reverend Francis Wayland, author of the most widely read work on political economy before the Civil War, came to the topic via this route. His *Elements of Political Economy*, first published in 1837, was a codification of lectures he had prepared in connection with his presidential duties at Brown University in Rhode Island. Wayland's approach to the subject matter was heavily influenced by his background as a clergyman. Within his perspective, the "invisible hand" should be understood as the "Divine hand."

Wayland drew heavily on the later classical tradition, as transmitted primarily by J.-B. Say and J. R. McCulloch. He accepted fully its conclusions about the beneficence of free markets and the wisdom of careful limits on governmental participation in economic activity. But his message was not just a clone of the European originals. On a number of significant points, he re-wrote standard doctrine.

His adaptation of European thought to the American environment banished later classicism's preoccupation with the dismal prospects associated with the approach of the stationary state. This outcome seemed inapplicable in the United States, where land scarcity posed no threat and the Malthusian population devil was nowhere in evidence. Classical teaching on the "unproductiveness" of labor in the services sector also required revision: those "laborers" engaged in the "industry of discovery and investigation" created knowledge that advanced the welfare of the community and were, therefore, productive. Ricardo's account of rent as flowing exclusively from the "natural and indestructible powers of the soil" was particularly objectionable. Rents were also determined by the attractiveness of land for commercial, industrial, and residential purposes. In addition, the Ricardian account of agricultural development – which presupposed that cultivation began on high-fertility acreages and was subsequently extended to inferior ones – was out of touch with the reality of America's westward expansion (Wayland, 1838, *passim*).

Imported ideas could thus provide an organizational frame for economic discourse. But when adapted to the perceived structural "facts" of the American economy and adjusted for ideological compatibility with the dominant religious tradition, much in the originals dropped out in translation. America offered the promise of a happy future in which uninterrupted progress and social harmony could prevail.

15.4   A RENEWED CALL FOR IMPORT REJECTION: THE CONTRIBUTION OF HENRY C. CAREY (1793–1879)

While bowdlerized versions of European classicism formed the orthodoxy in academic instruction, a vigorous statement of heterodoxy flowed from the pen of Philadelphia's Henry C. Carey. His central message amounted to an appeal for a "new" American approach to the economic process in which tariff shelter for home industries played a strategic role. When setting out his views, he took sharp aim at Malthus and Ricardo. This was a step beyond Raymond, who had focused on Smith and had ignored Ricardo. For Carey, Malthusian teaching on the causal linkage between population growth and subsistence wages was misguided. To refute it, he introduced a "principle of association" which held that enlarged populations – when concentrated geographically – promoted the division of labor, raised productivity, and brought benefits to all. The concept of "diminishing returns" should thus be replaced by one of "increasing returns." The Ricardian rent theory was also wrong. Carey asserted that extension of the cultivated area had proceeded historically from the inferior to the superior lands – the reverse of the Ricardian sequencing. Although he gave too much weight to this alleged "fact," his essential argument on this point was that productivity in agriculture could expand through time as a result of technological improvements and gains in labor efficiency. Clustering the manufacturing and agricultural sectors would generate mutually reinforcing growth and bring this result to pass.

The desired outcome, however, could not be accomplished under a regime of free international trade. In Carey's opinion, that position amounted to nothing less than a British conspiracy to lock the American economy (and much of the rest of the world, for that matter) into the dependent status of a primary producer. Not only did this suppress economic advance; it tended also to contaminate the "New World" with the class conflicts of the "Old World." The class divisions that had provided the organizing categories of Ricardian economics should have no place on the American continent. Instead, a "harmony of interests" should prevail. But it would have to be contrived through policy intervention to promote balanced expansion of industry and agriculture.

Carey was the first American to attract much attention abroad. Lots of it was unflattering. John Stuart Mill, for example, saw fit to denounce his muddles in his *Principles* (Mill, 1848, pp. 181–3, 922–5) and Marx attacked him as a "naive harmonizer" in *Das Kapital* (Marx, 1867, p. 563). In Germany, on the other hand, translations of his works found sympathetic audiences, aided in part by Friedrich List's efforts in promoting them. At the minimum, Carey did something to reduce America's trade deficit in the international traffic in economic ideas.

15.5 THE "PECULIAR INSTITUTION" AS PART OF THE NATIONAL REALITY BEFORE THE CIVIL WAR

American writers assigned high priority to social harmony and typically held that the United States offered unique opportunities for its realization. The institution of slavery in the Southern states meant, however, that American society had a fundamental disharmony imbedded in its very structure. To what extent, then, did this national reality influence American political economy in the first half of the nineteenth century? Whether one regarded the "peculiar institution" as malignant or benign, its existence was the overarching issue in political discourse prior to the Civil War.

Among authors of works on political economy, many who regarded slavery as repugnant chose to exclude it from their central purview, treating it instead as a moral and legal question. Wayland, for example, adopted this posture. He was not blind to abuses within the system, but argued that they should be corrected by uplifting the moral character of masters and slaves alike. Nor did he support proposals that Congress should legislate slavery out of existence. In his view, the federal government had no constitutional authority to do so: disposition of this matter properly belonged to the respective states.

Others insisted that slavery had to be dealt with head-on in American political economy. Raymond, for example, took this position, writing that "an American treatise would be very imperfect" if it "should omit so important a subject" (Raymond, 1820, p. 438). In his judgment, the slave system had a significant – and negative – impact on the growth of national wealth because it artificially suppressed the potential contribution of labor to production. This institution bred a mind-set in the South that encouraged laziness in its white population and also compromised labor efficiency among blacks. Raymond regarded the "peculiar institution" as a national blight and held that its elimination would remove a brake on economic progress.

Carey was even more outspoken in denouncing slavery and in insisting that its discussion belonged within the sphere of economic analysis. His approach was totally in character. The British commercial system, he maintained, was responsible for slavery's survival in the United States. Free trade had locked the South into an economic structure based on cheap labor to produce primary commodities for export. This evil could be remedied if Carey's "national system" were adopted. A climate of economic expansion – nurtured by protection to support the coordinated development of farm and factory – would raise the demand for labor. And, as he put it, "when two masters seek one laborer, the latter becomes free" (Carey, 1853, p. 303).

Slavery as a distinctive feature of the national reality conditioned the flow of American political economy in yet other ways. In the early decades of the nineteenth century, a number of Southern states were in the vanguard of the country's intellectual life. Largely immune from the theological correctness that was superimposed on political economy as presented in the Northeast, they had easier access to avant-garde European thought. This was particularly noteworthy in the 1820s in Jefferson's Virginia and in the state of South Carolina, where Thomas Cooper (1759–1839) and Jacob Nunez Cardozo (1786–1873) produced defenses of free trade, argued on Ricardian lines. The promising sparks in Southern political economy were soon snuffed out. Creative thinkers who could not subscribe to the regional "orthodoxy" on slavery were silenced or departed for more congenial surroundings. Those who accepted the "orthodoxy" dissipated intellectual energies in their attempts to defend the "peculiar institution."

15.6   A Special Case of Analytic Originality

While Americans conspicuously lagged Western Europeans in the creation of analytic breakthroughs, the environment of the New World was not inherently hostile to conceptual innovation in economics. A genuinely original advance in economic theorizing was published in Boston in 1834 under the title *Statement of Some New Principles on the Subject of Political Economy, Exposing the Fallacies of the System of Free Trade, and of Some Other Doctrines Maintained in "The Wealth of Nations."* The author, John Rae (1796–1872), was a Scotsman who had emigrated to Canada in 1822, where he found employment as a schoolmaster. As far as political economy was concerned, he was largely self-taught (though he had taken a degree at the University of Aberdeen and had studied medicine for several years at the University of Edinburgh). Despite the subtitle of his major work, the book was not a militantly protectionist tract. To the contrary, the qualifications to Adam Smith's case for free trade were argued primarily on "infant industry" grounds. From Rae's perspective, the "legislator" had a positive role to play in shaping policies to promote capital accumulation and to provide a climate favorable to economic progress. These conclusions emerged in the context of his inquiry into the "laws" regulating the increase or diminution of "wealth" in various nations of the world. Rae's agenda was clearly congruent with the spirit of classical economics in the tradition of Smith. What made Rae's position distinctive was the way he explained the process of capital accumulation.

Rae clearly broke new ground when analyzing the conditions that influenced "the effective desire of accumulation." An analogous conception in mainstream classical economics held accumulation to be primarily a function of saving arising from the profits of a capitalist class. Rae instead argued that the strength or weakness of the accumulative principle involved questions of intertemporal choice in which decisions about sacrificing present goods for future ones were heavily conditioned by social and cultural conditions. The moral of this part of the tale was that a society in which the accumulative principle was strong would create more capital instruments – and would thus grow faster – than one in which the accumulative principle was weak. In support of this proposition, he drew – among other things – on his observations of conditions in the New World. Much of the explanation of the apparent poverty of North American Indian tribes – and, he added, of Asians and Africans in general – could be traced to the weakness of the accumulative principle in their cultures. The condition of the accumulating societies (e.g., Britain, Holland, and Western Europe more generally) stood in marked contrast.

Rae's analysis identified the conceptual core of what would later become the accepted neoclassical theory of interest. This aspect of his thought left no mark in his lifetime and had to be rediscovered a quarter-century after his death. Although it is a bit of a stretch to count Rae as a contributor to American economics, his example at least demonstrates that valuable and fundamental economic ideas could germinate in the soil of the New World, despite the fact that they went unappreciated by his contemporaries.

15.7 THE LANDSCAPE OF THE LATE NINETEENTH CENTURY

After the Civil War, the contours of political economy in America shifted. Slavery was off the national agenda. The new threat to social harmony came from other directions. As the country moved into a mature phase of industrialization, strife between capital and labor took ugly turns. New questions emerged about both the efficiency and the fairness of a market system increasingly dominated by "bigness." Meanwhile, some lingering issues concerning the functioning of the nation's money and credit system, as well as America's place in the international monetary order, awaited resolution. Meanwhile, a long-standing controversy between advocates of free trade and advocates of protection had taken on an added dimension of complexity. As a central part of its program to finance mobilization during the Civil War, the Federal government had raised tariff schedules to unprecedented heights and the beneficiaries of that policy were determined to resist reductions in the shelters they had come to enjoy.

The events of the Civil War had bred a new consciousness about the potential of tooled knowledge to ameliorate social and economic problems. This sentiment motivated the creation of an American Social Science Association (ASSA) in 1865. This Boston-based organization was inspired in the post-bellum flush of enthusiasm for social reforms. Its organizers charted an ambitious program. As they set out the Association's overall purpose in the Constitution:

Its objects are, to aid the development of Social Science, and to guide the public mind to the best practical means of promoting the Amendment of Laws, the Advancement of Education, the Prevention or Repression of Crime, the Reformation of Criminals, and the Progress of Public Morality, the Adoption of Sanitary Regulations, and the diffusion of sound principles on questions of Economy, Trade, and Finance. (As quoted in Haskell, 1977, p. 161)

It was presupposed here that the collection and dissemination of facts on social and economic conditions would be sufficient to mobilize the public behind remedies for perceived ills. In the vernacular of the time, investigation should be accompanied by agitation and then by action. This initiative, it is worth noting, was applauded by the leading British economist of the day. In correspondence with the officers of the ASSA (who had invited him to be their guest in the United States), John Stuart Mill remarked:

What you say about the new start which the mind of America has been led to make by her long and arduous struggle, is exactly what I foresaw from almost the very beginning. I wrote in January, 1862, and often said in the years following, that if the war lasted long enough, it would very likely regenerate the American people, and I have been seeing more and more clearly since it closed, that to a considerable extent it has really done so, and in particular, that reason and right feeling on any public subject has a better chance of being favorably listened to, and of finding the national mind open to comprehend it, than at any previous time in American history. (Mill, 1870)

The post-bellum climate had clearly generated a substantially increased demand for expertise to guide the shaping of economic and social policies. Indeed, the ASSA took as part of its charge to investigate such topics as pauperism, the "relation of employers and employed," hours of labor, the national debt, tariffs and taxation, the control of markets, the value of gold, and "all questions connected with the currency." But there was a bottleneck on the supply side: the country then lacked a cadre of trained personnel equipped to deal dispassionately with these issues. And this, in turn, frustrated the ASSA's capacity to carry out its mission. The backgrounds of the few whom the organization identified to conduct economic studies will illustrate the nature of the problem. David A. Wells (1828–98), who was called to head one of ASSA's investigative departments, had moved from a prewar career as a successful author and distributor of scientific manuals – during which he had identified himself with Carey's brand of protectionism – to an appointment in 1866 as Commissioner of the Revenue in the Federal government. His experience in that post had convinced him that the wartime fiscal policy built around high tariffs had bred serious inefficiencies in the country's manufacturing sector and he then became one of the nation's most uncompromising champions of free trade. (Wells was to acquire a considerable international reputation: his various honors included election by the French Academy to the seat vacated by the death of John Stuart Mill.)

By 1874, the ASSA had managed to attract two men with professorial titles – William Graham Sumner (1840–1910) and Francis Amasa Walker (1840–97), both of Yale – to assist in its work. In view of the fact that academic appointments for specialists in political economy were then a rarity, this was noteworthy. Sumner's call to such a position was virtually by accident: he had been trained as a clergy-man and had been brought to Yale because a newly installed president had deputized him to deliver the custom-honored lectures to seniors on political economy/moral philosophy. Once there, Sumner became one of the nation's most outspoken advocates of a Spencerian version of Social Darwinism. Walker (whose father had written a political economy textbook that sustained the tradi-tion launched by the Reverend Francis Wayland) thus had an in-house exposure to the subject matter, but he also brought other qualities to the table: he had served as superintendent of 1870 Federal census (a job he was to repeat in 1880) and he had reached general officer rank in the Union Army at the prodigiously young age of 25.

Over time, the pool of competence in political economy was to grow. In the 1870s, three American institutions awarded a total of three doctorates in political economy; the decade of the 1880s saw the award of 11 such degrees by five institutions. But there was still a scarcity of home-grown Ph.D.'s. The major suppliers of advanced work in political economy to young Americans were the universities in Germany, to which they migrated in considerable numbers.

The "Germanization" of a significant body of recruits to political economy was to have formidable consequences. In the first instance, it sharpened a divide that was already latent among those engaged in serious work on economic issues. Those with a German exposure tended to identify themselves as members of a "new school." As the more militant among them saw matters, the methods and the conclusions of an "old school" that had looked to English political economy for inspiration should be denounced. Deductive reasoning in economics was held to be suspect: proper procedure called instead for direct empirical investiga-tion of economic reality. Similarly, the notion that economic "laws" could be identified – ones with universal validity throughout time and space – needed to be purged. No less important in the "new school" program was rejection of the "old school's" veneration of *laissez-faire*. The message that instead should be conveyed was that state intervention could make a constructive contribution to economic improvement. The mid-1880s witnessed escalation in the rhetorical warfare between members of these rival camps. This meant, in turn, that possession of an advanced degree in political economy was not itself an adequate badge of professional identification. One needed to inquire further into the particular "school" to which an aspiring professional belonged.

15.8   "NEW SCHOOLERS" VERSUS "OLD SCHOOLERS"
IN THE 1880s

The battle lines between the rivals in the American *Methodenstreit* of the 1880s were sharply drawn at the Johns Hopkins University, an institution founded in 1874 with the primary charge to compete with German universities (and all other comers, for that matter) in the production of graduate students with doctoral degrees in the liberal arts and sciences. Two strong personalities with interests in political economy were on the scene there. Simon Newcomb (1835–1919), an astronomer–mathematician economist, occupied a professorial chair in mathematics. He was a man with a flair for abstract model-building, whose wide-ranging interests included formulation of a sophisticated version of the quantity theory of money. His hostility toward governmental intervention in economic affairs had made him a natural leader of the "old school." Richard T. Ely (1854–1943), with a doctorate from the University of Heidelberg, held an appointment as an associate in political economy, an untenured position. Writing from the German historical perspective, he regarded himself as in the vanguard of the "new school" and called for the scholar to be actively engaged in setting the world to rights.

Hostilities between these two went public in 1884. Ely fired the opening salvo in an essay that attacked the sterility of the methods of the "English" school. He asserted that "mathematico-economic works" represented "a not very successful attempt to develop further the older abstract political economy" and that "works which have advocated the application of mathematics to economics form no essential part of the development of economic literature" (Ely, 1884, pp. 5–64). Newcomb's ire was aroused and he asked Daniel Coit Gilman, President of Johns Hopkins, for "an opportunity to say a few words about your department of political economy before the impulse which has been given me by Dr. Ely's pamphlet entirely dies out. It looks a little incongruous to see so sweeping and wholesale an attack upon the introduction of any rational or scientific method in economics come from a university whose other specialties have tended in the opposite direction" (Newcomb, 1884a). Newcomb indicted Ely's position in print in November 1884, characterizing Ely's work as an example of fundamental intellectual confusion and as an "irrational" proceeding (Newcomb, 1884b, pp. 291–301).

The two men re-aired their differences publicly in 1886 in *Science*, the journal of the American Association for the Advancement of Science. (It should be noted that the American Association for the Advancement of Science – following the lead of its British counterpart – created a section on Economic Science and Statistics that became operational in 1882.) Ely and Newcomb then restated familiar positions. Ely maintained that concern with what ought to be was inherent in the work of the political economist; that economists should seek to understand the "laws of Progress" and to show how they could be directed to promote the economic and social growth of mankind; and that the ethical ideal was "simply the Christian doctrine of talents committed to men, all to be improved" (Ely, 1886, pp. 529–33). Newcomb, on the other hand, maintained that it was a "contradiction in terms" to regard discussion of what should be as "science"; that the principle of "noninterference" in economic affairs also favored progress, but sought its achievement by giving individuals the widest possible latitude for choice; and that public intervention was suspect because governments were incapable of acting on "sound business principles" (Newcomb, 1886a, pp. 538–42). In an unsigned review of Ely's book, *The Labor Movement in America* (1886), Newcomb was even more outspoken in his denunciation of Ely's work, saying it displayed a "lack of logical acumen" and an "intensity of bias." Newcomb concluded with the following comment: "Dr. Ely seems to us to be seriously out of place in a university chair" (Newcomb, 1886b, pp. 293–94). Newcomb also informed Gilman privately of his negative appraisal of Ely's competence, advising him that "very little attention [was] paid to the analytic process" in Ely's teaching at Johns Hopkins (Newcomb, 1886d). After observing the performance of Ely's graduate students (whom he had been asked to examine in May 1886), Newcomb reported that "the main teaching seems to have been directed toward the administrative and economic policies of the leading countries of the world, especially Germany." In Newcomb's judgment, "the candidates showed an almost deplorable want of training in the power of logical analysis of the economic theories that move men and determine the course of our industry at the present time . . . [T]hey were amply able to grapple with the subject, had it only been presented to them, but that was quite new to their minds" (Newcomb, 1886c).

There could be no common ground between these positions in the *Methodenstreit* of the 1880s. "New school" advocates indicted members of the "old school" as "immoral," and "old schoolers" treated the "new school's" protagonists as "incompetent" and "unscientific." More was at stake here than just the outcome of a methodological dispute. For the "new schoolers" particularly, jobs also mattered. Most in their ranks were not yet in established careers. Given their sympathies for the rights of workers, they were in an exposed position at a time when public opinion was agitated about the threat to the social order posed by violent strikes.

These considerations influenced the timing of the formation of the American Economic Association in 1885. Ely seized the initiative in this matter by calling on the like-minded to join an organization that would be explicitly committed to combating the influence of "the Sumner, Newcomb crowd." Part of this effort represented an attempt on the part of "new schoolers" to strengthen their hand by consolidation, thereby reducing their vulnerability in the academic labor market. Ely also had a further objective in mind. The initiation of national scholarly organizations was an activity looked upon with favor by the administration at Johns Hopkins, and he had reason to believe that his involvement with AEA would bolster his quest for a permanent position there. (With regard to this expectation, he was disappointed and he moved to the University of Wisconsin in 1892.) It should be noted the AEA was not conceived of as a conventional scholarly body. On the contrary, it was designed as a vehicle to promote the "new school" program. This was apparent in the platform that Ely drafted for it, which advanced the following propositions: "we regard the state as an educational and ethical agency whose positive aid is an indispensable condition of human progress . . . (W)e hold that the doctrine of *laissez faire* is unsafe in politics and unsound in morals . . . We do not accept the final statements which characterized the political economy of a past generation . . . We hold that the conflict of labor and capital has brought to the front a vast number of social problems whose solution is impossible without the united efforts of church, state and science" (Ely, 1885; as reprinted in Ely, 1938, p. 163).

Meanwhile – despite the distractions created by the internecine warfare between the rival camps – some interesting substantive research was being conducted and finding an outlet. The AEA's initial activities included the sponsorship of a monograph series that published a memorable study, "The relation of the modern municipality to the gas supply," by "new schooler" Edmund J. James (1855–1925), in which he set out the case for public ownership of a natural monopoly. Another "new schooler," Henry Carter Adams (1851–1921), examined "The relation of the state to industrial action," in which he developed criteria for state intervention developed around the conception of industries subject to increasing, decreasing, and constant returns. In a book-length study, Yale's Arthur T. Hadley (1856–1930) – another veteran of the German postgraduate experience, but not a "new schooler" – produced an analysis of the railway industry which contained one of the first demonstrations that firms may operate at a loss so long as variable costs are covered. In 1884, Francis Amasa Walker – who was shortly to serve as the first president of the AEA, a post he held from 1885 to 1892 – published the first edition of a textbook that was to set the standard for the next decade.

15.9   THE FALL-OUT FROM THE AMERICAN *METHODENSTREIT*

The *Methodenstreit* was to leave a formidable mark on the subsequent flow of American economics. By the mid-1890s, economists on both sides of the barricades in the preceding decade concluded that it would be opportune to mute their differences. Further blood-letting – at least in public – would be unseemly and counterproductive. Economists of all persuasions were then eager to claim standing as "professionals," not least because they wished to solidify a secure position for the discipline in the expanding university system. This change in the climate was reflected in the restructuring of the American Economic Association. The polarizing language of Ely's original platform was expunged and Ely himself was removed from high office in the Association. By 1894, even Newcomb had seen fit to join the AEA, though Sumner continued to reject all invitations.

The success of some amateurs in capturing the popular imagination added urgency to this regrouping. To the aspiring professionals, it was humiliating when the untutored could move the public. Two examples merit attention. Henry George (1839–97), a journalist with only an elementary education, was particularly effective in mobilizing opinion. His *Progress and Poverty*, first issued in 1879, became a bestseller. There was an unmistakable native-soil quality to this work: George had been inspired to write it by his experience in California, where he had observed overnight fortunes created from the appreciation in land values as its territory was being rapidly settled. The "monopoly power" conveyed by private ownership of land, he concluded, was the root of all evil: unearned rents distorted income distribution and land speculation idled productive resources. The remedy was a "single tax" through which the state would appropriate these ill-gotten gains. Less significant – but still embarrassing – was the work of William Harvey (1851–1936), a lawyer, sometime silver miner, and subsequently a publisher in Chicago. His *Coin's Financial School*, published at the height of the highly charged national debate over bimetallism in the 1890s, insisted that permanent prosperity would be assured through free coinage of silver at a silver–gold ratio of 16 to 1. Harvey added liveliness to his argument by depicting an imaginary debate, in which a small child confounded a learned economist with the cogency of his case for a crude quantity theory of money. Altogether, it behooved the professionals to bury their differences and to defend common ground against "quacks."

Meanwhile, a number of subtle – but significant – shifts in position were occurring within the ranks of the professionals, particularly among those who had cut their teeth in the "new school." John Bates Clark (1847–1938), for example, had begun his career sympathetic to the ethical component of "new school" doctrine. His interest in the linkage between economics and ethics did not waver. By the mid-1890s, model-building could now be seen as having an essential role to play in understanding the "ethics" of income distribution. This consideration inspired his innovative contributions to marginal productivity theory which, in turn, won him a reputation as the first American to produce pure theory of world-class quality.

Ely's work also took a different turn. His interest in championing causes persisted. But he, in company with many who had joined his movement, was obliged to rethink the early enthusiasm for governmental intervention. An awkward national reality – one that sharply separated the United States from Germany – had to be faced squarely. America lacked a cadre of professional civil servants competent to administer an enlarged program of public regulation. Under the American "spoils system," expansion in the jurisdiction of the state would simply fatten the wallets of corruptible politicians. It is not in the least surprising that Ely chose to channel part of his abundant energy to lobbying for a merit system in the civil service, or that he regarded the School of Economics, Political Science and History which he built at the University of Wisconsin as a training ground for future civil servants.

Simultaneously, there were further signs of fundamental changes on the American economics scene. By the mid-1890s, some impressively able home-grown talents – that is, those who had studied the discipline entirely in the United States and who were thus innocent of direct exposure to doctrines espoused in foreign universities – had begun to emerge. The career of Irving Fisher (1867–1947) is a notable case in point. He obtained his undergraduate and graduate training at a single institution: Yale University. His doctoral dissertation – entitled *Mathematical Investigations in the Theory of Value and Prices*, and completed in 1891 – was a pioneering statement in mathematical economics and was to be recognized as a classic in that genre. In his subsequent career, Fisher went on to make internationally applauded original contributions to the theory of capital and interest, to monetary theory and policy, and to the theory and practice of index-number making.

The intellectual momentum of the 1890s also generated a reorientation toward another aspect of the original "new school" program: that is, its doubts about the usefulness of deductive theorizing. The skepticism lived on, but it found expression in other ways. Some of those who turned their backs on abstract theory elected to concentrate on the collection and analysis of statistical data. Empirical work of this type had been going on quietly for some time, building on foundations painstakingly laid through Francis Amasa Walker's liaison with the Federal Bureau of the Census. This line of investigation was now invigorated. Others sought to enrich the discipline through direct observation of the economic behavior of living people. John R. Commons (1862–1945), for example, began to move inquiry in that direction with his studies of the circumstances of workers. What came through was the finding that the labor movement in America was structured by "group consciousness," not "class consciousness." When the implications of that insight were assimilated, they helped to blunt the impact of another doctrine – namely, Marxism – that was available on the import market.

The 1890s also spawned a home-grown strain of radicalism in academic economics. Thorstein Veblen (1857–1929) picked up one of the threads of the "new school" – its disdain for model-building organized around *a priori* assumptions about human behavior. His idiosyncratic critique of marginalism placed him far outside the mainstream, yet his voice was surely that of an authentic American original. The practical impact of his message was delayed until the 1930s, when a group of "planners" inspired by his teaching acquired influential governmental positions. Had it not been for the tolerance for diversity conditioned by the fallout from the *Methodenstreit*, it is an open question whether or not Veblen would have been able to support himself adequately to press his ideas forward.

15.10 *Fin de siècle* Assessments

By 1900, American economics had moved a long way from where it began. This reflected transformations in the structure of the economy, as well as changes in the character of the international marketplace for economic ideas (and America's position within it). In the early going, American political economy had been heavily import-dependent, even though foreign ideas were altered to adjust their fit to circumstances in the "New World." Domestic production – though sometimes strident in its assertions of originality – was then viewed by most of the rest of the world as naive and unsophisticated.

It is perhaps ironic that the *Methodenstreit* of the 1880s – which began as a confrontation between advocates of German and British doctrines – should have given birth to a variety of new departures with clear American markings. No longer could American economics be dismissed as retarded. There was dynamism aplenty. A striking component of the new national reality was its very openness to pluralism.

By the close of the nineteenth century, the United States was about to become a net exporter of economic ideas. This reversal of fortunes had begun to catch the attention of perceptive foreign observers. Writing in 1898, Britain's Alfred Marshall, for example, observed: ". . . there are many signs that America is on the way to take the same leading position in economic thought, that she has already taken in economic practice." (Marshall, 1961 [1898], vol. II, pp. 760–1). This was quite a different note from the one Americans themselves had sounded in 1876.

Note

This chapter draws heavily on two earlier essays by the author: "The position of the United States in the international marketplace for economic ideas (1776–1900)," in M. Albertone and A. Masoero (eds.), *Political Economy and National Realities*, Fondazione Luigi Einaudi, Torino, 1994, and "Economists and professional organizations in pre-World War I America," in M. M. Augello and M. E. L. Guidi (eds.), *The Spread of Political Economy and the Professionalisation of Economics*, Routledge, London, 2001.

Bibliography

Carey, H. C. 1853: *The Slave Trade, Domestic and Foreign: Why It Exists and How It May Be Extinguished*. Philadelphia, PA: A. Hart.

Dunbar, C. F. 1876: Economic science in America, 1776–1876. *North American Review*, CXXII (January), 124–54.

Ely, R. T. 1884: The past and present of political economy. *Johns Hopkins University Studies in Historical and Political Science*, II, 5–64.

—— 1885: Platform of the American Economic Association. As reprinted in Ely, R. T. 1938: *Ground Under Our Feet: An Autobiography*. New York: Macmillan.

—— 1886: Ethics and economics. *Science*, VII, June 11, 529–33.

Haskell, T. L. 1977: *The Emergence of Professional Social Science: The American Social Science Association and the Nineteenth Century Crisis of Authority*. Urbana, IL: University of Illinois Press.

Marshall, A. 1961 [1898]: *Principles of Economics*, 9th (variorum) edn., vols. I and II. London: Macmillan.

Marx, K. 1967 [1867]: *Capital*, vol. I. New York: International.

Mill, J. S. 1926 [1848]: *Principles of Political Economy*, ed. W. J. Ashley. London: Longmans, Green.

—— 1874 [1870]: Letter dated 1870, published in *The Journal of Social Science*, V.

Newcomb, S. 1884a: Letter to President Gilman, May 14. Gilman Collection, Special Collections, Milton S. Eisenhower Library, Johns Hopkins University.

—— 1884b: The two schools of political economy. *The Princeton Review*, LX (November), 291–301.

—— 1886a: Aspects of the economic discussion. *Science*, VII, June 18, 538–42.

—— 1886b: Dr. Ely and the Labor Movement. *The Nation*, XLIII, October 7, 293–4.

—— 1886c: Letter to President Gilman, May 24. Gilman Collection, Special Collections, Milton S. Eisenhower Library, Johns Hopkins University.

—— 1886d: Letter to President Gilman, May 28. Gilman Collection, Special Collections, Milton S. Eisenhower Library, Johns Hopkins University.

Raymond, D. 1820: *Thoughts on Political Economy*. Baltimore; Fielding Lucas, Jrs.

Wayland, F. 1838: *The Elements of Political Economy*, 2nd edn. Boston: Crocker and Brewster/ New York: Robinson and Franklin.

CHAPTER SIXTEEN

English Marginalism: Jevons, Marshall, and Pigou

Peter Groenewegen

16.1 INTRODUCTION

English marginalism embraces a group of economists, active in the late nine-teenth and early twentieth centuries, who used the marginalist method for analyzing economic questions relating, in the first instance, to the theories of value and distribution, and later to a wider range of economic questions in the theories of money, fluctuations, income determination, and growth. Jevons, Marshall, and Pigou were major contributors to this "marginal revolution" in England, but not the only important pioneers. Edgeworth and Wicksteed (both contemporaries of Jevons and Marshall) and Marshall's Cambridge students, of whom Pigou was among the first, are also important. The "marginal revolution" had a well-known international dimension (see Horwitz, ch. 17, this volume; Walker, ch. 18, this volume) and its impact continues to reverberate in economic theory.

The concept of marginalism itself has received surprisingly little attention in the history of economics literature. The word was slow to creep into the language of English economics. As Howey (1972) indicates, it was first used by J. A. Hobson (1914, pp. 174–5, 331–2) in a derogatory manner. The original Palgrave *Dictionary of Political Economy* did not have an article on "marginalism." However, Edgeworth's second article on "margin" in its final paragraphs described the widespread use by mathematical economists of "margins" in economics in both its theories of consumption and production, to which "Jevons' exposition . . . forms an admirable introduction . . . [while their] fullest and most accurate exposition

... is to be found in Prof. Marshall's *Princ. of Econ.*" (Edgeworth, 1894, p. 691). The later *Encyclopaedia of the Social Sciences* (Seligman, 1948 [1930]) likewise contains no article specifically devoted to "marginalism." The same applies to the *New Palgrave Dictionary* (Eatwell et al., 1987), which contains articles on "marginal and average cost pricing," "marginal efficiency of capital," "marginal productivity theory," and "marginal utility of money" as well as an article on "marginalist economics." The last acknowledges "the almost total domination that marginalist economics has enjoyed for about a century" without igniting the "spark of an ultimate truth" (Campus, 1987, pp. 321–2). The second quoted remark is a comment from Sraffa (1926, p. 535), foreshadowing his prelude to a critique of the dominant marginalist method (Sraffa, 1960, esp. p. v).

This chapter is basically concerned with Jevons's application of the marginal method as one of its early pioneers; with Marshall's masterful exposition of marginalism, especially in his *Principles of Economics*; and with its elaboration by Marshall's official Cambridge successor, Pigou. The final section briefly refers to three other leading English economists of the period – Edgeworth, Sidgwick, and Wicksteed – and in addition raises selected post-Pigovian aspects in the history of English marginalism.

16.2 WILLIAM STANLEY JEVONS (1835–82)

Jevons was born in Liverpool, the ninth child in a large, middle-class family. He studied chemistry and engineering at London University in the early 1850s without taking his degree. In 1853 he went to Sydney (Australia) as assayer of its new mint, staying there for six years. On his return to London, he completed his degree. He also started working on a new, mathematical theory of political economy, on which he read a paper to Section F of the British Association for the Advancement of Science (Jevons, 1911a [1862]). Unlike his *A Serious Fall in the Value of Gold* (1863) and his subsequent book, *The Coal Question* (1865), this raised little interest. His major claim to intellectual fame, *Theory of Political Economy,* was published in 1871 (2nd edn., 1879). It elaborated his mathematical theory of political economy, based predominantly on the pleasure/pain (utility/disutility) principle and employing the marginalist method. In 1862 he was elected Fellow of the Royal Society. He was appointed Professor of Political Economy at London's University College in 1876, a post from which he retired in 1880 to have more time for writing. However, he died early from a swimming accident in 1882. In 1875 Jevons published *Money and the Mechanism of Exchange*, and in 1882 *The State in Relation to Labour* appeared posthumously. Volumes of essays appeared in 1883 (*Methods of Social Reform*) and 1884 (*Investigations in Currency and Finance*). Although Jevons's work as an economist was wide-ranging (for good surveys, see Black, 1981; Peart, 1996), this essay concentrates on his marginalist treatment of value, exchange, labor, and capital.

Jevons's (1911a [1862]) "Brief account of a general mathematical theory of value" was his first presentation of the marginalist method. After arguing that "a true theory of economy can only be attained by going back to the great springs of human action, *the feelings of pleasure and pain*" (Jevons, 1911a [1862], p. 304) which treated pleasure and utility as synonyms, Jevons focused attention on what he then called "the coefficient of utility," described as a "generally diminishing function of the whole quantity of the object consumed." This, in his view, provided the basis for "the most important law of the whole theory" (Jevons, 1911a [1862], p. 307). Earlier (Jevons, 1911a [1862], p. 306), the coefficient of utility had been defined as "the ratio between the last increment or infinitely small supply of the object, and the increment of pleasure which it occasions." This incrementalist, or marginalist, perspective was then used to explain the application of labor, the extent of exchange and the rate of interest. In the first, Jevons established that "labour will be exerted . . . until a further increment will be more painful than the increment of produce thereby obtained is pleasurable" (Jevons, 1911a [1862], p. 307). The theory of exchange was then deduced "from the laws of utility" by postulating that equality of the "increment of utility lost and gained at the limits of the quantities exchanged" determined the extent of trade, and that such findings based on a two individuals–two commodities case were easy to extend to "any number of commodities" and therefore applicable to "generalised trade . . . [and] international trade" (Jevons, 1911a [1862], pp. 308–10). Finally, the 1862 paper showed the universal determination of the rate of interest "by *the ratio which a new increment of produce bears to the increment of capital by which it was produced*," clearly foreshadowing a marginal productivity theory of interest.

The *Theory of Political Economy* elaborated the 1862 propositions without extending the principles and methods by which they had been originally derived. Hence it is difficult to treat Jevons's development of a marginalist method and its application to utility as part of a "marginalist revolution" in 1871 that was taking place simultaneously in two other European countries. The eight chapters of *Theory of Political Economy* reveal this formal similarity of contents with the 1862 paper. After an introduction (ch. 1), Jevons deals with the theory of pleasure, pain, and utility (chs. 2 and 3), exchange (ch. 4), labor, rent, and capital (chs. 5–7), and concluding remarks (ch. 8). The book displays its marginalist credentials explicitly without using the terminology. Thus, halfway through the work, while treating the theory of labor, it proclaims, "as in the other questions of Economics, all depends upon the final increments" (Jevons, 1911b [1871], p. 171), while the major elements of the subject are identified as "[u]tility, wealth, value, commodity, labour, land, capital" (Jevons, 1911b [1871], p. 1). The book likewise reasserts the mathematical quality of the subject, "*our science must be mathematical, simply because it deals with quantities*" (Jevons, 1911b [1871], p. 3), with the calculus as the basic mathematical tool, assisted by some Euclidean geometry (the *Theory* is extensively illustrated by diagrams). The problem of economics is defined (Jevons, 1911b [1871], p. 37) as the maximization of pleasure (minimization of pain), as is particularly clearly illustrated in Jevons's treatment of resource allocation, including that of labor. The quotation below neatly illustrates the marginalist nature of his approach to utility and his nonuse of words such as "margin" or "marginalist" therein:

We shall seldom need to consider the degree of utility except as regards the last increment which has been consumed, or, which comes to the same thing, the next increment which is about to be consumed. I shall therefore commonly use the expression *final degree of utility,* as meaning the degree of utility of the last addition. (Jevons, 1911b [1871], p. 51)

This "degree of utility" is defined as a diminishing function of the quantity of the commodity held, so that "*the degree of utility . . . decreases as that quantity increases*" (Jevons, 1911b [1871], p. 53). Optimum allocation in consumption then requires equalization of the final degree of utility of the commodities consumed (Jevons, 1911b [1871], p. 61), exchange equilibrium the equality of the price and the utility ratios (Jevons, 1911b [1871], p. 95), optimum duration of labor supply the equation of marginal pain (disutility) and marginal benefit (utility) of that labor (Jevons, 1911b [1871], p. 173), and the optimum allocation of capital the equalization of interest with the "advantage [in terms of product] of the last increment of capital [employed]" (Jevons, 1911b [1871], p. 256). Jevons (1911b [1871], pp. 212–13) also explicitly admitted that versions of the classical theory of rent, particularly those of James Mill (1821) and McCulloch (1838), were pieces of economic analysis using the incremental method. In this respect, Keynes (1972 [1936], p. 109) neatly identified Jevons's contribution as belonging "to the group of economists whose school of thought dominated the subject for the half-century after the death of Mill in 1873."

Jevons's economic writings encompass more than the marginalist theory of value and distribution. He made interesting contributions to monetary and business cycle theory, and to the economics of energy resource scarcity, which has a very a contemporary feel about it. The last issue was raised in his *The Coal Question,* which analyzed the implications of predictable shortages in the "present great supplies of coal," then "the material source of energy" for Great Britain, underpinning its great industrial strength that was so successfully built on steel (Jevons, 1906 [1865], pp. 2–3). Jevons's treatment raised geological as well as economic aspects of the problem (impacts on costs, prices, and imports, economizing the use of coal, and finding substitutes for coal). His conclusion emphasized the "momentous choice" facing the policy-maker "between brief but true greatness" from using available coal resources at a rate dictated by current technology, or a "longer [period] of continued mediocrity" if scarce coal resources were tightly rationed and industry was thereby effectively starved of its major energy source (Jevons, 1906 [1865], p. 460). Although marginalist methods could have been used to advantage in explaining this argument, Jevons did not do so. Neither did Jevons's writings on monetary and the associated business cycle theory, posthumously collected by H. S. Foxwell as *Investigations into Currency and Finance* (Jevons, 1884). This volume contains various versions of his famous sunspot theory of the cycle, as well as his 1863 monograph, *A Serious Fall in the Value of Gold.* Essays on social reform (Jevons, 1883) reveal Jevons's broad social concerns, ranging from the use (and abuse) of free public libraries and museums, to that of employing married women in factories, cruelty to animals, and the drink question, demonstrating that the noted marginalist theorist was also a wide-ranging social scientist. The splendid essays on Cantillon and on the future of political economy appended to his unfinished and posthumously published *Principles of Economics* (Jevons, 1905) show his gifts as a historian of economics.

16.3 ALFRED MARSHALL (1842–1924)

Born in Bermondsey (London) in 1842, Marshall was seven years younger than Jevons. He was educated at the Merchant Taylor School, where he gained a taste for mathematics: he subsequently completed the Cambridge Mathematical Tripos in 1865 as "second wrangler" (second in the first-class honors list), thereby securing a Fellowship at St John's College. He then gradually switched to the moral sciences, concentrating on economics from the early 1870s. His first book, *Economics of Industry* (1879, 2nd edn. 1881) was written jointly with his wife (a former student, whom he had married in 1877). That same year he privately published material on pure theory (Marshall, 1975b [1879]). After holding academic positions at Bristol and Oxford, in 1884 Marshall became Professor of Political Economy at Cambridge. He retired in 1908, when his student Pigou (discussed below) succeeded him. Marshall's major book, *Principles of Economics*, appeared in 1890 (eighth, definitive, edition in 1920; reprinted in 1961). During his retirement, he published supplementary volumes (*Industry and Trade*, 1919; *Money, Credit and Commerce*, 1923) as partial substitutes for a second volume of his *Principles*, which he never managed to complete.

Marshall is sometimes bracketed with Jevons (whose *Theory of Political Economy* he reviewed – Marshall, 1925 [1872]), Menger, and Walras as a participant in the marginal revolution. This is misleading, if only because his initial price analysis ignores utility considerations (Marshall, 1975a [1871]). He was, however, a very significant pioneer of marginal analysis following Cournot (1963 [1838]) and von Thünen (1966 [1826–63]), from whose work he had benefited at an early stage in his economic studies. Another differentiating factor from Jevons was that Marshall never showed strong hostility to his classical predecessors, instead incorporating part of their work within his own system. This is therefore appropriately described as neoclassical, a genuine merger of old and new doctrines. Marshall's work, including his *Principles*, also combined theory with much factual matter drawn from personal empirical observations and painstaking study of empirical and historical work. Again unlike Jevons, Marshall strongly disliked displaying mathematics in his theory – banishing his mathematical economics to an appendix and burying his diagrams in the footnotes of his *Principles*. Through his tremendous influence as a teacher, he founded the Cambridge school of economics. His economic principles based on supply and demand analysis endured until well after his death, the *Principles* surviving as a major university economics text until after World War II. Useful overviews of his economics are O'Brien (1981) and Whitaker (1987); Groenewegen (1995) presents a full-scale biography, including detailed assessment of his economic work.

As a trained mathematician, Marshall immediately took to the marginal method in analyzing economic problems, to which study of Cournot's and von Thünen's economics had introduced him. His early economic writings, published with editorial introductions in Whitaker (1975), clearly illustrate this. Examples are Marshall's stress on the "balancing of advantages" in the theory of decision-making as applied to money (Whitaker, 1975, vol. I, pp. 166–7) and his use of incrementalist diagrams for explaining the theory of rent (Whitaker, 1975, vol. I, p. 240). By the early 1870s, sophisticated incremental analysis guided Marshall's thinking on tolls, monopoly, and growth and enabled him to sketch a marginal productivity theory of distribution (Whitaker, 1975, vol. II, pp. 281–3, 284–5, 309–16, 323–5). This mathematical economics was completely hidden in the initial textbook presentation of the theory (Marshall and Marshall, 1879) but fully displayed in the privately printed pure theory of international trade and domestic value (Marshall, 1975b [1879], vol. II, pp. 117–81, 186–236).

At a higher level, much of this theory was carefully reworked for Marshall's *magnum opus, Principles of Economics* (Marshall, 1961 [1890]). This had been originally intended as a two-volume work, of which the second, never completed, volume, was at one stage to contain "foreign trade, money and banking, trade fluctuations, taxation, collectivism [and] aims for the future" (Groenewegen, 1995, p. 407; its chapter 10 presents a detailed discussion of the long haul of the *Principles* from 1881 to 1922). The first volume became a classic text on value, production, and distribution. From the second edition onward, its structure emphasized the "general relations of demand, supply and value" (book V), and their use for a theory of "the distribution of the national income" or of wages, rent, interest, and profit (book VI). These followed two preliminary books, the second of which was definitional, and two books that provided the foundations for the theory of value in the theory of demand (book III, "Of wants and their satisfaction") and of supply or production (book IV, "The agents of production, land, labour, capital and organisation"). In addition, later editions of the *Principles* contained 12 appendices (amounting to over 13 percent of the text) and a concise set of mathematical notes. The extent to which Marshall polished his *Principles* can be seen in the variorum edition painstakingly prepared by his nephew, C. W. Guillebaud (Marshall, 1961 [1890]), the edition used in what follows.

The preface to the first edition (reprinted in all subsequent editions) signaled the specific marginalist intent of the work, and provided a concise statement of Marshall's views on the essential role of mathematics in the elucidation of economic principles. The relevant paragraph can be quoted in full, since it also provides a clear acknowledgment of Marshall's mentors in marginal analysis and of how he saw Jevons's role in his economics education:

Under the guidance of Cournot, and in a less degree of von Thünen, I was led to attach great importance to the fact that our observations of nature, in the moral as in the physical world, relate not so much to aggregate quantities, and that in particular the demand for a thing is a continuous function of which the "marginal"* increment is, in stable equilibrium, balanced against the corresponding increment of its cost of production. It is not easy to get a clear full view of continuity in this aspect without the aid either of mathematical symbols or of diagrams. The use of the latter requires no special knowledge, and they often express the conditions of economic life more accurately, as well as more easily, than do mathematical symbols; and therefore they have been applied as supplementary illustrations in the footnotes of the present volume. The argument in the text is never dependent on them; and they may be omitted; but experience seems to show that they give a firmer grasp of many important principles than can be got without their aid; and that there are many problems of pure theory, which no one who has once learnt to use diagrams will willingly handle in any other way.

* The term "marginal" increment I borrowed from von Thünen's *Der Isolirte Staat*, 1826–63, and is now commonly used by German economists. When Jevons' Theory appeared, I adopted his word "final"; but I have been gradually convinced that "marginal" is the better.

(Marshall, 1961 [1890], p. x and n.1)

The "balancing of advantages" underlying both Marshall's theory of consumption (as, for example, done by "the primitive housewife" in book III, chapter V; Marshall 1961 [1890], p. 117) and his theory of production (for example, book V, chapter VIII; Marshall, 1961 [1890], p. 405) was shown to be particularly fruitful soil for the application of the marginal method. It was also crucial for the theory of distribution, where Marshall emphatically indicated that the marginal productivity theory applied the principle that "we must *go to the margin to study the action of those forces which govern* the value of the whole" (Marshall, 1961 [1890], p. 410). This applied with equal force to use of the margin in profit maximization (where the condition of equating marginal cost with marginal revenue is implied following the manner of Cournot) and use of consumer surplus for solving problems pertaining to social welfare. The book abounds with exhortations to "study the *margin of profitable expenditure*" (Marshall, 1961 [1890], p. 432), and portrays the resource allocation decision facing housewife and businessman as fundamentally the same, being designed to distribute their resources so "that they have the same marginal utility [benefit] in each use" (Marshall, 1961 [1890], pp. 358–9).

The economics of the *Principles,* it needs to be stressed, is not confined to the presentation, and solution, of static allocation problems in consumption and production as a way for highlighting the use of marginal method in expositing the theory of value and distribution. Just as Marshall was aware of the dangers in over-reliance on mathematics in economics, so he realized the complexity for the theorist of grasping the realities of economic life. In this quest, he held up biology as the mecca for the economist. This was a sign that the dynamics and the evolutionary processes by which the economic institutions of markets, firms, competition, and productive organization gradually altered and adapted, needed both induction (observation and study of facts) and deduction (logical, including mathematical analysis). The laws of economics were analogous to laws of the tides, not to the laws of physics, as represented by the law of gravitation. They referred to tendencies and not to precise truths (Marshall, 1961 [1890], book I, ch. III, esp. pp. 29, 32–33). This principle of Marshall's economics is evident in his specific treatment of virtually every economic question. It enabled him to reconcile competition and increasing returns, to introduce issues of family, education, arbitration, trades unions, and custom into his discussion of wages and labor; and to blend well-established insights into economic behavior from his favorite classical mentors (Smith, Ricardo, and J. S. Mill) with the tools of modern, marginalist reasoning. It created a spirit of eclectic tolerance in his views on scope and method, which makes present-day study of his great text still eminently worthwhile.

Marshall's mixed methodology is even more strikingly visible in his *Industry and Trade*, his last major completed book. It provided a careful, comparative, study of industrial techniques and business organization in the major industrialized countries of the early twentieth century, Great Britain, Germany, and the United States. It is an exercise in realistic economics, with theory mixed in at all the appropriate places. The book combines statics and dynamics, history and contemporary analysis, and examines competition as essentially a monopolistic phenomenon involving a finite and often rather small number of large firms, thereby rejecting the artificial construct of perfect competition so beloved by much contemporary theory. A great deal of it remains a rich source for the economic history of the late Victorian and Edwardian eras, because it reflected the insights gained from Marshall's *wanderjahre* in factories (see Groenewegen, 1995, ch. 8, esp. pp. 208–14). Its contents continue to be a source of inspiration to contemporary investigators of industrial organization. It shows to perfection the two sides of Marshall's skills in combining fact with theory.

Marshall's last book, *Money, Credit and Commerce* (Marshall, 1923) is little more than a pastiche of early work, and as such remains of interest. It brings together in one book the pure theory of international trade and reflections on monetary problems and business fluctuations presented to Royal Commissions and other government inquiries. It indicates what could have been, had less time been spent on perfecting the *Principles* (see Groenewegen, 1995, ch. 19). These later volumes also provide a clear link with what was to happen in Cambridge economics during the decades after his death – the "imperfect competition revolution" in the theory of the firm as business organization, and the "Keynesian revolution" in the theories of money, inflation, employment, and output.

As was the case with Jevons, Marshall's work in economics also covered social reform and practical policy matters. In later life, he claimed that his personal concern with the problem of poverty for sections of the working class, and with members of what he termed "the residuum," had initially sparked his interest in economic studies as a practical means of helping the lowest orders of society to gain access to the resources needed in order to enjoy a fruitful life. Some of these concerns are visible in the pages of the *Principles*, especially in the final chapter of its last editions. Specific policy contributions were edited by Keynes as *Official Papers of Alfred Marshall*. These reprinted his evidence to Royal Commissions and to other government inquiries, relating to monetary questions, to "depressions of trade and industry," to taxation policy, and to international trade. A supplement to Marshall's *Official Papers* (Marshall, 1996) provides easier access to Marshall's views on education as given to a Committee of Inquiry in 1880, substantial extracts from work for the Labour Commission (of which he was a member) that are directly attributable to him, as well as more monetary evidence and material on the fiscal question which (probably mistakenly) has been attributed to him. The economics of these volumes is not easily summarized (see Groenewegen,

1995, ch. 11). However, they more clearly reveal Marshall, the well-rounded economist and social scientist, competent to deal with a wide variety of policy issues not only in money, banking, the cycle, and trade policy to which Marshall (1926) drew attention, but also to education and, especially, to labor relations in all its manifold aspects. Like Jevons, Marshall was no narrow theorist of marginalist economics but a student of the subject as a whole, anxious to grapple with its various problems, human, social, and theoretical, using every conceivable method that assisted in the task.

16.4 ARTHUR CECIL PIGOU (1877–1959)

Pigou was born in 1877, in Ryde, on the Isle of Wight. He was Head of School at Harrow and won a scholarship for King's College, Cambridge. There he gained first-class honors initially in the History Tripos, and subsequently in the Moral Sciences, of which economics was then still a part. It made him a Fellow of King's, the Cambridge college with which Keynes was also associated. He began to teach economics in 1903, and succeeded Marshall as Cambridge Professor of Economics in 1908. Pigou did not retire until 1943. During World War I, he was a conscientious objector but worked close to the front as part of an ambulance team during the long university summer vacations. His wartime experiences may have turned him into the recluse that he became from the early 1920s (Pigou, 1952 [1939]; Johnson, 1978 [1960]; Collard, 1981, pp. 105–10).

Pigou's economics is now largely remembered for two things. First, and negatively, he is remembered for his quarrel with Keynes over the theory of employment, caused by Keynes's devastating critique of Pigou's own work on the subject (Pigou, 1933). This is particularly visible in his hostile review of *The General Theory* (Pigou, 1936), only partly retracted in a subsequent appraisal (Pigou, 1950). His analytic contribution to the real balance effect, sometimes called the Pigou effect, greatly assisted the "neoclassical synthesis" between Keynes's theory and marginalist equilibrium economics, of Clower and Patinkin, in the 1950s. More positively, and more importantly in the long run, was his path-breaking work on welfare economics. This expanded upon various hints on the subject left in Marshall's economics. Pigou's pioneering and highly original welfare economics was first published in *Wealth and Welfare* (Pigou, 1912). Its contents in turn spawned three major theoretical works in the 1920s: the *Economics of Welfare* (Pigou, 1920b), *Industrial Fluctuations* (Pigou, 1927), and *A Study of Public Finance* (Pigou, 1928). These books not only reveal his skills as a major marginalist economist but as a student of Marshall in the fullest sense of the word. Pigou (1920b, p. vii) expressed the view that economics provides the "instruments for the bettering of human life [by restraining] the misery and squalor that surround us, the injurious luxury of some wealthy families, the terrible uncertainty [from unemployment and business cycles] overshadowing many families of the poor [which constitute social] evils too plain to be ignored." This explicitly Marshallian credo was elaborated in his *Wealth and Welfare*, and more fully detailed in the three publications of the 1920s.

The essential concept in Pigou's broad perception of welfare was the national income or dividend. However, the marginal method tended to be employed in analyzing the welfare implications of changes in national income. Much of Pigou's welfare analysis was in fact conducted through balancing the advantages of various small changes in output in different industries, thereby equating costs and benefits at the margin. Business fluctuations of course also dealt with variations in national income, but of a different order. Public finance was largely a redistributive exercise channeling parts of national income to disadvantaged sections of society either by public expenditure or by tax and borrowing policies, hence maximizing welfare through bringing marginal utilities of money incomes closer to equality. Moreover, expenditure and tax policies also affected size of national income and output, either favorably or unfavorably.

An aspect of this last problem had a distinct, albeit limited, Marshallian pedigree. In his analysis of increasing and diminishing returns in the *Principles*, Marshall (1961 [1890], vol. I, pp. 467–70) had tentatively suggested that welfare (in terms of consumer surplus) could be increased if industries operating under increasing returns were encouraged to expand their output by means of a government bounty, while taxes could be levied to lower the output of diminishing returns industries. Social welfare gains arose from the cost and price consequences inherent in such changes in output. (Marshall later thought that Pigou had carried the tax/bounty analysis too far, partly because Pigou was attempting to treat the dynamic issues underlying increasing returns by the using tools specifically designed for static analysis.) Pigou's emphasis on measuring changes in national dividend as the index of welfare, thereby making his welfare analysis essentially an analysis of social product, was also innovative. Consequently, even if inadvertently, Pigou became an important and innovative pioneer in national income analysis well before regular official estimates of national income had become available.

The welfare implications of the national dividend had a production as well as a distributive aspect for Pigou. The size of the national income clearly influenced national welfare. Per capita growth of the national income therefore also enhanced national welfare, and Pigou did much to clear up potential ambiguities in growth measurement. This part of the welfare problem was a direct legacy of the British classical economics tradition from Smith to John Stuart Mill, with its focus on the growth of the wealth of nations. Such a legacy had been strongly preserved in the production analysis of Marshall's *Principles*. One ambiguity in growth measurement was that raised by the presence of externalities, a concept derived from Sidgwick's *Principles of Political Economy* (Sidgwick, 1887), but greatly refined by Pigou. His definition of such externalities has become classic:

> . . . the essence of the matter is that one person A, in the course of rendering some service, for which payment is made, to a second person B, incidentally also renders services or disservices to other persons C, D, and E, of such a sort that technical considerations prevent payment being exacted from the benefited parties or compensation being enforced on behalf of the injured parties. (Pigou, 1920b, p. 159)

A lighthouse benefiting the shipping in the area it serves, but not being able to exact payment from all these beneficiaries through the imposition of charges, was a clear example of such an "externality"; the smoke stack of a factory belching soot and noxious fumes into the atmosphere, for which those adversely affected rarely gained compensation, became a standard example of a negative externality, which needed to be deducted from the aggregate contribution to national output made by the factory in question. The implications of this for the analysis of contractual arrangements and property rights were never clearly presented by Pigou, but were clarified subsequently by economists such as Coase.

Fluctuations in the national dividend generated by business cycles had also grave welfare implications, particularly when income and employment levels declined during depressions. Remedies for cycle and unemployment were therefore significant for raising aggregate welfare. Pigou's work on industrial fluctuations is highly conscious of this fact: its division into two parts dealing with causation and remedies indicates that policy measures for reducing the size of fluctuations were a major reason for Pigou's study of this complex topic. Because it provided analysis of the dynamic forces influencing the national income – both of the broad movements over long periods and the short-term oscillations which were the essence of business cycles – Pigou was able to treat this part of his economic work as an important branch of his welfare economics. The prolonged unemployment that Britain experienced during the 1920s and 1930s, something which Pigou (1947) had chronicled in detail, raised profound issues for the welfare economist who was broadly contemplating the subject matter of the discipline. Pigou's enduring concern with unemployment explains his bitterness toward Keynes for his harsh criticism of Pigou's theoretical work on this subject (Keynes, 1973 [1936], pp. 272–9). Pigou subsequently made public amends for his early response to *The General Theory* (Pigou, 1950, esp. pp. 20, 61–6; and see Collard, 1981, pp. 122–32 for a detailed discussion).

There was a strong distributive element in Pigou's work, clearly illustrated in his twofold welfare criterion for judging whether welfare has increased in particular situations. Welfare increased if the social dividend increased but the poor were no worse off, *and* if the absolute dividend going to the poor increased but there was no decrease in the social dividend. Pigou's welfare criterion embodied utilitarian notions (as befitted a follower of Sidgwick, 1887) in that it attributed rising welfare to the higher utility attainable by the poor from an increase in their share of product at the expense of the wealthy.

Much active redistributive policy to raise social welfare is presented in Pigou's *Study of Public Finance* (Pigou, 1928). Its three parts deal, respectively, with principles of public expenditure, tax revenue, and public borrowing. The book did not cover all relevant aspects of public finance, given its intentional design of supplementing the earlier *Economics of Welfare* and *Industrial Fluctuations*. Together, they embodied "the main part of what I have to say on general economics" (Pigou, 1928, p. v).

The 1928 public finance text contained much marginalist analysis. Optimum size of aggregate government expenditure, for example, was achieved if expenditure was pushed "up to the point at which the satisfaction obtained from the last shilling expended is equal to the satisfaction lost in respect of the last shilling called up on government service [through taxation or public borrowing]" (Pigou, 1928, p. 52). This proposition clearly relied on interpersonal comparisons of utility. Optimal budget balance was to be achieved by equating satisfaction from expenditure of the last (marginal) shilling in each area of public endeavor.

Pigou's taxation theory relied on minimum aggregate sacrifice as its guiding principle. Ignoring excess burdens from taxation, this led to the view that, given uniform rates of declining marginal utility of income, equality of sacrifice (minimum aggregate sacrifice) produced steeply progressive personal income taxation. This, in fact, aimed at equating the utility of income at the margin for all taxpayers by chopping off all incomes above that level. Pigou admitted that such steeply progressive taxation could never be introduced because of the massive excess burdens that it created by distorting employment, saving, and investment decisions.

Pigou wrote many other books, including some studies directly related to World War I (*The Political Economy of War*, 1921, and *A Capital Levy and a Levy on War Wealth*, 1920a). He published various works on applied economics (Pigou, 1923, 1935b); an essay on *Marshall and Current Economic Thought* (1953); lectures on *Socialism and Capitalism* (1937); and a defense of "real" analysis in *The Veil of Money* (1948). Two more of his later books have greater theoretical significance. One analyzed the concept of stationary states, perceived as an "introductory prelude to economics [because it says nothing about] processes of change or conditions of disequilibrium" (Pigou, 1935b, p. v); the other addressed problems of employment and equilibrium in a macroeconomic manner, intended as a purely theoretical exercise. In sharp contrast to the applied works of the 1920s, these studies dealt analytically with "*fundamental economic problems*, with which every economist . . . *must* trouble himself" (Pigou, 1941, p. vii).

Pigou's ultimate standing in the history of economics will be judged by his welfare economics (Graaf, 1987; Middleton, 1998). The last describes Pigou's contribution as a "welfare economics revolution." Pigou's welfare analysis invariably used the marginal apparatus when deriving welfare criteria, therefore adapting these tools of marginalism designed originally to explain individual economic behavior to broad, social purposes. Pigou's views on optimal public sector size are identical in principle to Jevons's views on optimal individual labor supply and to Marshall's discussion of the "economizing" housewife. Pigou is therefore a key figure in English marginalist economics, in direct line of succession from Jevons, Sidgwick, and Marshall.

16.5   SOME FURTHER COMMENTS ON ENGLISH MARGINALISM

To complete this overview of English marginalism, some additional observations need to be made. These fall into two categories. First, some recognition has to be given to Sidgwick, Edgeworth, and Wicksteed. Secondly, the post-Pigovian phase of English marginalism needs brief mention as part of a summary overview of the subject.

Henry Sidgwick (1838–1900) was a co-founder of the Cambridge school of economics with Marshall, since he contributed to its teaching during its formative period. His *Principles of Political Economy* was based on the solid utilitarian foundations that likewise guided his philosophical views on ethics and politics. This book was partially Jevonian, but far more Millian in the organization of its contents. After a methodological introduction, its separate parts dealt with production, distribution, and exchange, in which discussions of international trade, money, and "the art of political economy" can also be found. Discussion of economic welfare issues appeared in the last, inspiring aspects of Pigou's work. However, Sidgwick (1887) was quickly overshadowed by the publication of Marshall (1961 [1890]), which henceforth dominated the economics textbook market in England.

Francis Ysidro Edgeworth (1845–1926) is often bracketed with Marshall (Newman, 1987, p. 84). He can be described as a hedonist first and a marginalist second, especially in *Mathematical Psychics*, his only book on economics, which had been briefly reviewed by Marshall (1975c [1881]). Following Jevons, Edgeworth (1881, pp. 1–3) staunchly defended mathematical economics, both from the quantitative nature of economics, and the usefulness of mathematical analysis in treating nonquantitative data. Its most important economic contributions were his demonstration of the indeterminacy of bilateral exchange contracts (a basic criticism of Jevons's theory of exchange) and his analysis of re-contracting. This introduced game-theoretic notions and aspects of the theory of coalitions, ideas not exploited until well after his death. Edgeworth's marginalism was constructively applied to taxation economics, the theory of international trade, and his many other contributions to economic theory (collected in Edgeworth, 1925; see also the detailed discussion in Creedy, 1986).

Philip Henry Wicksteed (1844–1927), described by Sraffa (1960, pp. v–vi) as the "purist of marginal theory," emphasized the association between the "marginal approach" and "change either in the scale of an industry or in the proportions of factors of production." As Jevons's major follower in economics, he made important contributions to economics. First, he solved the "adding-up problem" in marginal productivity theory by showing that total (value) product, under certain conditions, is precisely sufficient to pay the factors of production cooperating in production, when paid according to their marginal products (Wicksteed, 1894). Secondly, his textbook, *The Common Sense of Political Economy*, painstakingly developed the basic principles of the "marginal theory of economics" (Wicksteed, 1933 [1910], vol. I, p. xxix). Wicksteed had earlier criticized Marxian value theory by appealing to Jevons's marginal utility theory (Wicksteed, 1884, p. 715). Wicksteed staunchly defended the merits of mathematical economics, and his writings are most easily identifiable with Robbins's subsequent codification of marginalist economics through his definition of "*the* economic problem" (Robbins, 1932, esp. pp. xvi, 12–13). Wicksteed is therefore a particularly significant figure in English marginalism and his precise, analytic style is not infrequently preferred to the looser style of Marshall (for a sympathetic, brief account of Wicksteed, see Steedman, 1987).

During the 1930s, English marginalism continued to be developed with great rigor. A good example is the work on the theory of firm as "imperfect competition" by Joan Robinson at Cambridge, and in Hicks's translation into general equilibrium economics of the English marginal economics tradition (see Dimand, ch. 21, this volume). However, particularly in the context of the theory of the firm, and broadly in the spirit of Marshall's practice of empirical observation of business behavior, Oxford University studies in the price mechanism seriously questioned the usefulness of much of this marginal analysis of the firm in terms of profit maximization and cost minimization rules (equating costs and revenue at the margin). This type of research, however, never really replaced the dominant role of marginalist theory in English micro- and macroeconomics. The major legacy of the English marginalist pioneers – Jevons, Marshall, and Pigou – and their key collaborators and followers (Edgeworth and Wicksteed) remains the linchpin of much of what passes for economics in university classrooms.

Bibliography

Black, R. D. C. 1981: W. S. Jevons (1835–82). In O'Brien and Presley, op. cit., pp. 1–35.

Campus, A. 1987: Marginal economics. In Eatwell et al., op. cit., vol. 3, pp. 320–2.

Collard, D. 1981: A. C. Pigou (1877–1959). In O'Brien and Presley, op. cit., pp. 105–39.

Cournot, A. A. 1963 [1838]: *The Mathematical Principles of the Theory of Wealth*, trans. N. T. Bacon. Reprinted Homewood, IL: Richard D. Irwin.

Creedy, J. 1986: *Edgeworth and the Development of Neoclassical Economics*. Oxford: Blackwell.

Eatwell, J., Milgate, M., and Newman, P. (eds.) 1987: *The New Palgrave. A Dictionary of Economics*, 4 vols. London: Macmillan.

Edgeworth, F. Y. 1881: *Mathematical Psychics*. London: C. Kegan Paul.

—— 1894: Margin, In R. H. Inglis Palgrave (ed.), *Dictionary of Political Economy*, vol. 2. London: Macmillan, 691–2.

—— 1925: *Papers Relating to Political Economy*, 3 vols. London: Macmillan, for the Royal Economic Society.

Graaf, J. de V. 1987: A. C. Pigou (1877–1959). In Eatwell et al., op. cit., vol. 3, pp. 876–9.

Groenewegen, P. 1995: *A Soaring Eagle: Alfred Marshall 1842–1924*. Aldershot, UK: Edward Elgar.

Howey, R. S. 1972: The origins of marginalism. *History of Political Economy*, 4(2), 281–302.

Hobson, J. A. 1914: *Work and Wealth. A Human Evaluation*. London: Macmillan.

Jevons, W. S. 1875: *Money and the Mechanism of Exchange*. London: Kegan Paul, Trench, Trubner and Company.

—— 1882: *The State in Relation to Labour*. London: Macmillan.

—— 1883: *Methods of Social Reform and Other Papers*. London: Macmillan.

—— 1884: *Investigations in Currency and Finance*, edited with an introduction by H. S. Foxwell. London: Macmillan.

—— 1905: *The Principles of Economics. A Fragment of a Treatise on the Industrial Mechanism of Society, and Other Papers*, with an introduction by H. Higgs. London: Macmillan.

—— 1906 [1865]: *The Coal Question*, 3rd edn., revised and edited by A. W. Flux. London: Macmillan.

—— 1911a [1862]: Brief account of a general mathematical theory of political economy. In Jevons (1911b), op. cit., appendix III, pp. 303–14.

—— 1911b [1871]: *Theory of Political Economy*, 4th edn., with additional notes by H. S. Jevons. London: Macmillan.

Johnson, H. G. 1978 [1960]: Arthur Cecil Pigou 1877–1959: an obituary. *Canadian Journal of Economics*, 26, 150–5. Reprinted in Johnson, E. J. and Johnson, H. G. 1978: *The Shadow of Keynes*. Oxford: Blackwell, 173–80.

Keynes, J. M. 1972 [1936]: William Stanley Jevons. In D. Moggridge (ed.), *Essays in Biography, Collected Writings of John Maynard Keynes*, vol. 10. London: Macmillan, for the Royal Economic Society, 109–50.

—— 1973 [1936]: Appendix to chapter 19. Professor Pigou's "Theory of Unemployment." In D. Moggridge (ed.), *The General Theory of Employment, Interest and Money, Collected Writings of John Maynard Keynes*, vol. 7. London: Macmillan, for the Royal Economic Society, 272–9.

McCulloch, J. R. 1838: Introduction to Adam Smith, *An Enquiry into the Nature and Causes of the Wealth of Nations*, 3rd edn. Edinburgh: A & C Black.

Marshall, A. 1925 [1872]: Mr Jevons' theory of political economy. *Academy*, April 1. Reprinted in A. C. Pigou (ed.), *Memorials of Alfred Marshall*. London: Macmillan, 93–9.

—— 1919: *Industry and Trade*. London: Macmillan.

—— 1923: *Money, Credit and Commerce*. London: Macmillan.

—— 1926: *Official Papers*, ed. J. M. Keynes. London: Macmillan.

—— 1961 [1890]: *Principles of Economics,* variorum edition by C. W. Guillebaud. London: Macmillan.

—— 1975a [1871]: Essay on value. In Whitaker (1975), op. cit., vol. 1, pp. 125–59.

—— 1975b [1879]: The pure theory of international trade, the pure theory of domestic values. In Whitaker (1975), op. cit., vol. 2, pp. 117–81, 186–236.

—— 1975c [1881]: Review of F. Y. Edgeworth's *Mathematical Psychics*. In Whitaker (1975), op. cit., vol. 1, pp. 265–7.

—— 1996: *Official Papers. A Supplement,* ed. P. Groenewegen. Cambridge, UK: Cambridge University Press.

—— and Marshall, M. P. 1879: *Economics of Industry*. London: Macmillan.

Middleton, R. 1998: *Charlatans or Saviours?* Cheltenham, UK: Edward Elgar.

Mill, J. 1821: *Elements of Political Economy*. London: Baldwin, Cradock and Joy.

Newman, P. 1987: Francis Ysidro Edgeworth (1845–1926). In Eatwell et al., op. cit., vol. 2, pp. 84–98.

O'Brien, D. P. 1981: Alfred Marshall (1842–1924). In O'Brien and Presley, op. cit., pp. 36–104.

—— and Presley, J. R. (eds.) 1981: *Pioneers of Modern Economics in Britain*. London: Macmillan.

Peart, S. 1996: *The Economics of W. S. Jevons*. London: Routledge.

Pigou, A. C. 1912: *Wealth and Welfare*. London: Macmillan.

—— 1920a: *A Capital Levy and a Levy on War Wealth*. London: Oxford University Press.

—— 1920b: *The Economics of Welfare*. London: Macmillan.

—— 1921: *The Political Economy of War*. London: Macmillan.

—— 1923: *Essays in Applied Economics*. London: Macmillan.

—— 1927: *Industrial Fluctuations*. London: Macmillan.

—— 1928: *A Study in Public Finance*. London: Macmillan.

—— 1933: *The Theory of Unemployment*. London: Macmillan.

—— 1935a: *Economics in Practice*. London: Macmillan.

—— 1935b: *The Economics of Stationary States*. London: Macmillan.

—— 1936: Review of *The General Theory of Employment, Interest and Money*. *Economica*, 3, May, 115–32.

—— 1937: *Socialism and Capitalism*. London: Macmillan.

—— 1952 [1939]: Looking back from 1939. In A. C. Pigou, *Essays in Economics*. London: Macmillan, 1–9.

—— 1941: *Employment and Equilibrium*. London: Macmillan.

—— 1947: *Aspects of British Economic History 1918–1925*. London: Macmillan.

—— 1948: *The Veil of Money*. London: Macmillan.

—— 1950: *Keynes's General Theory: A Retrospective View*. London: Macmillan.

—— 1953: *Marshall and Current Economic Thought*. London: Macmillan.

Robbins, L. 1932: *The Nature and Significance of Economic Science*. London: Macmillan.

Seligman, E. R. A. (ed.) 1948 [1930]: *Encyclopaedia of the Social Sciences*. New York: Macmillan.

Sidgwick, H. 1887: *Principles of Political Economy*, 2nd edn. London: Macmillan.

Sraffa, P. 1926: The laws of returns under competitive conditions. *Economic Journal*, 36(4), 535–50.

—— 1960: *Production of Commodities by Means of Commodities. Prelude to a Critique of Economic Theory*. Cambridge, UK: Cambridge University Press.

Steedman, I. 1987: Philip Henry Wicksteed (1844–1927). In Eatwell et al., op. cit., vol. 4, pp. 915–19.

Thünen, J. H. von 1966 [1826–63]: *The Isolated State*, trans. C. Wartenberg, ed. P. Hall. Oxford: Pergamon Press.

Whitaker, J. K. (ed.) 1975: *The Early Economic Writings of Alfred Marshall 1867–1890*, 2 vols. London: Macmillan.

—— 1987: Alfred Marshall (1842–1924). In Eatwell et al., op. cit., vol. 3, pp. 350–63.

Wicksteed, P. H. 1884: The Marxian theory of value. *Today*, II, 388–409. Reprinted in Wicksteed (1933 [1910]), op. cit., vol. 2, pp. 705–24.

—— 1894: *An Essay on the Co-ordinations of the Laws of Distribution*. London: Macmillan.

—— 1933 [1910]: *The Common Sense of Political Economy*, 2 vols. London: Routledge and Kegan Paul.

CHAPTER SEVENTEEN

The Austrian Marginalists: Menger, Böhm-Bawerk, and Wieser

Steven Horwitz

17.1 INTRODUCTION

This chapter delineates the nature of the Austrian contribution to the marginalist revolution in the works of Carl Menger, Eugen Böhm-Bawerk, and Friederich Wieser. Although it will be unavoidably comparative, the focus will be on the origins and development of a distinct line of Austrian marginalism, particularly in the work of Menger. That is, the goal is not just to show that the Austrians marginalists were saying something different; rather, it is also to trace how those differences, which begin with Menger, were to play themselves out in the work of the next generation of Austrians. In particular, as the classic contributions of Erich Streissler (1972) and William Jaffé (1976) have noted, it was the *subjectivism* of the Austrians that distinguished them from the other marginalist revolutionaries. Subjectivism constitutes the thread that united the Austrian marginalists, although it is a thread that began to weaken with the work of Wieser and Böhm-Bawerk and was almost totally lost by the 1920s. It was to be rediscovered during the late 1930s and 1940s, when developments elsewhere in economics forced the Austrians of the time to reassess what both they and others were talking about with respect to "neoclassical" economics.

17.2   CARL MENGER'S SUBJECTIVIST MARGINALISM

The distinctly Austrian strand of the marginalist revolution begins with Carl Menger's path-breaking *Grundsatze*, or *Principles*, published in 1871. Like others of his time, Menger was steeped in the tradition of the older German historicists, and it is fairly clear that the *Principles* was Menger's attempt to bring that tradition forward. It is of note that the book is dedicated "with respectful esteem" to Wilhelm Roscher, then perhaps the leading thinker of the historical school. The final two paragraphs of the preface are a tribute to his German predecessors, where he refers to his own contribution as a "reform of the most important principles of our science" that is "built upon a foundation laid by previous work . . . of German scholars" (Menger, [1981] 1871, p. 49). He also goes to some length in the preface to make it clear that he wishes to claim that economic phenomena conform to "definite laws" and that the outcomes produced by economic activity are "entirely independent of the human will" (Menger, [1981] 1871, p. 48). The very first paragraph of the first chapter is a discussion of cause and effect, suggesting that he was attempting to counter the worst tendencies of historicism – namely, the idea that one can try simply to collect data and draw conclusions from them without the aid of some universalistic theoretical framework. From the start, Menger saw himself as building on and "reforming" the historicist tradition.

What would such a reform mean, particularly if his invoking of cause and effect suggests a critique of historicism? One reading is that Menger saw himself as providing the theoretical framework necessary to do the sort of detailed, applied economics so valued by the historicists. A detour into Menger's (1985 [1883]) other book on methodology (the *Investigations*) would take us too far from the topic at hand. However, it is worth noting that Menger (see also 1981 [1871], p. 47) was fairly clear in dividing up the tasks of economics into the theoretical (which dealt with laws) and the applied (where those laws were used to synthesize facts of the world into causal-genetic explanations of the emergence and evolution of economic and social phenomena). The rationale for theory is the doing of history, and the doing of (good) history requires a theoretical framework. To that degree, Menger appears to have seen himself as extending the ability of the historicists to do what they thought was right by providing them with the analytic framework he believed that they were missing.

Although the *Principles* is not focused on responding to English-language debates, it is clear in several places that Menger wished also to demonstrate the errors of that tradition with respect to its cost of production value theory. Friedrich von Hayek reports that Menger wrote the *Principles* in a "state of morbid excitement," suggesting that he had seen how he could both push forward his own tradition and respond to the theoretical difficulties the classicists had run into with cost-of-production theories of value (Hayek, 1981, p. 16).

17.2.1   The theory of goods

One notable aspect of Menger's presentation of marginal utility is that his discussions of value and the importance of the margin are not how he begins. Rather, he starts by defining what is meant by a good and how different sorts of goods might interrelate. These two discussions are important for Austrian marginalism as they bring to the fore several central themes. Menger (1981 [1871], p. 52) argues that a thing must meet four requirements to be considered a good:

1 There must be a human need for the thing.
2 The thing must be "capable of being brought into a causal connection with the satisfaction of this need."
3 Humans must know of this causal connection.
4 We must have enough command over the thing so that we can use it to satisfy the need.

Other than the second condition, which arguably refers to properties of the object itself, the conditions listed by Menger center not on the thing itself but on its relationship to humans. He speaks of human needs, human knowledge, and our ability to command the thing in question. From the start, Menger makes these concerns central to his conception of economics. As he later argues about value, what makes something a good is not a property of the good itself "but merely a relationship between certain things and men" (1981 [1871], p. 52, fn. 4). Ascribing the characteristic of being a "good" to the relationship between a thing and human beings is reflective of the distinctly subjectivist character of Austrian marginalism.

How far Menger was willing to carry that subjectivism is tested early on by his own example of "imaginary goods" (1981 [1871], p. 53). His example is a good where people *believe wrongly* that there is a causal connection between the good and the need, or where the need itself is not real. These things would remain "goods" but get their own category as "imaginary." Although distinguishing imaginary goods makes sense given Menger's four characteristics, it is worth asking, as von Mises (1976 [1933]) did, whether from an *economic* perspective this difference matters. If the goal is to explain observed market phenomena, then it will be what people believe about goods that will be the basis of their action in the marketplace and the social outcomes that they contribute to producing. The issue of whether the causal connection or the need is real is irrelevant, argued later subjectivists, to the economic analysis. Thus, despite the very subjectivist nature of Menger's version of marginalism, he did not necessarily extend it to its logical limits.

One of Menger's central contributions is the concept of the "ordering" of goods. He distinguishes among goods of various "orders," with goods of the "first" order being those that go directly to the consumer, and goods of "higher" orders being the inputs that go into making goods of the first order. As he (1981 [1871], p. 57) notes, goods of the higher orders are still goods because they still have a causal connection with satisfying a human need, even if that connection is an indirect one (via the good of the first order). This distinction among the orders of goods has two important roles within Austrian marginalism. First, it is a further example of the way in which the economic characteristics of goods are not inherent in the goods themselves, but in the ways in which humans make use of them. As Menger points out, what makes a good into a good of a particular order is not the physical properties of the good, but where it sits in the causal relationship with the satisfaction of a given human need (1981 [1871], p. 58). The same piece of bread might be a good of the first order when bought to make a lunch in a household, but a good of the second order when purchased by a restaurant to make a sandwich it sells to its customers. Despite being the same physical object, its economic importance depends on how it is used.

The importance of goods within human uses raises the second role that the ordering of goods plays within Austrian marginalism. Implicit in Menger's discussion of the ordering of goods is the idea that human actors formulate plans, and that the goods in question play roles within those plans. The reason why objects with the same physical properties can be goods of differing orders is that they play different roles in differing human plans. The piece of bread figures in the plan of the family residing in the household in a different way than it does in the plan of the restaurant owner. The centrality of "the plan" to Austrian thought was most fully developed by Ludwig Lachmann (1978 [1956]) more than 75 years after Menger, but the concept is there from the start.

The ordering of goods within human plans is also the foundation of the Austrian theory of capital and the related question of imputation. In the hands of Böhm-Bawerk and Wieser, these issues would be explored more completely. Menger did have much to say about the complementary nature of capital in the production of goods of the first order. He (1981 [1871], pp. 62–3) argues that for a second-order good to keep that goods-characteristic there must be available the goods complementary to it in the production of the first-order good in question. If those complementary second-order goods are not available, then the good in question loses its good-characteristic, because we have lost command of the goods necessary to produce the final good. We might have the need, the knowledge, and the physical capability, but we do not have the goods that we need to effect production of the final good. Menger also argues that the goods-characteristic of higher-order goods "derives" from the goods-character of the final good. Should the desire for some final good disappear, it would no longer be a good, as would also be true of all those higher-order goods used in producing it that could not be transferred to some other use. It is the subjective evaluation of final goods that determine whether or not the inputs needed to produce those goods are themselves economic goods.

17.2.2   Knowledge, time, and error

Embedded in Menger's conception of economic goods is the role of human knowledge, of both human needs and the causal connections between things and those needs. Once one stresses the importance of knowledge, one must take seriously the role of time and the possibility of error. Menger's earlier example of imaginary goods already suggests that error can play a role at the level of goods of the first order. However, he is also concerned to note that production processes take time, and where time passes, uncertainty is relevant and error can result. Menger (1981 [1871], p. 68) argues that the needs that give higher-order goods their goods-character must therefore not be the needs of today, but the needs of the future, at the point when the production process is complete. In other words, what makes them goods is the "human foresight" involved in bringing together various higher-order goods in anticipation of the needs of the future (cf., Kirzner, 1973). Once we recognize this point, then the uncertainty involved with the passage of the time means that our foresight is necessarily imperfect. The starting point of the economic process is the subjective plans of individuals, which are in turn based upon their own foresight about the future. In the Austrian version of marginalism, such plans can, and will often, be erroneous, leading to the readjustment of plans and further economic activity. This ceaseless flux of the market is characteristic of the disequilibrium orientation of the early Austrians.

17.2.3   Subjective value and Menger's margin

As Streissler and Jaffé have argued, not all versions of the marginalist revolution were the same, and the distinct contribution of Menger's marginalism was its subjectivism. Human beings are the ultimate source of economic value. Menger first makes this point by distinguishing "economic" from "non-economic" goods (1981 [1871], pp. 94–113). The distinction rests on whether or not the available quantity of the good is less than or greater than the human needs for the good. Economic goods are those where needs are greater than available quantities, necessitating that we "economize" on them. It is that process of economizing that forms the basis of Menger's exploration of value.

Menger defines value as "the importance that individual goods or quantities of goods attain for us because we are conscious of being dependent of command of them for the satisfaction of our needs" (1981 [1871], p. 115). Human "consciousness" is the key to value, in that our awareness of the linkage between an object and its ability to satisfy a need is what gives goods value. Our being "conscious" need not mean we are correct about that linkage. As Menger (1981 [1871], pp. 120–1) says later, "Value is thus nothing inherent in goods, no property of them, nor an independent thing existing by itself. It is a judgment economizing men make about the importance of the goods at their disposal for the maintenance of their lives and well-being." Human judgment is now substituted for being "conscious." We decide, using our judgment, whether things are believed to satisfy a need; thus we give them value. Value is therefore "entirely subjective in nature" (Menger, 1981 [1871], p. 121). This judgment of value is subject to the same sorts of concerns about time and error that we noted in the previous subsection.

For Menger, the subjectivity of value is what underlies his discussion of marginal utility. It is only after he has defined value that he moves on to talk about utility. In defining utility, he simply refers to it as "the capacity of a thing to serve for the satisfaction of human needs, and hence (provided the utility is recognized) it is a general prerequisite of goods-character" (1981 [1871], p. 119). In Menger's conception of marginalism, utility is not understood as a cardinal value that can be totaled up, nor is it even anything "measurable" in any meaningful way. It is, as Menger notes, understood as a "capacity," and one that is in the eye of the beholder. Utility is *not* the same as value, as value can only be applied to economic goods. Utility is therefore necessary for value, but it is not sufficient. Noneconomic goods have utility but not value, as they do not figure into the economizing decisions that humans make. More precisely, noneconomic goods are ones where "the satisfaction of human needs does not depend upon the availability of concrete quantities of [them]" (1981 [1871], p. 119). Noneconomic goods such as air do not have to be judged in terms of specific concrete quantities; rather, they are omnipresent in some sense.

It is around this set of points that Austrian marginalism departs from the other strands. For example, for Jevons, total utility was understood as some summable quantity (in the tradition of the English utilitarians) determined by a functional relationship with other variables, and marginal utility was simply the first derivative of that total utility function. For Jevons (and Walras), the "marginal" in "marginal utility" had a clearly mathematical meaning. For Menger, the notion of the margin was understood in different terms. As Hayek (1981, p. 18) points out, Menger does not even use the phrase "marginal utility" in the book, as it was first used in the Austrian tradition by Wieser. Instead, Menger had to resort to circumlocutions like those in the paragraphs above, particularly his references to "concrete quantities" of goods. By adding to the definition of value that is cited from Menger earlier ("the importance that individual goods or quantities of goods attain for us because we are conscious of being dependent of command of them for the satisfaction of our needs" – 1981 [1871], p. 115), the notion that we are talking about "concrete quantities" available for satisfying the "least valuable" of our needs, we obtain a Mengerian concept of marginal utility. In a later passage, Menger says:

> Accordingly, in every concrete case, of all the satisfactions secured by means of the whole quantity of a good at the disposal of an economizing individual, only those that have the least importance to him are dependent on the availability of a given portion of the whole quantity. Hence the value to this person of any portion of the whole available quantity of the good is equal to the importance to him of the satisfactions of the least importance among those assured by the whole quantity and achieved with an equal portion. (1981 [1871], p. 132)

This passage captures the essence of the Austrian version of marginal utility.

"Menger's margin" involves a notion of "marginal" that is clearly ordinal and not cardinal. Beyond that, it does not refer to the first derivative of a hypothesized utility function. Utility, for Menger and the Austrians more generally, is not a measurable quantity of pleasure (White, 1995). Utility is the "capacity," ascribed to a good by humans, to satisfy some need, not the hedonic sensation that a good produces when it satisfies that need. Thus, the "marginal utility" of a good is the capacity of a "concrete quantity" of that good to satisfy the least important specific need that it can satisfy. Faced with several buckets of water and several possible uses of that water (bathing, human consumption, animal consumption, and washing clothes), the marginal utility of water will be equal to the value of the least important of those needs that it is believed to have the capacity to satisfy. It is not a "feeling," nor is it the first derivative of a total utility function. It is the value attached to the specific need fulfilled by the specific amount of a good believed to have the capacity to satisfy that need. Only a few pages after the extracted definition above, Menger deploys it to solve the water–diamond paradox. As he (1981 [1871], p. 140) puts it there, the need that would be unmet by the loss of a concrete quantity of water would be of far less importance than that of the need unmet by the loss of a concrete quantity of diamonds, as diamonds are so few in quantity compared to water.

The Austrian conception of marginal utility marked out a very different path than did that of Jevons and Walras. Rather than pursuing the calculus-based notion of the margin, and the various equilibrium models that it enabled economists to construct, the Austrians continued to understand economizing behavior in terms of subjective judgments about specific goods and needs in a world full of error and uncertainty. Mengerian man was never the Vebelenian "lightning calculator of pleasures and pains"; rather, he was more like a sailor headed into a fog with a pretty good searchlight. He can see some things, but not others. He is also likely to bump into a few things that he could not have possibly been prepared for. And he does not know what he does not know. This Austrian conception of marginal utility leads fairly naturally to the emphasis on disequilibrium and discovery that marks the research agenda of modern Austrian economics since World War II. It also demonstrates, as Karen Vaughn (1990) has argued, that the rediscovery of what was distinct about Austrian economics during the late 1930s and 1940s in the work of Hayek and von Mises, and then again in the 1970s and 1980s with the Austrian revival, was really a journey back to roots of Austrian marginalism found in Menger.

17.2.4   The flow of value

Another crucial component of Austrian marginalism is the discussion of the flow of value and the concept of "imputation." Given the Austrian conception of value, and its subjectivist foundation, exploring the relationship between the value of the inputs and the value of an output was a straightforward proposition. In opposition to classical cost-of-production theories, where value flowed in the same direction as production, the Austrians argued that value flowed in the direction opposite of production. Rather than the inputs determining the value of the outputs (the same direction as production), it was the value that human beings ascribed to the outputs that determined the value of the inputs. The value of the inputs was "imputed" from the value of the outputs. As Menger (1981 [1871], p. 150, emphasis added) put it, with a particularly Austrian flavor, "On the contrary, it is evident that the value of the goods of higher order is always and without exception determined by the *prospective* value of the goods of lower order in whose production they serve."

The emphasis on "prospective" is the particular Austrian twist. Menger recognized from the start that the value of inputs was not something that could be ascertained deterministically. Knowing the current prices of outputs is not enough to determine the value of inputs, because the value of inputs depends on not the current prices of outputs, but the prospective prices, as envisioned by entrepreneurs. Those prospective prices are ultimately produced by the active minds of those entrepreneurs. This point is important because it once again suggests that the Austrian version of marginalism is not easily captured by equilibrium constructions. If the valuation of inputs is based on entrepreneurs' expectations of the value of outputs, then if and only if those expectations are mutually consistent and correct can the economy be characterized by equilibrium. In a Mengerian world in which subjectivity, uncertainty, and error are omnipresent, those conditions are unlikely to be met. Thus, input valuation is a competitive, disequilibrium, process. The ongoing clash of entrepreneurial judgments will constantly evaluate and reevaluate those inputs in nondeterministic ways. In addition, that process of imputation is institutionally dependent, in that only where certain institutional arrangements hold that allow entrepreneurs to compete in the formulation of production plans using privately owned capital will there be any assurance that inputs are being valued appropriately with respect to the value of output.

This point is central to Hayek's (1945) criticism of Schumpeter's understanding of the relationship between imputation and calculation under socialism. Hayek points out that Schumpeter's argument that even the socialist planner can impute the value of the inputs from the value of the outputs is true only if one assume that equilibrium holds. He also argues that the whole process of evaluation itself requires a competitive market order. Given that it is the prospective value of outputs that determines the value of inputs, it is only through the aforementioned clash of entrepreneurial expectations that the inputs get any value at all. Absent private property in capital, there is no way for them to be valued, from an Austrian perspective.

The Austrian emphasis on the structure of production and Menger's conception of the value of inputs being based on the prospective value of the outputs they produce leads to a further difference between Austrian presentations of marginalism and the Jevonian and Walrasian presentations. In the more equilibrium-oriented versions of marginalism, prices are seen as the independent variables into the utililty and production functions of actors, who then generate particular quantities consumed and produced as the dependent variables. The problem is to find the set of prices that will produce mutually consistent production and consumption choices. Although the *theorist* searches for a set of prices, the actors modeled are assumed to take those prices as given and to churn out quantity variables as a result.

In Menger's vision, prices are not independent variables; rather, they are the emergent result of the competitive economizing process we have described above. The order that Menger chooses to present his argument puts the theory of price in chapter five, well more than halfway through the book. It is the forward-looking consumption and production activities of economizing actors that produce prices: thus Menger has to describe carefully those economizing processes before he turns to the theory of price. Even there, how prices emerge depends up on the degree of competition among the buyers and sellers. He starts with price forma- tion under "isolated exchange" (what we might call "bilateral monopoly") and ends with a discussion of price formation under "bilateral competition." He notes how the range of possible market-clearing prices will be much narrower as the degree of competition on both sides increases (Endres, 1995). For Menger, it is also the case that this movement from bilateral monopoly to bilateral competition is part of the process of economic development and growth. Monopoly is seen as an early stage of development, with more rich competition being a sign of economic well-being (O'Driscoll, 1981).

17.2.5   Spontaneous order and Menger's marginalism

One overriding theme in Menger's Austrian marginalism is what Hayek would later term "spontaneous order." Economic phenomena emerge unintentionally from the economizing activity of human beings. We, as Menger argues, only aim to do the best with what we have, whether as consumers or producers, and in so doing, we set in motion chains of causality that produce economic value, market prices, and broader patterns of economic activity. These are the causes and effects that Menger begins the text with, as his way of improving on the work of his historical school predecessors. The very structure of the *Principles*, which puts prices and the emergence of money well into the argument, suggests the sort of causal-genetic explanations that Menger is interested in. It is these sorts of ex- planations that Menger thinks the earlier parts of the book make posssible. One needs to understand marginalism correctly in order to be able to offer sound spontaneous order explanations. If such explanations view human institutions and economic phenomena as "the product of human action but not human design" in Adam Ferguson's phrase co-opted by Hayek, then marginalism is the key to understanding the "human action" part of that formulation. The more strictly methodological arguments raised in the *Investigations* are further support for this interpretation.

Menger's theory of the origin of money is often pointed to as the exemplary spontaneous order explanation. Menger included that theory in the *Principles* and it follows his discussion of prices and the "commodity." This suggests that he sees the emergence of money as part of the same pattern of growth that animates his discussion of prices. In addition, he follows the discussion of the theory with a history of money, describing its uses in various eras and linking that to eco- nomic development more broadly. Having thoroughly described economizing behavior with the assistance of his notion of the margin, he can then move on to elucidating the emergence of economic institutions, such as money, and then use all of that to engage in the sort of historical analysis that his German pre- decessors valued so highly. He ends the *Principles* with the discussion of money not just because he needs the earlier theory to construct the theory of money's origin, but because it gives him the opportunity to show his own teachers that his theoretical advances enable him to tell *better* historical "stories" than they can. He goes to the length of describing how certain types of money are appropriate to certain particular historical eras (1981 [1871], pp. 262–71), which is precisely the sort of work that the historical school believed was so valuable. Menger too is interested such historical work, but appears to believe that it cannot be done (or at least not done well) without the theoretical tools of marginalism. If economic history is to be rendered intelligible, it will have to be through causal-genetic stories that begin with the economizing behavior of the human actors.

That the project of Austrian marginalism is to use a revised economic theory to offer causal-genetic interpretations of economic history is also clear from later work in the Austrian tradition. In a striking section of his *Human Action*, von Mises (1966 [1949], p. 405) discusses the "epistemological import" of Menger's theory of money. There he argues that the theory is to be taken as a sort of template for the methodology of economics, which is to construct such spontaneous order explanations of economic phenomena. It is worth noting that von Mises's discussion takes place not in the early methodological sections of the book, but later when he is into the material on what we would today characterize as "microeconomics." This is another example of Vaughn's (1990) claim that the revival of Austrian economics since World War II has involved a rediscovery of Mengerian themes. More generally, Menger's vision of marginalism and the task of economic theory was clearly different from that of the other marginalists.

17.3 WIESER'S EXTENSIONS OF AUSTRIAN MARGINALISM

Wieser's contributions to the marginalist revolution were numerous. They also represent a movement of the Austrians toward the marginalism seen in the other strands of the revolution. Here, we shall focus on two aspects: his contributions to value theory and his extension of Menger's fragmentary remarks on imputation. What we shall see is that Wieser's work helped to create a more unified and homogeneous body of theory that defined the marginalist revolution. By the time both he and Böhm-Bawerk had articulated their advances on Menger, the distinctiveness of Menger's work was beginning to be lost in the merging of the various strands of marginalism.

With respect to value theory, Wieser clarified the nature and importance of the "margin" for determining value. In his *Natural Value* (1956 [1889]), he explored in great detail what it meant to say that it was the utility of the least important use to which a homogeneous stock could be put that determined the value of any one unit of that stock (e.g., the buckets of water example from above). Wieser made use of a simple mathematical model to illustrate this point. That model also enabled him to distinguish between "utility" and "value," where value referred to "revenue." His model described how as the number of goods exchanged increased, the price per unit would fall (consistent with Menger's utility theory) and that the increase in utility from each good consumed would eventually become less and less. In addition, the total value/revenue received by the seller would not only add smaller increments, but would in fact decline in absolute terms as the price received fell with the sale of additional units. In essence,

Wieser plotted out the total utility and total revenue curves familiar from modern microeconomics.

Wieser assumed that the price paid for the marginal unit of the good would equal its utility to the consumer. So if one were to buy three units of a good, the total utility would equal the price one would pay for one unit, plus the price one would pay for a second unit, plus the price one would pay for a third. Note that this is not the same as the total expenditures/revenue that would come from the exchange of three units at a single market price. Wieser was really adding up the area under the demand curve, and he assumed that the demand curve also reflected utility. One of the core implications of the model was that total revenue would continue to rise as long as the utility (i.e., price) of the incremental unit sold was greater than the receipts lost by having to lower price on all units. Again, this is the inverted U-shaped marginal revenue curve. Wieser's contribution was not only to lay out those conditions carefully, but to link them to value through the assumption that the value of the marginal unit was equal to its market price.

One of Wieser's additional contributions to value theory was that he was first among the Austrians to actually use the term "marginal utility" to describe the value of the least important end to which a homogeneous stock was put. As the mathematical model discussed above suggests, Wieser was moving more toward the presentation of utility that was seen in the English and French marginalist traditions. As Vaughn (1994, p. 34) notes, Wieser placed Menger with Jevons, Walras, and Gossen as co-discoverers of the marginalist insight, without directly making any distinctions among them. In particular, his more utilitarian approach to utility, where he assumed, at least for the sake of convenience, that it could be summed into a total utility curve, represents an attempt to bring together Menger's work with that of Jevons. Thus, his use of the shorthand of "marginal utility" seems appropriate in a way that it might well not have been for Menger. The mathematics surely help to clarify aspects of utility theory, but do run the risk of losing some of the distinctive Austrian insights found in Menger's work.

In his later book *Social Economics*, Wieser makes use of the phrase "margin of utility" to describe Menger's concept of the least important use being the one that determines the value of any unit of a stock (Wieser, 1967 [1914], p. 88). That phrase has been lost from value theory in general and Austrian value theory in particular, which is unfortunate as it seems an effective way of getting around the circumlocutions of Menger and the potential misreading of Menger's contribution that can come from the more mathematically oriented "marginal utility."

Wieser's work on imputation is generally considered to be among his more important contributions to the development of economic thought. Here too, although he develops some essential Mengerian insights, he moves them in a direction that brings them closer to the other strands of marginalism. Wieser sharpens the Austrian view that it is the marginal utility of consumer goods that determine the value of the inputs that produce them. For one thing, Wieser argued that, at least where all resources are being utilized optimally, the value of the input will depend upon the various outputs that it could contribute to producing. Specifically, it will be the value of the least important good that it will produce that will determine the value of the input. In much the same way as the value of a consumption good is determined by the least important end to which it could be allocated, so the value of inputs depends upon the marginal output they could help to produce. Even more specifically, Wieser argued that value will depend upon both the marginal productivity of the input and the marginal utility of the output, rather than the marginal productivity and the *price*, as is the case in modern theory. It is also worth noting that in Wieser's Austrian presentation, there is no distinct role for "supply" in determining value. Inputs are valued by the marginal utility attached to what they produce, with opportunity cost determining the least important use. This is very much an Austrian point deriving from Menger: it is the actions of economizing actors that determine value of both outputs and inputs.

In developing the formal model for imputation, Wieser had to make two assumptions that pushed the analysis somewhat away from Menger's original perspective. One of those was the assumption of fixed proportions across production functions. This clearly makes the mathematics more tractable, but may not describe reality particularly well. Real-world entrepreneurial competition may be constantly discovering new methods of production that violate the fixed proportions assumption.

The second assumption is more important. Wieser assumed that the economy was in equilibrium, implying that the values of inputs could be calculated simultaneously. This assumption runs up against Menger's emphasis on causal-genetic explanations and the role of entrepreneurial expectations. For Menger, those input prices emerged out of the competitive process of entrepreneurs' forward-looking evaluations. This suggests that, at any moment in time, inputs may not be optimally allocated and that simultaneous equilibrium models will not be applicable. Wieser's work on imputation was important in clarifying the fact that it is the value of the outputs that determine the value of the inputs, but his decision to portray that as a simultaneous equilibrium model, though necessary for the mathematics, is one that took the Austrian strand of marginalism away from Menger's subjectivism and closer to that of Jevons and Walras.

17.4   BÖHM-BAWERK ON CAPITAL

A similar story can be told about Böhm-Bawerk's contributions to the Austrian strand of marginalism. His work on exchange forwarded Menger's marginalism, as did his contributions to capital theory. Böhm-Bawerk's (1922) famous horse market example made very clear the role of the marginal buyer and seller in determining the market-clearing price under conditions of bilateral competition. Specifically, that example drew important conclusions for doing exchange analysis with discrete supply and demand functions. Later neoclassical development of this work assumed an infinite number of buyers and sellers, or at least enough to treat both functions as continuous. In this sense, Böhm-Bawerk's analysis was an extension of Menger's focus on real human action (discrete buyers and sellers), rather than a calculus-oriented conception of utility. However, Böhm-Bawerk's capital theory also contained elements that worked against the subjectivist thrust of Menger's work. Here, as with Wieser, those elements worked toward the gradual crystallization of a more homogeneous neoclassical marginalism, while at the same time hiding what was distinct about the Austrian strand. That aspect of Böhm-Bawerk's capital theory demands distinct attention.

Two important advances that were part of Böhm-Bawerk's capital theory were the idea of the "roundaboutness" of production and the time-preference theory of the interest rate. Both of these were related to his theory of capital and were grounded in the subjectivism of Menger's marginalism. Roundaboutness referred to the fact that longer (more "roundabout") methods of production would generate more final output than shorter, less roundabout, ones. The key to this argument was that longer production processes, those that involved more "stages," enabled the increased use of capital (what Böhm-Bawerk called "produced means of production"), which would make the final output greater than otherwise. Longer production processes used more capital, creating higher capital to labor ratios, thus generating more output (although with diminishing marginal contributions).

Böhm-Bawerk's theory of interest is also a very important extension of Mengerian subjectivism. For Böhm-Bawerk, the payment of interest was clearly linked to capital, and capital, as we have seen, had a distinct time element to it. Why, then, did capital earn interest? Böhm-Bawerk's answer was that interest originates from the fact of human time preference. Humans, all other things equal, value the present more than the future. In order to get people wait for output in the future, they require additional compensation when that output arrives. Notice that this is consistent with the roundaboutness hypothesis: lengthening a process of production requires paying more interest to those who are waiting for the output, but such production processes also produce more output. Longer processes of production mean a longer period of time in which some people must go without output. Those who are being asked to wait longer (those who "financed" the production process) will require more compensation for their reduced ability to consume in the interim.

Böhm-Bawerk offered a number of reasons why we prefer the present to the future, but the one he put the most weight on was the fact that present goods were better able to satisfy human wants than future ones. Böhm-Bawerk links this to the roundaboutness hypothesis by arguing that starting a production process now will always generate more output than starting one in the future. However, one can also argue that the advantage that present goods carry is due to the sort of uncertainty that Menger identified in the *Principles*. One advantage of having a present good is that one can be certain about one's ability to consume it. Any future good inherently carries uncertainty with it, as events might intervene to prevent one from being able to consume it. All other things equal, present goods will thus be preferred to future ones. Although Böhm-Bawerk himself did not make this connection explicitly, it reflects another sense in which present goods are better able to satisfy human wants than are future goods.

It is also important to clear up a common misconception about Böhm-Bawerk's time-preference theory of the interest rate. This theory is intended only to explain the *origin* or the *existence* of interest, not the interest rate at any given moment in time. Market interest rates include the time-preference component, but also factors such as risk and inflation. Market rates will vary for reasons other than changes in time preferences. However, if one's goal is to explain why interest emerges at all (the Mengerian "essence" of interest), then one has to turn to the fact of time preference. This fits the Mengerian research agenda as well, as it provides a theoretical framework with which to look at actual market rates.

One of the problems with Böhm-Bawerk's theory is determining precisely what is meant by the "period of production," which might be used to measure the degree of roundaboutness in any production process. In his model, the flow of inputs was continuous, but outputs occurred at distinct points. Examples from nature where inputs are continually applied but the output "ripens" at particular moments in time capture the theory well. But with the continuous flow of inputs, what was the period of production? Suppose that one wanted to make something out of wood. The point of final output can be determined, but does the "period of production" extend all the way back to the seed that grew the tree 100 years earlier? If roundaboutness was to be measured by the period of production, Böhm-Bawerk seems to have a problem in determining precisely how to measure it.

Böhm-Bawerk tried to get around this problem by making use of an "average period of production" concept. He argued that one could weight the inputs according to how proximate they were to the final output. By summing these inputs, weighted by the number of periods they were used and then dividing through by the total number of inputs, one could calculate an "average" period of production. This was a significant move away from Mengerian subjectivism, as it necessitated that he assume that all inputs were homogeneous. It also forced him to assign weights somewhat arbitrarily – How could one know whether an output was more or less attributable to relatively recent or more distant inputs? What the "average period of production" concept overlooked, as was the case with Wieser's work on imputation, was the fact that the values for inputs were being determined by the subjective evaluations of entrepreneurs in a competitive market process. Finding an objectively definable average period might be useful to the theorist, but it was irrelevant to the entrepreneurs actually doing the valuing of inputs. All of the questions that the average period must answer are ones that cannot be answered "objectively" for any given production process. Entrepreneurs must compete through the use of monetary calculation to determine the values of those inputs and to determine the proper accounting of periods of production and contributions to output.

The average period of production concept was abandoned by later Austrian capital theorists (e.g., Hayek, 1941), and appropriately so. According to Schumpeter (1954), Menger called Böhm-Bawerk's use of the average period of production in his theory of capital "one of the greatest errors ever committed." However, Böhm-Bawerk's other contributions to capital theory that were more consistent with the distinctly Austrian strands of marginalism, in particular the time-preference theory of the interest rate and the notion of roundaboutness, were picked up and expanded upon by later generations of economists, both Austrian and otherwise.

Despite the flaws noted here, Böhm-Bawerk's work on capital is one of the enduring contributions to economic theory made by the Austrian marginalists.

17.5 Conclusion

The contributions of the Austrian marginalists represent both a distinct tradition in modern economics and a part of the family tree that comprises the consensus around which twentieth-century microeconomics was constructed. The consistency in those two characterizations is captured by the fact that the distinctiveness of the Austrian strand progressively began to weaken with the second and third generation of Austrian thinkers. As this chapter has argued, Wieser and Böhm-Bawerk surely pushed forward important ideas of Menger, but in some cases they did so in ways that left behind aspects of Menger's work that were notably different from those of his co-discoverers, Jevons and Walras. By the interwar years, that distinctiveness was largely gone, even in the eyes of the then-current generation of Austrian economists. It is only in the period around World War II and after that those original Mengerian themes began to be rediscovered and a distinctly Austrian version of marginalism began to be rearticulated. With the ongoing emphasis in modern microeconomics on questions of knowledge, information, and disequilibrium, and the push toward pluralism in economic methodology, the ideas and approaches of the Austrian marginalists remain of contemporary interest.

Note

The author thanks the editors for helpful suggestions.

Bibliography

Böhm-Bawerk, E. 1922: *Capital and Interest*. New York: Brentano's.

Endres, A. M. 1995: Carl Menger's theory of price formation reconsidered. *History of Political Economy*, 27(2), 261–87.

Hayek, F. A. 1941: *The Pure Theory of Capital*. Chicago: The University of Chicago Press.

—— 1945: The use of knowledge in society. Reprinted in *Individualism and Economic Order*. Chicago: The University of Chicago Press, 1948.

—— 1981: Introduction. In C. Menger, *Principles of Economics*. New York: New York University Press.

Jaffé, W. 1976: Menger, Jevons and Walras de-homogenized. *Economic Inquiry*, 14, 511–24.

Kirzner, I. M. 1973: *Competition and Entrepreneurship*. Chicago: The University of Chicago Press.

Lachmann, L. M. 1978 [1956]: *Capital and Its Structure*. Kansas City, MO: Sheed Andrews and McMeel.

Menger, C. 1981 [1871]: *Principles of Economics*. New York: New York University Press.

—— 1985 [1883]: *Investigations into the Method of the Social Sciences with Special Reference to Economics*. New York: New York University Press.

Mises, L. von 1966 [1949]: *Human Action: A Treatise on Economics*. Chicago, IL: Henry Regnery.

—— 1976 [1933]: *Epistemological Problems of Economics*. New York: New York University Press.

O'Driscoll, G. P. 1981: Monopoly in theory and practice. In I. M. Kirzner (ed.), *Method, Process, and Austrian Economics*. Lexington, MA: Lexington Books.

Schumpeter, J. A. 1954: *History of Economic Analysis*. New York: Oxford University Press.

Streissler, E. 1972: To what extent was the Austrian school marginalist? *History of Political Economy*, 4(3), 426–41.

Vaughn, K. 1990: The Mengerian roots of the Austrian revival. In B. Caldwell (ed.), *Carl Menger and His Legacy in Economics*. Annual supplement to *History of Political Economy*, 22. Durham, NC: Duke University Press.

—— 1994: *Austrian Economics in America*. Cambridge, UK: Cambridge University Press.

White, L. H. 1995: Is there an economics of interpersonal comparisons? *Advances in Austrian Economics* 2A. Greenwich, CT: JAI Press.

Wieser, F. von 1956 [1889]: *Natural Value*. New York: Kelley and Millman.

—— 1967 [1914]: *Social Economics*. New York: Augustus M. Kelley.

CHAPTER EIGHTEEN

Early General Equilibrium Economics: Walras, Pareto, and Cassel

Donald A. Walker

18.1 Léon Walras

18.1.1 Background

Walras, the founder of the modern theory of general economic equilibrium, was born on December 16, 1834 in Evreux, France, and christened Marie Esprit Léon. Despite his lack of formal credentials in economics, he obtained an appointment at the Academy (subsequently University) of Lausanne in 1870, and remained there for his entire career. He retired in 1892, and died on January 5, 1910 in Clarens, Switzerland (for biographical information, see Jaffé, 1935: for bibliographical information, see Walker, 1987; A. and L. Walras, 1987–).

18.1.2 Walras's mature comprehensive model

COMPETITION

Walras was the first economist to construct a complete general equilibrium model, the mature comprehensive model set forth in the second edition of the *Eléments* (1889). It is called "comprehensive" because it encompasses exchange, production, consumption, capital formation, and money; and "mature" to differentiate it from the models in the first and fourth editions. In that model, Walras not only expressed the belief that all economic phenomena are interrelated, which had been done by many economists before him, he also specified their interrelations, studied their disequilibrium behavior, and described their conditions of equilibrium.

One of Walras's fundamental methodological convictions was that the assumptions of a theory must be drawn very carefully from empirical reality (1896b, p. 10), and one of his principal objectives as an economic theorist was to understand the behavior of the markets that functioned in the economy of his time. His study of empirical reality convinced him that "free competition in regard to exchange is the almost universal regime" (Walras, 1965, vol. 2, letter 999, pp. 434–5), "practiced on all markets with more or less precision and therefore with less or more frictions" (Walras, 1895, p. 630), and so he drew the assumption of a purely competitive economy from the real economy. That is why he constructed a general equilibrium model of a freely competitive economy; not, as has been suggested (Jaffé, 1977), in order to design a utopia whose conditions necessitated the operation of that type of system. The specific type of real market from which he drew some characteristics was a freely competitive organized market, like a stock exchange or a wholesale market for an agricultural commodity (Walras, 1988, §41, pp. 70–1, cited because this is a variorum edition, with section numbers that enable the reader to find the passage in the 1954 English translation). In such markets, prices are determined by the forces of supply and demand without collusion and are changed by buyers and sellers in the same direction as the sign of the market excess demand (1988, §42, pp. 71–2), which is what Walras meant by the term "free competition." That feature, he contended, was also sufficiently true of unorganized competitive markets that the workings of free competition and its consequences can be attributed to them also (1988, §41, pp. 70–1). Regarding competition, he had "as a first step, reduced that mechanism to its essential elements." Subsequent steps should be taken, he argued, to create a progressively more realistic model, namely one infused with additional empirically derived conditions: "it is appropriate to introduce into [my] model one by one all the complications that reality presents" (1894, p. 624). Thus his general equilibrium model, he declared, was "not only the idea but the image" (1896a, pp. 469–70) of the real economy of his time.

MARGINAL UTILITY THEORY

Another of the fundamental building blocks of Walras's general equilibrium model is his idea of marginal utility and the maximization of total utility by each participant. Those concepts provided a motive for economic behavior and a condition of equilibrium, elements that were essential for the functioning of his model of general equilibrium. Instead of confining the marginal utility theory to the investigation of consumption and of simple exchange, Walras went far beyond the work of its other initiators by using it to analyze the behavior in multiple markets of a variety of participants undertaking different economic functions. In his model of consumer behavior (1988, §74, p. 107; §75, p. 111; §80, p. 116), Walras assumed that the utility a consumer derives from any commodity is independent of the amount he or she consumes of other commodities, that utility is cardinally measurable, and that each individual's demand for a commodity is, in principle, a function of the prices of all commodities. A consumer efficiently maximizes total utility by buying the quantity of each commodity that makes the utility received from the expenditure of a unit of money on it equal for every commodity purchased. Likewise, in Walras's models, professional traders and wholesale and retail merchants add to their holdings of each commodity, or sell out of their stocks of commodities, until they hold the batch of commodities that maximizes their utility. Entrepreneurs and capitalists strive to maximize utility by maximizing their profit and interest incomes respectively (1988, §188, p. 284).

EQUILIBRIUM IN THE MATURE COMPREHENSIVE MODEL

Walras studied the existence, uniqueness, and stability of general equilibrium in his model. He thought that he had proved that an equilibrium exists in it because he had described it with as many equations as there are unknowns (for example, 1988, §205, pp. 306–7). He then undertook a comparative static analysis in order to analyze how the solutions to the equations are affected by arbitrarily postulated or exogenously induced changes of their parameters, such as preferences, the quantity of money, and the quantity of a commodity held by the participants. Walras's proof was not valid, however, because he did not take account of the effect of disequilibrium processes on phenomena that are parameters in the equations, and because he did not establish that the solutions to the equations are economically admissible, as will be explained at the end of this essay. Nevertheless, his examination of the question went far beyond the analyses of other nineteenth-century economists, inasmuch as he dealt with a model of general rather than particular equilibrium. His study of uniqueness was limited to the consideration of isolated markets and a multi-market model of pure exchange, and his conclusion that "generally" multiple equilibria do not occur in the latter case was a statement rather than a proof (1988, §156, pp. 242–3).

DISEQUILIBRIUM BEHAVIOR IN REALITY AND IN THE MODEL

The basis of Walras's theoretical work on stability was his conception of the real economy as always undergoing processes of change (1988; §322, pp. 579–80). The disequilibrium adjustments, Walras maintained, continually move the real economy toward a position of general equilibrium. He called them the process of "tatonnement," a word that means "reiterated hesitant groping movements to find something." Walras set himself the task of modeling that behavior (Walras, 1965, vol. 2, letter 927, p. 364). Presenting his initial results in the years 1874–7, he thus became the first economist to study the stability of a general equilibrium model (1895, p. 630).

On every market day in the model, transactions of any particular commodity occur only at the price at which the supply and demand quantities are equal. Walras knew that was not true in many real markets, but believed that it was a "hypothesis that no scientific mind will hesitate to concede to the theoretician" (1895, p. 630). After attainment of that price, the market day in his model is nevertheless in disequilibrium if the price and the average cost of production of the commodity are not equal, or if the participants are affected by the prices subsequently determined in other markets. The aspect of the model's tatonnement that takes place with respect to new quantities manufactured is the progressive diminution of the difference between price and average cost of the product as a result of the changes of the price in the output market and of the prices of inputs. The rate of output in each industry is changed in the same direction as the sign of that difference. The aspect that takes place with respect to sales of each commodity is the progressive diminution of the difference between the quantity supplied and the quantity demanded. The price is changed in each market in the same direction as the sign of the excess demand quantity. "The system of new quantities manufactured and new prices . . . is closer to equilibrium than the previous one, and it is necessary only to continue the tatonnement in order to approach it more and more closely" (Walras, 1889, p. 241). In equilibrium, "prices are those at which the quantities demanded and supplied of each service or product are equal, and for which, moreover, the price of each product is equal to its average cost of production" (1988, p. 13). The mutually determined sets of prices, average costs, and quantities supplied and demanded are harmonious and fulfill the plans of all the participants in the model.

THE ENTREPRENEUR

Walras believed that entrepreneurs undertake essential functions in the real economy and therefore accorded them a role of crucial importance in the dynamic behavior of the mature comprehensive model (Walras, 1965, vol. 2, letter 800, p. 212). Entrepreneurs lead it to equilibrium. Walras portrayed them as relating input and output markets by buying labor, land services, capital-goods services, and raw and semi-finished goods, combining them to produce consumer commodities or capital goods, and selling them (1988, §189, pp. 287–8). One connection between input and output markets is established by the entrepreneur through the circumstance that the average cost of production is determined on the input side of the market and is an important part of the price charged on the output side. Entrepreneurs make a profit, which is their remuneration, as long as average cost is less than price and a loss in the opposite case. They adjust production from one disequilibrium rate to another, thereby altering average cost and price until they become equal. Profit is then zero and a state of equilibrium obtains (1988, §189, pp. 194–7). Another connection between input and output markets established by the entrepreneur is that they pay incomes to the owners of the economic resources that they hire and those incomes are spent by their recipients on consumer commodities and capital goods (1988, §§185–6, pp. 281–2).

CAPITAL FORMATION

Walras's treatment of savings and investment (1988, §§241–2, pp. 357–63) reveals yet another way in which entrepreneurs connect different economic sectors and markets. The incomes paid to owners of economic resources by entrepreneurs are partially saved by the recipients in their role as members of households, in which connection Walras formulated the first macroeconomic savings function. He developed a model of processes by which capitalists transfer their money savings to entrepreneurs through purchasing stocks and bonds (1988, §269, pp. 434–6), and explored those processes in studies of credit markets (1898, pp. 307–36). Walras showed how the capital goods that the entrepreneurs produce are priced and employed in the most profitable uses. He likewise constructed a model of the determination of the rate of net income generated by the use of capital goods, and of the determination of the market and equilibrium rates of interest (1988, §§231–71, pp. 345–436).

WELFARE ECONOMICS

Walras enunciated the principle of consumer sovereignty and modeled the way in which it operates to determine the set of commodities that are produced. The entrepreneur transmits the desires of consumers to the production side of the market, thus allocating resources so that the set of commodities produced is in accordance with the structure of consumer demands and hence reflects consumer preferences and purchasing power (1988, §188, pp. 283–4). On the basis of that analysis, Walras developed a thesis that became a central issue in the study of welfare economics, namely that free competition tends to generate a maximum of well-being for society (1988, §221, p. 334; §264, p. 424). The maximum is a relative one, because it depends upon the distribution of income and wealth and the dynamic characteristics of the model that result in it moving toward a particular set of equilibrium values. He emphasized that the maximum results from actions by economic agents to maximize utility, the establishment of a set of prices that equalizes supply and demand, the sovereignty of the consumer, and the other features of a competitive economy that he put into his model. The theory makes clear that "the mechanism of free competition leads precisely to the solution by tatonnement of this system of equations; from which it follows that the mechanism creates maximum satisfaction" (Walras, 1965, vol. 2, letter 928, pp. 364–5; and see Walras, 1988, §264, p. 424).

18.1.3   The written pledges sketch

The problem for Walras's exposition is that the equations that he wrote out have parameters that are actually endogenous variables in the tatonnement process in his model. He explained that production and exchange occur in disequilibrium in the mature comprehensive model, varying as prices change during the course of the adjustment of the markets toward their equilibrium set of variables (see, for example, 1889, pp. 235, 238, 294; 1988, §§209–12, pp. 315–19, §258, pp. 399–401). The phenomena that change as a result include the asset holdings of the participants, which alter as a function of the variations in hiring, production and sales that occur as entrepreneurs adjust levels of output in order to maximize profits; and they include the amounts of each type of capital good, which vary in accordance with changes in the amount and composition of investment, which in turn varies with changes of the prices, costs, and incomes of capital goods, and with the rate of interest and changing levels of saving. Other variables that are affected are the incomes of the participants. Since consumer demand functions depend on both asset holdings and income, they also change during the tatonnement. Consequently, the equations that Walras presented as relating to the mature model of general equilibrium do not in fact describe it. Their solutions – prices, rates of employment of resources, incomes, outputs, and quantities traded – are not the values toward which the model actually converges.

In 1899 and in the fourth edition of the *Eléments* (1900), Walras tried to design a virtual model that would eliminate this problem, thus abandoning his objective and method of trying to construct a realistic model. A virtual model is one in which no economic activities occur in disequilibrium, except for the quotation of prices and the manifestation of the associated desired supply and demand quantities. In that way he hoped that the parameters of his equations would represent conditions that are truly constant during the equilibrating process of his model. He thought that he could achieve the virtual property by assuming that suppliers of resources and other commodities do not produce disequilibrium amounts but, instead, make written pledges to provide the commodities. Walras stated that they vary the amounts offered as a function of a series of suggested prices until the set is found at which the desired supply and demand of every commodity become simultaneously equal in every market. Only then are other economic activities allowed to take place (1900, pp. VIII, 215, 224, 260, 298, 302; 1988, pp. 5–7, §§207, 213–14, 251, 273, 274; pp. 309, 323, 377, 441, 447). The written pledges construction, however, is an incomplete sketch, notably because would-be demanders of consumption goods do not make pledges and so have no means of expressing their desires (Walker, 1996, pp. 372–95). Of course, Walras asserted that there is a tatonnement and that equilibrium is found, but those were just unsupported statements, not a consequence of his assumptions, not an outcome of the structure of the sketch and the behavior of its participants. Furthermore, he did not carry out his plan (1900, p. VIII; 1988, pp. 5, 7) to convert into written pledges markets all the older sub-models that are supposed to play a role in the 1899 design – sub-models dating from his mature period of theorizing but that he left unchanged in the fourth edition of the *Eléments*. He therefore presented disequilibrium production and exchange as occurring in some markets but not in others, a situation contradicted by his equation system, which allows only for virtual behavior. Thus Walras did not construct a general equilibrium model in his last phase of theorizing. Neither the written pledges sketch alone, nor it and the collection of sub-models associated with it, contain a pricing process or any other economic activities. It does not constitute a functioning system and therefore has no dynamic path and no equilibrium.

Nevertheless, by 1889 Walras had a fully formed conception of the interrelatedness of economic phenomena and well-constructed sub-models of the important parts of a competitive economic system. The vitality of those contributions to economic theory was manifested by the strength of their influence on Vilfredo Pareto, to whose ideas we now turn.

18.2 VILFREDO PARETO

18.2.1 Background

Vilfredo Pareto's ideas are presented in this essay because he was, after Walras, the second most important economist in the early development of the theory of general equilibrium. Pareto was born on July 15, 1848 and christened

Federico-Vilfredo-Damaso. In the early 1880s he became interested in the application of mathematics to economic theory and policy formulation. Because of that approach (Walras, 1965, vol. 2, letter 1126, n. 3, pp. 553–4), and recommendations by Maffeo Pantaleoni and Walras, he was offered the position that Walras had held at the University of Lausanne and began his duties there in 1893. In the economic realm, he published his most important contributions in the *Cours d'économie politique* (1896/1897), *Manuale d'economia politica* (1906, 1909), and "Economie mathématique" (1911). After 1905, Pareto concentrated upon sociology. He retired in 1911, but continued making contributions to social science (see Pareto, 1963–2001). He died on August 19, 1923 (for biographical and bibliographical information, see Busino, 1987; Kirman, 1987).

18.2.2   The general equilibrium model

Walras's mathematical method and his conception of a multi-market competitive economy, of its equilibrating processes, and of general equilibrium, were extremely important in Pareto's economic reasoning (Walras, 1965, vol. 3, letter 1489, p. 154). He used Walras's mathematical form of expression of supply and demand, and regarded literary discussions of them as being useless and foolish (Pareto, 1909, ch. III, §181, p. 220). Pareto improved Walras's mature comprehensive model in some respects, and developed his own original theories. He agreed with Walras that the scope of pure economic theory is limited to facts and relationships regarding which free will does not play a part. He believed that the methods of positive science should be used in the study of all aspects of economics and of human behavior generally. Like Walras, he thought that the assumptions of a theory should be realistic (1916/1963, pp. 28–30). Inferences from them, he argued, should be evaluated by empirical studies, because "theories, their principles, their implications, are altogether subordinate to facts and possess no other criterion of truth than their capacity for picturing them" (1916/1963, p. 30). He also espoused the method of successive approximations of theory to the real economy, by which he meant the progressive introduction into a model of empirically derived considerations so as ultimately to achieve a high degree of realistic detail (1896/1897, vol. 1, pp. 16–17; vol. 2, pp. 15, 78).

THE THEORY OF DEMAND

Pareto's theory of consumer demand is a central pillar of his model of general equilibrium. He may have thought that it is not impossible, in principle, to measure utility objectively (see Kirman, 1987, p. 805), but he nevertheless observed that no one has "been able to succeed in demonstrating that pleasure can be measured, that it is a quantity, nor above all to discover how one could go about measuring it" (Pareto, 1909, appendix, §137, p. 661). He therefore made the important innovations of assuming that utility is ordinally measurable, the consumer being able to specify that he prefers one batch of commodities to another or is indifferent to them (1909, ch. III, §52, pp. 168–9), and of showing that his demand function can nevertheless be derived. Pareto also assumed that the utilities of different commodities are not independent. Some commodities are substitutes for each other, he noted, and others are complements (1909, ch. IV, §§12–14, pp. 253–56). Using calculus, Pareto then formulated a theory of consumer demand based on the Walrasian assumptions that the consumer wants to maximize his utility and knows how to do so, and that the quantity he demands of a commodity is a function of the prices of all consumer commodities, given his income and preferences (1896/1897, vol. 1, p. 35). Pareto also affirmed Walras's conclusion that the consumer achieves maximum utility by purchasing the amounts of any two commodities for which the ratio of their marginal utilities is equal to the ratio of their prices, although Pareto expressed that condition in the way appropriate for an ordinal indifference analysis (1909, appendix, §24, p. 559). Pareto's reformulation of Walras's model of consumer behavior was adopted by many continental economists and was developed into the modern theory of consumer demand.

THE EXISTENCE, UNIQUENESS, AND STABILITY OF EQUILIBRIUM

Like Walras, Pareto used a set of simultaneous equations in an effort to describe the characteristics of his model of general equilibration and equilibrium of a competitive economy, with the difference that he constructed a completely disaggregated version in which there is an equation for each consumer, for each resource supplier, and for each seller of output (1896/1897, vol. 1, pp. 44–61). Pareto believed that the dynamized version of his model was highly realistic (1897, p. 492). He asserted that equilibrium exists in his model because the number of independent equations equals the number of unknowns (1896/1897, vol. 1, pp. 26, 44–6, 61), and then discussed how the economy moves toward it.

In this connection, Pareto had studied Walras's attempts to show that his mature comprehensive model is stable and he naturally took its dynamics as his starting point – naturally, because that model, with all of its irrevocable disequilibrium processes and phenomena, is the one presented in the edition of the *Eléments* that Pareto studied in the 1890s. Pareto believed that the freely competitive tatonnement process featured in that model accurately described the disequilibrium behavior of the real market system. With respect to exchange, he contended that "Walras has shown that the bargaining that takes place in free competition is the means of solving the equations of exchange by repeated attempts" (1896/1897, vol. 1, pp. 24–5). "Mr Edgeworth has objected that that is only *one* means" by which markets move toward equilibrium. "He is right," Pareto declared, "but the way indicated by Mr Walras is truly the one that describes the largest proportion" of markets (1896/1897, vol. 1, p. 25). With respect to production, he argued that Walras's idea of tatonnement in that aspect of economic activity should also be adopted, and for the same reason, namely that it was an accurate description of what happened in the real economy: "Mr Walras has shown that the competition of entrepreneurs and traders is a means of solving the equations of the equilibrium of production through successive attempts. This idea, in general, seems very fruitful for economic science" (1896/1897, vol. 1, pp. 45–6). Pareto therefore used Walras's mature concept of tatonnement in his formulations of competitive economic adjustments in the 1890s, and he did not at any time pay any attention to the written pledges sketch. He made a minor addition to the analysis of what he called multiple equilibria by arguing that consumers might choose consumption patterns that lead them to the equilibrium that is best for them (1909, ch. III, §§128–9, pp. 197–8).

THE ENTREPRENEUR

Pareto followed Walras in arguing that speculators transmit price signals to the production side of the economy by buying or selling in response to price changes, and that they facilitate the process of transforming savings into new capital goods (Walras, 1880, pp. 370, 379; Pareto, 1896/1897, vol. 2, pp. 242–5). "The social function of speculators, insofar as they do not act directly on prices, is to solve the equations of economic equilibrium in the best and promptest manner possible" (Pareto, 1896/1897, vol. 2, p. 245). For the case of free competition, Pareto adopted Walras's theory of the entrepreneur, agreeing that their actions would lead to an equilibrium in which economic profits are zero. He extended the analysis of how entrepreneurs behave in the phase of disequilibrium, however, in two major ways. First, they make errors in their production decisions:

> It is necessary to produce commodities during a certain period of time – sometimes a very long time – before they are consumed. In order for there to be a perfect adaptation of production to consumption it would be necessary: 1° that consumer demand be predicted; 2° that the results of the process of production be accurately predicted. It is impossible to do these two things with precision. (1909, ch. IX, §76, p. 530)

The entrepreneurs try to correct their errors by changing production levels during the equilibrating phase of the economy. Secondly, entrepreneurs keep changing their profit goals, thereby repeatedly modifying the path taken to equilibrium, and as a result the equilibrium values of the variables change (1909, ch. V, §11, p. 289; §§74–5, p. 331). Thus, according to Pareto, path dependency results from disequilibrium transactions and disequilibrium production not only because they change the total amount of commodities and their distribution during the equilibrating process – causes of path-dependency in Walras's model – but also because of errors and revisions of expectations and plans on the part of the entrepreneurs (1896/1897, vol. 1, pp. 18–19).

Pareto also examined the behavior of firms in markets in which there is a lack of adequate competition. In that event, he noted, there is no tendency to reduce the profits made by an entrepreneur to zero. That gave rise to his analysis of a monopolistic entrepreneur who is able to restrict output and thereby to charge a price for his product that is greater than its average cost, which he would not be able to do if he were in a competitive industry (Pareto, 1896/1897, vol. 1, pp. 62–9, *passim*). Like most economists, Pareto argued that private monopolies are obstacles to an optimum allocation of resources and to efficient rates of their use. "It is easy to see that in all cases the monopolist's profit is obtained only by harming others" (1896/1897, vol. 1, p. 69).

Entrepreneurs are the central agents in Pareto's theory of production. He argued that some entrepreneurs choose a technology with variable coefficients of production and other choose one with fixed coefficients. He included both types in his theory of marginal productivity, thus producing a sophisticated version (1896/1897, vol. 2, pp. 84–90).

WELFARE ECONOMICS

Pareto supported the thesis that free competition generates a relative maximum of welfare for a society, and he sharpened the definition of that situation by stating that the "members of a group enjoy, in a certain state of the economy, a *maximum of utility* when . . . a small change . . . is agreeable to some, disagreeable to others" (1909, ch. VI, §33, p. 354); in other words, when it is impossible to make anyone better off without making someone worse off. Pareto also developed propositions about the welfare aspects of production and consumption of consumer commodities that were similar to Walras's theorem on the maximum utility of new capital goods (Walras, 1889, pp. 301–7; 1988, pp. 417–25). As a result of these formulations, Pareto became the first theorist to demonstrate, subject to various conditions, that a state of maximum efficiency can be achieved by an economy of the type that Walras described in his model. Pareto's formulation became the foundation of the "new welfare economics," which is the modern study of maximum efficiency and well-being. In recognition of his contribution, the optimum condition that he identified is known as a Pareto optimum.

Pareto's analysis of economic efficiency was powerful and general because he took account of the conditions for maximum efficiency in markets for all types of commodities, and in exchange, production, consumption, and capital formation. One of his notable contributions in this regard was to distinguish between the conditions for maximizing individual welfare and the conditions for maximizing the welfare of society as a whole. He showed that earlier economists sometimes erroneously assumed that because an individual can reach a higher level of well-being when he acts alone, all individuals can do so when they act simultaneously. In particular, he noted that if national income is constant, one person may be able to increase his welfare by acquiring more income, but all individuals obviously cannot do so.

Those who believe that the distribution of income should be changed have not been pleased with Pareto's law regarding it. He developed an equation that he believed describes the general aspects of the distribution of income in many different economies and times, showed the goodness of fit of the equation to the data for some economies, and concluded that the "distribution of income is not the effect of chance" (1897, p. 315). He argued that there are underlying laws of production and of the use of economic resources that cause the distribution of income to take that general form, thereby casting doubt on the possibility of altering the distribution of income by government policies. Even if it were true, however, that the functional distribution of income is largely unchangeable, Pareto should not be understood as implying that the personal distribution of income cannot be affected by taxes and transfer payments.

18.2.3 General socioeconomic equilibrium

Pareto's sociology was not an abandonment of economic analysis, but an attempt to provide a broad perspective which would enable a better comprehension of how the economy fits into the totality of human life, and which would therefore provide a better understanding of how the various aspects of social life must be taken into consideration in the formulation of policies which concern economic matters. He tried to show (1916) that, as most scholars have known, just as there are interconnections between economic variables, so also are there interconnections between noneconomic variables, and between them and the economic ones. Influenced by Auguste Comte's idea of a unified social science and by Herbert Spencer's application of Darwinism to an explanation of the development of civilizations, Pareto's objective was to achieve a theory of the general equilibrium of society as a whole. He was not able, however, to achieve a satisfactory synthesis of the diverse materials that enter into the problem. In particular, he was unable to show that a society tends to move toward a certain equilibrium configuration in its class relations, its judicial system, its political system, and so on, as well as toward an equilibrium of the economic variables in the manner described by Walras. The goal that he set himself was not only too ambitious for one scholar to attain but probably impossible, not just because of the great changes in fundamental conditions that continually occur, but because it is by no means clear – and certainly has never been demonstrated – that society as a whole is an equilibrating system. That should not diminish appreciation of the magnitude of Pareto's achievement in pointing out the many respects in which economic activities and the other aspects of private and social life are interrelated.

18.3   KARL GUSTAV CASSEL

18.3.1   Background

Karl Gustav Cassel is grouped with Walras and Pareto in this essay because he was also an important early general equilibrium theorist and because his work on general equilibrium is a lineal descendant of that of Walras. He was born in Sweden on October 20, 1866, attended Uppsala University and the University of Stockholm, and was appointed Professor of Economics and Financial Science at the latter institution in 1904. In addition to his work on general equilibrium, he contributed to the theory of interest and capital (1903), and his achievements in quantitative economics established his position as an exceptionally capable early econometrician (1935). He died on January 15, 1945 (for biographical and bibliographical information, see Myrdal, 1945; Gustafsson, 1987).

18.3.2   General equilibrium theory

APPROACH AND COMPONENTS

Cassel's approach to economics was consistently one of general equilibrium analysis. He disagreed, however, with a number of the components of the models that Walras and Pareto had developed. He rejected the marginal utility theory of value, whether based on cardinally or ordinally measurable utility (1918, p. 81). He argued that since the amount of commodities consumed could not be known until the set of equilibrium prices and quantities is determined with the use of a general equilibrium system of equations, the marginal need that is satisfied, and therefore the marginal utility to each consumer, could not be known until that set is determined. He concluded that "What we call 'marginal utility' – if we now wish to introduce this conception – thus occupies exactly the same place as an unknown in the problem as does price, and it is therefore obviously absurd to cite 'marginal utility' as a factor explaining price" (1932, p. 147). In place of that concept, Cassel wanted to substitute the principle of scarcity, in response to which Knut Wicksell commented that something is scarce

> . . . only in relation to wants, or to the extent it becomes an object of demand. And the degree of scarcity is measured in exactly the same way as marginal utility, by the strength of the next unsatisfied need, which first causes the commodity to be recognized as "scarce." In other words, scarcity and marginal utility are fundamentally one and the same thing. (Wicksell, 1934 [1918], p. 221)

Instead of using utility theory, Cassel assumed in his model of general equilibrium that demand functions are primitive constructions, which has led many commentators to declare that he anticipated revealed preference theory. Paul Samuelson (1993) has firmly rejected that view, arguing that Cassel instead had a "revealed *demand*" approach, which seems a reasonable assertion inasmuch as he denied the value of regarding demand functions as expressive of underlying preference functions.

Cassel did not accept the Walras–Pareto doctrine that maximum satisfaction is obtained by a perfectly competitive economy, arguing that large-scale enterprises are much more efficient than small-scale ones, but are "absolutely incompatible" with free c͏   ͏tion (1932, p. 129). Moreover, competition generates monopoly; it brings   ͏ing its own antithesis," so "to take free competition as the starting-r͏   ͏neral theory of prices is of very little use" (1932, p. 129). He thought͏   ͏oduction processes the factors of production are indivisible, ͏   ͏impossible to use less of one factor without throwing ͏   ?. p. 179). In his equation system, he consequently   ͏nologically fixed coefficients of production, which   ͏–Pareto theory of marginal productivity in which   ͏ts are variable, while suggesting in his literary account that substitution among factors is possible (1932, pp. 179–81).

Nevertheless, Cassel used Walras's conception of general economic equilibrium as a basis for his work, and carried a number of the specific constructions of Walras and Pareto forward in the stream of economic studies. His general equilibrium models were inferior to those of Walras and Pareto, for reasons that will be made clear, but they nonetheless made an original contribution to the subject. Moreover, his formulation was very influential. This was in large measure because his exposition was much more comprehensible than that of Walras, a feature that it owed to its highly simplistic character, and because he published it in German, the language spoken and written by the important continental general equilibrium theorists in the 1930s. The work of Walras and Pareto was not widely known, whereas Cassel's text, in German or English, was used in European universities and was considered to be the definitive statement of general equilibrium theory. It was standard reference material for the mathematicians and economists who were members of the Vienna Colloquium in the 1930s (Weintraub, 1983), becoming the starting point for the investigations of the existence of equilibrium undertaken by Karl Schlesinger and Abraham Wald. It was a stimulus to the work of John von Neumann on general equilibrium and, although of far less importance than the ideas of Walras and Pareto to J. R. Hicks, it was studied by him in either German, which he could read, or the English translation.

CASSEL'S THREE MODELS

Cassel presented three models using Walras's general equilibrium approach, which have consequently become known as Walras–Cassel models. The first was a model of pure exchange with fixed available amounts of the commodities (1932, pp. 138–40). Cassel constructed a demand function aggregated over all demanders for each commodity, the quantity demanded being a function of all prices. For each commodity, he set the demand function equal to the fixed supply and declared that there is an equilibrium set of prices because there are as many equations as unknowns. Inasmuch as the money expenditures of the consumers are given, absolute prices are determined. In the second, which he called a model of the stationary state because the quantities of the commodities produced are constant, Cassel assumed that the amounts of money to be spent by consumers, the quantities of the factors of production, and the technical coefficients are given. With great clarity and simplicity, he then constructed a system in which the demand and supply for each commodity produced are equated and similarly for each factor of production, and in which the output and the input sides of markets are linked. He then dropped the assumption that the incomes and expenditures of the consumers are given, and introduced equations that result from his identification of them as the owners of the factors of production. Their prices and quantities, and hence the incomes of their owners, are determined as part of the general equilibrium of an expanded system. In his third model, which he called a model of the uniformly progressing state, Cassel was concerned not with a position of equilibrium but with a path of growth, an interest that was probably inspired by Walras's investigation of some of the properties of a growing economy (Walras, 1988, pp. 447, 575–80). Cassel's reasoning and his exposition of this model were essentially literary. He discussed the modifications that were necessary to the equations of his second model and verbally deduced the consequences. He assumed that the amounts of the reproducible factors of production increase at a fixed rate (1932, pp. 152–5). As in the second model, they are always fully employed. The prices of the factors and of consumer commodities remain unchanged as the economy grows. Cassel deduced that exponential growth occurs: the production of each commodity increases at that rate, as do money incomes, demands, supplies, savings, investment, and consumption (1932, p. 153). The model thus introduced the concept of steady-state growth. Anticipating the Harrod–Domar model, it is an original early formulation of a multiplier–accelerator process.

THE CHARACTER AND LIMITATIONS OF THE MODELS

A serious limitation of Cassel's general equilibrium models is that they are devoid of behavioral content, and are therefore devoid of features, plausible or otherwise, to which his equations could have reference. Walras's and Pareto's models are vastly richer. They took pains to establish the institutions, procedures, technology, rules, and pricing processes in the markets that they analyzed, and only then did they try to describe many of those characteristics and their outcomes with equations. Walras, for example, used 116 pages for his theory of exchange alone. In contrast, Cassel used only 16 pages to present all three of his models. He made no mention of the characteristics of markets or the behavior of suppliers and demanders, offering no explanation of how prices are formed. His models are even more highly idealized systems than Walras's 1900 written pledges sketch. That was a sketch of a virtual model, but Walras described it as having disequilibrium states and, indeed, he introduced the device of written pledges with the intention that the model would be virtual but would also have a process of adjustments in disequilibrium that would lead it to general equilibrium. Cassel, on the other hand, constructed models that are not only virtual but that, he simply assumed, are always in equilibrium; they have no tatonnement process because he assumed that they do not. That greatly simplified the models, and therefore Cassel's theoretical task, because he had no reason to examine the questions of the existence of equilibrium or of stability, or whether or not there are multiple solution sets of the variables. It also means, however, that he did not provide any explanation of why his models should be considered theoretically interesting or empirically applicable.

18.4   A SUMMARY OF EARLY GENERAL EQUILIBRIUM ECONOMICS

General equilibrium theory has had a complicated history. Walras created the mature comprehensive model of general equilibration and equilibrium. It was a nonvirtual system; that is, one in which there are irrevocable disequilibrium transactions and disequilibrium production. He also created a sketch of a virtual hypothetical economy. Pareto amended and elaborated upon the nonvirtual model, replacing Walras's aggregative functions with disaggregated ones. Cassel chose to follow the virtual approach, added the assumption that the system is always in equilibrium, reverted to the use of aggregative functions, and developed a model of steady-state growth. Subsequently, some theorists used Cassel's assumption that the model is always in equilibrium, and John von Neumann followed his lead by developing a virtual purely competitive steady-state growth model which is also always in equilibrium, although with some different assumptions about consumption and savings.

For many years and down to the present day, however, most theorists have chosen to elaborate upon Walras's virtual sketch of a purely competitive economy. They have had one or another, or both, of two objectives. First, they wanted to determine whether equilibrium exists in such a model and whether the solutions sets are unique, realizing the incorrectness of the belief of Walras, Pareto, and

Cassel that the existence of equilibrium is assured simply by the equality of the number of equations and unknowns. It was recognized in the 1930s that because of the use of free inputs, such as air, sunshine, and rainwater may be, Walras's, Pareto's, and Cassel's equations of general equilibrium must be modified to include the possibility of zero prices, and that the solutions to the equations must be real numbers and cannot include negative prices or quantities. Secondly, since Walras's sketch of the use of written pledges is manifestly flawed and unworkable, general equilibrium theorists dispensed with his notion of written pledges and constructed a tatonnement process conducted by a central authority, flagrantly misnamed an "auctioneer." That personage, who does not conduct any auctions, quotes prices in all markets until he finds the set that would put them all simultaneously into equilibrium, whereupon he allows economic activities to take place at that set.

John Maynard Keynes's model was nonvirtual; its adjustments take place through irrevocable disequilibrium economic activities. It was not in the general equilibrium tradition, but it proved adaptable and assimilable to that tradition, which led to the creation of many nonvirtual macroeconomic general equilibrium models. In recent years many nonvirtual microeconomic general equilibrium models have also been devised, with the parentage of Walras's mature comprehensive model explicitly recognized by their creators (Walker, 2001, vol. 2, part III). Its workings have therefore found a secure place in economic thought. Similarly, Pareto's model gave rise to a disaggregative approach used by many economists, and especially to the new welfare economics, which was a central part of the revival of neoclassical economics in the 1930s and 1940s. Subsequently, Kenneth Arrow, Gérard Debreu, Frank Hahn, and other mathematical economists have used Walras's ideas about a virtual purely competitive model, Pareto's ideas about efficiency, concepts taken from game theory, and the notion of a central price-setter to develop the foundations of what has become known as the neo-Walrasian strand of general equilibrium theorizing.

Bibliography

Busino, G. 1987: Pareto, Vilfredo. In Eatwell et al., op. cit., vol. 3, pp. 799–804.

Cassel, K. G. 1903: *The Nature and Necessity of Interest*. London and New York: Macmillan.

—— 1918: *Theoretische Sozialökonomie*. Leipzig: C. F. Winter.

—— 1932: *The Theory of Social Economy*, translated by S. L. Barron from the 5th German edition. London: E. Benn. Reprinted New York: Augustus M. Kelley, 1967.

—— 1935: *On Quantitative Thinking in Economics*. Oxford: The Clarendon Press.

Eatwell, J., Milgate, M., and Newman, P. (eds.) 1987: *The New Palgrave. A Dictionary of Economics*, 3 vols. London: Macmillan.

Gustafsson, B. 1987: Cassel, Gustav. In Eatwell et al., op. cit., vol. 1, pp. 375–7.

Jaffé, W. 1935: Unpublished papers and letters of Léon Walras. *Journal of Political Economy*, 43, 187–207.

—— 1977: The normative bias of the Walrasian model: Walras versus Gossen. *Quarterly Journal of Economics*, 91, 371–87.

Kirman, A. P. 1987: Pareto as an economist. In Eatwell et al., op. cit., vol. 3, pp. 804–9.

Myrdal, G. 1945: Gustav Cassel in memoriam. *Ekonomisk revy*, 2, 3–13.

Pareto, V. 1896/1897: *Cours d'économie politique*, 2 vols, ed. G.-H. Bousquet and G. Busino. Geneva: Librairie Droz, 1964.

—— 1897: The new theories of economics. *Journal of Political Economy*, 5(4), 485–502.

—— 1909: *Manuel d'économie politique*, translated by Alfred Bonnet from the Italian *Manuale d'economia politica*. Milan: Società Editrice Libraria, 1906. Reviewed and corrected by the author, Paris: V. Giard & E. Brière. Translated by A. S. Schwier as *Manual of Political Economy*. New York: Augustus M. Kelley, 1971.

—— 1911: Economie mathématique. In *Encyclopédie des sciences mathématiques*, vol. 1. Paris: Teubner, Gauthier, Villars.

—— 1916: *Trattato di sociologia generale*, 4 vols. Florence: Barbera. Translated by A. Bongiorno and A. Livingston as *The Mind and Society; A Treatise on General Sociology*. New York: Dover, 1963.

—— 1963–2001: *Œuvres complètes de Vilfredo Pareto*, 31 vols, prepared under the direction of G. Busino. Geneva: Droz.

Samuelson, P. A. 1993: Gustav Cassel's scientific innovations: claims and realities. *History of Political Economy*, 25(3), 515–27.

Walker, D. A. (ed.) 1987: Bibliography of the writings of Léon Walras. *History of Political Economy*, 19(4), 667–702.

—— 1996: *Walras's Market Models*. Cambridge, UK: Cambridge University Press.

—— 2001: *The Legacy of Léon Walras*, 2 vols. In *Intellectual Legacies in Modern Economics*, series editor S. G. Medema. Cheltenham: Edward Elgar.

Walras, A. and Walras, L. 1987– : *Œuvres économiques complètes* [OEC], 14 vols, edited by P. Dockès, P.-H. Goutte, C. Hébert, C. Mouchot, J.-P. Potier, and J.-M. Servet, under the auspices of the Centre Auguste et Léon Walras. Paris: Economica.

Walras, L. 1874/1877: *Eléments d'économie politique pure ou Théorie de la richesse sociale*. Lausanne: Imprimerie L. Corbaz & Cie; Paris, Guillaumin & Cie; Basle, H. Georg; 2nd edn., 1889; 3rd edn., 1896a; 4th edn., 1900; 5th edn., 1926, translated by W. Jaffé as *Elements of Pure Economics or the Theory of Social Wealth*. Homewood, IL: Richard D. Irwin, 1954. For a comparative edition, see Walras (1988), op. cit.

—— 1880: La bourse, la spéculation et l'agiotage. *Bibliothèque Universelle et Revue Suisse*, 85th year, 3rd period, 5 (March), 452–76; 6 (April), 66–107.

—— 1894: Note on his own work and on Vilfredo Pareto's prepared for the latter's installation as professor at the University of Lausanne, in Walras (1965), op. cit., vol. 2, pp. 624–5.

—— 1895: Enclosure to letter from Léon Walras to Vilfredo Pareto, January 9, in Walras (1965), op. cit., vol. 2, pp. 628–32.

—— 1896b: *Etudes d'économie sociale (Théorie de la répartition de la richesse sociale)*. Lausanne: F. Rouge/Paris: F. Pichon. In Walras and Walras (1987–) [OEC], op. cit., vol. 9, 1990.

—— 1898: *Etudes d'économie appliquée (Théorie de la production de la richesse sociale)*. Lausanne: F. Rouge/Paris: F. Pichon. In Walras and Walras (1987–) [OEC], op. cit., vol. 10, 1992.

—— 1899: Equations de la circulation. *Bulletin de la Société Vaudoise des Sciences Naturelles*, 35(132), 85–103.

—— 1965: *Correspondence of Léon Walras and Related Papers*, 3 vols, ed. W. Jaffé. Amsterdam: North-Holland.

—— 1988 [1874/1877]: *Eléments d'économie politique pure ou Théorie de la richesse sociale*, ed. C. Mouchot. In Walras and Walras (1987–) [OEC], op. cit., vol. 8.

Weintraub, E. R. 1983: On the existence of a competitive equilibrium: 1930–1954. *Journal of Economic Literature*, 21(1), 1–39.

Wicksell, K. 1934 [1918]: Professor Cassel's system of economics. In *Lectures on Political Economy*, 2 vols, trans. E. Classen. London: Routledge and Kegan Paul; vol. 1, appendix 1, 219–57.

CHAPTER NINETEEN

The "First" Imperfect Competition Revolution

Maria Cristina Marcuzzo

19.1 THE LEADING PLAYERS

Imperfections and frictions in the workings of the forces of competition, such as institutional arrangements or monopolistic elements, have always been recognized by economists when representing market mechanisms (Cassells, 1937). However, it was believed that rigidities in the market mechanism did not seriously impede the working of competition and that it was therefore reasonable to make the general assumption of "perfect" or "pure" competition in the theory of markets, as a tolerably close approximation to the real world. In fact, the classical and neoclassical visions of the working of competition differed radically, as did their theories underpinning the price mechanism, but they were less distant as far as the generality of the assumption of abstracting from frictions and imperfections was concerned.

In the 1920s and 1930s a new wave of research gathered from the opposite presumption, namely that the perfect competition assumption lacked realism, drawing attention toward new market features and other forms of competition, and so specific apparatus to deal with them was sought after. However, like most intellectual "revolutions," imperfect competition was more a reaction *against* rather than an endorsement *of* a unifying research program; in fact, there was a greater consensus on the reasons for abandoning perfect competition than on how to represent the working of "imperfect" markets.

The "leading players" in the imperfect competition revolution in the 1920s and 1930s were many; according to Samuelson, the list includes Kahn, J. M. Clark, Viner, Sraffa, Hotelling, Robertson, Robbins, Shove, Austin and Joan Robinson,

Harrod, and Chamberlin (Samuelson, 1994, p. 55). While Marshall and Pigou certainly contain some "loose hints" to the "middle ground between monopoly and competition" (Whitaker, 1989, p. 189), it was the "new" generation of Cambridge economists who cultivated the new research ground. The path-breaking insights by Sraffa, the building up of a new theoretical system by Kahn and Robinson, and the extension of market imperfection to macroeconomics by Kalecki constitute the major achievements in the Cambridge (UK) tradition. On the other side of the Atlantic, in Cambridge, Massachusetts, Chamberlin and Triffin developed a system of thought that featured market competition based on strategic interdependence among sellers and product differentiation. While sharing with the other Cambridge authors mistrust in the perfect competition assumption, they were not ingrained in the Marshallian tradition and they drew their inspiration from different sources (Rheinwald, 1977).

By the early 1950s, after a heyday of nearly two decades, the imperfect competition revolution came under attack both by the Chicago school, which reinstated a free-market approach both to micro- and macro-issues and, surprisingly, also as a result of the lukewarm acceptance of the mark-up pricing approach within the Cambridge (UK) school (A. Robinson, 1950; Kahn, 1952). It was only in the 1980s that a "second" imperfect competition revolution took place, in reaction to the pervasiveness of the free competition assumption and in an attempt to give microeconomic foundation to the Keynesian approach to market failures. A new and rich literature, based on various types of imperfections and rigidities, has developed over the past 20 years, once again challenging the wisdom that competition can be treated in general as perfect. In the "second" imperfect competition revolution, uncertainty, asymmetric information, preferences, and nonincreasing costs have been given the central role in explaining the occurrence of imperfections and rigidities in the mechanism.

This chapter examines the development of the "first" imperfect competition revolution in the two Cambridges, briefly reviewing the work of the authors who were the major protagonists of a change in the economic representation of market mechanisms, and concluding with some thoughts on its legacy after the highs and lows of its fortunes.

19.2   PIERO SRAFFA

There can be no doubt that the real initiator of the imperfect competition revolution was Sraffa, in his article in the December issue of the *Economic Journal* of 1926, which set off a true "revolution" both for the novelty of the approach and for the implications it carried.

Sraffa gave two reasons why the hypothesis of perfect competition should be abandoned. First, he held that the *theory* in which that hypothesis was embedded was logically inconsistent; secondly, he argued that the behavioral descriptions implied in that hypothesis were at variance with the known facts.

The particular theory under attack was the Marshallian–Pigouvian representation of the working of individual markets. Drawing on his previous article, published in Italian (Sraffa, 1925), Sraffa showed that many of the assumptions upon which the theory rested were ill founded.

The assumption that long-period costs for the firm increase when conditions of perfect competition hold was the result of attributing to a single firm what was attributable, under particular circumstances, only to an industry. Since each firm is too small to have an appreciable influence on the price of its factors, the result of an increasing marginal cost for the firm can be obtained only by assuming that the number of firms is fixed within each industry and that each firm, as it expands production, experiences a decrease in productivity by a factor that is constant for the industry. But this can be justified only for an industry that happens to be the sole employer of a factor that cannot be augmented. Furthermore, the assumption that the number of firms within a given industry is fixed violates one of the postulates of perfect competition, namely the open entry and exit of firms from any industry.

The assumption of decreasing average costs is also shown to be inconsistent with the theory of perfect competition. If it is admitted that there is a firm whose costs per unit of output decrease when production increases, there is nothing to prevent that firm from expanding production indefinitely and becoming a monopolistic producer in that market.

If, on the other hand, it is assumed that firms operate with constant costs a further difficulty arises for the theory of perfect competition in the Marshall–Pigou tradition, which assumes that the firm faces a perfectly horizontal demand curve. In fact, given constant costs, either the equilibrium is undetermined or, if it is postulated that firms always produce as much as possible, the possibility of one single firm monopolizing the market cannot be ruled out.

The lack of realism in the assumption of perfect competition is revealed by the common knowledge that producers are not usually constrained by costs – which are normally diminishing for the producers of manufactured goods – but by demand. However, the theory of perfect competition assumes that while firms can sell any quantity whatsoever at the given market price, they are unable to lower prices or to increase marketing expenses in order to increase their market share. Unfortunately, quite the opposite behavior is observed in most markets.

On the other hand, while the producer cannot have any influence on price, the consumer is assumed to be indifferent as to the products of any given industry. The assumption of a perfectly elastic demand curve encapsulates the idea that products are homogeneous and therefore that there is perfect substitution or indifference in consumption.

Thus, in Sraffa, abandonment of the hypothesis of perfect competition means abandoning a *particular* theory; that is, a theory that sees competition as a situation in which expansion of firms is halted by rising costs. Far from being restricted to very special circumstances, the hypothesis that – within the Marshall–Pigou apparatus – firms should be regarded as single monopolies functions better than perfect competition, in accounting for the evidence; that is, that the expansion of firms is halted not by raising costs but by the limitation of demand. Sraffa's insight, "by showing how limited is the domain of applicability of perfect competition, and by breaking the spell, so to speak of the perfectly elastic demand that faces the perfect competitor" (Newman and Vassilakis, 1988, p. 41), carried with it a radical change of perspective.

19.3   RICHARD KAHN

The first to pursue the line of research opened by Sraffa was Kahn in his fellow-ship dissertation, *The Economics of the Short Period*, which was written between October 1928 and December 1929, but remained unpublished in English until 1989. The reason Kahn gave for abandoning the hypothesis of perfect competition was that the Marshallian–Pigouvian apparatus could not account for a fact observed during the Great Depression of the 1920s: that firms could earn a positive profit while working below capacity. If market conditions were perfectly competitive it would follow that, when price was greater than average cost, firms would be producing up to capacity output; when price fell below average cost, they should close down. On the contrary, in the 1920s Depression, when demand fell heavily, firms in the cotton and coal industries used "to close down the whole plant on some days and to work the whole plant a full shift on other days" (Kahn, 1989, p. 57.)

The explanation of this behavior was sought by Kahn in the shape of their prime cost curve, reflecting the technical method with which output could be varied in the short period. When the plant and machinery could not be altered, as is the case in the short period, the relevant segment of the marginal cost curve is horizontal, which is then equal to constant average prime cost until full capacity is reached, when it becomes infinite. The shape of the prime cost curve – a reverse L – and the evidence of short-time working are a serious challenge to the prediction that whenever the price exceeds the average cost curve, firms produce at full capacity level of output. If this were so, only inefficient firms would be working below capacity; but this went against the evidence that showed that short-time working was a consistent behavior across all firms in the 1920s. Moreover, a constant marginal cost curve loses its significance as a determinant of output when faced by a perfectly horizontal demand curve, as is the case in perfect competition. Kahn found the solution by assuming that each firm was in fact facing a down-sloping demand curve and that competition was in fact "imperfect."

The equilibrium level of output and price is then determined not, as in perfect competition, by the equality of price and marginal cost, but as in monopoly by the product of output and the difference between price and average prime cost, as far as output is concerned, and on the basis of elasticity of demand as far as price is concerned. Kahn resorted here to the standard definition of Marshall's "maximum monopoly net revenue" (Marshall, 1964, p. 397) – the point at which the difference between the monopolist supply price and demand price times output is a maximum – to determine the equilibrium level of output and price, and provided an ingenious method of measuring market imperfection (Marcuzzo, 1994, pp. 30–1). At the time the dissertation was written, marginal revenue remained an unnamed concept.

By introducing the imperfection of the market, Kahn was able to explain why at low levels of demand price does not fall to marginal cost, and why the equilibrium level of output is at less than full capacity.

19.4   JOAN ROBINSON

As in the case of Kahn's dissertation, the starting point of the *Economics of Imperfect Competition* is Sraffa's proposal "to re-write the theory of value, starting from the conception of the firm as a monopolist" (J. Robinson, 1969, p. 6); the aim of the book was to extend the marginal technique, enriched by the discovery of the new concept of "marginal revenue," to all market forms and to provide an answer to the challenge posed by Sraffa in questioning the consistency of the Marshall–Pigou apparatus.

The approach taken by Joan Robinson was to apply the technique based on average and marginal curves, incorporating various cost and demand conditions of commodities and factors of production, to all market forms. Perfect competition becomes a special case in a general theory of competition, allowing for various degrees of substitution and preferences on the part of consumers as captured by the value of the elasticity of demand for the firm. Perfect competition is then defined as a market condition characterized by a perfectly horizontal demand curve; that is, with infinite elasticity. On the supply side, various assumptions are allowed for in the behavior of costs, corresponding to increasing, decreasing, and constant cost cases. In fact, in an imperfect market, namely with a down-sloping demand curve facing each firm, *any* assumption about the shape of the marginal cost curve provides for the determinacy of equilibrium.

Full equilibrium conditions for any given industry are derived in both a perfect and an imperfect market: "An industry is said to be in full equilibrium when there is no tendency for the number of firms to alter. The profits earned by the firms in it are then normal" (J. Robinson, 1969, p. 93). Since profits are normal when price (average revenue, AR) is equal to average cost (AC) and firms are in individual equilibrium when marginal revenue (MR) equals marginal cost (MC), it follows that full equilibrium requires the double condition that MR = MC and AR = AC.

Proof is then given that the "double condition" can only be fulfilled when the individual demand curve of the firm is tangent to its average cost curve. Hicks neatly summarizes the main point: "Since the demand curve is downward sloping, the average curve must also be downward sloping at the equilibrium point. Equilibrium under monopolistic competition is only possible when average costs are diminishing; that is to say, the equilibrium output of a firm will be less than the output which would give minimum average costs – the output which would actually be reached under conditions of perfect competition" (Hicks, 1935, p. 140).

Therefore, comparison between equilibrium conditions of perfect and imperfect competition had a dismal welfare implication: in the former case marginal and average cost are equal at the point at which average cost is at a minimum, while in the latter case "the double condition of equilibrium can only be fulfilled for some output at which average cost is falling. The firms will therefore be of less than optimum size when profits are normal" (J. Robinson, 1969, p. 97).

19.5 KAHN VERSUS SRAFFA

With the change in perspective from seeing firms as identical and competing in a unified market to seeing them as single monopolies, each one with its individual market, the question arose as to whether "a world of monopolies" would imply different results as far as the determination of the equilibrium price was concerned. In other words, would price in an imperfect market be different from price in the case of monopoly?

This issue was at the heart of the contrast between Sraffa's approach and that of Kahn and Robinson. Kahn declared that there was "a serious error in Sraffa's exposition [in the 1926 article] since it implied that under conditions of uniformity among firms, provided that the market is slightly imperfect, the magnitude of the imperfection is irrelevant to the equilibrium price" (Sraffa, 1926, p. 549; Kahn, 1989, p. 94).

On the contrary, Kahn claimed that "a reduction of the amount of imperfection causes – in the short run at any rate – a fall in price and in profits" (Kahn, 1989, p. 94). He had reached this conclusion on the basis of an analysis of the individual demand curve facing each seller, indicating what the entrepreneur imagines to be the relation between his price and his output. The assumptions – "that are in the mind of the business man when he maximises his profit" (Kahn, 1989, p. 100) – are that when he alters his price or output, either the prices or outputs of the other firms remain constant, or they will react by varying their prices and outputs. In all three cases, Kahn argued, the aggregate demand curve of an industry in the hands of a single monopolist is steeper than the demand curve facing each in an oligopolistic industry. It therefore follows that "under conditions of polypoly the equilibrium price is less than under conditions of monopoly" (Kahn, 1989, p. 117), contrary to Sraffa's assertion.

Kahn claimed that Sraffa had acknowledged "the force of my [Kahn's] objection to his argument" (Kahn, 1989, p. 95). The extant evidence is not, however, to this effect. In the Lecture Notes of the course on Advanced Theory of Value, which Sraffa gave in Cambridge in 1928–31, in a note, added after Sraffa had read Kahn's dissertation, he says:

> To say that in imperfect competition price is always less than in monopoly, it means to fall into the [. . .] error, which is based on assumption that problem is independent of the relation between individual and collective elasticity of D[emand]. The point is that I assume a slight, but finite, degree of imperfection (elasticity of demand not infinite). But in this case, with the rise in prices, the elasticity decreases all the time, without limit. (see Marcuzzo, 2001, pp. 88–9)

Kahn based his analysis on conjectural demand curves whose slopes embody various assumptions made by each firm about the behavior of other firms within the industry. A change in price by any one firm does not leave the slope of the demand curves of all the other firms unchanged, because account is taken of the reactions of competitors. In general, when there is only one producer (as in monopoly), its demand curve is steeper than when there are many producers (as in oligopoly), because in that case the behavior of the other firms is not taken into account. Since the equilibrium price, for a given supply curve, is determined by the slope of the demand curve, it follows that price is higher in monopoly than in oligopoly.

On the contrary, Sraffa's argument is based on the degree of consumer preferences as shown by the value of the market elasticity of demand. Following an increase in price by one firm, demands for all firms are raised. Since the prices of substitutes go up, each buyer is willing to pay a higher price for the product of the firm from which he prefers to buy (Sraffa, 1926, p. 547). The limit to the price increase is given by the loss of customers to the market, not to the individual firm, since customers will return to the preferred firm when the other firms have also raised their price. Thus for Sraffa, unlike Kahn, "for an industry consisting of firms which are all similar and similarly situated" (Sraffa, 1926, p. 547) there is no reason why the price corresponding to the Marshall's "maximum monopoly revenue" should be different in monopoly and in oligopoly.

19.6   Sraffa versus Kahn and Robinson

As is well known, Sraffa lost interest in imperfect competition and soon abandoned the field, giving rise to much speculation. It has, for instance, been maintained that Sraffa's "profound objective" was to rid the analysis of all kind of subjective and mental determinants; it would have been the awareness that dealing with an imperfect market "renders the mental determinants of equilibrium unavoidable" (Dardi, 2000, p. 131) that estranged him from the entire problem. This hypothesis is not, it seems to me, ultimately convincing, since we have other examples of Sraffa's readiness to describe market behavior in terms of beliefs and expectations. Actually, Sraffa was opposed to the neoclassical representation of behavior in terms of demand and supply curves, based on preferences and utility, scarcity, and factors of production, and he favored an approach – such as that of the classical political economists – which anchored economic behavior in the condition of production, the pursuit of self-interest by agents, and an understanding of competition as a force leading to uniformity of the rate of profit (Clifton, 1977). It was the demand (and supply) functions, and their usage in the determination of equilibrium within a partial approach framework, to which Sraffa was objecting. Similarly, in the case of Keynes's theory of the liquidity preference, he was objecting not to taking into consideration individuals' preferences and convictions, but to representing them in the shape of a demand for money function.

Sraffa's estrangement from the theory of imperfect competition had more to do with his rejection of the theory that underpinned it than any refusal to deal with motivations and interactions among economic agents (Marcuzzo, 2001).

19.7 MICHAL KALECKI

Did working with the assumption of imperfect competition entail implications regarding the representation of the economic system as a whole? It is well known that Keynes remained unimpressed by the imperfect competition revolution he was witnessing, and worked his way through *The General Theory* without taking much notice of it; neither Kahn nor Joan Robinson made any attempt to bridge the two major events in Cambridge economics in the 1930s. In fact, it was Kalecki who "brought imperfect competition in touch with the theory of employment" (J. Robinson, 1969, p. viii) and who, in the second half of the 1930s, developed an approach based on imperfect perfect competition within a macroeconomic analysis of the economic system.

When Kalecki arrived in England in 1936 he had already worked with the imperfect competition assumption in his analysis of cartels in Poland and elsewhere (Sawyer, 2001, p. 246). At the end of 1937 he moved to Cambridge and became an active participant in Sraffa's Research Students seminar. Also, for two years he was involved in the Cambridge *Research Scheme of the National Institute of Economic and Social Research into Prime Costs, Proceeds and Output* (which was set up to keep him in Cambridge). Unfortunately, his results came in for very critical comments from Kahn and Joan Robinson, who objected in particular to his "degree of monopoly" concept: "[it] is not a thing in itself . . . [therefore] to say that there has been a 'change in the degree of monopoly' is never a final account of what has happened, and it is often unreasonable to expect a constant degree of monopoly in the face of other changes . . ." (R. F. Kahn's papers, King's College Archives, file 5/1). This criticism, while probably inducing Kalecki to resign from his Cambridge job, did not stop him from dedicating two articles (Kalecki, 1938, 1940) to working out the concept of the degree of monopoly within a macroeconomic framework, which did not rely on the assumption of free competition.

First, assuming that prices are formed by equating marginal cost to marginal revenue, market imperfection is defined by the elasticity of demand for the product of each firm as a function of the ratio between the price charged by the individual firm and the average price of the industry (an average of the prices charged by each firm, weighted according to their respective outputs). The degree of market imperfection is constant if, for each individual firm, the elasticity of demand is correlated solely with its price; otherwise, the degree of market imperfection varies.

Kalecki then drops the assumption that firms fix prices according to the equality of marginal cost and marginal revenue and examines the case of oligopoly. This case arises when the firm sets the price at a point at which marginal revenue is greater than marginal cost. The price is set at this particular level because each firm knows that a lower price would induce the rival firms to lower their prices, while a higher price would not make them raise it. Thus, in any given market, the degree of oligopoly is measured by the ratio of marginal revenue to marginal cost, which is, in general, greater than one (Kalecki, 1940).

Kalecki was highly original, although at the cost of simplification, in producing a methodology to study the *aggregate* effects of price policy by firms in a macro-economic representation of the economic system (Marcuzzo, 1996, pp. 11–12). Last but not least, he could explain why there need not be an inverse relationship between real wages and unemployment, forcing Keynes to acknowledge the point (Keynes, 1973, pp. 409 ff.).

19.8   Edward Chamberlin

Much has been said about the curious coincidence of two books bearing almost the same title and dealing with almost the same topic being published in the same year in the two Cambridges, on either side of the Atlantic (Samuelson, 1967). Chamberlin's *Theory of Monopolistic Competition* (1933), however, as repeatedly claimed by its author, was a book that did not draw its inspiration from Sraffa's criticism of the Marshallian value theory, nor was it concerned with extending marginal analysis to all market forms. It was the observation of what was actually happening in the real world that pointed the way to abandoning any idea of identical firms working in homogeneous markets. Diversity and nonuniformity of behavior was the rule, and this needed to be brought together in a new vision of the market.

Chamberlin's analysis is based on the recognition that each seller is a monopolist in the sense of having "complete control over the supply of a *distinguishable* product." Yet, like any monopolist, each seller faces substitutes for his product; therefore competition, rather than being pure or perfect, should be conceived as monopolistic. Furthermore, the entry or exit of sellers "carries with it an expansion or contraction in the number of *products* in the whole system instead of merely a change in the number of producers of some given product [. . .] Imperfection, although it may be made to include more by definition, has the strong connotation of *general* 'frictions', such as imperfect knowledge, irrationality or immobility, exerting an influence rather evenly over the entire market. But with the recognition of a different product and market for each seller presumptions as to uniformity in *any* sense disappear, and we have diversity . . ." (Chamberlin, 1961, pp. 526–7).

While in Joan Robinson's *Economics of Imperfect Competition* the key position is held by the industry, in Chamberlin's *Monopolistic Competition* the key position is held by groups, where each seller has a monopoly of his own distinguishable product and various types of group relationships between sellers are envisaged. Unlike Joan Robinson, who took preferences to be in the "minds of consumers," Chamberlin saw product heterogeneity as a "competitive weapon" (O'Brien, 1983, p. 35) actively used by sellers to differentiate their products.

This second strand of thought of the imperfect competition revolution is centered not so much on "irrational" consumers' preferences, or on decreasing costs, as on the idea of groups of sellers exploiting differences and diversity in their products to gain market power at each other's expense. Many of the analytic results are similar to those produced by Joan Robinson, but Chamberlin's analysis tries to escape the static, partial equilibrium framework without, however, succeeding in satisfactorily addressing the dynamic, strategic interdependence issues posed by oligopoly.

19.9 ROBERT TRIFFIN

Only a few years afterwards Triffin, in his Ph.D. thesis written under Chamberlin's supervision, was able to set up the agenda, if not the solution, posed by the theory of oligopoly as sketched out by Chamberlin.

He pointed out that the criterion for monopoly and competition is to be found in the nature of the relationship between firms, rather than in the situation characteristic of each firm as represented by the slope of its demand curve. This is why the approach taken by Chamberlin, who considers the set of reactions within a group of firms, is superior to that of Joan Robinson, who frames her analysis of identical firms within a partial equilibrium approach. In fact, in her approach changes in production by other firms in the industry are not taken into the picture, "but only entry or exit of firms and arbitrary shifts in the total demand for the commodity turned out by the industry" (Triffin, 1940, p. 44).

However, Triffin saw two aspects of the theory of imperfect competition as developed by Chamberlin and Robinson as equally unsatisfactory: (1) the reliance on ill defined concepts such as "group" or "industry," rather than a focus on the interdependence of firms; and (2) the assumption that the subjective demand curve, which expresses the expectations of the producers as to the relationship between the price they charge and the quantity the market will buy, is also an objective demand curve – "embodying the actual reactions of the market" (Triffin, 1940, p. 63).

For Triffin, the central concept is the elasticity of substitution between two products; when its value is not infinite, there is scope for an independent price policy by the producers of these two commodities and the question to be addressed becomes that of the general competitiveness between goods. "Only in the case of pure competition does the grouping of firms into one industry reduce to a more simple and more definite type of behaviour and reactions of sellers" (Triffin, 1940, p. 88).

In the work of Triffin, imperfect competition is rooted in the analysis of strategic behavior and the study of interdependence between firms. He rejected the classification of different forms of competition (pure or perfect, monopolistic or imperfect) based on the number of firms within a group or industry and on the differentiation of or absence of differentiation between the products of those firms, stressing the point that forms of competitions are a matter of relations between sellers. The difficulty in the treatment of forms of competition other than pure or perfect arises not only from the influence of one firm upon other firms, but also from the chain reactions of other firms affecting the firm.

In conclusion, for Triffin, the perfect elasticity of the demand curve is not a good test for perfect competition. The essential element in the definition is "the perfect dependence of the firm's sales upon the price charged by other sellers . . . plus the inability of the firm to influence the price decision of these sellers" (p. 138).

19.10 THE LEGACY

The strand of the theory of imperfect competition that originated in Cambridge, England, was an attack on the Marshallian cost and demand curves launched by Sraffa in his 1925 and 1926 articles on the ground of lack of consistency and realism. In the work done first by Richard Kahn and then by Joan Robinson, imperfect competition was a means to supplement the Marshallian approach rather than a reason to discard it. Perfect competition was shown to be a special case, rather than the general case prevailing in actual markets, when supply and demand curves have a particular shape; but the whole marginal apparatus, embodied in the average and marginal curves, was reinstated against Sraffa's criticism, in response to which particular assumptions and *ad hoc* definitions were fabricated.

Kalecki's attempt to incorporate market imperfection into a macroeconomic analysis of the system in order to integrate firms' behavior in a more realistic theory of price was only partially successful, but showed how to give more weight to effective demand, rather than to real wages, in determining the level of employment.

Chamberlin's contribution did not grow in that milieu; its main argument rested on product differentiation and strategic behavior as central to the representation of market. Triffin clarified the set of issues that should be tackled if a satisfactory theory of oligopoly within a general equilibrium framework was to be developed.

However, the "first" imperfect competition revolution did not outgrow into an alternative research program, nor did it seriously undermine the perfect-competition approach to economics. Nevertheless, the imperfect competition revolution jeopardized the argument that competition results in economic efficiency, shaking confidence in markets as the best means to allocate resources and allowing for intervention and institutional changes.

The reaction came, in the late 1940s and early 1950s, from several Chicago-based scholars – in the main, Milton Friedman and George Stigler (Keppler, 1994, 1998) – who formulated criticisms of monopolistic competition theory arguing against the claim that it was a more realistic model of the actual economy. The argument was that the value of a theory does not lie in the realism of its assumptions, but in the realism of its predictions. An example is provided not only by the famous 1949 article by Stigler in which he denounced imperfect competition as lacking generality and being empirically empty, but also in his attack on Paul Sweezy's work on the kinked demand curve (Sutton, 1989; Freedman, 1995).

The first imperfect competition revolution was a reaction against the lack of realism of the perfect competition assumption but, ironically, was attacked for its inability to stand up to the test of its predictions. It has been aptly said that "The effect (and surely the purpose) of Friedman's 1953 essay [Friedman, 1953] was to save the theory of value and distribution as logically consistent and widely applicable central core of economic theory and basis for applied economics" (Moss, 1984, p. 316).

Meanwhile, important articles and books based on market forms other than perfect competition continued to be written, but the main body of doctrine seemed to remain unscathed. Samuelson's defense of imperfect competition as a true "revolution" is set against this background: "Chamberlin, Sraffa, Robinson and their contemporaries have led economics into a new land from which their critics will never evict us" (Samuelson, 1967, p. 138).

In recent years, however, we have witnessed the rise of a "second" imperfect competition in modern micro- and macromodels, as a way of contrasting and enriching the basic perfect competition models (see Dixon and Rankin, 1994; Gabszewicz and Thisse, 2000). Emphasis has been put on various forms of price rigidities, accounted for by information asymmetries and limited rationality, acknowledging that some markets do not exist – or if they do, that the agents lack the perfect information and perfect knowledge to make them work. While some reservations are held against this New Keynesian way of attempting to contrast the New Classical reinstatement of free-market economics, there now seems to be a greater consensus than in the past that market forces should be seen as limited, partial, and imperfect in their working. Moreover, an alternative approach to the analysis of markets and to modeling interactions among various types of agents has been developed in game theory, which does not rely on the distinction between perfect and imperfect competition. It is widely held that this approach is best suited to deal with oligopoly and strategic behavior, and is capable of solving many of the difficult issues involved in these matters.

The question then arises as to what is the real legacy of the first imperfect competition revolution. Does the departure from the basic model in the forms of allowance for consumers' preferences, product differentiation, and strategic behavior in decision-making provide a real alternative to the case of perfect competition? Or is it, rather – as Sraffa probably meant it – that room has been made for a different price theory, which involves a different meaning of competition? The crux of the matter lies in the choice of either of the two diverging lines of research – in representing strategic decisions of agents or in developing a differently based theory of prices – which resulted from the "first" imperfect competition revolution.

I personally share the opinion expressed by a leading player in the theory of oligopoly that we should "try to identify such objective elements as may, in real situations, serve as basis for price determination. Otherwise, we would run the danger of remaining in the fantastic world of reaction curves and conjectural variations – a world where everything might and nothing need happen" (Sylos Labini, 1969, p. 34).

Bibliography

Cassells, J. M. 1937: Monopolistic competition and economic realism. *Canadian Journal of Economics*, 3(3), 376–93.

Chamberlin, E. H. 1933: *The Theory of Monopolistic Competition*. Cambridge, MA: Harvard University Press.

—— 1961: The origin and early development of monopolistic competition theory. *Quarterly Journal of Economics*, 74(4), 515–43.

Clifton, J. A. 1977: Competition and the evolution of the capitalist mode of production. *Cambridge Journal of Economics*, 1(2), 137–51.

Dardi, M. 2000: Why did Sraffa lose interest in imperfect competition? In R. Marchionatti and T. Cozzi (eds.), *Piero Sraffa's Political Economy. A Centenary Estimate*. London: Routledge.

Dixon, H. D. and Rankin, N. 1994: Imperfect competition and macroeconomics. *Oxford Economic Papers*, 46(2), 171–99.

Freedman, C. 1995: The economist as mythmaker – Stigler's kinky transformation. *Journal of Economic Issues*, 29(1), 175–209.

Friedman, M. 1953: The methodology of positive economics. In *Essays in Positive Economics*. Chicago: The University of Chicago Press.

Gabszewicz, J. J. and Thisse, J. F. 2000: Microeconomics theories of imperfect competition. *Cahiers d'Économie Politique*, 37, 47–99.

Hicks, J. R. 1935: Annual survey of economic theory: the theory of monopoly. *Econometrica*, 3(1), 1–20.

Kahn, R. F. 1952: Review of Oxford studies in prices mechanism. *Economic Journal*, 62(245), 119–30.

—— 1989: *The Economics of the Short Period*. London: Macmillan.

Kalecki, M. 1938: The determinants of distribution of the national income. *Econometrica*, 6(2), 97–112.

—— 1940: The supply curve of an industry under imperfect competition. *Review of Economic Studies*, 7(1), 91–122.

Keppler, J. H. 1994: *Monopolistic Competition Theory. Origins, Results and Implications*. Baltimore, MD: The Johns Hopkins University Press.

—— 1998: The genesis of "positive economics" and the rejection of monopolistic competition theory: a methodological debate. *Cambridge Journal of Economics*, 22(3), 261–76.

Keynes, J. M. 1973: Relative movements of real wages and output. Reprinted in D. Moggridge (ed.), *The Collected Writings of John Maynard Keynes*, vol. VII. London: Macmillan.

Marcuzzo, M. C. 1994: R. F. Kahn and imperfect competition. *Cambridge Journal of Economics*, 18(1), 25–40.

—— 1996: Alternative microeconomic foundations for macroeconomics: the controversy over the L-shaped cost curve revisited. *Review of Political Economy*, 8(1), 7–22.

—— 2001: Sraffa and Cambridge economics, 1928–1931. In R. Marchionatti and T. Cozzi (eds.), *Piero Sraffa's Political Economy: A Centenary Estimate*. London: Routledge.

Marshall, A. 1964: *Principles of Economics*, 8th edn. London: Macmillan.

Moss, S. 1984: The history of the theory of the firm from Marshall to Robinson and Chamberlin: the source of positivism in economics. *Economica*, 51(203), 307–18.

Newman, P. and Vassilakis, P. 1988: Sraffa and imperfect competition. *Cambridge Journal of Economics*, 12(1), 37–42.

O'Brien, D. P. 1983: Research programmes in competitive structure. *Journal of Economic Studies*, 10(4), 29–51.

Rheinwald, T. P. 1977: The genesis of Chamberlinian monopolistic competition. *History of Political Economy*, 9(4), 522–34.

Robinson, A. 1950: The pricing of manufactured products. *Economic Journal*, 60(241), 771–80.

Robinson, J. 1969: *The Economics of Imperfect Competition*, 2nd edn. London: Macmillan.

Samuelson, P. A. 1967: *The Monopolistic Competition Revolution*. In R. E. Kuenne (ed.), *Monopolistic Competition Theory: Studies in Impact*. New York: Wiley.

—— 1994: Richard Kahn: his welfare economics and lifetime achievement. *Cambridge Journal of Economics*, 18(1), 55–72.

Sawyer, M. 2001: Kalecki on imperfect competition, inflation and money. *Cambridge Journal of Economics*, 25(2), 245–61.

Sraffa, P. 1925: Sulle relazioni di costo e di quantità prodotta. *Annali di Economia*, II, 277–327.

—— 1926: The laws of returns under competitive conditions. *Economic Journal*, 36(144), 535–50.

Stigler, J. 1949: Monopolistic competition in retrospect. In *Five Lectures on Economic Problems*, London: Longman, 12–24.

Sutton, J. 1989: Is imperfect competition empirically empty? In G. R. Feiwel (ed.), *The Economics of Imperfect Competition and Employment*. London: Macmillan.

Sylos Labini, P. 1969: *Oligopoly and Technical Progress*, 2nd edn. Cambridge, MA: Harvard University Press.

Triffin, R. 1940: *Monopolistic Competition and General Equilibrium Theory*. Cambridge, MA: Harvard University Press.

Whitaker, J. K. 1989: The Cambridge background to imperfect competition. In G. F. Feiwel (ed.), *The Economics of Imperfect Competition and Employment. Joan Robinson and Beyond*. London: Macmillan.

CHAPTER TWENTY

The Stabilization of Price Theory, 1920–1955

Roger E. Backhouse

20.1 THE NEOCLASSICAL SYNTHESIS IN HISTORICAL PERSPECTIVE

In 1955, Paul Samuelson introduced the term "neoclassical synthesis" into his textbook:

> We shall again and again meet in later chapters what is called the "neoclassical synthesis." According to this: if modern economics does its task so well that unemployment and inflation are substantially banished from democratic societies, then its importance will wither away and the traditional economics (whose concern is the *wise* allocation of fully employed resources) will really come into its own – almost for the first time. (Samuelson, 1955, p. 11)

In this passage, Samuelson draws a contrast between the Keynesian theory of income determination, described simply as "modern economics," and "traditional" microeconomics. Samuelson's rhetoric concerning the neoclassical synthesis made it clear that it was one of the central points, if not the central point, that he wanted his readers to learn. Readers were told that it was important to "insist" on it (p. 659). Nations were everywhere discovering that it worked (p. 624) and problems of international economics could be solved if the world mastered it (p. 676). He even expressed gratitude that the Russians had not discovered it (p. 733).

The aspect of the neoclassical synthesis that has received most attention is the implied relationship between macroeconomics and microeconomics, and Samuelson's role in propagating the Keynesian revolution. Like Alfred Marshall before him, Samuelson clearly wanted to establish the scientific credentials of economics and one way to do this was to emphasize consensus within the profession and continuity with the past. This explains his frequent use of adjectives such as "traditional" and "classical." It is in this vein that he claimed that "neoclassical economics," namely the combination of "whatever is valuable in the older economics" and "modern theories of income determination," was "accepted in its broad outlines by all but about 5 per cent of extreme left-wing and right-wing writers" (Samuelson, 1955, p. 212). It is, therefore, hardly surprising that he presented microeconomics as though it were uncontroversial and settled.

One of the remarkable features of Samuelson's treatment of price theory is that, in complete contrast to the way he treated the theory of income determination, he played down the modernity of the theory that he was describing. He offered only minor hints that price theory had changed. For example, he wrote of the "kernel of truth in the older economics" having been separated from the "chaff of misleading applications" and about preserving "whatever is valuable" in the older economics (Samuelson, 1955, pp. 11, 212). The picture is one of older theories having been polished and refined, without any indication that this refinement might have involved a radical transformation of the subject.

It would have been much harder to justify such a claim in or around 1920. Between the 1920s and the 1950s, price theory had stabilized in the sense that a consensus had become established. However, this stabilization involved a series of intense controversies over issues that went to the heart of the subject. Furthermore, in all cases important economists remained unconvinced about the outcome. It is a picture with close parallels to what happened in macroeconomics (see Backhouse, 1985, chs. 16, 26; or Laidler, 1999). It is misleading to present the process as just a refinement or perfection of earlier theory. To see this, consider the elements on which the price theory of the neoclassical synthesis rested:

1 The organizing principle was competitive equilibrium of demand and supply. Competition was understood as the inability of individual agents to influence market price combined, in the long run, with freedom of entry and exit.
2 Demand was determined by consumers, who chose their most preferred bundle of goods, subject to their budget constraint. Preferences were assumed to exhibit nonsatiation, transitivity, and convexity. If a utility function was used, it was understood as a purely ordinal representation of preferences.
3 Firms were assumed to behave as if they maximized profit subject to a production function and the prices of factors and products.
4 Where problems clearly involved noncompetitive behavior, imperfections of competition were understood as violations of the price-taking assumption: agents were able to influence prices in the markets in which they were trading.
5 Welfare functions should be individualistic, containing as arguments the utilities (in the sense described above) of individual consumers. Given the absence of scientific grounds for comparing different individuals' utilities, the main welfare criterion was Pareto-efficiency or Pareto-optimality (the two terms being used interchangeably).

These assumptions cover several types of theory: "highbrow" theories used in the literature on proofs of the existence, uniqueness, and stability of general competitive equilibrium, as well as "lowbrow" theories used in introductory textbooks. They encompass the Chicago, MIT, and Arrow–Debreu versions of neoclassical economics (for example, as distinguished in Hands and Mirowski, 1998). Samuelson's textbook brilliantly integrated this diversity of theories, along with Keynesian macroeconomics, into an apparently seamless whole.

20.2   CONSUMERS AND DEMAND

In the 1920s, the idea that consumer behavior should be viewed as involving the maximization of utility subject to a budget constraint, with demands being determined by the relevant first-order conditions, was widely accepted. There was, however, no consensus on the way this should be interpreted. The "purest" approach was represented by Pareto. He used terms such as "pleasure," "utility," and his preferred term "ophelimity" but he made it clear that, though useful for exposition, they were not necessary to construct the theory (Pareto, 1971 [1906], p. 112). The theory rested on "the determination of the quantities of goods which constitute combinations between which the individual is indifferent" (p. 113). No metaphysical entity was required. He accepted Fisher's (1892) demonstration that sets of indifference curves could not, in general, be integrated to obtain utility functions. This was the mathematical counterpart of his view that terms such as "utility" were inessential to the theory.

In an article that was not widely cited until the 1930s, Slutsky claimed that the merit of Pareto's theory was "its purely formal character and its complete independence of all psychological and philosophical hypotheses" (1953 [1915], p. 28). He emphasized that, on Pareto's definition, there was "[no] *point of contact whatsoever* between economics and psychology" (ibid., emphasis in original). The theory was based solely on observations of behavior, or "facts of economic conduct" (1953 [1915], p. 54). He used it to derive the relationships between prices, quantities, and income. Of particular importance was what has come to be known as the Slutsky symmetry condition: that, if consumers are maximizing utility subject to a budget constraint,

> The residual variability of the j-th good in the case of a compensated variation of the price p_i is equal to the residual variability of the i-th good in the case of a compensated variation of the price p_j. (Slutsky, 1953 [1915], p. 43)

However, having built up his theory on this basis, Slutsky speculated on the implications of going beyond this, to assume that second derivatives of the utility function were negative. Such an assumption would require "internal evidence" relating to the "consciousness of economic conduct," or the "psychological aspect of utility" (1953 [1915], pp. 54–6). Laws derived on this basis would need to be tested experimentally. Although Slutsky considered this valuable, it would be valuable for the psychic and moral sciences rather than for the economic. In short, economics did not require investigation of the psychological aspects of utility (for further discussion of utility theory up to and including Slutsky, see Stigler, 1950).

Other economists attached much more importance to the psychological aspect of utility. Wicksell (1934 [1918], p. 221), in a critique of Cassel, made it clear that the psychological interpretation of utility was important in providing an explanation of *why* things were objects of demand. The economist who dispensed with psychology was like a stockbroker who dealt in railway stocks without knowing what a railway was. This was also the attitude of the Cambridge school. Although they had moved away from nineteenth-century utilitarianism, which viewed behavior in terms of pleasure and pain, they viewed the utility of goods as indicating their ability to satisfy wants (the relationship of their view to psychological hedonism is clearly discussed in Pigou, 1903, pp. 67–8). Wants provided the "motor-force" or "incentive to action" (Marshall, 1920 [1890], p. 13). Psychology, and hence utility, described the cause of behavior. This was stated even more explicitly by Pigou, who argued that "satisfactions and dissatisfactions" affected behavior through "desires and aversions" (Pigou, 1932 [1920], p. 23). Utility measures the intensity of desire.

A further reason why the Cambridge school attached importance to the psychological interpretation of utility was that they believed this allowed them to draw conclusions about welfare. Marshall's welfare economics was based on the concept of consumers' surplus, and to interpret this as a measure of welfare he needed to talk about the marginal utility of money. He appeared to have no hesitation in saying that a shilling might yield greater satisfaction to the same person at different times, or greater satisfaction to a poor person than to a rich one (Marshall, 1920 [1890], p. 15). For Pigou, the concept of welfare, and hence the psychological interpretation of utility, was even more important. Economics was about welfare, which had to be measured. Psychology provided the link between behavior and welfare.

At the other end of the spectrum were economists who wanted to dispense with utility altogether. Cassel (1932 [1923], p. 49) tried to replace the theory of value with a theory of pricing. The pure theory of marginal utility was superfluous and failed to extend our knowledge of actual processes (1932 [1923], p. 81). This was also the view of Moore (1914, pp. 66–7), who argued for statistical demand curves derived from regression analysis, and Mitchell (1925, pp. 4–5), who believed that economists would lose interest in nonquantitative models of behavior. In rejecting the idea of consumers who have ready-made scales of bid and offer prices, Mitchell will have been influenced by Veblen's lambasting of the notion that tastes could be taken as exogenous.

These examples illustrate the variety of interpretations of utility theory that existed around 1920. Other theories could be added to the list, such as Fetter's use of instinct-impulse psychology or Wieser's "Austrian" theory of value (see Mitchell, 1969). Marshall's was perhaps the most widely held approach, but there was no consensus on how consumers' behavior should be analyzed.

This situation began to change in the 1920s and 1930s as economists increasingly moved away from psychological interpretations of utility. At the London

School of Economics, Robbins (1932) attacked Marshallian theory, arguing that there was no scientific basis for the value judgments on which measurable utility rested. His younger colleagues, Hicks and Allen (1934), took up this program, taking Pareto as their starting point (see Hicks, 1983, ch. 31). Pareto had shown that it was possible to go from observable conduct to a scale of preferences, but it was not possible to go from there to a particular utility function. Hicks and Allen (1934, p. 26) argued that this meant that the subjective theory of value was transformed into "a general logic of choice." Pareto had realized this, but had not carried through the project of completely reworking the theory of value to take account of it. Hicks and Allen saw this as their task. They reformulated the theory of the consumer in terms of marginal rates of substitution and used the theory to analyze the relationship between preferences, income, and demand. After publishing this work, they discovered Slutsky's article, finding that it anticipated some of their results. Allen (1936, p. 127) argued that, though Slutsky's results were correct, his method (of using a utility function) could lead to misleading results "in the hands of a less sure mathematician."

Robbins (1932, p. 99) was skeptical about whether it would ever be possible to establish quantitative, statistical laws of demand and supply. In contrast, Henry Schultz set up a statistical laboratory in Chicago to help establish such laws. He was a student of Henry Moore, who was known for his discovery of a positively sloped demand curve for pig iron (Moore, 1914) which, he claimed, represented a new type of dynamic demand curve, relevant to the cycle (see Mirowski, 1990; Morgan, 1990, pp. 26–34, 143–5). Schultz carried on this work, but whereas Moore had rejected Marshallian theory, Schultz (1925, 1927b) used Marshall's elasticities of demand and supply as the framework for his statistical analysis.

However, although he used supply and demand analysis, Schultz came to reject the psychology on which the Cambridge economists considered it to rest. He objected to the notion that a change in one price should be seen as "causing" a change in the price of another commodity (Schultz, 1927a, p, 702): by ruling out interdependence of prices, it made a "realistic" treatment of some problems impossible. He referred to the "epoch-making discoveries of Walras and Pareto" (Schultz, 1927a, p. 703). These, however, were only static and needed to be made dynamic. The recent work of Moore (1925, 1926) and Roos (1927) had done this. The following year, Schultz made the methodology underlying his rejection of psychological theories clear:

> The formulas of geometry enable us to compute distances, areas and volumes; the formulas of economics have no such heuristic properties. This is due primarily to the fact that most economic laws or principles are expressed in terms of the *properties* of things or persons rather than in terms of operations. Thus we define "utility" as the *property* which a thing has to satisfy a want, and we talk of "keeping other things constant" without specifying the mental or physical operations by which this may be done. (Schultz, 1928, p. 647)

He went on to quote Percy Bridgman's view that "If a specific question has meaning, it must be possible to find operations by which an answer may be given to it" (Schultz, 1928, pp. 647–8). Economics could become an experimental science only by confining itself to concepts that could be made operational. Utility was superfluous.

Schultz also pointed out that demands could come from producers as well as consumers, and in this case there was no reason why demand curves should slope downwards. That was why, with the exception of Moore, economists had confined their statistical studies to the demand for foodstuffs. Given these interests, it is hardly surprising that Schultz took an interest in an article, published in the *Journal of Political Economy* under his editorship, by Hotelling (1932). Hotelling explored three models of demand. One of them was a model of entrepreneurs' demands, derived from maximization of net profit, $u(p_1, p_2, \ldots p_n) - p_1 q_1 - p_2 q_2 \ldots p_n q_n$, where u denoted sales revenue and the p's and q's the prices and quantities of n goods. He showed that the condition under which the function $u(.)$ could be obtained from observations of prices and quantities was that the cross-partial derivatives relating any pair of goods must be equal: that the effect of the price of good i on the quantity of good j must equal the effect of the price of good j on the quantity of good i. This can be called the Hotelling symmetry condition. Although it related to entrepreneurial demands, it would apply to consumers' demands if the marginal utility of income were constant, as might be the case when aggregating over individuals. This condition could be tested and, even before Hotelling's article had been published, Schultz used his statistical laboratory to calculate these derivatives for a variety of agricultural goods. The symmetry condition was not satisfied. In the same article, Hotelling related this model of demand to the traditional one, which imposed the condition that total spending be constant, limited by income. For the latter, it was impossible to derive the function $u(.)$ from observed data. Hands and Mirowski (1997) and Mirowski and Hands (1998) argue that Hotelling intended that his model of entrepreneurial demand might serve as a model of consumers' demand. In contrast, Hurwicz (1997) argues that Hotelling realized it was appropriate only for entrepreneurial demand and did not apply to the individual consumer. Hotelling's third model, which offered a statistical explanation for the slope and shape of the demand function, was neglected.

This marked the beginning of a period of cooperation between Schultz and Hotelling, during which they tackled the problem of demand, Hotelling emphasizing theory and Schultz empirical work. During this period, they discovered the work of Slutsky, Hicks, and Allen, and the condition that, for an income-constrained consumer, the cross-partial derivatives of the *compensated* demand function should be equal. The culmination of this line of research (which ended with Schultz's death in a car accident in 1938) was Schultz's *Theory and Measurement of Demand* (1938). In the final section of this book, Schultz tested the hypothesis of rational consumer behavior by testing both the Hotelling and Slutsky symmetry conditions for a range of agricultural products. The results were not encouraging – conflicting evidence meant that the demand relations between pork and mutton could not be determined from the data. Schultz tried to find a statistical explanation that saved the theory, but the project of establishing quantitative demand relations appeared unsuccessful.

From here, a variety of routes were followed. Knight (1944) defended the use of demand curves, but was very critical of attempts to test the underlying theory. In a dynamic economy, where incomes and psychological factors were changing continually, testing such theories was doomed to failure. Friedman, who had worked with Schultz, agreed with Knight that economists should not seek to go behind the demand curve. He argued that empirical work should move away from indifference curves toward analyzing direct relations between demand and factors such as income, wealth, prices, and personal characteristics. He described the theory underlying such work as a "Marshallian" demand curve (Friedman, 1949; cf., Friedman and Wallis, 1942). Interdependence of demands was played down. During the 1940s, Schultz's approach to demand was continued at Chicago, at the Cowles Commission under Marschak, who emphasized the interdependence of the economic system. From the late 1940s, this work led into both general equilibrium theory and econometric analysis of demand systems.

Indifference curve analysis was also rejected by Samuelson (1938), in his theory of revealed preference. Influenced, like Schultz, by operationalism, he sought to reduce consumer theory to what could be deduced from assumptions about observed choices. It turned out, however, that the differences between Samuelson's revealed preference theory and the Hicks–Allen ordinal utility theory were not significant. Thus, although there were important differences between the ways in which different economists tackled the theory of demand, there was a consensus on the underlying theory. The attempt to use utility theory as a psychological foundation for the theory of demand had been abandoned, and it was generally accepted that utility functions must be ordinal, describing rather than explaining choice.

20.3 MARKET STRUCTURE AND SUPPLY

In 1920, the standard theory of supply was that of Marshall's *Principles*. The main characteristic of this book is that Marshall used a formal mathematical structure as a framework for constructing an evolutionary theory. Neither the algebra of the appendix nor the graphical analysis of the footnotes matched the complexity of the text. Industries, the basic unit of analysis, comprised changing groups of heterogeneous firms. Markets were competitive ("free" competition) but not perfectly competitive – firms had their own special markets. Some industries faced increasing and others faced diminishing returns to scale. Even in the long run, firms and markets were not in equilibrium. And yet Marshall analyzed this complexity through supply and demand. Supply curves reflected marginal costs faced by the representative firm in each industry, this being the firm that was judged typical of the market being analyzed.

During the 1920s, the Marshallian structure was questioned on both sides of the Atlantic, in very different ways. In England, Clapham (1922) questioned the usefulness of Marshall's classification of industries according to whether they faced increasing or decreasing returns. No one, he pointed out, had filled in these "boxes." He questioned whether it was even possible to fill in the boxes, due to the difficulty of distinguishing between economies of scale and the results of invention. After a brief controversy (Pigou, 1922; Robertson, 1924), this was followed by an even more influential critique by Sraffa (1926). Sraffa questioned whether returns to scale could be anything other than constant in Marshall's theory. Increasing returns were consistent with competitive analysis only if they arose from economies of scale that were external to the firm but internal to the industry. It was impossible to find convincing examples. Decreasing returns, on the other hand, were inconsistent with partial equilibrium analysis, because they could arise only because of rising factor prices (assumed constant). Two years after that, Robbins (1928) launched an attack on Marshall's concept of the representative firm. Economics, he contended, no more needed a representative firm than it needed a representative worker or representative piece of land. It was the marginal firm that was relevant.

The effect of the "cost controversy," as the debate arising from the contributions of Clapham and Sraffa came to be known, led to the development of analytic tools to deal with the problem of monopoly. Following Harrod (1930), economists started to use the term "marginal revenue" to describe the first derivative of the revenue function, a concept understood by Marshall (and Cournot before him) but not identified with a specific name. Harrod pointed out that the firm's demand curve would not be the same as the industry demand curve and that abandoning perfect competition meant abandoning the supply curve. Supply would depend on the elasticity of demand facing the firm as well as on price. These new conceptual tools received their fullest expression in Joan Robinson's *Economics of Imperfect Competition* (1933), which virtually created the modern geometry of the theory of the firm, analyzing perfect and imperfect competition, monopoly, monopsony, and even the kinked demand curve (conventionally attributed to Sweezy, 1939).

Although Robinson was responsible for the development of a powerful "box of tools," to use her expression, to emphasize these is to neglect the most significant aspect of the change that was taking place. Marshall's dynamic, evolutionary theory was being replaced by static equilibrium analysis. The problems with returns to scale identified by Sraffa were problems with the concept of static equilibrium. Robbins's strictures against the representative firm were valid only if one was analyzing equilibrium. Robinson, in formalizing Marshall's reasoning, was making assumptions (such as identical firms and reversible cost curves) necessary to construct formal models of equilibrium. As Shove (1933) pointed out, her theory and Marshall's did not operate on the same terrain.

In the United States, a parallel movement took place. However, its character was radically different. Knight's *Risk, Uncertainty and Profit* (1921) spelled out in detail the assumptions needed to ensure perfect competition. It was clear that they were satisfied in very few real-world markets. There was awareness of increasing returns and their implications for competition. J. M. Clark (1923) wrote a book on the implications of "overhead costs," arguing that such costs, which made increasing returns likely, were an important feature of modern business. A competitive market could not function unless firms that took the initiative in changing prices gained a temporary advantage, which meant that variation in prices was necessary for competition to work. This ability to obtain a temporary advantage, therefore, should not be considered as an imperfection (Clark, 1923, pp. 416–20). Such competition was, however, different from "cut-throat" competition, where temporary price cuts were used to drive rivals out of business in an attempt to increase monopoly power. Problems such as "dumping" were widely discussed. There was thus a much greater emphasis on problems of business and real-world markets in the American literature than in the British.

This was the background out of which Chamberlin's *Theory of Monopolistic Competition* (1933), submitted as a Harvard Ph.D. thesis (supervised by Young) in 1927, emerged. Marshall's theory of the firm, had been developed in an age and in a country where it was possible to think of a firm as a family business, with fortunes linked to those of its owner–manager. This was a long way from the business conditions as observed in the United States in the 1920s. Chamberlin and his contemporaries were also aware of many business practices that were ruled out by perfect competition and were not taken into account by Marshall. They were, therefore, concerned with bringing Marshall's theory up to date, not with overthrowing it.

Chamberlin did use marginal revenue and marginal cost, and he derived the tangency condition for monopolistic competition but, unlike Robinson, did not regard it as central to his work. There were even occasions when he used average costs and revenues, closer to the way in which businessmen actually thought, in preference to marginal analysis. However, the radical differences between his work and Robinson's are evident from his contents page. After discussing value under "pure" competition (competition without monopoly elements), his chapter headings refer to oligopoly and duopoly, product differentiation, and selling costs. His argument was that product differentiation and selling costs such as advertising meant that meant that pure competition no longer described the way in which markets worked. The emphasis on oligopoly explains why Chamberlin chose to adopt the device of using two demand curves facing each firm. One corresponded to the case in which rivals kept their prices constant and the other to that in which they matched any price cut made by the firm concerned (the first would be much more elastic than the second). He used this to analyze the dynamics of price-cutting, entry, and exit, as well as equilibrium. The "tangency solution" referred merely to one special case (equilibrium where the number of firms was large).

Chamberlin assumed that firms produced products that were different from each other – product differentiation involved more than simply advertising and brand names. The result was that the concept of an industry became ambiguous and was replaced by that of the group. The logical conclusion of this approach, however, was that every firm produced a unique product – a world of competing monopolies. This meant that it proved difficult to extend Chamberlin's partial equilibrium theory to encompass general equilibrium (see Triffin, 1940).

The most important aspect of Chamberlin's work was that it opened up the field of market structure. He classified markets according to two characteristics: the number of firms and the degree of product differentiation, for each of which he analyzed how firms would behave. In the hands of Bain (1942, 1956), one of his students, this led directly into the structure–conduct–performance paradigm. This involved analyzing the structure of an industry (number of firms, degree of product differentiation, durability of product, and so on) and working out how firms would behave. Having determined this, conclusions could be drawn concerning the efficiency with which the industry performed. It was a thoroughly empirical approach to problems of market structure and supply.

Although he did not emphasize the fact, Chamberlin, like Marshall, never committed himself to the assumption that firms maximized profits. Others, however, launched more direct attacks on profit maximization. At Oxford, Hall and Hitch (1939), followed by Andrews (1949), undertook extensive surveys of how businessmen actually set prices (a methodological analysis of this work and the ensuing controversy is offered by Hausman and Mongin, 1998). On the basis of this evidence they advocated the "full-cost pricing" hypothesis. Businessmen, they argued, did not know what marginal costs were and instead set prices as a mark-up on average variable cost. They denied that firms maximized profits. In the United States, faced with the apparent inconsistency between Keynesian unemployment theory and the standard theory of factor demands, Lester (1946) surveyed manufacturing plants and came to the conclusion that wages were unimportant in influencing firms' employment decisions. This provoked a strong response from Machlup (1946) and later Friedman (1953). They made it clear that profit maximization was not intended as a theory of how businessmen thought but was a device by which economists could understand the outcomes of business decisions. Friedman expressed this by saying that firms behaved "as if" they maximized profits: whether or not they understood this was as irrelevant as whether or not a car driver understood the physics of velocity and acceleration. Machlup also tried to discredit the survey evidence on which criticisms of marginalist theories were based.

By the 1950s, the arguments of Friedman and Machlup had become widely accepted. Firms were modeled as being in profit-maximizing equilibrium, and short-run monopoly power was taken to depend on the elasticity of demand. There were differences: the "Harvard school" (including Bain) emphasized the range of market structures, while Chicago economists thought perfect competition and monopoly sufficient (perfect competition as the general case, monopoly for use in individual cases). However, such differences were largely swept into the field of industrial organization, leaving relative consensus in the core of price theory.

20.4   COMPETITION, THE PRICE SYSTEM, AND WELFARE

Price theory has always been closely linked to welfare. Walras (1954 [1874], p. 255) had reached the conclusion that "free competition" would, subject to two conditions, give "the greatest possible satisfaction of wants." This idea was developed by Pareto, who argued that free competition would produce "maximum ophelimity," which he defined in the following way:

We will say that members of a collectivity enjoy *maximum ophelimity* in a certain position when it is impossible to find a way of moving from that position very slightly in such a manner that the ophelimity enjoyed by each of the individuals of that collectivity increases or decreases. That is to say, any small displacement in departing from that position necessarily has the effect of increasing the ophelimity which certain individuals enjoy, and decreasing that which others enjoy, of being agreeable to some and disagreeable to others. (Pareto, 1971 [1906], p. 261)

In contrast, the Cambridge school adopted an aggregative, utilitarian approach. Marshall analyzed welfare using the concept of consumers' surplus. He used this to prove the doctrine that "every equilibrium of demand and supply may fairly be regarded as a position of maximum satisfaction" (Marshall, 1920 [1890], p. 390). However, he emphasized the limitations of the doctrine when some industries faced increasing returns. To remedy this he proposed a tax-bounty scheme, designed to shift production toward increasing returns industries, thereby increasing consumers' surplus. This was an aggregative approach to social welfare, focusing on the level and distribution of the national dividend (the value of output).

Pigou analyzed welfare in terms of the relationship between marginal private and social products rather than consumers' surplus, but his conception of welfare was essentially the same as Marshall's. The national dividend (national income) measured the group of satisfactions and dissatisfactions that could be measured in terms of money (Pigou, 1932 [1920], p. 23). Increases in the national dividend corresponded to increases in welfare, provided that the welfare of the poor was not reduced (Pigou, 1932 [1920], p. 82). It also followed that if income were unequally distributed, the marginal utility of income would be different for different individuals, implying that redistribution from the rich to the poor would raise overall welfare. The result was that Cambridge economists normally discussed the effects of changes on welfare on the assumption that the distribution of income was given. Pigou (1912), for example, organized his discussion of welfare under the headings of the size, distribution, and variability of the national dividend (he dropped the last of these in *The Economics of Welfare*).

Two things stimulated debate about the meaning of welfare. The first was that questioning the psychological basis for utility raised doubts about the Cambridge approach to welfare economics. If utility could be measured (albeit making assumptions about the marginal utility of money), it was clear what welfare economics was concerned with, but once that was abandoned, the meaning of social welfare became much less clear. Pareto, in the passage quoted above, wrote of "maximum ophelimity," but it was not clear what was being maximized. Thus one question that economists tried to answer in the 1920s and 1930s was: "In a social optimum, what is it that is optimized?" The answer was not clear. The second motivation for exploring welfare economics was the question, made more urgent by the existence of the Soviet Union, of socialism versus capitalism. Pareto, and following him Barone (1935 [1908]), had tackled this question, noting the formal similarity of the equations that had to be solved under both systems. After 1920, however, the question was more urgent.

What has become known as the Socialist Calculation debate started when von Mises (1935 [1920]) launched a critique of socialism. The background to this was the Bolshevik revolution in Russia and the attempt to establish a socialist state. In the period of "war communism," the Bolshevik government established a system of central planning in which markets and prices were abolished. Influenced by Marx, the idea was to eliminate the waste that was inherent in capitalism and to plan production on a rational basis. Von Mises responded to this by arguing that rational calculation required the coordination of different producers' and consumers' evaluations and that without markets and competitive prices, the information required would not be available. Changes in tastes, technical progress, and the complexity of modern economic systems meant that it would be impossible for any central planner to manage without free markets.

Socialists responded to this challenge by trying to develop mechanisms whereby socialist economies could allocate resources optimally. Because most such schemes involved having markets for labor and consumers' goods (with central planning confined to producers' goods and production), these schemes were known as "market socialism." This literature was important for two reasons. The first is that, in tackling this problem, the advocates of market socialism had to confront the same question as was raised by the new consumer theory: "What is optimized in a social optimum?" Different answers to this question led to the derivation of different optimum conditions. These were eventually developed into the so-called "new welfare economics" and the derivation of the conditions for what became known, in the 1950s, as a Pareto optimum. [A particularly helpful survey of the literature from the 1920s and 1930s is Bergson (1938). For a brief survey, see Backhouse (1985, ch. 24).]

The second is that the debate with von Mises and, later, Hayek, raised the question – which is central to price theory – about the nature of competition (for overviews of this debate, see Vaughn, 1980; Lavoie, 1985). The market socialists provided schemes whereby socialism could be organized so as to produce an allocation of resources that was identical to that which would occur under perfect competition. They argued that this proved socialism could, at least in principle, be efficient because the conditions for a social optimum would be satisfied. Arguing that socialism was efficient because it could be made to mimic capitalism clearly implied a different view of competition from that held by Marx, who had argued that the reason for socialism was to avoid the waste that arose when capitalists competed with each other. Hayek (1937) took up this theme, arguing that that competition should be seen as a process whereby knowledge was created and disseminated. Perfect competition, because it ignored this process, abstracted from the important features of competition. Market-socialist schemes could never work, because they failed to provide any alternative to the market as a means for creating and disseminating knowledge.

20.5 PERFECT COMPETITION AS THE PARADIGM FOR PRICE THEORY

Toward the end of the 1930s, perfect competition emerged as the paradigmatic case in price theory. In the same way that Hicks's work with Allen had developed Pareto's consumer theory, his *Value and Capital* (1939) provided an elegant restatement of general equilibrium theory. His account of the theory encompassed the new consumer theory and recent Swedish work on expectations (Myrdal, 1939 [1931]). The concept of temporary equilibrium provided a way to use general equilibrium theory to understand Keynesian macroeconomics. However, although Hicks achieved a wide readership, on both sides of the Atlantic, the book that provided the mathematical framework on which the microeconomics of the neoclassical synthesis rested, and virtually provided a manual in price theory for many economists in the 1950s, was Samuelson's *Foundations of Economic Analysis* (1947). (This was written in the late 1930s, but publication was delayed because of the war.) Samuelson later wrote that *Value and Capital* had prepared the ground for his more mathematical treatment of the subject. In *Foundations*, individual behavior became almost synonymous with constrained optimization.

Given the emphasis, during the 1930s, on imperfect competition, it is perhaps surprising that price theory stabilized around the concept of perfect competition. However, it is important to note that it took the literature on imperfect competition to crystallize the concept of perfect competition. One reason for this is that, as economists progressed with theories of monopoly, oligopoly, and imperfect competition, it became clear that general results were hard to find. This may explain Hicks's (1939, p. 83) remark that, "a general abandonment of the assumption of perfect competition . . . must have very destructive consequences for economic theory." Other theories were needed for specific problems (notably industrial organization), but the theory of perfect competition was seen as the only foundation on which price theory, understood as a general theory of what determined prices, could rest.

Separate from this transformation of Anglo-American price theory was the work in Vienna on the existence of general competitive equilibrium associated with Schlesinger, Wald, and von Neumann (the literature on general equilibrium theory is discussed elsewhere, which is why this paragraph is so over-condensed). When they were forced to leave Europe, many of these economists settled in the United States, where the Cowles Commission provided the main focus for mathematical economics in the late 1940s. Out of this arose the more abstract version of general equilibrium theory, the Arrow–Debreu model, summarized in Debreu's *Theory of Value* (1959). Although it is possible, somewhat Whiggishly, to construct a sequence comprising Walras–Pareto–Hicks–Samuelson–Arrow/ Debreu, to do this overlooks the substantially different intellectual origins of the last three. In the 1950s, however, the Arrow–Debreu (1954) model, even though work on it remained a minority activity, came to be regarded as the definitive statement of the most rigorous version of neoclassical price theory.

In the 1950s, price theory had come to be based on perfect competition. There were substantial differences between the Chicago (Friedman–Stigler), Cowles (Arrow–Debreu), and MIT (Samuelson) versions of the theory, but they were recognizably variations on a common theme. There were economists who did not accept the framework, but their work was consigned to "applied fields" outside the "core," such as industrial organization or development economics.

20.6   INTERPRETATION

Between 1920 and 1955, price theory was refined and clarified. However, simply to say this is to overlook crucial features of the story. The theory was simplified and made more precise, but in the process it was changed radically (for the argument that increased rigor inevitably changes a theory, see Backhouse, 1998). Certain lines of inquiry were ruled out. There were thus losses as well as gains. Consumer theory ceased to explain choices and merely described them: rationality came to be equated with consistent, transitive preferences (this is discussed, and similar arguments made with respect to the theory of distribution and welfare economics, in Mandler, 1999). The firm came to be modeled as maximizing profits, and aspects of the firm and markets (for which Marshall had provided evolutionary arguments) that could not be encompassed within this framework were abandoned. Competition came to be understood in terms of the inability of agents to influence price in markets that were devoid of any institutional features, defined only by the existence of a single price. The result was that process views of competition were ignored.

All aspects of this process were controversial and were debated. Economists later decided that many of the rejected lines of inquiry were important: evolutionary views of the firm; dynamic perspectives on competition; nonoptimizing behavior; and utilitarian welfare economics. Most economists, however, wrote as though no significant changes had taken place and did not even take seriously the critiques that had been made of the emerging synthesis. The history of consumer theory was presented as though nothing at all was lost in the move to purely ordinal theories. The standard account of the Socialist Calculation debate presented Hayek as conceding the market socialists' argument that central planning was theoretically possible. The conflation of Chamberlin's theory with Robinson's served to deflect attention from his discussions of oligopoly, selling costs, and price dynamics. Marshall was portrayed as being muddled rather than as offering an evolutionary perspective on markets. A common feature in this rewriting of history was the neglect of all arguments that could not be expressed using formal equilibrium models.

Many economists refused to accept the new consensus. To some extent, their limited competence at mathematics played a role (as with Robertson and J. M. Clark). However, many of them retained good reasons for objecting to the emerging synthesis. These included Robertson, J. M. Clark, Knight (though he was a key figure in the new Chicago school, he never accepted the consensus on competition), Hayek, and to some extent Chamberlin. The new synthesis became established with the emergence, from the 1950s, of a generation that was better trained in mathematical techniques than their predecessors. Robinson's "box of tools" became more prominent, to the extent that it became synonymous with theory. For earlier generations, mathematical models, when they were used, instantiated economic theory, whereas for the later one, they became the theory. Perspectives that could not be captured within the mathematical apparatus were no longer regarded as part of the theoretical core.

Bibliography

Allen, R. D. G. 1936: Professor Slutsky's theory of consumers' choice. *Review of Economic Studies*, 3, 120–9.

Andrews, P. W. S. 1949: A reconsideration of the theory of the individual business. *Oxford Economic Papers*, NS 1(1), 54–89.

Arrow, K. J. and Debreu, G. 1954: Existence of equilibrium for a competitive economy. *Econometrica*, 22, 265–90.

Backhouse, R. E. 1985: *A History of Modern Economic Analysis*. Oxford and New York: Blackwell.

—— 1998: If mathematics is informal, perhaps we should accept that economics is informal too. *Economic Journal*, 108, 1848–58.

Bain, J. S. 1942: Market classification in modern price theory. *Quarterly Journal of Economics*, 56, 560–74.

—— 1956: *Barriers to New Competition*. Cambridge, MA: Harvard University Press.

Barber, W. J. (ed.) 1997: *The Works of Irving Fisher*, 10 vols. London: Pickering & Chatto.

Barone, E. 1935 [1908]: The ministry of production in the collectivist state. In F. A. Hayek (ed.), *Collectivist Economic Planning*. London: Routledge.

Bergson, A. 1938: A reformulation of certain aspects of welfare economics. *Quarterly Journal of Economics*, 52, 310–34.

Cassel, G. 1932 [1923]: *The Theory of Social Economy*, trans. S.L. Barron. New York: Harcourt, Brace and World.

Chamberlin, E. H. 1933: *The Theory of Monopolistic Competition*. Cambridge, MA: Harvard University Press.

Clapham, J. H. 1922: Of empty economic boxes. *Economic Journal*, 32, 305–14.

Clark, J. M. 1923: *The Economics of Overhead Costs*. Chicago: The University of Chicago Press.

Debreu, G. 1959: *The Theory of Value: An Axiomatic Analysis of Economic Equilibrium*. New Haven and London: Yale University Press.

Fisher, I. 1892: Mathematical investigations in the theory of value and prices. *Transactions of the Connecticut Academy*, 9, 1–124. Reprinted in Barber, op. cit., vol. 1.

Friedman, M. 1949: The Marshallian demand curve. *Journal of Political Economy*, 57(6), 463–95.

—— 1953: The methodology of positive economics. In M. Friedman (ed.), *Essays in Positive Economics*. Chicago: The Chicago University Press.

—— and Wallis, W. A. 1942: The empirical derivation of indifference functions. In O. Lange, F. McIntyre, and T. O. Yntema (eds.), *Studies in Mathematical Economics and Econometrics*. Chicago: The University of Chicago Press, 175–89.

Hall, R. L. and Hitch, C. J. 1939: Price theory and business behaviour. *Oxford Economic Papers*, 2, 12–45.

Hands, D. W. and Mirowski, P. 1997: Harold Hotelling and the neoclassical dream. In R. E. Backhouse, D. M. Hausman, U. Mäki, and A. Salanti (eds.), *Economics and Methodology: Crossing Boundaries*. London: Macmillan, 322–97.

—— and —— 1998: A paradox of budgets: the postwar stabilization of American neo-classical demand theory. *History of Political Economy*, 30 (From Interwar Pluralism to Postwar Neoclassicism), 260–92.

Harrod, R. F. 1930: Notes on supply. *Economic Journal*, 40, 232–41.

Hausman, D. M. and Mongin, P. 1998: Economists' responses to anomalies: full-cost pricing versus preference reversals. *History of Political Economy*, 29 (Annual Supplement), 255–72.

Hayek, F. A. 1937: Economics and knowledge. *Economica*, 4, 33–54.

Hendry, D. F. and Morgan, M. S. 1995: *The Foundations of Econometric Analysis*. Cambridge, UK: Cambridge University Press.

Hicks, J. R. 1939: *Value and Capital*. Oxford: The Clarendon Press.

—— 1983: *Classics and Moderns: Collected Essays on Economic Theory*, vol. 3. Oxford: Blackwell.

—— 1984: *The Economics of John Hicks*, ed. D. Helm. Oxford: Blackwell.

—— and Allen, R. D. G. 1934: A reconsideration of the theory of value. *Economica*, 1, 52–76, 196–219. Reprinted in Hicks (1984), op. cit.

Hotelling, H. 1932: Edgeworth's taxation paradox and the nature of demand and supply functions. *Journal of Political Economy*, 40, 577–616.

Hurwicz, L. 1997: Comment. In R. E. Backhouse, D. M. Hausman, U. Mäki, and A. Salanti (eds.), *Economics and Methodology: Crossing Boundaries*. London: Macmillan, 398–416.

Knight, F. H. 1921: *Risk, Uncertainty and Profit*. Boston: Houghton Mifflin.

—— 1944: Realism and relevance in the theory of demand. *Journal of Political Economy*, 52, 289–318.

Laidler, D. 1999: *Fabricating the Keynesian Revolution: Studies in the Inter-War Literature on Money, the Cycle and Unemployment*. Cambridge, UK: Cambridge University Press.

Lavoie, D. 1985: *Rivalry and Central Planning*. Cambridge, UK: Cambridge University Press.

Lester, R. A. 1946: Shortcomings of marginal analysis for wage–employment problems. *American Economic Review*, 36(1), 63–82.

Machlup, F. A. 1946: Marginal analysis and empirical research. *American Economic Review*, 36(4), 519–54.

Mandler, M. 1999: *Dilemmas in Economic Theory: Persisting Foundational Problems of Microeconomics*. Oxford: Oxford University Press.

Marshall, A. 1920 [1890]: *Principles of Economics: An Introductory Volume*, 8th edn. London: Macmillan.

Mirowski, P. 1990. Problems in the paternity of econometrics: Henry Ludwell Moore. *History of Political Economy*, 22, 587–610.

Mises, L. von 1935 [1920]: Economic calculation in the socialist commonwealth. In F. A. Hayek (ed.), *Collectivist Economic Planning*. London: Routledge, 87–130.

Mitchell, W. C. 1925: Quantitative analysis in economic theory. *American Economic Review*, 15(1), 1–12.

—— 1969: *Types of Economic Theory: Mercantilism to Institutionalism*, 2 vols, ed. J. Dorfman. New York: Augustus M. Kelley.

Moore, H. L. 1914: *Economic Cycles: Their Law and Cause*. New York: Macmillan. Reprinted in Hendry and Morgan, op. cit.

—— 1925: A moving equilibrium of demand and supply. *Quarterly Journal of Economics*, 39, 357–71.

—— 1926: A theory of economic oscillations. *Quarterly Journal of Economics*, 41, 1–29.

Morgan, M. S. 1990: *The History of Econometric Ideas*. Cambridge, UK: Cambridge University Press.

Myrdal, G. 1939 [1931]: *Monetary Equilibrium*. London: W. Hodge.

Pareto, V. 1971 [1906]: *Manual of Political Economy*, trans. A. S. Schweier. New York: Augustus M. Kelley.

Pigou, A. C. 1903: Some remarks on utility. *Economic Journal*, 13, 58–68.

—— 1912: *Wealth and Welfare*. London: Macmillan.

—— 1922: Empty economic boxes: a reply. *Economic Journal*, 32, 458–65.

—— 1932 [1920]: *The Economics of Welfare*, 4th edn. London: Macmillan.

Robbins, L. C. 1928: The representative firm. *Economic Journal*, 38, 387–404.

—— 1932: *The Nature and Significance of Economic Science*. London: Macmillan.

Robertson, D. H. 1924: Those empty boxes. *Economic Journal*, 34, 16–30.

Robinson, J. V. 1933: *Economics of imperfect competition*. London: Macmillan.

Roos, C. F. 1927: A dynamical theory of economics. *Journal of Political Economy*, 35, 632–56.

Samuelson, P. A. 1938: A note on the pure theory of consumers' behaviour. *Economica*, 5, 61–72.

—— 1947: *Foundations of Economic Analysis*. Cambridge, MA: Harvard University Press.

—— 1955: *Economics: An Introductory Analysis*, 5th edn. New York: McGraw-Hill.

Schultz, H. 1925: The statistical law of demand as illustrated by the demand for sugar. *Journal of Political Economy*, 33, 481–504, 577–631.

—— 1927a: Mathematical economics and the quantitative method. *Journal of Political Economy*, 35, 702–6.

—— 1927b: Theoretical considerations relating to supply. *Journal of Political Economy*, 35, 437–64.

—— 1928: Rational economics. *American Economic Review*, 18, 643–8.

—— 1938: *Theory and Measurement of Demand*. Chicago: The University of Chicago Press.

Shove, G. 1933: The imperfection of the market. *Economic Journal*, 43(169), 113–24.

Slutsky, E. E. 1953 [1915]: On the theory of the budget of the consumer. In G. J. Stigler and K. E. Boulding (eds.), *Readings in Price Theory*. London: George Allen & Unwin, 27–56.

Sraffa, P. 1926: The laws of returns under competitive conditions. *Economic Journal*, 36, 335–50.

Stigler, G. J. 1950: The development of utility theory. *Journal of Political Economy*, 58, 307–27, 373–96.

Sweezy, P. M. 1939: Demand under conditions of oligopoly. *Journal of Political Economy*, 47, 567–73.

Triffin, R. 1940: *Monopolistic Competition and General Equilibrium Theory*. Cambridge, MA: Harvard University Press.

Vaughn, K. I. 1980: Economic calculation under socialism: the Austrian contribution. *Economic Inquiry*, 18, 535–54.

Walras, L. 1954 [1874]: *Elements of Pure Economics*, trans. W. Jaffé. Homewood, IL: Richard D. Irwin.

Wicksell, K. 1934 [1918]: *Lectures on Political Economy*, vol. 2, trans. E. Classen, appendices trans. S. Adler. London: Routledge.

CHAPTER TWENTY-ONE

Interwar Monetary and Business Cycle Theory: Macroeconomics before Keynes

Robert W. Dimand

21.1 INTRODUCTION

According to Francis X. Diebold, "A striking and easily forgotten fact is that, before Keynes and Klein, *there really was no macroeconomics*" (in Adams, 1992, p. 31, Diebold's emphasis). But the rich and varied traditions of monetary and business cycle theory forming the context for Keynes's *The General Theory* and the emergence of modern macroeconomics was much more than passing asides of classical and neoclassical value theorists. Economists analyzed the price level, real and nominal interest rates, and fluctuations in output and employment long before John Maynard Keynes's *The General Theory of Employment, Interest and Money* (1936) transformed the nature and language of their controversies, bringing the two bodies of literature focused on prices and cyclical fluctuations into a discourse centered on determining employment and national income.

The quantity theory of money, which holds that changes in the money supply will, for given demand for real money balances, eventually change prices in the same proportion, is "the oldest surviving theory in economics" (Blaug, 1995), antedating Adam Smith's classical economics by at least two centuries.

The Salamanca school and Jean Bodin used the quantity theory to explain the sixteenth-century "Price Revolution," the inflation following the silver inflow from the New World (Grice-Hutchinson, 1952; O'Brien, 2000). Douglas Vickers (1959) and Thomas Guggenheim (1989) reveal the contributions of John Locke, Richard Cantillon, and Isaac Gervaise to understanding velocity of circulation and international adjustment, and of John Law to banking. David Hume's 1752 specie-flow analysis of international monetary adjustment through changes in national price levels, with short-run changes in real output, was the high point of pre-classical monetary economics (Humphrey, 1986, pp. 128–33). While Hume linked each country's price level to the country's money stock and stressed relative price effects on trade balances, Adam Smith anticipated the monetary approach to the balance of payments by assuming purchasing power parity (with the world price level determined by world gold supply and world demand for real money balances) and stressing the direct effect on spending (and hence on the balance of payments and thus the money supply) of a country's excess demand or supply of money (Humphrey, 1986, pp. 180–7).

Keynes (1936) reconsidered the debate over a supposed general glut of commodities at the end of the Napoleonic Wars, regretting that David Ricardo's sharper analysis and invocation of Say's (or James Mill's) Law of Markets won out over what Keynes considered Thomas Robert Malthus's deeper insight that insufficient effective demand could cause an excess supply of labor without an excess demand for any good. Thomas Sowell (1972) shows that statements of the Law of Markets by classical economists were more varied and complex, often subtler, and sometimes confused and contradictory, than Keynes recognized. John Stuart Mill, among others, searched for a formulation that would be stronger than the truism now known as Say's Equality (if each market is in equilibrium, then the sum of excess demand over all commodity markets necessarily adds to zero) but weaker than Say's Identity, that excess demand for all commodity markets (that is, all markets except that for money) always sums to zero for any set of prices (which implies that the money market always clears for any prices, leaving absolute prices indeterminate). Jean-Baptiste Say himself endorsed public works to remedy unemployment, and criticized Ricardo for neglecting the hoarding of savings if investment opportunities were lacking (Hutchison, 1980, p. 3n). Ricardo preferred restoring gold convertibility of sterling at the depreciated parity rather than deflation to restore the prewar parity. Robert Link (1959) and Bernard Corry (1962) surveyed the macroeconomics of English classical economists and their critics, while Frank W. Fetter (1965) and Anna Schwartz (1987) elucidated more strictly monetary controversies. Denis O'Brien (1993) is a noteworthy monograph on Thomas Joplin, while Henry Thornton (1965 [1802]) attracts attention for his analysis of central banking and influence on the Bullion Report.

Outside mainstream classical economics, Karl Marx reflected on Quesnay's *Tableau économique* and composed schemes of simple and expanded reproduction, precursors of representations of circular flow and of multi-sector growth models. He rejected Say's Law to consider realization crises (but implicitly assumed it in other parts of *Capital*) and inspired generations of underconsumption and disproportionality crisis theorists (Howard and King, 1989–92). Also in the 1860s, William Stanley Jevons and Clément Juglar stimulated statistical and theoretical trade cycle studies, a literature extensively sampled in O'Brien (1997) and Hagemann (2001). Jevons's papers on cycles (collected posthumously in Jevons, 1884) did more than his marginal utility analysis to persuade the British Association for the Advancement of Science that economics was sufficiently scientific for Section F to remain. Jevons's view of sunspot cycles as driving trade cycles has been derided, to the neglect of his lasting contributions on seasonality and the application of index numbers to effects of gold discoveries. However, Peart (1996) shows that Jevons's procedure was reasonable for a largely agricultural economy. Meteorologists then believed that sunspots produced cycles in weather, which would affect harvests, and economists might accept the conclusions of meteorologists about meteorology.

As Mitchell (1927, p. 7) observed, "Before the end of the nineteenth century there had accumulated a body of observations and speculations sufficient to justify the writing of histories of the theories of crises." Hutchison (1953, p. 437) cites Eugen von Bergmann's *Die Wirtschaftskrisen: Geschichte der nationalökonomischen Krisentheorien* (Stuttgart, 1895) as "still an outstandingly valuable work covering the nineteenth century and going well back into the eighteenth" and Edward D. Jones's *Economic Crises* (New York, 1900) as "a short survey of the main theories with a useful bibliography." In 1909, the London School of Economics published a 71-page bibliography of unemployment.

21.2 WHO WERE THE LEADING INTERWAR MONETARY AND BUSINESS CYCLE THEORISTS?

Alfred Marshall, Knut Wicksell, and Irving Fisher appear on the cover of David Laidler's *The Golden Age of the Quantity Theory* (1991). Before 1914, these three laid the foundations for interwar developments in monetary theory, just as Jevons and Juglar did for interwar business cycle analysis. Marshall's *Money, Credit and Commerce* was not published until 1923, but incorporated manuscripts dating from the 1870s, while other contributions, collected in his *Official Papers* (1926), were presented to government inquiries before the turn of the century. The Cambridge cash balance approach to the quantity theory ($M = kPY$ in modern notation, relating desired cash balances to nominal income) and the Cambridge analysis of saving and investment followed from Marshall's work (Eshag, 1963; Bridel, 1987). Wicksell's distinction between market rate of interest and natural rate (which would equate desired saving to investment) and his analysis of cumulative inflation or deflation in a credit economy led to the Stockholm school's economic dynamics (Wicksell, 1935 [1915], 1962 [1898]; Jonung, 1991, 1993). The Fisher relation, expected inflation as the difference between real and money interest rates (Fisher, 1896), and the Fisher diagram, showing optimal consumption over two periods with present discounted value of expected lifetime income as the budget constraint (Fisher, 1907), are fundamental for later macroeconomics.

Citation counts of journal articles in English (Deutscher, 1990) confirm Cambridge, Stockholm, and American quantity theorists as leading sources of monetary economics between the wars, while Wesley Mitchell's National Bureau of Economic Research and the Vienna school were prominent in business cycle analysis. Outside the mainstream, some monetary heretics (notably Foster and Catchings) and the *émigré* Polish Marxist Michal Kalecki attracted attention.

21.3   CAMBRIDGE

For Keynes (1936), classical economics did not end with John Stuart Mill. In Keynes's usage, the "classical" economists were all those to whom he attributed acceptance of Say's Law (impossibility of insufficient aggregate demand), including Marshall and Pigou, professors of economics at Cambridge from 1885 to1908 and 1908 to 1943, respectively. Keynes (1936, appendix to ch. 19) took Pigou (1933) as his target, summarizing it in two classical postulates. Keynes (1936, ch. 2) accepted the first classical postulate, that the real wage equals the marginal product of labor (the economy is on the labor demand curve), but rejected the second, that utility of the real wage equals marginal disutility of labor (the economy is on the labor supply curve). Rather than typifying pre-Keynesian economics, Pigou was unusual in the extent to which he treated supply and demand for labor in real terms, introducing monetary factors late in his book. Even Mark Casson (1983, pp. 16–17, 157), seeing Pigou as pioneer of a "Pre-Keynesian" theory of structural unemployment, allows that Pigou's writing "degenerated into little more than analytical taxonomy in the 1930s . . . There is no standard work epitomizing Pre-Keynesian theory. Pigou was the person best equipped to write such a book, but instead he wrote *The Theory of Unemployment* (1933) – a taxonomy of the subject which makes the reader wonder how anyone could write anything so tedious and abstract in the middle of an economic crisis."

However, Michael Brady (1995) has shown that, accepting the first classical postulate, Keynes's exposition of the employment function (the inverse of the aggregate supply function) in chapters 20 and 21 of *The General Theory* was shaped by the Marshallian elasticity approach of Pigou (1933, part II, chs. 8–10). Those chapters indicate the value of Pigou's contribution and Keynes's proficiency as mathematician and microeconomist. Nahid Aslanbeigui (1992) dissents from Keynes's critique of Pigou (1933), presenting evidence, notably a letter from Pigou to Keynes in May 1937 (Keynes, 1971–89, vol. XIV, p. 54), that Pigou intended a reverse L-shaped labor supply schedule, not an upward-sloping one as attributed to Pigou (1933) by Keynes (1936). As Hawtrey remarked, "And how is any reader of the *Theory of Unemployment* to guess what Pigou has in mind, seeing that there is not a word about it from the beginning of the book to the end?" (Keynes, 1971–89, vol. XIV, p. 55).

Keynes, when young, was an orthodox Cambridge cash-balance theorist. *A Tract on Monetary Reform* (Keynes, 1923) and the articles leading to it analyzed inflation as a tax on the holding of money and government bonds, the resulting reduction of demand for real money balances (by 92 percent during the German hyperinflation) as a social cost of inflation, the consequent decline in inflation tax revenue beyond a revenue-maximizing inflation rate, and the nominal interest differential between two countries as the forward premium or discount on foreign exchange (Humphrey, 1986, pp. 38–48; Dimand, 1988, pp. 4–20; Flanders, 1989, pp. 160–9). Pigou's articles on the value of money and on the foreign exchanges lacked these standards of later monetarist analysis. Milton Friedman and Thomas Sargent, who have deep reservations about *The General Theory*, both admire Keynes's *Tract*. While Keynes developed covered interest parity, Fisher (1896) had introduced uncovered interest parity (interest rates in two standards differ by the expected rate of appreciation or depreciation). Patinkin (1982) concluded that Keynes and Pigou greatly exaggerated how the Cambridge cash-balance approach was more choice-theoretic and less mechanical than Fisher's $MV = PT$ equation of exchange.

Hicks (1937) interpreted what set Keynes (1936) apart from the "classics," and created the IS–LM diagram that long dominated macroeconomic teaching (on similar models of Champernowne, Reddaway, Harrod, and Meade, and how Hicks's two-good model differed from later one-good textbook IS–LM analysis, see Young, 1987). Samuelson (1946) even asserted that Keynes didn't understand his own theory until Hicks and others transformed it into diagrams and systems of simultaneous equations. Hicks did not share this view, holding that IS–LM captured only one side of Keynes's theory. Notes taken by students (Rymes, 1987) reveal that Keynes presented a four-equation model in his 1933 lectures but chose not to use it in his book. According to Hicks, in classical theory (as represented by Robertson's and Lavington's loanable funds theory of interest), interest equilibrates saving (loanable funds) and investment, while income is given by full employment of resources (a vertical aggregate supply curve at potential output). In the Keynesian liquidity preference theory, the interest rate equates money demand (liquidity preference) to money supply, while the level of income equates investment to saving. For Hicks, these become special cases of a more general theory in which investment, saving, and money demand depend on both national income and the interest rate, with those two endogenous variables simultaneously satisfying both the IS (investment = saving) and LM (liquidity preference = money supply) conditions. In equilibrium, it made no more sense to argue whether interest was determined by the IS curve or the LM curve than to argue whether demand or supply determines a good's price in Marshall's scissors diagram.

Keynes's student, colleague, friend, and rival Dennis Robertson was neglected, like Hawtrey, Hayek, Fisher, and Mitchell, during the high tide of Keynesian dominance, until his work was reexamined by Presley (1979), Laidler (1999, pp. 90–9), and Fletcher (2000). Like Pigou (1927), Robertson (1926) emphasized the influence of expectations on investment, and doubted how well the market coordinates intertemporal allocation. Despite the claims of Klein (1946) and Samuelson (1946), Pigou's and Robertson's policy views resembled Keynes's, as Keynes recognized. Keynes (1936) complimented the LSE deflationist Lionel Robbins (1934) for advocating policy consistent with his theory. As Patinkin (1982) argued, Keynes diverged from Pigou and Robertson in macroeconomic theory, not policy. Earlier, Robertson (1915) presented a real theory of fluctuations in national income, based on technology shocks and overinvestment, in contrast to the monetary theory of fluctuations of Fisher (with Brown, 1911) and Hawtrey (1913), and considered some fluctuations around trend "appropriate." Goodhart and Presley (1994) argue that Robertson (1915), together with Schumpeter (1934 [1912]) on bursts of entrepreneurial innovation, prefigured important aspects of real business cycle theory

Hawtrey stood out from his British contemporaries by opposing counter-cyclical fiscal policy on theoretical grounds (crowding out of private investment by public spending), and influenced the Treasury's opposition to such policy. Hawtrey (1913, 1919) advanced a monetary theory of fluctuations, and supported the active monetary policy for economic stabilization (Deutscher, 1990). In this, he differed from Robbins or Hayek at the LSE, who also opposed activist fiscal policy. Despite opposing fiscal policy, Hawtrey was among the developers of a finite-valued spending multiplier, with a numerical example with leakage into imports in a 1928 memorandum, another with leakage into saving in 1930, and an algebraic analysis published in Hawtrey (1932), a year after Richard Kahn's publication of the finite-valued multiplier (Davis, 1980; Dimand, 1988; Deutscher, 1990). A possible reconciliation of Hawtrey's multiplier contributions with his rejection of fiscal policy is suggested by his later identification of liquidity prefer-ence (money demand as a both function of interest and income) as Keynes's crucial advance. If money demand isn't interest-sensitive, fiscal policy will be crowded out even though monetary policy is still effective.

Endres and Fleming (1999a,b) examine the International Labour Organization (ILO) in Geneva as an innovative source of economic analysis and policy advice between the wars, including advocacy of deficit-financed public investment as a response to unemployment and depression. They discuss Bellerby (1923, 1925), a Cambridge lecturer in the early 1920s (joining with Keynes in opposing deflation and Britain's return to the prewar parity) and a leading ILO economist in the late 1920s. Bellerby will surely figure prominently in future accounts of Cambridge monetary economics.

In his University of Melbourne inaugural lecture, Giblin (1930), a graduate of King's College, Cambridge, derived a finite-valued spending multiplier with leakages into imports alone, so that it was only finite if rest-of-the-world income was exogenous. Copland (1960) and Milmow (2000) consider Giblin as a possible proto-Keynesian.

21.4 Stockholm and Lausanne

The Swedish monetary theorist Knut Wicksell participated in debates on deflation and cycles into the early 1920s (Boianovsky, 1995, 1998). Building upon Wicksell, Erik Lindahl (1939), Erik Lundberg (1937, 1994), Gunnar Myrdal (1939), and Bertil Ohlin (1978 [1933]), among others, contributed to macroeconomic dynamics (Uhr, 1990; Jonung, 1991, 1993). Myrdal was later confident that the Swedes could have produced *The General Theory* without Keynes, but Lundberg

(1996) rejected Schumpeter's claims for Lundberg as a rival to Keynes. Patinkin (1982) claimed the Swedes lacked Keynes's central message, the principle of effective demand (determination of a stable equilibrium level of income). They concentrated instead on price dynamics, not output or employment, although giving policy advice on unemployment. Ohlin was more Keynesian than Keynes in emphasizing income rather than price changes in his 1929 exchange with Keynes over the transfer problem. In 1933 Ohlin summed a geometric series to find the multiplier effect of public works (Wadensjo; in Jonung, 1991, p. 116 – the calculation was deleted from the memorandum before publication because of criticism by Dag Hammarskjöld), but in the *Economic Journal* in 1937 Ohlin rejected the stability of the consumption function and the usefulness of multiplier analysis. The Norwegian econometrician Ragnar Frisch also contributed to business cycle analysis in the 1930s (see Andvig, 1985; see also the Frisch–Tinbergen exchange reprinted in Hendry and Morgan, 1995). Denmark's Jens Warming brought leakages into saving into multiplier analysis in a 1932 comment on Kahn. Scandinavian economists did not invent Keynes's *The General Theory* independently, but they did contribute to macroeconomic dynamics and macroeconometrics.

The Lausanne school of general equilibrium theorists also discussed monetary and employment questions (about Pareto on employment, see Tarascio, 1969). Pascal Bridel (1997) examines problematic attempts by Walras and Pareto to incorporate money in general equilibrium analysis, an unresolved issue that became of wider interest to economists only after World War II, as Walrasian general equilibrium analysis became widespread.

21.5   THE AMERICANS: FISHER, CHICAGO, YOUNG, AND CURRIE

"The story of 20th century macroeconomics begins with Irving Fisher," declares De Long (2000, p. 83). The quantity theory goes back "to David Hume, if not before. But the equation-of-exchange and the transformation of the quantity theory of money into a tool for making quantitative analyses and predictions of the price level, inflation, and interest rates was the creation of Irving Fisher" (De Long, 2000, p. 85). Fisher (1896) stressed expected inflation as the difference between real and money interest (acknowledging J. S. Mill and Marshall), extending this analysis to uncovered interest parity and the expectations theory of term structure. The two-period consumption diagram (Fisher, 1907, p. 407), embodying consumption-smoothing and the present discounted value of expected lifetime disposable income as the budget constraint, is the basis for modern consumption theory. Fisher (1930) offered perhaps the first clear, correct statement of the marginal opportunity cost of holding money, but he did not incorporate this in his studies of velocity of circulation. Fisher's contributions ranged from "money illusion" (to be eradicated by education and by publishing price indexes) through indexed bonds and a price level rule for monetary policy to his "ideal index," but he never synthesized his monetary, capital, and general equilibrium theories. Fisher's reputation suffered from his dramatic mis-prediction of stock prices in 1929. Postwar textbooks caricatured Fisher as upholding a rigid, constant-velocity, constant-output version of the quantity theory. However, Fisher (with Brown, 1911, ch. 4) stressed output changes during "transition periods" between equilibria, driven by real interest fluctuations as nominal interest adjusted slowly and imperfectly to monetary shocks. Fisher (1926) was even reprinted in 1973 as "I discovered the Phillips curve." Fisher's causality from monetary shocks to a distributed lag of price changes to unemployment resembled the "Phillips curve" of later macroeconomics more closely than that of A. W. H. Phillips (whose causality ran from unemployment to wage changes). Hyman Minsky, James Tobin, and others rediscovered Fisher's debt-deflation theory of how some recessions turn into great depressions (Fisher, 1933). William Barber's edition (Fisher, 1997) and Loef and Monissen (1999) renewed interest in Fisher.

Don Patinkin (1981) contested Milton Friedman's claim that his restatement of the quantity theory continued a Chicago oral tradition of money theory and policy (see Tavlas, 1998; see also the Friedman–Patinkin exchange in Gordon, 1974). Patinkin, himself educated at Chicago, argued that Friedman's view of money demand as a stable function of a handful of variables owed more to Keynes and to non-Chicago quantity theorists than to Chicago oral tradition. Henry Simons endorsed monetary rules rather than discretion but, like the other Chicago economists of the 1930s, had neither written money demand as a function of the interest rate, as Keynes did, nor made use of Fisher's distinction between real and money interest, both central features of Friedman's monetarism (Simons, 1948). J. Ronnie Davis (1971) showed that Chicago economists of the early 1930s countenanced deficit-financed public works in the Depression, and that one, Paul Douglas, understood the multiplier before *The General Theory* was published (but, unnoticed by Davis, after the publication of multiplier analysis by Kahn in 1931 and 1933 and Keynes in a 1933 pamphlet, all cited by Douglas – see Dimand, 1988). If, as Patinkin (1981, 1982) argues, Keynes's innovation was in theory rather than in advocacy of public works or budget deficits, support of fiscal activism by Chicago economists or by some of their German contemporaries (Backhaus, 1997; Klausinger, 1999), however interesting, does not constitute anticipation of Keynes.

Allyn Young, who died in 1929, two years after leaving Harvard for a chair at the LSE, is belatedly recognized as a significant theorist. His 1928 Section F presidential address on "Increasing returns and economic progress" prefigures endogenous growth theory (Currie, 1997; Sandilands, 2000). Beyond his writings (Mehrling and Sandilands, 1999), Young was an important teacher, influencing Frank Knight at Cornell, Edward Chamberlin, Lauchlin Currie and Arthur Marget at Harvard, and Nicholas Kaldor at the LSE. Perry Mehrling (1997) argues for Young's importance in monetary economics, but Young's reputation rests on his contribution to growth theory. The promising beginning for modern growth theory suggested by independent publications in 1928 by Young, Cambridge philosopher Frank Ramsey, and Soviet central planner G. F'eldman (all reprinted in Dimand, 2002) was cut short by the deaths of Young and of Ramsey (aged 26) and F'eldman's disappearance in Stalin's purges.

Young's student Currie (1934) anticipated elements of the later Friedman and Schwartz interpretation of the Great Depression as a Great Contraction of the money stock, although Currie differed from Friedman and Schwartz (1963) over the money supply mechanism (Steindl, 1995; see also Brunner's introduction to the 1968 edition of Currie, 1934). In the later 1930s, Currie introduced Keynesianism ("Curried Keynes") into Washington policy discussions (Sandilands, 1990).

21.6　BUSINESS CYCLE INSTITUTES FROM NBER TO MOSCOW

The statistical approach to business cycles, decomposing time series into trends and cycles of assorted amplitude and length (Kitchin cycles, Juglar cycles, 20-year Kuznets cycles, and 55-year Kondratiev long waves, among others) with little *a priori* economic theory, flourished between the wars, particularly after Wesley Mitchell founded the National Bureau of Economic Research in 1920 (see Mitchell, 1913, 1927, 1951; Sherman, 2001). A Conjuncture Institute directed by Kondratiev opened in Moscow in 1921 (disappearing with its director in Stalin's purges). The Rockefeller Foundation partially funded similar institutes established in Berlin in 1925 and Vienna in 1927 (Craver, 1986; Kondratiev, 1998; Klein, 1999), as well as research on cyclical growth at the already established Kiel Institute of World Economics. Kalecki worked at Warsaw's Business Cycle Institute. There were others from Belgium to Bulgaria. The London and Cambridge Economic Service produced a business barometer in the manner of Warren Persons at Harvard.

Enough superimposed cycles can represent any time series as cyclical. Using an ancestor of spectral analysis called the periodogram, Beveridge decomposed wheat prices into 19 cycles with periods ranging from 2.735 years to 68 years, 11 of them very prominent. Such large numbers of cycles inspired skepticism about this statistical approach to business cycle analysis, as did Slutsky's 1927 demonstration that summation of random shocks could produce a series that looked cyclical (see Slutsky, 1937 [1927]). The relatively atheoretical statistical investigators of business cycles did not come into conflict with more theoretically oriented econometricians in the interwar period. Later, Koopmans (1947), research director of the Cowles Commission, criticized the NBER empiricism of Burns and Mitchell (1946) as "measurement without theory" (the controversy is reprinted in Hendry and Morgan, 1995). The vector autoregression (VAR) or "atheoretical macroeconometrics" associated with Sims (1980) marked a return to the NBER empirical approach to cycles, with modern statistical techniques.

The real business cycle stream of "The New Classical research program walks in the footprints of Joseph Schumpeter's *Business Cycles* (1939), holding that the key to the business cycle is the stochastic character of economic growth" (De Long, 2000, p. 83). Aghion and Howitt (1998) formalize Schumpeterian creative destruction, in which entrepreneurial innovation destroys the value of existing physical and human capital. Like Hayek, Schumpeter opposed policy activism during the Great Depression (Klausinger, 1995), but Schumpeter interpreted the severity of the Depression as the fortuitous coincidence of downturns in several cycles of differing periodicity (exacerbated by New Deal policies that restricted output to support prices).

The banker L. Albert Hahn, who taught part-time at the University of Frankfurt and later at the New School for Social Research (the "University in Exile") in New York, founded the Frankfurt Society for Research on Business Cycles in 1926. Going beyond Schumpeter (1934 [1912]), Hahn (1920) made strong claims for stimulus to real output by bank credit-creation. Hahn (1949, pp. 6–7) later declared that "all that is wrong and exaggerated in Keynes I said myself much earlier and more clearly" and reprinted critiques of his own 1920 volume by Ellis (1934) and Haberler, arguing that their objections also applied to Keynes (1936). Boudreaux and Selgin (1990) present Hahn as a precursor of both Keynes and monetarism. However, Hahn championed demand stimulus during the German hyperinflation of the 1920s, when Keynes (1923) analyzed the costs of inflation, and then turned to advocacy of hard money during the Great Depression, when Keynes urged demand stimulus to remedy mass unemployment. To say the least, Hahn's timing in matching his policy proposals to the current situation was unfortunate.

21.7 Vienna and the London School of Economics

The success of lectures delivered at the LSE by Friedrich Hayek (1931), then director of the Austrian Institute for Business Cycle Research, led to his election to a chair at the LSE at the age of 32, championing of Austrian trade cycle theory by another young LSE professor, Lionel Robbins (1934; and see introductions to Hayek, 1931; von Mises, 1935), and translation of other Austrian works. Austrian monetary overinvestment theory argued that expansionary monetary policy made subsequent depression inevitable by encouraging excessive lengthening of the average period of production (Ellis, 1934). The LSE–Austrian school rejected reasoning in terms of aggregates such as the price level, yet a key Austrian concept, the average period of production, became ensnared in capital theory paradoxes. The LSE–Vienna school was devastated by the loss to Keynesian or eclectic positions of promising young Hayekians studying or teaching at the LSE, with a few, notably Paul Sweezy, moving beyond Keynes to Marx (McCormick, 1992). Milton Friedman (in Gordon, 1974, pp. 162–3) argues that Keynes had more appeal to young economists at the LSE than at Chicago because at the LSE:

> the dominant view was that the depression was an inevitable result of the prior boom, that it was deepened by the attempts to prevent prices and wages from falling and firms from going bankrupt . . . that the only sound policy was to let the depression run its course, bring down money costs, and eliminate weak and unsound firms. By contrast with this dismal picture, the news seeping out of Cambridge (England) about Keynes's interpretation of the depression and the right policy to cure it must have come like a flash of light on a dark night. . . . It was the London School (really Austrian) view that I referred to in my "Restatement" when I spoke of "the atrophied and rigid caricature [of the quantity theory] that is so frequently described by the proponents of the new income-expenditure approach – and with some justice, to judge by much of the literature on policy that was spawned by the quantity theorists."

O'Driscoll (1977), Steele (1993), and Colonna and Hagemann (1994) renewed serious study of Hayek's analysis of how markets deal with the coordination problem, as Moss (1976) did for von Mises. The emphasis is on Hayek's development of Menger's concept of spontaneous order and his extension of von Mises's critique of the rationality of socialist planning, rather than his formal theorizing. As *The Economist* (March 31, 2001, p. 77) concludes, "Hayek was not much of a technical economist, as Keynes and Mr Friedman in their different ways understood. But he was a social philosopher of rare system and power."

W. H. Hutt (1977 [1939]), an LSE graduate teaching at the University of Cape Town, presented a search-theoretic explanation of unemployment as an alternative to Keynes (1936). An acerbic critic of union power, Hutt drew on both Hayek's Austrian emphasis on market process and discovery of information, and on Beveridge's analysis of unemployment as a frictional problem of market organization, though he dismissed Beveridge (1930) as "a beautifully written descriptive, empirical study with no analytical content" (on Beveridge (1930), see Dimand, 1999). Hutt (1977 [1939]), the culmination of LSE–Austrian theorizing about unemployment in the 1930s, has attracted little study. Leijonhufvud (1969, p. 31n) identified neglect of Hutt (1977 [1939]) on search as "the worst sin of omission" in Leijonhufvud (1968).

21.8   THE OUTSIDERS: MONETARY HERETICS

Monetary heretics, asserting some flaw in the automatic adjustment mechanism of a capitalist monetary economy, raised questions not faced by mainstream economists (not always well-posed questions by any means). During economic upheavals, they received a hearing or a reply from academic economists (King, 1988; Dimand, 1991), with Robertson and Hayek rebutting the underconsumptionism of Foster and Catchings, and Fisher, Hawtrey, and Keynes taking up Silvio Gesell's stamped scrip proposal. Keynes (1936, ch. 23) praised "the proud army of heretics," notably John Hobson, who had paid attention to effective demand in determining aggregate output. Bleaney (1976) surveys underconsumptionism. Nemmers (1956), Backhouse (1990, 1994), and Schneider (1996) study Hobson's macroeconomics.

21.9   KALECKI AND THE MARXIAN TRADITION

Marxian economics was even further from the mainstream than monetary heresies. Joan Robinson (1977), Lawrence Klein, and others credited Michal Kalecki with independently discovering Keynes's General Theory, building upon Marx and Rosa Luxemburg (1951 [1913]). Patinkin (1982) disputed this, holding that the central message of Kalecki's articles from 1932 to 1935 was investment cycles, unlike the General Theory's principle of effective demand, interpreted as IS goods-market equilibrium (both solution of the equilibrium equation $F(Y) = Y$ and demonstration of stability by the adjustment equation $dY/dt = G[F(Y) - Y]$, where $G' > 0$).

Chapple (1991) argues that Kalecki determined output consistently with the principle of effective demand in a 1933 article in Polish (Kalecki, 1990, pp. 165–74) that Patinkin (1982, p. 69n) dismissed in one sentence in a footnote for arbitrarily fixing the profit share. Chapple (1993) shows capitalist spending decisions determining aggregate income in another 1933 Kalecki essay, with a procyclical profit share, unitary marginal propensity to consume out of wages, and zero marginal propensity to consume out of profits. Chapple (1995a) shows that Kalecki's 1934 Polish journal article "Three systems" (Kalecki, 1990, pp. 201–19) had a three-equation model of goods and money markets and aggregate supply. Kalecki did not include "Three systems" among his translated selected articles in 1966 and 1971, or cite it later, or develop its static equilibrium method, preferring dynamic models where investment alters the capital stock. This may exclude "Three systems" from Kalecki's "central message," but the essays studied by Chapple (1991, 1993, 1995a,b) remain of great interest for what Kalecki was able to produce in the early 1930s working in the Marxian tradition (see also Feiwell, 1975; Sebastiani, 1994; King et al., 1999). Kalecki aside, Howard and King (1989–92, vol. II, p. 19) conclude that "Marxist analyses of the Depression proved deficient, and the ultimate reason is similar to that applying in the case of bourgeois economics: they lacked an adequate theory of effective demand."

21.10 CONCLUSION: MACROECONOMICS BEFORE THE GENERAL THEORY

Harry Johnson (Johnson and Johnson, 1978) and Laidler (1999) argued that for the Keynesian revolution or monetarist counter-revolution to capture the attention and allegiance of the profession and policy-makers, differences with previous theories had to be over-dramatized, terminology altered, and continuities under-played. This led to a period of neglect of the monetary theory flowing from the work of Marshall, Fisher, and Wicksell, and of business cycle theory following from Juglar and Jevons. This rich and varied body of writings included contributions linked to later developments (Robertson and Schumpeter to real business cycles, Schumpeter and Young to endogenous growth, Mitchell to VARs, and Fisher to much of later monetary macroeconomics). Keynes was steeped in Cambridge tradition, and also exposed to Fisher and Wicksell (but not the Lausanne general equilibrium school). Patinkin's concept of a central message helps to clarify where Keynes stood in relation to his predecessors, and to sort out the problem of multiple discoveries. While Keynes also stressed the uncertainty underlying volatile investment decisions, Keynes's central message, according to Patinkin, was the principle of effective demand, the determination and stability of equilibrium income and employment, displacing the central message of quantity theory about prices (with output affected during transition periods) and the message of business cycle analysis about dynamics. Keynes transformed macroeconomics, but a substantial and valuable body of macroeconomics already existed to be transformed.

Bibliography

Adams, F. G. (ed.) 1992: *Lawrence Klein's The Keynesian Revolution: 50 Years After*. Philadelphia: Department of Economics, University of Pennsylvania.

Aghion, P. and Howitt, P. 1998: *Endogenous Growth Theory*. Cambridge, MA: The MIT Press.

Andvig, J. 1985: *Ragnar Frisch and the Great Depression: A Study in the Interwar History of Macroeconomic Theory and Policy*. Oslo: Norwegian Institute of International Affairs.

Aslanbeigui, N. 1992: Pigou's inconsistencies or Keynes's misconceptions? *History of Political Economy*, 24(4), 413–33.

Backhaus, J. 1997: Keynes's German contenders 1932–1944: on the sociology of multiple discoveries in economics. *History of Economic Ideas*, 5(2), 69–84.

Backhouse, R. 1990: J. A. Hobson as a macroeconomic theorist. In M. Freeden (ed.), *Reappraising J. A. Hobson: Humanism and Welfare*, London: Unwin Hyman, 116–36.

—— 1994: Mummery and Hobson's *The Physiology of Industry*. In J. Pheby (ed.), *J. A. Hobson after Fifty Years: Freethinker of the Social Sciences*, London: Macmillan, 78–99.

Bellerby, J. R. 1923: *Control of Credit as a Remedy for Unemployment*. London: P. S. King.

—— 1925: *Monetary Stability*. London: Macmillan.

Beveridge, W. 1930: *Unemployment, a Problem of Industry (1909 and 1930)*. London: Longmans, Green.

Blaug, M. 1995: Why is the quantity theory of money the oldest surviving theory in economics? In M. Blaug, W. Eltis, D. O'Brien, D. Patinkin, R. Skidelsky, and G. Wood, *The Quantity Theory of Money From Locke to Keynes and Friedman*, Aldershot, UK: Edward Elgar, 27–49.

Bleaney, M. 1976: *Underconsumption Theories: A History and Critical Analysis*. New York: International.

Boianovsky, M. 1995: Wicksell's business cycle. *European Journal for the History of Economic Thought*, 2(2), 375–411.

—— 1998: Wicksell on deflation in the early 1920s. *History of Political Economy*, 30(2), 219–76.

Boudreaux, D. and Selgin, G. 1990: L. Albert Hahn: a precursor of Keynesianism *and* the monetarist counterrevolution. *History of Political Economy*, 22(2), 261–80.

Brady, M. 1995: A study of J. M. Keynes' Marshallian–Pigouvian elasticity approach in Chapter 20 and 21 of the GT. *History of Economics Review*, 24, 55–71.

Bridel, P. 1987: *Cambridge Monetary Thought: The Development of Saving-Investment Analysis from Marshall to Keynes*. London: Macmillan.

—— 1997: *Money and General Equilibrium Theory From Walras to Pareto (1870–1923)*. Cheltenham, UK: Edward Elgar.

Burns, A. F. and Mitchell, W. C. 1946: *Measuring Business Cycles*. New York: National Bureau of Economic Research.

Casson, M. 1983: *Economics of Unemployment: An Historical Perspective*. Oxford: Martin Robertson.

Chapple, S. 1991: Did Kalecki get there first? The race for the General Theory. *History of Political Economy*, 23(2), 243–61.

—— 1993: Kalecki's theory of the business cycle and the General Theory. *History of Economics Review*, 20, 120–39.

—— 1995a: Effective demand in Kalecki's early macroeconomics. *History of Economics Review*, 24, 43–54.

—— 1995b: The Kaleckian origins of the Keynesian model. *Oxford Economic Papers*, 47(2), 524–37.

Colonna, M. and Hagemann, H. (eds.) 1994: *The Economics of F. A. Hayek*, vol. 1: *Money and Business Cycles*. Aldershot, UK: Edward Elgar.

Copland, D. (ed.) 1960: *Giblin: The Scholar and the Man*. Melbourne: Cheshire.

Corry, B. 1962: *Money, Saving and Investment in English Economics 1800–1850*. London: Macmillan.

Craver, E. 1986: Patronage and the direction of research in economics: the Rockefeller Foundation in Europe, 1924–1938, *Minerva*, 24, 205–22.

Currie, L. 1934: *The Supply and Control of Money in the United States*. Cambridge, MA: Harvard University Press. Reprinted with introduction by K. Brunner, New York: Russell & Russell, 1968.

—— 1997: Implications of an endogenous theory of growth in Allyn Young's macro-economic concept of increasing returns, *History of Political Economy*, 29(3), 414–43.

Davis, E. G. 1980: The correspondence between R. G. Hawtrey and J. M. Keynes on the *Treatise*: the genesis of output adjustment models. *Canadian Journal of Economics*, 12(4), 716–24.

Davis, J. R. 1971: *The New Economics and the Old Economists*. Ames: Iowa State University Press.

De Long, J. B. 2000: The triumph of monetarism? *Journal of Economic Perspectives*, 14(1), 83–94.

Deutscher, P. 1990: *R. G. Hawtrey and the Development of Macroeconomics*. London: Macmillan.

Dimand, R. W. 1988: *The Origins of the Keynesian Revolution*. Aldershot, UK: Edward Elgar.

—— 1991: Cranks, heretics and macroeconomics in the 1930s. *History of Economics Review*, 16, 11–30.

—— 1999: Beveridge on unemployment and cycles before *The General Theory*. *History of Economic Ideas*, 7(3), 33–51.

—— (ed.) 2002: *The Origins of Macroeconomics*, 10 vols. London and New York: Routledge.

Ellis, H. 1934: *German Monetary Theory 1905–1933*. Cambridge, MA: Harvard University Press.

Endres, A. and Fleming, G. 1999a: Public investment programmes in the interwar period: the view from Geneva. *European Journal of the History of Economic Thought*, 6(1), 87–109.

—— and —— 1999b: The ILO and the League of Nations: a distinctive perspective on macroeconomic stabilization policy in the 1920s. In L. Pasinetti and B. Schefold (eds.), *The Impact of Keynes on Economics in the 20th Century*. Cheltenham, UK: Edward Elgar, 202–20.

Eshag, E. 1963: *From Marshall to Keynes: An Essay on the Monetary Theory of the Cambridge School*. Oxford: Blackwell.

Feiwell, G. 1975: *The Intellectual Capital of Michal Kalecki*. Knoxville: University of Tennessee Press.

Fetter, F. W. 1965: *The Development of British Monetary Orthodoxy 1797–1875*. Cambridge, MA: Harvard University Press.

Fisher, I. 1896: *Appreciation and Interest*. New York: Macmillan, for the American Economic Association.

—— 1907: *The Rate of Interest*. New York: Macmillan.

——, with Brown, H. G. 1911: *The Purchasing Power of Money*. New York: Macmillan.

—— 1926: A statistical relation between unemployment and price changes. *International Labour Review*, 13(6), 785–92. Reprinted 1973 as: Lost and found: I discovered the Phillips curve. *Journal of Political Economy*, 81(2), 496–502.

—— 1930: *The Theory of Interest*. New York: Macmillan.

—— 1933: The debt-deflation theory of Great Depressions. *Econometrica*, 1(3), 337–57.

—— 1997: *Works of Irving Fisher*, 14 vols, edited by W. J. Barber assisted by R. W. Dimand and K. Foster, consulting editor J. Tobin. London: Pickering & Chatto.

Flanders, M. J. 1989: *International Monetary Economics 1870–1960: Between the Classical and the New Classical.* Cambridge, UK: Cambridge University Press.

Fletcher, G. 2000: *Understanding Dennis Robertson: The Man and his Work.* Cheltenham, UK: Edward Elgar.

Friedman, M. and Schwartz, A. J. 1963: *A Monetary History of the United States 1867–1960.* Princeton, NJ: Princeton University Press for National Bureau of Economic Research.

Giblin, L. F. 1930: *Australia 1930.* Melbourne: Melbourne University Press. Reprinted in Dimand (2002), op. cit.

Goodhart, C. and Presley, J. 1994: Real business cycle theory: A restatement of Robertsonian economics? *Economic Notes Monte dei Paschi di Siena,* 23(2), 275–91.

Gordon, R. J. (ed.) 1974: *Milton Friedman's Monetary Framework: A Debate with his Critics.* Chicago: The University of Chicago Press.

Grice-Hutchinson, M. 1952: *The School of Salamanca: Readings in Spanish Monetary Theory, 1544–1605.* Oxford: The Clarendon Press.

Guggenheim, T. 1989: *Preclassical Monetary Theories.* London and New York: Pinter.

Hagemann, H. (ed.) 2001: *Business Cycle Theory: Selected Texts 1860–1939,* 4 vols. London: Pickering & Chatto.

Hahn, L. A. 1920: *Volkswirtschaftliche Theorie des Bankkredits.* Tübingen.

—— 1949: *The Economics of Illusion.* New York: Squier.

Hawtrey, R. 1913: *Good and Bad Trade.* London: Constable. Reprinted New York: Kelley, 1970 (with 1962 preface by author).

—— 1919: *Currency and Credit.* London: Longman.

—— 1932: *The Art of Central Banking.* London: Longman.

Hayek, F. A. 1931: *Prices and Production.* London: Routledge.

Hendry, D. and Morgan, M. (eds.) 1995: *Foundations of Econometric Analysis.* Cambridge, UK: Cambridge University Press.

Hicks, J. R. 1937: Mr Keynes and the classics: a suggested interpretation. *Econometrica,* 5(1), 147–59.

Howard, M. and King, J. 1989–92: *A History of Marxian Economics,* 2 vols. Princeton, NJ: Princeton University Press.

Humphrey, T. 1986: *Essays on Inflation,* 5th edn. Richmond, VA: Federal Reserve Bank of Richmond.

Hutchison, T. W. 1953: *A Review of Economic Doctrines 1870–1929.* Oxford: The Clarendon Press.

—— 1980: *The Limitation of General Theories in Macroeconomics.* Washington, DC: American Enterprise Institute.

Hutt, W. H. 1977 [1939]: *The Theory of Idle Resources.* London: Cape; 2nd edn. Indianapolis: Liberty Fund, 1977.

Jevons, W. S. 1884: *Investigations in Currency and Finance,* ed. H. S. Foxwell. London: Macmillan.

Johnson, E. S. and Johnson, H. G. 1978: *The Shadow of Keynes.* Chicago: The University of Chicago Press.

Jonung, L. (ed.) 1991: *The Stockholm School of Economics Revisited.* Cambridge, UK: Cambridge University Press.

—— (ed.) 1993: *Swedish Economic Thought.* London and New York: Routledge.

Kalecki, M. 1990: *Collected Works of Michal Kalecki, Volume I: Capitalism, Business Cycles and Full Employment,* ed. J. Osiatynski. Oxford: The Clarendon Press.

Keynes, J. M. 1923: *A Tract on Monetary Reform.* London: Macmillan.

—— 1936: *The General Theory of Employment, Interest and Money.* London: Macmillan.

—— 1971–89: *Collected Writings*, 30 vols, general eds. D. E. Moggridge and E. A. G. Robinson, volume eds. E. S. Johnson and D. E. Moggridge. London: Macmillan and New York: Cambridge University Press, for the Royal Economic Society.

King, J. E. 1988: *Economic Exiles*. London: Macmillan.

—— et al. 1999: Special issue on Kalecki, *Review of Political Economy*, 11(3), 251–371.

Klausinger, H. 1995: Schumpeter and Hayek: two views of the Great Depression re-examined. *History of Economic Ideas*, 3, 93–127.

—— 1999: German anticipations of the Keynesian revolution? The case of Lautenbach, Neisser and Röpke. *European Journal of the History of Economic Thought*, 6(3), 378–403.

Klein, J. 1999: The rise of "Non-October" econometrics: Kondratiev and Slutsky at the Moscow Conjuncture Institute. *History of Political Economy*, 31(1), 137–68.

Klein, L. 1946: *The Keynesian Revolution*. New York: Macmillan.

Kondratiev, N. D. 1998: *The Works of Nikolai D. Kondratiev*, 4 vols, ed. N. Makasheva, W. Samuels, and V. Barnett. London: Pickering & Chatto.

Koopmans, T. 1947: Measurement without theory. *Review of Economic Statistics*, 29, 161–72.

Laidler, D. 1991: *The Golden Age of the Quantity Theory*. Princeton, NJ: Princeton University Press.

—— 1999: *Fabricating the Keynesian Revolution: Studies of the Inter-War Literature on Money, the Cycle, and Unemployment*. Cambridge, UK: Cambridge University Press.

Leijonhufvud, A. 1968: *On Keynesian Economics and the Economics of Keynes*. New York: Oxford University Press.

—— 1969: *Keynes and the Classics*. London: Institute of Economic Affairs.

Lindhal, E. 1939: *Studies in the Theory of Money and Capital*. London: George Allen & Unwin.

Link, R. 1959: *English Theories of Economic Fluctuations 1815–1848*. New York: Columbia University Press.

Loef, H.-E. and Monissen, H. (eds.) 1999: *The Economics of Irving Fisher*. Cheltenham, UK: Edward Elgar.

Lundberg, E. 1937: *Studies in the Theory of Economic Expansion*. London: King.

—— 1994: *Studies in Economic Instability and Change*, edited with a postscript by R. G. H. Henrikson. Stockholm: SNS Forlag.

—— 1996: *The Development of Swedish and Keynesian Macroeconomic Theory and its Impact on Economic Policy*. Cambridge, UK: Cambridge University Press.

Luxemburg, R. 1951 [1913]: *The Accumulation of Capital*, translated by A. Schwarzchild, with an introduction by J. Robinson. New Haven, CT: Yale University Press, 1951.

Marshall, A. 1923: *Money, Credit and Commerce*. London: Macmillan.

—— 1926: *Official Papers of Alfred Marshall*, ed. J. M. Keynes. London: Macmillan.

McCormick, B. 1992: *Hayek and the Keynesian Avalanche*. New York: St. Martin's Press.

Mehrling, P. 1997: *The Money Interest and the Public Interest: American Monetary Thought 1920–1970*. Cambridge, MA: Harvard University Press.

—— and Sandilands, R. (eds.) 1999: *Money and Growth: Selected Papers of Allyn Abbott Young*. London and New York: Routledge.

Milmow, A. 2000: Revisiting Giblin: Australia's first proto-Keynesian economist? *History of Economics Review*, 31, 48–67.

Mises, L. von 1935: *The Theory of Money and Credit*, trans. H. Batson. London: Cape.

Mitchell, W. C. 1913: *Business Cycles*. Berkeley, CA: University of California Press. Reprinted New York: Burt Franklin, 1970.

—— 1927: *Business Cycles, the Problem and its Setting*. New York: National Bureau for Economic Research.

—— 1951: *What Happens During Business Cycles: A Progress Report.* New York: National Bureau of Economic Research.

Moss, L. (ed.) 1976: *The Economics of Ludwig von Mises.* Kansas City, MO: Sheed & Ward.

Myrdal, G. 1939: *Monetary Equilibrium,* trans. R. Bryce and N. Stolper. London: W. Hodge.

Nemmers, E. E. 1956: *Hobson and Underconsumption.* Amsterdam: North-Holland.

O'Brien, D. 1993: *Thomas Joplin and Classical Macroeconomics.* Oxford: The Clarendon Press.

—— (ed.) 1997: *Foundations of Business Cycle Theory,* 3 vols. Cheltenham, UK: Edward Elgar.

—— 2000: Bodin's analysis of inflation, *History of Political Economy,* 32(2), 267–92.

O'Driscoll, G. 1977: *Economics as a Coordination Problem: The Contributions of Friedrich A. Hayek.* Kansas City, MO: Sheed Andrews and McMeel.

Ohlin, B. 1978 [1933]: On the formulation of monetary theory. *History of Political Economy,* 10(3), 353–88.

Patinkin, D. 1981: *Essays on and in the Chicago Tradition.* Durham, NC: Duke University Press.

—— 1982: *Anticipations of the General Theory? And Other Essays on Keynes.* Chicago: The University of Chicago Press.

Peart, S. 1996: *The Economics of W. S. Jevons.* London and New York: Routledge.

Pigou, A. C. 1927: *Industrial Fluctuations.* London: Macmillan.

—— 1933: *Theory of Unemployment.* London: Macmillan.

Presley, J. 1979: *Robertsonian Economics.* London: Macmillan.

Robbins, L. 1934: *The Great Depression.* London: Macmillan.

Robertson, D. H. 1915: *A Study of Industrial Fluctuation.* London: King.

—— 1926: *Banking Policy and the Price Level.* London: King.

Robinson, J. 1977: Michal Kalecki on the economics of capitalism, *Oxford Bulletin of Economics and Statistics,* 39(1), 7–17.

Rymes, T. K. (ed.) 1987: *Keynes's Lectures, 1932–35: Notes of Students.* Ottawa: Department of Economics, Carleton University.

Samuelson, P. A. 1946: Lord Keynes and the General Theory, *Econometrica,* 14(2), 187–200.

Sandilands, R. 1990: *The Life and Political Economy of Lauchlin Currie.* Durham, NC: Duke University Press.

—— 2000: Perspectives on Allyn Young in theories of endogenous growth. *Journal of the History of Economic Thought,* 22(3), 309–28.

Schneider, M. 1996: *J. A. Hobson.* London: Macmillan.

Schumpeter, J. 1934 [1912]: *The Theory of Economic Development,* trans. R. Opie. Cambridge, MA: Harvard University Press.

—— 1939: *Business Cycles,* 2 vols. New York: McGraw-Hill.

Schwartz, A. J. 1987: Banking school, currency school, free banking school. In J. Eatwell, M. Milgate, and P. Newman (eds.), *The New Palgrave: A Dictionary of Economics,* London: Macmillan.

Sebastiani, M. 1994: *Kalecki and Unemployment Equilibrium.* London: Macmillan.

Sherman, H. 2001: The business cycle theory of Wesley Mitchell. *Journal of Economic Issues,* 35(1), 85–97.

Simons, H. 1948: *Economic Policy for a Free Society.* Chicago: The University of Chicago Press.

Sims, C. 1980: Macroeconomics and reality. *Econometrica,* 48(1), 1–48.

Slutsky, E. E. 1937 [1927]: The summation of random causes on the source of cyclic process. *Econometrica,* 5, 105–46.

Sowell, T. 1972: *Say's Law: An Historical Analysis.* Princeton, NJ: Princeton University Press.

Steele, G. R. 1993: *The Economics of Friedrich Hayek.* London: Macmillan.

Steindl, F. 1995: *Monetary Interpretations of the Great Depression*. Ann Arbor, MI: University of Michigan Press.

Tarascio, V. 1969: The monetary and employment theories of Vilfredo Pareto. *History of Political Economy*, 1(1), 101–22.

Tavlas, G. 1998: Retrospectives: Was the monetarist tradition invented? *Journal of Economic Perspectives*, 12(4), 211–22.

Thornton, H. 1965 [1802]: *An Enquiry into the Nature and Effects of the Paper Credit of Great Britain*, ed. F. Hayek. New York: Kelley.

Trautwein, H.-M. 1996: Money, equilibrium, and the business cycle: Hayek's Wicksellian dichotomy. *History of Political Economy*, 28(1), 27–55.

Uhr, C. 1990: Erik Lundberg's economic dynamics. *Journal of the History of Economic Thought*, 12(2), 222–35.

Vickers, D. 1959: *Studies in the Theory of Money 1690–1776*. New York: Chilton.

Wicksell, K. 1935 [1915]: *Lectures on Political Economy*, vol. II, trans. E. Claasen. London: Routledge.

—— 1962 [1898]: *Interest and Prices*, trans. R. Kahn. London: Macmillan, for the Royal Economic Society, 1936. Reprinted New York: Kelley.

Young, W. 1987: *Interpreting Mr Keynes: The IS–LM Enigma*. Cambridge, UK: Polity Press.

CHAPTER TWENTY-TWO

Keynes and the Cambridge School

G. C. Harcourt and Prue Kerr

22.1   INTRODUCTION

We start with Maynard Keynes's central ideas. We then discuss the strands that emerged in the work of others, some contemporaries, some followers, some agreeing and extending, others disagreeing and/or returning to ideas that Keynes sloughed off or played down. *The General Theory* is the natural starting point. We trace developments from and reactions to it, especially by people who were associated, at least for part of their working lives, with Cambridge, England. In the concluding paragraphs, we briefly discuss the contributions of those not geographically located in Cambridge who nevertheless worked within the tradition of Keynes and the Cambridge school.

22.2   KEYNES AND THE CLASSICS

The General Theory emerged as a reaction to the system of thought, principally associated with Alfred Marshall and A. C. Pigou, on which Keynes was brought up and which he was to subsume, misleadingly, under the rubric of the classical school. Keynes rationally reconstructed the classical system by setting out what, though it could not be found in the writings of any one "classical" economist, must have been assumed and developed if sense were to be made of their attitudes and claims. (Keynes's procedure could be equally well described as opportunistic.) In its most stark form, the classical system assumes a clear dichotomy between the real and the monetary, with the real the dominant partner, at least in the long period. In a competitive environment there is a tendency to market-clearing in all markets (including the labor market), again, at least in the long period. This determines the values of equilibrium normal long-period prices and quantities, including those for the services of the factors of production. It also provides the theoretical value of T in Irving Fisher's version of the quantity theory of money (QTM) (Y in Marshall's version) and, together with the assumption of an exogenous value of M and a given value of $V(k)$, makes the general price level (P) proportional to M. The natural rate of interest – a real concept – equilibrates real saving and investment, determining the composition of full-employment Y, itself determined by the full-employment equilibrium value of employment in the labor market. The money rate of interest has to adjust to the real rate, which rules the roost.

This is more a Marshallian than a Ricardian view of the world; it assumes Say's Law in a form in which the original classical political economists would never have stated it, as far as full employment of labor (as opposed to capital) is concerned.

This system underlay Keynes's *Tract* and *Treatise on Money*, though Keynes champed at the bit of its constraints, wishing to analyze short-period happenings to production and employment and propose policies appropriate for other than that long run in which we are all dead. Even in the *Treatise on Money*, long-period stock and flow equilibrium and its attainment dominated the core of the analysis. Keynes felt guilty analyzing short-period changes in output and employment, but he did allow himself the banana plantation parable, the analysis of which was incomplete because Kahn's multiplier analysis had not yet occurred.

These constraints were virtually completely removed in *The General Theory*. The real-money dichotomy was discarded; money and financial matters entered from the start of the analysis, fully integrated with real happenings. Money, analytically, had all its dimensions – a store of value as well as a medium of exchange and a unit of account. Emphasis moved from the long to the short period. Keynes's predilections in this regard were reinforced by the approach and work of his favorite pupil, now colleague, Richard Kahn, whose King's fellowship dissertation, "The economics of the short period," made the short period worthy of study in its own right – though, as we shall see, it is not unanimously agreed that *The General Theory* is or should be short period in emphasis. The switch from saving determining investment to investment determining saving, which was already occurring in Cambridge and elsewhere, became complete in *The General Theory*. The money rate of interest, now the price that equalized the demand for and supply of money, ruled the roost; the *General Theory* version of the natural rate of interest, the *mec* (it should have been the *mei*), had to measure up to it. The heretical concept of an unemployment equilibrium or rest state, the point of effective demand, emerged as the central proposition of *The General Theory*.

With Say's Law refuted, QTM no longer explained the general price level. Keynes substituted for it a macroeconomic version of Marshall's short-period supply curve. With marginal-cost pricing usually assumed to occur, there was an upward-sloping relationship between activity and the general price level in any given situation. Some of his closest colleagues and co-workers – Roy Harrod, Kahn, Austin and Joan Robinson, Gerald Shove, and Piero Sraffa – had helped to develop the then emerging theory of imperfect competition. Keynes noted this but did not think it of central importance for his new, different purposes – he took as given the degree of competition. (Michal Kalecki showed in his review article of *The General Theory* how right Keynes's instinct was. Nevertheless, Kalecki and, subsequently the post-Keynesians, for example, Nicholas Kaldor, Alfred Eichner, G. C. Harcourt and Peter Kenyon, Sydney Weintraub, and Adrian Wood, were to make mark-up pricing, replete with a theory of the determination of its size, an integral part of the theories of employment and distribution.) Crucially, Keynes's philosophical views, developed while he was still an undergraduate and most comprehensively expressed in his 1909 King's fellowship dissertation, *A Treatise on Probability* (subsequently published in 1921), are an integral aspect of the complex analysis of *The General Theory*. We refer to the modern writings on the significance of this in the concluding paragraphs.

We should also mention the sad happening that Keynes's closest collaborator in the development of monetary theory during the 1920s, Dennis Robertson, parted company with him as *The General Theory* emerged. Robertson was shocked by Keynes's disrespect for his elders and betters (read Marshall). He thought the policy implications were dangerous because Keynes's analysis did not capture the rich, inescapable dynamics of the interactions of the real and monetary sectors of industrialized economies. They implied cyclical developments, around which monetary and fiscal measures should attempt to fit like a glove but not try to remove, in order to preserve the potential of long-term rises in productivity and the standard of living generally. The rift was both a personal and professional tragedy (a superb account of the psychological and intellectual reasons for it can be found in Fletcher, 2000).

Kahn and Joan Robinson were always hostile to the IS–LM version of Keynes's system as it came down to the profession and the textbooks, principally through J. R. Hicks's famous 1937 article. They never said why in print, but it became clear in the postwar period that they thought it cut out Keynes's emphasis on how an environment of inescapable uncertainty affected how (usually) sensible people did the best they could when making economic decisions. They also thought it impossible to properly set out Keynes's new ideas within the framework of Hicks's adaptation of the Walrasian system. The latter underlay *Value and Capital* (1939), written while Hicks was teaching in Cambridge in the second half of the 1930s (it was conceived when he was at LSE), so that it was the natural framework within which for him to try to understand Keynes's new theory. Keynes, Kahn, and Austin and Joan Robinson were always resolutely Marshallian in method, even for macroeconomics. Yet passages in *The General Theory* – see, for example, page 173 – may legitimately be interpreted in terms of IS–LM. They show its great limitations as well as the basic insight that it gives (see Moggridge, 1976, pp. 171–4). The two relationships cannot be taken to be independent of one another; changes in the value of a parameter underlying one may often affect those underlying the other, leading to Keynes's shifting equilibrium model and to the modern analysis of path-dependence (which Kaldor initially set out in 1934!). Several of Keynes's closest allies did *The General Theory* in terms of IS–LM, admittedly in algebra or words, not diagrams. Thus Brian Reddaway's review, and Harrod's and James Meade's contributions to the session at the Oxford conference at which Hicks presented his paper are so set out. Indeed, Hicks read Harrod's and Meade's papers *before* he wrote his and produced the diagram (see Young, 1987).

22.3   KEYNES, KEYNESIANS, AND WORLD WAR II

Although a group of Keynesians dispute it (see pp. 351–2 below), those closest to Keynes regarded Keynes's core model as set in the short period. He was mostly concerned with the employment-creating effects of investment expenditure and virtually ignored its capacity-creating effects. He analyzed the conditions for the establishment of a rest state that could be associated with unemployment in a situation in which the existing stock of capital goods, supplies of skilled and unskilled labor, the quantity of money, and the degree of competition were given. He provided a sketchy analysis of the trade cycle in a later chapter and made some asides about prospects for long-term growth (or their lack), but never systematically examined them in *The General Theory* itself. He set out policy proposals for attaining full employment in the short term, starting from a deep slump but, again, only sketched in the difficulties associated with sustaining full employment – Kalecki (1943) analyzed the crucial difference between the political economy of getting to full employment and sustaining it. In wartime, Keynes and his ideas played a major role in getting the British economy through World War II without major inflationary problems. Keynes illustrated his theory's generality in *How to Pay for the War* (1940). There he introduced the concept of an inflationary gap – aggregate demand in real terms exceeding full-employment aggregate supply – and the steps to be taken to eliminate the gap to avoid prices rising, queues forming, and order books lengthening.

During the war, two of Keynes's closest associates, Meade and Richard Stone, developed a comprehensive system of national accounts based on the relationships in Keynes's theory to help the war effort by avoiding bottlenecks and shortages. Building on these foundations Stone developed the accounts uniformly and internationally. (He received the Nobel Prize in 1984 for these "fundamental contributions." Meade received it in 1977 for his contributions to international economics, also built on Keynesian foundations.) Economic historians – for example, Alec Cairncross, Phyllis Deane, Charles Feinstein, and Brian Mitchell – used the Keynesian system and national accounts to reinterpret aspects of the Industrial Revolution and, in the case of Deane, to analyze the problems of developing countries.

22.4   GROWTH AND DISTRIBUTION

In the postwar period, Kahn, Joan Robinson, and Sraffa, stimulated by Harrod's seminal prewar and early postwar writings on growth (1939, 1948) and by the problems of reconstruction and development generally, turned their attention to "generalising *The General Theory* to the long period." (They were later joined by

Kaldor and then Luigi Pasinetti.) They reached back over the neoclassical interlude of resource allocation and price theory generally to the preoccupations of the classical political economists and Marx with growth, distribution, and the role of technical progress, taking in the findings of the Keynesian revolution in the process. Harrod posed two fundamental problems: first, the instability of his warranted rate of growth, g_w – the rate of growth which, if attained, would be sustained because actual outcomes would persuade decision-makers concerning accumulation that they were doing the correct rates of accumulation. If it were not attained, the economy would give out destabilizing signals; the actual rate of growth, g, would tend to move further and further away from g_w in either direction, depending upon whether g was greater than or less than g_w. The second problem was whether there were forces at work that could bring g_w and g_n together, where g_n, the natural rate of growth, represented the supply potential of the economy associated with the rates of growth of its labor supply in quantity and quality. There was no reason why g_w should equal g_n, because g_w was concerned with accumulators achieving their desires, not wage-earners necessarily being fully employed, as they would be on g_n. The Cambridge Keynesian growth theorists addressed these two basic problems. (John Cornwall, much influenced by Kaldor's approach in particular and unwilling to accept Harrod's assumption that g_n was independent of g_w, has over the past 40 years and more, illuminated our understanding of the development of capitalist economies over time by analyzing how g_w and g_n feed back into one another: see Harcourt and Monadjemi, 1999.)

To illustrate significant differences in their approaches, we consider those of Kahn and Joan Robinson, on the one hand, and Kaldor, on the other. Both developed macroeconomic theories of distribution. Kaldor called them "Keynesian" because he found their origins in the passages in the *Treatise on Money* on the widow's cruse and because they incorporated the Keynesian view that investment led and saving responded to it. Kaldor initially argued that in the long period the economy grew at full employment along g_n; the role of the multiplier was to determine the distribution of income between profits and wages, supposing that the marginal propensity to save from profits, s_{II}, exceeded that from wages, s_w, and money prices were more flexible than money wages in the long period. If the economy were not saving the right amount to allow the provision of the accumulation needed to keep the economy on g_n, the gap between planned investment and saving would so change the distribution of income as prices change more rapidly than money wages, as to bring about an overall saving ratio equal to the required investment ratio in long-period full-employment income. (In the 1930s, Kalecki developed a similar theory for the short period, but did not require the economy to be at full employment. Saving therefore could be brought to equality with investment by changes in income *and* its distribution, and the resulting rest state could be associated with involuntary unemployment. Moreover, Kalecki explicitly linked pricing practices and their determinants in different sectors of the economy to the distribution of income.)

Kahn and Joan Robinson developed their arguments in two stages. First, they examined the properties of Golden Ages, so-called because they were mythical states, never to be realized in reality. Their aim was to make precise certain definitions – profits, capital, saving, investment – and relationships which could only be made so in Golden Ages (or "steady states," as the neoclassical growth theorists called them) where expectations and actuality always matched. They identified several variants of Golden Age, some with desirable properties, others not, such as Bastard Golden Ages, with sustained unemployment of labor. They then attempted to analyze processes occurring in historical time (as opposed to the logical time of Golden Age analysis), never completely successfully. Indeed, toward the end of her life, Joan Robinson sometimes despaired of ever achieving this, though in one of her last papers (coauthored with Amit Bhaduri: see Bhaduri and Robinson, 1980), she was less pessimistic than in her nihilistic paper of the same year, originally entitled "Spring cleaning" (Robinson, 1985 [1980]). There she argued that we should scrap everything and start anew.

Kaldor, though, was happy to use steady-state analysis in descriptive analysis of the real world, making sense in explanations of the occurrence of his famous "stylised facts" – near enough regularities over time to require explanation. He wrote a series of papers in the 1950s and 1960s, starting from his famous "Alternative theories of distribution" (1955–6). They were both Keynesian and classical, because he now introduced a technical progress function relating productivity growth to the rate of take-up through accumulation of the flow of new ideas through time. In the most refined version, investment is specifically related to embodiment at the margin of new ideas and to productivity growth. All incorporate Kaldor's (and, eventually, other Cambridge growth theorists') refusal to accept the neoclassical distinction between movements *along* a given production function (deepening) and movements *of* the production function due to technical progress. Kaldor regarded the distinction as incoherent – new accumulation carried with it, indissolubly, new ways of making products and, often, new products themselves.

Kaldor's and Joan Robinson's views were not *that* different from the pioneering work of Wilfred Salter on vintages in *Productivity and Technical Change* (1960), except that, at any moment of time, the *ex ante* production function of "best-practice" techniques was whittled down to one point, endogenously created to meet the needs of the moment (in the light of expectations about the future), while Salter allowed a choice of techniques to occur. Eventually, Kaldor rejected this approach. He ultimately thought that the problems of steady growth arose from the difficulty of keeping the growth of the availability of primary products in line with the growth of the absorptive capacity of the industrial sectors of the world. In his view neither the Keynesian nor the neoclassical models could handle the *complementarity* of an integrated world. A multi-sector model was required to tackle the mutual interdependence of the sectors, where the development of each depends upon and is stimulated by the development of others. Different pricing behavior as between the sectors tended to frustrate the emergence of harmonious interdependence. Kaldor's approach has been developed by his biographer, Tony Thirlwall, often with John McCombie (see, e.g., McCombie and Thirlwall, 1994). But we have run ahead of our story.

22.5 THE CAPITAL THEORY CRITIQUE

Simultaneously with these positive developments of classical cum Marxian cum Keynesian ideas occurred a critique of the foundations of neoclassical value, growth, and distribution theory associated with the so-called Cambridge controversies in the theory of capital. Starting as an attack on the capital variable in the aggregate production function, it developed, especially in the hands of Joan Robinson and Kahn, into a critique of the long-period method – comparisons of long-period positions with different values of a key parameter to analyze processes occurring in actual time. Summed up in Joan Robinson's phrase, "History versus equilibrium," it is the error of using differences to illuminate the results of changes. Another strand of the critique was precipitated into the public domain by Joan Robinson in 1953–4 (developed long before by Sraffa, it was revealed with the publication of *Production of Commodities* in 1960.) It questioned the robustness of the intuition that prices, including distributive prices, were reliable indexes of scarcity. This intuition was refuted in the 1960s by the capital-reversing and reswitching results. They destroyed the theoretical foundations of the inevitability of a downward-sloping demand curve for capital (outside the domain of one commodity models) and of negative relationships between the rate of profits (r), on the one hand, and capital-output ratios and sustainable levels of consumption per head, on the other. Indeed, the coherence of the concept of a marginal product of capital (outside the one commodity domain) was called into question. The marginal productivity theory of distribution became problematic, for reasons other than those adduced within the neoclassical framework (see Mandler, 1999).

In the 1950s Kahn and Joan Robinson extended Keynes's liquidity preference theory of the rate of interest to take in the stock market, adding equities to bonds as financial assets competing with the holding of money. They built on Keynes's 1937 papers (see Keynes, 1937a,b) setting out his insight of the *Treatise on Money*, lost sight of in *The General Theory*, that finance, not saving, was the ultimate constraint on the rate of accumulation, provided that expected profits were buoyant. (Depressed expected profits obviously bite in a slump, regardless of the state of finance – hence Keynes's pessimism about an effective role for easier credit terms *on their own* in revival from a slump.) Also associated with these developments were Kaldor's seminal ideas from the late 1930s about the operation of markets where stocks dominate flows and expectations of future price movements on both sides of the market dominate the impact of the usual determinants of prices.

22.6 PIERO SRAFFA'S *PRODUCTION OF COMMODITIES*

Sraffa had started long before the 1950s on a critique of the foundations of the neoclassical value and distribution theory. The first public inklings of this, as Joan Robinson saw it, were in the 1951 Introduction to the Ricardo volumes edited by Sraffa in collaboration with Maurice Dobb. She was then searching for a satisfactory theory of the origin and size of the rate of profits in her emerging work on growth theory. In the Introduction, Sraffa discussed Ricardo's theory, starting with a reconstruction, historical and rational, which involved the use of a corn model to explain Ricardo's early view that the profits of the farmer ruled the roost. This was to be replaced in the *Principles* by a labor-embodied theory of profits, an obvious link to Marx but without the concept of exploitation. (Smith and Ricardo recognized the existence of class war and the lack of harmony in the operation of capitalism.) Joan Robinson had been absorbing Marx's messages from the mid-1930s, encouraged first by her friendship with Kalecki and then in order to take her mind off the war.

When *Production of Commodities* was published (1960), a few reviewers sensed Sraffa's twofold purpose – to provide a prelude to a refutation of the conceptual and logical foundations of (neoclassical) economic theory and to revive the approach of the classical political economists and Marx to value and distribution theory. The latter was intended to make possible a coherent theory of the laws of motion of capitalist society, already potentially there in Marx's writings, but with errors removed and unfinished business completed. Such were the views of Dobb (the leading Marxist economist of his generation in the UK) and Sraffa, Joan Robinson (with reservations), Ronald Meek, and Kalecki. The core organizing concept is the surplus – its creation, extraction, distribution, and use. In the book, Sraffa examines production with a surplus in a system of single commodity industries; the determination, first, of r and long-period relative prices when the value of w is given and then of w and prices when the value of r is given; joint production systems in order to analyze fixed capital; land, in order to take in price-determined rent; and the choice of technique to complete the story *and* show the nonrobustness of the intuition of price as an index of scarcity in distribution theory. The system of Sraffa's book is a rigorous representation of the structure of the centers of gravitation associated with the natural prices of Smith and Ricardo and the prices of production of Marx. It is not one side of Marshall's demand and supply story of the determination of long-period equilibrium normal prices (it has been so interpreted by even such astute critics as Samuelson and Mandler).

Sraffa's method is seen by Sraffians as the examination of the outcome of persistent forces in establishing centers of gravitation of the economic system. It incorporates the classical political economists' insight that in a competitive environment there is a tendency toward equality of profit rates in all activities; thus a theory of the overall rate of profits to which they tend in value is needed, a macroeconomic theory because it "could not be otherwise" (Pasinetti, 1962, p. 277). It provides the basis for the revival of classical theory as well as a prelude to a critique of neoclassical theory. The initial critique was spelt out in the capital theory debates of the 1950s to 1970s (see Harcourt, 1972). Positive aspects of the rehabilitation may be found in, for example, Heinz Kurz and Neri Salvadori's work on long-period production (1995).

22.7 LONG-PERIOD KEYNESIANS

Sraffa, though a close friend of Keynes, was not bowled over by *The General Theory*. (He did defend Keynes's *Treatise on Money* against Friedrich von Hayek's attack, in the process using the concept of own rates of interest. Keynes used the concept to play a key role in the crucial, difficult chapter 17 of *The General Theory*. We suspect that Sraffa would not have approved, because he used the concept in an internal critique of Hayek's system, not to analyze actual economies.) Sraffa's followers embraced Keynes but argued that for his theory to be revolutionary, he must provide (or have provided) a *long-period* theory of effective demand purged of neoclassical leftovers in, for example, the *mec* of his investment theory which, they argue, is vulnerable to the capital theory critique (not so, according to Pasinetti). Murray Milgate (1982) is the most detailed argument for this viewpoint but there are prior articles by, for example, Pierangelo Garegnani, gathered together (including dissent from Joan Robinson) in the 1983 collection edited by John Eatwell and Milgate.

22.8 LUIGI PASINETTI, RICHARD GOODWIN, AND MICHAL KALECKI

The most original, ambitious, and sustained attempt to marry classical political economy (as revived by Sraffa) and Keynes's insights is found in the writings of Pasinetti, senior heir to the "pure" post-Keynesian school of economic thought now that the founding members are dead. His multi-sectoral growth model, originally developed in his Cambridge Ph.D. dissertation in the 1950s and 1960s, and reaching maturity in his 1981 book (and 1993 students' guide), is a *tour de force*. It absorbs Kahn's and Joan Robinson's Golden Age analysis, *The General Theory*'s principal insights, Kaldor's growth and distribution theories, and Sraffa's analysis of value, distribution, and production-interdependent systems. It takes in the principal issues of what Baumol called the magnificent dynamics of classical political economy. A principal distinction stands out: Pasinetti's insistence that we understand the principles of an institution-free system before we take into account the role of institutions and particular historical episodes. Pasinetti illustrated this distinction in his discussion of the principle of effective demand in Keynes's theory (1997).

The method of the long-period Keynesians was never acceptable to Joan Robinson and Kahn, or to Goodwin and Kalecki (who never explicitly engaged with it). Joan Robinson experimented with the long period in a Marshallian sense in the 1930s after *The General Theory*'s publication, to see whether Keynes's new results went through in this setting. She became increasingly dissatisfied with her findings, in the postwar period, repudiating Marshallian method and concepts as such. Keynes was arguing by the early 1940s that long-period equilibrium probably had no conceptual basis in his new theory. (He did not go as far as Joan Robinson in spelling out why.) The really innovative developments are associated with Kalecki and Goodwin. (Goodwin supervised Pasinetti's research in its early stages.) They increasingly refuted the notion of the trend and cycle as separable concepts, brought about by nonoverlapping determinants. Independently, they developed models of cyclical growth as characteristic of the movement of capitalist economies. The basic idea was put succinctly (as ever) by Kalecki: "The long-run trend [is] but a slowly changing component of a chain of short-period situations . . . [not an] independent entity" (Kalecki, 1968; 1971, p. 165). Goodwin, too, ultimately married production-interdependence models (as well as Sraffa, Leontief was a mentor at the other Cambridge) with aggregate, Keynes-type cyclical models that also had Marxian ingredients (he was Harrod's pupil at Oxford and Schumpeter's colleague at Harvard) (see, e.g., Goodwin and Punzo, 1987). Bhaduri and Joan Robinson (1980) entwined Kalecki and Marx with Sraffa. Sraffa's role was to provide thought experiments at a high level of abstraction, resulting in an acceptable theory of the rate of profits.

22.9   Frank Hahn at Cambridge

We have concentrated on the writings of, mostly, those closest to Keynes (or his ideas) as well as being influenced by the classicals and Marx, and becoming more and more disillusioned with neoclassical economics. But we also mentioned how others discerned in the IS–LM approaches the core of Keynes's system, at least as a starting point and a pedagogical device. Although the developments flowing from this were deplored by the first group, this way of "doing" Keynes has been most influential in teaching and the development of theory and policy. Some developments occurred in Cambridge itself. Perhaps the most original is associated with Frank Hahn (in his LSE Ph.D. thesis, published years later in 1972; he came to Cambridge in 1960). Hahn modified the IS portion of Hicks's apparatus to take in a macroeconomic theory of distribution in which the marginal propensity to save from profits exceeded that from wages and induced investment levels had to be matched by corresponding voluntary savings. This implied a relationship between income levels and the share of profits. He married this with a supply-side story whereby entrepreneurs, operating in an uncertain environment, could only be persuaded to accumulate at a rate that made the income levels feasible and to organize production and employment so as to bring them about if they received certain shares of national income as profits. The intersection of the two relationships was a stable, short-period rest state for income and distribution.

In Cambridge, Hahn collaborated with Robin Matthews to write a survey article on growth theory (1964), the role model for surveys ever afterwards. Matthews also published two books on the trade cycle that were Keynesian in their orientation, one an historical study, the other a wide-ranging textbook in the Cambridge Economic Handbooks series. The second book was full of original ideas. One of the most innovative came from his 1950s study of the saving function and the problem of trend and cycle. He reinterpreted Duesenberry's ratchet effect by relating spending and saving to previous lowest levels of unemployment in booms (rather than highest levels of income) so that the growth in productivity was taken into account. He also wrote on the financial aspects of the Keynesian multiplier working out over time.

After an interlude on general equilibrium theory and giving his name to a process in growth theory, Hahn became a leading critic of monetarism and the

New Classical macroeconomics of the 1970s on. He was aghast at their policies and even more so at what he regarded as their intellectual dishonesty in claiming that their theoretical analysis of how the economy worked justified their proposed policies. Although he never understood Marx, we think he would have had some sympathy with Thomas Balogh's quip that monetarism was the incomes policy of Karl Marx. In the 1980s and, with Robert Solow, in the 1990s, he courageously criticized the monetarists from within, attempting to provide alternatives which, using modern theoretical methods, came up with Keynes-type results (Hahn and Solow, 1995). But there are none so blind . . . ; we fear that their work has been ignored by those they attacked *and* by their potential allies, the post-Keynesians.

22.10   RICHARD STONE AND JAMES MEADE IN THE POSTWAR YEARS

Stone, the first Director (1945–55) of the Department of Applied Economics (DAE), developed in collaboration with J. A. C. Brown an eclectic growth model which was nevertheless inspired by Keynes's original ideas. Known as the Cambridge Growth Project, the aim was to design a model that allowed the expenditure and production-interdependence of the British economy to be tracked over the medium to longer term under different scenarios. Its origin was Brown's suggestion that they bring together previous work in the DAE on social accounting, input–output, and consumer behavior to build such a model for the British economy. (The complementarity with Pasinetti's contributions is not fanciful.) David Champernowne (Keynes's pupil when Keynes was writing *The General Theory*) also made fundamental contributions in the postwar period in his own independent way to our understanding of Keynes's theory in the short and long periods, and to growth and distribution theory.

We must also document Meade's postwar writings, not only on international trade (in a Keynesian setting) at LSE but also on growth theory when he succeeded Robertson in the Chair of Political Economy in 1957. His growth theory was neoclassical in the Solow/Swan sense, but he never forgot his Keynesian credentials. As with Solow and Swan (who never forgot their's either), he assumed that short-period effective demand puzzles had been taken care of by an all-wise government, so that the long-period effects of substitution between the factors of production responding to changes in the prices of their services and the effects of technical progress could be analyzed. As a side issue, Meade (sometimes with Hahn) clarified some of the issues raised in Pasinetti (1962), on the dependence of the long-period rate of profits solely on the saving propensity of a class of pure capitalists and the natural rate of growth. Meade's 1966 note, using geometry superbly as ever, allows the reader/viewer to discover easily the properties of Pasinetti Land and its dual MSM Land, where Harrod-type ideas rule and the capitalist class has ceased to exist. (MS stands for Modigliani and Samuelson, who wrote a long paper on the issues, while M stands for Meade.) In the 1980s Meade, in collaboration with a number of younger colleagues, worked on stabilization policies, incorporating the techniques of control engineering. (Meade was a great supporter of Bill Phillips's pioneering work on these issues with these techniques at LSE in the 1940s, 1950s, and after.) Meade's last book, published just before his death in 1995, was concerned with policies directed at the attainment of full employment and a just distribution of income and wealth: a fitting endpoint for a lifetime of service and decency, steeped in Keynes's tradition.

22.11   Kaldor and Keynes's Mantle

The person at postwar Cambridge who most took on Keynes's mantle was undoubtedly Nicholas Kaldor. We have referred to his contributions to growth theory in which, initially, the Keynesian influence was strong. But it was within the framework of Keynes's own system that he made the most direct contributions, including an internal critique of details of the system. First, Kaldor could not accept Keynes's microeconomic foundations of, in the main, Marshallian marginal cost pricing. In its place, Kaldor put his representative firm/industry model of a price-leading and -setting oligopolist surrounded by followers. In the 1960s and 1970s he developed aspects of these views, on their own and in macroeconomic settings, providing fertile suggestions for future research. (Wood's 1975 book is the most direct heir.) Kaldor's objections were related to his lifelong preoccupation with cumulative causation processes and his appreciation of an all-pervading influence of increasing returns, especially in manufacturing industry, so that he could not accept atomistic competition as a general pricing model (outside primary industries). Secondly, he thought that Keynes made a tactical mistake by departing from his otherwise lifelong view to treat the money supply in *The General Theory* as exogenous, not endogenous, or at least given (probably what Keynes did). This is a mistaken view of how the banking system and the Central Bank operated. It also proved to be a hostage to fortune as monetarists grew more and more influential. Kaldor was one of the few UK voices in the wilderness taking them on. He was a pioneer of the view that the money supply is endogenous, that it is overwhelmingly demand that creates the money supply. Here he was joined by James Trevithick, who also continued the Keynesian tradition in teaching and in two classic texts, on inflation and involuntary unemployment respectively. Like Keynes, Kaldor was active in policy – advising the UK Labour governments in the 1960s and 1970s and international governments too, sometimes with unexpected and startling results.

22.12   Other Cambridge Contributors in the Postwar Years

Another Cambridge economist who made seminal contributions in similar areas is Robin Marris. *The Economic Theory of "Managerial" Capitalism* (1964) is a highly original account of modern firm behavior, the path-breaking aspects of which are now being fully realized. His 1980s and 1990s writings on imperfectly competitive foundations of the Keynesian system are also strikingly original and controversial – he argues that only these microfoundations allow Keynes's macroeconomic results to go through.

Bob Rowthorn published the seminal paper on conflict inflation in 1977. It is the starting point in the modern literature for discussions of this process, the idea that sustained rates of inflation bring about an uneasy truce between capital and labor. Both fail to achieve completely their aspirations for accumulation and standards of living respectively.

What of Austin Robinson, who worked so closely with Keynes for many years (and whose 1947 obituary article of Keynes is required reading alongside the subsequent biographies – Harrod, Moggridge, and Robert Skidelsky's unmatchable three volumes)? Austin was an applied political economist *par excellence*. Armed with his deep and astute understanding of Marshall, Pigou, and Keynes, and with his wide knowledge of the real world in developed and developing countries, in government service, and as an advisor, he devoted much time in the postwar period to development problems. (Austin also stressed what he considered to be a neglected aspect of postwar Keynesian developments, detailed analysis and knowledge of individual firm and industry behavior, and of regional problems.) In his writings on developing economies he made wise diagnoses and put forward sensible, practical humane policy proposals that took into account the detailed cultural and sociological characteristics of the societies and the aspirations of all their citizens. In these pursuits he was joined by Brian Reddaway, whose writings on development and on the British economy reflect a similar highly intelligent, practical approach. Reddaway succeeded Stone as Director of the DAE in 1955; he did and supervised applied work that was clearly Keynesian-inspired in its approach and theoretical structure. Reddaway (who succeeded Meade in the Chair of Political Economy) was succeeded at the DAE by Wynne Godley. With Frances Cripps, other DAE officers, and Robert Neild, Godley brought an amalgam of Marshall and Keynes to his view of how the UK economy works and how to forecast in the short term. He developed a consistent set of flow and stock constraints associated with the interrelationship of real flows and stocks and their financial counterparts. These had their origins in Keynes's theory and the characteristics of Marshall's long period, modified for macroeconomic analysis.

Finally, we mention the highly original approaches of Ajit Singh to development problems, Frank Wilkinson to the understanding of the labor market, and Tony Lawson to methodological and philosophical issues, all of which add considerably to the traditions and achievements of Keynes and the Cambridge school. Singh is a major spokesman for views that are a creditable and decent alternative to those of the so-called Washington consensus on development strategies. Wilkinson has analyzed in much detail the functioning of labor markets, both individually and in relation to the economy as a whole. He takes an historical and institutional perspective, and shows great sympathy and understanding for wage-earners and unions. Lawson's writings on critical realism and open systems, vestiges of which he discerns in Keynes's writings, have opened up an international debate on the legitimacy of mainstream theory and econometric practice. They assume a closed system. Lawson argues that a discipline such as economics should be concerned with analysis of an open system.

With the retirement and then death of many of the main *dramatis personae*, the Cambridge Faculty has become more and more a clone of leading US schools.

The traditions outlined here are still carried on by a besieged minority, mostly centered around the *Cambridge Journal of Economics*. Some still have a foothold in the Faculty; others form a thriving colony in the Judge Institute of Management Studies or are scattered around in colleges, as college, not university, teachers. More optimistically, in centers other than Cambridge, Keynes and the Cambridge tradition are to be found under the wide embracing rubric of post-Keynesianism.

22.13 The Cambridge Tradition in Other Centers

We think especially of the writings of the late Athanasios (Tom) Asimakopulos, Avi Cohen, John and Wendy Cornwall, Omar Hamouda, Marc Lavoie, Tom Rymes, and – most of all – the late Lorie Tarshis in Canada; the late Keith Frearson, Robert Dixon, Peter Groenewegen, the essay's authors (when there!), Joseph Helevi, John King, Peter Kriesler, John Nevile, Ray Petrides, Colin Rogers (and his South African countryperson, Christopher Torr), Trevor Stegman, Michael White, and others in Australia; the late George Shackle, Philip Arestis, Victoria Chick, Sheila Dow, Douglas Mair, Peter Reynolds, Peter Riach, Malcolm Sawyer, Ian Steedman, and others in the UK; and of the late Sidney Weintraub, Allin Cottrell, Paul Davidson, Sandy Darity, Amitava Dutt, Gary Dymski, the late Al Eichner, John Kenneth Galbraith (and son James), Rick Holt, Jan Kregel, Michael Lawlor, Fred Lee, Stephen Marglin, the late Hyman Minsky, Basil Moore, Edward Nell, Steve Pressman, Roy Rotheim, Nina Shapiro, the late Paul Wells, and others in the USA.

There are strongholds in continental Europe, particularly for those who were influenced by Piero Sraffa, as well as by Keynes. We have mentioned Garegnani and Pasinetti in Italy. We add Alessandro Roncaglia, Neri Salvadori, Claudio Sardoni, Roberto Scazzieri, and Paolo Sylos-Labini (and many others of course). In Germany, Bertram Schefold is a major Sraffian scholar, as were Heinz Kurz and Christian Gehrke (they are now in Austria). There are other major contributors in Austria, especially Michael Landesmann, Kurt Rothschild, and the late Josef Steindl. In Switzerland, Mauro Baranzini has written fine books and essays that especially reflect Pasinetti's approach. Heinrich Bortis's magnificent monograph (1997) is a synthesis of the main strands of thought to be found under the post-Keynesian rubric; it exhibits a humane political philosophy and provides a guide to effective, decent policies. In India, Amit Bhaduri, the late Krishna Bharadwaj, and their colleagues, especially at JNU, and the late Sukhamoy Chakravarty at the Delhi school have made major contributions to the tradition. In addition, they applied the approach in their deep understanding of economic and political processes in developing economies. Pervez Tahir in Pakistan critically evaluated Joan Robinson's writings on development in general and China in particular. In Central and Latin America (especially in Brazil), pupils of Davidson, Harcourt, Kalecki, and Marglin are making significant contributions broadly within the tradition described in the essay.

22.14 ECONOMICS AND PHILOSOPHY

Most important for our present purposes is the work of the past three decades on the links between Keynes's philosophy and his economics. Many seminal writings on these themes started their lives as Ph.D. dissertations in Cambridge – Rod O'Donnell, Anna Carabelli, John Coates, Flavio Comim, and Jochen Runde, for example. An early, influential volume, edited by Lawson and Hashem Pesaran, was published in 1985. Subsequently, John Davis published a major monograph (1994a) and edited a major volume (1994b) on similar themes.

Three crucial aspects of Keynes's economic writings, especially in *The General Theory* and after, emanate from his philosophical understanding. The first is the realization that in the operation of an economic system, the whole may be more than the sum of the parts – hence his emphasis on the need in macroeconomic analysis to avoid the fallacy of composition, a lesson largely forgotten as representative agent models have come to dominate modern analysis. The second is that in a discipline such as economics there is a whole spectrum of relevant languages, according to which issues, or aspects of issues, are discussed. It runs from intuition and poetry through lawyer-like arguments to formal logic and mathematics. All have rightful places; none should have a monopoly – truth does not only come in the guise of a mathematical model. The third (derived from Marshall) is that we need to analyze how (usually) sensible people decide in situations of inescapable uncertainty, the one sure constant of all economic life and therefore another "incontrovertible" proposition of our "miserable subject" (Keynes to Bertil Ohlin, April 29, 1937; see Keynes, 1973, p. 190).

Note

We thank, but in no way implicate, the editors for their comments. We are indebted to Sheila Dow for allowing us to see a draft of her essay, "Postwar heterodox economics: Post Keynesian economics."

Bibliography

Bhaduri, A. and Robinson, J. 1980: Accumulation and exploitation: an analysis in the tradition of Marx, Sraffa and Kalecki. *Cambridge Journal of Economics*, 4, 103–15.

Bortis, H. 1997: *Institutions, Behaviour and Economic Theory. A Contribution to Classical-Keynesian Political Economy*. Cambridge, UK: Cambridge University Press.

Davis, J. B. 1994a: *Keynes's Philosophical Development*. Cambridge: Cambridge University Press.

—— (ed.) 1994b: *The State of Interpretation of Keynes*. Boston: Kluwer.

Eatwell, J. and Milgate, M. (eds.) 1983: *Keynes's Economics and the Theory of Value and Distribution*. London: Duckworth.

Fletcher, G. 2000: *Understanding Dennis Robertson. The Man and His Work*. Cheltenham, UK and Northampton, MA: Edward Elgar.

Goodwin, R.M. and Punzo, L. F. 1987: *The Dynamics of a Capitalist Economy. A Multi-Sectoral Approach*. Cambridge, UK: Polity Press.

Hahn, F. H. 1972: *The Share of Wages in the National Income*. London: Weidenfeld and Nicolson.

—— and Matthews, R. C. O. 1964: The theory of economic growth: a survey. *Economic Journal*, 74, 779–902.

—— and Solow, R. M. 1995: *A Critical Essay on Modern Macroeconomic Theory*. Oxford: Blackwell.

Harcourt, G. C. 1972: *Some Cambridge Controversies in The Theory of Capital*. Cambridge, UK: Cambridge University Press.

—— and Monadjemi, M. 1999: The vital contributions of John Cornwall to economic theory and policy: A tribute from two admiring friends on the occasion of his 70th birthday. In M. Setterfield (ed.), *Growth, Employment and Inflation. Essays in Honour of John Cornwall*. Basingstoke, UK: Macmillan, 10–23.

Harrod, R. F. 1939: An essay in dynamic theory. *Economic Journal*, 49, 14–33.

—— 1948: *Towards a Dynamic Economics*. London: Macmillan.

Hicks, J. R. 1937: Mr. Keynes and the "classics." *Econometrica*, 5, 147–59.

—— 1939: *Value and Capital*. Oxford: The Clarendon Press.

Kaldor, N. 1955–6: Alternative theories of distribution. *Review of Economic Studies*, 23, 83–100.

Kalecki, M. 1943: Political aspects of full employment. *Political Quarterly*, 14, 322–31. Reprinted in Kalecki (1971), op. cit., pp. 138–45.

—— 1968: Trend and business cycles reconsidered. *Economic Journal*, 78, 263–76. Reprinted in Kalecki (1971), op. cit., pp. 165–83.

—— 1971: *Selected Essays on the Dynamics of the Capitalist Economy 1933–1970*. Cambridge, UK: Cambridge University Press.

Keynes, J. M. 1937a: Alternative theories of the rate of interest. *Economic Journal*, 47. Reprinted in Keynes (1973), op. cit., pp. 201–15.

—— 1937b: The "ex ante" theory of the rate of interest. *Economic Journal*, 47. Reprinted in Keynes (1973), op. cit., pp. 215–23.

—— 1940: *How to Pay for the War*. London: Macmillan. Reprinted in Keynes, J. M. 1972: *The Collected Writings of John Maynard Keynes*, vol. IX, *Essays in Persuasion*, ed. D. Moggridge. London: Macmillan, pp. 367–439.

—— 1973: *The Collected Writings of John Maynard Keynes*, vol. XIV, *The General Theory and After. Part II. Defence and Development*, ed. D. Moggridge. London: Macmillan.

Kurz, H. D. and Salvadori, N. 1995: *Theory of Production. A Long-Period Analysis*. Cambridge, UK: Cambridge University Press.

Lawson, T. and Pesaran, H. (eds.) 1985: *Keynes' Economics: Methodological Issues*. London: Croom Helm.

Mandler, M. 1999: *Dilemmas in Economic Theory*. Oxford: Oxford University Press.

Marris, R. L. 1964: *The Economic Theory of "Managerial" Capitalism*. London: Macmillan.

McCombie, J. S. L. and Thirlwall, A. P. 1994: *Economic Growth and the Balance-of-Payments Constraint*. Basingstoke: Macmillan.

Meade, J. E. 1966: The outcome of the Pasinetti process: a note. *Economic Journal*, 76, 161–5.

Milgate, M. 1982: *Capital and Employment. A Study in Keynes's Economics*. London: Academic Press.

Moggridge, D. E. 1976: *John Maynard Keynes*. Harmondsworth: Penguin.

Pasinetti, L. L. 1962: Rate of profit and income distribution in relation to the rate of economic growth. *Review of Economic Studies*, 29, 267–79.

—— 1981: *Structural Change and Economic Growth*. Cambridge, UK: Cambridge University Press.

—— 1993: *Structural Economic Dynamics*. Cambridge, UK: Cambridge University Press.

—— 1997: The principle of effective demand. In G. C. Harcourt and P. A. Riach (eds.), *A "Second Edition" of The General Theory*, vol. I. London: Routledge, 93–104.

Robinson, E. A. G. 1947: John Maynard Keynes 1883–1946. *Economic Journal*, 57, 1–68.

Robinson, J. 1953–4: The production function and the theory of capital. *Review of Economic Studies*, 21, 81–106.

—— 1985 [1980]: The theory of normal prices and reconstruction of economic theory. In G. R. Feiwel (ed.), *Issues in Contemporary Macroeconomics and Distribution*. London: Macmillan, 157–65. The original 1980 paper was entitled "Spring cleaning."

Rowthorn, R. E. 1977: Conflict, inflation and money. *Cambridge Journal of Economics*, 1, 215–39.

Salter, W. E. G. 1960: *Productivity and Technical Change*. Cambridge, UK: Cambridge University Press.

Sraffa, P. 1951: Introduction. In *The Works and Correspondence of David Ricardo, Volume I, On the Principles of Political Economy and Taxation*, edited by P. Sraffa with the collaboration of M. H. Dobb. Cambridge, UK: Cambridge University Press, xiii–lxii.

—— 1960: *Production of Commodities by Means of Commodities. Prelude to a Critique of Economic Theory*. Cambridge, UK: Cambridge University Press.

Wood, A. 1975: *A Theory of Profits*. Cambridge, UK: Cambridge University Press.

Young, W. 1987: *Interpreting Mr. Keynes*. Cambridge, UK: Polity Press.

American Institutional Economics in the Interwar Period

Malcolm Rutherford

23.1   The Formation of Institutionalism as a Movement

The explicit identification of something called the "institutional approach" to economics, or "institutional economics," goes back only to 1918. In 1916, Walton Hamilton mentioned that Robert Hoxie had called himself an institutional economist, so the term was in verbal use by then (Hamilton, 1974 [1916]), but its first prominent use in the literature of economics occurred in 1918 with Hamilton's American Economic Association conference paper titled "The Institutional Approach to Economic Theory," published in the AEA proceedings in 1919 (Hamilton, 1919).

Hamilton's paper was clearly intended as a call for the economics profession at large to adopt what he called the "institutional approach." Hamilton argued that anything that "aspired to the name of economic theory" had to be (i) capable of giving unity to economic investigations of many different areas, (ii) relevant to the problem of control, (iii) relate to institutions as both the "changeable elements of economic life and the agencies through which they are to be directed," (iv) concerned with "process" in the form of institutional change and development, and (v) based on an acceptable theory of human behavior, one in harmony with the "conclusions of modern social psychology." According to Hamilton, only institutional economics could meet these tests. The "leaders" of this move to develop an institutional economic theory he identified as H. C. Adams and Charles Horton Cooley – both his own teachers at Michigan – and Thorstein Veblen and Wesley Mitchell. At the same session, J. M. Clark spoke on "Economic theory in an era of social readjustment" (Clark, 1919), and argued for an economics both "actively relevant to the issues of its time" and based on an "ideal of scientific impartiality." Walter Stewart (Hamilton's friend and colleague) chaired this session, and in his remarks commented on need to utilize the "most competent thought in the related sciences of psychology and sociology" and to build an economics "organized around the central problem of control." He also stated his belief that "an adequate analysis of many of our problems can be made only by a union of the statistical method and the institutional approach" (Stewart, 1919, p. 319), a reference to his own and Wesley Mitchell's quantitative work.

The exact timing of this effort to promote "institutional economics" as a distinctive approach likely had much to do with the end of World War I. The war had impressed upon many the great importance of improved economic data and policy analysis, and of the potential role of government in the economy. The period of reconstruction seemed to offer significant opportunities to bring changes to the conduct of economic research, education, and policy. In 1918, while still involved in wartime work, Hamilton and Harold Moulton planned the conference session (speaking to others such as Mitchell, Stewart, and Veblen) and even talked of the possibility of a "permanent reclamation of the American Economics Association" (Dorfman, 1974, p. 27).

The 1918 AEA session was followed by further efforts to promote institutional economics. Another AEA session critical of traditional theory was organized in 1920. This session featured J. M. Clark, who presented his paper "Soundings in non-Euclidian economics" (Clark, 1921), critical of orthodox theoretical propositions. In 1924 Mitchell gave his Presidential Address to the AEA, in which he argued that quantitative methods would transform economics by displacing traditional theory and leading to a much greater stress on institutions (Mitchell, 1925). Lionel Edie called this address "a genuine manifesto of quantitative and institutional economics," and one that stated "the faith of a very large part of the younger generation of economists" (Edie, 1927, p. 417). In the same year, Rexford Tugwell edited *The Trend of Economics*, a book again seen as something of an institutionalist manifesto, and which included papers from Mitchell and Clark as well as from younger people of institutionalist persuasion such as Tugwell himself, F. C. Mills, Sumner Slichter, Morris Copeland, and Robert Hale (Tugwell, 1971 [1924]; for a critical review, see Young, 1927 [1925]).

It needs to be remembered that in the 1920s in particular many economists on both sides of the Atlantic had considerable doubts concerning the usefulness and empirical applicability of the conceptual apparatus of neoclassical economics (see, e.g., Clapham, 1922), and during the interwar period institutionalism developed a significant following, with a concentrated presence at a number of schools and research institutes. In addition to Hamilton, Clark, and Mitchell, who were the most visible proponents of institutionalism, there was John R. Commons, whose *Legal Foundations of Capitalism* (1968 [1924]) led to his inclusion in institutionalist ranks, and many others (see Rutherford, 2000a,b). In terms of schools, Veblen and Hoxie had been an influence at Chicago, and although Veblen left in 1906 and Hoxie committed suicide in 1916, Chicago remained a department with a strong institutionalist element until J. M. Clark's departure for Columbia in 1926. Morris Copeland, Carter Goodrich, Hazel Kyrk, Sumner Slichter, and Helen Wright all obtained doctorates from Chicago in the early 1920s, as did Clarence Ayres (but in philosophy). Hamilton was at the center of groups that were shorter-lived, first at Amherst (1915–23) and later at the Robert Brookings Graduate School (1923–8). The Amherst group included Hamilton, Stewart, and Ayres on faculty, and undergraduate students such as Copeland, Goodrich, Willard Thorp, Louis Reed, Winfield Riefler, and Stacy May (and also Talcott Parsons). At Brookings, the staff included Helen Wright, and the doctoral students Riefler, May, Isador Lubin, Mordecai Ezekiel, Robert Montgomery, Max Lerner, and many others (Rutherford, forthcoming b). The organization of the Brookings Institution in 1928 resulted in the demise of the graduate school. Around 1930, a group formed at the Washington Square College in New York, with Willard Atkins, Louis Reed, Anton Friedrich, and several others. Other institutionalist groups existed at Texas, where Clarence Ayres joined Robert Montgomery in 1930, and in a number of other schools and colleges.

However, the two major centers for institutionalism in the interwar period were without doubt Columbia and Wisconsin, at that time two of the leading doctoral departments of economics in the country (Froman, 1942). Wisconsin's department included Commons (until he retired in 1933), E. E. Witte, Harold Groves, Martin Glaeser, Selig Perlman, and several others. Columbia was an even bigger center for institutionalism, with Mitchell, Clark, Rexford Tugwell, F. C. Mills, A. R. Burns, Joseph Dorfman, Leo Wolman, Goodrich, James Bonbright, and Robert Hale all in the economics department or Business School at various times, and Gardiner Means, Adolf A. Berle, and many other people of related views in other departments (Rutherford, forthcoming a). Bonbright, Dorfman, Hale, Mills, Reed, Taylor, and Thorp were all Columbia doctoral graduates, as were Simon Kuznets and A. F. Burns. The NBER was also closely associated with Mitchell's quantitative approach, and Mills, Wolman, Thorp, Kuznets, and A. F. Burns were all heavily involved with the NBER research program.

23.2 THE SOURCES AND APPEAL
OF INTERWAR INSTITUTIONAL ECONOMICS

Of course, the various elements that went to make up the core of the institutional approach as defined by Hamilton, Clark, and Stewart were all present in American economics before 1918. Institutionalism as it formed in the interwar period was an approach to economics that derived from several sources. While the single most significant source of inspiration for institutionalism was the work of Thorstein Veblen, it is important to understand that institutionalism was a blending of ideas taken from Veblen with those from others (Rutherford, 2001).

At the most basic level, the most important element in the institutionalist approach is the conception of the economic system as a set of evolving social institutions. In this, institutions are seen as much more than constraints on individual action. Social norms, conventions, laws, and common practices embody generally accepted ways of thinking and behaving, and they work to mold the preferences and values of individuals brought up under their sway. A good part of this orientation came from Veblen, but also from sociologists such as Charles Horton Cooley. For Cooley, the usual treatment of valuation in economics failed to go back of an individual's given wants, "it being assumed, apparently, that these wants spring from the inscrutable depths of the private mind," and not recognized that "they are the expressions of institutional development." Individual preferences are "molded by the market;" and the market "is a continuous institution in which the individual lives and which is ever forming his ideas" (Cooley, 1913). For Walton Hamilton, Cooley taught him "that business, as well as the state, is a scheme of arrangements, and that our choice is not between regulation and letting things alone, but between one scheme of control and another . . . he forced us to give up our common sense notions, led us away from an atomic individualism, made us see 'life as an organic whole,' and revealed to us 'the individual' and 'society' remaking each other in an endless process of change" (Hamilton, 1929, p. 185).

This overall conception was also seen as connecting studies of particular topics. Hamilton argued that the existing orthodox "value theory" was not utilized in many studies of particular applied areas, so that "for all the constraints of neo-classical theory, each of these subjects tends to develop an isolated body of thought." In contrast, the institutional approach, by providing a common context within which studies of different topics could be placed, could "unify" economics: "In describing in general terms economic organization it makes clear the kind of industrial world within which such particular things as money, insurance, and corporation finance have their being" (Hamilton, 1919, p. 312). The same point was made by Mitchell: "When, however, economic theory is made an account of the cumulative change of economic behavior, then all studies of special institutions become organic parts of a single whole" (Mitchell, 1971 [1924], p. 24).

On a more specific level, Veblen's framework, which stressed the role of new technology in bringing about institutional change (by changing the underlying ways of living and thinking) and the predominantly "pecuniary" character of the existing set of American institutions (that is, expressing the "business" values of pecuniary success and individual gain by money making), was widely influential among institutionalists. Within this framework Veblen developed his analyses of "conspicuous consumption" and consumption norms; the effect of corporate finance on the ownership and control of firms; business and financial strategies for profit-making, salesmanship, and advertising; the emergence of a specialist managerial class; business fluctuations; and many other topics (Veblen, 1924 [1899], 1975 [1904]).

Veblen's approach to existing institutions was a highly critical one. Existing institutions, due both to the inertia inherent in any established scheme and to the defensive activities of vested interests, tended to become out of step with new technological means and with the economic issues and social problems they generated. For Veblen, the existing legal and social institutions of America were outmoded and inadequate to the task of the social control of modern large-scale industry. What Veblen perceived was a *systemic* failure of "business" institutions to channel private economic activity in ways consistent with the public interest. Veblen attacked the manipulative, restrictive, and unproductive tactics used by business to generate income (including consolidations, control via holding companies and interlocking directorates, financial manipulation, insider dealing, sharp practices, and unscrupulous salesmanship), the "waste" generated by monopoly restriction, unemployment, conspicuous consumption, and competitive advertising, and he held out little hope of change short of a complete rejection of "business" principles.

On the other hand, Charles Horton Cooley also analyzed pecuniary institutions but in more measured tones, and it must be emphasized that many institutionalists, including Hamilton, J. M. Clark, John R. Commons, and Robert L. Hale placed a much greater emphasis on the evolution of legal institutions than did Veblen. Both Hamilton and Hale moved into law schools and had close connections with legal scholars of the realist school. The major sources of this emphasis on legal institutions were Richard Ely (who taught Commons) and H. C. Adams (who taught Hamilton). This greater emphasis on law and on legal evolution helped to shift the character of institutionalism away from Veblen's radicalism and connect it to a pragmatic philosophy, based primarily on the work of John Dewey, which looked to legislative and legal reform concerning such issues such as business regulation, labor law, collective bargaining, health and safety regulations, and consumer protection.

Thus, in the hands of institutionalists such as Hamilton, Clark, Mitchell, and Commons, the problem became one of supplementing the market with other forms of "social control" or one of "how to make production for profit turn out a larger supply of useful goods under conditions more conducive to welfare" (Mitchell, 1950 [1923], p. 148). In this way Hamilton could claim that the institutional approach related to institutions as the "changeable elements of economic life and the agencies through which they are to be directed" and was "relevant to the problem of control."

Another important claim concerned the linking of institutional economics with "modern psychology." Veblen had provided a particularly penetrating criticism of the hedonistic psychology implicit in marginal utility theory (Veblen, 1961 [1898]) and pointed to an alternative based on instinct/habit psychology. What was important for institutionalists, however, was less his specific formulation than the impetus he gave to the idea that economics might be reconstructed on the basis of a theory of human behavior in harmony with the "conclusions of modern social psychology." Particularly important in this was William McDougall's *An Introduction to Social Psychology* (1908), and John B. Watson's earlier work towards a "behaviorist" approach. Wesley Mitchell was prompted to write a long two-part article on "The rationality of economic activity" (1910a,b) that made much use of McDougall. Mitchell argued that "there is no logical need of positing an abstract human nature characterized by rationality" (Mitchell, 1910b, p. 216). Consistent with this, Mitchell regarded economic rationality as largely an institutional product, the result of habituation to pecuniary institutions and monetary calculation, and as an attribute that was "inculcated" to varying degrees in different areas of life (Mitchell, 1912).

Carleton Parker also became an enthusiastic proponent of the application of instinct theory to the issue of labor unrest (Parker, 1920). Parker argued that the "stabilizing of the science of psychology and the vogue among economists of the scientific method will not allow these psychological findings to be shouldered out by the careless a priori deductions touching human nature which still dominate our text books" (1920, pp. 131–2). Ideas such as these created great excitement at the time (Rutherford, 2001).

Finally, and of central importance to the attraction of institutionalism, was the claim that it represented the ideal of empirical science. The major influence here was Wesley Mitchell's combination of Veblenian ideas concerning the significance of the institutions of the "money economy" with the quantitative and statistical approach that he had absorbed as a student at Chicago. Mitchell's *Business Cycles* (1913) was enthusiastically received and widely regarded at the time as a paradigm for a scientific economics. Mitchell thought of business cycles as a phenomenon arising out of the patterns of behavior generated by the institutions of a developed money economy (Mitchell, 1927, pp. 61–188), and in his Presidential Address to the American Economic Association, and in other papers, he explicitly connected quantitative work and the institutional approach, arguing that it is institutions that create the regularities in the behavior of the mass of people that quantitative work analyses (Mitchell, 1925, 1971 [1924]). Mitchell's quantitative bent was shared by others such as Stewart, Mills, Copeland, and Thorp.

The institutionalist ideal of a scientific economics by no means excluded theory, but such theory was supposed to be closer to reality and more open to empirical testing than "orthodox" theory. Also, in the institutionalist vision, empirical evidence was not limited to quantitative and statistical methods. J. M. Clark, one of the leading theorists of the interwar period, argued that "economics must come into closer touch with facts and embrace broader ranges of data than 'orthodox' economics has hitherto done" and that "it must establish touch with these data, either by becoming more inductive, or by much verification of results, or by taking over the accredited results of specialists in other fields, notably psychology, anthropology, jurisprudence and history" (Clark, 1927, p. 221). It is also worth noting that several institutionalists, including Mitchell, criticized Veblen for being too speculative and for failing to empirically check his conclusions (Rutherford, 1999).

In this light, Hamilton's claims for the institutional approach could appear as not at all exaggerated. At that point, and through the 1920s, institutionalism could easily have seemed to be a very promising program – modern, scientific, pointing to a critical analysis of the existing economic system and its performance, in tune with the latest in psychological, social scientific, and legal research, established at leading universities and research institutes, and involved in important issues of economic policy and reform.

23.3   The Contributions of Interwar Institutionalism

Mark Blaug has stated that institutionalism "was never more than a tenuous inclination to dissent from orthodox economics" (Blaug, 1978, p. 712), and George

Stigler has claimed that institutionalism had "no positive agenda of research," "no set of problems or new methods," nothing but "a stance of hostility to the standard theoretical tradition" (quoted in Kitch, 1983, p. 170). This view still finds wide currency; for example, Oliver Williamson has recently argued that "unable or unwilling to offer a rival research agenda, the older institutional economics was given over to methodological objections to orthodoxy" (Williamson, 1998, p. 24). That institutionalists did have a positive program of research in mind should be clear from the above (see also Yonay, 1998). Not all of the elements of this program were pursued successfully, but there can be no doubt that institutionalists did make important positive contributions to economics in the interwar period.

First, following from their view of science, institutionalists took the issue of improving economic measurement seriously. The NBER not only produced many empirical studies relating to business cycles, labor, and price movements, but also played a vital role in the development of national income accounting, particularly through the work of Mitchell's student, Simon Kuznets. In conjunction with the Federal Reserve, the NBER also did much to develop monetary and financial data. Moreover, during the New Deal, institutionalists were heavily involved in the effort to improve the statistical work of government agencies (Rutherford, 2002).

Secondly, institutionalists made contributions to a number of key debates in economics on issues such as psychology and economics, the economics of the household, the pricing behavior of firms, ownership and control of corporations, monopoly and competition, unions and labor markets, public utilities and regulation, law and economics, various types of market failures, and business cycles.

As noted above, one of the most often repeated claims among institutionalists was that a "scientific" economics would have to be consistent with "modern" psychology. A typical argument was that economics "is a science of human behavior" and any conception of human behavior that the economist may adopt "is a matter of psychology" (Clark, 1918, p. 4). J. M. Clark made one of the most interesting efforts to develop the psychological basis of institutional economics in a paper published in 1918. Building on William James and Cooley, he argues that the "effort of decision" is an important cost. Clark here is considering both the costs of information gathering and of calculation. Taking into account such decision costs would mean that even a perfect hedonist "would stop calculating when it seemed likely to involve more trouble than it was worth." This point cannot be determined with exactness (Clark, 1918, p. 25), so that information and decision costs provide an explanation and an economic function for custom and habit. Custom and habit are methods of economizing on decision costs, but habits and customs are "quasi-static" and slow down the responses of consumers to changes in prices or quality. In a rapidly changing world habit and custom can quickly become outmoded (Clark, 1918, p. 30).

Many others contributed to the institutionalist literature on psychology and economics, including Tugwell (1922, 1930), Copeland (1958 [1930]), and Ayres (1918, 1921a,b, 1936). As noted above, many of the items written before the mid-1920s utilize instinct/habit psychology. Later work made more use of behaviorism, with particular reference to its focus on measurement, observable behavior, and its "natural science" character. In 1924 Mitchell argued that psychology was "moving rapidly toward an objective conception and a quantitative treatment of their problem," and that the psychologist's emphasis on stimulus and response, conditioned reflexes, performance tests, and experimental method favor the spread of the conception that all the social sciences have common aims, methods, and aspirations (Mitchell, 1925, p. 6). Similar views were expressed by Copeland (1958 [1930]).

Related to the work on psychology and economics were the economics of consumption and of the household, pursued by Hazel Kyrk in her *Theory of Consumption* (1923) and her *Economic Problems of the Family* (1933), and by Theresa McMahon in her *Social and Economic Standards of Living* (1925). Kyrk was highly critical of marginal utility theory as a basis for a theory of consumption and emphasized the social nature of the formation of consumption values. McMahon made use of Veblen's conception of emulation in consumption, while Kyrk echoed Mitchell's views that the "business man's calculation of profit and loss cannot be transferred to a field not controlled by pecuniary standards" (1923, p. 144). For both, the key idea is that consumption patterns relate to habitual "standards of living." Kyrk undertook to measure and critically analyze existing standards of living, and to create policy to help achieve higher standards of living. In her later work, Kyrk discussed the household in both its producing and consuming roles, the division of labor between the sexes, employment and earnings of women, adequacy of family incomes, and issues of risks of disability, unemployment, provision for the future and social security, and the protection and education of the consumer (Dorfman, 1959, pp. 570–8; Hirschfeld, 1998).

Following from the institutionalist conception of the economy as dominated by pecuniary or business institutions (at least outside of the household), a great deal of work was conducted by institutionalists on the behavior of business firms and on the functioning of markets. There was much discussion of the inadequacy of the standard models of perfect competition and pure monopoly, backed up by numerous industry case studies (Hamilton and Associates, 1938). The coal industry received much attention. In that industry, Hamilton and Wright (1925) found little that corresponded to the ideal of a competitive industry. The workings of competition were in actuality compromised by ignorance, customary practice, elements of monopoly, and a multiplicity of State and Federal regulations. Furthermore, even as compromised, the competition within the industry had resulted not in efficient low-cost production but in persistent excess capacity, inefficiency, irregular operation, poor working conditions, and low earnings (1925, p. 92). For Hamilton and Wright, this result was due to the impact of technological change that was too rapid to be made orderly by market forces (1925, p. 208). This represented a common institutionalist view that, particularly under modern conditions of rapid technological advance, competition could lead to chaos and inefficiency rather than to order and efficiency.

Beyond the coal industry, George Stocking's (1925) Columbia Ph.D. thesis dealt with common pool problems and was entitled "The oil industry and the competitive system: a study in waste." Ezekiel (1938) worked on agricultural pricing, including the cobweb model and its implications for the orthodox view of "self-regulating" markets.

A related theme was that technological change had altered the structure of costs faced by firms and had altered their behavior. This argument derived from J. M. Clark's *Overhead Costs* (1923). Overhead or fixed costs have to be covered in the long run, but the share of the overhead to be borne by any given part of the business is a matter of business policy. For Clark, the growth of overhead costs as a result of capital-intensive methods of production had resulted in price discrimination, an extension of monopoly, and an increase in price inflexibility over the cycle. A little later, Gardiner Means (1935) developed his theory of administered pricing, which sparked a vast literature on relative price inflexibility.

On issues of corporate finance and ownership, Bonbright and Means co-authored *The Holding Company* (1932), and Berle and Means (1932) *The Modern Corporation and Private Property* (1932). These works much extended Veblen's earlier discussions of corporate consolidation and the separation of ownership and control. Berle and Means' work raised important issues of agency, and whether managers would maximize profits.

On labor market issues, institutionalists concerned themselves with studying unions and the history of the labor movement (Commons et al., 1918), developing in the process both classifications of unions and explanations for the particular pattern of trade union development in America (Perlman, 1928). Mitchell's National Bureau also sponsored empirical studies on the growth of trades unions (Wolman, 1924), and on many other labor issues. Wage determination was also a problem that attracted the attention of institutionalists. Walton Hamilton's 1922 article on wages and 1923 book *The Control of Wages* (with Stacy May; see Hamilton and May, 1968 [1923]) attempted to outline the various factors that contributed to the determination of wages, and provide what he called a "functional theory of wages" (Hamilton and May, 1968 [1923], p. 112). Clark called Hamilton's work an "example of what the institutional point of view does when it enters the field of the theory of value and distribution." This is not to provide an "abstract formulation of the characteristic outcome" but a "directory of the forces to be studied" in any particular case. Such studies are a "proper sequel to orthodox laws of supply and demand" (Clark, 1927, pp. 276–7). Discussions of "the wage bargain" or "the labor bargain" were provided by other institutional labor economists such as Commons (1968 [1924]) and Sumner Slichter (1931). In this work, much attention was given to issues of collective bargaining and systems of conciliation and mediation.

Public utilities, including issues relating to the valuation of utility property and the proper basis for rate regulation, were major areas of institutionalist research. Concepts of intangible property and of goodwill were developed within this discussion. Clark devoted several chapters in *The Social Control of Business* (1926) to the topic, while Commons devoted considerable space to the concept of intangible property, goodwill, and valuation issues in his *Legal Foundations* (Commons, 1968 [1924], pp. 157–215). Bonbright's (1937) *Valuation of Property* dealt with the difference between commercial and social valuation, with an emphasis on issues of the valuation of public utilities. Bonbright (1937), Hale (1921), and Glaeser (1927) all wrote extensively on issues of public utility regulation, with Hale probably having the greatest impact on the direction of court decisions through his campaign of criticism of the "fair value" concept as a basis for rate regulation (Bonbright, 1961, p. 164).

In his *Social Control of Business* Clark argues that business cannot be regarded as a purely private affair. In Clark's words "it is sufficiently clear that industry is essentially a matter of public concern, and that the stake which the public has in its processes is not adequately protected by the safeguards which individualism affords" (Clark, 1926, p. 50). This idea of private business being broadly "affected with a public interest" was absolutely central to the institutionalist literature of this period. It was a major theme of the legal economic work of Robert Hale. For Hale, any business affected the public in numerous ways, so that to limit state regulation to those businesses "affected with a public interest" was no more limiting than the "notion of 'public welfare' itself" (Fried, 1998, p. 106). Clark expresses the same idea in his claim that "every business is 'affected with a public interest' of one sort or another" (Clark, 1926, p. 185), and the argument reappears in Tugwell's "The economic basis for business regulation" (Tugwell, 1921), and *The Economic Basis of Public Interest* (Tugwell, 1968 [1922]), and in Walton Hamilton's "Affectation with public interest" (Hamilton, 1930).

More general interconnections between law and economics and the operation of markets were addressed by Hamilton (1938), Hale (1923; see Samuels, 1973), and Commons (1934, 1968 [1924]). Commons's approach was the most developed and was built on his notions of the pervasiveness of distributional conflicts, of legislatures and courts as attempting to resolve conflicts (at least between those interest groups with representation), and of the evolution of the law as the outcome of these ongoing processes of conflict resolution. His view of the possibilities of legal evolution led him to reject Veblen's antithesis between business and industry. He developed his concept of the "transaction" as the basic unit of analysis. In turn, the terms of transactions were determined by the structure of "working rules," including legal rights, duties, liberties, and exposures, and by economic (bargaining) power. Market transactions were conceived of as a transfer of rights that took place in a context of legal and economic power, and always involving some degree of "coercion," in the sense of some degree of restriction upon alternatives (Commons, 1932; see also Hale, 1923). He also provided a theory of the behavior of legislatures based on "log-rolling," and a theory of judicial decision-making based on the concept of "reasonableness," a concept that included, but was not limited to, a concern with efficiency (Commons, 1932, pp. 24–5; 1934, pp. 751–5).

Within the period before the Great Depression, the institutionalist program dealing with business cycles was centered on Wesley Mitchell's work and that which he promoted through the NBER. As noted above, Mitchell explicitly placed his work on business cycles within an institutional context by associating cycles with the functioning of the system of pecuniary institutions. Mitchell's 1913 volume *Business Cycles*, with its discussion of the four-phase cycle driven by an interaction of factors such as the behavior of profit-seeking firms, the behavior of banks, and the leads and lags in the adjustment of prices and wages, became the standard institutionalist reference. Institutionalist work on business cycles, however, did not end, but only really began, with Mitchell's 1913 volume. At the NBER, Mitchell focused heavily on promoting work that would add to the understanding of business cycles, generating a stream of research studies far too long to list here, but contributing to the development of national income measures, business cycle indicators, and much more. In addition, J. M. Clark developed his concept of the accelerator out of his study of Mitchell's 1913 work, and the accelerator mechanism soon became a standard part of cycle theory (Clark, 1917). Clark's *Overhead Costs* (1923) also contributed to the discussion of cycles. This book contained one of the earliest suggestions that large capital-intensive firms may display less price flexibility over the course of a cycle, and thus exacerbate the fluctuation of output and employment. This was a point that found an empirical counterpart in Willford King's NBER study on employment in large and small firms (King, 1923), and in the work of F. C. Mills, again for the NBER, on price movements (Mills, 1927, 1929). Arguments about the role of price inflexibility were to play an important part in later institutionalist work on cycles and depressions by Tugwell (1931, 1932), Gardiner Means (1935), and others (see Rutherford, 1994; Woirol, 1999). Clark was to make many further contributions to business cycle research in the 1930s (Shute, 1997).

Of course, Mitchell's work was not the only approach to business cycles to be found within institutionalism. Many institutionalists, including Hamilton, had an interest in the work of J. A. Hobson, and Hobson's underconsumptionism became popular among institutionalists in the 1930s.

On issues of market failure, Clark (1926) discussed a large number of types of market failure in his *Social Control of Business*. These included monopoly, maintaining the ethical level of competition, protecting individuals where they are unable to properly judge alternatives, problems of agency, relief for people displaced by rapid economic and technological change, relief of poverty (including social security and minimum wages), regulation of advertising and the provision of information and standards, increasing equality of opportunity, externalities ("unpaid costs of industry"), public goods ("inappropriable services"), the wastes of "arms race" types of competition (such as competitive advertising), unemployment, the interests of posterity or future generations, and any other discrepancy between private and social accounting. Slichter (1971 [1924]) provided a list of market failures almost as long, including the pro-cyclical behavior of banks, overexploitation of natural resources, discrimination in employment, advertising and salesmanship, lack of market information, pollution and other external effects, uncertainty and unemployment, economic waste and inefficiency, and economic conflict. All of these problems were seen as justifying some additional "social control" of business activity.

Finally, and intimately related to the above, institutionalists made important contributions to policy in their roles in the development of unemployment insurance, workmen's compensation, social security, labor legislation, public utility regulation, agricultural price support programs, and in the promotion of government "planning" to create high and stable levels of output. Commons had pioneered public utility regulation, unemployment insurance, and workmen's compensation in Wisconsin, and the Wisconsin model was widely influential. Many institutionalists were active members of the American Association of Labor Legislation, and the AALL promoted many reforms to labor legislation. Medical insurance programs were also pursued by the AALL (Chasse, 1994), and also by the Committee on the Cost of Medical Care, which involved both Hamilton and Mitchell.

Institutionalists also had significant influence within the New Deal. Commons's students, such as Witte, Arthur J. Altmeyer, and Wilbur Cohen, played leading roles in the development of federal social security programs. Berle and Tugwell were two of Roosevelt's original "Brains Trust," and Tugwell and Means were the leading advocates of the "structuralist" or planning approach that had influence in the early part of the New Deal (Barber, 1996). Tugwell was Assistant Secretary of Agriculture. Means also worked as an economic advisor in the Department of Agriculture, and later led the industrial research group of the National Resources Committee, a group that also included Lubin, Ezekiel, and Thorp. Riefler became Economic Advisor to the Executive Council. Thorp served as Consumers' Division Director of the National Emergency Council and Chairman of the Advisory Council of the National Recovery Administration. Ezekiel became economic advisor to the Secretary of Agriculture and played a prominent role in the design of agricultural policy, and Lubin became Commissioner of Labor Statistics.

23.4 INSTITUTIONALISM IN THE 1930s AND BEYOND

The above represents a significant record of achievement, but even by the 1930s areas of weakness in the institutionalist program were beginning to become apparent and new challenges were emerging from elsewhere.

The difficulties internal to the institutionalist program were several. First, the effort to provide a foundation in "modern psychology" had met the problem that psychology was itself not anything like as stabilized as Parker had thought, and had moved from instinct/habit psychology to behaviorism. Although behaviorism was initially met with some enthusiasm by institutionalists such as Mitchell and Copeland, it became increasingly narrow and mechanistic in its application of stimulus–response. As a result, it came under serious criticism for ignoring the more active and creative aspects of human behavior and became increasingly suspect as an adequate basis for a theory of social behavior. The close linkages between institutional economics and behavioristic psychology foreseen by Mitchell did not develop, and institutionalism was left without clear social psychological foundations. Perhaps because of this, what was called institutional economics became more disparate over time, with internal disputes over the role of purpose and choice in the selection of institutions (Commons, 1934, p. 654; Copeland, 1936). By the 1930s critics were complaining that there was little in the way of an identifiable institutionalist school (Homan, 1932), and even institutionalists themselves began to wonder about the usefulness of the term (Rutherford, 2000a, p. 300).

Another area of difficulty concerned the institutionalist approach to cycles and depressions. In 1922 Mitchell had launched into a major project to update his 1913 work on business cycles with the aid of the NBER. This project was originally conceived of consisting of two main volumes "The problem and its setting," and a theoretical volume, "The rhythm of business activity," along with accompanying volumes of statistical data. At some point in the 1930s, the original two-volume conception became three volumes. The second was to be "Business cycles: the analysis of cyclical behavior," but the project became ever larger, and was eventually broken up, with different parts allocated to different researchers. The second volume was revised several times but there always seemed to be more to do, the project became seriously bogged down, and Mitchell kept on putting off the work on the theoretical volume (Rutherford, forthcoming a). Furthermore, the experience of the New Deal was not an entirely successful one for the institutionalists such as Tugwell and Means, who found their planning or structuralist agenda losing ground to other approaches.

These internal problems were compounded by developments outside of institutionalism. Keynesian economics provided an alternative to both the macroeconomic policy and business cycle research being conducted by institutionalists. With the postwar connection between Keynesian economics and econometrics, the challenge to the institutionalist program became even stronger, and culminated in Koopman's famous, if inaccurate, charge against Burns and Mitchell of "measurement without theory" (Koopmans, 1947).

It was also the case that, from the early 1930s onwards, neoclassical economics launched into new phases of development. Hick's revision of demand theory eliminated explicitly hedonistic language, and seemed to free economics from the shifting basis of psychology, while the work of Joan Robinson and Edward Chamberlin provided neoclassical economics with approaches to imperfect competition. The treatment of externalities was also much clarified.

These developments shifted attention back to theory of a neoclassical sort, and resulted in institutionalism becoming regarded as lacking in theory. Institutionalism, however, remained alive and well in the more applied field areas of the discipline, and in 1944 Clarence Ayres attempted a new statement of institutionalist principles (see Ayres, 1962 [1944]) – but to continue would take us beyond the scope of this essay, into the era that followed World War II.

Bibliography

Ayres, C. E. 1918: The epistemological significance of social psychology. *Journal of Philosophy, Psychology and Scientific Methods*, January 17, 35–44.
—— 1921a: Instinct and capacity – I. *Journal of Philosophy*, 18 (October 13), 561–5.
—— 1921b: Instinct and capacity – II. *Journal of Philosophy*, 19 (October 27), 600–6.
—— 1936: Fifty years' developments in ideas of human nature and motivation. *American Economic Review*, 26, 224–36.
—— 1962 [1944]: *The Theory of Economic Progress*, 2nd edn. New York: Schocken.

Barber, W. J. 1996: *Designs Within Disorder: Franklin D. Roosevelt, the Economists, and the Shaping of Economic Policy, 1933–1945*. New York: Cambridge University Press.

Berle, A. A. and Means, G. C. 1932: *The Modern Corporation and Private Property*. New York: Macmillan.

Blaug, M. 1978: *Economic Theory in Retrospect*, 3rd edn. London: Cambridge University Press.

Bonbright, J. C. 1937: *The Valuation of Property*. New York: McGraw-Hill.

—— 1961: *Principles of Public Utility Rates*. New York: Columbia University Press.

—— and Means, G. C. 1932: *The Holding Company*. New York: McGraw-Hill.

Chasse, J. D. 1994: The American Association for Labor Legislation: an episode in institutional policy analysis. *Journal of Economic Issues*, 25, 799–828.

Clapham, J. H. 1922: Of empty economic boxes. *Economic Journal*, 32, 305–14.

Clark, J. M. 1917: Business acceleration and the law of demand: a technical factor in business cycles. *Journal of Political Economy*, 25, 217–35.

—— 1918: Economics and modern psychology, I and II. *Journal of Political Economy*, 26, 1–30, 136–66.

—— 1919: Economic theory in an era of social readjustment. *American Economic Review*, 9, 280–90.

—— 1921: Soundings in non-Euclidean economics. *American Economic Review*, 11, 132–43.

—— 1923: *Studies in the Economics of Overhead Costs*. Chicago: The University of Chicago Press.

—— 1926: *Social Control of Business*. Chicago: The University of Chicago Press.

—— 1927: Recent developments in economics. In E. C. Hayes (ed.), *Recent Developments in the Social Sciences*. Philadelphia, PA: Lippincott, 213–306.

Commons, J. R. 1968 [1924]: *The Legal Foundations of Capitalism*. Madison, WI: University of Wisconsin Press.

—— 1932: The problem of correlating law, economics and ethics. *Wisconsin Law Review*, 8, 3–26.

—— 1934: *Institutional Economics: Its Place in Political Economy*. New York: Macmillan.

——, Saposs, D. J., Sumner, H. L., Mittleman, E. B., Hoagland, H. E., Andrews, J. B., and Perlman, S. 1918: *History of Labor in the United States*, 4 vols. New York: Macmillan.

Cooley, C. H. 1913: The institutional character of pecuniary valuation. *American Journal of Sociology*, 18, 543–55.

Copeland, M. A. 1936: Commons's institutionalism in relation to problems of social evolution and economic planning. *Quarterly Journal of Economics*, 50, 333–46.

—— 1958 [1930]: Psychology and the natural science point of view. Reprinted in *Fact and Theory in Economics*. Ithaca, NY: Cornell University Press, 11–36.

Dorfman, J. 1959: *The Economic Mind in American Civilization*, vols. 4 and 5. New York: Viking.

—— 1974: Walton Hale Hamilton and industrial policy. Introduction to W. H. Hamilton, *Industrial Policy and Institutionalism: Selected Essays*. Clifton, NJ: Augustus M. Kelley, 5–28.

Edie, L. D. 1927: Some positive contributions of the institutional concept. *Quarterly Journal of Economics*, 41, 405–40.

Ezekiel, M. 1938: The cobweb theorem. *Quarterly Journal of Economics*, 52, 255–80.

Fried, B. H. 1998: *The Progressive Assault on Laissez Faire: Robert Hale and the First Law and Economics Movement*. Cambridge, MA: Harvard University Press.

Froman, L. A. 1942: Graduate students in economics, 1904–1940. *American Economic Review*, 32, 817–26.

Glaeser, M. G. 1927: *Outlines of Public Utility Economics*. New York: Macmillan.

Hale, R. L. 1921: The "physical value" fallacy in rate cases. *Yale Law Journal*, 30, 710–31.

—— 1923: Coercion and distribution in a supposedly non-coercive state. *Political Science Quarterly*, 38, 470–94.

Hamilton, W. H. 1919: The institutional approach to economic theory. *American Economic Review*, 9, 309–18.

—— 1922: A theory of the rate of wages. *Quarterly Journal of Economics*, 36, 581–625.

—— 1929: Charles Horton Cooley. *Social Forces*, 8, 183–7.

—— 1930: Affectation with public interest. *Yale Law Journal*, 39, 1089–112.

—— 1938: Price – by way of litigation. *Columbia Law Review*, 38, 1008–36.

—— 1974 [1916]: The development of Hoxie's economics. Reprinted in W. H. Hamilton, *Industrial Policy and Institutionalism: Selected Essays*. Clifton, NJ: Augustus M. Kelley, 53–81.

—— and Associates 1938: *Price and Price Policies*. New York: McGraw-Hill.

—— and May, S. 1968 [1923]: *The Control of Wages*. New York: Augustus M. Kelley.

—— and Wright, H. R. 1925: *The Case Of Bituminous Coal*. New York: Macmillan.

Hirschfeld, M. L. 1998: Methodological stance and consumption theory: a lesson in feminist methodology. In J. B. Davis (ed.), *New Economics and its History*. Annual Supplement to *History of Political Economy*, 29. Durham, NC: Duke University Press.

Homan, P. T. 1932: An appraisal of institutional economics. *American Economic Review*, 22, 10–17.

King, W. I. 1923: *Employment, Hours, and Earnings in Prosperity and Depression*. New York: National Bureau of Economic Research.

Kitch, E. W. (ed.) 1983: The fire of truth: a remembrance of law and economics at Chicago, 1923–1970. *Journal of Law and Economics*, 26, 163–234.

Koopmans, T. C. 1947: Measurement without theory. *Review of Economic Statistics*, 29, 161–72.

Kyrk, H. 1923: *A Theory of Consumption*. Boston: Houghton Mifflin.

—— 1933: *Economic Problems of the Family*. New York: Harper and Brothers.

McDougall, W. 1908: *An Introduction to Social Psychology*. London: Methuen.

McMahon, T. 1925: *Social and Economic Standards of Living*. Boston: D. C. Heath.

Means, G. C. 1935: Industrial prices and their relative inflexibility. Senate Document 13, 74th Congress, 1st Session. Washington DC: US Government Printing Office.

Mills, F. C. 1927: *The Behavior of Prices*. New York: National Bureau of Economic Research.

—— 1929: Price movements and related industrial changes. In *Recent Economic Changes*, Report of the Committee on Recent Economic Changes of the President's Conference on Unemployment. New York: National Bureau of Economic Research.

Mitchell, W. C. 1910a: The rationality of economic activity, I. *Journal of Political Economy*, 18, 97–113.

—— 1910b: The rationality of economic activity, II. *Journal of Political Economy*, 18, 197–216.

—— 1912: The backward art of spending money. *American Economic Review*, 2, 269–81.

—— 1913: *Business Cycles*. Berkeley, CA: University of California Press.

—— 1925: Quantitative analysis in economic theory. *American Economic Review*, 15, 1–12.

—— 1927: *Business Cycles: The Problem and its Setting*. New York: National Bureau of Economic Research.

—— 1950 [1923]: Making goods and making money. In *The Backward Art of Spending Money and Other Essays*. New York: Augustus M. Kelley, 137–48.

—— 1971 [1924]: The prospects of economics. In R. G. Tugwell (ed.), *The Trend of Economics*. Port Washington, NY: Kennikat Press, 1–34.

Parker, C. H. 1920: *The Causal Laborer and Other Essays*. New York: Harcourt, Brace and Howe.

Perlman, S. 1928: *A Theory of the Labor Movement*. New York: Macmillan.

Rutherford, M. 1994: J. A. Hobson and American institutionalism: underconsumption and technological change. In J. Pheby (ed.), *J. A. Hobson After Fifty Years*. London: Macmillan, 188–210.

—— 1999: Institutionalism as "scientific" economics. In R. Backhouse and J. Creedy (eds.), *From Classical Economics to the Theory of the Firm: Essays in Honour of D. P. O'Brien*. Aldershot, UK: Edward Elgar.

—— 2000a: Institutionalism between the wars. *Journal of Economic Issues*, 34, 291–303.

—— 2000b: Understanding institutional economics: 1918–1929. *Journal of the History of Economic Thought*, 22, 277–308.

—— 2001: Institutional economics: then and now. *Journal of Economic Perspectives*, 15, 173–94.

—— 2002: Morris A. Copeland: a case study in the history of institutional economics. *Journal of the History of Economic Thought*, 24, 261–90.

—— forthcoming a: Institutional economics at Columbia University. *History of Political Economy*.

—— forthcoming b: On the economic frontier: Walton Hamilton, institutional economics, and education. *History of Political Economy*.

Samuels, W. J. 1973: The economy as a system of power and its legal bases: the legal economics of Robert Lee Hale. *University of Miami Law Review*, 27, 261–371.

Shute, L. 1997: *John Maurice Clark: A Social Economics for the Twenty-First Century*. New York: St. Martin's Press.

Slichter, S. H. 1931: *Modern Economic Society*. New York: H. Holt.

—— 1971 [1924]: The organization and control of economic activity. In R. G. Tugwell (ed.), *The Trend of Economics*. Port Washington, NY: Kennikat Press, 303–55.

Stewart, W. W. 1919: Economic theory – discussion. *American Economic Review*, 9, 319–20.

Stocking, G. W. 1925: *The Oil Industry and the Competitive System: A Study in Waste*. Boston and New York: Houghton Mifflin.

Tugwell, R. G. 1921: The economic basis for business regulation. *American Economic Review*, 11, 643–58.

—— 1922: Human nature in economic theory. *Journal of Political Economy*, 30, 317–45.

—— 1930: Human nature and social economy, I and II. *Journal of Philosophy*, 17, 449–57; 18, 477–92.

—— 1931: The theory of occupational obsolescence. *Political Science Quarterly*, 46, 171–227.

—— 1932: Flaws in the Hoover economic plan. *Current History*, 35, 525–31.

—— 1968 [1922]: *The Economic Basis of Public Interest*. New York: Augustus M. Kelley.

—— (ed.) 1971 [1924]: *The Trend of Economics*. Port Washington, NY: Kennikat Press.

Veblen, T. 1924 [1899]: *The Theory of the Leisure Class*. London: George Allen & Unwin.

—— 1961 [1898]: Why is economics not an evolutionary science? In *The Place of Science in Modern Civilisation*. New York: Russell & Russell, 56–81.

—— 1975 [1904]: *The Theory of Business Enterprise*. Clifton, NJ: Augustus M. Kelley.

Williamson, O. E. 1998: Transaction cost economics: how it works: where it is headed. *De Economist*, 146, 23–58.

Woirol, G. R. 1999: The contributions of Frederick C. Mills. *Journal of the History of Economic Thought*, 21, 163–85.

Wolman, L. 1924: *The Growth of American Trade Unions, 1880–1923*. New York: National Bureau of Economic Research.

Yonay, Y. P. 1998: *The Struggle Over the Soul of Economics: Institutionalist and Neoclassical Economists in America Between the Wars*. Princeton, NJ: Princeton University Press.

Young, A. A. 1927 [1925]: The trend of economics as seen by some American economists. Reprinted in *Economic Problems Old and New*. Boston: Houghton Mifflin, 232–60.

CHAPTER TWENTY-FOUR

Postwar Neoclassical Microeconomics

S. Abu Turab Rizvi

24.1 Introduction

Postwar neoclassical microeconomic theory was a curious mixture of successes and problems. Its successes include widespread use, as both a basis for all areas of economics and a growing method in other social sciences. The ideas that constrained optimization is the embodiment of individual rationality and that individually rational behavior should be the building block of all social theory have proved very popular. This popularity is belied, however, by very serious churning in the underlying formal theory of neoclassical microeconomics in the postwar period. Indeed, the formal theory can be characterized as having a series of impossibility results that imply a demonstrable lack of progress on the main problems set for the theory. The theory had to be reinvented regularly in response to problems, and applications of the theory are often tenuous inasmuch as the theory is not firm. While this protean character has allowed the theory to survive and become widespread, many of the main interests of microeconomists have been sidestepped. The overall result is breadth of application and use combined with troubling lack of depth. The resulting dynamic is best seen historically.

The topic is vast. In order to keep this presentation manageable, this chapter focuses on the main aspects of general equilibrium theory and the pluralist approaches that have come, increasingly, to replace it.

24.2 Samuelson's *Foundations* and its Setting

Postwar neoclassical microeconomics began confidently with Paul Samuelson's *Foundations of Economic Analysis* (1947). The book arose from Samuelson's Harvard

Ph.D. dissertation. As Samuelson's career advanced, the book's main mathematical device – the formulation of nearly every economic matter as a constrained optimization problem – became commonplace. Constrained optimization came to represent *the* economic problem, subsuming Lionel Robbins's formulation of economics as the allocation of scarce resources among competing ends. Scarcity was represented as constraint and the allocation process involved optimization. Constrained optimization had been a hallmark of neoclassical theory, at least since the work of Vilfredo Pareto, who stated: "The principal subject of our study is economic equilibrium. We shall see shortly that this equilibrium results from the opposition between men's tastes and the obstacles to satisfying them. Our study includes, then, three distinct parts: 1° the study of tastes; 2° the study of obstacles; 3° the study of the way in which these two elements combine to reach equilibrium" (Pareto, 1971 [1906], p. 106).

Maximization (of something good or valuable) and minimization (of something bad or undesirable) often imply goal-directed behavior; constrained optimization became seen as the embodiment of individually rational choice. As such, constrained optimization has reverberated and replicated throughout economics and into related fields (Heilbroner, 1991). The success of neoclassical microeconomics in taking over nearly all of economics and spreading into sociology, political science, and other areas not ordinarily seen as economic rested on the portability and usefulness of constrained optimization as an expression of individual rationality. The basic, fecund mathematical technique used by Samuelson in constrained optimization was the Lagrange multiplier method of differentiable calculus. An indication of Samuelson's influence is found in Robert Lucas' Nobel lecture:

> It was lucky for me that one of my undergraduate texts referred to Paul Samuelson's *Foundations of Economic Analysis* as "the most important book in economics since the war." Both the mathematics and the economics in *Foundations* were way over my head, but I was too ambitious to spend my summer on the second most important book in economics, and Samuelson's confident and engaging style kept me going. All my spare time that summer went in to working through the first four chapters, line by line, going back to my calculus books when I needed to. By the beginning of fall quarter I was as good an economic technician as anyone on the Chicago faculty. Even more important, I had internalized Samuelson's standards for when an economic question had been properly posed and when it had been answered, and was in a position to take charge of my own economic education. (Lucas, 1995)

As useful and original as Samuelson's work was, it might best be situated as part of a revival of neoclassical microeconomics that took place in the 1930s and 1940s. Mathematical microeconomics again became prominent after the initial activity – associated with Menger, Jevons, Walras, Pareto, and others – in the latter nineteenth and early twentieth centuries (Mirowski, 1989). This revival took place at Harvard and Chicago in the United States, at the London School of Economics, and as part of French planning. It was associated with the names of Oskar Lange, Harold Hotelling, John Hicks, Maurice Allais, Abba Lerner, and, of course, Samuelson. They and many other contributors published their works in the *Economic Journal*, the *Journal of Political Economy*, the *Review of Economic Studies*, and *Econometrica* – the prestigious publications in neoclassical economics.

The culminating statement of the results was Samuelson's *Foundations*. It derived demand curves from utility functions and based the production side of the economy on the profit-maximization decisions of firms, both using the calculus. Samuelson and his colleagues provided a basis for the demand and supply sides of the economy with a single method, constrained optimization. While these authors did not successfully solve the general equilibrium equations resulting from these optimizations, they were able to state them. They identified, though they did not successfully pursue, some of the key desiderata of microeconomic general equilibrium theory: the existence, stability, and uniqueness of equilibrium, and the long-sought relations thereof to the theories of money, capital, and growth. These issues were to centrally occupy neoclassical microeconomics for the next forty-odd years.

The establishment of equilibria of demand and supply is an important feature of neoclassical microeconomics. An equally important preoccupation has been the welfare properties of the equilibrium allocations. Prior to Samuelson's *Foundations*, Lerner, Lange, and Allais demonstrated what became known as the two Fundamental Theorems of Welfare Economics: that every competitive equilibrium is Pareto-optimal, such that no one can be made better off without making someone else worse off, and that any Pareto-optimal allocation can be achieved as a competitive equilibrium with some redistribution of the agents' initial endowments. Lerner and Lange had used these results to argue for economic planning and market-based socialism, and engaged with Austrian thinkers in what became known as the Socialist Calculation debate (Lavoie, 1985). But many Pareto-optimal allocations remained from which to choose; an important research project became the determination of the best Pareto optimum. The approach favored by Samuelson, building on the work of Abram Bergson (1938), posited a social welfare function ordering all allocations. The Bergson–Samuelson social-welfare-function approach was to receive a fatal blow, however, due to the Impossibility Theorem of Kenneth Arrow (1951b). Arrow and his associates, Gerard Debreu and Tjalling Koopmans, also challenged the use of calculus in microeconomic theory.

24.3 ARROW'S IMPOSSIBILITY THEOREM

Postwar activity in microeconomic theory began with Samuelson's *Foundations*. The 1950s were ushered in by Kenneth Arrow's *Social Choice and Individual Values* (1951b), also begun as a Ph.D. dissertation. Contributing to the Cowles Foundation monograph edited by Tjalling Koopmans on activity analysis (Arrow, 1951a), Arrow deployed the Cowles Foundation's axiomatic approach to economic theorizing. After moving to the Rand Corporation, he explored when supra-individual entities such as societies and nations could be said to have well-behaved preferences of the sort attributed to individuals in neoclassical economics (the importance of Cowles and Rand in the development of the economics of this period is discussed by Mirowski, 2002; see also Leonard, forthcoming). Arrow's exploration led him to his Impossibility Theorem, which concluded that under fairly innocuous conditions, including one on nondictatorship according to which no single individual's preferences would dominate the social ranking, there were no such well-behaved preferences. This proved to be a remarkably durable result.

It is also a negative result and has important consequences for the neoclassical project. Much of economics and politics – and social science generally – is concerned with making statements about collectivities: countries, societies, groups, and institutions. The hope that such statements could have solid microeconomic foundations in individual optimization was devastated by Arrow's Impossibility Theorem. It also had other important consequences. For example, the Bergson–Samuelson social welfare function – an attempt to make a statement about which economic allocations were best, as opposed to the imperfect ranking given by the Pareto criterion – was a direct casualty of the Impossibility Theorem. Neoclassical economics could not presume to say much about the overall ranking of allocations except in terms of the quite partial ordering implied by the First Welfare Theorem and its emphasis on (Pareto) efficiency. The usefulness of the Second Welfare Theorem was also limited: asserting that any competitive equilibrium could be obtained with a suitable configuration of endowments, the theory was unable to develop a coherent comparative statics by which changes in endowments could relate to changes in equilibria, and this assertion could never approach practical implementation.

Arrow's theorem announced two further troubling and interrelated themes for neoclassical theory. The first is its problem with the aggregation of individual economic relations; this surfaced in Arrow's theorem itself, in the capital controversies of the 1960s (Harcourt, 1972) and in the Sonnenschein–Mantel–Debreu results on the arbitrariness of aggregate excess demands (discussed in section 24.5). The inability to address aggregated economic relations means that the legitimate scope of the theory is circumscribed and its usefulness is bounded. The second, related problem is that the course of neoclassical theory has often been thwarted by internally generated impossibility results. By "internally generated" is meant that it is results of the neoclassical theorists themselves that often have shown the limits of the theory. But this is to get ahead of ourselves. The heady and confident days of neoclassical microeconomic theory continued, as general equilibrium theorists achieved successes in establishing the existence of competitive equilibrium.

24.4 THE EXISTENCE OF COMPETITIVE EQUILIBRIUM

Authors in the 1930s and 1940s did not pay much attention to rigorous demonstration of the existence of a general equilibrium. In the early 1950s, this issue received considerable attention. The existence issue had already been examined by the theorists of the Vienna Colloquium around 1930 (Weintraub, 1983), when they explored the equations that Gustav Cassell derived from Walras's work (this strand of general equilibrium theory is often called neo-Walrasian). Frederik Zeuthen, Hans Neisser, and Heinrich von Stackelberg noted problems with the Walras–Cassell equations, including the possibility that prices might be negative in a proposed solution. Karl Schlesinger proposed complementary slackness conditions, and Abraham Wald fashioned a general equilibrium proof using inequalities rather than equations. John von Neumann's work on other issues resulted in the introduction of fixed-point theorems into economics that would become important in existence proofs. The German invasion of Austria, however, meant the end of the Vienna Colloquium, whose members, in large part, fled Vienna into exile in the United Kingdom and the United States.

The efforts to demonstrate the existence of competitive equilibrium continued in the United States under the auspices of the Cowles Commission, which began in Chicago (later moving to New Haven). The general equilibrium theorists (Arrow, Debreu, Tjalling Koopmans, Lionel McKenzie, and others) used mathematical techniques resembling those employed by the Vienna group rather than the calculus methods of Hicks and Samuelson. The Cowles economists, including Arrow (1951b), used axiomatic reasoning (which had also played a prominent role in von Neumann and Morgenstern's 1944 *Theory of Games and Economic Behavior*). They also employed set theory, especially as it analyzed convex structures (Koopmans, 1957; Debreu, 1959). Many of the economic issues that they examined were similar to those considered by Samuelson: consumer theory, producer theory, and the theorems of welfare economics. These were reconsidered with the new mathematical methods, often exaggeratedly contrasted with the earlier calculus: Debreu wrote disparagingly of "calculus and other compromises with logic" (Debreu, 1959). The basic tenets of this approach were given in the methodological treatment of Koopmans (1957) and the summary statement of Debreu (1959).

These authors referred to existence proofs of Arrow and Debreu (1954), Lionel McKenzie (1954), David Gale (1955), and Hukukane Nikaido (1956). In these proofs, the general equilibrium theorists demonstrated the existence of competitive equilibrium using fixed-point theorems, such as that of Kakutani, which was related to the fixed-point theorem introduced to the economics literature by von Neumann (1937) in his growth model, printed in English translation in 1945. These accomplishments were important in moving the general equilibrium program forward. Problems were immediately recognized, however. For example, the economic models with which the theorists' demonstrated existence did not demonstrate the specialization taken for granted in market economies (Rizvi, 1991). However, the most important set of problems was that of the definiteness of the competitive equilibria.

While the existence proofs demonstrated that the general equilibrium equations had some solution, they did not show that there was just one equilibrium (uniqueness), that the economy would converge to an equilibrium if it were not in one or were perturbed while in one (stability), and that the precise characteristics of the equilibrium could be found once the data of preferences, endowments, and technology had been given (computability). These important concerns had been broached by Hicks (1939), Samuelson, and others, and then by the axiomatic general equilibrium school (Koopmans, 1957; Scarf, 1967). Other important concerns were not addressed in the existence work, but had to be if general equilibrium theory were to be a progressive research program. One was the issue of comparative statics, which answered the question: If an aspect of the data of the problem (preferences, endowments, or technology) changed in some direction, how would the equilibrium change and could we expect this change to be uniformly in a particular direction? This was clearly related to uniqueness. Other questions were: Could existence of equilibrium be proved for imperfectly competitive economies? Could the general equilibrium project help to identify econometric equations? Could general equilibrium theory underpin the theories of money and of macroeconomics more generally? What about capital and growth? In this sense, the demonstration of existence raised more questions than it answered.

It was difficult to make progress on these questions during the later 1950s and 1960s; many new ideas emerged, which nevertheless did not conclusively settle matters. For example, the stability of equilibrium was examined by Arrow and Leonid Hurwicz (1958), Arrow, Block, and Hurwicz (1959), and Lionel McKenzie (1960). No sooner had this work begun than counterexamples to the kind of stability sought began to appear: by Herbert Scarf (1960), for instance. The response was to reformulate the concept of stability, as in the work on non-*tâtonnement* stability (Frank Hahn and Takashi Negishi, 1962). A similar dynamic is seen in work trying to meld the theories of money and of general equilibrium. Donald Patinkin's (1956) initial attempt was criticized by Hahn (1965) along strictly general equilibrium lines. In response to his own critique, Hahn – along with others – tried to develop an equilibrium theory of money based on transaction costs and sequence economies (Hahn, 1971, 1973; Grandmont, 1977). Likewise, when Edmond Malinvaud (1953) was able to incorporate aspect of capital into the general equilibrium framework, he did so by incorporating an intertemporal equilibrium framework (Milgate, 1979). In each of these cases – from more usual stability concepts to non-*tâtonnement* stability, from straightforward approaches to money to transactions cost and sequence economy approaches, and from synchronous to intertemporal equilibrium – changes arose because of a lack of progress on the basis of the earlier, more clear-cut concepts. The result was a theory that became increasingly abstruse and rarefied, such that the average practitioner increasingly became disenchanted with and unable to understand or use general equilibrium theory. This process continued throughout the 1960s and 1970s and beyond, as conceptual innovation and ever-greater mathematical sophistication was applied to seemingly fundamental aspects of microeconomics for which clear and simple answers ought to have been available.

This trend bears some examination. In the pages of *Econometrica*, *Review of Economic Studies*, *Journal of Mathematical Economics*, and *Journal of Economic Theory*, numerous articles seemed to have little relevance to the main concerns of most economists. The mathematics employed was high-powered and arcane. One example was the many works aimed at demonstrating that the core of an economy would converge to its competitive equilibria as the number of agents in the economy increased without limit. In establishing this Edgeworthian conjecture, economists used the mathematically sophisticated tools of measure theory and nonstandard analysis. It was impossible for many economists to read this literature. Debreu and Scarf (1963) demonstrated this conjecture for a case where the set of agents was repeatedly replicated in its entirety. Robert Aumann (1964) did the same for a case in which the economy had a continuum of agents, akin to points on a line. A key mathematical device from measure theory, Lyapunov's Theorem, came to be widely used. Edgeworth's conjecture was developed for more and more general cases by Truman Bewley (1973), Werner Hildenbrand (1974), Donald Brown and Abraham Robinson (1972), and Robert Anderson (1978). With each development, the mathematics became harder to understand and the additional insight gained was arguably decreasing.

This pattern was seen in several other areas of general equilibrium endeavor. First, general equilibrium theorists became concerned with the existence of general equilibrium with an infinite number of goods. This meant the use of infinite-dimensional vector space theory. The problem was first set by Debreu (1954) and followed up by Truman Bewley (1991 [1969], 1972), Bezalel Peleg and Menahem Yaari (1970), and many others. Secondly, Debreu (1970) realized that some progress on uniqueness could be made if the differentiability assumptions he had once disparaged were applied in very particular settings. He employed Sard's Theorem from differentiable topology to demonstrate that, in such settings, equilibria are locally unique, such that there is usually a finite number of equilibria. Egbert Dierker (1974) and many others then applied the methods of global analysis to the problem of uniqueness. In these and many other cases, sophisticated mathematics, comprehensible to a few and used in very restricted domains, was employed to pursue a topic that did not really speak to the main concerns of economists.

Consequently, a pressing need existed for clarity and progress in general equilibrium theory. In an attempt to provide these, Arrow and Hahn (1971) wrote their epochal textbook, *General Competitive Analysis*, which heralded the beginning of a decade that was to prove fateful for microeconomic theory.

24.5   THE ARBITRARINESS RESULTS

In *General Competitive Analysis*, Arrow and Hahn restated and summarized the main results of the general equilibrium efforts of the 1950s and 1960s, and formulated a series of research questions that would have to be answered for the theory to make progress. The problems were stability, uniqueness, comparative statics, econometric identification, imperfectly competitive general equilibrium, and the microfoundations of macroeconomics.

This last topic shows how central microeconomic theory had become to all aspects of economics. In the neoclassical approach, theoretical development proceeded on the basis of individualist foundations. This implied that for a theory to be well founded, it had to have a microeconomic basis. Since all of the formal theory of economics was evidently at the microeconomic level, and formalist general equilibrium theory was microeconomics *par excellence*, no sub-field of economics could be said to have an adequate foundation without becoming, as it were, an applied field of general equilibrium theory. Thus macroeconomics – as a conceptually distinct field from microeconomics – nearly disappeared, except as serving as a label, during this time. E. Roy Weintraub (1979, p. 5) stated quite correctly for the time he wrote in that "even those few economists who argue that current microeconomics *does not generate* macroeconomics have been extremely shy in their attempts to convince their colleagues of the seriousness of their concerns." Allan Drazen (1980, p. 293) similarly expressed a common view when he held that "explanations of macroeconomic phenomena will be complete only when such explanations are consistent with microeconomic choice theoretic behavior and can be phrased in the language of general equilibrium theory." Many economists today recall the period of 1970–85 as one in which nearly every economic statement was considered suspect without some sort of microfoundations; this thinking continues in large measure to this day, albeit with significant exceptions (Rizvi, 1994b). A curious feature of this period was the reliance on representative agent models that purported to demonstrate microfoundations with the use of a single agent or very few types of agent. This particular approach has been criticized very effectively (Kirman, 1992).

Suffice it to say, general equilibrium theory as it emerged in the time following Arrow and Hahn's book had a very large burden to bear. It proved unequal to this task. Such became clear in a spectacular series of impossibility results that might be called Sonnenschein–Mantel–Debreu (SMD) theory after its main promulgators (Rizvi, 1994b, 1997b). In the 1970s, it was established that despite the availability of well-behaved axioms at the individual level, the aggregate excess demands arising in Walrasian formalist general equilibrium models were arbitrary, except that they satisfied Walras's Law and a form of continuity. These two properties were needed to establish existence of the general equilibrium solutions, but all of the Arrow–Hahn desiderata mentioned at the beginning of this section required well-behaved aggregate excess demands. Economists eventually came to see that there could be no general results on uniqueness (Mas-Colell, 1977), stability (Sonnenschein, 1973), comparative statics (Kehoe, 1985), econometric identification (Diewert, 1977; Stoker, 1984a,b), imperfectly competitive general equilibrium (Roberts and Sonnenschein, 1977; Grodal, 1996), and microfoundations of macroeconomics (Rizvi, 1994b). The SMD articles showed that formalist general equilibrium theory had reached a dead end: no general results beyond existence of equilibrium were possible.

Consequently, when SMD theory became well known by the early 1980s (for example, through the survey by Shafer and Sonnenschein, 1982), it became increasingly clear to many economists that general equilibrium theory could not fulfill a promise of over 30 years. This realization had serious and unsettling consequences. Werner Hildenbrand wrote that:

> When I read in the seventies the publications of Sonnenschein, Mantel and Debreu on the structure of the excess demand function of an exchange economy, I was deeply consternated. Up to that time I had the naïve illusion that the microeconomic

foundation of the general equilibrium model, which I had admired so much, does not only allow us to prove that the model and the concept of equilibrium are logically consistent (existence of equilibria), but also allows us to show that the equilibrium is well determined. This illusion, or should I say rather, this hope, was destroyed, once and for all, at least for the traditional model of exchange economies. (Hildenbrand, 1994, ix)

It is difficult to overstate the importance of the arbitrariness results for neo-classical microeconomic theory. Arrow's Impossibility Theorem meant that general progress on welfare economics in the neoclassical vein was unattainable; the SMD theory meant that microeconomics could not yield determinateness to general equilibrium. Importantly, it also meant that the project of providing aggregate phenomena with a basis in general equilibrium microeconomics had come to an end (Rizvi, 1994b). The results had an epoch-ending impact. Erst-while champions of general equilibrium theory have had to abandon the field. Christopher Bliss thus wrote, "The near emptiness of general equilibrium theory is a theorem of the theory" (Bliss, 1993, p. 227).

Once the arbitrariness results called into question the central status of general equilibrium theory, a stage of pluralism in microeconomics ensued (Rizvi, 1994a, pp. 2–6; 1997b, pp. 275–6). Strictly, the arbitrariness results put an end to neoclassical general equilibrium theory of the Arrow–Debreu–McKenzie variety. Many neoclassical ways of thinking – partial equilibrium arguments, textbook presentations, many applications, and much of economic practice – still persist, even if they might explicitly or implicitly make reference to an underlying general equilibrium model. More in keeping with the emphasis of this essay on theoretical developments, it is notable that rational-choice game theory, experi-mental economics, and other developments arose in the early- to mid-1980s. In each case, no significant theoretical or methodological innovations were deep enough to have caused this upsurge. Rather, general equilibrium theory vacated the dominant position it had enjoyed since the early 1950s, and these alternative approaches were able to develop and to receive a hearing on issues that the previous theory could not.

24.6 GAME THEORY AND EXPERIMENTAL ECONOMICS

The still-continuing wave of pluralism in economic theory, begun in the wake of general equilibrium theory's collapse, is seen in the work on complexity (Mirowski, 2002), experimental economics, the market demand approach championed by Hildenbrand, Grandmont, and others, and other approaches (Rizvi, 1997b). The most prominent of the pluralist approaches became rational-choice game the-ory. (Rational-choice game theory contrasts with game theory that emphasizes rule-following behavior, such as evolutionary game theory.) In the early 1980s, as increasing numbers of economists accepted the gravity of the arbitrariness results, game theory seemed to have certain things in its favor (see contributors to Weintraub, 1992). It dealt with strategic interactions, had a history of dealing with imperfect competition, and had recently been revivified with Harsanyi's

(1973) reinterpretation of mixed-strategy equilibrium and Rubinstein's bargaining result (1982). It is arguable, however, that its ascendance occurred mainly because of the vacuum created by the collapse of general equilibrium theory. An example illuminating this transition may be seen in comments by Sonnenschein – a key figure in establishing the problems with general equilibrium theory – who showed a way out of the older theory and toward game theory, despite reservations (Rizvi, 1994a). In commenting on a paper by Oliver Hart that surveyed the unsuccessful attempts at demonstrating an imperfectly competitive general equilibrium, Sonnenschein (1985, p. 176) argued that there was a need for "new blood" and that this was to be provided by rational-choice game theory. He also mentioned his students, Dilip Abreu, Vijay Krishna, David Pearce, Motty Perry, and Leo Simon – who were to be influential in the new trajectory – as influencing his thinking. Sonnenschein quite explicitly linked the need for game theory to the problems with general equilibrium. He wrote that game theory has ideas "that are useful for the theory of monopolistic competition . . . My feeling is that the Negishi line [of approaching imperfect competition via general equilibrium theory], which builds on the Arrow–Debreu–McKenzie theory, has been pretty much played out" (Sonnenschein, 1985, p. 176).

This turn toward the theory of games in economic theory gained enormous momentum at this time. Fisher (1989, p. 113) correctly asserted that "game theory [had come] to the ascendant as the premier fashionable tool of microtheorists. That ascendancy appears fairly complete." Very shortly after Fisher wrote, the textbooks and treatises by Kreps (1990a,b) and Fudenberg and Tirole (1991) cemented the position of game theory in economic theory. Rational-choice game theory reached beyond pure theory, however, transforming many fields, including industrial organization and international economics. Industrial organization in particular was thoroughly changed; Tirole's (1988) game-based treatment became the leading textbook in the field. This trend was documented by Peltzman (1991). Rational-choice game theory came to dominate microeconomics and its applied fields (Rizvi, 1994a).

Unfortunately, rational-choice game theory suffered from key foundational problems. Once again, the cycle of theoretical difficulty following theoretical transformation arose in neoclassical microeconomics. A key problem for rational-choice game theory was the very concept of rationality in a game-theoretic setting (Rizvi, forthcoming). The primary difficulty is that its common solution concepts (prescriptions as to how to play a game), such as Nash equilibrium, are burdened with extremely implausible common-knowledge assumptions (Brandenburger, 1992; Bicchieri, 1993). Common knowledge means that each player knows that each player knows that each player knows (and so on) each player's rationality and structure of the game. With such an immense structure of knowledge being assumed, the idea of strategizing, which involves guesswork in the face of a lack of knowledge, is nearly rendered incoherent.

Common knowledge also has important negative implications for the economics of asymmetric information, on which a large edifice has been built, usually in the context of game-theoretic models (Riley, 2001). Asymmetric information models are used to illuminate areas as diverse as incentives, auctions, insurance, and corporate governance, and many other issues in capital and labor markets. Yet Aumann's (1977) "Agreeing to disagree" result says that private information is negated by common knowledge. The implications for information economics are profound. This suspicion is confirmed by the startling no-trade theorems that assert that new information cannot induce trade between rational agents, even in the presence of asymmetric information, when common-knowledge assumptions are made (Milgrom and Stokey, 1982). This is indeed a startling result, since it is a common intuition that exchange – for example, in speculative assets – occurs precisely because buyers and sellers have heterogeneous beliefs about the worth of what is being transacted. There are also other, related problems with rationality in game theory (Rizvi, 1997a).

We see here a familiar pattern with neoclassical microeconomics. The requirements for coherence in the theory – in this case, common-knowledge assumptions – render its plausible applications – in this case, situations with asymmetric information – without theoretical foundation. Users of the theory undoubtedly want to be able to say something about auctions, incentives, corporate governance, and so on, but have an unpalatable choice: either continue to use models (involving asymmetric information) without adequate theoretical backing or abandon the fundamental theory on which the models were based. The more practically oriented economists (who are the larger group) tend to choose the first course. The more theoretically purist types tend to keep seeking a better foundation. This means that confusion reigns: many theoretically suspect models persist along with the pursuit for better foundations. The sheer proliferation of approaches is often mistaken for success, when it is better seen to be a result of difficulties. Still, the lively pursuit indicates a degree of health and promise: theoretical pluralism can be heuristically productive. Many might argue that applied models, even where they do not have adequate foundations, are capable of generating interesting hypotheses.

Partly because of its problems with rationality, and partly because incompatible experimental evidence dogged its commonly used models, rational-choice game theory has recently faced challenges from evolutionary game theory (Rizvi, 1997a). The contrary evidence concerns the theoretical predictions of the ultimatum bargaining game variant of the Rubinstein (1982) bargaining model that can be said to usher in the rational-choice game theory. In discussions of the issues following this development, some economists wondered if some players were simply not maximizers. This view opened the gate to evolutionary-type reasoning, which is amenable in principle to a multiplicity of player types (own-gain maximizers and those preferring equality, for example). In the words of Samuelson (1995), the response to this confusion was "to abandon the model of rational players optimizing against stable preferences" of whatever sort. "The result has been the development of evolutionary game theory."

In evolutionary game theory, dating from around 1990, agents are rule-following rather than maximizing, although one rule can be to maximize in a rudimentary way. As such, evolutionary game theory is a striking deviation from many of the main trends in postwar neoclassical microeconomics; it is closer to the bounded rationality models associated with Herbert Simon (Sent, 1998).

Yet, in contrast with boundedly rational agents, evolutionary players need not even try to be rational. The population of agent types evolves as more successful types replace less successful ones – usually interpreted as involving imitation. Nevertheless, evolutionary models mimic the biological survival of the fittest (Weibull, 1995; Samuelson, 1997). Equilibrium involves stability in population compositions. Evolutionary game theory shows how far contemporary neo-classical economics has come from a time when rationally maximizing behavior on the part of individuals was thought to be necessary for a coherent economic model. It should be emphasized, however, that in contrast with the more strictly rule-following approaches, many bounded rationality models remain faithful to the thrust of the maximization impulse by interpreting bounded rationality as maximization subject to an information-processing constraint.

Game theory methods show a two-step move from traditional rational arguments. First, rational-choice game theory keeps the rationality but adds the interactivity, hence the common-knowledge problems. Secondly, to a large extent, evolutionary game theory removes the rationality. Thus rational-choice game theory is an important intermediate stage in the change to the approach to rationality. To the extent that individual rationality might be seen as a defining characteristic of the neoclassical, this change (and other changes leading to pluralism) could be argued to be a change in microeconomics from the "neoclassical" to the "mainstream" (Mirowski, 2002; Davis, forthcoming).

Another example of pluralism following the demise of general equilibrium theory also shows departures from old methods: the quite impressive rise of experimental economics. The first review of experimental economics (Rapaport and Orwant, 1962) was able to cover the field in one article (Roth, in Kagel and Roth, 1995, p. 3). Roth (1987, p. 1) writes that "... when I began my own experimental work about a dozen years ago, it was most convenient to publish the results in journals of psychology and business ... Experimental work became well enough represented in the literature so that, in 1985, the *Journal of Economic Literature* established a separate bibliographic category, 'Experimental Economic Methods.'" As with rational-choice game theory, experimental economics rose in the wake of troubles with general equilibrium theory.

Experimental economics could not flourish, however, in the deductive, axiomatic atmosphere of general equilibrium theory. The experimental method is by nature inductive; users of the method need to be open to disconfirmation of axioms held to be true by introspection. This was not the case when general equilibrium theory was in its heyday and, for example, the concept of transitivity was employed centrally by Arrow and Debreu as an axiom (Arrow, 1951b; Arrow and Debreu, 1954). When Kenneth May (1954), a mathematician, presented experimental evidence that showed that transitivity was violated by many subjects, his results were ignored by the theorists. Hugo Sonnenschein, writing 17 years later, lamented that "the economics profession appears to be so well indoctrinated with the concept of transitive preference that statements about behavior arising from intransitive preferences are sometimes interpreted as making no sense. Indeed, such behavior is referred to as 'irrational.' Suffice it to say that the rationality of consumer behavior is not based on empirical observation." Instead, "Empirical observations or experimental results frequently indicate intransitivities of choices" (Sonnenschein, 1971, p. 223). This was the situation earlier. More recently, following general equilibrium theory's troubles with arbitrariness, we see a different landscape – a situation in which experiments helped to de-center rational-choice game theory in favor of evolutionary arguments.

These three examples of pluralism following the arbitrariness troubles with general equilibrium theory – rational-choice game theory, evolutionary game theory, and experimental economics – depart in different ways from the main neoclassical general equilibrium program. None deals centrally or at all with welfare issues, a long-time concern of economists. Rational-choice game theory focuses on strategic interaction to the exclusion of much else. Evolutionary models deviate from the neoclassical focus on rational agents. Experiments favor induction over deduction. They each contribute to the wide variety of approaches to economics gaining acceptance in the current setting.

24.7 CONCLUSION

Postwar microeconomic theory has undergone periodic transformations in response to serious and recurring difficulties. For each new difficulty, a novel method has been developed, such that important fields of inquiry were given up. General progress has been rare. Arrow's Impossibility Theorem meant that the hope for a general theory of welfare, at the level of collectivities of individuals, was abandoned. The lack of progress in general equilibrium theory beyond the demonstration of existence meant that theorists devoted much of their attention to the elaboration of variant concepts and the use of abstruse mathematics, which were far from the concern and understanding of most economists and users of economics. The arbitrariness results meant that broad progress in general equilibrium theory itself had come to an end. The idea of basing the study of aggregate economic relations on individualist microfoundations was therefore challenged. As competitive general equilibrium theory began to have problems, rational-choice game theory – even in the absence of significant theoretical innovation – came to the fore. The wholesale adoption of rational-choice game theory meant that implausible assumptions about agent knowledge had to be granted. These resulted in further conundrums, such as the no-trade theorems, which call into question an economics based on asymmetric information. The problems of rational-choice game theory led to the rise and acceptance of evolutionary game theory and experimental economics, even though rule-based behavior contradicts the long-held neoclassical assumption of rational maximization by agents. The experimental method similarly contradicts the long-held neoclassical deductive, often axiomatic, style of theoretical development prior to confrontation with facts. A constant factor in all of this theorizing, however, is the persistence of the mathematical mode of expression. While this aspect of microeconomic theorizing cannot be pursued here, it is worth noting that all of the postwar microeconomic work described has been stated mathematically. Even experimental economics, which is more inductive in nature, is nearly always testing an underlying mathematical model.

At the same time, neoclassical economics seems to require the very things – individual maximizing agents as a building block, deduction of everything else from that basis – that some of its thoughtful and long-time practitioners have now come to treat with mistrust. Recall Drazen's purist neoclassical remark that "explanations of macroeconomic phenomena will be complete only when such explanations are consistent with microeconomic choice theoretic behavior and can be phrased in the language of general equilibrium theory" (1980, p. 293). Even more absolute was Harsanyi's (1968, p. 321) pronouncement that "social norms should not be used as the basic explanatory variable in analyzing social behavior, but rather should themselves be explained in terms of people's individual objectives and interests." Yet many prominent economists now acknowledge significant exceptions. Kenneth Arrow (1994, p. 1) has announced that "social categories are in fact used in economic analysis . . . [as] absolute necessities of the analysis" and has cast a skeptical eye on the "touchstone of accepted economics that all explanations must run in terms of the actions and reactions of individuals." Despite these important examples, however, for the main body of economists, social regularities remain a category that must be explained with reference to individual behavior.

Neoclassical microeconomics therefore now combines pluralism with a measure of confusion. Very few of the troublesome parts of the theory have been thoroughly eliminated: social welfare functions, well-behaved aggregate demands, and Nash equilibria remain prominent in textbooks. Yet many theorists, realizing the significance of the problems, have gone on to seek firmer foundations. Their search has led them farther and farther from the easily recognizable neoclassical theory inherited from Jevons, Menger, Walras, and Pareto.

Note

In preparing this entry, I have benefitted enormously from reference works which have served as background and whose help I would like to acknowledge. These are, first, Arrow and Intriligator (1981, 1982, 1996); and, secondly, G. Fonseca and L. J. Ussher, *The History of Economic Thought Website*.

Bibliography

Anderson, R. M. 1978: An elementary core equivalence theorem. *Econometrica*, 46, 1483–7.
Arrow, K. J. 1951a: Alternative proof of the substitution theorem for Leontief models in the general case. In T. C. Koopmans (ed.), *Activity Analysis of Production and Allocation*. New York: John Wiley.
—— 1951b: *Social Choice and Individual Values*. New York: John Wiley.
—— 1994: Methodological individualism and social knowledge. *American Economic Review* (Papers and Proceedings), 84, 1–9.
—— and Debreu, G. 1954: Existence of an equilibrium for a competitive economy. *Econometrica*, 22, 265–90.
—— and Hahn, F. H. 1971: *General Competitive Analysis*. San Francisco: Holden-Day.

—— and Hurwicz, L. 1958: On the stability of the competitive equilibrium. *Econometrica*, 26, 522–52.

—— and Intriligator, M. D. (eds.) 1981, 1982, 1996: *Handbook of Mathematical Economics*, vols. I–III. Amsterdam: North-Holland.

——, Block, D. H., and Hurwicz, L. 1959: On the stability of the competitive equilibrium, II. *Econometrica*, 27, 82–109.

Aumann, R. J. 1964: Markets with a continuum of traders. *Econometrica*, 32, 39–50.

—— 1977: Agreeing to disagree. *Annals of Statistics*, 4, 1236–9.

Bergson, A. 1938: A reformulation of certain aspects of welfare economics. *Quarterly Journal of Economics*, 52, 310–34.

Bewley, T. F. 1972: Existence of equilibrium in economics with infinitely many commodities. *Journal of Economic Theory*, 4, 514–40.

—— 1973: Edgeworth's conjecture. *Econometrica*, 41, 425–54.

—— 1991 [1969]: A theorem on the existence of competitive equilibria in a market with a finite number of agents and whose commodity space is L_{inf}. Reprinted In M. Khan and N. Yannelis (eds.), *Studies in Economic Theory*. Berlin: Springer-Verlag.

Bicchieri, C. 1993: *Rationality and Coordination*. Cambridge, UK: Cambridge University Press.

Bliss, C. 1993: Oil trade and general equilibrium: a review article. *Journal of International and Comparative Economics*, 2, 227–42.

Brandenburger, A. 1992: Knowledge and equilibrium in games. *Journal of Economic Perspectives*, 6, 83–101.

Brown, D. J. and Robinson, A. 1972: A limit theorem on the cores of large standard exchange economies. *Proceeding of the National Academy of Sciences*, 69, 1258–60.

Davis, J. B. forthcoming: *The Theory of the Individual in Economics*. London: Routledge.

Debreu, G. 1954: Valuation and Pareto optimum. *Proceedings of the National Academy of Sciences*, 40, 588–92.

—— 1959: *Theory of Value: An Axiomatic Analysis of Economic Equilibrium*. New York: John Wiley.

—— 1970: Economies with a finite set of equilibria. *Econometrica*, 38, 387–92.

—— and Scarf, H. 1963: A limit theorem on the core of an exchange economy. *International Economic Review*, 4, 235–46.

Dierker, E. 1974: *Topological Methods in Walrasian Economics*. Berlin: Springer-Verlag.

Diewert, W. E. 1977: Generalized Slutsky conditions for aggregate consumer demand functions. *Journal of Economic Theory*, 15, 353–62.

Drazen, A. 1980: Recent developments in macroeconomic disequilibrium theory. *Econometrica*, 48, 283–306.

Fisher, F. 1989: Games economists play: a noncooperative view. *RAND Journal of Economics*, 20, 113–23.

Fonseca, G. L. and Ussher, L. J. *The History of Economic Thought Website*: http://cepa.newschool.edu/het/index.htm

Fudenberg, D. and Tirole, J. 1991: *Game Theory*. Cambridge, MA: The MIT Press.

Gale, D. 1955: The law of supply and demand. *Mathematica Scandinavica*, 3, 155–69.

Grandmont, J.-M. 1977: Temporary general equilibrium theory. *Econometrica*, 45, 535–72.

Grodal, B. 1996: Profit maximization and imperfect competition. In B. Allen (ed.), *Economics in a Changing World*, vol. 2. London: Macmillan.

Hahn, F. H. 1965: On some problems of proving the existence of an equilibrium in a monetary economy. In F. H. Hahn and F. Brechling (eds.), *The Theory of Interest Rates*. New York: Macmillan.

—— 1971: Equilibrium with transaction costs. *Econometrica*, 39, 417–39.

—— 1973: On transactions costs, inessential sequence economies, and money. *Review of Economic Studies*, 40, 449–62.

—— and Negishi, T. 1962: A theorem on non-*tâtonnement* stability. *Econometrica*, 30, 463–9.

Harcourt, G. C. 1972: *Some Cambridge Controversies in the Theory of Capital*. Cambridge, UK: Cambridge University Press.

Harsanyi, J. 1968: Individualistic versus functionalistic explanations in the light of game theory. In I. Lakatos (ed.), *Problems in the Philosophy of Science*. Amsterdam: North-Holland, 305–21, 327–48.

—— 1973: Games with randomly disturbed payoffs: a new strategy for mixed-strategy equilibrium points. *International Journal of Game Theory*, 2, 1–23.

Heilbroner, R. 1991: Economics as universal science. *Social Research*, 58, 457–74.

Hicks, J. R. 1939: *Value and Capital*. Oxford: The Clarendon Press.

Hildenbrand, W. 1974: *Core and Equilibria of a Large Economy*. Princeton, NJ: Princeton University Press.

—— 1994: *Market Demand*. Princeton, NJ: Princeton University Press.

Kagel, J. and Roth, A. 1995: *The Handbook of Experimental Economics*. Princeton, NJ: Princeton University Press.

Kehoe, T. J. 1985: Multiplicity of equilibria and comparative statics. *Quarterly Journal of Economics*, 100, 119–47.

Kirman, A. P. 1992: Whom or what does the representative individual represent? *Journal of Economic Perspectives*, 6, 117–36.

Koopmans, T. C. 1957: *Three Essays on the State of Economic Science*. New York: McGraw-Hill.

Kreps, D. 1990a: *A Course in Microeconomic Theory*. Princeton, NJ: Princeton University Press.

—— 1990b: *Game Theory and Economic Modelling*. Oxford: Oxford University Press.

Lavoie, D. 1985: *Rivalry and Central Planning: The Socialist Calculation Debate Reconsidered*. New York: Cambridge University Press.

Leonard, R. forthcoming: *From Red Vienna to Santa Monica: von Neumann, Morgenstern and Social Science, 1925–1960*. Cambridge: Cambridge University Press.

Lucas, R. E. 1995: Robert E. Lucas, Jr. – autobiography. Accessed on March 22, 2002, at http://www.nobel.se/economics/laureates/1995/lucas-autobio.html

Malinvaud, E. 1953: Capital accumulation and efficient allocation of resources. *Econometrica*, 21, 233–68.

Mas-Colell, A. 1977: On the equilibrium price set of a pure exchange economy. *Journal of Mathematical Economics*, 4, 117–26.

May, K. O. 1954: Intransitivity, utility, and the aggregation of preference patterns. *Econometrica*, 22, 1–13.

McKenzie, L. 1954: On equilibrium in Graham's model of world trade and other competitive systems. *Econometrica*, 22, 147–61.

—— 1960: Stability of equilibrium and the value of positive excess demand. *Econometrica*, 28, 606–17.

Milgate, M. 1979: On the origin of the notion of intertemporal equilibrium. *Economica*, 46, 1–10.

Milgrom, P. and Stokey, N. 1982: Information, trade and common knowledge. *Journal of Economic Theory*, 26, 17–27.

Mirowski, P. 1989: *More Heat than Light*. Cambridge, UK: Cambridge University Press.

—— 2002: *Machine Dreams: Economics as a Cyborg Science*. Cambridge, UK: Cambridge University Press.

Neumann, J. von 1937: Über ein ökonomisches Gleichungssystem und eine Verallgemeinerung des Brouwerschen Fixpunktsatzes. *Ergebnisse eines mathematischen Kolloquiums*, 8, 73–83.

—— and Morgenstern, O. 1944: *Theory of Games and Economic Behavior*. Princeton, NJ: Princeton University Press.

Nikaido, H. 1956: On the classical multilateral exchange problem. *Metroeconomica*, 8, 135–45.

Pareto, V. 1971 [1906]: *Manual of Political Economy*, trans. Ann Schwier. New York: Augustus M. Kelley.

Patinkin, D. 1956: *Money, Interest and Prices: An Integration of Monetary and Value Theory*. Evanston, IL: Row, Petersen.

Peleg, B. and Yaari, M. 1970: Markets with countably many commodities. *International Economic Review*, 11, 369–77.

Rapoport, A. and Orwant, C. 1962: Experimental games: a review. *Behavioral Science*, 7, 1–37.

Peltzman, S. 1991: *The Handbook of Industrial Organization*: a review article. *Journal of Political Economy*, 99, 201–17.

Riley, J. 2001: Silver signals: twenty-five years of screening and signaling. *Journal of Economic Literature*, 39, 432–78.

Rizvi, S. A. T. 1991: Specialisation and the existence problem in general equilibrium theory. *Contributions to Political Economy*, 10, 1–20.

—— 1994a: Game theory to the rescue? *Contributions to Political Economy*, 13, 1–28.

—— 1994b: The microfoundations project in general equilibrium theory. *Cambridge Journal of Economics*, 18, 357–77.

—— 1997a: The evolution of game theory. Paper presented to the Erasmus Institute of Philosophy and Economics, Erasmus University, Rotterdam, December 18.

—— 1997b: Responses to arbitrariness in contemporary microeconomics. *History of Political Economy*, 29, 273–88.

—— forthcoming: Rationality, evolution and games. In M. Colonna and A. Salanti (eds.), *Strategic Rationality in Economics: Recent Advances and Perspectives*. Oxford: Oxford University Press.

Roberts, J. and Sonnenschein, H. 1977: On the foundations of the theory of monopolistic competition *Econometrica*, 45, 101–13.

Roth, A. E. 1987: Introduction and overview In A. E. Roth (ed.), *Laboratory Experimentation in Economics: Six Points of View*. Cambridge, UK: Cambridge University Press.

Rubinstein, A. 1982: Perfect equilibrium in a bargaining model. *Econometrica*, 50, 97–109.

Samuelson, L. 1995: Bounded rationality and game theory. *Quarterly Review of Economics and Finance*, 36, 17–35.

—— 1997: *Evolutionary Games and Equilibrium Selection*. Cambridge, MA: The MIT Press.

Samuelson, P. A. 1947: *Foundations of Economic Analysis*. Cambridge, MA: Harvard University Press.

Scarf, H. S. 1960: Some examples of global instability of competitive equilibria. *International Economic Review*, 1, 157–72.

—— 1967: On the computation of equilibrium prices. In W. Fellner (ed.), *Ten Economic Studies in the Tradition of Irving Fisher*. New York: John Wiley, 207–30.

Sent, E.-M. 1998: Bounded rationality. In J. B. Davis, D. W. Hands, and U. Mäki (eds.), *The Handbook of Economic Methodology*. Cheltenham, UK: Edward Elgar, 36–40.

Shafer, W. and Sonnenschein, H. 1982: Market demand and excess demand functions. In K. J. Arrow and M. D. Intriligator (eds.), *Handbook of Mathematical Economics*, vol. 2. Amsterdam: North-Holland.

Sonnenschein, H. F. 1971: Demand theory without transitive preferences. In J. S. Chipman, L. Hurwicz, M. K. Richter, and H. F. Sonnenschein (eds.), *Preferences, Utility and Demand: A Minnesota Symposium*. New York: Harcourt Brace Jovanovich.

—— 1973: Utility hypothesis and market demand theory. *Western Economic Journal*, 11, 404–10.

—— 1985: Comment on Hart, O. D., Imperfect competition in general equilibrium: an overview of recent work. In K. J. Arrow and S. Honkapohja (eds.), *Frontiers of Economics*. Oxford: Blackwell.

Stoker, T. M. 1984a: Completeness distribution restrictions and the form of aggregate functions. *Econometrica*, 52, 887–907.

—— 1984b: Exact aggregation and generalized Slutsky conditions. *Journal of Economic Theory*, 33, 368–77.

Tirole, J. 1988: *The Theory of Industrial Organization*. Cambridge, MA: The MIT Press.

Weibull, J. W. 1995: *Evolutionary Game Theory*. Cambridge, MA: The MIT Press.

Weintraub, E. R. 1979: *Microfoundations: The Compatibility of Microeconomics and Macroeconomics*. Cambridge, UK: Cambridge University Press.

—— 1983: The existence of a competitive equilibrium. *Journal of Economic Literature*, 21, 1–39.

—— 1992: *Toward a History of Game Theory*. Durham, NC: Duke University Press.

The Formalist Revolution of the 1950s

Mark Blaug

25.1 INTRODUCTION

Something happened to economics in the decade of the 1950s that is little appreciated by most economists and even by professional historians of economic thought: the subject went through an intellectual revolution as profound in its impact as the so-called "Keynesian Revolution" of prewar years. I call it the Formalist Revolution after Ward (1972, pp. 40–1), who was the first to recognize the enormous intellectual transformation of economics in the years after World War II.

It is common to think of interwar economics in terms of a struggle between institutionalists and neoclassicists but, as Morgan and Rutherford (1998, pp. 21–5) have reminded us, "pluralism" is a more accurate description of the state of play in economics between the two world wars, reflecting the considerable variety that actually prevailed in modes of investigation, techniques of analysis, and types of policy advice. The extraordinary uniformity in the global analytic style of the economics profession that we nowadays characterize as neoclassical economics only dates from the 1950. The term "neoclassical economics" as a standard label for the mainstream of modern economics over the past century, going back as far as the Marginal Revolution of the 1870s, is confusing enough because the early pioneers of marginalism saw themselves as post-classicals, rejecting the classical economics of Smith, Ricardo, and Mill, and would have decisively rejected the label "neoclassical" that was invented by Veblen in 1900 (Aspromourgos, 1986). But to apply the same label to prewar and postwar orthodox economics is

doubly confusing because, faced with such leading monographs of the 1940s and
1950s as, say, Samuelson's *Foundations of Economic Analysis* (1947) and Arrow's
Social Choice and Individual Values (1951), and with Arrow and Debreu's "Existence of an equilibrium for a competitive economy" (1954), no prewar orthodox
economist could have made head or tail of them.

In short, economics underwent a metamorphosis in the late 1940s and 1950s
whatever one calls it. I call it a Formalist Revolution, after Ward, because it was
marked by extreme "formalism" – not just a preference, but an absolute preference for the form of an economic argument over its content – which frequently
(but not necessarily) implies reliance on mathematical modeling and whose
ultimate objective is, like the notorious Hilbert program in mathematics, the
complete axiomatization of economic theory. It is perfectly possible to employ
mathematics elegantly (like Cournot in 1938) or clumsily (like Walras in 1871)
and yet eschew formalism in the sense that the mathematics is employed not for
its own sake but in order to throw more light on certain aspects of economic
reality. It is also possible not to employ mathematics at all (like Joan Robinson in
1956) and yet be highly formalistic in that the logic of the analysis is emphasized
irrespective of whether it serves to illuminate economic phenomena. Economists
emerged from World War II covered in glory because their technical expertise
proved surprisingly useful in dealing with military problems, employing such
new optimizing techniques as linear programming and activity analysis (Mirowski,
1998; Goodwin, 1998). In all of these exercises, mathematics figured heavily and
yet the Formalist Revolution was much more than the application of mathematical techniques to economics. It was, rather, reveling in mathematical modeling
as an end in itself and treating the equilibrium solution of the economic model as
the final answer to the question that prompted the investigation in the first place.

The Formalist Revolution made the existence and determinacy of equilibrium
the be-all and end-all of economic analysis. But what is new in that? Surely,
pinning down the equilibrium solution of a model had always been the aim of
economic theory? Well, yes and no. Equilibrium is the end-state of a process that
we economists think of as competition, but economic analysis can emphasize
the nature of the end-state or the nature of the competitive process that may
converge on an end-state – but it can rarely do both in equal measure. What is
little understood about the Formalist Revolution of the 1950s is precisely that
the process-conception of equilibrium was so effectively buried in that period
that what is now called neoclassical orthodox, mainstream economics consists
entirely of end-state equilibrium theorizing, with process-analysis relegated
entirely to unorthodox Austrian economics or equally unorthodox evolutionary
economics. Let me explain.

25.2   The Arrow–Debreu Restatement of Walras

The centerpiece of my story is the famous 1954 paper by Arrow and Debreu, not
just because it is regarded to this day as a truly rigorous proof of the existence
of general equilibrium in a market economy, the fulfillment of Walras's dream

80 years earlier, but because it is the perfect example of how concentration on the precise nature of equilibrium can crowd out disequilibrium analysis. As soon as it appeared it was hailed for its bold use of new mathematical techniques, replacing differential calculus by convex analysis, characterizing equilibria by separation theorems instead of tangencies, and employing the then relatively new tools of game theory and Nash equilibria (Weintraub, 1991, pp. 104–7). What was little noticed at the time was that this was also one of the earliest dramatic uses in economics of the so-called "indirect proof method" of modern mathematics. Arrow and Debreu used Brouwer's "fixed-point theorem" to prove the existence of general equilibrium, and the essence of the fixed-point logic is to demonstrate a conclusion by showing that its violation involves an inconsistency by contradicting one or more axioms of the model. Such a "nonconstructive" proof jumps directly from the axioms of the model to its final outcome: instead of constructing an example of whatever it is that is being justified, in this case existence of equilibrium, it argues instead that equilibrium is logically implied by one or more of the axioms. Modern existence proofs *à la* Arrow and Debreu are nonconstructive in that they make no effort to show how equilibrium comes about, but merely that it is reasonable to conceive of the existence of equilibrium. One might say that they are possibility-of-existence proofs, not actual existence proofs.

Furthermore, Arrow and Debreu are perfectly frank in disavowing any claims that general equilibrium theory provides a descriptively accurate picture of the economy. By the end, they are compelled to assume the existence of forward markets for all goods and services traded, the absence of idle money balances held by economic agents, the absence of market-makers holding inventories, the absence of bank credit, and so on, in order to prove the existence of multi-market equilibrium, and even so they find that they can throw no light on the uniqueness or stability of general equilibrium. As they concede (Arrow and Debreu, 1954, p. 266): "The latter study [of stability] would require specification of the dynamics of a competitive market as well as the definition of equilibrium." No wonder, then, that they made use of Nash's relatively new concept of equilibrium to solve the game of "an abstract economy," because the justification for a Nash equilibrium is a negative one: a Nash equilibrium in a noncooperative game is such that each rational player's strategy maximizes his or her expected payoff against the given strategy of the other rational players; nothing other than a Nash equilibrium can be the solution of such a game. Note that this says nothing about the process whereby the equilibrium is obtained; it is absolutely silent about the expectations of the players, the revision of plans, their epistemic learning capacities, and so forth; equilibrium is simply imposed as a fixed point in which market adjustments have come to an end (Weintraub, 1991, p. 108).

It is not difficult to see that the Arrow–Debreu article is formalism run riot, in the sense that what was once an economic problem – Is simultaneous multi-market equilibrium actually possible? – has been transformed into a mathematical problem, which is solved, not by the standards of the economics profession, but by those of the mathematics profession. This is Bourbakism pure and simple, named after a changing group of French mathematicians who, since 1939, have been producing an encyclopedic work on mathematical structures that exemplifies the Hilbertian axiomatic method. Debreu was a self-declared Bourbakian and produced his own *Theory of Value* (1959), which carried the formalism of the Arrow–Debreu paper one step further: "Allegiance of rigor dictates the axiomatic form of the analysis where the theory, in its strict sense, is logically entirely disconnected from its interpretation" (Debreu, 1959, p. 3).

25.3 THE RISE AND FALL OF GAME THEORY

One of the historical puzzles that lies directly across our central decade of the 1950s is the virtual disappearance of game theory in the 1950s and 1960s after bursting on the scene in 1944 with the publication of *The Theory of Games and Economic Behavior* by von Neumann and Morgenstern. There is little doubt about the widespread disillusion among economists with early game theory, probably because it offered definite solutions only for two-person, constant-sum games, which are largely irrelevant for economics (Luce and Raiffa, 1957, pp. 10–11; Dorfman, Samuelson, and Solow, 1958, p. 445). After virtually passing into oblivion in the 1970s, game theory made an astonishing comeback in the 1980s; by 1985 game theory in general, and Nash equilibrium in particular, became just about the only language in economics with which to analyze the interactive behavior of rational agents. When we consider that game theory is perhaps the only example of a mathematical theory explicitly invented for the social sciences, its steady decline for something like a generation is almost as mysterious as its enthusiastic revival in the past two decades.

Giocoli (2000a,b) seems to me to provide a convincing explanation of the fall and rise of game theory in economics, which ties together a number of elements in our own story; namely, the disappearance of disequilibrium analysis, the increasing concentration on the end-state of equilibrium, and the sinister appearance of fixed-point logic in the treatment of equilibrium. Both interwar microeconomics and business cycle theory focused its analysis on what Giocoli calls the "how and why" of equilibrium. Equilibrium had long been represented in economics as a balance of forces, but it was Hayek in a number of essays in the 1930s who broke with this standard mechanical conception of equilibrium by introducing the essentially dynamic concept of equilibrium as a situation in which all the plans of agents are reconciled and made mutually consistent, such as to confirm their plans and expectations (Ingrao and Israel, 1990, ch. 8; Weintraub, 1991, chs. 2, 5). In short, what emerged as the central question in prewar economics was just how self-interested agents in a multi-period decision-making context learn to formulate and revise their plans. However, early game theory as summed up in von Neumann and Morgenstern's *opus* did not derive from these concerns in prewar orthodox economics, but from the mathematical formalism descended from Hilbert. The average economist in the 1950s and 1960s, despite Arrow and Debreu, could not quite grasp an equilibrium concept based on the formal logic of fixed-point proofs, lacking any positive interpretation in a process that was converging to equilibrium – and that is what accounts for the delayed acceptance of early game theory by the economic community. The delayed acceptance included the now ubiquitous Nash equilibrium concept because, as published in 1951, Nash's papers defended the idea of Nash equilibrium by a negative, fixed-point justification. In his doctoral dissertation, Nash (1996, pp. 32–3) offered a positive justification for his equilibrium concept in what he called "mass action," or what we now call an "evolutionary" interpretation (Milath, 1998): in an iterative adjustment process, boundedly rational players gradually learn to adjust their own strategies to get a higher payoff after observing other players, a process that eventually converges to a Nash equilibrium. However, Nash cut out the pages proposing this from the published version of the thesis in the 1951 *Annals of Mathematics*. Instead, he used the von Neumann–Morgenstern argument that if each player had perfect knowledge of the game structure and perfect rationality in the sense of instant computational powers, then equilibrium in a game would necessarily be a set of payoffs, whose violation would be inconsistent with rationality. This is precisely what we earlier called a negative justification for equilibrium. All the old criticisms that had been constantly hurled at classical duopoly theory – Why should duopolists continue myopically to assume constant reactions from their rivals irrespective of experience? – were swept away by Nash's invitation to leap directly to the final long-run equilibrium without regard to any process of adjustments converging on equilibrium. As Ken Binmore (Nash, 1996, p. xii) rightly observed: "Nash's 1951 paper allowed economists, not only to appreciate the immensely wide range of possible applications of the idea of a Nash equilibrium, it also freed them of the need they had previously perceived to tie down the dynamics of the relevant equilibrating process before being able to talk about the equilibrium to which it will converge in the long run."

When Arrow and Debreu employed game theory and the Nash equilibrium to prove the existence of general equilibrium in the 1950s, the Formalist Revolution was still in its early stages. It took another decade or more for formalism and Bourbakianism to break down all resistance to game theory and fixed-point proofs of noncooperative equilibria. It was only in the 1970s that Nash equilibrium was accepted as the basic equilibrium concept of neoclassical economics, when it was suddenly characterized as the very embodiment of the criterion of rationality that, it was now claimed, had always been an essential feature of economic theory.

25.4 BACK TO WALRAS

We have described the Arrow and Debreu paper as the capstone of the Walrasian program, but we must now try to appraise their achievement from the vantage point of a half-century later. The ascendancy of the end-state conception of equilibrium and the almost total disappearance of the process-conception of equilibrium, which is my language for what Arrow and Debreu managed to accomplish, has its roots in Walras himself who, in successive editions of his *Elements of Pure Economics*, allowed the existence-of-equilibrium question to drown the problems of uniqueness and stability of equilibrium.

Walras's original intention was to do much more than to demonstrate the existence, uniqueness and stability of general equilibrium: it was also to provide an abstract but nevertheless realistic study of the interdependence of markets in a capitalist economy, and he never completely lost sight of that aim through four editions of his *Elements* over a period of 26 years. Nevertheless, he fundamentally altered his *Elements* between the third (1896) and fourth (1900) edition, introducing a new *tâtonnement* process for the model of capital formation and the circulation of money. He had always eliminated disequilibrium transactions in his model of pure exchange, misleadingly labeling them as "false trading"; in the fourth edition he also eliminated disequilibrium production decisions, introducing the fiction that the transactors communicated, not orally or by the physical signals implied by the appearance of out-of-equilibrium production quantities, but by written pledges of their intentions to purchase or sell at various prices "cried randomly." Walras never explained why he made these changes but, apparently, he thought that genuinely to allow disequilibrium transactions threatened the cogency of the demonstration that there were always enough independent equations to solve for the unknown prices and quantities, which was his version of a proof of the existence of general equilibrium (Walker, 1996; Bridel, 1997, ch. 4; Costa, 1998, ch. 2; De Vroey, 1999). He never made any effort to prove "uniqueness" of the price vector that secures general equilibrium and in respect of either local or global stability of equilibrium, he seems to have blandly assumed that the *tâtonnement* process of price adjustments as a positive function of the excess demand for commodities is always proportional to the amount of excess demand, in which case equilibrium would indeed be stable whatever the length of the stabilizing process.

The fate of Walras's *Elements* is not unlike that of von Neumann and Morgenstern's *Theory of Games and Economic Behavior*: it suffered a gradual demise after Walras's death in 1910 and by, say, 1930 it is doubtful that there were more than a half-dozen economists in the world who had ever read Walras, much less understood him. From this state of total neglect began the rise, which eventually brought GE (general equilibrium) theory to the front ranks of economic theory in the postwar years. It was Hicks, Hotelling, Lange, and Samuelson who were responsible in the golden decade of the 1930s in bringing about this remarkable revival of GE theory (Blaug, 1997a, pp. 77–8; Samuelson, 1989, p. 1384n). In the writings of these earlier defenders of Walras, GE theory was treated as a quasi-realistic description of a market economy, which was perfectly capable of confronting practical questions, such as the feasibility of "market socialism." But in the work of contemporary Viennese mathematicians, such as Karl Schlesinger, Abraham Wald, and John von Neumann, GE theory began to undergo axiomatization, setting aside all concerns with verisimilitude, let alone empirical verification, leading directly to the Arrow–Debreu paper and Debreu's *Theory of Value* in which GE theory is boldly defended as a self-sufficient mathematical structure, having no necessary contact with reality, or at most, as in Arrow and Hahn's *General Competitive Analysis* (1971), representing a purely formal picture of the determination of economic equilibrium in an idealized decentralized competitive economy. Considering that this metamorphosis took less than a generation, this is really one of the remarkable *Gestalt*-switches in the interpretation of a major economic theory in the entire history of economic thought.

25.5   Is GE Theory Moribund?

Let us briefly consider how the neo-Walrasian research program has turned out some 50 years after Arrow and Debreu. The existence proof of Arrow and Debreu stands up today as it did in 1954, if only because the method of indirect proof that they employed is logically impeccable and is immune to revision on grounds of new evidence, being concerned with little else than the notional consistency of the trading plans of purely virtual agents. What it signifies, however, is another question. It is difficult to see how or why such negative proofs should ever have been thought to be of economic interest inasmuch as the method of proof bears no resemblance to any recognizable economic mechanism. Even if we suppose that disequilibrium prices are ruled out by assumption, the interesting question of how trading plans based on predetermined equilibrium prices can actually be carried out is never even raised. Indeed, the very idea of demonstrating a link between the mathematical solution of the existence problem and the outcome of market interaction was simply abandoned by Arrow and Debreu. In short, what is missing in GE theory and hence in Neowalrasian microeconomics is, quite simply, competitive rivalry between transactors in actual markets. We have forgotten that, as Clower (1994, p. 806) aptly put it, "the invisible hand also has 'fingers'" (see Costa, 1998, ch. 4).

So much, then, for the existence problem. As for uniqueness, it has been shown that general equilibrium entails one and only one price vector if and only if all commodities are gross substitutes for one another, an assumption that is, to put it mildly, highly unlikely to be true. Finally, there is the crucial question of stability. The static properties of equilibrium have no practical meaning, unless they persist in the face of small disturbances and emerge fairly quickly after the appearance of disturbances. To believe in GE theory is to rely on the dynamic stability of equilibrium (Fisher, 1983, p. 2). Now it is perfectly true that the hypothesis of relative stability possesses an inherent plausibility because as Samuelson (1947, p. 5) once said, "How many times has the reader seen an egg standing on its end?" But that is probably due to the presence of nonprice coordinating mechanisms, such as particular conventions and institutions, market rules and procedures, technological constraints, and the like, all of which do little to establish the stabilizing properties of GE pricing models. Despite a considerable literature on local and global stability, the upshot of the discussion so far is a more or less total impasse: not only are we unable to prove that competitive markets are invariably stable but we have gained little insight as to the features of markets that render them more or less stable (Ingrao and Israel, 1990, pp. 361–2).

We reach the curious conclusion that equilibrium in GE theory is known not to be either unique or stable, and that its very existence can only be demonstrated indirectly by a negative proof. Nevertheless, GE theory continues to be regarded

as the fundamental framework for theoretical discourse and the basis of computable macroeconomic models. It is even taken to be the essential basis of project
evaluations in welfare economics. Is this yet another example of an emperor who
has no clothes (Kirman, 1989)?

25.6 RESPONSES TO THE FAILURE OF GE THEORY

There have been a number of responses to the apparent failure of GE theory to
live up to its own promises: to deliver rigorous solutions to the problems of the
existence, uniqueness, and stability of equilibrium. One response is to claim that
GE theory, despite its limitations, can somehow be employed negatively to refute
certain widely held economic propositions. That was Frank Hahn's classic defense
and I have elsewhere argued against this ju-jitsu move (Blaug, 1990, ch. 8).
Another response is simply to hedge ones bets in the hope that any moment
now GE theory will suddenly be transformed by a dose of realism. Ingrao and
Israel's path-breaking study of the history of GE theory seems to take this route:
it actually praises Debreu for exposing the logical errors of the theory, complains
of the character of GE theory in its Arrow–Debreu version, and then expresses
the hope that the relations between theory and empirical reality will soon be
"re-examined" (Ingrao and Israel, 1990, p. 362).

More interesting than any of these is Weintraub's defense by way of
"constructivism." For Weintraub (1991, pp. 108–9), "equilibrium is a feature of
our models, not the world" and stability of equilibrium is not something "out
there" in the economy. His study of the stability literature is "constructivist":
knowledge in science, as well as knowledge about the history of science, is
socially constructed in the sense that it has meaning only within the discourse
of the relevant community, in this case that of economists. So, questions about
scientific validity, or empirical support for GE theory, have no meaning if only
because the theorists who played the Wittgenstein language game called GE
theory did not concern themselves with such questions. The book is studiously,
almost painfully, constructivist in never endorsing or criticizing the epistemic
claims of GE theory.

Weintraub is not always very clear as to the import of constructivism. Of
course, economic theories are constructed; of course, meanings are stabilized by
the language games that economists play. "Models and theorems and evidence
of various nature, empirical and formal and definitional," he notes (ibid., p. 127),
"are adduced to convince other members of the concerned community that some
meanings are preferable for the agreed purposes." Why is this truism worth
saying? Surely, what we want to know as historians of economic thought is why
some "evidence of various nature" and "some meanings" are regarded as more
persuasive than others. Are we really to believe that the claim that queues at
grocery stores are *ipso facto* proof of disequilibrium in food retail markets, or that
an economy with massive unemployment is not in macroeconomic equilibrium,
are just assertions about the logical properties of models and say nothing about
the state of the world? Whatever happened to the "correspondence rules" that all

of us attach to economic theories, explicitly or implicitly? When economists are told that a tax on butter will raise the equilibrium price of butter, they have learned from the "correspondence rules" of the theory of market equilibrium that to test this conjecture they will need to study the price elasticities of the demand for and supply of butter. They will regard the proposition in question as having considerable relevance for policy, because it involves definite assertion about the nature of reality and not just moves in a language game.

Notice how different is this defense of equilibrium from the one offered by Frank Hahn in 1973. The standard view of equilibrium was, according to Hahn (1973), to consider it as the outcome of a process, in which case it was useful only if economic processes could be shown to actually converge on equilibrium. Alternatively, it is useful because it is a set of simultaneous and mutually compatible plans in which all learning has ceased: it makes precise the limits of economic analysis since he claimed that we have no theory of learning. We can only specify a final equilibrium state because no rigorous general theory of disequilibrium is possible. So, an end-state conception of equilibrium is needed because we have no adequate process-conception that will tell us how actual expectations and plan revisions converge to the end-state (but see Weibull, 1995; Fudenberg and Levine, 1998). Now, Hahn's argument is unduly influenced by his mathematical notion of what constitutes an adequate rigorous theory, but he at any rate seems to believe that an end-state equilibrium is somehow "out there" and that it can be found in real time with the aid of certain "correspondence rules."

Weintraub's "constructivist" interpretation of equilibrium is the last stage in his long journey over several books and many years to an impregnable defense of GE theory. If general equilibrium is not an actual real state of affairs that could conceivably happen, but just a heuristic device, a point of reference, a way of talking, then to ask whether there are missing markets for some goods or whether agents have perfect foresight has the same sort of meaning as to ask whether there really are an infinite number of primes or whether the square root of a negative number does require the imaginary number i. If Weintraub is right, we need to reconstruct the entire subject of economics, because economists have apparently deceived themselves about economic theory for over four centuries.

25.7 PERFECT COMPETITION AND ALL THAT

There is one element in the story that we have so far ignored, but we must now bring it in to round off the argument about the shortcomings of GE theory. It is the concept of perfect competition, which, surprisingly enough, was invented *de novo* by Cournot in 1838 (Machovec, 1995, ch. 2; Blaug, 1997a, pp. 67–71). The concept itself and the analytic habits of thought associated with it, particularly the concentration on an end-state conception of competitive equilibrium in which firms appear solely as passive price-takers, was alien not just to the great economists of the classical past but even to the early marginalists in the last quarter of the nineteenth century (with the sole exception of Edgeworth). The perfectly competitive model which we now think of as standard neoclassical microeconomics made its debut in the writings of Frank Knight in the 1920s and then hardened into dogma by the spread of imperfect and monopolistic competition theory in the 1930s (Machovec, 1995, ch. 8; Blaug, 1997a, p. 68).

It involved the suppression of the idea that markets might adjust, not in terms of price but in terms of quantity, or at least more quickly in terms of quantity than in terms of price. Marshall and Walras never saw eye to eye in respect of the stability conditions of a competitive market, but neither made it clear that the disagreement was a disagreement about the concrete process of competition (Blaug, 1997, pp. 72–6). In Marshall it is the production economy in which sellers adjust output in response to excess demand price that is the paradigmatic case of market adjustment, whereas in Walras it is the exchange economy in which buyers adjust price offers in response to excess demand that is taken to be the typical case. The revival of GE theory in the 1930s buried the very idea of quantity adjustments even in labor markets, and once the Formalist Revolution got under way in the 1950s, the virtual ban on disequilibrium analysis completed the triumph of price adjustments as the only way that markets ever respond to shocks. In a brand of economics that was increasingly static, all the nonprice forms of competition – favorable locations, product innovations, advertising wars, quicker deliveries, improved maintenance and service guarantees, and so on – were assigned to such low-prestige subjects as marketing and business studies. Even industrial organization, the one sub-field in economics in which students of business behavior might expect to learn something about competitive rivalry, only survived as part of the standard curriculum offering of a university economics department in the 1970s and 1980s by adapting game theory as its principal analytic tool.

Perfect competition never existed, nor ever could exist, as all the textbooks agree (Blaug, 1997a, pp. 70–1), and yet the real world is said to be approximately like, not far from, or even very close to the idealized world of perfect competition. How do we know? Because historical comparisons tell us so and it is such informal, nonrigorous appraisals that convince us that competitive markets perform better than centrally planned economies. Market economies are informationally parsimonious, technically dynamic, and responsive to consumer demand, and that is why we rate capitalism over socialism despite periodic business depressions and unequal income distributions (Nelson, 1981). In short, we appraise the private enterprise system in terms of the consequences of market processes and leave all the beautiful statical properties of end-state equilibria to classroom examination questions.

25.8   A CONFIRMATION AND A COUNTER-EXAMPLE

Let us now come back to the 1950s. Almost in the same month that Arrow and Debreu published their seminal paper on the existence of general equilibrium, Joan Robinson (1953–4) precipitated the Cambridge–Cambridge debate in capital theory, at least when it was followed a decade later by Samuelson's surrogate production function article in 1962, the *Quarterly Journal of Economics* symposium on capital-reversing and capital-reswitching in 1962 and, finally, the Harcourt (1969) survey article in the *Journal of Economic Literature* in 1969. From the beginning, this debate was not about the workings of the economy, but about the logical properties of economic models: Is there a strictly monotonic relationship between a change in the rate of interest and the capital–labor ratio, and is the rate of interest a function of the relative scarcity of capital in the economy as alleged in the neoclassical theory of distribution? Now, one might have thought that the issue is essentially an empirical one – How likely is it for the reswitching of interest rates to occur? – but with few exceptions both parties in the debate insisted vehemently that a logical flaw in a comprehensive economic theory can never be repaired by empirical evidence (Blaug, 1990, ch. 10). This is not the place to adjudicate this famous dispute, but what is striking about this 20-year-long debate is its entirely formalistic character. No one, whether on one side of the Atlantic or the other, ever asked: What do we learn about the economy if we decide that reswitching does or does not occur, and what follows about economic policy?

Notice too the extraordinary resemblance of this discussion about capital theory to the Arrow–Debreu existence proof: once Cambridge US capitulated and agreed that reswitching is logically possible, the debate dried up, as if the uses of an essentially static equilibrium framework to address issues of dynamic processes had been fully exhausted. In a striking essay on the nature of economic science, Donald McCloskey (1991) wrote: "From everywhere outside of economics except the department of Mathematics the proof of the existence of competitive equilibrium . . . will seem strange. They do not claim to show that an actual existing economy is in equilibrium, or that the equilibrium of an existence economy is desirable. They show that certain equations describing a certain blackboard economy have a solution, but they do not give the solution to the blackboard problem, much less to an extant economy." The analogy with the reswitching debate is perfect: reswitching cannot logically be excluded from the neoclassical marginal productivity theory of distribution. So what?

That brings us to the one undisputed example of formalism in the 1950s: growth theory of the Solow–Swann variety that appeared full-blown in 1956 (Hacche, 1979). This was no "inquiry into the causes of the wealth of nations" but a study of the necessary features of steady-state growth – that is, equiproportionate increases in all the relevant economic variables of economic models into the indefinite future – whose ability to shed light on actual economies growing in real historical time was called into question by even its leading practitioners. Modern growth theory, John Hicks (1965, p. 183) admitted, "has been fertile in the generation of classroom exercises: and so far as we can yet see, they are exercises, not real problems. They are not even hypothetical real problems, of the type 'what would happen if?' where 'if' is something that could conceivably happen. They are shadows of real problems dressed up in such a way that by pure logic we can find solutions for them." Does this conclusion remind us of anything?

The next example is much more controversial: *The Production of Commodities by Means of Commodities* by Piero Sraffa, published in 1960 at the very close of the decade with which we have been concerned. The book begins with an economy in an end-state of long-run equilibrium and the author wastes no words telling us how we have got there, or what would happen if we departed from it: homogeneous labor is the only nonreproducible input, whose amount is given at the outset of the analysis; fixed input-coefficients prevail in all industries (firms are never mentioned) and, hence, production would obey constant returns to scale if output ever varied, a possibility that is explicitly ruled out; the profit rate is equalized between industries, from which we infer that producers maximize profits and minimize unit costs, but not a word is spent considering the motivation of individuals; and the economy is closed and the pattern of demand obviously plays no role in determining prices, although it must equally obviously affect the scales of output of each industry.

The mode of exposition of the book is entirely Walrasian, and by page 5 we are already counting equations and unknowns to see if they match as a means of ensuring ourselves that we have a determinate solution for prices and quantities. It turns out that to determine both relative prices and the rate of profit, we must take the rate of wages as given, a conclusion that is central to Sraffa's basic thesis that the theory of value or the determination of prices is divorced from the determination of income distribution, the latter depending essentially on a power struggle between capital and labor. Whether this is in fact the central conclusion of the book is itself controversial. The book is tightly argued and abounds in beautiful logical puzzles – the definition of "the standard system," the definition of "joint production," the distinction between basics and nonbasics, and so forth – and even now, 42 years later, the purpose of Sraffa's book is so opaquely expressed that commentators cannot agree on what it adds up to (Moseley, 1995, ch. 1); this may well be one of its central attractions. Its sub-title was "A prelude to a critique of economic theory," but this apparent aim of undermining neoclassical economics and recovering the classical political economy of Ricardo and Marx only confuses the issue of its aims still further, because classical economics was a theory of a moving equilibrium or, rather, a moving demand disequilibrium, since neither the labor market nor the capital market was imagined to be in the state of long-run equilibrium, which of course is why the rate of population growth and the rate of capital accumulation was assumed to be positive (Blaug, 1999).

Again, this is not the occasion to attempt to unravel the real meaning of Sraffa's gnostic text, but simply to underline its total commitment to formalism. The real world is referred to once in the whole book, and for the rest we are totally immersed in a logical world of Sraffa's own making, whose very connection with a previous intellectual tradition is problematic. It is no wonder that despite a considerable following, at least in Europe, the Sraffian Research Program has produced little more than analytic refinement of the original model and not a single substantial insight into any concrete economic problem (see Steedman's entirely negative defense in Moseley, 1995, pp. 18–19). If ever economics was guilty of being a language game rather like Scholastic philosophy, Sraffian economics is an almost perfect corroboration of the thesis.

I bring the argument to a close with a counter-example: the one clear example where adherence to the framework of GE theory brought an incontrovertible benefit: I refer to Don Patinkin's *Money, Interest and Prices* (1956). This book, which should have brought Patinkin the Nobel Prize twice over, not only integrated money and value theory, developed the notion of the real balance effect and recovered its pivotal role in the classical quantity theory of money, and unified GE theory with the Keynesian concept of "unemployment equilibrium," but made a number of pioneering contributions to the history of economic thought with a series of "Supplementary Notes" that were scandalously omitted from the second abridged edition, published in 1989. I have returned expectedly in the above to the steady omission of disequilibrium analysis, but that is one accusation of which Patinkin is innocent. The book is perhaps best known for its interpretation of Keynesian economics as a theory of unemployment, dealing not with a situation of static underemployment equilibrium, but with one of dynamic disequilibrium, in which markets adjust too slowly to bring about full unemployment in the time-span under consideration. The "neoclassical synthesis" was a label coined by Samuelson in the fifth edition of his *Economics* (1955), but Weintraub (1991, pp. 123–4) is quite right to hail Patinkin as the one who truly "created the neoclassical synthesis as we understand it." Even in his exegesis of nineteenth- and twentieth-century monetary theorists, Patinkin did more than anyone else to remind us that the nonneutrality of money in short-run disequilibrium was just as much part of the quantity theory of money as the much vaunted long-run neutrality of money, and perhaps even more so (Blaug, 1997b, pp. 615–16). Patinkin demonstrates that GE theory is not impelled by its logical structure totally to suppress the process of conception of equilibrium; it is simply a mixture that does not easily blend. It is true, however, that Patinkin carried the maddening tendency of Walrasians to settle real economic questions by counting equations and unknowns to its breaking point. His famous assault on the classical and neoclassical "dichotomization of the pricing process," by which relative prices are first determined in commodity markets and absolute prices are then determined subsequently in the money market, rested on Walras's Law that there cannot be an excess demand for goods without an excess supply for money. This wins an argument about the role of money in economic affairs by an algebraic demonstration without lifting the chalk off the blackboard. It was exactly like Hicks's (1939, pp. 160–2) habit of settling the great Keynesian debate between the liquidity preference and loanable funds theories of interest by asking which equation to drop, the money equation or the goods equation. It is precisely this rush to algebra so endemic in GE theory that dooms it to sterility.

25.9 CONCLUSION

The central question of orthodox prewar microtheory – How is market equilibrium actually attained? – has been shunted aside ever since the Formalist Revolution of the 1950s. In GE theory, the question of whether it is attained at all dominated the issue of convergence to equilibrium so successfully as to swallow it up entirely. Even game theory begged the question, because its definition of equilibrium as the solution of a game makes sense once we have arrived at the solution but in no way explains how we got there. That everything depends on everything else is no reason to think that it depends on everything else simultaneously and instantly, without the passage of real time, that neither prices or quantities are ever sticky, that since information is always symmetric for both sides of the market there are no missing markets, or that price-taking is just as universal out of equilibrium as in equilibrium – in short, that the metaphor of thinking about price determination in terms of the mathematics of solving simultaneous equations has proved in the fullness of time to be grossly misleading.

With the triumph of formalism, the economists' community began ever more to resemble the community of mathematicians: finding an elegant generalization of an established result, or a new application of a well-known concept, became the only desiderata of young aspirants in the subject; cleverness, not wisdom or a concern with actual economic problems, now came to be increasingly rewarded in departments of economics around the world. The past half-century has only seen a continuous onward march of this trend. The Formalist Revolution was a watershed in the history of economic thought, and the economists of today are recognizably the children of the revolutionaries of the 1950s.

Bibliography

Arrow, K. J. and Debreu, G. 1954: Existence of an equilibrium for a competitive economy. *Econometrica*, 22(3), 265–90.

Aspromourgos, T. 1986: On the origins of the term "neoclassical." *Cambridge Journal of Economics*, 10, 265–70.

Blaug, M. 1990: *The Methodology of Economics*, 2nd edn. Cambridge, UK: Cambridge University Press.

—— 1997a: Competition as an end-state and competition as a process. In *Not Only an Economist. Recent Essays*. Cheltenham, UK: Edward Elgar, 66–86.

—— 1997b: *Economic Theory in Retrospect*, 5th edn. Cambridge, UK: Cambridge University Press.

—— 1999: Misunderstanding classical economics: the Sraffian interpretation of the surplus approach. *History of Political Economy*, 31(2), 213–36.

Bridel, P. 1997: *Money and General Equilibrium Theory*. Cheltenham, UK: Edward Elgar.

Clower, R. C. 1994: Economics as an inductive science. *Southern Economic Journal*, 60(4), 805–14.

Costa, M. L. 1998: *General Equilibrium: Analysis and the Theory of Markets*. Cheltenham, UK: Edward Elgar.

Debreu, G. 1959: *Theory of Value. An Axiomatic Analysis of Economic Equilibrium*. New Haven, CT: Yale University Press.

De Vroey, M. 1999: Transforming Walras into a Marshallian economist: a critical review of Donald Walker's *Walras's Market Models*. *Journal of the History of Economic Thought*, 21(4), 413–36.

Dorfman, R., Samuelson, P. A., and Solow, R. M. 1958: *Linear Programming and Economic Analysis*. New York: McGraw-Hill.

Fisher, F. M. 1983: *Disequilibrium Foundations of Equilibrium Economics*. Cambridge, UK: Cambridge University Press.

Fudenberg, F. and Levine, D. 1998: *The Theory of Learning in Games*. Cambridge, MA: The MIT Press.

Giocoli, G. 2000a: Fixing the point. The contribution of early game theory to the tool box of modern economics. Unpublished paper, Department of Economics, University of Pisa.

—— 2000b: Equilibrium and rationality in modern economics: from the years of "high theory" to the foundation of modern game theory. Ph.D. thesis, Università degli Studi di Firenze.

Goodwin, C. D. 1998: The patrons of economics in a time of transformation. In M. S. Morgan and M. Rutherford (eds.), *From Interwar Pluralism to Postwar Neoclassicism*, Annual Supplement to vol. 30 of *History of Political Economy*, 53–87.

Hacche, G. 1979: *The Theory of Economic Growth*. London: Macmillan.

Hahn, F. 1973: *On the Notion of Equilibrium in Economics: An Inaugural Lecture*. Cambridge, UK: Cambridge University Press. Reprinted in Hahn, F. 1984: *Equilibrium and Macroeconomics*. Oxford: Blackwell, 43–71.

Harcourt, G. C. 1969: Some Cambridge controversies in the theory of capital. *Journal of Economic Literature*, 7(2), 369–405.

Hicks, J. R. 1939: *Value and Capital*. Oxford: The Clarendon Press.

—— 1965: *Capital and Growth*. Oxford: The Clarendon Press.

Ingrao, B. and Israel, G. 1990: *The Invisible Hand: Economic Equilibrium in the History of Science*. Cambridge MA: The MIT Press.

Kirman, A. 1989: The intrinsic limits of modern economic theory: the emperor has no clothes. *Economic Journal*, 99, 126–39.

Luce, R. D. and Raiffa, H. 1957: *Games and Decisions*. New York: John Wiley.

Machovec, F. M. 1995: *Perfect Competition and the Transformation of Economics*. London: Routledge.

McCloskey, D. N. 1991: Economic science: a search through the hyperspace of assumptions. *Methodus*, 3(1), 6–16. Reprinted in S. T. Ziliak (ed.) 2001: *Measurement and Meaning in Economics. The Essential Deirdre McCloskey*, vol. 3. Cheltenham, UK: Edward Elgar, 23–4.

Milath, G. J. 1998: Do people play Nash equilibrium? Lessons from evolutionary game theory? *Journal of Economic Literature*, 3(3), 1347–74.

Mirowski, P. 1998: Machine dreams: economic agents as cyborgs. In J. B. Davis (ed.), *New Economics and Its History*, Annual Supplement to vol. 29 of *History of Political Economy*, 13–40.

Morgan, M. S. and Rutherford, M. 1998: American economics: the character of the transformation. In M. S. Morgan and M. Rutherford (eds.), *From Interwar Pluralism to Postwar Neoclassicism*. Annual Supplement to vol. 30 of *History of Political* Economy, 1–26.

Moseley, F. 1995: *Heterodox Economic Theories. True or False?* Aldershot, UK: Edward Elgar.

Nash, J. F. 1996: *Essays in Game Theory*. Cheltenham, UK: Edward Elgar.

Nelson, R. R. 1981: Assessing private enterprise: an exegesis of tangled doctrine. *Bell Journal of Economics*, 2(1), 93–111. Reprinted in P. J. Boettke (ed.), *The Legacy of Friedrich von Hayek*, vol. III. Cheltenham, UK: Edward Elgar, 80–98.

Patinkin, D. 1956: *Money, Interest and Prices: An Interpretation of Money and Value Theory*. Evanston, IL: Peterson; 2nd edn. Harper & Row, 1965; 2nd edn. abridged, Harper & Row, 1989.

Robinson, J. 1953–4: The production function and the theory of capital. *Review of Economic Studies*, 21, 81–106. Reprinted in Robinson, J. 1960: *Collected Economic Papers*, vol. 2. Oxford: Blackwell, 114–31.

Samuelson, P. A. 1947: *Foundations of Economic Analysis*. Cambridge, UK: Cambridge University Press.

—— 1989: How *Foundations* came to be. *Journal of Economic Literature*, 36(3), 1375–86.

Walker, D. A. 1996: *Walras's Market Models*. Cambridge, UK: Cambridge University Press.

Ward, B. 1972: *What's Wrong with Economics?* London: Macmillan.

Weibull, J. 1995: *Evolutionary Game Theory*, Cambridge, MA: The MIT Press.

Weintraub, E. R. 1991: *Stabilizing Dynamics: Constructing Economic Knowledge*. Cambridge, UK: Cambridge University Press.

A History of Postwar Monetary Economics and Macroeconomics

Kevin D. Hoover

26.1   WORLD WAR II AS A TRANSITIONAL PERIOD

Despite a degree of arbitrariness, World War II provides a natural division in the history of macroeconomics. The macroeconomics of the interwar period was a rich tapestry of competing models and methodologies, pursued with a sophistication that was only gradually regained in the postwar period (see chs. 19 and 20; Laidler, 1999). John Maynard Keynes's *The General Theory of Employment, Interest and Money*, published in 1936, three years before the onset of war in Europe, appeared to many as an important, but not preeminent, contribution to the contemporary debates. Yet, by 1945, Keynesian macroeconomics was clearly ascendant.

Keynes provided a conceptual framework that greatly simplified professional discussions of macroeconomic policy. The main elements were: (i) an aggregative analysis – his key distinction between the economics of individual or firm decision-making, taking aggregate output as fixed, and the economics of output and employment as a whole supplies the content, if the not the name, of the now common distinction between microeconomics and macroeconomics; (ii) the determination of aggregate output by aggregate analogues to Marshallian supply and demand; (iii) the possibility (even likelihood) that aggregate supply and demand could determine a level of output at which resources were not fully employed; and (iv) the possibility that monetary and fiscal policies could boost aggregate demand to counteract unemployment.

The decade after the publication of *The General Theory* was a period of exploration, investigation, and consolidation – a period in which the Keynesian model was forged into the paradigm that guided mainstream macroeconomic analysis for the next three decades. John Hick's (1937) IS–LL model (later renamed the IS–LM model) emerged as the canonical representation of the Keynesian system. The downward-sloping IS curve represented combinations of interest rates and output for which planned savings (directly related to income or output) and planned investment (inversely related to interest rates) were equal. The upward-sloping LM curve represented combinations in which the demand for money (directly related to income and inversely related to interest rates) equaled the fixed supply of money. The crossing point determined the level of aggregate demand. Hicks placed little stress on aggregate supply, while Modigliani's (1944) influential Keynesian model offered a highly simplified aggregate-supply curve: perfectly elastic at the current price level up to full employment and inelastic at full employment – a reverse L-shaped curve in price/output space.

These models simplified Keynes's account in an effort to render it into a closed set of algebraic equations. They represented the core structure of *The General Theory*, but omitted many nuances. Alan Coddington (1983) stigmatized them – with some justice – as "hydraulic Keynesianism." What it lost in detail, hydraulic Keynesianism made up in its suitability for mathematical and structural econometric elaboration.

The war itself gave a boost to practical Keynesianism. Keynes had diagnosed the Great Depression of the 1930s as a massive failure of aggregate demand. The war represented an enormous boost to aggregate demand that finally ended the Depression and led governments to accept the legitimacy of deliberate interventions to direct the economy. The Beveridge Report of 1942 in Great Britain and the Employment Act of 1946 in the United States provided blueprints for government involvement in the macroeconomy along Keynesian lines. The war was financed through massive government borrowing. After previous wars, governments had generally placed a high priority on the repayment of these debts. This time, however, Abba Lerner's (1943) Keynesian notion of "functional finance" suggested that government fiscal policy should be judged for its effects on output, employment, and prices, rather than on accounting standards in which the balanced budget held a special place. Policy-makers were concerned that demobilization of the millions of men and women under arms could trigger a postwar recession, and they were prepared to respond with demand stimulus. Practical policy required good information on the state of the economy. Keynes's aggregative framework fitted well with the design of systematic national accounts due to Colin Clark, Simon Kuznets, and Meade and Stone. The collection of macroeconomic data accelerated rapidly after the war in most developed countries, which proved a boon for scientific research in macroeconomics as well as for practical policy-making.

26.2 THE ERA OF KEYNESIAN DOMINANCE, 1945–1970

For at least 25 years after the end of World War II, mainstream macroeconomics was predominantly Keynesian. *The General Theory* had collapsed the rich debates of the 1920s and 1930s into a static, short-run, aggregative model, concerned exclusively with a closed economy. One central plank on the agenda for macroeconomic research was to recover what was lost in Keynes's simplifications. A second was to use the newly available data sources to give empirical content to ever more detailed Keynesian models. A third was to explore the relationships between the now distinct categories of macroeconomics and microeconomics.

26.2.1   Long-run growth

Fluctuations in investment were the key to Keynes's analysis of aggregate demand and the business cycle, yet *The General Theory* contains no systematic account of its role in economic growth. To repair this omission, Roy Harrod, beginning in 1939, developed a theory in which labor and capital combined in fixed proportions to generate output.

Ignoring technical progress, the growth rate of the economy depended on the investment rate (misleadingly referred to as the savings rate) and the rate at which capital was converted into output. Harrod defined the *warranted rate of growth* as $g = s/v$ = *investment share in GDP/capital-output ratio*. He defined the *natural rate of growth* as the rate of growth of the labor force (n). So long as $g = n$, the economy will grow steadily. Evsey Domar independently constructed essentially the same model. The Harrod–Domar model displays "knife-edge" instability. If s is low enough, so that $g < n$, then unemployment in the economy will rise progressively; if it is great enough, any existing unemployment will be absorbed and, with no further labor available, the growth in output will be stymied.

Working independently, Robert Solow and Trevor Swan suggested in 1956 that the knife-edge property of the Harrod–Domar model resulted from the assumption of fixed technology (constant v). If firms could adjust their inputs to reflect relative factor prices, then progressively increasing unemployment, for example, would result in a falling real wage and a fall in the capital-output ratio, raising g and reestablishing a *balanced* or *steady-state* growth path at the natural rate (n).

The Solow–Swan (or *neoclassical* growth) model was easily adapted to include technical progress treated as a rescaling of its underlying constant-returns-to-scale production function. It formed the basis for Solow's accounting exercise in which the sources of US GNP growth were attributed to growth in the factors of production and to technical progress (total factor productivity). His conclusion that total factor productivity was overwhelmingly the dominant factor seemed to many to be counterintuitive. By the early 1960s, intellectual effort focused on developing the model, including adding endogenous technical progress, embodied in a capital stock differentiated by investment vintage, and extending it to multiple sectors. (For a contemporaneous survey of the growth literature, see Hahn and Matthews, 1964.)

Joan Robinson, Nicholas Kaldor, and other economists at the University of Cambridge (England) developed accounts of growth that were closely related to Harrod's and skeptical of the neoclassical approach. They tried to integrate the

Keynesian demand model and a Marxist or neo-Ricardian account of income distribution. Robinson, in particular, criticized the *aggregate* neoclassical, marginalist theory of distribution in which profits were the marginal product of capital. While the marginal analysis might work for a particular, homogeneous physical capital good and a single firm, aggregate capital was measured in monetary terms: the sum of the present discounted value of the expected profit streams of the physical means of production of all firms. The quantity and price (the rate of discount) of aggregate capital must be jointly determined. Aggregate capital was not, then, the sort of independent quantity that could have a well-defined marginal product, which in turn determined its rate of return. Robinson maintained that the very notion of aggregate capital was circular and absurd.

In the debate that came to be known as the "Two Cambridges Controversy," Paul Samuelson, Solow, and other economists associated with the Massachusetts Institute of Technology in Cambridge, Massachusetts, essentially conceded Robinson's point. Nonetheless, they maintained that, as an idealization or "parable," the distributional consequences of the Solow–Swan (or neoclassical) growth model pointed robustly in the right direction. Cambridge, England, won the debate on a technicality, demonstrating, that with heterogeneous physical capital goods, it was possible that there would not be a monotonic inverse relationship between wage and profit rates as predicted by the neoclassical parable. Cambridge, Massachusetts, however, won the larger battle: aggregate capital, aggregate production functions, and the Solow–Swan model remain workhorses of mainstream macroeconomics to this day (see Harcourt, 1972; Bliss, 1975).

The Solow–Swan model provided a framework for the analysis of long-run policy. The first efforts of Edmund Phelps and others took the maximization of consumption per head to be the policy goal. The so-called "golden rule" for growth called for investment policies that resulted in a rate of return on capital equal to the sum of the rate of growth of the labor force, the rate of technical progress, and the rate of depreciation. The analysis warned against overinvestment: capital–labor ratios higher than the golden rule level were inefficient in the comparative static sense that a lower level supported a higher consumption per head; and also in the dynamic, or Paretian, sense that movement toward the golden rule would free up capital for consumption and would permit higher consumption per head in *every* period along the transition to the golden-rule balanced-growth path. Because investment rates below the golden rule are dynamically efficient and not Pareto-rankable, growth theory from the mid-1960s on stressed optimal-growth models in which preferences over intertemporal consumption patterns are reflected in an aggregate utility function. Essentially, the investment rate (s) was treated as an endogenous variable rather than a given parameter.

In another extension, Robert Mundell and James Tobin incorporated money demand functions into the neoclassical growth model. The "Tobin–Mundell effect" in their models violates superneutrality: inflation raises the opportunity cost of holding money and encourages substitution into real capital, boosting output. In contrast, Miguel Sidrauski's monetary model, which introduces real money holdings into the utility function of an optimal-growth model, preserves superneutrality.

To this day, the optimal growth model forms the core of the account of long-run dynamics in mainstream macroeconomics – and is widely accepted by economists who disagree extensively over short-run and policy issues. By 1970, research into growth models had reached diminishing returns, and little advance was made until the advent of endogenous growth models in the work of Paul Romer and Robert Lucas, in the mid-1980s. These models widened the scope of macroeconomics to address important questions in economic development, but have little affected the larger course of macroeconomics. (For further references on growth, see Wan, 1971; Jones, 1998.)

26.2.2 Short-run dynamics

Interwar macroeconomics had included elaborate accounts of the short-run dynamics of the business cycle, but *The General Theory* offered only a static model. Substantial postwar research reintroduced dynamical features into every aspect of the Keynesian model. The two most significant areas, perhaps, were dynamical accounts of inflation and unemployment.

He was not the first to discern an inverse relationship between wage inflation and unemployment, but A. W. H. Phillips's (1958) study of nearly 100 years of data for the United Kingdom proved to be a landmark. Phillips's study was grounded in a vision of the Keynesian model as a system developing in real time and in Phillips's own research into the mathematics of optimal control. Unlike Keynes, Phillips modeled firms as wage-setters. In light of later developments, it is also worth noting that Phillips was careful to account for the role of trend inflation in such a way that he respected the distinction between real and nominal wages.

Development of the Phillips curve proceeded on three tracks. First, by the early 1960s Phillips curves were estimated for many countries, using both wage inflation and price inflation as dependent variables. Secondly, a number of economists, most notably Richard Lipsey, elucidated the microeconomic behavior that might account for the Phillips curve. And, thirdly, Paul Samuelson and Solow provided an analysis that treated the Phillips curve as a menu of policy choices in which higher inflation was the price of lower unemployment. Their notion of an exploitable tradeoff helped to place the Phillips curve in the center of practical policy analysis. Again, in light of later developments, it is worth noting that Samuelson and Solow were aware that the overly aggressive exploitation of the tradeoff might lead to an acceleration of trend inflation and an unfavorable shift of the tradeoff itself (see Wulwick, 1987).

By the beginning of the Kennedy Administration, Keynesian economic advisors dominated American government circles. One advisor, Arthur Okun, answered the question of how to guide aggregate-demand management with another empirical relationship. "Okun's Law" states that there is an approximately linear, inverse relationship between the growth of output and changes in the unemployment rate. Okun's Law has not received extensive theoretical investigation or development, but has remained an important rule of thumb for policy-makers.

26.2.3 Macroeconometric models

Structural macroeconometric modeling began before World War II (Tinbergen, 1939). Although Keynes was deeply skeptical of the econometric enterprise, the model-builders quickly incorporated the Keynesian framework. Nearly every postwar model is an elaboration on the simple IS–LM/aggregate-supply framework. In part, this is a testament to the flexibility and breadth of that framework and, in part, a reflection of the mutual adaptation of the Keynesian model and the national-accounting conventions that governed data collection.

The pivotal figure in the history of econometric model-building was Lawrence Klein, a close student of *The General Theory*. Klein took advantage of recent developments in structural econometrics due to Trygve Haavelmo and the Cowles Commission. Building on Tinbergen's work, by 1950 Klein formulated and estimated three models of the interwar US economy. Working with Arthur Goldberger, Klein developed a seminal model of the postwar US economy in 1955, a model with 20 stochastic equations and five identities that was used for forecasting and policy analysis. Meanwhile, Tinbergen supervised the creation of a series of increasingly sophisticated models of the Dutch economy. Working with a group at Oxford University, Klein developed a model for the UK economy. (For the early history of macroeconometrics, see Morgan, 1990; Hendry and Morgan, 1995.)

Macroeconometric model-building and its supporting activities (see section 26.2.4) dominated macroeconomic research in the 1960s. In both the USA and the UK, researchers continued to elaborate Klein's model. Three models represent pinnacles of American model-building in the late 1960s. The largest was the Social Science Research Council (SSRC)/Brookings model, which ultimately included about 400 stochastic equations. The MPS (Massachusetts Institute of Technology/University of Pennsylvania/SSRC) model was similar to the Brookings model, but included a rich financial sector. Finally, the Data Resources Incorporated (DRI) model – similar in scope to the other large models – was the most important commercial macroeconometric model. DRI found a significant market for model-based forecasts and policy analysis, as well as for the macroeconomic database that it maintained to support its model. By the early 1970s, macroeconometric models had been constructed for virtually all developed, and for many developing, countries (see Bodkin, Klein, and Marwah, 1991).

26.2.4 Microfoundations of macroeconomics: individual equations

In *The General Theory*, Keynes rationalized the key aggregate relationships such as the consumption function and the investment function with reference to individual behavior. In *The Keynesian Revolution* (1947), Klein emphasized the desirability of securing the microfoundational underpinnings of each of these functions. A reciprocal effort to develop the econometrics of individual equations of the large macromodels and their theoretical, microeconomic underpinnings was a substantial focus of research in this period.

The consumption function presents the clearest case. Keynes had admitted a large number of potential factors into the analysis of consumption and savings. These included precaution, bequests, time preference, considerations of expected, or life-cycle, income and consumption patterns, capital gains and losses, fiscal policy, expectations, and the average level of real wages (consumption and income were measured in wage units). But early attempts to model consumption empirically assumed that the static consumption was linear in disposable income and that the marginal propensity to consume was less than the average propensity to consume. This implied that over time – as the economy became richer – the average propensity to consume should be falling, and that cross-sectionally richer people should have a lower average propensity to consume than poorer people. Research by Simon Kuznets suggested that, while these implications might be true in the short run and cross-sectionally, in the long run (decade to decade) the marginal propensity to consume and the average propensity to consume were equal and approximately constant.

James Duesenberry (1949) reconciled the long-run time series with (i) the short-run time series and (ii) the cross-sectional data by modeling consumption as a function of individuals' past incomes and those of their social group. As income rises over time, individuals reset their standard of prosperity and so, on average, do not come to regard themselves as high income unless their income rises faster than those of their social peers. Despite the empirical evidence that he offered, the economics profession viewed Duesenberry's "relative-income hypothesis" as unsatisfactory because of its appeal to sociological facts that were not accounted for as the outcome of an explicit individual optimization problem. Building on joint work with Kuznets, Milton Friedman (1957) modeled consumption as an intertemporal optimization problem in which the budget constraint was the implicit return on the present value of all future income (labor and nonlabor). Almost simultaneously, Franco Modigliani and Richard Brumberg (1954) modeled consumption in a nearly equivalent manner, focusing on the stock of implicit wealth rather than the flow of income from the same present-value calculation.

On the assumption that people prefer consumption streams that are steadier than their income streams, the "permanent-income/life-cycle model" suggests that Kuznets's puzzles result from mismeasurement. The average and marginal propensities to consume from permanent income are equal and constant. Transitory fluctuations in income little change permanent income or consumption. Permanent income is not directly observed, as it depends on individuals' expectations of future income. The responsiveness of consumption to measured income is lower in the short run since transitory components dominate, and higher in the long run when they tend to cancel out. Similarly, in the cross-section, some observed individuals experience transitory income higher (lower) than their permanent income and so have lower (higher) consumption than individuals with permanently high (low) income. Thus, the measured marginal propensity to consume is lower than the permanent marginal and average propensity to consume that is observable in the long-run time series.

Friedman's investigation of the consumption function also revived interest in the role of expectations, largely ignored since Keynes's *The General Theory*.

Friedman's method of modeling expectations of future income through a geo-metrically weighted sum of past incomes proved easy to rationalize as partial adjustment to past prediction errors and was widely applied in other contexts.

Other constituent functions of the Keynesian macromodel received similar treat-ment in the 1950s and 1960s. William Baumol and Tobin, for instance, modeled the transactions and speculative demands for money (Laidler, 1993), while Dale Jorgenson, among others, modeled the microfoundations of investment.

Research into the microfoundations of individual relationships derived much of its cachet from its relation to research into large-scale macromodels. Both were driven from center stage with the emergence of general equilibrium micro-foundations as the dominant research program in macroeconomics, although they remain of considerable practical interest to this day.

26.2.5 Microfoundations of macroeconomics: general equilibrium

One of Keynes's main criticisms of the "classics" was their failure to account for the interdependence of production and consumption decisions. He offered instead an aggregate general equilibrium system. The IS–LM model reinforced the general equilibrium nature of the Keynesian model. Nevertheless, beginning with Wassily Leontief's early critique of *The General Theory*, many economists questioned the consistency of the Keynesian model with the microeconomic general equilibrium model.

Don Patinkin addressed the two main problems in his *Money, Interest, and Prices* (1956). First, the standard Walrasian general equilibrium model is essen-tially a barter model. Walras had introduced money through an aggregate relationship similar to a standard quantity-equation for money, but this did not account for the individual behavior of money holders in a manner analogous to other supply and demand relationships in the model. Patinkin argued that money was held for its services and should be valued like other real goods. Patinkin entered real money balances (M/p) into the individual utility functions of an otherwise Walrasian model. Patinkin wrote nearly simultaneously with the publication of the proofs of the existence of a general equilibrium in systems without money. He assumed – but did not prove – the existence of an equilib-rium with money. Frank Hahn later showed that, in general, there is no solution to Patinkin's system, because the price deflator can change discontinuously as relative prices adjust in the *tâtonnement* process through which equilibrium is established. Patinkin's solution has remained influential at an aggregate level, but was unsuccessful in providing true microfoundations (see Hoover, 1988).

Patinkin also isolated the second problem: the Walrasian system assumes that quantities adjust to prices under the assumption that no trades are made until a market-clearing price vector is established, yet the Keynesian model assumes that quantities respond to quantities (e.g., the consumption function relates consumption to income, not to prices) or that markets do not clear. Patinkin examined the labor market closely in light of these problems. They were taken up in more generality by Clower (1965). He argued that, if producers and consumers knew that markets would not clear, they would incorporate quantity constraints into their decisions. For example, a worker who knew that he could not purchase as many goods as he liked at the current price would supply less labor at a given real wage than he would if the goods supply were infinitely elastic at that price. Clower argued that prices are often set away from their market-clearing values, so that quantity rationing is the norm. Ubiquitous rationing accounts for such Keynesian relationships as the consumption function and the aggregate-supply function. Axel Leijonhufvud (1968) constructed an elaborate historical reinterpretation of Keynes's *The General Theory* on the basis of Clower's analysis.

Robert Barro and Herschel Grossman (1971) provided the most influential formal model of Clower's analysis. They simplified the analysis by assuming that prices were fixed by forces outside the model. Their "fixed-priced" model is notable for importing the representative-agent approach from growth theory. With no serious account of how to construct economy-wide aggregates from the choices of individual agents, this move was a serious retreat from the original goal of the microfoundational program. Although the fixed-price model was quickly supplanted in the United States, it became highly developed in Europe (e.g., Malinvaud, 1977) and remains influential.

26.3   The Debate Over Money and Monetary Policy, 1956–1982

26.3.1   Diminishing the importance of money

Although the title of Keynes's masterwork included *Money* and *Interest*, early postwar Keynesians emphasized fiscal policy over monetary policy. Although not accurate as exegesis, Hicks (1937) famously justified his judgment that "the General Theory of Employment is the Economics of Depression" by the "*special* form of Mr. Keynes's theory" in which the LM curve is infinitely elastic (later referred to as the "liquidity trap"). Empirical research in prewar Britain also suggested that the investment function and, hence, the IS curve were nearly interest-inelastic. A horizontal LM curve and a vertical IS curve together imply impotent monetary policy.

As well as underwriting the weakness of monetary policy, the Radcliffe Report to the British Parliament (1959) argued that the existence of numerous close substitutes for currency and checking accounts implied that the velocity of circulation for any narrow monetary aggregate would be highly unstable, rendering it both hard to define a practicable concept of money and to control the real economy with any particular monetary aggregate. The report advocated targeting interest rates as the only practical monetary policy.

The Radcliffe Report reflected the "new view" of money. John Gurley and Edwin Shaw (1960) and Tobin, among others, advocated replacing the simple money/bond dichotomy of the Keynesian system with a fuller account of the wide spectrum of financial assets. Tobin (1969) especially tried to link the financial system to the real economy through a variant on an idea of Keynes's that is often referred to as "Tobin's q": the ratio of the market value of a real asset to its replacement cost. When q is greater than unity, it pays to invest; when it is less than unity, it is better to hold financial assets. Working with William Brainard, Tobin engaged in a heroic attempt to adapt the new view to the econometric macromodel.

26.3.9 Emphasizing the importance of money

The University of Chicago was relatively immune to Keynesian ideas and, through the 1930s and 1940s, continued to teach the classical quantity theory of money, despite Keynes's criticisms. Milton Friedman reinvigorated the Chicago tradition in an edited volume, *Studies in the Quantity Theory of Money* (1956), and, especially, in his own contribution to it, "The quantity theory: a restatement." Rather than Irving Fisher's transaction version of the quantity theory, Friedman adopted the "Cambridge" or income version which, given the existence of national-income accounts, proved easier to implement empirically. In itself, Friedman's demand function for money is perfectly compatible with Keynesian analysis. The differences between Friedman and the Keynesians center on his insistence that: (i) markets clear in the long run; (ii) the demand for money is a stable function of a few variables, even if the unconditional velocity of circulation is highly variable; and (iii) the supply of money is easily controllable by the monetary authorities. The quantity of money is unimportant for real outcomes in the long run as markets clear, but most short-run cyclical real fluctuations can be blamed on bungled monetary policy.

Friedman and his colleague Anna Schwartz won many converts to their view that monetary policy is the principal cause of cyclical fluctuations with the magisterial *Monetary History of the United States* (1963). The *tour de force* was their account of the Great Depression as an unintended monetary contraction. Peter Temin (1976) argued that this explanation required that interest rates rise along with falling output, but that, in fact, interest rates fell. While no one Keynesian offered a complete reassessment of US monetary history, the debate in the 1960s was highly empirical, focusing on the stability of money demand compared to the stability of Keynesian multipliers, the predictive power of monetary policy compared to fiscal policy, and the independent controllability of the money supply. These heated debates often hinged on what counted as acceptable econometric methods and, in a climactic battle over the causal direction between money, on the one side, and output and prices, on the other, became intensively methodological.

26.3.3 Monetarism

In the end, the war was fought to a draw in the sense that neither side won many converts. Yet, under the sobriquet *monetarists*, the quantity theorists did establish themselves as an intellectually formidable alternative to the previously dominant Keynesians.

The monetarist assumption of the long-run neutrality of money stood in direct conflict to a long-run tradeoff between inflation and unemployment implied by a simple Phillips curve. In 1967 Edmund Phelps developed a model in which the Phillips curve emerged in an expectations-augmented form: aggregate demand stimulus accelerated inflation, but reduced unemployment only until expectations adapted to the new policy. Independently, in his presidential address to the American Economic Association that same year, Friedman argued that monetary policy could affect real output only in the short run. In the long run, the Phillips curve was vertical at a "natural rate of unemployment" determined by tastes, technology, resources, and institutions. The natural-rate hypothesis received a strong boost when, in the early 1970s, inflation and unemployment rose simultaneously in most developed economies.

Adopting an old Chicago theme due to Henry Simons, Friedman and other monetarists, such as Karl Brunner and Allan Meltzer, advocated that monetary policy be conducted according to simple, fixed rules. The rationale was partly libertarian (the government should not manipulate people's behavior), partly based in the Phillips curve (expectations are more accurately formed when policy is easily understood), and partly an expression of distrust in econometric models (the lags between monetary actions and their real effects are long, variable, and poorly modeled, and attempting to exploit them often leads to perverse outcomes). Monetarists preferred a rule that targets a relatively narrow monetary aggregate (the monetary base, or "M1"). Market interest-rate rules would, they argued, be unstable: if the target were too low, inflation would increase, cutting real interest rates and further increasing inflation.

Although much has been made over the differences between monetarists and Keynesians (see Mayer, 1978), monetarists were at ease with Keynes's highly aggregated framework and showed little interest in the effort to develop general equilibrium microfoundations. Mainstream Keynesians easily adopted the idea of the natural rate or – as many preferred to call it – the *n*onaccelerating *i*nflation *r*ate of *u*nemployment (*NAIRU*). The most important differences were (i) whether deviations from the natural rate – logically, belonging to the Marshallian short-run – in practice lasted a short time (as the monetarists thought) or a long time (as the Keynesians thought) and (ii) whether aggregate-demand policy could reliably and effectively offset these deviations.

Monetarism influenced – and continues to influence – central banks around the world. Especially important are the monetarist notions that monetary policy can effectively target only nominal quantities and, therefore, ought to target inflation, and that central banks should be independent of political control and follow transparent rules. Beyond this, a strict monetarism was attempted in the US only for a brief time between 1979 and 1982, as a response to high and accelerating inflation. The experiment collapsed as a result of the instability of the link between the target variable (the monetary base) and the money stock (M1) and the instability of the demand for money in the face of financial innovation (Judd and Scadding, 1982). While advocating some monetarist principles, the Federal Reserve resumed interest-rate targeting in 1982.

During Margaret Thatcher's premiership, monetarism became highly influential (and hotly contested) in the United Kingdom. In a paper that was circulated in British policy circles long before its publication, David Hendry and Neil Ericsson

(1991) launched a stinging attack on the empirical adequacy of Friedman and Schwartz's *Monetary Trends* (1982). This volume – a sequel to their earlier *Monetary History* that extended its reach to the UK – had given substantial support to British monetarists. Friedman and Schwartz's (1991) reply was equally biting – its tone recalling the American debates of the 1960s. As well as proving hard to implement, monetarism came to symbolize Thatcher's conservative economic policy – monetary and nonmonetary – generally.

26.4   THE BATTLE OF THE SCHOOLS, 1970–1990

26.4.1   The New Classical challenge

While monetarism challenged the Keynesian mainstream mainly over empirical judgments and policy prescriptions, the New Classical macroeconomics attacked its theoretical foundations. Its leading light, Robert Lucas, sought to combine the Chicago tradition in monetary policy with the developing program in general equilibrium microfoundations. Lucas and Leonard Rapping's intertemporal, market-clearing model of the labor market sought to show that fluctuations in employment could be analyzed without invoking rationing notions such as involuntary unemployment. Lucas, therefore, felt justified in rejecting the fixed-price approach and tying macroeconomics solidly to the dominant Walrasian general equilibrium model.

Lucas's program was clearly laid out in a paper presented to a Federal Reserve conference in 1970. Surprisingly, his first target was not the Keynesians, but his teacher – Milton Friedman. Lucas argued that if expectations were formed adaptively, as Friedman typically supposed, then during the infinite time it takes expectations to converge to the true values, there would continue to be real, though diminishing, effects on employment and output. A Phillips curve that is vertical only in the infinitely long run is not really vertical for policy purposes.

Lucas replaced adaptive expectations with John Muth's *rational-expectations hypothesis*. The rational-expectations hypothesis can be formulated in various ways. Lucas preferred to see it as "model-consistent expectations": what people are modeled to expect is what the model itself predicts. People with rational expectations would still make mistakes, but their mistakes would be unsystematic, uncorrelated, and therefore unpredictable. Adding the rational-expectations hypothesis to a simple monetarist macromodel eliminated persistent deviations from the natural rate, effectively collapsing the long run into the short run. In Lucas's account, only unanticipated money-supply shocks could have real effects.

Lucas and, later, Thomas Sargent and Neil Wallace, demonstrated in aggregate macroeconomic models with clearing factor markets and rational expectations that monetary policy was incapable of guiding the real economy. Policies controlling any nominal quantity could have real effects, but they could not have *systematic* real effects and were, therefore, useless to the policy-maker. Lucas took the argument further, constructing a model in which prices are the only conveyers of information and unsystematic monetary policy shocks can generate an apparent Phillips curve tradeoff between output and inflation.

Lucas demonstrated that rational expectations add force to a general result of the microfoundations program: as the underlying decision problems of individual agents changed, the estimated aggregate relationships captured in macroeconometric models would also change. Agents with rational expectations would incorporate changes in systematic monetary policy into their decision problems, so that the aggregate relationships would shift with each shift in policy. This argument, known as the "Lucas critique," was held by some to explain observed instabilities in macroeconometric models and was widely regarded as proof that microfoundations, in which the analysis was grounded in the fundamental parameters governing tastes and technology, were essential to a successful empirical macroeconomics. In practice, however, most New Classical models employ some variant on the representative agent and eschew serious microfoundations.

The business cycle, with its persistent (serially correlated) fluctuations in real output and employment, was a challenge for the New Classical macroeconomics. In 1975 Lucas showed that persistent fluctuations would be generated through the optimal readjustment of the capital stock to output deviations initiated by monetary shocks. By the early 1980s, the balance of empirical evidence failed to confirm that monetary surprises account for most real fluctuations. Following the lead of Finn Kydland and Edward Prescott, the New Classical school largely abandoned the monetary-surprise model of business cycles in favor of the real business cycle model, in which shocks to technology (total factor productivity) or other real factors are propagated through optimal capital adjustment and the intertemporal substitution of labor supply. (See Hoover (1988) for a survey of the New Classical macroeconomics and Hartley, Hoover, and Salyer (1998) on the real business cycle program.)

26.4.2   The VAR program

While the Lucas critique questioned the microfoundational basis of large-scale macroeconometric models, they were besieged on another front as well. The dominant econometric tradition relied on structural econometric models in which economic theory was used to identify (or render causally interpretable) the estimated relationships. Another tradition had long existed side-by-side structural models: time-series econometrics appealed less to *a priori* theory. Crude time-series methods had been used in support of monetarism in the 1960s. In 1972 Christopher Sims initiated a large literature when he applied Granger-causality tests to US data to demonstrate the temporal priority of money over output – a result widely interpreted to support monetarism.

Sims's manifesto of 1980, "Macroeconomics and reality," attacked structural macroeconometric models for relying on "incredible" identifying assumptions. He proposed instead to rely on unrestricted, dynamic, reduced-form specifications known as "vector autoregressions" (VARs). These were used to forecast the effects of shocks to various macroeconomic variables *ceteris paribus* (impulse responses) or to attribute the variance of a variable of interest to its own variance and that of other variables in the VAR (variance decomposition).

Thomas Cooley, Stephen LeRoy, and Edward Leamer, among others, pointed out that Sims employed implicit identification in adopting particular causal orderings among the contemporaneous variables in order to compute impulse responses and variance decompositions. These stood in as much need of justification as any identifying restrictions. Sims conceded the point. Since the mid-1980s "structural VARs" – that is, VARs with an explicit contemporaneous causal order – have become a mainstay of macroeconomic research. How to achieve credible identification of the contemporaneous structure remains a fraught question (the VAR program is surveyed by Hoover, 1988).

26.4.3 The Keynesian reaction

The early New Classical economics of Lucas, Sargent, and Wallace threatened the Keynesian conception of the economic problem as one of sub-optimal output and employment that could be mitigated by aggregate-demand management. The striking innovation of the rational-expectations hypothesis was, however, too attractive to dismiss: people may not form expectations precisely rationally, but could a serious economic analysis rely on easily corrected misperceptions of policy as its *modus operandi*? Keynesians first reacted by attacking the assumption that markets clear continuously. Stanley Fischer and Phelps and John Taylor presented models in which wages and prices could not adjust rapidly to clear markets because of preexisting contracts. This gave aggregate-demand policies real short-run effects, although money was neutral – and the Phillips curve was vertical – in the long run (Hoover, 1988).

The New Classicals asked why agents would enter into such sub-optimal contracts. While one response was to say – whether obviously optimal or not – such contracts do exist, by the early 1980s the "new Keynesians" felt an obligation to supply microeconomic rationales for various sticky prices. George Akerlof and Janet Yellen argued that small deviations from optimal prices would have only second-order effects on profits, although first-order effects on output and employment. Gregory Mankiw and others demonstrated that small costs of price adjustment ("menu costs") could turn Akerlof and Yellen's "near rationality" models into fully rational models in which prices were nonetheless sticky.

Solow, Akerlof, Joseph Stiglitz, and Carl Shapiro, among others, explored "efficiency-wage" models in which worker efficiency depends on the wage rate, giving employers an incentive to hire fewer workers but to pay them a higher-than-market-clearing wage. These models explain involuntary unemployment and sticky real wages but not sticky nominal wages, which is what is needed to explain effective aggregate-demand policies. Laurence Ball and David Romer showed that combining the real-wage stickiness with menu costs can produce larger – and more realistic – responses of output to aggregate-demand policy (on efficiency-wage models, see Akerlof and Yellen, 1986).

Stiglitz and Andrew Weiss initiated research into credit-rationing as an optimal market outcome. The central idea was that borrowers and lenders have differential information about the borrowers' risks of default. Lenders might prefer to charge lower interest rates but to ration available funds. Higher market-clearing rates could cause the most credit-worthy borrowers to withdraw, skewing the pool of remaining borrowers toward higher average risk. Monetary policy, on this view, operates not only through the opportunity cost of investment, but through a "credit channel" in which an increase in central bank reserves permits banks to relax their lending constraints and to finance the investment projects of firms with otherwise limited access to credit markets.

Although the new Keynesian program of finding microfoundations that explain various aspects of aggregate sub-optimality as consistent with individual optimization remains active, the new Keynesians have never offered a systematic vision or a comprehensive model of the economy analogous to that of the New Classicals or of Keynes himself. (For references on new Keynesian macroeconomics, see Mankiw and Romer, 1991.)

26.5   Macroeconomics at the Turn of the Millennium

It is probably too soon to attempt the history of macroeconomics in the past decade. Nevertheless, there appears to be a surprising *détente* in the battle of the schools. The New Classical insistence on microfoundations has been adopted by almost all mainstream macroeconomists. And most have accepted microfoundations in the form of the representative–agent model or some near variant, despite the fact that a plausible case has never been offered for how any such agent could legitimately represent millions of economic decision-makers (see Kirman, 1992; Hartley, 1997). New Classicals have generally been forced to concede that without sticky prices or wages their models cannot reproduce the empirical fluctuations observed in the economy, although how to explain this stickiness remains an open question.

Empirical methods also now transcend the schools. Structural VARs are widely employed by New Classicals, Keynesians, and even heterodox macroeconomists. "Calibration" methods, which eschew econometric estimation in favor of informal comparisons of summary statistics from numerical simulations to the analogous statistics for actual data, were first adopted by the real business cycle sect of the New Classical school. Although it remains controversial, calibration is no longer restricted to real business cycle modelers (for a discussion of calibration methods, see Hartley, Hoover, and Salyer, 1998).

Empirical methods are now divided more on geographic than ideological lines. European time-series methods are typically more structural than structural VARs, but derive much of that structure from attention to statistical properties rather than from highly refined theoretical considerations (for surveys of macroeconometric methods, see Hoover, 1995).

On macroeconomic policy, there is now general agreement that monetary policy can have important, systematic real effects in the short run. But there remains active disagreement over whether the economy is sufficiently self-adjusting in the short run that active management should be eschewed.

Finally, perhaps because the 1990s were less turbulent and more prosperous than the 1970s and 1980s, macroeconomists have turned their attention once more to the macroeconomics of growth and, especially, the role of technical change and social and political institutions in the growth process (for a survey, see Barro, 1997). So far, no clear scholastic divisions have appeared in the economics of growth similar to those that plagued the macroeconomics of the short run from the monetarist insurgency through the heyday of the new Keynesians.

Bibliography

Akerlof, G. A. and Yellen, J. L. (eds.) 1986: *Efficiency Wage Models of the Labor Market.* Cambridge, UK: Cambridge University Press.

Barro, R. J. 1997: *Determinants of Economic Growth: A Cross-Country Empirical Study.* Cambridge, MA: The MIT Press.

—— and Grossman, H. I. 1971: A general disequilibrium model of income and employment. *American Economic Review*, 61(1), 82–93.

Bliss, C. J. 1975: *Capital Theory and the Distribution of Income.* Amsterdam: North-Holland.

Bodkin, R. G., Klein, L. R., and Marwah, K. 1991: *A History of Macroeconometric Model Building.* Aldershot, UK: Edward Elgar.

Clower, R. W. 1965: The Keynesian counter-revolution: a theoretical appraisal. In F. H. Hahn and F. Brechling (eds.), *The Theory of Interest Rates.* London: Macmillan.

Coddington, A. 1983: *Keynesian Economics: The Search for First Principles.* London: George Allen & Unwin.

Duesenberry, J. S. 1949: *Income, Saving, and the Theory of Consumer Behavior.* Cambridge, MA: Harvard University Press.

Friedman, M. (ed.) 1956: *Studies in the Quantity Theory of Money.* Chicago: The University of Chicago Press.

—— 1957: *A Theory of the Consumption Function.* Princeton, NJ: Princeton University Press.

—— and Schwartz, A. J. 1963: *A Monetary History of the United States, 1867–1960.* Princeton, NJ: Princeton University Press.

—— and —— 1982: *Monetary Trends in the United States and the United Kingdom, Their Relation to Income, Prices, and Interest Rates, 1867–1975.* Chicago: The University of Chicago Press.

—— and —— 1991: Alternative approaches to analyzing economic data. *American Economic Review*, 81(1), 39–49.

Gurley, J. and Shaw, E. 1960: *Money in a Theory of Finance.* Washington, DC: Brookings Institution.

Hahn, F. H. and Matthews, R. 1964: The theory of economic growth: a survey. *Economic Journal*, 74(296), 779–902.

Harcourt, G. C. 1972: *Some Cambridge Controversies in the Theory of Capital.* Cambridge, UK: Cambridge University Press.

Hartley, J. E. 1997: *The Representative Agent in Macroeconomics.* London: Routledge.

——, Hoover, K. D., and Salyer, K. D. 1998: The limits to business cycle research. In J. E. Hartley, K. D. Hoover, and K. D. Salyer (eds.), *Real Business Cycles: A Reader.* London: Routledge, ch. 1.

Hendry, D. F. and Ericsson, N. R. 1991: An econometric analysis of U.K. money demand in monetary trends in the United States and the United Kingdom by Milton Friedman and Anna J. Schwartz. *American Economic Review*, 81(1), 8–38.

—— and Morgan, M. S. 1995: *The Foundations of Econometric Analysis*. New York: Cambridge University Press.

Hicks, J. R. 1937: Mr. Keynes and the classics. In *Critical Essays in Monetary Theory*. Oxford: The Clarendon Press, 1967.

Hoover, K. D. 1988: *The New Classical Macroeconomics: A Sceptical Inquiry*. Oxford: Blackwell.

—— (ed.) 1995: *Macroeconometrics: Developments, Tensions, and Prospects*. Boston: Kluwer.

Jones, C. I. 1998: *Introduction to Economic Growth*. New York: Norton.

Judd, J. P. and Scadding, J. L. 1982: The search for a stable money demand function: a survey of the post-1973 literature. *Journal of Economic Literature*, 20(3), 993–1024.

Keynes, J. M. 1936: *The General Theory of Employment Interest and Money*. London: Macmillan.

Kirman, A. P. 1992: Whom or what does the representative individual represent? *Journal of Economic Perspectives*, 6(2), 117–36.

Klein, L. R. 1947: *The Keynesian Revolution*. New York: Macmillan.

Laidler, D. E. W. 1993: *The Demand for Money: Theories, Evidence, and Problems*, 4th edn. New York: HarperCollins.

—— 1999: *Fabricating the Keynesian Revolution: Studies of the Inter-War Literature on Money, the Cycle, and Unemployment*. Cambridge, UK: Cambridge University Press.

Leijonhufvud, A. 1968: *On Keynesian Economics and the Economics of Keynes: A Study in Monetary Theory*. New York: Oxford University Press.

Lerner, A. 1943: Functional finance and the Federal debt. *Social Research*, 10(1), 38–51.

Malinvaud, E. 1977: *The Theory of Unemployment Reconsidered*. New York: John Wiley.

Mankiw, N. G. and Romer, D. (eds.) 1991: *New Keynesian Economics*. Cambridge, MA: The MIT Press.

Mayer, T. et al. 1978: *The Structure of Monetarism*. New York: Norton.

Modigliani, F. 1944: Liquidity preference and the theory of interest of money. *Econometrica*, 12(1), 44–88.

—— and Brumberg, R. 1954: Utility analysis and the consumption function: an interpretation of cross-section data. In K. Kurihara (ed.), *Post-Keynesian Economics*. New Brunswick, NJ: Rutgers University Press.

Morgan, M. S. 1990: *The History of Econometric Ideas*. Cambridge, UK: Cambridge University Press.

Patinkin, D. 1956: *Money, Interest, and Prices*. New York: Harper and Row.

Phillips, A. W. 1958: The relation between unemployment and the rate of change of money wages in the United Kingdom 1961–1957. *Economica*, NS, 25(100), 283–99.

Radcliffe Report 1959: *Report of the Committee on the Working of the Monetary System*. Cmnd. 827. London: Her Majesty's Stationary Office.

Temin, P. 1976: *Did Monetary Forces Cause the Great Depression?* New York: Norton.

Tinbergen, J. 1939: *Statistical Testing of Business-Cycle Theories*, vol. II: *Business Cycles in the United States of America, 1919–1932*. Geneva: League of Nations.

Tobin, J. 1969: A general equilibrium approach to monetary theory. *Journal of Money, Credit, and Banking*, 1(1), 15–29.

Wan, H. Y. 1971: *Economic Growth*. New York: Harcourt Brace Jovanovich.

Wulwick, N. J. 1987: The Phillips curve: Which? Whose? To do what? How? *Southern Economic Journal*, 53(4), 834–57.

CHAPTER TWENTY-SEVEN

The Economic Role of Government in the History of Economic Thought

Steven G. Medema

27.1 INTRODUCTION

The question as to the appropriate role for government within the economic system is as old as economic thought. For much of that history, the economy was seen as but one piece of a larger social system and the study of economics, or political economy, as one facet of a larger social theory. Only with the advent of commercial society and the organization of economic activity more overtly within the context of the market did the perception of the economy as a quasi-independent part of the social system begin to gain currency. This has a number of implications, but for present purposes one stands out: the earlier economic literature envisioned a system wherein government and economy are integrally linked aspects of the social system, whereas in later literature government and economy – or government and market – are often viewed as independent spheres of action, with corresponding questions as to how much one should "intrude" upon the other.

The perspectives that motivate or underlie the discussion of the appropriate economic role for government are many and diverse; the resulting analysis thus reflects diverse and often contradictory accounts of the appropriate economic tasks for government. This vast topic requires the selective adoption of an organizing principle, and that adopted here is "the economic role of government as a response to the forces of self-interest." While this necessarily excludes a variety of contributions and perspectives, it provides the vehicle for a useful analysis of how the economic role of government has been viewed throughout the history of economic thought and analysis, and the forces that have motivated these views.

27.2 PRE-CLASSICAL ECONOMICS

One defining characteristic of much pre-classical economic thought is its natural-istic, or natural law, orientation – an orientation reflected in the roles ascribed to government by these scholars. This *a priori* approach to the subject made the role of government something given rather than something to be worked out. We find here no deep theory of governmental behavior and no serious analysis of the ability of government to carry out the tasks ascribed to it by these authors. There is, rather, an assumed natural order of things and consequent statements of how government should act so as to facilitate the operation of a social–economic system that comports with the dictates of natural law.

27.2.1 The Greeks and Scholastics

The Greek contribution to economic thought arises primarily through the works of Plato (e.g., in *Republic* and *Laws*) and Aristotle (e.g., in *Politics* and *Ethics*). Their analysis centered around the *polis*, or city–state, and what, ideally, would constitute "the good life." An important aspect was justice, including the role to be played by the governing authority. The economic upheaval against which Plato and Aristotle discussed economic issues was seen to be a consequence of the surge in economic growth following the liberalization of commercial activity, including the expansion of international trading activity. Given what they saw as the undesirable effects of economic growth, their analysis centered on the estab-lishment of a relatively stationary state of economic activity accompanied by a reasonable standard of economic well-being.

For Plato and Aristotle, the most straightforward means of attaining their objectives for the ideal state was through relatively strict limits on commercial activity in which the state was to play a central role. A system of laws should be so structured as to facilitate a stationary state with a reasonable level of economic well-being for all citizens. Aristotle saw the market as a "creature of the state" (Lowry, 1987, p. 237); with this came prescriptions for the regulation of commer-cial dealings. For example, both Plato and Aristotle recognized that a satisfactory level of material well-being required the harnessing of the division of labor. This should be conducted such that natural roles were enforced (Plato) or at least given effect by government (condoning slavery, by Aristotle). Both Plato and Aristotle objected to the internationalization of the division of labor, which they believed introduced base influences into society; various government actions – such as separate domestic and international trading currencies – were recom-mended to mitigate incentives to seek private gain through foreign trade. Commercial activity in general was frowned upon, and at best was seen as a necessary evil to equalize needs and possessions. Policies – including prohibitions against lending at interest, the elimination of profits, and statutory fixation of prices – were recommended to control commercial activity.

Certain significant parallels existed between the respective analyses of the Greeks and the Scholastics, derivative of St. Thomas Aquinas's attempt to reconcile Church teachings with the work of Aristotle. Their analysis of the relationship between man and his creator, an aspect of which is the relation between individuals in a social context, led the Scholastics to consider commodity exchanges and monetary issues from a Christian moral perspective. The "economic problem," in a sense, was man's sinful nature, the effect of which, if left unchecked, was to promulgate outcomes contrary to the dictates of Christian justice if unchecked by religious and civil laws.

While viewing common property as the ideal (evidenced in communal monastic institutions), the Scholastics believed that private property was optimal for society as a whole, owing to the negative incentive effects that common property provides for sinful, worldly people – a religious variant of Aristotle's position. Unlike Plato and Aristotle, the Scholastics were more favorably disposed to commercial activity, generally believing that market outcomes would satisfy the dictates of justice in the absence of monopoly or fraud. Following Aquinas, the early Scholastics supported prohibitions on lending at interest, although this view slowly eroded as later scholars came to understand the opportunity cost of lending. Concern over the harmful effects on purchasing power that could come with macroeconomic fluctuations led many Scholastics to support some degree of price control – the regulation of prices within certain upper and lower limits – in order to mitigate fluctuations in the value of money.

For both Greek and Scholastic writers, relatively extensive government activity was a necessity to create a harmonious social–economic order. Instead of an over-arching theory of the state, there was a set of supposedly naturally ordained ends that government could (and should) assist society in attaining. In particular, the operation of self-interest was seen as promoting outcomes inconsistent with those prescribed by nature or by God; government action was necessary to prevent, or at least minimize, the more base impacts of self-interested behavior.

27.2.2 Mercantilism

Mercantilist political economy differed from its predecessors in the relative lack of emphasis given to questions of value and distribution, but the mercantilist goal of nation–state building, combined with their notion that national political–economic strength entailed running a trade surplus payable in bullion, engendered a view of government policy involving extensive regulation of economic affairs. Continuity with Greek and Scholastic thought is found in the view that individual self-interest, if given free reign, would run against the national interest, although moral qualms were replaced by the mercantilists' more worldly concerns. Self-interest was bound to engender excessive consumption of both domestic and foreign goods, thereby diminishing the quantity and raising the price of goods for export (reducing their competitiveness on world markets) and increasing imports – thus harming the trade balance and the nation's stock of precious metals.

Mercantilism melded political and economic policy under the nationalistic banner. That political and economic objectives were mutually reinforcing can be seen by noting that bullion accumulation was accompanied by the development of military (including naval) power, which protected both nation and trade shipments; the acquisition of colonies, which brought empire, sources of raw materials for manufacturing, and markets for exports; and the slave trade, which supplied low-cost labor. For the mercantilists the test of policy proposals was the effect on the nation's stock of precious metals. As Lars Magnusson (1993, pp. 6–8) has pointed out, mercantilism departed from previous thinking by viewing the economic system as "an independent territory with its own distinctive laws." Here, economic welfare "more than anything else depended upon the statesman's ability to rule according to the laws dictated by an independent economic realm;" such was necessary because of the inability of self-interested private action, as translated through the market mechanism, to maximize national wealth defined as stocks of precious metals.

This was to be accomplished through a scheme of economic policy of which import restriction and export promotion were only the most obvious components. Other policies included the regulation of precious metal exchanges, including prohibitions on bullion exports, exchange control, protecting the quality of coinage, and related regulations restricting the hoarding of bullion and its conversion into plate, jewelry, and so on in order to ensure sufficient circulating currency to fuel the nation's economic activity. Strategic policies favoring certain important national industries and protecting infant industries were popular, as were labor-related policies – including loose immigration and tight emigration rules, and subsidies to encourage workers to relocate to manufacturing centers – which served to keep labor supply up and wages low, thus facilitating the price-competitiveness of exports.

27.2.3 Physiocracy

The backlash against mercantilist thinking was first significantly found among the eighteenth-century French physiocratic thinkers who reacted against Colbert's policies promoting manufacturing at the expense of agriculture. These policies, combined with wars and high tax burdens, impoverished the agricultural peasant proprietors and retarded productivity advances in the agricultural sector.

The physiocrats saw the world as comprising a set of self-evident truths arising from natural law. These natural laws extended to the economic system, and physiocrats considered agricultural production the cornerstone of economic activity, arguing that it alone generated a net product – a surplus of output over input; manufacturing was sterile. The net product was the sole source of funds for investments in increased productivity. François Quesnay and the other physiocrats saw the maximization of this surplus as providing the means of advancing agricultural technology to match the production of other nations. Unchecked, consumers would make excessive expenditures on manufactured goods (*luxe de decoration*); this, combined with the mercantile system in place, worked to impede the growth of the net product.

All policy proposals were to be judged by their effect on net product. The physiocrats therefore were steadfastly against policies restricting agricultural production in favor of manufacturing – such as prohibitions on agricultural exports that kept food prices, and thereby manufacturing wages, low. Against mercantilist policy, Quesnay argued that the sole function of the state is the provision of security – national defense and the appropriate system of laws (those harmonizing with natural law). The physiocrats' opposition to government interference with commerce is evident from Quesnay's essay "Corn," where he argues that "all trade ought to be free . . . It is enough for the government to watch over the expansion of the revenue of the kingdom's property; not to put any obstacles in the way of industry; and to give the people the opportunity to spend as they choose . . ." (in Meek, 1962, p. 79; see also p. 237). This freedom entailed freedom in the production and circulation of goods, the reduction or elimination of transport tolls, improving transportation infrastructure, and eliminating the tax system oppressing agriculture in favor of a single tax on the net product.

But physiocratic support for *laissez-faire* was, in actuality, selective (Samuels, 1962; Steiner, 2002). In addition to the loosening of restrictions on agricultural production, they advocated agricultural price supports, legal limits on interest rates to minimize the cost of borrowing for agricultural proprietors, and restrictions on the export of manufactured products – because export promotion led to political pressures to hold down food prices in order to keep manufacturing wages/costs low. As Samuels (1962, p. 149) has pointed out, far from proposing a minimalist and inactive state, the physiocrats looked to achieve their aims "through the agency of the political state," the substitution for mercantilist policies of policies that favored the agricultural sector and the interests it represented – as evidenced in Quesnay's statement in "Maxims" that "the government's economic policy should be concerned only with encouraging productive [i.e., agricultural] expenditures and trade in raw produce . . ." (in Meek, 1962, p. 233). Quesnay's *Tableau* was deployed to "demonstrate" both the error of Colbert's policies and the benefits of physiocratic policy proposals.

27.3 CLASSICAL ECONOMICS

27.3.1 Adam Smith and the system of natural liberty

The physiocratic revolt against mercantilism was extended by Adam Smith in the *Wealth of Nations*. For Smith, the wealth of a nation consisted in the value of its produce rather than in the national stock of precious metals or the net product of agriculture, and government's role was to facilitate the growth of national wealth, so defined. In this sense, Smith demonstrated an important commonality with the mercantilist and physiocratic writers, but the accomplishment of the goal of maximizing the value of output required a very different role for government than that posited by earlier writers.

Smith's critiques of mercantilism and physiocracy were parallel; he saw their respective favoritisms as promoting flows of resources to the favored sectors in amounts greater than would otherwise obtain. The question is whether this is good for or harmful to the interests of society. Smith is unequivocal: "Every individual is constantly exerting himself to find out the most advantageous employment for whatever capital he can command. It is his own advantage, indeed, and not that of society, which he has in view. But the study of his own advantage naturally, or rather necessarily leads him to prefer that employment which is most advantageous to society" (Smith, 1776, p. 421). Self-interest is not something to be suppressed, as with the Greeks and Scholastics, nor even to be shunted down a particular road, as with the incentives offered by the mercantilists and physiocrats. Rather, the free play of self-interest is said to redound to the benefit of society as a whole. In Smith's view, the individual is "led by an invisible hand to promote an end which was no part of his intention" (p. 423). Given this propensity on the part of the individual and the associated positive (if unintended) consequences:

> The statesman, who should attempt to direct private people in what manner they ought to employ their capitals, would not only load himself with a most unnecessary attention, but assume an authority which could safely be trusted, not only to no single person, but to no council or senate whatever, and which would nowhere be so dangerous as in the hands of a man who had folly and presumption enough to fancy himself fit to exercise it. (p. 423)

But it is not simply a matter of government officials being, in Smith's view, incapable; for Smith, the market system does not require such overt direction. Attempts by government to channel self-interest in some direction inhibit rather than promote the growth of wealth (pp. 650–1) and, in doing so, enrich special interests at the expense of society as a whole. Smith states the basic framework of his view of the economic role of government as follows:

> All systems either of preference or restraint, therefore, being thus completely taken away, the obvious and simple system of natural liberty establishes itself of its own accord. Every man, as long as he does not violate the laws of justice, is left perfectly free to pursue his own interest his own way, and to bring both his industry and his capital into competition with those of any other man, or order of men. The sovereign is completely discharged from a duty, in the attempting to perform which he must always be exposed to innumerable delusions, and for the proper performance of which no human wisdom or knowledge could ever be sufficient; the duty of superintending the industry of private people, and of directing it towards the employments most suitable to the interest of society. (p. 651)

What, then, is the appropriate role for government within such a system? "According to the system of natural liberty, the sovereign has only three duties to attend to," the provision of national defense, the provision of civil justice, and "the duty of erecting and maintaining certain public works and certain public institutions" which could not be profitably provided by the private sector but which provide a net benefit to society (p. 651). These last include the standard roads, bridges, canals, and harbors – which serve to facilitate commerce – but also education, to counteract what he saw as the mind-numbing effects of the division of labor, temporary monopolies given to joint-stock companies to facilitate new trade avenues, and religious instruction for clergy. Smith also allows for exceptions to free trade to encourage and protect industries essential to national defense, to level the playing field for domestic products subject to tax at home, and retaliatory tariffs inducing other countries to lower their trade barriers.

Smith was not a doctrinaire advocate of *laissez-faire*. He was, on the one hand, in favor of doing away with the trade restrictions of the mercantilists, apprenticeship and settlement laws (which inhibited the free flow of labor), legal monopoly, and the laws of succession that impeded free trade in land. But, in addition to the basic governmental functions noted above, he supported regulation of public hygiene, legal ceilings on interest rates (to prevent excessive flows of financial capital into high-risk ventures), light duties on imports of manufactured goods, the mandating of quality certifications on linen and plate, certain banking and currency regulations to promote a stable monetary system, and the discouragement of the spread of drinking establishments through taxes on liquor (one of various regulations Smith advocated to compensate for individuals' imperfect knowledge – or diminished telescopic faculty). (For an excellent elaboration of Smith's rather broad-based conception of the appropriate functions for the state, see Skinner, 1996.)

Smith was inherently suspicious of government's ability to properly manage economic affairs, but he also recognized that there were various policies that could improve national welfare. Equally important, however, was Smith's recognition that the market does not operate without government; indeed, Smith calls political economy "a branch of the science of a statesman or legislator" (p. 397), making it, in part at least, a branch of jurisprudence. Smith found in the system of natural liberty a regulating mechanism not discerned by previous commentators – a coordinating force keeping self-interest from becoming totally destructive. But he also understood that governmental action supplies the legal–institutional process through and within which markets function. It was not government that Smith was opposed to; rather, he was after the appropriate set of policies to facilitate the growth of wealth.

27.3.2   The nineteenth-century classical economists and the program of economic reform

Many writers caricature both Smith and the nineteenth-century classical economists as rigorous adherents of *laissez-faire*. In both instances, the caricature is misleading. The classicals were strongly reformist, critical of numerous institutions of their time, and highly optimistic that the insights of political economy could be used to create socially beneficial economic policy.

The classicals, like Smith, were cognizant of the virtues of the market as an allocation mechanism, but they also understood that the market could only operate satisfactorily – harmonizing actions of self-interested agents with the interests of society as a whole – within a framework of legal, political, and moral restrictions. Seeming hostility to government is manifest throughout classical economics (a legacy of Smith's harsh critique of mercantilism), but a careful reading of the classical writings will reveal that the classicals had a relatively pragmatic view of the economic role of government (Robbins, 1952; Samuels, 1966; O'Brien, 1975). Witness J. R. McCulloch, who argued that "The principle of *laisser-faire* may be safely trusted to do in some things but in many more it is wholly inapplicable; and to appeal to it on all occasions savours more of the policy of a parrot than of a statesman or a philosopher" (McCulloch, 1848, p. 156; quoted in Robbins, 1952, p. 43). Likewise, Nassau Senior argued, "the only rational foundation of government, the only foundation of a right to govern and a correlative duty to obey is, expediency – the general benefit of the community" (Senior, 1928, vol. ii, p. 302; quoted in Robbins, 1952, p. 45). The classicals were concerned with determining the set of policies promoting society's best interests and were vociferously opposed to policies that they believed served the interests of particular groups at the expense of the larger population. Their consumption-oriented view led them to the belief that freedom of choice was desirable for consumers, and that freedom for producers was the most effective means of satisfying consumer desires. The impersonal forces of the market, working through the system of natural liberty, would then serve to harmonize these interests – at least to a greater and more beneficial extent than other systems.

The classical justification for private property (with its encouragement of industry) and security of contract (with its associated encouragement of exchange) is found in this general utility, rather than from some preconceived notion of natural rights or natural law. Robbins (1952, p. 56) even suggests that Smith's "invisible hand" is actually government itself: it "is not the hand of some god or some natural agency independent of human effort; it is the hand of the law-giver, the hand which withdraws from the sphere of the pursuit of self-interest those possibilities which do not harmonize with the public good." For the classicals, therefore, the state was neither a simple night watchman nor a broad planner. The most basic function of government was the establishment and enforcement of a system of law that would control, channel, and restrain individual action so that individual pursuit of self-interest would create the greatest happiness.

The accomplishment of this greatest happiness required far more than the establishment of a system of laws to facilitate the market, combined with the Smithian notion of defense, justice, and the provision of certain public works. Indeed, the scope for government action expanded as the classicals' period unfolded. The classicals *were* consistently opposed to monopoly, price (including interest rate) regulation, and taxation and regulation of the production process (especially foodstuffs). But numerous additional functions – varying across writers – were ascribed to government as necessary to the public interest, including public health regulations, public provision of medical care, building regulations (to combat the emerging industrial slums), industrial safety and health regulations and employer liability for injuries caused by the failure to meet standards, regulation of prices charged by public utilities, and factory legislation restricting the

work of children. The classicals generally supported the right of workers to form
trades unions, except to the extent that membership was mandatory and unions
had a monopolizing effect on the labor market (consistent with their general
opposition to monopoly). Malthus and Ricardo favored the abolition of the Poor
Laws, doing so largely because they believed the Poor Laws to be ineffective –
reducing industry and increasing the population. Later classicals advocated more
moderate Poor Law reforms, making the position of relief recipients inferior to
laborers in order to encourage work and reduce population pressure.

J. S. Mill's contribution in his *Principles* (originally published in 1848) is
emblematic of both the continuity within the classical tradition reaching back to
Smith and a transition toward the increasing recognition of market failures that
characterizes neoclassical economics. Mill's (1909 [1871], p. 800), criterion for the
boundaries of the appropriate functions of government was neither strict nor
a priori; it was "expediency." Mill's "necessary" functions of government, where
the case for expediency is obvious, are extremely broad; even things seemingly as
simple as the enforcement of property and contract cannot, according to Mill, be
as circumscribed as many would think. In the case of property:

> It may be imagined, perhaps, that the law has only to declare and protect the right
> of every one to what he himself has produced, or acquired by the voluntary consent,
> fairly obtained, of those who produced it. But is there nothing recognized as prop-
> erty except what has been produced? Is there not the earth itself, its forests and
> waters, and all other riches, above and below the surface? These are the inheritance
> of the human race, and there must be regulations for the common enjoyment of it.
> What rights, and under what conditions, a person shall be allowed to exercise over
> any portion of this common inheritance cannot be left undecided. No function of
> government is less optional than the regulation of these things, or more completely
> involved in the idea of civilized society. (p. 797)

Likewise, with contracts, "governments do not limit their concern . . . to a
simple enforcement [of the product of voluntary consent]. They take upon
themselves to determine what contracts are fit to be enforced" (p. 798).

In discussing the limits of *laissez-faire*, Mill criticized ideologues on both poles,
contending that the issue of the appropriate boundaries for government action
"does not . . . admit of any universal solution" (pp. 941–2). Mill found it important to distinguish between two forms of government action: the authoritative,
in which certain types of conduct are prescribed or proscribed, and the non-
authoritative, where government provides, for example, advice, information,
services, institutions, and so on, which are thereby available but do not impinge
upon freedom of choice and action. The former, he argues, "has a much more
limited sphere of legitimate action" and "requires a much stronger necessity to
justify it" (p. 942). Mill sees "a circle around every human being which no
government . . . ought to be permitted to overstep," and, for him, this circle should
include "all that part which concerns only the life . . . of the individual, and does
not affect the interests of others, or affects them only through the moral influence
of example" (p. 943). Mill is arguing for freedom of individual action where

externalities are not present; where externalities do exist, however, the situation is altered. People are not always the best judge, he says – for example, regarding education for either themselves or their children. He supports public provision of education (pp. 953–4), but he also maintains that government should not monopolize it. He adopts a similar view with regard to public charity, colonization, scientific exploration, and the maintenance of a learned class – functions that, as with public works, substantially further the interests of society but which, he argues, will not be provided in sufficient amounts through voluntary mechanisms.

In spite of his relatively extensive elaboration of legitimate governmental functions, Mill contends that government is poorly organized to carry out many of the tasks that people would wish it to undertake, and that, even if well organized, the related information issues and incentives are such as to make private efforts superior to governmental ones in carrying out many tasks (pp. 945–7). As such, a society should restrict "to the narrowest compass the intervention of a public authority in the business of the community," and the burden of proof should fall "on those who recommend, government interference" (p. 950). His prescription? "*Laisser-faire*, in short, should be the general practice: every departure from it, unless required by some great good, is a certain evil" (p. 950).

27.4 THE "INTERVENTIONIST" TURN: MARGINALISM AND THE DEVELOPMENT OF NEOCLASSICAL WELFARE ECONOMICS

The marginal revolution helped change how economists analyzed the economic role of government. Normative analysis faded from the scene; writings on public finance largely ceased to discuss the appropriate role of government and were confined to how to raise the revenues necessary for the operation of government (Baumol, 1952, p. 154). Discussion of the role of government shifted to the newly emerging welfare economics. More than positivist philosophy drove these developments. Externally, late-nineteenth- and twentieth-century economists saw the effects, both positive and negative, of widespread industrialization and increasing congestion. Internally, the *tools* of marginal analysis made possible the *demonstration* of the potential failings of the system of natural liberty and, therefore, the possibilities of governmental policy actions for promoting, rather than diminishing, social welfare.

27.4.1 Henry Sidgwick: dismantling the system of natural liberty

Mill's premonitions of externality-related market failure were further developed by Henry Sidgwick. Sidgwick (1901, p. 402) accepted that "the motive of self-interest does work powerfully and continually." Yet, he argued, the fact that the system works does not mean that it functions optimally in all times and places. "[E]ven in a society composed – solely or mainly – of 'economic men,'" he wrote, "the system of natural liberty would have, in certain conditions, no tendency to realize the beneficent results claimed for it" (pp. 402–3). Unlike Marx, who maintained that supposed governmental corrective policies would be ineffective at best and would in many instances even further destabilize the market system, Sidgwick stood with Mill, contending that governmental corrective actions could counter many of the negative effects of self-interested behavior.

In discussing the harmful nature of external effects, Sidgwick anticipated Ronald Coase's "The problem of social cost" (1960), writing that "In a perfectly ideal community of economic men all persons concerned would doubtless voluntarily agree to take the measures required to ward off such common dangers . . ." But in reality, he said, "the efforts and sacrifices of a great majority are liable to be rendered almost useless by the neglect of one or two individuals . . ." (1901, pp. 409–10). Sidgwick applied marginal analysis to the common pool fisheries problem to illustrate his point (p. 410), one example of the need for regulation of the use of natural resources when self-interested agents failed to take into account the full social impact of their activities (pp. 475–6). In Sidgwick's opinion, the general failure to properly account for the interests of future generations, even among parents, is a potentially serious source of market failure (pp. 412–13).

Freedom of action has other limitations as well. Sidgwick contends that people are at times unable to see their own bests interests or to take adequate care of themselves, thereby justifying certain paternalistic actions by government – hence the need for health regulations on foodstuffs, the licensing of physicians and other occupations, workplace safety regulations, and various limitations on freedom of contract (pp. 405–6, 425). He adopts a similar view with regard to monopoly – not just in the sense that monopoly reduces output and increases price, but also because the monopolist, by virtue of its privileged position, may not have any incentive to invest in the development of more economical production techniques. Sidgwick also suggests that there are many instances in which private enterprise will not provide goods and services owing to the inability to appropriate sufficient returns to justify the investment – for example, lighthouses, forests (with "their beneficial effects in moderating and equalizing rainfall"), worker training, inventions, and the "machinery of transfer" (things that facilitate transactions and exchange). This last instance provides a still more sophisticated case for governmental provision of traditional public works, including roads, canals and railways, telegraph and postal services, and light and water, as well as the provision of currency: government becomes the *facilitator* of commerce and the market rather than an impediment to it.

The widespread failure of public and social interests to coincide means that, in such cases, governmental interference needs to be regarded not merely as "a temporary resource, but not improbably [as] a normal element of the organization of industry" (p. 414). Sidgwick acknowledges that market failures do not inevitably imply the need for government corrective action because its drawbacks may be more severe than those of the market failure itself (p. 414). These "drawbacks and disadvantages" include government using its power for corrupt purposes; the desire to please special interest groups; "wasteful expenditures under the influence of popular sentiment;" supervisory problems, given the expanded range of government activities; the tax cost associated with these operations of government; and the lack of incentives for government workers to properly carry out their functions (pp. 414–15). But, Sidgwick argues, "moral and political progress [in society] may be expected to diminish" these disadvantages (p. 416), thereby eventually increasing the range of activities that government can carry out in a manner superior to market forces.

27.4.2 A. C. Pigou and Pigovian welfare theory

It was the triumph of A. C. Pigou to graft the analysis of the potential for market failure evidenced in Sidgwick to the emerging theoretical apparatus of marginal analysis (see O'Donnell, 1979). In his *Economics of Welfare* (1932), Pigou examined "how far the free play of self-interest, acting under the existing legal system, tends to distribute the country's resources in the way most favourable to the production of a large national dividend, and how far it is feasible for State action to improve upon 'natural' tendencies" (p. xii).

Of the various instances of divergence between private and social interests pointed to by Pigou, perhaps the most important, in terms of long-run impact on the literature, are situations in which "one person A, in the course of rendering some service, for which payment is made, to a second person B, incidentally also render services or disservices to other persons (not producers of like services), of such a sort that payment cannot be exacted from the benefited parties or compensation enforced on behalf of the injured parties" (p. 183). Pigou distinguishes between positive externalities, where "marginal private net product falls short of social net product, because incidental services are performed to third parties from whom it is technically difficult to exact payment" (pp. 183–4), and negative externalities, where, "owing to the technical difficulty of enforcing compensation for incidental disservices, marginal private net product is greater than marginal social net product" (p. 185). The former case includes lighthouses, parks, roads and tramways, afforestation, street lighting, pollution abatement, and scientific research; the latter category includes the effects of such things as congestion and destruction of amenity from new factories and from new buildings erected in crowded city centers, the damage to roads from automobiles, the production and sale of alcohol, and the effects on children from factory labor of women.

Pigou appreciated that divergences between private and social net products arising between contracting parties – for example, the principal–agent problems that result from tenancy situations – may be amenable to resolution by negotiation, but he denied negotiation as a viable possibility in situations of third-party effects. However, he says, the state can act "to remove the divergence in any field by 'extraordinary encouragements' or 'extraordinary restraints,'" such as taxes and subsidies (p. 192); in certain more complex cases, regulations – such as zoning ordinances – may be in order. Pigou is clearly of the mind that large-numbers externality problems are inevitable and that they invalidate the classicals' claims regarding the system of natural liberty: "No 'invisible hand' can be relied on to produce a good arrangement of the whole from a combination of separate treatments of the parts. It is, therefore, necessary that an authority of wider reach should intervene and should tackle the collective problems of beauty, of air and of light, as those other problems of gas and water have been tackled" (p. 195). In particular, "[i]n any industry, where there is reason to believe that the free play of self-interest will cause an amount of resources to be invested different from the amount that is required in the best interest of the national dividend, there is a *prima facie* case for public intervention" (p. 331). He goes on, however, to say that one must assess the government's qualifications for advantageous interference, noting that:

> It is not sufficient to contrast the imperfect adjustments of unfettered private enterprise with the best adjustment that economists in their studies can imagine. For we cannot expect that any public authority will attain, or will even wholeheartedly seek, that ideal. Such authorities are liable alike to ignorance, to sectional pressure and to personal corruption by private interest. A loud-voiced part of their constituents, if organised for votes, may easily outweigh the whole. (pp. 331–2)

One can hear echoes of the qualms of the classical economists. But, following Sidgwick, Pigou (pp. 333–5) suggests that these problems can often be satisfactorily avoided; his view is one of optimism rather than pessimism regarding the prospects for governmental improvement of the operation of the market.

The subsequent refinement of Pigou's analysis demonstrated with increasing analytic rigor the conditions necessary for market optimum, the factors and forces that would cause market outcomes to diverge from the optimum, and the means by which governmental action could correct these market failures. While Pigou had demonstrated the existence of market failure where private and social interests diverge, his attempts to demonstrate that positive or negative third-party effects *cause* market failure relied on logical argument, and his assertions that government could remove these divergences with appropriate policy measures were only assertions. But the groundwork had been laid, and it was not long before the burgeoning mathematical tools were employed by economists to establish the necessary conditions for optimality (Bergson, 1938; Lange, 1942; Debreu, 1954), demonstrating both that externalities did indeed cause departures from the social optimum and that taxes and subsidies (with rates set equal to the marginal cost or benefit of the external effect), and regulations, could lead the actions of private agents to harmonize with the social interest (see, e.g., Meade, 1952).

The quest for determinate, optimal solutions to questions of economic theory and policy is evidenced vividly in the Pigovian welfare analysis. The shortcomings of the system of natural liberty and the ability of government not only to improve upon the workings of the market but to generate optimal outcomes were "proven." The rhetorical, persuasive force of this analysis should not be underestimated. This theory demonstrated that perfect markets work perfectly, imperfect markets work imperfectly, and perfect government can cause imperfect markets to also function perfectly. This became the textbook model. Qualms regarding the ability of government to actually accomplish the correction of market failures, so evident in classical economics, had all but disappeared. The role of government *vis-à-vis* market was no longer an *a priori* set of assertions, nor an opinion based upon casual empiricism; it was demonstrable in the scientific sense.

27.5 FROM MARKET FAILURE TO GOVERNMENT FAILURE

Pigou's conceptualization remained orthodox through the latter part of the twentieth century, but the beginnings of a challenge emerged in the 1950s and 1960s. This challenge had multiple thrusts; a common thread was the failure of the received view to account for the potential imperfections associated with government policy – that neoclassical economics had a theory of market failure but no government failure.

The principal challenge was the theoretical one, exemplified most influentially in Ronald Coase's "The problem of social cost" (1960). Coase demonstrated that, under standard neoclassical assumptions, Pigovian corrective instruments were not necessary to resolve divergences between private and social costs. Coase argued that these divergences occurred owing to the failure of government to assign rights over the resources in question and that, once such rights were assigned, externalities would be efficiently resolved through negotiation – the now-famous Coase Theorem (see Medema and Zerbe, 2000). Coase did emphasize that transaction costs would almost inevitably preclude such efficient bargains in the real world. But that was not the point: rather, the theoretical apparatus that had demonstrated the failure of the market and the necessity for government intervention was shown to be wrong-headed.

A second challenge might be called "empirical" and took multiple forms. The underlying theme was that while neoclassical theory could demonstrate that government policies could be used to efficiently correct situations of market failure, real-world factors and forces, notably information costs, would prevent the attainment of the social optimum via these policy actions. Coase (1960), for example, argued that while transaction costs precluded efficient market solutions to externality problems, costs are also associated with the operation of government. These costs are relevant to assessing the efficiency of Pigovian solutions and might well result in the cure for market failure being worse than the disease. In a similar vein, the Chicago view of monopoly was that it is either transitory, an efficient response to market conditions, or exists only because its position is facilitated by government. Likewise, high levels of industrial concentration were not viewed as inherently harmful, since rivalrous behavior (e.g., price competition) on the part of a small number of firms could mimic the results of competition. As such, monopoly and highly concentrated oligopoly do not necessarily imply the need for government regulatory action. A further empirical strand was the questioning of the traditional "public goods" story – the inability of the market mechanism to provide certain goods in optimal amounts owing to the effects of nonrivalry and nonexcludability. Coase (1974), for example, pointed out that lighthouses – a classic example of supposed market failure – had been provided by the private sector in England until well into the nineteenth century. This literature, in a sense, reverted to the classical approach: policy analysis informed by a lack of confidence in the ability of government to actually get things right, in an efficiency sense. These asserted governmental deficiencies were due less to any underlying model of government behavior and more to beliefs, perhaps based on casual empiricism, that markets weren't as bad as some thought and government's potential not so great as the Pigovian theory would lead one to believe.

The third challenge to the efficacy of government came through public choice analysis, emanating largely from the Virginia school but also in part from Chicago. The focus was the examination, largely theoretical, of the operations of government and the political process generally, using the model of the self-interested rational actor. As with Pigovian welfare economics, the results indicated a wide range of divergences between private and social interests – here in the legislative, bureaucratic, and direct democratic voting processes. The demonstration was one of government rather than market failure, adding theoretical force to the pessimism of the classicals and their modern followers, and suggesting that Sidgwickian and Pigovian optimism regarding government intervention was unfounded. (For surveys of the public choice literature, see Mueller, 1989, 1997.)

This is not to say that by the end of the twentieth century the state of things had come full circle back to the classical view. Far from it. There was an acknowledgment (in certain quarters, at least) of the inefficiencies of both market and government. A heterogeneous normative view of the economic role of government developed, with individual positions as to the efficacy of markets versus government resting largely on one's perspective on whether the limitations of the market are, in a given set of circumstances, more or less severe than the limitations of government.

27.6   CONCLUSION

While the focus of this essay has been almost exclusively on "microeconomic" analyses of market failure and governmental responses to it, these movements have macroeconomic counterparts: Say's Law comported with the classicals' affirmative view of the system of natural liberty. Keynesian macroeconomics corresponded with Pigovian welfare economics in affirming a broad scope for activist government intervention. Rational expectations theory reinforced the microeconomic work of the Chicago and Virginia schools in gaining converts to macroeconomic noninterventionism. These parallels should not be surprising, given that the policy issues of macroeconomics – stabilization policy and incomes policy – are themselves responses to market failure: stability failure and distribution failure.

Views on the economic role of government in the history of economic thought have been, from the beginning, enmeshed in questions regarding the effects of the exercise of individual self-interest on society as a whole. Pre-classical commentators looked for a means to coordinate or restrain the base effects of self-interested behavior, and saw no means other than government regulation. Smith and the nineteenth-century classicals saw the system of natural liberty harmonizing, to a greater or lesser extent, self-interest and social interest, allowing markets to function with a minimum of direct control by government.

Neoclassical economics illuminated divergences that the market could not satisfactorily coordinate and showed how government could serve as a coordinating force. The backlash, led by Chicago and Virginia, showed that self-interested behavior also impacts the operation of government, and causes market failure and government failure alike.

Note

The author wishes to thank Warren Samuels, John Davis, Roger Backhouse, Tony Brewer, Bob Coats, Walter Eltis, Ian Steedman, participants in the 2001 UK History of Economic Thought Conference, and seminar participants at the University of Nice/LATAPSES for their insightful comments on earlier drafts of this essay.

Bibliography

Arrow, K. J. and Scitovsky, T. 1969: *Readings in Welfare Economics*. Homewood, IL: Richard D. Irwin, for the American Economic Association.

Baumol, W. J. 1952: *Welfare Economics and the Theory of the State*. London: London School of Economics and Political Science and Longmans, Green.

Bergson, A. 1938: A reformulation of certain aspects of welfare economics. *Quarterly Journal of Economics*, 52, 310–34.

Buchanan, J. M. 1960: La Scienza delle finanze: the Italian tradition in fiscal theory. In J. M. Buchanan, *Fiscal Theory and Political Economy: Selected Essays*. Chapel Hill, NC: University of North Carolina Press.

Coase, R. H. 1960: The problem of social cost. *Journal of Law and Economics*, 3, 1–44.

—— 1974: The lighthouse in economics. *Journal of Law and Economics*, 17, 357–76.

Debreu, G. 1954: Valuation equilibrium and Pareto optimum. *Proceedings of the National Academy of Sciences*, 40, 588–92.

Gordon, B. 1975: *Economic Analysis Before Adam Smith: Hesiod to Lessius*. New York: Harper & Row.

Lange, O. 1942: The foundations of welfare economics. *Econometrica*, 10, 215–28.

Lowry, S. T. 1987: *The Archaeology of Economic Ideas: The Classical Greek Tradition*. Durham, NC: Duke University Press.

Magnusson, L. 1993: Introduction. In L. Magnusson (ed.), *Mercantilist Economics*. Boston: Kluwer.

McCulloch, J. R. 1848: *A Treatise on the Succession to Property Vacant by Death: Including Inquiries into the Influence of Primogeniture, Entails, Compulsory Partition, Foundations, &c., over the Public Interests*. London: Longman, Brown, Green, and Longmans.

Meade, J. E. 1952: External economies and diseconomies in a competitive situation. *Economic Journal*, 62, 54–67.

Medema, S. G. 2001: Wicksell's reconciliation of the disparate elements of Italian public finance. University of Colorado at Denver, Department of Economics, Working Paper #2001–05.

—— and Zerbe, R. O., Jr. 2000: The Coase Theorem. In B. Bouckaert and G. De Geest (eds.), *Encyclopedia of Law and Economics*, vol. I. Cheltenham, UK: Edward Elgar, 836–92.

Meek, R. L. 1962: *The Economics of Physiocracy: Essays and Translations*. London: George Allen & Unwin. Reprinted Fairfield, NJ: Augustus M. Kelley, 1993.

Mill, J. S. 1871: *Principles of Political Economy*, 7th edn. London: Longmans, Green, 1909.

Mueller, D. C. 1989: *Public Choice II*. Cambridge, UK: Cambridge University Press.

—— 1997: *Perspectives on Public Choice*. Cambridge, UK: Cambridge University Press.

O'Brien, D. P. 1975: *The Classical Economists*. Oxford: The Clarendon Press.

O'Donnell, M. G. 1979: Pigou: an extension of Sidgwickian thought. *History of Political Economy*, 11(4), 588–605.

Pigou, A. C. 1932: *The Economics of Welfare*, 4th edn. London: Macmillan.

Robbins, L. 1952: *The Theory of Economic Policy in English Classical Political Economy*. London: Macmillan.

Samuels, W. J. 1962: The physiocratic theory of economic policy. *Quarterly Journal of Economics*, 76, 145–62.

—— 1966: *The Classical Theory of Economic Policy*. Cleveland: World.

Senior, N. W. 1928: *Industrial Efficiency and Social Economy*, original mss. arranged and edited by S. Leon Levy, 2 vols. London: P. S. King & Son.

Sidgwick, H. 1901: *The Principles of Political Economy*, 3rd edn. London: Macmillan.

Skinner, A. S. 1996: The role of the state. In *A System of Social Science: Papers Relating to Adam Smith*, 2nd edn. Oxford: Oxford University Press.

Smith, A. 1776: *An Inquiry into the Nature and Causes of the Wealth of Nations*. New York: Modern Library, 1937.

—— 1978: *Lectures on Jurisprudence*. Oxford: Oxford University Press.

Steiner, P. 2002: Wealth and power: Quesnay's political economy of the agricultural kingdom. *Journal of the History of Economic Thought*, 24, 91–110.

Stigler, G. J. and Boulding, K. E. 1952: *Readings in Price Theory*. Homewood, IL: Richard D. Irwin, for the American Economic Association.

Viner, J. 1927: Adam Smith and laissez faire. *Journal of Political Economy*, 35, 198–232. Reprinted in Viner, J. 1991: *Essays on the Intellectual History of Economics*. Princeton, NJ: Princeton University Press, 85–113.

—— 1937: *Studies in the Theory of International Trade*. New York: Harper & Brothers. Reprinted Clifton, NJ: Augustus M. Kelley, 1975.

Postwar Heterodox Economics

A   THE AUSTRIAN SCHOOL OF ECONOMICS, 1950–2000
Peter J. Boettke and Peter T. Leeson

28A.1   THE EARLIER HISTORY OF THE AUSTRIAN SCHOOL

The doctrines that comprise the Austrian school of economics have varied and the relative position of the school within the mainstream of economic thought has moved from the center to the fringe several times throughout the 130 years of its history. Carl Menger, in his *Grundsatze der Volkswirthshaftslehre* of 1871, substituted subjective marginal utility for the classicists' objective cost of production as the theory of value. Friedrich von Wieser introduced the idea of opportunity cost and emphasized its subjective and ubiquitous character. Eugen von Böhm-Bawerk engaged in applying Menger's theory of value to the theories of capital and interest. The next generation's leaders were Ludwig von Mises and Hans Mayer, who emphasized epistemic, ontological, and other philosophical themes. A fourth generation of Austrian economists emerged (most of whom would make their academic mark in the USA after World War II) that included such major economists as F. A. Hayek, Gottfried Haberler, Oskar Morgenstern, Fritz Machlup, and Paul Rosenstein-Rodan. Austrian economics flourished in the period immediately following World War I.

By the mid-1930s, however, the idea of a distinct Austrian program, even in the minds of the Austrians themselves, was seriously waning, in part because the mainstream more or less absorbed the important points the Austrians were making. Von Mises (1981 [1933], p. 214) had argued that while it is commonplace in modern economics to distinguish between the Austrian, Anglo-American, and Lausanne schools, "these three schools of thought differ only in their mode of expressing the same fundamental idea and that they are divided more by their terminology and by peculiarities of presentation than by the substance of their teachings." Hayek was even more explicit when he wrote as late as 1968 that while the fourth generation of Austrian economists continued to show their training in Vienna in the 1920s in terms of their style of thinking and theoretical interests, they could hardly be considered a separate school of thought anymore. "A school has its greatest success when it ceases as such to exist because its leading ideals have become a part of the general dominant teaching. The Vienna school has to a great extent come to enjoy such a success" (1968, p. 52). Yet by the period immediately after World War I, the basic insights of von Mises and Hayek were much less appreciated by their fellow economists.

The main tenets of the Austrian school that members of the fourth generation thought had been fully incorporated into the mainstream are clear. Fritz Machlup (1982, p. 42) emphasized that Austrian economists had never been uniform in their belief structure, intensely debating among themselves over the relative importance of concepts and tenets. Nevertheless, Machlup offered six "main tenets" which economists trained in the Austrian approach would accept:

1 *Methodological individualism.* Ultimately, we can trace all economic phenomena back to the actions of individuals; thus individual actions must serve as the basic building blocks of economic theory.
2 *Methodological subjectivism.* Economics takes man's ultimate ends and judgments of value as given. Questions of value, expectations, intent, and knowledge are created in the minds of individuals and must be considered in this light.
3 *Marginalism.* All economic decisions are made on the margin. All choices are choices regarding the last unit added or subtracted from a given stock.
4 *Tastes and preferences.* Individuals' demands for goods and services are the result of their subjective valuations of the ability of such goods and services to satisfy their wants.
5 *Opportunity costs.* All activities have a cost. This cost is the most highly valued alternative that is forgone because the means for its satisfaction have been devoted to some other (more highly valued) use.
6 *Time structure of consumption and production.* All decisions take place in time. Decisions about how to allocate resources for the purposes of consumption and production across time are determined by individuals' time-preferences.

Machlup offers two other tenets of the Austrian school that he considered "highly controversial":

7 *Consumer sovereignty.* In the marketplace, the consumer is king. Consumers' demands drive the shape of the market and determine how resources are used. Intervention in the marketplace stifles this process.
8 *Political individualism.* Political freedom is impossible without economic freedom.

Machlup also hinted at the Austrian view of markets as a process – that is, the adjustment process and path toward equilibrium – rather than the correctness and usefulness of equilibrium theory and the conditions of static equilibrium.

Machlup's six main tenets are all positions that are more or less embraced by mainstream economics. The key to what differentiates Austrian economics from mainstream economics in Machlup's eyes then seems to be the controversial tenets seven and eight. Unlike the previous six tenets, these two have a normative edge to them. Both, on some level or another, seem to be saying that free markets are superior to government intervention. Indeed, in his piece, Machlup points out that contrary to many Austrians who view their economic statements as *wertfrei*, "nevertheless, the label, 'Austrian economics' has come to imply a commitment to the libertarian program" (1982, p. 45). Thus, in Machlup's mind Austrian economics is neoclassical economics with a free market bent. No doubt Machlup is proud of his educational pedigree in Vienna, but even more so because it had proven so successful in getting its main teaching accepted as part of the dominant teaching in economics.

For Austrians like Machlup trained in the 1920s, the defining characteristics of Austrian economics are tenets held in common by the mainstream. But if we agree with this statement, how does the notion of an Austrian school of thought distinct from the mainstream make sense? The answer to this question lies in the advances that Austrian economics achieved after World War II, in particular in the unique contributions that Hayek and von Mises made in the 1940s in *Individualism and Economic Order* (Hayek, 1948) and *Human Action: A Treatise on Economics* (von Mises, 1949) respectively. For von Mises and Hayek, the ideas in these works were merely statements of "modern economics," but in the hands of the fifth (Rothbard, Lachmann, and Kirzner), sixth (e.g., Rizzo, Lavoie, Garrison, White, Block, and Salerno) and seventh (e.g., Selgin, Boettke, Horwitz, and Prychitko) generations of Austrian economists these ideas would become the framework for an alternative paradigm in economic science.

28A.2 REDRAWING THE LINES: MAINSTREAM AND AUSTRIAN ECONOMICS DEHOMOGENIZED

In the 1920s and 1930s, von Mises and Hayek were engaged in an intellectual battle with the socialists over the feasibility of socialism (see Boettke, 2000). The great debate that ensued between these two and the socialist's most prominent figure, Oskar Lange, came to be called the "Socialist Calculation debate." Von Mises maintained that since socialism, by definition, precludes the possibility of private ownership of the means of production, no market prices that reflect the relative scarcities of resources can emerge. Without market prices to guide production, he argued, socialism is unable to rationally allocate resources among competing ends. Strictly speaking, socialism is impossible.

Lange responded by claiming that market prices are unnecessary to rationally allocate resources. The socialist central planners need only establish shadow prices and then instruct industry managers to produce at that level of output which sets price equal to marginal costs, and minimize average costs. If the planning board selects the wrong prices, simple trial and error will quickly reveal the correct prices. Lange postulated an adjustment process within his model that is similar to the process that underlies the Walrasian model.

Hayek responded to Lange's rebuttal by pointing out that Lange's model assumes everything that it needs to prove. Only in a state of final equilibrium, where final prices are known, could the planners set price equal to marginal costs and minimize average costs. In the Walrasian model, equilibrium is guaranteed through a pre-reconciliation of plans. In equilibrium, agents' plans dovetail with one another so that all opportunities for mutual learning have been exhausted. The Walrasian model clarifies the conditions under which equilibrium could be said to be obtained, but the model is silent on how actors' plans could be adjusted in an equilibration process. The pre-reconciliation of plans is a defining characteristic of equilibrium, but the key theoretical question that economists must address is how in the absence of such pre-reconciliation individual actors will be led to reconcile their plans with one another. Hayek argued that individuals outside of the equilibrium state will be moved to discover the opportunities for mutual learning, since each unexploited opportunity represents possibilities for improvement in their lot in life. The ceaseless activity of the market is driven by the opportunities for mutual gain. If the data of the market were frozen this activity would converge quickly on a state of affairs where all mutual gains are exhausted. Due to the constantly changing nature of market conditions, this equilibrium is constantly shifting. What allows capitalism to discover the knowledge necessary to allocate resources effectively is the competitive market process. Only via this process can we generate the knowledge necessary to make rational allocation possible. Lange's model left no room for the activity of economic life and, as such, his model could not address the dynamic problems that socialist planning would have to confront in practice.

Later, von Mises buttressed Hayek's argument with his notion of the entrepreneur. The entrepreneur, von Mises stated, is the driving force of the market process. Entrepreneurs both create and respond to the changes in market conditions, and through their profit-seeking push the market in the direction of clearing. Absent the institutional framework of private property that allows entrepreneurs to appraise the economic situation via the price system, socialist planning must fail. While Hayek's work in response to the market socialists focused on fleshing out the importance of the market as a process that generates a price system that enables us to make use of dispersed knowledge, von Mises's subsequent work not only restated his argument on the impossibility of economic calculation under socialism, but also developed his notion of the entrepreneur as the driving force in the market economy.

It was only in the years following the Socialist Calculation debate, in the late 1940s, that von Mises and Hayek fully understood that their view of the nature of the economic process was fundamentally different from the view of the rest of the economics profession (see Kirzner, 1987). The increasing emphasis by von Mises and Hayek on uncertainty, entrepreneurship, knowledge, and market processes all emerged in the calculation debate. The calculation debate forced von Mises and Hayek to really elucidate their understandings of the market process, and it made them realize the implications of their own ideas. They were blind-sided by the fact that Lange (and Lerner) used neoclassical arguments to construct a defense of socialist economic organization. Although by the 1930s it seemed as though the mainstream had incorporated Austrian ideas rather fully, it became clear to those trained under them in the late 1940s and the 1950s that the von Mises and Hayek understanding of the economic process was very different, and far from being accepted by the profession at large. The dividing line between Austrian and mainstream ideas was redrawn and with it the Austrian school, as a distinct school of economic thought, reborn.

28A.3 THE PERSPECTIVE OF AUSTRIAN ECONOMICS AFTER WORLD WAR II

Against this backdrop grew the next generation of Austrian economists, who trained after World War II, in the 1950s. The tenets of market process theory and a focus on the importance of entrepreneurship are conspicuously absent in Machlup, who trained in the 1920s. Only after World War II did the importance of these elements to Austrian economics (along with several others, to be discussed later) emerge. How, then, did Austrians trained in the 1950s view Austrian economics?

We can see these differences most clearly by looking at the way in which an Austrian trained in the 1950s defined his school of thought, and then contrast them with Machlup's understanding. Kirzner (1986) acknowledges the correctness of Machlup's six tenets but points out that the existing list does not take into account the theoretical advances made in the 1940s by von Mises and Hayek.

In light of the contributions made by von Mises and Hayek in the Socialist Calculation debate, Kirzner believes that two more tenets must be added to Machlup's basic six to complete the list. These are:

(a) Markets as a process – the notion of markets and competition as learning and discovery processes.
(b) Radical uncertainty – uncertainty pervades all our actions and is the ubiquitous context in which all choice must be made.

While these ideas only become articulated in the postwar work of von Mises and Hayek, they were partly evident as far back as the early 1930s. Indeed, Kirzner points out that the Austrian critique of "functional price theories," and calling for "causal-genetic theories," was an early expression of the importance of market process theory (see Cowan and Rizzo, 1996). The Austrians were stressing the importance of understanding the sequence of events that cause prices to emerge over the sterile description of static equilibrium. But Austrians in the von Mises circle in Vienna, Kirzner says, did not recognize this insight as a radical departure from mainstream economic theory.

For Kirzner, it is this notion of market process and uncertainty that distinguishes Austrian economics from the mainstream. Kirzner's work, while emphasizing the uncertainty present in all human decision-making, has primarily focused on the entrepreneurial market process (e.g., Kirzner, 1973). Ludwig Lachmann, on the other hand, tended to emphasize the elements of radical subjectivism and radical uncertainty that are inherent in the economic process (e.g., Lachmann, 1977). The different emphases of these two scholars led to the internal theoretical debate within the Austrian school in the 1970s and 1980s on the equilibrating properties of the market process (see Vaughn, 1994). O'Driscoll and Rizzo's *The Economics of Time and Ignorance* (1985) sought to build on the twin themes of uncertainty and market process, and restated the theoretical contribution of the Austrian school of economics in relation to contemporary economic theory and policy. O'Driscoll and Rizzo's work appealed to an audience of heterodox economists, who found the emphasis on subjectivism, time, uncertainty, and indeterminancy within the economic process a welcomed relief from the sterile theory of neoclassical economics. The debate between Kirzner and Lachmann remains unsettled in the literature, but as much of modern mainstream theory has moved away from general equilibrium models, so have Austrians ceased to focus their theoretical attention on the issue of whether or not the market process converges to general competitive equilibrium.

28A.4   Beyond Microeconomics

Our story has emphasized the distinguishing characteristics of the Austrian approach in the field of microeconomic theory. The Austrian position with regard to macroeconomic theory can be summed up as follows: while there may indeed be macroeconomic problems (unemployment, inflation, business cycles), there are only microeconomic explanations and solutions. There are no aggregate relationships unmoored to individual choices that matter for economic analysis. This position, of course, brought the Austrians into opposition with a postwar economics dominated by Keynesianism and its emphasis on the relationship between aggregate variables. Hayek had identified this aggregation problem with Keynes' economics in his earlier debate with Keynes in the 1930s. He argued that aggregation masked the structural composition of an economy, which must be scrutinized if the economist hopes to understand overall economic performance (see Caldwell, 1995).

While their work on capital theory (e.g., Lachmann, 1956; Kirzner, 1966) provides a bridge between microeconomics and macroeconomics, Israel Kirzner and Ludwig Lachmann tended to emphasize the microeconomic tenets that constituted a unique Austrian understanding of the market economy, while the other fifth-generation economist, Murray Rothbard, tended to emphasize the macroeconomic analysis that would differentiate the Austrians from other schools of economic thought in the 1960s (see Rothbard, 1962, pp. 661–764, 832–9, 850–79). The key to this, in Rothbard's mind, was an explanation of the costs and consequences of government pursuing inflationary credit expansion. Rothbard argued that the "bust" in the business cycle was causally linked to the earlier government generated "boom." The market economy is self-correcting and will quickly eliminate the earlier government-generated errors in investment, unless the process of adjustment is interfered with by government policies.

Rothbard's message, like the similar message provided by von Mises and Hayek during the 1930s, was rejected by the majority of economists in the 1960s, who believed that the role of the economist was to provide sage advice to government policy-makers on how to maintain the economy in full employment. But for a generation of economists coming of age in the late 1960s and early 1970s, the earlier macroeconomics consensus was fracturing in light of the theoretical incoherence of the Keynesian synthesis and the empirical record of Keynesian demand management policy. The monetarist counter-revolution led by Milton Friedman, and the New Classical revolution led by Robert Lucas, effectively displaced the Keynesian hegemony in macroeconomics by the mid-1970s. In that mix, a resurgent Austrian school of economics must also be mentioned. Hayek was awarded the Nobel Prize in 1974, and his pre-Keynesian theories of the economic process started to be read more widely. A group of younger economists earning their Ph.D.'s precisely at this time, who were raised on Rothbard's writings, capitalized on the moment to pursue new work in macroeconomics.

Gerald O'Driscoll's *Economics as a Coordination Problem* (1977) was the first systemic examination of the work of F. A. Hayek that placed Hayek's work on monetary theory and the trade cycle within a broader unified framework of economics. Roger Garrison began to present the Austrian cycle within a standard model for a comparative analysis in the 1970s. Garrison's work culminated in his *Time and Money* (2000), where he argues for a switch from the labor-based macroeconomics of Keynesianism and monetarism to a capital-based macroeconomics championed by the Austrians. Peter Lewin's *Capital in Disequilibrium* (1998) and Steve Horwitz's *Microfoundations and Macroeconomics* (2000) are other contemporary contributions to Austrian macroeconomics.

In addition to the problems of the trade cycle, Rothbard's work emphasized the fraudulent and destructive force that the government represents with its monopoly position over the money supply. Hayek also wrote against government monopoly of the money supply and in the 1970s called for the *The Denationalization of Money* (1976). Again, young scholars raised on Rothbard's writings on the problems of government money were able to exploit the inflationary period of the 1970s and offer a radical argument for "free banking." Lawrence H. White's *Free Banking in Britain* (1984) led to a burgeoning literature on how a system of competitive currency would in fact operate. This "free banking" strain of modern Austrian economics has had considerable success in addressing the mainstream of the economics profession, and it is not uncommon for work in this field to be published in the leading professional journals (see, e.g., Selgin and White, 1994).

28A.5 ECONOMIC SYSTEMS AND ECONOMIC DEVELOPMENT

The collapse of the Soviet-type economies in the late 1980s was the most significant political economy event since the Great Depression. Standard models of optimal planning and the macroeconomic examination of Soviet economic growth proved to be unable to explain the collapse of the Soviet system and offer advice for the transition from socialism to capitalism. The Austrian economists had long been the most vocal critics of the socialist economic system within the economics profession. Don Lavoie's *Rivalry and Central Planning* (1985) was perfectly timed in order to capitalize on this historical situation. Lavoie's work demonstrated how the market socialist model of neoclassical economists diverted the debate into statics, and how a reexamination of the dynamic character of the market economy should transform economic research to focus on questions of the institutional environment and the entrepreneurial character of economic activity. Following up on Lavoie's work, Boettke (1990) addressed the origin of the Soviet political and economic system, and Prychitko (1991) took up the challenge of the workers' control model of socialism. The modern Austrian focus on the importance of institutions in providing the incentives for the acquisition and use of information and entrepreneurial innovation has merged considerably with the work of the New Institutional Economics of James Buchanan, Ronald Coase, Douglass North, Gordon Tullock, and Oliver Williamson (see Boettke, 1993, 2001).

Development economics has also been transformed in the wake of the collapse of communism. Scholars are now emphasizing the underlying institutional environment and cultural preconditions that enable countries to realize generalized prosperity (see Lal, 1999). Recent work in economic development is taking up the task of testing Hayek's claims about common-law traditions and the rule of law (Mahoney, 2001). In short, in the area of economic systems and development, Austrian ideas are making significant inroads into the mainstream of contemporary research.

28A.6 Conclusion

Contemporary Austrians straddle heterodoxy and orthodoxy within the economics profession. They offer a heterodox critique of formal theory, but contribute to the policy consensus that has emerged in the past 20 years, that has moved away from state-led development to a more *laissez-faire* position in international and domestic policy. But the intellectual battleground today is much more defined by methodological issues than ideological ones. Indeed, many of the policy wisdoms that flow from an Austrian analysis of the market economy are part of the common knowledge of market-oriented economists, but the Austrian methodological stance, and the theoretical agenda that generated that wisdom, are rejected by those who still pursue the model and measure research strategy in economic science. Thus, today, the Austrian school finds itself in a strange position with regard to its fellow economists. It believes that others have stumbled upon the right answers to many practical policy questions, but for the wrong reasons.

Note

We thank John Robert Subrick, Edward Stringham, Scott Beaulier, Ryan Oprea, and Warren Samuels for their comments on an earlier version.

Bibliography

Boettke, P. 1990: *The Political Economy of Soviet Socialism: The Formative Years, 1918–1928*. Boston: Kluwer.

—— 1993: *Why Perestroika Failed: The Politics and Economics of Socialist Transformation*. London: Routledge.

—— (ed.) 2000: *Socialism and the Market Economy: The Socialist Calculation Debate Revisited*, 9 vols. London: Routledge.

—— 2001: *Calculation and Coordination: Essays on Socialism and Transitional Political Economy*. London: Routledge.

Caldwell, B. (ed.) 1995: *The Collected Works of F. A. Hayek: Contra Keynes and Cambridge*. Chicago: The University of Chicago Press.

Cowan, R. and Rizzo, M. 1996: The casual genetic moment in economics. *Kyklos*, 49(3), 273–316.

Garrison, R. 2000: *Time and Money*. New York: Routledge.

Hayek, F. A. 1948: *Individualism and Economic Order*. Chicago: The University of Chicago Press.

—— 1968: Economic thought VI: The Austrian school of economics. In D. M. Sills and R. K. Merton (eds.), *International Encyclopedia of the Social Sciences*. New York: Macmillan.

—— 1976: *The Denationalization of Money*. London: Institute for Economic Affairs.

Horwitz, S. 2000: *Microfoundations and Macroeconomics*. New York: Routledge.

Kirzner, I. 1966: *An Essay on Capital*. New York: Augustus M. Kelley.

—— 1973: *Competition and Entrepreneurship*. Chicago: The University of Chicago Press.

—— 1986: The Austrian school of economics. In J. Eatwell, M. Milgate, and P. Newman (eds.), *The New Palgrave: A Dictionary of Economics*, 4 vols. London: Macmillan.

—— 1987: The socialist calculation debate: lessons for Austrians. *Review of Austrian Economics*, 2, 1–18.

Lachmann, L. 1956: *Capital and Its Structure*. London: London School of Economics.

—— 1977: *Capital, Expectations and the Market Process*. Kansas City, MO: Sheed and McMeel.

Lal, D. 1998: *Unintended Consequences*. Cambridge, MA: The MIT Press.

Lavoie, D. 1985: *Rivalry and Central Planning*. New York: Cambridge University Press.

Lewin, P. 1998: *Capital in Disequilibrium*. New York: Routledge.

Machlup, F. 1982: Austrian economics. In D. Greenwald (ed.), *Encyclopedia of Economics*. New York: McGraw-Hill.

Mahoney, P. 2001: The common law and economic growth: Hayek might be right. *Journal of Legal Studies*, 30(2), 503–25.

Mises, L. von 1949: *Human Action: A Treatise on Economics*. Chicago, IL: Henry Regnery.

—— 1981 [1933]: *Epistemological Problems in Economics*. New York: New York University Press, 1981.

O'Driscoll, G. 1977: *Economics as a Coordination Problem*. Kansas City, MO: Sheed and McMeel.

—— and Rizzo, M. 1985: *The Economic of Time and Ignorance*. Oxford: Blackwell.

Prychitko, D. 1991: *Marxism and Workers' Self-Management*. Westport, CT: Greenwood.

Rothbard, M. 1962: *Man, Economy and State*, 2 vols. Princeton, NJ: Van Nostrand.

Selgin, G. and White, L. H. 1994: How would the invisible hand handle money? *Journal of Economic Literature*, 32(4), 1718–49.

Vaughn, K. 1994: *Austrian Economics in America*. New York: Cambridge University Press.

White, L. H. 1984: *Free Banking in Britain*. New York: Cambridge University Press.

B   FEMINIST ECONOMICS
Janet A. Seiz

28B.1   Introduction

Beginning in the mid-1960s, feminists in most of the social sciences and humanities forcefully challenged their disciplines' treatment of issues related to women
and gender. By the mid-1980s, feminist scholarship had significantly altered many
disciplines. Feminist economists, however, had little progress to report: relatively
few feminist critiques of economics had appeared, and they had not been
influential. By the mid-1990s, the picture was changing. While economics had by
no means been transformed, feminist economists were much more numerous, and
far more explicitly feminist work was being published. Space constraints permit
here only a very rough sketch of this ongoing story, but references are provided for further reading (for more detailed surveys, see Beneria, 1995; Hewitson,
1999).

28B.2   How it Began

In the 1970s and 1980s, the economics profession appeared to welcome neither
women nor feminist ideas. Women received only 6 percent of the economics
Ph.D.'s awarded in the USA in 1970, about 14 percent in 1980, and just 20 percent
in 1990 (Kahn, 1995, p. 194; see also Albelda, 1997). "Most economists," wrote
Barbara Bergmann (1987, p. 132), were "hostile to any suggestion that the
economic position of women needs improvement." Economic literature had little
to say about gender. Economists "showed little interest in those segments of
the economy that have been largely the domain of women, namely household
production and volunteer work" and "generally ignored the extent to which
women were involved in the rest of the economy" (Ferber and Teiman, 1981,
p. 128). Using definitions of "work" modeled on men's experiences, economists
and statisticians greatly underestimated women's economic contributions
(Ciancanelli and Berch, 1987). Gender inequality was commonly treated as "beyond
the purview of economic analysis, either in the realm of biological givens or
sociological imponderables" (Folbre and Hartmann, 1988, p. 184). Economists'
discussions of policies regarding, for example, government budgets, economic
development, and international trade almost never addressed the effects of policy
choices on women or gender relations.

It was true that women's economic lives had at last received some serious
attention from labor economists, but the dominant writings in the field were read
as strongly antifeminist. The path-breakers in neoclassical work on gender –
Jacob Mincer, Gary Becker, and Solomon Polachek – collectively constructed a
tight "supply-side" account in which the differences between women's and men's
work and earnings appeared to be unproblematic. Starting in the mid-1960s,
Becker created a "new home economics" dealing with household production,

marriage, divorce, fertility, and the gender division of labor. In his scheme, men had comparative advantage in market work, and women in childrearing and housework, partly rooted in biology (Becker, 1981). Since having children typically interrupted labor-force participation, women invested less than men in market human capital and chose occupations that were relatively easy to leave and reenter. Their wages, accordingly, were lower than men's (Mincer and Polachek, 1974).

While feminists might have been glad that work on gender had reached the mainstream, most were appalled by that work's message. Ferber and Teiman (1981, p. 131) noted that "[t]he new tools developed for the economic analysis of the family . . . have to a considerable extent been used to tacitly endorse the status quo." Becker's work, lamented Bergmann (1987, p. 132), "explains, justifies, and even glorifies role differentiation by sex." Women's lower economic status appeared as a vicious circle of their own making: "women specialize in housework because they earn less in the labor market, and they earn less in the labor market because they specialize in housework" (Ferber and Birnbaum, 1977, p. 20). The comparative advantage model obscured the extent to which childrearing and housework were tasks "whose social imposition is one manifestation of gender hierarchy" (Ciancanelli and Berch, 1987, p. 245). "[T]he inferior labor market position of women [is presented as] something women have freely chosen, as a normal and generally benign adaptation to 'their responsibilities' for housework and childrearing. Low-wage work is seen as appropriate for people who behave as they do. The laws against discrimination . . . are, in this view, superfluous or of minor value" (Bergmann, 1989, p. 43).

Under feminist scrutiny, Marxist political economy was also found wanting. Marx and Engels had treated gender inequality primarily as a by-product of class relations. In capitalism, women's disadvantage arose from their economic dependence; the proletariat exhibited less gender inequality than the bourgeoisie, since its men were propertyless and its women usually worked for wages. Socialism would liberate women by making the means of production social property, collectivizing domestic work, and drawing women into the labor force (see Vogel, 1983).

In the late 1960s, leftist feminists in the UK and USA began to extend Marxist theory to search for the "material basis" of gender inequality. Most focused initially on women's work and the benefits that it produced for capitalists. Women's nurturing and socializing of children was essential for "social reproduction." Women's unwaged work in the home enabled families to subsist on lower wages, increasing capitalists' profits (on domestic labor, see Himmelweit, 1999; Jefferson and King, 2001). Women also constituted a "reserve army of labor," available for wage work if needed (e.g., in wartime) and easily ejected when the need disappeared.

Many feminists saw these analyses as useful but insufficient. Marxist theory did not convincingly address the noneconomic aspects of gender inequality or the varied ways in which women's disadvantage served men. Responding to these lacunae, Heidi Hartmann (1976, 1981) developed a "dual systems" theory in which capitalism and "patriarchy" constituted separate and semiautonomous systems. Capitalists benefited from women's subordination, but so did men. For instance, women's exclusion from large parts of the labor market both kept men's wages higher than they would otherwise be and ensured men the benefit of women's household services. Nancy Folbre (1982) posed Marxism another challenge, developing a model of exploitation within the household: a male worker, exploited at the workplace, might be an exploiter at home if the value of his wife's consumption fell too far short of that which her labor produced (for more on socialist feminist economics, see Albelda, 1997; Mutari, 2001).

Initially, these pioneering writers (both mainstream and leftist) typically depended on small circles of colleagues for intellectual support. Over time, however, mainstream, Marxian, and institutionalist feminists increasingly sought out and responded to each other's work. This openness, rare in economics, facilitated the rapid growth of feminist research (for feminist social theory informed by all three approaches, see Folbre, 1994).

Beginning in the late 1980s, a number of feminists argued that the "androcentrism" of economics showed not only in its treatment of women and gender, but also in its basic conceptual framework, delineation of its subject matter, and theoretical and empirical methods. [Important examples are collected in Ferber and Nelson (1993), Kuiper and Sap (1995), and Nelson (1996). See also Grapard (1999), Pujol (1992), and Seiz (1992).] For instance, neoclassical economics reproduced gender stereotypes by portraying behavior in the marketplace (seen as men's domain) as guided by the rational pursuit of self-interest, and behavior in the household (designated women's sphere) as guided by altruism (Folbre and Hartmann, 1988). It evaded central questions about gender by refusing to inquire into the origin of "preferences." It exaggerated the importance of individual choice, neglecting the often dramatically dissimilar constraints facing different social groups. It misrepresented the institutional setting of economic life, obscuring power relations by having outcomes determined in explicit or implicit competitive markets. It assumed interpersonal utility comparisons were impossible. And its "*Homo economicus*," the free and independent maker of self-interested choices, lived a life very unlike most women's: the persona fit a "separative" (masculine) image of selfhood that ignored emotional connections to others (England, 1993). It followed, said some, that the neoclassical framework was ill-suited for feminist inquiry: as Ferber and Nelson (1993, p. 6) put it, "models of free individual choice are not adequate to analyze behavior fraught with issues of dependence, interdependence, tradition and power."

Some of the features that feminists criticized could plausibly be viewed as emanating from male experiences and/or serving male interests, their presence symptomatic of women's absence from the discipline. A "standpoint epistemology" developed by feminist philosophers (e.g., Harding, 1986) explored ways in which individuals' beliefs might be shaped by their "social locations." Economists' gender, however, was clearly only part of the story: some of feminists' criticisms of neoclassicism were shared by male heterodox economists, and all inquirers were shaped by prevailing social beliefs about gender (Nelson, 1996). Furthermore, individuals often transcended or opposed the views associated with their social identities. Thus standpoint epistemology, though often illuminating, would by no means suffice for explaining or assessing economic ideas (Seiz, 1995).

Diana Strassmann (1993) extended the critique to the sociology of economics, showing how the "authorized" analytic framework helped to determine who would succeed in economics. Individuals whose thinking did not conform to the "core ideas of self-interested individualism and contractual exchange" (1993, p. 54) tended to be excluded from or silenced within the profession. "Although women and minorities commonly experience dissonance with the standard models of economics, only those who adhere to foundational metaphors are allowed to participate in the conversations of the mainstream" (1993, p. 57). Thus the discipline's social biases were perpetuated.

These critiques implied that the more homogeneous a group of inquirers was, the more "partial" (in both senses of the word) would its "knowledge" be. Bringing in new voices (including women's) was not just a matter of "equal opportunity" but also one of "truth": incorporating a wider range of perspectives would increase the reliability of research (Harding, 1995; Nelson, 1995, 1996).

28B.3   Gender and the History of Economics

When feminist economists began to investigate earlier economists' treatment of gender, they were struck by the paucity of material (Madden, 1972, p. 21): economists seemed to have paid scant attention to women, and intellectual historians had examined neither the discipline's handling of gender nor women's contributions to economics.

Both those areas were explored in Michèle Pujol's *Feminism and Anti-Feminism in Early Economic Thought* (1992), a path-breaking book that told a damning tale. Few major economists had shown interest in women's economic activities or problems. In their "principles" texts – their grand portraits of economic life – the classical "founding fathers" had made almost no reference to women. Many of the discipline's leaders – including Pigou, Marshall, Jevons, and Edgeworth – had strongly opposed women's participation in market labor.

Some challenges to gender inequality had appeared, in mostly "forgotten" economic writings by feminist women and men. Harriet Taylor, Pujol suggested, strongly influenced John Stuart Mill and was the more radical thinker. The "crowding hypothesis" (that women's wages were lower because they were crowded into a small number of occupations), usually credited to Edgeworth, was actually articulated earlier by Mill and Taylor, Barbara Bodichon, and Millicent Garrett Fawcett. Fawcett and Eleanor Rathbone conducted a fascinating and still timely debate over whether women would be better served by wider job opportunities or by family allowances paid to mothers.

Other feminist histories followed that of Pujol. Groenewegen (1994) included essays on Jevons, Marshall, Sidney and Beatrice Webb, and others. Forget (1997) assessed Say's views on gender, and Bodkin (1999) compared Smith, Taylor, and Mill. Robert Dimand (1995) described a wide array of women's economic writings and documented their neglect by historians. Dimand et al. (1995) covered

Jane Marcet, Harriet Martineau, Charlotte Perkins Gilman, Barbara Bodichon, and others, and offered several studies of women in the economics profession. Folbre (1998) related the experiences of some of the first US women to work as professional economists. The *Biographical Dictionary of Women Economists* (Dimand et al., 2000) assembled entries on more than 100 women, excluding women still employed as economists (for additional references, see Lewis, 1999).

28B.4   Feminist Economics Now

While women and feminist ideas have become more visible in economics, neither is a large presence. Women now receive just over 25 percent of economics Ph.D.'s in the USA, and they are still scarce on the faculties of Ph.D.-granting universities (see Kahn, 1995; Hammond, 1999; Olsen and Emami, 2002). A 1992 survey of American Economic Association members suggested that feminist work had had little impact on the profession (Albelda, 1997). Within a few years, however, feminist economists had a professional association and a journal of their own, and their research output grew rapidly. The International Association for Feminist Economics, founded in 1992, had in 1999 600 members from 38 countries (Shackelford, 1999). IAFFE's journal, *Feminist Economics*, has since 1995 published articles on a broad range of gender-related topics, its diverse content reflecting the geographic, methodological, and political heterogeneity of its audience.

Feminist economics now comprises a sizable literature. Noted here are a few of its many lines of research (see also Beneria, 1995; Strassmann, 1999):

- *Women's work in industrialized countries.* Feminists have challenged the "Chicago school" treatment of gender inequality on many fronts, developing richer analyses of women's labor-supply decisions, investigating the workings and extent of discrimination, and comparing situations across countries. Overviews of the emerging understanding of gender differentials – and associated policy discussions – may be found in Bergmann (1986), Blau et al. (2001), and Jacobsen (1998).
- *Economic development.* Women's work in less-industrialized countries has also been studied. Ester Boserup (1970) was the pioneer, arguing that modernization typically created attractive new economic opportunities open only to men. Subsequent research and practice initially focused largely on better "integrating" women into development; recent feminist contributions have included more critical analyses of development and its complex, varied, and often adverse effects on women (see references in Elson, 1995, 1999; Bakker, 1999; Mammen and Paxson, 2000).
- *Gender and property.* In both industrialized and "developing" nations, scholars and policy-makers concerned about women have focused mainly on employment and wages. Bina Agarwal (1994) argues that women's relationship to property can be even more important. In agrarian societies, "the gender gap in the ownership and control of property is the single most critical contributor to the gender gap in economic well-being, social status and empowerment"

(Agarwal, 1994, p. 264). This work has influenced discussions of women's property rights in many countries.

- *Households.* Economists have conventionally treated the household as a unified decision-maker, pooling resources and maximizing "household" well-being. Feminists (e.g., Folbre, 1986; Sen, 1990) strongly criticized the "unitary household" model for obscuring conflicts of interest over tasks and consumption. Moreover, empirical studies often find that it does matter for distribution which household member receives income. Many economists are exploring alternative representations, some of which draw upon game theory (see discussions in Lundberg and Pollak, 1996; Agarwal, 1997; Seiz, 1999; Woolley, 1999).
- *Caring labor.* The work of taking care of others, traditionally provided in the home, is increasingly being performed for pay. Feminist economists have analyzed the distinctiveness and importance of caring labor, and are studying how its supply and quality might change as women's market work continues to rise while men's household work increases very little. "Markets on their own," say Folbre and Nelson (2000, p. 138), "are unlikely to provide the particular volume and quality of 'real' care that society desires for children, the sick and the elderly." To "turn back the clock" by restricting women's labor market opportunities is neither possible nor desirable – so societies must find better ways to address this problem (Folbre, 1995; Himmelweit, 1995).
- *Macroeconomics.* Until recently, gender was almost entirely absent from macroeconomic analyses. Now feminists have investigated how macroeconomic events – including those associated with "globalization" and Structural Adjustment Programs – affect women and gender relations (see Bakker, 1994; Sparr, 1994; Cagatay et al., 1995; Berik, 1999; Beneria et al., 2000). Trade regimes and government budgets have differential effects because women and men do different work: some changes benefit women and others are clearly harmful. New macroeconomic models incorporating unwaged household labor promise to illuminate many policy issues.

28B.5 CONCLUSION

Feminist scholarship has (in my view) already affected economic thought and policy on many issues, including gender divisions of labor, income inequality, structural adjustment, national product measurements, household modeling, and women's property rights. Feminist economics is still evolving, and it may influence mainstream economics in other important ways. Intellectual historians might learn a great deal from following this story: its outcome will affect many lives, and it offers a rich case study of the two-way relationship between economics and the social discourses that surround it.

Bibliography

Agarwal, B. 1994: *A Field of One's Own: Gender and Land Rights in South Asia.* New York: Cambridge University Press.

—— 1997: "Bargaining" and gender relations: within and beyond the household. *Feminist Economics*, 3(1), 1–51.

Albelda, R. 1997: *Economics and Feminism: Disturbances in the Field.* New York: Twayne.

Bakker, I. (ed.) 1994: *The Strategic Silence: Gender and Economic Policy.* London: Zed Books.

—— 1999: Development policies. In Peterson and Lewis, op. cit., pp. 83–95.

Becker, G. 1981: *A Treatise on the Family.* Cambridge, MA: Harvard University Press.

Beneria, L. 1995: Toward a greater integration of gender in economics. *World Development*, 23(11), 1839–50.

——, Floro, M., Grown, C., and MacDonald, M. (eds.) 2000: Special issue on globalization. *Feminist Economics*, 6(3).

Bergmann, B. 1986: *The Economic Emergence of Women.* New York: Basic Books.

—— 1987: The task of a feminist economics: a more equitable future. In C. Farnham (ed.), *The Impact of Feminist Research in the Academy.* Bloomington, IN: Indiana University Press.

—— 1989: Does the market for women's labor need fixing? *Journal of Economic Perspectives*, 3(1), 43–60.

Berik, G. 1999: Globalization. In Peterson and Lewis, op. cit., pp. 402–11.

Blau, F., Ferber, M., and Winkler, A. 2001: *The Economics of Women, Men and Work.* Englewood Cliffs, NJ: Prentice-Hall.

Bodkin, R. 1999: Women's agency in classical economic thought: Adam Smith, Harriet Taylor Mill and J. S. Mill. *Feminist Economics*, 5(1), 45–60.

Boserup, E. 1970: *Women's Role in Economic Development.* New York: St Martin's Press.

Cagatay, N., Elson, D., and Grown, C. (eds.) 1995: Special issue on gender, adjustment, and macroeconomics. *World Development*, 23(11).

Ciancanelli, P. and Berch, B. 1987: Gender and the GNP. In B. Hess and M. Marx Ferree (eds.), *Analyzing Gender: A Handbook of Social Science Research.* Newbury Park, CA: Sage.

Dimand, M. A., Dimand, R., and Forget, E. (eds.) 1995: *Women of Value: Feminist Essays on the History of Women in Economics.* Brookfield, VT: Edward Elgar.

Dimand, R. 1995: The neglect of women's contributions to economics. In M. A. Dimand et al. (1995), op. cit., pp. 1–24.

——, Dimand, M. A., and Forget, E. (eds.) 2000: *Biographical Dictionary of Women Economists.* Brookfield, VT: Edward Elgar.

Elson, D. (ed.) 1995: *Male Bias in the Development Process.* Manchester: Manchester University Press.

—— 1999: Theories of development. In Peterson and Lewis, op. cit., pp. 95–107.

England, P. 1993: The separative self: androcentric bias in neoclassical assumptions. In Ferber and Nelson, op. cit., pp. 37–53.

Ferber, M. and Birnbaum, B. 1977: The "new home economics": retrospect and prospect. *Journal of Consumer Research*, 4(1), 19–28.

—— and Nelson, J. (eds.) 1993: *Beyond Economic Man: Feminist Theory and Economics.* Chicago: The University of Chicago Press.

—— and Teiman, M. 1981: The oldest, the most established, the most quantitative of the social sciences – and the most dominated by men: the impact of feminism on economics. In D. Spender (ed.), *Men's Studies Modified: The Impact of Feminism on the Academic Disciplines.* New York: Pergamon Press.

Folbre, N. 1982: Exploitation comes home: a critique of the Marxian theory of family labor. *Cambridge Journal of Economics*, 6(4), 317–29.

—— 1986: Hearts and spades: paradigms of household economics. *World Development*, 14(2), 245–55.

—— 1994: *Who Pays for the Kids? Gender and the Structures of Constraint*. New York: Routledge.

—— 1995: "Holding hands at midnight": the paradox of caring labor. *Feminist Economics*, 1(1), 73–92.

—— 1998: The "sphere of women" in early-twentieth-century economics. In H. Silverberg (ed.), *Gender and American Social Science, The Formative Years*. Princeton, NJ: Princeton University Press.

—— and Hartmann, H. 1988: The rhetoric of self interest and the ideology of gender. In A. Klamer, D. McCloskey, and R. Solow (eds.), *The Consequences of Economic Rhetoric*. New York: Cambridge University Press.

—— and Nelson, J. 2000: For love or money – or both? *Journal of Economic Perspectives*, 14(4), 123–40.

Forget, E. 1997: The market for virtue: Jean-Baptiste Say on women in the economy and society. *Feminist Economics*, 3(1), 95–111.

Grapard, U. 1999: Methodology. In Peterson and Lewis, op. cit., pp. 544–55.

Groenewegen, P. (ed.) 1994: *Feminism and Political Economy in Victorian England*. Brookfield, VT: Edward Elgar.

Hammond, C. 1999: Women in the economics profession. In Peterson and Lewis, op. cit., pp. 757–64.

Harding, S. 1986: *The Science Question in Feminism*. Ithaca, NY: Cornell University Press.

—— 1995: Can feminist thought make economics more objective? *Feminist Economics*, 1(1), 7–32.

Hartmann, H. 1976: Capitalism, patriarchy and job segregation by sex. *Signs: Journal of Women in Culture and Society*, 1(3 pt 2), 137–70.

—— 1981: The family as the locus of gender, class, and political struggle: the example of housework. *Signs*, 6(3), 366–94.

Hewitson, G. 1999: *Feminist Economics: Interrogating the Masculinity of Rational Economic Man*. Brookfield, VT: Edward Elgar.

Himmelweit, S. 1995: The discovery of "unpaid work": the social consequences of the expansion of "work." *Feminist Economics*, 1(2), 1–20.

—— 1999: Domestic labour. In Peterson and Lewis, op. cit., pp. 126–35.

Jacobsen, J. 1998: *The Economics of Gender*. Cambridge, MA: Blackwell.

Jefferson, T. and King, J. E. 2001: "Never intended to be a theory of everything": domestic labor in neoclassical and Marxian economics. *Feminist Economics*, 7(3), 71–101.

Kahn, S. 1995: Women in the economics profession. *Journal of Economic Perspectives*, 9(4), 193–205.

Kuiper, E. and Sap, J. (eds.) 1995: *Out of the Margin: Feminist Perspectives on Economics*. New York: Routledge.

Lewis, M. 1999: History of economic thought. In Peterson and Lewis, op. cit., pp. 433–43.

Lundberg, S. and Pollak, R. 1996: Bargaining and distribution in marriage. *Journal of Economic Perspectives*, 10(4), 139–58.

Madden, J. 1972: The development of economic thought on the "woman problem." *Review of Radical Political Economics*, 4(3), 21–38.

Mammen, K. and Paxson, C. 2000: Women's work and economic development. *Journal of Economic Perspectives*, 14(4), 141–64.

Mincer, J. and Polachek, S. 1974: Family investments in human capital. *Journal of Political Economy*, 82, S76–108.

Mutari, E. 2001: "As broad as our life experience": visions of feminist political economy, 1972–1991. *Review of Radical Political Economics*, 33(4), 379–99.

Nelson, J. 1995: Feminism and economics. *Journal of Economic Perspectives*, 9(2), 131–48.

—— 1996: *Feminism, Objectivity and Economics*. New York: Routledge.

Olsen, P. and Emami, Z. 2002: *Engendering Economics: Conversations with Women Economists in the United States*. New York: Routledge.

Peterson, J. and Lewis, M. (eds.) 1999: *The Elgar Companion to Feminist Economics*. Northampton, MA: Edward Elgar.

Pujol, M. 1992: *Feminism and Anti-Feminism in Early Economic Thought*. Brookfield, VT: Edward Elgar.

Seiz, J. 1992: Gender and economic research. In N. De Marchi (ed.), *Post-Popperian Methodology of Economics: Recovering Practice*. Boston: Kluwer.

—— 1995: Epistemology and the tasks of feminist economics. *Feminist Economics*, 1(3), 110–18.

—— 1999: Game theory and bargaining models. In Peterson and Lewis, op. cit., pp. 379–90.

Sen, A. 1990: Gender and cooperative conflicts. In I. Tinker (ed.), *Persistent Inequalities: Women and World Development*. New York: Oxford University Press.

Shackelford, J. 1999: International Association for Feminist Economics (IAFFE). In Peterson and Lewis, op. cit., pp. 486–9.

Sparr, P. (ed.) 1994: *Mortgaging Women's Lives: Feminist Critiques of Structural Adjustment*. London: Zed Books.

Strassmann, D. 1993: Not a free market: the rhetoric of disciplinary authority in economics. In Ferber and Nelson, op. cit., pp. 54–68.

—— 1999: Feminist economics. In Peterson and Lewis, op. cit., pp. 360–73.

Vogel, L. 1983: *Marxism and the Oppression of Women*. New Brunswick, NJ: Routledge University Press.

Woolley, F. 1999: Economics of family. In Peterson and Lewis, op. cit., pp. 328–36.

C INSTITUTIONAL ECONOMICS
Geoffrey M. Hodgson

28C.1 INTRODUCTION

The term "institutional economics" refers to the movement inspired initially by the work of Thorstein Veblen (1857–1929) and including leading American economists in the first half of the twentieth century such as John Rogers Commons (1862–1945), Wesley Mitchell (1874–1948), and John Maurice Clark (1884–1963). This movement reached the zenith of its influence in American academia in the 1920s and 1930s.

However, the original tradition of institutional economics survives and shows the signs of a revival today. Its renewal has in part been stimulated by the rise after 1975 of the so-called "new institutional economics" of Oliver Williamson, Richard Posner, Mancur Olson, and others. But the theoretical approach of the "new" institutional economics is closer to postwar mainstream economics and in some respects different from the school of thought examined here.

Section 28C.2 briefly outlines the common, underlying approach of the original tradition of institutional economics. Sections 28C.3 and 28C.4 discuss postwar institutionalism in America and Europe respectively. A number of tendencies and groupings are identified. The final section addresses the evolving agenda of modern institutional economics.

28C.2 WHAT IS THE ENDURING ESSENCE OF INSTITUTIONAL ECONOMICS?

At least one common theme pervades institutionalism, from the writings of Veblen in the 1890s to those of the present day. This is the notion that it is legitimate and important to take individual purposes and preferences as partly molded by circumstances (Hodgson, 2000).

In addition, institutionalism has always emphasized the importance of institutions in economic life. The focus is both on how institutions affect individuals and how institutions themselves change and evolve. Furthermore, American institutionalists in the interwar period were typically oriented toward reformist, redistributive, and interventionist economic measures (Rutherford, 1999). However, policy differences within American institutionalism have been enormous, and no single policy orientation can readily serve as a fundamental definition of institutionalism itself.

The acceptance of an idea of the institutionalized individual does not immediately rule out the possibility that institutionalism and some aspects of neoclassical economics may be complementary. Although Veblen was an exception, other institutionalists searched for some complementarity between neoclassical and institutional economics. This group included Commons, Mitchell, Clark, Paul Douglas, and Arthur F. Burns. Obversely, like the institutionalists, neoclassical economist Alfred Marshall brought changing preferences into his analysis. There is no clear or sharp boundary between institutionalism and Marshallian neoclassical economics, although subsequent versions of neoclassical economics have diverged considerably from institutionalism.

It is important to dispense with the mistaken view that the old institutional economics was atheoretical or against theory. Within institutional economics we can find many theoretical contributions (Rutherford, 1994, 2001). For example, Veblen's theoretical emphasis on the role of knowledge in economic growth is remarkably relevant for economic theory today; Commons was responsible for developing the theoretical interface between economics and law; Mitchell had a theory – and not merely a description – of the business cycle; Clark pioneered work on the interaction between the multiplier and the accelerator, and foreshadowed the concept of bounded rationality; and so on.

If institutional economics involves the acceptance of the malleability of preferences, then it is clear that a number of other schools of thought share these and other "institutionalist" views. For example, the Post Keynesian approach of Joan Robinson, Nicholas Kaldor, and others also sometimes regarded individual preferences as changeable. The same could be said of much Marxian economics, the German historical school, the French *régulation* school, the "evolutionary economics" of Richard Nelson and Sidney Winter (1982), and much else. These approaches all emphasize the importance of institutions, the need to place analyses in a historical context, and so on. However, for the purposes of this essay we shall confine ourselves largely to those approaches generally described as "institutional economics."

Within these confines, we shall discuss two broad postwar groupings within institutional economics, namely America institutionalism and European institutionalism. For reasons of restricted space, in the face of a large number of complex strands and influences, the narrative here must be confined to highly selective highlights and details.

28C.3   AMERICAN INSTITUTIONALISM

Clarence Ayres (1891–1972) was a leading American instutionalist in the postwar period. To understand Ayres's role and contribution, it is necessary to look at the context in which Ayres originally intervened and some aspects of his own thought. The original institutional economics of Veblen was partly founded on ideas from Darwinism, pragmatist philosophy, instinct–habit psychology, and cultural anthropology – from the works of Charles Sanders Peirce, William James, and several others. However, by the 1920s, Darwinism was being eschewed by social scientists, pragmatist philosophy was being challenged by the rise of positivism, and instinct–habit psychology was being displaced by behaviorism (Degler, 1991; Hodgson, 1999). Ayres (1921) rejected instinct–habit psychology. For Ayres, the influence of John Dewey was more important than that of the earlier pragmatists. However, Ayres did not place the same degree of emphasis as Dewey on the explanatory value of psychology. Furthermore, although Ayres endorsed Darwin's concentration on materialist causes and his rejection of religion, Ayres saw Darwin's particular theory, involving "survival of the fittest, natural selection, sexual selection" as obsolete (Ayres, 1932, p. 95).

Ayres's most influential work was his *Theory of Economic Progress* (1944). He argued that the driving force of economic development was technological change, and that institutions were the conservative brake or restraining block on this development. Ayres thus saw institutions as wholly constraining rather than also enabling in their function. Although Ayres claimed to be influenced by Veblen in the formulation of these ideas, in key respects their views were very different. For instance, Veblen saw institutions – even if they were typically conservative in character – as part of the indispensable framework of social life. Furthermore, Veblen's view of the driving role of technological change was much more qualified and circumspect than that of Ayres (Hodgson, 1998b).

In addition, Ayres saw the technological imperative as a solution to the ethical problems of welfare, evaluation, and progress. Partly influenced by Dewey, Ayres developed an "instrumental value theory" in which policy outcomes were judged according to their capacity to enhance technological progress and the provision of human material needs. Ayres not only provided a new welfare criterion based on instrumental rather than utilitarian principles, but also eschewed the need to develop an alternative theory of price and distribution. Technological dynamics, rather than the microeconomic analysis of human behavior, were at the foundation of his analysis.

In several respects, Ayres's ideas were well adapted for the prevailing American intellectual climate from the 1930s to the 1980s. He rejected instinct–habit psychology to endorse the rising behaviorism. He placed less emphasis on the explanation of human agency. He can thus be seen as part of an interwar and postwar movement within both economics and sociology to remove psychology from a position of doctrinal influence over the social sciences. Ayres also distanced his doctrines from Darwinism, thus reinforcing a trend to remove the social sciences from biology. His negative view of institutions as constraints fitted well with the American distrust of rules and authority, while he could also court American liberal opinion by endorsing measures of social reform. Finally, his positive view of technical change dovetailed well with the American culture of technophilia.

Located at the University of Texas from 1930 to 1968, Ayres proved to be hugely influential over a whole generation of American institutionalists. Marc Tool (1994, p. 16) has noted: "Ayres and his students have been among the most significant contributors to the development of institutional economics in the last half-century." Ayres ranks alongside Allan Gruchy (1906–90), Dudley Dillard (1913–91), and John Kenneth Galbraith (b. 1908) as one of the leading American institutionalists of the 1945–70 period.

Gruchy and Dillard were important for several reasons. In particular, they built strong links between institutionalism and the economics of Keynes. Gruchy (1948) emphasized the parallels between some philosophical aspects of Keynesianism and institutionalism, while Dillard (1948) produced a highly influential textbook that synthesized aspects of the Keynesian and institutionalist theory.

Through his extensive writings on modern capitalism, Galbraith (1958, 1969) had an enormous impact on the wider public, but proportionately less on academic economists. Nevertheless, his intellectual influence is highly significant, and he is also responsible for strengthening the links between institutionalism and Keynesianism. The analysis of the modern corporation, and its links with the consumer on one side and with the state and the military on the other, have been central to his analysis.

The Ayresian influence within American institutionalism prevailed alongside others of lesser strength, including a group at the University of Wisconsin, where in particular the ideas of Commons persisted (Bromley, 1994). This group was notable for its contribution to agricultural economics and to the hybrid discipline of economics and law. There were also internal developments within Ayresian institutionalism, particularly those of J. Fagg Foster and his students, who tried from the 1960s to develop the Ayresian approach in a more nuanced and less problematic manner (Tool, 2000).

As the postwar institutionalists progressively lost influence in the American Economic Association and their control of departments of economics in leading US universities, they eventually decided to form an association of their own. The Association for Evolutionary Economics (AFEE) was founded in 1965. Largely because of the Ayresian influence, Ayres's negative view of institutions, and his dislike of the term "institutionalist," the term "evolutionary" was adopted in the title. For the founders of AFEE, this term had broad and loose connotations. It had less to do with the specifically Darwinian ideas emphasized by Veblen.

One of the important events in the development of American institutionalism was the establishment of the *Journal of Economic Issues* by the Association for Evolutionary Economics in 1967. It has been edited successively by Warren Samuels, Marc Tool, Anne Mayhew, and Glen Atkinson.

Quite separately, another "evolutionary economics" emerged in the 1980s, under the leadership of Nelson and Winter (1982), with a more biologically oriented use of the adjective and a greater emphasis on theoretical microfoundations. This led to two separate networks of "evolutionary economists" in the USA, with relatively little interaction between them. Yet the work of Nelson and Winter is in some respects redolent of Veblen (Hodgson, 1993). This similarity has subsequently been acknowledged by these two modern authors (Hodgson, 1999).

28C.4   EUROPEAN INSTITUTIONALISM

In the nineteenth century, the German historical school of Wilhelm Roscher, Gustav Schmoller, Werner Sombart, and others spread its influence beyond Germany to Britain, France, Italy, and other European countries, as well as to America (Hodgson, 2001). However, the institutionalist label was never widely adopted in Europe, and institutionalism itself has always contained a diversity of ideas. For these reasons, the task of identifying institutionalist theory in the Old World can be little more than the identification of declared sympathizers and schools of thought that are similar to American institutionalism.

British economics was overshadowed by Adam Smith in the nineteenth century and by Alfred Marshall in the twentieth. In the postwar period the paramount influence was John Maynard Keynes. All three authors emphasized the role of institutions. Marshall, in particular, repeatedly emphasized the possibility of changing wants and preferences. In part, the towering influences of Smith, Marshall, and Keynes may help to explain why institutional economics never gained an explicit foothold in Britain, until very recently. In theoretical terms their conceptions were close enough to institutionalism to encourage and legitimate its ideas, and their conceptions of political economy or economics were sufficiently broad to admit institutionalism. But even Keynes was unfamiliar with the important works of leading American institutionalists.

It is in continental Europe that we find the three major figures with the closest and most explicit links with American institutionalism, namely K. William Kapp (1910–76, Germany and Switzerland), Gunnar Myrdal (1898–1987, Sweden), and Karl Polanyi (1886–1964, Austria and Hungary).

Kapp (1950) made major contributions to the theory of social cost and the environmental impact of business enterprise, as well to general institutional theory. Myrdal is well known for his additions to monetary theory, as well as his later applications of the theory of cumulative causation to studies of ethnic disadvantage, regional disparity and Third World underdevelopment (Myrdal, 1939, 1944, 1957, 1968). He also contributed to the discussion of the value-laden nature of science. In 1974, Myrdal was awarded the Nobel Prize for his work in economics. Polanyi made highly significant contributions to economic history, economic anthropology, and institutional theory. He argued that the development of the capitalist market system during the Industrial Revolution was not, and could not have been, entirely spontaneous but necessarily involved the legislation, regulation, and intervention of the state (Polanyi, 1944).

However, despite their contributions, none of these figures has left behind a thriving school of disciples with significant influence in the European universities. Strangely, it is outside their home countries that they are most recognized. In the case of Myrdal, for example, his ideas on cumulative causation were taken up most prominently by Nicholas Kaldor at the University of Cambridge in England. Polanyi eventually emigrated to the United States and established an important following there. Kapp spent most of his adult life teaching in the United States and in Switzerland. In sharp contrast to its American counterpart, Ayres's influence on European institutionalism has been negligible. Even Dewey, one of the giants of twentieth-century Western philosophy, is less prominent in the European intellectual scene. In terms of ethics and policy, neither Commons's "reasonable value" nor Ayres's "instrumental value" have as yet become rooted in European soil.

In addition, in the postwar period, many economists in or close to institutionalism in Europe have paid more attention to the development of alternative microfoundations. This is apparent in Polanyi's use of ideas from anthropology to develop basic categories of human interaction, Kapp's dissection of different aspects of social cost, and Myrdal's attention to the impact on individual preferences in the process of circular and cumulative causation. More recently, enduring influences in Europe, such as Alfred Marshall and Joseph Schumpeter, have inspired important institutionalist microdevelopments in the theory of human agency, technological innovation, and the theory of the firm (Dosi et al., 1988; Dosi, 2000).

These differences in emphasis, compared with the old American tradition of institutional economics, were apparent when the European Association for Evolutionary Political Economy and the International Joseph Schumpeter Association were founded in 1988. These associations have served as major forums for institutional and evolutionary economics in recent years.

28C.5   The Evolving Agenda for Modern Institutionalism

A number of developments in the 1990s, in Europe, America, and elsewhere, have created a new agenda for institutional economics and an opportunity for those working in the older institutionalist traditions to contribute to cutting-edge developments. The first point of note is that the study of institutions has become one of the major topics of research throughout the social sciences. The importance of institutions in both economic theory and policy is now widely recognized.

At the same time, however, the competing tradition of "new" institutionalism, despite its achievements, is facing internal problems and difficulties, especially concerning the explanation of the process of emergence and evolution of

institutions (Sened, 1997, pp. 179–80; Williamson, 2000, p. 595). Several important research questions remain to be answered.

A number of works have undermined some central ideas in the "new" institutionalism and paved the way for an "old" institutionalist revival. For example,
Alexander Field (1979) has advanced a fundamental criticism of the "new
institutionalist" idea that the explanation of the evolution of institutions can
start from given individuals in an institution-free "state of nature." Crucially, in
all attempts to explain institutions in this way, some elemental rules or institutions are assumed. Furthermore, human interaction requires rules of cognition
and communication involving language (Hodgson, 1988, 1998a). And language
itself is an institution.

These criticisms have affected some "new" institutional economists. Interestingly, as a result, aspects of the "new" institutionalist research program have
become closer to themes in the "old" institutionalism. For example, Jack Knight
(1992) has criticized much of the new institutionalist literature for neglecting the
importance of distributional and power considerations in the emergence and
development of institutions. Even more clearly, Masahiko Aoki (2001) has accepted
the impossibility of an institution-free world and has developed a novel, game-
theoretic approach. He has not only assumed individuals as given, but also a
historically bestowed set of institutions. With these materials, he has explored the
evolution of further institutions. The next step, which Aoki recognizes but does
not fully complete, is to develop a more evolutionary and open-ended framework
of analysis. We are reminded of Veblen's (1919, p. 37) search for "a theory of the
process of consecutive change, realized to be self-continuing or self-propagating
and to have no final term."

Another literature, from outside the "old" institutionalism, emphasizes the
role of institutional constraints over individual rationality in the understanding
of institutions (Gode and Sunder, 1993). These models suggest that ordered and
sometimes predictable behavior can result largely from institutional constraints.
In placing less emphasis on individual rationality, these models also create a
space for a revival of the "old" institutionalism (Mirowski, 2002).

The emergence of settled patterns of behavior may be either largely independent of the deliberation of the agents, or dependent on the existence of behavior
dominated by habit or inertia. This points to a research agenda focused on the
role of systemic constraints, on the reconstitutive effects of institutions on individuals, and on the degree to which institutional evolution may depend on
the formation of concordant habits. Again, all these themes are found in the
"old" institutionalism.

Remarkably, another recent theoretical development has revived a theme that
was prevalent in the German historical school, concerning the necessary role of
the state in consolidating and legitimating some institutions. Against the idea
that laws and property rights can evolve fully without the state, Itai Sened (1997)
argued that true individual rights are established only when a territorial institution establishes its monopoly over the use of force. Sened criticized the idea of
legal codes as epiphenomena, merely formalizing conventions of behavior that
have evolved out of individual interactions. Sened argued that the state plays

an essential role in maintaining law and order and providing a legal framework for individual actions. His essential point amounts to nothing less than the rehabilitation of a major theme of the German historical school and the "old" institutional economics.

Once it is recognized that human activity can only be understood as emerging in a context with some preexisting institutions, then we are more able to focus on the effects of institutional constraints and "downward causation" upon individuals, as well as to understand how interactions between individuals give rise to new institutional forms. The emergence and stability of some institutions may be enhanced by processes through which institutional channels and constraints lead to the formation of concordant habits of thought and behavior. In considering an open-ended evolution of both institutions and individual preferences, such arguments are again redolent of the "old" institutionalism.

Strikingly, with the decline of the research program that attempted to explain all institutions from individuals in an original, institution-free "state of nature," some of the former boundaries between the "old" and the "new" institutional economics have been eroded. The evolution of institutional economics in the final quarter of the twentieth century has created an exciting new agenda for both the "new" and the "old" institutional economics in the coming years.

Bibliography

Aoki, M. 2001: *Toward a Comparative Institutional Analysis*. Cambridge, MA: The MIT Press.

Ayres, C. E. 1921: Instinct and capacity. I: The instinct of belief-in-instincts. II: Homo Domesticus. *Journal of Philosophy*, 18(21–2), 561–5, 600–6.

—— 1932: *Huxley*. New York: Norton.

—— 1944: *The Theory of Economic Progress*. Chapel Hill, NC: University of North Carolina Press.

Bromley, D. W. 1994: Institutional economics, Wisconsin school of. In G. M. Hodgson, W. J. Samuels, and M. R. Tool (eds.) 1994: *The Elgar Companion to Institutional and Evolutionary Economics*, vol. 1. Aldershot, UK: Edward Elgar, 386–92.

Degler, C. N. 1991: *In Search of Human Nature: The Decline and Revival of Darwinism in American Social Thought*. Oxford and New York: Oxford University Press.

Dillard, D. 1948: *The Economics of John Maynard Keynes: The Theory of a Monetary Economy*. London: Crosby Lockwood.

Dosi, G. 2000: *Innovation, Organization and Industrial Dynamics*. Cheltenham, UK: Edward Elgar.

——, Freeman, C., Nelson, R., Silverberg, G., and Soete, L. L. G. (eds.) 1988: *Technical Change and Economic Theory*. London: Pinter.

Field, A. J. 1979: On the explanation of rules using rational choice models. *Journal of Economic Issues*, 13(1), 49–72.

Galbraith, J. K. 1958: *The Affluent Society*. London: Hamilton.

—— 1969: *The New Industrial State*. Harmondsworth, UK: Penguin.

Gode, D. K. and Sunder, S. 1993: Allocative efficiency of markets with zero-intelligence traders: market as a partial substitute for individual rationality. *Journal of Political Economy*, 101(1), 119–37.

Gruchy, A. G. 1948: The philosophical basis of the new Keynesian economics. *International Journal of Ethics*, 58(4), 235–44.

Hodgson, G. M. 1988: *Economics and Institutions: A Manifesto for a Modern Institutional Economics*. Cambridge, UK: Polity Press/Philadelphia, PA: University of Pennsylvania Press.

—— 1993: *Economics and Evolution: Bringing Life Back Into Economics*. Cambridge, UK: Polity Press/Ann Arbor, MI: University of Michigan Press.

—— 1998a: The approach of institutional economics. *Journal of Economic Literature*, 36(1), 166–92.

—— 1998b: Dichotomizing the dichotomy: Veblen versus Ayres. In S. Fayazmanesh and M. Tool (eds.) 1998: *Institutionalist Method and Value: Essays in Honour of Paul Dale Bush*, vol. 1. Cheltenham, UK: Edward Elgar, 48–73.

—— 1999: *Evolution and Institutions: On Evolutionary Economics and the Evolution of Economics*. Cheltenham, UK: Edward Elgar.

—— 2000: What is the essence of institutional economics? *Journal of Economic Issues*, 34(2), 317–29.

—— 2001: *How Economics Forgot History: The Problem of Historical Specificity in Social Science*. London and New York: Routledge.

Kapp, K. W. 1950: *The Social Costs of Private Enterprise*. Cambridge, MA: Harvard University Press.

Knight, J. 1992: *Institutions and Social Conflict*. Cambridge, UK: Cambridge University Press.

Mirowski, P. 2002: *Machine Dreams: Economics Becomes a Cyborg Science*. Cambridge, UK: Cambridge University Press.

Myrdal, G. 1939: *Monetary Equilibrium*, translated from the Swedish edition of 1931 and the German edition of 1933. London: Hodge.

—— 1944: *An American Dilemma: The Negro Problem and Modern Democracy*. New York: Harper and Row.

—— 1957: *Economic Theory and Underdeveloped Regions*. London: Duckworth.

—— 1968: *Asian Drama: An Inquiry into the Poverty of Nations*. Harmondsworth, UK: Penguin/ New York: Twentieth Century Fund.

Nelson, R. R. and Winter, S. G. 1982: *An Evolutionary Theory of Economic Change*. Cambridge, MA: Harvard University Press.

Polanyi, K. 1944: *The Great Transformation: The Political and Economic Origins of Our Time*. New York: Rinehart.

Rutherford, M. H. 1994: *Institutions in Economics: The Old and the New Institutionalism*. Cambridge, UK: Cambridge University Press.

—— 1999: Institutionalism as "scientific economics." In Backhouse, R. E. and Creedy, J. (eds.) 1999: *From Classical Economics to the Theory of the Firm: Essays in Honour of D. P. O'Brien*. Cheltenham, UK: Edward Elgar, 223–42.

—— 2001: Institutional economics: then and now. *Journal of Economic Perspectives*, 15(3), 173–94.

Sened, I. 1997: *The Political Institution of Private Property*. Cambridge: Cambridge University Press.

Tool, M. R. 1994: Ayres, Clarence E. In G. M. Hodgson, W. J. Samuels, and M. R. Tool (eds.) 1994: *The Elgar Companion to Institutional and Evolutionary Economics*, vol. 1. Aldershot, UK: Edward Elgar, 16–22.

—— 2000: *Value Theory and Economic Progress: The Institutional Economics of J. Fagg Foster*. Boston: Kluwer.

Veblen, T. B. 1919: *The Place of Science in Modern Civilisation and Other Essays*. New York: Huebsch.

Williamson, O. E. 2000: The new institutional economics: taking stock, looking ahead. *Journal of Economic Literature*, 38(3), 595–613.

D POST KEYNESIAN ECONOMICS
Sheila C. Dow

28D.1 Introduction

"Post Keynesian" is a category which was probably first used to refer to a distinctive approach to economics (rather than simply economics after Keynes) by Joan Robinson (1960, p. v) when referring to the work she had done in the 1950s. The range of subject matter in the volume provided an indication of the focus of Post Keynesian economics: the problems of development under capitalism and socialism, the accumulation of capital, imperfect competition, and interest and employment. The term "Post Keynesian," without a hyphen, was promulgated as something more particular than the general "economics since Keynes," for which the term "post-Keynesian" was for a time used.

The history, indeed definition, of a school of thought requires imposing categories on a more complex reality. The categorization of a school of thought both aids the historian in providing an account of a complex literature and plays a substantive part in the development of thought. The following traces the institutional and social arrangements that played an active part in the evolution of Post Keynesian economics.

In a further categorization, the postwar period is divided into three sub-periods. The first, spanning the 1950s and 1960s, saw the contemporaries and students of Keynes, Kalecki, and Sraffa continuing to develop their ideas, both in Cambridge and elsewhere. The next two decades saw, first, the significant spread of these ideas beyond the Cambridge and ex-Cambridge circle and, secondly, the creation of a range of institutional mechanisms that further extended both the influence of and influences on Post Keynesianism. The third period, which continues today from the 1990s, is the outcome of parallel developments in other heterodox schools of thought, and the resulting increased scope for, and interest in, ideas being developed in synthetic form across boundaries. For more detail on the history of Post Keynesian thought, see King (2002); for its treatment in the history of thought, see Ramadan and Samuels (1996); and for the current state of Post Keynesian economic theory, see Arestis (1996) and Holt and Pressman (2001).

28D.2 The Early Days of Post Keynesianism (1950s and 1960s)

Post Keynesian economics grew out of the work of Keynes's Cambridge contemporaries. Their focus was on the principle of effective demand. By the postwar period, much work had already been done by Keynes and his circle in developing the key ideas of *The General Theory* (Keynes, 1936): the income multiplier, the theory of liquidity preference, and the need for demand management to address problems of unemployment equilibrium. The focus next was on extending

Keynes's short-period analysis into the long period, and developing a theory of value and distribution that did not rely on competitive markets.

A key influence in pursuing these questions was another contemporary at Cambridge, Kalecki (1990, 1991). While Kalecki's macroeconomics also stressed effective demand, his earlier Marxian influences encouraged a focus on monopoly capital and distribution. Robinson accordingly developed a theory of cycles and growth that addressed the (unlikely) conditions for steady growth at full employment – the "golden age."

The Cambridge economists presented an explicit alternative to the neoclassical theory of value and distribution. The neoclassical synthesis had absorbed Keynes's macroeconomics into aggregative general equilibrium macroeconomics as a special case (whereas Keynes had presented the neoclassical result of full employment equilibrium as the special case). While demand management was implemented in policy circles, academic macroeconomists were refining a framework that would rule out unemployment equilibrium as anything other than an aberration. Full-employment equilibrium was assured by market forces, unless impeded by the liquidity trap or an imperfectly competitive labor market. Furthermore, economic growth and the distribution of income under competitive conditions were determined by factor supplies and technical conditions.

The early Post Keynesians endeavored to counter these results by demonstrating the weakness of the neoclassical theoretical framework itself, exposing its logical flaws. Sraffa (1960) made a key contribution, demonstrating the circularity of the neoclassical theory of value and distribution, since there was no unit of measurement independent of prices and distribution. Robinson, more concerned to find an independent unit by which to measure capital, also put forward the capital reversal, or reswitching, argument, that factor proportions could change in either direction as relative factor returns changed. The outcome of these critiques was the "capital controversies" between the Post Keynesians of Cambridge, England, and the neoclassicals of Cambridge, MA (Harcourt, 1972).

Robinson (1978) and Kaldor (1972) were quite clear that the critique was much broader than the reswitching issue. They questioned both the meaning of the aggregate "capital" and the meaning of equilibrium and its relation to the real world, or "history." The debate marked out and explicated Post Keynesianism as a distinctive approach to economics. By the end of this period, the community of Post Keynesians was still centered on Cambridge, but the influence of this view of Keynes had spread, both in the UK (in the work of Shackle, for example) and elsewhere, such as Italy, North America, and Australia (notably through Garegnani and Pasinetti, Tarshis and Asikmakopoulos, and Harcourt, respectively). Furthermore, Sidney Weintraub was an influential figure in the early development of Post Keynesianism, who had no direct Cambridge connection.

28D.3 THE SPREAD OF POST KEYNESIANISM (1970s AND 1980s)

Awareness of Post Keynesian arguments in the USA was increasing. A new generation (for example, Davidson, Eichner, Kregel, Nell, and Minsky), some with Marxian as well as Keynesian and Kaleckian influences, created a body of work that challenged the growing neoclassical orthodoxy (see Lee, 2000). A meeting between Robinson and sympathizers was organized at the ASSA meetings in New Orleans in 1971 by Eichner; a growing sense of identity as a school of thought was built up, finding expression in Eichner and Kregel's (1975) paper, and the founding of the *Journal of Post Keynesian Economics* in 1978 by Paul Davidson and Sidney Weintraub. Together with *Australian Economic Papers* (from 1963) and the Cambridge Journal of Economics (from 1977), this new journal communicated Post Keynesian ideas to an international audience. Also important was Eichner's (1979) edited guide, using articles from *Challenge*, in which he summarized the essential features of Post Keynesianism as:

1 The rate of investment as an explanation of growth and distribution.
2 A view of the economy as constantly in motion.
3 The fundamental role in the economic system of financial institutions.
4 Administered pricing in advanced economies.
5 Theory concerned with actual, rather than hypothetical, economic systems.

It is characteristic of this period that theory was highlighted first, and then empirical characteristics of the economy and methodology (nowadays the order would tend to be reversed).

Cambridge continued as the symbolic center of Post Keynesianism, with the presence of Robinson, Kahn, Pasinetti, Kaldor, and Goodwin, and later the leadership exerted by Geoff Harcourt and the editors of the *Cambridge Journal of Economics* and *Contributions to Political Economy*. Other institutional developments widened the range of Post Keynesians' meetings: the Kent Keynes Seminars (1971–91); the Trieste summer school for graduate students (1981–92); the Malvern conferences (1987–96); the UK Post Keynesian Economics Study Group (1988–); and the International Post Keynesian Workshop (held at Knoxville, Tennessee, in 1995–2000, and since then at University of Missouri at Kansas City). Furthermore, other journals were publishing heterodox economics, including Post Keynesian material, such as the *Economic Notes* of the Montei dei Paschi de Siena (1972–), *Thames Papers in Political Economy* (1974–90), *Metroeconomica* (after 1983), the *Review of Political Economy* (1989–) and *International Papers in Political Economy* (1993–).

These developments occurred against a background of growing support for monetarist economic policy, which relegated demand management to the role of inflation control through control of the money supply. Kaldor (1982), along with Balogh and Trevithick, led the sustained Post Keynesian critique of monetarism. Kaldor's argument, that the authorities could not control the money supply (whether or not the money supply actually had a causal role), cut across Keynes's theory of liquidity preference in a way that was not fully addressed until the end of this period.

The fact that Keynesian policies were being blamed for the stagflation of the latter 1970s, however, prompted a reconsideration of what exactly was meant by Keynesianism. Coddington's (1976) classification of Keynesianism served to clarify the distinction between the "hydraulic Keynesianism" which had provided the theoretical basis for demand management up to this time, the "reconstituted reductionists," drawing on the work of Clower, who were leading the drive for a complete general equilibrium system with macroeconomics founded on the principles of rational economic behavior, and the "fundamentalist Keynesians" such as Robinson, who emphasized the uncertainty of knowledge. While Coddington denigrated the last as leading to "nihilism," his article underscored the long-standing interpretation of Keynes that emphasized expectations issues. This challenged the emerging view that rational expectations theory was novel in reinstating expectations on the macroeconomic agenda.

The focus of the US Post Keynesians (notably Davidson) and of Post Keynesians in the UK outside Cambridge (notably Shackle and Chick) was on uncertainty, expectations, and liquidity preference. This represented a return to the short-period concerns of Keynes, but adding subsequent developments on the institutional structure of financial markets. Ramadan and Samuels (1996) draw attention to how this strand of thought departs from the concern with growth and distribution that was central to the first Post Keynesian period. Key publications were Davidson's (1972, 1982) books on domestic and international monetary theory, Minsky's (1975, 1982) accounts of the business cycle, Shackle's work on uncertainty, which dated back to the 1930s (for example, Shackle, 1972), Chick's (1983) systematic study and extension of *The General Theory* and a series of influential articles by Kregel who, like the others, maintained the methodological distinctiveness of Keynes (for example Kregel, 1976). In addition, Moore (1988) developed his theory of money supply endogeneity, drawing on Kaldor's work.

Between 1971 and 1989, the Royal Economic Society published what became a 30-volume collection of Keynes's writings. This provided scholars with a wealth of material on which to base new interpretations of Keynes's ideas, and new case-study material showing applications of his ideas. Furthermore, the first volume of Skidelsky's (1983) biography of Keynes helped scholars to understand the context in which he was writing, as a foundation for more refined interpretation of his economic ideas (as did the subsequent two volumes). But the most profound impact on the school of thought was felt as a result of work based on the reissue of Keynes's (1921) *Treatise on Probability*, the pioneers being the doctoral work of Carabelli (1988) and O'Donnell (1989), and Lawson and Pesaran's (1985) edited volume. This work both enriched the Post Keynesian theory on expectations and allowed for a fuller understanding of Keynes's economic methodology. It became conventional to see Keynes's methodology as following from his philosophy, while his philosophy itself evolved in the light of his economics (Davis, 1994). There was also a shift toward defining Post Keynesianism in terms of its methodology (Dow, 1985, 1990, 1991, 1998).

Not all Post Keynesians identified with this emphasis on issues of knowledge. Indeed, a difference of perspective (Keynesian and classical) was already evident at the Trieste summer schools. Efforts were made to compare the theoretical systems of Keynes and Kalecki (Reynolds, 1987), Keynes and Sraffa (Dutt and Amadeo, 1990), and Keynes and Ricardian economics (Bortis, 1996), and where possible to point the way to synthesis. But these works also brought out incompatibilities. Even within one strand, there could be a range of interpretations (see, for example, Roncaglia's 1991 account of different interpretations of Sraffa). An influential review by Hamouda and Harcourt (1988) implied that Post Keynesianism was inexorably divided (for his most recent views on these matters, see Harcourt, 2001). Post Keynesianism seemed to be struggling, in the face of both the strength of orthodox economics and its own internal incoherence.

28D.4   CONSOLIDATION AND OUTREACH (1990s ONWARD)

During the past decade, Post Keynesian economists addressed a changed intellectual and economic context. Neoclassical macroeconomics, which previously had been reasonably unified around the rationality principle within a general equilibrium framework, become increasingly fragmented. One branch developed around "new Keynesian" economics, and efforts were made by Post Keynesians to see how much scope existed for any synergy with Post Keynesianism (Rotheim, 1998). Furthermore, the confident monetarist stance of macroeconomic policy of the 1980s, aided by large macromodels, give way to an almost Keynesian concern with demand management and a pluralist use of a collection of models (see Bank of England, 1999). Finally, other heterodox schools of thought had been maturing and developing their own institutional structures. A common methodological thread running through much of the heterodoxy was an espousal of pluralism (for an explicit treatment, see Salanti and Screpanti, 1997).

A sense of common cause among heterodox economists led to the formation of informal and formal groupings of different heterodox approaches. Thus the UK Post Keynesian Study Group, for example, attracted a wider range of interests than a focus purely on Keynes, Kalecki, and Sraffa, and Post Keynesians took part in the activities of other organizations, such as the institutionalist organizations (the European Association of Evolutionary Political Economy and the Association for Evolutionary Economics); Arestis (1996) stresses the growing interface with institutionalism. The growing sense of common cause among groups unwilling to accept the monism of orthodox economics also encouraged the formation of umbrella heterodox organizations, such as the International Confederation of Associations for Pluralism in Economics (ICAPE), founded in 1993 as ICARE, the Association of Heterodox Economics (AHE) founded in 1999, and the campaign begun in 2000 by the Post-autistic Economics (PAE) Movement.

This development also spawned a concerted effort to develop further what was understood to be distinctively Post Keynesian. Ramadan and Samuels (1996) could still identify in the 1990s the diversity within Post Keynesianism that had concerned Hamouda and Harcourt (1988). There was a specific exchange on the question of whether or not Post Keynesianism is a coherent school of thought at all (see Chick, 1995; Walters and Young, 1997; Arestis, Dunn, and Sawyer, 1999). The focus was increasingly on Post Keynesianism as a distinctive methodological approach, applied to subject matter and pursuing ideas beyond those found in the original texts of Keynes, Kalecki, and Sraffa. The philosophical foundations and methodology of Post Keynesianism have also been discussed explicitly in terms of critical realism (see the Fall 1999 issue of the *Journal of Post Keynesian*

Economics). Built on the Keynes philosophy literature of the 1980s and early 1990s, a common thread has run from Keynes's philosophy to modern Post Keynesianism. Since this methodological work has increased the focus on uncertainty, which paradoxically plays no part in Sraffian economics, doubts are still expressed as to how far Sraffian economics can be compatible with the rest of Post Keynesian economics. Engagement continues between the different strands within Post Keynesianism.

Reflecting the increased methodological awareness among Post Keynesians, Chick (1995, p. 20) has defined Post Keynesianism as a distinctive mode of thought, encompassing the following elements:

1 to recover the insights of Keynes, Kalecki and their early disciples,
2 to extend those insights beyond the borders set by Keynes's *General Theory* . . . and thus
3 to complete the Keynesian Revolution.

Post Keynesian literature grew inexorably and was addressed to a range of audiences: self-identified Post Keynesians, other heterodox economists, and orthodox economists pushing against the boundaries of orthodox methodology to address policy issues. There has been a consolidation in textbook treatments (Arestis, 1992; De Carvalho, 1992; Lavoie, 1992; Palley, 1996; Lee, 1998; Deprez and Harvey, 1999) and survey articles (such as Cottrell's 1994 survey of Post Keynesian monetary theory, Arestis's 1996 more general survey, and Pasinetti's 2001 survey of growth and distribution theory). Further major developments were Sawyer's (1988) edited collection, King's (1995a,b) book of interviews and bibliography, Harcourt and Riach's (1997) two-volume "second edition" of *The General Theory*, Holt and Pressman's (2001) new guide to Post Keynesian economics, and King's (2002) history of Post Keynesian thought.

As to the content of Post Keynesian economics, the institutional arrangements that have brought heterodox economists together (in person and in the literature) have encouraged efforts, particularly among young scholars, to engage in synthetic developments, putting ideas together in new combinations (as, for example, in Fontana, 2000). Furthermore, while the earlier period had been dominated by study of Keynes's *Collected Writings*, attention has shifted toward new theoretical developments and addressing current policy issues, building on the new understandings of Keynes.

The design and operation of European Monetary Union, for example, has been the focus of policy application of a range of distinctive Post Keynesian theoretical developments. Arestis, McCauley and Sawyer (2001) offer a critique of an institutional structure based on orthodox theory with its separation of real and monetary variables, and argue for an alternative that takes account of:

- the interdependence of the monetary and the real, such that there is scope for more activist fiscal policy to tackle unemployment
- the endogenous nature of money-supply creation and the need for a strong lender-of-last-resort

- the distributional implications of macroeconomic policy and the need for policy tools to promote balanced growth across regions
- the nonmonetary sources of inflation and the need for institutional arrangements to address it.

Similarly, Post Keynesians have addressed such current policy issues as the design of the international financial system; for example, the relative merits of taxing speculative capital flows. Here we see evidence of both the focus of Post Keynesianism on developing theory in such a way as to allow policy issues to be addressed and the awareness, shared with institutionalists, of the importance of institutions.

28D.5   CONCLUSION

We have attempted a very brief account of the postwar evolution of thought loosely categorized as Post Keynesian. We have seen common threads of awareness of methodological distinctiveness from orthodox economics and of substantive-theoretical analysis of effective demand, unemployment, growth and development, and distribution, many emphasizing the role of financial markets, and the uncertainty of knowledge underpinning decision-making and institutions. As it happens, both threads (methodological and substantive-theoretical) correspond to recent concerns within orthodox economics. Indeed, at a time when the relevance to practical issues of the fictional orthodox theoretical scheme is a matter for wider discussion, Post Keynesian economics offers an increasingly well-developed alternative.

Note

The comments and suggestions of Philip Arestis, Victoria Chick, Geoff Harcourt, John King, and the Editors are gratefully acknowledged.

Bibliography

Arestis, P. 1992: *The Post Keynesian Approach to Economics*. Cheltenham, UK: Edward Elgar.

—— 1996: Post-Keynesian economics: towards coherence. *Cambridge Journal of Economics*, 20(1), 111–36.

——, Dunn, S. P., and Sawyer, M. 1999: Post Keynesian economics and its critics. *Journal of Post Keynesian Economics*, 21(4), 527–49.

——, McCauley, K., and Sawyer, M. 2001: An alternative stability pact for the European Union. *Cambridge Journal of Economics*, 25, 113–30.

Bank of England 1999: *Economic Models at the Bank of England*. London: Bank of England.

Bortis, H. 1996: *Institutions, Behaviour and Economic Theory*. Cambridge, UK: Cambridge University Press.

Carabelli, A. 1988: *On Keynes's Method*. London: Macmillan.

De Carvalho, F. J. C. 1996: *Mr Keynes and the Post Keynesians: Principles of Macroeconomics for a Monetary Production Economy*. Aldershot, UK: Edward Elgar.

Chick, V. 1983: *Macroeconomics After Keynes: A Reconsideration of the General Theory.* Deddington, UK: Philip Allan.

—— 1995: Is there a case for Post Keynesian economics? *Scottish Journal of Political Economy*, 42(1), 20–36.

Coddington, A. 1976: Keynesian economics: the search for first principles. *Journal of Economic Literature*, 14(4), 1258–73.

Cottrell, A. 1994: Post Keynesian monetary economics. *Cambridge Journal of Economics*, 18(6), 587–605.

Davidson, P. 1972: *Money and the Real World.* London: Macmillan.

—— 1982: *International Money and the Real World.* London: Macmillan.

Davis, J. B. 1994: *Keynes's Philosophical Development.* Cambridge, UK: Cambridge University Press.

Deprez, J. and Harvey, J. T. (eds.) 1999: *Foundations of International Economics: Post Keynesian Perspectives.* London: Routledge.

Dow, S. C. 1985: *Macroeconomic Thought: A Methodological Approach.* Oxford: Blackwell.

—— 1990: Post Keynesianism as political economy: a methodological discussion. *Review of Political Economy*, 2(3), 345–58.

—— 1991: The Post-Keynesian school. In D. Mair and A. Miller (eds.), *A Modern Guide to Economic Thought.* Cheltenham, UK: Edward Elgar, 176–206.

—— 1998: Post Keynesian methodology. In J. B. Davis, D. W. Hands, and U. Mäki (eds.), *The Handbook of Economic Methodology.* Cheltenham, UK: Edward Elgar, 378–82.

Dutt, A. K. and Amadeo, E. J. 1990: *Keynes's Third Alternative? The Neo-Ricardian Keynesians and the Post Keynesians.* Aldershot, UK: Edward Elgar.

Eichner, A. S. 1979: *A Guide to Post Keynesian Economics.* Armonk, NY: M. E. Sharpe.

—— and Kregel, J. A. 1975: An essay on Post Keynesian theory: a new paradigm in economics. *Journal of Economic Literature*, 13(4), 1293–314.

Fontana, G. 2000: Post Keynesians and circuitists on money and uncertainty: an attempt at generality. *Journal of Post Keynesian Economics*, 23(1), 27–48.

Hamouda, O. F. and Harcourt, G. C. 1988: Post Keynesianism: from criticism to coherence? *Bulletin of Economic Research*, 40(1), 1–33.

Harcourt, G. C. 1972: *Some Cambridge Controversies in the Theory of Capital.* Cambridge, UK: Cambridge University Press.

—— 2001: *50 Years a Keynesian and Other Essays.* London: Palgrave.

—— and Riach, P. (eds.) 1997: *A "Second Edition" of the General Theory*, vols. 1 and 2. London: Routledge.

Holt, R. P. F. and Pressman, S., 2001: *A New Guide to Post Keynesian Economics.* London: Taylor & Francis.

Kaldor, N. 1972: The irrelevance of equilibrium economics. *Economic Journal*, 82, 1237–55.

—— 1982: *The Scourge of Monetarism.* Oxford: Oxford University Press.

Kalecki, M. 1990: *Collected Works*, vol. 1, ed. J. Osiatynski. Oxford: The Clarendon Press.

—— 1991: *Collected Works*, vol. 2, ed. J. Osiatynski. Oxford: The Clarendon Press.

Keynes, J. M. 1921: *A Treatise on Probability.* London: Macmillan.

—— 1936: *The General Theory of Employment, Interest and Money.* London: Macmillan.

King, J. E. 1995a: *Conversations with Post Keynesians.* London: Macmillan.

—— 1995b: *Post Keynesian Economics: An Annotated Bibliography.* Cheltenham, UK: Edward Elgar.

—— 2002: *A History of Post Keynesian Economics 1936–2000.* Cheltenham, UK: Edward Elgar.

Kregel, J. 1976: Economic methodology in the face of uncertainty. *Economic Journal*, 86, 209–25.

Lavoie, M. 1992: *Foundations in Post Keynesian Analysis*. Cheltenham, UK: Edward Elgar.

Lawson, T. and Pesaran, H. (eds.) 1985: *Keynes's Economics: Methodological Issues*. London: Routledge.

Lee, F. S. 1998: *Post Keynesian Price Theory*. Cambridge, UK: Cambridge University Press.

—— 2000: The organizational history of Post Keynesian economics in America, 1971–95. *Journal of Post Keynesian Economics*, 23(1), 141–62.

Minsky, H. P. 1975: *John Maynard Keynes*. New York: Columbia University Press.

—— 1982: *Can "It" Happen Again? Essays on Instability and Finance*. Armonk, NY: M. E. Sharpe. Republished as Inflation, Recession and Economic Policy. Brighton, UK: Wheatsheaf.

Moore, B. J. 1988: *Horizontalists and Verticalists: The Macroeconomics of Credit Money*. Cambridge, UK: Cambridge University Press.

O'Donnell, R. M. 1989: *Keynes: Philosophy, Politics and Economics. The Philosophical Foundations of Keynes's Thought and their Influence on his Economics and Politics*. London: Macmillan.

Palley, T. J. 1996: *Post Keynesian Economics: Debt, Distribution and the Macro Economy*. London: Macmillan.

Pasinetti, L. 2001: Critique of the neoclassical theory of growth and distribution. *Banca Nazionale del Lavoro Quarterly Review*, 53, 383–432.

Ramadan, U. and Samuels, W. J. 1996: The treatment of Post Keynesian economics in the history of economic thought texts. *Journal of Post Keynesian Economics*, 18, 547–65.

Reynolds, P. J. 1987: *Political Economy: A Synthesis of Kaleckian and Post Keynesian Economics*. Brighton, UK: Wheatsheaf.

Robinson, J. 1960: Introduction. In *Collected Economic Papers*, vol. 2. Oxford: Blackwell, v.

—— 1978: History versus equilibrium. Reprinted in *Contributions to Modern Economics*. Oxford: Blackwell, 126–36.

Roncaglia, A. 1991: The Sraffian schools. *Review of Political Economy*, 3, 187–219.

Rotheim, R. J. (ed.) 1998: *New Keynesian Economics/Post Keynesian Alternatives*. London: Routledge.

Salanti, A. and Screpanti, E. (eds.) 1997: *Pluralism in Economics*. Cheltenham, UK: Edward Elgar.

Sawyer, M. (ed.) 1988: *Post-Keynesian Economics*. Cheltenham, UK: Edward Elgar.

Shackle, G. L. S. 1972: *Epistemics and Economics: A Critique of Economic Doctrines*. Cambridge, UK: Cambridge University Press.

Skidelsky, R. 1983: *John Maynard Keynes*, vol. 1: *Hopes Betrayed 1883–1920*. London: Macmillan.

Sraffa, P. 1960: *Production of Commodities by Means of Commodities*. Cambridge, UK: Cambridge University Press.

Walters, B. and Young, D. 1997: On the coherence of Post Keynesian economics. *Scottish Journal of Political Economy*, 44(3), 329–49.

E RADICAL POLITICAL ECONOMY
Bruce Pietrykowski

28E.1 Introduction

The postwar revitalization of the classical political economy of Ricardo and Marx as radical political economics developed an interdisciplinary approach to the economy, polity, and society. It offered an alternative to the neoclassical portrayal of the capitalist system. In so doing it often crossed into sociology, philosophy, and psychology. While modern radical political economics therefore is diverse, a historical portrait can be articulated. This depiction necessarily will be partial and focus on how radical political economics attends to issues of power and conflict. Not all radical economic theory is neo-Marxist in approach, but Marx's influence is the dominant force, as witnessed by the emergence of postwar Western Marxist economic (Howard and King, 1992) and social (Anderson, 1984) theory in Britain, North America, and Europe.

28E.2   Postwar Intellectual Roots

The self-defined radical political economy developed in distinct phases, driven by the institutional culture of the economics profession and the social and economic forces shaping capitalism. In the aftermath of World War II and the onset of Cold War anti-communism, there was precious little terrain upon which to establish a radical vision in the United States (Sweezy and Magdoff, 1988). With the exception of the journal *Monthly Review*, first published in 1942, and Steindl's *Maturity and Stagnation in American Capitalism* (1952), there was little in the way of contemporary radical economic analysis of capitalism. In contrast to neoclassical theory, radicals examined American corporations in terms of deliberative planning activities, imperfect competition, and monopoly power; and, following Marx, constructed a discourse opposed to neoclassical economic theory along two dimensions. The first consisted of a critique of neoclassical concepts and methods; and the second was a substantively different conceptual apparatus by which to understand the nature of capitalism. In Steindl's work, the dichotomies between plan and market, equilibrium and disequilibrium, are uprooted. Rather than viewing equilibrium as a tendency toward which economic agents move, radical political economists understand the market system as inherently destabilizing. The system is represented as a shifting set of competing and contradictory impulses, motivations, and constraints. This focus on conflict, tension, contradiction, and resolution that temporarily resolves an economic crisis while simultaneously sowing the seeds for future contradiction and tension is a hallmark of the radicals' approach to understanding advanced capitalism.

   The influence of Keynes and Kalecki appears in radical explanations of economic crisis and the tendency of advanced capitalist countries to systematically generate insufficient levels of aggregate demand. The postwar consolidation of US economic power and the establishment of managerial structures conducive to the growth of corporate profitability were identified as key institutional features of modern capitalism. Marketing, advertising, and increased government expenditures were necessary to facilitate purchases and regenerate the circuit of capital. Yet, in spite of these inducements, the productive capacity of the system has an inherent tendency to outrun demand (Baran and Sweezy, 1966). Sweezy, trained as a neoclassical economist at Harvard and LSE in the 1920s and 1930s, and an early postwar proponent of Marxism, reflected that "Marxian economics was not a very well-developed set of documents and ideas . . . I don't think that most of the Keynesian ideas are in any way incompatible with the basic Marxian ideas, but the Marxian ideas didn't carry a convincing usable theory of what was happening in the 1930s" (Colander and Landreth, 1996, pp. 78–9). This early postwar foray into radical political economy read Marx through a Keynesian lens.

28E.3   THE EMERGENCE OF THE NEW LEFT IN ECONOMICS

The birth and maturation of a self-consciously "radical" alternative to neoclassical economic theory can be traced to the social movements of the 1960s and 1970s. Civil rights, women's liberation, and Third World revolution, most notably in Vietnam, radicalized a generation of economists (Hymer and Roosevelt, 1972). Vietnam-era protests called attention to the poverty, inequality, and violence generated in the name of national interest and corporate profit. Students for a Democratic Society (SDS) arose to address these concerns. SDS included graduate economics students at such schools as the University of Michigan (Bluestone, 1979). At Harvard, Berkeley, MIT, and Columbia, students became radicalized by the events of the 1960s and sought to construct a critique of neoclassical theory (Arestis and Sawyer, 1992; Reich, 1995). They came to believe that neoclassical economics was incapable of adequately explaining contemporary social and economic life. Many took the next step and argued that the neoclassical framework sustains and helps to reproduce systems of power and oppression by legitimating the status quo and justifying an unequal distribution of the world's economic resources.

This critique was not initially motivated by a return to Marx. Nor was there a cadre of radical faculty from whom one could learn about Marx. These students were neoclassically trained; very few considered themselves Marxist (Bluestone, 1979). Through a process of investigation, critique, and dialogue many began to look to Marx and to those advancing a Western Marxist perspective critical of both US-style capitalism and Soviet authoritarian state socialism for a foundation upon which to build an alternative vision of economics (Gintis, 1982). In Britain the social movements of the 1960s expanded the space for dialogue between Leftist academics and activists. *New Left Review* and the *Bulletin of the Conference of Socialist Economists*, the latter founded in 1970 and later re-titled *Capital and Class*, proffered political commentary, theoretical debate, and policy critique. The intellectual history of radical political economics is inextricably tied to both the New Left political and social movements of the 1960s and 1970s, and the rejection of neoclassical method and analysis.

In December 1968, the Union for Radical Political Economics (URPE) held its first national conference in Philadelphia, in opposition to the American Economics Association (AEA) meeting in Chicago. Many economists felt that meeting in Chicago would be an endorsement of that city's violent police reaction to the anti-war protests held at the Democratic National Convention the previous summer. In response, a special AEA Executive Committee meeting, chaired by AEA President Kenneth Boulding, concluded that moving the meeting location would run counter to AEA policy of political neutrality (American Economic Association, 1969, p. 571). This appeal to neutrality was in marked contrast to the political advocacy of URPE.

Topics at the 1968 URPE conference included poverty, urban crisis and race relations, corporate/government power and the erosion of democratic rights, economic imperialism, and the political role of economists in society. Participants were deeply conscious of the need to critically assess the neoclassical paradigm. For example, Zweig (1968) argued that marginalist analysis was inherently biased against large-scale social change. The neoclassical claim to scientific objectivity also came under attack. The URPE prospectus declared, "modern economics deceives itself when it insists it is value-free. The values are there, perhaps hidden behind statements about objectivity and neutrality in economics. And these values conveniently find the status quo quite satisfying, or at least satisficing. Our quarrel is with both the nature of these values and the failure of economists to admit they are operating on certain value premises" (URPE Secretariat, 1968, p. 173). An illustration of how political analysis was woven into economic practice is Weeks' response to Zweig, published as the lead article of the first issue of the *Review of Radical Political Economics*. For Weeks, political ideology and not marginalist method is to blame for the reactionary nature of mainstream economics. This tension between political interests and scientific method repeatedly resurfaces in debates surrounding the development of the radical research program.

The attempt to reconstruct political economy as an alternative to neoclassical economics occurred at a time when the explanatory power of macroeconomics was coming under attack. In addition to the war in Vietnam, two of the most intractable domestic problems facing policy-makers were stagflation and urban poverty. The New Left movement directed economists back to Marx's works. They sought to simultaneously construct a contemporary economic analysis with Marxian-inspired concepts and methods and employ it to explain the problems inherent in contemporary capitalism.

Several Marxian concepts were incorporated into the radical perspective: the identification of class as the primary unit of analysis; the definition of profit in terms of economic surplus or surplus value; exploitation of labor as an active process of extracting labor from the commodity labor power; class power as a dominant economic ordering mechanism; and profits as determined by technical change, class struggle, and the institutional structure of society. The ensuing research program was broad, and marked by an exceptional variety of approaches, with wide variation in the degree to which radical political economists used Marxian categories to produce their analysis.

Some radical economists sought to rigorously define Marxian concepts to measure and explain profit trends and business cycles. They attempted to remedy some problematic features of Marx, notably the transformation problem whereby labor values are transformed into prices of production and market prices (Shaikh, 1977; Foley, 1982). The ability to connect market outcomes to the creative act of laboring in such a way that variations in labor time that are socially necessary to produce a good or service are a true reflection of market values was a critical endeavor for these Marxian economists. Measures of profit could then be adduced and used in the empirical estimation of profit; this work generated vigorous debates over the validity of Marx's theory of the tendency toward a falling rate of profit (Okishio, 1961; Shaikh, 1978; Weisskopf, 1979).

Another stream of radical political economics developed from a critique of neoclassical microeconomic theory. Influenced by sociological and psychological theories of socialization and social interaction, these economists looked to how institutions shaped individual preferences, group affiliation, and economic outcomes. Two institutions selected for analysis were schools and factories.

When students were challenging the underlying values of capitalist society, neoclassical economists were increasingly drawn to human capital explanations of education and income determination. In contrast, Bowles and Gintis (1976) argued that schools helped to socialize individuals into their class positions. The type of school attended determined the character traits conducive to the reproduction of one's class status. Rather than portraying schooling as the outcome of exogenous tastes and preferences, education was seen an adjunct to the capitalist production system in the sense that schools "produced" workers and shaped and/or reinforced individuals' willingness to accept patterns of inequality and power (Gintis, 1972).

Apropos of the factory system, radical political economists elaborated upon Marx's distinction between labor and labor power. Instead of analyzing labor as an interchangeable factor of production, they identified labor's unique role in production. This does not require adherence to a labor theory of value (Gintis and Bowles, 1981); rather, it rests on the analytic distinction between labor and labor power. Labor power is the object of the contract between capital and labor; it specifies a general capacity to perform laboring activity. Labor represents the concrete effort involved in transforming objects into useful products or services. The extraction of labor from labor power is inherently conflictual and contingent, since the objectives of workers and capitalists are different. This framework is a central feature of modern radical political economy.

Initial applications of this approach consisted of historical studies of the labor extraction process. Firms adopted scientific management to detach conception from execution (Braverman, 1974, p. 114) and corporations utilized bureaucratic rules and incentives to instill obedience and loyalty (Edwards, 1979). As workers became increasingly alienated and powerless, managers, in turn, became essential. Although later criticized for underemphasizing worker resistance, this account of the rise of managerial systems of control was widely influential. Together with Ollman's (1971) study of alienation, Hymer's (1970) notion that multinational corporations spatially separate the locus of production from administration, and Burawoy's (1979) exploration of the ways in which workers create meaning for themselves while performing alienating work, "labor process" studies helped to create space for Marxist analysis. They established the legitimacy of the radical approach in the social sciences; the task remained to demonstrate both that capitalism was predicated on the creation and reconstitution of institutions of power, oppression, and control and that the system was profitable yet inefficient. The subversive goal of the radicals was to call into question the identification of profit-maximizing behavior with efficiency (Gordon, 1976), propelling radical political economists toward engagement with neoclassical theory.

A number of 1970s studies suggested that managerial control was one of many potentially efficient production techniques. Marglin (1974), for example, saw technological change determined by how technology complemented systems of managerial power. The factory predated the introduction of new technology, not vice versa. Bosses were necessary to ensure the distribution of income to the owner in the form of profit.

28E.4 Power, Difference, and Deconstruction in Radical Political Economics

The decade of the 1980s was characterized by: (1) an institutionalist Marxist account of historical change through a "social structure of accumulation" (SSA) model; and (2) a microeconomic analysis of the inefficiency of capitalist production.

An SSA is a long period during which the social, economic, and political institutions supportive of capitalist accumulation are: (a) explored; (b) established and successfully reproduced; and (c) threatened by internal contradictions within the institutional structure, calling forth a period of decay and exploration (Gordon, Edwards, and Reich, 1982). The model traces its intellectual lineage to Marx, Keynes, and the American institutionalists. Aglietta (1979) advanced a similar framework in his account of the establishment of a "Fordist" regime of accumulation. First published in French in 1976, *A Theory of Capitalist Regulation* identified the ensemble of institutional mechanisms governing production and consumption necessary to regulate the US system of capital accumulation. Whereas the SSA approach was grounded in an attempt to ascertain key characteristics necessary for long waves of economic growth, the regulation school theorists provide an account of the ways in which national/regional politics and history combine to establish particular growth regimes (Boyer, 1990).

The SSA approach sought to explain the evolution of systems of labor control. In the postwar regime of "labor market segmentation" workers are allocated to positions in the labor market based in part on racial and gender identity. Capitalists use race and gender to segment the labor market and reduce the likelihood that workers will organize across segments (Reich, 1980). Proponents of the SSA approach attended – albeit incompletely (Albelda and Tilly, 1994) – to the way in which gender and race were used by employers to reproduce power and privilege.

The postwar SSA was described in terms of class relations (capital–labor accord), capitalist global expansion (Pax Americana), social movements (capital–citizen accord), and inter-capitalist competition. The analysis now included institutional factors not hitherto incorporated into formal radical models of economic change. Nevertheless, as a descriptive historical account it lacked the discursive legitimacy that mainstream economics afforded econometric models. In 1983 Bowles, Gordon, and Weisskopf advanced a social econometric model of aggregate productivity growth to explain the US productivity decline. Publication of their research in the *Brookings Papers* secured an audience of policymakers. One particularly novel feature of this work rested on the empirical measurement of class conflict and its effect on productivity. The "cost of job loss" established a monetary measure of the imbalance of power between capital and labor. Productivity decline was correlated with decreases in the cost of job loss and the intensity of supervision in the workplace. By entering the productivity debate, radicals adopted the methods of mainstream economics: empirical measurement, model specification, and explanatory power of regression results. Echoing Weeks' 1969 position, Bowles, Gordon, and Weisskopf claim, "the mainstream economists' inability to solve the productivity puzzle reflects a failure of vision, not of technique" (1990, p. 98). Throughout the 1980s and 1990s, these radical political economists sought to enter into a dialogue with mainstream economists.

At the microeconomic level, radicals argued that the institutional structure of production not only generates outputs but also reproduces worker dispositions toward work. Shirking is therefore a rational response to alienated labor (Bowles and Gintis, 1993). If an alternative organizational structure exists that workers perceive as more just and less alienating, it may be possible to elicit the same level of work effort with fewer supervisory resources, thereby improving technical efficiency (Bowles, 1985). In addition, the cost of job loss explained why labor would be systemically underutilized inasmuch as a full-employment economy would undermine the threat of job loss (Bowles and Boyer, 1988). This analysis provided a microeconomic basis for earlier radical critiques of macropolicy. The microanalytic discourse of radical political economy complemented the research of economists and political scientists utilizing neoclassical general equilibrium and game theory to develop "analytical Marxism" (Roemer, 1986).

If the development of a microfoundations for radical political economics signaled a partial *rapprochement* with neoclassical economics, the 1980s also witnessed a reorientation of Marxian social and economic theory. It emerged in attempts to interpret Marx as a social economist intent on embedding analyses of the economy in society, culture, and anthropology (Heilbroner, 1985). It also appeared in efforts to locate the logic of capitalism in relation to a reciprocal logic of self-definition and social recognition, thereby affording market-based need satisfaction a status irreducible to the material forces of production (Levine, 1988). The result of these forays was to destabilize the dominant narrative of class conflict and technical change in the sphere of production – a theme elaborated upon by "anti-essentialist" Marxism (Resnick and Wolff, 1987).

Influenced by the twentieth-century Marxist philosopher Louis Althusser and represented in the journal *Rethinking Marxism*, first published in 1988, anti-essentialist Marxists oppose empiricism and rationalism as the proper basis for a Marxian epistemology. They maintain that culture, politics, and society over-determine economic processes which, in turn, help to shape culture, polity, and social life. They proceed to deconstruct Marxian concepts, notably class. Eschewing a binary class framework, they examine processes of surplus production and distribution to both reveal a multiplicity of class positions and economic relationships and illustrate the complexity and fragility of the capitalist economy and the possibility for noncapitalist forms of community and economic life. By recasting Marx as a postmodern theorist of disjuncture, uncertainty, and instability, they question the inevitability of capitalist economic crisis inscribed in modern, rationalist, scientific Marxism (Amariglio and Ruccio, 1994).

28E.5 CONCLUSION

By the 1990s, a wide variety of perspectives aligned with the Marxian legacy. URPE's *Review of Radical Political Economics* remained a leading publication outlet. In addition, graduate departments of economics at the University of Massachusetts-Amherst, the New School for Social Research, the University of Utah, the University of California at Riverside, the University of Notre Dame, and the American University each employed a core of radical political economists on their faculty.

The convergence of radical economics with both neoclassical and Keynesian economics was but one of the major trends. The classical Marxian perspective – represented through analyses of the tendency for the rate of profit to fall, labor theory of value, and capitalist crisis theory – continues to engage many scholars. Feminist and Marxist–feminist accounts of the gender division of labor and the economic impact of household work added greatly to the scope and rigor of radical political economic analysis (Albelda, 1997). With the feminist critique of the reductionism of traditional Marxism, a postmodern critique of essentialism led to a critical reassessment of economics method and practice (Amariglio, Resnick, and Wolff, 1990). Taken together, these contesting visions of radical economics continue to define the field.

Bibliography

Aglietta, M. 1979: *A Theory of Capitalist Regulation*. London: Verso.

Albelda, R. 1997: *Economics and Feminism*. New York: Twayne.

—— and Tilly, C. 1994: Towards a broader vision: race, gender, and labor market segmentation. In D. M. Kotz, T. McDonough, and M. Reich (eds.), *Social Structures of Accumulation*. New York: Cambridge University Press, 212–30.

Amariglio, J. and Ruccio, D. F. 1994: Postmodernism, Marxism, and the critique of modern economic thought. *Rethinking Marxism*, 7(3), 7–35.

——, Resnick, S., and Wolff, R. 1990: Division and difference in the "discipline" of economics. *Critical Inquiry*, 17, 108–37.

American Economic Association 1969: Annual Business Meeting, December 29, 1968. *American Economic Review*, 59(2), 571.

Anderson, P. 1984: *In the Tracks of Historical Materialism*. Chicago: The University of Chicago Press.

Arestis, P. and Sawyer, M. 1992: *A Biographical Dictionary of Dissenting Economists*. Brookfield, VT: Edward Elgar.

Baran, P. A. and Sweezy, P. M. 1966: *Monopoly Capital*. New York: Monthly Review Press.

Bluestone, B. 1979: Oral history, Department of Economics, University of Michigan-Ann Arbor. Bentley Historical Library. Accession #Bimu C26 2, Box 5.

Bowles, S. 1985: The production process in a competitive economy. *American Economic Review*, 75(1), 16–36.

—— and Boyer, R. 1988: Labor discipline and aggregate demand. *American Economic Review*, 78(2), 395–400.

—— and Gintis, H. 1976: *Schooling in Capitalist America*. New York: Basic Books.

—— and —— 1993: The revenge of Homo Economicus. *Journal of Economic Perspectives*, 7(1), 83–102.

——, Gordon, D. M., and Weisskopf, T. E. 1983: Hearts and minds: a social model of US productivity growth. *Brookings Papers on Economic Activity*, 2, 381–441.

——, ——, and —— 1990: *After the Wasteland: A Democratic Economics for the Year 2000*. Armonk, NY: M.E. Sharpe.

Boyer, R. 1990: *The Regulation School: A Critical Introduction*. New York: Columbia University Press.

Braverman, H. 1974: *Labor and Monopoly*. New York: Monthly Review Press.

Burawoy, M. 1979: *Manufacturing Consent*. Chicago: The University of Chicago Press.

Colander, D. C. and Landreth, H. 1996: Paul Malor Sweezy. In *The Coming of Keynesianism to America*. Brookfield, VT: Edward Elgar, 73–84.

Edwards, R. 1979: *Contested Terrain*. New York: Basic Books.

Foley, D. K. 1982: The value of money, the value of labor, and the Marxian transformation problem. *Review of Radical Political Economics*, 14(2), 37–47.

Gintis, H. 1972: Consumer behavior and the concept of sovereignty. *American Economic Review*, 62(2), 267–78.

—— 1982: The reemergence of Marxian economics in America. In B. Ollman and E. Vernoff (eds.), *The Left Academy*. New York: McGraw-Hill, 53–81.

—— and Bowles, S. 1981: Structure and practice in the labor theory of value. *Review of Radical Political Economics*, 12(4), 1–26.

Gordon, D. M. 1976: Capitalist efficiency and socialist efficiency. *Monthly Review*, 24 (July–August), 19–39.

——, Edwards, R., and Reich, M. 1982: *Segmented Work, Divided Workers*. Cambridge, UK: Cambridge University Press.

Heilbroner, R. L. 1985: *The Nature and Logic of Capitalism*. New York: Norton.

Howard, M. C. and King, J. E. 1992: *A History of Marxian Economics; Volume II, 1929–1990*. Princeton: Princeton University Press.

Hymer, S. 1970: The efficiency (contradictions) of multinational corporations. *American Economic Review*, 60(2), 441–8.

—— and Roosevelt, F. 1972: Comment – symposium on the political economy of the New Left. *Quarterly Journal of Economics*, 86(4), 644–57.

Levine, D. P. 1988: *Needs, Rights, and the Market*. Boulder, CO: Lynne Rienner.

Marglin, S. A. 1974: What do bosses do? *Review of Radical Political Economics*, 6(2), 60–112.

Okishio, N. 1961: Technical change and the rate of profit. *Kobe University Economic Review*, 85–99.

Ollman, B. 1971: *Alienation*. Cambridge, UK: Cambridge University Press.

Reich, M. 1980: *Racial Inequality and Class Conflict*. Princeton, NJ: Princeton University Press.

—— 1995: Radical economics: successes and failures. In F. Moseley (ed.), *Heterodox Economic Theories: True or False?* Aldershot, UK: Edward Elgar, 45–70.

Resnick, S. A. and Wolff, R. D. 1987: *Knowledge and Class*. Chicago: The University of Chicago Press.

Roemer, J. 1986: *Analytical Marxism*. Cambridge, UK: Cambridge University Press.

Shaikh, A. 1977: Marx's theory of value and the "transformation problem." In J. Schwartz (ed.), *The Subtle Anatomy of Capitalism*. Santa Monica, CA: Goodyear, 106–39.

—— 1978: Political economy and capitalism. *Cambridge Journal of Economics*, 2(2), 233–51.

Steindl, J. 1952: *Maturity and Stagnation in American Capitalism*. Oxford: Blackwell.

Sweezy, P. and Magdoff, H. 1988: Marxism in America. *Rethinking Marxism*, 1(1), 87–207.

URPE Secretariat 1968: The Union for Radical Political Economics: a prospectus. In *The Conference Papers of the Union for Radical Political Economics*. Ann Arbor, MI: URPE, 173–4.

Weeks, J. 1969: Political economy and the politics of economists. *Review of Radical Political Economics*, 1(1), 1–10.

Weisskopf, T. E. 1979: Marxian crisis theory and the rate of profit in the postwar U.S. economy. *Cambridge Journal of Economics*, 3(3), 341–78.

Zweig, M. 1968: New Left critique of economics. In *The Conference Papers of the Union for Radical Political Economics*. Ann Arbor, MI: URPE, 46–54.

PART II

Historiography

CHAPTER TWENTY-NINE

Historiography

Matthias Klaes

29.1   INTRODUCTION

The term "historiography," literally "the writing of history," carries two distinct meanings. On the one hand, it refers to historical accounts of the past, in contrast to the past itself. On the other hand, the term is used in a meta-theoretical sense as the reflection on how historians account for the past. Historiography in this second sense has two aspects. It may refer either to the particular historical methods employed by the historian, or to a broader reflection on the methodology underlying her historical research. According to the broader interpretation, historiography is to the practice of the history of economics what the methodology of economics is to the practice of economics. An additional complexity arises because both history and methodology of economics are meta-discourses (cf., Emmett, 1997) in respect to the discipline of economics, which increasingly draw upon one another. For the remainder of this contribution, the term "historiography" will be used to refer to the methodology, as opposed to the methods, of historical research. Finally, the relevance of historiography as a meta-theoretical reflection on the methodology of historical research in economics is of course not restricted to disciplinary history of economics but is equally relevant to economic history as the history of the economy, although this dimension will not be further explored here.

Among the various ways in which one could discuss historiographic issues in the history of economics, two seem to suggest themselves in particular. One could provide a comparative overview of different historiographies that are currently employed or hotly debated in the history of economics. Alternatively, one could embark on a historical account of the development of the various approaches. The first perspective is much better served by the present volume as a whole than by any single work of survey. The second, further discussed below, suffers the handicap that so far at least, it refers to largely uncharted territory. This chapter therefore follows a different strategy, approaching historiographic reflection in the history of economics in the context of selected wider debates in general history, philosophy, and the history of science. The ambition is not to aspire to comprehensive coverage of these debates, but to eclectically concentrate instead on a selection of themes that resonate with important recent historiographic developments in the history of economics. In what follows, the reader should also be warned that for the most part, historiography is discussed on the basis of the Anglo-American literature, notwithstanding the rich and longstanding historiographic traditions of continental Europe, for example.

29.2 Historiography as Meta-Discourse of Historical Research

Historiographic reflection in the history of economics can proceed in several directions. What is it that distinguishes history of economics from the history of science, for example, or from general history, cultural and social history, intellectual history, the philosophy and methodology of economics, economic history, and, finally, economics itself? Related, although not strictly of a historiographic nature, are attempts to justify the pursuit of the history of economics, especially *vis-à-vis* the economics profession at large. On a more particular level, one may ask how the history of economics *could* be pursued, *should* be pursued, or *is* being pursued. Of this triad, the first inquiry typically takes the form of trying to identify dimensions by which histories of economics could differ from each other in principle. Historiographic debate has approached this question on the basis of various binary oppositions, such as relativist versus absolutist history, historical versus rational reconstruction, presentism versus contextualism, internal versus external, thick versus thin, or social versus conceptual history (cf., Backhouse, 1994, pp. 1–9).

Once potential differences in historical approach are identified, it is only a short step to engage in normative appraisal of these differences. Historiography turns thus into a project of establishing how the history of economics should be pursued. Answers to this question tend to depend on one's particular position regarding the nature of the history of economics, and on one's underlying philosophical view on economics (Weintraub, 1999). A particular offshoot of this normative reflection has been the issue of "Whiggism" in the history of economics: the focus on the progressive perfection of economics as a disciplinary body of knowledge. Most contributions to this debate have dismissed Whig history of economics, but as a genre it continues to be alive and well in the field.

Finally, historiography may engage in positive reflection upon the history of economics. The question would no longer be how history of economics could or should be practiced, but how it actually is being practiced. With few exceptions (e.g., Popescu, 1964; and more recently Backhouse, 2001) this approach to historiography has not been pursued at any notable scale in the history of economics, in contrast, for example, to the situation in general history (White, 1973). In many respects, positive historiography follows from the suspicion that many historians and sociologists of science have developed toward traditional normative methodology. The equivalent argument within economics has been most forcefully put forward by the "rhetoric of economics" literature (McCloskey, 1985, 1990; Klamer, 1988). In reflection of these post-foundationalist developments both in the philosophy of science and the methodology of economics, and in contrast to the normative strands of the historiography of economics, positive historiography looks at the writings of historians who are trying to identify empirically how the ongoing enterprise of history of economics has developed and changed over time.

29.3   HISTORIOGRAPHY IN GENERAL HISTORY

In general history, introductions to historiography frequently start with a reference to the Prussian historian Leopold von Ranke (for a commendable short introduction to general historiography, see Arnold, 2000). Used as an exemplar, Ranke is typically described as the "father of modern historiography" (in this context, see Smith, 1995) for his insistence that the task of the historian should be the strict presentation of facts to establish "what actually happened," based on close study of historical sources and abstaining from sweeping attempts to judge the past (Ranke, 1874 [1824], pp. v–viii; and abused, see Repgen, 1982). This appeal to historical evidence and the historical method, reacting to German idealism, was meant to place history on a scientific footing and distinguish it from a more liberal attitude toward historical detail by Enlightenment thinkers such as Voltaire.

Fidelity to its sources is still regarded as the virtue *sine qua non* of professional historical scholarship. In that respect at least, Ranke's program of objective history has survived to this day. Whether a continuous detailed unearthing of historical facts will accumulate to historical truth is a more controversial issue. Once a distinction between the past and the account of it in historical scholarship is acknowledged, a one-to-one mapping between the two must become problematic. All that is ever accessible to the historian are the records of the past, not the past itself. Arguably, due to the complexity of the available source material, historians are likely to find more than one plausible way to reconstruct the past from its archives. Moreover, it is debatable whether the compilation of a chronicle, as a mere compilation of historical facts, exhausts the objective of historical scholarship. To the extent that the historian is supposed to provide a richer account of the past, be it in terms of historical context, interpretation of periods of transition, or historical explanation, she has to decide on the relative significance of particular events of the past. Let us refer to this one-to-many relationship between the corpus of historical sources and the historian's rendering of the past as the "historiographic hiatus."

Rankean historiography has had an important impact on the history of economics through Butterfield's (1965 [1931]) attack on the "Whig interpretation" of history. The term "Whig" originated as a term of abuse against political opponents, in particular in the context of seventeenth-century English reform movements, where it was applied to supporters of the Calvinist tendencies in the Anglican Church. Butterfield, in drawing from the traditional usage, employed "Whig" as a disparaging term against a nineteenth-century historiographic tradition – epitomized by the historical work of the Whig politician Thomas Babington Macaulay – which described English constitutional history as the progressive perfection of liberal parliamentary democracy. In a similar way, "Whiggism" in the history of economics is typically used to discredit accounts that are informed by a commitment to rational or scientific progress in the development of economic theory, and exhibit a tendency to evaluate past theories in the light of present-day knowledge. As charges of Whiggism in the history of economics are in danger of replacing serious debate with ambiguous knock-down arguments, it is worth bearing in mind from which side of the historiographic debate these charges were initially made.

According to Butterfield (1965 [1931], p. v), the Whig interpretation of history consists of "the tendency in many historians to write on the side of Protestants and Whigs, to praise revolutions provided they have been successful, to emphasise certain principles of progress in the past and to produce a story which is the ratification if not the glorification of the present." The crucial ingredient of Whig history is its subordination of the past to the present. As the archetypical example, Butterfield refers to the Whig historian's quest for origins as a naive search of the past for analogies to the present. Proper historical research, according to Butterfield, should proceed in the descriptive tradition of Ranke. The unfolding of historical events is too complex to be amenable to macroscopic explanations or generalizations. Instead of reading the present into the past, the historian should make the past her present. Accusations of Whig history have thus a certain reactionary connotation, in spite of their use in the history of economics to bolster "new" historiographic approaches.

With the advent of the linguistic turn in historiography and the emergence of a "new history" in the 1970s and 1980s, general history is marked by a more general opposition between a traditional paradigm on the one hand, and a diversity of new approaches on the other (Kozicki, 1993; Burke, 2001). This opposition has provoked a number of traditionally minded historians to paint dark pictures of intellectual crisis (e.g., Evans, 1997). What is at issue can again be approached via the historiographic hiatus. What constitutes a historical source needs to be historicized in the first place (Jenkins, 1995, pp. 16–25). Put differently, the notion of "source" is not innocent but a historically constructed entity itself.

Traditional history had been concerned with politics, largely based on official documents located in archives. This traditional constraint can be relaxed twofold. On the one hand, the question regarding what is central to the historical account may be answered differently, opening up the whole breadth of different topics currently found in social and cultural history, such as the history of madness (Foucault, 1961; Hacking, 1995), the climate (Grove, 2001), truth (Shapin, 1994), or the body (Porter, 2001). On the other hand, and related to the opening up of the historical field of investigation, what counts as a legitimate source for historical inquiry may be interpreted more broadly, extending beyond official documents to include other types of evidence such as literary sources or oral evidence (cf., Burke, 2001). Given that what counts as respectable historical subject matter and valid source material is subject to historical contingency itself, the more general point which follows from the observation of such broadening of historical research is that the historian's account turns out to be inextricably bound to her own historical locus, being thus subject to the same processes of social negotiation that she is studying herself with reference to the past. It is important to realize that this aspect of the historical hiatus precedes any hermeneutic issues involved in accessing the past.

The reaction to the traditional paradigm of descriptive historical research can furthermore be divided into two different branches, depending on how historians have approached the tension stemming from the historiographic hiatus. Historians associated with the French *Annales* school for example, one of the most important challengers of traditional history, emphasized long-term structural change over myopic event history (e.g., Braudel, 1949; cf., Burke, 1990). The goal of the historian turns into the quest of the underlying reasons for a particular development. Depending on the status given to the explanations obtained in this way, one may thus arrive at a historical project distinct from Rankean history, but nevertheless with a claim to scientific objectivity.

Objective history may also be regarded as unattainable in principle. This undercurrent in the new approaches to history has led to unsettled calls of a looming intellectual crisis. Traditional historiography shows awareness of the limitations inherent to uncovering historical facts in a comprehensive and unbiased way. Nevertheless, striving for an incremental uncovering of the truth about events of the past remains the guiding ideal. In contrast to this, the literary branch of the reaction to historical objectivity, for example, maintains that historical writing is subject to an inescapable fictional component. Similar to the rhetoric-of-economics literature, this branch has emphasized the narrative aspects of historical research, and in particular the role of figures of speech, such as analogies and metaphors (White, 1973; cf., Megill and McCloskey, 1987). This second branch is typically regarded as the "postmodern" successor to the modernist projects of both the *Annales* school and Rankean historiography (cf., Jenkins, 1995).

Postmodern historiography has provoked sharp reactions (Monas, 1993). Literary approaches to historiography are often accused of promoting an "anything goes" approach to the past, in which historians, and ultimately society, replace the reconstruction of the past with its invention. Although few historians with postmodern sympathies are committed to an anti-realist position regarding events of the past, these charges of idealist history have received renewed attention in the context of "holocaust denial" (Shermer and Grobman, 2000). If history has a fictional component that is essential to it, and not merely accidental, then the tension between traditional history and some of the more recent approaches appears indeed to reduce to a binary opposition between idealist and realist commitments to the past, quite in the same way as it is found in recent disputes in the philosophy and sociology of science (cf., Bloor, 1996). But, similar to the realist sociologist of scientific knowledge (Bloor, 1999), or Mäki's (1988) realist position in the methodology of economics, historians may accept inescapable fictionality in their accounts of the past without having to give up a realist commitment to the past.

It is interesting to note at this point that the most overtly idealist approach in general history, intellectual history or the history of ideas, has little to do with the "new" histories of recent years. With the advent of the descriptive approach to history advocated by Ranke and his followers, the history of ideas developed as a pursuit distinct from general history, continuing the more broadly oriented and speculative elements found in the historical writings of the Enlightenment scholars from whom Ranke tried to break away. In the history of ideas, concepts are regarded as the "immutable mobiles" (cf., Latour, 1987, p. 227) of historical analysis.

Take, for example, Lovejoy's (1960 [1936]) classic study of the history of the idea of the "great chain of being," which starts with Plato and ends with Friedrich E. D. Schleiermacher and eighteenth-century German romanticism. As a stable entity, the idea is traced through time and space in its journey from one author to the next. Residing in the collective mental realm, it catches the attention of the historian only once it has manifested itself in particular expressions or concepts. These vary across contexts, literatures, and epochs. The historian is thus bound to tie the heterogeneous appearance of concepts in her corpus together into a coherent whole. The only criterion that she can apply is a prior understanding of the idea the history of which she wants to trace. Thus, her historiographic approach may closely resemble the Whig interpretation of history that Butterfield had so vehemently criticized (see, however, Samuels, 1974).

From the perspective of the history of economics, intellectual history provides a crucial link to the more general historiographic debate. The 1960s act as a watershed in this regard. This period saw the emergence of new approaches to history, some of whose proponents fiercely attacked the history of ideas (e.g., Foucault, 1969). In addition, several historians of political thought, notably Skinner (1969), called for a rethinking of how their discipline approached intellectual history. Many historians of economics studied their subject from a perspective of traditional conceptual history. Closely related to the history of ideas, this historiography concentrates on locating precursors of currently relevant concepts and theories. The more general discussions around intellectual history were thus of direct relevance. So were the contemporary events in the history of science, where Kuhn's (1970 [1962]) analysis of the role of paradigm shifts created sufficient upheaval to itself induce a paradigm shift. For more detailed appreciation of historiography in the history of science, in particular regarding the cross-connection to intellectual history and the history of ideas, the reader is referred to Kragh (1987).

The first issue of *History of Political Economy* reflected these currents of the 1960s. The founding editors, conscious of their responsibility in shaping the self-understanding of the emerging subdiscipline, were adamant that the journal should not just be dedicated to "history of economic thought" (Goodwin, Spengler, and Smith, 1969, p. 1): "We wish to count among our contributors not only those devoted to unravelling the intricacies of the development of economic analysis but also scholars who explore the relations of theory and analysis to policy, to other disciplines, and to social history in general."

This spirit was most clearly expressed in the lead article of the first issue. Coats (1969, p. 12) criticized his colleagues in the history of economics for their insufficient commitment to the past, and their predominant interest in the "succession of particular theorems, theories or individuals." Kuhn's influence was openly acknowledged, and Coats tried to convince his readers that "[f]or the present generation of scholars the most fruitful research topics are the relationship of economic thought to policy and the sociology of economics." (Coats, 1969, p. 14). The consolidation of the field around the new journal went thus hand in hand with an acknowledgment of and dissatisfaction with the different way of pursuing the history of economics which went before.

29.4   THE SYSTEMATIC RELEVANCE OF DISCIPLINARY HISTORY

While the promotion of new approaches to the history of economics formed an important impetus to the 1970s emergence of the history of economics subdiscipline in the Anglo-American realm, the underlying motivation was a growing loss of interest in the field by economic practitioners. More than four decades ago, Paul Samuelson (1954, p. 380) noted with contempt that it was those economists who were not sufficiently competent to follow the mathematical revolution of postwar economics who were seeking shelter in the history of economic thought. A little later, Donald Winch (1962) wrote a well-known essay expressing the worry that the history of economics was becoming as irrelevant for the discipline of economics as the history of physics for the practicing physicist. For Boulding (1971), it was of little surprise that postwar economics, with its aspirations to copy the style and success of the natural sciences, had turned away from the study of the "wrong opinions of dead men."

According to a common perception, the history of economics formed an essential part of economics in the 1930s and before (cf., Samuelson, 1987, pp. 181–2). The decline of the disciplinary standing of the history of economic thought, while an interesting phenomenon in its own right, points to the underlying question of the relationship between a given discipline and its history. On the one hand, one can cite the case of the natural sciences. The history of science has become an independent academic discipline and is largely housed outside the science faculties. There is little controversy over the question of whether an aspiring young physicist should read Newton's *Principia*, for example. The consensus is that she is better advised to invest her intellectual energies in more contemporary pursuits, leaving Newton to the historians, although even this very clear division of labor has not provided for a trouble-free relationship between scientists and historians of science (cf., Reingold, 1981). In philosophy, on the other hand, no student will escape detailed study of the classical authors.

It is interesting to note, though, that the relationship between philosophy and its history is as controversial as in the case of economics. Gracia (1992) has provided a comprehensive analysis of this debate. His classification of the different reasons for doing history is applicable beyond the realm of philosophy and will serve as the framework for the present discussion. Gracia points out that by asking for a justification of the history of philosophy one implicitly acknowledges that philosophy and history of philosophy are compatible in principle. He distinguishes this position from incompatibilism and historicism.

Incompatibilists deny any relation between philosophy and its history. Philosophy is concerned with the truth-value of propositions, while its history is concerned with the beliefs of past philosophers, independent of their truth-value. According to this view, the past is an obstacle to clarity. Philosophy should not be concerned with the errors of the past, but should always start from scratch. Historicists, on the other hand, deny a cut between the present and the past. Philosophy is concerned with the continuous rearticulation of a view about ourselves and the world. In order to get over the presumptions of the model in which one operates, it is necessary to uncover its origins. In its extreme form, this position holds that philosophy is inextricably trapped in its history. To do philosophy means to study past philosophers.

Applying Gracia's further discussion to economics, it will be granted for a moment that economics and its history are neither incompatible nor identical pursuits. This makes it possible to ask for the value of the history of economics from the perspective of a practicing economist. According to what Gracia calls the "negative" view, the history of economics does not offer more to economics than does the history of physics to physics. It is of little value for economic research because it stultifies creativity, encourages antiquarianism, and takes up precious time – which is already too short for keeping up with the rapid developments of the present, and, if one is lucky, with some relevant aspects of economic history. The history of economics is thus only of interest to historians of economics, and possibly to historians of science and related fields of general history. This view is exemplified in economics by Hahn (1992, p. 165): "What the dead had to say, when of value, has long since been absorbed, and when we need to say it again we can generally say it much better."

The "affirmative" view, on the other hand, defends the value of history for practicing economists. Gracia distinguishes among three different strategies of justification. The rhetorical justification sees history as a source of inspiration, support, and respectability (cf., Landreth and Colander, 1994, p. 16). Past economists can serve as role models for the current generation or may teach us humility. Moreover, "by standing on the shoulders of giants we can appear to be very tall indeed" (Gracia, 1992, p. 142; cf., Schumpeter, 1994 [1954], p. 4). According to the second strategy, which Gracia calls the "pragmatic" justification, history provides case studies of good and bad reasoning from which we can learn, or which we can utilize to teach the subject to students (cf., Screpanti and Zamagni, 1993, p. v). Furthermore, those who do not know the past are condemned to repeat it (cf., Blaug, 1985, pp. vii, 711). Finally, history may play a liberating role in making us aware of our presuppositions (Roll, 1992, p. 2). It may even offer a therapy in the face of a sick and confused present (Gracia, 1992, p. 148), which may partly explain the strong interest in history of economics among heterodox schools.

Gracia's third strategy of justification provides theoretical reasons for the beneficial nature of history. A systematic study of the past may give us important clues for the understanding of present trends and future developments in economics, which may influence our personal research strategy. Investigations of this kind could perceivably be pursued within the new economics of science if applied to economics itself (cf., Sent, 1999). Furthermore, there are positions that justify the history of economics independently from its systematic relevance. Apart from references to human curiosity, there is the example of Schumpeter (1994 [1954], p. 5) who suggests that the study of disciplinary history reveals the working of the human mind. Backhouse (1985, p. 2; 1995, pp. 44–5) defends the view that history can and should be used to evaluate and appraise the economics of both the present and the past.

Returning to Gracia's initial distinction between incompatibilism, compatibilism, and historicism, there is one way to argue in favor of the history of economics which constitutes an important variation of the last of those three positions. According to the historicist position, present thinking is inextricably bound to its past. In other words, the only way to philosophize would be to engage in the history of philosophy. Similarly, the only way to do economics would be to engage in history of economics. While no historian of economics would want to subscribe to such a radical formulation, historicism in the historiography of economics may be defended in a qualified sense. The historicist points out that even the present that we study is already part of the past. In the history of economics, Boulding (1971, p. 227) has reversed this position by introducing the "principle of the extended present." The disciplinary present is defined as that interval during which a given debate is not yet closed. To the extent that the historian of economics works within this interval, she actually engages in the current discussion. This amounts to the following "weak" version of the historicist position. While studying the past is not the only way, it nevertheless represents one way to do economics, at least in the confines of the extended present.

One precondition for contributing to an ongoing economic debate is, however, that the work of the historian exhibit a "conceptual" dimension (cf., Klaes, 2001). A second prerequisite relates to the type of history being pursued. A social history of the discipline of economics that pays little or no attention to economic content is an unlikely candidate for contributing directly to a debate. This is not to deny, though, any indirect influences that such an account may eventually have on the self-understanding of the profession. On the other hand, there are examples like Sraffa, whose close reading of the works of Ricardo led him to formulate a new interpretation of his theory of value and distribution that inspired a neo-Ricardian tradition in modern economics.

29.5 (RE)CONSTRUCTING HISTORICAL RECONSTRUCTION

As indicated in the introduction, historiographic reflection on how to approach the history of economics has frequently resorted to mobilizing a number of binary oppositions. Probably the most prominent one has been the absolutism–relativism dichotomy: "The relativist regards every single theory put forward in the past as a more or less faithful reflection of contemporary conditions [. . .]; the absolutist has eyes only for the strictly intellectual development of the subject, regarded as a steady progression from error to truth" (Blaug, 1985, p. 2; cf., Skinner, 1969). An absolutist approach to the history of economics will result in the writing of history from the perspective of a set of economic insights and theories that are accepted as valid standards of judgments for the insights and theories encountered in the historical interval considered. These standards may be drawn from "state-of-the-art" economics, in which case the resulting history is likely to read as Whig history. A relativist approach, on the other hand, strives to assume an agnostic stance toward the validity of past theories.

Within historiographic discussions in economics, there has been an unfortunate tendency to run debates about the absolutism–relativism distinction together with the general issue of adequate exegesis of historical source material, and thus with aspects of the historiographic hiatus discussed above. The historian of economics, the argument goes, is bound to read the past from the present because her ultimate frame of reference for understanding the past must be her own temporal location in the present. Interestingly this argument, intended to support the absolutist position, unwittingly acknowledges the relativist proposal of a hiatus between sources and historical account. By rejecting the idea of an "objective" reading of a given source, the temporal location of the historian becomes decisive for the unlocking of the past.

For economists and historians of economics, this should not come as a surprise. Long and arduous debates on the "correct" interpretation of the work of prominent economists abound. But to read past texts from the perspective of a given theory – as required by an absolutist historiography – is not quite the same as the requirement imposed on us by the inescapable hermeneutical circle of approaching any given text on the basis of only a provisional level of understanding. In his influential article, Skinner (1969) has called the tendency of absolutist historiography to retrieve from sources of the past instances of the putative application of present-day concepts the "mythology of doctrine." In the history of economics, the mythology of doctrine has been forcefully exposed by Tribe's (1978) study of the sharp discontinuities of interpretation between, for example, the economic concept of "labor" in the seventeenth and twentieth centuries, which puts into question absolutist historicizing in its attempts to construct an *a priori* continuity of understanding between the present and the past. Properly considered, this continuity should be regarded as a hypothesis that must stand up to historical scrutiny itself, lest the absolutist reconstruction of the past risks turning into an ahistorical construction.

A further confusion easily results from uncritically running together Whig history with absolutist historiography. While Whiggism presupposes absolutism, an absolutist stance as such contains no commitment to a history of progress. By relaxing Whiggism to teleological historicizing one may, for example, engage in a project inverse to Whig history by describing historical developments in terms of progressive decline, but still judged from an absolutist perspective. Heterodox histories of economics occasionally come near this temptation of telling the emergence of modern economics from the perspective of a past Golden Age.

To complicate matters, many historians, following Blaug (1990; cf., Rorty, 1984), have begun to replace the absolutist–relativist terminology with that of rational versus historical reconstruction. Historical reconstruction should interpret past theories such that their original authors would recognize and accept them

(Skinner, 1969, p. 28), while rational reconstruction should ideally be able to convince them that – and where – they went wrong. This acknowledges the fundamental hermeneutical circularity of historical exegesis in that any reading is caught in acts of "reconstruction" of something bygone and needs to be aware of its own horizon of interpretation.

As a result of what has become known as the Popper–Kuhn debate (for its general reception in the history and methodology of economics, see Blaug, 1992; Caldwell, 1994), these terms have acquired a distinct and rather more specific meaning in the history and philosophy of science. For Popper (1959), science comprises a rational pursuit for knowledge that, while fallible, merits trust because it consists of conjectures that have so far withstood our attempts to refute them. In contrast, Kuhn (1970 [1962]) celebrated the path-dependent cultural enterprise of normal science, where refutations of the scope envisaged by Popper play only a marginal role. Kuhn's account has stirred trouble. Allegedly, it depicts science as an irrational undertaking based on the dangerous doctrine of relativism. As a response, Lakatos (1970, 1971) expanded Popper's framework into a historiography aimed at reconciling the rich material forthcoming from historical case studies, with the portrayal of science as a rational pursuit.

At the same time, the Popper–Kuhn debate also served as inspiration for a new (i.e., post-Mertonian) sociology of scientific knowledge, based on a productive reception of Kuhn's account of normal science (cf., Bloor, 1976; Barnes, 1982), which has been attracting increasing attention in the history and methodology of economics (Mirowski, 1989, 1994; Weintraub, 1991; Mäki, 1992; Hands, 1997). The Mertonian program was premised on a distinction between a disinterested search for truth on the one hand, and the influence of social factors external to this rational process on the other hand. While Merton emphasized that these external factors had some role to play in steering the general direction of scientific development, he regarded the short-term problem-solving activity internal to science as largely autonomous (Merton, 1938, p. 75). The task of the historian of science was thus to follow the internal development of science, while the sociologist of science should study the influence of external factors (cf., Shapin, 1992).

Lakatos's rational reconstruction can be regarded as a particular interpretation of the rationalist commitment underlying both Mertonian "internal" history and Blaug–Rorty rational reconstruction. It is precisely Lakatos's aim to make the criteria explicit by which the historian decides how to reconstruct past science. Rational reconstruction rests on a particular philosophy of rational progress in science: the historian adopting such an approach "will omit everything that is irrational in the light of his rationality theory" (Lakatos, 1971, p. 106). If the historian happens to implement Lakatos's methodology of scientific research programs, she will thus concentrate on the development of the hard core of these programs.

Conversely, it would thus seem that the sociology of science and its domain of external factors correspond to Lakatos and Blaug–Rorty historical reconstruction. The crucial distinction between the Lakatosian interpretation of historical reconstruction and Mertonian externalism, first noted by Kuhn (1971), was that, in the framework of Lakatos, external factors, by definition, distort the rational scientific quest for truth. Historical reconstruction has in fact turned into the residual category of rational reconstruction. The task of historical reconstruction is to recount "how actual history 'misbehaved' in the light of its rational reconstruction" (Lakatos, 1971, p. 107). The historical reconstruction of "actual history" is thus unintelligible without reference to the rational reconstruction of the latter, in the same way as footnotes – an analogy very aptly chosen by Lakatos – relate to the main body of a text.

It is here that the move from the absolutism–relativism distinction to rational versus historical reconstruction becomes problematic. Rational reconstruction as inherited from the absolutist approach is committed to an underlying continuity in the history of economics, stretching backward from the present. Lakatosian rational reconstruction proposes a particular interpretation of that continuity. However, Lakatosian historical reconstruction is discontinuous to the relativist reading of the past. Its scope is restricted to account for error and irrationality, and thus it is clearly in conflict with Skinner's criterion for Blaug–Rorty historical reconstruction, as an account intelligible and acceptable to the author of the past. Only with the hindsight of rational reconstruction should this author be able to recognize her errors: "We need to think that, in philosophy as in science, the mighty dead look down from heaven at our recent successes, and are happy to find that their mistakes have been corrected" (Rorty, 1984, p. 51).

Historical reconstruction in the Lakatosian sense is thus something quite different from historical reconstruction as inherited from the absolutist–relativist distinction. It is not at all relativist, but depends on an absolutist reading of the past. Take away the main text, and the collection of footnotes becomes unintelligible. Lakatos has in fact turned the sociology of scientific knowledge into a sociology of scientific error (Bloor, 1976, p. 12). It has been the legacy of the new sociology of science (Barnes et al., 1996) to reverse this conclusion, by reading Kuhn as demonstrating the inherently social nature of the internal processes hitherto ascribed to the operation of disinterested scientific rationality. As a result, the internalism–externalism divide of Mertonian sociology of science dissolves (Barnes and Shapin, 1979, p. 9; Shapin, 1992), as does the foundation for Lakatosian rational reconstruction. Instead of being a sociology only of error, historical reconstruction would turn into a relativist account of both error and truth.

29.6   CONCLUSION

Where does this leave the opposition of rational versus historical reconstruction and thus of absolutism and relativism in the history of economics? Even if one accepts Lakatosian rational reconstruction as a convincing conceptualization of the broader usage of "rational reconstruction," the two contrasting interpretations of "historical reconstruction" that we have identified, in terms of a sociology of scientific error on the one hand, and a sociology of scientific knowledge on the other, strongly suggest that a more consistent terminology is advisable. While "absolutism" may, with the just-mentioned proviso, translate into Lakatosian "rational reconstruction," "relativism" fails to translate into the Lakatosian pendant of "historical reconstruction." Given the relatively infrequent invocation of Lakatosian historical reconstruction, the onus should be on those who are discussing it to flag their narrow interpretation of the term, so that Blaug–Rorty historical reconstruction, in the sense of contextualism, and with possible relativist implications, may reign. We could then generally speak of the reconstruction of past economics, with the terms "historical" and "rational" indicating which horizon of understanding we have tried to approach. Depending on the dimensions of the relevant "extended present" and our conceptual focus or its absence, we might on that basis aim to directly contribute to economics or to appraise it, and in that respect we would quite happily endure possible charges of Whiggism.

Incidentally, Butterfield (1949) himself displayed surprisingly Whiggish tendencies when writing on the history of science, as opposed to general history. This only reinforces the suspicion that the more pressing historiographic question is whether or not to embrace a relativist position, similar to the debates surrounding the historiography of the "new" approaches in general history. And similar to the sense of crisis provoked there, the "science wars" that followed the Sokal affair have polarized current discourse (cf., Anon., 1997). Again, at stake is what counts for real, there in terms of our access to the past, here in terms of our access to the present and future. At the bottom of the Popper–Kuhn debate lurks the same challenge, of confronting the idealist dimension that is present in any relativist account of knowledge. As in general history, some versions of relativism in the history of science are compatible with a fundamentally realist commitment. Unfortunately, in the heat of what is frequently an emotionally highly charged debate, the finer points and distinctions risk getting lost.

Compared to these debates in general history and the history of science, historiographic discussion in the history of economics has been encouragingly heterogeneous and peaceful. Real differences exist (cf., Klaes, 2001), and occasionally do come to light in public debate – see, for example, the Birken (1988, 1994)–Lipkis (1993) exchange, or the online discussion in reaction to Henderson (1996). On the other hand, defenders of the rationalist cause in the history of economics have, at least so far, displayed an attitude of open-mindedness that is deplorably lacking in the more viciously fought controversies in general history and the field of science studies. There are, however, some indications of a growing and worrying rift between prominent economists and the historians studying them and their work, which can largely be attributed to conflicting views on historiography.

Be this as it may, one important corollary follows from Weintraub (1999). Due to their underlying philosophical commitments, historiographic choices are never innocent. Even if they do not force their proponents ultimately to one side or the other of the Popper–Kuhn debate, or one of its more recent or ancient incarnations, the upshot is that the historiographies that we adopt as individual historians of economics, while certainly there for us to study and self-critically investigate, are less the result of a disinterested matching of means from the pluralist historiographic toolbox to our research ends than we might like to admit.

Note

Thanks to Roger Backhouse, Mark Blaug, Tony Brewer, Annette Fräger, Martin Kusch, Heino Heinrich Nau, and the three Editors for crucial feedback on draft versions of this chapter.

Bibliography

Anon. 1997: Science wars and the need for respect and rigour. *Nature*, 385(6615), 373.

Arnold, J. H. 2000: *History. A Very Short Introduction*. Oxford: Oxford University Press.

Backhouse, R. 1985: *A History of Modern Economic Analysis*. Oxford: Blackwell.

—— 1994: *Economists and the Economy*. New Brunswick, NJ: Transaction.

—— 1995: *Interpreting Macroeconomics*. London: Routledge.

—— 2001: History of economics, economics and economic history in Britain, 1824–2000. Mimeo.

Barnes, B. 1982: *T. S. Kuhn and Social Science*. London: Macmillan.

—— and Shapin, S. 1979: *Natural Order*. Beverly Hills, CA: Sage.

——, Bloor, D., and Henry, J. 1996: *Scientific Knowledge. A Sociological Analysis*. London: Athlone.

Birken, L. 1988: From macroeconomics to microeconomics: the marginalist revolution in sociocultural perspective. *History of Political Economy*, 20, 251–64.

—— 1994: Intellectual history and the history of economic thought: a reply to J. M. Lipkis. *History of Political Economy*, 26, 501–8.

Blaug, M. 1985: *Economic Theory in Retrospect*. Cambridge: Cambridge University Press.

—— 1990: On the historiography of economics. *Journal of the History of Economic Thought*, 12, 27–37.

—— 1992: *The Methodology of Economics*. Cambridge: Cambridge University Press.

Bloor, D. 1976: *Knowledge and Social Imagery*. Chicago: The University of Chicago Press.

—— 1996: Idealism and the Sociology of Knowledge. *Social Studies of Science*, 26, 839–56.

—— 1999: Anti-Latour. *Studies in the History and Philosophy of Science*, 30, 81–112.

Boulding, K. 1971: After Samuelson, who needs Adam Smith? *History of Political Economy*, 3, 225–37.

Braudel, F. 1949: *Méditerranée et le monde méditerranéen à l'époque de Philippe II*. Paris: Colin.

Burke, P. 1990: *The French Historical Revolution: The Annales School, 1929–1989*. Cambridge, UK: Polity Press.

—— (ed.) 2001: *New Perspectives on Historical Writing*, 2nd edn. Cambridge, UK: Polity Press.

Butterfield, H. 1965 [1931]: *The Whig Interpretation of History*. New York: Norton.

—— 1949: *The Origins of Modern Science, 1300–1800*. London: Bell.

Caldwell, B. 1994: *Beyond Positivism*. London: George Allen & Unwin.

Coats, A. W. 1969: Research priorities in the history of economics. *History of Political Economy*, 1, 9–18.

Emmett, R. 1997: Reflections on "breaking away": economics as science and the history of economics as history of science. In W. J. Samuels and J. Biddle (eds.), *Research in the History of Economic Thought and Methodology*. Greenwich, CT: JAI Press, 15.

Evans, R. J. 1997: *In Defence of History*. London: Granta.

Foucault, M. 1961: *Folie et déraison. Histoire de la folie à l'âge classique*. Paris: Plon.

—— 1969: *L'Archéologie du savoir*. Paris: Gallimard.

Goodwin, C. D. W., Spengler, J. J., and Smith, R. S. 1969: Avant-propos. *History of Political Economy*, 1, 1–4.

Gracia, J. 1992: *Philosophy and its History*. Albany, NY: State University of New York Press.

Grove, R. H. 2001: Environmental history. In Burke (2001), op. cit., pp. 261–82.

Hacking, I. 1995: *Rewriting the Soul*. Princeton, NJ: Princeton University Press.

Hahn, F. H. 1992: Autobiographical notes with reflections. In M. Szenberg (ed.), *Eminent Economists*. Cambridge, UK: Cambridge University Press.

Hands, D. W. 1997: Conjectures and reputations: the sociology of scientific knowledge and the history of economic thought. *History of Political Economy*, 29, 695–739.

Henderson, J. P. 1996: Whig history of economics is dead – now what? *History of Economics Society Discussion List Archive*. <eh.net/HE/hes_list/>.

Jenkins, K. 1995: *On "What is History."* London: Routledge.

Klaes, M. 2001: *Begriffsgeschichte*: between the Scylla of conceptual and the Charybdis of institutional history of economics. *Journal of the History of Economic Thought*, 23, 153–79.

Klamer, A. 1988: Economics as discourse. In N. De Marchi (ed.), *The Popperian Legacy in Economics*. Cambridge, UK: Cambridge University Press, 259–76.

Kozicki, H. (ed.) 1993: *Developments in Modern Historiography*. Basingstoke: Macmillan. Reprinted in 1998 by The Open University and Palgrave.

Kragh, H. 1987: *An Introduction to the Historiography of Science*. Cambridge, UK: Cambridge University Press.

Kuhn, T. 1970 [1962]: *The Structure of Scientific Revolutions*, 2nd edn. Chicago: The University of Chicago Press.

—— 1971: Notes on Lakatos. In R. C. Buck and R. S. Cohen (eds.), *Boston Studies in the Philosophy of Science*, vol. 8. Dordrecht: Reidel, 137–46.

Lakatos, I. 1970: Falsification and the methodology of scientific research programmes. In J. Worrall and G. Currie (eds.), *The Methodology of Scientific Research Programmes*, vol. 1. Cambridge: Cambridge University Press, 8–101.

—— 1971: History of science and its rational reconstructions. In R. C. Buck and R. S. Cohen (eds.), *Boston Studies in the Philosophy of Science*, vol. 8. Dordrecht: Reidel, 91–136.

Landreth, H. and Colander, D. C. 1994: *History of Economic Thought*. Boston: Houghton Mifflin.

Latour, B. 1987: *Science in Action*. Cambridge, MA: Harvard University Press.

Lipkis, J. 1993: Historians and the history of economic thought: a response to Lawrence Birken. *History of Political Economy*, 25, 85–113.

Lovejoy, A. O. 1960 [1936]: *The Great Chain of Being*. New York: Harper and Row.

Mäki, U. 1988: How to combine rhetoric and realism in the methodology of economics. *Economics and Philosophy*, 4, 89–109.

—— 1992: Social conditioning of economics. In N. De Marchi (ed.), *Post-Popperian Methodology of Economics: Recovering Practice*. Boston: Kluwer, 65–104.

McCloskey, D. N. 1985: *The Rhetoric of Economics*. Madison, WI: University of Wisconsin Press.

—— 1990: *If You're So Smart*. Chicago: The University of Chicago Press.

Megill, A. and McCloskey, D. N. 1987: The rhetoric of history. In J. S. Nelson, A. Megill, and D. N. McCloskey (eds.), *The Rhetoric of the Human Sciences*. Madison, WI: University of Wisconsin Press, 221–38.

Merton, R. 1938: *Science, Technology and Society in Seventeenth Century England*. New York: Fertig.

Mirowski, P. 1989: *More Heat Than Light*. Cambridge: Cambridge University Press.

—— 1994: The realms of the natural. In P. Mirowski (ed.), *Natural Images in Economic Thought*. Cambridge, UK: Cambridge University Press, 451–83.

Monas, S. 1993: Contemporary historiography: some kicks in the old coffin. In Kozicki, op. cit., pp. 1–16.

Popescu, O. 1964: On the historiography of economic thought: a bibliographical survey. *Journal of World History*, 8, 168–209.

Popper, K. 1959: *The Logic of Scientific Discovery*. London: Hutchinson.

Porter, R. 2001: History of the body reconsidered. In Burke (2001), op. cit., pp. 233–60.

Ranke, L. von 1874 [1824]: *Geschichten der romanischen und germanischen Völker von 1494 bis 1514*, 2nd edn. Leipzig, Duncker and Humblot.

Reingold, N. 1981: Science, scientists, and historians of science. *History of Science*, 19, 274–83.

Repgen, K. 1982: Über Rankes Diktum von 1824. *Historisches Jahrbuch*, 102, 439–49.

Roll, E. 1992: *A History of Economic Thought*. London: Faber and Faber.

Rorty, R. 1984: The historiography of philosophy: four genres. In R. Rorty, J. B. Schneewind, and Q. Skinner (eds.), *Philosophy in History*. Cambridge, UK: Cambridge University Press, 49–75.

Samuels, W. J. 1974: The history of economic thought as intellectual history. *History of Political Economy*, 6, 305–23.

Samuelson, P. 1954: Some psychological aspects of mathematics and economics. *Review of Economics and Statistics*, 36, 380–6.

—— 1987: Out of the closet: a program for the Whig history of economic science. In M. Blaug (ed.), *The Historiography of Economics*. Aldershot, UK: Edward Elgar, 181–90.

Schumpeter, J. A. 1994 [1954]: *History of Economic Analysis*, ed. E. B. Schumpeter. London: Routledge.

Screpanti, E. and Zamagni, S. 1993: *An Outline of the History of Economic Thought*. Oxford: The Clarendon Press.

Sent, E. 1999: Economics of science: survey and suggestions. *Journal of Economic Methodology*, 6, 95–124.

Shapin, S. 1992: Discipline and bounding: the history and sociology of science as seen through the externalism–internalism debate. *History of Science*, 30, 333–69.

—— 1994: *A Social History of Truth*. Chicago: The University of Chicago Press.

Shermer, M. and Grobman, A. 2000: *Denying History. Who Says the Holocaust Never Happened and Why Do They Say It?* Berkeley, CA: University of California Press.

Skinner, Q. 1969: Meaning and understanding in the history of ideas. *History and Theory*, 8, 3–53.

Smith, B. G. 1995: Gender and the practices of scientific history: the seminar and archival research in the nineteenth century. *American Historical Review*, 100, 1150–76.

Tribe, K. 1978: *Land, Labour and Economic Discourse*. London: Routledge and Kegan Paul.

Weintraub, E. R. 1991: *Stabilizing Dynamics*. Cambridge, UK: Cambridge University Press.

—— 1999: How should we write the history of twentieth-century economics? *Oxford Review of Economic Policy*, 15, 139–52.

White, H. 1973: *Metahistory*. Baltimore, MD: Johns Hopkins University Press.

Winch, D. 1962: What price the history of economic thought? *Scottish Journal of Political Economy*, 9, 193–204.

CHAPTER THIRTY

The Sociology of Economics and Scientific Knowledge, and the History of Economic Thought

A. W. Bob Coats

30.1 INTRODUCTION

The title of this essay conveys only a hint of the terminological and substantive confusion, yet also the promise, suggested by the loosely interlinked network of subjects (disciplines, sub-disciplines, and fields) to which it refers. Some of these subjects are venerable and comparatively static, whereas others, of more recent origin, are not merely rapidly expanding and overlapping, but also changing their shape and content. (Current general terminology includes "the sociology of knowledge," "the sociology of science," "the sociology of scientific knowledge," "social studies [or theories] of science," "science as social knowledge," "science studies [or theory]," "the science of science," and "social economics." More specific terms such as "the economics of science" and the "economics of scientific knowledge" suggest possibilities for further, perhaps even endless, terminological proliferation. However, in recent years there seems to have been an increasing tendency to use the portmanteau term "science studies.") This state of affairs may be stimulating to scholars working or specializing in these branches of knowledge, but it is somewhat bewildering to newcomers and students who are trying to take their bearings and find their way through the substantial volume of relevant literature.

The following account is subdivided into five sections:

- Section 30.2 is a brief introduction to Schumpeter's conception of economic sociology, which originated in 1912, and its relationship to sociology, economic history, and the history of economic thought. His unfinished posthumous *History of Economic Analysis* (1994 [1954]) covers a much broader territory than the title suggests.
- Between Schumpeter's death in 1950 and the extraordinary impact of Thomas Kuhn's *The Structure of Scientific Revolutions* (1970 [1962]), the most influential American version of the sociology of science was Robert Merton's functionalism. His most significant writings appeared between the late 1930s and *The Sociology of Science: Theoretical and Empirical Investigations* (1973). The discussion of Merton's ideas in section 30.3 leads to a brief consideration of Kuhn's account of scientific revolutions and the "social conditioning" of economics.
- From the early 1970s the Mertonian approach was gradually superseded by new developments that can be loosely grouped under the general heading of "the sociology of scientific knowledge" (SSK). In section 30.4, attention will be focused on only one of the two principal "first-generation" species of SSK – social constructivism – because the second approach, known as the "Strong Programme" and associated with the so-called Edinburgh school, is less directly relevant to the history of economic thought.
- A "second-generation" example of SSK – "the economics of science," or "the economics of scientific knowledge" (ESK) – is the main subject of the short penultimate section 30.5.
- Finally, section 30.6 is devoted to general reflections on the past and future of the subjects discussed in the previous sections.

30.2   Schumpeter's Economic Sociology

As this *Companion* focuses on the history of economic thought, it is appropriate to begin by considering the views of that outstanding master of the discipline, Joseph A. Schumpeter, the first major economist to examine what he termed "economic sociology." Schumpeter's works provide a direct intellectual link between the founders of economic sociology – Max Weber, Emile Durkheim, and Georg Simmel, in the period 1890–1920 – and the renaissance of that subject since the later 1970s. As early as the first (1912) edition of his *Theorie der Wirtschaftlichen Entwicklung*, Schumpeter outlined his conception of a universal social science that would combine the sociology, methodology, and history of science – of which the history of economic analysis would constitute an integral part. [Shionoya notes that Schumpeter's conception of the research program of a universal science has been neglected because the relevant chapter (7) of the first edition of his *Theorie der Wirtschaftlichen Entwicklung* was omitted from subsequent editions (Shionoya, 1998, p. 436). The present account draws heavily on Shionoya's work, including Shionoya (1996, 1997).] Although he did not participate in the famous *Methodenstreit* or "battle of methods" between the Austrian and German economists, Schumpeter was inspired by the controversy, and recognized virtues and limitations on both sides in the debate. Indeed, throughout his life he endeavored to develop an approach that would integrate theory and history. He viewed the history of economics as exploring the relationship between the economy and ideas, a field in which the sociology and methodology of science converge. Economic dynamics, he argued, should be based on economic statics, and combined with economic sociology to provide an analysis of changes in the institutional framework of the economy. He viewed economic sociology as one of the principal specialized fields in economics (together with theory, history, and statistics), describing it as "a sort of generalized, or typified or stylized economic history" (Schumpeter, 1994 [1954], p. 20). "Of these fundamental fields, economic history [he said] . . . is by far the most important," adding that if "starting afresh," and having to choose only one field, it would be economic history (Schumpeter, 1994 [1954], p. 12, cf., p. 13). It is obvious why Schumpeter's "all encompassing" approach is attractive to an economic historian with a special interest in the institutional history of economics.

In the uncompleted part I of his posthumously published *magnum opus*, *The History of Economic Analysis*, Schumpeter left only brief and tantalizing glimpses of how he might have developed his views on economic sociology (Schumpeter, 1994 [1954], pp. 20–1, "Economics and sociology," pp. 25–7, and "The scientific process: vision and rules of procedure," pp. 41–7). As Mark Perlman has observed, he "wanted a vision which embraced and bound together the permanent and exogenous with the sociological–transitory and indigenous [*sic*], and he failed to find it" (cf., Perlman, 1996, p. 200). Nevertheless, his magisterial volume contained many suggestions and *aperçus* that have stimulated a considerable volume of research on the sociology of economic knowledge (science). To cite a single example of Schumpeter's penetrating insights, see the *History* (1994 [1954], p. 47):

> the professionals that devote themselves to scientific work in a particular field and even all the professionals who devote themselves to scientific work in any field tend to become a sociological group. This means that they have other things in common besides the interest in scientific work or in a particular science per se . . . The group accepts or refuses to accept co-workers for reasons other than their professional competence or incompetence.

Remarks of this kind have had a lasting influence on research into the sociology and professionalization of economics.

It is often difficult to identify clear turning points in the history of economic and social ideas, and the present case is no exception. In more senses than one, the timing of Schumpeter's posthumous *History* was unfortunate for, as Richard Swedberg has noted: "from the 1920's to the 1960's economists and sociologists have completely ignored each other and have gone about their business as though the other science did not exist" (Swedberg, 1990, p. 4). Of course, there were some exceptions to this sweeping generalization, such as the American Talcott

Parsons, and numerous non-American authors. But for much of the three decades after Schumpeter's death in 1950, the climate of opinion was no more receptive than it had been earlier, although with hindsight it is clear that Thomas Kuhn's *The Structure of Scientific Revolutions* (1970 [1962]) was the harbinger of a new era.

30.3 Robert Merton's Functionalism

Prior to the publication of Kuhn's path-breaking study of scientific revolutions, the leading American sociologist of science was the functionalist Robert K. Merton, whose publications spanned the period from the late 1930s to the late 1970s. Unlike the Marxist tradition in science studies – which had a direct, if limited, impact on economic ideas – the Mertonian writings were only indirectly relevant to economics, although they were influential in shaping the prevailing view of the essential characteristics of science, the social and cultural context of scientific knowledge, and the scientist's distinctive role in Western society. Starting with the seventeenth century, Merton traced the historical process whereby science had acquired and maintained its twentieth-century cultural hegemony, and emphasized the importance of four central norms:

a) *Universalism*: the criteria for scientific evaluation are not specific to any particular individual or group. Scientific standards are independent of the author and applicable to all.
b) *Communism*: science is an intellectual commune. Scientists share their results and data with the wider scientific community.
c) *Disinterestedness*: scientists (qua scientists) are disinterested in the impact of their work. They do not seek political or financial rewards for their work and can therefore follow an argument wherever it leads.
d) *Scepticism*: no scientific result is accepted without scrutiny by empirical and logical criteria. Scientists refuse to believe any result until it has been demonstrated by scientific standards.

(Hands, 2001, p. 181)

During what can loosely be termed the "Mertonian era" in the sociology of science, philosophers, sociologists, and historians of science devoted considerable energy to discussing the relative importance of "external" and "internal" influences on the development of science. Of course, the two sides in the debate were not as clearly demarcated as this description might suggest, but on the whole the Mertonians were externalists, whereas the intellectual pendulum subsequently shifted toward internalist explanations – for example, with the philosopher of science Imre Lakatos, and the leading writers in the sociology of scientific knowledge movement (to be considered below; see section 30.4).

According to a leading latter-day Mertonian sociologist of science, Joseph Ben David, historical studies in the field should be focused on external events, because "the influence of internal disciplinary traditions is permanent and ubiquitous," whereas "the sociological influences upon the actual products of scientific inquiry can only be tenuous and sporadic," therefore presenting few research opportunities (Ben David, 1984 [1971], pp. ix, xxii). As Jan Golinski has observed:

> The Mertonian model gives institutions a central, but strangely occluded role in the sociology of science . . . [they] arise when they mirror a broader cultural acceptance of the scientific ethos . . . and become vehicles for imparting the norms to initiates, hence sustaining scientific practice over time; [and yet] they remain curiously insubstantial entities. Although dysfunctional organizations can hinder growth, properly functioning institutions are simply channels to convey the fertilizing values that irrigate the field of science.

In an important sense, Ben David's work is "a sociological history that aims to show how scientists attained independence from social forces." Three stages can be identified: the creation of a "social role" for the scientist; the achievement of "intellectual autonomy" for science; and the construction of "organizational autonomy in institutions devoted to the subject" (Golinski, 1998, pp. 50, 51; sentence order slightly changed).

In what might be termed the "late Mertonian period," the focus of attention among sociologists of science shifted away from consideration of the norms of science to investigations of "the interplay between social formations of scientists and cognitive developments in the field of science" (Hands, 2001, p. 185). Statistical methods were often utilized in citation analysis, content analysis, and historical analysis, in addition to the study of empirical ideas, such as the self-fulfilling prophesy, the Matthew effect, and the nature and significance of multiple discoveries. Mertonians undertook valuable studies of the organization of science, university institutionalization, the role of scientific associations, and the significance of generation differences among scientists (Coats's work was similar, though not self-consciously Mertonian). Merton himself never questioned the high intellectual status of science, but in the tension between the "technocratic" and the "critical" approaches, J. D. Bernal and the Marxists were in the latter camp (Hands, p. 185).

Generally speaking, the Mertonians were moderates, emphasizing the importance of the social and cultural factors that shaped the development of science while avoiding the cruder versions of social or economic determinism to be found in some Marxist writings, and in the works of the sociologist Karl Mannheim. More careful and subtle interpretations of social conditions are now available, for example in the writings of Uskali Mäki, who has suggested that at least three distinct kinds of social conditioning are implied in the recent sociology of science literature:

1 The content of accepted theory or belief (or its metaphysical and epistemological presuppositions) is caused (in an unspecified way) by social factors (such as cultures or interests internal or external to science). Here, a social fact causally generates an aspect of science (namely, scientific knowledge).
2 The goals of scientists' actions are social states or processes (such as credibility or power and their growth). Here a social fact constitutes an aspect of science (namely, scientists' goals).

3 The process of the justification of scientific claims is a social process of negotiation and rhetorical persuasion. Again a social fact constitutes an aspect of science
   (namely, the process of justification).

                                                          (Mäki, 1992, pp. 65–104)

Of these, Mäki adds, point 1 has been endorsed by the so-called "Strong
Programme" of the Edinburgh school, while points 2 and 3 have been more
emphatically studied by the so-called "social constructivists" in ethnographic and
anthropological approaches (cf., Mäki, 1992, p. 66; see also the "Commentary" by
Coats, ibid., pp. 105–10; and Mäki, 1993b, pp. 76–109).

In place of the established Mertonian "uniformitarian" or incrementalist view
of the progress of science, Kuhn substituted a "castastrophist" interpretation,
centering on the impact of revolutionary paradigm changes. The details of Kuhn's
account are by now familiar and need not be recounted here. For the present
purpose, it is sufficient to recall the remarkable intellectual stimulus provided by
his synthesis of history, philosophy, epistemology, the sociology of science, and
the study of science as a profession. In the longer term, as D. Wade Hands has
observed, since Kuhn:

> No longer is science examined from a purely philosophical perspective; it is now
> investigated from a much wider range of historical and empirical viewpoints. The
> result of these changes has been the elaboration of a vision of science that is anti-
> foundationalist, fundamentally social, much less uniform and much more amenable
> to a naturalistic mode of inquiry . . . These changes have radically undermined the
> traditional philosophical approach to scientific knowledge, and opened the door
> for other, more sociological, approaches that take the collective nature of scientific
> activity as their starting point. (Hands, 1998, p. 474)

Kuhn was, of course, primarily interested in the history of the natural sciences.
Nevertheless, his ideas had a considerable impact on a wide range of other
disciplines including economics, and there were a variety of attempts to provide
a Kuhnian account of the general development of the discipline. Research on the
economist's role and function in society and government was directly stimulated
by Kuhn's ideas.

30.4 The Sociology of Scientific Knowledge

In recent years, students of the sociology of economics and economic methodology have drawn a distinction between the older "sociology of science" and the
more recent "sociology of scientific knowledge" (SSK), arguing that whereas the
former focused on the changing social and cultural *context* of science, the latter
has been more radical, and focused on the *content* of science (Hands, 2001,
pp. 183–4). In accordance with the positivistic, rules-based (so-called "Received
View") of scientific (and economic) methodology, the sociology of science "does
not really question the objective validity of science," whereas "much of the contemporary [SSK] literature considers even the content of science to be socially

constituted and contingent (*thus neither universal nor distinctive*)" (Hands, 2001, p. 183; emphasis added). However, Hands cautions that the distinction between the sociology of science and SSK "is not as crisp as it initially sounds, and it can be difficult to apply in specific cases . . . [thus] it is a useful, but imperfect conceptual tool" (p. 184). Broadly speaking, the same is true of the difference between the earlier general concepts of the sociology of scientific development (sometimes referred to as *Weltanschauungen* analyses) and the predominantly local concerns of SSK. Here too, the shift of focus should not be overstated. For example, the earlier "sociology of science (knowledge)" in Schumpeter and later writings considered numerous less general topics, such as the nature and significance of "schools" of economic thought, changes in the academic and other institutions that provided research opportunities, and the functions and control of scientific journals and other publication outlets – matters on which broad national, or even international, patterns have been established, with an obviously translocal range and significance. These can be termed the "institutional," or "organizational," structures of science. [See, for example, the numerous research possibilities mentioned in Coats (1993a, pp. 13, 24ff.) and Coats (1993b, pp. 38–48). These papers were originally published in 1984 and 1985, respectively. For pertinent reservations about the concept of professionalization, see Golinski (1998, pp. 67–9).]

In the post-Mertonian social constructivists' accounts, it is recognized that scientific concepts and institutions have been constructed – that is, they are "the outcome of interactions and negotiations among those who participate in them as well as of larger-scale forces affecting society as a whole." Moreover, "organizations are not regarded as inflexible determinants of individual behavior" (Golinski, 1998, p. 55). Such a view obviously has radical implications for the conception of the role of scientific knowledge and organizations in society, especially as applied to the natural sciences. According to Hands (2001, p. 176), the "Strong Programme" (or the Edinburgh school – hereinafter SP) and the social constructivists together constituted the first generation of SSK authors, beginning in the 1970s. In the following account, however, attention will be focused exclusively on the latter category, since exponents of the SP, unlike the social constructivists, have displayed no direct interest in the history of economic thought. According to Golinski (1998, p. 5), the SP "provided an important inspiration" for the SSK. [Hands treats the terms "constructivism" and "social constructivism" as interchangeable, attributing the latter to Berger and Luckman (1996). He also occasionally describes the exponents of these views as "constructionists."]

In one sense, the relevance of sociological influences to economic ideas and economists' practices is only too obvious, and too often disconcerting, for it is easy to poke fun at the economists' scientific pretensions and the claims of "economics imperialism." Most economists are well aware of the troubled relationship between economic ideas and policy, and few of them cherish the illusion that they are immune from societal pressures and temptations. Nevertheless, they cling to an ideal of scientific autonomy while, at the same time, in many cases seizing the available opportunities to participate in public policy discussion and/or decision-making. Sociological analysis can provide a bridge that links economic methodology with the history of economics. This is especially the case when methodology is viewed as the study and evaluation of the procedural rules, heuristic principles, and scientific conventions utilized by economists, and the history of economics is focused on the origins, development, and significance of changing styles of professional activity, rather than merely the study of disembodied ideas or outstanding individual contributors to the discipline. However, this is not the place to pursue these matters further (cf., Coats, 1993a, pp. 23ff.).

With the more recent influence of constructivism, there has been a discernible shift of emphasis in the history of economics literature from "economic thought to economists' practices" (Emmett, 2001, p. 262). Ross Emmett maintains that constructivism "is not a new form of intellectual history. Rather, it is the application of certain sociological methods to the explanation of scientific activity" (ibid.). In the constructivist writings, five aspects of scientific practices are singled out:

a) How scientists and their communities identify themselves and discipline their conduct;
b) the sites of scientific production;
c) the rhetorical devices scientists use;
d) the use of tools, models and representations of nature; and
e) the relation between science and culture.

(Emmett, 2001, pp. 262–3)

Hands has summarized the characteristics of constructivist literature succinctly, as "hands on, micro, no tight priors, everything negotiable, impotence of nature, and the debunking of the traditional view of scientific knowledge" (2001, p. 93). For a somewhat different list of Golinski's "five themes," see Sent (2001, p. 69).

In a brief essay, it is obviously impossible to cover the entire range of SSK and constructivist writings. I shall therefore focus on three very different examples that are directly relevant to the history of economic thought, authored by E. Roy Weintraub, Esther-Mirjam Sent, and Yuval P. Yonay.

Weintraub has been the most vigorous and outspoken proponent of constructivism in economics in a number of writings, but especially in his book *Stabilizing Dynamics* (1991a) and in a conference paper with the same title (1991b). The book is an outgrowth of his work on Imre Lakatos's philosophy of science – the Lakatos of *Proofs and Refutations* (1976) rather than his *Methodology of Scientific Research Programmes* (1978). In his brief "Comment on Weintraub" (in De Marchi and Blaug, 1991, p. 291), Philip Mirowski (1991) claimed that Weintraub's work "on the construction of the idea of economic stability within the neoclassical research program will stand as one of the milestones in the history of economic thought in the twentieth century" (for serious criticisms of Weintraub's work, see Hands, 2001, pp. 293–5).

Weintraub's research called for a rare combination of technical expertise in abstract economic theory and an impressive dedication to historical reconstruction. A brief statement of his *credo* is the following:

> We must accept that history is not presented to us raw, as a neutral case or data source on which we can perform tests of our methodological theories of how scientific

knowledge is gained. History is not "out there" waiting to answer our questions or corroborate our hypotheses. History is not found; history is written. It is an authorial construction to some purpose or other and is itself as much a creative enterprise as is the "theory" it is often "meant" to describe. (Weintraub, 1991a, p. 4)

Weintraub attaches paramount importance to the fact that economics, like other disciplinary activities, is undertaken in "interpretive communities," and is necessarily a social activity:

... historians of economics seem to have as an audience not only the methodology community but also a community of sociologists who study science as a social enterprise. There is not, however [at least yet!] a subdiscipline within economics based on the sociology of science that corresponds to that subdiscipline called methodology that is based on the philosophy of science. Whether this is because economists in the end disbelieve in sociology as, in Leijonhufvud's phrase "a lesser tribe without a modl as totem," or whether this is because it is too difficult for neoclassical economists to think about groups as social actors is in the end of no matter. There are not many historians of economics who have an interest in the sociology of the economics profession. (Weintraub, 1991a, pp. 8–9)

Nevertheless, in the decade since that passage was published the situation has changed substantially, and for the better.

Whereas the central feature of Weintraub's constructivist approach has been the analysis of sequences of research papers on specific problems in mathematical economic theory (for example, the "existence" of a competitive equilibrium, general equilibrium analysis, and stability theory), Sent's book is designed to trace and account for sequential phases in the research of a single individual: the rational expectations theorist, Thomas J. Sargent.

Using the framework constructed by the sociologist of science Andrew Pickering, Sent provides a subtle and detailed account of Sargent's succession of intellectual and technical "free moves" (under his own control), "forced moves" (beyond his control), resistance (when significant obstacles are encountered), and the dialectic of resistance and accommodation (Pickering, 1995, p. 52; Sent, 1998, p. 16; for a valuable account of the application of Pickering's work to economics, see Davis, 1998). Sent's approach is:

inspired by the increased interest of science studies scholars in scientific culture and practice . . . , where culture is defined as a heterogeneous multiplicity of skills, social relations, concepts, theories, and so on, and practice involves cultural extension. (Sent, 1998, p. 14)

Sent seeks to identify, understand, and explain the significance of the specific alternatives available to Sargent, the choices that he made, and the consequences of those decisions. They show that even the treatment of rational expectations by this one particular economist had many faces (Sent, 1998, p. 13).

In her innovative Introduction, from which the above quotations have been taken, Sent describes ten different "stories" about the rise of rational expectations –

related to availability of new data or use of new techniques or natural development
from existing theories or problems with existing theories or linking of theory and
econometrics. (Sent, 1998, p. 2)

– a task to which Sargent attached great importance. He was seeking to develop
a universal economic science "by establishing a tie between neoclassical economic
theory and econometrics." His search was driven more by narrow technical concerns than by philosophical goals, for he was not a "big picture" theorist (Sent,
1998, p. 14). Sent obviously does not believe that there is one "true" story of
Sargent's quest for knowledge.

As Sheila Dow remarks in her perceptive review, Sent's promise of an "assessment" of Sargent's "achievements" is not incompatible with the post-positivist
rejection of "external" standards, because Sargent's work is assessed by reference
to his own standards, "and this is an important step before proceeding to apply
different criteria" (Dow, 2001, p. 424). Dow's comment recalls the central principle in Bruce Caldwell's advocacy of "methodological pluralism" (Caldwell,
1982, ch. 13).

Sent's book is so rich in detail, so well written, and so boldly and effectively organized, that it is especially valuable to the nontechnical, primarily
historical, reader. It sets new standards in the sociology of economic science
literature.

The third example of the application of SSK to the history of economic thought
– Yuval P. Yonay's book, *The Struggle over the Soul of Economics: Institutionalists
and Neoclassical Economists in America between the Wars* – is very different. As an
avowed constructionist, Yonay rejects the conventional historiography of the discipline "built on clear definitions of schools and approaches," since it characterizes "any two movements . . . either as completely contradictory or as compatible."
[This is, of course, a caricature. Are there no intermediate cases?] By contrast, the
constructivist "treats intellectual schools as labels fluidly assigned to groups either
by themselves or by others," so that the resulting "map of the discipline . . .
depends on negotiation among different definitions of the situation" (Yonay,
1998, p. 70; cf., pp. 75, 195).

Yonay is an enthusiastic (and uncritical) advocate of the sociological actor-
network analysis (hereinafter ANA; alternatively known as ANT – actor-network
theory) proposed by Michael Callon and Bruno Latour (1981). This emphasizes
the diversity and complexity of the sciences, and denies that there is any absolute
standard by which to judge scientific enterprises. A network consists of a *mélange*
of "facts, people, money, methodological principles, theories, instruments, machines, practices, organizations, and so forth," and these elements are mutually
reinforcing. "Consequently, it is difficult to undermine any single link of the
network without undermining the others" (Yonay, 1998, p. 22). Admittedly, Yonay
adds,

it is absolutely [*sic*] possible that the whole network is based on shaky foundations,
but such a claim can be made only by other scientists and scholars who must base
their claim on another network, stronger or weaker. (Yonay, 1998, p. 22)

This conflict of networks is reminiscent of the contest between rival paradigms as depicted by Kuhn, a thinker whom Yonay dismisses. But unfortunately he muddies the waters by adding that "the network concept" overlaps in some degree institutional bodies such as disciplines, schools, paradigms, and research programs (Yonay, 1998, p. 22), and both incorporates and extends some features of the rhetorical approach. He concedes that all this is too comprehensive and complex to be handled in his study, which is therefore not a "full blown ANA," and therefore feels obliged to focus on "scholastic and cognitive arguments only." Consequently, his book centers on the structure of methodological controversies (Yonay, 1998, p. 26) – a much more "conventional" topic, it must be said.

Yonay retains the familiar institutionalist and neoclassical labels in order to "keep this project manageable" and make the main thesis comprehensible (Yonay, 1998, pp. 26–7), while acknowledging that there were divisions within each camp. As a constructivist, he recognizes that his interpretation of the "story" is not "objective," since it is influenced by his desire to "establish a general thesis about the history of economics." While admitting that his work is probably influenced "by my prior knowledge of sociology and economics and by my ideological inclinations and preferences as a sociologist," he claims that his task has been undertaken "in good faith, and offers . . . a plausible way to read these texts." Presumably this is the strongest claim that a constructivist can make, for "nobody knows what 'the Truth' is before the trials of strength are concluded" (Yonay, 1998, pp. 21, 28) – or, indeed, even then?

A striking feature of Yonay's account is his enthusiastic adoption of Latour's militaristic terminology, with its references to struggles, fights, skirmishes, attacks, the mobilization and recruitment of allies, victory, and how "the old-fashioned neoclassicists . . . fought for their lives" (Yonay, 1998, p. 194). The opponents in these campaigns were not just people, but also concepts, for an ally "can be anything that bears upon the strength of the contribution in question" (Yonay, 1998, p. 21), including all the persuasive arguments employed by controversialists. No wonder Yonay cannot cover the entire network required for a "full blown ANA." Unfortunately, his use of Latour's framework and terminology is far too crude to reveal the more subtle and intricate aspects of the story that he has undertaken to tell.

30.5 The Economics of Science, or the Economics of Scientific Knowledge

It is now time to turn from SSK to the economics of science and the economics of scientific knowledge (ESK). As Hands suggests, although the development of an economic version of SSK may seem "a rather obvious next step in the study of science," that move has wider philosophical implications that will leave many economists feeling uncomfortable (see Hands, 1994, pp. 81, 96–8). Even when authors are not consciously attempting to apply economic analysis to science, the arguments offered do sound very much like economic arguments, especially when "science is viewed as analogous to a capitalist market economy in which agents are maximizing producers who competitively and greedily pursue their self-interest" (Hands, 1994; quoting Mäki, 1992, p. 79).

However, while it is important not to assume that "unbounded" economic rationality is the same thing as scientists' rationality (cf., Hands, 2001, pp. 386–7), this is not the place to consider the various and subtle differences between bounded and unbounded rationality – a matter of significance in any consideration of ESK or the economics of science.

Mäki maintains that the authors who employ such "quasi-economic argumentation" (for example, Latour and Woolgar, and Karin Knorr-Cetina) are not in fact applying economics to science. On the contrary, they probably "consider neoclassical economics to be naively reductionist, narrowly individualist, and in general a quite uninteresting approach to studying (any) social process." (Mäki, 1992, p. 83). James Wible provides an excellent example of the naive reliance on simple marginal analysis in his observation on fraud in science: "If the marginal return to fraudulent activities increases relative to legitimate activities, then the individual would be expected to increase the proportion of time spent on illegitimate activities." This argument is essentially tautological. [See Wible (1992, p. 19; cf., Wible, 1998a, ch. 3) for a more elaborate analysis. Also his survey article on "The economics of science" in Davis, Hands, and Mäki (1998, pp. 145–52).] Pickering's approach is "self-consciously constructivist," for he focuses on the intricate details of the "dynamics of practice" rather than the more general "social interests" highlighted in SSK research. Even so, Pickering's contribution is sometimes attacked as fundamentally economic on the same grounds as philosophers of science – such as Alexander Rosenberg – attack economics (see Hands, 1994, p. 85).

G. Radnitzky and W. W. Bartley are among the authors who have intentionally utilized familiar "invisible hand" arguments in explaining how scientific knowledge emerges from the competitive process of scientific criticism, in exactly the same way that economic welfare supposedly emerges from the competitive market process. And there were striking anticipations of this idea in the writings of the American "pragmaticist" C. S. Peirce, in 1879 (Hands, 1994, pp. 86, 89; Wible, 1998a, ch. 4).

30.6 Concluding Reflections

At this point, it is hardly necessary to reemphasize that the foregoing account covers only a limited part of the substantial and still rapidly growing science studies literature (that is, the sociology of science/knowledge, SSK, and the economics of science and ESK). Rather than adding more details or examples from this literature, it will be more useful to focus on two widely recognized problems in the field – reflexivity and relativism.

Hands has briefly characterized these problems in his contributions to the recent *Handbook of Economic Methodology*, as follows:

i) *Realism versus relativism*: if scientists' beliefs are caused by their social interests (strong programme) or the contingent social context (constructivism), what is the role of nature, or the material world, in the formation of our scientific beliefs? Are all scientific beliefs equally valid or valid only relative to the particular community that has proposed them?

ii) *Reflexivity*: if all scientific theories are the product of the interests of the scientists who propose them, then why should not interest also govern the beliefs of the sociologists doing the sociology of scientific knowledge?

iii) *SSK and the traditional philosophy of science*: does SSK replace the traditional (epistemically normative) study of scientific knowledge with a purely descriptive analysis of the practice of scientists, or simply provide a new set of answers to the traditional epistemic questions? In other words, is SSK revolutionary . . . or reformist (providing new, perhaps radical answers to the traditional questions)?
(adapted from Hands, 1998a–c; see also his articles on reflexivity and relativism in the same volume, pp. 413–16, 416–18)

These issues are directly relevant not only to economists' current practices, but also to economic methodology and the historiography of the discipline. Generally speaking, the question of reflexivity has been recognized only comparatively recently, as a byproduct of the conflicted methodological situation following the demise of positivism. However, reflexivity (or self-reference) is likely to become an increasingly important issue in the future (see, for example, Wible, 1998a, especially ch. 11; also the discussion in Sent, 2001, p. 277ff., in terms of the symmetry thesis). Relativism, on the other hand, is a much more venerable problem as, for example, in the famous *Methodenstreit* mentioned earlier (see above, p. 509). Some of the German historical economists accused the British classical school of cosmopolitanism and perpetualism; that is, the claim that their doctrines were true of all places and all times. (Strangely enough, among the "orthodox" figures mentioned in this essay, both Schumpeter and Sargent viewed economics as in some sense a universal science.)

According to Ross Emmett,

> Given the close connection . . . between historians of economics and the discipline they study one might suspect that some historians of economics would suggest that an *economics of scientific knowledge* is better suited to their needs than a *sociology of scientific knowledge*. [Yet] while there are aspects of recent economic theory that could enrich our analysis of the actions of economists and scientists within constrained settings, there are also reasons to be wary of narrowing the field from the concerns of science studies to those of economics. As John Davis (1997) has argued . . . the goals of science studies have been to dethrone the notion of an ahistorical and universal science, and to broaden the explanatory scope of the historian. On the other hand, economics, at least in its mainstream form, affirms the universality of economics and, in a reductionist fashion, seeks to explain all human action as economic. Despite the discomfort some historians of economics may feel toward a sociology of scientific knowledge . . . the questions addressed here are ones which promise interesting and rewarding research. (Emmett, 2001, pp. 264–5; emphasis in original)

At the present time there is an active debate about the possibilities and risks for historians of economic thought as a result of the new developments in SSK,

ESK, and other branches of science studies. There is concern among historians of economics that SSK's focus on economists' practices will foster an unduly narrow conception of the field and a corresponding loss of contact with the broader, more conventional, interests of historians. Likewise, a concentration on ESK and the economics of science may lead to an unduly economistic approach of the kind favored by advocates of economics imperialism, who seem to be more pre-occupied with expanding economics' explanatory reach than in enhancing our understanding of human behavior. These are merely examples of contemporary concerns, which in some respects reflect the influence of post-positivist and even postmodernist tendencies in the historical disciplines.

In the absence of any single voice to express the stresses and opportunities inherent in the present situation, it may be appropriate to conclude with the appeal of a leading, if somewhat controversial, member of the sociology of science community of scholars, H. M. Collins, issued a decade ago at a distinguished gathering of economists, historians, philosophers, and sociologists who had assembled at a conference to assess the influence of Imre Lakatos's ideas on the problems and possibilities involved in the appraisal of economic theories:

> unlike historians and sociologists of natural science, most historians of economics already practice the subject that they want to describe. They work in university departments of economics as economists while their history takes only part of their time . . . And yet many historians of economics seem to want to throw away these advantages, preferring to do the sort of history of economics which does not require any special *understanding* of the subject. With a few exceptions, historians adopt the distanced viewpoint of rational reconstruction as their perspective . . .
>
> Part of the reason for this must be the very institutional location of historians of economics which confers upon them such a potential advantage. The professional reference-group for historians of economics is not historians of science but other economists. The judges of good work in the history of economics are likewise economists, rather than historians of science in general. That, I suppose, is why only a few historians of economics have been caught up with the changes that have happened in the history of science over the last two decades. In addition, being on the outside of these debates, perhaps they remain enchanted with the idea of science and disenchanted with their own economics. Like the scientists in the war stories, they may still believe that what they do is not real scientific economics; the real economics can be found on the next hilltop. Perhaps, even if they have never seen the canonical model of economic science at work, they believe it is just over the horizon. (Collins, 1991, pp. 496–7; emphasis added)

Bibliography

Ben David, J. 1984 [1971]: *The Scientist's Role in Society. A Comparative Study*, 2nd edn. Chicago: The University of Chicago Press.

Berger, P. L. and Luckman, T. 1966: *The Social Construction of Reality. A Treatise in the Sociology of Knowledge*. New York: Anchor.

Caldwell, B. 1982: *Beyond Positivism: Economic Methodology in the Twentieth Century*. London: George Allen & Unwin.

Callon, M. and Latour, B. 1981: Unscrewing the big Leviathan: how actors macro-structure reality and how sociologists help them to do so. In K. Knorr-Cetina and A. V. Cicourel (eds.), *Advances in Social Theory and Methodology*. Boston: Routledge.

Coats, A. W. 1955: Review of Joseph Schumpeter: *A History of Economic Analysis*, Oxford University Press. *Economica*, N.S., May, 171–4.

—— 1992: Commentary [on Mäki]. In N. De Marchi (ed.), *Post-Popperian Methodology of Economics. Recovering Practice*. Boston: Kluwer, pp. 105–10.

—— 1993a: The sociology of knowledge and the history of economics. In A. W. Coats (ed.), *The Sociology and Professionalization of Economics: British and American Economic Essays*, vol. II. London: Routledge, 11–36.

—— 1993b: The sociology of science and its application to economics. Ibid., pp. 37–57.

—— 2000: Review of Yuval P. Yonay: *The Struggle over the Soul of Economics. Institutionalists and Neoclassical Economists in America between the Wars. The European Journal of the History of Economic Thought*, 7(1), 169–71.

Collins, H. M. 1991: History and sociology of science and methodology of economics. In De Marchi and Blaug, op. cit., pp. 492–8.

Davis, J. B. 1997: The fox and the henhouses: the economics of scientific knowledge. *History of Political Economy*, 29(4), 741–6.

—— 1998: New economics and its history: a Pickeringian view. In J. B. Davis (ed.), *New Economics and its History:* Annual Supplement to *History of Political Economy*, 29. Durham, NC: Duke University Press, 289–308.

——, Hands, D. W., and Mäki, U. (eds.) 1998: *The Handbook of Economic Methodology*. Cheltenham, UK: Edward Elgar.

De Marchi, N. and Blaug, M. 1991: *Appraising Economic Theories. Studies in the Methodology of Research Programs*. Aldershot, UK: Edward Elgar.

Dow, S. 2001: Review essay of E. M. Sent's *The Evolving Rationality of Rational Expectations: An Assessment of Thomas Sargent's Achievements. Journal of Economic Methodology*, 8(3), 423–8.

Emmett, R. B. 2001: "Where else would you look? Constructivism and the historiography of economics. *Journal of the History of Economic Thought*, 23(2), 262–5.

Golinski, J. 1998: *Making Natural Knowledge, Constructivism and the History of Science*. Cambridge, UK: Cambridge University Press.

Hands, D. W. 1994: The sociology of scientific knowledge: some thoughts on the possibilities. In R. Backhouse (ed.), *New Directions in Economic Knowledge*. London: Routledge, 75–106.

—— 1997: Conjectures and reputations: the sociology of scientific knowledge and the history of economic thought. *History of Political Economy*, 29, 695–741.

—— 1998a: Reflexivity. In Davis et al., op. cit., pp. 413–16.

—— 1998b: Relativism. In Davis et al., op. cit., pp. 416–18.

—— 1998c: The sociology of scientific knowledge. In Davis et al., op. cit., pp. 474–7.

—— 2001: *Reflection Without Rules. Economic Methodology and Contemporary Science Theory*. Cambridge, UK: Cambridge University Press.

Kuhn, T. S. 1970 [1962]: *The Structure of Scientific Revolutions*. Chicago: The University of Chicago Press.

Lakatos, I. 1976: *Proofs and Refutations*. Cambridge, UK: Cambridge University Press.

—— 1978: Methodology of scientific research programmes. Reprinted in his *Philosophical Papers*, vol. 1. Cambridge, UK: Cambridge University Press.

Mäki, U. 1992: Social conditioning of economics. In N. De Marchi (ed.), *Post-Popperian Methodology of Economics. Recovering Practice*. Boston: Kluwer, 65–104.

—— 1993a: Economics with institutions: agenda for methodological enquiry. In U. Mäki, B. Gustafsson, and C. Knudsen (eds.), *Rationality, Institutions and Economic Methodology*. London: Routledge, 3–42.

—— 1993b: Social theories of science and the fate of institutionalism in economics. In U. Mäki, B. Gustafsson, and C. Knudsen (eds.), *Rationality, Institutions and Economic Methodology*. London: Routledge, 76–109.

Merton, R. K. 1973: *The Sociology of Science: Theoretical and Empirical Investigations*. Chicago: The University of Chicago Press.

Mirowski, P. 1991: Comments on Weintraub. In De Marchi and Blaug, op. cit., pp. 291–3.

Perlman, M. 1996: *The Character of Economic Thought, Economic Characters, and Economic Institutions. Selected Essays*. Ann Arbor, MI: University of Michigan Press.

Pickering, A. 1995: *The Mangle of Practice: Time, Agency and Science*. Chicago: The University of Chicago Press.

Schumpeter, J. A. 1912: *Theorie der Wirtschaftlichen Entwicklung*. Leipzig: Duncker and Humblot.

—— 1994 [1954]: *History of Economic Analysis*. New York: Oxford University Press. Reprinted London: Routledge.

Sent, E.-M. 1998. *The Evolving Rationality of Rational Expectations: An Assessment of Thomas Sargent's Achievements*. Cambridge, UK: Cambridge University Press.

—— 2001: Making economic knowledge: review of Jan Golinski's *Making Natural Knowledge. Journal of the History of Economic Thought*, 23(2), 267–75.

Shionoya, Y. 1996: The sociology of science and Schumpeter's ideology, In L. S. Moss (ed.), *Joseph A. Schumpeter, Historian of Economics. Perspectives on the History of Economic Thought*. Selected papers from the History of Economics Society Conference, 1994. London: Routledge, 279–316.

—— 1997: *Schumpeter and the Idea of a Social Science. A Metatheoretical Study*. Cambridge, UK: Cambridge University Press.

—— 1998: Schumpeterian evolutionism. In Davis et al., op. cit., pp. 436–9.

Swedberg, R. 1990: *Economics and Sociology. Redefining their Boundaries: Conversations with Economists and Sociologists*. Princeton, NJ: Princeton University Press.

—— 1998: Economic sociology. In Davis et al., op. cit., pp. 134–8.

Weintraub, E. R. 1991a: *Stabilizing Dynamics. Constructing Economic Knowledge*. Cambridge, UK: Cambridge University Press.

—— 1991b: Stabilizing dynamics. In De Marchi and Blaug, op. cit., pp. 23–90.

Wible, J. R. 1992: Fraud in science: an economic approach. *Philosophy of the Social Sciences*, 22, 5–27.

—— 1998a: *The Economics of Science. Methodology and Epistemology as if Economics Really Mattered*. London: Routledge.

—— 1998b: Economics of science. In Davis et al., op. cit., pp. 145–53.

Yonay, Y. P. 1998. *The Struggle for the Soul of Economics. Institutionalists and Neoclassical Economists in America between the Wars*. Princeton, NJ: Princeton University Press.

CHAPTER THIRTY-ONE

Exegesis, Hermeneutics, and Interpretation

Ross B. Emmett

31.1 INTRODUCTION

Before you on the desk sits an economics text. It may be the most recent article in a journal or a classic book in the discipline. If you are like most readers, your concern as you read is to make sense of what the text says. This is the central task of textual interpretation: to make sense of the meaning of a text.

The other two words of our title are closely associated with interpretation, although they are used less frequently in economics than in the humanities. "Exegesis" refers to the *critical analysis of a text*, and hence is an integral part of the interpretive task. Exegesis takes us beyond reading the text to attending to its genre, style, form, word choice, model assumptions, internal logic, and contextual issues. Because the exegetical task forces one to pay close attention to the text, an exegesis usually focuses on one particular passage (or, in the case of contemporary economics texts, one model) in an author's work. "Hermeneutics," on the other hand, most often refers to the study of the methods or principles of interpretation. It may be thought of as the *methodology of interpretation*. Because this essay will focus on the methodologies of interpretation in the history of economics, it is primarily an essay in hermeneutics.

The close relation of methodological studies to philosophy has led to a hermeneutic tradition in philosophy, which assumes the primacy of the interpretive stance. Hermeneutic philosophy is founded on the notion that all knowledge, not only knowledge of the meaning of a text, is a process of interpretation – there are only interpretations and their reinterpretations. While its philosophic roots lie in the nineteenth century, especially in the work of Wilhelm Dilthey (1976), twentieth-century hermeneutic philosophy is dominated by the contrast between the work of Hans-Georg Gadamer (1989) and Jacques Derrida (1976; see also Michelfelder and Palmer, 1989). Banished from economics during the positivist orientation of the postwar period, hermeneutic philosophy has made some inroads into contemporary economics, especially among Austrian economists. The inter-action of hermeneutic philosophy and economics lies outside the scope of this essay, but the interested reader can consult Lavoie (1991) and Gerard (1993).

But let us return to the text before you. Most readers obtain a satisfactory understanding of a text by reading it for themselves. Even if the text is written in a style that is unfamiliar to the modern reader, or uses some specific tools and terminology unique to a sub-field of the economics discipline, you probably picked it up with the confidence that its meaning would be clear to you, even if you have to do a bit of exegetical work to ferret the meaning out.

Yet, while making sense of a text's meaning seems to be a simple process, it can be fraught with difficulty. One of the prime difficulties was expressed well by the Christian reformer Samuel Werenfels, about 400 years ago, with reference to the Bible: "Men ope this book, their favourite creed in mind; Each seeks his own, and each his own doth find." Werenfels's observation is as true of the reading of canonical texts in economics as it is of sacred religious texts. One can find in many of the seminal works of economics passages that lend credence to any number of economic theories. And the literature of the history of economic thought is filled with "new" interpretations of classic texts which demonstrate how a historical author agrees with one or another contemporary theory. Invariably, the contemporary theory the classical text is said to "anticipate" is the author's own! How can we distinguish between what we think these authors' works mean, and what they really mean?

31.2   STIGLER'S PRINCIPLE OF SCIENTIFIC EXEGESIS

One starting point for answering that question is found in the work of George Stigler. In "Textual exegesis as a scientific problem," Stigler (1965) addressed the problem of choosing among competing interpretations of a portion of an author's work. Stigler clearly has Werenfels's problem in mind when he points out that one can find in many authors' works individual passages that seem to support widely different theoretical conclusions. How should those passages be inter-preted? Which of them should be given prominence? Stigler likens the problem of textual exegesis in this regard to the problem of the single fact in statistical work. In order to increase your confidence in a statistical test, you increase the sample size. Similarly, in order to increase your confidence in a particular inter-pretation of a text, you increase the amount of the author's work taken into consideration. "We increase our confidence in the interpretation of an author by increasing the number of his main theoretical conclusions which we can deduce from (our interpretation of) his analytical system" (Stigler, 1965, p. 448).

Stigler goes on to provide a method for applying his "principle of scienti-fic exegesis" (Stigler, 1965, p. 448), illustrated in figure 31.1. First, the "general

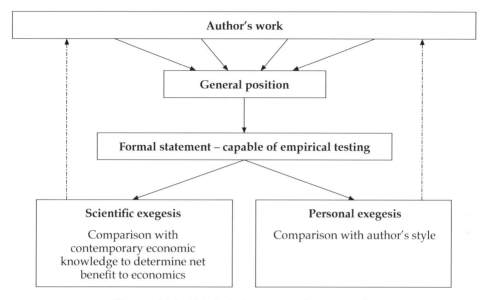

Figure 31.1 Stigler's hermeneutic approach

position" of the author under study is established. A general position is the theoretical core of an author's work, restated in a manner compatible with contemporary economic theory. The general position will probably not be formally stated in the author's own work, but will have to be constructed by interpreters from the various elements of the author's work. Nevertheless, Stigler appears confident that, at any given time, the economics community will recognize what the general positions of past economists are, especially in the case of significant figures such as Adam Smith, David Ricardo, Karl Marx, Léon Walras, or John Maynard Keynes. Once the author's general position is identified, it can be stated in "a strong form capable of contradictions by the facts" (Stigler, 1965, p. 448).

At this point, Stigler argues that two different interpretive activities can occur. First, contemporary theorists can examine the relation between the author's general position and what the modern discipline knows about the economy. The interpretation of the author's general position allows us to evaluate how it can be (has been) amended or improved to explain a greater portion of modern economic life. If the author's general position survives comparison with contemporary economic knowledge, we can say that the author has had a net positive impact on the modern discipline. On the other hand, if the modern discipline's knowledge falsifies the author's general position, the interpretation allows us to say that the author's work has made no lasting contribution to economics.

The other interpretive activity which can occur once the author's general position has been stated in a strong form is the evaluation of the consistency of the author's own conclusions. Theorists often make logical mistakes, or hold beliefs that are later proven false. Should the classical economists' "iron law of wages," or Stanley Jevons's sunspot theory of the business cycle, lead us to reject their entire theoretical work? Certainly not. While economic science may winnow this chaff through the process of testing the author's general position, some inter- preters may be interested in figuring out exactly what the original author really did believe, even when it is wrong by today's standards. Where contradictory passages in an author's work are encountered during this type of interpretive work, Stigler says his principle of scientific exegesis provides no guidance, because the net benefit to modern economics is not the interpreter's concern. In its place, he suggests that the interpreter choose as "decisive" an interpretation that fits well with the author's "style" of thought. Stigler calls this rule "the principle of per- sonal exegesis" (Stigler, 1965, p. 448). We will return to the theme of personal exegesis later in the essay.

31.3   STIGLER AND THE HERMENEUTIC CIRCLE

Stigler's principle of scientific exegesis provides a strong hermeneutic program for the evaluation of the contribution of past economic work to the current discip- line. However, there is a fly in Stigler's exegetical ointment. Notice in figure 31.1 the prominent role that the author's "general position" plays. While this theoret- ical framework is derived from the author's work, it also plays a governing role in the interpretation of specific passages in the author's work (note the feedback loop from the general position to the author's work through both personal and scientific exegesis). Which comes first, the text or the general position?

In Stigler's formulation, there is an implicit assumption that the interpreter already knows the author's "general position" before she begins to interpret a specific passage of the text. A seemingly innocuous assumption, this actually points to one of the central issues in hermeneutics, which has generated much of the most interesting work in hermeneutic theory. Put differently, Stigler assumes that if you are to make sense of any portion of the text before you, you need to have some prior understanding of what the text is generally about. But how are you to acquire a general understanding of the text without understanding all the passages within the text? We call this dilemma the "hermeneutic circle": understanding any portion of a text requires knowledge of all of the text, under- standing all of the text requires knowledge of every portion of the text.

Methodologically, the problem posed by the hermeneutic circle is a question of how you break out of the hermeneutic circle. Is there a means of avoiding the trap? Stigler's assumption that the interpreter has prior knowledge of the author's general position comes quite close to the answer to this question provided by Paul Ricoeur (1981) in his synthesis of hermeneutic philosophy. Drawing upon the hermeneutic tradition of Dilthey, Gadamer, Martin Heidegger (1962), and others, Ricoeur accepts the dilemma expressed in the problem of the hermeneutic circle, but suggests that the dilemma's resolution lies not in the metaphor of "breaking out" but, rather, in one's "entrance into" the circle. He argues that the interpreter must enter the circle with the *right* pre-understanding of the text. You come to the text before you with an anticipation of what it may hold; an anticipation shaped by your familiarity with other texts and with an interpretive community. Quoting Heidegger, Ricoeur (1981, p. 58) says, "what is decisive is not to get out of the circle but to come into it in the right way." But this only pushes our methodological question back one level, for now we have to ask: What is the "right way" to come into the hermeneutic circle?

Stigler's response to the question of the "right way" for an economist to gain a pre-understanding of economics texts is best expressed in another essay (Stigler, 1982). There, in an investigation of the possible uses of biography in the study of the history of economics, Stigler argues that the meaning of a text is determined not by the individual interpreter or even the original author, but by the scientific community of economists, as they read and re-read the text over time: "The recipients of a scientific message are the people who determine what the message is . . ." (Stigler, 1982, p. 91). *For economists*, then, the *right* pre-understanding of authors' general positions is provided to the interpreter by the economics profession. That scientific community is best positioned, Stigler argues, to understand the scientific meaning of a text. So the modern interpreter enters the hermeneutic circle as an economist with the profession's pre-understanding of the scientific meaning of the author's work in hand.

We have come full circle with Stigler. The methodological principle of scientific exegesis calls for us to use the author's text as a testing ground for the analytic framework that the economics profession has identified with the author. If we can show that the author's theoretical conclusions are deducible from the general position ascribed to the author, and these theoretical conclusions stand up against what the modern profession knows of the economy, we can say that the author has made a positive net contribution to modern economics. Where these conclusions need modification or improvement, we can show that the economics profession has progressed beyond the author's original work. Both history and progress, then, emerge from the exegetical work associated with identifying the author's general position.

31.4 The Mythology of Coherence

Stigler's argument that the interpreter's pre-understanding of an economics text should depend upon the general position ascribed to the author by the economics profession is, however, problematic. The first reason we should be suspicious of Stigler's notion regarding the pre-understanding of the general position focuses on the problematic nature of the "general position" itself. Where does one find the general position within the author's work? It is rarely said to be in one specific passage; rather, one finds pieces of it scattered over the length and breadth of the author's career. But why choose those pieces and not others? What do you do with statements that modify parts of the general position, or with other statements that we can show to contradict the general position? We are, of course, right back to Stigler's original problem – the hermeneutic circle. But, why, we ask, did the author not simply make her general position clear herself?

To use Stigler's own statistical style of discourse, the central problem with the notion of distilling a general position from an author's work is one of over-determination. Just as there are several hypotheses that can account for a specific set of data, there are always several possible general positions that can be constructed from any author's work. Increasing the sample size (the range of the author's work taken into consideration) simply increases the probability that competing general positions cannot be ruled out.

A general position, therefore, is an *abstraction* from the texts that comprise the author's work. In keeping with Stigler's characterization, Don Patinkin (1982, p. 17) once described it as the attempt "to pass a regression line through a scholar's work that will represent its central message." Ignoring the author's own interests and audience, the interpreter abstracts a general position from an author's texts; giving the author's work a coherent meaning that the author never actually thought at any particular moment in time and could in fact disagree with. The search for a coherent general position for the purpose of evaluating scientific progress is labeled by Quentin Skinner (1988) as the construction of a "mythology of coherence." While we may assume that no author deliberately contradicts herself in order to make her contemporary or future interpreters confused, we must also accept the fact that no author's work is handed down to us from "on high" – written in a single moment and with a God-like recognition of all the interconnections among the work's many parts. Skinner remarks that such mythologies become histories "not of ideas at all, but of abstractions: a history of thoughts which no one ever actually succeeded in thinking, at a level of coherence which no one ever actually attained" (Skinner, 1988, p. 40).

If we take the passage of time in an author's work seriously, and reconstruct specific passages on their own merits (even when they are at odds with passages written earlier or later in the author's life), it is unlikely that we will end up creating a mythical general position. Anthony Waterman caught Skinner's point well when he remarked, in responding to a criticism of his interpretation of a particular passage in Malthus:

> There is a great temptation to tidy up the creative mess left behind by men like Malthus. But Quentin Skinner . . . has warned historians of ideas to resist that temptation. For to succumb to what he called the "mythology of coherence" would be to impose a far greater distortion upon the material than that minimum that must inevitably be inflicted when we attempt to pin down *a coherent subset* of our author's work. Those of us who accept this methodological rule will content ourselves with lots of little snapshots, like "Mr. Keynes and the Classics"; and will remain unrepentantly sceptical of all attempts to inform us of "What Malthus (Keynes, Marx, et al.) Really Meant." (Waterman, 1988, pp. 206–7)

31.5   INTERLUDE: "LITTLE SNAPSHOTS" – RATIONAL RECONSTRUCTION

While there are a couple more problems with the search for general positions that need to be examined, Waterman's suggestion that we "content ourselves with lots of little snapshots" provides an opportunity to point out a positive hermeneutic application of Stigler's principle of scientific exegesis. You may, in fact, already have thought to ask this question: What if the interpretive goal is more modest than the construction of a general position that spans the author's entire work? What if you simply want to bring a subset of the author's work – one particular text, or a small group of texts – into dialogue with current economics? Could we thereby avoid the mythology of coherence trap that is inherent in a general position? In order to distinguish this less ambitious interpretive task from the construction of general positions, we will give it the label "rational reconstruction." Originally introduced by Richard Rorty (1984), the term rational reconstruction is used here in a narrower sense than it is by Blaug (1990), who applies it to any interpretation adopting the concerns of current economics as its primary hermeneutic stance, including the search for past authors' general positions.

As interpretive exercises, rational reconstructions differ from the construction of general positions in four important ways. First, rational reconstructions, as suggested by Waterman's phrase, focus on a subset of a past author's work. Whether it is one book or article, or a group of articles written at about the same time, the text chosen for a rational reconstruction is not chosen because it best represents the author's general position; the interpreter's goal is simply to bring that particular text into dialogue with present-day concerns. A narrower focus prevents abstractions that move too far away from the texts under consideration. In this sense, a rational reconstruction is still governed by the texts in a way that a general position may not be.

Secondly, the interpreter's task in a rational reconstruction is not the construction of a theoretical position from the past author's work that can be contrasted with current knowledge but, rather, the reconstruction of the past author's argument in a modern theoretical framework. Mathematical modeling techniques and theoretical concepts unknown to the original author may appear in the rational reconstruction, and aspects of the author's argument that the interpreter knows to be mistaken may be replaced with more defensible propositions. Reconstruction, then, is an appropriate term for this interpretive exercise: the author's work will not appear as it did in the original, but will be rendered intelligible to the modern economic theorist.

Thirdly, the selection of techniques and concepts used to cast the author's work in modern garb by each interpreter implies that multiple rational reconstructions of an author's work may be possible. We saw earlier that the possibility of multiple general positions from an author's work poses a problem for interpreters who are seeking an abstract coherent theoretical framework from the entirety of an author's work. In the case of rational reconstructions, the existence of differing interpretations emerges from the choices made by the interpreter. If one were to compare rational reconstructions, the relevant comparison would be which reconstruction makes the original author's work more useful to the needs of the modern economics community (Emmett, 1997).

Finally, because rational reconstructions focus on particular parts of authors' work and bring that work into dialogue with contemporary scholarship, they are less likely to be used as an indicator of the degree of scientific progress from the past to the present. The connection between Stigler's principle of scientific exegesis, the search for general positions, and the notion of scientific progress will be mentioned in a subsequent section. Rather than setting the past author up for a damning comparison, a rational reconstruction makes the author our contemporary, and forces us to confront the fact that we may not know something that she did. Because rational reconstructions deliberately rewrite past authors' work in the language of current science in order to challenge current theory, we might think of them as the use of the past to advance toward the future, rather than a judgment upon the past from the standpoint of the present.

31.6 HERMENEUTIC AUTHORITY AND THE HERMENEUTICS OF SUSPICION

A second reason why Stigler's notion of the pre-understood general position is problematic emerges from the role that it assigns to the economics profession as the final arbiter of meaning. If the economics profession governs the pre-understanding that we bring to the text before us, will that scientific community be willing to give a legitimate hearing to a new interpretation of a well-known text? ("We" know Adam Smith, and this is not the Smith "we" know.) Can a new interpretation of an author cause the profession to reevaluate a canonical author's position relative to contemporary work? Ricardo serves as a good example, because Stigler himself assumes that we "know" Ricardo. Yet, even in Stigler's lifetime, a fundamental reinterpretation of Ricardo's work was under way, led by Samuel Hollander (1979). The new "Ricardo" is at odds with Stigler's own "Ricardo," and would likely be judged to have had a greater net contribution to modern economic thought than Stigler might have allowed. Stigler also dismissed the contribution of American institutionalists to postwar economics, but more recent studies have created linkages between them and the emergence of the New Institutionalism (Rutherford, 1994). If the scientific community determines the meaning of the text, can these studies change the community's pre-understanding?

The notion of the economics profession as the final arbiter of meaning is problematic, therefore, because it gives *hermeneutic authority* to one specific interpretive community (see Fish, 1980). On what basis are we to accept the authority of the economics profession as an arbiter of meaning for economics texts? Are we to accept its authority because of the validity of current economics theory, its practioners' knowledge of the texts, their interpretive skills and balanced appreciation for the net benefit of past theorists' work – or simply because we are economists? These questions were raised in an interesting way several years ago, when an English professor at Harvard University held a conference on Adam Smith. The title of the conference was "Who Owns Adam Smith?" and only a few historians of economics were among the invited speakers.

Similarly, why should economists yield hermeneutic authority to other disciplines over texts that might contribute to our understanding of economics? Historians of economics have sometimes been reluctant to accept the contribution of "noneconomics" texts to the history of economics. This reluctance may stem from another implication of Stigler's principle: economists are not the recipients of the message of noneconomics texts, and therefore are unqualified to interpret them. Unpublished manuscripts, correspondence, government reports, magazine articles, and teaching materials provide a rich resource for understanding the meaning of published texts (Weintraub et al., 1998), but were often ignored until recently, because historians of economics accepted Stigler's argument that biographical material would divert them from the task of assessing the scientific validity of the abstracted general position (Stigler, 1982). In like manner, nonscholarly dialogue by economists and others on public policy has often also been ignored by historians of economics, because neither the economists' contributions nor other commentary were "economics" proper. The acceptance of this artificial dichotomy between economics and noneconomics texts left historians of economics handicapped in their efforts to interpret texts, because they missed opportunities to study sources that might assist them. A recent study of the origins of the "dismal science" by one of Stigler's former students provides an excellent example of the implications of our ignorance of this dichotomy (Levy, 2001).

Even within the community of economists, there are problems with the hermeneutic authority of mainstream economics' interpretation of particular authors. The magisterial voice that Stigler adopts suggests to the historian of economics that the pre-understanding of an economics text comes from the economics profession because that scientific community speaks with one voice. However, the notion of *one community, one voice* is as problematic as that of hermeneutic authority. The various schools of economics interpret past authors quite differently, and historians of economics in the past 40 years have shown remarkable diversity in their interpretations of past economists' writings. The past is often the stage on which the debates of the present are contested. Once again, the interpretation of Ricardo is a good example, with at least two, if not three, different Ricardian theoretical frameworks articulated in the literature. Furthermore, the differences among these different "general positions" usually parallel the theoretical differences between different schools of economics (for a plea to make this contest the center of the history of economics, see Roncaglia, 1996).

Is there a way to avoid the proliferation of "general positions" ascribed to canonical texts among competing contemporary schools of economics? As long as the focus of interpretation is on the construction of a general position that can be used to identify the author's net benefit to modern economics (Stigler's hermeneutic principle), the answer is probably "No." However, we can gain something by turning this question around somewhat, and looking at the issue from a different angle. Rather than looking at the various general positions ascribed to an author by the different schools of economics and arguing over their relative merits, we might ask of any particular general position the following questions: What aspects of the author's work does this interpretation obscure from view? What does it hide? These questions engage the reader in what, following Ricoeur (1970, pp. 32–3), might be called the "hermeneutics of suspicion." If interpretation is the act of focusing attention on certain themes in a work, then necessarily it is also the act of leading one's attention away from other themes in the work. One task an interpreter can undertake is that of uncovering in an author's work that which the "general position" ascribed to the author has missed.

31.7   WHIG HISTORY

The third problem with Stigler's hermeneutic program relates to the issue of scientific progress and the present-day scientific community's appreciation of the past on its own terms. Stigler's mentor in the history of economics, Frank H. Knight, began his essay on classical economics with the words: "On the assumption that the primary interest in the 'ancients' in such a field as economics is to learn from their mistakes, the principal theme of this discussion will be the contrast between the 'classical' system and 'correct' views" (Knight, 2000, p. 237). Stigler's principle of scientific exegesis articulates the hermeneutic program behind these words, a program designed to interpret the contribution of authors and key works to the progress of economic science. By identifying the key interpretive question as the determination of an author's net benefit to modern economic science, Stigler implicitly sets a standard for scientific progress: present-day theory stands as the judge of the past. More than likely, no past author will escape the interpreter's knife entirely (for contrasting views of the importance of progress for the historian of economics, see Winch, 2000; Hynes, 2001).

A history that allows present-day theory to be the judge of the past is often called a *Whig history*. The term, picked up from Herbert Butterfield's (1931) study, has been a subject of debate among historians of economics since Paul Samuelson (1987) first introduced it. Much of the discussion has been complicated by the conflation of two different problems. The first, often called *presentism*, refers to a theme already introduced in this essay; namely, the practically inevitable present-day concerns embedded in a pre-understanding that the interpreter brings with her to the study of past texts. But Butterfield's concern was not with presentism *per se*; he acknowledged that all history shares this problem, and that present-day concerns often do provide a motivation for historical investigation. Whig history is a particular type of presentism; one that makes the historian's present-day perspective the judge of the past. In a Whig history, the goal of the interpreter is to praise those who have significant net contributions and to condemn those whose contributions have been discarded on the waste heaps of historical progress. Although Stigler's principle of scientific exegesis need not be used for Whiggish purposes (rational reconstructions usually avoid the charge of Whig history), it often is. As Frank Hahn recently said: "What the dead had to say, when of value, has long since been absorbed, and when we need to say it again we can generally say it much better" (Hahn, 1993, p. 165). Stigler would not have put it better.

31.8   ABANDONING WHIG HISTORY, AND THE SEARCH FOR GENERAL POSITIONS

So far, we have asked what sense *you as a member of the contemporary community of economists* can make of a past economist's work. Stigler's principle of scientific exegesis was our starting point, and we have examined the pitfalls such as mythologies of coherence and Whig history into which it may lead us. While the legitimacy of general positions, Whig history, and notions of progress in the history of economics remain topics of debate (see Henderson, 1996; see also the discussion on history of economics readers in the August 2001 and September 2001 archives of the HES email list), some historians of economics have abandoned the attempt to assess the past in terms of the present, and opted instead for what has been called "historical reconstruction" (Rorty, 1984). Choosing to make the past their present, these historians of economics focus on reconstructing the meaning of texts at specific moments in time in the past (for a contribution that helped to turn historians' attention in this direction, see Weintraub, 1991).

Until recently, studies that focused on a text's relation to its own context were considered to be "external" or "relativist" history (Blaug, 1985). The critics of external history condemned the deterministic linkage made in such studies between a text and its social, political, cultural, and intellectual contexts (for example, that Keynes's *The General Theory* arose from the Great Depression). Ideas, it was said, have their own history; telling the story of an idea's development was "internal" or "absolutist" history (Blaug, 1985). However, there is a difference between arguing that ideas are determined by their context and interpreting the historical meaning of texts. Rather than seeking the link between ideas and historical events, historical reconstructions seek to reconstruct the sense (meaning) that someone gave a particular text at some historical point. The most obvious form of historical reconstruction is the effort to understand the original author's meaning. But there are other forms of historical reconstruction as well. For example, we might want to ask what sense public policy-makers in the 1940s made of Keynes *The General Theory*, or what Piero Sraffa (1951) made of David Ricardo. We might also be interested in what contemporaries of the original author made of the text when it appeared. Our interest in these questions leads us to try to make sense of the meaning that *someone other than ourselves* (and in many cases, other than a present-day economist) gave to a text.

To examine the hermeneutic issues related to historical reconstruction, we will focus on the reconstruction of the original author's meaning. The same principles apply to other historical reconstructions. We can ask initially if Stigler's aforementioned principle of personal exegesis provides the basis for the historical reconstruction of the original author's meaning. Although we have concluded that scientific exegesis is problematic, might personal exegesis yet help us to construct a coherent account of the author's own theoretical conclusions (wrong as they may be!)?

Stigler, you may remember, suggested that after determining an author's general position, it would be possible to go back and examine whether the conclusions of the general position match up with the author's own conclusions. Putting aside the issues that we have already addressed regarding the determination of a general position, we will focus here instead on Stigler's suggestion that the appropriate guide to follow in personal exegesis is the author's "style." Economists are not accustomed to analyzing a writer's style as part of their exegetical work, but style has reentered economics discourse in the rhetorical work of D. N. McCloskey (1998). McCloskey points out that every writer adopts an "ethos" or *persona* in her writing. A writer's "style" emerges from the authority or trustworthiness of the ethos to which she appeals. Nineteenth-century writers wrote in a plain style: educated readers addressing their equals. Modern economists adopt a style that deflects attention from the writer toward the authority of the "scientific ethos" provided by the community of economists (McCloskey, 1998, pp. 10–11).

Because style depends, at least in part, upon the author's rhetorical community, Stigler's notion of personal exegesis naturally takes us into an examination of the author's intellectual and social context. What concerns the interpreter interested in historical reconstruction is the range of meanings of words and concepts that were available to the author at the time she wrote her text. The term "uncertainty," for example, has a more specific meaning within economics today than it did in the early twentieth century, when Frank Knight (1921) wrote his famous treatise on the subject. If we wish to reconstruct Knight's treatment of uncertainty historically, we will have to make ourselves aware of the range of meanings that he may have drawn on, rather than assuming that he shared the current discipline's understanding of the term (Emmett, 1997). While we may not be willing to go as far as Michel Foucault (1972, p. 129) in arguing that the linguistic structure in which Knight operated governed the possible meanings that could be assigned to his text, we can agree that the disciplinary discourse of uncertainty in the 1910s will have to be placed in the context of the term's meaning within a larger social and philosophic discourse (for examples, see Kloppenberg, 1986). J. G. A. Pocock (1962, 1985) has made this type of linguistic contextualism the cornerstone of his historiography, which has made significant inroads into the history of economics, especially the history of its early period (see Winch, 1996).

While we may agree with Pocock and Foucault that the discursive context and linguistic structure within which a past author worked limit the range of meanings and usages to which the author had access, the key issue for most historians of economics is what the author *did* with the meanings at her disposal. It is not just the meaning of concepts and structure of the language that are important, but their use. To return to the example of Knight's notion of uncertainty, we recognize that he took notions of indeterminacy and voluntary action that were attached to the notion of uncertainty outside the realm of economics and brought them together in the introduction of a new concept within economics. A historical reconstruction of his work would then recognize the new use within economics of a term previously associated with other discourses. Hence, while we as interpreters cannot avoid the examination of an author's intellectual and linguistic context in the process of writing an historical reconstruction, we must in the final analysis make sense of the particular way in which the author used those concepts and spoke within that linguistic context to communicate to her contemporaries what she meant.

The guiding hermeneutic principle of historical reconstruction is Quentin Skinner's: "The relevant logical consideration is that no agent can eventually be said to have meant or done something which he could never be brought to accept as a correct description of what he had meant or done" (Skinner, 1998, p. 48). To make it clear that hermeneutic authority is given here to the original agent, Skinner adds that his principle requires that "any plausible account" the interpreter may provide "of what the agent meant must necessarily fall under, and make use of, the range of descriptions which the agent himself could at least in principle have applied to describe and classify what he was doing" (Skinner, 1998, p. 48). While this principle bears some resemblance to Stigler's principle of personal exegesis, Skinner argues that one should examine the author's *use* of words rather than the author's style (for comparison of Skinner's approach to Pocock and others, see Tully, 1988; Bevir, 1999). Skinner's question is: What was the author trying to do by using the words she used?

Answering Skinner's question often requires a richly textured study of the text that examines its relation to the author, the author's discursive community, and the social context within which the author lived at the time of writing the text. A wide variety of literature will assist the interpreter; including published texts (scholarly and otherwise), unpublished manuscripts, correspondence, curricular materials, pictures, interviews, and other materials. The anthropologist Clifford Geertz (1973) has called such studies "thick" descriptions; the term is an appropriate contrast to the thin abstractions of general positions.

31.9 CONCLUSION

At the beginning, we considered an economics text sitting on the desk in front of you. Making sense of that text appeared to be a straightforward problem of reading carefully. By now, however, you may wonder what sense, or how many senses, you can make of the text! The problems that we have considered challenge any interpretation you may attempt, be it the construction of a general position along Stiglerian lines, a rational reconstruction, or a historical reconstruction. In conclusion, then, perhaps it is appropriate to summarize and emphasize the positive aspects of the issues we have considered.

First, as interpreters, we cannot escape the concerns of the times in which we live. We live in the present, and our historical interests are often animated by our present-day concerns. But the interpreter does have a choice as to whether she will interpret the text from the perspective of the present. Where the interpreter's interest is in bringing an historical author's work into dialogue with current economics, Stigler's principle of scientific exegesis is an appropriate guide. However, there is a thin line between rationally reconstructing the author's work in a way that enables the interpreter to identify its relation to modern thought and adopting the judgmental voice of Whig history. The latter should be avoided when the former is undertaken.

Secondly, whether the interpreter seeks to reconstruct the contemporary meaning of a text (rational reconstruction) or a historical meaning (historical reconstruction), less is more. The creation of a general statement of the author's position inevitably leads the interpreter to create a mythology; an abstraction from the author's work that will be upheld by appeal to some texts, but almost certainly falsified by others. Careful exegesis of specific texts, considering the range of meanings that they might have, the context in which they were created, and the purposes to which the author (or past interpreter) may have put them, will serve the interpreter well. Ironically, perhaps, abstract general positions turn out to be thinner representations of an author's work than either the contemporary rendering provided by a good rational reconstructions or the richly textured accounts that emerge from a good historical reconstruction.

Finally, the act of interpretation is a humbling experience. When we recognize the contingencies that shape the texts that we interpret, we also realize that our own ideas are limited by the context in which we live. And when the past speaks to us, we learn that others thought well – sometimes even better than we do.

Note

The author wishes to thank Bruce Janz and Anthony Waterman for conversations that enriched the views expressed here.

Bibliography

Bevir, M. 1999: *The Logic of the History of Ideas*. Cambridge, UK: Cambridge University Press.

Blaug, M. 1985: *Economic Theory in Retrospect*. Cambridge, UK: Cambridge University Press.

—— 1990: On the historiography of economics. *Journal of the History of Economic Thought*, 12, 27–37.

Butterfield, H. 1931: *The Whig Interpretation of History*. London: Pelican.

Derrida, J. 1976: *Of Grammatology*. Baltimore, MD: Johns Hopkins University Press.

Dilthey, W. 1976: *Selected Writings*. Cambridge, UK: Cambridge University Press.

Emmett, R. B. 1997: Reflections on "breaking away": economics as science and the history of economics as history of science. *Research in the History of Economic Thought and Methodology*, 15, 221–36.

Fish, S. 1980: *Is There a Text in This Class? The Authority of Interpretive Communities*. Cambridge, MA: Harvard University Press.

Foucault, M. 1972: *The Archaeology of Knowledge*. London: Tavistock.

Gadamer, H.-G. 1989: *Truth and Method*, 2nd revised edn. New York: Crossroad.

Geertz, C. 1973: *The Interpretation of Culture: Selected Essays*. New York: Basic Books.

Gerrard, B. 1993: The significance of interpretation in economics. In W. Henderson, T. Dudley-Evans, and R. Backhouse (eds.), *Economics and Language*. London: Routledge, 51–63.

Hahn, F. 1993: Autobiographical notes with reflections. In M. Szenberg (ed.), *Eminent Economists*. Cambridge, UK: Cambridge University Press.

Heidegger, M. 1962: *Being and Time*, revised edition. New York: Harper & Row.

Henderson, J. 1996: Whig history of economics is dead – Now what? http://www.eh.net/HE/hes_list/Editorials/henderson.php

Hollander, S. 1979: *The Economics of David Ricardo*. Toronto: University of Toronto Press.

Hynes, A. 2001: Economics' past and present: historical analysis and current practice. *Journal of the History of Economic Thought*, 23, 181–95.

Kloppenberg, J. 1986: *Uncertain Victory: Social Democracy and Progressivism in European and American Social Thought 1870–1920*. New York: Oxford University Press.

Knight, F. H. 1921: *Risk, Uncertainty, and Profit*. Boston: Houghton Mifflin.

—— 2000: The Ricardian theory of production and distribution. In R. B. Emmett (ed.), *Selected Essays by Frank H. Knight*, vol. 1: *"What is Truth" in Economics?* Chicago: The

University of Chicago Press, 237–89. Originally published in the *Canadian Journal of Economics and Political Science*, 1 (February and May 1935), 3–25 and 171–96.

Lavoie, D. (ed.) 1991: *Economics and Hermeneutics*. London: Routledge.

Levy, D. M. 2001: *How the Dismal Science Got Its Name: Classical Economics & the Ur-Text of Racial Politics*. Ann Arbor, MI: University of Michigan Press.

McCloskey, D. N. 1998: *The Rhetoric of Economics*. Madison, WI: University of Wisconsin Press.

Michelfelder, D. P. and Palmer, R. E. (eds.) 1989: *Dialogue and Deconstruction: The Gadamer–Derrida Encounter*. Albany, NY: State University of New York Press.

Patinkin, D. 1982: *Anticipations of The General Theory?* Oxford: Blackwell.

Pocock, J. G. A. 1962: The history of political thought: a methodological enquiry. In P. Laslett and W. Runciman (eds.), *Philosophy, Politics and Society*, second series. Oxford: Blackwell, 183–202.

—— 1985: State of the art. In *Virtue, Commerce and History*. Cambridge, UK: Cambridge University Press, 1–34.

Ricoeur, P. 1970: *Freud and Philosophy: An Essay on Interpretation*. New Haven, CN: Yale University Press.

—— 1981: *Hermeneutics and the Human Sciences*. Cambridge, UK: Cambridge University Press.

Roncaglia, A. 1996: Why should economists study the history of economic thought? *The European Journal of the History of Economic Thought*, 3, 296–309.

Rorty, R. 1984: The historiography of philosophy: four genres. In R. Rorty, J. B. Schneewind, and Q. Skinner (eds.), *Philosophy in History: Essays on the Historiography of Philosophy*. Cambridge, UK: Cambridge University Press, 49–75.

Rutherford, M. 1994: *Institutions in Economics: The Old and the New Institutionalism*. Cambridge, UK: Cambridge University Press.

Samuelson, P. 1987: Out of the closet: a program for the Whig history of science. *History of Economics Society Bulletin*, 9 (Fall), 51–60.

Skinner, Q. 1988: Meaning and understanding in the history of ideas. In J. Tully (ed.), *Meaning and Context: Quentin Skinner and His Critics*. Princeton, NJ: Princeton University Press, 29–67. Originally published in *History and Theory*, 8 (1969), 3–53.

Sraffa, P. 1951: Introduction. In *The Works and Correspondence of David Ricardo*. Cambridge, UK: Cambridge University Press, for the Royal Economic Society.

Stigler, G. J. 1965: Textual exegesis as a scientific problem. *Economica*, 32, 447–50.

—— 1982: The scientific uses of scientific biography, with special reference to J. S. Mill. In *The Economist as Preacher and Other Essays*. Chicago: The University of Chicago Press. Originally published in Robson, J. M. and Laine, M. (eds.) 1976: *James and John Stuart Mill: Papers of the Centenary Conference*, Toronto: Toronto University Press.

Tully, J. (ed.) 1988: *Meaning and Context: Quentin Skinner and His Critics*. Princeton, NJ: Princeton University Press.

Waterman, A. M. C. 1988: Malthus on long swings: a reply. *Canadian Journal of Economics*, 21, 206–7.

Weintraub, R. 1991: Stabilizing *Dynamics: Constructing Economic Knowledge*. Cambridge, UK: Cambridge University Press.

Weintraub, R., Meardon, S. J., Gayer, T., and Banzhaf, H. S. 1998: Archiving the history of economics. *Journal of Economic Literature*, 36, 1496–501.

Winch. D. 1996: *Riches and Poverty: An Intellectual History of Political Economy in Britain, 1750–1834*. Cambridge, UK: Cambridge University Press.

—— 2000: Does progress matter? *The European Journal of the History of Economic Thought*, 7, 465–84.

CHAPTER THIRTY-TWO

Textuality and the History of Economics: Intention and Meaning

Vivienne Brown

32.1 INTRODUCTION

To say that studying the history of economics involves interpreting economics works and associated archival materials that were written in the past may seem uncontroversial, but such an apparently simple formulation of what is done in studying the history of economics is far from straightforward. Issues of interpretation have been the subject of intense debate over recent decades, and these debates have spanned (at least) philosophy, literary theory, history, and cultural studies. This essay will focus on just one aspect of these debates by engaging with arguments about the objective of reconstructing the author's intended meaning, and it will relate these arguments to the notions of "text" and "textuality." Given the high opportunity costs of engagement in such apparently arcane theoretical debate, economists may well wonder whether there is any particular potential payoff for their understanding of the history of their own discipline. A presupposition of this essay is that these theoretical debates do have something to contribute to the history of economics in helping to explain how different interpretations of the same works keep being produced, and so have implications for the ways in which the history of economics may be understood.

It is a commonsense presupposition that correctly interpreting a work gives us the meaning that its author intended; correctly reading Adam Smith's works, for example, gives us the meaning that Smith intended. To query this commonsense presupposition may seem to some to imply that we have already crossed the Rubicon that separates rational from irrational discourse, but two questions may be raised at this stage which should caution against such a hasty conclusion.

First, to what extent is it to be expected that the history of economics should be characterized by a high or increasing degree of consensus over the meanings of the works that constitute its object of study? [See Brown (1997a) for a survey of the range of interpretations relating to Adam Smith.] This raises the question of how it is – if all are seeking to recover the same thing, the author's intended meaning – that historians of economics (and other intellectual historians) can reach contrary interpretive conclusions on the basis of reading the same works. Secondly, what are the procedures, criteria, and evidence for assessing the relative validity of different interpretations? If a correct interpretation of a work gives the author's intended meaning, how is it established which ones of those on offer do indeed give that intended meaning, or approximate in some way to it? This raises the question of evidence, since in order to apply criteria for an assessment of the comparative merit of rival interpretations it is necessary to know what the evidence is to which those criteria relate.

It is part of the present argument that these two apparently simple questions are not at all simple, and that trying to answer them has some radical implications for the way in which the history of economics, or any other form of intellectual history, is understood. In engaging with arguments that intellectual history should study (or should include the study of) authors' intended meanings, section 32.2 will address the first component of this notion by examining different notions of "intention," and section 32.3 will address the second component by examining notions of "meaning." In section 32.4 the notions of "text" and "textuality" will be discussed as a means of overcoming some of the difficulties outlined in sections 32.2 and 32.3 concerning an author's intended meaning. The essay concludes by very briefly returning to the two questions raised in the previous paragraph, concerning the heterogeneity of different interpretations in the history of economics and the evidence that might be relevant for evaluating them.

32.2   INTENTION

Although historians of economics may think of the notion of "intention" as intuitively straightforward, this notion has been the subject of considerable philosophic and literary debate (e.g., Newton-de Molina, 1976; Davidson, 1980a; Patterson, 1990; Iseminger, 1992; Anscombe, 2000 [1957]). One categorization of notions of intention that are relevant for interpretive debates has been proposed by the philosopher Donald Davidson, as follows:

> There are, I think, three sorts of intention which are present in all speech acts. First of all, there are ends or intentions which lie as it were beyond the production of words, ends that could at least in principle be achieved by nonlinguistic means. Thus one may speak with the intention of being elected mayor, of amusing a child, of warning a pilot of ice on the wings; one may write with the intention of making money, of proving one's cleverness, to celebrate the freedom of the will, or to neutralize a plaguing memory or emotion. Such ends do not involve language, in the sense that their description does not have to mention language. I call these intentions

"ulterior." . . . Second, every linguistic utterance or inscription is produced with the intention that it should have a certain force: it is intended to be an assertion, or command, a joke or question, a pledge or insult. There can be borderline cases, but only when straddling a border is intended: so it is possible to intend an utterance of "Go to sleep" as somewhere between an order and the expression of a wish, or to intend the remark "See you in July" as part promise and part prediction. Third, it is a necessary mark of a linguistic action that the speaker or writer intends his words to be interpreted as having a certain meaning. These are the strictly semantic intentions. (Davidson, 1993, pp. 298–9)

This threefold categorization of "intention," as ulterior intention, intention in saying something (illocutionary force), and semantic intention, will be followed below in examining the role of the author's intentions in defining the meaning of utterances or works.

The first category of intention is the ulterior intention in writing x. In Davidson's description, this is an intention that could in principle be achieved by nonlinguistic means. A related, though not identical, notion of intention is given in Wimsatt and Beardsley (1954) as the "design or plan in the author's mind" such that intention has affinities for "the author's attitude towards his work, the way he felt, what made him write" (p. 4). This article criticized what it termed "the intentional fallacy" by arguing that the "design or intention of the author is neither available nor desirable as a standard for judging the success of a work of literary art" such as poetry (p. 3). This is an argument about poetic evaluation that is based on an account of meaning as internal to the poem (rather than, say, based on the author's aspirations or the socio-historical context of writing), and so is discoverable by means of studying the poem's semantics, syntax, figuration, and so on, according to the critic's knowledge of a public language and its literature. The poet's prior intentions, if actually carried out, are regarded as redundant and, if not executed, are regarded as irrelevant; the thoughts and attitudes of the poem are therefore to be imputed to its *persona* or dramatic speaker, not to the actual author. This anti-intentionalist attack on Romantic aesthetics from the standpoint of New Criticism launched a major debate about literary intentionalism that spread far beyond its initial concern with poetic evaluation.

The second category of intention in Davidson's classification is what is meant *by* saying something, or what someone is doing *in* saying something. This category of intention derives from the work of J. L. Austin (1975 [1962]), in which utterances are conceived as speech acts or linguistic acts, and so are a form of action rather than something counterposed to action. Illocutionary acts are speech acts in which something is done or performed in saying something. For example, saying "I promise," according to certain conventions of promise-making, is just to make a promise; and saying "I name this . . . X" is, under certain conventions, just to name something as X. More generally, in any speech act the author or speaker *is doing something* intentionally in writing or speaking, such as asserting, promising, or threatening, and this point or force of the writing or speaking is the intended illocutionary force. Speaking or writing with a certain intended illocutionary force is thus to perform an act, an illocutionary act, the point of the illocutionary act being the intended illocutionary force. Successful performance of an illocutionary act requires that there is "uptake" of the act, in the sense that the audience or readership understands the intended illocutionary force of the utterance or work.

This approach has been developed in the work of Quentin Skinner in the history of political thought and has achieved a wide influence in intellectual history by this route (Skinner, 1988a–c; also critical articles in Tully, 1988). It is argued that to recover the *historical* meaning of a work it is necessary to recover the intended illocutionary force of the work in addition to understanding its sense and reference; or, alternatively, that to understand a work's sense and reference in historical context it is necessary also to recover its intended illocutionary force. To understand the historical meaning of a work it is therefore necessary to understand what the author was doing in writing such a work, and to achieve this it is necessary to recover the author's intentions in writing such a work, by placing it in its relevant historical context of argument and counter-argument as framed by the recognized linguistic conventions of the time. In an early statement of this position, it was argued that "the essential question which we therefore confront, in studying any given text, is what its author, in writing at the time he did for the audience he intended to address, could in practice have been intending to communicate" (Skinner, 1988a, p. 65). To answer this question requires the decoding of the author's intentions by placing that utterance in the context of the linguistic conventions of the time, which would have been taken for granted by the intended audience, and with respect to which the author's intentions in making that utterance would have been understood by those who were cognizant of those conventions. It was also argued in this paper that this historical approach requires that those intentions should be describable in terms that could have been accepted as correct by the author, even though the historian may be able to give a fuller or more convincing account of the author's intentions than the author could have given, thus ruling out the use of later conceptual criteria that were not available to the author (1988a, p. 48).

To embed the history of ideas in the intentions of the author as an historical figure purports to give a decidedly historicist inflexion to the history of ideas, but this has been somewhat displaced in later statements of Skinner's position, where it is argued that an interpreter does not have to take the author's statements about his intentions as a final authority on what those intentions (really) were. Whatever the hazards of overriding the author in any particular case, it is accepted in principle that sometimes the historian may have to discount an author's statements about the meaning of a work, since the author may be "self-deceiving" or "incompetent" in this respect (Skinner, 1988b, p. 77). It is thus not the author but the interpreter who is the "final authority" concerning what the author was doing in a particular work (p. 77). This raises the question of the relationship between the *intended* illocutionary force and the *actual* illocutionary force of an utterance as interpreted by the historian. If establishing the actual illocutionary force of an utterance, or what is meant by an author's saying x, is, ultimately, not determined by what the author thought was meant in saying x, then it is the actual, not the intended, illocutionary force of an utterance that is taken to constitute the meaning of that utterance or what the author was actually doing in the work. If it is the interpreter who is the final authority on what the author was doing in a particular piece of work, then the author's intentions are inferred from what that interpreter takes to be the actual illocutionary force.

It follows from this that the actual illocutionary force of a work (as identified by the interpreter) may be intended or unintended by the author of the work, and that which of the two it is thought to be is an issue of interpretive judgment with respect to the texts concerned, rather than the result of some privileged information regarding the author's actual intentions. This is indeed recognized in Skinner's later reply to critics, where it is accepted that what the interpreter is in fact concerned with is the actual illocutionary force of an utterance; and that the meaning and context of the utterance are sufficient to determine its illocutionary force "regardless of whether the speaker issued the utterance with that intended force" (Skinner, 1988c, p. 277). This is consistent with an earlier argument of Skinner's that the author's intentions in writing a work are in some sense "inside" the work; this contrasts with what is presented above as the first category of intention, which is held to lie "outside" the work in a merely contingent relationship with it (Skinner, 1988b, p. 74). Skinner's conclusion, that "the best hypothesis to adopt at this stage will usually be to assume that he [the author, in this case Machiavelli] was doing what he was doing intentionally" (Skinner, 1988c, p. 277), thus simply assumes that the actual illocutionary force of an utterance or piece of writing was intended in that an author was indeed intentionally doing whatever it was that he or she is taken to have been doing. Such a response, however, effectively cedes the criticism directed against Skinner's intentionalist position that, if the authority of the texts is held to be definitive in establishing what is meant by an author in saying x, then appeals to the author's intentional doing of something in saying x become strictly redundant to establishing that it is x that is being said. This is related to the point that there are no grammatical tests for verbs of action to establish agency in terms of intentional doing: "No grammatical test I know of, in terms of the things we may be said to do, of active or passive mood, or of any other sort, will separate out the cases here where we want to speak of agency" (Davidson, 1980b, p. 120). In other words, a person's "doings" may be intentional or not; and so a problem with Austin's and Skinner's accounts of illocutionary force is that interpreting what an author was doing in saying x is not sufficient to establish that it was an intentional doing on the author's part (for this point, see Austin, 1975 [1962], pp. 105–7). The acceptance that this approach "leaves the traditional figure of the author in extremely poor health" (Skinner, 1988c, p. 276) thus acknowledges that the role of the author's intentions in writing x is not after all the "main focus" of interpretive attention, which must instead be directed to the appropriate forms of discourse and their contextually determined conventions.

The third category of intention in Davidson's list is "semantic intention"; that is, the speaker or writer intends his or her words to be interpreted as having a certain meaning. An early statement of semantic intentionalism argued that it was the author's intentions or determining will that provides a determinate object for interpretation, since a text has to "represent *somebody's* meaning – if not the author's, then the critic's" (Hirsch, 1967, p. 3). Given the many different interpretations that could conceivably be made of a piece of writing, the only one compelling normative principle of interpretation is the one of understanding what the author meant, since "if a text means what it says, then it means nothing in particular. Its saying has no determinate existence but must be the saying of an author or reader" (p. 13). The author's "verbal meaning" is, by contrast, reproducible and determinate, and it is this that is represented by the text and forms the determinate object for analysis. It is acknowledged that there can be no certainty that any particular interpretation is the author's intended verbal meaning, and so the central issue for the *validity* of an interpretation hinges on a probabilistic judgment as to whether it is the author's intended meaning.

If the author's verbal meaning which is represented by a text is the determinate object of analysis for an interpreter, the notion of intended verbal meaning has to be developed in such a way that it may be accessible to interpreters – and here lies a central difficulty with this version of intentionalism that is similar to the one faced by Skinner's intentionalism. Early in the book, it is said that "*meaning is that which is represented by a text; it is what the author meant by his use of a particular sign sequence; it is what the signs represent*" (Hirsch, 1967, p. 8), but the crucial issue is the relationship between the first two propositions in this passage and the third one; that is, between what the author meant by using a particular sign sequence and what that sign sequence represents (or is taken to represent by an interpreter). What the sign sequence represents is taken to be determined by the author's determining will, but yet the construal of an author's willed meaning is then explained with reference to a linguistic account of the probable implications of utterances within a system of "types" and "genres" of which the interpreter is required to have had prior experience. It thus turns out that author and interpreter are required to have a "shared" understanding of what is to be the relevant framework of interpretation, and this shared requirement is registered in the shifts in Hirsch's definitions of author's verbal meaning from that which is subject to the determining will of the author to that which is shared by author and interpreter (pp. 31, 49, 66, 77). It is this shared framework, denominated in terms of types and genres, that is used to establish the author's unconscious as well as conscious verbal meanings; in the knowledge of the appropriate types and genres, the interpreter attributes the author with intending the unattended as well as attended meanings of the text, on the basis that these are the meanings that are implied by the text. An author may not be fully self-conscious in that he or she may not be paying full attention to all the implications of what is being uttered, but the criteria for construing the author's unconscious verbal meanings are the same as for the conscious ones, since both are held to be part of the intended verbal meaning. Thus what the author is thought to have intended (whether consciously or not) is inferred from what are construed to be the linguistic implications of the signs.

Arguments concerning the author's will and self-consciousness thus turn out to be redundant, since what really matters for interpretation and the assessment of the validity of interpretation is the proposed linguistic analysis of implication, types, and genres, and so on, and this is illustrated in the later discussion (in chapter 5) of the evidence required for the probabilistic process of validation which is concerned solely with issues of textual construal, but which ends by acknowledging that interpretation in the end amounts to "guessing what the author meant" (Hirsch, 1967, p. 207). The inherent weakness of pinning interpretation to a refined process of guessing the author's intentions lies in the fundamental distinction between what the author intended to do and what the author did (whether or not these are construed as conscious or unconscious), but these two notions are elided right at the beginning, where it is written: "that a man may not be conscious of all that he means is no more remarkable than that he may not be conscious of all that he does" (p. 22). The problem here is not just that intentionalism needs to encumber interpretation with theories of unconscious doings, but that, as observed above, not all doings are intentional.

A recent study reformulates this intentionalist argument by combining post-analytic philosophy, semantic holism, procedural individualism, and pyscho-analytic theory (Bevir, 1999, 2000; see the Round Table discussion in *Rethinking History*, 4(3) (2000), 295–350). According to this "weak intentionalism," authorial intentions are "the final intentions of authors as they make an utterance" and so they are equated with the meaning that the utterance had for the author at the point of writing the work rather than being prior to the utterance (1999, p. 69). For readers, hermeneutic meaning is the meaning that they ascribe to a work, and so the main difference between authors and readers is only that authors "appear to play a more active role than readers," such that whereas authors "intend to convey meaning," readers "merely happen to grasp meaning" (1999, pp. 53–4). Meaning is thus attributed to works by individuals and does not inhere in the work; it is the meaning a work has for a specific individual and not something that the work has independently of individuals (1999, pp. 54, 74). To be a *historical* meaning this hermeneutic meaning has to have been a meaning for an individual who was a historical figure in the past. It follows that the historian of ideas studies the beliefs that were expressed by the author in writing the work (or readers later reading it) such that "when people make an utterance, they express ideas or beliefs, and it is these ideas or beliefs that constitute the objects studied by historians of ideas" (1999, p. 142). Bevir's account of weak individualism is used to criticize Skinner's conventionalism and the contextualism of J. G. A. Pocock (e.g., Pocock, 1985).

Bevir's argument also needs to address the issue of the relation between conscious and unconscious intentions. It is argued that, since sincerity is logically prior to insincerity, the conscious is logically prior to the unconscious, and rationality is prior to irrationality, the historian of ideas should presume that the author's beliefs that are expressed in the work are sincere, conscious, and rational. It turns out, however, that this is an initial presumption only, and that historians should acknowledge that the author's beliefs may be insincere, unconscious, or irrational. An author's intentions may thus include pre-conscious intentions (which are unknown to the author) and unconscious intentions (about which the author may be wrong) as well as conscious intentions. In this case, the beliefs expressed by the author are not his or her actual beliefs, and so the historian of ideas should study not the beliefs that are expressed by the author but the actual beliefs of the author, since "when people's actual beliefs differ from their expressed ones, historians have to go beyond the expressed beliefs if they are to recover the actual ones" (Bevir, 1999, p. 267). But in this case the actual beliefs are those expressed by the work, not those expressed by the author (Bevir, 1999, p. 71). But how may the historian decide that the author's expressed beliefs are insincere, unconscious, or irrational? The injunction to the historian is to make sense of the material, since "the logic of their [the historians'] discipline remains such that they should invoke insincerity, the unconscious, or the irrational only if they cannot make sense of the material without doing so" (Bevir, 1999, p. 173), but the material that has to be made sense of here is not the expressed beliefs of the author but the works themselves. The reasons for deciding whether the author's expressed beliefs are sincere and so on are based on the historian's injunction to make sense of the material. The logic of the historian's discipline is thus that the work has to be made sense of by invoking whatever authorial beliefs – sincere or insincere, conscious or unconscious, rational or irrational – are thought necessary to achieve this (Brown, 2002).

Bevir's weak intentionalism thus requires attributing beliefs to authors which they may not have been aware of having, or which they might even have rejected as not their own, and in this respect his account is similar to Skinner's. In casting the author's pre-conscious and unconscious intentions as intentions none the less, the historian is required to provide a rationalized reconstruction of the author that relies on some modern understanding of psychoanalytic theory, and which may not correspond with the self-consciousness of the actual historical figure, even though it is the historical experience of that figure that ostensibly ensures that the intended meaning is an historical meaning. As with Skinner's and Hirsch's accounts, what drives the interpretation of the work is the need to attend to the actual beliefs (or actual illocutionary force or actual implications) as interpreted in the work under study, and any imputation of author's meaning is an inference based on that interpretive requirement. What is missing in such talk of the dependence of the work's meaning on the intentions of the author is any evidence of the author's intentions independently of the interpretations of the works (and other archival materials) that are being proposed by the historian. This is another instance of the difficulty faced by Skinner's and Hirsch's approach, that there is but one entity – the works and other archives in question – and so there is no evidence of the author's conscious and unconscious intentions independently of the interpretations being offered of the works, and which could be called upon to assess the extent to which any particular interpretation is a valid reconstruction of those intentions (cf., Hirsch, 1967, p. 165). Bevir's argument that objectivity is achieved by comparing rival interpretations with respect to various criteria does not meet this point, since what are being compared – according to his account – are rival interpretations of the works, not rival interpretations of the author's expressed beliefs.

This section has considered examples of the three different categories of authorial intentions that are presented in Davidson's passage, and it has argued that none of these provides a coherent account of the argument that the meaning of works is given by the (conscious and unconscious) intentions of their authors. This is not to say that accounts of authorial intentions would not be interesting or worth having if they could be found. The difficulty that is common to such approaches is (at least) twofold. First, there is the issue of the evidence of what those intentions were. If such evidence does not exist independently of the interpretations of the works and other archives that are at issue, then there is no independent evidence in principle relating to the author's intentions – as opposed to the evidence relating to the interpretation of the works. This implies that such claims about providing knowledge of the author's intentions are epistemologically empty. Secondly, imputing particular intentions to the author on the basis of an interpretation of the works may involve an interpretive reconstruction of the author's intentions, which the author as historical agent neither would nor could have assented to if they were put to him or her. This implies that such reconstructions of the author's alleged intentions cannot make claim to be invoking the historical author's intentions as they existed in time for him or her as a self-conscious agent, and so the strictly *historical* significance of such interpretations is open to question. What remains of such claims to have discovered or recovered the author's intentions thus amounts either to a rhetorical (in the narrow sense of merely persuasive) gesture, or a complimentary gesture bestowed upon valued interpretations which are simply supposed to have successfully reconstructed the author's intentions (cf., Ankersmit, 2000, pp. 325–6).

32.3 MEANING

The intentionalist approaches reviewed in section 32.2 have in common the argument that the meaning of a work is given by the psychological or mental state (or content of the mental state) of the author, whether this is construed in terms of the author's intentions, determining will, beliefs, or viewpoint. The meaning of the work is thus determined by some psychological or mental entity that exists in a relation of exteriority to the works but yet is held to determine the proper interpretation of those works. This meaning, determined externally, is then somehow intrinsic to the work and so can be "grasped," "found," "uncovered," or "recovered" in the act of interpretation. It is this that explains the tension in intentionalist arguments between the exteriority of the source of meaning with respect to the author's intention and the interiority of that same meaning with respect to the work itself. Caught between these two alternative sites for the definitive center of a work's meaning, these intentionalist arguments inevitably have to recognize that it is indeed the latter that is definitive but, as argued above, this renders precarious the notion of author's intention.

There is one version of the intentionalist argument, however, that does not encounter this problem. This version *identifies* the author's intended meaning with the interpretation of the work such that what emerges from a process of interpretation just is the author's intended meaning, since that just is what interpretation delivers (Knapp and Michaels, 1985; for a discussion, see Mitchell, 1985). Instead of positing the author's intended meaning as something which has or did have an independent existence *vis-à-vis* the work, the author's intended meaning is by definition held to be that which an interpretation renders. This version of the intentionalist argument overcomes the problems outlined in the previous section, since there is no longer any claim that the author's intention had a historical existence independently of interpretations of the work or that it is something that the author as a historical figure could have recognized or identified as his or her own. Such an argument is therefore not subject to the criticisms advanced in section 32.2, but this is achieved by making the argument tautologous. If any interpretation is by definition a rendering of the author's intended meaning, then the significance of its being so is surely lost. If its being the author's intended meaning no longer operates as a constraint on what may be claimed in an interpretation (over and above what the evidence of the work can sustain), then surely there is no longer any point in claiming it to be so.

According to Hirsch's argument, once the assumption of an author's intended meaning is removed, then no interpretation can correspond to *the* meaning of the text, because the text itself has no determinate meaning and can say different things to different readers (Hirsch, 1967, pp. 5, 11). Similarly, according to Bevir's argument, meanings cannot be ascribed to texts in themselves; unless the interpreter specifies for whom the text had that particular meaning, then the interpreter is merely saying how he or she chooses to read the text, and in this case "we should not make the mistake of assuming he is offering us an interpretation of the text itself; we might enjoy his reading, but we should not bother to ask ourselves whether it is true or not for there is no object of which it seeks to give an adequate account" (Bevir, 2000, p. 391). If the notion of author's intended meaning according to these intentionalist arguments is not accepted, however, this implies that all there can be are meanings that are the product of different readings. According to intentionalist arguments such as Hirsch's and Bevir's, such readings suffer the lack of not offering an account of the author's meaning, but if the author's meaning (as something other than an interpretation of the work) is not accessible, then the notion of a reading is a more coherent notion than author's meaning. What is construed as a weakness from within an intentionalist argument is thus regarded as a strength once that intentionalist argument is recognized as deeply problematic. Furthermore, it is not the case that there is no "object" of which a reading seeks to give an adequate account, since that object is provided by the text/work. Indeed, even within intentionalist accounts this has to be the case, since there is no object apart from the works of which an account can be given. As argued above, even according to the intentionalist accounts of Skinner, Hirsch, and Bevir, all that the interpreter can do is governed by the text: for Skinner, the historian seeks to give an account of the actual illocutionary force; for Hirsch, the interpreter seeks to construe the implications of the text; and for Bevir, the historian of ideas seeks to make sense of the materials. Inevitably, all that intentionalist interpretations can ever hope to achieve is to provide readings of the texts/works, and this is made evident in their own writings.

The differences between these various positions may be illustrated by reference to the issue of the "symmetry" or "asymmetry" of information between the analyst and the agent being studied (e.g., Sent, 1998). In the case of interpreting works in intellectual history, the analyst is the intellectual historian and the agent is the author of the work. Is there symmetry of information between the historian and the author? The author presumably has some access to the contents of his or her own mind that is denied to the historian. In addition, the author's information about the biographical, historical, and intellectual circumstances of the writing of the work is different from the historian's information about these topics. Both may have equal information about the contents of the works, however, on the assumption that there are no significant problems with missing or corrupted editions of the work (an assumption that is not always appropriate). Assuming that the historian and author have the same information about the contents of the work, there seems to be a major asymmetry in terms of knowledge of the author's mind and knowledge of the circumstances of writing the work. How do the different approaches to the relation between intention and meaning discussed above deal with this? Hirsch's argument provides discussion of the ways in which the interpreter may gain knowledge of the author's intended meaning but concedes that, in the end, interpretation amounts to refined guesswork. This suggests that the asymmetry is such that the historian's information is inferior to the author's. Skinner's and Bevir's arguments, however, reverse this asymmetry; each one privileges the interpreter's information, as the interpreter may have a better understanding of the author's intentions than the author has him- or herself, whether this superior information is based on the superiority of modern historical research or on modern psychoanalytic theory. The argument put by Knapp and Michaels, however, collapses the information relation between interpreter and author into one of identity; as an interpretation of the work just is the author's meaning, there can be no difference in principle between the two. The argument of this essay, by contrast, is that the asymmetry in information between interpreter and author is insuperable, as the interpreter cannot gain access to the mental state of authors who are now deceased. The proper object of interpretation is the work itself and not an inaccessible mental state, and so the issues raised by a/symmetry of information do not apply.

32.4 Textuality

There are various senses in which a piece of writing may be said to be a "text." The word "text" itself is the past participle stem of the Latin verb *texere*, to weave, intertwine, plait, or (of writing) compose. The English words "textile" and "texture" also derive from the same Latin word. This etymology of the word "text" is apparent in expressions that refer to the "weaving" of a story, the "thread" of an argument, or the "texture" of a piece of writing. A "text" may thus be taken to be a weaving or a network of analytic, conceptual, logical, and theoretical relations that is woven with the threads of language. This implies that language is not a transparent medium through which arguments are expressed, the invisible and self-effacing carrier of a message from the mind of the author to the mind of the reader, but is interwoven with or provides the very filaments of the substantive arguments themselves. Construing a piece of writing as a "text" in this sense thus foregrounds the issue of the relation between the weaving of the argument and the linguistic threads and filaments by means of which the text is woven. Issues of language – style, figuration, rhetoric, the polysemy of words – are thus not extraneous to the meaning ascribed to the text in the process of reading but are a constitutive part of it. Reading a text thus requires a practice of "close reading" that examines the woven network of textual relations and how the substantive, logical, and linguistic aspects of the text may be intertwined. This is uncontroversial for overtly literary writings, but its implications are not always taken into account for nonliterary writings (for an attempt at such a reading of Adam Smith's works, see Brown, 1994, 1995, 1997b).

In examining the texture of a piece of writing, it is thus an issue for investigation as to what kinds of linguistic threads there are and how they might be interwoven. The various threads may well be drawn from different "languages," such that different historical moments may be interlaced with different analytic, conceptual, and axiological systems. An issue for investigation is the extent to which a text may be an ordered text with a determining structure, logic, or language, or whether it is a tissue (also deriving from *texere*) of heterogeneous languages and hence internally differentiated or textured. Also, there is the question of whether and to what extent the text is laid open, smooth, and without creases or marks, or whether it is folded in upon itself so that the patterning or texture is subject to breaks or introversions. Furthermore, the text may not have finished or clearly defined edges, since the threads may be left hanging loose or interwoven with other texts.

Texts function within contexts of interpretation. To suggest that a text needs to be read in terms of a context is, however, not to prescribe a single method of reading but, rather, to open up some of the issues that might be involved in any particular method. To suggest that the context should be a *historical* one, in order to generate a historical reading, is also not to prescribe a single kind of reading, since there may be no single authentic historical moment that coincides with the originary moment of the creation of the text and which determines a single appropriate historical context for reading it. If a given text incorporates different historical threads, it is thus still an issue as to how these threads are to be followed in pursuing a reading. Such threads may also relate in different ways to what is known (if at all) of the biography or the stated intentions of the author, or of the economic, social, political, philosophic, theological, artistic, cultural, or intellectual motifs of the time. As more is learnt about the possible historical contexts that may assist a reading of a text, so there may be a plurality of possible contexts – different interweavings or different forms of intertextuality – and an increase in the possible readings of a work which may be justified by the textual evidence. This plurality may well sit uneasily with a single discipline's conception of the canonic status of an exemplary author's works, as such disciplinary readings may tend to promote a unilinear or monologic notion of the work even though such works may still be liable to competing interpretations within the discipline. A discipline's "conversation" with its own canonic authors may thus turn out to be more dialogical, more multi-voiced, more open-ended, and less discipline-based, than canonic presuppositions might suggest (Brown, 1993). (The argument of these paragraphs derives from a large literature, which includes writings by Bakhtin, Barthes, De Man, Derrrida, Fish, Foucauld, and LaCapra.)

The notion of a "text" as a woven network of arguments and language is, however, itself only a metaphor. Its usefulness derives from the way in which it focuses on the need for a close reading of argument and language (which need not exclude attention to conceptual clarity, logical rigor, and analytic coherence). Exploring the resources of the text thus helps to prevent the abuse of claiming an unknowable authorial intention to buttress particular interpretations. But there are also limits to the applicability of this metaphor. The study of a woven cloth is conducted in a medium that is different from the medium of the cloth; in the case of written texts, the study is conducted in the same medium as the text itself. There is thus no meta-language for analyzing the language and argument of a text; and each interpreter is in turn an author, each interpretation in turn another work.

Any work, any piece of connected writing, however, is a self-referential entity. Words and expressions refer backward and forward; an argument makes a point, leads into another or draws to a conclusion; and narrative structures provide commentary or a sense of direction on what is being argued or concluded. The language of a piece of writing thus seems to instantiate intentional agency in that it is self-referentially engaged in doing something all the while; and this helps to explain how a piece of writing seems to have its own "voice" or "persona," even when that voice or persona is being disrupted or displaced by the workings of the language of the piece. This may be illustrated by the ways in which purposive argument is ascribed to a piece of writing. Instead of saying that author A meant such-and-such, or that author A argued such-and-such, it could be said (as in this essay) that the work or text says such-and-such, or that it argues such-and-such, thereby ascribing purposive argument to the work or text rather than to the author. Expressing the arguments of the text in the passive voice (such as "it is argued that" or "the argument is offered that") does not seem to eliminate this implied agency either, since the actions of "arguing" and "offering an argument" – even when expressed in the passive voice – still seem to presuppose agency of some sort; in this sense, the passive voice still seems to register the "voice" of an argumentative agent. This suggests that a form of agency is still being registered as present to the text even when the interpretation being offered of the text is not one cast in terms of the author's intentions. Intentionalist arguments about meaning thus mistake this generalized intentionality of language for the intention of a particular author of an individual work. In other words, that intentionality is registered in language as a signifying system does not imply that the meaning of any particular piece of writing is determined by the intentions of the author of that piece. Sections 32.2 and 32.3 have outlined some of the difficulties involved in sustaining intentionalist arguments, and this section has tried to present an alternative approach to interpretation or reading. The rejection of authorial intended meaning as determining the meaning of a text is thus not a criticism of all notions of agency or intentionality, but represents an alternative way of trying to understand the ways in which complex notions of agency are inscribed within language, irrespective of, or even contrary to, the intentions of individual writing subjects. In this sense, the structures of language do not simply mirror the ways of the self, but form part of the context in which complex notions of the self are negotiated, refracted, contested, and sublimated.

32.5 Conclusion

In the Introduction to this essay, two issues of interpretation were raised: To what extent is it to be expected that the history of economics should be characterized by a high or increasing degree of consensus, and what are the procedures and criteria for assessing the relative validity of different interpretations? These are large issues that can hardly be addressed satisfactorily in a conclusion. To the extent that the assumption that interpretation seeks the recovery of the author's intended meaning suggests that progress in the history of economics ought to be associated with some sort of convergence of interpretations, the relinquishment of that assumption might provide some reasons why such convergence is not necessarily to be expected, and so might provide an explanation of the increasing range of interpretations in the history of economics. But such a relinquishment does not imply a loose conception that "anything goes." On the contrary, the emphasis on close readings suggests that textual analysis should become more – not less – rigorous, and that increasingly high standards of textual evidence should be expected in defense of any interpretation. And on the question of the appropriate evidence for an interpretation, there is no evidence of the author's intention that is independent of the interpretation being offered of the works. This suggests that intentionalist interpretation cannot in practice be sustained.

Note

I would like to thank the Editors for their comments on an earlier draft of this essay. I am especially indebted to John Davis for raising the issue of symmetry of information.

Bibliography

Ankersmit, F. R. 2000: Comments on Bevir's *The Logic of the History of Ideas. Rethinking History*, 4, 321–31.

Anscombe, G. E. M. 2000 [1957]: *Intention*. Cambridge, MA: Harvard University Press.

Austin, J. L. 1975 [1962]: *How to Do Things with Words*. Oxford: The Clarendon Press.

Bevir, M. 1999: *The Logic of the History of Ideas*. Cambridge, UK: Cambridge University Press.

—— 2000: Meaning and interpretation: a defense of procedural individualism. *New Literary History*, 31, 385–403.

Brown, V. 1993: Decanonizing discourses: textual analysis and the history of economic thought. In W. Henderson, T. Dudley-Evans, and R. Backhouse (eds.), *Economics and Language*. London: Routledge.

—— 1994: *Adam Smith's Discourse: Canonicity, Commerce and Conscience*. London: Routledge.

—— 1995: The moral self and ethical dialogism: three genres. *Philosophy and Rhetoric*, 28, 276–99.

—— 1997a: "Mere inventions of the imagination:" a survey of recent literature on Adam Smith. *Economics and Philosophy*, 13, 281–312.

—— 1997b: Dialogism, the gaze and the emergence of economic discourse. *New Literary History*, 28, 697–710.

—— 2002: On some problems with weak intentionalism for intellectual history. *History and Theory*, 41, 198–208.

Davidson, D. 1980a: *Essays on Actions and Events*. Oxford: The Clarendon Press.

—— 1980b: The logical form of action sentences. In *Essays on Actions and Events*. Oxford: The Clarendon Press, 105–22.

—— 1993: Locating literary language. In R. W. Dasenbrock (ed.), *Literary Theory after Davidson*. Philadelphia, PA: Pennsylvania State University Press, 295–308.

Hirsch, E. D., Jr. 1967: *Validity in Interpretation*. New Haven, CN: Yale University Press.

Iseminger, G. (ed.) 1992: *Intention and Interpretation*. Philadelphia, PA: Temple University Press.

Knapp, S. and Michaels, W. B. 1985: Against theory. In W. J. T. Mitchell (ed.), *Against Theory: Literary Studies and the New Pragmatism*. Chicago: The University of Chicago Press, 11–30.

Mitchell, W. J. T. (ed.) 1985: *Against Theory: Literary Studies and the New Pragmatism*. Chicago: The University of Chicago Press.

Newton-de Molina, D. (ed.) 1976: *On Literary Intention*. Edinburgh: Edinburgh University Press.

Patterson, A. 1990: Intention. In F. Lentricchia and T. McLaughlin (eds.), *Critical Terms for Literary Study*. Chicago: The University of Chicago Press, 135–46.

Pocock, J. G. A. 1985: *Virtue, Commerce, and History*. Cambridge, UK: Cambridge University Press.

Sent, E.-M. 1998: Sargent and the unbearably lightness of symmetry. *The Journal of Economic Methodology*, 5, 93–114.

Skinner, Q. 1988a: Meaning and understanding in the history of ideas. In Tully, op. cit., pp. 29–67. First published in *History and Theory*, 8 (1969), 3–53.

—— 1988b: Motives, intentions and the interpretation of texts. In Tully, op. cit., pp. 68–78. First published in Newton-de Molina, op. cit., 210–21.

—— 1988c: A reply to my critics. In Tully, op. cit., pp. 231–88.

Tully, J. (ed.) 1988: *Meaning and Context: Quentin Skinner and his Critics*. Cambridge, UK: Polity Press.

Wimsatt, W. K. and Beardsley, M. C. 1954: The intentional fallacy. In W. K. Wimsatt (ed.), *The Verbal Icon: Studies in the Meaning of Poetry*. London: Methuen, 3–18. Reprinted in Newton-de Molina, op. cit.

CHAPTER THIRTY-THREE

Mathematical Modeling as an Exegetical Tool: Rational Reconstruction

A. M. C. Waterman

33.1 TERMINOLOGY

33.1.1 Rational reconstruction

Rational reconstruction (hereinafter, RR) will be understood in this essay in the sense used by Imre Lakatos (1978, ch. 2) in reference to the history of science. According to Lakatos, RR is equivalent to what he calls *internal history*: a putatively diachronic account of what counts as "growth of knowledge" or "progress in science" – as "progress" is adjudicated by the particular normative methodology favored by the historian. Lakatos's *external history* is confined to social and economic conjuncture, the tastes, ideologies, and metaphysics of the scientists, and other circumstances that "explain the residual non-rational factors." Thus "external history is irrelevant for the understanding of science" (Lakatos, 1978, pp. 118, 102).

It is apparent that there must be at least as many rational reconstructions of any particular episode as there are methodologies. Thus an historian who accepts the criteria of scientific progress proposed by "conventionalism" will offer a very different internal history of some important scientific innovation from that of another historian whose criteria are those specified by Lakatos's own methodology of "scientific research programmes." It also appears that those who accept Thomas Kuhn's account of *The Structure of Scientific Revolutions* (1962) must disqualify themselves from attempting any kind of RR. For "*In Kuhn's view there can be no logic, but only psychology of discovery*": hence "*scientific revolution is irrational, a matter for mob psychology*" (Lakatos, 1978, pp. 90, 91; italics in original).

Some historians of economic thought (e.g., Blaug, 1990) have preferred Richard Rorty's seemingly more open-ended usage of "rational reconstruction" (never clearly defined) to identify one of the four "genres" of the historiography of philosophy; the others being "historical reconstruction" and "*Geistesgeshichte*" (literally, a study of the "spirit" of the times) each of which, like RR, is legitimate and useful, and "doxography" (praise of dead philosophers), which is neither (Rorty, 1984). For Mark Blaug, RR corresponds to his own "economic theory in retrospect," which he described as "absolutist" history in contrast with "relativist" history – the latter being "almost the same" as Rorty's "historical reconstruction" (Blaug, 1997, pp. 1–2, 7–8). But in fact it more closely resembles Lakatos's "external history." Rorty himself, pretending to believe that modern philosophers know and understand some things that the greatest of their predecessors did not, defended RR as "self-consciously letting our own philosophical views dictate the terms in which to describe the dead" (Rorty, 1984, p. 50). By doing this, Rorty claimed, we are "able to see the history of our race as a long conversational interchange":

> We need to think that, in philosophy as in science, the mighty mistaken dead look down from heaven at our recent successes, and are happy to find that their mistakes have been corrected. (p. 51)

It would appear from this that Rorty believes that there can be and is "progress" in philosophy, that criteria exist to determine what counts as progress, and hence that we can reconstruct parts at least of the "long conversational interchange" in terms "dictated by our own philosophical views." To this extent, Rorty's fuzzier usage of RR is congruent with, if not identical to, Lakatos's more rigorously specified definition.

The reason for preferring Lakatos's definition with reference to the history of economic thought (hereinafter, HET) lies in an obvious difference between the "conversation" of economists and that of philosophers. For Rorty was less than wholly serious in his claim that there can be "progress" in philosophy. "We hesitate [to say that Aristotle or Leibniz or Descartes were ignorant of what now count as 'facts' in philosophy] because we have colleagues who are themselves ignorant of such facts, and whom we courteously describe not as 'ignorant', but as 'holding different philosophical views'" (Rorty, 1984, pp. 49–50). It is at least as plausible, therefore, to regard philosophy as a continual recycling of old ideas, and none the worse for that. Although there is undoubtedly some element of this in economics too (Waterman, 1997), it is obvious that economists have a far more highly developed sense of "progress" or "growth of knowledge" in their discipline than do philosophers. Theories are formulated, models constructed, and hypotheses tested in a way that closely resembles the method of the natural sciences. Most economists believe that they can explain a wider range of social phenomena with modern theory than was possible for Smith and Ricardo, Walras and Edgeworth, or Wicksell and Keynes. And because what motivates many is the desire to produce knowledge that is "useful" in that it can be applied to improve public policy and legislation, any serious doubt about that possibility – either among economists themselves or among those who pay for their services – would drastically reduce, if not eliminate, the profession. Philosophy, however, thrives on self-doubt.

33.1.2 Mathematical modeling

Economic analysis is inconceivable without the use of models, either implicit or explicit. For example, the "mental experiment" at the heart of David Hume's essay "Of the balance of trade" (1994 [1752]) can only be conducted when aggregative concepts such as "money," "the price of all labour and commodities," and "the art and industry of each nation" have been abstracted from the real world of commerce, implicitly quantified, and related to one another in the imaginary world of the analyst's model. Likewise, when Adam Smith states that "the demand for men, like that for any other commodity, necessarily regulates the production of men" (1976 [1776], book I, p. 98), he is manipulating abstractions and implying an imaginary causal nexus of other abstractions – the growth-rate of "population" in relation to that of "capital," and so on – some of which are discussed in *Wealth of Nations* I.viii. Therefore the term *model* will be used in this essay to denote a formal arrangement of abstractions constructed to represent, emblematically or figuratively, some supposed system of cause and effect existing in the real world of human societies. By use of models, economists explain and predict social phenomena.

Whether or not there could be explanatory and predictive economic models that successfully resisted all attempts to represent them in mathematical form, most economic theorizing today is in fact conducted in explicitly mathematical terms. However, although exceptions exist as far back as the eighteenth century (Theocharis, 1961), this was not the case for most economic theorizing before Walras's *Eléments* (1954 [1874]). And between the 1870s and the 1940s much economic theory continued to be "literary." It is a question for HET, therefore, whether the seemingly implicit mathematical reasoning in much literary economic theory invites explicit mathematical treatment; and, if so, whether the resulting "translation" of literary theorizing into mathematics can tell us anything that the author did not reveal in his text, and which – were we able to bring him back to life – he might be brought to agree that he had really intended to say. It is the purpose of this essay to address that question. Meanwhile, it is sufficient to define *mathematical modeling* (hereinafter, MM) in the historiography of economic thought as the representation in mathematical terms of what seem to be the most important elements in literary economic theory. The precise relation between MM and RR will be considered below.

33.1.3   Exegesis

The term, which is derived from the Greek verb $\epsilon\xi\eta\gamma\acute\epsilon o\mu\alpha\iota$ = "I narrate, explain," originated in connection with the study of sacred Scripture, and may be defined as "the art of explaining a text." In scriptural exegesis at any rate, "the explanation may include a *translation, paraphrase,* or commentary on the meaning" (ODCC, 1977; italics added). There is no reason to exclude any of these possibilities from the exegesis of nonscriptural texts. Now if translation be undertaken at all, any paraphrase will presumably be written in the language of translation. And if the MM of literary economic theorizing may indeed be regarded as *paraphrase* written in the "language" of mathematics, then MM can properly be employed as an "exegetical tool" in HET. But since translation is prior, the question is whether translation into mathematics of an economic argument originally formulated in some natural language is possible; and whether, even if possible, there may be either or both a significant loss in content and a significant distortion of meaning. This question raises further ones. Is mathematics a "language" at all? Does economic theory possess any nonmathematical components, essential to its proper understanding, that resist translation? Are there any good criteria of "correct" translation between *any* two languages?

Paul Samuelson (e.g., 1947, 1952) has argued strongly for the equivalence of mathematical and literary theorizing, and for the greater efficiency of the former in economics. George Stigler (1949, p. 45) assumed the possibility of translation, which, he asserted, "is absolutely necessary, not merely desirable." Contributors to the symposium on mathematical economics in the *Review of Economics and Statistics* (1954, pp. 357–86) took the possibility of translation for granted. Whether they were justified in so doing was later contested (Dennis, 1982). Meanwhile, W. V. Quine (1960) showed that without some generally agreed set of rules for translation, it is possible that two equally "good" translations from any one language into any other may be mutually incompatible. In this essay, it will simply be assumed that translation of literary into mathematical economic theory is usually sufficiently reliable for the attempt to be worthwhile; and hence that a paraphrase of the former in the language of mathematics might be a useful "exegetical tool." Quine's objection holds against all forms of translation and therefore against all use of translation and paraphrase in exegesis: including the attempt to translate the original Hebrew and Greek of the scriptural texts first into Latin and then into modern languages. In this respect at any rate, exegesis of *Wealth of Nations* beginning with a "translation" into mathematics is on all fours with exegesis of the Book of Genesis beginning with a translation into English.

33.2   Mathematical Modeling, Rational Reconstruction, and History

It is obvious that MM is not RR as Lakatos understands the latter, for MM is synchronic and RR diachronic. Consider the first example of MM in Takashi

Negishi's *History of Economic Theory* (1989), which addresses John Locke's concept of "vent" and its function in Locke's value theory. A simple model of supply is constructed which takes account of limited information, search for buyers and sellers, and both buying and selling costs. Negishi uses the model to show that John Law (1966 [1705]) and all who followed him were wrong to interpret Locke's "vent" as "demand"; that Karen Vaughn (1980) was correct to interpret Locke's price theory based on "vent" as the microeconomic foundation of his version of the Quantity Theory; and that Locke's results are sensitive to the range of certain parameters. There is, however, no connection between this piece of MM and anything that follows. We have not been offered an account of a "progressive problem shift" (supposing that we have chosen to understand growth of knowledge in terms of Lakatos's methodology): simply a snapshot – or X-ray photograph – of what the Quantity Theory "scientific research programme" looked like in 1691.

Yet it would seem that MM is well suited to be a tool of RR. Provided that we can model the theory of a dead economist by means of the symbols and functions that we had used to model that of his predecessors, we can show exactly what theoretical value added – if any – was contributed by the former. Consider an extremely simple example. Let us model Keynesian macroeconomic equilibrium, following J. R. Hicks (1937), as:

$$Y = Z(Y, r, \Delta),\qquad(33.1)$$

$$M = P.L(Y, i),\qquad(33.2)$$

where $i = r + d/dt(P^e)$ and expected price level, $P^e = P$, the actual price level assumed to be constant. M and Δ are shift parameters. Let $-\infty \leq \partial L/\partial i \leq 0$. It is then obvious that equilibrium Y will be invariant with respect to Δ if $\partial L/\partial i = 0$. Hicks regarded this as a "classical assumption," and so was able to illustrate part of Keynes's claim to have "generalized" classical macroeconomics. For the novel doctrine of "liquidity preference" makes the demand for money a decreasing function of i, the bond yield (that is, $\partial L/\partial i < 0$). *In general*, therefore, equilibrium Y would be responsive to any change in the shift parameter Δ. In this example, MM formulates precisely what Lakatos (1970, p. 118) called a "theoretically progressive problem shift," and is therefore part of the rational reconstruction of a putative step forward in macroeconomic theory.

Negishi's MM of Locke's value theory shows that MM can be a *tool of exegesis*. We understand Locke's text better as a result of Negishi's model, and we can use the model to criticize and appraise the merely literary exegesis of other authors. The Hicksian MM of Keynes's macroeconomic theory shows that MM can be a *tool of RR*. We understand more clearly why Keynes claimed to have provided a "general" theory that exhibited the results of what he called "classical" theory as a special case. It is possible to imagine an "internal" history of economic theorizing based on a temporal sequence of related and commensurable mathematical models. But before going further it is important to consider the relation of MM and RR to *history*.

Economics is more akin to physics than it is to philosophy (and more like ecology than either). But it does resemble philosophy, especially political philosophy, in one important respect. Its central ideas refer to human consciousness in human society, and are formulated in a language of discourse generated by the entire range of "humane" studies available to its authors: theology, philosophy, history, and the arts and letters. In order to write a satisfactory *intellectual history* (hereinafter, IH) of the production and significance of economic ideas, we must imagine ourselves eavesdropping upon a bygone conversation: inward with the language and literature, religion and politics, tastes and morals, of those we are observing. We put ourselves in the position of our subjects and look in the same direction, and with the same eyes, as they. The fact that this is strictly impossible does not absolve the historian from the obligation to attempt it (Blaug, 1997, p. 8). This sense of IH was classically enounced by Quentin Skinner (1969). However, Lakatos (1978, p. 102, n. 1) reported that in his discipline "internal history" is usually defined as "intellectual history"; "external history" as "social history." In his own, "unorthodox, new demarcation," what was meant by "internal history" is simply RR as explained above. But Lakatos's "external history" is a mere residual and is not to be taken as IH in the Skinnerian sense necessary for a truly "historical" HET.

It has lately been suggested (Waterman, 1998a) that HET be regarded as synonymous with "history of political economy," and as a catch-all for any and all "historical" studies of economic thought. Then IH (of economic thought) is a subset of HET (or, more generally, the intersection of IH in general with HET) concerned with the past "as it really was." It includes both "historical reconstruction" and "*Geistesgeschichte*" in Rorty's senses. Each of these in turn includes, but is not exhausted by, Lakatos's "external history." What is known as *history of economic analysis* (hereinafter, HEA) is then what Blaug correctly describes as *Economic Theory in Retrospect* (1997), which is "internal history" in Lakatos's "unorthodox, new" sense, or simply RR. Its purpose is to trace the lines of descent of leading analytic themes in economics, and account for their articulation. HEA is like a topological diagram of the kind that helps us get from Uxbridge to Charing Cross on the London Underground. But IH is like a genuine, scale map of London. We cannot superimpose the former on the latter without distorting geographical truth.

It is important to note that just as a topological diagram can be a cartographic tool, so HEA can be a tool of IH. For by attending to the internal logic of the conversation we are observing we enrich our understanding of what is being said and why. Since it has been argued above, therefore, that MM can be a tool of RR [= HEA], it follows that MM may have a part to play in IH as a component of the relevant HEA. And since it has also been shown that even when MM is *not* used in RR it can be an exegetical tool, it may also have an "autonomous" use in IH. The complex relations among (1) IH, (2) HET, (3) HEA [= RR = "internal history"], (4) "historical reconstruction," (5) "*Geistesgeschichte*," (6) MM, and (7) "external history" may be illustrated in the Venn diagram of figure 33.1.

Set (1) is IH in general, which of course includes much more (10) than simply the IH of economic thought (12). Set (2) is HET, some of which is IH (12 and its

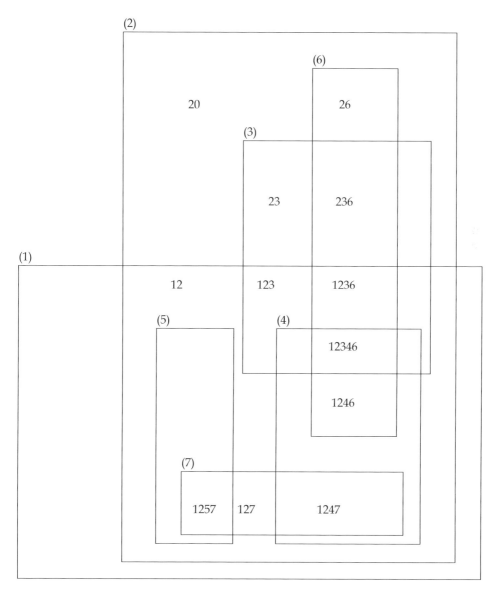

Figure 33.1 The relations among mathematical modeling (MM), rational reconstruction (RR), intellectual history (IH), and the history of economic thought (HET). (1) Intellectual history (IH); (2) history of economic thought (HET); (3) rational reconstruction (RR) or history of economic analysis (HEA); (4) historical reconstruction; (5) "*Geistesgeschichte*"; (6) mathematical modeling (MM); (7) "external history"

subsets) and some not (20, 23, and 236). Both "historical reconstruction" (124) and "*Geistesgeschichte*" (125) belong to the IH of HET (12). Set (3), which is HEA = RR, intersects in part with IH (123, 1236, 1246, and 12346) and in part does not (23 and 236). Set (7) is Lakatos's "external history" and belongs wholly in IH, intersecting with "historical reconstruction" (1247), with "*Geistesgeschichte*" (1257), and with neither (127). *Mathematical modeling* is represented as set (6). It may be merely an exegetical tool of HET (26); a tool of RR (236); an exegetical tool of "historical reconstruction" (1246); a tool of RR used in the service of IH (1236); or either or both an exegetical tool and a tool of RR used as a tool of "historical reconstruction," itself a component of the intellectual history of economics (12346).

In what follows, some attempt will be made to identify in terms of this taxonomy the historiographic function of the examples of MM reported and appraised.

33.3 EXAMPLES OF MATHEMATICAL MODELING IN THE HISTORY OF ECONOMIC THOUGHT

The earliest example of an author's using MM in HET is that of William Whewell (1971b [1831]), who produced a "mathematical exposition" of "some of the leading doctrines" in Ricardo (1851 [1817]). It was Whewell's belief, expressed in an earlier lecture on mathematical economics, that:

> Some parts of this science of Political Economy . . . may be presented in a more systematic and connected form, and I would add, more simply and clearly, by the use of mathematical language than without such help; and moreover to those accustomed to this language, they may be rendered far more intelligible and accessible than they are without it. (Whewell, 1971a [1829], p. 1)

It is remarkable that Whewell identifies, in this passage, the most important claims advanced by Samuelson (1947, 1952) with respect to the use of mathematics in economics: (a) mathematics is a "language"; (b) it is possible to translate "some parts . . . of Political Economy" (i.e., "the elements and axioms which are its materials," Whewell, 1971a [1829], p. 3) into "mathematical language"; (c) such translation may achieve the greater rigor of "a more systematic and connected form"; and (d) it presents economic theory "more simply and clearly," so rendering it "far more intelligible and accessible."

It was Whewell's purpose in the two lectures which comprised this article "to trace the consequences" of "the principles which form the basis of Mr. Ricardo's system," and which Whewell himself believed to be without justification (1971b [1831], pp. 2, 3). In this case, MM was simply an exegetical tool of HET (26). Although his mathematics was "awkward and sometimes simply 'incorrect,'" Whewell is judged by a modern commentator to have discovered, through his mathematical reconstruction of Ricardo, several important analytic concepts usually attributed to the "marginal revolution" of the 1870s (Cochrane, 1970). A few years later, one of Whewell's Cambridge colleagues, John Edward Tozer, published two papers on mathematical economics (Tozer, 1838, 1841 [1840]), the first of which applied MM to analytic work of Barton, Sismondi, M'Culloch, and Ricardo, with the object of criticizing their arguments (Gehrke, 2000).

Alhough important work in mathematical economics was published in the first half of the nineteenth century by Heinrich von Thünen (1966 [1826, 1850, 1863] and Augustin Cournot (1838), there appears to have been no further attempt at the MM of other authors' work after Tozer's until Alfred Marshall busied himself in 1867 with translating "Ricardo's reasoning into mathematics" (Keynes, 1972 [1933], p. 181). Not only did Marshall never publish this work, however: he exerted his powerful influence to discourage mathematical methods in economics except as a preliminary and private, ground-clearing exercise. For "... it seems doubtful whether anyone spends his time well in reading lengthy translations of economic doctrines into mathematics, that have not been made by himself" (Marshall, 1952 [1890], p. ix). Three generations of English-speaking economists, enthralled by Marshall's doctrine, spent their time instead in the "laborious literary working over of essentially simple mathematical concepts" (Samuelson, 1947, p. 6). Sophisticated and far-reaching developments in mathematical economics (e.g., Ramsey, 1928; Leontief, 1936; Neumann and Morgenstern, 1944; Neumann, 1945–6 [1938]) went largely unnoticed by the profession. Even the (elementary algebraic) general equilibrium theory of Walras (1954 [1874]) was widely ignored until its popularization by J. R. Hicks (1939). And such HET as then existed (e.g., Roll, 1938; Gide and Rist, 1944 [1909]) was entirely literary. All this was changed quite suddenly by the publication of Samuelson's *Foundations of Economic Analysis* (1947).

From the parochial standpoint of this essay, the most important thing about *Foundations* is that it contains – in passing and merely to illustrate a mathematical idea – what may be the first published example of genuine MM in HET since Whewell and Tozer. Samuelson (1947, p. 297) noted that in his *Essay on Population* (1798), "Malthus implicitly and explicitly assumed the law of diminishing (per capita) returns." Hence we may write:

$$f = \varphi(N), \quad \varphi'(N) < 0, \tag{33.3}$$

where $f \equiv F/N$ is per capita real income, F is the total production of "the means of subsistence" or "food," and N is the total population. Now equation (33.3) implies the (diminishing *marginal* returns) aggregate production function of "food" in the agricultural economy assumed by Malthus and Ricardo:

$$F = F(N), \quad F' > 0, \quad F'' < 0. \tag{33.4}$$

Equation (33.3) is a simple example of MM as an exegetical tool: a straightforward translation into mathematical language of Malthus's assumption (1798, pp. 25–6) that the ratio of "population" to "the means of subsistence" increases as the former rises.

But equation (33.4) may be regarded as the RR of a theoretically progressive problem-shift. For it was a short step from Malthus's original argument of 1798 to the implicit formulation in 1815 and 1817 of a diminishing-returns aggregate production function (Malthus, 1815; Ricardo, 1815, 1951 [1817]). It is also the starting point of a series of mathematical models of the "classical" theory of growth and distribution, beginning with Peacock (1952). One of the most interesting is that of Stigler (1952), in which it is shown that Malthus's "ratios" imply a production function of the form $F = L \ln N$, where L is a shift parameter that captures land availability, capital–labor ratios, and technique. The concept of an aggregate production function of the general form (33.4) has been much employed since the 1950s in MM of the "classical" authors, in particular Malthus and Ricardo. L. L. Pasinetti's (1960) influential formulation of "the Ricardian System" begins with (33.4). Samuelson's (1959) two-part "Modern treatment" is chiefly concerned to employ linear-programming ideas to explore Ricardo's value theory, but diminishing returns in agriculture enter the picture. Samuelson (1959) is genuine RR in that its object is to show that "Poor as our knowledge and insights are, they are way ahead of those of our predecessors" (1959, p. 231). The most famous of all such production-function models, however, is Samuelson's "Canonical classical model of political economy" (1978). Inputs into the productive process are "doses" of V, "made up of balanced proportions of L and K applied to a fixed vector of lands" (1978, p. 1418); where L is labor (represented as N in (33.4) above) and K capital. By means of this model, we can see that "Adam Smith, David Ricardo, Thomas Robert Malthus, and John Stuart Mill shared in common essentially one dynamic model of equilibrium, growth and distribution" (Samuelson, 1978, p. 1415). The "canonical classical model" is clearly a case of RR, for "within every classical economist there is to be discerned a modern economist trying to be born" (Samuelson, 1978, p. 1415).

The production-function approach allows macroeconomic growth modeling, originally devised for neoclassical theory (Solow, 1956), to be extended to the classical authors by adding a fixed factor (land) and by making population growth endogenous (Swan, 1956, pp. 340–2). This line of inquiry was pursued by Walter Eltis in a series of papers between 1972 and 1981, incorporated in his monograph (Eltis, 1984), which includes MM of the growth theory of Quesnay, Smith, Malthus, Ricardo, and Marx. Eltis's work inspired an important MM of "Malthus's theory of wages and growth" (Costabile and Rowthorn, 1985).

The concept of a diminishing-returns aggregate production function, so illuminating when applied to the Malthus–Ricardo doctrine of rent, is less helpful in the MM of other aspects of classical political economy. In the first place, despite Samuelson's (1978) assumption, not only Marx but also Adam Smith and his contemporaries ignored "the limitation of land and natural resources" in their analyses (Hollander, 1980; Waterman, 1999, 2001). Secondly, much light can be thrown on classical and pre-classical value theory and growth theory by the modeling assumption of many goods, produced interdependently by processes with constant inputs. Thirdly, so far as Adam Smith at any rate is concerned, neglect of increasing returns to scale must seriously impair the exegetical credentials of any "Smithian" model.

Few attempts, if any, have been made to deal rigorously with the third topic. Smith's analysis seems to assume the persistence of competition, which pervasive IRS must undermine (however, see Negishi, 1989, pp. 89–95). Only informal, *ad hoc* treatment has from time to time been suggested (e.g., Barkai, 1969). Willingness to abstract from land scarcity and diminishing returns, however, has afforded opportunity for a great variety of linear models deriving ultimately from Leontief (1936) and Neumann (1945–6 [1938]), ranging from the elementary algebra of Samuelson's "dissection" of Marx as a "minor Post-Ricardian" (Samuelson, 1957, p. 911) to the relative sophistication of Morishima's more flattering account of the same dead economist as "one of the authors of the Marx–von Neumann model" deserving to be "ranked as high as Walras in the history of mathematical economics" (Morishima, 1973, pp. 3 and 1).

A fundamental building block in all such models is the replacement of the aggregate production function, equation (33.4), with a technique matrix:

$$A \equiv [a_{ij}], \quad i = 1, \ldots, n, \quad j = 1, \ldots, n, \tag{33.5}$$

where $a_{ij} \geq 0$ is the input of commodity i per unit of output of commodity j and there are n sectors of production. It is obvious that matrix (33.5) can only be "viable" if net output in all sectors is nonnegative. At the relatively small cost of abstraction from resource scarcity and choice of technique, models incorporating (33.5) have been constructed to investigate various aspects of the economic analyses of Quesnay, Smith, Ricardo, and Marx.

Although early Leontief-type MM of Ricardo and Marx was produced by Kenneth May (1949–50) and Burgess Cameron (1952), perhaps the most widely known and discussed has been that of Piero Sraffa (1960). In contrast to Neumann's original formulation, which treated workers like "farm animals" (Champernowne, 1945–6, p. 12), Sraffa separated human from nonhuman inputs. But in order for Sraffa's version to generate relative prices in a Ricardo-like manner, either the profit rate or the wage rate must be exogenous. Although Sraffa himself chose the former, most of those who have used the model follow (some passages of) Ricardo in assuming that human inputs are supplied at a constant, exogenously determined wage rate: hence the economic implications are the same as those of Neumann. The linear MM of other classical authors includes a much-simplified Neumann growth model applied to Adam Smith and subsequently to Malthus (Negishi, 1989, pp. 83–9; 1993); and an ambitious "vindication" by Samuelson (1977) of Smith's value-added analysis of the natural price as against Marx's criticism.

Although MM of classical and pre-classical authors has been conducted largely in terms of (33.4) or (33.5), attempts have also been made to model in other ways classical monetary theory (e.g., Becker and Baumol, 1952), Hume's specie-flow mechanism (e.g., Anderson and Takayama, 1977; Negishi, 1989), Bentham's felicific calculus (Lapidus and Sigot, 2000), Say's Law (e.g., Becker and Baumol, 1952; Negishi, 1989), some "demand-led" aspects of pre-classical economic analysis (Waterman, 1996, 2001), and various other topics. Computer simulation has been employed by J. F. Berdell (1995, 2001) to model long-run dynamics and path-dependency in Hume, Smith, Ricardo, and Malthus.

Because most neoclassical authors expressed their ideas in at least implicitly mathematical form, there has been far less MM of post-1870 HET, although – for example – Robert Dorfman (2001) and Paul Samuelson (2001) have each recently reported on Böhm-Bawerk. The obvious exception is J. M. Keynes (1883–1946), who though, like Marshall, a trained mathematician was deeply imbued with Marshall's distrust of mathematical economics. Ever since the original formulations by W. B. Reddaway (1936) and J. E. Meade (1937), therefore, Keynes (1936) has invited MM.

33.4 USES OF MATHEMATICAL MODELING IN THE HISTORY OF ECONOMIC THOUGHT

In most of the examples reported in section 33.3, MM has been used as a simple tool of exegesis (26); less frequently in the strict, Lakatosian sense of RR employed in this essay (236); and hardly at all in IH (1236, 1246, and 12346).

It is certainly the case that Samuelson's MM is almost always employed in the cause of "Whig history" and therefore *implies* the RR of a series of progressive problem-shifts. See, for example, Samuelson (1957, 1959, 1978), discussed above, in which the classical authors are shown to have been doing modern economics, but not as well as we do it now because of their primitive and defective analytic tools. It is also clear that early MM of Keynes (1936) was usually intended to show how that work "generalized" the macroeconomics of its predecessors. Perhaps because economics is less triumphantly progressive than the physical sciences, however, at least some MM has been employed to show that the replacement of old theories by new has sometimes led to losses, as well as gains, in knowledge (e.g., Waterman, 2001). At any rate, it is certainly the case that recent historians who have employed MM to describe a temporal series of economic theories (e.g., Eltis, 1984; Negishi, 1989) have made little attempt to unify their models by common notation, and none to connect them sequentially in order to exhibit "growth of knowledge."

In principle, MM might be a tool of IH, either in RR of some episode during which contemporaries believed that knowledge had increased (1236 and 12346), or simply used exegetically to display the logical structure of an argument and so to throw light on its contemporary reception (1246). An example of the latter is Waterman (1991, 1992), in which a diagrammatic model based on an explicit mathematical structure is used to explain how it was that Malthus's contemporaries could read the first *Essay* as a defense of private property rather than an attack on "perfectibility." But in practice few intellectual historians find mathematical methods congenial; and few economists attempt intellectual history.

The merely exegetical use of MM seems to have had one or more of three objects: (a) that of testing other historians' literary exegesis (e.g., Negishi, 1989); (b) that of testing the logical validity and internal consistency of the primary text (e.g., Samuelson, 1959; Waterman, 1998b); and (c) that of implementing the aims of Stigler's (1982 [1965]) "scientific exegesis." The purpose of (c) is to identify an author's "net scientific contribution" and to "state it in a strong form capable of contradiction by the facts" (Stigler, 1982 [1965], p. 69). Hence the possibility of RR is assumed in this case, if seldom pursued.

The most obvious historiographic difficulty raised by mathematical exegesis is that the same text can be made to yield very different results. Eltis (1984, ch. 5) and Costabile and Rowthorn (1985) use Keynesian macroeconomic categories to elucidate an "optimum propensity to save" at which the recurrent possibility of a "general glut" is avoided. Negishi (1993), however, uses a Neumann-type "Smithian growth model" to represent Malthus "not so much as an underconsumptionist as a supply sider" (Negishi, 1989, p. 152). Incompatible appraisals of Marx afforded by Samuelson (1957) and Morishima (1973) have been noted above. Moreover, Morishima's (1973, ch. 4) and Samuelson's (1971) MM of the "transformation problem" are also in conflict. Waterman (2001) contradicts the MM of *Wealth of Nations* in Samuelson (1978). Examples could be multiplied. It is therefore important to decide whether these evident and frequent disagreements are a fatal objection to the use of MM in HET, or whether they can be explained and accommodated.

If most MM were employed in the service of RR, and if those engaged in the latter employed different methodologies to rationalize the growth of knowledge (Lakatos, 1978), then we should expect their results to differ. But this has not been the case. Or if the rules for translating English, for example, into mathematics were not generally agreed upon (Quine, 1960), that instead might explain some of the variation in "translation." But although there has been little discussion of this problem by historians of economic thought, it would seem unlikely that uncertainty of translation is a large part of the explanation. The classical authors and their eighteenth-century predecessors formulated their analyses in terms of causal nexi between putatively scalar, aggregative magnitudes. Another explanation that locates the problem in the historian rather than in the data sees the motive for mathematical exegesis as a desire to confirm and rationalize the historian's prior understanding of a text. Thus Morishima (1989, p. 122) objects that Samuelson's (1978) "canonical classical model" is "nothing but Samuelson in the garb of Ricardo." But a reviewer observed that parts of Morishima's own book "represent Morishima in the garb of Ricardo" (Maneschi, 1992, p. 761). Although it is difficult to imagine that any historian, whether mathematical or not, could be wholly self-effacing, we may trust to competitive reviewing to minimize this vice.

It would seem more fruitful, therefore, to seek the explanation of divergent mathematical exegeses in the texts themselves rather than in their exegetes. A promising line of inquiry is suggested by the title of Samuelson (1957): "Wages and interest: a modern *dissection* of Marxian models" (italics added).

When a zoological specimen is "dissected" in the laboratory, the biologist cuts away all that obscures the particular tissue to be studied. The knowledge so obtained is genuine but partial. In order to understand the organism as a whole, we must supplement our (anatomical) knowledge of the pulmonary system with that of our fellow investigators' knowledge of viscera, muscles, tendons, nerves, and glands. And anatomical knowledge must be supplemented by general systemic (physiological) knowledge.

In like manner, the economist who employs the scalpel of MM to "dissect" out some particular line of argument in a predecessor's text obtains genuine but partial knowledge. Suppose that an analyst models elements of Adam Smith's argument in book I, chapter viii of *Wealth of Nations*, to obtain:

$$W^* = S + \alpha.gK, \quad \alpha > 0, \tag{33.6}$$

where W^* is the equilibrium or "natural" wage rate, S is a socially determined subsistence requirement, gK is the exponential rate of capital accumulation in steady state, and α is a population growth parameter (Waterman, 1998b, pp. 574–5). Equation (33.6) exhibits correctly that single "strand" in the rich texture of Smith's thought which leads to a famous conclusion:

> . . . it is in the progressive state, while the society is advancing to the further acquisition, rather than when it has acquired its full complement of riches, that the condition of the labouring poor . . . seems to be the happiest and most comfortable. It is hard in the stationary, and miserable in the declining state. (Smith, 1976, p. 99)

There is more to *Wealth of Nations*, even to that chapter, than equation (33.6). But in conjunction with other "dissections" – and the results of other kinds of textual study – (33.6) can be used in building up a complete picture of the whole organism.

It is now obvious why mathematical exegeses of the same text may differ. Analysts may, and often do, "dissect" different tissues from the same dead rat. Thus Pasinetti (1960) attends to diminishing returns and rent in Ricardo's *Principles*: Sraffa (1960) to labor inputs and relative values. Such differences may be apparent or real. They are *apparent* when the diverse results of MM could in principle be harmonized in a more general model that has correctly captured, and exhibited the relation among, all elements of the text that have so far been "dissected." They are *real* when this is not possible, because the incompatibility of various mathematical exegeses arises from inconsistency or incoherence in the original text.

Whether real differences are useful to the historian depends upon which type of history is in view. If the object is a "Whig history" that illustrates "progress" in economic analysis by means of at least implicit RR, then Stigler's "scientific exegesis" is an important historiographic technique. The analyst must select only those mutually compatible mathematical models of the text that together maximize "the number of [the author's] main theoretical conclusions which we can deduce from (our interpretation of) his analytic system" (Stigler, 1982, p. 69). Models that are incompatible with the author's "central theoretical position" are a nuisance and must be discarded. But if the object is IH (and until or unless some more powerful analysis is discovered that turns "real" into an "apparent" differences), all mathematical exegeses, however divergent in their results, are valuable. For by displaying clearly any inconsistency and logical error in the author's text, they protect the historian from the "mythology of coherence" (Skinner, 1969, pp. 16–18; see Waterman, 1998b), and allow us to report truthfully all we can now know about our author and his works.

That other kinds of textual study are needed to supplement and round out the knowledge we can acquire by MM has been noted by Morishima (1973, p. 6), who discovered that although his own MM of Marx's "transformation problem" was "surprisingly similar" in its mathematical form to that of Samuelson (1971), yet his appraisal of the economic significance of the results differed: "This is an interesting example of the non-univalence of the correspondence between economics and mathematics" (Morishima, 1973, p. 6, n. 4).

Bibliography

Anderson, R. K. and Takayama, A. 1977: Devaluation, the specie flow mechanism and the steady state. *Review of Economic Studies*, 44, 347–61.

Barkai, H. 1969: A formal outline of a Smithian growth model. *Quarterly Journal of Economics*, 83, 396–414.

Becker, G. S. and Baumol, W. J. 1952: The classical monetary theory: the outcome of the discussion. *Economica*, 19, 355–76.

Berdell, J. F. 1995: The present relevance of Hume's open economy monetary dynamics. *The Economic Journal*, 105, 1205–17.

—— 2001: *International Trade and Economic Growth in Open Economies: The Classical Dynamics of Hume, Smith, Ricardo and Malthus*. Cheltenham, UK: Edward Elgar.

Blaug, M. 1990: On the historiography of economics. *Journal of the History of Economic Thought*, 12(1), 27–37.

—— 1997: *Economic Theory in Retrospect*, 5th edn. Cambridge, UK: Cambridge University Press.

Cameron, B. 1952: The labour theory of value in Leontief models. *The Economic Journal*, 62, 191–7.

Champernowne, D. G. 1945–6: A note on J. v. Neumann's article on "A model of economic equilibrium." *Review of Economic Studies*, 13, 10–18.

Cochrane, J. L. 1970: The first mathematical Ricardian model. *History of Political Economy*, 2, 419–31.

Costabile, L. and Rowthorn, R. E. 1985: Malthus's theory of wages and growth. *The Economic Journal*, 95, 418–37.

Cournot, A. 1838: *Recherches sur les principles mathématique de la théorie des richesse*. Paris: Hachette.

Dennis, K. 1982: Economic theory and the problem of translation. *Journal of Economic Issues*, 16, 691–712, 1039–62.

Dorfman, R. 2001: Modernizing Böhm-Bawerk's theory of interest. *Journal of the History of Economic Thought*, 23(1), 37–54.

Eltis, W. 1984: *The Classical Theory of Economic Growth*. London: Macmillan.

Gehrke, Ch. 2000: Tozer on machinery. *The European Journal of the History of Economic Thought*, 7, 485–506.

Gide, C. and Rist, C. 1909: *Histoire des doctrines économiques depuis les physiocrates jusqu'à nos jours*. Paris: Recueil Sirey.

Hicks, J. R. 1937: Mr Keynes and the classics: a suggested interpretation. *Econometrica*, 5, 147–59.

—— 1939: *Value and Capital. An Inquiry into some Fundamental Principles of Economic Theory*. Oxford: The Clarendon Press.

Hollander, S. 1980: On Professor Samuelson's canonical classical model of political economy. *Journal of Economic Literature*, 18, 559–74.

Hume, D. 1994 [1752]: Of the balance of trade. In *Political Essays*, ed. K. Haakonssen. Cambridge, UK: Cambridge University Press.

Keynes, J. M. 1936: *The General Theory of Employment, Interest and Money*. London: Macmillan.

—— 1972 [1933]: *Essays in Biography*. Reprinted in E. Johnson and D. Moggridge (eds.) *The Collected Writings of John Maynard Keynes*, vol. X (of 25 vols). London: Macmillan.

Kuhn, T. S. 1962: *The Structure of Scientific Revolutions*. Princeton, NJ: Princeton University Press.

Lakatos, I. 1970: Falsification and the methodology of scientific research programmes. In I. Lakatos and A. Musgrave (eds.), *Criticism and the Growth of Knowledge*. Cambridge, UK: Cambridge University Press.

—— 1978: *The Methodology of Scientific Research Programmes*. Philosophical Papers, vol. I, ed. J. Worrall and G. Currie. Cambridge, UK: Cambridge University Press.

Lapidus, A. and Sigot, N. 2000: Individual utility in a context of asymmetric sensitivity to pleasure and pain: an interpretation of Bentham's *Felicific Calculus*. *The European Journal of the History of Economic Thought*, 7, 45–78.

Law, J. 1966 [1705]: *Money and Trade Considered*. New York: Kelley.

Leontief, W. 1936: Quantitative input–output relations in the economic system of the United States. *Review of Economics and Statistics*, 18, 105–25.

[Malthus, T. R.] 1798: *An Essay on the Principle of Population as it Affects the Future Improvement of Society . . .* London: Johnson.

Malthus, T. R. 1815: *An Inquiry into the Nature and Progress of Rent, and the Principles by which it is Regulated*. London: Murray.

Maneschi, A. 1992: Review of Morishima (1989) and Reid (1989). *History of Political Economy*, 24, 760–2.

May, K. 1949–50: The structure of classical value theory. *Review of Economic Studies*, 17, 60–9.

Marshall, A. 1952 [1890]: *Principles of Economics. An Introductory Volume*, reprint of 8th edn. (1920). London: Macmillan.

Meade, J. E. 1937: A simplified model of Mr Keynes' system. *Review of Economic Studies*, 4, 98–107.

Morishima, M. 1973: *Marx's Economics: A Dual Theory of Value and Growth*. Cambridge, UK: Cambridge University Press.

—— 1989: *Ricardo's Economics: A General Equilibrium Theory of Distribution and Growth*. Cambridge, UK: Cambridge University Press.

Negishi, T. 1989: *History of Economic Theory*. Amsterdam: North-Holland.

—— 1993: A Smithian growth model and Malthus's optimal propensity to save. *The European Journal of the History of Economic Thought*, 1, 115–27.

Neumann, J. von 1945–6 [1938]: A model of general economic equilibrium (trans. G. Morgenstern). *Review of Economic Studies*, 13, 1–9.

—— and Morgenstern, O. 1944: *The Theory of Games and Economic Behavior*. Princeton, NJ: Princeton University Press.

ODCC 1997: *The Oxford Dictionary of the Christian Church* (ed. F. L. Cross), 3rd edn., ed. E. A. Livingstone. Oxford: Oxford University Press.

Pasinetti, L. L. 1960: A mathematical formulation of the Ricardian system. *Review of Economic Studies*, 27, 77–98.

Peacock, A. T. 1952: Theory of population and modern economic analysis. *Population Studies*, 6, 114–22.

Quine, W. V. 1960: *Word and Object*. New York: John Wiley.

Ramsey, F. P. 1928: A mathematical theory of saving. *Economic Journal*, 38, 543–59.

Reddaway, W. B. 1936: The General Theory of Employment, Interest and Money. *Economic Record*, 12, 28–36.

Ricardo, D. 1815: *An Essay on the Influence of a Low Price of Corn on the Profits of Stock . . .* London: Murray.

—— 1951 [1817]: *Principles of Political Economy, and Taxation.* In P. Sraffa (ed.), *The Works and Correspondence of David Ricardo*, vol. I (of 11 vols). Cambridge, UK: Cambridge University Press.

Roll, E. 1938: *A History of Economic Thought.* London: Faber & Faber.

Rorty, R. 1984: The historiography of philosophy: four genres. In R. Rorty, J. B. Schneewind, and Q. Skinner (eds.), *Philosophy in History.* Cambridge, UK: Cambridge University Press.

Samuelson, P. A. 1947: *Foundations of Economic Analysis.* Cambridge, MA: Harvard University Press.

—— 1952: Economic theory and mathematics: an appraisal. *American Economic Review*, 42, 56–66. Reprinted in Stiglitz, op. cit., vol. 2, no. 126.

—— 1957: Wages and interest: a modern dissection of Marxian economic models. *The American Economic Review*, 47, 884–912. Reprinted in Stiglitz, op. cit., vol. 1, no. 29.

—— 1959: A modern treatment of the Ricardian economy. *Quarterly Journal of Economics*, 73, 1–35, 217–31. Reprinted in Stiglitz, op. cit., vol. 1, nos. 31 and 32.

—— 1971: Understanding the Marxian notion of exploitation: a summary of the so-called transformation problem between Marxian values and competitive prices. *Journal of Economic Literature*, 9, 399–431.

—— 1977: A modern theorist's vindication of Adam Smith. *American Economic Review*, 67, 42–9.

—— 1978: The canonical classical model of political economy. *Journal of Economic Literature*, 16, 1415–34.

—— 2001: A modern post-mortem on Böhm's capital theory: its vital normative flaw shared by pre-Sraffian mainstream capital theory. *Journal of the History of Economic Thought*, 23, 301–17.

Skinner, Q. 1969: Meaning and understanding in the history of ideas. *History and Theory*, 8, 1–53.

Smith, A. 1976 [1776]: *An Inquiry into the Nature and Causes of the Wealth of Nations*, ed. R. H. Campbell, A. S. Skinner, and W. B. Todd, 2 vols. Oxford: The Clarendon Press.

Solow, R. M. 1956: A contribution to the theory of economic growth. *Quarterly Journal of Economics*, 70, 65–94.

Sraffa, P. (ed.) 1951–73: *The Works and Correspondence of David Ricardo*, 11 vols. Cambridge, UK: Cambridge University Press.

—— 1960: *Production of Commodities by Means of Commodities.* Cambridge, UK: Cambridge University Press.

Stigler, G. 1949: *Five Lectures on Economic Problems.* London: Longman.

—— 1952: The Ricardian theory of value and distribution. *The Journal of Political Economy*, 60, 187–207.

—— 1982 [1965]: Textual exegesis as a scientific problem. *Economica*, 32(128), 447–50. Reprinted in *The Economist as Preacher.* Oxford: Blackwell, ch. 6.

Stiglitz, J. E. (ed.) 1966: *The Collected Scientific Papers of Paul A. Samuelson*, 2 vols. Cambridge, MA: The MIT Press.

Swan, T. W. 1956: Economic growth and capital accumulation. *Economic Record*, 32, 334–61.

Theocharis, R. D. 1961: *Early Developments in Mathematical Economics.* London: Macmillan.

Thünen, J. H. von 1966 [1826, 1850, 1863]: *Der isolierte Staat in Beziehung auf Landwirtschaft und Nationalökonomie.* Darmstadt: Wissenschaftliche Buchgesellschaft.

Tozer, J. E. 1838: Mathematical investigation of the effect of machinery on the wealth of a community in which it is employed and on the fund for the payment of wages. *Transactions of the Cambridge Philosophical Society*, 6, 507–22. Reprinted in Tozer (1968), op. cit.

—— 1841 [1840]: *On the Effect of the Non-Residence of Landlords on the Wealth of a Community*. Cambridge: printed at the Pitt Press by J. W. Parker, printer to the University. Reprinted in Tozer (1968), op. cit.

—— 1968: *Mathematical Investigation of the Effect of Machinery on the Wealth of a Community and On the Effect of the Non-Residence of Landlords on the Wealth of a Community*, edited with an introduction by D. A. Collard. New York: Augustus M. Kelley.

Vaughn, K. 1980: *John Locke: Economist and Social Scientist*. Chicago: The University of Chicago Press.

Walras, L. 1954 [1874]: *Elements of Pure Economics*, trans. W. Jaffé. London: George Allen & Unwin.

Waterman, A. M. C. 1991: *Revolution, Economics and Religion: Christian Political Economy, 1798–1833*. Cambridge, UK: Cambridge University Press.

—— 1992: Analysis and ideology in Malthus's *Essay on Population*. *Australian Economic Papers*, 31, 203–15.

—— 1996: Why William Paley was "the First of the Cambridge Economists." *Cambridge Journal of Economics*, 20, 673–86.

—— 1997: Recycling old ideas: economics among the humanities. *Research in the History of Economic Thought and Methodology*, 15, 237–49.

—— 1998a: Reappraisal of "Malthus the Economist," 1933–97. *History of Political Economy*, 30, 293–334.

—— 1998b: Malthus, mathematics, and the mythology of coherence. *History of Political Economy*, 30, 571–99.

—— 1999: Hollander on the "canonical classical growth model": a comment. *Journal of the History of Economic Thought*, 21, 311–13.

—— 2001: Notes towards an un-canonical, pre-classical model of political œconomy. In E. L. Forget and S. Peart (eds.), *Reflections on the Classical Canon in Economics: Essays in Honor of Samuel Hollander*. London: Routledge.

Whewell, W. 1971a [1829]: Mathematical exposition of some doctrines of political economy. *Transactions of the Cambridge Philosophical Society*. Reprinted in *Mathematical Exposition of Some Doctrines of Political Economy*. New York: Augustus M. Kelley.

—— 1971b [1831]: Mathematical exposition of some of the leading doctrines in Mr. Ricardo's "Principles of Political Economy and Taxation." *Transactions of the Cambridge Philosophical Society*. Reprinted in *Mathematical Exposition of Some Doctrines of Political Economy*. New York: Augustus M. Kelley.

Economic Methodology since Kuhn

John B. Davis

34.1 INTRODUCTION

This chapter surveys contemporary thinking about economic methodology subsequent to Thomas Kuhn's *Structure of Scientific Revolutions* (1962), in an effort to explain its recent development, current nature, and possible future. Economic methodology since Kuhn might be characterized as having been in something of a state of permanent revolution. Before Kuhn, most economists adhered to a relatively small number of enduring methodological views: Lionel Robbins's conception of economics (Robbins, 1932), Milton Friedman's instrumentalism (Friedman, 1953), and verificationist views that arose out of logical positivism. Of course, there were methodological debates in the years immediately before Kuhn (cf., Blaug, 1992 [1980]; Caldwell, 1982) – Terence Hutchison versus Fritz Machlup, Friedman versus Richard Lester and the critics of marginalist analysis, and Tjalling Koopmans versus Friedman and Robbins (and indeed even older debates such as the famous *Methodenstreit*) – but these debates did little to change thinking about economic methodology prior to 1960. Subsequent to Kuhn, however, the situation changed dramatically. Although new views prevailed for brief periods – Karl Popper's falsificationism, Imre Lakatos's methodology of scientific research programs, D. McCloskey's rhetoric of economics approach – it cannot be said that these new views came even close to acquiring the lasting status and breadth of appeal that their pre-Kuhnian predecessors had possessed. Currently, no methodological views enjoy widespread acceptance either among economists or economic methodologists. At the same time, the very volume of methodological thinking about economics today significantly exceeds, in both quantity and diversity of ideas, the total of all the methodological thinking about economics that predates Kuhn (cf., Hands, 2001). What happened to bring about his change?

One fact stands out. Prior to Kuhn, there were very few individuals who specialized in economic methodology as a relatively independent field of investigation, and economic methodology was, rather, only one area of concern for practicing economists within the general field of economics. But in the years that followed this was less and less the case, as the field of economic methodology, along with the history of economics, gradually became a distinct sub-discipline and the province of a new set of specialists – particularly after 1980, with the first appearance of books devoted explicitly to the field (Stewart, 1979; Boland, 1982; Caldwell, 1982; Blaug, 1992 [1980]). This had two important consequences for the relationship between economic methodology and economics as a whole. First, since most economists were not current with the new developments in methodology – and were often aware that they weren't – they either abandoned interest in the field or continued to half-heartedly support old pre-Kuhnian ideas. Secondly, economic methodologists, cut loose as a relatively independent sub-discipline from a more inertially evolving economics, were free to explore a whole range of new ways of thinking about economics. In fact, this new thinking took the form of reasoning in epistemological, historical, and sociological terms about economics. After Kuhn, then, economic methodologists increasingly turned away from reasoning *in terms* of economics to, rather, reasoning *about* economics in epistemological, historical, and sociological terms – a form of thinking that was unfamiliar and uninteresting to most economists.

The high rate of change in methodological thinking since Kuhn's book, combined with the considerable diversity in ideas that now characterizes the field, alone justifies our saying that the field is currently in a state of permanent revolution. But the separation between economics and economic methodology since Kuhn suggests that the field of economic methodology is also in a state of permanent crisis. On the one hand, economic methodologists since Kuhn have developed a multitude of competing and intriguing new perspectives on economics with which to explain the nature and practice of economics. On the other hand, these new perspectives have been consistently devalued in virtue of their rejection or – perhaps even worse – their simple disregard and neglect by those in the field to which they apply. The crisis in the field of economic methodology, then, is a crisis of "exciting irrelevance"; that is, one that comes of an unwillingness to give up on any of a multitude of intriguing new perspectives, combined with a nagging sense that they may ultimately all constitute uninteresting, if not mistaken, pathways.

This state of affairs has created considerable pluralism in economic methodology regarding the nature and direction of the field, a situation that is likely to persist for the foreseeable future. This pluralism can be seen in terms of a number of unresolved issues that have divided and seem to continue to divide methodologists: (1) whether economic methodology should be prescriptive or descriptive; (2) whether economics should be understood as a natural science or a social science; and (3) whether economic methodologists, together with historians of economics, should shift their focus more toward a general history and philosophy of science framework. These three debates are addressed in the next three sections, followed by concluding remarks on the state of contemporary economic methodology in the fifth and concluding section.

34.2 SHOULD ECONOMIC METHODOLOGY BE PRESCRIPTIVE OR DESCRIPTIVE?

Thinking on this issue has gone from the idea that economic methodology should be prescriptive through the idea that it should be descriptive to contemporary views that mix both postures in different ways. The opening phase in this sequence is most evident in the logical positivism of the 1930s, which employed a highly prescriptive verificationist criterion of meaning that asserted that the only meaningful (and thus scientific) propositions were those that could be empirically verified. Although there was much debate over how to formulate this criterion, it was widely agreed that its purpose – to demarcate science from nonscience (often disparagingly termed "metaphysics") – was necessary to the advancement of science. By 1960, pre-Kuhnian philosophy of science and economic methodology was almost entirely demarcationist in attempting to set out rules for identifying good science (Hands, 2001). Even those not fully in the empiricist tradition shared this general aim. In the marginalist controversy involving Lester and Machlup, regarding whether actual businesses maximize profit (cf., Mongin, 1998), Machlup argued that good economics needs to employ theoretical assumptions that are not themselves empirically verifiable, but which enable us to reject empirical results that may be at odds with our theories (Machlup, 1955). Alternatively, in connection with the same debate, Friedman argued that we make good theoretical assumptions even when they are unrealistic if they nonetheless allow us to make reliable empirical predictions (Friedman, 1953). For both Machlup and Friedman, then, demarcating the practices of good economics was the core principle of economic methodology.

However, the high point for prescriptivist economic methodology was Popper's falsification criterion, which was perhaps even more focused on demarcating good and bad science than the verification criterion had been, since it (at least in its simplest form) makes entire theories answer to a single disconfirming test. Indeed, Popper coined the term "demarcation," and used it to distinguish science and "pseudo-science," examples of which, for him, included Marxism and Freudianism (Popper, 1963, p. 255). In fairness to Popper, identification of his methodological views with the falsification criterion overlooks the critical rationalist side to his thinking and the "Socratic Popper" (Boland, 1997, p. 263). But the traditional Popperian view was nonetheless for a time thought by many to embody the highest virtues in economic methodology (e.g., Blaug, 1992 [1980]). One measure of the significance of Kuhn's book, then, was that it was seen not only as discrediting Popperianism, but also as having cast doubt on the entire prescriptivist project of formulating demarcation criteria for science (e.g., Laudan, 1983).

As an historian of science, Kuhn's goal was to examine the actual historical development of scientific theories. Thus his aim was to describe how scientific theories came to be accepted, rather than to judge which ones deserved the label "scientific." Moreover, his particular view of the historical developmental process in science emphasized revolutionary transformations in thinking, in which one paradigm replaced another. How one paradigm replaced another, however, was left largely unexplained, in large part because Kuhn saw this process as historically contingent. Scientists worked within paradigms, doing "normal" science and ignoring empirical anomalies that were at odds with the reigning paradigms, until an accumulation of these somehow precipitated the movement of (usually a new generation of) scientists to a new paradigm. That this involved a "revolution" not only implies that there were no rules by which competing paradigms might be judged, but also that paradigms were incommensurable. External criteria for judging the scientificity of a paradigm, then, simply did not exist. Kuhn's views were also taken to support the idea that observation is theory-laden, thus undermining the reliance that both the logical positivists and falsificationists had placed on judging theories according to how they measured up to evidence.

The major response to Kuhn in the prescriptivist tradition (indeed, one adopted by many of those who abandoned Popperianism) was Lakatos's methodology of scientific research programs (MSRP) strategy. Rather than a single theory, Lakatos focused on networks of interconnected theories, or "research programs," which could be characterized in terms of "hard cores" surrounded by "protective belts" (Lakatos, 1978). The former were not subject to criticism, but developments with respect to the latter could be characterized with hindsight as either progressive or degenerating. A research program is progressive if it is both theoretically progressive – new theories include new empirical content – and empirically progressive – this new content is corroborated and involves the prediction of "novel" facts (Lakatos, 1970, p. 118). Lakatos thus accommodated Kuhn's historical emphasis while yet retaining elements of a demarcationist approach. However, this combination was not to be sustained, primarily because few agreed that Lakatos's account of progressivity was adequate, especially in connection with his emphasis on novel facts. Indeed, after Kuhn the entire demarcation project was increasingly looked upon more skeptically. While Kuhn's own views about scientific revolutions were also subjected to criticism, nonetheless left standing by the 1970s was a new emphasis on descriptive, historical accounts of science. It was on this basis that the sociology of scientific knowledge literature developed as the first genuinely post-Kuhnian approach.

The literature on the sociology of scientific knowledge has gone through a number of stages, but rather than attempt to describe these in any detail (although cf., Hands, 1997; 2001, pp. 175ff.) I rely here on a brief account of the original Edinburgh Strong Programme to show the fundamental change in direction that the sociology of scientific knowledge brings to the philosophy of science and economic methodology. In the first place, the Strong Programme "is concerned with knowledge, including scientific knowledge, purely as a natural phenomenon" (Bloor, 1991 [1976], p. 5). By this, Bloor meant that we should study the causal processes underlying scientists' adoption of their beliefs rather than focus upon the epistemological foundations of those beliefs, as was done in traditional philosophy of science. This involved examining scientists' actual behavior and, in particular, explaining the role that social interests played in the determination of their beliefs. Thus scientific theories were not thought to be adopted on logical grounds but, rather, because historical social forces supported the emergence of certain ideas. For example, were a group of scientists to find that governmental resources existed for certain types of research, they would be expected to find it in their interest to pursue that type of research. This does not imply that the content of science reduces to underlying social forces, but it does imply that the direction of development in science cannot be separated from an understanding of the historical social forces operating upon scientists. But then, as with Kuhn, the question was not whether there were rules that prescribed how to do good science but, rather, what were the practices and social contexts of the scientists involved.

Thus, in much of the later literature that followed a sociology of scientific knowledge approach, detailed studies of scientists' laboratories and practices were a dominant focus (e.g., Collins, 1992 [1985]). But very little in the way of prescriptive comment on the nature of science in general could emerge from such studies. Indeed, even the emphasis on social interests became too blunt a tool for most research that used this approach, since to argue that social interests were always at play suggested that there might be an appropriate or good sort of methodology based on the analysis of social forces that might be universally applied in the study of science. At the same time, the emphasis on detailed studies of scientists' laboratories and practices helped to bring out that there was much that was not transcontextual about science. Harry Collins investigated scientists' practice of replicating experiments to establish the legitimacy of their results, and found that not only was replication not systematically practiced, but that the terms on which it was practiced varied considerably from one scientific context to another (Collins, 1992 [1985]). Thus even scientists themselves eschewed the sorts of legitimation procedures that might enable us to prescribe rules for good science.

However, more recently there has been something of a backlash among sociologists of science against the strongest anti-prescriptivist views, leading to approaches that aim to be nonevaluative as a whole, while nonetheless ruling out views thought to be relativist and/or idealist. Thus, Collins has been charged with "methodological idealism" and with failing to adequately expose "the social element in knowledge," because his methods "invite us to make unchecked suppositions about the scope and role of social factors without providing any controls on them" (Barnes, Bloor, and Henry, 1996, p. 15). His error, it is argued, is in proceeding "*as if* the natural world, and our experience of it, played no significant role in the production of knowledge" (ibid., p. 13). But what seems rather more reasonable is to say that there is a relative stability and autonomy to perception that helps to explain scientists' success in achieving consensus when creating instruments for socially accepted methods of observing the world. Thus, in the attempt to understand science, it is not enough to simply describe what scientists do. "Good" description of science involves giving proper weight to the role that observation plays in science. It follows that "good" science may itself be identified according to the role that observation – even when socially determined – plays in the formation of scientific theories.

This argument in turn raises the question of whether realism constitutes a necessary component of scientific methodology. To answer this question in the affirmative would reintroduce a prescriptivist methodological theme, in the form of the argument that science ought to be evaluated according to how well it represents what really exists. Sociologists of science known as "constructivists" argue along Collins's lines that the real exerts no fundamental influence on science. They do not deny the existence of the material world "out there," since it resists what we and scientists attempt to do, but they argue that "for these resistances to make sense, they have to be interpreted [and] [t]he very moment you interpret them, you enter the real of the social world" (Knorr-Cetina, in Callebaut, 1993, p. 185). Against this, however, it has also been argued that we are better off abandoning the representational idiom and employing a performative image of science, in which scientists and nature are engaged in a "dialectic of resistance and accommodation" that combines an "interactively stabilized" human *and* material agency (Pickering, 1995). The idea here is that nature and the world play an even larger role in determining scientific thinking than is normally allowed by those who emphasize interpretation and the influence of the social world permit. This allows for a "pragmatic realism" that requires that we understand science in terms of how knowledge relates to the world, without employing traditional realist notions such as correspondence. Again, description is moderated by views of what constitutes "good" science.

Although these arguments have been made within the sociology of science community, they have not gone unnoticed by methodologists of economics. An example of the ambivalence over whether methodology should be descriptive or prescriptive from the latter is Daniel Hausman's account of the methodology of economics (Reuten, 1996). To begin with, Hausman doubts that a science – perhaps especially economics – that operated according to the prescriptivist standards of "either Popper's or Lakatos' methodology could exist" (Hausman, 1992, p. 204). He then characterizes economic methodology as a deductive *a priori* method (in the tradition of J. S. Mill and Robbins), and states that "[a]lthough the methodological rules of the method *a priori* . . . cannot be defended, I shall nevertheless defend the existing practices of theory assessment among economists" (ibid., p. 206). That defense proceeds by recognizing questionable methodological commitments in neoclassical economics, followed by assertions such as that "economists have good reason to be committed to them," they do "not do much harm," and that there "is a good deal of truth to them" (ibid., p. 210). At the same time, however, he concludes that while proceeding on an *a priori* basis is "not unjustifiably dogmatic, there is a serious risk" to setting aside empirical anomalies and being unwilling to "consider alternatives" (ibid., pp. 210–11).

We can understand these remarks in terms of the kind of methodological approach that Hausman recommends. By building on Mill's *a priori* method, Hausman frees economics of the responsibility of directly addressing empirical evidence. This weakens the prescriptivist side of his account, since theory assessment acquires special force in connection with whether theories measure up to evidence, while at the same time giving weight to Hausman's project of describing the current practice of economics. But in setting out a new methodological framework in terms of an inexact deductive method, Hausman has still generated criteria for theory assessment. Thus he cannot but doubt at times that neoclassical economics lives up to the standards of "good" economics. In effect, his dilemma is not unlike that faced by those writing in the field of the sociology of science. When they emphasize how social practices among scientists influence observation, they de-emphasize the empirical. But faced with the task of explaining what counts as reasonable sociology of science, they too reintroduce normative criteria for the sciences that they examine. I turn in the conclusion below to how these developments may be linked to the gap between economists and economic methodologists.

34.3   SHOULD ECONOMICS BE UNDERSTOOD AS A NATURAL OR A SOCIAL SCIENCE?

Before Kuhn, this question was better phrased as follows: Do all sciences operate on the same general principles, or do the social sciences operate on distinct principles? In the 1950s, the majority view among philosophers of science and those interested in economic methodology was the former one. Logical empiricism, the dominant philosophy of science, required that all scientific theories – whatever their subject matter – be translatable into empirical observation language. Scientific inquiry was structured according to the hypothetico-deductive method: from a general hypothesis and statements of initial conditions, predictive statements were deduced that could then be evaluated according to empirical evidence. On this view, scientific theories that were successful did not actually explain but, rather, simply described our empirical observations. Scientific "explanation," then, involved applying the covering law or deductive–nomological (D–N) model, in which a particular observed event was accounted for by being subsumed under a general law together with a set of initial conditions (Hempel and Oppenheim, 1948). This general conception emphasized the existence of scientific laws, framing these laws in terms of empirical evidence such as could be collected through experimentation, and seeing science as an objective enterprise that was independent of the sort of socio-historical forces that operated in most other domains of human life.

After Kuhn, these ideas came increasingly under attack. Although Popper's *Logik der Forschung* originally appeared in 1934, its later English translation (Popper, 1959) gave timely weight to Kuhn's claims that science did not develop inductively through the production of general laws. Popper pointed out that universal statements can never be confirmed by singular statements, but can always be falsified by them. Rather than aiming at producing laws, then, science aimed at producing reasonable conjectures that might stand up to potentially falsifying empirical tests. Consequently, science was, rather, a process of continually abandoning general propositions that did not stand up to empirical evidence. One reason why this was important to economic methodologists was that, while economics seemed to include a variety of laws (Gresham's Law, the law of demand, the law of diminishing returns, Okun's Law, and so on), these laws were generally imprecise by comparison with, say, the laws of physics. Popper's thinking was thus influential among economic methodologists who thought that he offered an approach that was more suitable to economics. But if economics as a social science was not nomological in the fashion of physics, did this not also imply that empirical evidence had a different status in economics?

One of the most important ideas in Kuhn's book was the claim that empirical observation is theory-laden. Logical empiricism assumed that experiment and observation were theoretically presuppositionless. Kuhn argued, however, that scientists "see" things in terms of the paradigms in which they operate, and that this meant that science needed to be explained in terms of sociological and historical perspectives that accounted for paradigm emergence and development. But this made the progress of natural science depend upon categories that were far removed from its traditional understanding – making a place, for example, for concepts such as interpretation, which have been argued to be the basis for treating social science as distinct from natural science (e.g., Winch, 1990 [1958]). Effectively, this also reversed the question with which we began this section. Rather than asking whether all sciences operate on the same general principles, or whether the social sciences operate on distinct principles, the question now became one of whether all sciences operate on the same general principles or whether the *natural* sciences operate on distinct principles.

A number of new initiatives in economic methodology gave an affirmative answer to the first part of this new question and a negative answer to the second part, in the process rewriting the methodology of economics in the language of interpretation. Perhaps most radically, McCloskey argued that the methodology of economics was the practice of rhetoric and persuasion, thus substituting the classical idea of a skill or an art for the modernist, epistemological idea of science as a body of knowledge (McCloskey, 1985). McCloskey was influenced by the American philosopher Richard Rorty (Davis, 1990), whose neo-pragmatist philosophy critiqued another key idea behind the traditional logical empiricist view of science, namely that – philosophically speaking – science "mirrored" nature (Rorty, 1979). Rorty understood interpretation in reflexive terms as entering the hermeneutic circle, and viewed science and philosophy as an historical social practice that lacked certainty-producing epistemic foundations. This was consonant with parallel developments in the sociology of science (discussed above) that described how science emerged in concrete communities whose character reflected scientists' interests. In the strongest versions of this latter literature, science was a socially constructed phenomenon that placed the real world behind a barrier to interpretation.

Yet the momentum behind these developments did not go unresisted. Economic methodologists since Kuhn have also defended the view that economics should be seen as a science on the order of the natural sciences. Perhaps the strongest position of this sort has been advanced by the philosopher of economics Alexander Rosenberg, who has argued that economics cannot become a science until it abandons its long-standing reliance on "folk psychology" (Rosenberg, 1992). Folk psychology explains human action as the effect of our desires working in combination with our beliefs, such as is involved in the analysis of utility maximization. More broadly, folk psychology involves the domain of intentionality or the subject of human mental life. For Rosenberg, mental entities have no place in scientific explanation, because they cannot be explained in the rigorous material terms that are characteristic of natural science. However, it ought not to be thought of as an insurmountable difficulty for economics to address this problem. Human mental states can be re-described and identified as neural or brain states – a view sometimes called "eliminative materialism." Were economists to abandon their characterization of mental states in intentional terms, and treat them behaviorally as brain states, economics might then function as a natural science, and perhaps qualify as a science.

Another way of reconfiguring economics as a natural science – also related to the issue of how we understand the mind – derives from the work of Herbert Simon. Simon is best known for developing the idea that human rationality involves "satisficing" behavior and a bounded rationality in which individuals make use of limited information and a limited computational capacity. But Simon's thinking about bounded rationality and human beings' reliance on "rules of thumb" and "heuristics" in decision-making also served as the basis for his later thinking about how to model artificial intelligence systems (Simon, 1957 [1945]; cf., Sent, 1997). Computers, he demonstrated, could be designed to employ the same "rules of thumb" and "heuristics" as are generally observed in human decision-making. But this implied that if computers are information-processing systems, then the human mind could also be conceived as essentially an information-processing system. Simon's original work in this regard long antedated Kuhn's, but it gained new life with the rise of cognitive science in the 1980s. Cognitive science – the general view that human beings are information-processing systems – has found many applications, but in a philosophy of science context was instrumental to the development of a "naturalized" epistemology inspired by natural science (e.g., Goldman, 1986).

The concept of "naturalized epistemology" originated in connection with Willard Van Orman Quine's postwar philosophic views (e.g., Quine, 1969). Quine had earlier argued that scientific theories are "underdetermined" by the evidence offered in their support (Quine, 1980 [1951]). How, then, were we to explain the attachment to scientific views that we observe among scientists? Rather than asking ourselves traditional epistemological questions regarding how theories are justified, Quine proposed that we engage in a purely descriptive account of science, and – in order to carry out this descriptive inquiry – rely on what the sciences themselves offer. More specifically, the science of psychology – indeed, behaviorist psychology – provides a method of conducting this inquiry as well as a naturalized alternative for investigating how scientific views are adopted and maintained in general. Quine's views have been quite influential in philosophy of science, but not as much so in economic methodology, most likely on account of his tendency toward behaviorist psychology. Nonetheless, the basic idea that economic methodology might employ the principles of natural science is entertained by some economic methodologists in connection with accounts of economics that are couched in terms of evolutionary science.

Evolutionary views in economics go back to Thorstein Veblen, and have recently enjoyed a considerable revival in connection with the idea that the economy undergoes a process of Darwinian evolution, although there is also considerable debate regarding whether biological metaphors are appropriate in economics (e.g., Nelson and Winter, 1982; Hodgson, 1993; Vromen, 2001). Relatedly, evolutionary epistemology relies on the idea a that science such as economics develops much like the process of Darwinian evolution. Although there is a large literature from this perspective in philosophy of science, much of it is not familiar to most economic methodologists. Nonetheless, some have considered this approach as a strategy of analysis via acquaintance with the later evolutionary views of Popper (1972), whose work in general has been of sustained interest to methodologists. Popper's evolutionary epistemology follows from his earlier thinking about scientists practicing a falsificationist methodology. The basic idea is that, in a selection process that constantly puts up new theories in much the same way as new organisms appear, falsified propositions fail. Theories whose propositions withstand a falsificationist selection process are adapted to their environment. Although this notion of adaptation is like the neo-pragmatist ideas that Rorty advanced in his own critique of traditional epistemology, here of course the critique comes from natural science. The fact that related arguments regarding the process of theory change can come from two such very different sources is strong evidence that economic methodology is ambivalent regarding whether economics is a natural science or social science.

Finally, there are methodological views that treat economics as a natural science, but make important concessions to concepts and ideas long associated with the interpretivist view of social science. One is the work of Harold Kincaid, which combines naturalism and holism (Kincaid, 1996). Kincaid believes that the standards of science are those that were historically established by natural science, but that many of the concepts and concerns of social science do not appear in natural science. For example, Karl Marx is said to have operated with a natural science methodology, especially in developing what has since become known as Marxian sociology, but his concerns with the relationships between classes and individuals required formulation of new conceptual tools. Holism is a macrosociological notion that helps in this regard, particularly when confronting theory strategies such as reductionism and supervenience. Reductionism is the idea that properties or descriptions in one domain of theory can be fully translated into or reduced to properties or descriptions in another domain of theory; in contrast, supervenience concerns how one domain of properties or descriptions is irreducible to, or supervenes on, a second domain. Interestingly, the concept of supervenience can be meaningfully applied to disputes in natural science, such as arise in connection with understanding the relationship between biology and chemistry. This all gives further evidence of the pluralistic views in economic methodology over whether the field's roots are in natural or social science.

34.4 SHOULD ECONOMIC METHODOLOGISTS SHIFT THEIR FOCUS TOWARD THE HISTORY AND PHILOSOPHY OF SCIENCE?

If economic methodology today is, as suggested above, "excitingly irrelevant" because of the gulf between economics and economic methodology, there seem to be two ways in which the field might develop in the future. On the one hand, methodologists might shift their focus more toward what appear to be preeminent concerns of economists, such as empirical modeling, in an effort to join their investigations to those of economists (cf., Boumans and Morgan, 2001; Hoover, 2001). On the other hand, methodologists might give up their attempts to communicate with economists and, rather, increasingly ally themselves with the independent community of historians and philosophers of science (cf., Mirowski, 2001). Essentially this same issue was debated by historians of economics in connection with an examination of their relation to economics in a symposium published in *History of Political Economy* (Weintraub, 1992). The debate was revisited in a subsequent volume on the "Future of the history of economics" (Weintraub, 2002). Since economic methodology arose as a sub-field of the history of economics, and since concern with the practice of the history of economics is itself one form of economic methodology (historiography), it will be helpful to review this debate in connection with the question of how the field of methodology should relate to economics as a whole.

The original debate was initiated by Margaret Schabas, who looked at the matter from the point of view of an historian of science (Schabas, 1992). Schabas observed that the history of economics had traditionally been pursued as a history of economic *ideas*, and this seemed to be at the expense of a fuller historical examination of the conditions and circumstances under which ideas are produced and maintained. Moreover, the history of ideas approach was more the sort of thing that economists would approve of (were they to pay attention to the field), while the history of science approach was less likely be approved of by economists, if only because its socio-historical approach explains ideas in terms of the conditions in which they arise, often not representing science as the sort of noble, disinterested affair that most scientists, economists included, prefer to believe it is. For Schabas, however, the separation between economists and historians of economics was something to be desired, not regretted, since it would lay the basis for better historical work in the history of economics. But much the same reasoning might be extended to the field of economic methodology – that is, methodologists would do better to turn to philosophy of science, both to take advantage of its general resources and also for the comparisons that this would permit between economics and other sciences.

There were many responses to Schabas, most of which granted that it would be desirable for historians of economics to pay additional attention to the practices and methods of the history and philosophy of science. But many of even Schabas's more sympathetic respondents thought that historians and methodologists of economics ought to retain close ties to economics (even where not reciprocated), and not just for practical reasons such as maintaining their employment. One argument recalled the debate here over whether economics ought to be seen as a natural or social science. If the history and philosophy of science were dominated by a concern with natural science, and yet economics was better thought of as a social science, then closer contact with economics was to be preferred. Another argument was that a close knowledge of economics was necessary in order to produce good history of economics. Many in the history of science had extensive training in the sciences whose histories they wrote, and thus even though they were institutionally separated from those sciences, their concerns were still not simply general history and philosophy of science concerns.

For economic methodologists, the issue of whether economic methodology should be seen as a prescriptive or descriptive enterprise turned out to be central. Those who favored a prescriptive view of methodology tended to draw more heavily on the philosophy of science, because it provided independent standards for how science of any sort ought to be pursued. For example, Popperian and Lakatosian methodological arguments came from *outside* economics, and were then applied *to* economics. Implicitly, the prescriptivists' argument was that older, pre-Kuhnian methodological approaches generated by economists themselves – such as Robbins's mixture of introspection and *a priori* deductivism, or Friedman's prediction-favoring instrumentalism – were Whig methodologies, too often put to the task of legitimating whatever economic theory happened to prevail. In contrast, methodological views that had developed in connection with an understanding of science in general possessed leverage *vis-à-vis* any science. Philosophies of science or methodologies of economics external to science were thus prescriptive by nature. Like Schabas, methodologists of this persuasion saw separation from economics as an advantage in providing an independent basis for understanding – and in this case assessing – the theories and claims of economics.

In contrast, economic methodologists who favor a descriptive approach have argued both for and against a closer connection between methodology and economics. McCloskey, who characterizes the methodology of economics as rhetoric and the art of persuasion, distinguishes between *Methodology* and *methodology*; the first involves an epistemological evaluation of economics pursued from an elevated philosophic vantage point external to economics, while the second involves descriptive examination of all the concrete methods by which economists seek to persuade one another of their arguments. To carry out the latter sort of investigation, one needs to have close contact with the practice of economics. Not surprisingly, then, at first economists expressed moderate support for McCloskey's methodological approach, seeing – perhaps for the first time since Kuhn – some attention on the part of methodologists to what economists saw themselves as doing. (This now seems less the case, as McCloskey has become more critical of economics in her later views.)

Among economic methodologists who favor a descriptive approach to the field, but who argue against a close connection between methodology and economics, the most prominent is Roy Weintraub. For Weintraub, economists constitute a distinct interpretive community that is relatively independent from other interpretive communities (Weintraub, 1990). Every interpretive community possesses its own unique goals, practices, conventions, and presuppositions and, accordingly, it makes little sense for individuals in one community to criticize what goes on in another. For this reason, Weintraub agrees with McCloskey that economic methodology must be descriptive (indeed, both were influenced by Rorty), but in fact he draws precisely the opposite conclusion to McCloskey, in calling on historians of economics to develop a stronger affiliation with the history of science. Weintraub is even prepared to go so far as to abandon the field of economic methodology altogether, as being hopelessly intertwined with the old prescriptivist program of Popper and Lakatos, and to call for a science studies approach to the study of economics that eschews methodological arguments.

One thing, then, that this array of positions on the question of the closeness of the desired connection between economic methodology and economics tells us is that methodologists are likely both to agree with one another for different reasons and also disagree with one another for different reasons. But, as I suggest in the concluding section, disagreements within agreements may be a sign of good health in the field of economic methodology. In any event, there is little reason to expect the sorts of differences described here to go away in the foreseeable future, since the different views described in this section are generally rooted in their authors' deeper theoretical and philosophic commitments.

34.5   THE STATE OF CONTEMPORARY ECONOMIC METHODOLOGY

What is characteristic of economic methodology since Kuhn is, to borrow Schabas's expression, the field's "breaking away" from economics through a process of increasing specialization. Before Kuhn, methodology was almost entirely the province of economists; after Kuhn, methodology largely became the concern of individuals for whom it was their primary specialization. My suggestion above, that this made the field "excitingly irrelevant," is meant to emphasize how the separation of economics and methodology removed the anchoring effect that economics had on methodology, creating a crisis in direction of development for the latter. But there is also a positive side to this crisis, associated with the rich proliferation of ideas in methodology that would likely not have occurred had a closer connection to the field been sustained. How, then, should one evaluate the state of economic methodology since Kuhn? In closing, I address this question by characterizing the relationship between economics and economic methodology in a manner analogous to the relationship between economics and the economy. My model for the latter is one of the most influential contributions to economics in the postwar period, namely Robert Lucas's famous critique of empirical macroeconomics (Lucas, 1976).

The Lucas critique was based on the idea that when people in the economy make choices, they take into account government policy regarding the economy and the theory on which it is based. The large econometric forecasting models of the macroeconomy, however, relied on equations that were assumed to be stable through changes in policy regimes. Lucas used the concept of rational expectations to argue that these models failed to predict how the economy would respond to policy changes, because they assumed that people would continue to expect old policies rather than adjust to new policies. Before Lucas, economists had operated on the premise that the economy as an object of investigation was not influenced by economic theory. With rational expectations, however, since people were now understood to operate with the very models that economists created, macroeconomics had to be reformulated (for Lucas, as the New Classical economics) to include this reflexive relationship between the economy and its theory. No longer could one assume that the economy was an object of investigation that was separate from the investigator; rather, the object being investigated was now influenced by the act of investigation, and this in turn influenced the nature of the investigation.

Of course, the degree to which, and the manner in which, reflexivity operates in connection with the macroeconomy has since been much debated, especially in regard to the concept of rational expectations. But the Lucas critique has been widely accepted, and remains part of contemporary macroeconomics. Thus it is interesting that reflexivity is essentially a *methodological* principle. Not only does it refer to the relationship between economics and the economy – and thus concern the definition and scope of economics – but it also recalls one of the more radical post-Kuhn methodological approaches, namely the pragmatist thinking of Rorty and the hermeneutic circle. Note that one of Rorty's key ideas is that the traditional philosophic approach that sought certain epistemic foundations for science is misguided. In the absence of such foundations, Rorty argues that we must look at how our beliefs become established and how this influences the formation of further beliefs.

What does this tell us, then, about the relationship between economics and economic methodology? Just as economics investigates the workings of the economy, so economic methodology investigates the workings of economics. My claim, then, is that just as the relationship between economics and the economy has reflexive elements, so also the relationship between economic methodology and economics has reflexive elements. Economic methodology, that is, cannot suppose that economics, its object of investigation, is *not* influenced by work in economic methodology, or indeed that this influence does not have its own effects on the practice of economic methodology. In saying this, I do not, of course, mean to suggest that something on the order of the tightness of fit that rational expectations assumes in connection with the economy and economics applies in this case to economics and economic methodology. Rather, the point is the more general one involved in the Lucas critique, that reflexivity implies the existence of feedback relationships between economics and methodology.

First, then, how might one argue that economics has indeed been influenced by economic methodology, despite economists' general ignorance of developments in the field? Let me suggest that although most economists could say very little about the content of recent methodological thinking, many are nonetheless aware of Kuhn and his idea that there may be such a thing as a "scientific revolution"; are aware that, since Kuhn, economic methodology has become an active domain of specialization; and are aware that, by and large, economic methodologists have a critical view of the methodological practices of economists. The combination of these points, in fact, gives us reason to believe that the separation between economics and economic methodology is also due to defensiveness on the part of economists. Since methodology had previously come from the ranks of economists, but now comes largely from outside their ranks, this has encouraged economists to distance themselves from the subject of economic methodology – particularly in the climate of skepticism about science brought about by Kuhn. But this cannot be a comfortable situation for economists, despite their disclaiming any interest in methodology, since it coincides with the loss of their monopoly over self-evaluation.

Secondly, how has this state of affairs reverberated back upon methodologists? On the one hand, the separation between economics and methodology has helped to make the former an object of the latter. As economists distance themselves from the field of economic methodology, this reinforces the relative autonomy of the field, thus giving methodologists confidence that their investigations are of value. On the other hand, this motivated separation also creates doubts among methodologists regarding the value of their explanations, stimulating them – it also seems – to ask whether their work ought not to draw more closely on the practice of economics. These "push" and "pull" forces, I suggest, are intrinsic to the field of economic methodology as a now relatively distinct form of investigation. Consequently, the tension between these two forces is likely to remain, and to continue to characterize debates in the field. From this perspective, the three controversies discussed above reflect a pluralism that should probably be considered normal fare in the field of economic methodology. In effect, fundamental differences will continue to obtain among economic methodologists, because the field is no longer internal to economics as a whole.

Thus the field of economic methodology is likely to persist in a state of permanent revolution. Is that state also one of crisis, a crisis of "exciting irrelevance"? The answer to this question, it seems, depends upon which side of the "push–pull" story one is most strongly attracted to. Those who emphasize the relative autonomy of the field presumably favor the proliferation in ideas and theories that separation permits economic methodologists. Those who doubt that methodology is sufficiently in touch with the practices of economists presumably favor closer proximity to economics. Apparently, however, both camps will continue to operate in the field.

Bibliography

Barnes, B., Bloor, D., and Henry, J. 1996: *Scientific Knowledge*. Chicago: The University of Chicago Press.

Blaug, M. 1992 [1980]: *The Methodology of Economics: Or How Economists Explain*, 2nd edn. Cambridge, UK: Cambridge University Press.

Bloor, D. 1991 [1976]: *Knowledge and Social Imagery*, 2nd edn. Chicago: The University of Chicago Press.

Boland, L. 1982: *The Foundations of Economic Method*. London: George Allen & Unwin.

—— 1997: *Critical Economic Methodology: A Personal Odyssey*. London: Routledge.

Boumans, M. and Morgan, M. 2001: *Ceteris paribus* conditions: materiality and the application of economic theories. *Journal of Economic Methodology*, 8(1), 11–26.

Caldwell, B. 1982: *Beyond Positivism: Economic Methodology in the Twentieth Century*. London: George Allen & Unwin.

Callebaut, W. 1993: *Taking the Naturalistic Turn*. Chicago: The University of Chicago Press.

Collins, H. 1992 [1985]: *Changing Order: Replication and Induction in Scientific Practice*, 2nd edn. Beverly Hills, CA: Sage.

Davis, J. 1990: Rorty's contribution to McCloskey's understanding of conversation as the methodology of economics. *Research in the History of Economic Thought and Methodology*, 7, 73–85.

Friedman, M. 1953: The methodology of positive economics. In *Essays in Positive Economics*. Chicago: The University of Chicago Press, 3–43.

Goldman, A. 1986: *Epistemology and Cognition*. Cambridge, MA: Harvard University Press.

Hands, D. 1997: Conjectures and reputations: the sociology of scientific knowledge and the history of economic thought. *History of Political Economy*, 29, 695–739.

—— 2001: *Reflection without Rules: Economic Methodology and Contemporary Science Theory*. Cambridge, UK: Cambridge University Press.

Hausman, D. 1992: *The Inexact and Separate Science of Economics*. Cambridge, UK: Cambridge University Press.

Hempel, C. and Oppenheim, P. 1948: Studies in the logic of explanation. *Philosophy of Science*, 15, 135–75.

Hodgson, G. 1993: *Economics and Evolution: Bringing Life Back Into Economics*. Ann Arbor, MI: University of Michigan Press.

Hoover, K. 2001: *The Methodology of Empirical Macroeconomics*. Cambridge, UK: Cambridge University Press.

Kincaid, H. 1996: *Philosophical Foundations of the Social Sciences*. Cambridge, UK: Cambridge University Press.

Kuhn, T. 1962: *The Structure of Scientific Revolutions*. Chicago: The University of Chicago Press.

Lakatos, I. 1970: Falsification and the methodology of scientific research programmes. In I. Lakatos and A. Musgrave (eds.), *Criticism and the Growth of Knowledge*. Cambridge, UK: Cambridge University Press, 91–196.

—— 1978: *The Methodology of Scientific Research Programmes: Philosophical Papers*, vol. I, ed. J. Worrall and G. Currie. Cambridge, UK: Cambridge University Press.

Laudan, L. 1983: The demise of the demarcation problem. In R. Cohen and L. Laudan (eds.), *Physics, Philosophy and Psychoanalysis*. Dordrecht: Kluwer.

Lucas, R. 1976: Econometric policy evaluation: a critique. In K. Brunner and A. Meltzer (eds.), *The Phillips Curve and Labor Markets*. Amsterdam: North-Holland.

Machlup, F. 1955: The problem of verification in economics. *Southern Economic Journal*, 22, 1–21.

McCloskey, D. 1985: *The Rhetoric of Economics*. Madison, WI: University of Wisconsin Press.

Mirowski, P. 2001: *Machine Dreams: Economics Becomes a Cyborg Science*. Cambridge, UK: Cambridge University Press.

Mongin, P. 1998: The marginalist controversy. In J. Davis, D. Hands, and U. Mäki (eds.), *The Handbook of Economic Methodology*. Cheltenham, UK: Edward Elgar, 277–81.

Nelson, R. and Winter, S. 1982: *An Evolutionary Theory of Economic Change*, Cambridge, MA: Harvard University Press.

Pickering, A. 1995: *The Mangle of Practice*. Chicago: The University of Chicago Press.

Popper, K. 1959 [1934]: *The Logic of Scientific Discovery*. London: Hutchinson. Originally published as *Logik der Forschung*. Vienna: Springer-Verlag.

—— 1963: *Conjectures and Refutations: The Growth of Scientific Knowledge*. New York: Harper.

—— 1972: *Objective Knowledge*. Oxford: Oxford University Press.

Quine, W. 1980 [1951]: Two dogmas of empiricism. Reprinted in *From a Logical Point of View*. Cambridge, MA: Harvard University Press, 20–46.

—— 1969: Epistemology naturalized. In *Ontological Relativity and Other Essays*. New York: Columbia University Press, 69–90.

Reuten, G. 1996: A revision of neoclassical economics methodology – appraising Hausman's Mill-twist, Robbins' gist and Popper's whist. *Journal of Economic Methodology*, 3(1), 39–67.

Robbins, L. 1932: *An Essay on the Nature and Significance of Economic Science*. London: Macmillan.

Rorty, R. 1979: *Philosophy and the Mirror of Nature*. Princeton, NJ: Princeton University Press.

Rosenberg, A. 1992: *Economics – Mathematical Politics or Science of Diminishing Returns*. Chicago: The University of Chicago Press.

Schabas, M. 1992: Breaking away: history of economics as history of science. *History of Political Economy*, 24(1), 187–203.

Simon, H. 1957 [1945]: *Administrative Behavior*, 2nd edn. New York: Macmillan.

Sent, E.-M. 1997: Sargent versus Simon: bounded rationality unbound. *Cambridge Journal of Economics*, 21, 323–38.

Stewart, I. 1979: *Reasoning and Method in Economics: An Introduction to Economic Methodology*. London: McGraw-Hill.

Vromen, J. 2001: Ontological commitments of evolutionary economics. In U. Mäki (ed.), *The Economic World View*. Cambridge, UK: Cambridge University Press, 189–224.

Weintraub, E. 1990: Methodology doesn't matter, but history of thought might. In S. Honkapohja (ed.), *The State of Macroeconomics*. Oxford: Blackwell, 263–79.

—— (ed.) 1992: Minisymposium: the history of economics and the history of science. *History of Political Economy*, 24(1), 185–247.

—— (ed.) 2002: The future of the history of economics. Annual Supplement to *History of Political Economy*, 34, forthcoming.

Winch, P. 1990 [1958]: *The Idea of a Social Science*, 2nd edn. London: Routledge.

Biography and the History of Economics

D. E. Moggridge

35.1   INTRODUCTION

Biographies of economists are as old as the genre, which dates from Samuel Johnson's *Lives of the Poets*, the first four volumes of which appeared in 1779, and James Boswell's *Life of Johnson*, which appeared in 1791. One need only think of Dugald Stewart's *Account of the Life and Writings of Adam Smith* (1980 [1793]). Economists' autobiographies date from about the same time – from Hume (1980 [1777]), which is "important historically as one of the first extended accounts by a writer of his literary progress" (Pascal, 1960, p. 15). The flow has continued: in the case of Smith, four members of the editorial team of the Glasgow edition of the *Works and Correspondence* have contributed to new lives (Campbell and Skinner, 1982; Raphael, 1985; Ross, 1995). Autobiography also continues apace: the *Journal of the History of Economic Thought*, the organ of the History of Economics Society recently commissioned a number of autobiographical essays, as have the *Banca Nazionale del Lavoro Quarterly Review* (some of which were collected in book form by Jan Kregel, 1988, 1989) and the *American Economist* (some of which appear in Szenberg, 1992, 1998), and individual editors have compiled collections (Breit and Spencer, 1986; Heertje, 1993, 1995, 1997, 1999). Still more recently, Roger Backhouse and Roger Middleton have collected together (with additions) the autobiographical introductions to the publisher Edward Elgar's series "Economists of the Twentieth Century" as *Exemplary Economists* (2000). There are also collections of "autobiographical" interviews such as *Hayek on Hayek* (Kresge and Wenar, 1994) and Keith Tribe's *Economic Careers: Economics and Economists in Britain 1930–1970* (1997). There is also a literature of interviews with practicing economists on the state of particular sub-disciplines (Ibanez, 1999; Snowden and Vane, 1999), or on their development (see the interviews with the founders of cliometrics in the *Newsletter of the Cliometric Society*, beginning with Lance Davis in July 1990), or on particular historical processes such as Keynes's coming to America (Colander and Landreth, 1996). Even the *Journal of Economic Perspectives* is getting in on the act (Krueger, 2000, 2001).

In this discussion I will concentrate, with exceptions, on material published since 1990. For a partial list of earlier biographical material, see Moggridge (1989), which excludes autobiographies such as Hoover (1965), Dulles (1980), and the various autobiographical writings of Harry Johnson (Johnson and Johnson, 1978). The years since 1990 have seen two new biographies of Keynes (Moggridge, 1992; Felix, 1999), as well as the completion of Robert Skidelsky's trilogy (1983, 1992, 2000) – not to mention his Oxford "Past Masters" contribution on the same subject (1996). There have also been biographies of Edwin Cannan (Ebenstein, 1997), John Bates Clark (Henry, 1995), John Maurice Clark (Schute, 1997), Ronald Coase (Medema, 1994), Irving Fisher (Allen, 1993), John Kenneth Galbraith (Stanfield, 1996), Robert Hall (Jones, 1994), Friedrich von Hayek (Ebenstein, 2001), John Hicks (Hamouda, 1993), J. A. Hobson (Schneider, 1996), Nicholas Kaldor (Turner, 1993), John Neville Keynes (Deane, 2001), N. D. Kondratiev (Barnett, 1998), John Law (Murphy, 1997), Alfred Marshall (Groenewegen, 1995), Karl Marx (Wheen, 1999), Gunnar Myrdal (Dostaler, Ethier, and Lepage, 1992), John Nash (Nasar, 1999), Dennis Robertson (Fletcher, 2000), Austin Robinson (Cairncross, 1993), Joseph Schumpeter (Allen, 1991; März, 1991; Swedberg, 1991; Stolper, 1994), G. L. S. Shackle (Ford, 1994), Piero Sraffa (Potier, 1991; Roncaglia, 2000), Thorsten Veblen (Jorgensen and Jorgensen, 1999; Edgell, 2001), and Allyn Young (Blitch, 1995). A biography of Lionel Robbins, whose famous autobiography (1971) is much used for biographies of other economists, is in preparation. There was also Perry Mehrling's intellectual biography of a group of American monetary economists (1997). There have also been collective volumes on German-speaking *émigré* economists after 1933 (Hagemann, 1997), *Adam Smith's Daughters* (Polkinghorn and Thomson, 1998), "neglected" northwest European economists (Samuels, 1998), and Italian economists (Meacci, 1998), and biographical dictionaries of women economists (Dimand, Dimand, and Forget, 2000) and dissenting economists (Arestis and Sawyer, 1992; Holt and Pressman, 1998).

In the realm of autobiography, as well as the contributions to the two journals and collective volumes mentioned above, and mixed collections of memoir and autobiography such as Coase (1994) and Harcourt (2001), there have also been volume-length accounts by James Buchanan (1992), Alec Cairncross (1999), S. Herbert Frankel (1992), Milton and Rose Friedman (1998), Benjamin Higgins (1992), Charles Kindleberger (1991), Raymond Mikesell (2000), and Franco Modigliani (2001), as well as substantial, autobiographical commentaries in I. M. D. Little's collection of his previously published papers (1999).

Economists' biographies and autobiographies have become sufficiently common for novelists, who often use the construction of a biography as the core of their plot (see, e.g., Byatt, 1990, 2000), to remark on the phenomenon. Chick, the narrator of Saul Bellow's *Ravelstein* (2000), is engaged in a study of John Maynard Keynes and fascinated by his memoir of "Melchior" (Keynes, 1949). Characteristically, perhaps, Bellow takes liberties (p. 8) with the story of Lloyd George and the French Minister of Finance, Louis-Lucien Klotz.

The relation between biography and the history of economic thought has generated a small literature (Jaffé, 1965; Stigler, 1982c [1976]; Walker, 1983a, 1983b (ed.); Breit, 1987; Moggridge, 1989). [Denis O'Brien (2000) has a section entitled "biography" but it is predominantly about editing economists.] With autobiography, there is no such literature: we are limited to editorial introductions such as Tribe (1997) and Backhouse and Middleton (2000). At least initially, I shall consider the two genres separately.

35.2 ECONOMISTS' BIOGRAPHERS ON THE ROLE OF BIOGRAPHY

In the many biographies, even those published during the past decade, there is little mention of this literature, the exceptions being Moggridge (1992, pp. xvi–xxvi) and Groenewegen (1995, p. xii). This is not surprising, as biography stands on its own as a genre – one with its own scholarly infrastructure, including the journal *Biography*, which is now in its 24th year. With economists, there are number of possible justifications for the exercise. One is "nobody has ever written a full biography of the man" – the justification used, for example, by Patricia James – possibly with a subsidiary task of setting the record straight (James, 1979, p. 1). This is the primary justification used by Peter Groenewegen (1995, p. xii), to which he added his subject's relevance to general Victorian intellectual and social history (ibid., p. 2). A similar justification is used for Robert Hall, most of whose career was in Whitehall: "His character and achievements are not widely known. This memoir is designed to tell more people about him" (Jones, 1994, p. 1). There is the related justification "here was an interesting man who lived at an interesting time" (Weatherall, 1976, p. v). Another justification, ignoring Stigler (see below) is that "By knowing a thinker's life and times better, one may obtain a greater insight into his thought" (Ebenstein, 2001, p. 1). This echoes Roy Harrod's view of Keynes, that "an understanding of the background to his thought is indispensable for a correct interpretation of his conclusions" (1951, p. v). Or, as Ian Simpson Ross put it more carefully with Adam Smith (1995, p. xvii), "Plausible reconstruction of the meaning of Smith's discourses from an historical standpoint can be helpfully contextualised by the life story." There may also be a similar logic of justification in Harrod's *The Life of John Maynard Keynes*, written within a few years of its subject's death:

> I cannot conceive how a future student, however conscientious and able, who had first hand knowledge neither of Keynes nor of the intellectual circles which formed his environment could fail to fall into grievous errors of interpretation. (1951, p. v)

This comment displays remarkable contempt for the craft of the professional historian.

There is also what Robert Skidelsky, in his "review of reviews" of the English edition of the first volume of his Keynes trilogy, which included a Stigleresque review by Maurice Peston, called "the itch to explain" (1985, p. xvii). There may be a disciplinary agenda, as revealed in Robert Skidelsky's last substantive sentence in his introduction to the third volume of his trilogy:

If this biography has rescued Keynes from the economists, and placed him in the world of history where it properly belongs, it will have achieved its aim. (2000, p. xxii).

Given Harrod's claim quoted above, it might be a plausible aim. However as his immediate predecessor (Felix, 1999), cited *once* to correct *one* error (2000, p. 11n), was a professional historian, and as the biographer before that (Moggridge, 1992) was an historian of economics, the claim is forced. It is clear (e.g., 1983, pp. xv–xxii; 2000, pp. 491–8) that Skidelsky has a "thing" about Harrod.

In addition to "the conviction that the life and work of this great social scientist instructs us in the working of the human mind and the ways of the human spirit," there is an explanatory purpose in Robert Allen's biography of Joseph Schumpeter that "It . . . informs us of how progress in the analysis of society and the economy takes place" (1991, p. xix).

Finally, there is what one might call the moral purpose, clearest perhaps with the Victorians, such as Leslie Stephen, who in his biography of Henry Fawcett, after mentioning several memorials to his subject, continued as follows:

> Such monuments are but outward symbols of the living influence still exercised upon the hearts of his countrymen by a character equally remarkable for masculine independence and generous sympathy. My sole aim has been to do something towards enabling my readers to bring that influence to bear upon themselves. (1885, p. 468)

Thus we have a story to tell and something to explain or illuminate. In many cases, the interests of the biographer extend well beyond the discipline. Indeed, in some cases, such as Alan Ebenstein's recent biography of Hayek (Ebenstein, 2001), it could be argued that the last thing to interest the author is economics! The volume provides no indication of how Hayek as an economist was able to win a Nobel Prize for economics. The volume has even led at least one reader to raise the question as to how historians of economics should treat nonhistorians' biographies. The simple answer is "with care." One can think of wonderfully useful contributions to the history of economics by noneconomists; in the case of Keynes, for example, the work of Peter Clarke (1988) and Warren Young (1987). On the other hand, one can think of the case of Robert Skidelsky, where the treatments of both Keynes's own ideas and of other elements of the history of thought leave something to be desired (Laidler, 2002).

35.3   BIOGRAPHY AND THE HISTORY OF ECONOMICS: THE LITERATURE

The conversation on the relation between biography and the history of economic thought began with William Jaffé (1965) attacking the view that some "historians of our science think that it a virtue to overlook . . . [biographical material] as if the personal aspects of it were a contaminating substance about which the less said the better" (p. 224). He attempted to make a case, with examples from his work on Walras, "for the importance of biography in the understanding of analysis" (p. 226). He reported that the notion that biographical material might be useful had first occurred to him after he found the letters and papers in *Memorials of Alfred Marshall* (Pigou, 1926) helpful in understanding the *Principles*. Its full implications came to him during his long studies of Walras, when "it gradually dawned on me that his general equilibrium theory must be understood as a work of art, and that, like all works of art, it was marked with the personality of its creator" (Jaffé, 1965, p. 226). And he was prepared to argue:

> What is true of Walras' contribution is equally true of all the great innovations in our science, whether it be that of Adam Smith, Malthus or Ricardo, that of Cournot, Pareto or Marshall, or that of John Maynard Keynes. . . . Consequently we must miss some essential trait of an argument, or of a theory, or of a description in economics, if we ignore the distinctive individuality of its author. (pp. 226–7)

He stressed that he was talking of "the fundamental individual discoveries which from time to time modify the corpus [of economic science] in some essential way and give it a new aspect" (p. 227).

After emphasizing the importance of evidence such as oral traditions, the opinions of others, and notes and jottings in the economist's own papers, he proceeded to his examples from Walras. All of these related either to the genesis of particular Walrasian ideas in the work of Louis Poinsot, Achille-Nicolas Isnard, Paul Picard, and Herman Amstein, or to "the influences and circumstances that led him to devote himself to purely theoretical pursuits" (p. 230).

Jaffé's plea for the use of biography met with a reaction. George Stigler, an avid consumer of biographies, had little to say about Jaffé's arguments. Stigler did not confront Jaffé's examples: the targets of his rhetorical scorn – "The hand picked example, the implicit absurdity, the abhorrence of evidence" (Stigler, 1982c [1976], p. 86) – were all authors dealing with J. S. Mill. Stigler *did not* discuss the genesis of economic ideas. But he argued that if "science consists of the arguments and evidence that lead *other* men to accept or reject scientific views," then:

> Science is a social enterprise, and those parts of a man's life which do not affect the relationship between that man and his fellow scientists are strictly extra-scientific. When we are told that we must understand a man's life to understand what he really meant, we are being invited to abandon science. . . . The recipients of a scientific message are the people who determine what the message is, and no flight of genius which does not reach the recipients will ever reach and affect the science. (1982c [1976], p. 91)

In other words, Stigler did not believe that biographical information – or at least very much biographical information – played a role if one was concerned with "the *scientific* role these men played in the evolution of economic theory: that role was played with the words they wrote, not with the ideas they intended to express" (p. 92). Biographical information might help in the study of the sociology of the discipline, but that was another matter. This view, Stigler acknowledged (1982c [1976], p. 92) was characteristic of the physical sciences.

In later unpublished papers reported on by Walker (1983a, pp. 43–7; 1983b (ed.), pp. 2–3), Jaffé made his views more explicit. He saw three roles for biographical information: helping to explain the genesis of ideas; helping to elucidate the meaning the author wished to convey (what others have called the "vision"); and assisting in the process of acceptance of a theory (the activities of the economic scientist directed toward the dissemination or acceptance of his theories).

Donald Walker then entered the conversation (1983), with a taxonomy of the ways in which biography – or, more accurately, different types of biographical information (personal, professional, and bibliographic) – could be used for the history of economic thought. He accepted Stigler's views as to how economics worked. (This meant that the reinterpretation of an economist's work using material not available to all – or at least some – contemporaries represented a separate, later item from the one originally created.) Developing and filling in his taxonomy, he suggested that for modern economists ("who wrote since 1770") it was "ordinarily not necessary to have biographical information to establish the meaning of theories" (p. 55). The main argument here was that "we already know the meaning of the specific words and terms and techniques that . . . [the economist] used or can establish it from the context of his writing" (p. 55) – a position that many economist–intellectual historians, such as Donald Winch (1976, 1996), would dispute. Walker claimed to be unable to find a single example of where the sort of environmental information provided by a biography had helped to establish an author's meaning, although he was prepared to accept that it might be the case with someone. Similarly, he suggested that such information was unnecessary for an account of the intellectual evolution of economics as a discipline. Rather, he followed Stigler in suggesting that the major role of biographical information lay in its assisting our understanding of the sociology of the subject. He allowed such information a subsidiary role in the study of the genesis of an author's ideas, but even here he was inclined, despite Jaffé's papers on Walras which he had just edited (Walker, 1983b (ed.)), to believe that the possibilities were limited. His problem with Jaffé in the single case that he discussed was that the evidence was "circumstantial" (1983b (ed.), p. 52). This does not, however, destroy its value as evidence. Difficulties, he suggested, arose from an absence of information and the fact that investigations into the process of creation of new ideas were "more like psychology than a study of the evolution of economic thought" (1983b (ed.), p. 52) – that is, difficult.

Other than my own, there has been one other discussion of biography and the history of economics, William Breit's "Biography and the making of economic worlds" (1987). Breit saw three possible roles for biography in the study of the history of economics; heuristic, therapeutic, and scientific. The first two – the stimulation of interest in the subject and the guiding of further investigation (p. 824) and "the lessons learned about the life-styles and work-habits of scholars" (p. 825) – were unimportant, except, perhaps, in the classroom. The third arose from Breit's view of economics and other social sciences as not being dominated by single paradigms at any particular time. Rather:

economic science . . . proceeds by the formation of enclaves of consensus and these competing enclaves exist side-by-side, each governed by its unique and individual world-view. These enclaves are what we perceive as schools of thought, or what I would prefer to call "interpretive communities." (p. 827)

He turned to the consensual glue that holds these communities together and found it in a suggestion of George Stigler's (1982a [1969], p. 116):

A school within a science is a collection of affiliated scientists who display a considerable higher degree of agreement upon a particular set of views than the science as a whole displays. It is essential to a school that there be many scientists outside it, or the school would have no one with which to argue.
. . .
   A school must have a leader, because the consensus of its members will normally be achieved and maintained by major scientific entrepreneurs. In some instances, such as the Ricardian school, the chief bond has, in fact, been admiration for the leader. I doubt whether a scientific school based upon substantive scientific views can long survive the death of its leader, except in the improbable event of the appearance of a new leader of comparable stature. New analytical and empirical challenges will continue to emerge and only a strong leader can provide generally acceptable responses to these challenges.

According to Breit, understanding the process by which such entrepreneurial or charismatic leaders emerge required the use of biographical data. In "economics the proper analogy is not so much science as art and the role of the historian of economics is much closer to that of the art historian than to the historian of science" (1987, p. 829). Exactly what difference that made to the use of biographical material in the history of economics was not elaborated on.

Breit proceeded to provide an illustration of how biographical material can illuminate the process though which successful scientific entrepreneurs create schools or worlds, taking the example of Ricardo replacing Malthus as the dominant figure in English economics. To do so, he latched onto Keynes's conjecture in *The General Theory* as to the reasons for Ricardo's success (Keynes, 1973a [1936], pp. 32–3):

It must have been due to a complex of suitabilities in the doctrine to the environment into which it was projected. That it reached conclusions quite different from what the ordinary uninstructed person would expect, added, I suppose, to its intellectual prestige. That its teaching, translated into practice, was austere and often unpalatable, lent it virtue. That it was adapted to carry a vast and consistent logical superstructure gave it beauty.

Thus there is a disjuncture between the reasons biographers of economists give for their enterprises and the literature on the uses of biographical materials about economists in the history of economics. Nonetheless, I think that the discussion of the uses of biographical material can be moved a little further, taking yet another cue from Stigler.

35.4   Further Considerations

In his autobiography, *Memoirs of an Unregulated Economist* (1988), although Stigler admitted that he "cannot be confident that it would be profitable for a young scholar to study the history of the subject," especially if that scholar was likely to be an innovator (pp. 215, 216), he made a powerful case for the history of economic thought as both a humane and a scientific enterprise. He accepted that personal knowledge is an advantage in understanding an economist's ideas. Inevitably, he had to accept that one "surprising feature taught by intellectual history is the persistence of uncertainty as to what a person really meant" (p. 216). It is the existence of this uncertainty that earlier in the book led him, in his discussion of the advantages, not only for students but for the professorate, of concentrating work at the frontiers of the subject in a limited number of departments, that, over and above the stimulation of very able colleagues and the earlier discovery of error, was the advantage of easy communications. He continued (pp. 36–7):

> Even though Jones and I have always spoken English and may even have gone to the same graduate school, each of us thinks somewhat differently; we each have a different order in which we think and probably a different pace in expressing ideas. Family members use words which have special meanings for them. . . . So it is with every person, and that is why intimate association makes communication between people efficient and accurate. If I had known David Ricardo, I would be better able to understand his written words. That would be a help, because to this day the meanings of this theories are much debated.

Even with the conception of the discipline as a box of tools, this moves the discussion forward. The fact that economists were writing for their fellow professionals (more and more so as the discipline became "professionalized") and were subject to certain rules of the game, does not mean that the products of their pen were anonymous "economese." Anyone who has read pieces by Maynard Keynes, Dennis Robertson, Ralph Hawtrey, and A. C. Pigou and was presented another example with the name removed would almost certainly know to whom it belonged. There was a distinctive style, at least initially. The style disappeared as "time, experience and the collaboration of a number of minds" found the "best way" of expressing the ideas (Keynes, 1937, p. 111) and ideas were, in David Laidler's (1999) phrase, "fabricated" for incorporation into the general body of run-of-the-mill economics.

The initial style as such is important. It encapsulated not only the formal elements of the author's theory but, particularly when the ideas appeared in book form, an associated bundle of intuitions and hunches. As Keynes repeatedly emphasized – from early papers for Cambridge discussion societies through his 1924 memoir of Marshall to his posthumously published 1942 lecture "Newton the man" – at the center of the act of creation is an intuition or insight that allows the scientist to "see through the obscurity of the argument or of the apparently unrelated data," as a result of which "the details will quickly fall into a scheme of arrangement, between each part of which there is a real connection" (Keynes, 1909, p. 5). Then comes the problem of formalization and tidying up. But the intuition came first and normally ran ahead of the formal analysis. The original text will carry the mixture. This is important for two reasons: (i) the factual historical one that this was the package originally presented to the profession which, perhaps with supplementary supporting papers, persuaded it that there was something to "fabricate"; and (ii) the inevitable fact that whenever two historians of economics dispute the meaning of X's thought they are forced back to the original text, with its mixture of formalism and intuition – of fully and less fully worked out ideas. In these circumstances, in the absence of personal contact, it would seem folly not to make what use one can of the alternative supplements to scientific publications – personal knowledge in the case of the living, or, in the case of the dead, the raw materials of biography, perhaps even mediated by a biographer. Biographical materials or the biography may, with luck, for the historian of economics produce the equivalent of Stigler's desire to have Ricardo as a colleague. Of course the biographer cannot reproduce the inner world or his of her subject. But, after seeing his or her subject's mind operate on occasion after occasion, the biographer is able to describe or illuminate its workings more completely. That may be of some use to the historian of analysis. These are certainly good grounds for making efficient use of biographical information.

At this point, I should discuss one other source of biographical information – the biographical memoir. For British economists the best, long-standing source of these is the *Proceedings of the British Academy*. The *Economic Journal* followed its American counterparts in the 1980s and early 1990s in eschewing such material. One of the victims of this change in practice was George Stigler. In the 1990s the *EJ* revived the economist's obituary, briefly with a defined editor. There are also dictionaries of national biography. Twenty-four volumes of a new *American National Biography* appeared in 1999. A *New DNB* is to replace the *Dictionary of National Biography* in the UK in 2004, with essays recast or revised as necessary. The reworking allows the inclusion of new material and the treating of the subject in a less respectful manner than was formerly the case, particularly when volumes were dealing with the recently deceased. The new material will also have the advantage of being (a) machine readable and searchable and (b) having supporting supplementary biographical information available in a standardized format – a boon for both synthetic and comparative studies of the profession. Among the stock of *EJ* biographies are Keynes's memoir of Marshall (1924), which Schumpeter regarded as "the most brilliant life of a man of science I have ever read" (1946, p. 503, n. 12) – a piece that Ronald Coase has demonstrated (1984, 1990) also shows the extent to which the dead can influence their biographical treatment – Austin Robinson's memoir of Keynes (Robinson, 1947), and Henry Phelps Brown's memoir of Roy Harrod (Brown, 1980). Phelps Brown also wrote Harrod's memoir for the British Academy (1979) – in a series that includes other notable memoirs, such as R. D. C. Black's *Ralph George Hawtrey* (Black, 1977) and James Tobin's *Harry Gordon Johnson* (Tobin, 1978).

35.5 AUTOBIOGRAPHY

Thus far, I have only discussed biographies. Given their status as raw material for biographers and others and their recent efflorescence, autobiographies also merit attention. At the heart of any autobiography is the memory of the subject, supplemented by other external evidence. Given the importance of memory in many walks of life and the consequences of memory loss, psychologists and others have been concerned with its characteristics for decades. In the 1920s, F. C. Bartlett conducted a number of experiments, which included the use of a North American native folk-tale, "The war of the ghosts," adapted from a translation by Franz Boas. Bartlett's conclusions were of some interest:

1. It appears that accuracy of reproduction, in a literal sense, is the rare exception . . .
2. In a chain of reproductions obtained from a single individual, the general form or outline is remarkably persistent . . .
4. With frequent reproduction the form and items of remembered detail very quickly become strengthened and thereafter suffer little change.
5. With infrequent reproduction, omission of detail, simplification of events and structure, and transformation of items into more familiar detail may go on almost indefinitely, or so long as unaided recall is possible.
6. . . . [I]n long-distance remembering, elaboration becomes more common in some cases; and there may be increasing importation, or invention . . .
8. Detail is outstanding when it fits in with a subject's pre-formed interests and tendencies. It is then remembered, though often transformed and it tends to take a progressively earlier place in successive reproductions . . .
10. In all successive rememberings, rationalisation, the reduction of material to a form which can be readily and "satisfyingly" dealt with is very prominent.

(Bartlett, 1932, pp. 93–4)

More recent studies of autobiographical memory suggest that the accuracy of memories is highest for lists of words – as the memory has to deal with more complex situations, it becomes less accurate. Autobiographical memories are constructed out of various components, and final construction will be "guided by the person's goals at the time of retrieval, as well as by the goals at the time of encoding [the components, so that] changes in what is remembered should be expected" (Rubin, 1996, p. 4). Such memories are not always accurate, but perhaps because of the presence of specific details, individuals may believe that the remembered event occurred even in cases where there is independent evidence that it did not (ibid., p. 5). High degrees of emotional stress increase recall, while depression leads to the recall of general, rather than specific, events (ibid., p. 10).

Autobiographical memories are constructed and maintained by a central process in the working memory. It would appear that such memories are put together from the autobiographical knowledge stored in the long-term memory. The knowledge is itself indexed by "personally meaningful and self-relevant themes" (Conway, 1996, p. 72). Such themes, central to psychoanalysis, may be period specific – for example, to transitions such as university or the achievement of specific possible selves. Autobiographical memories are constructed by sampling autobiographical knowledge. Such knowledge is only selectively encoded so that memories are never "complete." Some events may never enter the long-term memory:

> Events that do not impinge upon the current themes, plans and goals of the self, and that do not correspond to existing autobiographical knowledge structures, may simply not be encoded in long-term memory. Thus, event knowledge is only incompletely retained and events themselves are only retained to the extent that they are self-relevant and/or compatible with the relevant pre-existing long-term knowledge. (ibid., pp. 87–8)

But if memories are not complete, it does not follow that they are inaccurate. They are likely to be fairly accurate if only because if autobiographical memory exists to provide some record of past selves, one needs records of relevant episodes such as the attainment of particular goals.

Such is the state of memory, which may be supplemented by external evidence. These elements are combined in the process of creating an autobiography. Autobiography is the past seen from the present and "later experience will sift the past and determine what was important and worth talking about from what merely seemed important then" (Pascal, 1960, p. 69). The perspective is important, as is the fact that autobiography relates not facts "but experiences – i.e. the interaction of a man and facts or events. By experience we mean something with meaning and there can be many varieties and shades of meaning" (ibid., p. 16). Moreover, in addressing the past from the present, the autobiographer runs the risk of linking them too continuously or logically: "We not only tend consciously to rationalise our lives, but memory, as Maurois points out operates unconsciously to the same end" (ibid., p. 15; Maurois, 1929, p. 161). It is the standpoint of the moment at which the author reviews his relationship (or mis-relationship) between himself and the outside world that is of importance to our present concerns. No matter what the avowed purpose of the exercise is, autobiography is "a kind of apologetics" (Gusdorf, 1980, p. 39). Lionel Robbins's *Autobiography of an Economist* (1971) is a good example:

> In the final analysis . . . the prerogative of the autobiography consists in this: that it shows us not the objective stages of a career – to discern these is the task of the historian – but that it reveals instead the effort of a creator to give the meaning of his own mythic tale. (Gusdorf, 1980, p. 49)

Yet it is a tale, once told, that the author will have to live with; so one might expect some circumspection about contemporaries or recent events.

All of this suggests that autobiographical material should be used carefully. It is useful evidence but it may not always be sound, particularly as regards discussions of motivation or cause (Moggridge, 2001). Yet most collections of autobiographical essays are unreflective on their contents. The exceptions are

Kregel (1988, 1989), Szenberg (1992, 1998), Tribe (1997), and Backhouse and Middleton (2000). Some do not even discuss the principles on which their subjects were approached, although in others, such as Breit and Spencer (1986), it is self-evident. The more reflective, such as Backhouse and Middleton (2000), from whom the examples below are taken, attempt to draw out common threads in career paths which, despite such events as graduate school and – for one still-surviving generation – wartime service, are extremely heterogeneous, except for the important role that change or serendipity plays in many cases; for example, Dick Lipsey choosing LSE over Chicago because of the latter's French language requirement, or Wilfrid Beckerman's choice of a Ph.D. topic on Anglo-Danish trade so that he could visit a Danish girlfriend. They also trace the remarkably broad influence of Harry Johnson, first at Cambridge and Manchester (Beckerman, Brittan, Eltis, Corden, and Lipsey), then at Chicago (Laidler, Hamada), and finally at the LSE (Lal, Laidler, Lazonick) – not to mention his editorial work for the *Review of Economic Studies* and the *Journal of Political Economy*. Keith Tribe also reflects on his interviewees: his introduction drew me to the work of psychologists on memory [Bartlett (1932) and an earlier Rubin (1986) survey]. He also noted examples of repetition across sources, most notably in the case of the contributions of Kenneth Boulding to the *Banca Nazionale del Lavoro Quarterly Review* and the Szenberg collection (1998, pp. 6–7). In fact, one of the less remarked upon features of the collections is the amount of repetition in requests for autobiographical memoirs. In the collections edited by Kregel (1988, 1989), Szenberg (1992, 1998), Breit and Spencer (1986), and Backhouse and Middleton (2000), the interviews undertaken by Tribe (1997), and the uncollected essays in the *Banca Nazionale del Lavoro Quarterly Review*, the *American Economist*, and the *Journal of the History of Economic Thought*, there are 198 essays. Of these, 30 represent cases in which the authors concerned made two – or, in five cases, three – autobiographical contributions.

The existence of this growing stock of autobiographical memoirs can play a useful role in the history of economics. In particular, given the absence of manuscript records in many universities in the UK (and probably elsewhere), such memoirs may prove prime supplements to university calendars in tracing the development of particular departments though much of the postwar period (Tribe, 1997, pp. 5–6). Their value will increase as the stock of memoirs moves beyond the heady days of the postwar consolidation and 1960s expansion of economics to more recent, and more troubled, times. Longer, autobiographical volumes should provide useful supplements to these shorter pieces, but one can think of less enlightening counter-examples, such as that of Robbins (1971). Fortunately, the LSE has good records! Autobiographies and interviews as published in the *Journal of the History of Economic Thought* or the *Newsletter of the Cliometric Society* may also prove useful to historians of sub-disciplines in economics.

This brings me back to the uses of biography in the history of economic thought. It can perform the same sociological functions as autobiography, as a possible supplement to the possibilities of understanding the development of economic analysis that I have already discussed. However, economists do not just develop pieces of analysis for reasons internal to the profession and then try, with varying degrees of success, to sell them to their professional colleagues. Economists have also attempted to change the world. Here, changing analysis and persuading one's colleagues is an important part of the process, but there is also the matter of persuading others – public servants, politicians, and the general public. What is possible, even in economic matters, is a matter of persuasion. And there are good examples of such exercises in the biographical literature, such as Skidelsky on Keynes on prewar finance or the campaign surrounding *How to Pay for the War* (Skidelsky, 2000). Professional persuasion, and consensus, was an important part of the process (Sayers, 1956, pp. 2–3). Keynes's failure to persuade, and the accompanying professional disarray in the case of *A Treatise on Money* and the related policy package in the Macmillan Committee and the Economic Advisory Council, played an important part in his lack of success in 1930–1 (Howson and Winch, 1977, pp. 46–81; Clarke, 1988, chs. 4–7). Professional disarray also reduced the impact of the economists' 1903 "manifesto" on trade policy, organized by Edgeworth (Groenewegen, 1995, p. 382ff.). Such persuasive exercises are also part of the history of economics.

35.6 CONCLUSION

In conclusion, I should emphasize a few points. First, although there are outstandingly good examples of biographical treatments of economists – Smith, Wicksell (Gärdlund, 1996 [1958]), Marshall, and Keynes – as a discipline, economics has not always been well served. To some extent, it is its own fault: to judge by most journals, economists do not value it, even to the extent that they once did. In the case of autobiographies, again there are classics such as Mill (1989 [1873]) and there has been a recent efflorescence, the impact and implications of which the discipline has not as yet absorbed. Secondly, perhaps because economists have relatively few good studies that use biographies, they tend to undervalue and misunderstand such exercises within the discipline. Economists understand the usefulness of biographical "facts" for their enterprises, but they are relatively uncritical users of those facts, perhaps as a result of the declining emphasis on historical skills in their training. They also behave in public, despite continuous disputes about "what X actually meant," as if the history of technical economics is some sort of scientific process where individual peculiarities count for little in the end. In the long sweep of history, this should be the case, but the history of economics suggests that the short periods where the contrary might be true can last for decades – a generation or more – which is a long time. Thirdly, in attempting to be scientific, economists tend to ignore useful evidence and to forget that facts do not speak for themselves. Selection and arrangement do matter – for purposes of both persuasion and enlightenment – even when arguments are constrained by formal "rules of the game." In dealing with individuals and their achievements, peculiarities are important. If they were not, why would George Stigler think it useful to have Ricardo as a colleague? Given that he could not, perhaps the role of biographical materials in the history of economics is more important than many have been prepared to allow.

Bibliography

Allen, R. L. 1991: *Opening Doors: The Life and Work of Joseph Schumpeter*, 2 vols. New Brunswick, NJ: Transaction.

—— 1993: *Irving Fisher: A Biography*. Cambridge, MA: Blackwell.

Arestis, P. and Sawyer, M. C. (eds.) 1992: *A Biographical Dictionary of Dissenting Economists*. Aldershot, UK: Edward Elgar.

Backhouse, R. and Middleton, R. (eds.) 2000: *Exemplary Economists*. Cheltenham, UK: Edward Elgar.

Barnett, V. 1998: *Kondratiev and the Dynamics of Economic Development: Long Cycles and Industrial Growth in Historical Context*. Basingstoke, UK: Macmillan.

Bartlett, F. C. 1932: *Remembering: A Study in Experimental and Social Psychology*. Cambridge, UK: Cambridge University Press.

Bellow, S. 2000: *Ravelstein*. New York: Viking.

Black, R. D. C. 1977: Ralph George Hawtrey, 1879–1975. *Proceedings of the British Academy*, 63, 364–97.

Blitch, C. P. 1995: *Allyn Young: The Peripatetic Economist*. Basingstoke, UK: Macmillan.

Breit, W. 1987: Biography and the making of economic worlds. *Southern Economic Journal*, 53, 823–33.

—— and Spencer, R. (eds.) 1986: *Lives of the Laureates: Seven Nobel Economists*. Cambridge MA: The MIT Press. Subsequent editions in 1990 and 1995 increased the number of "lives" to 10 and 13.

Brown, E. H. P. 1979: Henry Roy Forbes Harrod, 1900–1978. *Proceedings of the British Academy*, 75, 653–96.

—— 1980: Sir Roy Forbes Harrod: a biographical memoir. *Economic Journal*, 90, 1–33.

Buchanan, J. M. 1992: *Better than Ploughing and Other Personal Essays*. Chicago: The University of Chicago Press.

Byatt, A. S. 1990: *Possession: A Romance*. London: Chatto and Windus.

—— 2000: *The Biographer's Tale*. London: Chatto and Windus.

Cairncross, A. 1993: *Austin Robinson: The Life of an Economic Adviser*. Basingstoke, UK: Macmillan.

—— 1999: *Living with the Century*. Countess of Moray's, Fife: inyx.

Campbell, R. A. and Skinner, A. S. 1982: *Adam Smith*. London: Croom Helm.

Clarke, P. 1988: The Keynesian Revolution in the Making, 1924–1936. Oxford: The Clarendon Press.

Coase, R. H. 1984: Alfred Marshall's father and mother. *History of Political Economy*, 16, 519–27. Reprinted in Coase (1994), op. cit., pp. 119–29.

—— 1990: Alfred Marshall's family ancestry. In R. McWilliams-Tullberg (ed.), *Alfred Marshall in Retrospect*. Aldershot, UK: Edward Elgar. Reprinted in Coase (1994), op. cit., pp. 130–50.

—— 1994: *Essays on Economics and Economists*. Chicago: The University of Chicago Press.

Colander, D. and Landreth, H. 1996: *The Coming of Keynesianism to America: Conversations with the Founders of Keynesian Economics*, Cheltenham, UK: Edward Elgar.

Conway, M. 1996: Autobiographical knowledge and autobiographical memories. In Rubin (1996), op. cit., pp. 67–93.

Deane, P. 2001: *The Life and Times of J. Neville Keynes: A Beacon in the Tempest*. Cheltenham, UK: Edward Elgar.

Dimand, R. W., Dimand, M. A., and Forget, E. (eds.) 2000: *A Biographical Dictionary of Women Economists*. Cheltenham, UK: Edward Elgar.

Dostaler, G., Ethier, D., and Lepage, L. 1992: *Gunnar Myrdal and his Works*. Montreal: Harvest House.

Dulles, E. L. 1980: *Chances of a Lifetime: A Memoir*. Englewood Cliffs, NJ: Prentice-Hall.

Ebenstein, A. 1997: *Edwin Cannan: Liberal Doyen*. London: Routledge.

—— 2001: *Friedrich Hayek: A Biography*. New York: Palgrave.

Edgell, S. 2001: *Veblen in Perspective: His Life and Thought*. Armonk, NY: M. E. Sharpe.

Felix, D. 1999: *Keynes: A Critical Life*. Westport, CT: Greenwood Press.

Fletcher, G. 2000: *Understanding Dennis Robertson: The Man and His Work*. Cheltenham, UK: Edward Elgar.

Ford, J. L. 1994: *G. L. S. Shackle: The Dissenting Economist's Economist*. Aldershot, UK: Edward Elgar.

Frankel, S. H. 1992: *An Economist's Testimony: The Autobiography of S. Herbert Frankel*. Oxford: Centre for Postgraduate Hebrew Studies.

Friedman, M. and Friedman, R. 1998: *Two Lucky People: Memoirs*. Chicago: The University of Chicago Press.

Gärdlund, T. 1996 [1958]: *The Life of Knut Wicksell*. Stockholm: Almquist & Wicksell/ Cheltenham, UK: Edward Elgar.

Garraty, J. A. and Carnes, M. C. (eds.) 1999: *American National Biography*. New York: Oxford University Press.

Groenewegen, P. 1995: *A Soaring Eagle: Alfred Marshall, 1842–1924*. Aldershot, UK: Edward Elgar.

Gusdorf, G. 1980: Conditions and limits of autobiography. In Olney, J. (ed.) 1980: *Auto-biography: Essays Theoretical and Critical*. Princeton, NJ: Princeton University Press.

Hagemann, H. 1997: *Zur Deutschsprachigen Wirtschaftswissenschaftlichen Emigration nach 1933*. Marburg: Metropolis-Verlag.

Hamouda, O. F. 1993: *John R. Hicks: The Economist's Economist*. Oxford: Blackwell.

Harcourt, G. C. 2001: *50 Years a Keynesian and Other Essays*. Basingstoke, UK: Palgrave.

Harrod, R. F. 1951: *The Life of John Maynard Keynes*. London: Macmillan.

Heertje, A. (ed.) 1993: *The Makers of Modern Economics*, vol. I. Hemel Hempstead, UK: Wheatsheaf.

—— (ed.) 1995: *The Makers of Modern Economics*, vol. II. Aldershot, UK: Edward Elgar.

—— (ed.) 1997: *The Makers of Modern Economics*, vol. III. Cheltenham, UK: Edward Elgar.

—— (ed.) 1999: *The Makers of Modern Economics*, vol. IV. Cheltenham, UK: Edward Elgar.

Henry, J. F. 1995: *John Bates Clark: The Making of a New-Classical Economist*. Basingstoke, UK: Macmillan.

Higgins, B. H. 1992: *All the Difference: A Development Economist's Quest*. Montreal: McGill University Press/Kingston: Queen's University Press.

Holt, R. P. F. and Pressman, S. (eds.) 1998: *Economics and its Discontents: Twentieth Century Dissenting Economists*. Cheltenham, UK: Edward Elgar.

Hoover, C. B. 1965: *Memoirs of Capitalism, Communism and Nazism*. Durham, NC: Duke University Press.

Howson, S. and Winch, D. 1977: *The Economic Advisory Council 1930–1939: A Study of Economic Advice during Depression and Recovery*. Cambridge, UK: Cambridge University Press.

Hume, David 1980 [1777]: *My Own Life*. In E. C. Mossner, *The Life of David Hume*, 2nd edn. Oxford: The Clarendon Press, 612–15.

Ibanez, C. U. 1999: *The Current State of Macroeconomics: Leading Thinkers in Conversation*. Basingstoke, UK: Macmillan.

Jaffé, W. 1965: Biography and economic analysis. *Western Economic Journal*, 3, 223–32.

James, P. 1979: *Population Malthus: His Life and Times*. London: Routledge.

Johnson, E. S. and Johnson, H. G. 1978: *The Shadow of Keynes: Understanding Keynes, Cambridge and Keynesian Economics*. Chicago: The University of Chicago Press.

Jones, K. 1994: *An Economist Among Mandarins: A Biography of Robert Hall (1901–1988)*. Cambridge: Cambridge University Press.

Jorgensen, E. W. and Jorgensen, H. I. 1999: *Thorsten Veblen: Victorian Firebrand*. Armonk NY: M. E. Sharpe.

Keynes, J. M. 1909: Science and art. February 20, 1909, King's College, Cambridge, Keynes Papers, UA/10/1.

—— 1924: Alfred Marshall. *Economic Journal*, XXXIV (September). Reprinted in Keynes (1972), op. cit., pp. 161–231.

—— 1937: The general theory of employment. *Quarterly Journal of Economics*, LI (February). Reprinted in Keynes (1973b), op. cit., 109–23.

—— 1947 [1942]: Newton: the man. In Royal Society of London (ed.), *Newton Tercentenary Celebrations, 15–19 July 1946*. Cambridge, UK: Cambridge University Press. Reprinted in Keynes (1972), op. cit., pp. 363–74.

—— 1949: Melchior: a defeated enemy. In *Two Memoirs*. London: Rupert Hart-Davis. Reprinted in Keynes (1972), op. cit., pp. 389–439.

—— 1972: *The Collected Writings of John Maynard Keynes*, vol. X, *Essays in Biography*, ed. D. E. Moggridge. London: Macmillan, for the Royal Economic Society.

—— 1973a [1936]: *The General Theory of Employment, Interest and Money*. London: Macmillan, for the Royal Economic Society.

—— 1973b: *The Collected Writings of John Maynard Keynes*, vol. XIV, *The General Theory and After. Part II. Defence and Development*, ed. D. E. Moggridge. London: Macmillan, for the Royal Economic Society.

Kindleberger, C. P. 1991: *The Life of an Economist: An Autobiography*. Oxford: Blackwell.

Kregel, J. A. (ed.) 1988: *Recollections of Eminent Economists*, vol. I. Basingstoke, UK: Macmillan.

—— (ed.) 1989: *Recollections of Eminent Economists*, vol. II. Basingstoke, UK: Macmillan.

Kresge, S. and Wenar, L. (eds.) 1994: *Hayek on Hayek: An Autobiographical Dialogue*. Chicago: The University of Chicago Press.

Krueger, A. B. 2000: An interview with Zvi Griliches. *Journal of Economic Perspectives*, 14, 171–89.

—— 2001: An interview with William J. Baumol. *Journal of Economic Perspectives*, 15, 211–31.

Laidler, D. 1999: *Fabricating the Keynesian Revolution: Studies of the Inter-war Literature on Money, the Cycle and Unemployment*. Cambridge, UK: Cambridge University Press.

—— 2002: Skidelsky's Keynes: a review essay. *European Journal of the History of Economic Thought*, 9, 97–110.

Little, I. M. D. 1999: *Collection and Recollections: Economic Papers and their Provenance*. Oxford: The Clarendon Press.

März, E. 1991: *Joseph Schumpeter: Scholar, Teacher and Politician*. New Haven, CN: Yale University Press.

Maurois, A. 1929: *Aspects of Biography*, trans. S. C. Roberts. New York: Appleton.

Meacci, F. (ed.) 1998: *Italian Economists of the Twentieth Century*. Cheltenham, UK: Edward Elgar.

Medema, S. G. 1994: *Ronald H. Coase*. Basingstoke, UK: Macmillan.

Mehrling, P. G. 1997: *The Money Interest and the Public Interest: American Monetary Thought, 1920–1970*. Cambridge, MA: Harvard University Press.

Mikesell, R. F. 2000: *Foreign Adventures of an Economist*. Eugene, OR: University of Oregon Press.

Mill, J. S. 1989 [1873]: *Autobiography*, ed. J. Robson. London: Penguin.

Modigliani, F. 2001: *Adventures of an Economist*. New York: Texere.

Moggridge, D. E. 1989: Economists and biographers. *Bulletin of the History of Economics Society*, 11, 174–89.

—— 1992: *Maynard Keynes: An Economist's Biography*. London: Routledge.

—— 2001: H.G. J. as a biographer's subject: some autobiographical writings. *American Journal of Economics and Sociology*, 60, 651–66.

Murphy, A. 1997: *John Law: Economic Theorist and Policy-Maker*. Oxford: The Clarendon Press.

Nasar, S. 1999: *A Beautiful Mind: A Biography of John Forbes Nash Jr., Winner of the Nobel Prize in Economics, 1994*. London: Faber.

O'Brien, D. P. 2000: History of economic thought as a discipline. In A. E. Murphy and R. Pendergast (eds.), *Contributions to the History of Economic Thought: Essays in Honour of R. D. C. Black*. London: Routledge.

Pascal, R. 1960: *Design and Truth in Autobiography*. London: Routledge.

Pigou, A. C. 1926: *Memorials of Alfred Marshall*. London: Macmillan.

Polkinghorn, B. and Thomson, D. L. 1998: *Adam Smith's Daughters: Eight Prominent Women Economists from the Eighteenth Century to the Present*. Cheltenham, UK: Edward Elgar.

Potier, J.-P. 1991: *Piero Sraffa: Unorthodox Economist (1898–1983)*. London: Routledge.

Raphael, D. D. 1985: *Adam Smith*. Oxford: Oxford University Press.

Robbins, L. 1971: *Autobiography of an Economist*. London: Macmillan

Robinson, E. A. G. 1947: John Maynard Keynes, 1883–1946. *Economic Journal*, 57, 1–68.

Roncaglia, A. 2000: *Piero Sraffa: His Life, Thought and Cultural Heritage*. London: Routledge.

Ross, I. S. 1995: *The Life of Adam Smith*. Oxford: The Clarendon Press.

Rubin, D. C. (ed.) 1986: *Autobiographical Memory*. Cambridge, UK: Cambridge University Press.

—— (ed.) 1996: *Remembering Our Past: Studies in Autobiographical Memory*. Cambridge, UK: Cambridge University Press.

Samuels, W. (ed.) 1998: *European Economists of the Early Twentieth Century, I, Studies of Neglected Thinkers of Belgium, France, The Netherlands and Scandinavia*. Cheltenham, UK: Edward Elgar.

Sayers, R. S. 1956: *Financial Policy, 1939–1945*. London: Her Majesty's Stationery Office and Longmans Green.

Schneider, M. 1996: *J. A. Hobson*. Basingstoke, UK: Macmillan.

Schumpeter, J. A. 1946: John Maynard Keynes, 1883–1946. *American Economic Review*, 36, 495–518.

Shute, L. 1997: *John Maurice Clark: A Social Economics for the Twenty-First Century*. Basingstoke, UK: Macmillan.

Skidelsky, R. 1983: *John Maynard Keynes: Hopes Betrayed, 1883–1920*. London: Macmillan.

—— 1985: *John Maynard Keynes: Hopes Betrayed, 1883–1920*. New York: Viking.

—— 1992: *John Maynard Keynes: The Economist as Saviour, 1920–1937*. London: Macmillan.

—— 1996: *Keynes*, Oxford: Oxford University Press.

—— 2000: *John Maynard Keynes: Fighting for Britain, 1937–1946*, London: Macmillan.

Snowden, B and Vane, H. 1999: *Conversations with Leading Economists: Interpreting Modern Macroeconomics*. Cheltenham, UK: Edward Elgar.

Stanfield, J. R. 1996: *John Kenneth Galbraith*. Basingstoke, UK: Macmillan.

Stephen, L. 1885: *Henry Fawcett*. London: Macmillan.

Stewart, D. 1980 [1793]: *Account of the Life and Writings of Adam Smith LLD*, ed. I. S. Ross. Reprinted in Smith, A. 1980: *Essays on Philosophical Subjects*, ed. W. P. D. Wightman and C. J. Bryce. Oxford: The Clarendon Press, 269–351.

Stigler, G. J. 1982a [1969]: Does economics have a useful past? *History of Political Economy*, 1. Reprinted in Stigler (1982b), op. cit., pp. 107–18.

—— 1982b: *The Economist as Preacher and Other Essays*. Oxford: Blackwell.

—— 1982c [1976]: The scientific uses of biography with special reference to J. S. Mill. In J. M. Robson and M. Laine (eds.), *James and John Stuart Mill: Papers of the Centenary Conference*. Toronto: University of Toronto Press. Reprinted in Stigler (1982b), op. cit., pp. 86–97.

—— 1988: *Memoirs of an Unregulated Economist*. New York: Basic Books.

Stolper, W. F. 1994: *Joseph Alois Schumpeter: The Public Life of a Private Man*. Princeton, NJ: Princeton University Press.

Swedberg, R. 1991: *Joseph A. Schumpeter: His Life and Work*. Cambridge: Polity Press. Published in the United States as *Schumpeter: A Biography*. Princeton, NJ: Princeton University Press.

Szenberg, M. (ed.) 1992: *Eminent Economists: Their Life Philosophies*. Cambridge, UK: Cambridge University Press.

—— (ed.) 1998: *Passion and Craft: Economists at Work*. Ann Arbor, MI: University of Michigan Press.

Tobin, J. 1978: Harry Gordon Johnson, 1923–1977. *Proceedings of the British Academy*, 64, 443–58.

Tribe, K. 1997: *Economic Careers: Economics and Economists in Britain, 1930–1970*. London: Routledge.

Turner, M. S. 1993: *Nicholas Kaldor and the Real World*. Armonk, NY: M. E. Sharpe.

Walker, D. A. 1983a: Biography and the study of the history of economic thought. *Research on the History of Economic Thought and Methodology*, I, 41–59.

—— (ed.) 1983b: *William Jaffé's Essays on Walras*. Cambridge, UK: Cambridge University Press.

Weatherall, D. 1976: *David Ricardo: A Biography*. The Hague: Martinus Nijhoff.

Wheen, F. 1999: *Karl Marx*. London: Fourth Estate.

Winch, D. 1976: *Adam Smith's Politics: An Essay in Historiographic Revision*. Cambridge, UK: Cambridge University Press.

—— 1996: *Riches and Poverty: An Intellectual History of Political Economy in Britain, 1750–1834*. Cambridge, UK: Cambridge University Press.

Young, W. F. 1987: *Interpreting Mr. Keynes: The IS–LM Enigma*. Cambridge, UK: Polity Press.

Economics and Economists in the Policy Process

Craufurd D. W. Goodwin

36.1　ECONOMICS AND POLICY IN THE PREHISTORY OF ECONOMICS

Economists have usually been anxious to influence policy, varying only in their ability to do so and their willingness to admit it. Before the development of a recognized economic science and an economics profession, they had difficulty being taken seriously. Until perhaps the eighteenth century no separate body of economics or applied economics literature was recognized. Earlier, it was necessary for economic thought to enter policy discussion through either another discipline, such as philosophy or theology, or debate over current events. It was soon discovered that unlike the physical or biological sciences, where policy could be based upon confident predictions about the behavior of key variables, the main economic actors were both difficult to predict and likely to change their behavior over time.

Prior to the eighteenth century, the economy was thought to be less a potential source of progress and advance in human welfare than a cause of retrogression and danger. Humans were seen as vicious and passionate creatures that could be at their worst in the economy. Unless restrained, they could do damage to others and to themselves. Greek philosophers feared that human selfishness could lead to monopoly, exploitation, maldistribution of income, envy, corruption, and the downfall of a just and efficient city–state devoted to the good life of its citizens. Humans, therefore, had to be constrained in their economic activity. Even rule by a benevolent aristocracy could change quickly under economic pressures to tyranny or to mob rule.

In the Middle Ages, Christian theologians added to the political hazards the danger that free-wheeling economic actors would encourage sin among selfish, jealous, and misguided humans, and preclude salvation. Economic activities seen today as efficient were viewed as sources of social conflict and injustice: in particular, free market exchange, the taking of interest, and the accumulation of wealth without limit.

Distinctive characteristics of the early policy process must be considered when assessing the impact of economic ideas on policy. Until the nineteenth century, with few exceptions, government was personal and authoritarian, and the policy process consisted of a monarch, aristocrat, or tribal chieftain deciding how to solve a problem and taking action. Representative legislatures and bureaucracies were unimportant. Economic thinking could enter the policy process when someone was able to get to the key decision-maker and present a persuasive case. This was done successfully by Plato and Aristotle through education (one of Aristotle's students was Alexander the Great) and through a philosophic literature that had economic policy injunctions embedded within it. The Greek philosophers also acted as consultants to the state on various economic questions.

The Christian Church later looked to the Greek philosophers for answers to economic questions, and theology replaced philosophy as the primary transmission belt for economic ideas, through papal edicts, the confessional, treatises such as Thomas Aquinas's *Summa Theologica*, and direct intervention by individual clerics. Attention was directed to property rights, the taking of interest, and how to achieve a "just" price in the market. The notion of all-encompassing laws, whether eternal, natural, or human, lay behind the policy judgments of the "Scholastic doctors" of this era.

During the late Middle Ages and the Renaissance, policy problems due to consolidation of nation–states and growing international trade faced economic thinkers, and their involvement in policy-making became close. Indeed, most could not have imagined why anyone would engage in economic inquiry other than to seek influence. Commentators, including self-interested participants in the controversies of the moment and personal advisers to political authorities, extended understanding of the economy by exploring tariffs, subsidies, colonies, public transport, monopoly, paper money, and different forms of taxation. These topics were more macro than micro, embedded in issues of growth, national security, price stability, and employment.

Some early literature has been called a "mirror for princes," because it was constructed to tell a prince what he wanted to see, in all its implications. Ideas did not begin in science and move to policy. They went the other way. Later commentators gave these early economic writers the title "mercantilist" and viewed them with distaste and suspicion. Pioneering insights from such authors as Bernard Mandeville, Thomas Mun, and Dudley North have been clouded by the perception that they mixed inappropriately economic self-interest with policy debate.

36.2 CLASSICAL ECONOMICS AND POLICY

During the eighteenth-century "Enlightenment," the first coherent formulations of an economic system emerged, without qualification for time and place. The norm underlying these systems, in contrast to earlier concerns with state-building and salvation, was the production of goods and services for the satisfaction of human wants, consistent with individual and social morality. It now became possible to discern policy implications and construct policy instruments with specific reference to a system. Charges against earlier thinkers that proposals were too *ad hoc*, too entwined with advocates' self-interest, or dependent on metaphysics or religion to be persuasive could now be answered with the argument that good economic policy was rooted in scientific economic theory.

An early expression of such a system came from the French physiocrats, led by the Court physician François Quesnay and A. R. J. Turgot. The physiocratic economic model emphasized uninterrupted flows of funds throughout the system and the interconnectedness of all sectors, as illustrated in the *Tableau économique*. It emphasized the distribution of the economic surplus (*produit net*) from agriculture, the accumulation of capital (*avances*), economies of scale (*grand culture*), taxes that would not interfere with production (*impôt unique*) and suitable market prices (*bon prix*). The physiocrats denounced feudal and mercantilist restrictions, especially taxes that distorted flows of funds. They wanted state revenue to come from landowners, the only ones that commanded a surplus. The physiocrats happily accepted positions of influence within government, as their mercantilist predecessors had done. But to a greater degree they mistrusted the state and made famous the celebrated and enduring injunction to leave markets alone: "*laissez faire, laissez passer*." The physiocrats impacted numerous policy areas, including international trade, the administration of colonies, and even the debate over the constitution for the new United States of America. Like the earlier Scholastics, the physiocrats looked for actions and policies in the economy that were "just" and "natural."

Another great Enlightenment vision of a distinct economic system appeared in Scotland, first in the essays of David Hume and then in the great treatise of Adam Smith, *An Inquiry into the Nature and Causes of the Wealth of Nations* (1776). This Scottish vision drew heavily on the physiocrats, especially for an understanding of the role of capital, but it focused more on how individual buyers and sellers in unregulated markets unintentionally achieved social goals. Smith provided an answer to the question posed by economic thinkers of the previous century about how the natural selfishness of humans could be reconciled with the common good. Smith's answer was that competition in the marketplace directed selfish suppliers to produce goods at least cost and in quantities desired by demanders. Smith also studied complex "noneconomic" social forces, such as the "sympathies" of its members, and he insisted that these too needed to be included in policy-making. Smithian doctrine implied a role for economic advisers in the state, but a more detached and consultative role than an activist one. Economists, or "political economists," challenged innumerable inherited practices and institutions that prevented market efficiency: monopolies, colonies, guilds, protective tariffs, subsidies, and endowments for education. The conception of a scholar of the economy newly emerged, removed somewhat from the world of affairs but able to extract policy lessons from a generalized model. In principle, this advice was uncorrupted by personal self-interest or superstition of any kind. The practice was rather different. Smith himself was far from being a hermit. He was a close observer of public affairs, an enthusiastic clubman, and a willing adviser to government. But his influence came from his detachment from the particularities of issues and his evident commitment to the public interest. His appointment as commissioner of customs came after his reputation as policy sage was well established.

The tradition of close attention to, but scholarly distance from, the hurly-burly world of public policy continued, in principle at least, into the nineteenth century. A seeming paradox persisted, however: despite the classical economists' commitment to principle and to detachment from activities that might corrupt their policy judgment, they were not ivory-towered scholars. With few exceptions, they were not engaged in full-time research or teaching, but were fully embedded in the institutions that made up the economy, and about which they wrote: T. R. Malthus as well as James and John Stuart Mill with the East India Company, David Ricardo as a successful stockbroker, Henry Thornton a banker, Robert Torrens a Member of Parliament, Richard Whateley an archbishop, and so on. They seldom functioned as modern professional economists in, or at the ear of, government. Their response to any charge of partiality was that they explored questions from first principles and thought of themselves as having no client, except perhaps the broad community of producers and consumers. The diverse locations of classical political economists mirrored the milieu in which policy was then formed. There was no large centralized government; makers of policy were embedded mainly in the private sector of agricultural producers and financial corporations, the professions, the aristocracy, the Church, and local government. The apparent dispersion of classical economists throughout economy and society reflected this prevailing dispersion of political power.

The policy subjects that interested the classical economists, and on which they advised government, grew from their theories: population and emigration, land settlement, monopoly, commercial restriction and subsidy, money supply, public finance, national security, and empire. They also had valuable things to say on other current issues, from public education to the Factory Acts and treatment of paupers.

During the classical period, several important devices emerged by which political economists might influence policy. Decisions that influenced the economy were made in both Parliament and institutions such as local councils, guilds, the army, and the Church. Policy influence required that these institutions be reached in the best ways possible. The political economists gave serious attention to issues and ideas through discussion groups with eclectic memberships – the Political Economy Club of London, the London Statistical Society (later the Royal Statistical Society), and The British Association for the Advancement of Science, to mention only several of the most prominent. Many periodicals began to mobilize the educated middle classes to think seriously about the economy and other subjects. The most influential paper on economic topics was the weekly London *Economist*, published still today, but there were also daily papers (The *Morning Chronicle, The Scotsman*, and so on) that specialized in economic policy discussion, and monthlies and quarterlies that addressed subjects in greater depth, often from varied ideological or methodological perspectives (the *Westminster Review,*

Quarterly Review, Blackwood's, North British Review, and so on). For the lower reaches of society, fiction – as in the novelettes of Harriet Martineau – conveyed policy lessons on economic questions: whether to join a trade union, how much to work and save, or how many children to bring into the world. Fiction was used also by the critics of classical economics, such as Charles Dickens and Thomas Love Peacock. Throughout most of the nineteenth century, the Church remained sympathetic to many of the policy conclusions of classical political economy, and Church materials of various kinds were another medium through which economists could be heard.

36.3 FROM THE ART TO THE SCIENCE OF POLITICAL ECONOMY

The great classical political economists – Smith, Bentham, Ricardo, Malthus, Torrens, and the two Mills – viewed the construction of economic policy as an art. They appreciated the complexity of the process. The objectives might be several; there were innumerable parties at interest to be taken into account; various actors had to be mollified or foiled; and new policy mechanisms had to be imagined. Colonial policy is an example. Here was the problem of balancing the interests of the metropolis and the colonies against each other. Political economists agreed that the large monopoly companies had been deeply problematic and they recoiled at more bureaucracy. Yet there was little inclination to give up India or the possessions still governed by companies. How about the American colonies? Where exactly was their benefit to the mother country? The classical economists answered "in trade," but that trade did not require a dependent relationship. Smith envisioned something like the loose British Commonwealth that ultimately emerged to unite metropolis with dependencies. But there were competing visions. Bentham saw the colonies as an exciting laboratory for reform. Some disciples of Malthus welcomed a haven for excess population. The Ricardians worried about a diversion of scarce capital to the colonies. Edward Gibbon Wakefield discerned a fortuitous symbiosis between old and new countries, through which the excess people and capital in one could find outlet in the other. All of these ideas required creative policy thinking that went beyond any simple interpretation of a single model that demonstrated the gains from trade.

The mid-nineteenth century presented economists with exciting policy challenges that required vision and imagination. Several young economic theorists sought to transform economics into a more serious science, self-contained and rigorous, in the image of the physical and biological sciences, which were themselves then being transformed. Aspects of this transformation from classical political economy to what would come to be known as neoclassical economics included academicizing the subject via enclosure within colleges and universities. Curricula, departments, chairs, textbooks, faculties, and arcane terminology were used to define the subject. And just as the tradition had been long established that lawyers talk only to lawyers, so in economics noneconomists were increasingly excluded from "serious" conversation. No more, as with classical political economy, could archbishops (Whateley) or postmasters general (Fawcett) become pillars of the profession. This transformation had at least three outcomes for economic policy. First, the range of policy issues perceived as legitimate for scientific discussion was narrowed. For example, consumer tastes now lay outside the limits of scientific inquiry in economics, as did population growth and relations among social classes. Economists thought they had much to say about how production and exchange could achieve maximum efficiency; but how the product was then used was somebody else's business. Secondly, in the English-speaking world at least, with memories of the mercantilists, leaders of the profession insisted that economists not become dangerously close personally to policy areas where they offered advice. Their recommendations must remain untainted by special interest. In particular, they should not normally seek or take up posts in government. The situation in the German-speaking world was somewhat different. Responsible economic advisers elsewhere might serve on special committees or commissions of inquiry, testify before the legislature, and occasionally deliver carefully balanced public utterances. But they should not become co-opted or reach a position where their scientific judgment might become clouded or silent. Thirdly, economists should expect that since they have all supposedly mastered the same analytic tools, and they all have access to the same data, they should all reach the same policy conclusions. The cacophony of voices and free-wheeling debate with noneconomists on almost any topic during the classical period could no longer be tolerated. In the English-speaking world, Alfred Marshall did much to specify this new stance. His own position was that the competitive market system could solve most economic problems spontaneously and without outside intervention, and that many of the system's most serious problems came from meddlers, either self-interested rent-seekers or well-meaning government officials. Professional economists should not worsen the situation with their own meddling. Marshall's successor at the University of Cambridge, Arthur Pigou, developed the field of welfare economics that attempted to specify the limits within which economists might contemplate intervention in markets. The notion of utility that was central to the new neoclassical economics, the very personal objective of the self-interested economic actor, played an important part in constraining market interference. Since it could not be demonstrated that individual utilities were in any way commensurable, beyond an efficiency condition that came to be known as Pareto optimality, no legitimate case could be made using economic theory for governmental intervention or for redistribution of income and wealth. This restrained posture toward policy was extended by disciples of Marshall and others, notably leaders of the University of Chicago tradition such as Henry Simons, Frank Knight, Milton Friedman, George Stigler, and Gary Becker.

36.4   A MORE ACTIVE ROLE FOR THE ECONOMIST IN ECONOMIC POLICY

While the restrained Marshallian role for government and the economist was refined during the late nineteenth and early twentieth centuries, other attitudes emerged among economists.

Ironically, disciples of the revolutionary thinker Karl Marx, most of whom had a deep interest in public affairs, were enjoined by their master from contributing to policy that was incremental, remedial, and directed to problems of the moment. The Marxian view was that inexorable change was always taking place in the means of production, and therefore the capitalist market system, like all systems before it, was becoming increasingly obsolete, and indeed was beyond repair. The mounting "contradictions of capitalism" would necessarily lead sooner or later to the only real solution to economic problems, revolutionary change in the system. A good Marxist economist should not become involved in policy that might impede the onset of the revolution by ameliorating the conditions that would impel the change. The Marxian policy agenda was to watch problems become worse in the short run so that they could become better in the long run. But this left the Marxian economist out of the policy loop.

Beside the Marshallian and Marxian postures toward the appropriate place for economists in public policy, both of which coached restraint, other positions emerged that counseled a stronger role for the economist. One tradition came to be associated with the politics of social democracy, which claimed that the capitalist market system was unfair to many of its members. Economists, therefore, had a responsibility to work with politicians and bureaucrats to rectify imbalances and injustices. On the European continent, this tradition led to experiments with national health insurance and what is now called in the United States "social security." In Britain, detailed surveys of conditions of poverty during the depressed 1890s provided the impetus for the Fabian Society, which included economists among its members, to call for various programs to change the patterns of income and wealth distribution – to "level up and level down."

A substantial number of economists during the nineteenth century approached the "economy" as a concept limited to a particular time and place, and continually changing because of technological and cultural movement as well as accidents of history. The potential role for the state, and for the economist as a guide for the state, seemed virtually limitless. These "historical" economists called for careful empirical study of particular circumstances and the preparation of proposals for reform. This tradition was given impetus in both Germany and the United States by Friedrich List's *National System of Political Economy* (1841). It supported varied policies toward economic development through a series of "stages," each requiring distinct treatment. The German historians' position implied a rich and creative role for economists in government, and they served as central bankers and ministers of finance, identified in a derogatory way by their critics as "socialists of the chair."

In the United States, a distinctive body of economic thought emerged in the twentieth century that called for an active role for economists in policy, influenced by both the ideas of the German historical school and an evolutionary perspective on economic change generated by Thorstein Veblen and his disciples. These American institutionalists, as they were called, suggested that just as a physician treated diseases and genetic faults in the human body, so they as physicians to the body politick should work with governments to make the economy better. Wesley C. Mitchell, John R. Commons, Clarence Ayres, Rexford

Tugwell, John Kenneth Galbraith, and other economists in the institutionalist tradition advised legislators and bureaucrats and accepted short-term assignments in government. Much complex economic legislation on such topics as labor relations, farm price supports, worker health and safety, and anti-trust, as well as the institutional infrastructure that emerged from President Roosevelt's New Deal, bore the stamp of these economists' work. FDR's "Brains Trust" was one of the first advisory bodies to a head of state that contained prominent economists.

36.5 THE POLICY CHALLENGE OF
TWO WORLD WARS AND DEPRESSION

Two developments in the twentieth century prompted economists to rethink their participation in the making and implementation of economic policy: conflict on a massive scale between highly complex market economies, and global stagnation that seemed unwilling to disappear on its own.

World War I was fought mainly without the participation of professional economists in positions of real power. Businessmen, personified in the United States by the financier Bernard Baruch, were the main advisers to government, and as a result they took much of the blame for the inflation, ineffectiveness, and corruption that seemed to characterize economic aspects of the war effort. World War II was very different; then economists took much of the credit for success. Similarly, the Great Depression was initially little understood by economists. Businessmen, especially those in the Hoover administration and to some extent also in the Roosevelt administration, were again given the first opportunity to find a solution. By the time their efforts failed, some economists, at least, were confident that they had the answer.

A critical factor in the new positions and reputations gained by economists in government by the onset of World War II was the theoretical contribution of John Maynard Keynes. Keynes's macroeconomics emphasized the importance and possibility of controlling, or at least affecting, aggregate demand to restrain inflation in wartime and to sustain employment in recession. Many economists were uncomfortable with what seemed an entirely new perspective. Others found it an exhilarating new policy frontier and perceived that they might be useful as never before. Most importantly, few other economists had good ideas to challenge the Keynesian position on how to mobilize the economy successfully for war and how to keep the workforce employed when war ended. The Keynesians insisted that government needed to determine both how to manipulate the components of aggregate demand and precisely how much manipulation should be undertaken. To the extent that these questions had previously been asked in government at all, they had been addressed mainly by central bankers and ministers of finance. The Keynesian economists' argument was that these questions could best be answered by professional experts, who were detached from political controversy. Some insisted that the voting public should participate in this inquiry that affected them so much. Keynes postulated an economic system that depended heavily on economic actors' psychological behavior throughout inter-locking markets, and readily conceded that this could not easily be understood. Humans were not some kind of rational automatons responding to utility and pro-duction functions in easily predictable ways. Rather, they were a heterogeneous mass, or herd, responding to various behavioral imperatives, some of which, like King Midas's thirst for gold, might lead to their self-destruction. Keynes portrayed a system with serious pathological flaws, but one that was correctable through judicious public intervention in what the prominent journalist and interpreter of Keynes in America, Walter Lippmann, called "the compensated economy."

Between the two world wars, several private philanthropies actively supported economists' early efforts to discover ways of restoring prosperity and reducing the likelihood of war. Even before World War I, The Carnegie Endowment for International Peace had started a program on the relationship between the eco-nomy and conflict, headed by the distinguished Columbia University economist John Bates Clark. The Rockefeller Foundation, in attempts to make economics more useful to society, supported projects across Europe and America to under-stand better the nature of business cycles. In the United States the economics discipline responded enthusiastically to these offers of financial support, and sev-eral professional bodies mobilized to manage the resources, notably the National Bureau of Economic Research, the Social Science Research Council, and the American Council of Learned Societies. The business magnate Robert Brookings endowed his Brookings Institution in Washington, for research and the training of economists directed to such priority areas as improved government budgeting and foreign economic policy. These philanthropic initiatives by the private sector led to more involvement of economists in government: for example, Wesley Mitchell, founder of the National Bureau, helped to sort through the pros and cons of some centralized economic planning; and Leo Pasvolsky, head of the research program at Brookings on international economic relations, became an important senior adviser to Secretary of State Cordell Hull, who was active in planning the new United Nations.

36.6   WAR AND DEPRESSION CONCENTRATE THE ECONOMIC MIND

In the prosecution of World War II – and in contrast to that of World War I – economists were employed throughout government: in both macroeconomic agen-cies such as the Federal Reserve, the Treasury, and the Budget Bureau, where Keynesian notions of demand management seemed demonstrably useful; and in many new institutions created specifically to wage war, where the problems were mainly microeconomic in nature, such as how to arrange for the production and distribution of strategic materials, and how to ease back into an unregulated market economy when war ended. Some of the most enthusiastic young converts to macroeconomic doctrine, exposed to Keynes's ideas in Alvin Hansen's seminar at Harvard University and elsewhere, quickly found themselves in positions of great policy influence: for example, Lauchlin Currie at the Board of Governors of the Federal Reserve, and later in the Roosevelt White House; and John Kenneth

Galbraith as deputy director of the Office of Price Administration. In the military services, wartime also revealed new roles for economists, in the formulation of strategy and even in the selection of targets for air raids, a task assigned to the young international economist Charles Kindelberger, among others. Micro-economics as the study of optimization subject to constraints demonstrated how it could offer valuable, even counterintuitive, guidance on such prosaic questions as how to aim a machine gun.

The onset of serious recession in both Europe and America in the 1920s and 1930s, decades bracketed by the world wars, provided an auspicious moment for economists to claim a stronger voice in policy-making. These years yielded a stream of questions about which they, more than any others, could be expected to have some answers. But there was not the steady progress in making their voice heard that happened later in World War II. In both Britain and the United States, various committees and commissions were appointed on which economists sat to seek an end to the depression: for example, the Committee on Social Trends appointed by President Hoover, on which Wesley Mitchell was an influential member; and the Economic Advisory Committee appointed by British Prime Minster Ramsey McDonald, that included Keynes. The problem then may have been, in part, that economists were far from speaking with one voice. At one extreme, some economists concluded that no action should be taken and that the economy would heal itself; at the other extreme, other economists insisted that the depression had demonstrated that the capitalist market system was hopelessly flawed, and it would be only through radical structural reform, such as that proposed under the National Recovery Administration, introduced as part of the first New Deal, that the system could again be made to work. It would take the new status gained by economists during World War II and the increasing authority of Keynesian doctrine to cause their ideas about employment, inflation, and growth to be taken very seriously.

In the 1930s and 1940s, in addition to questions of war and depression, worries persisted about the treatment of natural resources. Over all hung the image of the dust bowl, with clouds of topsoil drifting away from the farm belt forever, contrasted with devastating floods that every year hit the Midwest and South. Americans saw the closing of the real and symbolic frontier and came to appreciate that they no longer had the option of dealing with destruction of the landscape through the slogan "Go West, young man." Worries about the potential loss of natural resources forever were reflected in the creation of national parks, dam construction, land reclamation, and planning in the context of river valleys, as in the case of the Tennessee Valley Authority. The presence of many special interests in these developments strengthened the case for independent experts, and economists presented themselves as prime candidates. Nagging questions were asked repeatedly in debates over natural resources, in which increasingly the economists took part, including the following: Were the nation's resources being squandered by a careless society? Would there be enough farmland, water, petroleum, coal, and rare minerals for the current generation's children and grandchildren to live the good life? Could we ever fight a world war again after so many of our key resources had moved offshore? Could we now be held up by potential enemies who controlled these resources? Might the Great Depression, indeed, even be explained in part by our mistreatment of natural resources? The final question was: Could economists suggest a persuasive course of action to respond to these troubling questions?

The National Resources Planning Board (NRPB) was established in the 1930s by President Roosevelt to address resource and related questions. It commissioned much research that was relevant to policy, especially by younger economists who were badly in need of employment – some of whom, such as Milton Friedman, achieved great prominence later in their careers. But the main challenge faced by the NRPB was to gain the attention of those who actually made and implemented policy. Economists were still learning how to leave behind their scholarly voice and to write for an audience with a much more practical agenda. Most of the NRPB research seems to have languished unread on library shelves, a lesson well remembered by later economists who sought influence. After World War II, the continuing concern with natural resources was taken up by economists in the Interior Department, and then by the widely publicized President's Materials Policy Commission, which included such prominent economists as Harvard's Edward Mason. The Commission reported in 1953 and led to the establishment of the private nonprofit research institution Resources for the Future, which has since been involved in illuminating policy issues relating to natural resources.

36.7   CLARIFYING THE ECONOMIST'S ROLE IN POLICY

At the end of World War II, the prospects were brighter than ever before for the close involvement of economists in the policy process. Economists had come to believe that now they had the answers to many pressing problems – and, based on their performance during the war, the citizenry was prepared, by and large, to let them prove it. The main remaining question was how best to construct institutions to use economists effectively while guarding their professional integrity. Several models from the 1930s were reviewed and rejected, such as the "Brains Trust" and the NRPB. In the end, a number of paths were followed. In the United States, after extensive debate, the Employment Act of 1946 established the Council of Economic Advisers as a staff agency of the President, and a Joint Economic Committee intended to increase sophisticated macroeconomic understanding in Congress. Another model tried in other countries, including Canada, Germany, and The Netherlands, was a semi-independent council of economic experts, charged to interpret economic science for current problems. Still a third path, influenced by the first two, was to embed economists widely throughout the governmental bureaucracy somewhat in the way lawyers gained their positions decades earlier. In the same way that lawyers were said to speak only to lawyers, so that whenever there was a lawyer present, every part of government needed one, as soon as "econospeak" became firmly established in government, every government agency had to have its own economist in order to be admitted to the conversation.

Another path for economists in the policy discussion after World War II, in addition to participation in government, was through the institutions of the private sector and of civil society. Just as more and more governmental agencies discovered that they needed economists after World War II if they were to take part in the important debates over the economy, so major corporations, trade associations, and even trades unions reached the same conclusion. There, economists were given several roles: to conduct market forecasts in a systematic way, to discover for their employers the implications of the macroeconomic and microeconomic policies of government, to undertake strategic planning, and to clarify the implications of public policy options so that corporate interests could be defended. Business economists, like academic and governmental economists, formed their own associations, journals, and other trappings of professional identity.

In addition to business, finance, and the trades unions, various groups in civil society looked for a voice in economic conversation and discovered that to achieve this they needed the help of economists. Churches, voters' organizations, women's groups, environmental bodies, and many others found that access required expertise. Philanthropic foundations that, during the first half of the twentieth century, had supported economics as an emerging academic profession with relevance to public policy, now helped to coordinate and assist a response across a much wider front. In particular, from the 1950s the Ford Foundation joined the Rockefeller Foundation, the Carnegie Corporation, and other philanthropies in funding a much broader involvement of economists in policy.

From at least the early nineteenth century, prominent economists writing in the mass media served as translators of economic theory, and the implications of theory for policy. In Britain, J. R. McCulloch, Nassau Senior, and Walter Bagehot were among the most prominent. Journalists, among others, had convictions both that a widening franchise in a democracy required sophisticated economic understanding among voters and that economic principles should guide citizens in their daily lives. Journalists pointed out that citizens should understand the gains that could be expected from free trade, that fiscal deficits were not necessarily terrible, and that in the long run increasing wages depended more on rising productivity than on struggles with other income recipients. By the mid-twentieth century sophisticated commentators emerged in the media, who were journalists first and economists second. Walter Lippmann was the leading example in the first half of the century; while Leonard Silk of the *New York Times*, Hobart Rowan of the *Washington Post*, and Sam Brittan of the *Financial Times* were prominent examples in the second half. Well-known academic economists joined the professional journalists in providing sophisticated commentary, often providing simplified versions of methodological, theoretical, and ideological controversies that were earlier played out in professional journals. That such published controversy continues suggests that the media's audience welcomes it. A wider public is, in any event, admitted to conversations over vital policy questions that concern them – whether over recession policy, globalization, healthcare provision, or environmental protection. Whereas nineteenth-century economists tended to speak with one voice on large issues (for example, in opposition to an imperial tariff scheme), in the twentieth century they generated a cacophony. Examples of celebrated economists who, through their articles, editorials, and "op eds" have enlightened public debate over economic policies, include Milton Friedman, Paul Samuelson, Herbert Stein, Gary Becker, and Paul Krugman. Consumers of the media presumably learned that what happened in the domestic and global economies was not inevitable and could be affected by citizen input, thereby stimulating attention to the interpretation of economic events.

Nongovernmental institutions that applied economic science to economic policy either newly appeared after World War II or extended their roles substantially. Typically, they maintained some professional economists on permanent appointment; provided a forum for economists between positions; and engaged, as part-time associates, economists who had permanent appointments at academic institutions. These institutions caused the boundaries between government, media, the private sector, and civil society to be far more porous for economists in the United States than they had been before the war, and than they were in most other countries even after the war. Indeed, the "in-and-outer" economist became an important element in the American public policy process. Institutions that served the in-and-outers came to be known collectively as "think tanks," ranging from the venerable Brookings Institution, the American Enterprise Institute for Public Policy Research, and the Council on Foreign Relations to the newer Center for Strategic and International Studies, the Policy Studies Institute, The Institute for International Economics, Resources for the Future, and the Cato Institute. Their style ranged from highly academic, such as the "new" National Bureau of Economic Research and the Woodrow Wilson International Center for Scholars, to intensely practical, such as the International Institute for Strategic Studies, and avowedly political, such as the Heritage Foundation. Most of these institutions depended heavily on the enlarged private philanthropic sector that appeared after World War II; some, such as Brookings, Resources for the Future, and the Institute for International Economics, enjoyed a substantial private endowment; some, such as the RAND Corporation and the Urban Institute, depended primarily on government grants and contracts; and some lived hand to mouth. A few institutions, such as Brookings, covered a wide range of topical areas. Most had a well-defined, narrow focus; for example, World Resources Institute and Worldwatch on natural resource issues, and the Overseas Development Council on problems of Third World growth. The increasing number and sophistication of these organizations possibly helps to explain some decline in the employment of business economists by large corporations. If a business executive could turn for advice and commentary on policy questions that ranged from clean-air legislation to NAFTA to a trusted think tank that required only a modest annual contribution, why maintain expensive in-house economists?

36.8 THE RISE AND FALL OF THE ECONOMIST'S PRESTIGE

The high point for economists' influence in the policy process came in the 1960s and 1970s, in the administrations of Presidents Kennedy, Johnson, Nixon, Ford, and Carter. In addition to their roles – which were well established by this time – as public administrators and advisers, economists began to appear as high-ranking political appointees and elected officials. Their apparent success in showing how to respond to recession, and in preparing for such domestic challenges as President Johnson's War on Poverty, led economists to be thought of almost as Plato's Guardians, well-trained and protected by their academic or in-and-outer careers from dangerous temptations. They could be trusted to perceive the public interest correctly and to pursue it indomitably. Moreover, the positive perception of economists was not confined to either the political Left or the Right. Cabinet and sub-cabinet appointments of prominent economists were as common in the Ford as in the Kennedy years, and it was President Nixon who proclaimed in the 1970s, "We are all Keynesians now." One need only recall some of the prominent professional economists who served as cabinet members and agency heads during these decades: George Shultz, John Dunlop, James Schlesinger, Juanita Kreps, Michael Blumenthal, David Bell, Ray Marshall, and others. Admiration for economists in high policy positions was not limited to the United States. In Britain, Prime Minister Harold Wilson was an economist, as was Chancellor Helmut Schmidt in Germany.

The fall in the reputation of economists was as fast as their rise. The New Deal economists had given the impression of radicalism. They frightened people with talk of planning and redistribution, and were banished to the back room. The postwar economists promised too much. Their fate was tied to the condition of the economy, for whose successes they gladly took credit. By the end of the 1970s, disillusionment with the performance of the economy was intense, and economists were compelled to take the blame. Persistent unemployment, combined by the late 1970s with inflation and stagnation, suggested that economists lacked some answers. They did not seem to have the tools to cope with a sudden crisis such as the OPEC oil embargo or the "stagflation" that followed. It was increasingly suggested some economic problems were actually due to interventionist economists who had neglected the "supply side" of the economy and the health of the business sector while fixated on aggregate demand, environmental costs, problems of poverty, and other distributional issues. Economists were charged with complicity in introducing various restrictions that prevented free markets from working. After the 1960s and 1970s, when several prominent economists had unsuccessfully advised on ways in which to control inflation, from exhortation to controls – none of which were apparently effective – only a firm contraction in the rate of growth of the money supply by the Federal Reserve Board in 1979–80 seemed to achieve the desired result. So where was the need for professional economists?

Ronald Reagan entered office in 1980 with a neoliberal agenda and a doctrine of supply-side economics that called for a substantial reduction in intervention. Margaret Thatcher in the United Kingdom followed a similar policy. There were no professional economists in Reagan's cabinet, and even his Council of Economic Advisers was given the ambivalent charge, in part, to step aside and let business people who really understood the economy formulate policy. The tradition concerning the proper role for the economist in policy that appealed most to the Reaganites was that of Alfred Marshall, sustained at the University of Chicago, which said that the proper place for prominent economists was at home, where they might declaim on policy if they felt moved, but only from afar. This prescribed policy role for economists in government was strengthened by a new theoretical tradition in macroeconomics, led by Robert Lucas at Chicago, that argued that under assumptions of "rational expectations," there is little that an interventionist economist in government can accomplish anyway.

The extreme neoliberal policy stance, with its very limited role for economists in government, was relaxed somewhat under the administration of George Bush Sr. The two terms of President Bill Clinton exhibited some return to a conventional Keynesian posture toward macroeconomic problems. Even under a Democratic regime, however, it seemed that economists had permanently lost the luster of the 1960s and 1970s. Seen now as mere professionals with important skills for policy-making, but no more so than any other group, they were now seldom invited to have a voice at the highest levels of policy-making in the cabinet or elsewhere. In the words of the old adage, they were on tap but no longer on top.

Paradoxically, just when professional economists were losing their newfound prominence in the policy-making circles of government in the 1980s and 1990s, they were gaining new authority in various international organizations. Economists were present in the World Bank, the regional development banks, the International Monetary Fund, the OECD, the UN, and other international bodies from their beginning, but they rose to positions of real significance only during the last quarter of the century. It is possible to suggest a few reasons for this success. First, as the problems of development in new countries came increasingly to appear intractable, attention turned to the economic structures in these countries. Economists insisted that, as with the macroeconomic problems of Western countries in the 1960s, they had the solutions. They now claimed that responsibility for stagnation lay with restrictions imposed on free market growth, and with irresponsible regimes and their maladministration of public finance and foreign exchange flows. These diagnoses by economists in international organizations were given weight by the fall of the Soviet Union in 1989 and the rejection of socialist planning as the road to development by most new countries. Nobel Prize winner Joseph Stiglitz, for a time chief economist of the World Bank, has been the most prominent critic of the performance of economists in international organizations. He claims that they do not grasp the problems correctly and, as a result, have prescribed the wrong medicine for most of the ills of the 1990s. As the world entered the new century, it was still too soon to tell whether hubris had again overtaken economists engaged in policy formation, and whether a sober reappraisal of the economists' advice in international organizations might lead to the same disillusionment that was evident in the 1980s.

Bibliography

Barber, W. J. 1985: *From New Era to New Deal: Herbert Hoover, the Economists, and American Economic Policy, 1921–1933*. Cambridge, UK: Cambridge University Press.

—— 1996: *Designs within Disorder: Franklin D. Roosevelt, the Economists, and the Shaping of American Economic Policy, 1933–1945*. New York: Cambridge University Press.

Blustein, P. 2002: *The Chastening: Inside the Crisis that Rocked the Global Financial System and Humbled the IMF*. New York: Public Affairs.

Coats, A. W. (ed.) 1971: *The Classical Economists and Economic Policy*. London: Methuen.

Fetter, F. W. 1980: *The Economist in Parliament, 1780–1868*. Durham, NC: Duke University Press.

Furner, M. O. and Supple, B. (ed.) 1990: *The State and Economic Knowledge: The American and British Experiences*. Cambridge, UK: Cambridge University Press.

Goodwin, C. (ed.) 1975: *Exhortation and Controls: The Search for a Wage-Price Policy 1945–1971*. Washington, DC: Brookings Institution Press.

—— 1981: *Energy Policy in Perspective*. Washington, DC: Brookings Institution Press.

Gordon, B. 1975: *Economic Analysis before Adam Smith*. London: Macmillan.

—— 1977: *Political Economy in Parliament, 1819–1823*. New York: Barnes & Noble.

Hall, P. (ed.) 1989: *The Political Power of Economic Ideas: Keynesianism across Nations*. Princeton, NJ: Princeton University Press.

Hirschman, A. O. 1977: *The Passions and the Interests: Political Arguments for Capitalism before Its Triumph*. Princeton, NJ: Princeton University Press.

Howson, S. and Winch, D. 1977: *The Economic Advisory Council, 1930–1939: A Study in Economic Advice during Depression and Recovery*. Cambridge, UK: Cambridge University Press.

Langholm, O 1998: *The Legacy of Scholasticism in Economic Thought*. Cambridge, UK: Cambridge University Press.

Lowry, S. T. 1987: *The Archaeology of Economic Ideas*. Durham, NC: Duke University Press.

Meek, R. L. 1962: *The Economics of Physiocracy: Essays and Translations*. London: George Allen & Unwin.

—— 1967: *Economics and Ideology and Other Essays: Studies in the Development of Economic Thought*. London: Chapman & Hall.

Nathan, R. P. 2000: *Social Science in Government: The Role of Policy Researchers*. New York: Rockefeller Institute Press.

O'Brien, D. P. 1975: *The Classical Economists*. Oxford: The Clarendon Press.

Perry, G. L. and Tobin, J. (eds.) 2000: *Economic Events, Ideas, and Policies: The 1960's and After*. Washington, DC: Brookings Institution Press.

Robbins, L. 1976: *Political Economy, Past and Present: A Review of Leading Theories of Economic Policy*. New York: Columbia University Press.

Rutherford, M. 1994: *Institutions in Economics: The Old and the New Institutionalism*. Cambridge, UK: Cambridge University Press.

Samuels, W. 1966: *The Classical Theory of Economic Policy*. Cleveland, OH: World Publishing.

Stein, H. 1969: *The Fiscal Revolution in America*. Chicago: The University of Chicago Press.

Tribe, K. 1988: *Governing Economy: the Reformation of German Economic Discourse, 1750–1840*. Cambridge, UK: Cambridge University Press.

—— (ed.) 1997: *Economic Careers: Economics and Economists in Britain, 1930–1970*. London: Routledge.

Winch, D. 1969: *Economics and Policy: A Historical Study*. London: Hodder & Stoughton.

—— 1996: *Riches and Poverty: An Intellectual History of Political Economy in Britain, 1750–1834*. Cambridge: Cambridge University Press.

The International Diffusion of Economic Thought

José Luís Cardoso

37.1   THE HISTORIOGRAPHIC LEGACY

Nowadays, any mention of the problem of the international diffusion of economic thought would seem to dispense with the need for justification or explanation. Indeed, the very conditions and forms under which economic knowledge is produced and circulated inevitably imply processes of creation and sharing in which geographical and language barriers have been progressively eliminated. The standardized levels of conceptual formalization and the almost unanimous acceptance of similar techniques and instruments of analysis have made a decisive contribution toward the formation of universal languages with a high potential for international communication. Above all, attention needs to be drawn to the ease with which new research avenues and hypotheses are transmitted and disseminated, together with new experiments and results, and new knowledge about economic reality.

There is nothing original in claiming that the international transmission of economic thought is a normal and recurrent phenomenon. Almost half a century ago, this diagnosis was presented by T. W. Hutchison:

> With the vastly increased number of translations and of widely circulating specialist journals, including international journals, and with the increasingly mathematical character of advanced economic analysis, it seems, on the whole, very unlikely that good new ideas, whenever or wherever they do arise, will not have a reasonably fair chance of being heard and of making their way . . . Economists are now part, even

often from their undergraduate years, of large, organised, internationally-linked academic machines, with their subjects closely organised and defined and their questions and categories ready formulated. (1955, pp. 14–15)

If we consider the dramatic growth in communication instruments at the disposal of the academic community over the past half-century, Hutchison's words would appear to be somewhat self-evident.

This does not mean that the problem should not be mentioned or is no longer worthy of discussion. Even if the international diffusion of economic thought may be seen today as relatively unproblematic, this has not always been the case. The processes of and barriers to the international diffusion, transmission, and appropriation that took place in the past have to a great extent contributed to shaping and structuring the development of economic thought in ways that are worth trying to understand.

To overcome any remaining skepticism about the relevance of such an endeavor, it is sufficient to bear in mind the vast range of topics associated with the expression "economic thought." In fact, this term embraces matters relating not only to the ideological, doctrinal, or normative frameworks within which economic thinkers operate, but also to the methods, concepts, and techniques of analysis that they use, as well as to the implications of their theories in the definition of economic policy guidelines. In other words, the subjects being studied show that economics as a field of scientific inquiry is not immune to presuppositions based on value judgments; nor is it in any way unaffected by the applications and uses to which it is inevitably put. These are already more than enough reasons to explain both the historical dimension of the subject and the added importance of the process involved in the international transmission of economic thought, inasmuch as it allows for a strengthening of the already close link between the formation and diffusion of economics and the social environments and contexts that give rise to its use and appropriation.

This is a subject that has generally been discussed without any visible antagonisms. In fact, it is even possible to note a certain consensus of interpretation that has allowed authors with quite distinct views on economic science and its history to converge in their approaches.

Given the importance of the *Wealth of Nations* for the foundation and shaping of political economy as an autonomous field of scientific inquiry, it is only natural that the diffusion of Smith's work has been one of the earliest case studies that brought to light a certain concern with the issue of the international transmission of economic doctrines and theories. The limited impact of Smithian principles of *laissez faire* in Germany at the end of the eighteenth century – as well as the discussion of the meaning of some of the Smithian concepts concerning value and distribution by his contemporary German translators and reviewers – was the main topic of a pioneering essay by C. W. Hasek (1925). A few years later, the subject was enriched with an overall picture of the theme (Palyi, 1928), providing examples from several European countries and showing how Smithian influences went hand in hand with other simultaneous influences, such as French physiocracy and German cameralism.

In spite of the innovative, groundbreaking nature of these essays, the question of the international diffusion of economic thought only gained particular visibility with the organization of a session devoted to this very theme at the Annual Conference of the American Economic Association in 1954. The contributions to this session, later published in the special Papers and Proceedings issue of the *American Economic Review* in 1955, include the already mentioned paper by T. W. Hutchison (1955), a text by Joseph Dorfman (1955), and a summary of the conference discussion, with comments by J. Letiche, G. Hildebrand, and W. Jaffé.

Hutchison and Dorfman's texts provide detailed analyses of research situations that relate to specific periods and schools of economic thought. In Hutchison's case, his attention is concentrated on the genesis and diffusion of the theoretical principles of the so-called marginalist revolution and neoclassical economics, especially in regard to their Marshallian component. In Dorfman's case, the subject under analysis is the spread of the doctrinal principles of the German historical school in the United States, laying emphasis on explaining the adaptations made to some of the ideas imported, in order to make them better suited to addressing the problems of American economic reality.

Regardless of the added value brought by these texts, which have made it possible to look more deeply into new research subjects, they are also important in terms of the minimum methodological framework that they seek to provide for studying the phenomenon of the diffusion of economic ideas. More precisely, they announce certain heuristic concerns about the formation, change, and succession of economic ideas, and about the favorable conditions, acceleration factors, and obstacles that can hinder the processes that govern their subsequent transmission and diffusion. Other aspects implicitly contained in the pioneering reflections of these texts are those that relate to the constraints dictated by different levels of economic development and by the greater or lesser degree of cultural and political cosmopolitanism, which, because they are inevitably found in any society taken as the reference for such analysis, determine both the opportunity for, and depth of, the diffusion processes.

Two authors who took a closer look at the methodological guidelines outlined earlier deserve special mention. The first is Joseph J. Spengler, for his presentation of an embryonic information theory model (Spengler, 1970), in which the author discusses the specific problems (arising whenever economic ideas are being transmitted) that confront the source country, the receiver country, the media of transmission, and the content transmitted.

The second author is Craufurd D. Goodwin, for two thorough contributions to the discussion of the problem of the transfer of economic ideas. In one of these papers (Goodwin, 1972), a general attempt is made to explain the relationship between the spread of ideas and the prevailing social and political organization, with a view to finding explanations for the diffusion of economic thought amongst those different agents (professional economists, policy-makers, nonprofessional public opinion) who use it for the development of social action. In another text (Goodwin, 1973), after providing an overview of the main features of the diffusion of marginalism in the English-speaking "New World" countries (Australia, Canada, and the United States), Goodwin stresses the similarities and the differences among the three major revolutions in economics (the Smithian, marginal, and Keynesian revolutions) and their spread on a worldwide scale. He argues that the differences concerning the technical content of economic theories, and the links that these "scientific revolutions" had with economic policy issues, social thought and philosophy, and the degree of development of the economics profession, provide useful explanations to understand how economic ideas may develop and mature in different environments. The focus on these topics is a natural sequence to the case studies previously analyzed by the same author (Goodwin, 1961, 1966, 1968).

A notable effort to systematize these subjects was made by Ernest Lluch (1980) in a text which, because it was written in Spanish, ended up falling prey to one of the very problems that he discusses in relation to the obstacles hindering the transmission of innovative economic thought; that is, the lack of knowledge caused by language barriers.

The main novelty introduced by Lluch's text is the link that it establishes between the analysis of international transmission and the definition of the specificities of a national history of economic thought. In this type of approach, the premise is maintained that cultural interchange at an international level is a natural feature of everyday experience in both academic and professional life. However, the smoothness of such an interchange may be subject to different kinds of constraints.

One type of constraint relates to the development of the media of transmission, such as the speed of circulation of foreign books, easy access to leading journals in the field, overall familiarity with foreign languages, the quantity and quality of translations, and facilities for private and institutional international contacts. It also relates to the level of scientific autonomy or academic recognition that, in given historical circumstances, economics may have attained in a certain country or group of countries. It further relates to differences in economic development between the source country and the receiver country, which may be more or less apparent in different historical periods.

A second type of constraint is basically to be found in the existence of long-lasting disequilibrium relationships between countries that have a tradition of innovation and creation in economics and others that have no choice other than to use and adapt a scientific discourse created abroad. One may be tempted to assume that, in countries that have never been at the forefront of theoretical developments, the history of economics is reduced to a mere succession of foreign influences. But even if knowledge of, and familiarity with, what is done abroad is a healthy sign of cosmopolitanism, it does not follow that the receiver country has to accept the greater part of those ideas, analytic principles, and practical recipes which only make sense in other historical settings. This means that the ease or difficulty with which economic doctrines, theories, and policies are accepted is always constrained by the particularities of the economic reality, social and political institutions, and scientific environment in the receiver country. It is precisely the way in which a country uses and adapts the influences received that makes the study of the history of economic thought worthwhile from a national point of view.

This standpoint easily applies to the experience of many countries, for which the distinctive features of a national thought stem from the complementary facets of foreign influences and processes of original creation and adaptation. Examples of this kind of approach are provided by Almodovar and Cardoso (1998), Boylan and Foley (1992), Dasgupta (1993), Faccarello (1998), Groenewegen and MacFarlane (1990), Morris-Suzuki (1989), Neill (1991), Quintana (1999–2001, vol. I), Sandelin (1991), Sugiyama and Mizuta (1988), and Van Daal and Heertje (1992). According to the available studies, nationality or place of residence or publication are criteria regarded as necessary but not sufficient to determine the national character of economic thought. Diffusion and reception are uneven and selective, in accordance with the specific problems for which specific solutions are required; it is when these problems are faced and solved that innovative, genuinely national forms of economic thought may emerge. However, it should be noted that they are still an outcome of international diffusion phenomena.

Returning once again to this brief historiographic review, it is now time to mention another compulsory reference in establishing the general framework for studying the processes involved in the diffusion of economic ideas. This is the introduction of the book edited by David Colander and A. W. Coats (1989), in which the authors present the major questions raised by the creation of general models that explain the phenomenon under consideration here. Their approach is based on three fundamental models: the infectious disease model, according to which the spread of an idea can be likened to the spread of a disease; the information theory model; and the model of the marketplace for ideas.

As far as the last model is concerned, one of the most notable aspects is the way in which the authors implicitly adhere to the approach presented by George J. Stigler (1983) for examining the reasons why, at a certain period, economic ideas may be accepted, ignored, recycled, or rejected. In other words, it is a model that subjects the process of transmission and appropriation to an approach identical to the one used for the study of any other type of market. The texts gathered together by Colander and Coats, however, pay scant attention to the problem of the international diffusion of economic ideas. Most attention is paid to the processes of communication and diffusion between professional economists, and between these and the public at large, as well as policy-makers.

Spengler's information theory model was improved by Uskali Mäki (1996), who provided an historiographic framework that explains a variety of aspects related to the processes of transmission, selection, and adaptation of economic ideas and their conditioning by different kinds of internal and external factors.

The methodological guidelines inspired by Stigler's work with the model of the market for ideas were further developed and coherently applied by Vicent Llombart (1995) in a study of the critical reception afforded to physiocratic thought in Spain.

37.2 SOME CASE STUDIES

Physiocracy is precisely one of the schools of economic thought that has been studied more frequently from the perspective of the processes involved in its international diffusion. This was, in fact, the subject underlying the organization of a conference, whose papers were later published in Delmas, Demals, and Steiner (1995), and whose original aim was a comparison of different countries in relation to the specific question of the assimilation and critical use of the analytic, doctrinal, and political legacy bequeathed to us by this school of economic thought.

The main conclusion arising from the contributions to this volume is that there is a fundamental distinction to be made between countries that were receptive to the theoretical features of physiocracy – namely the notions of *produit net*, capital, and circular flow – and countries for which the diffusion of physiocratic discourse was mainly conceived as a banner for a program of gradual reform of *ancien régime* economic and social institutions. For the latter, the ideals of economic liberalism inspired changes, but were primarily conceived as instruments to reinforce social cohesion and were not meant to attack the established political systems of enlightened despotism.

Since the publication of the above-mentioned pioneering essays on the diffusion of Adam Smith across Europe (Hasek, 1925; Palyi, 1928), many other contributions have addressed the influences exerted by the author of the *Wealth of Nations*. The books edited by H. Mizuta and C. Sugiyama (1993) and by Cheng-chung Lai (2000) put together different sets of articles and chapters of books dealing with the peculiarities of the motives for diffusion, the processes and speed of reception and assimilation, the quality of translations, and the impact on decision-makers in different countries, namely Germany, France, Italy, Spain, Portugal, Denmark, Sweden, Russia, the United States, India, China, and Japan. A complementary survey is also provided by the conference volume *Smithian and Neo-Smithian Political Economy* (Béraud, Gislain, and Steiner, forthcoming).

When facing these different case studies, our main concern should be to find patterns that allow us to establish parallels, divergences, and complementary relationships in the development of certain currents of economic thought in different countries. This means that comparative studies are one of the most important vehicles for analyzing the processes involved in the international diffusion and assimilation of economic thought.

Such importance was clearly illustrated by the international project that culminated in the conference held at San Miniato (Florence) in 1986, under the title of "The Institutionalisation of Political Economy: Its Introduction and Acceptance into European, American and Japanese Universities." The main results of this meeting were made known through a number of autonomous publications that looked at experiences in the teaching and dissemination of political economy in various countries, particularly during the nineteenth century.

The San Miniato project served as a model for the realization of other projects at a national level, involving different dimensions of the institutionalization process. The Italian case was the most fruitful in terms of published results. In fact, extensive volumes were published of proceedings from specific conferences held about university chairs (Augello et al., 1988), about journals (Augello et al., 1996), and about professional associations and societies of economists (Augello and Guidi, 2000). Besides providing detailed information about Italy, the conferences that gave rise to these publications also made it possible to collect testimonies about other national experiences, providing us with exercises in comparative studies that were later afforded their own autonomous dissemination (Augello and Guidi, 2001). Another interesting example is a volume of proceedings dedicated to the analysis of the influences of nineteenth-century French economists on other geographical horizons, which opens up the debate to an international analysis of the subject conducted from a comparative viewpoint (Dockès et al., 2000).

It was in Italy once again, in 1992, that yet another initiative was made involving scholars from different countries who were interested in engaging in a global discussion on the theme of the relationship between *Political Economy and National Realities*. The central problem under analysis at this conference was again that of the role played by historical and intellectual environments in the process of constructing, transmitting, and assimilating economics, based on the experiences of different countries analyzed from a comparative viewpoint (Albertone and Masoero, 1994). Such experiences teach us that it is worthwhile to highlight the methodological relevance of interdisciplinary studies that contribute to the historical reconstruction of economic theory, in a way that takes into account the national distinctive features of past cultural styles and traditions.

The same aim can be seen in another crucial work for the analysis of these subjects, this time limited to the study of the penetration and impact of Keynesian ideas in Europe, the United States, and Japan (Hall, 1989). This collection of essays serves to clarify and explain the full bearing of John Maynard Keynes's famous statement: "The ideas of economists and political philosophers, both when they are right and when they are wrong, are more powerful than is commonly understood" (1936, p. 383). The central question analyzed in this collection involves a comparison of the experiences of political decision-making and the management of economic policy in the main economies of the capitalist world between the end of the 1930s and the end of the 1960s with the theoretical and doctrinal support provided by Keynes's work and its use for managing economic fluctuations.

The international spread of economic ideas was the underlying topic covered by a set of articles published in *Research in the History of Economic Thought and Methodology* (vol. 14, 1996), devoted to two main themes: the introduction and assimilation of marginal analysis in countries that did not play a relevant role in the original advent of marginalism and neoclassical economics (such as Denmark, Finland, The Netherlands, and Japan); and the internationalization and development of economics in the post-1945 period in peripheral countries such as South Korea and Brazil. This second topic was considerably enriched in two collections of essays edited by A. W. Bob Coats (1997, 2000). Together, they represent a sequential and integrated work that demonstrates the enormous potentialities of international comparative studies of the dissemination and assimilation of economic ideas, theories, and policies.

In both volumes, the separate contributions provide both quantitative and qualitative information on the development of higher education systems (at the level of both undergraduate and graduate studies), the relevance and impact of specialized journals, and the themes and areas of basic and applied research, as well as the various association and professionalization processes followed by economists and their integration in the various segments of the labor market. Other aspects also given attention relate to the participation of economists in technical committees linked to international organizations. Such an approach makes it possible to gain a better understanding of the conditions and factors that have proved indispensable for the universal spread of the theories and practices used by economists, particularly through the adoption of the various languages, methodologies, techniques, and analytic concepts that are in recurrent use.

One of the most important components of the studies produced relates to the recording and presentation of the main theoretical models – basically embedded in both neoclassical and Keynesian frameworks – that have been used and developed in each country. The continuation of certain traditions in doctrine and thought, or the emergence of new fashions and paradigms, are essential conditions not only for appreciating the status that economics has acquired as a science, but also for understanding the disputes fought over the right to lead the task of reflecting upon the profoundly changing economic reality in most postwar European, as well as Latin American and Asian, countries. One final aspect that should also be stressed is the importance attached to the implications of the work of economists in defining the aims and tools of economic policy, taking into account the increasingly important role that economists have been called upon to play in the decision-making processes of governments.

37.3 CONCLUSIONS AND TEACHINGS

The examples mentioned in the previous section, as well as the brief discussion in section 37.1 about the way in which the historiography of economic thought has dealt with this subject, make it possible to sketch out some teachings and draw some conclusions.

One of the first aspects that should be highlighted is the strengthening of the belief that analysis of the processes of international transmission goes far beyond the limited scope of conventional approaches in the history of economics, especially the perspective that is centered upon the rational reconstruction of the internal contents of its theoretical and analytic components. In fact, interest in the questions of the transmission, assimilation, and adaptation of economic thought does not imply just eliminating frontiers between distinct economic spaces that communicate and interact in an ever more open and globalized manner. It also implies tearing down barriers between the disciplinary territories that have to be passed through if one is to achieve an adequate understanding of the historical, institutional, political, and cultural contexts that frame the circulation of economic ideas at an international level. In this way, the healthy proliferation of international comparative studies represents a very positive contribution toward the revitalization of, and innovation in, research into the history of economics.

Just when it seems as though everything has already been said about the significance of the most recondite chapter of one of the less important books of an only moderately famous author, it is perhaps useful to extend the research into less restricted horizons. Thus, for example, discussion of the way in which the works of Adam Smith, Karl Marx, John Maynard Keynes, or Milton Friedman were and are read, translated, and appropriated in different countries and in distinct historical contexts is not a matter that relates only to a local or national history of the processes involved in the assimilation of doctrines, theories, and economic policies. Above all, it is a subject that makes it possible to extend and enrich our available knowledge about the very authors that have been, or are being, appropriated. This means that the partial and selective reading of a renowned author – that is, the use made of the author as a symbol of authority to guarantee the validity of certain theoretical bases or practical recipes – similarly represents an addition to our available knowledge about this same author.

The great masters may not only be assessed by what they really said, but also by the diverse, idiosyncratic, and sometimes abusive use that has in fact been made of their work, when transmitted and disseminated internationally. It is always possible to sift through the more or less innovative or conservative features to be found in each author, and these ideas are then manipulated or capitalized upon in the light of the fame and popularity that such an author enjoyed, and on the basis of local conditions in receiver countries.

Another attribute that is inherent in the study of these transmission processes is the review of different viewpoints about the role that was effectively played by supposedly forgotten or ignored anticipators and precursors. It is not easy to accept the idea that certain theories, normally identified with the originality of a scientific discovery perfectly located in the work of a certain author or group of authors, may have undergone a different and previous gestation process. An approach that gives preference to the study of transmission processes may help to elucidate the circumstances leading to settings that favor the occurrence of multiple and simultaneous discoveries, which themselves make it necessary to attenuate and relativize the importance given to agents who, prior to this, were seen as unquestionable innovators (cf., Niehans, 1995). On the other hand, the problem may cease to be one of a simple dispute over the correct attribution of pioneering ideas, and become centered upon the analysis of the factors and reasons behind autonomous developments in the conceptual framework of economic theory.

Stress should also be laid on the fact that studies on the international flow of economic thought, especially when seen from the viewpoint of the receiver country, allow for a different attitude toward recognizing the importance and impact of heterodox currents or schools of thought. One reason for the sense of dissatisfaction experienced by anyone who reads or consults general histories of economic thought lies in the dominant character of all that has survived in comparison with what did in fact exist. The "official authorized" history of economic thought continues to be largely based on the contributions that were considered to be decisive in the formation of normal science or scientific research programs of undisputed value. It goes without saying that the introduction of a different scale of appreciation will help to reappraise the impact enjoyed by authors who have long since been forgotten, or have been considered to be minor contributors to the development of economics – because, in many cases, their influence and international diffusion went far beyond the limited repercussions of the main-stream orthodoxy.

The study of the processes of international transmission also allows for the formation of a critical view of the attempts to create overly rigid schemes that tend to divide authors into distinct periods, or to classify them according to schools or streams of thought. In fact, such attempts have always warned against the difficulty of establishing single definitive categories or typologies. If we look at the problem through the looking glass of international transmission, it is quite common for authors who are rarely joined together in their country or countries of origin to be jointly and simultaneously imported or assimilated into a different country. Such a phenomenon forces us to reflect on both the reasons for their joint effectiveness and the criteria implicit in the association of discourses, which, despite the fact that they are entirely independent, would suggest that they share a similar meaning or common objective.

All of these issues relating to the study of international transmission processes also apply in noninternational contexts, and may be seen as a way of enhancing the national histories and traditions of economic thought (Cardoso and Lluch, 1999). The introduction of a national dimension does not seek to deny the universal character of economics but, rather, to demonstrate the relevance of different adaptive processes in the spread of economic theories and ideas. The pertinence of a particular model for explaining reality does not depend only on the theoretical and doctrinal discourse, but also – and, indeed, very particularly – upon the successful adaptation to this same reality of the political presuppositions and consequences that are inherent therein. And this is essentially the reason why the international dissemination of economic thought is a powerful instrument, both for improving our understanding of the process involved in the formation of economics and for increasing our awareness of its implications about the way in which economic and social reality both functions and changes.

In conclusion, it can be said that this type of approach implies enlarging certain presuppositions that support a strictly positivist analysis of the evolution of economics as a science, based on rational reconstruction procedures. If we believe that the history of economics is also the history of the worldwide spread of doctrines, ideas, practices, theories, and analytic tools, and of the way in which they are subject to screening and selection, as well as the forms of appropriation and usage to which they are liable, then both the issues of international diffusion and the national dimension of economic problems must perforce be taken into consideration. By upholding the legitimacy and relevance of this path of research, one is helping to save the history of economic thought from the clutches of interpretive monolithism.

Note

The author acknowledges the comments and suggestions provided by the Editors of this *Companion*. The usual disclaimer applies. My interest in this subject owes a great deal to the teachings of Ernest Lluch, who was murdered by ETA terrorists in November 2000. This text is dedicated to his memory.

Bibliography

Albertone, M. and Masoero, A. 1994: *Political Economy and National Realities*. Torino: Fondazione Luigi Einaudi.

Almodovar, A. and Cardoso, J. L. 1998: *A History of Portuguese Economic Thought*. London: Routledge.

Augello, M. and Guidi, M. (eds.) 2000: *Associazionismo Economico e Diffusione dell'Economia Politica nellItalia dell'Ottocento*. Milano: F. Angeli.

—— and —— (eds.) 2001. *Economic Societies, Popular Enlightenment and the Rise of the Economic Profession*. London: Routledge.

Augello, M., Bianchini, M. and Guidi, M. (eds.) 1996: *Le Rivisti di Economia in Italia (1700–1900)*. Milano: F. Angeli.

——, ——, Gioli, G., and Roggi, P. (eds.) 1988: *Le Cattedre di Economia Politica in Italia. La Diffusione di una Disciplina Sospetta (1750–1900)*. Milano: F. Angeli.

Béraud, A., Gislain, J.-J., and Steiner, P. forthcoming: *L'Economie Politique Néo-Smithienne en France, 1803–1848*.

Boylan, T. A. and Foley, T. P. 1992: *Political Economy and Colonial Ireland. The Propagation and Ideological Function of Economic Discourse in the Nineteenth Century*. London: Routledge.

Cardoso, J. L. and Lluch, E. 1999: Las teorías económicas contempladas a través de una óptica nacional. In Quintana, op. cit., vol. 1, pp. 477–84.

Coats, A. W. Bob (ed.) 1997: *The Post-1945 Internationalisation of Economics*. Annual Supplement to *HOPE*, 28. Durham, NC: Duke University Press.

—— (ed.) 2000: *The Development of Economics in Western Europe since 1945*. London: Routledge.

Colander, D. C. and Coats, A. W. Bob 1989: *The Spread of Economic Ideas*. Cambridge, UK: Cambridge University Press.

Dasgupta, A. 1993: *A History of Indian Economic Thought*. London: Routledge.

Delmas, B., Demals, Th., and Steiner, P. 1995: *La diffusion internationale de la physiocratie (XVIIIe–XIXe)*. Grenoble: Presses universitaires.

Dockès, P., Frobert, L., Klotz, G., Potier, J.-P., and Tiran, A. (eds.) 2000: *Les traditions economiques françaises*. Paris: Editions CNRS.

Dorfman, J. 1955: The role of the German historical school in American economic thought. *American Economic Review*, 45(2), 17–28.

Faccarello, G. (ed.) 1998: *Studies in the History of French Political Economy. From Bodin to Walras*. London: Routledge.

Goodwin, C. D. 1961: *Canadian Economic Thought. The Political Economy of a Developing Nation, 1814–1914*. Durham, NC: Duke University Press.

—— 1966: *Economic Inquiry in Australia*. Durham, NC: Duke University Press.

—— 1968: Economic ideas in the development of Jamaica. In C. D. Goodwin and I. B. Holley, Jr. (eds.), *The Transfer of Ideas*. Durham, NC: Duke University Press, 138–69.

—— 1972: Economic theory and society: a plea for process analysis. *American Economic Review*, 62(2), 409–15.

—— 1973: Marginalism moves to the New World. In R. D. C. Black, A. W. Coats, and C. D. Goodwin (eds.), *The Marginal Revolution in Economics. Interpretation and Evaluation*. Durham, NC: Duke University Press, 285–304.

Groenewegen, P. and McFarlane, B. 1990: *A History of Australian Economic Thought*. London: Routledge.

Hall, P. A. (ed.) 1989: *The Political Power of Economic Ideas*. Princeton, NJ: Princeton University Press.

Hasek, C. W. 1925: *The Introduction of Adam Smith's Doctrines into Germany*. New York: Columbia University Press.

Hutchison, T. W. 1955: Insularity and cosmopolitanism in economic ideas. *American Economic Review*, 45(2), 1–16.

Keynes, J. M. 1936: *The General Theory of Employment, Interest and Money*. London: Macmillan.

Lai, Cheng-chung (ed.) 2000: *Adam Smith Across Nations: Translations and Receptions of The Wealth of Nations*. Oxford: Oxford University Press.

Llombart, V. 1995: Market for ideas and reception of physiocracy in Spain: some analytical and historical suggestions. *The European Journal of the History of Economic Thought*, 2(1), 29–51.

Lluch, E. 1980: Sobre la historia nacional del pensamiento economico. Introduction to A. Florez Estrada, *Curso de Economia Política (1828)*. Madrid: Instituto de Estudios Fiscales (reprint).

Mäki, U. 1996: Economic thought on the outskirts: toward a historiographical framework for studying intellectual peripheries. *Research in the History of Economic Thought and Methodology*, 14, 307–23.

Mizuta, H. and Sugiyama, C. (eds.) 1993. *Adam Smith: International Perspectives*. London: Macmillan.

Morris-Suzuki, T. 1989: *A History of Japanese Economic Thought*. London: Routledge.

Neill, R. 1991: *A History of Canadian Economic Thought*. London: Routledge.

Niehans, J. 1995: Multiple discoveries in economic theory. *The European Journal of the History of Economic Thought*, 2(1), 1–28.

Palyi, M. 1928: The introduction of Adam Smith on the continent. In J. M. Clark (ed.), *Adam Smith 1776–1926: Lectures to Commemorate the Sesquicentennial of the Publication of The Wealth of Nations*. Chicago: The University of Chicago Press.

Quintana, E. F. (ed.), 1999–2001. *Economia y Economistas Españoles*, 8 vols. Barcelona: Galaxia Gutemberg.

Sandelin, B. 1991: *The History of Swedish Economic Thought*. London: Routledge.

Spengler, J. A. 1970: Notes on the international transmission of economic ideas. *History of Political Economy*, 2(1), 133–51.

Stigler, G. J. 1983: Nobel Lecture: The process and progress of economics. *Journal of Political Economy*, 91(4), 529–45.

Sugiyama, C. and Mizuta, H. (eds.) 1988: *Enlightenment and Beyond. Political Economy Comes to Japan*. Tokyo: University of Tokyo Press.

Van Daal, J. and Heertje, A. (eds.) 1992: *Economic Thought in the Netherlands: 1650–1950*. Aldershot, UK: Avebury.

CHAPTER THIRTY-EIGHT

The History of Ideas and Economics

Mark Perlman

38.1 INTRODUCTION

Ideas are intellectualized concepts. Some seem so attractive that they are benchmarks, or "authority-statements." Different authority-statements develop, intermingle, and mature into comprehensive "authority-systems." Several have thoroughly revolutionized physics and chemistry. The task for anyone using a single authority-system is easy; the economists' world is full of conflicting authority-statements, with each school of economic thought embracing multiple (frequently contradictory) authority-statements.

For economists, there are three types of authority-systems: Faith, Science, and public policy.

38.2 IDEAS EMANATING FROM THIRTEENTH-CENTURY ROMAN CATHOLICISM

Modern secularists consider religious Faith as superstition, albeit a potent authority-system. For some religions Faith is sufficient, for others it is a necessity, and for still others (those based on ethical conventions) Faith is irrelevant. Nonetheless, all schools of economic thought draw on authority-systems that are derived originally from religious Faith, or from a system that was once intertwined with religious Faith.

38.2.1 The background

Until early in the thirteenth century, the long-established dominant Roman Catholic theological authority-system was anchored to St. Augustine's belief that

"Absolute Truth" (i.e., the Eucharist) was necessarily an abstraction; that is, beyond sensory perceptions. That belief stemmed from Neo-Platonism, a third-century Hellenic philosophy that melded ideas from pre-Socratic schools, Plato, Aristotelian metaphysics, and Stoicism with an oriental theory of emanation. Neo-Platonism rejected mathematics as a form of "Absolute Truth."

38.2.2 Scholasticism: Aristotle rediscovered

By 1240 two Dominicans, Albertus Magnus (1200–80) and Thomas Aquinas (1225–74) were teaching in the Faculty of Theology of the University of Paris. Departing from Augustinian orthodoxy, the two contended that sensory experience should be incorporated into theology as an additional form of "Truth." The proposal came from their reading Aristotle, a literature long-lost but recently translated from Arabic into Latin by Averröes. For conventional theologians, their proposal spelled danger. Would it not encourage Dual-Truth conflicts between real "Theological Truth" and mere philosophical truth? Aquinas's ready-if-putative answer was that such conflict was unlikely; if ever the two "differed," the explanation could only be an as-yet-undiscovered philosophers' logical error. Dual-truth Averröism interested some in the theology faculty; it also became an anti-theology rallying point among those in the Faculty of Philosophy.

Aquinas's fame mushroomed. By 1258 he was called to Rome to serve as the adviser on theology for four successive popes. In 1268, the Archbishop of Paris demanded his return, to undo his "damage." That task was overtaken by Thomas's death in 1274. Notwithstanding the Archbishop's assessment, the Church canonized him in 1323, declared him a Church Father in 1567, and by 1900 Thomism had become accepted Roman Catholic theology.

Besides introducing sensory perceptions to Catholic theology, the two reintroduced another Aristotelean thought, namely Aristotle's distinction between what is "just-by-law" and what is "just-by-nature." The latter ("Natural Law") was taken to be the manifestations of God through sensory perceptions of the world's regularities (for example, seasonal change or lunar phases). In Catholic theology, Natural Law became the virtual equivalent of Scripture.

38.2.3 Problems with the Scholastic tradition

Scholasticism credited a presumption of religious authority to everything found in Aristotle. Our reading of Aristotle is different; much was true, but much was palpably false. The Holy Inquisition, administered after 1233 by the Dominicans, eventually adopted a religious zeal that considered as heresy any criticism of the Aristotelean *summa*. The *Zeitgeist* of the Renaissance included bitter intolerance. Both the Inquisition and zealous Protestants burned their victims, reflecting angers that were only partly attributable to theology – rising nationalism was another factor.

38.2.4 The Reformation and developments in Britain

THEOLOGICAL CHANGES

After the thirteenth century, the Church's political hegemony began to totter. Instability affected every European institution. Land-wasting wars and population-killing epidemics were frequent. Also a variety of instability-causing inventions – for example, gunpowder, navigation discoveries that opened up the New World, and the impact of book printing – changed people's thinking. The Catholic bishops, long-accustomed to thwarting pietists' demands for internal reforms, now faced strong armies driven by nationalism, and intent on controlling land and wealth. Withal, the Reformation was theologically and politically an attack on the hegemony of Roman Catholicism's authority-system. Luther, Knox, and Calvin, the leading Protestant theological reformers, did more than attack the hierarchy's wealth and (personal) sins; they proposed to replace Catholicism's interposition-theology, *God–Church–Man*, with a direct *God–Man* nexus.

The roots of Protestant pietism were old. In 1208, Pope Innocent III authorized a "domestic" Crusade against the reform-minded Cathers (Albigensians) living in Southwest France. In 1382 John Wiclif, a pietist as well as an Oxford don, translated the Bible into English, believing that the Word should be pondered by everyone. The Bohemian university pietist, John Huss, became so popular a threat that he was burned at the stake in 1415, a fate that Martin Luther (1483–1546) escaped only because of a German nobleman's protection.

BRITAIN AND THE PROBLEMS OF THE CROWN

An anomaly ties Luther to the English King Henry VIII. Henry took full credit for writing the *Assertion of the Seven Sacraments* (1521), an anti-Luther screed probably drafted by Erasmus. For this, Pope Leo X awarded him the title *Defender of the Faith*. Yet in 1532 (after only 13 years, but two popes later) Clement VII refused Henry VIII the divorce thought necessary to ensure the future of his dynasty. Henry's reaction was royal; England divorced Rome in 1534. Personally controlling "his" Church of England thereafter, Henry enriched the treasury by confiscating the properties held by monastic orders. Henry preferred conventional theology, but the vagaries of his marital adventures turned him into a religious wild-card – authorizing the publication of the pietistic Tindale vernacular English Bible in 1536, and yet also issuing the Statute of Six Articles in 1539, which narrowly defined and punished heresy. Further vagaries left him married to Catherine Parr, a pietist with whose theological arguments he so violently disagreed that, at the time of his death, she feared for her life. Henry's immediate successors (the Protestant Edward VI and the devoutly Catholic Mary I) reigned sequentially, giving England a decade of religious conflict. Elizabeth I, after ascending the throne in 1558, trod cautiously on religious topics, a need that soon passed. The principal problem was Parliament's centuries-old reluctance to raise and appropriate revenues. However, Henry VII (the first Tudor) artfully bypassed Parliament's powers by creating in 1487 the Star Chamber, a special court that operated in camera, that generally found his enemies guilty of High Treason, and that invariably included in their punishment the seizure of their lands for the Crown. Used carefully, the threat of indictment with trial in the Star Chamber brought Parliament members to heel. Nonetheless, Parliaments continued to be elected, sit, deliberate, and vote taxes with reluctance.

The Stuart accession in 1604 exacerbated the Crown's tax problems. As King of Scotland, James I levied taxes easily; his Edinburgh problems were with pietistic Scottish Presbyterians. Arriving in London in 1603, James found a fully cooperative English episcopacy, but relations with Parliament were otherwise. Parliament was jealous of its rights and voted funds reluctantly. Charles I trumped James's Scottish ecclesiastical and his English parliamentary problems. Ill-advised by his Archbishop of Canterbury (William Laud), Charles proposed an English-type episcopacy for the Presbyterians. Reacting to Parliament's repeated refusals for money, Charles overdid the Star Chamber route. Nothing worked. After fleeing Scotland, which had been enraged by his episcopacy proposal, he faced an urgent need to pay for an enlarged army. Proffered concessions to Parliament were always too late and too small. Charles turned desperate, and his maneuvers of trying to play off his Scottish against his English enemies became ever more clumsy, turning crises into disasters. Civil war followed. Charles was twice captured, and Parliament eventually authorized a trial. He was immediately found guilty and beheaded (January 1648).

Parliament then declared Britain a Commonwealth. Oliver Cromwell, the successful leader of the Parliamentary Army, served as Lord Protector until his death. Richard, his son, was unable to maintain Puritan power. Thus, in 1660, the new leader of the Parliamentary Army, George Monk (a quondam Royalist who had served Oliver Cromwell loyally), invited the Stuart Pretender back, as King Charles II.

Why all this English history? In order to put the development of scientific induction into perspective, one must know something about the monarchs and their attitudes regarding the purpose of education.

THE PURPOSES OF KNOWLEDGE

Henry VIII, Elizabeth I, and James I had quick minds and boasted of their personal intellectual attainments. But theirs was a conventional knowledge – language fluency and some mastery of the seven Liberal Arts; that is, Porphyry's *quadrivium* (arithmetic, geometry, music, and astronomy) and the *trivium* (grammar, rhetoric, and logic). Their self-pride was in their "knowledge-for-its-own-sake."

Puritan theology included as a *sine qua non* universal Scriptural education. Their thinking was that after Man's Expulsion from Eden, all children, cursed by being born totally ignorant, had to be educated so that they could understand God's Word. But knowledge of Scripture, although necessary, was insufficient. As per the Prophets, additional knowledge was required:

> But thou, O Daniel, shut up the words, and seal the book, even to the time of the end; *many shall run to and fro, and knowledge shall be increased.* (*Daniel*, XII:4, italics added)

This meant that the acquisition of knowledge had a purpose aside from its own possession; "knowledge-for-its-own-sake" was replaced by "knowledge-for-social betterment." There it is: two views about the purpose of knowledge – a conventional Tudor–Stuart interest in the traditions of the seven liberal arts, and a Puritan religious obligation that justified education as a social necessity.

By 1600, these conflicting knowledge authority-statements were creating serious rifts. Oxford and Cambridge became hotbeds of factionalism, with Archbishop Laud (also Chancellor of the University of Oxford) expelling all teachers and students known to favor Puritanism in the 1640s; the Puritans replying in kind in the 1650s.

With the Restoration, Oxbridge returned to the old seven liberal arts curriculum, and although religious factionalism continued, it was muted. The college dons were careful about what they said and wrote. Even Isaac Newton, who thought his best work was in Unitarian theology, hid it with a difficult cipher.

Religious warfare ended when the Protestants in Parliament forced the abdication of the openly Catholic James II, just after his second wife gave birth to his first son. They replaced him with his Protestant oldest daughter (Mary II) and her Dutch husband (William III) to reign jointly. They passed legislation that required the monarch to be a member of the Church of England.

38.3   Idea-Sets About Science

We come now to Science and its relationship to religious Faith (e.g., Scholasticism), and the seminal contributions of Francis Bacon, René Descartes, and Isaac Newton.

38.3.1   Bacon's Scientific Method

Francis Bacon, who came from an established family with Puritan connections, complained even while a Cambridge undergraduate that the conventional *trivium* and *quadrivium* curriculum was intellectually sterile. After his graduation and further legal training at Grey's Inn, Bacon turned to a political career that was accurately characterized as brilliant and cynical. In Elizabeth's time when his sponsor Essex fell from favor, Bacon protected his own career by joining the group that prosecuted Essex to his death.

The accession of James I offered new opportunities. Bacon used the occasion to get the king's attention by appending an obsequious dedication to his major treatise *The Advancement of Learning* (1605). The ploy succeeded. Bacon became James's favorite – resulting in many, ever-increasing honors, including the Lord Chancellorship. Criticizing him for doing James's dirty work – that is, cynically maneuvering Parliament – Bacon's many enemies eventually discovered instances of his taking substantial bribes while adjudicating cases. Parliament then impeached him. He was tried, convicted, fined, and imprisoned. That finished his public career. Yet, James's friendship survived – in good part because the king, no slouch when it came to learning, had considerable respect for Bacon's intellect and his contributions to philosophy. Bacon's prestigious *Novum Organon* (1620) was published just prior to his disgrace. It is an extremely readable summary (in aphorism form) of his accumulated wisdom. He intended it along with *The Advancement of Learning* and some still-unfinished work to be his *magna summa*, tentatively entitled the *Great Instauration*.

Contemptuous of the traditional organization of Porphyry's *quadrivium* and *trivium*, and turning to Aristotle's early efforts to organize the body of knowledge, Bacon came up with his own tabular Tree of Knowledge. Regularly revised, his Tree serves as the point of departure for modern epistemology – with the *Propaedia* of the current (15th) edition of the *Encyclopedia Britannica* being a recent example.

Skepticism about authority-statements came naturally to Bacon. Specifically, he questioned logical argumentation as the basis for establishing truth. Instead, turning to Aristotle's endorsement of sensory cognition, he set about creating a standard system (i.e., an authority-statement) for using sensory impressions. As formulated, Bacon's system counseled iterative observations followed by tentative generalizations until the $(n - 1)$th and nth generalizations were identical – making it conditionally true – but only until some later observations replaced it. Bacon called this procedure the "Scientific Method." It remains the foundation of induction, a second perception of "Science."

38.3.2   Science as Cartesian modeling

René Descartes (1596–1650) was by profession a soldier and only by avocation a philosopher and a mathematician. He took Roman Catholicism seriously, but had no sympathy for Scholasticism's endorsement of Aristotle. His book *Discours de la Méthode* (1637) articulated a "new" system. Personally dubious about Truth coming from anything so unreliable as sensory perceptions, he turned to abstract idea-sets that antedated Augustinian neo-Platonism and Aristotle. What emerged first was a conviction that the meaning of life, itself, was the act of thinking (*cogito, ergo sum*). Secondly, completely rejecting the anti-mathematical biases of the neo-Platonists and St. Augustine, he found in Plato's acceptance of mathematics as Truth exactly what he sought.

Use of the term Science has problems – for Descartes, Science is defined as any part of the spectrum of learning that can be mathematically formulated. Hence, just as the queen is the mother of all of the bees in a hive, so mathematics becomes the "Queen of the Sciences."

As a philosopher, Descartes is credited with laying the foundations of modern rationalism. His credentials as a mathematician come from his inventing coordinate (analytic) geometry. His record as a soldier was mostly that he kept out of trouble.

To summarize: mathematical statements are logical models, and accordingly mathematically correct models share a communality, "Truth." The test of a Cartesian model is not what it predicts, but that it is immanently correct. For Cartesians any proposition in correct mathematical form is scientific. Some naive Cartesian modeling has proven useful in spite of its incomplete or totally incorrect assumptions; for example, marine navigation models work well even though they postulate the Earth to be the center of the universe. By contrast, Newton's theory of gravitation and equilibrium of forces, a model that had passed repeated tests of immanence, seems to have been incompletely specified. Since Edwin H. Hubble's spectrography results, it now seems that Willem de Sitter's theory of the expanding nature of the universe is valid, and the universe is not a balance between centrifugal and centripetal forces.

38.3.3   The Royal Society

Even prior to the Commonwealth, a group of intellectuals, most of whom had University of Oxford connections, met informally but regularly in London to discuss their ideas. Eventually, the group named itself "The Philosophical Club," but it was known as "The Invisible College." By the late 1650s, William Petty was its leader. Just after the Restoration, Petty along with others approached Charles II petitioning for a Royal charter. Charles was enthusiastic, and the Royal Society was chartered in 1662.

From the outset, election was based solely on intellectual merit; social status was irrelevant. The Society's interests broadened – it became an amalgam of the Stuart "knowledge-for-its-own-sake" and the Puritan "knowledge-for-social-betterment" traditions. It became the locus for scientific reporting, and when something new was to be announced the Royal Society in London, rather than in Oxford or Cambridge, was the preferred site. Members carefully eschewed discussions of anything that involved theology or theological conflict. Their concern was limited to *how* and *when* natural phenomena occurred; for the most part, questions of *why* (God's purpose) were omitted as being essentially theological. Papers were delivered and the best of them were eventually published in the Society's *Proceedings*. Much of the Society's early work, clearly in the Bacon mold, dealt with geographical and cosmological discovery that involved reports of new flora and fauna as well as the mapping of the universe. What resulted was a residual, "Science," by which they seem to have meant "studies of natural systems."

At first, the members seemingly favored Bacon's perception of what scientists should do. These include an early paper by William Petty, "A treatise on taxation" (1662) – it manifested Petty's instinctive feel for random sampling and was the first of many economic studies later lumped under the heading of the "Political Arithmetic School." Another by an early member, John Graunt, was "Some observations on the London bills of mortality," which "created" modern medical epidemiology. And Edmond Halley, even as a stripling Oxford student, interrupted his college years to travel to the island of St. Helena, and reported to the Society on his mapping of the stars seen in the Southern Hemisphere.

As the membership also included major mathematicians, papers that reflected the Cartesian approach to Science were also regular fare. One by Edmond Halley built on something that he had been told, namely that Breslau (Germany) had a constant population. This point absorbed, Halley speculated that if its age distribution also remained stable, he could easily calculate both age-specific death rates and normal survival rates by age. These estimates, he opined, could serve as the bases for further calculations about the amounts of money necessary to pay off life annuities and life insurance policies. (So persuasive was his presentation that some traders began to sell policies. Alas, Halley lacked knowledge of sampling, and speculators were economically ruined!)

Early influential members included William Wallis and Robert Boyle, both mathematicians of note. However, it was another mathematician, Isaac Newton, elected to the Society in 1671–2, who eventually reshaped the Society's program.

38.3.4   Fusions of the two systems of Science

THE NEWTON CRUCIAL TEST

Some claim that Isaac Newton (1642–1727), one of the two inventors of the calculus, was the all-time greatest physicist – if only because afterwards there remained so much less to invent. Yet, what was truly his and how much he "borrowed" from others remains hard to tell – Trinity College (Cambridge) lore is full of gossipy stories. Part of Newton's record must be his neurotic (possibly psychotic) personality: jealousies, hatreds, and a love of manipulation. Nonetheless, his personal brilliance dominated the Royal Society's activities for the last 40 years of his life.

Newton was an autodidact. Trinity College did not appreciate his abilities during his undergraduate years (even though that was when he invented "fluxions," his version of the calculus). Thereafter, he began work on his theory of mechanics, which eventually matured into his laws of motion. From these laws, he (or perhaps someone else) derived a theory of the celestial equilibration of forces. It took years for him to refine their presentation, but when they were eventually published as *De Motu Corporum*, and later much expanded as *Philosophiae Naturalis Principia Mathematica*, his preeminence was universally recognized. These were conceived as abstract mathematical models – clearly in the Cartesian tradition.

Newton's later study of optics, including findings about the color spectrum, was in the Bacon tradition. His procedure has become for many the standard for declaring a proposition to be scientific – namely, a scientific theory is the result of a hypothetico-deductive model being subsequently confirmed by a great empirical test (for example, Eddington's 1919 confirmation of Einstein's general theory of relativity). What this leaves open, of course, is doubt as to whether the test is absolute; it may be a special case.

THE GREAT NEW PARADIGMS

Turning to the great scientific advances during the latter half of the second millennium, there is consensus that they started with Nicholas Copernicus's *De Revolutionibus* (1543), which proved that the Earth revolved around the Sun (not the reverse, as Aristotle had believed). By 1600, what had been heresy was becoming orthodoxy; by 1700, it was canon. However, in spite of it being thought canon, Newton's celestial mechanics-in-equilibrium theory was wrong. Edwin P. Hubble's crucial experiment "confirmed" a theory advanced by Willem de Sitter (1872–1934) that the universe was infinitely expanding. Orthodoxies are not necessarily permanent!

The period includes displacement of the Aristotelian and alchemist phlogiston theory, that the four source materials of all earthly matter were fire, earth, air, and water. The great names were Robert Boyle (1627–91), Joseph Black (1728–99), Henry Cavendish (1731–1810), Antoine Lavoisier (1743–94), and Joseph Priestly (1733–1804). Later, in 1805, John Dalton (1766–1844) offered a general theory of the chemical elements. A theory of their "Periodic Table" was proposed by John Newlands in 1863, but remained unconfirmed until 1869, when some predictive experiments were made by Dmitri Mendeleyeef (1834–1907).

This panoply of post-Scholastic brilliance has been considered from another standpoint. Thomas Kuhn calls the suddenness and totality of authority-system change the emergence of New Scientific Paradigms, by which he means a conceptually new *Weltanschauungen* built on formal modeling, data-accumulation, and classic (i.e., crucial) experiments using tested methods (cf., *The Structure of Scientific Revolutions*, 1962).

However, even if our minds boggle at the number of scholarly fields enjoying such new paradigms, it does not follow that all fields can expect changes of such magnitude. Kuhn himself opined that those who looked for New Scientific Paradigms in the social sciences were going to be disappointed. There, the advance of knowledge was likely to be of the bit-at-a-time variety – Alfred Marshall's *Natura non facit sultum*.

Pursuing that topic, in his controversial 1959 Rede Lecture *Two Cultures and the Scientific Revolution*, the quondam physicist–science-administrator-turned-novelist Charles Snow asserted that what divides the sciences from the humanities is that science's virtue is that it is forward-looking; the humanities' failing is that it is backward-looking. A more appropriate distinction would be that science has been looking at how *things are*, while the humanities are studying how *human thought expresses itself*. In the former case, the evidence yields to systematic observation of mostly factual phenomena – with the biggest problem being accuracy of measurement. Fields of evidence in the case of human thought, largely records of subjective choices, are generally to be found in old libraries, where the big problem is not measurement but how to infer the loci of human understanding (Perlman, 1996, pp. 35–46).

38.3.5 Summary: Science and Faith

THE HISTORY OF SCIENCE

Although it is common to date modern thought to the series of wide-ranging seventeenth- to nineteenth-century discoveries in the many sub-fields of physics, chemistry, medicine, and biology, I believe that the Scholastic contribution, which opened scholars' eyes to taking in all of the information offered by each of the five senses, has a special claim to being the foundation of modern thought. Why? Because the Scholastics broadened Faith to include phenomena that were not explicitly Scripture-related.

Irrespective of Bacon's careful eschewing of any discussions that could reveal his choice between his mother's Puritanism and his patron's High Church religion, and Descartes's skirting of Roman Catholic hierarchical questions, their legacies were two new general authority-systems, each calling itself Science. Bacon's Science was an inductive method. Descartes's Science was a system that established Truth and integrated certain parts of Natural Law. Newton's Science, which fused the other two, was both mathematical and empirical. As we have noted, for many only what passes Newton's test is said to be scientific.

TYPES OF FAITH

The period from the mid-sixteenth to the early eighteenth century was one of budding authority-systems. Conflicts between scientists were rife, but questions relating to variations because of religious Faith were increasingly avoided. Indeed, by 1700 the idea that among scientists there should be religious toleration was born and was growing apace. Many avoided specific references to God (a theological entity) and, as Deists, they chose secularly neutral synonyms such as "the invisible hand" or "nature," terms meant to posit an ordered universe – even if they felt uncertain about the details of its making.

The atheism of the French Revolution served for many to separate conviction from cant. For many scientists (a self-description often pertaining to members of a profession that accepted only the Newton test), Science and religion were unrelated concepts. Both were perceived as authority-systems, each of which had its own brand of faith. The faith of scientists was in the logic and regularity of natural phenomena; while religious Faith often embraced an irregularity of natural phenomena – that is, miracles.

However, what emerged clearly in the nineteenth century was attempts to divorce completely scientific work from any religious foundations. This shift did not vitiate the role of faith – as an act. For many, faith in regularities explained by Science came to be their principal authority-system.

Several philosophers wanted something more material than religious Faith. Auguste Comte, the father of sociology, invented Positivism, a creed – somewhat in the original Bacon induction tradition – that facts, as perceived through the senses, are the source of information. Comte advised taking that knowledge and using deduction to extend one's reasoned conclusions. Accepting Bentham's utilitarianism as a way of discovering ethics, Comte added a set of his own social objectives, including the elimination of all ecclesiastically determined social norms, and the creation of an egalitarian society with some socialization of property and the means of production and distribution. Comte's Positivism was further formalized in the early twentieth century by a group of Viennese philosophers (the Vienna Circle) into a more sophisticated methodology, "Logical Positivism." They combined a logical model with empirical testable properties (including reference to statistical probabilities that affected observational errors) to find seemingly stable conclusions, if not exactly any final truths. Karl Popper's version is termed "falsificationism" (cf., Blaug, 1980).

Others, such as John Stuart Mill, seemingly had their faith grounded in their own cultural ethics. With them, their cultural ethics, specifically, and their underlying cultural traditions, generally, became their preferred standards, which – because father-figures are traditionally authoritative – I term Cultural or Patristic Authority-Systems (cf., Perlman and McCann, 1998, 2000). Some economists insist that studies of cultural authority-systems, which deal with nonrational considerations, are accordingly beyond the scope of their discipline (e.g., Pareto), and that they properly belong to the provinces of sociology and cultural anthropology. Alternatively, because rationality is itself a complex and elusive concept, other economists (for example, even John Maynard Keynes and his epistemics) see the differences between economics and those disciplines as more apparent than real.

In sum, Science is a complex of authority-systems; some including, but others abstracting from – and even others denying – religious Faith. But none denies faith in something. Even John Stuart Mill's faith was firmly grounded – in his case, in the cultural experiences of his class of British intellectuals – not what Oliver Wendall Holmes Jr. called "the life of the people" but, rather, what Mill might have called the ethics of his kind of Brit.

38.4 HOBBES'S *THE LEVIATHAN* AS THE FOUNDATION OF SOCIAL THEORY

38.4.1 Thomas Hobbes

Some date modern social theory, of which economics is a part, with the appearance of Niccolò Macchiavelli's *Il Principe* (1532) or Jean Bodin's *Les six livres de la République* (1576). Both were quasi-revolutionary, treating governmental rule not as an ethical but as an economic efficiency problem. That said, I choose Hobbes's *The Leviathan* (1651) as our point of departure, because his contribution went far beyond discussing morality and efficiency.

An assessment of Hobbes (1588–1679) starts by admiring how adroitly he survived his 91 years. Successfully switching sides twice during Britain's Civil War, he managed to remain influential – and that in spite of his "Guinness Book of Records" vinegar-saturated tongue and pen. Nonetheless, Hobbes had even "enjoyed" direct personal contact with virtually everyone of scholarly importance in the secular world: including, as friends, Francis Bacon, Charles II, Galileo, Ben Jonson, Marin Mersenne (the center of Descartes's intellectual circle), and William Petty; and, as personal enemies, several mathematicians (Descartes and John Wallis), the astronomer Seth Ward, and the chemist–physicist Robert Boyle. His "secret" was an insouciance about vitriolic disputation.

38.4.2 *The Leviathan*

Hobbes, swinging with the British political winds, went into exile in 1640 with the Royalists. Soon after the establishment of the Commonwealth, he returned to London, and in 1651 he published *The Leviathan*, a lengthy conjecture of how communities become organized.

Starting with a crucial *fact* (that is, man's inherent selfish individualism), he deduced that every man feared every other man. Accordingly, before any community existed what everyone faced was a world with "No arts, no letters, no society, and which is worst of all, continual fear and danger of violent death, and the life of man solitary, poor, nasty, brutish, and short" (*The Leviathan*, part I, ch. xviii).

Man, he conjectured, fortuitously had a capacity to reason imaginatively. Considering his situation, man realized the advantages of making agreements with other men. One was Social Contract; and, that established, the other would be a Government Contract. The Social Contract involved a general agreement – "If you will not harm me (and mine) I will not harm you and yours." Once that Contract was executed, an agreement about sanctions was required. It specified that I will recognize the authority of a dominant force – that is, *The Leviathan* – if it will protect me and mine from anyone who violates the Social Contract. Implicit was the Leviathan's right to make rules necessary to provide social order (safety). Explicit was Hobbes's belief that if and when the Leviathan did not provide safety, then its Government Contract had been voided. Briefly put, Hobbes was justifying his change from loyalty to the Crown to loyalty to Cromwell's Commonwealth by asserting that force, not morality, gave legitimacy to governmental power.

The book offered much beyond this rather simple message. Personal contact with Bacon led Hobbes to thinking about a need for evidence. Its opening chapters on how information is acquired, processed, and developed as language make "sense" – something easily accepted as authoritative. But Hobbes was not truly in the Bacon Science tradition; rather, what he employing was conjectural history (*histoire raisonée*), not what Bacon would have called evidence. Accordingly, *The Leviathan* consisted of logical deductions from an assumed premise. The rub comes because *The Leviathan* deals not with abstractions but with the sensory consequences of public-policy administration.

38.4.3 Hobbes's leading critics

As historically important as Hobbes's views were, equal or more so were several reactions that they elicited:

- The book was an atheist's attack on Christianity. Hobbes failed to grasp the Protestant (religious) "Truth" anent the God–Man nexus – God created all men with certain rights. One of these was a right to ownership of that part of whatever was attributable to his own labor input (cf., John Locke's *Treatise on Government*).
- Hobbes's assumptions regarding man's basic nature were observably wrong. Dispassionate systematic observation revealed that man was basically communitarian – often generous to his neighbors. Moreover, every normal man has a conscience (Smith's "impartial spectator") and is able to judge the morality of his choices (cf., Smith's *The Theory of Moral Sentiments*). Given the repaired assumption, it follows that men cooperate not out of fear but out of a reasoned recognition that job specialization leads to greater consumption (cf., Smith's *Wealth of Nations*).

- Hobbes's conclusion that the Government Contract was necessarily unconditional had no basis. To the contrary, that Contract could specify both powers
granted and powers withheld (Locke's *Treatise on Government*).

Was Hobbes was an atheist? The last part of the book dealt at length, and sympathetically, with the role of religion and the Church:

- For Royalists and the ecclesiastical supporters of the Divine Right of kings,
Hobbes's denying the centrality of the Church's anointing of kings was indicative of his failure to grasp that only when everyone accepted God's Will
regarding the clockwork nature of social organization would Augustine's
Rome become His City of God (cf., Joseph, Bishop Butler).
- Moreover, Hobbes's seeming lack of religious Faith suggests a general skepticism about faith – but did not he and everyone else accept on faith that even
when they are not in the forest to observe the phenomenon, a falling tree still
makes a noise (cf., George, Bishop Berkeley)?
- Anthony Ashley Cooper (not a bishop, but a nobleman – the Third Earl of
Shaftesbury) employed another tack. Questioning Hobbes's conjecture that
men were inherently totally selfish, Shaftesbury conjectured, presumably on
the basis of Scripture as much as anything else, that all normal men were born
with had a moral sense, a natural endowment that permitted them to hear that
"still small voice" cited in *1 Kings*, XIX:12 – that there were six, not five, senses.
That sixth sense was the "moral sense."
- As for Hobbes's theory of government, it provoked John Locke's arguments
for democratic constitutionalism. Locke derived his views from his Protestantism. Whether modern-day acceptance of all men having innate rights to life,
liberty, and estate stems from accepting Locke's Protestant authority-system
or from accepting American cultural history as the authority-system becomes
a problem when explaining to others who are foreign to both why we believe
as we do.

Given the foregoing, we can then better understand the two analytic derivations
from Locke's assertion about the right to estate (property). First, from it derives
the whole fabric of property rights, modified occasionally by referring to what
has been ceded to the government in the Second Contract. And, secondly, it was
the basis of the labor theory of value, the cornerstone of classical economics.

38.5 THE IMPACT OF IDEAS ON THE EVOLUTION OF ECONOMIC UNDERSTANDING

Economic knowledge overlaps other disciplines. Generally, schools of economic
thought are classifications of idea-sets. Most schools embrace multiple idea-sets,
and to decide their priorities is not simply a matter of intellectual exploration but
involves questions of personal leadership and the issues of the moment that are
claiming attention. A school's tenets, which comprise its authority-system, are

invariably complex and often a bit contradictory – particularly if several policy questions are involved.

38.5.1 The impact of ideas involving pure Faith and ideology

Again, I treat Faith as beliefs that are unconditionally accepted as Truth, whether divinely revealed, or Kantian categorical imperatives, or as historically necessary ideologies. Accordingly, there are many points of contact between Faith and the foundations of modern economics:

- For religion-based Faiths, note the authority-systems in Scholasticism; Locke's theory of property rights as a Protestant interpretation of Natural Law; and Christian socialist communitarianism, including the redistribution of wealth and income.
- For Kantian "categorical imperatives" serving as ethical foundations, note the authority-systems of Bentham's utilitarianism, including John Stuart Mill's faith in higher thinking; Comte's anti-ecclesiastical but strongly ethical Positivism; and integrated programmatic beliefs such as utilitarianism or socialism.
- For faith tied up with historical inevitability, note the complexities of authorities in Marx's scientific socialism, including its Bernstein–Menshevik revisions.

Faith-based authority-systems generally are intellectually nonnegotiable, because such faith is a personally endowed art-form – some people have it, others do not. For those who have it, it is powerful.

38.5.2 The impact of Science idea-sets

BACON'S SCIENTIFIC METHOD

The Bacon tradition ranges from Petty's 1664 *Verbum Sapienti* estimation of the national wealth and income of Britain to numerous contributions by Wesley Clair Mitchell and the American institutionalists. What distinguishes them is their concentration on amassing statistical data, organizing them, and then inferring generalizations that are applicable to answering problems.

However, the quintessential representative types are William Newmarch's six-volume *History of Prices and the State of Circulation from 1793 to 1837* (1838–57) and Adolphe Quetelet's 1835 pioneering effort on population characteristics, *A Treatise on Man and the Development of his Faculties* (as translated in 1842).

SCIENCE AS CARTESIAN MODELING

This approach, often termed *hypothetico-deductive* modeling, uses the authority-system of logic. Many of the earliest writers, however – Cantillon, Quesnay, and Say – eschewed formal mathematical display. Later, von Thünen and Cournot improved the standards of presentation with mathematically formulated models, particularly in Cournot's *Researches into the Mathematical Principles of the Theory of Wealth* (1963 [1838]). The French formalistic tradition in economics came to full-flower with Walras's model of static general equilibrium.

The list of English-language economic "greats" is longer. Among the better known were Jevons (*The Theory of Political Economy*, 1871), Edgeworth (*Mathematical Psychics*, 1881; *Metretike*, 1887), and Irving Fisher (*Mathematical Investigations in the Theory of Value and Price*, 1892).

Publication of the 1944 *Theory of Games and Economic Behavior* by von Neumann and Morgenstern, Samuelson's 1947 *Foundations of Economic Analysis*, and Gary Becker's 1976 *The Economic Approach to Human Behavior*, alone, mark the transformation of mainstream professional economics from descriptive generalizing to mathematical modeling. Samuelson's defense of this transition is pert: "[Willard] Gibbs, not a loquacious man, . . . made a four-word speech: 'Mathematics is a language.' I have only one objection to that statement: I wish he had made it 25 per cent shorter . . . Mathematics *is* language." (quoted in Machlup, 1991, p. 350).

There are currently several schools of economic thought that are seemingly devoted totally to Cartesian modeling: Game Theory, Public Choice, and Rational Expectations.

In one important tangential deviation, Carl Menger, historically deduction's flag-bearer in the *Methodensteit*, eschewed the use of mathematics because his models were built on subjective (nonrational) individual preference choices.

Like Menger's, Maynard Keynes's system also involved nonrational foundations. But by the time Keynes wrote, mathematics had advanced, and Keynes's use of probability distributions could be phrased as mathematical abstractions.

Whether even more recent developments in mathematics – for example, chaos theory – will revolutionize economics to the point of Kuhnian Paradigmatic Change remains an interesting speculation.

NEWTON-TYPE FUSIONS

Newton's hypothetico-deduction with empirical verification clearly underlay Malthus's decision to follow up his *Essay on Population* (1798) with many (failed) efforts at empirical validation.

Although Alfred Marshall nominally allocated to Neville Keynes, his quondam student, the responsibility for defining the methodology of economics, it was both Marshall's *Principles of Economics*, including its geometry in the footnotes, and its methodological and mathematical appendices, and his *Industry and Trade* (1920), with its considerable episodic and quantitative empirical materials, that served as the optimal examples of the fusion of deduction and induction. However, Marshall was skeptical of any mathematical formulation of economic relationships being able to stand up to a Crucial Experiment; indeed, Marshall's purpose was to explain the factors involved in the economic process rather than to try to weigh their importance or make predictions about outcomes.

Pareto's mathematically formulated (log-normal) Law of Wages has stood up in repeated Crucial Experiments, but it was derived inductively and lacks any deductive core.

Clearly, econometrics is the optimal example of the fusion that Newton had in mind. It offers a plethora of mathematically formulated models, with preliminary empirical sensitivity-test refinements, that seem to be closest to what Newton had in mind. But often the tests are inconclusive, rather than either passed or failed (cf., Perlman, 1979; Lipsey, 2000).

38.5.3 Political economy as a variety of authority-statements and authority-systems

For generations, economic literature prepared by pamphleteers (pens-for-hire), as distinguished from the philosophically wise (Schumpeter's "Consultant-Administrators"), offered advice designed to persuade the decision-makers (in England the Parliament, elsewhere the Crown) on virtually everything. Why these English scribblers thought of themselves as brilliantly competing openly in the market of ideas, while Schumpeter thought of them as "intellectual harlots," reveals much about differences in culture-associated authority-systems.

Table 38.1 illustrates the complexities of identifying schools of thought with specific issues, the methods employed, the foci, and the choices of underlying authority-statements and authority-systems. Would that economics were a simpler subject. Frank Knight once remarked that as it took several millennia for us to realize that stones do not have free will, it might take a millennium or two for economists to realize that men do. Several terms may need amplification:

- *Reason*, a synonym for reflective judgment, involves observation, combining induction (experience reviewed for significance) and some small-scale deduction (cf., the judicial "rule of reason").
- *Rationality* involves more than logic or even reason. It is best grasped by comparing it to irrational (against reason), nonrational (without reason), and super-rational (beyond reason, as in "miracles" or religious Faith).

Schools of economic thought and their principal writers are chosen arbitrarily. The choice of the key issues is also arbitrary, and it explains only the immediate reason for listing a particular writer; von Thünen's work on cooperatives, for example, has nothing in common with the Austrian/epistemic school.

The number of analytic methods, although small, is clearly one reason why economics has no Kuhnian Paradigm – there is as yet no discipline-wide agreement about the efficiency of any single method.

The "Foci" and "Authority-statements and authority-systems" groupings are, of course, the rationale for this whole exercise.

There are many explanations for the evolution of the economics discipline. It is not simply that there is no agreement on the appropriate tests for methods. Rather, what we have are various expressions of commitment to faith (religious or Spinoza-like regularities) and to such philosophic principles as individualism and communitarian responsibility. Underlying many writings is the author's belief that the universe is or is not ordered (that is, not a "heap"). Critical too is an author's idiosyncratic combination of optimism, pessimism, cynicism, and skepticism in terms of a *Weltanschauung*, or according to a specific topical issue.

Table 38.1 Selected schools of economic thought: issues, methods, foci, authority-statements, and systems

School	Principal names	Key issues	Analytic methods	Foci	Authority-statements and authority-systems
SCHOLASTIC	Albertus, Aquinas	Just wage, just price, usury	Religious Faith, abstraction	Distributive justice, usury	Christian theology, Aristotle
Mercantilist British	Malynes, Missenden, Child, Mun	National monetary and trade policies	Reason	Monopoly profits and saving, merchants – political power	Faith – trade optimal industry with zero-sum international competition
	Steuart	Balanced development	Reason	National welfare and fisc, monopoly profits and saving, sumptuary laws	Faith – trade optimal industry with zero-sum international competition
French, Austrian, cameralist	Montchrétien, Colbert, van Horningk, Justi	Balanced development	Reason	Monetary-fiscal policies	Natural Law, trade optimal industry with zero-sum international competition
SMITHIAN Pro-empiric	Mandeville	Benevolent consequences of greed, *laissez faire*	Reason	Paradox; private vice–public weal, anti-labor	Induction, individualism, hedonic amoralism
Smithian – TMS	Smith, Hutcheson, Malthus	Normativism, empathy, communitarianism	Reason	Individual morality, communitarian identification	Natural Law, rationality
Smithian – *Wealth of Nations*	Smith, Hume	Development, individualism, division of labor, self-regulating markets, free trade	Reason	Self-regulating markets, free trade, individual self-determination, labor welfare	Natural Law, individualism, property rights, labor value theory, rationality
CLASSICAL	James Mill, Ricardo, Say, Senior	Utilitarianism, self-regulating markets, free trade, overpopulation, labor theory of value, wages fund	Abstraction, reason	Economic efficiency, free trade	Utilitarianism, internationalism, rationality, property rights
	J. S. Mill	As above, universal education, normativism	Abstraction, reason	Normativism (higher cultural ethics), redistributive justice	Deductive–inductive logic, rationality, normativism, liberalism
	Marx	As per James Mill, inevitability of capitalism's depressions	Materialist–Hegelian dialectic		Materialist-Hegelian dialectic

Category		Concept	Method	Economics	Characteristics
UTILITARIANISM					
Hedonistic	Bentham	Hedonic calculus: rationality and reason	Abstraction, reason	Hedonism, "greatest good for greatest number," property rights, usury	Methodological individualism, logic, rationality; anti-Natural Law
Ethical	J. S. Mill	Ethical calculus, reason	Abstraction, reason	Economic principles of an ethical society	Deductive–inductive logic, rationality, normativism
Scientific	Jevons	Hedonic calculus: rationality	Abstraction, reason	Scientific deductive theory	Deductive–inductive logic, Positivism, methodological individualism
MARGINALIST					
Utilitarian	Jevons	Hedonic calculus: rationality	Abstraction, reason	Static microeconomics	Methodological individualism, mathematics
Psychological	Carl Menger	Epistemics	Nonrational foundations underlying logic	Static microeconomics	Rationality, methodological individualism, liberalism
Mathematical	Walras	*Tâtonnement*	Deduction	Static general equilibrium	Mathematics, methodological individualism
AUSTRIAN/EPISTEMIC	Cantillon	Entrepreneur, uncertainty	Abstraction, reason	Static microeconomics	Property rights, deduction, rationality
	von Thünen	Risk and uncertainty	Abstraction, reason	Static microeconomics	Deduction, rationality
	Menger, Böhm-Bawerk, Wieser, von Mises	Market efficiency	Nonrational foundations underlying logic	Static microeconomics	Reason, methodological individualism
	John Maynard Keynes	Uncertainty, economic stagnation	Abstraction, reason	Static microeconomics	Probability mathematics
	Hayek	Market institutions	Abstraction, reason	Static macroeconomics	Natural Law, individualism
	Shackle	Uncertainty ("unknowledge")	Reason	Dynamic macroeconomics	Reason
CAMBRIDGE, UK	Marshall	Partial equilibrium, elasticities, time-markets, consumer surplus, quasi-rents	Abstraction, reason, induction	Formalized static microeconomic analysis, historico-descriptive microeconomic dynamics	Mathematics, methodological individualism, normativism
	Pigou	Welfare – equity, unemployment	Abstraction, reason	Macroeconomics, economic stability, redistributive justice	Normativism, communitarianism
	Keynes	Uncertainty, business cycles	Abstraction, reason	Static macroeconomics, economic stability, monetary and fiscal policies	Communitarianism, rationality, mathematics

Table 38.1 (cont'd)

School	Principal names	Key issues	Analytic methods	Foci	Authority-statements and authority-systems
FRENCH RATIONALIST	Cantillon	Entrepreneur, uncertainty	Abstraction, reason	Static microeconomics	Property rights, rationality, logic
	Physiocrats	Social efficiency, fiscal revenue, laissez faire	Abstraction, reason	Static macroeconomics, circular-flow model, fiscal policy	Natural Law, logic, rationality
	Cournot and Deduit	Tax policy	Deduction	Static microeconomics, fiscal policy	Mathematics
	Walras, Allais	Welfare economics	Deduction	Static macroeconomics	Mathematics
STATISTICAL					
Political arithmeticians	Petty, Graunt	Economic inventory	Induction	Social welfare	Empiricism, rationality
Social statisticians	Quetelet, Galton	Economic inventory	Induction	Social welfare	Empiricism, rationality
Economic statisticians	Moore, Mitchell	Economic inventory	Induction	Business cycles	Empiricism, rationality, probability theory
Econometrics	Frisch, Tinbergen	Economic inventory and theory	Induction, probability	Verification of theory	Fusion of two "Sciences"
HISTORICAL–INSTITUTIONALIST					
German	Roscher → Schmoller	Social progress, development	Induction, reason	Macroeconomics	Communitarianism, Hegelianism
American	Veblen	Anti-theoretic statics	Irony	Utilitarian culture	Instinctive psychology
	Commons	Welfare economics	Induction, reason	Redistributive justice	Natural Law, normativism, property rights
	Mitchell	Business cycles	Induction, reason	Economic stabilization	Natural Law, probability theory
Schumpeter	Schumpeter	Economic development	Induction, reason	Macroeconomics	Natural Law, probability theory
Neo-institutionalist	Richter, North, Williamson	Economic development	Induction, probability	Dynamic macroeconomics	Deduction–induction, probability theory
NEOCLASSICAL SYNTHESIS	Hicks, Samuelson	Varied, including value theory, trade	Deduction	Macroeconomics	Mathematics
	Arrow, Debreu	Formalizing economic theory of competition	Deduction	Macroeconomics	Mathematics
RATIONAL EXPECTATIONS	Muth, Lucas	Tax policy and individual agency	Deduction	Macroeconomics	Deductive logic
PUBLIC CHOICE	Buchanan, Arrow	Government policy	Deduction	Comprehensive choice systems	Logic, methodological individualism

Source: Derived from Marietta and Perlman (2000), pp. 151–89.

In all, what emerges is an absence of simplicity; rather, economic thought is a rich intellectual jungle. Some dream that in the future that jungle will be tamed and with the proper principles can be cultivated; others see it as the organic source of more rather than fewer authority-statements and systems.

38.6 CONCLUSION

Using history, we traced changes in Roman Catholic theology that led to entirely new systems of knowledge, which also in time developed their own dogmas. And the economics that we know reflects the conflicts between the dogmas (Truths or truths) of the different types of knowledge considered, the cultural preferences of the purveyor and customer of economic thought, and the problems involved. Ideas, including scientific ideas, take several "forms," ranging from Platonic abstract essences to cognitively observed forms, ideal types, principles, and things as ephemeral as notions. How anyone chooses idea-sets reflects their personal capacity, their experiences, and the believer's trust in the accuracy or relevance or appropriateness of the source of the idea. That said, what does it mean?

Given the importance of free will, is there any other approach to making sense of the past?

Bibliography

Becker, G. S. 1976: *The Economic Approach to Human Behavior*. Chicago: The University of Chicago Press.

Blaug, M. 1980: *The Methodology of Economics: or, How Economists Explain*. Cambridge, UK: Cambridge University Press.

Cournot, A. A. 1963 [1838]: *Researches into the Mathematical Principles of the Theory of Wealth*, with Irving Fisher's original notes. Homewood, IL: Richard D. Irwin.

Edgeworth, F. Y. 1996 [1881]: *Mathematical Psychics, an Essay on the Application of Mathematics to the Moral Sciences*, ed. C. R. McCann, Jr. Cheltenham, UK: Edward Elgar.

Fisher, I. 1925 [1892]: *Mathematical Investigations in the Theory of Value and Prices*. New Haven, CN: Yale University Press.

Jevons, W. S. 1911 [1871]: *The Theory of Political Economy*, with notes and an extension of the bibliography of mathematical economic writings, 4th edn. London: Macmillan.

Kuhn, T. S. 1962: *The Structure of Scientific Revolutions*. Chicago: The University of Chicago Press.

Lipsey, R. G. 2000: The famous Phillips curve article. In R. Leeson (ed.), *A. W. H. Phillips: Collected Works in Contemporary Perspective*. Cambridge, UK: Cambridge University Press.

Machlup, F. 1991: *Economic Semantics*, 2nd edn., with a new introduction by Mark Perlman. New Brunswick, NJ: Transaction.

Marietta, M. and Perlman, M. 2000: The uses of authority in economics: shared intellectual frameworks as the foundation of personal persuasion. *American Journal of Economics and Sociology*, 59(2), 151–89.

Neumann, J. von and Morgenstern, O. 1944: *Theory of Games and Economic Behavior*. Princeton, NJ: Princeton University Press.

Newmarch, W. 1838–57: *History of Prices and the State of Circulation from 1793 to 1837*, 6 vols. London: Longman, Orme, Brown, Green, and Longmans.

Perlman, M. 1979: One man's Baedeker to productivity growth discussions. In W. Fellner (ed.), *Contemporary Economic Problems*. Washington, DC: American Enterprise Institute, 79–113.

—— 1996: *The Character of Economic Thought, Economic Characters, and Economic Institutions: Selected Essays by Mark Perlman*. Ann Arbor, MI: University of Michigan Press.

—— 2000: *Pillars of Economic Thought: Factors and Markets*. Ann Arbor. MI: University of Michigan Press.

Perlman, M. and McCann, C. R., Jr. 1998: *Pillars of Economic Thought: Ideas and Traditions*. Ann Arbor, MI: University of Michigan Press.

Quetelet, A. 1969 [1835]: *A Treatise on Man and the Development of his Faculties*, a facsimile reproduction of the English translation of 1842, with an introduction by S. Diamond. Gainesville, FL: Scholars' Facsimiles & Reprints.

Samuelson, P. A. 1947: *Foundations of Economic Analysis*. Cambridge, MA: Harvard University Press.

Snow, C. P. 1959: *Two Cultures and the Scientific Revolution*. New York: Cambridge University Press.

—— 1969: [*Two Cultures and the Scientific Revolution.*] *The Two Cultures: and A Second Look: An Expanded Version of "Two Cultures and the Scientific Revolution."* London: Cambridge University Press.

CHAPTER THIRTY-NINE

Research in the History of Economic Thought as a Vehicle for the Defense and Criticism of Orthodox Economics

John Lodewijks

It is almost impossible to attend a gathering of North American historians of economic thought without getting the uncomfortable feeling that many are there to grieve over the corpse. Many come to lament a time when economics was different, when it was better, and when it had not been perverted by formalism and higher mathematics. Many grieve for John Maynard Keynes and Commons, for Friedrich Hayek and Mitchell and Ludwig von Mises.

> *Bradley W. Bateman (in Morgan and Rutherford, 1998, p. 29)*

It is a striking fact that conferences in history of economic thought attract Austrians, Marxists, Radical political economists, Sraffians, institutionalists and post-Keynesians in disproportionate numbers, all non-neoclassicals or even anti-neoclassicals who have no place else to go to talk to scholars outside their narrow intellectual circles.

> *Mark Blaug (2001, p. 147)*

39.1   BALANCING THE HISTORY OF ECONOMICS

Many students throughout the world were introduced to the history of economics through Robert Heilbroner's immensely popular *The Worldly Philosophers,* originally published in 1953 and now in its seventh edition, with over four million copies sold to date. Geoffrey Harcourt (2001, p. 167) claims that it is the best introduction to the lives and contributions of the great economists ever written. The chapters on Marx and Veblen are delightfully entertaining and beautifully crafted. But is it a "balanced" history of economics? It was written by an author who, in this work and in numerous other publications, displays a highly critical stance toward mainstream economics. Heilbroner (1979, p. 197) alleges that modern economics "is shallow and poor rather than deep and rich" and disappointing in comparison with the economics of earlier periods. Modern economics "has nothing to compare with the 'magnificent dynamics' of the Classicists" and Heilbroner cannot discover in modern economics a depth or breadth comparable with earlier periods, or any great overall vision that illuminates issues. Critics maintain that his history is biased, focusing too heavily on the economics of socialists, Marxists, and the "Underworld of Economics."

Mark Skousen (2001) wrote *The Making of Modern Economics* specifically to "right" this imbalance. Like Heilbroner, this text is also provocative and entertaining, with scandals of various sorts embellishing the lives of the great thinkers. Yet it would be difficult to call this a balanced history either. It is an Austrian history of economics, where Adam Smith's self-regulating system of natural liberty and competition triumphs against the forces of socialist interventionism. Each episode in the history of economics is evaluated in terms of what was added or subtracted from Smith's system, and in so doing the "power of neo-classical analysis" is revealed. The title of chapter six is "Marx madness plunges economics into a new dark age," and there Marx is chastised as a "demonic genius," an "anti-semitic Jew" who wrote "satanic verses," and ultimately a "dismal failure." In chapter seven, "Menger and the Austrians reverse the tide" and resurrect Smith's system of natural liberty. In chapter thirteen, "The Keynes mutiny: capitalism faces its greatest challenge," one might be excused for presuming that capitalism's greatest challenge was the Great Depression. Not so. It is Keynes. Skousen begins the chapter with a quote that claims that "Keynesian economics is . . . the most serious blow that the authority of orthodox economics has yet suffered." It was then left to Milton Friedman "to reverse the Keynesian tide and reestablish the virtues of neoclassical economics" (Skousen, 2001, p. 397).

Should we be concerned about the way in which these histories of thought are written? For example, there is not even a mention of the seminal research of either Samuel Hollander or Philip Mirowski in the Skousen book. Nor is the intellectual history of Adam Smith, written by Jacob Viner and Donald Winch, acknowledged. Winch's work is explicitly against attempts to recruit Smith retroactively into some ideological category and association with extreme *laissez-faire* and libertarianism. One response is to note that Heilbroner and Skousen provide introductions to the subject, written in provocative ways, to entice students toward further study where they then go on to do "real" history of economics. Skousen (2001, p. 5) freely admits that his "book is not a normal history. It is candidly, an irreverent, passionate, sometimes humorous, and often highly opinionated account of the lives and theories of famous economists." A related point is that these texts relate to the teaching of the history of economics, not research at the frontier of the sub-discipline. Alternatively, our friends from literary criticism might also argue that all history is socially constructed and there is no objective truth out there to be discovered. The writing of histories is a creative enterprise and the texts above presumably satisfy the needs of their interpretive communities. Finally, perhaps the concern about balance and objectivity is a storm in a teacup. Will not students easily discern the biases of these texts and take them with a grain of salt? Students of Warren Samuels's history of thought class could clearly discern the ideological agenda behind texts by E. K. Hunt and Ray Canterbery. These texts were intentionally and explicitly critical of the way in which economic thought has developed. In contrast, Henry Spiegel's *The Growth of Economic Thought* was perceived to have no agenda to push and no intention to promote any particular school of thought (Medema and Samuels, 2001, p. 295).

39.2 RESEARCH IN THE HISTORY OF ECONOMICS

One could tell a story of how research in the history of economics has been colored by the stance that various scholars have taken toward orthodox economics. The written history could then be regarded as a vehicle for the defense or criticism of orthodoxy. The work of Terence Hutchison seems a natural place to start. Since *The Significance and Basic Postulates of Economic Theory* first appeared in 1938, the central methodological themes of Hutchison's research has remained essentially unchanged (Hands, 2001, pp. 536–40). For example, part I of his 1953 *Review of Economic Doctrines, 1870–1929,* was entitled "The architects of equilibrium economics and their main critics" and in the *Preface* he was again alluding to "a lessening in the realism and relevance" of economic analysis. Hutchison has long complained of the failure of economics to conform to the canons of positive science. Economic theory rests on weak epistemological foundations, employs highly unrealistic assumptions, and is therefore incapable of generating empirically falsifiable predictions. Practitioners are too preoccupied with refinements and elaborations of abstract general theories. These themes were highlighted in his 1977 *Knowledge and Ignorance in Economics* and in numerous other publications. Hutchison, an outsider to the profession, has been intensely critical of economics.

Mark Blaug has followed in Hutchison's footsteps. Blaug had two supervisors – George Stigler and Terence Hutchison – at Columbia and both were mentors of sorts. Blaug is highly critical of the current state of economic knowledge, and emphasizes the need for more determined efforts to produce theories that yield unambiguously refutable implications and then to confront those implications with the facts. He rails against the disease of formalism in modern economics, where the form of an argument dominates substance and content. Modern theory then ceases to make any descriptive claim about actual economic systems, and becomes a purely formal apparatus, a mathematical thought-experiment. Blaug (2001, p. 160) alleges that Debreu's *Theory of Value* is "probably the most arid and pointless book in the entire literature of economics" and that the "history of general equilibrium theory from Walras to Arrow–Debreu has been a journey down a blind alley, and it is historians of economic thought who seem to have finally hammered down the nails in this coffin."

Two aspects of Blaug's work in this context are interesting to observe. First, while Blaug is critical of orthodoxy, he has very limited sympathy with heterodox critics. His damning critique of the Marxian and Sraffian research programs is well known. He also has little time for post-modernist approaches. Secondly, Roger Backhouse (in Medema and Samuels, 2001, p. 21) has charted Blaug's intellectual journey through the various editions of his *Economic Theory in Retrospect*. What is interesting is Blaug's "change of mind" over the years on Ricardo, Sraffa's interpretation of Ricardo, macroeconomics, and the value of general equilibrium analysis. Blaug on general equilibrium, for example, has moved from supporter to critic. (A similar "change of mind" over Ricardo happened to Samuel Hollander. At one time he subscribed to Sraffa's reading of Ricardo, but the "weight of evidence" led him to abandon this interpretation.)

Philip Mirowski's *More Heat than Light* (1990) has generated enormous interest in the field and considerable controversy (see De Marchi, 1993). Mirowski highlights deep conceptual problems in the foundations of economic science through its perverse attempts to emulate physics. His account of the marginal revolution is one of the delayed and distorted adoption of ideas from the physical sciences. His book is a severe historical critique of neoclassical economics, which claims that economics today is outdated physics and that economics should abandon physics (see Leonard, in De Marchi, 1993). Rizvi has outlined what he calls Mirowski's "palpable and very personal opposition to mainstream economics" (p. 215). The almost mocking attitude to Paul Samuelson is a clear example of this. Mirowski notes that he "fully anticipated the wrath of the orthodox neoclassical economics profession. Had I been trying to ingratiate myself with that crew, I should have done things differently . . ." (De Marchi, 1993, p. 306).

In sharp contrast to the above critiques of economics, but no less controversial, stands the work of Samuel Hollander. Hollander's thesis is that the history of economics shows strong continuity. Classical and neoclassical economists both share essentially the same approach to pricing, distribution, and allocation theory. Hollander claims, for example, that Ricardo's "cost-price analysis is pre-eminently an analysis of the allocation of scarce resources, proceeding in terms of general equilibrium, with allowance for final demand, and the interdependence of factor and commodity markets." Hollander's interpretation of classical economics has irked reviewers from the Sraffian camp and from the anti-Neo-Ricardians, such as Denis O'Brien, Terry Peach, and Terence Hutchison, the latter commenting on Hollander's "extraordinary capacity . . . for dismissing, disregarding, or devaluing evidence, however plain and unambiguous, that conflicts with the Hollander interpretation" (Lodewijks, 1995, p. 143).

A large part of the furor over Hollander's approach is its identification with "Whig" history. The clearest exponent of this is Paul Samuelson (1987, p. 52), who proposes "that history of economics more purposefully reorient itself toward studying the past from the standpoint of the present state of economic science." He alleges that "within any classical economist there is to be discerned a modern economist trying to be born." The implicit assumption is that knowledge is cumulative, and you judge past scholars in terms of how much they contributed to the present state of understanding. Others who adopt this framework are

George Stigler, Donald Walker, and A. M. C. Waterman. Critics of Whig history say that it is a distorted historical reconstruction, where thinkers are examined out of context. Moreover, it serves to justify and legitimize modern economics with a search for pedigrees and precursors.

The research in the history of economics undertaken by Hutchison, Blaug, Mirowski, and Hollander has been pathbreaking. These scholars also have established very strong positions as either defenders or critics of modern economics. If our craft is identified with attacks on mainstream economics, this may partly explain our declining fortunes in the profession. It may generate an overall negative impression of our research and confirm suspicions about the field. The end result is that it reduces the chances of graduate students gaining some acquaintance with the history of their discipline as an essential component of their training and some familiarity with exemplary work in the field. Also, if one comes to the history of economics with a view that economics is fundamentally misguided or, alternatively, that we can find a supply-and-demand model in every past thinker if we look hard enough, then that colors the historical interpretation. In the next section, we deal with schools of thought where these concerns have added importance.

39.3 HETERODOXY AND THE HISTORY OF THOUGHT

Roy Weintraub has taken a strong position that work in the Austrian, Marxian, institutionalist, or post-Keynesian tradition cannot be regarded as legitimate history of economic thought. In his view, citing long-dead economists and employing historical references does not generate historical scholarship. Weintraub notes that the history of the discipline is being increasingly told by those who are hostile to the discipline and its major contributors, and is being used to justify or criticize the role of individuals or schools. The history of economics has become a home for heterodox traditions that are antithetical to the mainstream. Many of these issues were explored in a conference on "The future of the history of economics" held at Duke University in April 2001 (Weintraub, 2002).

A survey of British historians of economic thought undertaken by Roger Backhouse for the conference revealed that 54 percent identified themselves as heterodox, but only 11 percent identified themselves as neoclassical. Many entered the history of economics due to dissatisfaction with conventional economics. One implication is that university funding in Britain, which depends on a research assessment exercise that ranks research, will discriminate against historians of thought and heterodox economists who do not publish in mainstream "top" journals.

Aiko Ikeo delivered a paper that showed that the majority of historians of thought in Japan were also critical of mainstream economics, while in many Eastern European countries the history of economics was taught in the Marxist tradition. Anthony Brewer examined the Marxist tradition and concluded that "Much, perhaps most, of the literature on Marx's economics . . . is therefore of little use to the historian of economics." Ronald Meek and Maurice Dobb are two well-known Marxist historians of thought. Meek was initially an uncritical Marxist and a supporter of Joseph Stalin, who later was skeptical of Marxism, and became more an intellectual historian, albeit one strongly influenced by Marxian themes and approaches. The transformation can be documented in the various editions of his *Studies in the Labour Theory of Value*. Dobb regarded economics "as a tool of the working people in their struggle for social liberation" (Medema and Samuels, 2001, p. 83). His *Theories of Value and Distribution since Adam Smith* was the first history-of-thought text in the light of the Sraffian revolution. Sraffa's "corn model" interpretation of Ricardo led to a rational reconstruction of the history of economics to demonstrate that there was a "surplus" tradition, in sharp contrast to mainstream economics. Among Sraffians, this interpretation of Ricardo is an integral part of their attempt to overthrow neoclassical value, distribution, and growth theory.

The Sraffian approach to classical economics, often labeled neo-Ricardian, has elicited much debate, and this continues in trenchant claims of bias in *The New Palgrave Dictionary of Economics* and, more recently, in the *Elgar Companion to Classical Economics* (Blaug, 1999; Peach, 1999; Hollander, 2000). The conference paper by Christina Marcuzzo and Annalisa Rosselli illustrated how Italian history of thought from the late 1960s to the early 1980s was strongly influenced by Marx and Sraffa. History of thought in Italy became synonymous with doing nonmainstream economics. Indeed, it is alleged that the neo-Ricardians have cornered some of the leading European academic journals in the field.

Malcolm Rutherford (1994) has written extensively on old and new American institutionalism. Post-Keynesian approaches, broadly interpreted, have long been popular in many other countries. Sheila Dow takes a more upbeat perspective on the use of history by post-Keynesians and on heterodox economics generally. She notes that some heterodox economists may use history of thought as a vehicle for supporting their views, but most use it to understand historical ideas better and to assist the development of theory. Post-Keynesians embed the history of economics in their theoretical and policy discussions. Sraffians more than post-Keynesians make contributions to the history of economics; the latter rarely go back earlier in time than the contributions of Keynes and Kalecki. Harcourt (2001) contains various intellectual biographies, tributes, and eulogies in the post-Keynesian tradition. Post-Keynesianism, he says, "is an extremely broad church. The overlaps at each end of a long spectrum of views are marginal, reflecting little more than a shared hostility towards mainstream neoclassical economics and methodology" (2001, p. 263). Harcourt provides glimpses of the intellectual history of Joan Robinson and her circle – Austin Robinson, Richard Kahn, Piero Sraffa, Nicholas Kaldor, Michal Kalecki, Dick Goodwin, Maurice Dobb, Luigi Pasinetti, and, of course, John Maynard Keynes. Yet in the essays one finds very few critical comments on the contributions of this "circle." Indeed, it is quite a challenge to find any. Whereas for the orthodox economist the research frontier is clearly being advanced in the near present, for some heterodox schools the research frontier is still largely discernible in the works of the founders or their immediate followers. At some point, as the approach becomes less popular, the profession's attention moves away from developing and elaborating the key insights of the founders. Scholars sympathetic to heterodoxy then have to go back in time to "pick up the torch" and run with it.

Peter Boettke has been quite critical of the use made by Austrians of the history of economics. He thinks that it is often used for ideological purposes and hagiography, and that it is too passionate and committed. Murray Rothbard's treatment of Adam Smith is best viewed as a libertarian diatribe, rather than a careful examination of Smith's system. However, he also gives examples of where Austrians have produced high-quality history of thought, and mentions the work of Karen Vaughn, Bruce Caldwell, and Laurence Moss. Boettke calculates that 5 percent of *History of Political Economy* articles and 6.8 percent of *Journal of the History of Economic Thought* articles have been written by or about Austrian economists. He also estimates that around one in four to one in five articles in specialist Austrian economics journals are works in the history of economics. Many of the books written by Austrian school economists contain substantial historical material (Medema and Samuels, 2001, pp. 117–28).

Mark Blaug (2001) argues that the history of economics appeals to a different type of mind from that of the average mainstream economist. It attracts the more philosophic, less mathematically inclined mind and the more policy-relevant economist, who feels that the discipline has a rationale of improving society. In other words, the sub-discipline is a haven for heterodoxy! Is this inherently undesirable? Certainly, in an increasingly homogenized discipline, it provides an avenue through which dissent can be expressed. Perhaps it is one role of historians of thought to provide discomfiture: "The task of the historian of social theory is not . . . either to celebrate, to bury – or even merely to understand – the past; its task is to discomfort the present" (Lowry, 1991, p. 136). Historians of thought present the work of a Nobel Laureate in an historical perspective that is at variance with the (self-serving) recollections of the Nobelist himself. Or they outline the historical antecedents and developments that have been hidden, or rewritten in more palatable forms, in textbooks that show a basic continuity of research endeavor that leads to the present. Or they raise uncomfortable questions about the military origins of game theory.

Criticism may help to reform the discipline, but if the history of the subject is being increasingly told by those who are hostile to the discipline and its major contributors, then it should come as no surprise that the history of economic thought will be increasingly marginalized in the profession. Conversely, the smaller number of historians of thought who are sympathetic to modern economics seem to have a greater proclivity at placing their research in mainstream journals. John Creedy, who works on technical issues relating to the historical development of neoclassical economics, is a case in point. Samuel Hollander is another obvious example. Overall, the erosion of the position of the history of economics in the larger discipline of economics is clear. The subject is no longer taught at many institutions. However, there is a tricky issue of causality here. Is the history of economic thought marginalized because it is dominated by heterodox economists, or are heterodox economists naturally attracted to nonorthodox, and hence marginalized, research endeavors? Indeed, some could argue that we should be making more overtures to heterodox economists, as they at least appreciate our craft while the profession as a whole turns away from any historical interest. Since orthodox scholars tend to be more Whiggish, perhaps those with a heterodox approach have a comparative advantage in our field, as better-quality history of thought results from those who do not begin with Whig history. One could ask why there are not more orthodox scholars in the sub-discipline. One hypothesis, yet to be fully explored, relates to the nature of Ph.D. research. Is it the case that those who completed a mainstream thesis topic, and who were relatively successful in terms of publications and citations in mainstream journals, are more likely to defend orthodoxy when they later are persuaded to work in the history-of-thought field? I can think of a few counter-examples, but not that many.

The issues of objectivity and bias still remain. Look at Groenewegen and McFarlane (1990). The strength of the book is undoubtedly its emphasis on the diversity of sources and dissent in Australian economics. Australian economics sprang from a varied mixture of sources – academics, public servants, gifted amateurs, and cranks. The book covers in detail heterodox and other contributions to the subject from outside academe. Yet this coverage comes at a cost. One complaint is that the authors have overemphasized the work of "radicals, outsiders, cranks, and heretics" and in the process omitted major themes in the development of economic analysis in Australia. The neglected contributions include the development of the computable general equilibrium models to analyze commercial policy, Australia's system of centralized wage-fixing, and the contributions of agricultural economists.

The counsel of perfection is that an author should be frank about (or at least implicitly conscious of) the way in which his or her ideological position colors the analysis, or try to be as objective as possible. Warren Samuels says that we should attempt to explain and interpret history with minimal ideological content, and without any intention to advance a political agenda, or without legitimizing and privileging any particular school of thought. Irrespective of these good intentions, others such as Martin Bronfenbrenner saw Samuels as an unmitigated critic of neoclassicism!

Is quality history of thought produced by heterodox economists? History of thought has always been used by economists (either trained in history of thought or not) in theoretical debates about mainstream economics. Blaug (2001, pp. 154–5) documents the examples of J. M. Keynes and Robert Lucas. Persuasion involves appeal to historical argument. But is an article on how Hayek would have analyzed the process of Eastern European transition, or how Minsky would have explained the Asian Crisis, a contribution to historical scholarship? Roy Weintraub would say no. Donald Walker (1988) would agree, but for different reasons. For Walker, the factor that determines whether or not economic writings are treated as part of the history of thought is not how long ago they were written but the approach of the person who is dealing with them. Walker proceeds to explain that an economist treats either present-day writings or older ones as history of thought when he examines them in order to establish their characteristics, interprets them, and evaluates them. He may or may not relate current doctrine to past doctrine, or examine past doctrine to see how it evolved into a subsequent state. But the historian "does not attack the doctrine as part of a debate over what current economic theory should be. Nor does he incorporate the doctrine into a new theory or modify it. The historian of economic thought cannot add to the unalterable body of past writings with which he deals. In contrast the contributor to current theory changes the subject on which he is writing so as to produce a new body of theory" (Walker, 1988, pp. 99–100). The issues raised in this section are not straightforward and often bewitched by terminological minefields, which we now enter.

39.4 A TORTUOUS MAZE OF TERMINOLOGY

Let us start with the term "orthodox" economics. This term is often used interchangeably with mainstream, modern, or neoclassical economics. It is questionable how useful these terms are, especially the latter one. Colander (2000) argues that neoclassical economics is not synonymous with modern mainstream economics. Even when Veblen coined the term, "it was not meant as a description of mainstream economics" (p. 131). Certain aspects of neoclassical economics remain as part of modern economics, but "modern economics is fundamentally different from neoclassical economics" (p. 133). Arguably, neoclassicism has the following characteristics: methodological individualism, subjective utility, rational economic man, efficient resource allocation, a general equilibrium conception of the economy, and a focus on the margin. Modern economics, says Colander, has departed from strict adherence to these modeling attributes. Hence we should stop using the term "neoclassical." Even more recently, John Davis (2002) has foreshadowed the "death" of "mainstream" economics. The mainstream is not a unified research program: many strands exist within the mainstream, such as game theory, and experimental and evolutionary economics. Unlike the neoclassical program of old, these are fragmented research programs. What holds these programs together is a shared methodology. Furthermore, the mainstream only achieves its prominence in a small set of North American hierarchical institutions.

If we leave the maze of the present, even in earlier times it is sometimes difficult to locate a ruling orthodoxy. Morgan and Rutherford (1998) show this clearly for the interwar period in America. Pluralism was the order of the day. There was no hegemony of method. Furthermore, a school or individual may be orthodox at one point in history and heterodox the next, and eventually return to the fold. Take Hayek, for example (Cockett, 1994).

The definition of heterodox economics is another bugbear. Colander (2000) again treads where angels fear to go. He lists several leading economists who have worked outside the orthodox framework, but they would not be regarded as "heterodox." He suggests that "If the term heterodox is to be considered meaningful, it should be defined as an approach to problems that is not accepted as legitimate. Thus, my litmus test of heterodox economists is their ability to get jobs at major graduate schools. Marxists and Institutionalist economists are heterodox economists" (p. 137). Note how centered on North American and how ahistorical this demarcation principle is. It apparently means that almost all historians of thought are heterodox. In fact, most of the economics profession would be heterodox, as there are only a small number of top graduate schools – perhaps 20, or as many as 50? Warren Samuels at Michigan State would not be classified as heterodox, even though he was long-time editor of the *Journal of Economic Issues*. What about Joan Robinson, Piero Sraffa, or Geoffrey Harcourt at Cambridge, or Hayek at the London School of Economics. Were they not heterodox?

Colander further confuses issues by attempting to characterize the central attributes of modern economics. We are told that content does not define modern economics. The modeling approach to problems is the central element of modern economics. So far, so good. Then he states that the "modelling is not seen as an end in itself; there is a continual discussion of the need to empirically test, and the formal modelling is undertaken in large part to make the models empirically testable, and applicable to policy, with formal statistical techniques" so that "the major thrust of modern economics is on formal empirical testing of the models" (Colander, 2000, pp. 137, 140). Hutchison, Stigler, Blaug, and a host of commentators would take issue with these statements.

In the very next article in the same journal issue in which Colander published his piece, we have a distinguished historian of thought, A. W. Coats, leading a round table on heterodox economics. Coats (2000) says that economics is such a heterogeneous discipline that, alongside the formalist uniformity, "there is also within the subject a number of dissenting or deviant doctrinal schools, rival methodological approaches, and innovative developments designed to remedy its defects and/or overcome its limitations" (p. 145). Many of the criticisms and remedies come from prominent economists with impeccable professional credentials. Their criticisms threaten the discipline's foundations and are a species of "orthodox subversion" (p. 146), and many are compatible with heterodoxy. He broadly defines heterodox as encompassing all nonorthodox ideas and approaches, including experimental, behavioral, social, and evolutionary economists. Coats lists the following as heterodox (that is, idiosyncratic, maverick, or deviant, but not necessarily dissident): George Akerlof, Robert Frank, Albert Hirschman, Mancur Olson, James Buchanan, Harvey Leibenstein, Thomas Schelling, Amartya Sen, Vernon Smith, Richard Thaler, and Oliver Williamson. Note that these economists are or were associated with "top" graduate schools!

Roger Backhouse's contribution to the round table is to provide a dividing line between dissent within orthodoxy and dissent from orthodoxy. He offers a very strict definition of heterodoxy. Economists are heterodox if they "self-consciously claim to be working in a way that does not fit in with the dominant way of doing economics, or to be offering an alternative that is incompatible with this." They have different core beliefs about the economy, publish in their own journals, go to their own conferences, and cite fellow travelers. Backhouse says that real business cycle and new institutional economics fails at least some of these criteria, and that only Marxian, post-Keynesian, old institutionalist, radical, and Austrian economics satisfy all of the criteria (p. 149).

Clearly, who is and who is not "heterodox" is a tricky issue, and will vary over time and space. Much of the discussion seems to implicitly assume that what now goes on in the "top" North American graduate schools defines orthodoxy.

This offends historians of thought in other countries and is simply ahistorical. What is surprising is that commentators who otherwise fiercely oppose Whig history will strongly oppose heterodoxy from modern economics – as if the present orthodoxy will last forever! Craufurd Goodwin thinks that we should abandon the orthodox and heterodox labels, as they "belong almost to another age." Malcolm Rutherford believes that modern orthodoxy has become more diverse and that it will discuss almost anything, as long as it is presented using a formalist modeling approach. Furthermore, much of the "progress in orthodox economics has come from taking over problems and issues originally explored within heterodox traditions" (p. 185). Again, perhaps the issue of heterodoxy is another storm in a teacup. Rutherford notes the decline in membership of the Association for Evolutionary Economics. The Sraffians in Italy are fighting a rearguard action. The Marxists are very thin on the ground. Heterodoxy can become moribund; very inward-looking, defensive, and not open to new ideas. The heterodox "bubble" in the history of economics may not last long. As for the Austrian school, some of its members do not even regard themselves as heterodox, but as part of the neoclassical tradition, because of shared aspects of a research program that is striving for universal explanation on the basis of marginal utility analysis.

Finally, one might think that the phrase "research in the history of economic thought" would be clear-cut. But is it research in economic thought or the history of economics? The latter is preferred by Mirowski, Weintraub, and those interested in history-of-science approaches. Leaving this squabble aside, we take it that research means publications in book form and in academic journals. This does raise issues about the relative quality of book publishers and whether certain outlets, such as Edward Elgar, are more sympathetic to criticisms of orthodoxy. It does appear that those with sizeable history-of-thought lists also have substantial heterodox listings or are aimed at a market (Japanese) that is more receptive to heterodoxy. With respect to journals, do we consider refereed journal publication in the leading journals and the specialist history-of-thought journals, or do we also include the *Cambridge Journal of Economics*, the *Journal of Economic Issues*, the *Journal of Austrian Economics*, and other outlets associated with heterodox schools of thought?

These conceptual muddles are compounded when the philosophers of science enter the scene.

39.5 METHODOLOGICAL INTERLUDE

One contentious area in the history of economics relates to economic methodology and the history and philosophy of science. Methodologists such as Bruce Caldwell, Wade Hands, and Larry Boland are prominent at the American history-of-thought meetings. The methodologists have journals of their own – *Economics and Philosophy* and the *Journal of Economic Methodology* – and publish their work in quality mainstream journals. The relevance of this approach for our craft is that there have been numerous attempts to apply ideas from the philosophy of science to the history of economics. We can be brief here, as John Davis (ch. 34, this volume) explores these issues in detail. What is clear is that many economic methodologists have been critical of modern economics. Roy Weintraub is one of the very few who has taken the methodologists on at their own game and developed a sophisticated methodological defense of the neoclassical general equilibrium research program. Even he, though, has come around to the view that the issue of what constitutes a good theory is not a matter of comparing the theory to some standard of scientific goodness (derived from the philosophy of science). He suggests that it makes no sense to view the history of economic thought through methodological spectacles. Historians should lose their interest in methodology, in terms of falsificationism, and in terms of general philosophy-of-science methods of appraisal.

Orthodox general equilibrium theory brought forth a barrage of philosophic attacks (as did marginal productivity distribution theory). General equilibrium theory was seen as the fullest culmination of neoclassical economics. As such, it attracted the ire of Hutchison, Blaug, and numerous other critics. There is now a feeling that this war is over and that the general equilibrium research program has ultimately failed. Rizvi (in Davis, 1997) outlines how the microfoundations of systematic aggregate phenomena could not be found in general equilibrium models. On a positive note, the failure of the program unleashed a greater diversity of approaches in microeconomics, including game theory, experimental economics, organizational theory, and evolutionary modeling. The critics may now have less of a central target to focus on. The heterodox schools will feel vindicated, although each school will have a different account of why the program failed.

39.6 CONCLUDING REMARKS

The history of economics can be used as defensive, critical, or neutral with reference to mainstream economics. The influx of critics of modern economics into the craft reflects broader currents in the profession that relate to research funding and corporatization of universities. History of thought is seen as an escape route from an increasingly abstract and technical profession, or one increasingly shaped by free market ideology. In earlier times, these refugees would have migrated to economic history (before cliometrics), to public finance (before public choice, Stiglitz and Atkinson, and the optimal tax literature), to development economics (before it became applied microeconomics), to industrial organization (before game theory), or finally to labor (before Chicago triumphed over institutionalism). But this movement to our sub-discipline may decline with time as these groups are further marginalized. To the extent that this intermingling continues, historians of thought are further isolating themselves from developments in the profession.

Should there be a purge that only leaves "legitimate" historians of thought to pursue intellectual history and historical reconstruction according to the standards of historians? Should we abandon current debates and rational reconstructions? This would narrow participation in the field; membership would be less open. Barriers to entry would inhibit many heterodox and other economists – although some wear multiple hats and can "do" quality history of thought as well as policy papers using historical argument. John Davis and Steve Medema have said that we need openness and inclusion, perhaps at some sacrifice to quality. They would rather celebrate diversity than homogenize the field. There is a place for all approaches – Mirowski, Blaug, Walker, and even Samuelson.

A key issue is whether there is a systematic bias in the way in which a large number of historians of economics pursue their craft. Is it ideologically based? Is the research motivated by a broader agenda of criticism of orthodoxy? Criticism may be used to reform the discipline or as a means to support alternative schools of thought. To the extent that we do not work in the dominant mathematical discourse of the profession, what we do will have little effect on economics as currently practiced. Indeed, the few North American Ph.D. programs that place greater emphasis on history of thought – the New School, Amherst, Colorado State, and Riverside – do it within the context of a focus on heterodoxy. One could argue that the field as a whole is not biased, but that there are many contributing to the field with explicit or implicit purposes that might lead to results that are arguably "biased." History done for the purpose of defending or criticizing some approach to economics is likely to be, as history, less reliable than, or inferior to, the work of an author who at least tries to maintain an objective or disinterested stance toward the material. We would like to think that historians of thought would quickly pounce on any bias or lack of objectivity, as they have in the past. To paraphrase Joan Robinson, we study the history of economics so as not to be fooled by historians of economic thought.

Note

I would like to acknowledge the helpful comments made by Warren Samuels, John Davis, and Jeff Biddle on an earlier draft of this chapter.

Bibliography

Blaug, M. 1999: Misunderstanding classical economics: the Sraffian interpretation of the surplus approach. *History of Political Economy*, 31(2), 213–36.

—— 2001: No history of ideas, please, we're economists. *Journal of Economic Perspectives*, 15(1), 145–64.

Coats, A. W. Bob et al. 2000: Roundtable: the progress of heterodox economics. *Journal of the History of Economic Thought*, 22(2), 145–90.

Cockett, R. 1994: *Thinking the Unthinkable: Think-Tanks and the Economic Counter-Revolution, 1931–1983*. London: HarperCollins.

Colander, D. 2000: The death of neoclassical economics. *Journal of the History of Economic Thought*, 22(2), 127–43.

Davis, J. B. (ed.) 1997: *New Economics and Its History*. Durham, NC: Duke University Press.

—— 2002: The emperor's clothes. *Journal of the History of Economic Thought*, 24(2), 141–54.

De Marchi, N. (ed.) 1993: *Non-Natural Social Science: Reflecting on the Enterprise of More Heat than Light*. Durham, NC: Duke University Press.

Groenewegen, P. and McFarlane, B. 1990: *A History of Australian Economic Thought*. London: Routledge.

Hands, D. W. 2001: Review of Hutchison, *On the Methodology of Economics and the Formalist Revolution. Journal of the History of Economic Thought*, 23(4), 536–40.

Harcourt, G. C. 2001: *50 Years a Keynesian and Other Essays*. New York: Palgrave.

Heilbroner, R. L. 1979: Modern economics as a chapter in the history of economic thought. *History of Political Economy*, 11(2), 192–8.

Hollander, S. 1987: *Classical Economics*. Oxford: Blackwell.

—— 2000: Sraffa and the interpretation of Ricardo: the Marxian dimension. *History of Political Economy*, 32(2), 187–232.

Hutchison, T. W. 1953: *A Review of Economic Doctrines 1870–1929*. London: Oxford University Press.

Lodewijks, J. 1995: Relevance, scholarship and the historian of economics. *History of Economic Ideas*, III(2), 131–55.

Lowry, S. T. 1991: Are there limits to the past in the history of economic thought? *Journal of the History of Economic Thought*, 13(2), 134–43.

Medema, S. G. and Samuels, W. J. (eds.) 2001: *Historians of Economics and Economic Thought: The Construction of Disciplinary Memory*. London: Routledge.

Mirowski, P. 1990: *More Heat than Light*. New York: Cambridge University Press.

Morgan, M. S. and Rutherford, M. (eds.) 1998: *From Interwar Pluralism to Postwar Neoclassicism*. Durham, NC: Duke University Press.

Peach, T. 1999: Surplus to requirements: Kurz and Salvadori's *The Elgar Companion to Classical Economics*. *Journal of the History of Economic Thought*, 21(4), 449–62.

Rutherford, M. 1994: *Institutions in Economics: The Old and the New Institutionalism*. Cambridge, UK: Cambridge University Press.

Samuelson, P. 1987: Out of the closet: a program for the Whig history of economic science. *History of Economics Society Bulletin*, 9(2), 51–60.

—— 1988: Keeping Whig history honest. *History of Economics Society Bulletin*, 10(2), 161–7.

Skousen, M. 2001: *The Making of Modern Economics: The Lives and Ideas of the Great Thinkers*. Armonk, NY: M. E. Sharpe.

Walker, D. A. 1988: Ten major problems in the study of the history of economic thought. *History of Economics Society Bulletin*, 10(2), 99–115.

Weintraub, E. R. (ed.) 2002: The future of the history of economics. *History of Political Economy*, 34, forthcoming.

Name Index

Subject Index